Feb 95

Neuropsychology of Memory
SECOND EDITION

Neuropsychology of Memory

SECOND EDITION

Edited by
LARRY R. SQUIRE *and* **NELSON BUTTERS**
University of California at San Diego School of Medicine
Department of Veterans Affairs Medical Center, San Diego

THE GUILFORD PRESS
New York   London

© 1992 The Guilford Press
A Division of Guilford Publications, Inc.
72 Spring Street, New York, NY 10012

Printed in the United States of America

This book is printed on acid-free paper.

Last digit is print number: 9 8 7 6 5 4 3 2 1

Library of Congress Cataloging-in-Publication Data
Neuropsychology of memory / edited by Larry R. Squire and Nelson
  Butters. — 2nd ed.
      p.   cm.
    Includes bibliographical references and index.
    ISBN 0-89862-881-4 — ISBN 0-89862-158-5 (pbk.)
    1. Amnesia 2. Memory—Physiological aspects. 3. Memory—Effect
  of drugs on. 4. Neuropsychology. I. Squire, Larry R.
  II. Butters, Nelson.
    [DNLM: 1. Amnesia. 2. Memory. 3. Memory Disorders.
  4. Neuropsychology. WM 173.7 N494]
  RC394.A5N48   1992
  616.85′232—dc20
  DNLM/DLC
  for Library of Congress   92-1431
                                                                  CIP

*To my teachers, Samuel H. Barondes
and Hans-Lukas Teuber.—
L. R. S.*

*To all my teachers: Morton Wiener,
H. Enger Rosvold, Mortimer
Mishkin, Harold Goodglass, and
Edith Kaplan; and to my wife,
Arlene, for her love, warmth, and
friendship for the past 35 years.—
N. B.*

Contributors

Marilyn S. Albert, PhD, Departments of Psychiatry and Neurology, Massachusetts General Hospital, Harvard Medical School, Boston, Massachusetts

Alan D. Baddeley, PhD, Medical Research Council Applied Psychology Unit, Cambridge, England, United Kingdom

William B. Barr, PhD, Departments of Neurology and Psychiatry, Hillside Hospital, Long Island Jewish Medical Center, The Long Island Campus of The Albert Einstein College of Medicine, Glen Oaks, New York

Russell M. Bauer, PhD, Center for Neuropsychological Studies, Department of Clinical and Health Psychology, University of Florida, Gainesville, Florida

William W. Beatty, PhD, Alcohol Research Center, Department of Psychiatry and Behavioral Sciences, University of Oklahoma Health Sciences Center, Oklahoma City, Oklahoma

Edward L. Bennett, PhD, Department of Psychology, University of California at Berkeley, Berkeley, California

Patricia A. Bernstein, MA, Department of Psychology, University of Colorado, Colorado Springs, Colorado

Jason Brandt, PhD, Department of Psychiatry and Behavioral Sciences, The Johns Hopkins University School of Medicine, Baltimore, Maryland

Nelson Butters, PhD, Psychology Service, Department of Veterans Affairs Medical Center, San Diego, California; Department of Psychiatry, University of California at San Diego School of Medicine, La Jolla, California

Laird S. Cermak, PhD, Psychology Research, Department of Veterans Affairs Medical Center, Boston, Massachusetts; Neurology Department, Boston University School of Medicine, Boston, Massachusetts

Han Soo Chang, MD, Department of Physiology, University of Tokyo School of Medicine, Hongo, Tokyo, Japan

Andrea A. Chiba, BS, Department of Psychology, University of Utah, Salt Lake City, Utah

Gregory A. Clark, PhD, Department of Psychology, Princeton University, Princeton, New Jersey

Paul J. Colombo, MA, Department of Psychology, University of California at Berkeley, Berkeley, California

Terry J. Crow, PhD, Department of Neurobiology and Anatomy, University of Texas Medical School, Houston, Texas

Hasker, P. Davis, PhD, Department of Psychology, University of Colorado, Colorado Springs, Colorado

Michael Davis, PhD, Ribicoff Research Facilities of the Connecticut Mental Health Center, Department of Psychiatry, Yale University School of Medicine, New Haven, Connecticut

Stephen B. Dunnett, PhD, Department of Experimental Psychology, University of Cambridge, Cambridge, England, United Kingdom

Howard Eichenbaum, PhD, Department of Psychology, University of North Carolina, Chapel Hill, North Carolina

Howard M. Eisenberg, MD, Division of Neurosurgery, University of Texas Medical Branch, Galveston, Texas

David Gaffan, PhD, Department of Experimental Psychology, Oxford University, Oxford, England, United Kingdom

Karen A. Gallie, MA, Department of Psychology, University of British Columbia, Vancouver, British Columbia, Canada

Paul E. Gold, PhD, Department of Psychology and Neuroscience Graduate Program, University of Virginia, Charlottesville, Virginia

Elkhonon Goldberg, PhD, Departments of Psychiatry and Neurology, Medical College of Pennsylvania/Eastern Pennsylvania Psychiatric Institute, Philadelphia, Pennsylvania

Peter Graf, PhD, Department of Psychology, University of British Columbia, Vancouver, British Columbia, Canada

Robert D. Hawkins, PhD, Center for Neurobiology and Behavior, and Howard Hughes Medical Institute, College of Physicians and Surgeons of Columbia University, New York, New York

William C. Heindel, PhD, Department of Psychiatry, University of California at San Diego School of Medicine, La Jolla, California

Ramona O. Hopkins, MS, Department of Psychology, University of Utah, Salt Lake City, Utah

Larry L. Jacoby, PhD, Department of Psychology, McMaster University, Hamilton, Ontario, Canada

Eric R. Kandel, MD, Center for Neurobiology and Behavior, and Howard Hughes Medical Institute, College of Physicians and Surgeons of Columbia University, New York, New York

Timothy E. Kennedy, PhD, Department of Anatomy, University of California at San Francisco, San Francisco, California

Raymond P. Kesner, PhD, Department of Psychology, University of Utah, Salt Lake City, Utah

Susan M. Koger, MA, Department of Psychology, University of New Hampshire, Durham, New Hampshire

Michael D. Kopelman, PhD, Academic Unit of Psychiatry, United Medical and Dental Schools of Guy's and St. Thomas's Hospitals, St. Thomas's Hospital, London, England, United Kingdom

Mark Kritchevsky, MD, Department of Neurosciences, University of California at San Diego School of Medicine, La Jolla, California; Neurology Service, Department of Veterans Affairs Medical Center, San Diego, California

Philip J. Langlais, PhD, Department of Psychology, San Diego State University, San Diego, California; Research Service, Department of Veterans Affairs Medical Center, San Diego, California

Joseph LeDoux, PhD, Center for Neural Science, New York University, New York, New York

Diane W. Lee, BA, Department of Psychology, University of California at Berkeley, Berkeley, California

Harvey S. Levin, PhD, Division of Neurosurgery, University of Texas Medical Branch, Galveston, Texas

Matthew A. Lilly, BS, Division of Neurosurgery, University of Texas Medical Branch, Galveston, Texas

D. Stephen Lindsay, PhD, Department of Psychology, McMaster University, Hamilton, Ontario, Canada

Robert G. Mair, PhD, Department of Psychology, University of New Hampshire, Durham, New Hampshire

Hans J. Markowitsch, PhD, Department of Psychology, University of Bielefeld, Bielefeld, Germany

Alicja L. Markowska, PhD, Neuromnemonics Laboratory, Department of Psychology, The Johns Hopkins University, Baltimore, Maryland

Alex Martin, PhD, Laboratory of Clinical Science, National Institute of Mental Health, Bethesda, Maryland

Joe L. Martinez, Jr., PhD, Department of Psychology, University of California at Berkeley, Berkeley, California

Andrew R. Mayes, DPhil, Department of Psychology, University of Liverpool, Liverpool, England, United Kingdom

James L. McGaugh, PhD, Center for the Neurobiology of Learning and Memory, and Department of Psychobiology, University of California at Irvine, Irvine, California

Yasushi Miyashita, PhD, Department of Physiology, University of Tokyo School of Medicine, Hongo, Tokyo, Japan

John W. Moore, PhD, Department of Psychology, University of Massachusetts, Amherst, Massachusetts

Koichi Mori, MD, PhD, Department of Physiology, University of Tokyo School of Medicine, Hongo, Tokyo, Japan

Morris Moscovitch, PhD, Department of Psychology, Erindale College, University of Toronto, Mississauga, Ontario, Canada; Rotman Research Institute, Baycrest Centre for Geriatric Care, North York, Ontario, Canada

Mark B. Moss, PhD, Departments of Anatomy and of Neurobiology and Neurology, Boston University School of Medicine, Boston, Massachusetts

Robert D. Nebes, PhD, Department of Psychiatry and Western Psychiatric Institute and Clinic, University of Pittsburgh, Pittsburgh, Pennsylvania

Mary Jo Nissen, PhD, Department of Psychology, University of Minnesota, Minneapolis, Minnesota

David S. Olton, PhD, Neuromnemonics Laboratory, Department of Psychology, The Johns Hopkins University, Baltimore, Maryland

J. M. Ordy, PhD, Fisons Pharmaceuticals, Rochester, New York

Marlene Oscar-Berman, PhD, Division of Psychiatry and Department of Neurology, Boston University School of Medicine, Boston, Massachusetts; Psychology Research Service, Department of Veterans Affairs Medical Center, Boston, Massachusetts

Tim Otto, PhD, Department of Psychology, University of North Carolina, Chapel Hill, North Carolina

Andrew Papanicolaou, PhD, Division of Neurosurgery, University of Texas Medical Branch, Galveston, Texas

Alan J. Parkin, DPhil, Laboratory of Experimental Psychology, University of Sussex, Brighton, England, United Kingdom

William W. Pendlebury, MD, Department of Pathology, University of Vermont College of Medicine, Burlington, Vermont

John K. Robinson, PhD, Unit on Behavioral Neuropharmacology, Experimental Therapeutics

Branch, National Institute of Mental Health, Bethesda, Maryland

Steven P. R. Rose, PhD, Brain and Behaviour Research Group, Open University, Milton Keynes, England, United Kingdom

Mark R. Rosenzweig, PhD, Department of Psychology, University of California at Berkeley, Berkeley, California

J. A. Saint-Cyr, PhD, Departments of Psychology and Anatomy and Cell Biology, University of Toronto, Toronto, Ontario, Canada; Department of Psychology and Playfair Neuroscience Unit, The Toronto Hospital (Western Division), Toronto, Ontario, Canada

David P. Salmon, PhD, Department of Neurosciences, University of California at San Diego School of Medicine, La Jolla, California

Erin M. Schuman, PhD, Department of Psychology, Princeton University, Princeton, New Jersey (Current address: Department of Molecular and Cellular Physiology, Stanford University, Stanford, California)

Peter A. Serrano, MA, Department of Psychology, University of California at Berkeley, Berkeley, California

David F. Sherry, PhD, Department of Psychology, University of Western Ontario, London, Ontario, Canada

Paul R. Solomon, PhD, Department of Psychology and Program in Neuroscience, Williams College, Williamstown, Massachusetts

Larry R. Squire, PhD, Department of Psychiatry, Department of Veterans Affairs Medical Center, San Diego, California; Department of Psychiatry, University of California at San Diego School of Medicine, La Jolla, California

A. E. Taylor, PhD, Department of Medicine, University of Toronto, Toronto, Ontario, Canada; Department of Psychology and Playfair Neuroscience Unit, The Toronto Hospital (Western Division), Toronto, Ontario, Canada

Leon J. Thal, MD, Neurology Service, Department of Veterans Affairs Medical Center, San Diego, California; Department of Neurosciences, University of California at San Diego School of Medicine, La Jolla, California

Garth J. Thomas, PhD, Department of Neurobiology and Anatomy, University of Rochester, Rochester, New York

Jeffrey P. Toth, PhD, Department of Psychology, McMaster University, Hamilton, Ontario, Canada

Mieke Verfaellie, PhD, Neurology Department, Boston University School of Medicine, Boston, Massachusetts

D. Yves von Cramon, MD, Department of Neuropsychology, City Hospital Bogenhausen, Munich, Germany

Norman M. Weinberger, PhD, Center for the Neurobiology of Learning and Memory, and Department of Psychobiology, University of California at Irvine, Irvine, California

Daniel B. Willingham, PhD, Department of Psychology, Williams College, Williamstown, Massachusetts

Barbara A. Wilson, PhD, Medical Research Council Applied Psychology Unit, Cambridge, England, United Kingdom

Gordon Winocur, PhD, Department of Psychology, Trent University, Petersborough, Ontario, Canada; Rotman Research Institute, Baycrest Centre for Geriatric Care, North York, Ontario, Canada

Stuart Zola-Morgan, PhD, Research Service, Department of Veterans Affairs Medical Center, San Diego, California; Department of Psychiatry, University of California at San Diego School of Medicine, La Jolla, California

Preface to the First Edition

The past 20 years have witnessed an exponential growth in studies of the neuropsychology of memory. Even for the avid student of this area, it has been impossible to keep abreast of the entire field and to integrate the findings of human and animal studies. While this difficulty with integration is due partially to the vast volume of investigations published each year, some of the problems appear to us to be related to a lack of understanding of investigators' implicit underlying assumptions about memory. For this reason, we have assembled in this volume contributions from a group of scientists who have assessed the neuropsychology of memory from the molecular as well as the molar perspective; have employed physiological, anatomical, pharmacological, and behavioral techniques; and have dealt with the complexities of memory in animals and humans. The contributors were assigned the task of reaching beyond their empirical data and currently favored theories and of making explicit their long-term programmatic goals. To facilitate the reader's appreciation of the various chapters, we have organized this volume into three sections: "Studies of Normal and Abnormal Memory in Humans"; "Studies of Memory in Nonhuman Primates"; and "Studies of Memory in Nonprimates: Physiology, Pharmacology, and Behavior." Within each of these three sections, the chapters have been further ordered to provide additional continuity and cohesion of the subject matter.

L. R. S.
N. B.

Preface to the Second Edition

In the 8 years since publication of the first edition of *Neuropsychology of Memory*, significant progress has been made in how we understand the organization of memory and its neurological foundations. Unmistakable shifts have occurred in the kinds of questions being asked and in the kinds of studies being carried out. For example, animal models of human memory impairment, available only since the early 1980s, are now being applied systematically to the task of identifying brain structures and connections important for memory. Progress in the fundamental problem of classification has emerged from a recognition that memory is not a single faculty but is composed instead of several different systems. In addition, in several areas of research a rapprochement has occurred for the findings from rats, monkeys, and humans. Because of these changes in the shape of the discipline, we have once again invited scientists to describe in brief chapters their current approaches to the study of memory, to make explicit their assumptions and objectives, and to summarize what has been learned. We have endeavored to include as broad as possible a spectrum of contemporary work on the neuropsychology of memory. To help the reader, we have organized the volume into three sections: "Studies of Normal and Abnormal Memory in Humans"; "Studies of Monkeys and Rodents"; and "Studies in Birds and Invertebrates." Each section is prefaced by an introductory comment, and the chapters within each section have been ordered to provide additional structure. We hope readers will find the result interesting and that comparisons to the first edition will provide both an indication of the direction of the discipline and an explicit measure of progress.

L. R. S.
N. B.

Contents

Neuropsychology of Memory

SECOND EDITION

Studies of Normal and Abnormal Memory in Humans

The neuropsychology of memory has undergone major changes during the last 20 years. Important advances have been made in isolating the specific medial temporal, diencephalic, and basal forebrain structures mediating memory. The role of the hippocampus and related cortex has now been well established, thanks to major advances in neuroanatomical and neuroimaging techniques. On the cognitive front there have been significant shifts of emphasis. The 1970s were characterized by theories focusing on storage, retrieval, and various executive functions (e.g., encoding) in the anterograde amnesia of amnesic patients. Both neuropsychologists and neuroscientists were committed to the exploration of what these patients could *not* learn and retain. In marked contrast, the 1980s and early 1990s have been dominated by studies of what the amnesic patient *can* learn and retain. The episodic–semantic, declarative–procedural, and explicit–implicit dichotomies have all stressed a core of memory paradigms on which amnesic patients and intact control subjects cannot be differentiated. Studies demonstrating normal learning by amnesic patients of motor, perceptuomotor, and cognitive skills, as well as normal performance on tests of repetition, lexical, semantic, and perceptual priming, can now be found in virtually every issue of the major neuropsychology journals. During the past few years cognitive neuropsychologists have begun to turn their attention to the specific mechanisms underlying these "preserved memory systems." Debates are in progress concerning the role of semantic and presemantic perceptual processes in the mediation of implicit memory. Similarly, investigations are now appearing that explore the influence of central motor programs in skill learning and in certain types of priming and perceptual adaptation.

These changes in theoretical emphasis have been paralleled by changes in the patient populations being studied. Whereas the investigation of abnormal memory in the 1970s and early 1980s rarely ventured beyond the traditional "hippocampal" and "diencephalic" amnesic patient, there has been a growing interest in the late 1980s and early 1990s in the pattern of memory deficits associated with various forms of dementia (e.g., Alzheimer's disease, Huntington's and Parkinson's disease, multiple sclerosis, and head trauma). This extension of patient populations deemed worthy of study has been partially driven by critical clinical needs involving early detection and the differentiation of one form of dementia from another. However, studies of the memory disorders of demented patients have frequently been motivated by a desire to understand the role of various cortical and subcortical structures in memory. Because demented patients are often impaired on semantic, procedural, and implicit memory tasks, their performance may offer important clues concerning the specific brain structures mediating the "preserved memory systems" of amnesic patients. It also has become apparent that these patient populations may help answer some questions about the cognitive mechanisms underlying these memory systems.

Given these rapid changes in the study of normal and abnormal memory in recent years, it is not surprising that the topics and concerns of the second edition of this volume are quite different from those of the first edition (published 1984). Although the first seven chapters in this section do address theoretical issues pertaining to anterograde and retrograde amnesia, several chapters raise important conceptual and clinical issues about the defining features of implicit memory and about the semantic and perceptual processes that may underlie this type of memory.

Chapters 8 and 9 review issues pertaining to the localization of amnesic patients' memory dysfunctions, and describe some of the advances that have been made in this arena.

Chapters 10–13 explore the nature of the anterograde and retrograde amnesias of several types of memory disorders. Chapter 10 presents new data and theoretical concepts concerning differences between the memory disorders of diencephalic and hippocampal amnesic patients. Chapter 11 continues a prominent theme from the first edition—that is, the factors contributing to the severe anterograde and retrograde memory disorders of alcoholic patients with Korsakoff's syndrome. It also notes some of the similarities and differences between patients with Korsakoff's syndrome and amnesic patients in the early stages of Alzheimer's disease. Chapters 12 and 13 discuss the features and etiology of transient global amnesia and of functional amnesias, respectively. In many ways, the reader will find these four chapters an updating of issues mentioned prominently in the first edition of this book.

Chapters 14–17 are grouped together because of their concern with procedural memory and skill learning. These chapters all deal with the neurological and/or psychological processes involved in normal skill learning, and three (Chapters 15, 16, 17) address the possible role of structures in the neocortex and basal ganglia in this type of memory. These chapters also consider some of the differences between priming and skill learning, and contrast the performance of patients with "cortical" and "subcortical" dementias on various skill learning tasks.

Chapters 18–23 are concerned with the memory disorders associated with Alzheimer's disease and normal aging. Two of the chapters (19 and 20) present strikingly different theoretical interpretations of the semantic memory deficits of patients with Alzheimer's disease, and one (18) describes the most useful memory measures for detecting this disease in its earliest stages. The possible neuro-chemical bases of these memory and other cognitive disorders are presented in Chapter 24. Chapters 21 and 22 suggest important distinctions between explicit and implicit memory, and then evaluate the utility of this distinction in elderly subjects. Chapter 23 reviews the findings of recent studies on the disruption of classical conditioning in normal and abnormal aging. These studies employ both humans and experimental animals, and attempt to assess several etiological factors that have been proposed for Alzheimer's disease. Readers of the first edition will note that there have been considerable gains in our knowledge about the memory disorders of patients with Alzheimer's disease.

Chapter 25 is concerned with the memory disorders of patients with multiple sclerosis, as well as the ways in which these impairments compare with those reported for other types of dementia. The final three chapters of this section focus upon the memory disorders frequently reported after severe head injury. Chapter 26 utilizes concepts borrowed from cognitive psychology to compare the explicit memory deficits of these patients with those of amnesic and demented patients. Chapters 27 and 28 also employ currently popular concepts in cognitive psychology (e.g., working memory) not only for assessment purposes but also for exploring their application to memory rehabilitation. The possibility that these patients' intact memory and executive capacities may be used to help them adapt to their daily environments has also attracted much attention in recent years.

1

A Neuropsychological Model of Memory and Consciousness

MORRIS MOSCOVITCH

Introduction

In my contribution to the first edition of this volume, I avoided speculating about different kinds of memory. Instead, I concentrated on identifying the sufficient conditions for distinguishing between memory tests on which performance of amnesic patients is relatively intact and those on which it is impaired (Moscovitch, 1984). Those conditions are the basis of the current distinction between explicit and implicit tests of memory (Graf & Schacter, 1985). In the years since the book appeared, the theoretical and empirical literature on this topic has burgeoned as no other has done in cognitive psychology and neuropsychology. One of the main consequences of this enterprise has been a growing appreciation both of the varieties of memory and of the component cognitive processes and neurological mechanisms that underlie them (Richardson-Klavehn & Bjork, 1988; Roediger & Craik, 1989). The operational, descriptive approach I adopted in my previous chapter is still useful in classifying memory tests, but it is no longer adequate in dealing with the rich theoretical and empirical literature we now have. I therefore supplement it with (in fact, subordinate it to) theoretical speculations about the varieties of memory in normal and brain-damaged people.

Classification of Tests

Memory is not a unitary process. It is possible to distinguish between two broad classes of memory tests, "explicit" and "implicit," performance on which is probably mediated by different neural structures (Graf & Schacter, 1985; Moscovitch, 1984; Richardson-Klavehn & Bjork, 1988). Explicit tests of memory, such as recognition and recall, depend on the conscious recollection of previously experienced events. On implicit tests, memory is inferred from the effects that experience or practice has on behavior; the subject is not required to refer to the past in performing the test.

Both implicit and explicit tests of memory can each be subdivided further into two subtypes. One type of implicit test is "procedural" and the other is "item-specific."

Procedural implicit tests involve the acquisition and retention of general skills, procedures, or rules, such as learning motor tasks, reading novel scripts, or solving rule-based puzzles (e.g., the Tower of Hanoi). Item-specific tests, on the other hand, are concerned with the acquisition and retention of a particular type of information, such as a word, face, or object. On such tests, the increased accuracy or speed with which a previously seen item is identified on repetition, known as the "repetition priming effect," is a measure of item-specific memory.

Explicit tests can be classified as "associative/cue-dependent" or as "strategic." Associative tests are those in which the cue is sufficient to bring the memory to mind. As I argue here, this process is relatively automatic and mandatory if the cue is appropriate. To give a sense of what I mean, it is the episodic memory equivalent of the response "Guildenstern" to the cue "Rosencrantz." Possible examples are "Have you been to Jerusalem?" or "Did you ever meet Hebb or Luria?" Strategic tests, on the other hand, are those in which the cue does not immediately give rise to an associative response, but rather initiates a memory search that is not unlike problem solving. Such a process is often set in motion by questions that have a temporal component, such as "What did you do three weekends ago?"

One purpose of this chapter is to speculate about the nature of the processes and structures involved in each of these tests. The scheme for classifying memory tests in each of these categories, however, is imperfect. One reason is that the defining features of each test are not sufficiently specific, and the other is that few tests are process-pure (Mandler, 1980; Jacoby, 1991). The classificatory scheme therefore describes the ideal type, of which the actual test is at best only a close approximation.

With these provisos in mind, I outline a neuropsychological model or framework of conscious and nonconscious processes in memory that accounts for performance of normal and memory-impaired people on each of these four types of tests. The model is derived from a critical examination of Fodor's (1983, 1985) ideas on modules and central systems, and the ways in which these can be applied to neuropsychology (for more details, see Moscovitch, 1989, and Moscovitch & Umilta, 1990, 1991).

Input Modules and Central Systems

According to Fodor, cognition arises from the operation of modules and central systems. Modules and central systems are computational devices that are distinguished from each other by the following criteria: domain specificity, informational encapsulation or cognitive impenetrability, and shallow output. Modules must satisfy all three criteria, whereas central systems satisfy none. Modules process information only from a specific domain, whereas central systems integrate information across superficially dissimilar domains. Modules are informationally encapsulated, so that higher-order cognitive information cannot penetrate them and influence their operation. Central systems, on the other hand, are open to—indeed, invite—top-down influences. It is through them that knowledge, expectancies, and motivation make their presence felt in cognition. Finally, modular output is shallow, in that it is not semantically interpreted and provides no information about its source. Meaning and relevance are assigned to modular output by central systems, which relate the output to stores of general knowledge as well as to current cognitive and motivational states. The output of central systems is deep, and their source or derivation is often available to conscious inspection.

Modules are therefore special-purpose devices that have evolved to pick up domain-specific information; to process it efficiently and automatically, without the distorting influence of expectancies and motivation; and to deliver a precise, but shallow and presemantic, message to a central system for interpretation. In short, they are "stupid" but efficient systems, necessary for "representing the world veridically, and making it accessible to thought" (Fodor, 1983, p. 40), which in its multifaceted aspects is a product of the typically "slow, deep, global, and voluntary" operations of "intelligent" central systems.

At the neuropsychological level, domain specificity is satisfied in part by evidence of localization of function; informational encapsulation is satisfied by evidence that the function in question is impervious to the effects of gross intellectual decline; and shallow output is satisfied by evidence of normal, domain-specific performance without any ability to interpret semantically the information pertaining to that domain (see Moscovitch & Umilta, 1990, 1991, for details and examples).

The Model (see Figure 1.1)

Cortical Input Modules: The Perceptual and Semantic Records

Memory begins with registration of information in cortical input modules. Environmental events are picked up by the input modules, which are involved in decoding and classifying the information at a perceptual, presemantic level. Their output is conveyed to central system structures, where they receive a semantic interpretation (meaning is assigned). These processes leave a record of their activity in the input modules and central semantic systems, both of which are presumed to be located in the posterior and midlateral neocortex. I use the terms *perceptual records* and *semantic records* (Kirsner & Dunn, 1985) to refer to the modification of the neural circuitry of input modules and central semantic systems, respectively. Records preserve information about the stimulating event and have processing consequences, so that identical and perhaps related events can be processed more quickly on subsequent presentation. It is the reactivation of perceptual and semantic records that accounts for repetition priming effects and sustains performance on item-specific implicit tests of memory (see also Tulving & Schacter, 1990; Schacter, 1990). The term *engram* refers to the informational content of the record.

The Hippocampal Component: A Memory Module

Only the output of modules can be made accessible to consciousness, although it can also drive procedural or action systems directly without first gaining access to consciousness (see Moscovitch, 1989; Schacter, 1989). If the output is consciously apprehended by virtue of its being delivered to working memory (see Moscovitch &

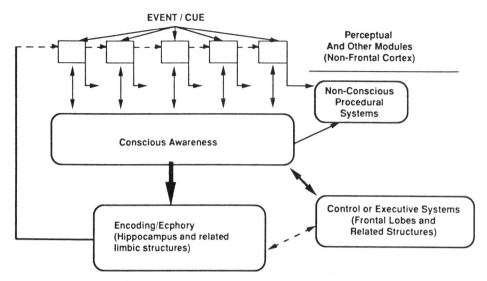

FIGURE 1.1. A sketch of the interaction of modules and central system structures in a neuropsychological model of memory (see text). Consciousness has yet to be localized. It may emerge as a product of the interaction between cortical and subcortical systems. From "Confabulation and the Frontal System: Strategic vs. Associative Retrieval in Neuropsychological Theories of Memory" (p. 154) by M. Moscovitch, 1989, in H. L. Roediger III and F. I. M. Craik (Eds.), *Varieties of Memory and Consciousness: Essays in Honor of Endel Tulving* (pp. 133–156). Hillsdale, NJ: Erlbaum. Copyright 1989 by Lawrence Erlbaum Associates. Reprinted by permission.

Umilta, 1990, 1991, for a discussion of working memory and consciousness), it is picked up automatically by the hippocampal component, which is a functional unit that comprises the hippocampus and related limbic structures in the medial temporal lobe and diencephalon.[1] Thus, only consciously experienced, usually semantically interpreted events, or signals related to them, are channeled automatically to the hippocampal component. This component, in turn, mandatorily binds the information it receives with the engrams in the modules and central systems whose activities gave rise to the conscious experience. This process is probably mediated by reciprocal pathways connecting the hippocampus to the neocortex via the entorhinal cortex and adjacent cortical areas (Squire, 1987; Hyman, Van Hoesen, & Damasio, 1990). This hippocampally mediated collection of bound engrams constitutes a *memory trace* (Hayman & Tulving, 1989), which is encoded as an index or file entry within the hippocampus. *Memory consolidation* refers to this entire hippocampal process.

Conscious recollection of an event occurs when a cue, either externally presented or internally generated, gains access to working memory (consciousness), activates the hippocampal index, and interacts with the memory trace. The outcome of that interaction is in turn delivered to consciousness (working memory). The process by which retrieval information is brought into interaction with stored information (Tulving, 1983) is called *ecphory* (Semon, 1921, cited in Schacter, Eich, & Tulving, 1978). Both ecphory and consolidation are rapid, automatic, and mandatory processes to which we

---

[1]The component has been designated "hippocampal" in deference to its most prominent structure and because the functions of the other structures have yet to be differentiated clearly from the memory function of the hippocampus.

have no conscious access. What is available to us is only the input and shallow output of the hippocampal system. Because of this, we consider the hippocampal component to constitute a memory module analogous in its operation and essential features to input modules. Because it is modular, because its representations (memory traces) consist of indices to bound or associated engrams, and because retrieval is automatic to cues associated with the memory trace, we refer to the hippocampal component as "associative"—a term that also describes the explicit memory tests mediated primarily by it.

The associative/ecphoric component of memory, with the hippocampus at its core, automatically encodes consciously apprehended information and, in response to the appropriate cue, automatically delivers ecphoric information back to consciousness as a memory. Being modular, this component lacks intelligence. If the cue does not elicit a memory directly, it cannot conduct a search on its own. Even if a memory is elicited, the information that is delivered may not be veridical, because the cue may activate the wrong trace or may interact inappropriately with existing traces to deliver partial, or even implausible and distorted, memories to consciousness. Lacking intelligence, the hippocampal component is not adequate for distinguishing these imposters from the genuine articles. Also, because the component's memory is associative, it lacks organization beyond associations that memory traces have formed with one another and with cues.

The Frontal Lobes: A Central System Structure

Strategic processes mediated by the frontal lobes and its related structures (the frontal component) are necessary for endowing memory with "intelligence"—that is, for organizing the information in consciousness that serves as the input to the hippocampal component, for evaluating hippocampal output to determine whether it is veridical, for monitoring the output so that it is consistent with the requirements of the test, and for placing the retrieved memories in a proper spatiotemporal context with other memories. In short, through "working-with memory" (Moscovitch & Winocur, 1992, in press), strategic processes make memory goal-directed. Unlike the associative/ecphoric processes of the hippocampus, strategic, frontal processes entail conscious awareness; as a result, they can be brought under conscious control and mediate performance on strategic, explicit tests of memory.

Item-Specific Implicit Tests and Input Modules

The Perceptual Record

According to the present model (Moscovitch, 1989; Moscovitch & Umilta, 1990, 1991), perceptual records in input modules are what support performance on many item-specific, implicit tests of memory. In many of these tests, retention of target items is measured by the presence of repetition priming effects. Such effects, as noted earlier, are obtained when stimuli are processed more accurately or more efficiently when they are repeated than when they were presented for the first time. Repetition priming effects are found in a variety of tasks involving words, pictures, and nonsense shapes (for reviews, see Moscovitch & Umilta, 1991; Tulving & Schacter, 1990; Richardson-Klavehn & Bjork, 1988). Because conscious recollection of the past is not required in any of these tasks, repetition priming effects serve as an implicit or nonconscious test of memory for the repeated target. Because the test is implicit, and mediated only by cortical input modules, amnesic patients with damage to the hippocampal component often perform normally on these tasks (Moscovitch & Umilta, 1991; Shimamura, 1986; Tulving & Schacter, 1990). So do demented patients with Alzheimer's disease (Keane, Gabrieli, Fennema, Growdon, & Corkin, 1991; Moscovitch, 1985).

To understand the relation between input modules and perceptual repetition priming effects requires at least a nodding acquaintance with some neuropsychological syndromes related to perception. One of the criteria of modularity is that only the module's shallow output is available to conscious inspection. Many neuropsychological deficits of perception, such as some forms of prosopagnosia, dyslexia, aphasia, neglect, and blindness, can be described as impairments that arise from a decoupling of perception from conscious awareness (for review, see Schacter, McAndrews, & Moscovitch, 1988).

For example, prosopagnosic patients can distinguish familiar from unfamiliar faces implicitly, as indicated by their galvanic skin response, but not explicitly, as indicated by conscious report either verbally or by pointing to the correct item (Bauer, 1984; Tranel & Damasio, 1985). To acquire such item-specific knowledge, input modules that do not have access to consciousness must have the capacity to be modified by experience; that is, they must be capable of storing perceptual records of the activity involved in decoding stimulus events or of the representations that ensue. Working with a prosopagnosic patient, Greve and Bauer (1990) presented strong evidence that modules dissociated from consciousness can store new information. When they tested retention for newly presented unfamiliar faces implicitly by asking their patient to choose the face he preferred between the target and the lure, he chose the target at a rate significantly above chance level, though on explicit tests no savings was noted (see also De Haan, Young, & Newcombe, 1987). Together, these studies suggest that if an input module is relatively intact, it can store new information as a perceptual record, but its shallow output cannot gain access to consciousness.

According to the present model, the information that perceptual records contain about the initial stimulating event enables identical (and, perhaps, related) stimuli to be processed more efficiently by the module when they are repeated. The information contained in the record must be at the level of abstraction specific to the domain in which the module operates. For example, if the perceptual record stores information in a specific modality, a stimulus that is repeated in a different modality will not reactivate the record, and therefore will not be processed more efficiently.

Our knowledge of the type of information that input modules store, though rudimentary, is sufficient to permit the formulation of some broad hypotheses about the variables that affect repetition priming effects. The hypotheses are derived from studies of patients with neuropsychological disorders that either affect modules or isolate them from other systems. For example, studies of patients with acquired dyslexia indicate that the visual word form system or module represents information at the level of visual, graphemic properties of words, but not at the level of specific features of letters such as font, size, script, and so on (Schwartz, Saffran, & Marin, 1980; Saffran & Marin, 1977). Visual repetition priming effects for words should therefore be sensitive to changes in modality, but not to changes in physical features. Except for completion of word stems and fragments (see Tulving & Schacter, 1990), which seems to be especially sensitive to variation in physical features, the results from many other tests, such as reading, lexical decision, and perceptual identification, are consistent with the prediction (Carr, Brown, & Charalambous, 1989; Jacoby, 1983; Scarborough, Cortese, & Scarborough, 1977). Because visual word forms are presemantic, higher-order semantic processes should have little or no influence on repetition priming effects. The literature is generally consistent with this prediction (Tulving & Schacter, 1990; Roediger, 1990; Richardson-Klavehn & Bjork, 1988; but see Bentin & Moscovitch, 1988).

The factors influencing repetition priming effects for line drawings of real or imaginary objects are also consistent with how objects are represented in input modules. Because the information stored is a visually structured, nonsemantic representation of a particular object, and not of a generic object (Riddoch & Humphreys, 1987; Schacter, Cooper, Delaney, Peterson, & Tharau, 1990; Warrington & Taylor, 1978), repetition priming effects are sensitive to changes in the token but not to variations in size or orientation, and are not influenced by semantic encoding processes (Schacter et al., 1990; Cooper, Schacter, Ballesteros, & Moore, 1992; Musen & Treisman, 1990; Jacoby, Baker, & Brooks, 1989; Warren & Morton, 1982; Jolicoeur, 1985; Jolicoeur & Milliken, 1989; Bartram, 1974). Similar consistencies are also found between studies of repetition priming effects for faces and neuropsychological evidence about the nature of face identity modules (Bentin & Moscovitch, 1988; Bruce & Young, 1986; Ellis, Young & Flude, 1990; Ellis, Young, Flude, & Hay, 1987; McNeil & Warrington, 1991).

The Semantic Record and Repetition Priming Effects

Not all repetition priming effects are immune to semantic influences. Small, but reliable, influences of higher-order conceptual processes are found on implicit tests in which a taxonomic category, a related word, or a question serves as a cue to elicit the target word (Blaxton, 1989; Roediger, 1990). Much smaller, but nonetheless also reliable, effects are also found for word stem and fragment completion (Roediger, 1990; Schwartz, 1989). That these tests are truly implicit is attested by the fact that performance on them is independent from performance on explicit tests in normal people, and by the fact that amnesic patients can perform normally on them (Schacter, 1987; Gardner, Boller, Moreines, & Butters, 1973; McAndrews, Glisky, & Schacter, 1987).

The existence of *conceptual* repetition priming effects suggests that central systems involved in interpreting the shallow output of modules can store a semantic record of their activity or representations. Like the perceptual record in modules, the semantic record is reactivated by the appropriate semantic input. If conceptual repetition priming effects are mediated by semantic central systems, they should be absent or reduced in patients with damage to those structures. Recent evidence that conceptual, but not perceptual, repetition priming effects are absent in patients with Alzheimer's disease (Butters, Heindel, & Salmon, 1990) and in patients with left temporal lobectomy (Blaxton, in press) supports this prediction.

Procedural Implicit Tests

The acquisition and retention without conscious awareness of motor and cognitive skills, such as mirror-image drawing and learning to read transformed script, have been noted in amnesic patients with various etiologies (Corkin, 1968; Milner, 1966; Milner, Corkin, & Teuber, 1968; Cohen & Squire 1980; Martone, Butters, Payne, Becker, & Sax, 1984; Moscovitch, Winocur, & McLachlan, 1986). Even rules necessary to solve such cognitive puzzles as the Tower of Hanoi can also be acquired implicitly and retained by patients with severe memory disorder (Saint-Cyr, Taylor, & Lang, 1988), though the effect is not always reliable (Butters, Wolfe, Martone, Granholme, & Cermak, 1985).

Recent studies, primarily by Butters et al. (1990) on patients with Huntington's and Parkinson's disease, suggest that the basal ganglia are critical for mediating performance on procedural implicit tests that have a strong sensorimotor component (Heindel, Salmon, & Butters, 1991). These patients, unlike amnesics or patients with Alzheimer's disease, do not show the normal improvement with practice on pursuit-rotor tasks and mirror drawing.

Performance on nonmotor procedural tests may be impaired following damage to some basal ganglia structures but not others. Patients with Huntington's disease have difficulty learning to read mirror-transformed script (Martone et al., 1984), but Parkinson's patients do not (Huberman, Freedman, & Moscovitch, 1988; Heindel, Salmon, Shults, Walicke, & Butters, 1989; Bondi & Kaszniak, 1991). The critical structure may be the caudate nucleus, which is directly affected in Huntington's disease, but only indirectly in Parkinson's disease.

Acquisition of the recursive rules for solving the Tower of Hanoi is impaired in Parkinson's disease patients and in Huntington's disease patients with moderate, but not mild, dementia (Saint-Cyr et al., 1988; Butters et al., 1985). The critical structures in this case may not be the basal ganglia at all, but rather the frontal lobes, since patients with focal frontal lesions are also impaired on this task (Shallice, 1982) and Parkinson's and Huntington's patients are known to have frontal dysfunction (Brown & Marsden, 1990).

Consistent with the neurological literature is our finding that procedural rule-learning memory and item-specific memory act independently in normal people. Using an anagram-solving task, a colleague and I (McAndrews & Moscovitch, 1990) showed that implicit acquisition and retention of a solution rule (the sequence in which the letters had to be rearranged) improved the speed and accuracy of anagram solution, independently of prior exposure to the target item. The procedural rule-learning and item-specific components of memory were additive.

Associative/Ecphoric Explicit Tests and the Hippocampal Component

In presenting this model, I have noted that the formation (consolidation) and retrieval (ecphory) of memory traces through the hippocampal component are automatic, mandatory processes that are initiated by conscious apprehension of targets and cues. If the hippocampal component acts like a module, as I have proposed, it should satisfy the three criteria of modularity: domain specificity, informational encapsulation, and shallow output. The available evidence, though sparse, is consistent with this proposal.

Domain Specificity

The domain of the hippocampal component is consciously apprehended information. Information that is not attended to, and is therefore not fully registered in consciousness, should not be consolidated or retrieved on explicit tests of memory. This fact has long been known to laypeople and is supported by well-controlled experiments (Craik & Byrd, 1982). It is significant that the information that is unavailable to the hippocampal component, either because attention is diverted from it (input interference) or because the input is unconsciously perceived, is picked up nonetheless by input modules and supports performance on implicit tests for the very same material that is unavailable on explicit tests (Eich, 1984; Forster, Booker, Schacter, & Davis, 1990; Forster & Davis, 1984; Kihlstrom, Schacter, Cork, Hurt, & Behr, 1990; Merikle & Reingold, 1991; Parkin, Reid, & Russo, 1990).

The neuropsychological criterion of domain specificity is satisfied by evidence showing that damage to the hippocampal component can produce memory loss with relatively preserved cognitive functions, whereas damage to other cortical structures can impair various aspects of cognition without affecting memory (Neary, Snowden, Northern, & Goulding, 1988; Milner, 1966, 1974). In short, there is ample evidence of double dissociation between hippocampal memory functions and cognitive functions mediated by other cortical structures.

Informational Encapsulation

According to the criterion of informational encapsulation, the hippocampal component, from the time it receives its input until it emits its output, should be resistent to higher-order influences, and its operation should be cognitively impenetrable to consciousness. Because the input to the component is consciously apprehended information that is highly processed and interpreted, and because its output is necessarily similar (see below for shallow output), it is difficult to determine from experiments on normal people whether this criterion is satisfied. The best evidence may be available from studies of retrieval. If the operation of the component is immune to higher-order influences, concurrent interfering tasks should have little effect on ecphoric processes necessary for retrieval. Indeed, there is a wealth of evidence that interference at study impairs memory, presumably by preventing the information from being fully registered in consciousness (Craik & Byrd, 1982). Judging from the dearth of reports, comparable effects are very difficult to obtain at test (see Baddeley, Lewis, Eldridge, & Thomson, 1984), probably because the ecphoric process is triggered automatically by the appropriate cue and delivers its output to consciousness without effort. When interference effects are obtained, they are probably affecting strategic rather than associative ecphoric processes (for further discussion, see the "Cognitive Resources . . ." section, below).

Neuropsychological evidence from demented patients may prove more useful than studies of normal people. Consistent with the criterion of informational encapsulation, memory loss is not a feature of dementia if the neuropathology causing it does not affect the hippocampal component (Neary et al., 1988). DeRenzi, Liotti, and Nichelli (1987) report a case of a patient with semantic memory loss caused by a focal lesion in whom episodic memory is not affected as severely. In short, the hippocampal component seems to be able to operate independently of other cognitive central systems.

Shallow Output

Umilta and I (Moscovitch & Umilta, 1991) proposed that the shallow output of the hippocampal component consists of memory of an event that is not placed in its proper spatiotemporal context; that is, it is recognized as a memory of the past, but it cannot be interpreted properly within the context of other past or current events without the involvement of central systems. Temporal order is not coded in the hippocampal component. Order information is dependent only on associations between events. The memory, therefore, consists of content without context; in its purer form, it is memory based on familiarity and stripped of explicit information about its source.

A dramatic demonstration of how memory operates when it relies only on the shallow output of the hippocampal component is provided by patients with large bilateral lesions of the frontal lobes and related structures, caused by anterior communicating artery aneurysms. Their performance on tests of recognition is relatively spared, though recall, which may have a strategic component, is impaired (Moscovitch, 1989; but see Delbecq-Derouesné, Beauvois, & Shallice, 1990). Many of these patients also confabulate (Berlyne, 1972; Moscovitch, 1989). Their confabulations, however, are rarely pure fabrications, but seem to consist of memories that unchecked ecphoric processes deliver to consciousness. Often they combine accurate memories without regard to their internal consistency or even plausibility. Though such patients sometimes recognize, and even recall, individuals and events, they place them in inappropriate contexts. Memory for temporal order is grossly impaired even when memory for the particular events is preserved. It is significant that when the hippocampal component is damaged but the frontal system is intact, memory for content is severely impaired, but what remains can be placed into context normally (Milner, Petrides, & Smith, 1985; Shimamura, Janowsky, & Squire, 1990).

In normal people, dissociations of content from context have been observed in experimental demonstrations of source amnesia (Schacter, Harbluk, & McLachlan, 1984), of independence between recognition and list differentiation (Jacoby, Woloshyn, & Kelley, 1989), and of independence between recognition based on familiarity and recognition based on strategic retrieval (Mandler, 1980; Gardiner & Java, 1989). The links to neural structures involved in strategic and associative/ecphoric aspects of memory are only now beginning to be made (Moscovitch, 1989; Schacter, 1987; Shimamura, Janowsky, & Squire, 1991).

Strategic Explicit Tests and the Frontal Lobes

The frontal lobes contribute to organizational aspects of memory at encoding and retrieval. It is not involved directly with consolidation and ecphoric processes, as is the hippocampal component. As prototypical central system structures, the frontal lobes are essential for organizing the input to the hippocampal system, evaluating its shallow output, placing it in its proper spatiotemporal context, and using the resulting information either to guide further mnemonic searches or to direct thought and plan future actions.

With the involvement of the frontal lobes, remembering is converted from an essentially reflexive process mediated by the hippocampal component to an intelligent, goal-directed activity. Frontal damage therefore does not lead to memory loss for the target if the cue is sufficient to specify it. Instead, deficits are noted on tests that are not cue-driven—tests in which additional strategic search processes are necessary for retrieving the target or for placing it in its spatiotemporal context. Thus, tests sensitive to frontal damage include judgments of recency (Milner, 1974) and temporal order (Moscovitch, 1989; Shimamura et al., 1990), conditional associative learning and self-ordered pointing (Petrides, 1985; Petrides & Milner, 1982), frequency estimation (Smith & Milner, 1988), memory for sources (Schacter, 1987; Janowsky, Shimamura, & Squire, 1989), and list differentiation (Moscovitch, 1982). Performance on delayed response and delayed alternation in both humans and monkeys (Goldman-Rakic, 1987; Freedman & Oscar-Berman, 1986a, 1986b) also depends on remembering spatiotemporal context from trial to trial, and consequently is impaired following frontal lesions. Even recognition and recall may suffer if organization at encoding (Incissa della Rochetta, 1986) or strategic search and monitoring at retrieval are prominent features of the task (Delbecq-Derouesné et al., 1990; Mayes, 1988; Moscovitch, 1989; see also Dywan & Jacoby, 1990, for controlled and automatic processes in recognition and list differentiation). Similar deficits are also noted in patients with Parkinson's or Huntington's disease (Brown & Marsden, 1990; Saint-Cyr et al., 1988; Vriezen & Moscovitch, 1990), and in "normal" elderly people, many of whom show symptoms of frontal dysfunction (for review, see Moscovitch & Winocur, 1992).

Because the frontal lobes, unlike the hippocampus, are central system structures, their operation is not domain-specific. Frontal impairments, when they occur, extend to a variety of domains. Deficits associated with frontal damage are not restricted therefore only to recently acquired, episodic memories. Remote memory and semantic memory seem to be affected as well (Moscovitch, 1989; Sagar, Cohen, Sullivan, Corkin, & Growdon, 1988; Shimamura et al., 1990). Even performance on implicit tests may be impaired, particularly those that may have a search component and those involved in learning and applying rules and procedures (Shallice, 1982; Saint-Cyr et al., 1988). Frontal memory deficits are often accompanied by deficits in strategic, organizational processes in other domains such as motor sequencing (Kolb & Milner, 1981; Luria, 1966) and problem solving and attention (Milner, 1964; Shallice, 1982, 1988; Stuss & Benson, 1986).

My colleagues and I have chosen the term *working-with memory* (Moscovitch & Winocur, 1992, in press; Moscovitch, 1992) to describe the memory functions of the frontal lobe. We prefer the more neutral, descriptive term over the theoretically loaded "working memory," a term that Baddeley (1986) and Goldman-Rakic (1987) favor. *Working-with memory* captures the essence of frontal contributions to memory, and carries no commitment to endorse everything that theories of "working memory" entail. It also avoids the confusion between different uses of the term "working memory" in the animal and human literature.

Cognitive Resources: Cortical Modules, the Frontal System, and the Hippocampal System

Because modules, including the hippocampal system, process information automatically, they are likely to require few cognitive resources for their operation. Interference with ecphoric retrieval processes by a concurrent task should be minimal. Interference with strategic processes by such a task at test, on the other hand, should be quite noticeable, since they are under voluntary control and are likely to draw on available cognitive resources (see Moscovitch & Umilta, 1990, 1991, on the interaction of central systems with a limited-capacity central processor). There is little evidence in the literature that addresses this issue directly. Of the few studies that reported concurrent-task interference effects on retrieval, almost all used tests that were sensitive to frontal damage or dysfunction: verbal fluency (Baddeley et al., 1984), recognition that requires list differentiation (Jacoby, Woloshyn, & Kelley, 1989; Dywan & Jacoby, 1990), and recall of categorized lists (Park, Smith, Dudley, & Lafronza, 1989).

To test the retrieval-interference hypothesis directly, I (Moscovitch, 1991) designed experiments that compared the effects of concurrent interference on memory tests sensitive to hippocampal damage with those on tests sensitive to frontal damage. The tests were administered either without interference, or with interference at study, at test, or on both occasions. The concurrent, secondary task was sequential finger tapping (index, ring, middle, small), which the subjects attempted to perform continuously and without error throughout the designated phase of the experiment. The prediction was that performance would suffer more on the frontal than on the hippocampal tests.

In the first experiment, subjects were administered the California Verbal Learning Test, which is a test of free recall and learning of a 16-item categorized list that consists of four items from each of four categories. In patients with frontal damage or dysfunction, recall is impaired on this list, because subjects fail to take full advantage of the organization inherent in the list. Clustering by category at recall is reduced. Concurrent interference at study and test, but at neither alone, reduced overall recall and clustering (see Figure 1.2), but had little effect on learning—a pattern consistent with frontal, but not hippocampal, dysfunction.

In another set of experiments, we examined the effects of interference on release from proactive inhibition (PI) (Craik & Birtwistle, 1971; Wickens, 1970). The locus of the release effect has been shown to occur at retrieval (Gardiner, Craik, & Birtwistle, 1972) in normal people. Consistent with this is the observation that release is often reduced in patients with frontal damage or dysfunction, though overall recall during the buildup of PI is normal (Moscovitch, 1982; Squire, 1982; Winocur, Kinsbourne, & Moscovitch, 1981; Moscovitch & Winocur, 1983; but see Freedman & Cermak, 1986;

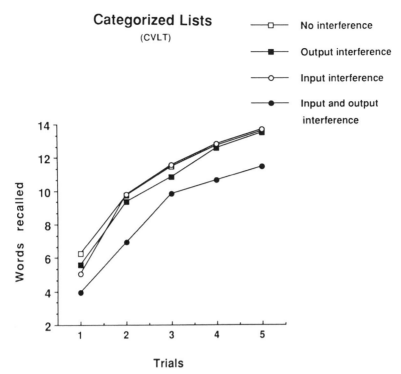

FIGURE 1.2. Recall of categorized lists: Average number of words recalled by college students in various concurrent interference conditions.

Janowsky, Shimamura, Kritchevsky, & Squire, 1989). The reverse is found after lesions of the hippocampal component (Moscovitch, 1982). As predicted, concurrent interference at both study and test, but at neither alone, reduced release from PI but had little effect on overall recall on the prerelease trials.

Because the frontal lobe's functions are not restricted to memory, concurrent interference should also affect performance on frontal tests in other domains. We found that sequential finger tapping led to a reduction of about 25% on a letter fluency task, which is sensitive to left frontal damage (Milner, 1964; Benton, 1968), but to less than a 5% reduction on category fluency, which is more sensitive to left temporal damage (Newcombe, 1969) (see Figure 1.3).

Although the results are not conclusive, since alternative interpretations are possible, the experiments on concurrent interference support the hypothesis that strategic mnemonic processes mediated by the frontal lobes are resource-demanding, whereas associative, hippocampal processes are relatively effortless. These findings are also consistant with the view that frontal lobes are central system structures and the hippocampus is modular.[2]

---

[2]Performance on item-specific implicit tests should be resistant to interference even at study. The evidence indicates this to be so (see "Associative/Ecphoric Tests and the Hippocampal Component," above). Performance on procedural implicit tests, insofar as they involve the frontal lobes, may also be susceptible to interference, but no relevant data are available on this topic.

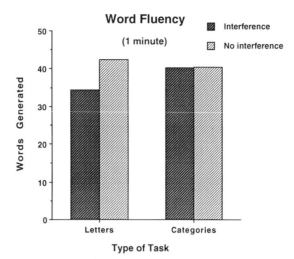

FIGURE 1.3. Average number of words generated in 1 minute in a letter (phonemic) and category fluency task with, and without, a concurrent interfering task.

ACKNOWLEDGMENTS

The research reported in this chapter was supported by the Medical Research Council of Canada. I thank Marlene Behrmann, Endel Tulving, Anne Triesman, Carlo Umilta, and Gordon Winocur for their helpful comments. I am also indebted to Nelson Butters, Fergus I. M. Craik, Larry L. Jacoby, Brenda Milner, Mortimer Mishkin, Daniel L. Schacter, Arthur P. Shimamura, and Larry R. Squire. Readers can easily recognize the influence of their work on my own.

REFERENCES

Baddeley, A. D. (1986). Working memory. Oxford: Oxford University Press.

Baddeley, A. D., Lewis, V., Eldridge, M., & Thomson, N. (1984). Attention and retrieval from long-term memory. *Journal of Experimental Psychology: General, 113,* 518–540.

Bartram, D. (1974). The role of visual and semantic codes in object naming. *Cognitive Psychology, 10,* 325–356.

Bauer, R. M. (1984). Autonomic recognition of names and faces in prosopagnosia: A neuropsychological application of the guilty knowledge test. *Neuropsychologia, 22,* 457–469.

Bentin, S., & Moscovitch, M. (1988). The time course of repetition effects for words and unfamiliar faces. *Journal of Experimental Psychology: General, 117,* 148–160.

Benton, A. L. (1968). Differential effects of frontal lobe disease. *Neuropsychologia, 6,* 53–60.

Berlyne, N. (1972). Confabulation: *British Journal of Psychiatry, 120,* 31–39.

Blaxton, T. A. (1989). Investigating dissociations among memory measures: Support for a transfer appropriate processing framework. *Journal of Experimental Psychology: Learning, Memory, and Cognition, 15,* 657–668.

Blaxton, T. A. (in press). Dissociations among memory measures in memory-impaired subjects: Evidence for a processing account of memory. *Memory and Cognition.*

Bondi, M. W., & Kaszniak, A. W. (1991). Implicit and explicit memory in Alzheimer's disease and Parkinson's disease. *Journal of Clinical and Experimental Neuropsychology, 13,* 339–358.

Brown, R. G., & Marsden, C. D. (1990). Cognitive function in Parkinson's disease: From description to theory. *Trends in Neurosciences, 13,* 21–29.

Bruce, V., & Young, A. (1986). Understanding face recognition. *British Journal of Psychology, 77,* 305–327.

Butters, N., Heindel, W. C., & Salmon, D. P. (1990). Dissociation of implicit memory in dementia: Neurological implications. *Bulletin of the Psychonomic Society, 28,* 359–366.

Butters, N., Wolfe, J., Martone, M., Granholme, E., & Cermak, L. (1985). Memory disorders associated with Huntington's Disease: Verbal recall, verbal recognition and procedural memory. *Neuropsychologia, 23,* 729-743.

Carr, T. H., Brown, J. S., & Charalambous, A. (1989). Repetition and reading: Perceptual encoding mechanisms are very abstract but not very interactive. *Journal of Experimental Psychology: Learning, Memory, and Cognition, 15,* 763-779.

Cohen, N. J., & Squire, L. R. (1980). Preserved learning and retention of pattern-analyzing skill in amnesia: Dissociation of "knowing how" and "knowing that." *Science, 210,* 207-209.

Cooper, L. A., Schacter, D. L., Ballesteros, S., & Moore, C. (1992). Priming and recognition of transformed three-dimensional objects: Effects of size and reflection. *Journal of Experimental Psychology: Learning, Memory, and Cognition, 18,* 43-57.

Corkin, S. (1968). Acquisition of motor skill after bilateral medial temporal-lobe excision. *Neuropsychologia, 6,* 255-266.

Craik, F. I. M., & Birtwistle, J. (1971). Proactive inhibition in free recall. *Journal of Experimental Psychology, 91,* 120-123.

Craik, F. I. M., & Byrd, M. (1982). Aging and cognitive deficits: The role of attentional resources. In F. I. M. Craik & S. Trehub (Eds.), *Aging and cognitive processes.* New York: Plenum Press.

DeHaan, E. H. F., Young, A., & Newcombe, F. (1987). Face recognition without awareness. *Cognitive Neuropsychology, 4,* 385-415.

Delbecq-Derouesné, J., Beauvois, M. F., & Shallice, T. (1990). Preserved recall versus impaired recognition: A case study. *Brain, 113,* 1045-1074.

DeRenzi, E., Liotti, M., & Nichelli, P. (1987). Semantic amnesia with perseveration of autobiographic memory: A case report. *Cortex, 23,* 575-597.

Dywan, J., & Jacoby, L. L. (1990). Effects of aging on source monitoring: Differences in susceptibility to false fame. *Psychology and Aging, 5,* 379-387.

Eich, E. (1984). Memory for unattended events: Remembering with and without awareness. *Memory and Cognition, 12,* 105-111.

Ellis, A. W., Young, A. W., & Flude, B. M. (1990). Repetition priming and face processing: Priming occurs within a system that responds to the identity of a face. *Quarterly Journal of Experimental Psychology, 42A,* 495-512.

Ellis, A. W., Young, A. W., Flude, B. M., & Hay, D. C. (1987). Repetition priming of face recognition. *Quarterly Journal of Experimental Psychology, 39A,* 193-210.

Fodor, J. A. (1983). *The modularity of mind.* Cambridge, MA: MIT Press.

Fodor, J. A. (1985). Multiple review of *The modularity of mind. Behavioral and Brain Sciences, 8,* 1-42.

Forster, K., Booker, J., Schacter, D. L., & Davis, C. (1990). Masked repetition priming: Lexical activation or novel memory trace. *Bulletin of the Psychonomic Society, 28,* 341-345.

Forster, K. I., & Davis, C. (1984). Repetition priming and frequency attenuation in lexical access. *Journal of Experimental Psychology, 10,* 680-698.

Freedman, M., & Cermak, L. S. (1986). Semantic encoding deficits in frontal lobe disease and amnesia. *Brain and Cognition, 5,* 108-114.

Freedman, M., & Oscar-Berman, M. (1986a). Selective delayed response deficits in Parkinson's and Alzheimer's disease. *Archives of Neurology, 43,* 886-890.

Freedman, M., & Oscar-Berman, M. (1986b). Bilateral frontal lobe disease and selective delayed response deficits in humans. *Behavioral Neuroscience, 100,* 337-342.

Gardiner, J. M., Craik, F. I. M., & Birtwistle, J. (1972). Retrieval cues and release from proactive inhibition. *Journal of Verbal Learning and Verbal Behavior, 11,* 778-783.

Gardiner, J., & Java, R. I. (1989). Measuring conscious awareness in recognition memory. *Bulletin of the Psychonomic Society, 27*(6), 509.

Gardner, H., Boller, F., Moreines, J., & Butters, N. (1975). Retrieving information from Korsakoff patients: Effects of categorical cues and reference to the task. *Cortex, 9,* 165-175.

Goldman-Rakic, P. S. (1987). Circuitry of primate prefrontal cortex and regulation of behavior by representational memory. In F. Plum (Ed.), *Handbook of physiology: Section 1. The nervous system. Vol. 5. Higher functions of the brain* (pp. 373-417). Bethesda, MD: American Physiological Society.

Graf, P., & Schacter, D. L. (1985). Implicit and explicit memory for new associations in normal and amnesic subjects. *Journal of Experimental Psychology: Learning, Memory, and Cognition, 11,* 501-518.

Greve, K. W., & Bauer, R. M. (1990). Implicit learning of new faces in prosopagnosia: An application of the mere-exposure paradigm. *Neuropsychologia, 28,* 1035-1042.

Hayman, C. A. G., & Tulving, E. (1989). Is priming in fragment completion based on a "traceless" memory system? *Journal of Experimental Psychology: Learning, Memory, and Cognition, 15,* 941-956.

Heindel, W. C., Salmon, D. P., & Butters, N. (1991). The biasing of weight judgements in Alzheimer's and Huntington's disease: A priming or programming phenomenon? *Journal of Clinical and Experimental Neuropsychology, 13,* 189-203.

Heindel, W. C., Salmon, D. P., Shults, C. W., Walicke, P. A., & Butters, N. (1989). Neuropsychological evidence for multiple implicit memory systems: A comparison of Alzheimer's, Huntington's, and Parkinson's disease patients. *Journal of Neuroscience, 9,* 582-587.

Huberman, M., Freedman, M., & Moscovitch, M. (1988). *Performance on implicit and explicit tests of memory in patients with Parkinson's and Alzheimer's disease.* Paper presented at the International Society for the Study of Parkinson's Disease, Jerusalem.

Hyman, B. T., Van Hoesen, G. W., & Damasio, A. R. (1990). Memory-related neural systems in Alzheimer's disease: An anatomic study. *Neurology, 40,* 1721-1730.

Incissa della Rochetta, A. (1986). Classification and recall of pictures after unilateral frontal or temporal lobectomy. *Cortex, 22,* 189-211.

Jacoby, L. L. (1983). Remembering the data: Analyzing interactive processes in reading. *Journal of Verbal Learning and Verbal Behavior, 22,* 485-508.

Jacoby, L. L. (1991). A process dissociation framework: Separating automatic from intentional uses of memory. *Journal of Memory and Language, 30,* 513-541.

Jacoby, L. L., Baker, J. G., & Brooks, L. R. (1989). Episodic effects on picture identification: Implications for theories of concept learning and theories of memory. *Journal of Experimental Psychology: Learning, Memory, and Cognition, 15,* 275-281.

Jacoby, L. L., Woloshyn, V., & Kelley, C. M. (1989). Becoming famous without being recognized: Unconscious influences of memory produced by dividing attention. *Journal of Experimental Psychology: General, 118,* 115-125.

Janowsky, J. S., Shimamura, A. P., Kritchevsky, M., & Squire, L. R. (1989). Cognitive impairment following frontal lobe damage and its relevance to human amnesia. *Behavioral Neuroscience, 103,* 548-560.

Janowsky, J. S., Shimamura, A. P., & Squire, L. R. (1989). Source memory impairment in patients with frontal lobe lesions. *Neuropsychologia, 27,* 1043-1056.

Jolicoeur, P. (1985). The time to name disoriented natural objects. *Memory and Cognition, 13,* 289-303.

Jolicoeur, P., & Milliken, B. (1989). Identification of disoriented objects: Effects of context of prior presentation. *Journal of Experimental Psychology: Learning, Memory, and Cognition, 15,* 200-210.

Keane, M. M., Gabrieli, J. D., Fennema, A. C., Growdon, J. H., & Corkin, S. (1991). Evidence for a dissociation between perceptual and conceptual priming in Alzheimer's disease. *Behavioral Neuroscience, 105,* 326-342.

Kihlstrom, J. F., Schacter, D. L., Cork, R. C., Hurt, C. A., & Behr, S. E. (1990). Implicit memory following surgical anaesthesia. *Psychological Science, 1,* 303-306.

Kirsner, K., & Dunn, D. (1985). The perceptual record: A common factor in repetition priming and attribute retention. In M. I. Posner & O. S. M. Marin (Eds.), *Attention and performance XI* (pp. 547-566). Hillsdale, NJ: Erlbaum.

Kolb, B., & Milner, B. (1981). Performance of complex arm and facial movements after focal brain lesions. *Neuropsychologia, 19,* 491-504.

Luria, A. R. (1966). *Higher cortical functions in man.* New York: Basic Books.

Mandler, G. (1980). Recognition: The judgment of previous occurrence. *Psychological Review, 87,* 252-271.

Martone, M., Butters, N., Payne, M., Becker, J., & Sax, D. S. (1984). Dissociations between skill learning and verbal recognition in amnesia and dementia. *Archives of Neurology, 41,* 965-970.

Mayes, A. R. (1988). *Human organic memory disorders.* Cambridge, England: Cambridge University Press.

McAndrews, M. P., Glisky, E. L., & Schacter, D. L. (1987). When priming persists: Long-lasting implicit memory for a single episode in amnesic patients. *Neuropsychologia, 25,* 497-506.

McAndrews, M. P., & Moscovitch, M. (1990). Transfer effects in implicit tests of memory. *Journal of Experimental Psychology: Learning, Memory, and Cognition, 16,* 772-788.

McNeil, J. E., & Warrington, E. K. (1991). Prosopagnosia: A reclassification. *Quarterly Journal of Experimental Psychology, 43A,* 267-287.

Merikle, P. M., & Reingold, E. M. (1991). Comparing direct (explicit) and indirect (implicit) measures to study unconscious memory. *Journal of Experimental Psychology: Learning, Memory, and Cognition, 17,* 224-233.

Milner, B. (1964). Some effects of frontal lobectomy in man. In J. M. Warren & K. Akert (Eds.), *The frontal granular cortex and behavior* (pp. 313-331). New York: McGraw-Hill.

Milner, B. (1966). Amnesia following operation on the temporal lobe. In C. W. M. Whitty & O. L. Zangwill (Eds.) *Amnesia.* London: Butterworths.

Milner, B. (1974). Hemispheric specialization: Scope and limits. In F. O. Schmitt & F. G. Worden (Eds.), *The neurosciences: Third research program*. Cambridge, MA: MIT Press.

Milner, B., Corkin, S., & Teuber, H.-L. (1968). Further analysis of the hippocampal amnesic syndrome. *Neuropsychologia, 6*, 267–282.

Milner, B., Petrides, M., & Smith, M. L. (1985). Frontal lobes and the temporal organization of memory. *Human Neurobiology, 4*, 137–142.

Moscovitch, M. (1982). Multiple dissociations of function in amnesia. In L. S. Cermak (Ed.), *Human memory and amnesia*. Hillsdale, NJ: Erlbaum.

Moscovitch, M. (1984). The sufficient conditions for demonstrating preserved memory in amnesia: A task analysis. In L. R. Squire & N. Butters (Eds.), *Neuropsychology of memory* (1st ed., pp. 104–114). New York: Guilford Press.

Moscovitch, M. (1985). Memory from infancy to old age: Implications for theories of normal and pathological memory. *Annals of the New York Academy of Sciences, 444*, 78–96.

Moscovitch, M. (1989). Confabulation and the frontal system: Strategic vs. associative retrieval in neuropsychological theories of memory. In H. L. Roediger III & F. I. M. Craik (Eds.), *Varieties of memory and consciousness: Essays in honor of Endel Tulving* (pp. 133–156). Hillsdale, NJ: Erlbaum.

Moscovitch, M. (1991). Cognitive resources and retrieval interference effects in normal people: The role of the frontal lobes and hippocampus. *Bulletin of the Psychonomic Society, 29*, 485. (Abstract)

Moscovitch, M. (1992). Memory and working-with-memory: A component process model based on modules and central systems. *Journal of Cognitive Neuroscience, 4*.

Moscovitch, M., & Umilta, C. (1990). Modularity and neuropsychology: Modular and central processes in attention and memory. In M. F. Schwartz (Ed.), *Modular deficits in Alzheimer type dementia* (pp. 1–59). Cambridge, MA: MIT Press/Bradford Books.

Moscovitch, M., & Umilta, C. (1991). Conscious and nonconscious aspects of memory: A neuropsychological framework of modules and central systems. In R. G. Lister & H. J. Weingartner (Eds.), *Perspectives on cognitive neuroscience*. Oxford: Oxford University Press.

Moscovitch, M., & Winocur, G. (1983). Contextual cues and release from proactive inhibition in old and young people. *Canadian Journal of Psychology, 37*, 331–344.

Moscovitch, M., & Winocur, G. (1992). The neuropsychology of memory and aging. In T. A. Salthouse & F. I. M. Craik (Eds.), *The handbook of aging and cognition*. Hillsdale, NJ: Erlbaum.

Moscovitch, M., & Winocur, G. (in press). Frontal lobes and memory. In L. R. Squire (Ed.), D. L. Schacter (Section Ed.), *The encyclopedia of learning and memory: Neuropsychology*. New York: Macmillan.

Moscovitch, M., Winocur, G., & McLachlan, D. (1986). Memory as assessed by recognition and reading time in normal and memory impaired people with Alzheimer's disease and other neurological disorders. *Journal of Experimental Psychology: General, 115*, 331–347.

Musen, G., & Treisman, A. (1990). Implicit and explicit memory for visual patterns. *Journal of Experimental Psychology: Learning, Memory, and Cognition, 16*, 127–137.

Neary, D., Snowden, J. S., Northern, B., & Goulding, P. (1988). Dementia of frontal lobe type. *Journal of Neurology, Neurosurgery and Psychiatry, 51*, 353–361.

Newcombe, F. (1969). *Missile wounds of the brain*. London: Oxford University Press.

Park, D. C., Smith, D. A., Dudley, W. N., & Lafronza, V. N. (1989). Effects of age and a divided attention task presented during encoding and retrieval on memory. *Journal of Experimental Psychology: Learning, Memory, and Cognition, 15*, 1185–1191.

Parkin, A. J., Reid, T., & Russo, R. (1990). On the differential nature of implicit and explicit memory. *Memory and Cognition, 18*, 307–314.

Petrides, M. (1985). Deficits on conditional associative-learning tasks after frontal and temporal-lobe lesions in man. *Neuropsychologia, 23*, 601–614.

Petrides, M., & Milner, B. (1982). Deficits on subject-ordered tasks after frontal- and temporal-lobe lesions in man. *Neuropsychologia, 20*, 249–262.

Richardson-Klavehn, A., & Bjork, R. A. (1988). Measures of memory. *Annual Review of Psychology, 39*, 475–543.

Riddoch, M. J., & Humphreys, G. W. (1987). Visual object processing in optic aphasia: A case of semantic access agnosia. *Cognitive Neuropsychology, 4*, 131–186.

Roediger, H. L., III. (1990). Implicit memory: Retention without remembering. *American Psychologist, 45*, 1043–1056.

Roediger, H. L., III, & Craik, F. I. M. (Eds.). (1989). *Varieties of memory and consciousness: Essays in honor of Endel Tulving*. Hillsdale, NJ: Erlbaum.

Saffran, E. M., & Marin, O. S. M. (1977). Reading without phonology: Evidence from aphasia. *Quarterly Journal of Experimental Psychology, 29*, 515–525.

Sagar, J. J., Cohen, N. J., Sullivan, E. V., Corkin, S., & Growdon, J. H. (1988). Remote memory in Alzheimer's disease and Parkinson's disease. *Brain, 111,* 185-206.

Saint-Cyr, J. A., Taylor, A., & Lang, A. (1988). Procedural learning and neostriatal dysfunction in man. *Brain, 111,* 941-959.

Scarborough, D. L., Cortese, C., & Scarborough, H. S. (1977). Frequency and repetition effects in lexical memory. *Journal of Experimental Psychology: Human Perception and Performance, 3,* 1-17.

Schacter, D. L. (1987). Memory, amnesia, and frontal lobe dysfunction. *Psychobiology, 15,* 21-36.

Schacter, D. L. (1989). On the relation between memory and conciousness: Dissociable interactions and conscious experience. In H. L. Roediger III & F. I. M. Craik (Eds.), *Varieties of memory and consciousness: Essays in honor of Endel Tulving.* Hillsdale, NJ: Erlbaum.

Schacter, D. L. (1990). Perceptual representational systems and implicit memory: Toward a resolution of the multiple memory systems debate. *Annals of the New York Academy of Sciences, 608,* 543-571.

Schacter, D. L., Cooper, L. A., Delaney, S. M., Peterson, M. A., & Tharan, M. (1990). Implicit memory for possible and impossible objects: Constraints on the construction of structural descriptions. *Journal of Experimental Psychology: Learning, Memory, and Cognition, 17,* 3-19.

Schacter, D. L., Eich, J. E., & Tulving, E. (1978). Richard Semon's theory of memory. *Journal of Verbal Learning and Verbal Behavior, 17,* 721-743.

Schacter, D. L., Harbluk, J. L., & McLachlan, D. R. (1984). Retrieval without recollection: An experimental analysis of source amnesia. *Journal of Verbal Learning and Verbal Behavior, 23,* 593-611.

Schacter, D. L., McAndrews, M. P., & Moscovitch, M. (1988). Access to consciousness: Dissociations between implicit and explicit knowledge in neuropsychological syndromes. In L. Weiskrantz (Ed.), *Thought without language* (pp. 242-278). Oxford: Oxford University Press.

Schwartz, B. L. (1989). Effects of generation on indirect measures of memory. *Journal of Experimental Psychology: Learning, Memory, and Cognition, 15,* 1119-1128.

Schwartz, M. F., Saffran, E. M., & Marin, O. S. M. (1980). Fractionating the reading process in dementia: Evidence for word-specific print-to-sound associations. In M. Coltheart, K. E. Patterson, & J. C. Marschall (Eds.), *Deep dyslexia.* London: Routledge & Kegan Paul.

Shallice, T. (1982). Specific impairments of planning. *Philosophical Transactions of the Royal Society of London, B298,* 199-209.

Shallice, T. (1988). *From neuropsychology to mental structure.* Cambridge, England: Cambridge University Press.

Shimamura, A. P. (1986). Priming effects in amnesia: Evidence for a dissociable memory system. *Quarterly Journal of Experimental Psychology, 38A,* 619-644.

Shimamura, A. P., Janowsky, J. S., & Squire, L. R. (1990). Memory for temporal order in patients with frontal lobe lesions and patients with amnesia. *Neuropsychologia, 28,* 803-813.

Shimamura, A. P., Janowsky, J. S., & Squire, L. R. (1991). What is the role of frontal lobe damage in memory disorders? In H. S. Levin, H. M. Eisenberg, & A. L. Benton (Eds.), *Frontal lobe function and dysfunction.* Oxford: Oxford University Press.

Smith, M. L., & Milner, B. (1988). Estimation of frequency of occurrence of abstract designs after frontal or temporal lobectomy. *Neuropsychologia, 26,* 297-306.

Squire, L. R. (1982). Comparisons between forms of amnesia: Some deficits are unique to Korsakoff's syndrome. *Journal of Experimental Psychology: Learning, Memory, and Cognition, 8,* 560-571.

Squire, L. R. (1987). *Memory and brain.* New York: Oxford University Press.

Stuss, D. T., & Benson, D. F. (1986). *The frontal lobes.* New York: Raven Press.

Tranel, E., & Damasio, A. R. (1985). Knowledge without awareness: An autonomic index of facial recognition by prosopagnosics. *Science, 228,* 1453-1454.

Tulving, E. (1983). *Elements of episodic memory.* Oxford: Clarendon Press.

Tulving, E., & Schacter, D. L. (1990). Priming and human memory systems. *Science, 247,* 301-306.

Vriezen, E., & Moscovitch, M. (1990). Temporal ordering and conditional associative learning in Parkinson's disease. *Neuropsychologia, 28,* 1283-1294.

Warren, C., & Morton, J. (1982). The effects of priming on picture recognition. *British Journal of Psychology, 73,* 117-129.

Warrington, E. K., & Taylor, A. M. (1978). Two categorical stages of object recognition. *Perception, 7,* 695-705.

Wickens, D. D. (1970). Encoding strategies of words: An empirical approach to meaning. *Psychological Review, 22,* 1-15.

Winocur, G., Kinsbourne, M., & Moscovitch, M. (1981). The effect of cueing on release form proactive interference in Korsakoff amnesic patients. *Journal of Experimental Psychology: Human Learning and Memory, 7,* 56-65.

2

What Are the Functional Deficits
That Underlie Amnesia?

ANDREW R. MAYES

Introduction

A major aim of research into organic amnesia is to identify what psychological processes are disrupted. A second major aim is to identify the brain structures, damage to
which causes these disruptions. Achievement of these aims will be facilitated by
developing hypotheses about what psychological processes are disrupted—hypotheses
that make clear predictions about the pattern of cognitive and mnemonic performance
that amnesics should show. In the near future, it should become possible to test and
refine these hypotheses, using neural network models that honor the architecture and
physiology of the brain structures in question. To the extent that these major aims are
met, we should gain an understanding of how the brain mediates recall and recognition
of experienced facts and events.

Although much has been learned in the past decade about the pattern of cognitive and mnemonic performance shown by amnesics, it is far less clear that this new
information distinguishes between different theoretical accounts of the functional
deficits underlying the condition. In my view, amnesia research needs to be more
theory-driven. This will require that relevant hypotheses be more fully articulated and
that tests of their predictions be carried out in a more considered manner. This chapter
represents an initial move in the desired direction.

The Main Hypotheses about the Functional Deficits Underlying Amnesia

Currently, three main groups of hypotheses about amnesia are influential. Perhaps the
most dominant of these is the view that amnesics have some kind of storage or
consolidation deficit for all those kinds of information for which their recall and
recognition is impaired (see, e.g., Squire, Shimamura, & Amaral, 1989; Zola-Morgan &
Squire, 1990). According to this hypothesis, amnesics' deficit in recognizing and recalling experienced facts and episodes arises because memories about facts and episodes
are not properly stored in patients. A diametrically opposed disconnectionist view has

been advanced by Schacter (1990), who has suggested that amnesics may store information about facts and episodes normally, but are unable to achieve aware memory (i.e., recognition and recall) of this information. This inability could arise because the intact memory system for facts and events is disconnected from a general-purpose "conscious awareness system" or from a system that generates aware memory, or because this memory awareness system is damaged. The third group of hypotheses may be regarded as intermediate between the other two. They propose that amnesics have a primary and severe deficit in aware memory for contextual information, and that this causes a secondary and less severe deficit in aware memory for the facts and episodes that typically fall at the focus of attention during learning (target information) (see Mayes, Meudell, & Pickering, 1985; Mayes, 1988; Schacter, 1990). Variants of this group of context-memory deficit hypotheses (CMDHs) differ with respect to the kinds of contextual information for which amnesics are postulated to have a primary deficit in aware memory, and with respect to whether this deficit is caused by an encoding, storage, or retrieval failure. They all agree, however, in postulating that amnesics store target information normally.

There are two variants of the storage deficit hypothesis. According to the more popular variant, memories are initially stored in the structures damaged in amnesics (most notably the hippocampus) and later transferred to association neocortex (Zola-Morgan & Squire, 1990). In amnesics, initial storage cannot occur, at least not at normal levels, so later transfer will be diminished at least proportionately. Consistent with this view, Hyman, Van Hoesen, and Damasio (see Damasio, Tranel, & Damasio, 1989) have proposed that the profound retrograde amnesia apparent in the early stages of Alzheimer's disease is associated with the degeneration of association cortex storage sites, such as those of the anterior temporal lobe and insula. An alternative but less popular variant would be that the structures implicated in amnesia normally facilitate storage of memories, which only occurs in association neocortex (see Mayes, 1988). It is possible that the former variant is true of amnesia caused by temporal lobe lesions, whereas the latter is true of amnesia caused by medial diencephalic or basal forebrain lesions. What predictions about amnesia do these hypotheses make? First, they predict the preserved intelligence and short-term memory found in pure amnesia. Second, they predict the preservation of simple classical condtioning (Daum, Channon, & Canavan, 1989) and various forms of skill learning (see Shimamura, 1989) that have been reported in amnesics, because these forms of memory are believed to be processed and stored in brain systems that are intact in amnesics. The remaining predictions of the storage deficit hypotheses are, however, much less clear-cut.

The first of these unclear predictions concerns whether amnesic recall and recognition deficits should be equally severe for all information relevant to aware memory of facts and episodes. The assumption has generally been that impairments should be of equal severity, but it can be argued that disruption will be greater when information has to be stored at a faster rate (A. D. Baddeley, personal communication, 1990). If this argument is correct, then, assuming that memory tasks that require a faster rate of storage are more difficult (as seems likely), amnesics should be more impaired at memory tasks that are more difficult for this reason. It is uncertain, however, that the argument is correct. It might be validated by showing that damage to a realistic neural network model of the storage view produces greater disruption of a task that requires information to be stored at a faster rate. Until this is shown, it is probably safer to assume that the hypotheses predict equally severe deficits for all kinds of aware memory.

The second unclear prediction concerns what, if any, kinds of priming should be preserved in amnesics, where priming is regarded as a form of item-specific unaware memory, mediated by relatively automatic processes, and tapped best by indirect tests of memory. The problem arises because there is no generally accepted account of priming, which may well be a heterogeneous phenomenon. If the priming of previously familiar information depends on the continued activation of existing memories, then amnesics should show preserved priming of previously familiar information. If priming depends on automatically accessing episodic memories even for recently experienced familiar information, as Jacoby has suggested (see Jacoby & Kelley, 1991), then amnesics should not show priming of previously familiar information. This issue needs to be resolved. With respect to the priming of information that was previously novel, the issue is also not completely clear-cut. If such priming depends on creating memory representations that form the basis of aware memory for facts or episodes, then novel information priming should be impaired in amnesics. If, however, novel information priming depends on a kind of cortically based memory representation that is distinct from the kind that underlies aware memory, then such priming *may* be preserved in amnesics. The properties of two distinct memory representation systems for the *same* information should be very different, so, for example, one might expect memories in the two systems to decay at different rates. Most plausibly, novel information priming should fade more rapidly than aware memory.

The predictions of the storage deficit hypotheses of amnesia with respect to rate of forgetting have not been properly considered, although several studies have found forgetting rate to be pathologically fast in amnesics or Alzheimer patients (see, e.g., Welsh, Butters, Hughes, Mohs, & Heyman, 1991). If amnesia involves a failure to modulate cortical storage, then it seems probable that amnesics will forget pathologically fast, in addition to showing impaired aware memory following a brief distraction. This is because their ability to consolidate information into store will be deficient—an impairment that will become more apparent as consolidation proceeds. The time course of accelerated forgetting will depend on the time course of the affected consolidation processes, which is unknown. The prediction of the alternative variant of the storage deficit hypothesis, which postulates initial storage in the structures damaged in amnesics, is less clear. A deficit should be apparent immediately following distraction, which is presumably when structures like those in the medial temporal lobes that may be damaged in amnesics become essential for the mediation of aware memory. Whether this deficit should increase in the relatively short term depends on whether the hypothesis predicts that consolidation of memories into their initial storage sites will be impaired in amnesics. In addition, the hypothesis may predict that forgetting in amnesics may be accelerated over a much longer period (perhaps of weeks or months), because transfer of memories from their initial storage sites to their storage sites in association cortex may be reduced in efficiency. These two predictions are unclear, because this variant of the storage deficit hypothesis does not specify explicitly whether initial consolidation should be impaired and whether subsequent transfer of storage will also be less effective.

Traditionally, the storage deficit hypotheses of amnesia have been regarded as giving a fair account of the phenomena of anterograde amnesia, but as failing to account for retrograde amnesia that extends back for years or even for decades. This clearly applies to the view that amnesics do not modulate cortical storage properly, because it is not credible to argue that this process continues for years. The other variant predicts some degree of impairment in memories that have not been completely transferred to association cortex before relevant brain damage occurs. It could be argued that this process takes about 4 weeks, at least in monkeys, on the basis of Zola-Morgan and Squire's (1990) finding that amnesic monkeys with lesions that include the hippocampus and parahippocampal cortex show a retrograde amnesia of this duration (although this result needs replicating with a larger premorbid memory data set). This leaves unexplained retrograde amnesias that extend back for decades, such as those that have been reported in patients with both medial temporal lobe and medial diencephalic damage. These might be explained by postulating either additional damage to the longer-term storage sites in the association cortex or damage to structures involved in retrieval. If severe retrograde amnesia has a prolonged temporal gradient, as has been claimed (see Mayes, 1988, for a discussion), both of these alternatives run into difficulties. One possibility would be that complex memories undergo progressive reorganization and transfer (see Butters & Cermak, 1986; Cermak, 1984), first from the structures implicated in amnesia to anterior temporal association cortex (N. Kapur, personal communication, 1991), and then to distributed sites in association cortex.

How do the predictions of the storage deficit hypotheses differ from those made by the disconnectionist accounts of amnesia? Both groups of hypotheses predict preservation of intelligence, classical conditioning, and skill learning, but disconnectionist accounts can only predict the preservation of short-term memory and aware memory for remote, overrehearsed information by making additional ad hoc assumptions. This is because both kinds of memory are aware, so it is hard to see why disconnection from or destruction of an awareness system should not disrupt them. On similar grounds, disconnectionist accounts should predict equal severity of impairment of long-term aware memory of all kinds as a central feature of anterograde amnesia. Disconnectionist views also predict that amnesics will forget at a normal rate. They differ most clearly from storage accounts with respect to their predictions concerning priming. Disconnectionist accounts predict that priming of both previously novel and previously familiar information of all kinds should be preserved in amnesia. In fact, the only easy way that a disconnectionist account can explain preservation of a form of aware memory is by supposing that the form of memory in question is held in a distinct brain region that is *not* disconnected from the system that gives awareness to memories. As it is assumed that the memory representations underlying aware memory are unaffected in patients, disconnectionist accounts would also predict that some kinds of item-specific unaware memory will be preserved in amnesics at long delays of days or weeks, where it becomes plausible to argue that a common memory representation subserves both priming and aware memory.

The CMDHs have no difficulty predicting preservation of intelligence, short-term memory, classical conditioning, and skill learning in amnesics. This group of hypotheses can predict preservation of remote memories in retrograde amnesia by supposing that as memories age and are rehearsed, they become semanticized and thus free of context (see Cermak, 1984). This possibility needs to be elaborated and its assumptions properly tested. Even so, it is hard to see how it can explain both short and long temporal gradients of retrograde amnesia, so the CMDHs may be unable to explain all patterns of retrograde amnesia that can be observed. Predictions of the CMDHs about rate of forgetting in amnesia depend on which of the variant hypotheses is adopted. Only if it is assumed that patients do not store contextual information properly because of a failure to modulate its consolidation will it be predicted that amnesics should show abnormally fast forgetting. The degree to which forgetting will be pathologically accelerated might also be predicted to be greater for memories of contextual information than for recognition of information attended to during learning. Free recall of this information might also be expected to fade more rapidly, as is discussed in the next section. The central prediction of the hypothesis is that patients will be more impaired in aware memory for context than in recognition of target information. Depending on the CMDH variant adopted, the disproportionately severe deficit will include aspects of independent context (information about spatiotemporal location and manner of presentation of target material that does not affect its meaningful interpretation), such as temporal or spatial location; all kinds of independent context; interactive context (information typically falling on the periphery of attention that affects the meaningful interpretation of target material); or both independent and interactive context. A corollary prediction is that amnesics should be more impaired at target free recall than at target recognition, because the former is more dependent on context retrieval, as indicated by context-dependent forgetting effects (see Davies & Thomson, 1988). The CMDHs also predict that the extent of these disproportionate deficits should correlate with the severity of amnesia. Finally, the predictions of the CMDHs with respect to amnesic priming are not clear, largely because there is no agreed-upon theory of how priming works. If priming involves the automatic retrieval of contextual information, then CMDH variants postulating that context is not stored should predict that no kind of amnesic priming will be preserved. In contrast, variants postulating a failure of aware retrieval of context should predict, like disconnectionist views, that all kinds of priming will be preserved in amnesia. If, however, priming to target material does not require the retrieval of context, then amnesics should show preserved priming of previously novel target material as well as of previously familiar target information in all CMDH variants. Nevertheless, they should not be able to show normal priming of contextual information if the impairment in aware memory for context is caused by a storage failure.

Although the three groups of hypotheses about amnesia differ considerably from one another, it can be seen that their predictions do not distinguish among them as clearly as is desirable. The rest of this chapter looks more closely at the predictions concerning whether all forms of aware memory are equally impaired in amnesics, at predictions concerning priming, and at problems in assessing these predictions. But this is preceded by a brief discussion of the putative heterogeneity of amnesia and the problem of amnesic forgetting rates.

Functional Heterogeneity and Forgetting Rates in Amnesia

If more than one form of amnesia exists, or more than one functional deficit underlies all severe cases of amnesia, none of the individual theoretical accounts just considered will be sufficient to explain the disorder. The preceding section has suggested that there may be more than one functional deficit underlying retrograde amnesias of differing temporal duration. This is an attractive idea, but remains unproven. Future work should correlate measures of retrograde amnesia with MRI measures of structural brain damage (see, e.g., Press, Amaral, & Squire, 1989), as well as assessments of neural metabolism based on the use of challenge procedures with PET (see, e.g., Petersen, Fox, Posner, Mintun, & Raichle, 1988). Lower levels of activation in association cortex during remote memory retrieval in amnesics when compared with normal people would provide weak support for the idea that a retrieval deficit contributes to temporally extensive retrograde amnesia. If evidence is forthcoming that different brain lesions cause retrograde amnesias that vary in temporal extensiveness, it will be important to identify whether they also cause anterograde amnesias of different severity.

Some researchers have long argued that medial temporal lobe lesions cause a functionally different amnesia from medial diencephalic lesions (see Mayes, 1988). The majority of workers are skeptical of this distinction, partly because of the paucity of evidence and partly because there are a number of circuits involving the structures in the two regions, such that damage to either region would break the same circuits. However, the circuit that projects from entorhinal cortex to hippocampus and back is damaged only by medial temporal lobe lesions, so it is feasible that medial diencephalic lesions would not disrupt the functions of this circuit. The possibility requires investigation.

Most interest about functional differences between temporal lobe and medial diencephalic amnesia has focused on the issue of forgetting rates. It has been argued that only temporal lobe amnesics show pathologically accelerated forgetting rates (see Mayes, 1988). The procedure used for assessing amnesic forgetting rates was developed by Huppert and Piercy (1978); it involves matching recognition in amnesics and their controls at an initial delay (usually 10 minutes) and then testing at longer delays of up to a week or more. The matching procedure produces a bias against finding accelerated amnesic forgetting, which increases with severity of amnesia. This is because matching is achieved by giving amnesics longer exposures to items during learning, so their mean item-presentation-to-test delay is longer than that of their controls. The result is that controls' forgetting rate is exaggerated relative to that of the amnesics (see Mayes, 1986). In addition, the procedure typically does not match at delays shorter than 10 minutes, so forgetting immediately after learning is not assessed. Interestingly, when matching was achieved at a shorter delay, faster forgetting was reported in Alzheimer's disease patients, who would have had medial temporal lobe damage (Hart, Kwentus, Harkins, & Taylor, 1988). This finding needs replicating, using the modification of the matching procedure proposed (Mayes, 1986) to avoid the bias discussed above. It also needs to be determined whether amnesics with medial diencephalic lesions show a similarly accelerated forgetting rate when this procedure is used. Nevertheless, when patients and controls are tested under identical conditions so that the problems of the matching procedure are obviated, there is evidence that

Alzheimer patients (with medial temporal lobe damage) show faster loss of free-recall ability at delays beyond 15 seconds than either Korsakoff patients, who have medial diencephalic damage (Moss, Albert, Butters, & Payne, 1986), or normal subjects (Welsh et al., 1991). This accords with the clinical impression that rapid loss of the ability to freely recall recently experienced things is the earliest sign of Alzheimer's disease in elderly individuals.

A colleague has recently used the matching procedure with story free recall and recognition in a mixed group of mild amnesics (Isaac, 1991). Matching was achieved after a filled delay of 15 seconds, and memory was tested with delays of up to 10 minutes for free recall and 1 hour for recognition. The patients did not show accelerated forgetting with recognition. It must be remembered, however, that the patients were only mildly amnesic, so Isaac's study does not exclude the possibility that more severely amnesic patients will show accelerated loss of recognition memory over delays between 15 seconds and 1 hour. In contrast, all the patients showed much faster loss of free recall than did any of the controls. There was no strong evidence in her study that patients with medial temporal lobe damage forgot faster than patients with medial diencephalic lesions (but, as indicated above, this may have been because the patients tested were only mildly amnesic). Isaac's finding that amnesics show a greater pathological acceleration of free recall than of recognition is consistent with a storage variant of the CMDHs. If free recall depends more than recognition on the retrieval of contextual information (as context- and state-dependent forgetting effects suggest), and amnesics fail to modulate the consolidation of contextual information, then exactly this would be predicted. Interestingly, Smith and Milner (1989) have reported that patients with right hippocampal damage show normal initial spatial memory, but an impairment after a delay. Isaac has also used her procedure to assess proactive and retroactive interference in amnesics, and has found no evidence that patients are more susceptible to interference when their levels of memory match those of controls, although they do make more intrusion errors. This finding has implications for interference theory as well as amnesia. For example, it may mean that much interference is not caused by the confusion of the contexts of different memories.

In summary, there is not yet compelling evidence that temporal lobe amnesics but not diencephalic amnesics show accelerated forgetting. The matching procedure (Mayes, 1986) needs to be used with matches at shorter delays, to determine whether there are circumstances when recognition as well as recall shows accelerated forgetting in patients.

Impairments of Aware Memory

Attempts to compare degree of impairment in amnesics for different kinds of aware memory use a procedure in which amnesics are tested under easier conditions than their controls, in order to get a match on at least one of the memory tasks. This procedure is followed because otherwise floor and ceiling effects would probably occur; even if these were avoided, scaling effects could be operating, because patients and controls would be scoring at very different levels. As will be discussed, however, there are problems with the matching procedure as well.

Matching amnesic and control target recognition or words by giving amnesics longer learning exposures or testing them at shorter delays, Hirst and colleagues (Hirst et al., 1986; Hirst, Johnson, Phelps, & Volpe, 1988) found that under the same conditions, patients performed worse on target free recall. They inferred that amnesics are more impaired on target free recall than on recognition. We (Shoqeirat & Mayes, 1991) found a similar result with object free recall and recognition, but there was a correlation between the extent of patients' disproportionate impairment on free recall and their performance on tests sensitive to frontal lobe lesions. This suggests that the disproportionate amnesic free-recall deficit may have been caused by incidental frontal lobe damage. In a further series of experiments, MacAndrews (1989) failed to replicate the findings of Hirst and his colleagues. Her procedure differed from that of Hirst and his colleagues in that her amnesics were tested at shorter delays. This is interesting, because the results of Isaac mentioned above suggest that amnesics will only be more impaired on target free recall than on recognition after a delay of several minutes.

Investigators using the matching procedure have reported greater deficits in aware memory both for temporal order information involving list discrimination (Squire, 1982; Kopelman, 1989) and for source of target information (Schacter, Harbluk, & McLachlan, 1984; Shimamura & Squire, 1987). There is, however, strong reason for supposing that the disproportionate source memory deficit is caused by incidental frontal lobe damage occurring in some amnesics (Janowsky, Shimamura, & Squire, 1989), although the situation with temporal order memory is more controversial. In unpublished work (Mayes, Meudell, MacDonald, & Pickering, 1990) my colleagues and I have found a disproportionate temporal order memory deficit in a mixed group of amnesics, but like Kopelman (1989) and unlike Squire (1982), we have found no association between this deficit and signs of frontal lobe damage. Shimamura, Janowsky, and Squire (1990) have reported that Korsakoff patients are more impaired than patients with hippocampal lesions at a different kind of temporal ordering memory task, but they are matched on item recognition. Patients with selective frontal lobe lesions were also impaired at the temporal ordering task, despite showing normal item recognition; however, like the Korsakoff patients and unlike the non-Korsakoff amnesics, they were impaired on the Initiation and Perseveration Index of the Dementia Rating Scale. It could be that any patient who shows similar signs of dementia (which may typically be caused by frontal lobe lesions) will be impaired at this temporal order memory task, because it requires the planned, active ordering of 15 items. The issues are complex because different temporal memory tasks tap different processes, some of which may be sensitive to "nonamnesic" lesions.

In other work using the matching procedure, we (Pickering, Mayes, & Fairbairn, 1989) have found that Korsakoff patients appear to be more impaired at cued recall of the modality of presentation of targets than at target recognition, and that the deficit was associated more strongly with severity of amnesia than signs of frontal lobe damage. We have since replicated this finding with a larger, mixed group of amnesics. In several studies, we have found that aware memory for spatial location in amnesics seems to be more impaired than their aware memory for targets (usually tested by recognition), and that the deficit is more closely associated with severity of amnesia than with signs of frontal lobe damage (Pickering, 1987; Mayes, Meudell, & Mac-

Donald, 1991; Shoqeirat & Mayes, 1991). Cave and Squire (1991) have reported, however, that Korsakoff patients and amnesics with medial temporal lobe damage seem equally impaired at two forms of spatial memory and both recall and recognition of targets in a matching paradigm, so the truth remains uncertain. Finally, in further work (Mayes, MacDonald, Donlan, Pears, & Meudell, in press), we have found that amnesics seemed to be more impaired at recognition of interactive context than at recognition of target material. However, although this disproportionate deficit was not associated with signs of frontal lobe damage, it was not clear that it was essential to amnesia.

At first blush, the results above seem most consistent with some version of the CMDHs. There are, however, problems of interpretation. First, context memory was sometimes tested by cued recall, whereas target memory was usually tested by recognition. If cued, like free, recall is more impaired than recognition in amnesics, then the apparent disproportionate deficits in context memory would be trivial consequences of this fact. Nevertheless, there is some evidence that cued recall is not more impaired than recognition in amnesics (Shimamura & Squire, 1989). Second, the results could have arisen because amnesia was accompanied by incidental damage to the frontal lobes, which caused a selective disruption of target free recall and aware context memory. This may apply to free recall, but it seems unlikely to apply to, for example, memory for spatial location and modality of presentation. Third and most important, the illusory appearance of a disproportionate deficit may be produced if the matching manipulation has a greater effect in normal subjects on the apparently less impaired kind of memory. For example, the appearance of greater amnesic impairment on memory for modality of presentation would be produced if the matching manipulation we used (Pickering et al., 1989) had a greater effect on target recognition than modality memory. This possible artifact is very difficult to control for, but it should be borne in mind that it can also operate so as to produce the illusion of equal deficits on two memory measures in amnesics, even when in reality they are more impaired on one of the measures (this occurs when the matching manipulation affects the more impaired measure to a greater extent in normal subjects). The apparent conflict between our results with spatial memory and those of Cave and Squire (1991) probably relates to differences in the effects of the matching manipulations on spatial relative to target memory across the two sets of experiments. Interpretation of tests of the central prediction of the CMDHs is therefore very hard at present, and future work will need to thoroughly assess the effects of matching manipulations on contrasted memory measures in amnesic control subjects.

Priming in Amnesia

Schacter (1991) has summarized current evidence as indicating that amnesics show preserved priming of previously familiar information; little evidence of priming of novel verbal information; and quite good evidence of preserved priming of novel nonverbal information. It is very unlikely that this fair summary of the current picture reflects reality, because no theory of amnesia or priming would predict it. More data are needed to resolve the puzzle.

There is good evidence that amnesics show preserved priming of previously familiar verbal information (see Mayes, 1991). We (Paller, Mayes, Thompson, et al., 1992) recently found that amnesics showed normal priming of familiar nonverbal information in a task that involved showing pairs of famous faces on two separate occasions and asking subjects to judge whether the pictures were of one person or two. On second exposure, amnesics' judgments were made faster to the same extent as those of controls. All the familiar information-priming tasks at which amnesics show preservation can be interpreted as indicative of more fluent or efficient processing of target items (Jacoby & Kelley, 1991). In another recent study, we (Paller, Mayes, McDermott, Pickering, & Meudell, 1991) showed preserved amnesic priming in a paradigm originally used by Witherspoon and Allan (1985), in which subjects are shown words twice (the second time briefly) and are asked to judge for how long the repeated words are shown. Like normal people, amnesics judged the repeated words to have been shown for longer than similar nonrepeated words. It has been argued that this effect depends on making an automatic inference that words were shown for longer because they were processed more easily (see Jacoby & Kelley, 1991). This is of interest because Jacoby and Mandler (see, e.g., Mandler, Hamson, & Dorfman, 1990) have suggested that recognition depends on two independent processes: an effortful recollective process that may require contextual retrieval, and an automatic familiarity process. Jacoby (see Jacoby & Kelley, 1991) has argued that familiarity depends on an automatic attribution of "pastness" based on increased ease of processing. The results of Paller, myself, and my colleagues suggest that amnesics may show relative preservation of this familiarity process, at least for words.

Most of the negative evidence about amnesic priming of novel verbal information is based on paradigms that depend on learning new associations between words, such as "baby–bishop." There is little evidence in amnesics for enhanced word completion priming of the kind originally reported by Graf and Schacter (1985) (see, e.g., Mayes & Gooding, 1989). The evidence about speeded reading of repeated novel word pairs is controversial (Moscovitch, Winocur, & McLachlan, 1986; Musen, Shimamura, & Squire, 1990). Finally, Paller and Mayes (submitted), using a new paradigm, found that perceptual identification priming was enhanced in normals, but not in amnesics, by recent exposure to previously unrelated word pairs. In contrast, we have found that amnesics do show preserved speeded reading of novel pronounceable nonwords (Mayes, Poole, & Gooding, 1991).

Preserved priming of nonverbal novel information in amnesics has been demonstrated with tasks that do not involve the learning of new associations between previously familiar material such as words (see, e.g., Gabrieli, Milberg, Keane, & Corkin, 1990). These tasks have also only shown preserved priming in amnesics at short delays, which is true at present of all tasks that have shown normal priming in amnesics. In future, it will be interesting to see whether novel nonverbal information priming can be demonstrated in amnesics when it depends on learning new associations, such as those between previously unrelated famous faces. It may be that automatic, unaware memory, like aware memory for new associations, only becomes apparent after multiple learning trials in normal as well as amnesic subjects (see Musen & Squire, in press). It is even more important to determine whether amnesics can show preserved novel (or indeed familiar) information priming at long delays, so as to provide a better test between the competing theories. Testing at long delays also removes the risk that the appearance of amnesic normality is an illusion arising from the fact that the priming test is less sensitive to differences than are aware memory tests.

The points above suggest that convincing and theoretically relevant novel information priming remains to be shown in amnesics. When preserved "priming" is not found in a task, however, it is always possible that this is because it is not occurring, and normal subjects are showing an effect because they are using aware memory unavailable to amnesics. The severity of this problem should never be underestimated, and it may have a solution in the form of a procedure for estimating the contributions to performance of aware memory and unaware memory that can be derived from the work of Jacoby (see Jacoby & Kelley, 1991). We are currently using this procedure with the paradigm of McAndrews, Glisky, and Schacter (1987) that involves interpreting puzzle sentences. They were able to show priming in severe amnesics after a 1-week delay, although they were unable to establish whether this priming was actually preserved because normal performance was strongly mediated by aware memory.

It must be concluded that available evidence still does not discriminate clearly among the main theories of amnesia. This will only be achieved by more rigorous testing of the predictions that differ most obviously between the theories, and by refining these predictions.

REFERENCES

Butters, N., & Cermak, L. S. (1986). A case study of the forgetting of autobiographical knowledge: Implications for the study of retrograde amnesia. In D. Rubin (Ed.), *Autobiographical memory*. New York: Cambridge University Press.

Cave, C. B., & Squire, L. R. (1991). Equivalent impairment of spatial and nonspatial memory following damage to the human hippocampus. *Hippocampus, 1*, 329–340.

Cermak, L. S. (1984). The episodic–semantic distinction in amnesia. In L. R. Squire & N. Butters (Eds.), *Neuropsychology of memory* (1st ed.). New York: Guilford Press.

Damasio, A. R., Tranel, D., & Damasio, H. (1989). Amnesia caused by herpes simplex encephalitis, infarctions in basal forebrain, Alzheimer's disease and anoxia/ischemia. In F. Boller & J. Grafman (Eds.), *Handbook of neuropsychology* (Vol. 3). Amsterdam: Elsevier.

Daum, I., Channon, S., & Canavan, A. G. M. (1989). Classical conditioning in patients with severe memory problems. *Journal of Neurology, Neurosurgery and Psychiatry, 52*, 47–51.

Davies, G. M., & Thomson, D. M. (1988). *Memory in context: Context in memory*. Chichester, England: Wiley.

Gabrieli, J. D. E., Milberg, W., Keane, M. M., & Corkin, S. (1990). Intact priming of patterns despite impaired memory. *Neuropsychologia, 28*, 417–427.

Graf, P., & Schacter, D. L. (1985). Implicit and explicit memory for new associations in normal and control subjects. *Journal of Experimental Psychology: Learning, Memory, and Cognition, 2*, 501–518.

Hart, R. P., Kwentus, J. A., Harkins, S. W., & Taylor, J. R. (1988). Rate of forgetting in Alzheimer's-type dementia. *Brain and Cognition, 7*, 31–38.

Hirst, W., Johnson, M. K., Kim, J. K., Phelps, E. A., Risse, G., & Volpe, B. T. (1986). Recognition and recall in amnesics. *Journal of Experimental Psychology: Learning, Memory, and Cognition, 12*, 445–451.

Hirst, W., Johnson, M. K., Phelps, E. A., & Volpe, B. T. (1988). More on recognition and recall in amnesics. *Journal of Experimental Psychology: Learning, Memory, and Cognition, 14*, 758–762.

Huppert, F. A., & Piercy, M. (1978). Dissociation between learning and remembering in amnesia. *Nature, 275*, 317–318.

Isaac, C. (1991). [Rate of forgetting in organic amnesia: A comparison of recall and recognition]. Unpublished data.

Jacoby, L. L., & Kelley, C. (1991). Unconscious influences of memory: Dissociations and automaticity. In A. D. Milner & M. D. Rugg (Eds.), *The neuropsychology of consciousness*. London: Academic Press.

Janowsky, J. S., Shimamura, A. P., & Squire, L. R. (1989). Source memory impairment in patients with frontal lobe lesions. *Neuropsychologia, 27,* 1043–1056.

Kopelman, M. D. (1989). Remote and autobiographical memory, temporal context memory and frontal atrophy in Korsakoff and Alzheimer patients. *Neuropsychologia, 27,* 437–460.

MacAndrews, S. B. G. (1989). *The structure of recall in amnesia.* Unpublished doctoral dissertation, University of Warwick, England.

Mandler, G., Hamson, C. O., & Dorfman, J. (1990). Tests of dual process theory: Word priming and recognition. *Quarterly Journal of Experimental Psychology, 42A,* 713–739.

Mayes, A. R. (1986). Learning and memory disorders and their assessment. *Neuropsychologia, 24,* 25–39.

Mayes, A. R. (1988). *Human organic memory disorders.* Cambridge, England: Cambridge University Press.

Mayes, A. R. (1991). Automatic memory processes in amnesia: How are they mediated? In A. D. Milner & M. D. Rugg (Eds.), *The neuropsychology of consciousness.* London: Academic Press.

Mayes, A. R., & Gooding, P. (1989). Enhancement of word completion priming in amnesics by cueing with previously novel associates. *Neuropsychologia, 27,* 1057–1072.

Mayes, A. R., MacDonald, C., Donlan, L., Pears, J., & Meudell, P. R. (in press). Amnesics have a disproportionately severe memory deficit for interactive context. *Quarterly Journal of Experimental Psychology.*

Mayes, A. R., Meudell, P. R., & MacDonald, C. (1991). Disproportionate intentional spatial memory impairments in amnesia. *Neuropsychologia, 29,* 771–784.

Mayes, A. R., Meudell, P. R., MacDonald, C., & Pickering, A. (1990). *Disproportionately impaired temporal order memory in amnesics with several aetiologies.* Unpublished manuscript.

Mayes, A. R., Meudell, P. R., & Pickering, A. D. (1985). Is organic amnesia caused by a selective deficit in remembering contextual information? *Cortex, 21,* 313–324.

Mayes, A. R., Poole, V., & Gooding, T. (1991). Increased reading speed for words and pronounceable nonwords: Evidence of preserved priming in amnesics. *Cortex, 27,* 403–415.

McAndrews, M. P., Glisky, E. L., & Schacter, D. L. (1987). When priming persists: Long-lasting implicit memory for a single episode in amnesic patients. *Neuropsychologia, 25,* 497–506.

Moscovitch, M., Winocur, G., & McLachlan, D. (1986). Memory as assessed by recognition and reading time in normal and memory-impaired people with Alzheimer's disease and other neurological disorders. *Journal of Experimental Psychology: Learning, Memory, and Cognition, 12,* 331–347.

Moss, M. B., Albert, M. S., Butters, N., & Payne, M. (1986). Differential patterns of memory loss among patients with Alzheimer's disease, Huntington's disease, and alcoholic Korsakoff's syndrome. *Archives of Neurology, 43,* 239–246.

Musen, G., Shimamura, A. P., & Squire, L. R. (1990). Intact text-specific reading skill in amnesia. *Journal of Experimental Psychology: Learning, Memory, and Cognition, 16,* 1068–1076.

Musen, G., & Squire, L. R. (in press). Amnesic patients and normal subjects exhibit implicit learning of novel associations after multiple but not after single trials. *Journal of Experimental Psychology: Learning, Memory, and Cognition.*

Paller, K. A., & Mayes, A. R. *New-association priming of word identification in normal and amnesic subjects.* Manuscript submitted for publication.

Paller, K. A., Mayes, A. R., McDermott, M., Pickering, A. D., & Meudell, P. R. (1991). Indirect measures of memory in a duration-judgement task are normal in amnesic patients. *Neuropsychologia, 29,* 1007–1018.

Paller, K. A., Mayes, A. R., Thompson, K. M., Young, A. W., Roberts, J., & Meudell, P. R. (1992). Priming of face matching in amnesia. *Brain and Cognition, 18,* 46–59.

Petersen, S. E., Fox, P. T., Posner, M. I., Mintun, M., & Raichle, M. E. (1988). Positron emission tomographic studies of the cortical anatomy of single-word processing. *Nature, 331,* 585–589.

Pickering, A. D. (1987). *Does amnesia arise from a specific deficit in memory for contextual information.* Unpublished doctoral dissertation, University of Manchester, England.

Pickering, A. D., Mayes, A. R., & Fairbairn, A. F. (1989). Amnesia and memory for modality information. *Neuropsychologia, 27,* 1249–1259.

Press, G. A., Amaral, D. G., & Squire, L. R. (1989). Hippocampal abnormalities in amnesic patients revealed by high-resolution magnetic resonance imaging. *Nature, 341,* 54–57.

Schacter, D. L. (1990). Toward a cognitive neuropsychology of awareness: Implicit knowledge and anosognosia. *Journal of Clinical and Experimental Neuropsychology, 12,* 155–178.

Schacter, D. L. (1991). Consciousness and awareness in memory and amnesia: Critical issues. In A. D. Milner & M. D. Rugg (Eds.), *The neuropsychology of consciousness.* London: Academic Press.

Schacter, D. L., Harbluk, J. L., & McLachlan, D. R. (1984). Retrieval without recollection: An experimental analysis of source amnesia. *Journal of Verbal Learning and Verbal Behavior, 23,* 593–611.

Shimamura, A. P. (1989). Disorders of memory: The cognitive science perspective. In F. Boller & J. Grafman (Eds.), *Handbook of neuropsychology* (Vol. 3). Amsterdam: Elsevier.

Shimamura, A. P., Janowsky, J. S., & Squire, L. R. (1990). Memory for the temporal order of events in patients with frontal lobe lesions and amnesic patients. *Neuropsychologia, 28,* 803–813.

Shimamura, A. P., & Squire, L. R. (1987). A neuropsychological study of fact memory and source amnesia. *Journal of Experimental Psychology: Learning, Memory, and Cognition, 13,* 464–473.

Shimamura, A. P., & Squire, L. R. (1989). Long-term memory in amnesia: Cued recall, recognition memory and confidence ratings. *Journal of Experimental Psychology: Learning, Memory, and Cognition, 15,* 763–770.

Shoqeirat, M. A., & Mayes, A. R. (1991) Disproportionate incidental spatial memory and recall deficits in amnesia. *Neuropsychologia, 29,* 749–769.

Smith, M. L., & Milner, B. (1989). Right hippocampal impairment in the recall of location: Encoding deficit or rapid forgetting? *Neuropsychologia, 27,* 71–82.

Squire, L. R. (1982). Comparisons between forms of amnesia: Some deficits are unique to Korsakoff patients. *Journal of Experimental Psychology: Learning, Memory, and Cognition, 8,* 560–571.

Squire, L. R., Shimamura, A. P., & Amaral, D. G. (1989). Memory and the hippocampus. In J. Byrne & W. Berry (Eds.), *Neural models of plasticity.* New York: Academic Press.

Welsh, K., Butters, N., Hughes, J., Mohs, R., & Heyman, A. (1991). Detection of abnormal memory decline in mild cases of Alzheimer's disease using CERAD neuropsychological measures. *Archives of Neurology, 48,* 278–281.

Witherspoon, D., & Allan, L. G. (1985). The effect of a prior presentation on temporal judgements in a perceptual identification task. *Memory and Cognition, 13,* 101–111.

Zola-Morgan, S., & Squire, L. R. (1990). The primate hippocampal formation: Evidence for a time-limited role in memory storage. *Science, 250,* 288–290.

3

The Role of Fluency in the Implicit and Explicit Task Performance of Amnesic Patients

LAIRD S. CERMAK and MIEKE VERFAELLIE

In the previous edition of this text, the distinction between "episodic" and "semantic" memory was used to differentiate those instances in which amnesic patients can learn and retrieve new information from those in which they cannot (Cermak, 1984). It was proposed that instances of successful retrieval do not reflect episodic retention, but instead reflect the operation of an intact semantic memory system. For instance, amnesics' ability to retrieve studied items in response to a strong associative cue was ascribed to the operation of associative links in semantic memory. Likewise, amnesics' ability to retrieve an occasional isolated item, as if "out of the blue," was thought to reflect temporary activation of its lexical or semantic representation. In both instances, activation of information already represented in memory was thought to mediate the amnesics' performance, whereas memory for a specific episode seemed to have no discernible effect at all.

Initial research efforts directed at evaluating the episodic–semantic hypothesis met with genuine success, and for some time it appeared that the distinction between episodic and semantic memory had captured the essence of the amnesic syndrome to a far greater extent than had any other dichotomy. Subsequently, however, a number of observations have cast doubt on the notion that amnesics' performance is mediated exclusively by the operation of semantic memory. Instead, performance has come to be viewed as a function of the specific processes involved in encoding and retrieval of episodic information. This has led to the thesis to be developed in this chapter: that the amnesics' performance may vary, depending on the extent to which specific episodic memory functions rely on automatic or controlled processes. Specifically, it is hypothesized that judgments that are relatively automatic, such as those based on familiarity (Mandler, 1980; Jacoby & Dallas, 1981), may be preserved in amnesia. In contrast, judgments based on conscious recollection of an episode, such as those required to attribute familiarity to its correct source, are impaired in amnesia. The steps we have followed in arriving at this conclusion from a strict episodic–semantic independence position are outlined here in a series of experiments conducted at the Memory Disorders Research Center.

Semantic Activation as an Explanation of Implicit Memory Effects in Amnesia

One of the early demonstrations of implicit memory in amnesia was based on the finding that in a perceptual identification task, patients were able to identify briefly presented words at a lower exposure duration when they had previously been presented on a study list than when they had not been previously presented (Diamond & Rozin, 1984; Cermak, Talbot, Chandler, & Wolbarst, 1985). Thus, some implicit retention appeared to occur, even though amnesic patients had very poor recognition of the studied words.

Two dichotomies were invoked to explain these priming effects. According to the procedural–declarative dichotomy (Cohen & Squire, 1980; Cohen, 1984), the improved performance was thought to result from a reinstatement of procedures and operations engaged in during initial stimulus presentation. Since the perceptual identification task reinstates the operations the amnesic patient engages in when initially reading the word, performance is facilitated, even though the patient may not have any record of the results of these operations. According to the semantic–episodic alternative outlined above, this facilitation was thought to reflect the temporary activation of a word's lexical or semantic referent. This activation sensitizes the patient to that particular word, which then becomes more readily reactivated under conditions of brief exposure.

To distinguish between these alternative accounts, we used pronounceable pseudowords, instead of real words, as stimuli in a perceptual identification task (Cermak et al., 1985). It was hypothesized that if the procedural learning hypothesis is correct, then amnesic patients ought to show implicit memory for novel materials as well as for materials with a pre-established semantic representation, since in either case the procedures at the time of study and test are kept constant. However, if the semantic activation theory is correct, then amnesics ought to perform significantly below normal when pseudowords are used, since no semantic representation exists for these stimuli. The results confirmed the latter prediction. The control subjects demonstrated significant priming for pseudowords, as indicated by their faster identification of targets compared to fillers, but amnesics did not. This result was interpreted as meaning that no new learning had occurred for amnesics. Thus, for performance to be facilitated, the information had to be already represented in memory.

Although these results clearly favored the hypothesis that priming in amnesia depends upon activation of semantic memory, we realized that the plausibility of a semantic activation hypothesis depended critically on the assumption that the representation and organization of information in semantic memory is intact in amnesia. We had already reported (Cermak, Reale, & Baker, 1978) that amnesic patients' search through lexical memory was normal, suggesting intact lexical organization. But we had also reported (Cermak et al., 1978) that a similar search through conceptual semantic memory was impaired. This could mean either that the organization of a conceptual semantic network was impaired, or that the search through this network was deficient. Consequently, our next series of tasks directly examined the integrity of the structure and organization of semantic memory in Korsakoff patients, independently of their ability to access this knowledge. This was done using semantic memory tasks that do not require active search for stored information (Verfaellie, Cermak, Blackford, & Weiss, 1990).

The first two tasks again used a perceptual identification paradigm in which patients had to identify briefly presented targets, but this time targets were preceded by the presentation of an associatively or a categorically related prime at an exposure duration above threshold. Associatively related primes were either highly associated with the target (e.g., "hungry-food") or moderately associated (e.g., "sour-apple"). Categorical primes were followed by exemplars of high (e.g., "vehicle-car") or moderate (e.g., "cloth-velvet") prototypicality. In both these tasks, Korsakoff patients identified targets faster when they were preceded by related primes than when they were preceded by neutral or unrelated primes. This was true for primes that were moderately related to the target as well as for primes that were highly related, suggesting that amnesics show normal sensitivity to associative and categorical links between words. However, it is obvious that in addition to automatic activation of semantic representations, priming in both these tasks could also reflect the operation of strategic processes. Even though the task did not require that the patients actively search for a specified word, the prime might allow them to anticipate likely target words. These anticipated words could then be matched to a partial visual input. To eliminate this strategic possibility, a third experiment was designed to assess the automatic spread of activation through semantic memory more directly. This was done using a lexical decision paradigm in which, on some trials, associatively related primes preceded the target word. To eliminate the use of strategic processes, the proportion of related prime-target pairs was deliberately kept small, and the stimulus onset interval between prime and target was kept short. These two factors were thought to minimize the possibility that patients would use the prime to direct their attention consciously to a limited set of related items. On this task the Korsakoff patients again demonstrated intact priming, leading to the conclusion that the organization of their semantic memory was not disrupted by brain injury. Instead, it was suggested that impaired performance on semantic search tasks must be the result of an impairment in the patients' ability to perform an internally directed memory search.

Contextual Effects on the Amnesics' Implicit Memory Performance

Now that we had established that the organization of semantic memory is intact in amnesics, we returned to a closer examination of the amnesics' priming of real words versus pseudowords. One of the differences between pseudowords and real words that we had previously emphasized was the fact that pseudowords lack a semantic representation. However, we realized that another important difference between the two types of stimuli is the fact that pseudowords also have unfamiliar orthography and phonology. To determine which of these features, perceptual familiarity or semantic activation, accounted for the difference between amnesics' real-word and pseudoword priming, two further perceptual identification experiments (Cermak, Verfaellie, Milberg, Letourneau, & Blackford, 1991) were performed. These priming experiments used as stimuli pseudohomonyms—that is, stimuli such as "phaire," which do not have an existing orthographic representation but share their phonology with real words, and as such indirectly allow access to meaning. The first experiment demonstrated that when all stimuli in the experimental list were pseudohomonyms, amnesics showed priming at a level comparable to that obtained for real words. Importantly, in this experiment some priming was also obtained (albeit below normal) when pseudowords were used as stimuli. Actually, the facilitation for pseudowords in this task was quite similar in magnitude to that obtained in the initial pseudoword identification task (described above). In that prior report, however, this finding was overshadowed by the fact that control subjects showed much larger repetition priming effects for pseudowords. Nonetheless, these two findings taken together suggest that even for amnesics, some priming of pseudowords (albeit below normal) does occur, even when their recognition memory for these same stimuli is at chance levels.

One reason why amnesics may show smaller repetition priming effects for pseudowords than controls do, could relate to their differential use of explicit memory. For control subjects, unlike amnesics, memory for the specific stimuli presented on the study list could support performance on the identification task. That is, previously presented items could be consciously anticipated during the identification trials, magnifying the distinction between repeated and unrepeated items. This would be most likely to occur for pseudowords, since these stimuli are the hardest to identify initially.

In an attempt to minimize reliance on explicit memory, a second experiment presented pseudowords, pseudohomonyms, and/or real words within the same study list. Since under these conditions the nature of a test stimulus could no longer be predicted, it was thought that the effectiveness of active recollection might be reduced. In this experiment, amnesics again showed some priming for pseudowords, but the magnitude of this priming remained below normal. Of equal importance was the finding that the presentation of mixed lists also affected the priming of pseudohomonyms. When pseudohomonyms were mixed within the same list as pseudowords, Korsakoff patients' priming for pseudohomonyms now became nonsignificant. The fact that pseudohomonyms have a familiar auditory word form seemed to be concealed by the unfamiliar orthography of *all* stimuli on the list. Consequently, pseudohomonyms lost their semantic salience and simply looked like pseudowords. When pseudohomonyms were mixed with real words, Korsakoff patients' priming for pseudohomonyms also became significantly lower than was the case for the alcoholic controls. Clearly, the semantic processing of pseudohomonyms critically depended on the patients' realization that the orthographically unfamiliar stimuli in the study list actually corresponded phonemically to real words. This was more likely to occur when all the stimuli shared this characteristic than when stimulus types were mixed within a list. Thus, the pseudohomonym findings in this experiment suggested that, at least for Korsakoff patients, priming depends on the conceptual salience of the stimuli. For real words, access to meaning may well occur automatically, resulting in normal repetition priming effects regardless of task manipulations. But, for pseudohomonyms, activation of meanings does not occur automatically. Instead, the presence and magnitude of priming effects are affected by contextual variables, which influence the manner in which information is processed.

Reinstating Processing Demands at Study and Test: Effects of Fluency

The finding that performance on the pseudohomonym identification task depends on the patients' strategy at the time of encoding led us to suggest that factors other than automatic activation of semantic memory mediate priming in amnesia. In order to get some indication as to the nature of these factors, we turned to a closer examination of the large body of studies examining priming in normal individuals. Generally, these studies have indicated that repetition priming effects are highly specific. For instance, changes in modality or presentation format significantly attenuate the magnitude of priming, as do changes in local context (for a review, see Richardson-Klavehn, & Bjork, 1988). To accommodate these findings, models of word repetition have been advanced that incorporate the contribution of unitized representations of words in the lexicon, as well as the contribution of episodic traces for particular events. Feustel, Shiffrin, and Salasoo (1983), for instance, suggest that the processing advantage of real words over pseudowords reflects the availability of unitized representations, whereas the repetition effect itself is thought to reflect episodic influences.

   Given the role of episodic memory in normal repetition priming effects, it became even more important to examine its possible contribution to the amnesics' performance. For this purpose, we used a lexical decision task in which words and nonwords were repeated following different lags, determined by the number of items intervening between repetitions (Verfaellie, Cermak, Letourneau, & Zuffante, 1991). It was thought that this task would be most likely to capture episodic effects on the amnesics' performance, since the processing demands at the time of study and test were carefully matched. In a first experiment, we established that Korsakoff patients were sensitive to previous presentations of words, as indicated by faster lexical decision times to words on their second presentation compared to their first. Korsakoff patients showed facilitation of a magnitude similar to that obtained for the alcoholic controls at all but a lag of 0 (i.e., no words intervened between repetitions), and it remained highly significant at a lag of 15 (i.e., 15 words intervened between repetitions).

   Next, to distinguish between semantic activation effects and episodic effects of fluency, we performed a lexical decision experiment that compared priming for high- and low-frequency words. As Scarborough, Cortese, and Scarborough (1977) had demonstrated, low-frequency words benefit more from repetition than do high-frequency words. This finding, referred to as the "frequency attenuation effect," reflects the fact that whereas high-frequency words are responded to faster than low-frequency words on their first presentation, this difference largely dissipates by the second presentation. Lexical access theories ascribe differences in response time to the existence of a relatively stable frequency hierarchy in the lexicon, in which high-frequency items are being searched first (Becker, 1979; Forster, 1976). However, the finding that a single presentation of an item can eliminate differences in response time, and thus apparently alter the organization of the lexicon, is difficult to account for by this hypothesis. Consequently, it has been claimed that the frequency attenuation effect reflects some form of episodic memory for the first presentation of the word (Forster & Davis, 1984). Consistent with this claim, these authors showed that when a word was masked on its first presentation to minimize the availability of its episodic representation, the frequency attenuation effect disappeared.

It was anticipated that if amnesics had truly forgotten the episode in which words were initially presented, the effects of frequency on their performance would be similar to those Forster and Davis (1984) obtained in their masked condition. Instead, we found that Korsakoff patients, like controls in an unmasked condition, showed larger repetition priming effects for low-frequency words than for high-frequency words. This finding implies that amnesic patients can use some level of episodic memory to facilitate their performance on an implicit memory task. However, their explicit recognition memory for the same material was, as usual, significantly impaired.

This outcome led us to speculate on the possibility that many of the judgments required in implicit memory tasks, including lexical decisions, are largely data-driven and can occur without "conscious" awareness of a past episode (Roediger & Blaxton, 1987; Jacoby, 1991). Instead, these judgments are based on the fluency with which the event in question is processed, as well as on the feeling of familiarity such fluency produces (Jacoby, 1978; Jacoby & Dallas, 1981). Of course, perceptual fluency can also serve as a basis for recognition judgments, but basing recognition on familiarity alone may be misleading (see Jacoby, Kelley, & Dywan, 1989). A more reliable basis for recognition judgments involves respecifying the context in which an event was initially encoded. This respecification process seems to be what is impaired in amnesia, leaving the patient with poor recognition memory, but normal performance on repetition priming tasks.

A further study (Cermak, Verfaellie, Jacoby, & Letourneau, 1992), which reinforced our conceptualization of amnesic performance in terms of episodic memory processes, used pictorial stimuli in the context of a clarification task analogous to that used by Jacoby, Baker, and Brooks (1989). In this task patients were exposed to fragmented pictures that could be gradually clarified by pressing a key on the computer. Later, pictures were again presented for clarification. Some of the pictures were identical to those seen earlier, some shared the same name, and some were completely different. The performance of Korsakoff patients was compared to that of a group of alcoholic controls tested immediately, as well as to that of a group of alcoholics tested following a 1-week delay. Of critical importance was performance on the same-name pictures. If amnesics required fewer key presses to identify identical than same-name pictures, this would provide evidence that specific memories of individual past experiences contribute to their performance. In contrast, no difference between the identification of identical and same-name pictures would be expected if savings in picture identification reflect the activation of an abstract semantic or conceptual representation. All groups identified identical pictures faster than same-name pictures, and these in turn were identified faster than new pictures—a finding favoring an episodic account. However, Korsakoff patients demonstrated smaller savings than did the alcoholic controls tested immediately. This reduction in savings was accompanied by poor, but far from zero, recognition memory. Delaying the memory performance of the alcoholic controls also produced a reduction in clarification performance and likewise reduced the accuracy of recognition performance, creating a pattern of results similar to that obtained by the amnesics. Overall, then, the pattern of results appeared to be one of association between picture clarification and recognition, rather than dissociation.

This outcome is exceedingly important, because it demonstrates that either associations or dissociations between implicit and explicit memory tasks can be obtained, depending on the nature of the processes involved. In the context of the lexical decision results described above, we suggested that performance on implicit memory tasks may be based largely on perceptual fluency, whereas explicit memory tasks such as recall and recognition may require active reconstruction of the study episode. In contrast, the present results suggest that performance on a picture clarification and recognition task can be based on the same processes. It is likely that both tasks depend to a large extent on the fluency with which specific visual details of a picture are processed. However, the ability to actively reconstruct previously studied pictures may not only contribute to recognition, but may also allow subjects to anticipate the identity of partially presented pictures.

Dissociating the Effects of Fluency and Recollection: Use of Oppositional Tasks

The finding that performance on implicit tests, as well as on explicit tests, may be mediated by a combination of automatic fluency and conscious recollection causes a significant interpretative problem for traditional implicit memory tasks. Since in these tasks, fluency and recollection influence performance in the same direction, impaired performance may result from an impairment in either one of the contributing processes. To distinguish impairments in automatic fluency from those in conscious recollection, a manipulation is needed that allows one to separate their effects, so as to isolate the contribution of each to the performance of amnesics and control subjects.

Following Jacoby and Kelley (1991), we have recently done so by creating a situation in which the effects of fluency and conscious recollection on task performance were directly opposed to each other. In this experiment, names randomly selected from a phone book were presented to patients, who were asked merely to pronounce each name as it was presented. This was followed by a fame judgment task, in which previously presented nonfamous names were intermixed with new nonfamous names as well as with names that were indeed famous (albeit relatively obscure). Before performing the fame judgment task, patients were told that the names they had just read were not famous, and if one now was presented, they should respond "no" to it. We referred to this task as an "exclusion" task, because patients were instructed to exclude names that might be processed more fluently because of their previous encounter. The results of this task revealed that, overall, amnesics were less accurate at making fame judgments than were controls. However, even when their overall level of accuracy was taken into account, amnesics and controls responded very differently to the exclusion instructions. Whereas alcoholic controls were equally likely to endorse an old or a new nonfamous name as being famous, amnesic patients were much more likely to endorse an old than a new nonfamous name. Since exclusion required conscious recollection that a name had been presented on the study list, we concluded from these findings that amnesics were unable to use conscious processes to oppose automatic effects of memory.

Can amnesics use conscious processes to enhance the effects of automatically generated fluency? To address this question, we performed a second experiment, designed so that the effects of conscious recollection and fluency would affect performance in the same direction. Here, subjects were told that the names presented on the study list were indeed famous (but obscure), and ought now to be responded to positively in the fame judgment task. Because of these instructions, we referred to this task as an "inclusion" task. In contrast to the results of the previous experiment, alcoholic patients now endorsed significantly more old nonfamous names than did the amnesics. In fact, the amnesics' performance on the inclusion task was only slightly and nonsignificantly higher than that on the exclusion task, whereas the alcoholics showed a striking and highly significant effect of task instructions. We concluded from these experiments that the amnesics' performance was mediated largely, if not exclusively, by the effects of fluency. The alcoholic controls, in contrast, could use conscious recollection either to enhance or to counteract the effects of fluency.

More recently, we have also used the oppositional process approach illustrated above in the context of a task frequently considered to be a prototypical implicit task (Cermak, Verfaellie, & Sweeney, in press). Subjects participated in a novel stem completion task, in which they were asked *not* to use the words that had been presented on a previously presented study list to complete the word stems (an exclusion task). In this condition, amnesics provided substantially more words from the study list than did the alcoholic controls. We also compared performance on the exclusion task with that on a standard stem completion task, in which patients were told to complete the stem with the first word that came to mind (an inclusion task). As in the fame experiments, the exclusion instruction had very little effect on the performance of amnesics, whereas it sharply decreased the number of study list words used as stem completions by the alcoholic controls. These findings provide further support for the hypothesis that amnesics are deficient in their ability to consciously recollect words that were previously studied.

Of further interest was the finding that on the standard word completion task, amnesics consistently provided more study list completions than did the alcoholic controls. This seemed to reflect the fact that the alcoholic controls, having more conscious control over their performance, chose to complete stems with words other than those on the study list. The amnesics, in contrast, may have been more responsive than controls to the fluency with which items were processed, because they were less capable of determining its source. Interestingly, when five study trials were given prior to word completion, the controls became more drawn to this fluency and increased their inclusion responses to the level of the amnesics. In contrast to the amnesics, however, they also had almost complete conscious control over their performance, as indicated by their ability to exclude previously studied items when the task required them to do so.

Conclusions

This series of experiments began as an attempt to determine which dichotomy of memory systems, procedural-declarative or semantic-episodic, better explains the phenomena of successful priming in amnesia. The early tasks seemed to favor semantic activation, since only pre-existing knowledge could be primed in amnesics. However, subsequent investigations suggested that the processing strategy utilized by the patients at the time of encoding also plays an important role, and this seemed to favor a more episodic explanation. Procedural explanations fell short even when procedural learning was defined to include cognitive processing, because later experiments disclosed that effects of repetition are not always dissociable from effects on explicit memory tasks. Instead, it appears that in some instances, performance on implicit and explicit tasks may be mediated by the same processes. In an attempt to dissociate the contribution of fluency and conscious recollection, we observed in the final experiments that amnesics respond to fluency, regardless of the task instructions. These findings suggest that amnesics are unable to attribute fluency to its correct source—a defect that probably underlies many of the amnesics' other characteristics, such as perseveration and source errors. In addition, it seems to explain the phenomena of priming better than other theories. In situations in which the feeling of familiarity associated with increased fluency can support performance, the patients appear to perform normally. When the feeling of familiarity needs to be consciously opposed, it results in errors.

ACKNOWLEDGMENTS

The research reported herein was supported by National Institute of Neurological Disorders and Stroke Program Project Grant No. NS26985 and National Institute on Alcohol Abuse and Alcoholism Grant No. AA00187 to Boston University School of Medicine, and by the Medical Research Service of the Department of Veterans Affairs.

REFERENCES

Becker, C. A. (1979). Semantic context and word frequency effects in visual word recognition. *Journal of Experimental Psychology: Human Perception and Performance, 5,* 252-259.

Cermak, L. S. (1984). The episodic-semantic distinction in amnesia. In L. R. Squire & N. Butters (Eds.), *Neuropsychology of memory* (1st ed., pp. 55-62). New York: Guilford Press.

Cermak, L. S., Reale, L., & Baker, E. (1978). Alcoholic Korsakoff patients' retrieval from semantic memory. *Brain and Language, 5,* 215-226.

Cermak, L. S., Talbot, N., Chandler, K., & Wolbarst, L. R. (1985). The perceptual priming phenomenon in amnesia. *Neuropsychologia, 23,* 615-622.

Cermak, L. S., Verfaellie, M., Jacoby, L. L., & Letourneau, L. (1992). *Episodic effects on picture clarification for alcoholic Korsakoff patients.* Manuscript submitted for publication.

Cermak, L. S., Verfaellie, M., Milberg, W. P., Letourneau, L. L., & Blackford, S. (1991). A further analysis of perceptual identification priming in alcoholic Korsakoff patients. *Neuropsychologia, 29,* 725-736.

Cermak, L. S., Verfaellie, M., & Sweeney, M. (in press). Fluency versus conscious recollection in the word completion performance of amnesic patients. *Brain and Cognition.*

Cohen, N. J. (1984). Preserved learning capacity in amnesia: Evidence for multiple memory systems. In L. R. Squire & N. Butters (Eds.), *Neuropsychology of memory* (1st ed., pp. 83-105). New York: Guilford Press.

Cohen, N. J., & Squire, L. R. (1980). Preserved learning and retention of pattern-analyzing skill in amnesia: Dissociation of knowing how and knowing that. *Science, 210*, 207–210.

Diamond, R., & Rozin, P. (1984). Activation of existing memories in anterograde amnesia. *Journal of Abnormal Psychology, 93*, 98–105.

Feustel, T. C., Shiffrin, R. M., & Salasoo, A. (1983). Episodic and lexical contributions to the repetition effect in word identification. *Journal of Experimental Psychology: General, 112*, 309–346.

Forster, K. I. (1976). Accessing the mental lexicon. In R. J. Wales & E. Walker (Eds.), *New approaches to language mechanisms* (pp. 257–287). Amsterdam: North-Holland.

Forster, K. I., & Davis, C. (1984). Repetition priming and frequency attenuation in lexical access. *Journal of Experimental Psychology: Learning, Memory, and Cognition, 10*, 680–698.

Jacoby, L. L. (1978). On interpreting the effects of repetition: Solving a problem versus remembering a solution. *Journal of Verbal Learning and Verbal Behavior, 17*, 649–667.

Jacoby, L. L. (1991). A process dissociation framework: Separating automatic from intentional uses of memory. *Journal of Memory and Language, 30*, 513–541.

Jacoby, L. L., Baker, J. G., & Brooks, L. R. (1989). Episodic effects on picture identification: Implications for theories of concept learning and theories of memory. *Journal of Experimental Psychology: Learning, Memory, and Cognition, 15*, 275–281.

Jacoby, L. L., & Dallas, M. (1981). On the relationship between autobiographical memory and perceptual learning. *Journal of Experimental Psychology: General, 110*, 306–340.

Jacoby, L. L., & Kelley, C. (1992). Unconscious influences of memory: Dissociations and automaticity. In A. D. Milner & M. D. Rugg (Eds.), *The neuropsychology of consciousness* (pp. 201–233). London: Academic Press.

Jacoby, L. L., Kelley, C. M., & Dywan, J. (1989). Memory attributions. In H. L. Roediger III & F. I. M. Craik (Eds.), *Varieties of memory and consciousness: Essays in honor of Endel Tulving* (pp. 391–422). Hillsdale, NJ: Erlbaum.

Mandler, G. (1980). Recognizing: The judgement of previous occurrence. *Psychological Review, 87*, 252–271.

Richardson-Klavehn, A., & Bjork, R. A. (1988). Measures of memory. *Annual Review of Psychology, 39*, 475–543.

Roediger, H. L., III, & Blaxton, T. A. (1987). Retrieval modes produce dissociations in memory for surface information. In D. Gorfein & R. R. Hoffman (Eds.), *Memory and cognitive processes: The Ebbinghaus Centennial Conference* (pp. 349–379). Hillsdale, NJ: Erlbaum.

Scarborough, D. L., Cortese, C., & Scarborough, H. (1977). Frequency and repetition effects in lexical memory. *Journal of Experimental Psychology: Human Perception and Performance, 3*, 1–17.

Verfaellie, M., Cermak, L. S., Blackford, S., & Weiss, S. (1990). Strategic and automatic priming of semantic memory in alcoholic Korsakoff patients. *Brain and Cognition, 13*, 178–192.

Verfaellie, M., Cermak, L. S., Letourneau, L. L., & Zuffante, P. (1991). Repetition effects in a lexical decision task: The role of episodic memory in the performance of alcoholic Korsakoff patients. *Neuropsychologia, 29*, 641–657.

4

Awareness, Automaticity, and Memory Dissociations

JEFFREY P. TOTH, D. STEPHEN LINDSAY, and LARRY L. JACOBY

There has been considerable recent interest in the relationship between direct and indirect tests of memory (e.g., Richardson-Klavehn & Bjork, 1988). On a direct test, such as recall or recognition, subjects are specifically instructed to consciously recollect a prior episode. On an indirect test, such as word fragment completion or exemplar generation, memory for the target episode is inferred from its effects on task performance (e.g., facilitated fragment completion for previously studied words). Indirect tests are intended to measure automatic influences of memory—that is, effects of memory that are not mediated by intentional retrieval and are not accompanied by a subjective experience of remembering—whereas direct tests are intended to measure intentional, aware uses of memory. The exciting finding is that performance on these two types of memory tests can be independent. For example, Weiskrantz and Warrington (1975) reported that amnesic subjects, who performed very poorly on a direct test of recognition memory, gained as much benefit from prior exposure to solution words on fragment completion as did control subjects.

It is tempting to assume that there are direct one-to-one correspondences (1) between the type of test subjects are given and the underlying memory system that supports test performance, and (2) between the underlying memory system and subjective experience. For example, subjects given an indirect test might use memory for a prior episode without having the subjective experience of remembering that episode, and such effects might reflect the operation of a special implicit memory system or process (Schacter, 1987). Most researchers have made these assumptions, if only tacitly, and treated deviations from these one-to-one correspondences as matters of measurement error. In what follows, we argue that the linkage among kind of test, kind of subjective experience, and kind of underlying memory process is not so fixed. Drawing a parallel between memory and attention, we argue that performance on any memory test is a joint product of controlled and automatic uses of memory, and propose that the subjective experience that accompanies task performance (e.g., remembering) is the product of an interpretive process by which current mental events are attributed to specific sources (e.g., memory) on the basis of evidence. One implication of these claims is that particular memory processes cannot be identified with particular tasks, because all tasks draw on multiple processes. As an alternative to identifying processes with tasks, we describe a "process dissociation procedure" that allows one to separate the contributions of different processes to performance on a given task. We believe that these procedures, developed in studies with normal under-graduates, will prove useful for specifying the nature of memory deficits suffered by patient populations.

Subjective Experience

Although cognitive psychology has been defined as "the science of the mental life" (e.g., Miller, 1966), most contemporary theorists pay scant attention to subjective experience (but see Bowers & Hilgard, 1988; Gardiner, 1988; Johnson, 1988). This is unfortunate, because people often act on the basis of their subjective interpretation of events. One possible reason for the neglect of subjective experience is that it is often viewed as simply reflecting the activation of underlying memory representations or systems; for instance, the subjective experience of remembering is assumed to arise from activation of episodic memory traces. An alternative view is that subjective experience reflects an inference or interpretation, created to make sense of the way people interact with the world around them. In such a constructive view of conscious-ness (Jacoby & Kelley, 1987; Mandler & Nakamura, 1987; Marcel, 1983), there is no necessary correspondence between subjective experience and form of underlying representation. For example, people can have the subjective experience of remember-ing in the absence of a corresponding "episodic" memory trace (as in *déjà vu*), and can use memories of specific past events without being aware of doing so (as in involuntary plagiarism; Brown & Murphy, 1989). We propose that subjective experience is based on qualitative aspects of how an event is processed, coupled with the (subjectively assessed) demands present in the current situation (Kelley & Jacoby, 1990).

It is reasonable to propose that qualities of current mental events provide a basis for memory judgments, because the use of memory does in fact influence the nature of current processing. One common effect of past experience is to make processing in the present more efficient, rapid, or fluent. For example, prior experience can enhance the perception of briefly flashed words or visually degraded pictures (Jacoby & Brooks, 1984; Jacoby & Dallas, 1981), the completion of word fragments (Tulving, Schacter, & Stark, 1982), the ability to solve problems or answer questions (Jacoby & Kelley, 1987; Kelley & Lindsay, 1992; Needham & Begg, 1991), and the speeded reading of text (Kolers, 1976).

Fluent processing is generally a reliable cue to the use of memory, because past experience so often does facilitate later performance, and these transfer effects are remarkably specific (Jacoby, Kelley, & Dywan, 1989). However, fluent processing can arise from sources other than memory. If oriented to the past, people may mistake ease of processing for an indication of prior occurrence. Consistent with this hypothesis, illusions of remembering have been produced by manipulating the visual clarity of memory test items (Whittlesea, Jacoby, & Girard, 1990) and the ease of completing word fragments presented as recall cues (Lindsay & Kelley, 1991). Similarly, Jacoby and Whitehouse (1989) found that unconscious perception of a new word prior to its presentation as a test item increased the probability of its being falsely recognized as old. Presumably, the unconsciously perceived presentation facilitated processing of the subsequent test word. In turn, the relative ease of processing produced a feeling of familiarity that was attributed to the prior study list. Importantly, when subjects were made aware of the flashed word (by increasing its duration), the probability of false recognition *decreased*. Being aware that the new test item was recently presented, subjects could discount or correctly attribute the source of their fluent processing. Finding qualitatively different effects for aware and unaware conditions is crucial for establishing the existence of unconscious perception (Cheesman & Merikle, 1986; Dixon, 1981; Holender, 1986). More generally, the strategy of placing conscious and unconscious processes in opposition allows one to isolate their separate contributions to performance. We discuss this strategy in greater detail in a later section.

Illusions of memory such as those described above show that one can have the experience of remembering in the absence of an underlying memory representation. Perceptual illusions have been helpful in uncovering the environmental cues that are used to construct perceptual experience (e.g., Brunswik, 1956). Similarly, memory illusions can be used to specify the cues that support an attribution of pastness (Jacoby, Kelley, & Dywan, 1989; Kelley & Jacoby, 1990). Our results suggest that fluency of processing is one such cue, and that subjects' current orientation influences their interpretation of variations in fluency. In each of the experiments described above, subjects were not informed of manipulations of fluency; instead, they were directed to make fine discriminations concerning a past event. Under these conditions, relatively small differences in processing fluency were interpreted as resulting from prior experience. However, if subjects are made aware of the source of these processing differences, illusions of remembering disappear (Jacoby & Whitehouse, 1989; Whittlesea et al., 1990). These results suggest that subjective experience is sensitive to current task demands as well as to prior experience.

Additional support for an attributional basis of subjective experience is provided by studies showing that unconscious influences of memory can be misattributed to the present. Fluent processing as a result of prior exposure can lengthen the apparent duration of a word that is flashed (Witherspoon & Allan, 1985), can lower the background noise accompanying the presentation of a sentence (Jacoby, Allan, Collins, & Larwill, 1988), and can increase the apparent fame of nonfamous names (Jacoby, Kelley, Brown, & Jasechko, 1989). Jacoby, Woloshyn, and Kelley (1989) had subjects study a list of nonfamous names under conditions of either full or divided attention. Later, subjects were asked to make fame judgments on a list of names, some of which were the nonfamous names they had read earlier. Subjects were told that all of the names read earlier were nonfamous. Nevertheless, in comparison to a set of new names, more of the old names were judged as famous in the divided-attention group. This can clearly be interpreted as an unconscious influence of memory, because if subjects could consciously recollect a name's prior occurrence, they could be sure it was not famous. It appears that, like a brief presentation, dividing attention reduces the ability to consciously recollect the past, thus increasing susceptibility to unconscious influences.

An analogous point is made by recent studies investigating the "mere-exposure effect" (Zajonc, 1968). Presentation of geometric shapes (Kunst-Wilson & Zajonc, 1980; Seamon, Brody, & Kauff, 1983a, 1983b) and photographs of human faces (Bornstein,

Leone, & Galley, 1987) at exposure durations too short to support above-chance-level recognition performance can nevertheless positively influence subsequent preference judgments (see Johnson, Kim, & Risse, 1985, for related work with Korsakoff patients). Interestingly, exposure effects in the absence of recognition are not specific to preferences, but can also influence judgments of contrast (Merikle & Reingold, 1991), brightness or darkness (Mandler, Nakamura, & Van Zandt, 1987), and even "familiarity" (Bonanno & Stillings, 1986). These findings reinforce our belief that subjective experience reflects an interpretive process, rather than being an inherent characteristic of the memory representation.

The subjective experience of remembering is often a valid indication of previous occurrence. However, the use of the past is often unconscious (Jacoby & Kelley, 1987) or misattributed to the present (Jacoby, Kelley, & Dywan, 1989). Moreover, as shown by illusions of memory as well as by confabulation in certain clinical cases (Baddeley & Wilson, 1986; Johnson, 1991; Moscovitch, 1989; Stuss & Benson, 1986), a feeling of remembering does not require an underlying memory trace. These observations are inconsistent with the assumption that subjective experience resides in memory traces or particular memory systems (e.g., Tulving, 1985). A related assumption—the notion that a memory test can be treated as a pure measure of a specific memory process—is discussed below.

The Factor-Pure Assumption

"There is no such entity as a 'pure' behavioral task, that is, a task that reflects only a single process or capacity" (Weiskrantz, 1989, p. 102). Weiskrantz offered this statement as one of several "dogmatic propositions with which most practicing neuropsychologist would agree" (p. 102), and we too would endorse it. Yet, despite this apparent consensus, neuropsychologists and others who study cognition often interpret tasks as though they were factor-pure measures of particular processes. Indeed, a good deal of the psychological literature could be characterized as an attempt to develop (or to criticize others' attempts to develop) factor-pure measures (Holender, 1986; Richardson-Klavehn & Bjork, 1988).

Because tasks are not factor-pure measures of processes, memory researchers often rely on findings of task dissociations. The current interest in indirect memory tests owes much to the discovery that amnesic subjects can show retention performance equivalent to that of normals (e.g., Weiskrantz & Warrington, 1975; Shimamura, 1986), and to subsequent findings of task dissociations in normals (e.g., Jacoby & Dallas, 1981; Tulving et al., 1982). Indeed, dissociations between performance on direct and indirect tests have led some researchers to propose a distinct area of research, the focus of which is "implicit memory," the form of memory revealed on indirect tests (Schacter, 1987). A task dissociation constitutes evidence that the tasks differ in at least one underlying process (Dunn & Kirsner, 1989), but could only necessitate postulating distinct forms of memory if retention tests were factor-pure. Tasks are not factor-pure; multiple processes can contribute to performance on any given task. This is evidenced by the variable relationship between tasks across experiments: The studies mentioned above reported dissociations between direct and indirect memory tests, but other studies have reported parallel effects between direct and indirect measures (Hunt & Toth, 1990; Jacoby & Dallas, 1981; Rappold & Hashtroudi, 1991; Schacter & Graf, 1986; Toth & Hunt, 1990) and dissociations between different indirect measures (Hunt & Toth, 1990; Roediger, Weldon, & Challis, 1989; Witherspoon & Moscovitch, 1989). This complex pattern of findings clearly indicates that a factor-pure interpretation of retention measures is untenable.

The theoretical issues surrounding interpretation of "implicit" memory effects are similar to those encountered in discussions of automaticity. We believe that comparisons between direct and indirect tests of memory are best understood as members of a larger class of task manipulations that have been used to explore the distinction between intentional and automatic processes (Jacoby, 1991; Jacoby & Kelley, 1991; Klatzky, 1984; Logan, 1990). Attention researchers have long been concerned with separating the contributions of automatic and controlled processes to task performance. We have found it useful to think of memory in this framework. Direct tests of memory may be described as requiring more controlled processes, whereas indirect tests may reflect more automatic uses of memory. It is becoming increasingly clear, however, that performance is never purely automatic or controlled (Allport, 1989; Neumann, 1984). Viewing task performance as the joint product of automatic and controlled processes provides an alternative to identifying tasks with specific processes or systems. Furthermore, this approach encourages research designed to separate automatic from controlled processes within a single task. In what follows, we describe a technique for accomplishing this goal.

Advantages of Opposition

Most indirect memory tests (e.g., fragment completion) can be described as "facilitation paradigms," in that the use of memory facilitates performance of a task (e.g., prior exposure to solution words facilitates fragment completion). One major problem with facilitation paradigms is that both automatic and intentional uses of memory for studied items can facilitate task performance. How can one be sure that a particular finding reflects unaware rather than aware uses of memory? One approach is to ask subjects to report on their awareness. A problem with this method is that it relies on subjects' definitions of "awareness" (Merikle, 1984). Furthermore, asking subjects to describe their subjective experience while taking the test (e.g., Gardiner, 1988) may affect that experience as well as performance, and posttest recollections of awareness during the test (e.g., Bowers & Schacter, 1990) may not be accurate or easy to interpret.

An alternative approach to demonstrating automatic influences of memory is to use an interference paradigm instead of a facilitation paradigm. In an interference paradigm, the situation is set up so that aware remembering will have an effect opposite to that of automatic influences of memory. Thus any effect of the study episode can be attributed to automatic effects of memory. For example, in Jacoby, Woloshyn, and Kelley's (1989) "false fame" studies, we know that the effect of prior exposure to nonfamous names on subsequent fame judgments reflected an automatic influence of memory, because subjects were told that the studied names were not famous. Likewise, it is clear that Jacoby and Whitehouse's (1989) subjects did not consciously perceive the briefly presented previews of recognition test items, because aware perception of preview items in a long-exposure condition had an opposite effect to that obtained with brief exposures. As a final example, by telling subjects at test not to report any postevent information, Lindsay (1990) provided unambiguous evidence that misleading postevent suggestions can impair ability to recall event details (e.g., Loftus, Miller, & Burns, 1978).

Interference paradigms allow one to demonstrate the existence of automatic effects of memory. However, those effects are underestimated because they are countervailed by controlled uses of memory. Also, interference paradigms do not yield quantitative estimates of separate processes, and so cannot be used to detect invariances in a particular kind of process across different conditions or populations. For example, early evidence suggested that performance on indirect memory tests does not decline with age, but more recent studies have reported age-related deficits in performance (see Hultsch & Dixon, 1990). This lack of consistency across studies may reflect differential contributions of automatic and controlled processes to different indirect tasks. In order to answer a question such as "Are automatic retrieval processes invariant across age?", one must be able to estimate the separate contributions of different processes to task performance. In the next section, we describe how interference and facilitation paradigms can be combined to yield separate quantitative estimates of automatic and controlled processes.

A Process Dissociation Procedure

Dual-process theories of recognition (e.g., Atkinson & Juola, 1974; Jacoby & Dallas, 1981; Mandler, 1980) propose that conscious recollection and judgments of familiarity are alternative bases for recognition memory decisions. Compared with recollection, judgments of familiarity are relatively automatic, in that they tend to be faster, less effortful, and less reliant on intention. It follows that, as with indirect tests of memory, performance on direct tests such as recognition is jointly determined by controlled and automatic uses of memory.

Jacoby (1991) has introduced a method for obtaining separate estimates of the contributions of familiarity and recollection to recognition memory judgments. The procedure involves comparing performance in a facilitation or "inclusion" test condition (in which familiarity and recollection have the same effect) with performance in an interference or "exclusion" test condition (in which familiarity and recollection have opposing effects). For example, to assess the separate contributions of recollection and familiarity to recognition of a visually presented list of words, subjects may be given two lists at input—one presented visually, the other presented aurally. In an inclusion test condition, subjects are told to accept (say "yes" to) all old items regardless of presentation list, and to reject only new items. Because to-be-included items could be correctly accepted on the basis of either familiarity or recollection, the probability of accepting a to-be-included item is the sum of the probability of the item being familiar (F) and the probability of the item being recollected (R), minus the intersect (F $*$ R):

$$P(\text{accept}|\text{to-be-included}) = F + R - (F \cdot R)$$

In contrast, an exclusion test condition asks subjects to accept *only* items that were heard and to reject items from the visual list as well as new items. Subjects are correctly told that if they can recollect an item as one that they saw, they can be certain that the word was *not* presented in the list that they heard. Thus, to-be-excluded items that subjects incorrectly accept (i.e., visual items) must be familiar (F) but not be recollected $(1 - R)$; otherwise, subjects would not accept them. The probability of incorrectly accepting a to-be-excluded item can therefore be expressed as follows:

$$P(\text{accept}|\text{to-be-excluded}) = F \cdot (1 - R) = F - (F \cdot R)$$

These equations and the observed probabilities permit estimates of the contributions of recollection and familiarity to be derived with simple algebra. For example, Jacoby (1992; see Jacoby & Kelley, 1991) explored the effects of dividing attention at study on subsequent recollection and familiarity. Subjects judged the relatedness of word pairs under conditions of full or divided attention, then heard a second list of words. At test, subjects in the inclusion condition were to accept any word presented in either of the earlier phases, whereas subjects in the exclusion condition were to accept only heard words. The results are presented in Table 4.1. In the inclusion conditions, subjects correctly accepted more words from related than from unrelated pairs, and dividing attention at study decreased correct recognition. In the exclusion conditions, on the other hand, subjects incorrectly accepted more words from unrelated than from related pairs, and dividing attention at study increased erroneous acceptance. The observed probabilities are sufficient to permit the conclusion that recollection was greater for words from related pairs, and that dividing attention impaired the use of recollection. However, without separate estimates of the two processes, these proba-

TABLE 4.1. Observed Probabilities of Accepting Test Items and Estimated Probabilities of Recollection and Familiarity as a Function of Attention at Study, Item Type, and Test Instructions

| | Observed probabilities | | Estimated probabilities | | | |
| | Item type | | Recollection | | Familiarity | |
	Rel.	Unrel.	Rel.	Unrel.	Rel.	Unrel.
Full attention						
Inclusion	.83	.70	.52	.32	.646	.558
Exclusion	.31	.38				
Divided attention						
Inclusion	.75	.61	.28	.12	.652	.557
Exclusion	.47	.49				

Note. Estimated recollection = P(accept|to-be-included) − P(accept|to-be-excluded). Estimated familiarity = P(accept|to-be-excluded)/(1 − recollection). From *Separating Automatic and Intentional Bases for Recognition Memory: Attention, Awareness, and Control* by L. L. Jacoby, 1992, manuscript submitted for publication.

bilities do not allow definitive conclusions concerning the effects of relatedness and attention on familiarity.

Using the process dissociation formulas described above, Jacoby (1992) estimated the separate contributions of familiarity and recollection to recognition responses on words studied in related and unrelated pairs. These estimates, presented in Table 4.1, can be derived from the equations presented at the bottom of the table. For example, the recollection (R) value of words from related pairs in the full-attention condition can be obtained by subtracting the probability of accepting to-be-excluded items from the probability of accepting to-be-included items (.83 − .31 = .52). Familiarity (F) can then be calculated by dividing the probability of accepting to-be-excluded items by the inverse of recollection (.31/[1 − .52]). Applying this same procedure to each set of conditions yields separate estimates of R and F.

As predicted, dividing attention at study dramatically reduced estimates of recollection (from .52 to .28 for words from related pairs, and from .32 to .12 for words from unrelated pairs), but had absolutely no effect on estimates of familiarity (.646 and .652 for words from related pairs, and .558 and .557 for words from unrelated pairs). Similar results were obtained by Jacoby (1991); estimations of familiarity were found to fit the observed probabilities of erroneously accepting to-be-excluded old items when attention was divided at test. These studies suggest that dividing attention at study or at test can block subjects' use of recollection as a basis for recognition judgments, thus leaving familiarity-based responding relatively unopposed. Most important, the invariance in familiarity across conditions could not have been established by equating processes with tasks and then examining task dissociations, because tasks are rarely process-pure.

The above-described findings suggest that dividing attention has effects similar to those seen in certain amnesic syndromes. Speculatively, amnesia may produce deficits in controlled processing (e.g., recollection) while leaving automatic influences of memory (e.g., familiarity) in place. However, the effects of dividing attention do not always parallel those of amnesia (e.g., Nissen & Bullemer, 1987). This may be because some secondary tasks act to change the segmentation of the primary task or break up its continuity, thereby influencing automatic as well as controlled processing. To understand the effects of divided attention on memory along with its relation to amnesia, it will probably be necessary to specify the relation between primary and secondary tasks more fully (Allport, 1989; Broadbent, 1989; Neisser, 1980). Without a method for separating automatic from controlled uses of memory, any selective impairments produced by either amnesia or divided attention cannot be clearly identified.

We believe that the process dissociation procedure is an important methodological tool that can be used to investigate a number of problems confronting memory researchers. For example, in the experiment described above, Jacoby (1992) found that words studied in related pairs were later more familiar than words studied in unrelated pairs (Table 4.1). Similarly, Jacoby (1991) obtained higher estimates of familiarity on items studied as anagrams to be solved than on items studied as words to be read aloud. These are important findings, because familiarity has previously been described as reflecting the match between study and test in perceptual characteristics (Jacoby & Dallas, 1981; Mandler, 1980). The results described here show that familiarity is not totally reliant on perceptual characteristics, but, rather, can also reflect prior conceptual processing.

The ability to compare a particular cognitive process in different populations and conditions is an important goal for memory researchers. Similar to signal detection theory (Swets, Tanner, & Birdsall, 1961), the process dissociation procedure separates the contribution of different processes to task performance, allowing one to discern invariance in one process across variations in another. In the studies reported above, for example, recollection was shown to be greatly impaired by dividing attention, whereas familiarity remained invariant across manipulations of attention. That invariance could not be shown without a procedure for separately estimating the processes contributing to performance.

The formulas described above were designed to separate the contributions of controlled and automatic processes to recognition memory judgments, but they can be applied to any domain in which two processes are hypothesized to make independent contributions to performance. One assumption of the process dissociation procedure is that similar judgment criteria are used in the inclusion and exclusion conditions. We know that this assumption was met in Jacoby (1991), because performance in the two conditions was nearly identical on heard and new items; Jacoby (1992) avoided criterion differences by using a forced-choice test. In other experiments, however, we have sometimes encountered differences in judgment criteria. Thus, as the approach is extended to other domains, details of the experimental conditions and/or formulas may need to be modified. For example, we are currently using process dissociation procedures to explore cued recall, stem and fragment completion, unconscious perception, and Stroop (1935) effects. Preliminary results in each of these areas are very encouraging.

Summary and Conclusions

In this chapter, we have challenged the notion that there are direct one-to-one mappings between tasks and processes and between processes and subjective experiences. Our argument is that the linkage among kind of test, kind of underlying representation, and kind of subjective experience is a rather loose one. One implication of this view is that subjective experience involves an unconscious inference whereby current mental events are attributed to sources on the basis of evidence. Another implication is that particular cognitive processes cannot be identified with particular tasks, because virtually all tasks involve the integration of multiple processes. Finally, we have described a "process dissociation procedure" that allows one to derive separate estimates of the different processes contributing to performance on a task. Application of the procedure in studies of recognition memory provided support for a dual-process model of recognition (Jacoby & Dallas, 1981; Mandler, 1980) and evidence that familiarity-based responding can reflect prior conceptual as well as perceptual processing.

We have described the process dissociation procedure in some detail, because we believe that it will prove useful for specifying the nature of cognitive deficits caused by neurological damage. For example, a process dissociation might reveal that frontal lobe patients have deficits in recollection but retain normal levels of familiarity. Other studies might show parallel disruptions in different clinical populations (e.g., frontal damage vs. normal aging). Findings of this sort would be important, not only for illuminating the consequences of neurological insult, but also for suggesting approaches to rehabilitation.

ACKNOWLEDGMENTS

Preparation of this chapter was supported by the North Atlantic Treaty Organization and the National Science Foundation under a grant awarded in 1990 to Jeffrey P. Toth; a Natural Science and Engineering Research Council (NSERC) postdoctoral fellowship to D. Stephen Lindsay; and an NSERC operating grant to Larry L. Jacoby. We thank Debra Jared, Colleen Kelley, and John Reeder for their very helpful comments on an earlier version of this chapter.

REFERENCES

Allport, A. (1989). Visual attention. In M. I. Posner (Ed.), *Foundations of cognitive science* (pp. 631–682). Cambridge, MA: MIT Press.

Atkinson, R. C., & Juola, J. F. (1974). Search and decision processes in recognition memory. In D. H. Krantz, R. C. Atkinson, R. D. Luce, & P. Suppes (Eds.), *Contemporary developments in mathematical psychology: Vol. 1. Learning, memory and thinking* (pp. 243–293). San Francisco, CA: W. H. Freeman.

Baddeley, A., & Wilson, B. (1986). Amnesia, autobiographical memory, and confabulation. In D. C. Rubin (Ed.), *Autobiographical memory* (pp. 225–252). Cambridge, England: Cambridge University Press.

Bonanno, G. A., & Stillings, N. A. (1986). Preference, familiarity, and recognition after repeated brief exposures to random geometric shapes. *American Journal of Psychology, 99*(8), 403–415.

Bornstein, R. F., Leone, D. R., & Galley, D. J. (1987). The generalizability of subliminal mere exposure effects: Influence of stimuli perceived without awareness on social behavior. *Journal of Personality and Social Psychology, 53,* 1070–1079.

Bowers, J. S., & Schacter, D. L. (1990). Implicit memory and test awareness. *Journal of Experimental Psychology: Learning, Memory, and Cognition, 16,* 404–416.

Bowers, K. S., & Hilgard, E. (1988). Some complexities in understanding memory. In H. M. Pettinati (Ed.), *Hypnosis and memory* (pp. 3–18). New York: Guilford Press.

Broadbent, D. E. (1989). Lasting representations and temporary processes. In H. L. Roediger III & F. I. M. Craik (Eds.), *Varieties of memory and consciousness: Essays in honour of Endel Tulving* (pp. 211–227). Hillsdale, NJ: Erlbaum.

Brown, A. L., & Murphy, D. R. (1989). Cryptomnesia: Delineating inadvertent plagiarism. *Journal of Experimental Psychology: Learning, Memory, and Cognition, 15,* 432–442.

Brunswik, E. (1956). *Perception and representative design of psychological experiments.* Berkeley: University of California Press.

Cheesman, J., & Merikle, P. M. (1986). Distinguishing conscious from unconscious perceptual processes. *Canadian Journal of Psychology, 40,* 343–367.

Dixon, N. F. (1981). *Preconscious processing.* Chichester, England: Wiley.

Dunn, J. C., & Kirsner, K. (1989). Implicit memory: Task or process? In S. Lewandowsky, J. C. Dunn, & K. Kirsner (Eds.), *Implicit memory: Theoretical issues* (pp. 17–31). Hillsdale, NJ: Erlbaum.

Gardiner, J. M. (1988). Functional aspects of recollective experience. *Memory and Cognition, 16,* 309–313.

Holender, D. (1986). Semantic activation without conscious identification in dichotic listening, parafoveal vision, and visual masking: A survey and appraisal. *Behavioral and Brain Sciences, 9,* 1–23.

Hultsch, D. F., & Dixon, R. A. (1990). Learning and memory and aging. In J. E. Birren & K. W. Schaie (Eds.), *Handbook of the psychology of aging* (3rd ed.). San Diego: Academic Press.

Hunt, R. R., & Toth, J. P. (1990). Perceptual identification, fragment completion, and free recall: Concepts and data. *Journal of Experimental Psychology: Learning, Memory, and Cognition, 16,* 282–290.

Jacoby, L. L. (1991). A process dissociation framework: Separating automatic from intentional uses of memory. *Journal of Memory and Language, 30,* 513–541.

Jacoby, L. L. (1992). *Separating automatic and intentional bases for recognition memory: Attention, aware-ness, and control.* Manuscript submitted for publication.

Jacoby, L. L., Allan, L. G., Collins, J. C., & Larwill, L. K. (1988). Memory influences subjective experience: Noise judgments. *Journal of Experimental Psychology: Learning, Memory, and Cognition, 14,* 240-247.

Jacoby, L. L., & Brooks, L. R. (1984). Nonanalytic cognition: Memory, perception and concept learning. In G. H. Bower (Ed.), *The psychology of learning and motivation: Advances in research and theory* (Vol. 18, pp. 1-47). New York: Academic Press.

Jacoby, L. L., & Dallas, M. (1981). On the relationship between autobiographical memory and perceptual learning. *Journal of Experimental Psychology: General, 3,* 306-340.

Jacoby, L. L., & Kelley, C. M. (1987). Unconscious influences of memory for a prior event. *Personality and Social Psychology Bulletin, 13,* 314-336.

Jacoby, L. L., & Kelley, C. M. (1991). Unconscious influences of memory: Dissociations and automaticity. In A. D. Milner & M. D. Rugg (Eds.), *The neuropsychology of consciousness* (pp. 201-233). London: Academic Press.

Jacoby, L. L., Kelley, C. M., Brown, J., & Jasechko, J. (1989). Becoming famous overnight: Limits on the ability to avoid unconscious influences of the past. *Journal of Personality and Social Psychology, 56,* 326-338.

Jacoby, L. L., Kelley, C. M., & Dywan, J. (1989). Memory attributions. In H. L. Roediger III & F. I. M. Craik (Eds.), *Varieties of memory and consciousness: Essays in honour of Endel Tulving* (pp. 391-422). Hillsdale, NJ: Erlbaum.

Jacoby, L. L., & Whitehouse, K. (1989). An illusion of memory: False recognition influenced by unconscious perception. *Journal of Experimental Psychology: General, 118,* 126-135.

Jacoby, L. L., Woloshyn, V., & Kelley, C. M. (1989). Becoming famous without being recognized: Uncon-scious influences of memory produced by dividing attention. *Journal of Experimental Psychology: General, 118,* 115-125.

Johnson, M. K. (1988). Discriminating the origin of information. In T. F. Oltmanns & B. A. Maher (Eds.), *Delusional beliefs: Interdisciplinary perspectives.* New York: Wiley.

Johnson, M. K. (1991). Reality monitoring: Evidence from confabulation in organic brain disease patients. In G. Prigatano & D. L. Schacter (Eds.), *Awareness of deficit after brain injury* (pp. 176-197). New York: Oxford University Press.

Johnson, M. K., Kim, J. K., & Risse, G. (1985). Do alcoholic Korsakoff's syndrome patients acquire affective reactions? *Journal of Experimental Psychology: Learning, Memory, and Cognition, 11,* 22-36.

Kelley, C. M., & Jacoby, L. L. (1990). The construction of subjective experience: Memory attributions. *Mind and Language, 5*(1), 49-68.

Kelley, C. M., & Lindsay, D. S. (1992). *Remembering mistaken for knowing: Ease of retrieval as a basis for confidence in answers to general knowledge questions.* Manuscript submitted for publication.

Klatzky, R. L. (1984). *Memory and awareness.* New York: W. H. Freeman.

Kolers, P. A. (1976). Reading a year later. *Journal of Experimental Psychology: Human Learning and Memory, 2,* 554-565.

Kunst-Wilson, W. R., & Zajonc, R. B. (1980). Affective discrimination of stimuli that cannot be recognized. *Science, 207,* 557-558.

Lindsay, D. S. (1990). Misleading suggestions can impair eyewitnesses' ability to remember event details. *Journal of Experimental Psychology: Learning, Memory, and Cognition, 16,* 1077-1083.

Lindsay, D. S., & Kelley, C. M. (1991). *Ease of generation during recall induces a feeling of remembering.* Poster presented at the meeting of the American Psychological Society, Washington, DC.

Loftus, E. F., Miller, D. G., & Burns, H. J. (1978). Semantic integration of verbal information into visual memory. *Journal of Experimental Psychology: Human Learning and Memory, 4,* 19-31.

Logan, G. D. (1990). Repetition priming and automaticity: Common underlying mechanisms. *Cognitive Psychology, 22,* 1-35.

Mandler, G. (1980). Recognizing: The judgment of previous occurrence. *Psychological Review, 87,* 252-271.

Mandler, G., & Nakamura, Y. (1987). Aspects of consciousness. *Personality and Social Psychology Bulletin, 13,* 299-313.

Mandler, G., Nakamura, Y., & Van Zandt, B. J. S. (1987). Nonspecific effects of exposure on stimuli that cannot be recognized. *Journal of Experimental Psychology: Learning, Memory, and Cognition, 13,* 646-648.

Marcel, A. J. (1983). Conscious and unconscious perception: An approach to the relations between phenomenal experience and perceptual processes. *Cognitive Psychology, 15,* 238-300.

Merikle, P. M. (1984). Toward a definition of awareness. *Bulletin of the Psychonomic Society, 22,* 449-450.

Merikle, P. M., & Reingold, E. M. (1991). Comparing direct (explicit) and indirect (implicit) measures to study unconscious memory. *Journal of Experimental Psychology: Learning, Memory, and Cognition*, *17*, 224-233.

Miller, G. A. (1966). *Psychology: The science of mental life*. Harmondsworth, England: Penguin.

Moscovitch, M. (1989). Confabulation and the frontal systems: Strategic versus associative retrieval in neuropsychological theories of memory. In H. L. Roediger III & F. I. M. Craik (Eds.), *Varieties of memory and consciousness: Essays in honour of Endel Tulving* (pp. 133-156). Hillsdale, NJ: Erlbaum.

Needham, D. R., & Begg, I. M. (1991). Problem-oriented training promotes spontaneous analogical transfer: Memory-oriented training promotes memory for training. *Memory and Cognition*, *19*, 543-557.

Neisser, U. (1980). The limits of cognition. In P. Jusczyk & R. Klein (Eds.), *The nature of thought: Essays in honor of D. O. Hebb* (pp. 115-132). Hillsdale, NJ: Erlbaum.

Neumann, O. (1984). Automatic processing: A review of recent findings and a plea for an old theory. In W. Prinz & A. F. Sanders (Eds.), *Cognition and motor processes* (pp. 255-293). Berlin: Springer-Verlag.

Nissen, M. J., & Bullemer, P. (1987). Attentional requirements of learning: Evidence from performance measures. *Cognitive Psychology*, *19*, 1-32.

Rappold, V. A., & Hashtroudi, S. (1991). Does organization improve priming? *Journal of Experimental Psychology: Learning, Memory, and Cognition*, *17*, 103-114.

Richardson-Klavehn, A., & Bjork, R. A. (1988). Measures of memory. *Annual Review of Psychology*, *39*, 475-543.

Roediger, H. L., III, Weldon, M. S., & Challis, B. H. (1989). Explaining dissociations between implicit and explicit measures of retention: A processing account. In H. L. Roediger III & F. I. M. Craik (Eds.), *Varieties of memory and consciousness: Essays in honour of Endel Tulving* (pp. 3-41). Hillsdale, NJ: Erlbaum.

Schacter, D. L. (1987). Implicit memory: History and current status. *Journal of Experimental Psychology: Learning, Memory, and Cognition*, *13*, 501-518.

Schacter, D. L., & Graf, P. (1986). Effects of elaborative processing on implicit and explicit memory for new associations. *Journal of Experimental Psychology: Learning, Memory, and Cognition*, *12*, 432-444.

Seamon, J. G., Brody, N., & Kauff, D. M. (1983a). Affective discrimination of stimuli that are not recognized: Effects of shadowing, masking, and cerebral laterality. *Journal of Experimental Psychology: Learning, Memory, and Cognition*, *9*, 544-555.

Seamon, J. G., Brody, N., & Kauff, D. M. (1983b). Affective discrimination of stimuli that are not recognized: Effects of delay between exposure and test. *Bulletin of the Psychonomic Society*, *21*, 187-189.

Shimamura, A. P. (1986). Priming effects in amnesia: Evidence for a dissociable memory function. *Quarterly Journal of Experimental Psychology*, *38A*, 619-644.

Stroop, J. R. (1935). Studies of interference in serial verbal reactions. *Journal of Experimental Psychology*, *18*, 643-662.

Stuss, D. T., & Benson, D. F. (1986). *The frontal lobes*. New York: Raven Press.

Swets, J. A., Tanner, W. P., & Birdsall, T. G. (1961). Decision processes in perception. *Psychological Review*, *68*, 301-340.

Toth, J. P., & Hunt, R. R. (1990). Effect of generation on a word-identification task. *Journal of Experimental Psychology: Learning, Memory, and Cognition*, *16*, 993-1003.

Tulving, E. (1985). How many memory systems are there? *American Psychologist*, *40*, 385-398.

Tulving, E., Schacter, D. L., & Stark, H. A. (1982). Priming effects in word-fragment completion are independent of recognition memory. *Journal of Experimental Psychology: Learning, Memory, and Cognition*, *8*, 336-342.

Weiskrantz, L. (1989). Remembering dissociations. In H. L. Roediger III & F. I. M. Craik (Eds.), *Varieties of memory and consciousness: Essays in honour of Endel Tulving* (pp. 101-120). Hillsdale, NJ: Erlbaum.

Weiskrantz, L., & Warrington, E. K. (1975). The problem of the amnesic syndrome in man and animals. In R. L. Isaacson & K. H. Pribram (Eds.), *The hippocampus* (Vol. 2). New York: Plenum.

Whittlesea, B. W. A., Jacoby, L. L., & Girard, K. A. (1990). Illusions of immediate memory: Evidence of an attributional basis for feelings of familiarity and perceptual quality. *Journal of Memory and Language*, *29*, 716-732.

Witherspoon, D., & Allan, L. G. (1985). The effects of a prior presentation on temporal judgments in a perceptual identification task. *Memory and Cognition*, *13*, 101-111.

Witherspoon, D., & Moscovitch, M. (1989). Stochastic independence between two implicit memory tasks. *Journal of Experimental Psychology: Learning, Memory, and Cognition*, *15*, 22-30.

Zajonc, R. B. (1968). Attitudinal effects of mere exposure. *Journal of Personality and Social Psychology Monograph*, *9*(2, Pt. 2), 1-27.

5

Memory Dissociations: A Cognitive Psychophysiology Perspective

RUSSELL M. BAUER and MIEKE VERFAELLIE

Recent studies of memory dissociations embodied within the distinction between "implicit" and "explicit" memory have resulted in new ways of thinking about and measuring memory performance in normal and amnesic populations (Jacoby, 1984). It now seems clear that memory manifests itself in multiple parallel ways, some of which are not reflected in measures of conscious recollection. Recent studies of perceptual priming (Cermak, Talbot, Chandler, & Wolbarst, 1985) and skill learning (Cohen & Squire, 1980) have clearly demonstrated that a substantial amount of learning takes place outside of awareness, and that in most cases such learning appears relatively intact in amnesia (Schacter, 1987). Schacter (1987; Schacter, McAndrews, & Moscovitch, 1988) noted important conceptual similarities among (1) sparing of implicit memory in amnesia, (2) spared recognition abilities in agnosia and hemianopia (Geschwind, 1965; Weiskrantz, 1986), and (3) dissociations between memory and awareness in normals (Nisbett & Wilson, 1977; Zajonc, 1980). In all these examples, performance in one response domain is dissociated from performance in another, leaving the impression that the patient/subject "knows" more than he or she can "tell." Different answers to the question "What does the patient know about X?" would be given, depending upon which response domain is examined (Moscovitch, 1984).

Our approach to memory dissociations has focused on dissociations between verbal and psychophysiological correlates of recognition, and is based on the fact that verbal, motor, and visceroautonomic response domains are often poorly correlated even in normal states. For example, low verbal–autonomic correlations are the rule in autonomic conditioning studies that examine the relationship between verbal awareness of the conditioned stimulus–unconditioned stimulus (CS-US) contingency and autonomic differentiation between CS+ and CS− (Ohman, 1983). Such "imperfect coupling" also has significant implications for clinical assessment of emotional disorders, where low or moderate correlations among verbal, motor, and physiological indicators of emotional disturbance raise real issues about which response domain should be regarded as the most "valid" target of assessment (Lang, Rice, & Sternbach, 1972). For example, extreme fear of public speaking may persist after treatment, despite vastly improved behavioral performance, reduced avoidance of speaking engagements, and low physiological reactivity (Sallis, Lichstein, & McGlynn, 1980).

In our view, memory dissociations of the implicit–explicit type are, for the most part, clear demonstrations of the general principle of imperfect response coupling. Our strategy has been to explore such dissociations by focusing on the relationships between (1) explicit measures of verbal recognition and (2) psychophysiological responses that are time-locked to the presentation of to-be-remembered (TBR) information. In this chapter, we first describe our approach and show that physiological responses to TBR information (so-called "autonomic recognition") can occur in both global and selective forms of memory disorder, and that such responses are in some cases not dependent on explicit verbal recognition. We then comment on factors that seem to influence the strength of this effect, and on the important (and as yet unresolved) issue of where autonomic recognition fits in the distinction between implicit and explicit memory.

Psychophysiological "Detection of Information"

Our studies of autonomic recognition in amnesic and agnosic patients are based on an applied psychophysiological technique known generally as the "detection of information" (DOI) paradigm (Ben-Shakhar, 1977; Ben-Shakhar & Furedy, 1990; Davis, 1961; Lieblich, Kugelmass, & Ben-Shakhar, 1970) and its applied variant, known specifically as the "guilty knowledge test" (GKT; Lykken, 1959, 1974, 1979). The GKT was introduced as a way of detecting whether a criminal suspect has specific information about crime details. Such procedures are necessary in situations where, because of the suspect's unwillingness to confuss such knowledge, verbal report is of limited value in determining what is known about the crime.

The GKT begins with the assumption that "a guilty subject will show some involuntary psychophysiological response to stimuli related to *remembered details* of the crime" (Lykken, 1959, p. 258; italics added). During the GKT, a series of multiple-choice items, each containing a single relevant (crime-related) alternative, is presented. Differential responses to crime-related information, which are expected to occur consistently only in a guilty suspect, result because the correct alternative supposedly represents a singular piece of significant information among the irrelevant alternatives. Because of its distinctive significance, the relevant alternative elicits an orienting response (OR) (Barry, 1977; Berlyne, 1960; Bernstein, Taylor, & Weinstein, 1975).[1]

The GKT has not attained wide use in criminology, because its reliance on highly detailed crime information places a burden on investigative resources and because its successful application requires the formal interrogation of suspects who are fully naive to crime details. However, the GKT has been used in experimental "guilt detection" investigations, in which psychophysiological responses are used along with verbal report to ascertain, what, if any, episodic information a subject has about a staged or

[1]In this respect, the DOI/GKT is different from the more widely known and more controversial practice of "lie detection," which is based primarily on the ability of such questions as "Did you kill John Brown?" to elicit defensive reactions (Podelsny & Raskin, 1978).

"mock" crime. In these studies, one group of subjects is made "guilty" (by learning of details surrounding a specific crime or by performing an experimentally sanctioned theft), while another group of subjects remains naive to the target information. The "guilty" and "innocent" subjects are then exposed to a GKT while verbal and psychophysiological responses are recorded. In most of these studies, electrodermal measures have been remarkably accurate in detecting "guilty" subjects (Ben-Shakhar, Lieblich, & Kugelmass, 1975 [60–78%]; Davidson, 1968 [98%]; Raskin, 1979 [89%]; Kykken, 1974). Similarly impressive results have been obtained using familiar personal information (Ben-Shakhar et al., 1975) and card selection procedures, in which subjects are shown a series of items, one of which they had previously chosen without the knowledge of the experimenter.

In most applications of DOI/GKT methodology, subjects say "no" to each alternative (thus denying guilt or knowledge of the relevant alternatives). This practice leaves open the question of whether orienting to the relevant information is a result of its intrinsic "signal value" or of the act of lying. Early reviews of the mechanism(s) responsible for DOI/GKT suggested that either emotional factors related to deception or motivational incentives for escaping detection were responsible for larger reactions to relevant alternatives (Gustafson & Orne, 1963). However, subsequent studies have clearly shown that the efficacy of DOI/GKT does not depend on the specific verbal response given to the question; equivalent rates of detection occur whether the subject is instructed to affirm, to deny, or to give no response to each item (Elaad & Ben-Shakhar, 1989). Since the information content of relevant items remains constant under all these response conditions, it is now generally agreed that DOI is based on the degree to which the information contained within the relevant alternatives can elicit ORs because of its "signal value" in relation to surrounding alternatives (Elaad & Ben-Shakhar, 1989; Gati & Ben-Shakhar, 1990; Lykken, 1974).

A fundamental characteristic of these studies is that some subjects are exposed to episodic information in the form of instructions or activities (e.g., a mock crime). Psychophysiological measures are then employed to detect which subjects have been so exposed. As such, DOI/GKT is an episodic recognition task. It is generally assumed that the "signal value" of relevant information derives from the fact that such information is distinctively recognized as part of the recently encountered episode (see Mandler, 1980). It is traditionally assumed that such recognition is necessary and sufficient for producing an OR to that item. Although this appears to be a prominent assumption, verbal memory is rarely tested directly, and recent data with normal subjects suggest that orienting to relevant items in DOI can proceed normally even when the subjects are unable to explicitly identify or recognize target itwms (Sackheim & Gur, 1979; Bauer, 1979). That is, the application of the DOI/GKT approach does not require the subject to consciously discriminate items or identify them as relevant.

In an example of this "covert recognition effect" (Bauer, 1979), college students made audiotapes of their own voices after having been told they were participating in a test of "verbal expressiveness." Two weeks later, they returned for an unannounced test of voice recognition, in which they listened to brief voice samples and decided whether each voice was their own or that of a stranger. Electrodermal responses (EDRs) and heart rate responses (HRRs) to each voice were continuously recorded. Physiological responses were almost twice as large on trials containing a subject's own voice than they were on "stranger" trials. Subjects were selected to have little experience hearing themselves on tape, and, as a result, many failed at least once to identify their own recorded voices. Importantly, EDRs and HRRs remained as strong on these trials as when correct self-identifications occurred. It was as if subjects' autonomic nervous system "recognized" their own voices even when verbal report failed.

If such dissociations can be made to occur in normals (and, in so doing, reveal something about the way in which such response variables are normally organized), then they might also be expected to characterize the way in which memory abilities become selectively impaired in amnesic states. In the past few years, we have been applying adaptations of this basic method to the study of amnesic and agnosic patients. We have attempted, in a DOI framework, to use psychophysiological measures as a way of determining whether amnesic subjects can discriminate between "targets" (studied or familiar stimuli) and "distractors" (not-studied or unfamiliar stimuli) in a recognition paradigm. In our view, such discrimination would provide evidence that, at least at a psychophysiological level, amnesics can "recognize" target information encountered during a learning episode.

Autonomic Recognition in Agnosia and Amnesia

Studies of Prosopagnosia

Our first attempt to formally apply the DOI paradigm to a neuropsychological syndrome concerned the evaluation of spared and impaired face recognition abilities in prosopagnosia, an acquired inability to recognize the faces of previously familiar persons (Damasio, Damasio, & Van Hoesen, 1982). The disorder is thought to result from an impairment in the normal process by which visual perception gains access to stored structural representations of faces, acquired through specific experience with others.

Despite a total inability to identify the faces they view, many prosopagnosics can demonstrate an extensive amount of intact facial processing if the task does not require conscious face identification and if the results of such processing are assessed indirectly (see Bruyer, 1991, for a review). We used a variant of the GKT to assess the presence of "covert" facial recognition abilities in a prosopagnosic patient (Bauer, 1984). We wanted to know whether autonomic responses could reveal knowledge of facial identity that was not reflected in verbal report. The patient (L. F.) was shown famous faces or faces of immediate family members while alternative names, only one of which was correct, were serially presented in a five-alternative forced-choice format. After all names were presented, L. F. chose the one he thought was correct. EDR was continuously recorded. Results are presented in Figure 5.1. On the "famous faces" task, the patient failed to name any of the faces spontaneously, and performed at no better than chance level with the multiple-choice format (20%). In contrast, he displayed the largest EDR to the correct name 60% of the time ($p < .05$). Normal controls showed significantly higher rates of spontaneous naming (90%) and multiple-choice recognition (100%), but accuracy of EDR recognition (80%) was equivalent to that seen in the prosopagnosic. Similar results occurred with L. F.'s family faces, though controls showed chance levels of verbal and autonomic recognition of these faces, since they were unfamiliar with them. These results suggest that EDRs can index knowledge of

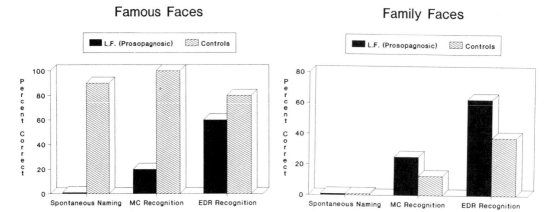

FIGURE 5.1. Verbal and EDR recognition accuracy on DOI/GKT with famous faces (left panel) and faces from L. F.'s family (right panel).

facial identity not reflected in verbal report. Tranel and Damasio (1985) replicated and extended these findings using a slightly different procedure, and the same basic pattern of results has been recently extended to the domain of event-related potentials (Renault, Signoret, Debruille, Breton, & Bolgert, 1989).

In a subsequent study with a second prosopagnosic patient (Bauer & Verfaellie, 1988), this finding was replicated with faces that had been learned prior to illness onset, but this patient did *not* show EDR recognition of newly learned faces, suggesting autonomic recognition only in situations in which a previously stored facial representation exists in memory.[2] This interpretation is consistent with at least one recent conceptualization of the priming effect in amnesia—namely, that it may primarily involve activation of previously stored memory representations (but see Graf & Schacter, 1987, for a recent exception).

It should be noted that in certain patients and under specific conditions, covert recognition is not found (Bauer, 1986; Newcombe, Young, & DeHaan, 1989). Most of these cases involve patients whose prosopagnosia is secondary to profound perceptual dysfunction, and the absence of autonomic recognition in such instances has been interpreted as a failure of perception to activate stored facial representations. However, Etcoff, Freeman, and Cave (1991) have shown that autonomic recognition of familiarity can be impaired in the absence of a perceptual defect. Thus, more needs to be learned about the boundaries of the phenomenon in agnosic patients.

Studies of Amnesia

Because our approach shares several features with the broader class of "implicit" memory measures, we began applying this general technique to the study of global

---

[2]It should be noted that this patient suffered substantial perceptual impairment and thus may have had difficulty extracting structural features from faces in order to encode new representations. Autonomic (Tranel & Damasio, 1985) and behavioral (Greve & Bauer, 1990) evidence of implicit learning of new faces does exist in other prosopagnosics, though the specific differences between those who do and do not show such "anterograde" effects remains unclear.

amnesic syndromes and asked whether amnesics could distinguish between targets and distractors even in cases of poor verbal recognition performance.

We first applied this method to the study of a new learning in a single patient with profound amnesia resulting from a left retrosplenial lesion (Verfaellie, Bauer, & Bowers, 1991). The patient, T. R., described by Valenstein et al. (1987), had a sudden onset of disorientation and severe headache. On admission, he had a profound verbal memory disturbance. CT scan revealed a left retrosplenial and ventricular hemorrhage. The patient underwent left occipito-parietal craniotomy to remove an arteriovenous malformation. Postoperative neuropsychological exams revealed a Wechsler Adult Intelligence Scale—Revised Verbal IQ of 115 and a Wechsler Memory Quotient of 80. Language and frontal functions were intact. Recent memory was dramatically impaired on all verbal tasks, but relatively normal on nonverbal tasks. Six months after surgery, we administered a task involving learning of a word list, followed after 30 minutes by a DOI/GKT procedure. In the learning phase, 32 words were projected for 2 seconds each. Thirty minutes later, 16 randomly selected targets were shown, embedded in sets of four distractors. The serial position of the target was counterbalanced across trials but it never occurred in the first position (Graham, 1973). EDR was continuously measured during recognition, and responses were individually determined for each word. Two healthy men matched to the patient for age ($\overline{X} = 37$ years) and education ($\overline{X} = 14.9$ years) participated as controls. As seen in the left panel of Figure 5.2, the patient correctly recognized only 44% of the targets (controls recognized 91%), but showed EDR recognition similar to controls. Because T. R. showed a larger range of EDR magnitudes than did controls, EDRs to the individual alternatives in each item were ranked by magnitude (Lykken, 1959), with 1 representing the smallest EDR and 4 representing the largest. As the data in the right panel of Figure 5.2 indicate, both T. R. and controls exhibited larger responses to targets than to distractors ($p < .01$). Even on trials in which verbal recognition was faulty, EDRs to targets in both T. R. and controls were significantly larger than those to distractors ($p < .01$). The patient also showed normal repetition priming on a mirror-image reading task adapted

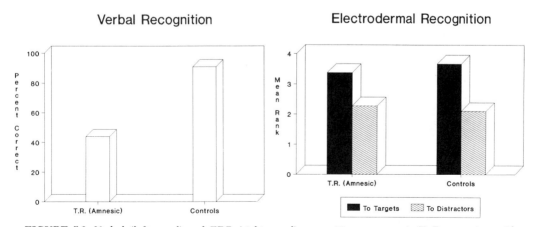

FIGURE 5.2. Verbal (left panel) and EDR (right panel) recognition accuracy in T. R., a patient with retrosplenial amnesia.

from Cohen and Squire (1980) and on a perceptual identification task adapted from Jacoby and Dallas (1981). These results again suggested that information not available to verbal report was present in the memory system but not reflected in explicit memory measures.

In a recent group study (Bauer et al., 1992), patients with alcoholic Korsakoff's disease (AK), patients with early Alzheimer's disease (AD), and two groups of controls (normals [NC] and alcoholics [AC]) learned the same 32-item word list and were later tested for multiple-choice recognition while EDRs were recorded. An additional group of controls was tested with a 4-week study–test delay to decrease explicit recognition accuracy (more is said about this group later). Results are presented in Figure 5.3. Figure 5.3A shows that although amnesics performed more poorly than the NC and AC groups on verbal measures of recognition accuracy, there were no group differences in accuracy of EDR recognition. Data from the long-delay control (LDC) group

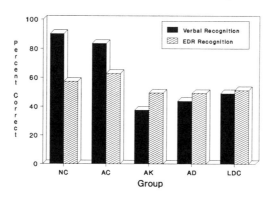

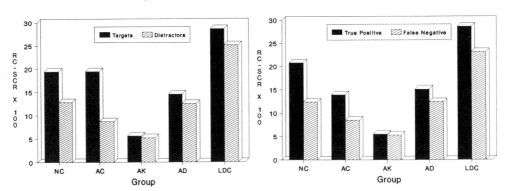

FIGURE 5.3. (**A**) Verbal and EDR recognition accuracy in amnesics and controls. (**B**) Range-corrected EDRs (skin conductance responses, or SCRs) to targets and distractors in amnesics and controls. In range correction (Lykken, 1972), each response is represented as a percentage of the difference between the subject's largest and smallest EDR during the experimental session (i.e., $\{EDR/[EDR_{max} - EDR_{min}] \times 100\}$). This correction is performed on a subject-by-subject basis. (**C**) Range-corrected EDRs to chosen (true-positive) and rejected (false-negative) targets in amnesics and controls.

suggested that imposing a 4-week study–test delay had a deleterious effect on verbal recognition, but had no apparent impact on EDR recognition accuracy. Also evident from Figure 5.3A is the fact that, in some instances, verbal recognition accuracy exceeded that seen in the EDR measure. This is an important finding that is discussed in detail in the next section. Figure 5.3B shows that both groups of amnesics showed larger EDRs to targets than to foils, even in instances where they failed to verbally recognize the targets. Among amnesics, this effect was significant only for the AD patients, though AK patients also tended to respond more strongly to targets than to distractors as well. As seen in Figure 5.3C, EDR recognition in this paradigm was sensitive not only to the actual status of words as targets or foils, but also to subjective choices ("target" or "foil") made by subjects. Although EDR discrimination proceeded normally in AK patients, one feature of their responses consistently stood out: They showed significantly smaller EDR magnitudes ($\bar{X} = 0.090$ μS) than did the other groups (NC = 0.286 μS; AC = 0.214 μS; AD = 0.242 μS; LDC = 0.248 μS), suggesting impairments in effort- and attention-related arousal (Markowitsch, Kessler, & Denzler, 1986; Oscar-Berman & Gade, 1979).

The Nature of Autonomic Recognition

We began our journey by asking whether DOI might yield evidence of "implicit" memory performance in agnosia and amnesia. The answer to this question appears to be "yes," but some qualifications are necessary, and much remains to be learned about the relationship between autonomic recognition and other indirect memory effects. In this section, we discuss two issues that have emerged, sometimes uninvited, in our attempts to apply DOI methodology to the study of neuropsychological syndromes.

What Is "Autonomic Recognition" Recognition Of?

Our original hypothesis was that EDR recognition, which reflects orienting to a "significant" stimulus, reflects the presence of a "trace" or record of the TBR item in memory. This hypothesis predicts that explicitly recognized items should always be associated with large EDRs. Interestingly, this is not always the case; on some trials, correct explicit recognition takes place without EDR recognition (e.g., see performance of the NC group in Figure 5.3A). This phenomenon is more likely to take place when recognition is immediate and confidence in the recognition judgment is high, suggesting that some factor related to the ease of memory "retrieval" may contribute to EDR activity during the modified DOI/GKT.

Recently, an information-processing model of the OR has emerged that serves as a useful framework within which to consider these results (Ohman, 1979). Ohman states that there are two conditions in which an OR will be elicited: (1) A stimulus can elicit an OR because it matches a memory representation primed as "significant" (our original hypothesis), and (2) an OR can be elicited when initial evaluation of the stimulus fails to find a matching representation in memory. This OR signals a call for processing in a central, limited-capacity information-processing channel, evoking subject-controlled, effortful (Kahneman, 1973) memory search.

Memory "mismatch" and the identification of a significant stimulus activate a common path linking the initial stages of stimulus processing (*à la* Sokolov, 1969) and the central channel. Because EDR is sensitive to cognitive effort (Kahneman, 1973), a skin conductance OR may "reflect not only the call but also part of the answer to the call" (Ohman, 1979, p. 454). Thus, the OR is not just a "significance detector," but also may signal a call for effortful processing that enhances memory retrieval (see also Mandler, 1975). If this view is correct, the electrodermal OR may be stronger and more reliable in conditions in which the representation of an item is not immediately available and must be effortfully retrieved from the long-term store. This effect is evident in generally larger range-corrected EDR in the LDC group (see Figures 5.3B and 5.3C), who presumably spent more effort in the recognition task because of the long study–test interval. Viewed in this way, the autonomic recognition phenomenon becomes more complex than initially conceived; our original view was that it reflected an implicit form of "activation" (cf. Graf, Squire, & Mandler, 1984) in the sense that it could proceed independently of explicit verbal recognition. Now it seems apparent that EDR recognition is additionally related to constructs relevant to explicit memory.

Autonomic Recognition and the Implicit–Explicit Distinction

One important consideration relates to the status of EDR recognition as an "implicit" memory effect. Recently, Schacter (1987, p. 510) has distinguished between "implicit" and "involuntary explicit" memory, and has suggested that some "implicit memory" effects could result from involuntary, yet conscious, explicit recall—cases in which test cues (e.g., word stems or subliminal words presented for perceptual identification) lead to unintentional reminding of the previous episode. This raises the possibility that the electrodermal OR, as an "involuntary" autonomic response to contextually significant items, may be more directly associated with explicit than with implicit memory effects.

Traditionally, questions about the relationship between implicit and explicit memory effects have been addressed in two ways: (1) by demonstrating stochastic independence of separate memory measures (cf. Tulving, Schacter, & Stark, 1982; Squire, Shimamura, & Graf, 1985, 1987), and (2) by demonstrating that functional parameters (e.g., encoding manipulations) designed to affect explicit memory have little or no effect on implicit memory (e.g., Graf & Schacter, 1985, 1987). In our study of EDR recognition in retrosplenial amnesia (Verfaellie et al., 1991), we demonstrated that verbal and autonomic reactions were statistically independent. In the group study just described (Bauer et al., 1992), we performed an analysis similar to that described by Tulving et al. (1982), which asserts that two memory measures are stochastically independent if the joint probability of their occurrence does not significantly exceed the product of their independent probabilities. Table 5.1 presents the results of this analysis, which suggest that verbal and EDR recognition can function independently in the DOI/GKT.

In an attempt to provide data relevant to the *functional* separation of verbal and electrodermal measures, we (Bauer et al., 1991) examined the effects of a levels-of-processing (Craik & Lockhart, 1972) manipulation on verbal and EDR recognition in AK and AD patients and in controls (NC and AC groups). Subjects were shown

TABLE 5.1. Stochastic Independence between Verbal and Electrodermal Recognition

Group	Item type	Simple probabilities		Joint probability	Stochastic independence
		R_n	Max	(R_n, Max)	$(R_n \times Max)$
NC	Old	.902	.440	.413	.397
	New	.098	.638	.042	.063
AC	Old	.835	.377	.326	.315
	New	.165	.705	.125	.116
AK	Old	.375	.253	.080	.095
	New	.625	.763	.463	.475
AD	Old	.438	.286	.148	.125
	New	.562	.731	.432	.411

Note. R_n = probability of "yes" response in recognition; Max = probability of maximum EDR to given word type; R_n, Max = joint probability of "yes" and maximum EDR. From *Autonomic Detection of Information without Verbal Recognition in Alcoholic Korsakoff and Alzheimer's Disease Patients* by R. M. Bauer, M. Verfaellie, S. Rediess, C. Schramke, D. Bowers, and R. T. Watson, 1992, manuscript submitted for publication.

a group of 30 words, each accompanied by questions designed to focus attention on orthographic, phonemic, or semantic attributes. In the orthographic condition, subjects were asked, "Is this word printed in upper-case letters?" In the phonemic condition, subjects were asked, "Does this word rhyme with _____?" In the semantic condition, the question was "Is this word a type of _____?" Equal numbers of "yes" and "no" questions were asked. Thirty minutes later, each of the targets was embedded in a five-alternative multiple-choice item, and verbal and EDR recognition was recorded. Figure 5.4 shows the results of this experiment. We found a strong levels effect in the NC and AC groups for verbal recognition only, but no levels effect in any group in

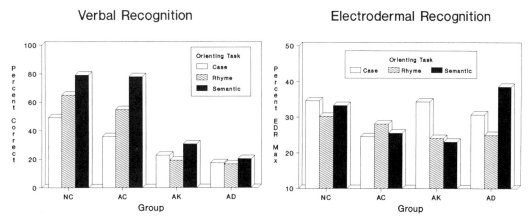

FIGURE 5.4. Effects of a levels-of-processing manipulation on verbal (left panel) and autonomic (right panel) recognition in amnesics and controls.

EDR recognition. Thus, we have both statistical and functional evidence that EDR recognition can be independent of verbal report, but additional work needs to be done on verbal–EDR relationships before we can be confident of this conclusion. One important need is to evaluate EDR activity during more traditional "indirect" memory tasks, to determine its relationship with overt behavioral measures of implicit memory.

Conclusions

Our approach to the study of memory dissociations has borrowed methods from cognitive psychophysiology and has attempted to capitalize on naturally occurring dissociations between verbal and autonomic responses in recognition paradigms. We and others have demonstrated that autonomic responses are capable of distinguishing target from nontarget information in recognition tasks, and that such discrimination does not require conscious, verbal recognition of targets as such. We have used the term "autonomic recognition" to refer to this phenomenon, though no claim is yet made that it necessarily reflects the operation of a distinct ability or memory system. In fact, evidence exists that electrodermal measures in particular are capable of reflecting both "involuntary" aspects of explicit memory and the relatively automatic "activation" of stored memory representations characteristic of some forms of implicit memory. At this stage in our understanding, it seems possible that both the reconstructive aspects of memory and the automatic activation implied in accounts of implicit memory function may drive electrodermal responding in recognition paradigms. Thus, the precise location of autonomic recognition along the continuum between explicit and implicit memory remains to be determined. An evaluation of autonomic "activation" in the context of traditional measures of implicit memory seems an important first step in addressing this issue.

ACKNOWLEDGMENTS

Preparation of this chapter was supported in part by National Institute on Alcohol Abuse and Alcoholism Grant No. 1 RO1 AA06203 to the University of Florida (Russell M. Bauer) and by National Institute of Neurological and Communicative Disorders and Stroke Program Project Grant No. NS 26985 to Boston University School of Medicine (Mieke Verfaellie). We thank Laird Cermak for allowing us to test alcoholic Korsakoff patients in the greater Boston area, and for his support and encouragement of this line of research. Betsy Tobias provided comments on an earlier draft, and Kevin Greve, Sharilyn Rediess, Carol Schramke, and Rae Hendlin provided help in data collection and statistical analysis. Their various talents and contributions are greatly appreciated.

REFERENCES

Barry, R. J. (1977). The effect of 'significance' upon indices of Sokolov's orienting response: A new conceptualization to replace the OR. *Physiological Psychology, 5,* 209–214.
Bauer, R. M. (1979). *Self-deception, self-description, and multiple cognitive control.* Unpublished doctoral dissertation, Pennsylvania State University.

Bauer, R. M. (1984). Autonomic recognition of names and faces in prosopagnosia: A neuropsychological application of the guilty knowledge test. *Neuropsychologia, 22,* 457–470.

Bauer, R. M. (1986). The cognitive psychophysiology of prosopagnosia. In H. Ellis, M. Jeeves, F. Newcombe, & A. Young (Eds.), *Aspects of face processing* (pp. 253–267). Dordrecht, The Netherlands: Martinus Nijhoff.

Bauer, R. M., & Verfaellie, M. (1988). Electrodermal recognition of familiar but not unfamiliar faces in prosopagnosia. *Brain and Cognition, 8,* 240–252.

Bauer, R. M., Verfaellie, M., Greve, K. W., Bowers, D., Rediess, S., & Schramke, C. (1991, February). *Verbal and autonomic responses to a levels of processing manipulation in Korsakoff and Alzheimer's disease patients.* Paper presented at the 19th Annual Meeting of the International Neuropsychological Society, San Antonio, TX.

Bauer, R. M., Verfaellie, M., Rediess, S., Schramke, C., Bowers, D., & Watson, R. T. (1992). *Autonomic detection of information without verbal recognition in alcoholic Korsakoff and Alzheimer's disease patients.* Manuscript submitted for publication.

Ben-Shakhar, G. (1977). A further study of the dichotomization theory in detection of information. *Psychophysiology, 14,* 408–413.

Ben-Shakhar, G., & Furedy, J. J. (1990). *Theories and applications in the detection of deception.* New York: Springer-Verlag.

Ben-Shakhar, G., Lieblich, I., & Kugelmass, S. (1975). Detection of information and GSR habituation: An attempt to derive detection efficiency from two habituation curves. *Psychophysiology, 12,* 283–288.

Berlyne, D. E. (1960). *Conflict, arousal, and curiosity.* New York: McGraw-Hill.

Bernstein, A. S., Taylor, K. W., & Weinstein, E. (1975). The phasic electrodermal response as a differentiated complex reflecting stimulus significance. *Psychophysiology, 12,* 158–169.

Bruyer, R. (1991). Covert face recognition in prosopagnosics: A review. *Brain and Cognition, 15,* 223–235.

Cermak, L. S., Talbot, W., Chandler, K., & Wolbarst, L. R. (1985). The perceptual priming phenomenon in amnesia. *Neuropsychologia, 23,* 615–622.

Cohen, N. J., & Squire, L. R. (1980). Preserved learning and retention of pattern analyzing skill in amnesia: Dissociation of knowing how and knowing that. *Science, 210,* 207–210.

Craik, F. I. M., & Lockhart, R. S. (1972). Levels of processing: A framework for memory research. *Journal of Verbal Learning and Verbal Behavior, 11,* 671–684.

Damasio, A. R., Damasio, H., & Van Hoesen, G. W. (1982). Prosopagnosia: Anatomic basis and behavioral mechanisms. *Neurology, 32,* 331–342.

Davidson, P. O. (1968). Validity of the guilty knowledge technique: The effects of motivation. *Journal of Applied Psychology, 52,* 62–65.

Davis, R. C. (1961). Physiological responses as a means of evaluating information. In A. D. Biderman & H. Zimmer (Eds.), *The manipulation of human behavior* (pp. 142–168). New York: Wiley.

Elaad, E., & Ben-Shakhar, G. (1989). Effects of motivation and verbal response type on psychophysiological detection in the guilty knowledge test. *Psychophysiology, 26,* 442–451.

Etcoff, N. L., Freeman, R., & Cave, K. R. (1991). Can we lose memories of faces? Content specificity and awareness in a prosopagnosic. *Journal of Cognitive Neuroscience, 3,* 25–41.

Gati, I., & Ben-Shakhar, G. (1990). Novelty and significance in orientation and habituation: A feature-matching approach. *Journal of Experimental Psychology: General, 119,* 251–263.

Geschwind, N. (1965). Disconnexion syndromes in animals and men. *Brain, 88,* 237–294, 585–644.

Graf, P., & Schacter, D. L. (1985). Implicit and explicit memory for new associations in normal and amnesic subjects. *Journal of Experimental Psychology: Learning, Memory, and Cognition, 11,* 501–518.

Graf, P., & Schacter, D. L. (1987). Selective effects of interference on implicit and explicit memory for new associations. *Journal of Experimental Psychology: Learning, Memory, and Cognition, 13,* 45–53.

Graf, P., Squire, L. R., & Mandler, G. (1984). The information that amnesic patients do not forget. *Journal of Experimental Psychology: Learning, Memory, and Cognition, 10,* 164–178.

Graham, F. K. (1973). Habituation and dishabituation of responses innervated by the autonomic nervous system. In H. V. S. Peeke & M. J. Herz (Eds.), *Habituation: Behavioral studies* (pp. 163–218). New York: Academic Press.

Greve, K. W., & Bauer, R. M. (1990). Implicit learning of new faces in prosopagnosia: An application of the mere-exposure paradigm. *Neuropsychologia, 28,* 1035–1041.

Gustafson, L. A., & Orne, M. T. (1963). Effects of heightened motivation on the detection of deception. *Journal of Applied Psychology, 47,* 408–411.

Jacoby, L. L. (1984). Incidental versus intentional retrieval: Remembering and awareness as separate issues.

In L. R. Squire & N. Butters (Eds), *Neuropsychology of memory* (1st ed., pp. 145–156). New York: Guilford Press.

Jacoby, L. L., & Dallas, M. (1981). On the relationship between autobiographical memory and perceptual learning. *Journal of Experimental Psychology: General, 110*, 306–340.

Kahneman, M. (1973). *Attention and effort*. Englewood Cliffs, NJ: Prentice-Hall.

Lang, P. J., Rice, D. G., & Sternbach, R. A. (1972). Psychophysiology of emotion. In N. S. Greenfield & R. A. Sternbach (Eds.), *Handbook of psychophysiology* (pp. 623–643). New York: Holt, Rinehart & Winston.

Leiblich, I., Kugelmass, S., & Ben-Shakhar, G. (1970). Efficiency of GSR detection of information as a function of stimulus set size. *Psychophysiology, 6*, 601–608.

Lykken, D. T. (1959). The GSR in the detection of guilt. *Journal of Applied Psychology, 43*, 385–388.

Lykken, D. T. (1972). Range correction applied to heart rate and GSR data. *Psychophysiology, 9*, 373–379.

Lykken, D. T. (1974). Psychology and the lie detector industry. *American Psychologist, 29*, 725–738.

Lykken, D. T. (1979). The detection of deception. *Psychological Bulletin, 86*, 47–53.

Mandler, G. (1975). *Mind and emotion*. New York: Wiley.

Mandler, G. (1980). Recognition: The judgment of previous occurrence. *Psychological Review, 87*, 252–271.

Markowitsch, J. H., Kessler, J., & Denzler, P. (1986). Recognition memory and psychophysiological responses to stimuli with neutral or emotional content: A study of Korsakoff patients and recently detoxified and longterm abstinent alcoholics. *International Journal of Neuroscience, 29*, 1–35.

Moscovitch, M. (1984). The sufficient conditions for demonstrating preserved memory in amnesia: A task analysis. In L. R. Squire & N. Butters (Eds), *Neuropsychology of memory* (1st ed., pp. 104–114). New York: Guilford Press.

Newcombe, F., Young, A., & DeHaan, E. H. F. (1989). Prosopagnosia and object agnosia without covert recognition, *Neuropsychologia, 27*, 179–191.

Nisbett, R. E., & Wilson, T. D. (1977). Telling more than we can know: Verbal reports on mental processes. *Psychological Review, 84*, 231–259.

Ohman, A. (1979). The orienting response, attention, and learning: An information-processing perspective. In H. D. Kimmel, E. VanOlst, & J. F. Orlebeke (Eds.), *The orienting reflex in humans* (pp. 443–471). Hillsdale, NJ: Erlbaum.

Ohman, A. (1983). The orienting response during Pavlovian conditioning. In D. Siddle (Ed.), *Orienting and habituation: Perspectives in human research* (pp. 315–369). New York: Wiley.

Oscar-Berman, M., & Gade, A. (1979). Electrodermal measures of arousal in humans with cortical or subcortical brain damage. In H. D. Kimmel, E. VanOlst, & J. F. Orlebeke (Eds.), *The orienting reflex in humans* (pp. 665–676). Hillsdale, NJ: Erlbaum.

Podelsny, J. A., & Raskin, D. C. (1978). Effectiveness of techniques and physiological measures in the detection of deception. *Psychophysiology, 15*, 344–359.

Raskin, D. C. (1979). Orienting and defensive reflexes in the detection of deception. In H. D. Kimmel, E. H. VanOlst, & J. F. Orlebeke (Eds.), *The orienting reflex in humans* (pp. 587–605). Hillsdale, NJ: Erlbaum.

Renault, B., Signoret, J. L., Debruille, B., Breton, F., & Bolgert, F. (1989). Brain potentials reveal covert facial recognition in prosopagnosia. *Neuropsychologia, 27*, 905–912.

Sackheim, H. A., & Gur, R. C. (1979). Self-deception: A concept in search of a phenomenon. *Journal of Personality and Social Psychology, 37*, 147–169.

Sallis, J. F., Lichstein, K. L., & McGlynn, F. D. (1980). Anxiety response patterns: A comparison of clinical and analogue populations. *Journal of Behavior Therapy and Experimental Psychiatry, 11*, 179–183.

Schacter, D. L. (1987). Implicit memory: History and current status. *Journal of Experimental Psychology: Learning, Memory, and Cognition, 13*, 501–518.

Schacter, D. L., McAndrews, M. P., & Moscovitch, M. (1988). Access to consciousness: Dissociations between implicit and explicit knowledge in neuropsychological syndromes. In L. Weiskrantz (Ed.), *Thought without language* (pp. 242–278). Oxford: Oxford University Press.

Sokolov, E. N. (1969). The modeling properties of the nervous system. In M. Cole & I. Maltzman (Eds.), *A handbook of contemporary Soviet psychology* (pp. 671–704). New York: Basic Books.

Squire, L. R., Shimamura, A. P., & Graf, P. (1985). Independence of recognition memory and priming effects: A neuropsychological analysis. *Journal of Experimental Psychology: Learning, Memory, and Cognition, 11*, 37–44.

Squire, L. R., Shimamura, A. P., & Graf, P. (1987). Strength and duration of priming effects in normal subjects and amnesic patients. *Neuropsychologia, 25*, 195–210.

Tranel, D., & Damasio, A. R. (1985). Knowledge without awareness: An autonomic index of facial recognition by prosopagnosics. *Science, 228*, 1453–1454.

Tulving, E., Schacter, D. L., & Stark, H. A. (1982). Priming effects in word-fragment completion are independent of recognition memory. *Journal of Experimental Psychology: Learning, Memory, and Cognition, 8,* 336-342.

Valenstein, E., Bowers, D., Verfaellie, M., Heilman, K. M., Day, A., & Watson, R. T. (1987). Retrosplenial amnesia. *Brain, 110,* 1631-1646.

Verfaellie, M., Bauer, R. M., & Bowers, D. (1991). Autonomic and behavioral evidence of 'implicit' memory in amnesia. *Brain and Cognition, 15,* 10-25.

Weiskrantz, L. (1986). *Blindsight: A case study and implications.* Oxford: Clarendon Press.

Zajonc, R. B. (1980). Feeling and thinking: Preferences need no inferences. *American Psychologist, 35,* 151-175.

6

Selective Knowledge Loss in Activational and Representational Amnesias

ELKHONON GOLDBERG and WILLIAM B. BARR

It is widely acknowledged that the scope of memory loss in amnesia is never complete. The structure of knowledge representation can be elucidated by studying specific patterns of knowledge loss and perseveration in amnesia. It has been suggested that in most amnesic syndromes, context-free information is better preserved than context-dependent information, and skills are better preserved than facts (Kinsbourne & Wood, 1975; Cohen & Squire, 1980). Although the phenomenal distinction between these categories of knowledge is widely accepted, consensus is lacking as to whether these knowledge types are mediated by neurally distinct mechanisms.

It is also acknowledged that amnesia is not a unitary construct and that at least several types of amnesias probably exist. Recently, it has become popular to specify two primary types of the amnesias: medial temporal lobe and diencephalic (Huppert & Piercy, 1978, 1979; Squire, 1986, 1987). Although valuable insights have been offered into the nature of this classification (Squire, Cohen, & Nadel, 1984), a wide range of amnesic phenomena remain unexplained by the distinction between these two types of amnesias.

In this chapter, we argue that many of our limitations in understanding the amnesias result from a failure to consider the full set of amnesic syndromes. We first specify a distinction between two types of knowledge that are selectively disturbed in amnesias. We then outline a distinction between two broad classes of memory processes, which are be referred to as "activational" and "representational" aspects of memory. The goal of the chapter is to demonstrate that activational amnesias and representational amnesias constitute two distinct types of memory disorders, caused by the respective breakdown of complementary knowledge types.

Singular and Generic Knowledge

Two fundamental dichotomies have been instrumental in delineating the scope of amnesia. The first one is Tulving's (1972) distinction between "episodic" and "semantic" memory. Episodic memory is typically defined as a system for storing temporally dated events and the spatiotemporal relations among them, whereas semantic memory is described as context-free knowledge of language, concepts, and facts.

The episodic–semantic dichotomy has been widely used in describing the scope of retrograde amnesia (RA). Kinsbourne and Wood (1975) and Schacter and Tulving (1982) have proposed that in classical amnesias episodic memory suffers, whereas semantic memory remains intact. Other authors, however, claim that in various forms of RA the scope of memory deficit is not limited to episodic memory, but also involves certain aspects of semantic memory. This has been demonstrated in patients with head injury (Goldberg et al., 1981; Goldberg & Bilder, 1986), alcoholic Korsakoff's syndrome (Butters & Cermak, 1986; Zola-Morgan, Cohen, & Squire, 1983), and herpes simplex encephalitis (DeRenzi, Liotti, & Michelli, 1987), as well as in patients who have undergone unilateral temporal lobectomies (Barr, Goldberg, Wasserstein, & Novelly, 1990).

The second distinction used in characterizing the scope of amnesia is that between "procedural" and "declarative" knowledge, defined respectively as "knowing how" and "knowing that" (Cohen & Squire, 1980; Squire, 1986). Declarative memory includes "facts, episodes and routes of everyday life," whereas procedural memory includes "motor, perceptual and cognitive skills" (Squire, 1986, p. 1614). It is commonly held that in amnesia only declarative memory suffers, whereas procedural memory is invulnerable to disease (Cohen & Squire, 1980). This is not disputed as a general rule, although it has been demonstrated that procedural memory also suffers in patients with certain subcortical disorders, such as Huntington's disease (Heindel, Butters, & Salmon, 1988; Martone, Butters, Payne, Becker, & Sax, 1984).

The heuristic value of the episodic–semantic and declarative–procedural dichotomies for the neuropsychology of memory is hard to overestimate. They have been utilized by a number of authors to capture the fact that the scope of memory loss in amnesia is never complete. In this chapter, we introduce a different but related dichotomy—a distinction between "singular" and "generic" knowledge. By "singular" knowledge, we are referring to knowledge of specific facts, which lack intrinsic temporal quality and represent information about individual, unique entities (e.g., "Paris is the capital of France"). Singular knowledge also includes knowledge of public and personal events, which have intrinsic temporal quality; that is, they occurred in time and represent information about one's personal life (e.g., "Nixon resigned in 1974," or "I attended High School No. 5 in Chicago").

With the term "generic" knowledge, we are referring to knowledge for general facts that lack intrinsic temporal quality and that represent information about large, possibly infinite classes of entities (e.g., "Squares have four sides," "Tomatoes are usually red"). Generic knowledge is not limited to verbal knowledge, since it also includes nonverbal generic representations. Even in its verbal aspect, generic knowledge is not limited to lexical knowledge, since it also includes peripheral aspects of meanings (e.g., "Dogs do not fly").

The relations among the taxonomies of knowledge discussed in this chapter are summarized in Figure 6.1. Singular knowledge, by definition, includes all episodic and singular semantic knowledge. Generic knowledge includes all procedural knowledge and generic semantic knowledge. In the following discussion, we argue that amnesias for singular and generic knowledge constitute two phenomenally and neuroanatomically distinct sets of syndromes.

A.

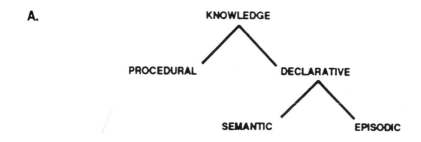

B.

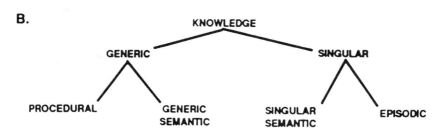

FIGURE 6.1. Taxonomies of knowledge: (**A**) Traditional taxonomy; (**B**) proposed taxonomy.

Activational and Representational Aspects of Memory

In terms of underlying mechanisms and neuroanatomical components, it is useful to distinguish two broad categories of memory processes: distribution of engram storage, and activational mechanisms required for consolidation of and access to engrams (Goldberg et al., 1981; Goldberg, 1984). We refer to these processes as "representational" and "activational" aspects of memory.

The activational component is critical for engram consolidation and accessibility. It does not serve as the "locus of engrams," but provides a range of modulatory effects necessary to form and access them (to ensure coordinated consolidation and retrieval). The activational component is mediated by various subcortical structures whose damage leads to classical amnesias. In a similar vein, Squire (1986) proposed that "the capacity for long-term memory requires the integrity of the medial temporal and diencephalic regions, which must operate in conjunction with the assemblies of neurons that represent stored information" (p. 1613).

Goldberg and colleagues (Goldberg et al., 1981; Goldberg, 1984) have proposed a hierarchical organization of the activational system involved in memory. This system begins with the ventral mesencephalic reticular formation, whose influences are characterized by a lack of regional specificity of impact. It also includes the nonspecific thalamic system at the diencephalic level, and the mammillary bodies and hippocampi at the limbic level. It has been proposed elsewhere (Goldberg et al., 1981) that the limbic component of the activational system is critical in both consolidation and retrieval, and that the mesencephalic component is particularly critical in retrieval and less critical in consolidation. This functional difference between the mesencephalic and limbic components of the activational memory system may account for clinical dissociations between anterograde amnesia and RA.

The representational component of memory involves the cerebral distribution of engrams. Contrary to the previously popular point of view, which held that engrams are evenly distributed throughout the brain (Lashley, 1950), it has been recently proposed that the engrams of the external world are localized in those brain structures involved in perceptual processing of the corresponding aspects of the world, and that the code of engrams is the same as the code involved in perceptual processing (Mishkin, 1982; Squire, 1986; Goldberg & Tucker, 1979; Goldberg, 1984). This is the only logical hypothesis if we believe that engrams are formed as patterns of synaptic modifications, since otherwise we would have to postulate that information is processed in one "locus" and then moved to another "locus" of the brain, which seems like a rather redundant proposititition.

This implies that engrams are distributed throughout particular areas of neocortex and possibly also throughout various subcortical systems directly involved in perceptual and motor integration, such as certain thalamic nuclei (e.g., dorsomedial and pulvinar), striatum, and cerebellum. Since our knowledge about various objects and events of the external world is usually multimodal, composite knowledge of an object or event is represented through multiple engrams, each corresponding to a specific sensory aspect and localized in a particular, sensory-specific neocortical and/or thalamic region. As Squire (1986) pointed out, engrams of real objects or events are indeed distributed, yet not throughout the whole brain but predominantly within neocortex and thalamus. However, every sensory-specific component of such a composite engram is tied to a particular neocortical and/or thalamic region. This is consonant with the view of Damasio (1985), who proposed that "the myriad modal memories that constitute the basis of knowledge must be stored in the sensory association cortices, bilaterally and according to modality" (p. 259). Motor memories are presumed to be tied to particular neocortical, neostriatal, and possibly cerebellar systems. The representational component of memory processes—the locus of engrams—is therefore associated with the neocortex, thalamus, and various subcortical motor systems.

It is reasonable to assume that engrams may vary in the degree of their robustness. Although it is far beyond the scope of this chapter to discuss the neural and synaptic engram characteristics, we can speculate that the robustness of an engram depends on the frequency with which it is evoked, the number of associative links into which it is embedded, the strength of synaptic connections, the number of different contexts in which it has been formed, and the mode of its formation (single-exposure precipitous, or multiple-exposure incremental). If this is the case, then generic knowledge is represented by more robust engrams than is singular knowledge. The foregoing comparison of singular and generic knowledge then becomes similar to the distinction between "memories" and "habits" made by Mishkin and his associates (Mishkin, 1982; Mishkin & Petri, 1984) in the monkey; the former is comparable to singular knowledge, and the latter to generic knowledge. Engram robustness will also be a function of engram "longevity," since the engram will be embedded into an increasing number of contexts with time, because of its increasing number of uses.

Amnesias for Singular and Generic Knowledge

Our initial distinction between the singular and generic knowledge was ontological in nature, based on the types of reality they represent. We are saying now that a relationship exists between this ontological dimension and the neurophysiology of the engrams: Generic knowledge is likely to be mediated by more robust engrams than is singular knowledge. Although the ontological distinction between singular and generic knowledge is categorical and dichotomous, engram robustness is viewed as a graded, continuous quality. To state it in other terms, singular and generic types of knowledge represent two extreme points on the continuum of the degree of redundancy of cortico-thalamic representations of information. The relationship between the singular–generic dimension and engram robustness is probabilistic rather than absolute. Instances of generic knowledge represented by relatively nonrobust engrams can be easily found (e.g., "Llamas have long necks"), but they are usually more likely to have been formed and are more robust than thematically matched instances of singular knowledge (e.g., "La Paz is the capital of Bolivia").

We propose that the more robust the engram, the less the access to it depends on the integrity of the activational machinery. Therefore, the integrity of the activation machinery is more critical for retrieval of singular than of generic knowledge. The more generalized and context-free particular knowledge is, the less does the access to its cortico-thalamic representation depend upon the integrity of the reticulo-limbic activational system. To put it in other words, damage to the activational aspects of memory will have a more adverse effect on access to singular than to generic knowledge. If this assumption is true, then we may logically conclude that most classical amnesias (e.g., mediotemporal and diencephalic) are caused by the breakdown of activational rather than representational aspects of memory, since they are characterized by a deficit in singular but not in generic knowledge. Obviously, an extreme breakdown of activational machinery will cause the failure to access both singular and generic knowledge. Such an extreme condition will result, however, in an altered consciousness level and confusional state, and will not be considered an amnesia, narrowly defined. We may also logically conclude that damage to activational machinery will have more adverse impact on access to relatively recent memories than on access to very old memories, since the latter are more robust. This is reflected in the temporal gradient that often characterizes RA.

Why are classical activational amnesias characterized by the impairment of singular but not generic knowledge? Our understanding of any condition is benefited by the availability of contrasting conditions. If activational amnesias are characterized by deficits in singular but not in generic knowledge, is it possible to identify conditions characterized by deficits in generic memory? We believe that this is the case.

A class of cortical neuropsychological syndromes exist that can be conceptualized as "representational amnesias," and that involve both generic and singular knowledge loss. These syndromes, albeit rare, are well known, and they are traditionally classified as "agnosias." The syndromes in question are the so-called "associative agnosias" or "asymbolias." The deficit inherent in associative agnosias entails an inability to identify an object as a member of a generic category, in the absence of a basic perceptual disorder. Although an object is "perceived," its interpretation in term of generic class membership fails. Teuber (1968) referred to these agnosias as "a percept that has somehow been stripped of its meaning" (p. 293). Associative agnosias are modality-specific and may take the forms of either visual object agnosia (Lissauer, 1890; McCarthy & Warrington, 1986), pure astereognosia (Wernicke, 1960; Hecaen & Albert, 1978), or auditory associative agnosia (Kleist, 1928; Spinnler & Vignolo, 1966). Ideational apraxia (Liepmann, 1900; DeRenzi & Lucchelli, 1988) also entails a loss of generic knowledge and can be considered as an amnesia for overlearned, object-oriented movements. The procedural knowledge lost in ideational apraxia is generic, since it entails the ability to manipulate a large (potentially infinite) class of similar, but not identical, objects under diverse metric circumstances.

It can be argued that the traditional designation of these syndromes as forms of agnosia rather than of amnesia reflects nothing other than the arbitrariness of taxonomic borders between agnosias and amnesias, and that substantively these syndromes can be very naturally understood as deficits of semantic memory. The heuristic value of studying associative agnosias in order to "gain insight into long-term semantic knowledge" has been emphasized by Zaidel (1986, p. 549) and Warrington (1975).

The critical, mandatory lesions leading to associative agnosias and ideational apraxias share the same general territory—the posterior portion of the left hemisphere. Both ideational apraxia and associative agnosias constitute deficits in generic knowledge. A consistent and parsimonious picture emerges of these syndromes as cortical amnesias for generic knowledge, both semantic and procedural. Their shared neuroanatomical territory is consistent with the notion of the left hemisphere's being the repository of compact codes and well-established categorical representations, both verbal and nonverbal (Goldberg & Costa, 1981; Goldberg, 1989, 1990; Kosslyn, 1987).

How are the well-known symbolic agnosias, which have been reinterpreted here as cortical or "generic" amnesias, related to classic amnesias? First, do they co-occur with classic amnesias? The answer to this question is a matter of definitions. According to traditional definitions, by "amnesias" we usually mean memory deficits that (1) are primary (i.e., unassociated with perceptual deficits), and (2) are characterized by a certain degree of generality of deficit (in other words, are not limited to too narrow a stimulus class). When memory deficit is superimposed upon perceptual deficit in the same modality, it is usually considered secondary to faulty input processing and thus is not regarded as amnesia.

As are most cortical syndromes, "asymbolias" are associated with deficient learning of new information in corresponding modalities: Visual learning is impaired in "visual object agnosia," and somatosensory learning is impaired in "pure astereognosia" (Luria, 1975). This learning deficit can be clearly demonstrated in the episodic domain by asking a patient to memorize a group of visually (tactually) presented stimuli (Luria, 1975). Barbizet (1970) talks about cortical, narrow-spectrum, modality-specific amnesias. In Warrington's (1975) case, the episodic amnesic deficit affected both visual and verbal domains, but the patient had combined deficits (visual object agnosia and anomia). Therefore, at least a limited-scope "episodic" anterograde amnesia is present in these syndromes. However, since it is superimposed upon a presumably perceptual deficit, and since the scope of it (the type of sensory input affected) coincides with the one affected by the "agnostic" component of the syndrome, the episodic learning deficit in these cases is usually not regarded as primary amnesia.

Conclusions

Damage to the two types of areas (reticulo-limbic vs. neocortical) will have two radically different types of impact on memory, resulting respectively in classical, predominantly activational amnesias for singular knowledge, and representational amnesias for generic knowledge. Medial temporal lobe amnesia and diencephalic amnesia are examples of activational amnesias. Associative agnosias and ideational apraxia are examples of representational amnesias. Severe amnesic disorders caused by progressive dementing illnesses such as Alzheimer's disease represent a combination of activational and representational amnesias.

Damage to the limbic systems most commonly implicated in memory will produce a relatively broad-spectrum memory deficit associated with more than one type of sensory modality, predominantly affecting access to singular knowledge without producing a perceptual deficit. Access to generic (semantic or procedural) information will be spared. The deficit will be caused not by the destruction of engram sites, but rather by the failure of activational prerequisites of consolidation and/or retrieval. It will adhere closely to the classical definition of "primary" amnesia.

Damage to the representational aspects of memory will have adverse effects on both generic and singular knowledge, since the "representational" amnesias caused by posterior neocortical lesions reflect damage to the engram sites. Any given modality-specific form of associative agnosia entails damage to the storage site of the corresponding sensory dimension of the total engram. This leads to a narrow, modality-specific deficit in generic knowledge (manifested as an associative agnosia or ideational apraxia), in combination with the deficit in learning new singular information in the corresponding modality (Barbizet, 1970; Luria, 1975).

The generic–singular knowledge distinction appears to be particularly well-suited to reflect the relationship between engram robustness and differential vulnerability of memory domains in "activational" amnesias. Generic knowledge is, by definition, embedded into multiple and strong associative links. It is pertinent to multiple contexts, is frequently used by virtue of its scope, and is likely to be acquired incrementally rather than on the basis of a single exposure. Singular knowledge, on the contrary, is embedded into fewer associative links and contexts. It is more likely to have been acquired on the basis of a single exposure, and in many cases is only occasionally evoked, accounting for weaker associative links. The difference between the two types of knowledge is merely in their accessibility, and thus the degree to which their access depends on the activational machinery. This, in turn, is the function of relative engram robustness, defined in terms of the number and strength of synaptic associations involved. Thus, the proposed generic–singular distinction not only accounts for the phenomenon of amnesias, but interrelates cognitive and physiological aspects of memory.

REFERENCES

Barbizet, J. (1970). *Human memory and its pathology*. San Francisco: W. H. Freeman.
Barr, W. B., Goldberg, E., Wasserstein, J., & Novelly, R. A. (1990). Retrograde amnesia following unilateral temporal lobectomy. *Neuropsychologia, 28*, 243-255.

Butters, N., & Cermak, L. S. (1986). A case study of the forgetting of autobiographical knowledge: Implications for the study of retrograde amnesia. In D. Rubin (Ed.), *Autobiographical memory* (pp. 253–272). New York: Cambridge University Press.

Cohen, N. J., & Squire, L. R. (1980). Preserved learning and retention of pattern-analyzing skills in amnesia: Dissociation of knowing how and knowing that. *Science, 210*, 207–210.

Damasio, A. R. (1985). Prosopagnosia. *Trends in Neurosciences, 8*, 132–135.

DeRenzi, E. D., Liotti, M., & Michelli, P. (1987). Semantic amnesia with preservation of autobiographic memory: A case report. *Cortex, 23*, 575–597.

DeRenzi, E., & Lucchelli, F. (1988). Ideational apraxia. *Brain, 111*, 1173–1185.

Goldberg, E. (1984). Papez circuit revisited: Two systems instead of one? In L. R. Squire & N. Butters (Eds.), *Neuropsychology of memory* (1st ed., pp. 183–193). New York: Guilford Press.

Goldberg, E. (1989). Gradiental approach to neocortical functional organization. *Journal of Clinical and Experimental Neuropsychology, 12*, 489–517.

Goldberg, E. (1990). Associative agnosias and the functions of the left hemisphere. *Journal of Clinical and Experimental Neuropsychology, 12*, 467–484.

Goldberg, E., Antin, S. P., Bilder, R. M., Gerstman, L. J., Hughes, J. E. O., & Mattis, S. (1981). Retrograde amnesia: Possible role of mesencephalic reticular activation in long-term memory. *Science, 213*, 1392–1394.

Goldberg, E., & Bilder, R. M. (1986). Neuropsychological perspectives: Retrograde amnesia and executive deficits. In L. Poon (Ed.), *The handbook of clinical memory assessment in older adults* (pp. 55–68). Washington, DC: American Psychological Association.

Goldberg, E., & Costa, L. D. (1981). Hemisphere differences in the acquisition and use of descriptive systems. *Brain and Language, 14*, 144–173.

Goldberg, E., & Tucker, D. (1979). Motor perseveration and long-term memory for visual forms. *Journal of Clinical Neuropsychology, 1*, 273–288.

Hecaen, H., & Albert, M. L. (1978). *Human neuropsychology*. New York: Wiley.

Heindel, W. C., Butters, N., & Salmon, D. P. (1988). Impaired learning of a motor skill in patients with Huntington's disease. *Behavioral Neuroscience, 102*, 141–147.

Huppert, F. A., & Piercy, M. (1978). Dissociation between learning and remembering in organic amnesia. *Nature, 275*, 317–318.

Huppert, F. A., & Piercy, M. (1979). Normal and abnormal forgetting in organic amnesia: Effect of locus of lesion. *Cortex, 15*, 385–390.

Kinsbourne, M., & Wood, F. (1975). Short-term memory process and the amnestic syndrome. In D. Deutsch & J. A. Deutsch (Eds.), *Short-term memory* (pp. 259–291). New York: Academic Press.

Kleist, K. (1928). Gehirnpathologische und lokalisatorische Ergebnisse uber Horstorungen, Gerausch-Taubheiten und Amusien. *Mschr. Psychiat. Neurol., 68*, 853–860.

Kosslyn, S. M. (1987). Seeing and imagining in the cerebral hemispheres: A computational approach. *Psychological Review, 94*, 148–175.

Lashley, K. S. (1950). In search of the engram. *Symposium of the Society for Experimental Biology, 4*, 454–482.

Liepmann, H. (1900). *Das Krankheitsbild der Apraxie ('motorischen Asymbolie')*. Berlin: Karger.

Lissauer, H. (1890). Ein Fall von Sedenblindheit nebst einen Beitrag Zur Theorie derselben. *Archiv für Psychiatrie, 21*, 222–270.

Luria, A. R. (1975). *The neuropsychology of memory*. Washington, DC: Winston Press.

Martone, M., Butters, N., Payne, M., Becker, J. T., & Sax, D. S.(1984). Dissociations between skill learning and verbal recognition in amnesia and dementia. *Archives of Neurology, 41*, 965–970.

McCarthy, R., & Warrington, E. K. (1986). Visual associative agnosia: A clinico-anatomical study. *Journal of Neurology, Neurosurgery and Psychiatry, 49*, 1233–1240.

Mishkin, M. (1982). A memory system in the monkey. *Philosophical Transactions of the Royal Society of London, B298*, 85–95.

Mishkin, M., & Petri, H. L. (1984). Memories and habits: Some implications for the analysis of learning and retention. In L. R. Squire & N. Butters (Eds.), *Neuropsychology of memory* (1st ed., pp. 287–296). New York: Guilford Press.

Schacter, D. L., & Tulving, E. (1982). Memory, amnesia and the episodic–semantic distinction. In R. L. Isaacson & N. E. Spear (Eds.), *The expression of knowledge* (pp. 35–65). New York: Plenum Press.

Spinnler, H., & Vignolo, L. A. (1966). Impaired recognition of meaningful sounds in aphasia. *Cortex, 2*, 337–348.

Squire, L. R. (1986). Mechanisms of memory. *Science, 232*, 1612–1619.

Squire, L. R. (1987). *Memory and brain*. New York: Oxford University Press.

Squire, L. R., Cohen, N. J., & Nadel, L. (1984). The medial temporal region and memory consolidation: A new hypothesis. In H. Weingartner & E. S. Parker (Eds.), *Memory consolidation: Psychobiology of cognition* (pp. 185-210). Hillsdale, NJ: Erlbaum.

Teuber, H. L. (1968). Alteration of perception and memory in man. In L. Weiskrantz (Ed.), *Analysis of behavioral change* (pp. 268-375). New York: Harper & Row.

Tulving, E. (1972). Episodic and semantic memory. In E. Tulving & W. Donaldson (Eds.), *Organization of memory* (pp. 381-403). New York: Academic Press.

Warrington, E. K. (1975). The selective impairment of semantic memory. *Quarterly Journal of Experimental Psychiatry, 27,* 635-657.

Wernicke, C. (1960). *Grundriss der Psychiatrie in Klinischen Vorlesungen* (2nd rev. ed.). Leipzig: Thieme.

Zaidel, D. W. (1986). Memory for scenes in stroke patients. *Brain, 109,* 547-560.

Zola-Morgan, S., Cohen, N. J., & Squire, L. R. (1983). Recall of remote episodic memory in amnesia. *Neuropsychologia, 21,* 487-500.

7

The Contributions of Emotional and Motivational Abnormalities to Cognitive Deficits in Alcoholism and Aging

MARLENE OSCAR-BERMAN

Introduction

The global objective of the research my colleagues and I have conducted during the past decade has been to understand the nature and cerebral bases of neurobehavioral abnormalities resulting from neurological disorders. In our past research, we have concentrated on describing a wide variety of functional changes, particularly those subserved by neuroanatomical systems of the frontal and temporal lobes (e.g., Freedman & Oscar-Berman, 1989; Oscar-Berman, McNamara, & Freedman, 1991; Oscar-Berman & Zola-Morgan, 1980). Results of that work have been helpful in differentiating the cognitive consequences of Alzheimer's disease, Parkinson's disease, anterior communicating artery disease, olivopontocerebellar atrophy, chronic alcoholism, and normal chronological aging (e.g., Freedman & Oscar-Berman, 1986a, 1986b, 1986c, 1987, 1989; Kish et al., 1988; Oscar-Berman, 1980, 1984, 1988, 1990).

In recent years, we have examined specific facets of emotional and motivational functions that may have an impact on cognitively based performance. In this most recent work, detoxified alcoholics (with and without clinical signs of Korsakoff's syndrome) and chronologically aging normal subjects have been the principal groups studied. Tasks sensitive to the pathophysiology of both alcoholism and aging have been selected. As Goldstein and his colleagues (Noonberg, Goldstein, & Page, 1985) and others (e.g., see Parsons, Butters, & Nathan, 1987) have cautioned, it is important to select tasks sensitive to both alcoholism and aging, because use of tests sensitive to one but not the other may yield results that imply either alcohol-related deficits alone or age-related deficits alone. Likewise, the concepts "emotion" (affect) and "motivation" (conation) have been operationally defined in terms of subjects' responses and the specific experimental procedures used to measure them; in this way, explicit behaviors are manipulated and measured under controlled laboratory conditions.

In the present chapter, I review the main findings of our research group's most recent approach to understanding the neuropsychology of alcoholism and aging. I begin with a summary of our findings on affective changes, followed by a summary of our findings on conative changes. A basic assumption underlying all of the work to be described is that emotional and motivational factors play a key role in cognition (including memory). If emotional and motivational systems are not normal, deleterious consequences for cognitive functioning are likely.

Affective Changes

Emotional changes have been noted to accompany long-term chronic alcohol abuse (e.g., see Parsons et al., 1987, and Oscar-Berman & Ellis, 1987, for reviews). In the most extreme case, alcoholics who have developed the severe neurological syndrome of Korsakoff's disease display a spectrum of affective changes reminiscent of patients with bilateral frontal lobe damage (Lhermitte & Signoret, 1976) or patients with right-hemisphere damage (Kaplan, 1988). Thus, events that normally would hold affective significance may elicit no emotional response in these patients, who in addition, may generate little spontaneous affectively oriented behavior. Interpersonally, these individuals appear dull, apathetic, and emotionally flat (Bedi & Halikas, 1985; Lezak, 1983; Lishman, 1978). Talland (1965), in describing a possible mechanism for the severe anterograde amnesia accompanying Korsakoff's syndrome, commented that the patients' failure to sustain emotional involvement in ongoing events is an important factor. Non-Korsakoff alcoholics also have been observed to have abnormal affective responses (Oscar-Berman, Hancock, Mildworf, Hutner, & Weber, 1990), and the acute administration of alcohol has been shown to influence the perception of emotional stimuli (Borrill, Rosen, & Summerfield, 1987).

Other investigators concerned with neuropsychological changes in alcoholics have made reference to the large body of work done on the neuropsychology of aging, as well as to "the premature-aging hypothesis" of alcoholism (Grant, 1986; Noonberg et al., 1985; Parsons et al., 1987; Riege, 1987; Ryan, 1982; Ryan & Butters, 1980). Briefly, the premature-aging hypothesis (in its various versions) suggests that alcoholism accelerates aging, beginning either at the onset of heavy drinking (usually in the teens or early 20s), or later in life, after the normal manifestations of aging have begun to appear (in the early 50s). A salient characteristic of normal chronological aging is decline in memory abilities (Albert & Moss, 1988; Poon, 1986). In the elderly, emotional changes (especially increases in depression) may accompany memory changes; however, the research literature on whether affective changes have significantly detrimental effects upon memory is equivocal and controversial (Jenike, 1988; Kelley, 1986; Newmann, 1989; Raskin, 1986).

A number of our recent studies have focused on the relationship between emotion and cognitive functions (including memory) in alcoholism and aging (Ellis, 1990; Ellis & Oscar-Berman, 1989; Oscar-Berman, Hancock, et al., 1990; Smith & Oscar-Berman, 1990, in press). Specifically, we employed diverse experimental paradigms to measure the ability of aging and alcoholic individuals (with and without Korsakoff's syndrome) to process and remember emotional stimuli. It was reasoned that disturbances related to emotional perceptual abilities would be reflected in poor performance on tasks relying primarily upon such skills, whereas deficits in short-term memory would be manifested principally under conditions requiring the processing and storage of information, regardless of emotional content.

Our studies of affective functions have explored the perception of emotional materials from two disparate perspectives, each to be described in turn. With one approach (see "Studies of Emotional Perception and Memory," below), we examined participants' abilities to identify, classify, and recognize particular types of emotional expressions (employing both visual and auditory input modalities), as well as their capacity for performing competing tasks (requiring focused attention). With the other approach (see "Right-Hemisphere Contributions to Functional Deficits," below), we concentrated on contributions of the right hemisphere to the processing of stimuli. The tasks used in both approaches were selected chiefly because of their sensitivity to the functions and structures under study. Perceptually based functions have a strong cortical influence; emotionally based functions have limbic, prefrontal, and right-hemisphere influence; and memory functions rely upon interactions among cortical and subcortical structures (e.g., the limbic system and the basal forebrain). Furthermore, tests of cerebral specialization can disclose right-hemisphere dysfunction, and tests involving dual-task methodologies can assess prefrontal integrity (as well as hemispheric specialization). Predictions with respect to the premature-aging hypothesis of alcoholism were that aging mainly would affect cortically mediated functions (especially perception and memory), whereas alcoholism would affect limbic functions (e.g., emotion) as well as cortically mediated behaviors. It was expected that alcoholic Korsakoff patients, with lesions in limbic, basal forebrain, and cortical systems, would evidence the most profound deficits with emotionally charged materials and with interference generated in dual-task experimental conditions. Hemispheric asymmetries were expected to be normal in Korsakoff patients, although overall performance levels were expected to be low.

Studies of Emotional Perception and Memory

We tested the following hypotheses: (1) Alcoholic Korsakoff patients would be seriously impaired on tasks of emotional perception and memory; (2) normal aging subjects would be impaired only on tests of affective memory (not emotional perception); (3) non-Korsakoff alcoholics would perform more poorly on tests of emotional perception than on tests of emotional memory; and (4) aging alcoholics would show a pattern of results resembling that of the Korsakoffs, but the impairment would be quantitatively less severe. As it turned out, results of these studies confirmed hypotheses related both to Korsakoff's syndrome and to aging, but did not unequivocally confirm hypotheses regarding the separate effects of alcoholism or the combined effects of alcoholism and aging. That is, Korsakoff patients exhibited the predicted deficits in emotional perception and memory, and they had difficulty with concurrent tasks; older subjects, whether alcoholic or not, were impaired on many tasks, but the deficits were less severe than those of the Korsakoff patients; and by and large, non-Korsakoff alcoholics did not differ from age-matched nonalcoholic subjects. The experiments that measured emotional processing are now summarized in detail (Oscar-Berman, Hancock, et al., 1990), followed by the experiments that measured dual-task divided attention and the affective valence of words (Smith & Oscar-Berman, 1990, in press).

In one study, we assessed emotional perception and memory (Oscar-Berman, Hancock, et al., 1990). The ability to identify and recognize emotional materials was examined in alcoholic Korsakoff patients, non-Korsakoff alcoholics, and nonalcoholic controls across a wide age range (23 to 77 years). Eight different experimental procedures were employed to evaluate the functions of interest. Stimulus materials were presented in two sensory modalities, visual and auditory. The materials were photographs of faces expressing one of four emotions (happy, sad, angry, or neutral), and recordings of sentences with emotional intonations or semantic meanings expressing those same four emotions. The visual tasks required subjects to identify the emotional expression of each photograph; to rate the intensity of the emotions being expressed; and, after a 30-minute break, to recognize familiar photographs from a series containing all of the previous photographs intermixed with a new set of photographs not previously presented ("foils"). The auditory tasks required subjects to identify only the emotional intonation or only the emotional content of spoken sentences, and, after a 30-minute break, to recognize the sentences that were heard before (from a series of new and old sentences). All of the foils, visual as well as auditory, contained the same emotional information as the target stimuli. Results of the experiments showed consistent abnormalities by the Korsakoff patients on the emotional tasks, and only minor aberrations in the non-Korsakoff alcoholics. Thus, whether the emotional materials were presented in the visual modality or in the auditory modality, the Korsakoffs generally made fewer correct identifications, and had poorer delayed-recognition scores, than age-matched nonalcoholic and/or non-Korsakoff alcoholic control subjects. Interestingly, the Korsakoffs did not differ significantly from the non-Korsakoff alcoholics on ratings of the intensities of the facial emotional expressions; both groups rated the expressions as being more intense than did the normal controls. Similarly, the Korsakoff and non-Korsakoff alcoholic groups did not differ from each other on accuracy of identifying the emotional intonations or on the semantic content of the spoken sentences (although alcoholics were not significantly different from normals on these measures). By and large, however, alcoholism—in the absence of Korsakoff's syndrome—was associated with only minor impairments in identifying and recognizing the emotional materials. The relative sparing of emotionally related perceptual and memory functions held, despite high scores by the alcoholics on the Beck Depression Inventory (Beck, Ward, Mendelson, Mock, & Erbaugh, 1961). Thus, the alcoholics were more depressed than the nonalcoholics, but this did not seriously affect their ability to perceive emotional materials accurately.

Other investigators have studied emotional perception in Korsakoff and non-Korsakoff alcoholic patients, and the results have been similar to those of the Oscar-Berman, Hancock, et al. (1990) study. For example, Butters and his colleagues (Davidoff et al., 1984; Granholm, Wolfe, & Butters, 1985) orally presented short stories with emotional themes (aggressive, sad, happy, sexual, or neutral) to Korsakoff and non-Korsakoff alcoholic patients (as well as to other groups of subjects), and measured immediate and delayed recall of the stories. The authors reported that Korsakoff patients' performances were influenced by the emotional content, but only when the stories contained a sexual theme. In that case, immediate—but not delayed—recall was enhanced slightly. They concluded that "failures in affective-arousal factors influence the Korsakoffs' performance rather than their actual learning (i.e., storage) processes" (Granholm et al., 1985, p. 331). In another study (Biber, Butters, Rosen, Gerstman, & Mattis, 1981), enhanced recognition was obtained from Korsakoff patients when they were required to make judgments of the likability of people, based upon photographic portraits. Again, the improvement in performance was attributed to increased affective/motivational arousal.

In our study of emotional perception and memory (Oscar-Berman, Hancock, et al., 1990), we also found that the older subjects, whether or not they had a history of alcoholism, exhibited significant deficits on most of the tasks, but the impairments were not so severe as those of the Korsakoff patients. By contrast to the alcoholics, older subjects—regardless of their history of alcoholism—were impaired on six of the eight experimental measures. Specifically, the older subjects correctly identified fewer facial and intonational expressions of emotion; they recalled fewer faces and fewer sentences after the 30-minute delay; and they matched fewer faces with the correct verbal labels. Older subjects did perform normally in two experimental conditions, however. First, the older subjects gave typical ratings of the intensity of facial expressions of emotion; second, they correctly matched the emotional content of spoken sentences with verbal labels of the emotions. In summary, the age-related deficits were not restricted to measures of delayed recognition, a finding that argues against an impairment restricted to memory functions. (The Beck scores of the older subjects were higher than those of the younger subjects, and may be related in some way to their poor performance; see Jenike, 1988; Kelley, 1986. However, as was the case for the alcoholics, the direct influence of depression was taken into account in the statistical analyses of the data.) It should be emphasized that the deficits of the older subjects, although quite reliable, were mild compared to the Korsakoff patients'. This difference probably reflects the relative sparing of damage to areas within the limbic system in the non-Korsakoff subjects. Instead, atrophy of neocortical regions, especially in prefrontal regions (Albert & Moss, 1988; Butters, Jernigan, & Cermak, 1991; Harper & Kril, 1989, 1990; Oscar-Berman, Hutner, & Bonner, in press; Oscar-Berman et al., 1991), probably accounts for some of the deficits common to the aging subjects and the Korsakoff patients. The limbic system damage in the Korsakoff patients would have additional direct effects upon affective functions (Lhermitte & Signoret, 1976; Oscar-Berman, 1980; Ryan & Butters, 1980), or indirect effects through disturbances in arousal and attention (Oscar-Berman, 1984, 1990; Pribram & McGuinness, 1975).

Finally, results of the study did not provide strong support for the premature-aging hypothesis of alcoholism, which suggests that aging is accelerated by long-term alcohol abuse (Ellis & Oscar-Berman, 1989; Noonberg et al., 1985; Parsons et al., 1987; Ryan, 1982). Thus, in only one of our experimental conditions (matching faces to appropriate verbal labels) could the results be taken to suggest a synergism of alcoholism and aging. In that instance, the younger normal subjects were performing significantly better than older normals, while the younger and the older alcoholics alike were performing at the level of the older normals.

In other studies, we examined the effects of long-term chronic alcoholism on the ability to perceive the affective significance of words, and on repetition priming effects for familiar and unfamiliar materials (Smith & Oscar-Berman, 1990, in press).

One of the studies (Smith & Oscar-Berman, in press) had been designed originally to test the possibilities that long-term chronic alcoholism, normal chronological aging, or both disproportionately impair functions of the right cerebral hemisphere. The topic of hemispheric functioning is addressed directly in the next section of the present chapter. For now, suffice it to say that there were no group differences in hemispheric asymmetries. However, the results provided support for the notion that attentional functions were diminished in alcoholics; since Korsakoff patients were not included in that study, the relationship of attentional deficits to affective/motivational arousal in amnesia (Davidoff et al., 1984; Granholm et al., 1985) was not measured (but see Ellis & Oscar-Berman, 1989, and Oscar-Berman, 1988, for reviews). In our study (Smith & Oscar-Berman, in press), detoxified long-term alcoholics and normal controls across a wide age span were required to classify foveally presented, emotionally loaded words according to their affective valence (positive or negative). (The emotional words were interspersed with foveally presented blanks [_____], serving as control stimuli requiring no classification.) The research participants were required concurrently to detect randomly occurring visual probe stimuli presented parafoveally in either the right or left visual hemifield. For alcoholic and control subjects alike, accuracy in affective judgments was higher when probe stimuli were presented to the left hemifield (right hemisphere) than when probes were presented to the right hemifield (left hemisphere). Alcoholics displayed a general response slowing in all task conditions, but failed to show any specific deficit in affective valence judgments, nor any abnormal lateral asymmetries in response speed or accuracy in the probe detection task. These results confirmed previous findings of divided-attention deficits in alcoholics (see Oscar-Berman & Ellis, 1987, for a review). It should be noted that Korsakoff patients were not included in this experiment because they failed to master the concurrent dual-task procedure; perhaps Korsakoff patients' inability to handle interference generated in the dual-task condition reflects damage to prefrontal cortical systems (Butters et al., 1991; Harper & Kril, 1989, 1990; Kopelman, 1991; Oscar-Berman et al., 1991, in press).

In another of our studies (Smith & Oscar-Berman, 1990), the effect of a concurrent processing load was measured in a different experimental context than in the previous study. Here, the repetition priming demonstrated by normal subjects performing a lexical decision task was compared between well-learned stimuli having pre-existing representations (words) and novel stimuli (pseudowords). (We had intended originally to compare priming effects for words differing in emotional valence, along with the pseudowords. However, we observed no differential effects across emotional word types. Nonetheless, the results for repetition priming of words vs. pseudowords are important, and deserve elaboration.) It is well established that the type of learning that supports performance on recall and recognition tests requires the availability of some limited-capacity working memory or attentional resource. In particular, numerous investigators have shown that subjects engaged in a concurrent attention-demanding task during the time in which target items were available for inspection displayed lower episodic recall or recognition scores for the targets than during focused-attention conditions (e.g., Baddeley, 1986; Kellogg & Dare, 1989; Murdock, 1965). Possibly, some resource-sensitive learning mechanism (e.g., episodic memory) normally reduces ability to elaborately encode stimuli (Craik & Byrd, 1982). If divided-attention conditions also reduced repetition priming effects, this would suggest that those effects are mediated by processes similar to those that permit conscious recollection. Furthermore, activation of existing representations (words) probably does not require attentive processes at input, whereas new learning (demonstrated by priming effects with pseudowords) does. To test that, in Experiment 1 we compared the effects of focused and divided attention on priming for words and pseudowords. We reasoned that when limitations are placed on resources during input, both types of stimuli should be affected if early attentive processing is necessary. Normal control subjects were required to perform a lexical decision task with either focused or divided attention—that is, either as a separate task or concurrently with a secondary task (counting the occurrence of a spurious event). In the single-task condition, repetition priming was observed in reaction times both for words and for pseudowords. By contrast, in the dual-task condition, priming was observed only for the words.

In Experiment 2 of the same study, the factors mediating the repetition priming of the two stimulus types (words and pseudowords) were examined in a between-subjects comparison. If patients who are impaired in their ability to form new episodic representations (Korsakoffs) were unable to demonstrate priming, it might suggest that episodic memory and repetition priming are mediated by similar mechanisms. If, instead, word priming was found to be preserved, but not priming for pseudowords in Korsakoff patients, it would suggest that word priming reflects the activation of pre-existing representations, whereas pseudoword priming depends upon episodic memory. Finally, if priming of pseudowords was found to be preserved in amnesia, this would suggest that such priming effects are mediated by a nonepisodic learning mechanism. With that reasoning in mind, lexical decision performance on the single-task condition was compared between Korsakoff and non-Korsakoff alcoholic subjects.

Priming was observed for both types of stimuli (words and pseudowords) in the non-Korsakoff group, but only for words in the Korsakoff patients. Thus, under the control conditions of this study (the single-task condition in Experiment 1, and non-amnesic subjects in Experiment 2), repetition speeded responses to both stimulus types. Experimental conditions that minimized the contribution of episodic memory to task performance (the dual-task demands of Experiment 1, as well as amnesia in Experiment 2) eliminated reaction time priming for pseudowords but not for words. However, in these same conditions, repetition increased the likelihood that pseudowords would be incorrectly classified. These results indicated that preserved repetition priming effects in amnesia do not solely reflect activation of representations in semantic memory.

Right-Hemisphere Contributions to Functional Deficits

As noted above, we have been intrigued by the "right-hemisphere hypothesis"—that is, the idea that functions usually associated with an intact right hemisphere are selectively disrupted with long-term alcohol abuse and/or with chronological aging (Noonberg et al., 1985; Parsons et al., 1987; Ryan, 1982). The topic of right-hemisphere integrity is important not just from the standpoint of contributions to cognitive functions (e.g., visuospatial skills), but also because of the role of the right hemisphere in emotion (Gainotti, 1972). Studies of right-hemisphere contributions to visuospatial functions in alcoholism and aging have been reviewed extensively elsewhere (e.g., Ellis & Oscar-Berman, 1989; Oscar-Berman, 1988) and are not summarized again here. In general (and as was true of the Smith & Oscar-Berman [in press] findings, noted earlier in the present chapter), the cumulative results of most of the research in this area have not provided unequivocal support for the hypothesis that either alcoholism or aging differentially affects the functioning of the two cerebral hemispheres. A brief description of one recent experiment employing a dichotic listening paradigm will suffice as exemplary of the findings (Ellis, 1990). An important feature of Ellis's study was that patients with right-hemisphere disease were included to establish baseline comparisons with the other groups.

Ellis (1990) used a complementary pair of dichotic laterality tasks to compare his groups on functional asymmetries for "verbal" (words) and "nonverbal" (tonal patterns) auditory stimuli. The groups included right-hemisphere patients, detoxified alcoholics, and normal controls across a wide age range (25 to 74 years). Another important feature of the study was that the laterality performances of the groups were compared with their scores on standard neuropsychological tests that classically reveal visuospatial abnormalities (e.g., Performance subscales of the Wechsler Adult Intelligence Scale). The right-hemisphere patients demonstrated a rightward shift on both laterality tests (exaggerated with the word stimuli), as well as the expected visuospatial deficits on standardized clinical tests. Although results of neuropsychological testing in the alcoholic and aging subjects replicated previous findings regarding a selective decline in visuospatial nonverbal abilities, perceptual laterality effects did not differ according to age or history of alcohol abuse. These data confirmed other findings that pervasive or selective right-hemisphere damage does not underlie the altered patterns of visuospatial test performance often observed. Rather, bilateral cerebral compromise or cross-callosal transfer deficiencies may be present both in aging individuals and in heavy drinkers (Harper & Kril, 1989, 1990; Miller & Saucedo, 1983), and nonverbal skills may simply be more vulnerable to the ensuing brain dysfunction. Alternatively, lateralized processing of emotional materials may be compromised without affecting the processing of nonemotional (e.g., visuospatial) information, but this issue was not addressed directly by Ellis's study.

Conative Functions

Another focus of our research has been on conative or motivational changes in alcoholism and aging. Like the study of emotion, this area of research—compared to the study of cognitive dysfunction—has received little attention from experimentalists concerned with alcoholism and aging. The terms "conation" and "motivation" are used broadly to refer to the role of reinforcement in associative functions during habit acquisition and performance (Bower & Hilgard, 1981). In our initial work with conative functions (see Ellis & Oscar-Berman, 1989, and Oscar-Berman, 1984, for reviews), we demonstrated abnormalities by alcoholics in responding to changing reward contingencies (Oscar-Berman, Sahakian, & Wikmark, 1976), and in probability learning (Oscar-Berman, Heyman, Bonner, & Ryder, 1980; Oscar-Berman et al., 1976). It was not clear whether the abnormalities were directly related to appreciating the value of reinforcements, to associating reward with stimulus attributes, or to some other experimental variables. In an attempt to clarify the nature of the deficits, we first examined visual associative learning and memory (Oscar-Berman & Pulaski, 1984; Pulaski & Oscar-Berman, 1984), and then we examined cross-modal associative functions (Oscar-Berman, Pulaski, Hutner, Weber, & Freedman, 1990). These studies are described in turn.

Visual Associative Learning and Memory

Visual associative learning and memory rely heavily upon inferotemporal cortical systems, and deficits in appreciating stimulus–reward associations may result from combined damage of the amygdala and hippocampus (Mishkin & Appenzeller, 1987). Mishkin has suggested that the two structures—amygdala plus hippocampus—serve as a functional unit through which cortical areas interact with subcortical targets essential for intact associative memory. Mishkin based his claims on findings that monkeys with combined amygdala–hippocampal lesions (Mishkin, 1982; Mishkin & Spiegler, 1978) showed impairments on tasks of associative memory in which reward–nonreward aspects of stimuli could be dissociated (Gaffan, 1974). Using experimental paradigms modeled after Gaffan's (1974), we tested Mishkin's notions about the nature of stimulus–reward associative deficits in human amnesia as results of alcoholism; we also looked for deficits related to aging and/or alcoholism in the absence of anterograde amnesia.

We conducted two experiments. In the first (Oscar-Berman & Pulaski, 1984), the procedure we employed required a series of acquisition trials and a series of retention trials (Gaffan, 1974; Mishkin & Spiegler, 1978); the stimuli were presented on the central panel of three adjacent stimulus–response panels. In the acquisition trials, 10 different visual stimuli were presented successively, one at a time. Responses to a random half of the 10 stimuli were reinforced. Retention was tested by requiring the subjects to discriminate the stimuli that were associated in memory with reward from those that were not. During the retention trials, the same 10 stimuli were presented again, but on the right-side panel only; the left panel always contained a dark circle on a white background in order to provide a constant alternative response choice. In the retention test, the stimuli that were rewarded in the acquisition trials were rewarded again; responses to stimuli that were not rewarded in the acquisition trials were not rewarded in the retention test, and when a nonrewarded stimulus was presented, a press to the left key (circle) was rewarded. To maximize reward in the retention test, subjects had to respond to those stimuli that were rewarded in the acquisition trials, and refrain from responding to the stimuli that were not. Rewarded and nonrewarded stimuli were equally familiar items, and reward and nonreward were equally familiar events. We found that Korsakoff patients were severely impaired in comparison to all other groups. In other words, Korsakoffs were clearly deficient in discriminating between stimuli that had been directly associated with reward and those that had been associated with no reward. The older subjects, with and without a history of alcohol abuse, showed similar impairments during retention compared to younger subjects, but the impairments were not as severe as those of the Korsakoffs.

In the second experiment (Pulaski & Oscar-Berman, 1984), we used the same apparatus and procedures as in the previous experiment, except that only five rewarded stimuli and no nonrewarded stimuli were presented in the acquisition trials. This allowed the rewarded and the nonrewarded stimuli to be discriminable during retention tests by their familiarity alone. It should be noted that, on retention trials, the nonrewarded distractor items from which the familiar rewarded items were to be distinguished were different. Furthermore, the time between trials during acquisition in this experiment was double that of the previous experiment, in order to equate times between acquisition and retention. The results of this second experiment indicated once more that Korsakoff patients had the most severe impairments, followed by older subjects with and without an alcohol history. Results of the two experiments combined supported suggestions that (1) the ability to associate stimulus information with reward and (2) the ability to recognize familiar stimuli (regardless of reward value) are impaired in alcohol-related amnesia, just as is the case for monkeys with hippocampal lesions (Mahut, Zola-Morgan, & Moss, 1982). Furthermore, the results again did not favor the notion that aging and alcoholism are synergistic, at least not with regard to their effects upon reward sensitivity and recognition memory.

Cross-Modal Associative Functions

Brain regions often implicated in cross-modal associative functions are the amygdala and the left angular gyrus at the parieto-temporo-occipital junction (Aitken, 1980; Ettlinger & Garcha, 1980; Mishkin & Appenzeller, 1987; Petrides & Iversen, 1976). The amygdala is a polysensory area within the limbic system, receiving inputs from all sensory systems through a series of primary sensory fields enroute to the temporo-insular region (Turner, Mishkin, & Knapp, 1980). The association of reward value with stimulus features is thought to converge (for polysensory cross-modal learning) in the amygdala (Mishkin, 1982; Murray & Mishkin, 1985), and damage to the hippocampal–amygdala complex has been suggested as the basis for anterograde amnesia (Mishkin & Appenzeller, 1987). The left angular gyrus is a language-related neocortical area where sensory information converges (Davenport, 1977). Geschwind (1965) drew attention to the left angular gyrus in cross-modal functions by proposing that certain features of language taking place there were dependent upon intersensory associations mediated by polysynaptic connections among the sensory systems. Cross-modal deficits have been associated with deficits in naming ability in Alzheimer's and Parkinson's diseases (Freedman & Oscar-Berman, 1992).

Although neither alcoholism nor aging has been related specifically to damage of the left angular gyrus, both conditions have been linked to diffuse, generalized damage of the entire cortical mantle (e.g., see Parsons et al., 1987, and Albert & Moss, 1988). The damage usually leaves alcoholics and normal elderly individuals free of severe dementia, although some language and visuospatial abnormalities have been reported (Ellis & Oscar-Berman, 1989; Albert & Moss, 1988). In our continued explorations of conative functions in alcoholic and aging subjects, we studied cross-modal associations in these groups (Oscar-Berman, Pulaski, et al., 1990). In that study, two experiments were designed in which separate aspects of cross-modal functioning were measured: (1) matching and (2) utilization of concepts. In one of the experiments, cross-modal equivalence matching was measured—that is, the ability to select in a second modality (e.g., vision) the same stimulus that was first presented in a different modality (e.g., touch). In the other experiment, cross-modal transfer of information about stimulus dimensions was measured—that is, the ability to recognize and use the concepts of texture and form, based upon prior experience in solving tactual problems, to solve visual problems. Normal and alcoholic subjects between the ages of 28 and 71 years participated in the research.

Results indicated, first, that aging was associated with a decline in tactual discrimination ability; these impairments were attributed to diffusely distributed cortical atrophy, including parietal cortex involved in tactual functions. Cross-modal functions were found to be compromised by alcoholic Korsakoff's disease. The Korsakoffs' deficits were linked to probable damage of the amygdala (Turner et al., 1980). Unlike the findings from our studies on emotional functions, our findings in regard to conative functions bore out predictions with respect to the premature-aging hypothesis of alcoholism. Thus, older alcoholics showed patterns of cross-modal deficits that were similar to Korsakoff patients', but the impairments of the former group were not as severe as those of the Korsakoffs. In considering these results, as well as results from other studies (Oscar-Berman et al., 1976, 1980; Oscar-Berman & Pulaski, 1984; Pulaski & Oscar-Berman, 1984), we concluded that alcoholic Korsakoff's disease produces deficiencies on a wide range of conative measures (e.g., associating reward with stimulus properties, recognizing shifts in reinforcement value, and making cross-modal associations; see Oscar-Berman, 1980, 1984, 1990, and Oscar-Berman & Ellis, 1987, for reviews).

Summary

For the most part, results of our recent studies of conative functions parallel those obtained from the studies of affective functions. That is, alcoholic Korsakoff patients evidenced the greatest deficits on many tasks; this probably reflects extensive brain damage, including damage to the neocortical, basal forebrain, and limbic regions. Aging subjects—with and without a history of alcoholism—also displayed deficits, but the impairments were not as severe or as extensive as those of the Korsakoff patients; deficits in aging subjects may be directly related to decreased sensory (tactual and visual) processing abilities controlled by neocortical regions. Aging alcoholics demonstrated greater deficits than their nonalcoholic peers on only a few occasions; these results cannot be taken to suggest a strong synergism of alcoholism and aging. However, when synergistic effects are observed, they probably reflect a combination of diffuse cortical atrophy with damage to other brain regions (e.g., the limbic system and the basal forebrain). Whatever the neuroanatomical substrates may be, it is important to recognize that specific facets of emotional and motivational functions may have an impact upon cognitively based neuropsychological performance in alcoholic and aging research participants.

ACKNOWLEDGMENTS

The research reported in this chapter was supported by a grant from the National Institute on Alcohol Abuse and Alcoholism (No. AA07112), by a grant from the National Institute of Deafness and Communicative Disorders (No. NS06209), and by funds from the U.S. Department of Veterans Affairs.

REFERENCES

Aitken, P. G. (1980). Lesion effects on tactual to visual cross-modal matching in the Rhesus monkey. *Neuropsychologia, 18,* 575–578.

Albert, M. S., & Moss, M. B. (Eds.). (1988). *Geriatric neuropsychology.* New York: Guilford Press.

Beck, A. T., Ward, C. H., Mendelson, M., Mock, J. E., & Erbaugh, J. (1961). An inventory for measuring depression. *Archives of General Psychiatry, 4,* 561–571.

Baddeley, A. D. (1986). *Working memory.* Oxford: Oxford University Press.

Bedi, A. R., & Halikas, J. A. (1985). Alcoholism and affective disorder. *Alcoholism: Clinical and Experimental Research, 9,* 133–134.

Biber, C., Butters, N., Rosen, J., Gerstman, L., & Mattis, S. (1981). Encoding strategies and recognition of faces by alcoholic Korsakoff and other brain-damaged patients. *Journal of Clinical Neuropsychology, 3,* 315–330.

Borrill, J. A., Rosen, B. K., & Summerfield, A. B. (1987). The influence of alcohol on judgement of facial expressions of emotion. *British Journal of Medical Psychology, 60,* 71–77.

Bower, G. H., & Hilgard, E. R. (1981). *Theories of learning* (5th ed.). Englewood Cliffs, NJ: Prentice-Hall.

Butters, N., Jernigan, T., & Cermak, L. S. (1991). Reduced grey matter observed in alcoholics using magnetic resonance imaging (MRI). *Journal of Clinical and Experimental Neuropsychology, 13,* 444.

Craik, F. I. M., & Byrd, M. (1982). Aging and cognitive deficits: The role of attentional resources. In F. I. M. Craik & S. Trehub (Eds), *Aging and cognitive processes.* New York: Plenum Press.

Davenport, R. K. (1977). Cross-modal perception: A basis for language? In D. M. Rumbaugh (Ed.), *Language learning by a chimpanzee: The Lana project.* New York: Academic Press.

Davidoff, D. A., Butters, N., Gerstman, L. J., Zurif, E., Paul, I. H., & Mattis, S. (1984). Affective/motivational factors in the recall of prose passages by alcoholic Korsakoff patients. *Alcohol, 1,* 63–69.

Ellis, R. J. (1990). Dichotic asymmetries in aging and alcoholic subjects. *Alcoholism: Clinical and Experimental Research, 14,* 863–871.

Ellis, R. J., & Oscar-Berman, M. (1989). Alcoholism, aging, and functional cerebral asymmetries. *Psychological Bulletin, 106,* 128–147.

Ettlinger, G., & Garcha, H. S. (1980). Cross-modal recognition by the monkey: The effects of cortical removals. *Neuropsychologia, 18,* 685–692.

Freedman, M., & Oscar-Berman, M. (1986a). Bilateral frontal lobe disease and selective delayed-response deficits in humans. *Behavioral Neuroscience, 100,* 337–342.

Freedman, M., & Oscar-Berman, M. (1986b). Selective delayed response deficits in Alzheimer's and Parkinson's disease. *Archives of Neurology, 43,* 886–890.

Freedman, M., & Oscar-Berman, M. (1986c). Comparative neuropsychology of cortical and subcortical dementia. *Canadian Journal of Neurological Science, 13,* 410–414.

Freedman, M., & Oscar-Berman, M. (1987). Tactile discrimination learning deficits in Alzheimer's and Parkinson's disease. *Archives of Neurology, 44,* 394–398.

Freedman, M., & Oscar-Berman, M. (1989). Spatial and visual learning deficits in Alzheimer's and Parkinson's disease. *Brain and Cognition, 11,* 114–126.

Freedman, M., & Oscar-Berman, M. (1992). *Language breakdown and cross-modal functions in dementia.* Manuscript submitted for publication.

Gaffan, D. (1974). Recognition impaired and association intact in the memory of monkeys after transection of the fornix. *Journal of Comparative and Physiological Psychology, 86,* 1100–1109.

Gainotti, G. (1972). Emotional behavior and hemispheric side of the lesion. *Cortex, 8,* 41–55.

Geschwind, N. (1965). Disconnexion syndromes in animals and man, Part I. *Brain, 88,* 237–294.

Granholm, E., Wolfe, J., & Butters, N. (1985). Affective-arousal factors in the recall of thematic stories by amnesic and demented patients. *Developmental Neuropsychology, 1,* 317–333.

Grant, I. (1986). *Neuropsychiatric correlates of alcoholism.* Washington, DC: American Psychiatric Press.

Harper, C. G., & Kril, J. (1989). Patterns of neuronal loss in the cerebral cortex in chronic alcoholic patients. *Journal of Neurological Sciences*, 92, 81–89.

Harper, C. G., & Kril, J. J. (1990). Neuropathology of alcoholism. *Alcohol and Alcoholism*, 25, 207–216.

Jenike, M. (1988). Depression and other psychiatric disorders. In M. S. Albert & M. B. Moss (Eds.), *Geriatric neuropsychology*. New York: Guilford Press.

Kaplan, E. (1988). A process approach to neuropsychological assessment. In T. Boll & B. K. Bryant (Eds.), *Clinical neuropsychology and brain function: Research, measurement and practice*. Washington, DC: American Psychological Association.

Kelley, C. M. (1986). Depressive mood effects on memory and attention. In L. W. Poon (Ed.), *Handbook for clinical memory assessment of older adults*. Washington, DC: American Psychological Association.

Kellogg, R. T., & Dare, R. S. (1989). Explicit memory for unattended information. *Bulletin of the Psychonomic Society*, 27, 409–412.

Kish, S. J., El-Awar, M., Schut, L., Leach, L., Oscar-Berman, M., & Freedman, M. (1988). Cognitive deficits in olivopontocerebellar atrophy: Implications for the cholinergic hypothesis of Alzheimer's dementia. *Annals of Neurology*, 24, 200–206.

Kopelman, M. D. (1991). Frontal dysfunction and memory deficits in the alcoholic Korsakoff syndrome and Alzheimer-type dementia. *Brain*, 114, 117–137.

Lezak, D. L. (1983). *Neuropsychological assessment*. New York: Oxford University Press.

Lhermitte, F., & Signoret, J. L. (1976). The amnesic syndrome and the hippocampal–mammillary system. In M. R. Rosenzweig & E. L. Bennett (Eds.), *Neural mechanisms of learning and memory*. Cambridge, MA: MIT Press.

Lishman, W. A. (1978). *Organic psychiatry*. Oxford: Blackwell Scientific.

Mahut, H., Zola-Morgan, S. M., & Moss, M. (1982). Hippocampal resections impair associative learning and recognition memory in the monkey. *Journal of Neuroscience*, 2, 1214–1229.

Miller, W. R., & Saucedo, C. F. (1983). Assessment of neuropsychological impairment and brain damage in problem drinkers. In C. J. Golden, J. A. Moses, Jr., J. A. Coffman, W. R. Miller, & F. D. Strider (Eds.), *Clinical neuropsychology: Interface with neurologic and psychiatric disorders*. New York: Grune & Stratton.

Mishkin, M. (1982). A memory system in the monkey. *Philosophical Transactions of the Royal Society of London*, B298, 85–95.

Mishkin, M., & Appenzeller, T. (1987). Anatomy of memory. *Scientific American*, 256, 80–89.

Mishkin, M., & Spiegler, B. J. (1978). Evidence for the participation of inferior temporal cortex and amygdala in stimulus–reward learning. *Society for Neuroscience Abstracts*, 4, 263.

Murdock, B. B., Jr. (1965). The effect of a subsidiary task on short-term memory. *British Journal of Psychology*, 56, 413–419.

Murray, E. A., & Mishkin, M. (1985). Amygdalectomy impairs cross-modal association in monkeys. *Science*, 228, 604–606.

Newmann, J. P. (1989). Aging and depression. *Psychology and Aging*, 4, 150–165.

Noonberg, A., Goldstein, G., & Page, H. A. (1985). Premature aging in male alcoholics: "Accelerated aging" or increased vulnerability? *Alcoholism: Clinical and Experimental Research*, 9, 334–338.

Oscar-Berman, M. (1980). Neuropsychological consequences of long-term chronic alcoholism. *American Scientist*, 68, 410–419.

Oscar-Berman, M. (1984). Comparative neuropsychology and alcoholic Korsakoff's disease. In L. R. Squire & N. Butters (Eds.), *Neuropsychology of memory* (1st ed.). New York: Guilford Press.

Oscar-Berman, M. (1988). Normal functional asymmetries in alcoholism? *Aphasiology*, 2, 369–374.

Oscar-Berman, M. (1990). Severe brain dysfunction: Alcoholic Korsakoff's syndrome. *Alcohol Health and Research World*, 14, 120–129.

Oscar-Berman, M., & Ellis, R. J. (1987). Cognitive deficits related to memory impairments in alcoholism. In M. Galanter (Ed.), *Recent developments in alcoholism* (Vol. 5). New York: Plenum Press.

Oscar-Berman, M., Hancock, M., Mildworf, B., Hutner, N., & Weber, D. (1990). Emotional perception and memory in alcoholism and aging. *Alcoholism: Clinical and Experimental Research*, 14, 383–393.

Oscar-Berman, M., Heyman, G. M., Bonner, R. T., & Ryder, J. (1980). Human neuropsychology: Some differences between Korsakoff and normal operant performance. *Psychological Research*, 41, 235–247.

Oscar-Berman, M., Hutner, N., & Bonner, R. T. (in press). Visual and auditory spatial and nonspatial delayed-response performance by Korsakoff and non-Korsakoff alcoholic and aging individuals. *Behavioral Neuroscience*, 106.

Oscar-Berman, M., McNamara, P., & Freedman, M. (1991). Delayed-response tasks: Parallels between experimental ablation studies and findings in patients with frontal lesions. In H. S. Levin, H. M. Eisenberg, & A. L. Benton (Eds.), *Frontal lobe function and injury*. New York: Oxford University Press.

Oscar-Berman, M., & Pulaski, J. L. (1984). *Association memory in amnesia, alcoholism, and aging.* Paper presented at the annual convention of the American Psychological Association, Toronto.

Oscar-Berman, M., Pulaski, J. L., Hutner, N., Weber, D. A., & Freedman, M. (1990). Cross-modal functions in alcoholism and aging. *Neuropsychologia, 28,* 851–869.

Oscar-Berman, M., Sahakian, B. J., & Wikmark, G. (1976). Spatial probability learning by alcoholic Korsakoff patients. *Journal of Experimental Psychology: Human Learning and Memory, 2,* 215–222.

Oscar-Berman, M., & Zola-Morgan, S. M. (1980). Comparative neuropsychology and Korsakoff's syndrome: II. Two-choice visual discrimination learning. *Neuropsychologia, 18,* 499–512.

Parsons, O. A., Butters, N. M., & Nathan, P. (Eds.). (1987). *Neuropsychology of alcoholism: Implications for diagnosis and treatment.* New York: Guilford Press.

Petrides, M., & Iversen, S. D. (1976). Cross-modal matching and the primate frontal cortex. *Science, 192,* 1023–1024.

Poon, L. W. (Ed.). (1986). *Handbook for clinical memory assessment of older adults.* Washington, DC: American Psychological Association.

Pribram, K. H., & McGuinness, D. (1975). Arousal, activation, and effort in the control of attention. *Psychological Review, 82,* 116–149.

Pulaski, J. L., & Oscar-Berman, M. (1984). *Recognition memory in amnesia, alcoholism, and aging.* Paper presented at the annual convention of the American Psychological Association, Toronto.

Raskin, A. (1986). Partialing out the effects of depression and age on conative functions: Experimental data and methodologic issues. In L. W. Poon (Ed.), *Handbook for clinical memory assessment of older adults.* Washington, DC: American Psychological Association.

Riege, W. H. (1987). Specificity of memory deficits in alcoholism. In M. Galanter (Ed.), *Recent advances in alcoholism* (Vol. 5). New York: Plenum Press.

Ryan, C. (1982). Alcoholism and premature aging: A neuropsychological perspective. *Alcoholism: Clinical and Experimental Research, 6,* 79–96.

Ryan, C., & Butters, N. (1980). Learning and memory impairments in young and old alcoholics: Evidence for the premature-aging hypothesis. *Alcoholism: Clinical and Experimental Research, 4,* 288–293.

Smith, M. E., & Oscar-Berman, M. (1990). Repetition priming of words and pseudowords in divided attention and in amnesia. *Journal of Experimental Psychology: Learning, Memory, and Cognition, 16,* 1033–1042.

Smith, M. E., & Oscar-Berman, M. (in press). Resource-limited information processing in alcoholism. *Journal of Studies on Alcohol.*

Talland, G. A. (1965). *Deranged memory.* New York: Academic Press.

Turner, B. H., Mishkin, M., & Knapp, M. (1980). Organization of the amygdaloid projections from modality-specific cortical association areas in the monkey. *Journal of Comparative Neurology, 191,* 515–543.

8

The Problem of "Localizing" Memory in Focal Cerebrovascular Lesions

D. YVES von CRAMON and HANS J. MARKOWITSCH

Introduction

H. Damasio and A. R. Damasio begin the second chapter of their book (*Lesion Analysis in Neuropsychology*, 1989) with a brief definition: "The essence of the lesion method is the establishment of a correlation between a circumscribed region of damaged brain and changes in some aspect of an experimentally controlled behavioral performance" (p. 7). This definition seems to us useful because it makes no assumptions as to any specific model of the organization of cerebral function, and thus allows for the possibility of accepting various models.

The localizationist/associationist approach assumes that certain relatively independent neural networks corresponding to the various "components" of the (human) memory system actually exist. This approach hypothesizes an increasingly complex flow in information processing: Elementary subprocesses have to be concluded before information is referred to higher integrative centers. Thus, complex memory functions may be conceived of as the result of a sequential/hierarchical "assembly line" process. The definition above is also compatible with the microgenetic/holistic approach as put forward by Brown (1977, 1979), which sees brain functions as complete from the moment of their origin, developing along a quasi-phylogenetic hierarchy of brain structures.

In the localizationist approach, focal damage to memory-relevant brain structures induces an interruption in a constantly advancing, sequential/hierarchical information-processing system. According to the microgenetic/holistic model, circumscribed cerebral lesions cause a restructuring of memory functions on a less elaborated level, which might have been appropriate to earlier phylogenetic stages in development. In this forced regression, normally "buried and submerged" primordial memory functions are re-emphasized.

At length, Deacon's (1989) suggestion for a "countercurrent analogy" may prove useful. Based on a well-accepted principle in biology and the engineering sciences, this analogy attempts to utilize the neuroanatomical fact that the majority of intercortical circuits, as well as numerous non-cortico-cortical circuits, demonstrate bidirectional projections with a typical (i.e., laminary) organization of their target areas (see Deacon, 1989). As a consequence, simultaneous activities in "antidromic" projections may constitute the basis of cerebral information processing. Through the interaction of "counter-currents" in such bidirectionally cooperating neuronal populations, gradations in activity may arise, which may be abolished or critically altered by focal cerebral lesions.

Performing lesion studies today requires the workers to discuss their results in the light of such theoretical models of the organization of brain functions. The fact that an anterior (polar) thalamic lesion induces impairments in learning and memory measures has been sufficiently documented to date. Thus, the essential question now concerns the manner in which that focal loss of thalamic tissue alters the flow of information in a memory network that extends to practically all parts of the central nervous system (CNS).

We believe that lesion studies remain essential for expanding our knowledge of the "memory-relevant wiring" in the brain. Especially until we learn more about the topographical–functional organization of (telencephalic) medullary compartments, we cannot afford to give up on lesion work, no matter what methodological problems are inherently involved (see below).

Problems of Method

Visibility of Brain Damage

The theoretical and methodological standards for lesion research must be improved substantially. The "background noise" so apparent in contradictory results in the clinical literature certainly has one of its causes in a long series of methodological problems, some of which could well be avoided.

Prior to the introduction of modern imaging techniques, lesion work was based on the macro- and microscopic examination of autopsy material, with the undeniable advantage that such postmortem studies could give an exact description of the nature, extent, and localization of a brain lesion. But there were also several disadvantages. First, observing and measuring the brain functions of mostly severely ill patients were not only subject to (ethical) limitations; they could not coincide with the neuropathological examination. Further preterminal damage to cerebral tissue also contaminated the relationship between brain lesion and subsequent functional deficit. In addition, an artifact in sample selection was unavoidable as long as subjects prevailed who were of advanced age and suffering from chronic disease.

Recent neuroimaging techniques have introduced the possibility of conducting lesion studies *in vivo*, repeatedly, and concurrently with the behavioral examination. At the same time, it must not be forgotten that the techniques presently available still only offer indirect evidence for brain lesions by means of various physical parameters (such as density and signal intensity).

Useful material for the lesion method can be found in the cerebrovascular diseases, as they are both frequent and fairly easy to demonstrate. Because of regularities in vascular supply areas (though not necessarily in angioarchitecture), tissue damage has a relatively high degree of interindividual uniformity and thus comparability. Lesions in vascular tissue are found in a large number of regions in the CNS, though not in all with the same frequency, so that a good many cortical and medullary areas can be tested for their memory relevance (for a limitation on this point, see below). In regard to the reliability of *in vivo* cerebrovascular lesion studies, the following methodological aspects are of particular importance:

- The neuroimaging technique.
- The time after injury.
- The selectivity of brain lesions.
- The amount of tissue damage in an individual brain structure.
- The morphological nature of the lesion.

The Technique of Investigation

MRI has to be recognized today as the standard method for studying focal cerebrovascular lesions. Compared to CT scans, its most salient advantages include high-quality sections in all three planes, a better chance of detecting vascular micro-lesions (more than 1 mm in diameter), and a higher degree of specifity for visualizing fine tissue differences (e.g., necrosis vs. gliosis).

For precise localization of focal brain lesions, the reference system chosen is also decisive. Those lines of reference that vary only slightly with the stereotaxic anterior commissure–posterior commissure (AC-PC) line, such as the glabella–inion line or the fronto-occipital line (see Fox, Perlmutter, & Raichle, 1985; Tokunaga, Takase, & Otani, 1977), should be given preference over those that are oriented on the skull. The orbito-meatal line deviates considerably from the longitudinal axis of the brain (Hebel & von Cramon, 1987). For a description of the standard procedure used in our laboratory for analyzing MRI, see Damasio and Damasio (1989).

Time since Brain Damage

We prefer lesion studies done in the chronic stage. Six months after injury, the borders of a vascular lesion are clearly marked, and processes of tissue repair are recognizable. In this chronic phase lesion-dependent impairments of memory func-tioning may be considered stable, although to the observer the functional handicap may still seem subject to change because of various cerebral reorganization processes or avoidance ("learned nonuse"), or because of reduction in the individual level of performance demands.

Selectivity of Brain Damage

There is abundant neuropathological evidence to show that single vascular le-sions are the exception rather than the rule; far more frequently the "critical brain lesion" is associated with additional tissue damage, usually in several different brain structures. Nonetheless, even fairly recent publications often fail to mention and

discuss those additional lesions, or do so only tangentially. A comprehensive reconstruction of the "lesion status" requires a consideration of all detectable tissue damage,
and not just of the one brain structure claimed to be critical. (Moreover, microlesions
with a diameter of less than 1 mm or hypoxic cell damage may well go undetected.)
The main point here is to understand the correspondence between certain critical brain
lesions and whatever memory deficits are demonstrable, keeping the impact of associated tissue loss firmly in view. And this in turn will help overcome the prejudice
against lesion studies as merely a simplified "look at holes in the brain."

Volume of Brain Damage

The present level of our understanding precludes giving precise information on
how much (of the volume) of any particular brain structure has been destroyed by a
focal vascular lesion. However, animal studies give indication that a functional deficit
is actually dependent on whether 90% or only 30% of a given brain structure is lesioned.
The difficulty in reliably estimating the amount of tissue damage in a particular brain
structure may explain some of the contradictory results mentioned above.

Pathophysiology of Brain Damage

As mentioned above, the MRI technology available today provides not only an
improved possibility for localization, but also a better view of different tissue components in focal vascular lesions. This fact should have decidedly positive effects on the
progress of lesion studies. We are able now to differentiate pseudocystic necrotic areas
(in which all the neuropil has been destroyed) from incomplete necrosis with consecutive gliotic and/or mesenchymal scarring or from hemorrhagic residues (hemosiderin
deposits). In the future, differences observed and measured after changes in memory
functions will be correlated with more exact assumptions on the morphological condition of a vascular cerebral lesion, and not just its volume and localization.

Investigation of Memory Processes in the Presence
of Additional Neuropsychological Deficits

The assessment of memory functions in brain-damaged individuals is usually under-
taken in the presence of additional behavioral disturbances that may affect mnemonic
functioning and that can be controlled for or at least determined to some degree. The
elapse of a period of several months between the occurrence of the damage and the
time of testing will only diminish but not nullify the contribution of lesion-dependent
changes in personality factors to memory test results (Walker, Caveness, & Critchley,
1969). We furthermore have to bear in mind that there is no single, unitary memory
function, but that anatomically related subcategorizations of memory may well exist
(e.g., "declarative" vs. "nondeclarative" memory; see Squire & Zola-Morgan, 1988).
Aside from these cognitive changes, there are both more general and more specific

changes that can accompany brain injury and broadly affect personality or else alter the expression of specific functions.

A recent example of interactive effects between mood and memory in vascular pathology stems from a patient with a reversible bilateral cerebral vein thrombosis in the region of the dorsal thalamus (Peper, Seier, Krieger, & Markowitsch, 1991). Clinically, there was an immediate improvement. Repeated CT and MRI scans revealed that the thrombotic area shrank considerably within 7 days and was reduced after 1 month to a tiny spot in the region of the mediodorsal thalamic nucleus. On the neuropsychological level, however, the patient remained quite depressed; though she still was motivated to have her behavioral status examined, it seems possible (if not likely) that her emotional condition—which after 15 months resulted in a suicide attempt—caused a deterioration in her mnemonic performance.

This particular case clearly illustrates frequent effects of vascular lesions. It shows both their immediate and their lasting impact on a variety of personality dimensions, including attention, mood, spontaneous activity, and motivation.

Brain damage may, of course, have a number of consequences for the subject's ability to encode, store, or retrieve information. An altered state of awareness may result in an impaired ability (or even the complete inability) to acknowledge even a severe memory impairment (e.g., Delbecq-Derouesné, Beauvois, & Shallice, 1990; Schacter, 1990). Increased distractibility or lack of concentration, reduced states of vigilance, chronic states of disinhibition, reduced information-processing rates, emotional instability, and an impairment in attention (confusion) have all been found after brain damage. Each may interfere with otherwise preserved mnemonic abilities (e.g., von Cramon, Brinkmann, & Schulz, 1975; Geschwind, 1982; Mattson & Levin, 1990; Sandson et al., 1988).

Certain kinds of brain injury may affect specific aspects of mnemonic behavior. Aside from basic sensory and/or motor changes, the understanding and expression of language will influence memory functions (e.g., Kempler et al., 1990). On the anatomical side, some of the thalamic relay stations are of importance for both language and memory, or may, in addition, be involved in attentional mechanisms (LaBerge & Buchsbaum, 1990). Judgment and inference impairments have been regarded as "both necessary and sufficient for unawareness of intellectual and memory impairments" (Levine, 1990, p. 269).

From these examples it follows that it is not possible simply to assess a range of memory functions in a focally lesioned patient; one has to try carefully to separate specific from less specific memory impairments by determining and evaluating possible concomitant changes. Brain lesions may affect various aspects of mental competence (Alexander, 1988), and focal vascular lesions may have remote effects on cerebral blood flow and metabolism (Pawlik et al., 1985).

The Contribution of Focal White Matter Lesions to an Understanding of the Human Memory System

The human nervous system contains a larger volume of fibers than of neurons, and several thousand fiber endings may terminate on a nerve cell. These relations; the fact that most areas are not more than five or six synapses away from any other region in the brain; and the fact that, of the more than 100 billion neurons, only about 30% are directly engaged in information processing (Kolb & Whishaw, 1989) all point to the dominance of the fiber systems in memory organization. Further examples of arguments for the importance of fiber systems in memory processing are Irle's (1990) recent analysis of the correlation of lesion size, localization, and behavioral effects in 283 monkey studies, from which she concluded that "lesion size alone is a poor predictor of the behavioral performance" (p. 203), and John's (1972) hypothesis that memory retrieval is dependent on a widespread interconnected network of neuron–fiberassemblies. Thus, it may be expected that damage to portions of the brain's fiber system will alter information processing significantly (see von Cramon & Hebel, 1989; Markowitsch, 1991).

Over the last few decades, there has been a continuous shift and backshift in the extent to which mnemonic disturbances have been related to the damage of particular brain structures, with gray matter regions dominating. To take the medial temporal lobe area as an example, Scoville and Milner (1957) stressed the hippocampus and parahippocampal gyrus, but de-emphasized the amygdala; Mishkin (1978) highlighted the combined role of amygdala and hippocampus; and more recently Zola-Morgan and coworkers again de-emphasized the memory-related role of the amygdala (Zola-Morgan, Squire, & Amaral, 1989) and of the temporal stem (Zola-Morgan, Squire, & Mishkin, 1982), and stressed that of field CA1 of the hippocampus proper (Zola-Morgan, Squire, & Amaral, 1986). Finally, in this tour through the temporal lobe, the perirhinal and parahippocampal cortices are considered as centrally important for memory processing (Zola-Morgan, Squire, Amaral, & Suzuki, 1989).

The damage of gray matter structures is usually easier to determine or to estimate than that of fiber systems, which are frequently not only tinier in volume but also more hidden, so that sometimes only an indirect approach is possible. One example of such an approach is comparing lesion locus and extent in several cases and dividing these into those in which damage includes specific fiber systems (and leads to persistent amnesia) and those in which this is not the case (von Cramon, Hebel, & Schuri, 1985). A further complication lies in the difficulty of evaluating how much of a fiber system may be damaged, and whether and within which limits partial fiber damage is "sufficient" to cause lasting memory problems. (The parallel question has been raised, for example, by Kritchevsky, Graff-Radford, & Damasio, 1987, with respect to the necessity of critical volume reduction for amnesia in medial thalamic damage.)

For most of the above-listed fiber systems of the medial and basolateral limbic circuits, little is known about their individual contribution to memory processing (see, e.g., von Cramon, in press). This holds especially true for fiber systems of the basolateral limbic circuit—namely, the bandeletta diagonalis and the stria terminalis.

A Case with Damage to Fibers of a "Subcortical Memory System"

A patient with a small left-sided infarction in the territory of the anterior perforating arteries (those arising from the C1 segment of the carotid artery) showed considerable verbal memory and learning deficits (Markowitsch, von Cramon, Hofmann, Sick,

& Kinzler, 1990). Repeated CT and MRI analyses revealed that the principal lesion lay within the "knee" of the internal capsule, obviously in front of the anterior thalamus (Figure 8.1). T1- and T2-weighted MRIs disclosed a triangular pseudocystic lesion centered on the genu of the left internal capsule. It seemed most likely that both the anterior and inferior thalamic peduncles were affected. Furthermore, partial damage of the fornical columns and of the stria terminalis could not be ruled out.

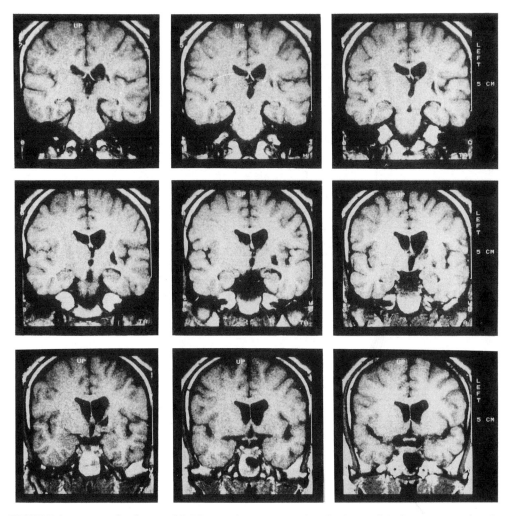

FIGURE 8.1. T1-weighted coronal MRI scans (Magnetom, 1.0 Tesla, SE mode), done 4 years after the patient suffered an infarct in the territory of the left anterior perforating arteries (top left to bottom right is from posterior to anterior). As to the verbal memory impairment, the triangular lesion centered on the genu of the left internal capsule (third row, left scan) seems to be most relevant; it presumably disrupted the anterior and inferior thalamic peduncle, the fornical column, the stria terminalis, and the anterior commissure, and injured the medial portion of the globus pallidus. From "Verbal Memory Deterioration after Unilateral Infarct of the Internal Capsule in an Adolescent" (p. 600) by H. J. Markowitsch, D. Y. von Cramon, E. Hofmann, C.-D. Sick, and P. Kinzler, 1990, *Cortex*, *26*, 597–609. Copyright 1990 by *Cortex*. Reprinted by permission.

This case was remarkable because the damage was small, circumscribed, and unilateral, and the "memory-relevant" structures that were damaged consisted of a small number of fibers. It shows that one small and even unilateral vascular lesion, if centered at a nodal point of information transfer, may affect memory processing, and that the resulting interruption of long-term information processing may be severe and continuous.

White Matter Damage

Fiber tracts, more so than distinct nuclear centers, may be regarded as nodal points, crossroads, or strategic links that, when damaged, may have drastic and enduring deleterious effects on mnemonic behavior. Although evidence of the consequences of combined damage to hippocampal-related and amygdala-related subsystems is presently equivocal (see, e.g., Graff-Radford, Tranel, Van Hoesen, & Brandt, 1990; Markowitsch, 1988; Squire, Amaral, & Press, 1990), it is the fiber systems that connect the two, and that, with refined diagnostic methodology, are increasingly recognized as important with respect to their involvement in long-term information processing.

Though much of the evidence at present appears to suggest that, even in focal cerebrovascular white matter lesions, memory functions can hardly be clearly specified, reality demonstrates that we can nevertheless be reasonably definitive if the above-mentioned precautions are recognized (see the examples above). More than most of the other kinds of brain damage, vascular lesions with fiber involvement provide a not-to-be-underestimated opportunity to combine anatomical with neuropsychological knowledge and to relate individual facets of memory disturbances to distinct neuronal damage. Ultimately, we may look forward to unraveling the brain's code of mnemonic information processing by collecting and comparing carefully investigated single cases with circumscribed cerebrovascular damage.

What Is Not Yet Known about the Three-Dimensional Components of the Human Memory System

We know that a simple structural lesion may affect the activity of regions far remote from the pathological site. Furthermore, psychological and social factors profoundly influence cerebral function (Reynolds, 1990, p. 488). Because evidence that damage in a single crucial region leads to amnesia is sparse, if it exists at all (Markowitsch, 1984), it has been stated repeatedly that the combined damage of several regions may lead to a chronic amnesic state (Mishkin, 1978; Squire et al., 1990). The idea of the necessity of combined structural damage supports the hypothesis that damaged fibers and therefore the communicating links between structures play a major role in long-term information processing. Though this is likely to be the case, a number of questions still remain. Among these are questions on the critical extent of damage (Grafman, Salazar, Weingartner, Vance, & Amin, 1986; Irle, 1990; Turkheimer, Yeo, & Bigler, 1990); on the critical amount of damage per defined area, nucleus, or fiber tract (e.g., Kritchevsky et al., 1987); on the localizability of stored information (e.g., Petersen, Fox, Snyder, & Raichle, 1990; Posner, Petersen, Fox, & Raichle, 1988); and on the modes of information processing by the brain, starting from the processes of encoding to the processes of retrieval.

To simplify, we can argue that in principle there are two views of information storage: one assuming the existence of a widespread network of information storage, in which the importance of any individual element is nearly negligible (e.g., John, Tang, Brill, Young, & Ono, 1986), and the other assuming the existence of single centers that are of critical importance, so that one can create a "brain map" of cognitive functions. It is likely that a combination of both views will approach reality most closely, and that different degrees of localization may correspond to functions of different complexity (cf. Mesulam's [1981] Figure 4, giving "four approaches to the cortical localization of complex function"). It is obvious that regions are functionally specialized, but cannot act on their own. For the passage of (declarative) mnemonic information, the "fixed wired" units of the limbic system apparently are particularly suitable. Nevertheless, even within this system task sharing occurs; for example, the amygdaloid clearly acts differently from the hippocampal complex.

Although we are considerably certain about the importance of several of these structures in memory processing, we do not know to what degree they interact and how information is coded *within* them. Here, a number of questions await answers. For instance, are the left and right medial mammillary nuclei functionally equipotential? Does a nucleus or region principally act as a whole; are clusters of macro- or micro-columns united; or is there a specific topographical or functional split within a nucleus, region, or fiber tract? Do monitoring regions such as portions of the prefrontal cortex (see Damasio & Damasio, 1990; Shallice, 1982) exist, interact, and control the memory-processing regions? How do limbic and striatal regions interact (see, e.g., Nauta, 1979)? To what degree are consciousness, a concept of time, and other more general variables prerequisites for successful information processing (e.g., Crick & Koch, 1990; Damasio, 1990; Glynn, 1990)? To what extent is it possible to predict, from the degree of an initial deficit after vascular damage, the subsequent amount of recovery (see Dikmen, Reitan, & Temkin, 1983)?

Although some of the more general questions cannot be solved in the near future, the contribution of individual brain portions to information processing may be elucidated further in the foreseeable future by findings obtainable with modern brain-scanning techniques. The contribution of portions of the cingulate gyrus, of individual nuclei of the basal forebrain, or of some of the fiber systems within the medial and basolateral limbic system is largely *terra incognita* (see von Cramon, in press).

REFERENCES

Alexander, M. P. (1988). Clinical determination of mental competence: A theory and a retrospective study. *Archives of Neurology, 45*, 23-26.
Brown, J. (1977). *Mind, brain, and consciousness.* New York: Academic Press.
Brown, J. (1979). Language representation in the brain. In H. Steklis & M. Raleigh (Eds.), *Neurobiology of social communication in primates* (pp. 133-195). New York: Academic Press.
Crick, F., & Koch, C. (1990). Towards a neurobiological theory of consciousness. *Seminars in the Neurosciences, 2*, 263-275.

Damasio, A. R. (1990). Synchronous activation in multiple cortical regions: A mechanism for recall. *Seminars in the Neurosciences, 2,* 287-296.

Damasio, H., & Damasio, A. R. (1989). *Lesion analysis in neuropsychology.* Oxford: Oxford University Press.

Damasio, H., & Damasio, A. R. (1990). The neural basis of memory, language and behavioral guidance: Advances with the lesion method in humans. *Seminars in the Neurosciences, 2,* 277-286.

Deacon, T. W. (1989). Holism and associationism in neuropsychology: An anatomical synthesis. In E. Perecman (Ed.), *Integrating theory and practice in clinical neuropsychology* (pp. 1-47). Hillsdale, NJ: Erlbaum.

Delbecq-Derouesné, J., Beauvois, M. F., & Shallice, T. (1990). Preserved recall versus impaired recognition. *Brain, 113,* 1045-1074.

Dikmen, S., Reitan, R. M., & Temkin, N. R. (1983). Neuropsychological recovery in head injury. *Archives of Neurology, 40,* 333-338.

Fox, P. T., Perlmutter, J. S., & Raichle, M. E. (1985). A stereotactic method of anatomical localization for positron emission tomography. *Journal of Computer Assisted Tomography, 9,* 141-153.

Geschwind, N. (1982). Disorders of attention: a frontier in neuropsychology. *Philosophical Transactions of the Royal Society of London, B298,* 173-185.

Glynn, I. M. (1990). Consciousness and time. *Nature, 348,* 477-479.

Graff-Radford, N.-R., Tranel, D., Van Hoesen, G. W., & Brandt, J. P. (1990). Diencephalic amnesia. *Brain, 113,* 1-25.

Grafman, J., Salazar, A., Weingartner, H., Vance, S., & Amin, D. (1986). The relationship of brain-tissue loss volume and lesion location to cognitive deficit. *Journal of Neuroscience, 6,* 301-307.

Hebel, N., & von Cramon, D. Y. (1987). Der Posteriorinfarkt [The posterior infarct]. *Fortschritte der Neurologie und Psychiatrie, 55,* 37-53.

Irle, E. (1990). An analysis of the correlation of lesion size, localization and behavioral effects in 283 published studies of cortical and subcortical lesions in Old World monkeys. *Brain Research Reviews, 15,* 181-215.

John, E. R. (1972). Switchboard versus statistical theories of learning and memory. *Science, 177,* 850-864.

John, E. R., Tang, Y., Brill, A. B., Young, R., & Ono, K. (1986). Double-labeled metabolic maps of memory. *Science, 233,* 1167-1175.

Kempler, D., Metter, E. J., Riege, W. H., Jackson, C. A., Benson, D. F., & Hanson, W. R. (1990). Slowly progressive aphasia: Three cases with language, memory, CT and PET data. *Journal of Neurology, Neurosurgery and Psychiatry, 53,* 987-993.

Kolb, B., & Whishaw, I. Q. (1989). *Fundamentals of human neuropsychology* (3rd ed.). San Francisco: W. H. Freeman.

Kritchevsky, M., Graff-Radford, N.-R., & Damasio, A. (1987). Normal memory after damage to medial thalamus. *Archives of Neurology, 44,* 959-962.

LaBerge, D., & Buchsbaum, M. S. (1990). Positron emission tomographic measurements of pulvinar activity during an attention task. *Journal of Neuroscience, 10,* 613-619.

Levine, D. N. (1990). Unawareness of visual and sensorimotor defects: A hypothesis. *Brain and Cognition, 13,* 233-281.

Markowitsch, H. J. (1984). Can amnesia be caused by damage of a single brain structure? *Cortex, 20,* 27-45.

Markowitsch, H. J. (1988). Diencephalic amnesia: A reorientation towards tracts? *Brain Research Reviews, 13,* 351-370.

Markowitsch, H. J. (1991). Memory disorders after diencephalic damage: Heterogeneity of findings. In M. C. Corballis, K. White, & W. Abraham (Eds.), *Memory mechanisms: A tribute to G. V. Goddard* (pp. 175-194). Hillsdale, NJ: Erlbaum.

Markowitsch, H. J., von Cramon, D. Y., Hofmann, E., Sick, C.-D., & Kinzler, P. (1990). Verbal memory deterioration after unilateral infarct of the internal capsule in an adolescent. *Cortex, 26,* 597-609.

Mattson, A. J., & Levin, H. S. (1990). Frontal lobe dysfunction following closed head injury. *Journal of Nervous and Mental Disease, 178,* 282-291.

Mesulam, M.-M. (1981). A cortical network for directed attention and unilateral neglect. *Annals of Neurology, 10,* 309-325.

Mishkin, M. (1978). Memory in monkeys severely impaired by combined, but not by separate removal of amygdala and hippocampus. *Nature, 273,* 297-298.

Nauta, W. J. H. (1979). Expanding borders of the limbic system concept. In T. Rasmussen & R. Marino (Eds.), *Functional neurosurgery* (pp. 7-23). New York: Raven Press.

Pawlik, G., Herholz, K., Beil, C., Wagner, R., Wienhard, K., & Heiss, W.-D. (1985). Remote effects of focal lesions on cerebral flow and metabolism. In W.-D. Heiss (Ed.), *Functional mapping of the brain in vascular disorders* (pp. 59-83). Berlin: Springer-Verlag.

Peper, M., Seier, U., Krieger, D., & Markowitsch, H. J. (1991). Impairment of memory in a patient with reversible bilateral thalamic lesions due to internal cerebral vein thrombosis. *Restorative Neurology and Neuroscience, 2*, 155-162.

Petersen, S. E., Fox, P. T., Snyder, A. Z., & Raichle, M. E. (1990). Activation of extrastriate and frontal cortical areas by visual words and word-like stimuli. *Science, 249*, 1041-1044.

Posner, M. I., Petersen, S. E., Fox, P. T., & Raichle, M. E. (1988). Localization of cognitive operations in the human brain. *Science, 240*, 1627-1631.

Reynolds, E. H. (1990). Structure and function in neurology and psychiatry. *British Journal of Psychiatry, 157*, 481-490.

Sandson, J., Crosson, B., Posner, M. I., Barco, P. P., Velozo, C. A., & Brobeck, T. C. (1988). Attentional imbalances following head injury. In J. M. Williams & C. J. Long (Eds.), *Cognitive approaches to neuropsychology* (pp. 45-59). New York: Plenum.

Schacter, D. L. (1990). Toward a cognitive neuropsychology of awareness: Implicit knowledge and anosognosia. *Journal of Clinical and Experimental Neuropsychology, 12*, 155-178.

Scoville, W. B., & Milner, B. (1957). Loss of recent memory after bilateral hippocampal lesions. *Journal of Neurology, Neurosurgery and Psychiatry, 20*, 11-21.

Shallice, T. (1982). Specific impairments of planning. *Philosophical Transactions of the Royal Society of London, B298*, 199-209.

Squire, L. R., Amaral, D. G., & Press, G. A. (1990). Magnetic resonance imaging of the hippocampal formation and mammillary nuclei distinguish medial temporal lobe and diencephalic amnesia. *Journal of Neuroscience, 10*, 3106-3117.

Squire, L. R., & Zola-Morgan, S. (1988). Memory: Brain systems and behavior. *Trends in Neurosciences, 11*, 170-175.

Tokunaga, A., Takase, M. & Otani, K. (1977). The glabella-inion line as a baseline for CT-scanning of the brain. *Neuroradiology, 14*, 67-71.

Turkheimer, E., Yeo, R. A., & Bigler, E. D. (1990). Basic relations among lesion laterality, lesion volume and neuropsychological performance. *Neuropsychologia, 28*, 1011-1019.

von Cramon, D. Y. (in press). Focal cerebral lesions damaging (subcortical) fiber projections related to memory and learning functions in man. In G. Vallar (Ed.), *Neuropsychological disorders associated with subcortical lesions.* Oxford: Oxford University Press.

von Cramon, D. Y., Brinkmann, R., & Schulz, H. (1975). Entwicklung eines Messinstrumentes zur Bestimmung der Aufmerksamkeit bei Patienten mit cerebralen Läsionen und Funktionsstörungen [Development of a method of measuring the attention of patients with cerebral lesions]. *Journal of Neurology, 208*, 241-256.

von Cramon, D. Y., & Hebel, N. (1989). Lern- und Gedächtnisstörungen bei fokalen zerebralen Gewebsläsionen [Memory and learning disturbances in focal cerebral tissue lesions]. *Fortschritte der Neurologie und Psychiatrie, 57*, 544-550.

von Cramon, D. Y., Hebel, N., & Schuri, U. (1985). A contribution to the anatomical basis of thalamic amnesia. *Brain, 108*, 993-1008.

Walker, A. E., Caveness, W. F., & Critchley, M. (1969). *The late effects of head injury.* Springfield, IL: Charles C. Thomas.

Zola-Morgan, S., Squire, L. R., & Amaral, D. G. (1986). Human amnesia and the medial temporal region: Enduring memory impairment following a bilateral lesion limited to field CA1 of the hippocampus. *Journal of Neuroscience, 6*, 2950-2967.

Zola-Morgan, S., Squire, L. R., & Amaral, D. G. (1989). Lesions of the amygdala that spare adjacent cortical regions do not impair memory or exacerbate the impairment following lesions of the hippocampal formation. *Journal of Neuroscience, 9*, 1922-1936.

Zola-Morgan, S., Squire, L. R., Amaral, D. G., & Suzuki, W. A. (1989). Lesions of perirhinal and parahippocampal cortex that spare the amygdala and hippocampal formation produce severe memory impairment. *Journal of Neuroscience, 9*, 4355-4370.

Zola-Morgan, S., Squire, L. R., & Mishkin, M. (1982). The neuroanatomy of amnesia: The amygdala-hippocampus vs. temporal stem. *Science, 218*, 1337-1339.

9

Learning and Memory in Humans, with an Emphasis on the Role of the Hippocampus

RAYMOND P. KESNER, RAMONA O. HOPKINS, and ANDREA A. CHIBA

The Data-Based Memory System and the Attribute Model

The literature on the neurobiological basis of memory in humans is voluminous. Many models have been proposed to account for a possible mnemonic contribution of the hippocampus. The most prominent theoretical models suggest that the hippocampus plays a role either in consolidating new information (Milner, 1970) or in encoding and retrieving all information within episodic memory (Tulving, 1987; Kinsbourne, 1987), event memory (Weiskrantz, 1987), declarative memory (Squire, 1987), or explicit memory (Schacter, 1987). The emphasis of episodic, event, and explicit memory is on specific personal or autobiographical experiences that involve conscious awareness. Declarative memory includes episodic memory, but, in addition, it includes memory for factual knowledge and experiences.

In a slightly different formulation of hippocampal mediation of memory, Kesner (1990), by integrating the above-mentioned models, has suggested that the hippocampus mediates information within a data-based memory system. This data-based memory system is primarily concerned with short- or intermediate-term memory storage, but not long-term memory storage, of *new* incoming information concerning the present. There is an emphasis on facts, data, and events that are usually personal and that occur within specific external and internal environmental contexts. From a dynamic point of view, the emphasis of the data-based memory system is on "bottom-up" processing. This system is likely to involve temporary memory representations allowing for "controlled" attentional and elaborative rehearsal (consolidation-dependent) or maintenance rehearsal processes.

In addition, it is proposed that memories within the data-based memory system can be subdivided into multidimensional representations in the form of attributes. Based on earlier suggestions by Underwood (1969) and Bower (1967), the attribute model of memory proposes that any specific memory is composed of a set of features or attributes that are specific and unique for each learning experience. There are at least six salient attributes that characterize the structural representation of information within the data-based memory system. These attributes are space, time, language, sensory perception, response, and affect.

A spatial attribute within this data-based framework involves the coding and temporary storage of specific stimuli representing spatial locations, directions, and distances, which are usually independent of a subject's own body schema. A temporal attribute involves the encoding and temporary storage of specific temporally separated stimuli as part of an episode, marking or tagging its occurrence in time—that is, separating one specific episode from previous or succeeding episodes. In addition to the temporal order component of the temporal attribute, there are also duration and time perspective (past, and present) components.

A linguistic attribute involves the coding and temporary storage of linguistic information, including lexical and syntactical components. A sensory-perceptual attribute involves the encoding and temporary storage of a set of varied sensory stimuli that are organized in the form of information content of a specific experience. A response attribute involves the encoding and temporary storage of information based on feedback from responses that occur in specific situations, as well as the selection of appropriate responses. An affect attribute involves the encoding and temporary storage of reinforcement contingencies that result in positive or negative emotional experiences.

The organization of these attributes can take many forms, utilizing both serial and parallel systems. Within this attribute/data-based memory system framework, it is assumed that generally the *right* hippocampus encodes *only* spatial and temporal attributes, and that generally the *left* hippocampus encodes *only* linguistic and temporal attributes. This proposal suggests that the hippocampus codes only a limited, albeit important, set of attributes. It is thus predicted that the hippocampus is less involved in mediating sensory-perceptual, response, and affect attributes (see Table 9.1). In contrast, the other models mentioned above would predict hippocampus involvement with all attributes. In order to test the attribute model, we have examined data-based memory performance during tasks that test specific attributes in patients with right and left temporal lobe lesions including the hippocampus, and in patients who have suffered a severe hypoxic episode resulting in bilateral hippocampal damage.

TABLE 9.1. Predictions of Hippocampal Mediation of Attributes within the Data-Based and Expectancy-Based Memory Systems, Based on Kesner's Attribute Model of Memory

Attributes	Data-based	Expectancy-based
Space	Yes (right)	No
Time	Yes (right and left)	No
Language	Yes (left)	No
Response	?	No
Sensory-perceptual	?	No
Affect	?	No

Memory for Verbal and Spatial Information in Patients with Temporal Lobectomies

As an extension of the notion of hippocampal lateralization of different modalities, we have designed parallel tests of episodic memory for verbal and spatial information. In order to test item recognition for spatial location, ×'s appear on a computer screen that is divided into a grid including 16 possible spaces. During the study phase of each trial, 6 stimulus locations (×'s) are randomly selected from a set of 16 and presented in a sequential manner. Each stimulus is presented for a period of 5 seconds. Immediately following the study phase, the test phase is presented. During the test phase, two items are simultaneously presented on the screen—one that occurred in the study sequence and one that did not. The subject is asked to choose the item he or she saw in the previous list. The test choices are counterbalanced across serial positions. The test of item recognition for verbal information is similar to that for spatial location. Each trial of the study phase contains sequential presentations of 6 words, randomly selected from a set of 16 possible choices. Each word is presented for a period of 5 seconds. During the study phase, two words are simultaneously presented on the screen—one that occurred in the study phase and one that did not. Again, the subject is requested to select the word that he or she saw in the study phase.

The order recognition tests of spatial location and of verbal information are comprised of study phases identical to those of the item tests. In each instance, the study phase is followed by a test phase in which two stimuli, both of which occurred in the study phase, are simultaneously presented on the screen. In the order recognition test for words and for spatial locations, the test stimuli are always sequentially or temporally adjacent to each other. The test phase of each condition requires that the subject indicates which of the two stimuli occurred earlier in the study sequence. For each of the item recognition tasks, 24 trials are presented per test session in order to obtain 4 observations per serial position. For each of the order recognition tests, 20 trials are presented per session in order to obtain 4 observations per serial position. Using one test session per trial for all of the tasks reduces output interference, while ensuring that the tasks are analogous to those used in testing animals. On both spatial and verbal recognition tasks, chance-level performance is indicated by 50% correct choices. A performance level of 75% correct choices is significantly better than chance.

In one study (Chiba, Kesner, Matsuo, & Heilbrun, 1990), 12 subjects who had undergone unilateral temporal lobectomy for control of refractory complex partial epilepsy of temporal lobe origin were tested on the item and order recognition tests for words and for spatial locations. The extent of tissue resected for each subject typically included 3-5 cm of the anterior temporal lobe, 1-4 cm of the hippocampus, and varying amounts of surrounding mesial temporal structures unilaterally. Subjects were tested 4 months to 2 years after surgery. Eight matched preoperative control subjects with refractory complex partial epilepsy of temporal lobe origin, and 10 college student control subjects, were also tested.

Results for item and order recognition memory for words and spatial locations averaged across all serial positions are shown in Figures 9.1 and 9.2. College student and epileptic control subjects performed well across all tasks. The performance of epileptic control subjects did not differ significantly from that of college student

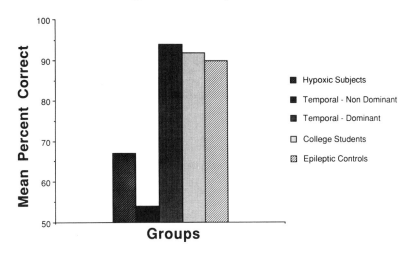

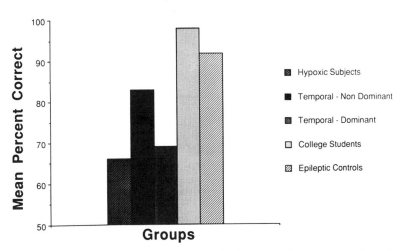

FIGURE 9.1. Mean percentage of correct performance for hypoxic subjects, temporal–nondominant patients, temporal–dominant patients, college students, and epileptic control subjects on item recognition for spatial location and words.

controls across all tasks. Temporal lobectomy subjects were impaired on tests of item and order recognition memory either for verbal or for spatial information, according to the site of temporal lobectomy relative to the subjects' language lateralization (dominant vs. nondominant). Subjects ($n = 5$) who had undergone temporal lobe removal of the language-dominant hemisphere displayed item and order recognition memory deficits for verbal information in the absence of spatial impairment. Subjects ($n = 6$) who had undergone temporal lobe removal of the nondominant hemisphere showed item and order recognition memory deficits for spatial information in the absence of

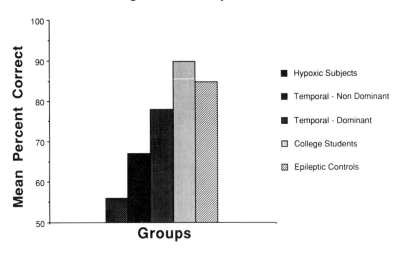

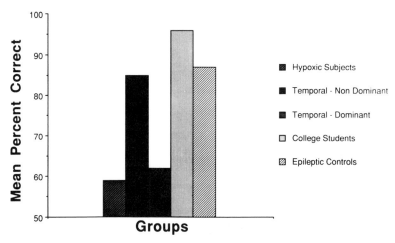

FIGURE 9.2. Mean percentage of correct performance for hypoxic subjects, temporal–nondominant patients, temporal-dominant patients, college students, and epileptic control subjects on order recognition for spatial location and words.

verbal impairment. Thus, subjects had a deficit either for spatial or for verbal information following unilateral temporal lobectomy, such that a dissociation existed within each subjects' verbal and spatial memory abilities.

These data extend previous findings of Smith and Milner (1981), Milner (1954), and Jones-Gotman (1986), who have also shown that the right hippocampus mediates spatial location or spatial design information, whereas the left hippocampus mediates language information. It should also be noted that similar deficits have been found for item and order recognition memory for spatial locations in rats with large lesions of the hippocampus (Kesner, 1990; Kesner, Crutcher, & Beers, 1988). Thus, these data support the proposal that in humans lateralization of spatial and temporal information, and of linguistic and temporal information, exists in the hippocampus.

Memory for Verbal, Spatial, and Motor Information in Hypoxic Subjects

Research has shown that the hippocampus can be affected by hypoxic or ischemic episodes. Previous work by Zola-Morgan, Squire, and Amaral (1986) showed that an individual who had experienced a hypoxic episode had pyramidal cell loss in the CA1 region of the hippocampus. This cell loss was correlated with an observable memory loss. It was thus of real interest to study individuals ($n = 10$) who had experienced a hypoxic episode and a control group of college students ($n = 10$) on tasks for item and order recognition memory (Hopkins & Kesner, 1990). The hypoxic episodes were based on a variety of etiologies, including respiratory arrest, cardiac arrest, and carbon monoxide poisoning. Testing was conducted 9 months to 2 years following the hypoxic event. A quantitative analysis of MRI data from hypoxic and control subjects was carried out, using the method developed by Press, Amaral, and Squire (1989). The results indicated that relative to control subjects, the hypoxic subjects had a significantly smaller hippocampus, but did not differ in the size of the parahippocampal gyrus or temporal lobe.

All subjects were assessed with the Denman Neuropsychology Memory Scale, which incorporates standard memory tests for use in clinical assessment of memory impairments (Denman, 1987). The Denman Neuropsychology Memory Scale is divided into subtests covering the following areas: story recall, delayed story recall, paired-associate learning, delayed paired-associate learning, digit span, remote verbal information, copy, immediate and delayed recall of the Rey–Osterrieth complex figure, musical tones and melodies, memory for faces, and remote nonverbal information. Hypoxic subjects were impaired on all subtests relative to control subjects, with the exception of digit span (forward and backward), musical tones and melodies, memory for faces, and remote nonverbal information.

The subjects were then asked to perform specific data-based memory tasks. The tasks consisted of lists of words, spatial locations, and hand positions (a motor response task). For each modality, both item and order recognition tasks were given. The word and spatial location recognition tasks have been described above. The motor response task is identical to the other tasks for both the study and test phases. Each trial of the study phase contains sequential presentations of 6 hand positions randomly selected from a set of 16 possible choices. During the presentation of each picture, the subject is required to imitate the hand position; there is no time limit. Half of the pictures require the use of the right hand, and the other half require the use of the left hand. During the test phase of the item recognition for motor responses, two pictures showing hand positions are simultaneously presented on the screen—one that occurred in the study phase and one that did not. The subject is required to select the picture that he or she saw and imitated in the study phase. There are 24 trials, which result in 4 observations for each serial position on the list. The order recognition test is identical to the item recognition test, except that two hand positions both seen in the study phase are shown. The subject is asked to choose the picture that occurred earlier in the sequence. There are 20 trials, which result in 4 observations for each serial position. The average performance for item and order recognition memory for words and spatial locations across all serial positions is shown in Figures 9.1 and 9.2, and indicates a total deficit for item and order recognition memory for both words and spatial location information.

Performance based on each specific serial position for item and order recognition memory for words, spatial locations, and hand positions is shown for hypoxic subjects and controls in Figures 9.3 and 9.4. On the tasks of item and order recognition for words, hypoxic subjects were impaired across all serial positions compared to control subjects. On the tasks of item and order recognition for spatial location, hypoxic subjects were impaired on all serial positions with the exception of the last position, indicating an intact recency effect. On the tasks of item and order recognition for hand position, hypoxic subjects showed both an intact primacy effect and an intact recency effect (Hopkins & Kesner, 1990). It should be noted that there were no significant differences in performance among all three of the item and order tests for control subjects.

The observation of intact recency and primacy effects, with poor memory performance for the middle items (hand positions) within the list, suggests that hypoxic subjects displayed enhanced interference for the middle items in remembering hand positions. Nevertheless, the intact memory for the end positions, especially the first position, suggests a disproportionately smaller deficit for motor memory compared to word or spatial location memory. The small memory impairment for hand positions is consistent with normal motor skill learning observed in amnesic subjects (Brooks & Baddeley, 1976; Cohen & Squire, 1980; Corkin, 1968; Milner, 1962). Not many studies have reported the results of explicit memory tests for specific motor responses in amnesic subjects. One study, carried out by Leonard and Milner (1991), demonstrated that patients with right or left temporal lobe damage and large hippocampal lesions are not impaired in the ability to remember the correct distance based on a previous movement of a lever. Leonard and Milner (1991) showed that in their memory-for-distance task, subjects with large right frontal lobe lesions were markedly impaired. In a different study in our laboratory, it has been shown that patients with bilateral or right frontal cortex lesions are impaired on item recognition for hand positions, whereas item recognition for words or spatial location is intact (Kesner, Hopkins, & Fineman, submitted).

Additional information regarding the temporal organization of episodic informa-tion demonstrates that animals and humans, when tested for spatial location informa-tion, display what is known as the "temporal distance effect" (Chiba & Kesner, 1989; Madsen & Kesner, 1989). Temporal distance is determined by the number of items that occur between any two test items during their sequential presentation in the study phase. Temporal distance was studied using a word and a spatial location task. The subjects were presented with a list of eight items, in an identical format and manner to the item and order recognition tasks described above; the only difference was that the distance between items was varied from 0 to 6. The test contained 56 trials, with 8 observations for each temporal distance.

Data for temporal distances obtained in previous experiments showed that col-lege students had difficulty at a temporal distance of 0, but little difficulty at distances

ITEM RECOGNITION

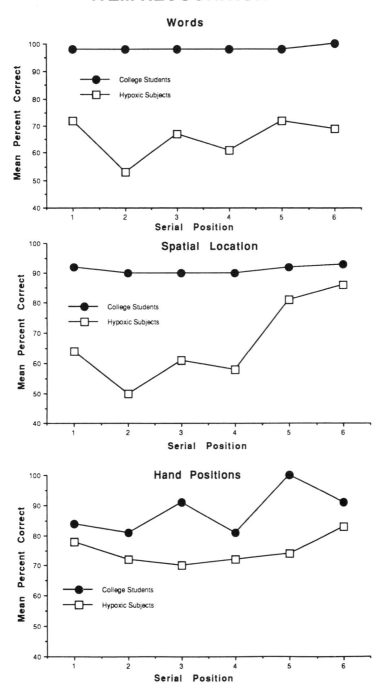

FIGURE 9.3. Mean percentage of correct performance for hypoxic subjects and college students on item recognition for words, spatial location, and hand positions across serial positions.

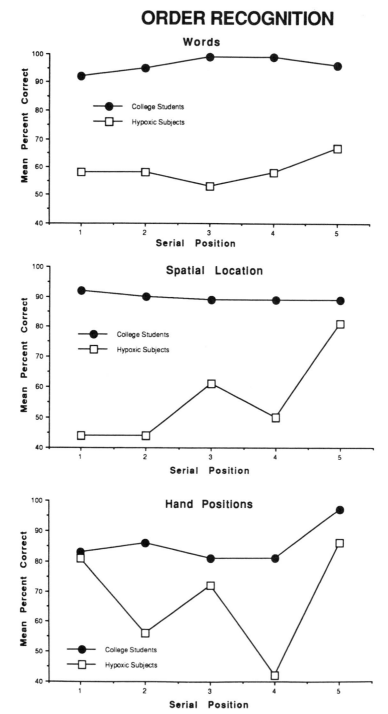

FIGURE 9.4. Mean percentage of correct performance for hypoxic subjects and college students on order recognition for words, spatial location, and hand positions across serial positions.

of 1 or greater. Subjects with mild Alzheimer's disease were impaired at all temporal distances, with the exception of 5 and 6 (Madsen & Kesner, 1989). Results obtained from hypoxic subjects ($n = 8$) and age-matched controls ($n = 8$) for temporal distance of words and spatial location are shown in Figure 9.5 and indicate that the hypoxic subjects were impaired across all temporal distances when compared to control subjects for both words and spatial locations (Hopkins & Kesner, 1991). Rats with large hippocampal lesions, on a parallel spatial location task, performed at chance level for all temporal distances (0 to 6) (Chiba & Kesner, 1989).

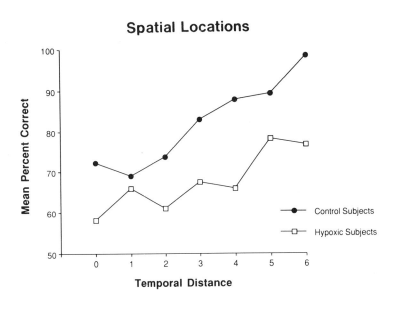

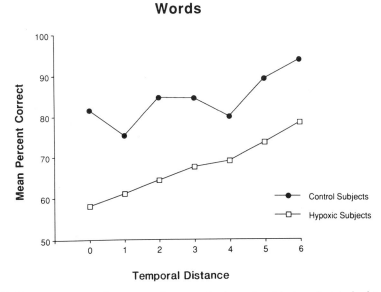

FIGURE 9.5. Mean percentage of correct performance for hypoxic subjects and control subjects on spatial locations and words as a function of temporal distance.

The deficits observed in hypoxic subjects relate to spatial, temporal, and linguistic coding of information. Since the current view of the hippocampus is that it codes spatial and linguistic data-based information in humans, these data support the attribute model. The data also suggest that there is some differential sparing of memory for motor responses and that memory for motor responses may be coded by another neural region besides the hippocampus, possibly the caudate nucleus. Kesner (1991), in other work, has shown that rats with caudate lesions were impaired on a task involving memory for a motor response, but that animals with hippocampal lesions were not impaired on this task.

Dissociation between Memory for Different Attributes

Empirical evidence suggests a dissociation between memory for objects and their spatial locations. Smith and Milner (1981) tested patients with right temporal lobectomies, patients with left temporal lobectomies, and normal controls on incidental recall of objects and their locations. Subjects were required to estimate the prices of several objects, which were organized as an array of visual stimuli on a test board. Subjects were then asked to recall the objects seen in the pricing task. All subjects showed good performance for immediate recall of objects. However, when asked to recall the objects after a 24-hour delay, the left temporal subjects were impaired relative to the right temporal and control subjects, and the right temporal subjects were also impaired relative to control subjects.

Following the test of object recall, subjects were asked to recall the absolute location (mean displacement) of the objects within the original array on the board. Left temporal and control subjects performed well on this task, both for immediate recall of the object locations and for a 24-hour delayed test of recall. Right temporal subjects were impaired both for immediate recall and for delayed recall relative to left temporal subjects and control subjects.

A dissociation between memory for objects and memory for spatial locations was also reported by Shoqeirat and Mayes (1991). In this study, amnesic subjects of different etiologies were tested on a task similar to that used by Smith and Milner. Disproportionate deficits of spatial memory relative to object memory were found between different groups of amnesics. In a more recent study, Cave and Squire (1991) also used a paradigm similar to that described by Smith and Milner. However, they found that their patients with bilateral hippocampal damage due to a history of anoxia or ischemia, relative to controls, had an impairment in both object memory and spatial memory performance. Since objects can be coded by both verbal (left hippocampus) and nonverbal (right hippocampus) representations, the deficits seen in hypoxic patients could result from an impairment in verbal labeling (mediated by the left hippocampus) or nonverbal representations (represented in the right hippocampus). Thus, it is possible that the deficit in object (nonspatial) recall is due to an impairment in coding linguistic information. It should be noted that a similar dissociation between object memory (intact) and spatial location memory (deficit) has been found following hippocampal lesions in rats (Kesner, 1991).

Is it also possible to find a dissociation between attributes of affect and language or affect and spatial location in subjects with hippocampal damage? In one study, Johnson, Kim, and Risse (1985) showed Korsakoff subjects pictures of two young men and asked the subjects to give their impression of each by rating them on several characteristics. Subjects were then read fictional biographical information depicting one man as the "good guy" and the other as the "bad guy." Following a 20-day retention interval, Korsakoff subjects were virtually unable to recall any biographical information. In contrast, upon reviewing the pictures, 78% of the Korsakoff subjects preferred the "good guy" over the "bad guy," and impression ratings were less favorable for the "bad guy." Thus, the subjects were able to draw upon affective attribute information without access to linguistic attribute information.

In summary, within the data-based memory system, the right hippocampus appears to code memory for both spatial and temporal attributes, and the left hippocampus appears to code memory for both linguistic and temporal attributes. The above-mentioned studies suggest that the right and the left hippocampus may be somewhat less involved in coding memory for visual objects (sensory-perceptual attributes), motor responses (egocentric spatial or response attributes), or memory for linguistic stimuli based on an evaluation of preference for these stimuli (affect attributes). These conclusions support the predictions of the attribute model (Table 9.1), but they support to a lesser extent the prediction of the episodic, event, declarative, and explicit memory models—namely, that there should be a deficit for all the attributes, including sensory-perceptual, response, and affect. Clearly, more research is needed to resolve the issue of the nature of data-based memory representation in the hippocampus.

Data-Based versus Knowledge-Based Memory and the Hippocampus

Even though it is assumed that the hippocampus encodes and retrieves information within episodic, event, declarative, or explicit memory, it is also assumed that the hippocampus does not encode or retrieve information based on semantic (Tulving, 1987; Kinsbourne, 1987), knowledge (Weiskrantz, 1987), procedural (Squire, 1987), or implicit (Schacter, 1987) memory. The emphasis of semantic and knowledge-based memory is on general knowledge of the world. It allows one to make abstract or concrete mental models of the world, and it can operate in the absence of critical incoming data. In agreement with Tulving's, Kinsbourne's, and Weiskrantz's positions, Kesner (1990) has also suggested that the hippocampus does not mediate information within an expectancy- or knowledge-based memory system. The expectancy-based memory system is primarily concerned with long-term memory storage of information in the form of a set of cognitive maps and their interactions, which are unique for each memory. The exact nature and organization of knowledge structures within each cognitive map need to be determined. From a dynamic point of view, the emphasis of the expectancy-based memory system is on "top-down" processing. This system is likely to involve permanent memory representations allowing for "automatic" attention, implicit memory activation, and the elicitation of rules and strategies. In addition, it is proposed that memories within the expectancy-based memory system can be subdivided into a multidimensional representation in the form of attributes. These attributes are the same as those suggested for the data-based memory system; however, they differ from the data-based system in that they involve the encoding and storage of permanent rather than temporary representations, and they are mediated by different neural substrates. To the cognitive map representation of the linguistic attribute, one would add semantic representations, and to that of the temporal attribute, one would add a role for a time perspective involving the future. The attribute model suggests that the hippocampus does not mediate temporal, spatial, or linguistic attributes within the expectancy-based memory system (Table 9.1), which is in agreement with the other models presented above. Support for this assumption comes from findings that amnesic patients with presumed hippocampal damage can learn and remember a semantic rule (Oscar-Berman, 1973) and can apply the Fibonacci principle to a numerical series (Kinsbourne & Wood, 1975).

However, few if any studies have reported a dissociation between data-based and knowledge-based memory based on hippocampal dysfunction, using comparable tasks that differentially emphasize the expectancy-based versus data-based memory systems. We designed another study to address this issue (Hopkins & Kesner, 1991).

The tests for assessing temporal distance described thus far are based on new data-based information, but do not assess the knowledge-based memory system. One way to assess whether the temporal distance effect occurs within the general knowledge system is to examine scripts. According to Schank and Abelson (1977), "scripts" are defined as "standardized generalized episodes" (p. 37). Scripts are overlearned, stereotyped memories for events that share the same theme and contain a composite of all the proposed attributes. In addition, some scripts have a strong sequence of temporal order, in which one event is causal or sets up conditions for the next event (a structured sequence). Other scripts do not have a strong temporal order, and the events can occur in an arbitrary sequence (an unstructured sequence).

In the Hopkins and Kesner (1991) study, hypoxic subjects ($n = 8$) and controls ($n = 8$) who were matched for age, education, and sex were tested for temporal distance within the context of data-based (unstructured) and knowledge-based (structured) scripts. The subjects were given eight scripts. The structured scripts included going to a restaurant, a movie, a grocery store, and a doctor's office. The unstructured scripts included a birthday party, house cleaning, going to a parade, and going to a circus. During the study phase, subjects were given a story of each script that contained eight events. They were asked to pay attention to the order of events. Each event was presented for a 5-second period. Immediately after the presentation of the last event, subjects were given four consecutive tests during which they were shown two of the events in the scripts, with a randomly presented temporal distance (number of items between events) of 0, 2, 4, or 6; they were asked to select the event that occurred earlier in the sequence. The structured and unstructured scripts were presented in an alternation sequence. The presentation of all eight scripts resulted in a total of four observations for each distance for both structured and unstructured scripts.

The results from hypoxic and control subjects for both structured and unstructured scripts as a function of temporal distance are shown in Figure 9.6. The graph shows that both groups of subjects performed very well for all distances for structured

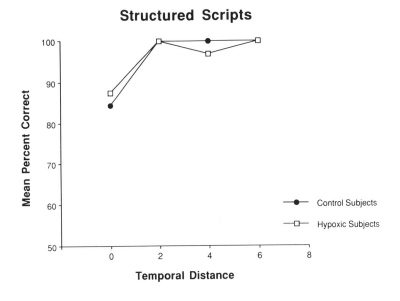

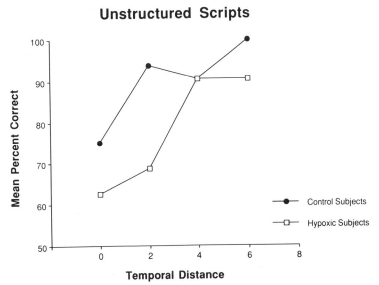

FIGURE 9.6. Mean percentage of correct performance for hypoxic subjects and control subjects on structured and unstructured scripts as a function of temporal distance.

scripts (expectancy- or knowledge-based memory). However, for unstructured scripts (data-based memory), the graph shows that relative to controls the hypoxic subjects were impaired at a temporal distance of 0 and 2, but performed similarly to controls at temporal distances of 4 and 6. These data suggest that the hippocampus plays an important role in processing or encoding data-based script information, but does not play a role in processing or encoding knowledge-based script information, supporting the predictions of the attribute model (Table 9.1).

Conclusion

In conclusion, it appears that the hippocampus is primarily involved in mediating spatial, temporal, and linguistic attributes within the data-based memory system, but not within the expectancy- or knowledge-based memory system. The advantage of the attribute model is that it can provide a heuristic to uncover different neuroanatomical substrates that mediate different attributes associated with memory representation, and thus can provide a means to uncover a larger number of memory attribute dissociations.

REFERENCES

Bower, G. H. (1967). A multicomponent theory of the memory trace. In K. W. Spence & J. T. Spence (Eds.), *The psychology of learning and motivation: Advances in research and theory* (pp. 230–327). New York: Academic Press.

Brooks, D. N., & Baddeley, A. (1976). What can amnesic patients learn? *Neuropsychologia, 14,* 111–122.

Cave, C. B., & Squire, L. R. (1991). Equivalent impairment of spatial and nonspatial memory following damage to the human hippocampus. *Hippocampus, 1,* 329–340.

Chiba, A. A., & Kesner, R. P. (1989). The role of the hippocampus and the medial prefrontal cortex in the temporal coding of spatial location. *Society for Neuroscience Abstracts, 15,* 608.

Chiba, A. A., Kesner, R. P., Matsuo, F., & Heilbrun, P. M. (1990). A dissociation between verbal and spatial memory following unilateral temporal lobectomy. *Society for Neuroscience Abstracts, 16,* 286.

Cohen, N. J., & Squire, L. R. (1980). Preserved learning and retention of pattern-analyzing skill in amnesia: Dissociation of knowing how and knowing that. *Science, 210,* 207–210.

Corkin, S. (1968). Acquisition of motor skill after bilateral medial temporal lobe excision. *Neuropsychologia, 6,* 255–265.

Denman, S. B. (1987). *Denman Neuropsychology Memory Scale.* Charleston, SC: Author.

Hopkins, R. O., & Kesner, R. P. (1990). Data based (episodic) memory for motor responses in hypoxic patients. *Society for Neuroscience Abstracts, 16,* 286.

Hopkins, R. O., & Kesner, R. P. (1991). Data-based and knowledge-based memory for temporal distances in hypoxic brain injured subjects. *Society for Neuroscience Abstracts, 17,* 136.

Johnson, M. K., Kim, J. K., & Risse, G. (1985). Do alcoholic Korsakoff's syndrome patients acquire affective reactions? *Journal of Experimental Psychology: Learning, Memory, and Cognition, 11,* 22–36.

Jones-Gotman, M. (1986). Memory for designs: The hippocampal contribution. *Neuropsychologia, 24,* 193–203.

Kesner, R. P. (1990). Learning and memory in rats with an emphasis on the role of the hippocampal formation. In R. P. Kesner & D. S. Olton (Eds.), *Neurobiology of comparative cognition* (pp. 179–204), Hillsdale, NJ: Erlbaum.

Kesner, R. P. (1991). The role of the hippocampus within an attribute model of memory. *Hippocampus, 1,* 279–282.

Kesner, R. P., Crutcher, K., & Beers, D. R. (1988). Serial position curves for item (spatial) information: Role of the dorsal hippocampus and medial septum. *Brain Research, 454,* 219–226.

Kesner, R. P., Hopkins, R. O., & Fineman, B. *Item and order dissociation in humans with prefrontal cortex damage.* Manuscript submitted for publication.

Kinsbourne, M. (1987). Brain mechanisms and memory. *Human Neurobiology, 6,* 81–92.

Kinsbourne, M., & Wood, F. (1975). Short-term memory processes and the amnesic syndrome. In D. Deutsch & J. A. Deutsch (Eds.), *Short-term memory* (pp. 258–293). New York: Academic Press.

Leonard, G., & Milner, B. (1991). Contribution of the right frontal lobe to the encoding and recall of kinesthetic distance information. *Neuropsychologia, 29,* 47–58.

Madsen, J., & Kesner, R. P. (1989). Temporal order information in normal subjects and patients with dementia of the Alzheimer's type. *Society for Neuroscience Abstracts, 15,* 728.

Milner, B. (1954). Intellectual function of the temporal lobes. *Psychology Bulletin, 51,* 42–62.

Milner, B. (1962). Les troubles de la mémoire accompagnant des lesions hippocampiques bilatérales. In P. Passouant (Ed.), *Physiologie de l'hippocampe* (p. 257). Paris: Centre National de la Recherche Scientifique.

Milner, B. (1970). Memory and the medial temporal regions of the brain. In K. H. Pribram & D. E. Broadbent (Eds.), *Biology of memory* (pp. 29–50), New York: Academic Press.

Oscar-Berman, M. (1973). Hypothesis testing and focusing behavior during concept formation by amnesic Korsakoff patients. *Neuropsychologia, 11,* 191–198.

Press, G. A., Amaral, D. G., & Squire, L. R. (1989). Hippocampal abnormalities in amnesic patients revealed by high-resolution magnetic resonance imaging. *Nature, 341,* 54–57.

Schacter, D. L. (1987). Implicit memory: History and current status. *Journal of Experimental Psychology: Learning, Memory, and Cognition, 13,* 501–508.

Schank, R. C., & Abelson, R. P. (1977). *Scripts, plans, goals and understanding: An inquiry into human knowledge structures.* Hillsdale, NJ: Erlbaum.

Shoqeirat, M. A., & Mayes, A. R. (1991). Disproportionate incidental spatial memory and recall deficits in amnesia. *Neuropsychologia, 29,* 749–769.

Smith, M. L., & Milner, B. (1981). The role of the right hippocampus in the recall of spatial location. *Neuropsychologia, 19,* 781–793.

Squire, L. R. (1987). *Memory and brain.* New York: Oxford University Press.

Tulving, E. (1987). Multiple memory systems and consciousness. *Human Neurobiology, 6,* 67–80.

Underwood, B. J. (1969). Attributes of memory. *Psychological Review, 76,* 559–573.

Weiskrantz, L. (1987). Neuroanatomy of memory and amnesia: A case for multiple memory systems. *Human Neurobiology, 6,* 93–105.

Zola-Morgan, S., Squire, L. R., & Amaral, D. G. (1986). Human amnesia and the medial temporal region: Enduring memory impairment following a bilateral lesion limited to field CA1 of the hippocampus. *Journal of Neuroscience, 6,* 2950–2967.

10

Functional Significance of Etiological Factors in Human Amnesia

ALAN J. PARKIN

An intriguing feature of human amnesia is that it can arise from damage to either of two distinct brain regions: the medial temporal lobes or the midline diencephalic nuclei (e.g., Parkin & Leng, 1992). This has led some to propose that, despite general psychometric similarities between patient groups, there are two qualitatively different forms of amnesia: "bitemporal" and "diencephalic." An argument against the "two amnesias" viewpoint is that the medial temporal and diencephalic structures associated with memory function—the hippocampus, mammillary bodies, mammillo-thalamic tract, and dorsomedial thalamic nucleus—comprise part of the limbic system and may therefore form a memory circuit (Warrington & Weiskrantz, 1982). However, even if linked structures are involved in memory function, it does not follow, *ipso facto*, that each limbic site has the same underlying function; passage of information from one limbic site to another may correspond to different stages in the memory process.

Behavioral Evidence for Two Forms of Amnesia

A number of studies (e.g., Lhermitte & Signoret, 1972) have proposed that bitemporal amnesics forget information more rapidly, but doubts about the methodological soundness of these studies (e.g., Parkin, 1984), as well as demonstrations of comparable forgetting rates (e.g., Freed & Corkin, 1988), have undermined this argument. Moreover, specifying a difference between patient groups in terms of forgetting rate is essentially a quantitative hypothesis, and thus vulnerable to the risk that any observed difference arises from a failure to match subjects on severity measures. However, this itself may be a self-defeating exercise, because a proposed difference in severity might reasonably be expected to manifest itself in exactly those measures used to equate severity. A second difference between bitemporal and diencephalic patients concerns their performance on the Brown–Peterson (BP) task. Before this can be discussed, however, a brief digression is required.

Amnesia and Frontal Lobe Function

Our own investigations of etiological variation in human amnesia (see below) center on Wernicke–Korsakoff syndrome (WKS) patients as examples of diencephalic amnesics, and survivors of herpes simplex encephalitis (HSE) as our primary examples of bitemporal amnesics. The primary lesion focus of WKS lies within the midline diencephalic nuclei (e.g., Victor, Adams, & Collins, 1989), and the primary lesion in HSE arises in the medial temporal lobe (Baringer, 1978). However, patients in neither of these groups are "pure" amnesics because both types exhibit other cognitive deficits, particularly involving malfunction of the prefrontal cortex. Prefrontal dysfunction adversely affects many cognitive tasks, including memory (Stuss & Benson, 1986), so any theory proposing fundamental differences in the amnesia arising from bitemporal and diencephalic lesions must demonstrate that these differences are not just a consequence of differential frontal involvement.

Etiological Factors and the Brown–Peterson Task

Investigations have shown that bitemporal amnesics perform the BP task far better than diencephalic amnesics do (see Leng & Parkin, 1988, for a review). The only exceptions have been the normal BP performance in Mair, Warrington, and Weiskrantz's (1979) WKS patients, and only marginally impaired performance in Kopelman's (1985) WKS patients. A colleague and I (Leng & Parkin, 1989) examined whether the observed difference between the groups was attributable to memory ability per se or to differences in frontal involvement. Memory ability failed to predict performance in either group, but in WKS patients, poorer BP performance was correlated with increased errors on WCST. We (Leng & Parkin, 1989) suggested that this frontal involvement reflected a retrieval component in the BP task. The presence of a frontal component in BP performance has been shown in several other studies (e.g., Parkin & Walter, 1991) and may also explain why Mair et al. (1979) failed to observe poor BP performance in their two WKS patients, because both were uncharacteristically free of frontal damage.

Comparative Studies of Contextual Influences on Short-Term Memory

Defined briefly, "context" can be considered as those features associated with a to-be-remembered stimulus that allow its discrimination from other similar traces. Most commonly context is defined in terms of extrinsic factors, such as the temporal or spatial attributes of presentation, but it can also relate to intrinsic manipulations such as associative context.

Mayes and his colleagues (Mayes, 1988) have shown that alcoholic WKS patients have highly defective memory for context. The logic of our first study was that if contextual manipulations affected the short-term memory of temporal lobe patients in the same way as that of alcoholic WKS patients, the case for functional heterogeneity, in terms of contextual deficit theory, would not be supported. We (Parkin, Leng, & Hunkin, 1990) presented patients with a 2×2 array of pictures and tested immediate recall until retention was perfect. Following a 60-second-delay, patients identified these items from a 16-picture array. This procedure was repeated three more times, except that items that had been targets became distractors and distractor items became targets. The subjects' task was then to identify the items they were asked to remember most recently. By trial 4, each picture had been a target once and a distractor three times. Thus, after trial 1, some record of temporal context had to be made if correct identification was to occur. WKS patients showed a marked drop in performance from trial 2 onward—a deficit wholly expected in patients unable to encode the contextual relations of a set of items. The temporal lobe group, however, performed better overall; in statistical terms, a significant drop in their performance did not occur until trial 4.

In a second experiment, we (Hunkin & Parkin, 1991a) examined whether the difference between WKS and HSE patients on the recency task results from the former's well-known sensitivity to proactive interference effects per se (Butters & Cermak, 1980) or stems from the specific manipulation of target–distractor familiarity. The recency experiment was therefore repeated in its original form and in a second version, using completely different sets of items on each trial. Figure 10.1 shows that there was only significant deterioration in performance, as a function of trials, for WKS patients in the original condition. These findings point to an important difference between alcoholic WKS patients and patients with post-HSE amnesia. Alcoholic WKS patients were more adversely affected by the contextual manipulation than the post-HSE patients. Furthermore, because the measure of short-term memory involved recognition memory, the measure we would consider least sensitive to retrieval factors, it would seem that the WKS patients' deficit arises from a failure to encode contextual information rather than to process it effectively at retrieval.

This interpretation of group differences is supported by a further study (Hunkin & Parkin, 1991b), which compared the groups on two variants of the list discrimination paradigm used by Squire, Nadel, and Slater (1981). In version 1 subjects were shown two sets of target sentences separated by 3 minutes of conversation. Recognition of the target sentences was then tested by means of a yes–no recognition procedure, and when a "yes" response was given, subjects were further required to say whether the sentence occurred in list 1 or list 2. In version 2 a single list of sentences was presented, with half the items being randomly placed to the left of the subject and the remainder to the right. Recognition was tested in a similar manner, but discrimination involved remembering the location (left or right) of each target. Overall levels of recognition and discrimination were comparable in the two groups; what differed was the relation between discrimination and recognition. For WKS patients, there was no significant correlation between the recognition and discrimination measures ($r = .13$). For the HSE patients, however, the correlation between the two measures was significant ($r = .68$). The former data are consistent with Squire's (1982) study of WKS patients, which also found no correlation between individual scores on recognition and temporal discrimination. Unlike Squire, however, we found no correlations between discrimination performance and frontal test scores.

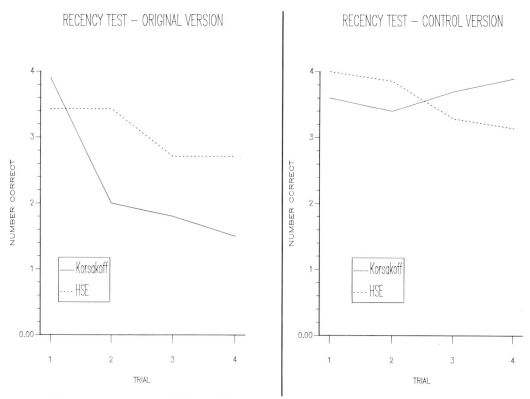

FIGURE 10.1. Performance of WKS and HSE patients on the original and control versions of the recency experiment. From *Recency Judgements in Different Forms of Human Amnesia* by N. M. Hunkin and A. J. Parkin, 1991, manuscript submitted for publication.

The absence of any necessary relationship between frontal measures and contextual encoding deficits is confirmed by our investigations of two patients with purely diencephalic lesions. Table 10.1 shows the performance of R. K. (hypothalamic glioma) and J. R. (left thalamic infarction) on recognition and temporal discrimination. R. K.'s recognition memory has improved following treatment of his tumor, but, despite this, his temporal discrimination has remained poor. J. R. has been tested using verbal and nonverbal stimuli; because of his left-lateralized lesion, his recognition of verbal material is poorer, but his recency judgment is equally impaired for both types of material. Impaired temporal discrimination without, or independent of, frontal involvement is also supported by case T. R. (Bowers, Verfaellie, Valenstein, & Heilman, 1988). This patient had a discrete left retrosplenial lesion and performed poorly on list discrimination involving verbal and nonverbal stimuli. Kopelman (1989), using a variant of Huppert and Piercy's (1979) paradigm, found poorer memory for temporal context in both WKS and Alzheimer patients, but no correlation with frontal test scores. Finally, Shimamura, Janowsky, and Squire (1990) demonstrated impaired memory for temporal order in frontal lobe patients, WKS patients, and other amnesic patients, but failed to find any correlation with Wisconsin Card-Sorting Test (WCST) scores.

TABLE 10.1. Performance of R. K., J. R., and Controls on Tests of Temporal Discrimination

Subject	Verbal		Nonverbal	
	Recognition (d')	Discrimination (z)	Recognition (d')	Discrimination (z)
R. K. (1)	1.75	1.15	—	—
R. K. (2)	1.50	−0.28	—	—
R. K. (3)	2.80	0	—	—
R. K. (4)	2.19	1.04	—	—
Control	2.98[a]	2.91[b]	—	—
J. R.	0.20	−0.38	1.39	−0.71
Control	2.04	1.44	1.02	0.62

[a] $SD = 0.65$.
[b] $SD = 1.71$.

Bitemporal versus Diencephalic Amnesia: A Theoretical Interpretation

Investigations of amnesia embrace a fundamental distinction between "context" and "target" memory. Context memory corresponds to memory attributes that allow a re-presented stimulus to be categorized along some spatiotemporal dimension such as list membership. Target memory has not been formally defined, but, operationally, it corresponds to memory attributes that allow a re-presented stimulus to be categorized as "previously encountered." Tasks that assess target and context memory for the same stimulus assume, methodologically, that contextual memory is contingent on target memory—simply because context memory is only measured once target memory has been established. This assumed contingency may be false. On the assumption that contextual attributes evoked by a re-presented stimulus may provide a basis for recognition, target memory may arise from the evocation of context, the activation of target memory, or both. In contrast, context memory requires the specific retrieval of contextual attributes and cannot be facilitated by target memory. Thus, contrary to the assumptions implicit in the methodology, target memory can be a redundant feature of context memory but not vice versa.

Rolls (1988) has described the cytoarchitecture of the hippocampus and related this to memory function. CA3 of the hippocampus receives inputs from many regions of the neocortex via the parahippocampal gyrus, and within CA3 there is a high level of recurrent collaterals, which Rolls interprets as evidence for an "autoassociation matrix." The functional significance of this matrix is that it can "detect conjunctions of events even when these are widely separated in information space, with their origin from quite different cortical areas" and can allocate "neurons to code efficiently for these conjunctions probably using a competitive learning mechanism (CA1)" (Rolls, 1988, p. 301). The "conjunction of events" encoded by CA3 (which are then returned to the neocortex by back projections involving the subiculum, entorhinal cortex, and parahippocampal gyrus) may constitute the context associated with a particular event. Indeed, Rolls states:

> The CA3 autoassociation system is ideal for remembering particular episodes, for, perhaps uniquely in the brain, it provides a single autoassociation matrix which

receives from many different areas of the cerebral association cortex. It is thus able to make almost any arbitrary association, including association to the context in which a set of events occurred. (pp. 301–302)

Rolls proposes "that the hippocampus is specialised to detect the best way in which to store information" (p. 301). This supposes that the hippocampus plays an "executive" role, and, by implication, that the neocortical input to CA3 is relatively unstructured. This view may be incorrect. Memory encoding represents only a small percentage of total information available to the organism at any time. Attentional factors and strategic influences, both functions associated with higher cortical structures, are assumed to influence this process, and it seems plausible that the determination of context is an important consequence of this activity. Within this framework, the role of the hippocampus may therefore be to consolidate rather than to determine the contextual elements associated with an event.

Contextual processing cannot, however, be an entirely neocortical function. Our patients R. K. and J. R. both show poor temporal context memory following disruption to purely diencephalic structures. The critical structures underlying the encoding of temporal context may be projections arising in the midline diencephalon, and terminating in the dorsolateral prefrontal cortex. Case T. R. (Bowers et al., 1988) also supports subcortical involvement in memory for temporal context, because his retrosplenial lesion was thought to "interrupt input from the anterior and lateral thalamic nuclei to retrosplenial cortex and medial temporal lobe" (Valenstein et al., 1987, p. 1639).

Within this framework, one can offer a tentative explanation of the observed differences between WKS and HSE patients on measures of context memory. WKS patients have lesions affecting projections from the midline diencephalon to the dorsolateral prefrontal cortex. The main consequence of this deficit should be an inability to organize appropriate contextual processing for a stimulus, resulting in an inadequate input to the hippocampus, which itself is largely unaffected in WKS. In HSE the primary lesion lies within the medial temporal lobe, with the hippocampus likely to be the most badly damaged structure. In contrast, midline diencephalic damage is uncommon, and frontal damage in HSE tends to be orbito-frontal rather than dorsolateral (Baringer, 1978)—a conclusion supported by the relatively good performance of HSE patients on the WCST, a test considered particularly sensitive to dorsolateral frontal lesions (Leng & Parkin, 1988). HSE patients could therefore have two bases for context memory: any memory ability intrinsic to the neocortical input itself, and the residual ability of hippocampal mechanisms to integrate and consolidate this contextual input. These two sources may be sufficient to support the levels of context memory observed in the HSE patients. A problem, however, is the equal level of target memory in our two groups. One might argue, on the grounds that target memory can arise from both target and context attributes, that the HSE patients should fare better on recognition, because their available target memory should be enhanced by the additional contextual memory that may be available. Failure to find a recognition differences may be merely a statistical fluke or may reflect the insensitivity of recognition measures. An alternative, however, is that equal levels of recognition performance, as well as contrasting memory performance, arise partly because the temporal lobe amnesics have a deficit in target memory.

Recently Sagar, Gabrielli, Sullivan, and Corkin (1990) have reported some intriguing data on the temporal lobe amnesic H. M. Memory for temporal context was measured using verbal and nonverbal recency discrimination and a frequency estimation task. Event memory was examined under comparable conditions, using a forced-choice recognition procedure. In both recency and frequency tests, H. M. showed above-chance-level and near-normal memory for temporal context under conditions where recognition of the same stimuli was close to, or at, chance level.

Although one must still explain why the information available for temporal context judgments could not be utilized for recognition memory, these data suggest that information about context can be available at a time when information concerning target memory is unavailable. If we assume that a similar state of affairs exists in our HSE patients, a more refined interpretation of their memory data is possible. On recognition, any advantage over the WKS group is undermined by a deficit in target memory. Recency judgments are better because some contextual memory is available and because "context-free" target memory is depleted, therefore reducing interference problems caused by general familiarity. Similarly, on temporal and spatial discrimination, the high degree of association between target and context memory could be attributed to the greater role that context plays in both tasks. Thus, on list discrimination, there may be a greater tendency for the recognition response to be based on the contextual elements evoked by the stimulus; for this reason, it is predictable that a correct list discrimination will be highly correlated with that response.

Two final questions are these: (1) What constitutes target memory? (2) If we are to talk of its depletion, how might that be independently assessed? One possibility is that target memory constitutes some mnemonic capability of the permanent cognitive representational systems that underlie our interactions with the external environment. It can be argued that these structures (e.g., the word recognition or picture recognition systems) can register patterns of activation, which in turn can serve as the basis for a memory response. Proposals of this kind have recently been invoked to account for various implicit memory phenomena and recognition memory in the absence of conscious recollection of temporal context (Gardiner & Parkin, 1990). Following on from this, measures of target memory depletion might be obtained by examining patients' performance on nonmemory measures, such as naming and identification. In our own sample of HSE patients, anomia is a common additional problem (e.g., Stewart, Parkin, & Hunkin, 1992) and one that has been noted in other studies of HSE (Gordon, Selnes, Hart, Hanley, & Whiteley, 1990).

ACKNOWLEDGMENTS

This chapter was prepared while I was Raine Visiting Professor of Psychiatry and Behavioural Science, University of Western Australia. I would like to thank Nikki Hunkin and John Dunn for helpful discussions.

REFERENCES

Baringer, J. R. (1978). Herpes simplex virus infections of the nervous system. In P. J. Vinken & G. W. Bruyn (Eds.), *Handbook of clinical neurology* (Vol. 34, pp. 145–159). Amsterdam: Elsevier.

Bowers, D., Verfaellie, M., Valenstein, E., & Heilman, K. M. (1988). Impaired acquisition of temporal information in retrosplenial amnesia. *Brain and Cognition, 8,* 47-66.

Butters, N., & Cermak, L. S. (1980). *Alcoholic Korsakoff's syndrome.* New York: Academic Press.

Freed, D. M., & Corkin, S. (1988). Rate of forgetting in H. M.: 6 month recognition. *Behavioral Neuroscience, 102,* 823-827.

Gardiner, J. M., & Parkin, A. J. (1990). Attention and recollective experience. *Memory and Cognition, 18,* 579-583.

Gordon, B., Selnes, O. A., Hart, J., Hanley, D. F., & Whiteley, R. J. (1990). Long-term cognitive sequelae of acyclovir-treated herpes simplex encephalitis. *Archives of Neurology, 47,* 646-647.

Hunkin, N. M., & Parkin, A. J. (1991a). *Recency judgements in different forms of human amnesia.* Manuscript submitted for publication.

Hunkin, N. M., & Parkin, A. J. (1991b). *Recognition versus temporal and spatial discrimination in different forms of human amnesia.* Manuscript submitted for publication.

Huppert, F. A., & Piercy, M. (1979). Normal and abnormal forgetting in organic amnesia: Effect of locus of lesion. *Cortex, 15,* 385-390.

Kopelman, M. D. (1985). Rates of forgetting in Alzheimer-type dementias and Korsakoff's syndrome. *Neuropsychologia, 23,* 623-638.

Kopelman, M. D. (1989). Remote and autobiographical memory, temporal context memory and frontal atrophy in Korsakoff and Alzheimer patients. *Neuropsychologia, 27,* 437-460.

Leng, N. R. C., & Parkin, A. J. (1988). Double dissociation of function in the frontal components of the human amnesic syndrome. *British Journal of Clinical Psychology, 27,* 359-362.

Leng, N. R. C., & Parkin, A. J. (1989). Aetiological variation in the amnesic syndrome: Comparisons using the Brown–Peterson task. *Cortex, 25,* 251-259.

Lhermitte, F., & Signoret, J. L. (1972). Analyse neuropsychologique et differentiation des syndromes amnésiques. *Revue Neurologique, 126,* 161-178.

Mair, W. G. P., Warrington, E. K., & Weiskrantz, L. (1979). Memory disorder in Korsakoff's psychosis. *Brain, 102,* 749-783.

Mayes, A. R. (1988). *Human organic memory disorders.* Oxford: Oxford University Press.

Parkin, A. J. (1984). Amnesic syndrome: A lesion specific disorder? *Cortex, 20,* 478-508.

Parkin, A. J., & Leng, N. R. C. (1992). *Neuropsychology of amnesic syndromes.* Basingstoke, England: Taylor & Francis.

Parkin, A. J., Leng, N. R. C., & Hunkin, N. (1990). Differential sensitivity to contextual information in diencephalic and temporal lobe amnesia. *Cortex, 26,* 373-380.

Parkin, A. J., & Walter, B. (1991). Short-term memory, ageing, and frontal dysfunction. *Psychobiology, 19,* 175-179.

Rolls, E. G. (1988). Parallel distributed processing in the brain: Implications of the functional architecture of neural networks in hippocampus. In R. G. M. Morris (Ed.), *Parallel distributed processing: Implications for psychology and neurobiology* (pp. 286-308). Oxford: Clarendon Press.

Sagar, H. J., Gabrielli, J. D. E., Sullivan, E. V., & Corkin, S. (1990). Recency and frequency discrimination in the amnesic patient H. M. *Brain, 113,* 581-602.

Shimamura, A. P., Janowsky, J. S., & Squire, L. R. (1990). Memory for the temporal order of events in patients with frontal lobe lesions and amnesic patients. *Neuropsychologia, 28,* 803-813.

Squire, L. R. (1982). Comparisons between forms of amnesia: Some deficits are unique to Korsakoff's syndrome. *Journal of Experimental Psychology: Learning, Memory, and Cognition, 8,* 560-571.

Squire, L. R., Nadel, L., & Slater, P. C. (1981). Anterograde amnesia and memory for temporal order. *Neuropsychologia, 19,* 141-146.

Stewart, F., Parkin, A. J., & Hunkin, N. M. (1992). Naming impairments following recovery from herpes simplex encephalitis: Category-specific? *Quarterly Journal of Experimental Psychology, 44A,* 261-284.

Stuss, D. T., & Benson, D. F. (1986). *The frontal lobes.* New York: Raven Press.

Valenstein, E., Bowers, D., Verfaellie, M., Heilman, K. M., Day, A., & Watson, R. T. (1987). Retrosplenial amnesia. *Brain, 110,* 1631-1646.

Victor, M., Adams, R. D., & Collins, G. H. (1989). *The Wernicke-Korsakoff syndrome* (2nd ed.) Philadelphia: F. A. Davis.

Warrington, E. K., & Weiskrantz, L. (1982). Amnesia: A disconnection syndrome? *Neuropsychologia, 20,* 233-248.

11

The "New" and the "Old": Components of the Anterograde and Retrograde Memory Loss in Korsakoff and Alzheimer Patients

MICHAEL D. KOPELMAN

Introduction

> The disorders and maladies of [memory], when classified and properly understood, are no longer to be regarded as a collection of . . . anecdotes of only passing interest. They will be found to be regulated by certain laws which constitute the very basis of memory, and from which its mechanism is easily laid bare.

> The progressive destruction of memory follows a logical order—a law . . . it begins with the most recent recollections which, being . . . rarely repeated and . . . having no permanent associations represent organization in its feeblest form.

These two quotations from Ribot (1882) illustrate an approach and a hypothesis. The first proposes what might now be called a "cognitive" approach to the study of amnesia, and my only quibble is that Ribot overestimated the "ease" with which the "mechanism" would be "laid bare." Modern neuropsychological research can be viewed as conforming to this approach. The second quotation suggests that Ribot believed that a progressive destruction of memory stores produces both anterograde and retrograde amnesia. This is a perfectly tenable hypothesis, but the burden of the present chapter is that it is probably not correct.

My own research has focused upon the nature of the explicit memory deficits in the alcoholic Korsakoff syndrome and Alzheimer dementia, with particular reference to short-term and long-term forgetting rates, temporal context memory, and the nature and characteristics of retrograde amnesia.

A particular focus of my attention has been upon the purported role of cholinergic depletion in producing such memory deficits. Cholinergic depletion is the most severe and consistently obtained neurotransmitter abnormality in Alzheimer dementia (Rossor, Iversen, Reynolds, Mountjoy, & Roth, 1984; Kopelman, 1986a). Although its purported role in Korsakoff syndrome (Arendt, Bigl, Arendt, & Tennstedt, 1983; Butters, 1985) has not been replicated (Mayes, Meudell, Mann, & Pickering, 1988), basal forebrain lesions implicating septo-hippocampal cholinergic projections have been shown to produce anterograde amnesia in both animals and humans (Damasio, Graff-Radford, Eslinger, Damasio, & Kassell, 1985; Damasio, Eslinger, Damasio, Van Hoesen, & Cornell, 1985; Salazar et al., 1986; Irle & Markowitsch, 1987; Phillips, Sangalang, & Sterns, 1987; Arendt et al., 1988).

As I hope to show, an appeal of the cognitive approach to memory disorders is that it does allow examination of the functional significance of purported biological abnormalities—not only cholinergic depletion, but structural lesions within the limbic-diencephalic circuits and the frontal lobes. The purpose of the present chapter is to review these findings, using concepts delineated elsewhere (e.g., Squire, 1987; Mayes, 1988; Baddeley, 1990).

Working Memory in Korsakoff and Alzheimer Patients

Span Tests

Traditionally, "primary memory" referred to the ability to hold small quantities of information for a few seconds only (James, 1890), whereas the modern notion of "working memory" emphasizes that material can be held temporarily, manipulated, and transformed in tasks such as speech comprehension and problem solving (Baddeley, 1983, 1990). Span tests represent the easiest and most commonly employed assessment of primary or working memory. In my own studies (Kopelman, 1985, 1991a), a group of mildly to moderately impaired Alzheimer patients showed a statistically significant decrement on both digit and block span, whereas Korsakoff patients showed intact performance. Many other studies have produced consistent results (Miller, 1973; Butters & Cermak, 1980; Corkin, 1982; Morris, 1984). Morris (1984) contended that the pattern of the decrement on letter and word span argued for the intactness in Alzheimer patients of the verbal "articulatory loop" of Baddeley's (1983) model of working memory, and he inferred that the dysfunction must involve the "central processor" component of working memory.

Verbal Short-Term Forgetting

One possible measure of central processor function is performance at "short-term" forgetting tests involving a distractor task, such as the Brown–Peterson test (Baddeley, 1986, 1990). I have examined verbal short-term forgetting in 14 Korsakoff and 14 Alzheimer patients between 2 and 20 seconds' delay following visual presentation of words (Kopelman, 1985). Korsakoff patients generally showed only a mild (nonsignificant) degree of impairment, although there was considerable variability between individual subjects in their performance, and the overall mean curve was beginning to deviate from that of healthy controls at 20 seconds' delay. Similar variability has been reported by Mayes et al. (1988) in two pathologically confirmed Korsakoff cases, one of whom showed substantial impairment at this test, whereas the other did not show impairment until a 15-second delay. By contrast, I found substantial impairment in Alzheimer patients across all delay intervals and a predominance of omission errors in this group (Kopelman, 1985). The clinical validity of the test was demonstrated by the fact that, whereas younger healthy subjects of high IQ performed best at this test, younger Alzheimer patients performed particularly poorly, consistent with the greater severity of their expected neuropathological and neurochemical changes (Bondareff, Mountjoy, & Roth, 1982; Mann, Yates, & Marcyniuk, 1984). The correlation with intelligence was maintained in the Alzheimer group, despite their much lower general level of IQ; that is, the most demented patients performed the worst. Furthermore, there were consistent correlations with two measures of the degree of cortical atrophy on CT scan, such that patients with more severe atrophy or larger ventricles performed worse on this test (Kopelman, 1985, 1991a). The Alzheimer findings were broadly consistent with those obtained in other studies by Corkin (1982), Morris (1986), and Dannenbaum, Parkinson, and Inman (1988).

Nonverbal Short-Term Forgetting

Sullivan, Corkin, and Growdon (1986) developed a nonverbal analogue of the Brown–Peterson test, requiring delayed retention of Corsi block sequences while the blocks were covered and the subject was required to perform a finger-tapping distractor task. I employed this same test, requiring subjects to retain either two or three blocks (titrated against block span) over 2- to 20-second delays (Kopelman, 1991a). In both studies, Alzheimer patients were impaired across all conditions, except for immediate recall. In my own study, this was the case whether the scoring was in terms of total blocks recalled in any order (Figure 11.1a) or blocks recalled in the correct

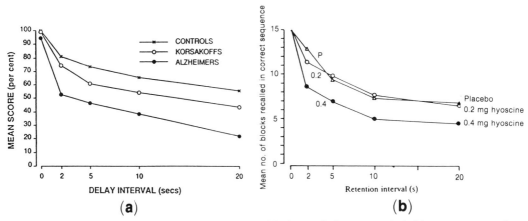

FIGURE 11.1. (a) Nonverbal short-term forgetting (blocks recalled in *any* order). Mean scores at each delay interval on the nonverbal short-term forgetting task by healthy controls, Korsakoff patients, and Alzheimer patients. From "Non-Verbal, Short-Term Forgetting in the Alcoholic Korsakoff Syndrome and Alzheimer-Type Dementia" (p. 740) by M. D. Kopelman, 1991, *Neuropsychologia, 29*, 737–747. Copyright 1991 by Pergamon Press. Reprinted by permission. (b) Cholinergic blockade: Nonverbal short-term forgetting (blocks recalled in *correct* sequence). P, placebo. Drug: hyoscine/scopolamine. From "Cholinergic 'Blockade' as a Model for Cholinergic Depletion: A Comparison of the Memory Deficits with Those of Alzheimer-Type Dementia and the Alcoholic Korsakoff Syndrome" (p. 1089) by M. D. Kopelman and T. H. Corn, 1988, *Brain, 111*, 1079–1110. Copyright 1988 by Oxford University Press. Reprinted by permission.

sequence. This study also included a sample of Korsakoff patients, who showed a level of performance intermediate between that of the healthy controls and that of the Alzheimer patients, the impairment relative to the controls being statistically significant (Figure 11.1a). Performance at this test was correlated with two measures of cortical atrophy on CT scan, and also with a measure of right-hemisphere dysfunction (picture arrangement errors; McFie & Thompson, 1972). This was interpreted as indicating that right-hemisphere atrophy might underlie the deficit on this test, and it was also suggested that left-hemisphere atrophy might account for the impairment on the (verbal) Brown–Peterson test.

Cholinergic Blockade

A colleague and I employed verbal and nonverbal versions of the short-term forgetting tests in healthy subjects, who had been administered a cholinergic antagonist (hyoscine/scopolamine) as a model for the effect of cholinergic depletion in patients (Kopelman & Corn, 1988). We found that cholinergic blockade (at a dose of 0.4 mg scopolamine i.v.) mimicked the impairment of Alzheimer patients on the verbal test, but *only* when the distractor task (information-processing load) was made more difficult (cf. Rusted, 1988) in a manner analogous to that used by Morris (1986), and it also mimicked the impairment on the nonverbal test (Figure 11.1b). In short, the model would suggest that cholinergic depletion within the neocortex may contribute in part to the Alzheimer patients' impairment on these tests.

Nature of the Impairment

Kinsbourne and Wood (1975) proposed that to demonstrate unequivocally accelerated forgetting on the Brown–Peterson test, it is necessary to show a significant group $\times$ interval interaction effect at points beyond the zero delay interval, because of a qualitative difference in the task between immediate recall (where there is often a ceiling effect) and after delays involving either rehearsal or distraction. Most of the studies cited above either failed to obtain a significant interaction effect beyond the first data point or obtained only very equivocal evidence of one (Corkin, 1982; Kopelman, 1985, 1991a; Sullivan et al., 1986). Morris (1986) appeared to obtain accelerated forgetting in two of his conditions (tapping and articulation) but not in two others (digit addition and reversal), although this was not commented upon. Kinsbourne and Wood (1975) argued that such a pattern of performance is most likely to reflect an encoding or a retrieval deficit, and I have suggested that a reduction in available processing resources may produce this encoding–retrieval deficit (Kopelman, 1991a). However, the possibility of very rapidly accelerated forgetting (between the first and second data points) cannot be completely excluded. Consistent with the encoding–retrieval hypothesis, Money, Kirk, and McNaughton (1992) recently obtained parallel curves for Alzheimer patients and controls on a nonverbal delayed-matching-to-sample test during delays between 0 and 32 seconds.

Secondary Memory in Korsakoff and Alzheimer Patients

Free Recall and Priming

In organic amnesia, performance on explicit tests of learning, such as free recall, is by definition severely impaired. On the other hand, one of the most clearly established findings is that the response to priming—for example, on word completion tasks—is remarkably preserved (Warrington & Weiskrantz, 1970; Shimamura, 1986). In their classic study, Graf, Squire, and Mandler (1984) showed that, whereas amnesic patients performed normally in a priming condition, they were significantly impaired in a cued-recall condition, in which they were aware of performing a memory task. On the other hand, various studies have shown impaired priming in Alzheimer patients, even on word completion tasks (e.g., Shimamura, Salmon, Squire, & Butters, 1987; Salmon, Shimamura, Butters, & Smith, 1988; Keane, Gabrieli, Fennema, Growdon, & Corkin, 1991). However, Partridge, Knight, and Feehan (1990) controlled for initial orientation to the stimuli, and found the same pattern as Graf et al. (1984) had obtained in amnesic patients—that is, normal priming and impaired cued recall. Other studies have also reported normal priming in Alzheimer patients when a more demanding orientation task is employed (Christensen & Birrell, 1991) or after controlling for the contribution of explicit memory to a word completion task (Randolph, 1991).

A colleague and I administered a cholinergic antagonist (scopolamine) to healthy subjects as a model for the effect of cholinergic depletion in patients (Kopelman & Corn, 1988). Figure 11.2 shows that our results neatly replicated those obtained by Graf et al. (1984) and Partridge et al. (1990) in amnesic and Alzheimer patients; that is, there was a severe impairment in free recall and in cued recall in two drug groups relative to a placebo group ($p < .001$ in each case), whereas there was no significant difference between the drug groups and the placebo group in the primed condition. Furthermore, we found that cholinergic blockade did not produce any impairment on the rate of learning of a mirror-reading task as a measure of procedural memory, although it did produce impairment on a variety of explicit tests of verbal and nonverbal recall and recognition.

Memory for Context

Currently, there are three main hypotheses concerning the relationship of contextual memory deficits to the impairment of target or explicit memory in amnesic patients. The first is that contextual memory deficits represent an additional dysfunction, superimposed upon the core amnesic syndrome and probably resulting from frontal lesions or atrophy (Squire, 1982; Schacter, Harbluk, & McLachlan, 1984; Schacter, 1987). The second is that the contextual memory deficit might even be the fundamental basis of the explicit memory impairment in the organic amnesic syndrome (Huppert & Piercy, 1976, 1982; Winocur & Kinsbourne, 1978; Hirst, 1982; Parkin, 1987; Mayes, 1988). Third, the contextual memory deficit may be only a particular attribute of the explicit memory deficit, disproportionately affected because

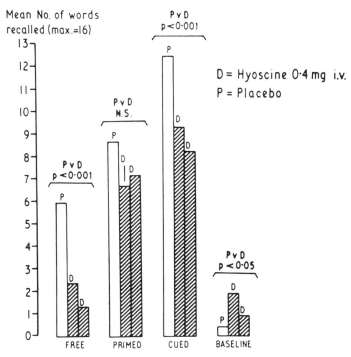

FIGURE 11.2. Word list recall in free, primed, cued, and baseline conditions. Open bars, placebo; hatched bars, hyoscine (scopolamine), where D = drug (scopolamine) administered on day 1 and P = placebo on day 1. From "Cholinergic 'Blockade' as a Model for Cholinergic Depletion: A Comparison of the Memory Deficits with Those of Alzheimer-Type Dementia and the Alcoholic Korsakoff Syndrome" (p. 1089) by M. D. Kopelman and T. H. Corn, 1988, *Brain, 111*, 1079–1110. Copyright 1988 by Oxford University Press. Reprinted by permission.

it is an especially "difficult" component of memory even in healthy subjects (Huppert & Piercy, 1978a; Baddeley, 1982, 1990).

I conducted a study designed to investigate the relative importance of frontal dysfunction and the severity of anterograde memory loss upon performance at three tests of temporal context memory in 32 Korsakoff and Alzheimer patients (Kopelman, 1989). The Korsakoff patients could be subdivided into those who had a substantial degree of frontal atrophy on CT scan and those who had only minimal frontal atrophy, according to a computerized pixel count of the size of the anterior interhemispheric fissure (Baldy et al., 1986). Three temporal context tests were employed—first, a retrograde test, requiring dating to the appropriate decade of correctly recognized pictures of news events; second, an anterograde test, which matched recognition performance for pictures from magazines by prolonging the exposure times to the test material for the patient groups, and then required the subjects to identify whether each correctly recognized picture had been seen in the first or second of two series; and third, a current orientation scale, involving items concerning orientation in time, place, and person. In brief, the three groups of patients (Korsakoff patients with or without substantial frontal atrophy and a group of Alzheimer patients) were all significantly impaired at each of these tasks, relative to healthy controls. On the other hand, there was virtually no difference in the performance of those Korsakoff patients with a greater or a lesser degree of frontal atrophy on CT scan at any of the tasks. Within the total patient group, there were weak and generally nonsignificant correlations (r's = approximately .10 to .30) between performance at the three temporal context tests and eight measures of frontal function. By contrast, there were statistically significant correlations ($r = .33$, $p < .05$, to $r = .60$, $p < .01$) between temporal context test performance and a measure of the severity of anterograde memory impairment. In short, it appears that the deficit in temporal context memory is more closely related to the severity of anterograde amnesia than to frontal function. The contextual memory deficit may therefore be a direct consequence of diencephalic or hippocampal pathology, although an additive effect of frontal and limbic–diencephalic lesions remains a possibility in these groups of patients (cf. Shimamura, Janowsky, & Squire, 1990).

Consistent with this finding, Mayes and colleagues have found that memory for other aspects of context also appear to be more closely related to the severity of the explicit memory impairment than to measures of frontal function, including memory for the modality of presented information and memory for spatial location (Pickering, Mayes, & Fairbairn, 1989; Shoqeirat & Mayes, 1991; Mayes, Meudell, & MacDonald, 1991). However, the correlations between the severity of memory impairment and context memory scores tend to be relatively low, suggesting that the contextual memory deficit may be one particular component of the explicit memory disorder, rather than the core feature.

Intermediate- and Long-Term Forgetting

"Long-term forgetting" refers to the rate of loss from secondary memory after learning has been accomplished (Kopelman, 1992a). Huppert and Piercy (1978b) described a picture recognition test, in which exposure times to the pictures could be manipulated in order to "match" the initial recognition scores of amnesic or dementing patients to those of healthy controls. Using this test, Huppert and Piercy (1978b), as well as various other researchers (Squire, 1981; Kopelman, 1985; Martone, Butters, & Trauner, 1986) have obtained normal forgetting rates in Korsakoff patients once learning has been accomplished. On the other hand, Huppert and Piercy (1979) claimed that the bitemporal lobectomy patient H.M. forgot faster than either controls or Korsakoff patients, suggesting that the temporal lobes may mediate long-term retention. However, this latter finding in H.M. was not replicated in a more detailed study by Freed, Corkin, and Cohen (1987).

I used the Huppert–Piercy test in Alzheimer patients, who show extensive pathology within the hippocampi and temporal lobes (Kopelman, 1985). The Alzheimer group's performance at initial recognition after 10 minutes was matched to that of a Korsakoff group and was only a little below that of a healthy control group, and their forgetting rate over a week was *the same* as that of the other two groups, whether scoring was in terms of percentage correct scores (Figure 11.3a), recognition scores as a proportion of scores at 10 minutes, or d'. Taken together with the Freed et al. (1987) finding, this result would appear to indicate that in Alzheimer dementia, as in the Korsakoff syndrome, the principal problem is in acquiring (or retrieving) new information rather than in long-term retention, and that temporal lobe pathology is *not*

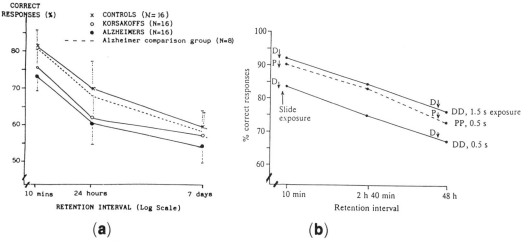

FIGURE 11.3. (a) Long-term forgetting. Mean percentage of pictures correctly identified as target or distractor (true positive + true negative) by Alzheimer patients (●), Korsakoff patients (○), and controls (×) on the Huppert–Piercy test (± 1 *SD*). From "Rates of Forgetting in Alzhiemer-Type Dementia and Korsakoff's Syndrome" (p. 631) by M. D. Kopelman, 1985, *Neuropsychologia, 23*, 623-638. Copyright 1985 by Pergamon Press. Reprinted by permission. (b) Cholinergic blockade: Long-term forgetting (Huppert–Piercy test). Two groups viewed the slides for 0.5 seconds each, and the third group for a mean of 1.5 seconds per slide. Group PP and both DD groups received an initial infusion of placebo or scopolamine, respectively, at 0 minutes on day 1 and a "shot" of placebo 60 minutes later (5 to 7 minutes after the end of recognition test 1). Continuous line, drug/scopolamine; broken line, placebo. From "Cholinergic 'Blockade' as a Model for Cholinergic Depletion: A Comparison of the Memory Deficits with Those of Alzheimer-Type Dementia and the Alcoholic Korsakoff Syndrome" (p. 1095) by M. D. Kopelman and T. H. Corn, 1988, *Brain, 111*, 1079-1110. Copyright 1988 by Oxford University Press. Reprinted by permission.

especially conducive to accelerated forgetting. Subsequently, Freed, Corkin, Growdon, and Nissen (1989) published a study that used a forced-choice version of the Huppert–Piercy test in Alzheimer patients; they also failed to find any overall difference between the mean forgetting rate of their patient group and that of the controls.

Consistent with this, we employed the Huppert–Piercy test in healthy subjects who had received a cholinergic antagonist (scopolamine) (Kopelman & Corn, 1988). We found that cholinergic blockade neatly mimicked the findings in Korsakoff and Alzheimer patients; that is, the drug impaired acquisition scores at initial recognition testing, but when this effect was overcome by prolonging exposure times to the drug group, the rate of forgetting over 48 hours was normal (Figure 11.3b).

Other studies have examined forgetting rates during intervals falling between what are conventionally regarded as "short-term" and "long-term" forgetting, or during periods encompassing aspects of both short-term (primary) and long-term (secondary) memory. In patients with left or bilateral hippocampal lesions, Frisk and Milner (1990) and Parkin and Leng (1988) have reported accelerated forgetting between immediate or 1-minute recall and subsequent delays, but these results were confounded by ceiling effects at criterion. Moss, Albert, Butters, and Payne (1986) found that Alzheimer patients appeared to forget faster between 15 seconds and 2 minutes than Korsakoff and Huntington's disease patients on a word recall test, although this finding was qualified by the fact that the Alzheimer patients manifested a lower initial (15-second) level of performance, and there was no attempt to match initial learning. Hart, Kwentus, Taylor, and Harkins (1987) reported accelerated forgetting rates in Alzheimer patients between a 90-second and a 10-minute delay, relative to depressed patients and healthy controls. However, a much briefer (and easier) test was given to match the subjects at 90 seconds than was administered at 10 minutes or subsequent delays (2 hours and 48 hours), making the memory load of the task much greater at these later delays. In studies not involving matching, I showed impaired delayed recall of a paragraph and of a name and address (Kopelman, 1986b), and others have also reported severe impairment on measures of delayed recall or "savings scores" (Knopman & Ryberg, 1989; Welsh, Butters, Hughes, Mohs, & Heyman, 1991; Delis et al., 1991); however, these unmatched findings remain difficult to interpret (Kopelman, 1992a).

On the other hand, Becker, Boller, Saxton, and McGonicle-Gibson (1987) found no evidence of accelerated forgetting in Alzheimer patients when they compared savings scores of immediate and delayed verbal and nonverbal recall with those of normal elderly subjects. Butters et al. (1988) found that the savings scores of Alzheimer patients did not differ from those of healthy controls on two paired-associate tests, or from those of organic amnesic patients on tests of immediate and delayed logical memory and visual reproduction, although the patient groups differed significantly from controls for these latter two tasks. Moreover, 11 Korsakoff patients and 5 patients with hippocampal lesions also failed to show any significant differences in savings scores across any of the four tests. However, the findings in both these latter studies were confounded by the absence of any matching procedure for initial learning across the subject groups, and by the probable presence of ceiling and floor effects in some of the tests.

In short, those studies, which have employed the appropriate and necessary matching procedures, have generally found normal long-term forgetting in amnesic or dementing patients (Kopelman, 1992a). The finding that there is an initial acquisition deficit, but no subsequent effect on long-term retention once learning has been accomplished, can be mimicked by cholinergic blockade administered as a model for cholinergic depletion (Kopelman & Corn, 1988), and can also be modelled within a "spreading-activation" framework of neuronal functioning (Cohen & Stanhope, 1991). There is a suggestion that forgetting rates may be accelerated in Alzheimer patients between approximately 15 seconds' delay and 10 minutes' delay, which would imply that such delays are critical for some physiological process of memory consolidation; however, this finding needs to be replicated using appropriate matching procedures.

Retrograde Amnesia and Autobiographical Memory

Temporal Gradients of the Retrograde Amnesia

If accelerated forgetting of newly acquired memories does not occur, once learning has been accomplished for as long as 10 minutes, it would appear unlikely that retrograde memory loss results from accelerated forgetting of "old" memories or a destruction of memory storage, as Ribot's (1882) law of regression suggested. More recently, various authors have suggested that the loss of "remote" or "autobiographical" memories may result from either a progressive anterograde disorder, preceding the diagnosis of a disease, or a generalized retrieval deficit, or some combination of these (Sanders & Warrington, 1971; Albert, Butters, & Levin, 1979; Cohen & Squire, 1981). The slope of the "temporal gradient" has commonly been interpreted as providing a clue to the underlying mechanism of the retrograde loss, but recent studies suggest little or no difference in the temporal gradients of patients with an acute or more insidious onset of their amnesia (Kopelman, Wilson, & Baddeley, 1989; Squire, Haist, & Shimamura, 1989). Relatively few studies have examined retrograde amnesia across a number of different aspects, including memory for remote public information, and for "personal semantic" facts and "autobiographical" incidents about oneself.

I conducted a series of such tests in Korsakoff and Alzheimer patients (Kopelman, 1989). In the recall of famous news events and of autobiographical facts and incidents, Alzheimer patients showed a gentle temporal gradient, with relative sparing of their earliest memories (cf. Sagar, Cohen, Sullivan, Corkin, & Growdon, 1988; Beatty, Salmon, Butters, Heindel, & Granholm, 1988), and Korsakoff patients showed a significantly steeper gradient on all three tests (Figures 11.4a and 11.4b). The Korsakoff group's impairment relative to healthy controls extended back 20 to 30 years from the

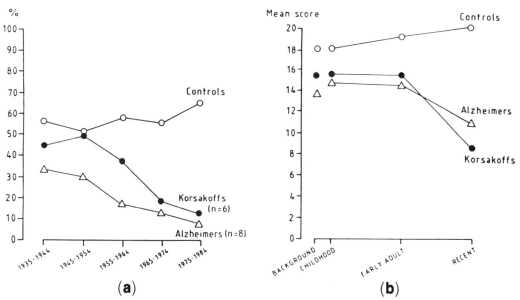

(a)   **(b)**

FIGURE 11.4. (a) News Events Test (recall): Age-matched comparison. Results obtained from the six oldest Korsakoff patients (mean age = 62.8 ± 2.0) and an age-matched subsample of the Alzheimer group (n = 8) (mean age = 64.5 ± 4.1). Mean age of control group = 61.75 ± 13.1. From "Remote and Autobiographical Memory, Temporal Context Memory, and Frontal Atrophy in Korsakoff and Alzheimer Patients" (p. 447) by M. D. Kopelman, 1989, *Neuropsychologia, 27,* 437–460. Copyright 1989 by Pergamon Press. Reprinted by permission. (b) Personal Semantic Memory Schedule (autobiographical facts). Maximum score = 21. n = 16 in each group. From "Remote and Autobiographical Memory, Temporal Context Memory, and Frontal Atrophy in Korsakoff and Alzheimer Patients" (p. 450) by M. D. Kopelman, 1989, *Neuropsychologia, 27,* 437–460. Copyright 1989 by Pergamon Press. Reprinted by permission.

time of testing; as the mean duration of the illness in this group was 5.75 years, this implied a retrograde component to the amnesia of 15 to 25 years (Figure 11.4a). On a recognition version of the News Events Test, both the Alzheimer and the Korsakoff patients showed a remarkably good response to the cues provided by recognition testing, with a significantly greater improvement (in terms of recognition minus recall scores) in both groups than in the healthy controls.

The Nature of the Deficit

These findings were taken as indicating a retrieval component to the deficit, in that both patient groups showed a marked improvement on recognition testing for the News Events Test (relative to recall performance), even for events long preceding the onset of the amnesia. The relative sparing of the very earliest memories, occurring in both the Alzheimer and the Korsakoff groups, was assumed to result from the greater salience and degree of rehearsal of these memories, providing some degree of protection against this retrieval deficit. The steeper temporal gradient in the Korsakoff than in the Alzheimer group was interpreted as indicating a *superimposed* progressive anterograde component to the amnesia during the period of the former group's heavy drinking (Kopelman, 1989). Although this latter factor might seem to contrast with the Kopelman et al. (1989) finding of no difference in the temporal gradients of patients with an acute or insidious onset, it should be noted that the period of heavy drinking in the Korsakoff group (13 to 37.5 years; mean = 23 years) was much more extensive than the insidiousness of the onset (1 to 6 years of the amnesic patients) in the Kopelman et al. (1989) study.

In general, there was only 21% shared variance between performance on retrograde and anterograde tests (Kopelman, 1989, 1991b). Moreover, cholinergic blockade mimics the anterograde but not the retrograde component of amnesia (Kopelman & Corn, 1988). Furthermore, various studies have described amnesic patients who have lesions confined to the limbic circuits or basal forebrain, in whom there is a severe anterograde amnesia, but only a brief or even absent retrograde loss (Russell & Nathan, 1946; Winocur, Oxbury, Roberts, Agnetti, & Davis, 1984; Damasio, Eslinger, et al., 1985; Damasio, Graff-Radford, et al., 1985; Salazar, et al., 1986; Zola-Morgan, Squire, & Amaral, 1986; Phillips et al., 1987; Hodges & Ward, 1989; Squire, Amaral, Zola-Morgan, Kritchevsky, & Press, 1989; Graff-Radford, Tranel, Van Hoesen, & Brandt, 1990; Dusoir, Kapur, Byrnes, McKinstry, & Hoare, 1990).

Consequently, I sought to examine whether the temporally extensive retrograde memory loss in Korsakoff and Alzheimer patients was related either to CT scan measures of frontal or general cortical atrophy or to measures of frontal dysfunction (Kopelman, 1989, 1991b). There was only very weak evidence of an association with the CT measures of either frontal atrophy (Kopelman, 1989) or more generalized cortical atrophy (Kopelman, 1991b). On the other hand, there did appear to be good evidence of a correlation between performance on frontal tests and an overall retrograde memory quotient (RMQ), but little relationship with an overall anterograde memory quotient (AMQ). Table 11.1 shows that six out of eight frontal tests

TABLE 11.1. Correlations between Frontal Tests and RMQ, AMQ, and Retrograde–Anterograde Difference Scores: Total Patient Sample ($n = 32$)

Frontal tests	RMQ	AMQ	Retrograde–anterograde difference
FAS Verbal Fluency	.52**	.27	.36*
Miller Correction	.10	−.24	.29
Birds and Colours	.59***	.26	.43**
Modified Weigl	.33*	.08	.29
Card-sorting categories	.51**	−.00	.56***
Card-sorting: % perseverations	−.40*	−.02	−.42**
Cognitive estimates	−.64***	−.48**	−.32*
Picture arrangement errors	−.21	−.22	−.06

Note. From "Frontal Dysfunction and Memory Deficits in the Alcoholic Korsakoff Syndrome and Alzheimer-Type Dementia" (p. 129) by M. D. Kopelman, 1991, *Brain, 114,* 117-137. Copyright 1991 by Oxford University Press. Reprinted by permission.
*$p < .05$, one-tailed. **$p < .01$, one-tailed. ***$p < .001$, one-tailed.

correlated significantly with RMQ and five out of eight correlated significantly with the retrograde–anterograde difference score (indicating relative sparing of retrograde memory), but only one out of eight frontal tests correlated significantly with AMQ. Moreover, Table 11.2 shows that this pattern of correlations held good across four individual measures of retrograde memory (News Events Test recognition and recall scores, Personal Semantic Memory Schedule scores, and Autobiographical Incidents Schedule scores). The only test for which it did not hold good was one that required only familiarity judgments concerning famous names (Famous Personalities Test; Stevens, 1979). Moreover, whereas AMQ predicted only 21% of the variance in RMQ scores, a regression equation based on three of the frontal tests accounted for 57% of the variance in Alzheimer patients, 68.5% in Korsakoff patients, and 64% in the total group.

This finding led me to suggest that the *combination* of frontal dysfunction and limbic–diencephalic pathology produces the temporally extensive retrograde loss seen in Alzheimer and Korsakoff patients and in other patients with extensive cortical damage (Kopelman, 1991b, 1992b). Moreover, Baddeley and Wilson (1986) have reported impoverished retrieval of autobiographical memories in some patients with apparently isolated frontal lesions, and disorganized, confabulated retrieval in other patients with frontal damage—a finding that has recently been replicated in a group of radiologically confirmed frontal patients by Della Sala, Laiacona, Spinnler, and Trivelli (1992). It seems likely that frontal lesions produce this extensive retrograde loss by a disruption of the organization of retrieval processes, causing impoverished recall in some patients and (less commonly) "spontaneous confabulation" in others (Stuss & Benson, 1986; Baddeley & Wilson, 1986; Kopelman, 1987, 1991b; Della Sala et al., 1992).

TABLE 11.2. Correlations between Individual Retrograde (Remote Memory) Tests and Individual Frontal Tests: Total Patient Sample ($n = 32$)

Frontal tests	News Event Test recognition	News Event Test recall	Famous Personalities Test	Personal Semantic Memory Schedule	Autobiographical Incidents Schedule
FAS Verbal Fluency	.41	.45**	.39*	.34*	.36*
Miller Correction	.23	.14	.00	-.01	.07
Birds and Colours	.43**	.43**	.19	.38*	.62***
Modified Weigl	.16	.27	.04	.31*	.38*
Card-sorting categories	.41*	.47**	.09	.33*	.49**
Card-sorting: % perseverations	-.43**	-.27	-.15	-.30*	-.24
Cognitive estimates	-.51**	-.49**	-.59***	-.50**	-.36*
Picture arrangement errors	-.15	-.19	-.18	-.20	-.15

Note. From "Frontal Dysfunction and Memory Deficits in the Alcoholic Korsakoff Syndrome and Alzheimer-Type Dementia" (p. 130) by M. D. Kopelman, 1991, *Brain, 114,* 117–137. Copyright 1991 by Oxford University Press. Reprinted by permission.
*p < .05, one-tailed. **p < .01, one-tailed. ***p < .001, one-tailed.

Conclusion

The amnesic syndrome, as exemplified in the alcoholic Korsakoff syndrome, involves a severe impairment of explicit memory for "new" verbal and nonverbal material, with preserved word completion priming, procedural memory, and long-term forgetting once learning has been accomplished. Many of these features are also evident in Alzheimer dementia, and they can be mimicked by administering a cholinergic antagonist (scopolamine) as a model for the effects of cholinergic depletion. It has been argued that the deficit in memory for context represents just one aspect of this explicit memory impairment—a particular attribute, but neither the core nor a superadded feature of the amnesia. Impairments in working memory (on span tests and short-term forgetting tasks) are much more pronounced in Alzheimer than in Korsakoff patients, perhaps because diminished processing resources in the Alzheimer group result in a short-term encoding or retrieval deficit. There is also evidence to suggest that the impairment on verbal short-term tasks is related to left-hemisphere cortical atrophy, and the deficit on nonverbal short-term tasks to right-hemisphere atrophy, and that cholinergic depletion within the hemispheres may make a partial contribution to these impairments. On the other hand, the temporally extensive retrograde loss, seen in both Alzheimer and Korsakoff patients but not in some other amnesias, may result from the concurrence of frontal atrophy and limbic–diencephalic pathology, resulting in a disruption of the retrieval processes for "old" memories.

REFERENCES

Albert, M. S., Butters, N., & Levin, J. (1979). Temporal gradients in the retrograde amnesia of patients with alcoholic Korsakoff's disease. *Archives of Neurology, 36*, 211–216.

Arendt, T., Allen, Y., Sindon, J., Schugens, M. M., Marchbanks, R. M., Lantos, P. L. & Gray, J. A. (1988). Cholinergic-rich brain transplants reverse alcohol-induced memory deficits. *Nature, 332*, 448–450.

Arendt, T., Bigl, V., Arendt, A. & Tennstedt, A. (1983). Loss of neurons in the nucleus basalis of Meynert in Alzheimer's disease, paralysis agitans and Korsakoff's disease. *Acta Neuropathologica, 61*, 101–108.

Baddeley, A. D. (1982). Amnesia: A minimal model and an interpretation. In L. S. Cermak (Ed.), *Human memory and amnesia*. Hillsdale, NJ: Erlbaum.

Baddeley, A. D (1983). Working memory. *Philosophical Transactions of the Royal Society of London, B302*, 311–323.

Baddeley, A. D. (1986). Working memory. Oxford: Oxford University Press.

Baddeley, A. D. (1990). Human memory: Theory and practice. Hillsdale, NJ: Erlbaum.

Baddeley, A. D., & Wilson, B. (1986). Amnesia, autobiographical memory, and confabulation. In D. C. Rubin (Ed.), *Autobiographical memory*. Cambridge: Cambridge University Press.

Baldy, R. E., Brindley, G. S., Ewusi-Mensah, I., Reveley, M. A., Turner, S. W., & Lishman, W. A. (1986). A fully-automated computer-assisted method of CT brain scan analysis for the measurement of cerebrospinal fluid spaces and brain absorption density. *Neuroradiology, 28*, 109–117.

Beatty, W. W., Salmon, D. P., Butters, N., Heindel, W. C. & Granholm, E. L. (1988). Retrograde amnesia in patients with Alzheimer's disease or Huntington's disease. *Neurobiology of Aging, 9*, 181–186.

Becker, J. T., Boller, F., Saxton, J., & McGonicle-Gibson, K. L (1987). Normal rates of forgetting of verbal and non-verbal material in Alzheimer's disease. *Cortex, 23*, 59–72.

Bondareff, W., Mountjoy, C. Q., & Roth, M. (1982). Loss of neurons of origin of the adrenergic projection to the cerebral cortex (nucleus locus ceruleus) in senile dementia. *Neurology, 32*, 164–168.

Butters, N. (1985). Alcoholic Korsakoff's syndrome: Some unresolved issues concerning etiology, neuropathology, and cognitive deficits. *Journal of Clinical and Experimental Neuropsychology, 7*, 181–210.

Butters, N., & Cermak, L. S. (1980). *Alcoholic Korsakoff's syndrome: An information-processing approach to amnesia*. New York: Academic Press.

Butters, N., Salmon, D. P., Munro Cullum, C., Cairns, P., Tröster, A. I., Jacobs, D., Moss, M., & Cermak, L. S. (1988). Differentiation of amnesic and demented patients with the Wechsler Memory Scale—Revised. *Clinical Neuropsychologist, 2,* 133-148.

Christensen, H., & Birrell, P. (1991). Explicit and implicit memory in dementia and normal ageing. *Psychological Research, 53,* 149-161.

Cohen, G., & Stanhope, N. (1991, July). *A spreading activation model of age differences: Evidence from set size effects.* Paper presented at the International Conference on Memory, Lancaster University, Lancaster, England.

Cohen, N. J., & Squire, L. R. (1981). Retrograde amnesia and remote memory impairment. *Neuropsychologia, 19,* 337-356.

Corkin, S. (1982). Some relationships between global amnesias and the memory impairments in Alzheimer's disease. In S. Corkin, K. L. Davis, J. H. Growdon, E. Usdin, & R. J. Wurtman (Eds.), *Alzheimer's Disease: A report of research in progress.* New York: Raven Press.

Damasio, A. R., Eslinger, P. J., Damasio, H., Van Hoesen, G. W., & Cornell, S. (1985). Multimodal amnesic syndrome following bilateral temporal and basal forebrain damage. *Archives of Neurology, 42,* 252-259.

Damasio, A. R., Graff-Radford, N. R., Eslinger, P. J., Damasio, H., & Kassell, N. (1985). Amnesia following basal forebrain lesions. *Archives of Neurology, 42,* 263-271.

Dannenbaum, S. E., Parkinson, S. R., & Inman, V. W. (1988). Short-term forgetting: Comparisons between patients with dementia of the Alzheimer-type, depressed, and normal elderly. *Cognitive Neuropsychology, 5,* 213-233.

Delis, D. C., Massman, P. J., Butters, N., Salmon, D. P., Cermak, L. S., & Kramer, J. H. (1991). Profiles of demented and amnesic patients on the California Verbal Learning Test: Implications for the assessment of memory disorders. *Psychological Assessment: A Journal of Consulting and Clinical Psychology, 3,* 19-26.

Della Sala, S., Laiacona, M., Spinnler, H., & Trivelli, C. (1992). *Impaired autobiographical recollection in some frontal patients.* Manuscript submitted for publication.

Dusoir, H., Kapur, N., Byrnes, D. P., McKinstry, S., & Hoare, R. D. (1990). The role of diencephalic pathology in human memory disorder: Evidence from a penetrating paranasal injury. *Brain, 113,* 1695-1706.

Freed, D. M., Corkin, S., & Cohen, N. J. (1987). Forgetting in H. M.: A second look. *Neuropsychologia, 25,* 461-472.

Freed, D. M., Corkin, S., Growdon, J. H., & Nissen, M. J. (1989). Selective attention in Alzheimer's disease: Characterizing cognitive subgroups of patients. *Neuropsychologia, 27,* 325-339.

Frisk, V., & Milner, B. (1990). The role of the left hippocampal region in the acquisition and retention of story content. *Neuropsychologia, 28,* 349-359.

Graf, P., Squire, L. R., & Mandler, G. (1984). The information that amnesic patients do not forget. *Journal of Experimental Psychology: Learning, Memory, and Cognition, 10,* 164-178.

Graff-Radford, N. R., Tranel, D., Van Hoesen, G., & Brandt, J. P. (1990). Diencephalic amnesia. *Brain, 113,* 1-25.

Hart, R. P., Kwentus, J. A., Taylor, J. R., & Harkins, S. W. (1987). Rate of forgetting in dementia and depression. *Journal of Consulting and Clinical Psychology, 55,* 101-105.

Hirst, W. (1982). The amnesic syndrome: Descriptions and explanations. *Psychological Bulletin, 91,* 435-460.

Hodges, J. R., & Ward, C. D. (1989). Observations during transient global amnesia: A behavioural and neuropsychological study of five cases. *Brain, 112,* 595-620.

Huppert, F. A., & Piercy, M. (1976). Recognition memory in amnesic patients: Effect of temporal context and familiarity of material. *Cortex, 12,* 3-20.

Huppert, F. A., & Piercy, M. (1978a). The role of trace strength in recency and frequency judgements by amnesic and control subjects. *Quarterly Journal of Experimental Psychology, 30,* 347-354.

Huppert, F. A., & Piercy, M. (1978b). Dissociation between learning and remembering in organic amnesia. *Nature, 275,* 317-318.

Huppert F. A., & Piercy, M. (1979). Normal and abnormal forgetting in organic amnesia: Effect of locus of lesion. *Cortex, 15,* 385-390.

Huppert, F. A., & Piercy, M. (1982). In search of the functional locus of amnesic syndromes. In L. S. Cermak (Ed.), *Human memory and amnesia.* Hillsdale, NJ: Erlbaum.

Irle, E., & Markowitsch, H. J. (1987). Basal forebrain-lesioned monkeys are severely impaired in tasks of association and recognition memory. *Annals of Neurology, 22,* 735-743.

James, W. (1890). *Principles of psychology* (Vol. 1). New York: Holt.

Keane, M. M., Gabrieli, J. D. E., Fennema, A. C., Growdon, J. H., & Corkin, S. (1991). Evidence for a dissociation between perceptual and conceptual priming in Alzheimer's disease. *Behavioral Neuro-science, 105*, 326–342.

Kinsbourne, M., & Wood, F. (1975). Short-term memory processes and the amnesic syndrome. In D. Deutsch & J. A. Deutsch (Eds.), *Short-term memory*. New York: Academic Press.

Knopman, D. S., & Ryberg, S. (1989). A verbal memory test with high predictive accuracy for dementia of the Alzheimer type. *Archives of Neurology, 44*, 141–145.

Kopelman, M. D. (1985). Rates of forgetting in Alzheimer-type dementia and Korsakoff's syndrome. *Neuropsychologia, 23*, 623–638.

Kopelman, M. D. (1986a). The cholinergic neurotransmitter system in human memory and dementia: A review. *Quarterly Journal of Experimental Psychology, 38A*, 535–573.

Kopelman, M. D. (1986b). Clinical tests of memory. *British Journal of Psychiatry, 148*, 517–525.

Kopelman, M. D. (1987). Two types of confabulation. *Journal of Neurology, Neurosurgery and Psychiatry, 50*, 1482–1487.

Kopelman, M. D. (1989). Remote and autobiographical memory, temporal context memory, and frontal atrophy in Korsakoff and Alzheimer patients. *Neuropsychologia, 27*, 437–460.

Kopelman, M. D. (1991a). Non-verbal, short-term forgetting in the alcoholic Korsakoff syndrome and Alzheimer-type dementia. *Neuropsychologia, 29*, 737–747.

Kopelman, M. D. (1991b). Frontal dysfunction and memory deficits in the alcoholic Korsakoff syndrome and Alzheimer-type dementia. *Brain, 114*, 117–137.

Kopelman, M. D. (1992a). Storage, forgetting, and retrieval in the anterograde and retrograde amnesia of Alzheimer dementia. In L. Backman (Ed.), *Memory functioning in dementia*. Amsterdam: Elsevier.

Kopelman, M. D. (1992b). The neuropsychology of remote memory. In F. Boller & H. Spinnler (Eds.), *The handbook of neuropsychology* (Vol. 8). Amsterdam: Elsevier.

Kopelman, M. D., & Corn, T. H. (1988). Cholinergic 'blockade' as a model for cholinergic depletion: A comparison of the memory deficits with those of Alzheimer-type dementia and the alcoholic Korsakoff syndrome. *Brain, 111*, 1079–1110.

Kopelman, M. D., Wilson, B. A., & Baddeley, A. D (1989). The Autobiographical Memory Interview: A new assessment of autobiographical and personal semantic memory in amnesic patients. *Journal of Clinical and Experimental Neuropsychology, 11*, 724–744.

Mann, D. M. A., Yates, P. O., & Marcyniuk, B. (1984). Alzheimer's presenile dementia, senile dementia of Alzheimer-type, and Down's syndrome in middle age form an age related continuum of pathological changes. *Neuropathology and Applied Neurobiology, 10*, 185–207.

Martone, E., Butters, N., & Trauner, D. (1986). Some analyses of forgetting of pictorial material in amnesic and demented patients. *Journal of Clinical and Experimental Neuropsychology, 8*, 161–178.

Mayes, A. R. (1988). *Human organic memory disorders*. Cambridge: Cambridge University Press.

Mayes, A. R., Meudell, P. R., Mann, D., & Pickering, A. (1988). Location of lesions in Korsakoff's syndrome: Neuropsychological and neuropathological data on two patients. *Cortex, 24*, 367–388.

Mayes, A. R., Meudell, P. R., & MacDonald, C. (1991). Disproportionate intentional spatial memory impairments in amnesia. *Neuropsychologia, 29*, 771–784.

McFie, J., & Thompson, J. A. (1972). Picture arrangement: A measure of frontal lobe function? *British Journal of Psychiatry, 121*, 547–552.

Miller, E. (1973). Short- and long-term memory in presenile dementia (Alzheimer's disease). *Psychological Medicine, 3*, 221–224.

Money, E. A., Kirk, R. C., & McNaughton, N. (1992). Alzheimer's dementia produces a loss of discrimination but no increase in rate of memory decay in delayed matching to sample. *Neuropsychologia, 30*, 133–144.

Morris, R. G. (1984). Dementia and the functioning of the articulatory loop system. *Cognitive Neuropsychology, 1*, 143–57.

Morris, R. G. (1986). Short-term forgetting in senile dementia of the Alzheimer's type. *Cognitive Neuropsychology, 3*, 77–97.

Moss, M. B., Albert, M. S., Butters, N., & Payne, M. (1986). Differential patterns of memory loss among patients with Alzheimer's disease, Huntington's disease and alcoholic Korsakoff's syndrome. *Archives of Neurology, 43*, 239–246.

Parkin, A. J. (1987). *Memory and amnesia: An introduction*. Oxford: Blackwell.

Parkin, A. J., & Leng, N. R. C. (1988). Comparative studies of human amnesia: Syndrome or syndromes? In H. Markowitsch (Ed.), *Information processing by the brain*. Toronto: Hans Huber.

Partridge, F. M., Knight, R. G., & Feehan, M. J. (1990). Direct and indirect memory performance in patients with senile dementia. *Psychological Medicine, 20*, 111–118.

Phillips, S., Sangalang, V., & Sterns, G. (1987). Basal forebrain infarction—a clinicopathological correlation. *Archives of Neurology, 44*, 1134–1138.

Pickering, A., Mayes, A. R., & Fairbairn, A. F. (1989). Amnesia and memory for modality information. *Neuropsychologia, 27,* 1249-1259.

Randolph, C. (1991). Implicit, explicit, and semantic memory functions in Alzheimer's disease and Huntington's disease. *Journal of Clinical and Experimental Neuropsychology, 13,* 479-494.

Ribot, T. (1882). *Diseases of memory.* New York: Appleton.

Rossor, M. N., Iversen, L. L., Reynolds, G. P., Mountjoy, C. Q., & Roth, M. (1984). Neurochemical characteristics of early and late onset types of Alzheimer's disease. *British Medical Journal, 288,* 961-964.

Russell, W. R., & Nathan, P. W. (1946). Traumatic amnesia. *Brain, 69,* 280-300.

Rusted, J. M. (1988). Dissociative effects of scopolomine on working memory in healthy young volunteers. *Psychopharmacology, 96,* 487-492.

Sagar, H. J., Cohen, N. J., Sullivan, E. V., Corkin, S., & Growdon, J. H. (1988). Remote memory function in Alzheimer's disease and Parkinson's disease. *Brain, 111,* 185-206.

Salazar, A. M., Grafman, J., Schlesselman, S., Vance, S. C., Mohr, J. P., Carpenter, M., Pevsner, P., Ludlow, C., & Weingartner, H. (1986). Penetrating war injuries of the basal forebrain: Neurology and cognition. *Neurology, 36,* 459-465.

Salmon, D. P., Shimamura, A. P., Butters, N., & Smith, S. (1988). Lexical and semantic priming deficits in patients with Alzheimer's disease. *Journal of Clinical and Experimental Neuropsychology, 10,* 477-494.

Sanders, H., & Warrington, E. (1971). Memory for remote events in amnesic patients. *Brain, 94,* 661-668.

Schacter, D. L. (1987). Memory, amnesia and frontal lobe dysfunction. *Psychobiology, 15,* 21-36.

Schacter, D. L., Harbluk, J. L., & McLachlan, D. R. (1984). Retrieval without recollection: An experimental analysis of source amnesia. *Journal of Verbal Learning and Verbal Behavior, 23,* 593-611.

Shimamura, A. P. (1986). Priming effects in amnesia: Evidence for a dissociable memory function. *Quarterly Journal of Experimental Psychology, 38A,* 619-644.

Shimamura, A. P., Janowsky, J. S., & Squire, L. R. (1990). Memory for the temporal order of events in patients with frontal lobe lesions and amnesic patients. *Neuropsychologia, 28,* 803-813.

Shimamura, A. P., Salmon, D. P., Squire, L. R., & Butters, N. (1987). Memory dysfunction and word priming in dementia and amnesia. *Behavioral Neuroscience, 101,* 347-351.

Shoqeirat, M. A., & Mayes, A. R. (1991). Disproportionate incidental spatial memory and recall deficits in amnesia. *Neuropsychologia, 29,* 749-770.

Squire, L. R. (1981). Two forms of human amnesia: An analysis of forgetting. *Journal of Neuroscience, 1,* 635-640.

Squire, L. R. (1982). Comparisons between forms of amnesia: Some deficits are unique to Korsakoff's syndrome. *Journal of Experimental Psychology: Learning, Memory, and Cognition, 8,* 560-572.

Squire, L. R. (1987). *Memory and brain.* Oxford: Oxford University Press.

Squire, L. R., Amaral, D. G., Zola-Morgan, S., Kritchevsky, M., & Press, G. (1989). Description of brain injury in the amnesic patient N. A. based on magnetic resonance imaging. *Experimental Neurology, 105,* 23-35.

Squire, L. R., Haist, F., & Shimamura, A. P. (1989). The neurology of memory: Quantitative assessment of retrograde amnesia in two types of amnesic patients. *Journal of Neuroscience, 9,* 828-839.

Stevens, M. (1979). Famous Personality Test: A test for measuring remote memory. *Bulletin of the British Psychological Society, 32,* 211.

Stuss, D. T., & Benson, D. F. (1986). *The frontal lobes.* New York: Raven Press.

Sullivan, E. V., Corkin, S., & Growdon, J. H. (1986). Verbal and non-verbal short-term memory in patients with Alzheimer's disease and in healthy elderly subjects. *Developmental Neuropsychology, 2,* 387-400.

Warrington, E. K., & Weiskrantz, L. (1970). Amnesic syndrome: Consolidation or retrieval? *Nature, 228,* 628-630.

Welsh, K., Butters, N., Hughes, J., Mohs, R., & Heyman, A. (1991). Detection of abnormal memory decline in mild cases of Alzheimer's disease using CERAD neuropsychological measures. *Archives of Neurology, 48,* 278-281.

Winocur, G., & Kinsbourne, M. (1978). Contextual cueing as an aid to Korsakoff amnesics. *Neuropsychologia, 16,* 671-682.

Winocur, G., Oxbury, S., Roberts, R., Agnetti, V., & Davis, C. (1984). Amnesia in a patient with bilateral lesions to the thalamus. *Neuropsychologia, 22,* 123-143.

Zola-Morgan, S., Squire, L. R., & Amaral, D. G. (1986). Human amnesia and the medial temporal region: Enduring memory impairment following a bilateral lesion limited to field CA1 of the hippocampus. *Journal of Neuroscience, 6,* 2950-2967.

12

Transient Global Amnesia

MARK KRITCHEVSKY

Transient global amnesia (TGA) is a short-lasting neurological condition in which memory impairment is the prominent deficit. It was first described by Bender (1956) and Guyotat and Courjon (1956), and later named and extensively characterized by Fisher and Adams (1958, 1964). Subsequent reports have dealt extensively with the neurological features of TGA and have discussed the neuropsychological profile of the TGA patient during and after the episode.

The Clinical Picture

The typical TGA episode is a 10-hour period of severe anterograde amnesia with some associated retrograde amnesia (Kritchevsky, 1987). The episode usually begins suddenly, lasts for at least several hours, and gradually resolves over several hours to a day. Most episodes last 2 to 12 hours (Caplan, 1985; Kritchevsky, 1989; Miller, Petersen, Metter, Millikan, & Yanagihara, 1987). One-third of TGA episodes are precipitated by physical or psychological stress (Fisher, 1982; Miller et al., 1987). The patient with TGA is often believed to be "confused" by family members. Nonetheless, careful neurological examination during the episode reveals that the patient has a relatively isolated amnesic syndrome and confirms that nearly all abnormal behavior during the episode is attributable to the amnesia (Donaldson, 1985; Gordon & Marin, 1979; Patten, 1971; Shuttleworth & Wise, 1973). Immediate memory is normal, and the patient has normal forward digit span. In contrast, he or she can recall little or no new verbal or nonverbal material a few minutes after being instructed to remember this material, and he or she characteristically asks the same question several or many times because of inability to recall the response. During TGA the patient also has a patchy loss of recall for events dating from several hours to many years before the attack. Personal identity is never lost. The patient often is unusually quiet and passive during the episode, but may be agitated. He or she frequently is aware of a problem and may repeat, "I think something is the matter with me," or "What's wrong? Have I had a stroke?" Mental status examination is otherwise normal, and the general neurological examination reveals no abnormality of the visual, auditory, somatosensory, or motor systems.

TGA is not uncommon, and it is a benign condition. Most TGA patients are over 50, and 75% are 50 to 69 years old (Caplan, 1985; Fisher, 1982; Miller et al., 1987). The estimated incidence of TGA is 5–10 per 100,000 per year for persons of all ages and 23–32 per 100,000 per year for persons older than 50 years (Koski & Marttila, 1990; Miller et al., 1987). The TGA patient has a good prognosis. Since TGA has a recurrence rate of 3–5% per year for at least 5 years after the first attack, some patients will have TGA more than once (Hinge, Jensen, Kjaer, Marquardsen, & Olivarius, 1986; Miller et al., 1987; Nausieda & Sherman, 1979; Shuping, Rollinson, & Toole, 1980). However, the TGA patient does not have an increased incidence of subsequent stroke (Hinge et al., 1986; Miller et al., 1987), or of serious or significant permanent memory deficit or other cognitive dysfunction (Kritchevsky, 1989; but see also Hodges & Oxbury, 1990).

The Neuropsychological Picture

The neuropsychological characterization of the patient with TGA has been difficult because of the temporary nature of the condition. Probably fewer than half of TGA patients see a physician during the episode, and of these, only a fraction see a neurologist or neuropsychologist while the amnesia is still severe. Moreover, neurologists know that TGA is benign and do not refer the TGA patient for neuropsychological testing, particularly during the episode. It is therefore not surprising that only 23 patients with TGA have been examined with formal neuropsychological tests during the episode of amnesia (Gallassi, Lorusso, & Stracciari, 1986; Hodges & Ward, 1989; Kritchevsky & Squire, 1989; Kritchevsky, Squire, & Zouzounis, 1988; Meador, Loring, King, & Nichols, 1988; Regard & Landis, 1984; Stillhard, Landis, Schiess, Regard, & Sialer, 1990; Stracciari, Rebucci, & Gallassi, 1987; Wilson, Koller, & Kelly, 1980). In addition, a patient with TGA can only be studied for 1 to 2 hours during the episode because of the onset of patient fatigue and the spontaneous resolution of the condition.

My colleagues and I have tested 11 patients during an attack of TGA (Kritchevsky & Squire, 1989; Kritchevsky et al., 1988; also discussed in Kritchevsky, 1989). The patients were tested between 2 and 11 hours after the onset of TGA, and all patients had severe memory problems at this time. We also tested 10 normal subjects on the tests of anterograde amnesia. These subjects averaged 68.8 years of age (65.4 for the TGA patients) and 12.0 years of education (12.8 for the TGA patients).

Three tests of anterograde amnesia were used. Two forms of each of these tests were employed—one during TGA and the other after TGA. We administered the two forms in one order to six of the patients and in the opposite order to the other five patients. In the story recall test, subjects were read a short prose passage (Gilbert, Levee, & Catalano, 1968) with the instruction, "When I am finished I want you to tell me as much of it as you can remember." Immediately thereafter, and again after a delay of 10–20 minutes, subjects attempted to recall the passage. The score was the number of story segments correctly recalled (maximum score = 19 or 21 segments). In the paired-associate learning test, we presented 10 unrelated noun–noun pairs (e.g., "army–table") on index cards at the rate of 6 seconds per pair, on each of three study trials (Jones, 1974). Following each study trial, we asked subjects to recall the second word of each pair upon seeing the first. For each trial the word pairs were presented in a different order. The maximum score for each trial was 10. In the diagram recall test, subjects were asked to copy either the Rey–Osterrieth (Osterrieth, 1944) or Taylor (Milner & Teuber, 1968) diagram. After a 10- to 20-minute delay, without forewarning, we asked them to draw the diagram from memory. The maximum score was 36 points.

All 11 patients had severe anterograde amnesia for verbal and nonverbal material. Figure 12.1 shows performance on the test of story recall. Immediate recall was impaired during TGA, in comparison both with the performance after TGA, $t(10) = 2.2$, $p = .05$, and with the performance of control subjects, $t(19) = 2.2$, $p < .05$. Impaired performance on the test of immediate recall reflects the fact that, for stories as long as these (three lines of text), immediate recall tests both immediate memory and the form of long-term memory that is impaired in amnesia. Delayed recall of verbal material also was impaired during TGA in comparison both with performance after TGA, $t(10) = 8.9$, $p < .01$, and with the performance of control subjects, $t(19) = 9.6$, $p < .01$.

Figure 12.2 shows performance on the test of paired-associate learning. A two-way analysis of variance (during or after TGA $\times$ three learning trials) showed that learning was impaired during TGA, $F(1, 10) = 31.9$, $p < .01$. The effect of trials was also significant, $F(2, 20) = 38.3$, $p < .01$, as was the interaction of TGA $\times$ trials, $F(2, 20) = 12.2$, $p < .01$. The trials effect indicates that some learning occurred across trials, and the interaction indicates that more learning occurred after TGA than during the episode. The performance of patients during TGA also was impaired compared with the performance of the control group, $F(1, 19) = 26.5$, $p < .01$.

Figure 12.3 shows performance on the diagram recall test. The ability to reconstruct the diagram from memory was impaired during TGA in comparison both with

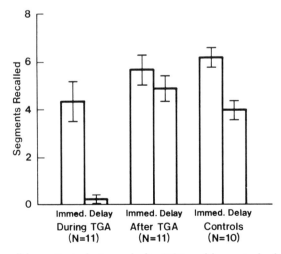

FIGURE 12.1. Story recall by patients during and after TGA and by control subjects. Recall was tested immediately after presentation of the story (Immed.) and again after a delay of 10–20 minutes (Delay). Brackets show standard errors of the mean. The data are from Kritchevsky and Squire (1989) and Kritchevsky et al. (1988). The figure is from "Transient Global Amnesia" (p. 174) by M. Kritchevsky, 1989, in F. Boller and J. Grafman (Eds.), *Handbook of Neuropsychology* (Vol. 3, pp. 167–182). Amsterdam: Elsevier. Copyright 1989 by Elsevier Science Publishers. Reprinted by permission.

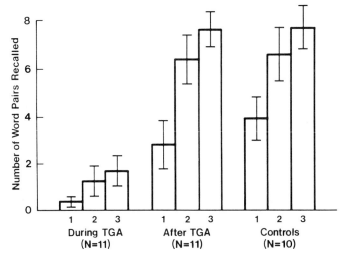

FIGURE 12.2. Paired-associate learning by patients during and after TGA and by control subjects. Ten word pairs were presented on each of three study trials. After each study trial, the first word of each pair was presented, and subjects attempted to recall the second word of the pair. Brackets show standard errors of the mean. The data are from Kritchevsky and Squire (1989) and Kritchevsky et al. (1988). The figure is from "Transient Global Amnesia" (p. 175) by M. Kritchevsky, 1989, in F. Boller and J. Grafman (Eds.), *Handbook of Neuropsychology* (Vol. 3, pp. 167-182). Amsterdam: Elsevier. Copyright 1989 by Elsevier Science Publishers. Reprinted by permission.

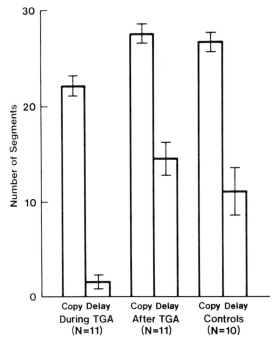

FIGURE 12.3. Copy and recall of a diagram by patients during and after TGA and by control subjects. Reconstruction of the figure was attempted 10-20 minutes after copying it. Brackets show standard errors of the mean. The data are from Kritchevsky and Squire (1989) and Kritchevsky et al. (1988). The figure is from "Transient Global Amnesia" (p. 175) by M. Kritchevsky, 1989, in F. Boller and J. Grafman (Eds.), *Handbook of Neuropsychology* (Vol. 3, pp. 167-182). Amsterdam: Elsevier. Copyright 1989 by Elsevier Science Publishers. Reprinted by permission.

performance after TGA, t (10) = 7.0, $p < .01$, and in comparison with the performance of control subjects, t (19) = 4.0, $p < .01$.

Two other points concern the anterograde amnesia of our TGA patients. First, there appeared to be a correlation of severity of anterograde amnesia with time of onset since TGA (Kritchevsky & Squire, 1989). Second, performance after TGA was fully recovered on all three tests of anterograde amnesia. The scores of the TGA patients were not noticeably different from the scores of the control subjects (all p's $> .10$).

Three tests were used to assess the retrograde amnesia of our TGA patients. The public events recall and recognition tests were administered to six patients between July 1, 1987 and December 31, 1987 (Kritchevsky & Squire, 1989). These tests consisted of questions about public events that had occurred from 1950 to 1985. We presented the recall test orally and then presented the recognition test in a four-alternative, multiple-choice format to be completed by the subject. Two alternate forms of the recall and recognition tests were used. Each form consisted of 9 to 15 items on the four decades covered by the tests. During TGA we gave three patients one form of the recall and recognition tests, and three the other form. After TGA we administered both forms to all patients. An extensive personalized test of past memory was given to three patients (Kritchevsky & Squire, 1989). (A shorter version of this test was given to five previous TGA patients, described in Kritchevsky et al., 1988.) The examiner asked questions concerning specific public or personal events that could be dated either to a recent day or month or to a more remote time period. The three patients were asked an average of 81 questions, selected on the basis of their interests and experiences. Only those questions answered correctly after TGA (mean = 67 questions) were considered in the analysis of memory function during TGA. Seventy-nine percent of the questions concerned public events. (These questions differed from those used in the public events recall and recognition tests.) The other 21% of the questions concerned personal events. Questions that could not be answered after TGA were considered to be outside a patient's fund of knowledge.

All 11 TGA patients had retrograde amnesia (Kritchevsky & Squire, 1989; Kritchevsky et al., 1988), and those patients who were studied most intensively all had a temporally graded retrograde amnesia covering at least 20 years prior to the onset of TGA (Kritchevsky & Squire, 1989). Performance on the public events recall test is shown in the left panel of Figure 12.4. A two-way analysis of variance (during or after TGA × four time periods) revealed a significant main effect of TGA, F (1, 5) = 22.2, $p < .01$, indicating that recall was impaired during TGA compared with after TGA. The effect of time period was also significant, F (3, 15) = 4.3, $p < .05$, reflecting that older memories were better recalled overall than recent ones. The interaction of TGA × time period was not significant ($p > .10$). Post hoc paired t tests showed that recall during TGA was impaired compared with recall after TGA for the time periods 1980 to 1985, t (5) = 3.9, $p < .05$; 1970 to 1979, t (5) = 4.3, $p < .01$; and 1960 to 1969, t (5) = 4.6, $p < .01$. Recall for events of the time period 1950 to 1959 was similar during and after TGA ($p > .10$).

Performance on the public events recognition test is shown in the right panel of Figure 12.4. A two-way analysis of variance (during or after TGA × four time periods) yielded a significant main effect of TGA, F (1, 5) = 11.7, $p < .05$. Recognition of

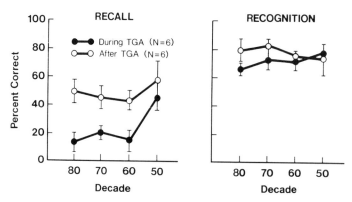

FIGURE 12.4. Performance during and after TGA on public events recall and recognition tests. Patients were asked questions about public events that had occurred from 1950 to 1985 (left panel). They then attempted to recognize the correct answers to the same questions on a four-alternative multiple-choice test (right panel). Brackets show standard errors of the mean. Patients were tested in 1987. From "Transient Global Amnesia: Evidence for Extensive, Temporally Graded Retrograde Amnesia" (p. 215) by M. Kritchevsky and L. R. Squire, 1989, *Neurology, 39*, 213–218. Copyright 1989 by Edgell Communications. Reprinted by permission.

public events was impaired during TGA compared with after TGA. There was no main effect of time period and no TGA × time period interaction. Post hoc paired *t* tests showed that recognition during TGA was impaired compared with after TGA for the time period 1980 to 1985, t (5) = 2.5, $p < .05$, but not for the other time periods (p's > .10).

Table 12.1 shows a similar pattern of retrograde amnesia for the three patients who were given the extensive personalized test of past memory. Retrograde amnesia was most severe for events that occurred during the 1½ years preceding the TGA. It was present for events that occurred in the 25 years before this time period, although fewer memories were affected. There was little evidence of retrograde amnesia before

TABLE 12.1. Results of the Personalized Test of Past Memory

	1986–1987	1980–1985	1970–1979	1960–1969	1940–1959	1930–1939
Case 1	14% (22)	28% (21)	50% (14)	80% (10)	100% (3)	83% (6)
Case 2	36% (22)	63% (27)	64% (11)	67% (6)	100% (4)	50% (2)
Case 3	42% (19)	61% (18)	60% (5)	100% (3)	100% (2)	100% (7)
Public events	27% (48)	48% (54)	57% (30)	86% (14)	100% (7)	86% (7)
Personal events	40% (15)	67% (12)	— (0)	60% (5)	100% (2)	88% (8)

Note. The percentage scores show the proportion of memories that could be recalled from each time period during TGA. The numbers in parentheses indicate the total number of memories queried in each time period that could be recalled after TGA. The row labeled "Public events" sums the data for all questions about public events that were asked during TGA. The row labeled "Personal events" sums the data for all questions about autobiographical material that were asked during TGA. Patients were tested in 1987. From "Transient Global Amnesia: Evidence for Extensive, Temporally Graded Retrograde Amnesia" (p. 216) by M. Kritchevsky and L. R. Squire, 1989, *Neurology, 39*, 213–218. Copyright 1989 by Edgell Communications. Reprinted by permission.

1960. Also, the retrograde amnesia affected both personal and public events, and it was patchy, as all patients were able to recall some events that had occurred within the time interval affected by retrograde amnesia.

Two other points deserve comment. First, permanent retrograde amnesia may have occurred for events occurring several hours to several days prior to TGA onset (Kritchevsky & Squire, 1989; Kritchevsky et al., 1988). Second, for five patients there appeared to be a correlation of the extent of retrograde amnesia with the severity of anterograde amnesia (Kritchevsky et al., 1988).

In general, our findings are consistent with the observations of other investigators. Twelve other patients examined during TGA with neuropsychological tests of new learning ability also had anterograde amnesia for verbal and, when tested, nonverbal material (Gallassi et al., 1986; Hodges & Ward, 1989; Meador et al., 1988; Regard & Landis, 1984; Stillhard et al., 1990; Stracciari et al., 1987; Wilson et al., 1980). Five of these patients also had a temporally graded retrograde amnesia during TGA (Hodges & Ward, 1989). In contrast to our findings, Hodges and Ward (1989) found no correlation between severity of anterograde and retrograde amnesia in their five patients, and Hodges and Oxbury (1990) suggested that there may be mild residual impairment of verbal memory and remote memory after TGA. Further investigations will clarify these issues.

The Cause

TGA is probably due to temporary dysfunction of bilateral medial temporal lobe or medial diencephalic structures important for memory. Indeed, single-photon emission computed tomography and positron emission tomography studies generally have supported temporal lobe dysfunction in TGA (Croisile & Trillet, 1990; Stillhard et al., 1990). This dysfunction is probably mediated by hypoperfusion of these brain regions, although the cause of this decreased blood flow remains unknown (see discussions in Caplan, 1985, and Kritchevsky, 1989). Thus, the benign course of TGA makes transient ischemic attack, due to thrombotic or embolic blockage of one or more blood vessels of the brain, an unlikely cause of TGA. Transient migrainous vasospasm of posterior circulation vessels could result in an episode of amnesia. Yet migraine is an unlikely cause of TGA because most TGA patients have neither a history of migraine nor evidence of ongoing migraine during the episode of amnesia. Caplan (1985) proposed that acute arterial dyscontrol, manifested as a transient period of altered vascular tone in the arteries of the vertebrobasilar territory, could result in the benign, temporary amnesic syndrome seen in TGA. This phenomenon may be similar to migraine and would explain the occasional presence during TGA of headache and other migrainous manifestations.

Summary

The goal of this chapter has been to characterize the amnesia of patients with TGA and to compare the performance of TGA patients with the performance of other amnesic patients who were administered the same memory tests. My colleagues and I have found that patients with TGA have severe anterograde amnesia for verbal and nonverbal material, and temporally graded retrograde amnesia covering at least 20 years before the onset of amnesia. All patients have had a complete recovery of memory functions after the episode, except for permanent amnesia for most of the time period of the episode and possible permanent retrograde amnesia for events that occurred several hours to several days before TGA onset.

The amnesia of TGA patients is similar to that of many other well-studied amnesic patients with known bilateral medial temporal or medial diencephalic lesions (Kritchevsky & Squire, 1989). Thus, our characterization of the amnesia of patients with TGA supports the idea that TGA is caused by temporary dysfunction of bilateral medial temporal lobe or medial diencephalic structures important for memory. On the other hand, patient R. B., who had damage limited to field CA1 of the hippocampus, had severe anterograde amnesia for verbal and nonverbal material but did not exhibit significant retrograde amnesia (Zola-Morgan, Squire, & Amaral, 1986). Because TGA patients have extensive retrograde amnesia, the area of dysfunction in TGA, if medial temporal, must involve more than just the CA1 region of the hippocampus.

REFERENCES

Bender, M. B. (1956). Syndrome of isolated episode of confusion with amnesia. *Journal of the Hillside Hospital, 5,* 212-215.

Caplan, L. B. (1985). Transient global amnesia. In J. A. M. Frederiks (Ed.), *Handbook of clinical neurology* (Vol. 1, pp. 205-218). Amsterdam: Elsevier.

Croisile, B., & Trillet, M. (1990). Cerebral blood flow and transient global amnesia. *Journal of Neurology, Neurosurgery and Psychiatry, 53,* 361.

Donaldson, I. M. (1985). "Psychometric" assessment during transient global amnesia. *Cortex, 21,* 149-152.

Fisher, C. M. (1982). Transient global amnesia: Precipitating activities and other observations. *Archives of Neurology, 39,* 605-608.

Fisher, C. M., & Adams, R. D. (1958). Transient global amnesia. *Transactions of the American Neurological Association, 83,* 143-145.

Fisher, C. M., & Adams, R. D. (1964). Transient global amnesia. *Acta Neurologica Scandinavica, 40*(Suppl. 9), 1-83.

Gallassi, R., Lorusso, S., & Stracciari, A. (1986). Neuropsychological findings during a transient global amnesia attack and its follow-up. *Italian Journal of Neurological Sciences, 7,* 45-49.

Gilbert, J. G., Levee, R. F., & Catalano, F. L. (1968). A preliminary report on a new memory scale. *Perceptual and Motor Skills, 27,* 277-278.

Gordon, B., & Marin, O. S. M. (1979). Transient global amnesia: An extensive case report. *Journal of Neurology, Neurosurgery and Psychiatry, 42,* 572-575.

Guyotat, J., & Courjon, J. (1956). Les ictus amnésiques. *Le Journal de Médecine de Lyon, 37,* 697-701.

Hinge, H. H., Jensen, T. S., Kjaer, M., Marquardsen, J., & Olivarius, B. (1986). The prognosis of transient global amnesia: Results of a multicenter study. *Archives of Neurology, 43,* 673-676.

Hodges, J. R., & Oxbury, S. M. (1990). Persistent memory impairment following transient global amnesia. *Journal of Clinical and Experimental Neuropsychology, 12,* 904-920.

Hodges, J. R., & Ward, C. D. (1989). Observations during transient global amnesia: A behavioural and neuropsychological study of five cases. *Brain, 112,* 595-620.

Jones, M. K. (1974). Imagery as a mnemonic aid after left temporal lobectomy: Contrast between material-specific and generalized memory disorders. *Neuropsychologia, 12,* 21-30.

Koski, K. J., & Marttila, R. J. (1990). Transient global amnesia: Incidence in an urban population. *Acta Neurologica Scandinavica, 81,* 358-360.

Kritchevsky, M. (1987). Transient global amnesia: When memory temporarily disappears. *Postgraduate Medicine, 82,* 95-100.

Kritchevsky, M. (1989). Transient global amnesia. In F. Boller & J. Grafman (Eds.), *Handbook of neuropsychology* (Vol. 3, pp. 167-182). Amsterdam: Elsevier.

Kritchevsky, M., & Squire, L. R. (1989). Transient global amnesia: Evidence for extensive, temporally graded retrograde amnesia. *Neurology, 39,* 213-218.

Kritchevsky, M., Squire, L. R., & Zouzounis, J. A. (1988). Transient global amnesia: Characterization of anterograde and retrograde amnesia. *Neurology, 38,* 213-219.

Meador, K. J., Loring, D. W., King, D. W., & Nichols, F. T. (1988). The P3 evoked potential and transient global amnesia. *Archives of Neurology, 45,* 465-467.

Miller, J. W., Petersen, R. C., Metter, E. J., Millikan, C. H., & Yanagihara, T. (1987). Transient global amnesia: Clinical characteristics and prognosis. *Neurology, 37,* 733-737.

Milner, B., & Teuber, H.-L. (1968). Alteration of perception and memory in man: Reflections on methods. In L. Weiskrantz (Ed.), *Analysis of behavioral change* (pp. 268-375). New York: Harper & Row.

Nausieda, P. A., & Sherman, I. C. (1979). Long-term prognosis in transient global amnesia. *Journal of the American Medical Association, 241,* 392-393.

Osterrieth, P. A. (1944). Le test de copie d'une figure complexe. *Archives de Psychologie, 30,* 206-356.

Patten, B. M. (1971). Transient global amnesia syndrome. *Journal of the American Medical Association, 217,* 690-691.

Regard, M., & Landis, T. (1984). Transient global amnesia: Neuropsychological dysfunction during attack and recovery in two "pure" cases. *Journal of Neurology, Neurosurgery and Psychiatry, 47,* 668-672.

Shuping, J. R., Rollinson, R. D., & Toole, J. F. (1980). Transient global amnesia. *Annals of Neurology, 7,* 281-285.

Shuttleworth, E. C., & Wise, G. R. (1973). Transient global amnesia due to arterial embolism. *Archives of Neurology, 29,* 340-342.

Stillhard, G., Landis, T., Schiess, R., Regard, M., & Sialer, G. (1990). Bitemporal hypoperfusion in transient global amnesia: 99m-Tc-HM- PAO SPECT and neuropsychological findings during and after an attack. *Journal of Neurology, Neurosurgery and Psychiatry, 53,* 339-342.

Stracciari, A., Rebucci, G. G., & Gallassi, R. (1987). Transient global amnesia: Neuropsychological study of a "pure" case. *Journal of Neurology, 234,* 126-127.

Wilson, R. S., Koller, W., & Kelly, M. P. (1980). The amnesia of transient global amnesia. *Journal of Clinical Neuropsychology, 2,* 259-266.

Zola-Morgan, S., Squire, L. R., & Amaral, D. G. (1986). Human amnesia and the medial temporal region: Enduring memory impairment following a bilateral lesion limited to field CA1 of the hippocampus. *Journal of Neuroscience, 6,* 2950-2967.

13

Detecting Amnesia's Impostors

JASON BRANDT

The amnesic syndrome, a severe and relatively pure impairment in new learning as a result of brain damage, has several classes of impersonators. The first class is composed of organic mental disorders in which memory is impaired, but not out of proportion to other cognitive functions. Primary degenerative dementia (e.g., that produced by Alzheimer's disease) is probably the most common of these disorders. It should be noted, however, that patients with early Alzheimer's disease often have isolated memory dysfunction, and may therefore be described as having an amnesic syndrome before they meet criteria for a dementia syndrome. The second class of impostors is composed of the somatoform and dissociative disorders. In these conditions, there may be prominent disturbances of memory in the absence of documentable brain lesions. The third class, and the focus of this chapter, is composed of malingered and factitious amnesia. In these conditions, there is the deliberate feigning of memory impairment in the setting of obvious external incentives (malingering) or in the absence of such incentives (factitious disorder).

Why should a volume on the neuropsychology of memory contain a chapter on malingered amnesia?[1] First, probably every practicing neuropsychologist has encountered patients who appear to be exaggerating, or totally fabricating, a memory impairment. Patients claiming amnesia usually maintain that they cannot remember one or more specific items of information (especially when seen in a forensic setting), or that they have more pervasive cognitive impairments (Rubinsky & Brandt, 1986). Thus the number of patients who claim a pure amnesic syndrome is probably relatively small. Nonetheless, being able to distinguish real from malingered memory impairment is of clinical value, as it will direct treatment efforts. (For a debate on treatment implications of this distinction, see Pankratz & Erickson, 1990.) Another reason for interest in malingering is that in studying how people fake amnesia, we may learn something about the structure and processes of normal memory. That is, the malingerer's mental model of memory and his understanding of the fractionation of memory that takes place in the amnesic syndrome are revealed by his or her task performances (Brandt, 1988).

---

[1]Because a patient's motivation to appear "ill" may not always be knowable to the clinician, and for the sake of simplicity of exposition, the terms "malingered" and "malingering" are used to describe deliberate efforts to appear memory-impaired, whether in the presence of obvious incentives or otherwise.

Choice of Research Subjects

A major obstacle to research on malingering is that the research subjects of greatest interest (patients seen in a clinical context who are actually feigning symptoms) rarely confess their deceitfulness, even when confronted with evidence. Therefore, most of the descriptions have been of *suspected* or *assumed* malingerers—subjects whose complaints are so incompatible with the available evidence as to be unbelievable. This approach is not, of course, without difficulty, since the range of possible neuropsychological presentations is not fully known. What might today appear to be an impossible constellations of behavioral–cognitive signs and symptoms might be shown in the future to be a genuine syndrome. One might easily imagine how a patient with blindsight, who reports seeing nothing in his or her "blind" field but can nonetheless avoid hazards, might be labeled a malingerer by those unfamiliar with this syndrome. Similarly, before the sparing of certain learning and memory abilities of patients with organic amnesia became well known, it is conceivable that some amnesic patients who were observed to improve their task performances with practice might have been thought to be feigning their disability.

An alternative research approach to the use of assumed malingerers is to use simulators—that is, healthy subjects who are instructed to feign amnesia. The assumption underlying studies of simulators is that the average person holds inaccurate beliefs about amnesia that can be detected with appropriate measures. An advantage of this type of study is that the researcher knows who is faking and who is not. A disadvantage is that the motivation of subjects to perform convincingly and deceive the examiner is rarely as strong as that of a criminal defendant claiming incompetence to stand trial, for example, or that of the plaintiff in a large personal injury suit. Recent data (discussed below) suggest that suspected malingerers and simulators actually perform quite differently on some tasks designed to detect feigned memory impairment.

Interview-Based Methods

It is a basic assumption in forensic psychology and psychiatry that inconsistencies in a patient's responding during an interview suggest malingering (Rogers, 1988). However, the recent discoveries that patients with true organic amnesia can recall information under some conditions and not under others, and that the differences between the two conditions may be as subtle as the wording of retrieval instructions (Graf, Squire, & Mandler, 1984), call into question the assumption that variability in responding to the same question asked in different ways is a sign of malingering.

A colleague and I (Wiggins & Brandt, 1988) developed a 14-item autobiographical interview composed of questions judged to be very simple even for moderately amnesic patients. We administered this interview to 4 amnesic patients, 27 normal control subjects, and 48 healthy people asked to simulate amnesia.[2] The interview has recently been administered to another 9 true amnesic patients. As seen in Table 13.1,

---

[2]Three different "amnesia-inducing" scenarios were presented to independent subgroups of simulators. Since the test performances of the subgroups did not differ, their results were pooled.

TABLE 13.1. Percentage of Patients Giving Incorrect, Implausible, or "I Don't Know" Responses on Autobiographical Interview

Question	Nomals (n = 27)	Amnesics (n = 13)	Simulators (n = 48)
1. "What is your name?"	0	0	25
2. "What is your age?"	0	31	35
3. "What is your date of birth?"	0	0	42
4. "What is your home telephone number?"	0	38	42
5. "What is your home address?"	0	0	12
6. "What is your Social Security number?"	4	38	48
7. "What is/was your mother's first name?"	0	0	17
8. "What is/was your mother's maiden name?"	0	0	29
9. "What is/was your father's first name?"	0	0	17
10. "What are/were your brothers' and/or sisters' names?"	0	0	23
11. "What did you have for breakfast this morning?"	0	23	25
12. "What did you have for dinner last night?"	0	61	42
The following two questions were asked 24 hours later:			
13. "What is my [the examiner's] name?"	0	77	37
If #13 failed, ask:			
14. "Choose my name from among these four choices . . ."	n/a	38	10

Note. Adapted from "The Detection of Simulated Amnesia" (p. 65) by E. C. Wiggins and J. Brandt, 1988, *Law and Human Behavior, 12,* 57–78. Copyright 1988 by Plenum Publishing Corp. Adapted by permission.

the simulators overplayed the role and performed more poorly than the genuine amnesics on most items, especially those of personal identity. The only items on which they demonstrated better memory than the real amnesics were the delayed-recall and delayed-recognition items. These were precisely the items that were most difficult for the genuine amnesics.

Very Simple Tasks

Another strategy often used to detect malingered amnesia is to administer a task that is actually very simple but disguised as a difficult task. The person motivated to perform poorly may do so on such a task. Perhaps the most widely used task for this purpose is the Rey 15-Item Memory Test (Rey, 1964; Lezak, 1983). The subject is shown a card on which there are 15 symbols and is given 10 seconds to memorize the material. Since the symbols are related ("A, B, C," "1, 2, 3," etc.), the task is actually very easy. Lezak (1983) has suggested that anyone scoring 9 or below either is "significantly deteriorated" or "consciously or unconsciously wishes to appear impaired" (p. 618). Although this task appears to enjoy widespread use, and the performance of various patient groups on the task has been described (Goldberg & Miller, 1986; Bernard & Fowler, 1990), its validity as a test of malingering has been assumed rather than demonstrated.

Recently, we (Schretlen, Brandt, Krafft, & Van Gorp, 1991) examined performance on this test in nine groups of subjects (total $n = 304$). Five groups were composed of genuine patients: those with traumatic brain injury, primary dementia, amnesic syndrome (several etiologies), severe mental illness (mostly schizophrenia with mental retardation), and mixed neuropsychiatric illnesses. Two groups were composed of subjects instructed to malinger, faking either amnesia or "insanity." A group of seven suspected malingerers and a normal control group were also included. The performance of the nine groups on the Rey 15-Item Memory Test is shown in Figure 13.1. It is noteworthy that the patients suspected of faking performed the most poorly, but not more so than patients with genuine amnesia. In contrast, normal subjects instructed to feign amnesia were unable to do so; they performed as well as the normal control subjects. These data suggest that the Rey 15-Item Test may not be as useful in the detection of malingered amnesia as previously believed. They also illustrate that paying healthy people a small sum of money does not produce the same tendency to dissimulation as does having a strong intrinsic motivation to do so (e.g., a pending legal decision).

Symptom Validity Testing

A general strategy that has gained widespread acceptance as an indicator of malingering is "symptom validity testing" (Pankratz, 1983). This technique examines the patient's forced-choice recognition of material he or she has been presented. With such a procedure, chance performance (i.e., guessing) can easily be determined statistically. With a sufficient number of trials, the patient who is trying to appear amnesic will find

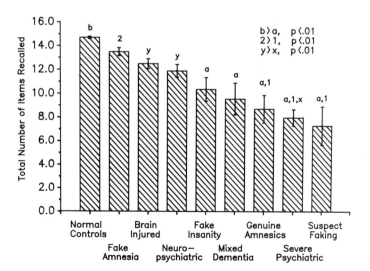

FIGURE 13.1. Performance on the Rey 15-Item Memory Test in nine groups of subjects. Means (± standard errors). From "Some Caveats in Using the Rey 15-Item Memory Test to Detect Malingered Amnesia" (p. 669) by D. Schretlen, J. Brandt, L. Krafft, and W. Van Grop, 1991, *Psychological Assessment, 3*, 667–672. Copyright 1991 by the American Psychological Association. Reprinted by permission.

it difficult to keep track of his or her responses, and may actually perform more poorly than chance. Thus, for example, with 100 two-alternative trials, no memory at all should yield approximately 50 correct responses. Deviation from this level of performance by as few as 10 trials (i.e., 40 correct, 60 incorrect) is extremely unlikely to occur by chance ($p < .03$) (Siegel, 1956). The poor performance can thus be assumed to be motivated (Binder & Pankratz, 1987; Hiscock & Hiscock, 1989).

We (Brandt, Rubinsky, & Lassen, 1985) demonstrated how a 20-item verbal recall and two-choice recognition test could be used to detect malingered amnesia. Three out of 10 college students instructed to simulate amnesia (but 0 out of 19 patients with genuine memory impairment) had recognition test performances worse than chance. A criminal defendant suspected of malingering amnesia (and other cognitive impairments) scored 3 out of 20 correct, significantly worse than chance.

In another study (Wiggins & Brandt, 1988), we administered a slightly different version of this verbal memory task, which we have come to call the Recall–Recognition Test, to three groups of subjects: 25 memory-disordered patients (15 of whom were recovering from closed head injuries), 48 healthy subjects simulating amnesia, and 27 nonsimulating normal control subjects. A 20-word list was presented for free recall, followed by two-alternative forced-choice recognition. One of two word lists was used for each subject, with the words from the unpresented list serving as the recognition foils. This version of the test rarely yields performances worse than chance. However, the relative performance on the recall and recognition portions was instructive. Simulators routinely underestimated the recall difficulties of amnesics and overestimated their recognition difficulties (see Figure 13.2). The genuinely memory-disordered patients improved most with the recognition procedure (mean increase of 12.52 words [$SD = 2.55$]), and the simulators improved least (mean increase of 9.02 words [$SD = 2.67$]), $t (71) = 5.40$, $p < .001$.

Recently, the Recall–Recognition Test was administered to 11 patients with severe amnesic syndromes and 4 patients who were suspected malingerers. The malingerers were patients who were referred for neuropsychological evaluation to the Cortical Function Laboratory of The Johns Hopkins Hospital. In all four cases, extensive examinations and neuroradiological tests failed to reveal any organic bases for the patients' cognitive complaints. In addition, each patient's symptoms were very severe, and the symptom patterns did not conform to any known neurological or psychiatric disorder. Finally, the results of other neuropsychological tests suggested deliberate attempts to "look bad." It is important to note that although the neuropsychological test results were considered in designating a patient an assumed malingerer, the data from other sources were convincing in and of themselves. They became only more overwhelming when the neuropsychological data were added.

The amnesic patients and assumed malingerers performed nearly identically on the free-recall portion of the Recall–Recognition Test. However, there was a large difference between the groups on the two-alternative, forced-choice recognition portion of the test. A group × condition (recall, recognition) mixed-design analysis of variance revealed a nonsignificant group effect; a significant condition effect, $F (1, 13) = 117.37$, $p < .0001$; and a significant group × condition interaction, $F (1, 13) = 8.66$, $p = .01$. The malingerers chose target words significantly less often than did the true amnesics, $t (13) = 2.69$, $p = .02$. In 9 of the 11 amnesic patients, two-choice recognition

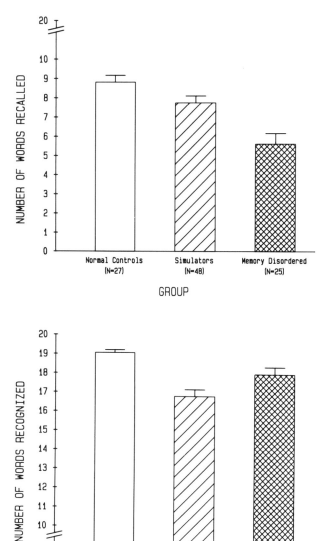

FIGURE 13.2. Performance on the free-recall (top panel) and two-alternative forced-choice recognition (bottom panel) portions of the Recall–Recognition Test in memory-disordered patients, healthy subjects simulating amnesia, and nonsimulating normal control subjects. Data from Wiggins and Brandt (1988). Bottom panel from "Malingered Amnesia" (p. 77) by J. Brandt, 1988, in R. Rogers (Ed.), *Clinical Assessment of Malingering and Deception.* New York: Guilford Press. Copyright 1988 by The Guilford Press. Reprinted by permission.

was at least nine words better than free recall. None of the four malingerers displayed an increase of this magnitude with recognition testing (Fisher's exact probability = .01).

Use of Implicit Memory Tasks

A recent approach to the detection of malingered amnesia involves exploiting the preserved learning and memory capacities of amnesic patients. The naive malingerer is assumed not to know that amnesic patients display their deficits most profoundly when explicit tests of memory are used, and can perform almost normally on tests of skill acquisition, perceptual priming, and the like. Thus, it is assumed that they would overplay the role and perform very poorly on tests of implicit memory as well as tests of explicit memory.

We (Wiggins & Brandt, 1988) had groups of simulators, normal control subjects, and a small group of genuinely amnesic patients attempt free recall of a 20-item word list. We administered a word stem completion task immediately thereafter and again 24 hours later. As on the Recall–Recognition Test, the recall performance of the simulators on this test was intermediate between that of the amnesics and normal controls. However, the simulators were less likely to complete the word stems with target words than were the other two groups, especially on delayed testing (see Figure 13.3).

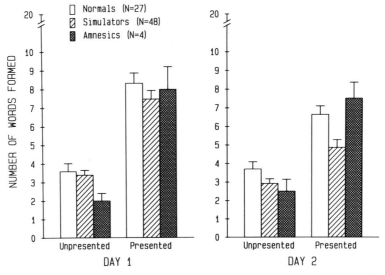

FIGURE 13.3. Performance on a word stem completion test by amnesic patients, normal subjects simulating amnesia, and normal control subjects. "Presented" denotes performance for the words that were presented on the to-be-remembered list. "Unpresented" refers to performance on a control list that the subjects had not heard before; this served as a baseline for guessing. From "The Detection of Simulated Amnesia" (p. 67) by E. C. Wiggins and J. Brandt, 1988, *Law and Human Behavior, 12,* 57–78. Copyright 1988 by Plenum Publishing Corp. Reprinted by permission.

On two other tests of implicit memory (reading of perceptually degraded words and naming of perceptually degraded pictures), the simulators displayed as much improvement over trials as did the amnesics. These results may suggest that the average naive person "knows" (implicitly) that improvement with practice on perceptual tasks is a different sort of memory from that which is impaired in amnesia. Alternatively, these implicit memory phenomena may be so automatic and effortless that they are difficult to inhibit willfully.

Qualitative Features of Explicit Memory Performance

Although there are few clear demonstrations of the utility of implicit memory tasks for distinguishing real from feigned amnesia, one aspect of explicit memory has proven useful repeatedly in our research: the serial position effect in free recall. It is reasonably well established that amnesic patients display either an attenuated or an absent primacy effect in free recall, arguably as a result of differential impairment in long-term memory (Baddeley & Warrington, 1970). When simulators perform free-recall tasks, their performance is lower overall, but they still produce the normal serial position function (Wiggins & Brandt, 1988) (see Figure 13.4).

Among other aspects of explicit memory that may be useful for the detection of malingered amnesia, but as yet remain unexamined, are imagery, meaningfulness, and semantic clustering effects in word list learning.

Conclusions and Caveats

At the present time, no individual test allows the detection of malingering with certainty in all cases. A combination of methods, possibly including the Wiggins and Brandt (1988) interview to assess malingered autobiographical amnesia and the Recall–Recognition Test to assess malingered anterograde amnesia, is recommended. Symptom validity testing is probably one of the most valuable general paradigms, because it allows a statistical probability to be placed on the likelihood that a given performance is that of a person with no memory for the material in question. However, its specificity (i.e., the probability that a true amnesic will test "negative") is almost certainly higher than its sensitivity (i.e., the probability that a malingerer will test "positive"). In addition, the predictive value and clinical utility of all test procedures for the detection of malingered amnesia will depend, to a great extent, on the base rate of malingering in the population being assessed. Clearly, those clinicians working in forensic settings or evaluating patients who are involved in personal injury litigation may expect higher rates of malingering than those in other clinical settings.

None of the available procedures allows a differentiation of malingered amnesia from factitious disorder or from "psychogenic" amnesia (dissociative disorder). The differentiation among these conditions depends on the patient's awareness of his or her motivations and on his or her will to deceive—aspects of the mental state that we have inadequate methods to assess. Indeed, some have questioned the usefulness of the distinction among these conditions altogether.

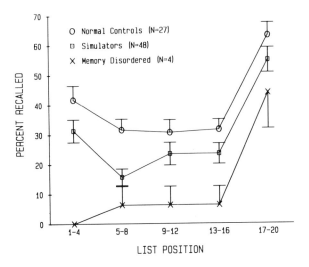

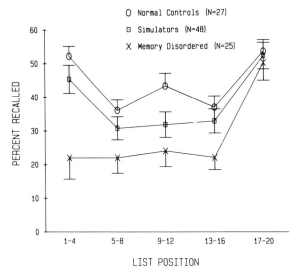

FIGURE 13.4. Serial position curves from free-recall portions of the Recall–Recognition Test (top panel) and a word stem completion test (bottom panel) for amnesic patients, simulators, and normal control subjects. From "The Detection of Simulated Amnesia" (pp. 66 and 73) by E. C. Wiggins and J. Brandt, 1988, *Law and Human Behavior, 12*, 57–78. Copyright 1988 by Plenum Publishing Corp. Reprinted by permission.

All the studies reviewed in this chapter compared suspected malingerers and simulators to genuine amnesics as if the latter were a homogeneous category. In fact, the various etiologies of organic amnesia produce syndromes with somewhat different cognitive characteristics (e.g., Butters & Miliotis, 1985; Heindel, Salmon, Shults, Walicke, & Butters, 1989; Squire, Haist, & Shimamura, 1989). However, these qualitative features have not yet been applied systematically in attempts to uncover malingering. Finally, it should be emphasized that the discovery that a patient is fabricating amnesia does not preclude the simultaneous existence of subtler, genuine memory impairment. In fact, it might be argued that malingerers have a higher-than-average likelihood of having psychiatric disorders (such as antisocial personality disorder) that predispose them to suffer minor brain damage (e.g., through head injuries or substance abuse). The clinician is cautioned against declaring a patient neuropsychologically "well" simply because that patient is being deceitful.

ACKNOWLEDGMENTS

I am extremely grateful to Elizabeth Wiggins, PhD, JD, Ralph H. B. Benedict, PhD, David Schretlen, PhD, and Laura Krafft, BA, for their invaluable assistance with several aspects of this research. June Corwin, PhD, and Phillip R. Slavney, MD, made very helpful comments on the chapter. This work was supported in part by National Institutes of Health Grants No. P50-AG05146 and No. P01-NS16375.

REFERENCES

Baddeley, A., & Warrington, E. K. (1970). Amnesia and the distinction between long and short-term memory. *Journal of Verbal Learning and Verbal Behavior, 91*, 176–189.

Bernard, L. C., & Fowler, W. (1990). Assessing the validity of memory complaints: Performance of brain-damaged and normal individuals on Rey's task to detect malingering. *Journal of Clinical Psychology, 46*, 432–436.

Binder, L. M., & Pankratz, L. (1987). Neuropsychological evidence of a factitious memory complaint. *Journal of Clinical and Experimental Neuropsychology, 9*, 167–171.

Brandt, J. (1988). Malingered amnesia. In R. Rogers (Ed.), *Clinical assessment of malingering and deception.* New York: Guilford Press.

Brandt, J., Rubinsky, E., & Lassen, G. (1985). Uncovering malingered amnesia. *Annals of the New York Academy of Sciences, 44*, 502–503.

Butters, N., & Miliotis, P. (1985). Amnesic disorders. In K. Heilman & E. Valenstein (Eds.), *Clinical neuropsychology* (2nd ed.). New York: Oxford University Press.

Goldberg, J. O., & Miller, H. R. (1986). Performance of psychiatric inpatients and intellectually deficient individuals on a task that assesses the validity of memory complaints. *Journal of Clinical Psychology, 42*, 792–795.

Graf, P., Squire, L. R., & Mandler, G. (1984). The information that amnesic patients do not forget. *Journal of Experimental Psychology: Learning, Memory and Cognition, 10*, 164–178.

Heindel, W. C., Salmon, D. P., Shults, C. W., Walicke, P. A., & Butters, N. (1989). Neuropsychological evidence for multiple implicit memory systems: A comparison of Alzheimer's, Huntington's and Parkinson's disease patients. *Journal of Neuroscience, 9*, 582–587.

Hiscock, M., & Hiscock, C. K. (1989). Refining the forced-choice method for the detection of malingering. *Journal of Clinical and Experimental Neuropsychology, 11*, 967–974.

Lezak, M. (1983). *Neuropsychological assessment* (2nd ed.). New York: Oxford University Press.

Pankratz, L. (1983). A new technique for the assessment and modification of feigned memory deficit. *Perceptual and Motor Skills, 57*, 367–372.

Pankratz, L., & Erickson, R. C. (1990). Two views of malingering. *Clinical Neuropsychologist, 4*, 379–389.

Rey, A. (1964). *L'examen clinique en psychologie.* Paris: Presses Universitaires de France.

Rogers, R. (Ed.). (1988). *Clinical assessment of malingering and deception.* New York: Guilford Press.

Rubinsky, E. W., & Brandt, J. (1986). Amnesia and criminal law: A clinical overview. *Behavioral Sciences and the Law, 4*, 27–46.

Schretlen, D., Brandt, J., Krafft, L., & Van Gorp, W. (1991). Some caveats in using the Rey 15-Item Memory Test to detect malingered amnesia. *Psychological Assessment, 3*, 667–672.

Siegel, S. (1956). *Nonparametric statistics for the behavioral sciences.* New York: McGraw-Hill.

Squire, L. R., Haist, F., & Shimamura, A. P. (1989). The neurology of memory: Quantitative assessment of retrograde amnesia in two groups of amnesic patients. *Journal of Neuroscience, 9*, 828–839.

Wiggins, E. C., & Brandt, J. (1988). The detection of simulated amnesia. *Law and Human Behavior, 12*, 57–78.

14

Systems of Motor Skill

DANIEL B. WILLINGHAM

The last 20 years have seen growing interest in taxonomies of memory, in which memory has been viewed not as a unitary faculty but as a number of systems. Each system handles different memory tasks and can operate independently of other systems. The systems are also thought to be anatomically separate. But what memory tasks does each system perform? The answer to that question has been the subject of debate (see Schacter, 1987, and Richardson-Klavehn & Bjork, 1988, for reviews). Despite the disagreements, all researchers appear to agree that motor skill learning can be viewed as a unitary faculty; that is, that all motor skills may be handled by the same memory system. I contend that there are actually independent systems of motor skill acquisition, and delineate three systems: one that learns mappings between perceptual and motor events, one that learns high-level motor plans, and one that learns to make movements spatially and temporally invariable. This chapter develops the reasoning for this proposal and offers evidence supporting it. The evidence is not conclusive, but is encouraging.

What Constitutes Proof for Multiple Memory Systems?

Neuropsychologists have pointed to neuroanatomical dissociations as evidence for multiple memory systems. For example, amnesic patients are impaired in tests of recognition and recall, but show the effect of previous experience on tests of repetition priming (e.g., Graf, Squire, & Mandler, 1984; Warrington & Weiskrantz, 1970) and perceptuomotor skill learning (Corkin, 1968; Nissen & Bullemer, 1987), and there are supporting data from animal models of amnesia (Mishkin, Malamut, & Bachevalier, 1984; Zola-Morgan & Squire, 1985). Nevertheless, some researchers assert that these findings do not compel different processes and/or representations at a cognitive level of description (Roediger, Rajaram, & Srinivas, 1990; Crowder, 1989). Some have suggested that the neuroanatomical data indicate a single, complex memory system with multiple dissociable components (Humphreys, Bain, & Pike, 1989). Indeed, the sharing of processes and representations very likely occurs in the execution of memory tasks that are supposedly handled by different systems, for there would be great redundancy otherwise; for example, there would be a lexicon for repetition priming and a second lexicon for reading.

If there is sharing among subsystems of processes or representations, why favor a multiple-systems framework over a framework positing one system with components? I propose that the multiple-systems view is useful if systems are defined functionally: A memory system is a set of processes and representations, instantiated in particular neural structures, that together serve a memory function. A particular process or representation may participate in more than one system, but there is little if any flexibility in the way they are used to solve memory tasks; they always operate the same way, but may be used in conjunction with different processes and representations as part of another memory system.

If memory systems are defined functionally, these functions dictate constraints on the way systems operate; fulfilling a particular function entails solving problems, and these problems can provide clues as to how the system is designed (see Marr, 1982, and Kosslyn, 1987, for further development of these ideas in research on vision and imagery). For example, some motor skills (such as using a computer mouse) require learning a new mapping between perceptual cues and motor responses. Learning a new mapping entails the solution of problems: How can a new perceptuomotor mapping be learned without disrupting existing mappings that are used in other situations? Recognition that this problem must be solved imposes constraints on theories of motor skill.

Finally, if different motor skill tasks pose very different problems for the motor skill system, one might expect that different rules of operation or different representations will be used to solve these problems. This implies that careful consideration of the problems the motor skill system must solve in learning different skills can help delineate systems of motor skill acquisition.

One would expect that the putative systems derived from a computational analysis would be corroborated by other methods—for example, dissociations between systems in brain-damaged patients, and strong neuroanatomical connections among brain sites that are part of the same system. In sum, one expects that separate systems (1) can operate independently; (2) serve different functions; and (3) have different neural bases. The challenge is to understand the problems to be solved by the motor skill system and to seek neuroanatomical evidence for separation of motor skill learning along the lines dictated by the computational analysis.

I begin with the assumption that the problems to be solved by the motor skill system may be inferred from the problems to be solved by the motor control system. This assumption is made because it appears that the brain sites underlying motor control are also the sites of plasticity in the system; it seems likely that motor skill processes are based directly on motor control processes. There is no clear evidence for separation of the generation of a motor response and the improvement of that response with practice. This contrasts with other systems of memory, in which there appear to be brain structures such as the hippocampus that, if damaged, disrupt memory but not other cognitive functions.

Three key problems have been outlined in motor control: perceptuomotor integration, excess degrees of freedom, and serial ordering (Pew & Rosenbaum, 1988). The goal is to examine these three problems as a potential taxonomy of motor skill. Are there separate brain mechanisms for the solution of these motor control problems, and do these mechanisms underlie separate systems of motor skill?

Perceptuomotor Integration

There are at least two ways that perceptual information must be integrated with motor information. In a visuomotor association, perceptual information dictates which movement should be made. For example, a red light when driving indicates that one should depress the brake pedal. Clearly, this sort of visuomotor association must be learned, because the visual stimulus is arbitrary.

The second perceptuomotor integration function is visual guidance. Visual information may provide feedback about an ongoing movement—for example, information about the car's position on the road helps one adjust the steering wheel. This guidance function also requires learning. For example, when one is learning to drive a car, the relationship between specific movements (mostly of the arms) and the resulting change in the car's position must be learned. More generally, learning occurs whenever the relationship of movements and their effect on the environment, as provided by visual feedback, is not known.

Visual guidance and visuomotor associations can be separated functionally, but, as will be seen, there is not yet strong evidence that they are separate neuroanatomically. Both functions seem to rely on the integrity of the premotor cortex (PMC), the posterior parietal cortex, and possibly the cerebellum.

Visuomotor Associations

Petrides (1982, 1985a, 1985b, 1986) and Passingham and his associates (Passingham, 1985, 1987; Halsband & Passingham, 1982; Halsband & Freund, 1990) have demonstrated that the PMC is important in associating arbitrary visual cues with motor responses. Monkeys and humans with PMC lesions are unable to learn such associations, though visual discrimination and motor control are adequate to perform the task, and other simple associations can be learned. In a typical experiment (Halsband & Passingham, 1982), a monkey is required to pull or twist a handle, depending on the color of a cue light. The monkey is trained to criterion, and the PMC is then lesioned. The monkey has difficulty in relearning the task, though associations other than visuomotor associations can be learned.

Single-cell recording studies also implicate the PMC in this function. Cells in the PMC fire differentially, depending on the motor act that a visual stimulus signifies (Godschalk, Lemon, Kuypers, & van der Steen, 1985; Mitz, Godschalk, & Wise, 1991; Weinrich & Wise, 1982; Wise & Mauritz, 1985). For example, Mitz et al. (1991) showed colored ASCII characters to monkeys; the response was movement of a joystick in one of three directions, or withholding movement. Neural activity was compared before and after training and to trials using untrained stimuli. They found learning-related changes in over half of the PMC neurons tested.

Visual Guidance

A number of researchers have implicated the posterior parietal cortex (Andersen, Essick, & Siegel, 1987; Jeannerod, 1986; Mountcastle, Lynch, Georgopoulos, Sakata, & Acuna, 1975; Taira, Mine, Georgopoulos, Murata, & Sakata, 1990) or the PMC (Wise, 1984, 1985) in the visual guidance of movement. Mountcastle et al. (1975) used a reaching paradigm and found a group of neurons in areas 5 and 7 that selectively fired when a monkey projected its arm into extrapersonal space, and another group that fired selectively when the monkey manipulated an object. Taira et al. (1990) found that, of the neurons in area 7 related to object manipulation, the majority (38 of 55) were less active in the dark than in the light. Furthermore, complex visually guided movements are disrupted by ablation of the PMC (see Wise, 1984, for a review), by ablation of the posterior parietal cortex (Lamotte & Acuna, 1978), or by disconnection of the PMC from visual cortex (Haaxma & Kuypers, 1975).

Although the details of a circuit mediating visuomotor associations and/or visual guidance is unclear, the PMC does receive projections directly from area 7a (Petrides & Pandya, 1984). The cortico-cortical pathway from area 7a to the PMC may not be the only important one, however. The posterior parietal cortex, in particular area 7a, projects to visually responsive cells in the pons (Glickstein et al., 1980; Glickstein, May, & Mercier, 1985; Schmahmann & Pandya, 1989). These pontine cells project to the contralateral cerebellar hemisphere (Mower, Gibson, Robinson, Stein, & Glickstein, 1980), and the PMC receives cerebellar input via nucleus X of the ventrolateral thalamus (Schell & Strick, 1984).

There are indications that humans with cerebellar abnormalities are impaired in integrating visual and motor information. Beppu and colleagues (Beppu, Suda, & Tanaka, 1984; Beppu, Nagaoka, & Tanaka, 1987) showed that cerebellar patients are deficient in a slow tracking task. Indeed, after some training, patients actually perform better without visual feedback (Beppu et al., 1987). A number of studies also implicate the cerebellum in an individual's learning to make accurate arm movements while wearing prism spectacles (Baizer & Glickstein, 1974; Gauthier, Hofferer, Hoyt, & Stark, 1979; Weiner, Hallett, & Funkenstein, 1983), and dentate inactivation also disrupts eye–hand coordination (Vercher & Gauthier, 1988).

Although these studies are consistent with a cerebellar role in the integration of visual and motor information, it should be noted that cerebellar damage leads a wide range of motor control difficulties, including disruption of movements that do not integrate feedback (Lamarre & Jacks, 1978), loss of motor synergies (Brooks & Thach, 1981; Thach, Goodkin, & Keating, 1992), and disruption of precise timing (Ivry, Keele, & Diener, 1988). The cerebellum has also been implicated in a wide range of learning processes, not all of them related to perceptuomotor integration (see Lalonde & Botez, 1990, for a review).

In summary, area 7a and the PMC are important in the integration of perceptual and motor information, whether the integration is a visuomotor association or the visual guidance of an ongoing motor act. The cerebellum may be important in either or both of these functions. The circuit subserving these functions may be the basis of a motor skill system.

Degrees of Freedom

An almost infinite number of trajectories will accomplish even a simple reaching movement. This flexibility brings with it a problem: How is a trajectory selected for execution from all these possibilities? This motor control problem can be cast as a skill-learning problem as well, because the challenge of some motor skills is to reduce the spatial and temporal variability of a movement. The goal of a bowler, a dancer, or a martial arts expert is to stereotype a movement.

Neuropsychologists have not viewed the acquisition of motor skill as a reduction of degrees of freedom. Still, some studies of motor control bear on this issue, using three basic approaches to reduction of excess degrees of freedom in the motor system. First, there may be a basis by which the efficiency of a movement is evaluated by the system—for example, the motor system may seek to minimize jerk (Hogan, 1984)—and the effort to minimize one attribute of a trajectory reduces the number of possible trajectories. A second approach is to use the mechanical properties of the limb to reduce or eliminate the computations necessary to specify a trajectory; for example, the spring-like properties of the muscles may be used (Polit & Bizzi, 1978). Third, groups of muscles may be linked in synergies, so that each muscle typically moves as part of a group (Bernstein, 1967). Neuropsychologists have rarely investigated the first and second approaches. There has been more interest in the neural basis of motor synergies.

The motor system reduces degrees of freedom by organizing action in terms of muscle groups rather than individual muscles in at least some movements—for example, locomotion (see Shik & Orlovsky, 1976, for a review) and mastication (see Luschei & Goldberg, 1981, for a review). There is also some evidence that stimulation of individual cortico-spinal neurons leads to the activation of not one but several muscles, which is potentially the basis of a muscle synergy (Buys, Lemon, Mantel, & Muir, 1986; Cheney, Fetz, & Palmer, 1985). Indeed, Humphrey (1986) has suggested that stimulation of single primary motor cortex neurons can cause simultaneous flexion and extension of the wrist muscles, to fix the wrist's position in preparation for a finger movement.

The cerebellum has also been implicated in the use of synergies. Horak and Nashner (1986) have demonstrated that humans make use of a very limited number of motor synergies in different combinations in order to maintain posture. Nashner has studied the ability of patients with cerebellar lesions (Nashner & Grimm, 1978) to respond to perturbations in their visual surroundings or in the platform on which they stood. Patients were impaired in maintaining stance under these perturbations, apparently because of a disruption in the process that establishes the temporal and spatial pattern of activation of muscle contractions.

Kane, Mink, and Thach (described in Thach et al., 1992) tested monkeys' ability to engage in single-joint and multiple-joint movements after inactivation of one of the deep cerebellar nuclei. Different movements were disrupted by inactivation of each nucleus, but overall the multiple-joint movements were more affected than the single-joint movements. These data fit well with clinical interpretations of cerebellar ataxia as a degeneration of motor synergies (Brooks & Thach, 1981; Holmes, 1939).

Although these data are suggestive, they do not provide a firm understanding of how the degrees-of-freedom problem is solved. Rather, the data suggest that synergies may operate at several levels, from the rather simple conjunction of muscle flexions that fix the wrist in preparation for a finger movement to the more complex synergies involving timing, direction, and amplitude to maintain posture or to locomote. A still more complex level is Schmidt's (1975) concept of a generalized motor program, in which one program has multiple synergies embedded within it. A program is a memory representation that contains the essential features of a class of movements— for example, throwing a ball. Control of different movements within the class is achieved by applying different parameters (e.g., force) to the invariant features of the movement. The cerebellum may play a role in all of these synergies—as the executor of some, or as a modulator of synergies stored in the brainstem or spinal cord (Thach et al., 1992).

In summary, there is little evidence for a motor skill system responsible for developing synergies. Though it is very likely that the motor system uses synergies to reduce the degrees of freedom and that this strategy might be used in skill learning, the research on how new synergies are acquired is lacking.

Serial Order

The final motor control problem is serial order. Movements must not simply be executed; they must be executed in the correct order. This fact is especially apparent in control problems that call for a large number of simple movements, such as typing. Evidence from a number of sources indicates that a basal ganglia–supplementary motor area (SMA) loop is critical for the adequate sequencing of motor information. This loop is one of several basal ganglia–thalamo-cortical loops described by Alexander, DeLong, and Strick (1986). The SMA projects mostly to the ventral and medial aspects of the putamen, which projects to the ventrolateral two-thirds of the internal and external segments of the globus pallidus, and to the substantia nigra, pars reticulata (SNr). The circuit closes on the SMA again, via the oral and medial aspects of the ventrolateral nucleus of the thalamus.

Patients with Parkinson's disease (PD), who suffer dopamine depletion to the striatum, and patients with Huntington's disease (HD), who suffer striatal atrophy, seem to have particular difficulties with sequencing motor acts. Beatty and Monson (1990) found impairment in PD patients in a simple sequencing task of hand gestures; Harrington and Haaland (1991) found that PD patients have difficulty assembling a complex program of hand postures. Benecke and colleagues (Benecke, Rothwell, Dick, Day, & Marsden, 1987; Thompson et al., 1988) have used a task in which patients must perform simple movements (moving a lever or squeezing a bulb) or perform them simultaneously or sequentially. HD and PD patients have much greater difficulty performing them simultaneously or sequentially. Stelmach, Worringham, and Strand (1987) found that PD patients do not show normal sequence length programming; their time to initiate a sequence of five simple movements is no longer than their time to initiate a sequence of two simple movements, indicating that they do not program the entire sequence in advance.

The striatum is but one station in this basal ganglia–thalamo-cortical loop. The SMA should also be involved in the sequencing of motor acts, and there is evidence that it is. Dick, Benecke, Rothwell, Day, and Marsden (1986) found that, like patients with striatal dysfunction, a patient with a right SMA infarct had great difficulty performing the lever movement and bulb squeeze sequentially. Gaymard, Pierrot-Deseilligny, and Rivaud (1990) found that in patients with left SMA infarcts, saccades made to a sequence of remembered positions were grossly impaired, whereas saccades to a single remembered position were only mildly impaired, and saccades to a visible target were normal. Monkeys with surgical lesions to SMA also have difficulty remembering a sequence of motor movements in the absence of vision (Halsband, 1987). Mushiake, Inase, and Tanji (1990) recorded from SMA in two monkeys and found a group of SMA neurons that were active when a monkey pressed a sequence of three buttons from memory, but were inactive when the sequence was guided by visual signals. These data are in line with Passingham's (1987) suggestion that the SMA is critical for movements using proprioceptive cues. This proposal, in turn, is sensible in light of the heavy inputs from the somatosensory cortex, and the paucity of visual cortical input, to the basal ganglia (Graybiel & Ragsdale, 1979; Kunzle, 1977).

How do these motor control data bear on motor skill-learning data? A number of studies have demonstrated that PD and HD patients are impaired on tracking tasks (such as pursuit rotor) that use a repetitive track (Flowers, 1978a; Heindel, Butters, & Salmon, 1988; Heindel, Salmon, Shults, Walicke, & Butters, 1989; Harrington, Haaland, Yeo, & Marder, 1990). According to the current explanation, patients are impaired because control subjects learn the specific sequence of movements for the repetitive track, but patients cannot. This implies that patients should show intact performance on a tracking task that uses a random instead of a repetitive track, and at least one study indicates that they are (Flowers, 1978a). HD patients are also impaired in learning a sequence of motor responses in a speeded-choice response task (Knopman & Nissen, 1991; Willingham & Koroshetz, 1990). In this paradigm one of four lights appears on a computer screen, and the subject pushes a button directly below the light. Unknown to the subject, the lights appear in a repeating sequence. Learning is evidenced by decreasing response times, and then an abrupt increase in response times when the lights appear randomly. Though HD patients do not show normal sequence learning on this task, they learn normally a different version of the task in which the lights always appear randomly, but the subject must learn a new and incompatible stimulus-response mapping (Willingham & Koroshetz, 1990).

Still, it is an oversimplification to say that the basal ganglia, in conjunction with the SMA, constitute a motor sequence-learning system. Patients with abnormalities of the striatum seem to have trouble generally with motor acts that are not guided by information in the environment. Stern, Mayeux, Rosen, and Ilson (1983) asked PD patients to trace designs (e.g., a sawtooth) with their fingers. After familiarizing the patients with the designs, the experimenters degraded some of the designs. Patients were impaired in tracing those parts of the design that were missing, while normal subjects could trace where the line should have been. Flowers (1978b) found that PD patients were impaired in tracking through the gaps in a ramp pattern that had been degraded.

These results led to the general hypothesis that PD patients could not make use of information in the environment on which to base future motor actions—so-called "predictive movements." Day, Dick, and Marsden (1984) refuted that idea by demonstrating that PD patients improve on a tracking task using a predictable track when they are aware of the predictability; Bloxham, Mindel, and Frith (1984) also argued that PD patients could use predictive information in a predictable tracking task. But, as pointed out by Haaland and Harrington (1990), the interpretation of Day et al.'s (1984) results is clouded by a possible floor effect, and Bloxham et al. (1984) used a performance-based selection criterion for their PD patients.

Several studies have used response time measures to assess PD patients' abilities to use predictive information. PD patients show no advantage in a situation where they are able to program a motor response in advance because they know which response will be called for, over a situation in which they do not know which response to make until a "go" signal (Evarts, Teravainen, & Calne, 1981; Sheridan, Flowers, & Hurrell, 1987). Other studies have failed to find such a deficit. Stelmach, Worringham, and Strand (1986) and Rafal, Inhoff, Friedman, and Bernstein (1987) did not find abnormal sequence length programming. These two findings indicate that PD patients may be able to program movements without strong environmental cues, but Haaland and Harrington (1990) point out that subjects in both studies practiced the required movements a great many times. This interpretation is borne out by a recent study (Worringham & Stelmach, 1990) that systematically varied the amount of practice in a simple aiming task. The results showed that PD patients could benefit from the opportunity to preprogram movements, but only with practice.

Thus, two aspects of the basal ganglia–thalamo-cortical loop's function may be delineated: (1) It participates in the sequencing of movements, and (2) it does so not on the basis of visual feedback or cues. These two functions may be related, in that if a sequence of movements is planned, it may often be in the absence of visual cues because these cues are not yet available. A plan implies knowledge of movements to be made without a reliance on perceptual feedback to direct the movements. Thus the basal ganglia–SMA loop may better be described as a high-level planner than as a sequencer of motor actions. The characterization of those plans (how specific they are in terms of effectors, coordinates, timing, etc.) must be the subject of future research.

That the motor control functions supported by this basal ganglia–SMA loop also support motor skill acquisition may be inferred from data indicating that patients with striatal abnormalities have difficulty learning some types of motor skills, and that those skills might be characterized as ones requiring learning a sequence of motor responses.

Conclusion

Three characteristics of multiple systems are offered at the outset of this chapter: the systems should be able to operate independently, they should serve different functions, and they should have different neural bases. This chapter has presented evidence regarding the third characteristic, and used as a starting point a set of problems in motor control laid out by Pew and Rosenbaum (1988): perceptuomotor integration, excess degrees of freedom, and serial ordering. There seems to be evidence suggestive of multiple, anatomically separate systems of motor skill, but the evidence cannot be considered conclusive.

Perceptuomotor integration seems to be handled in part by area 7a and the PMC, possibly in conjunction with the cerebellum. The circuit may involve direct connections between the two cortical regions and/or an indirect route linking area 7a, pons, cerebellum, thalamus, and PMC. The integration may take the form of a direct association between a visual cue and a motor response, or a new relationship between visual cues and motor responses, as in a tracking task. Whether these two types of perceptuomotor integration are separate neurally as well as functionally is not known.

Sequencing per se seems not to constitute a separate motor system. Rather, the basal ganglia and SMA are key structures in a circuit that seems important in high-level motor planning. This planning entails sequences of movements to be made before there are cues in the environment that can guide these movements.

The reduction of degrees of freedom in movement control, and the neural basis of the stereotyping of movements in a motor skill situation, remain unknown. Synergies clearly play a role in the control of some movements—for example, locomotion—and the anatomical loci of these synergies have received some attention. It is possible that the cerebellum helps establish these or other synergies, or that it influences their output in normal movement. Thus far, there has been little effort to study the development of new synergies.

In sum, there appears to be some evidence for anatomical separation of motor skills, but the evidence is inconclusive. It is inconclusive not because of mixed results from many experiments, but because of a lack of work directed toward the question, particularly in regard to reducing the degrees of freedom of a complex motor act with practice. Whether the particular description of motor skill systems described here proves fruitful will become clear as research progresses.

ACKNOWLEDGMENTS

I thank Joe Steinmetz and Tom Thach for helpful suggestions on this topic, and John Gabrieli, David Rosenbaum, Larry Squire, Elizabeth H. Willingham, and Steve Wise for many helpful comments on an earlier version of this chapter.

REFERENCES

Alexander, G. E., DeLong, M. R., & Strick, P. L. (1986). Parallel organization of functionally segregated circuits linking basal ganglia and cortex. *Annual Review of Neuroscience, 9,* 357–381.

Andersen, R. A., Essick, G. K., & Siegel, R. M. (1987). Neurons of area 7 activated by both visual stimuli and oculomotor behavior. *Experimental Brain Research, 67,* 316–322.

Baizer, J. S., & Glickstein, M. (1974). Role of cerebellum in prism adaptation. *Journal of Physiology, 236,* 34–35.

Beatty, W. W., & Monson, N. (1990). Picture and motor sequencing in Parkinson's disease. *Journal of Geriatric Psychiatry and Neurology, 3,* 192–197.

Benecke, R., Rothwell, J. C., Dick, J. P. R., Day, B. L., & Marsden, C. D. (1987). Performance of simultaneous and sequential movements in patients with Parkinson's disease. *Brain, 110,* 361–379.

Beppu, H., Nagaoka, M., & Tanaka, R. (1987). Analysis of cerebellar motor disorders by visually-guided elbow tracking movement. *Brain, 110,* 1-18.

Beppu, H., Suda, M., & Tanaka, R. (1984). Analysis of cerebellar motor disorders by visually guided elbow tracking movement. *Brain, 107,* 787-809.

Bernstein, N. (1967). *The coordination and regulation of movements.* Oxford: Pergamon Press.

Bloxham, C. A., Mindel, T. A., & Frith, C. D. (1984). Initiation and execution of predictable and unpredictable movements in Parkinson's disease. *Brain, 107,* 371-384.

Brooks, V. B., & Thach, W. T. (1981). Cerebellar control of posture and movement. In V. B. Brooks (Ed.), *Handbook of physiology: Section 1. The nervous system. Vol. 2. Motor control* (Part 2, pp. 877-946). Bethesda, MD: American Physiological Society.

Buys, E. J., Lemon, R. N., Mantel, G. W. H., & Muir, R. B. (1986). Selective facilitation of different hand muscles by single corticospinal neurons in the conscious monkey. *Journal of Physiology* (London), *381,* 529-549.

Cheney, P. D., Fetz, E. E., & Palmer, S. S. (1985). Pattern of facilitation and suppression of antagonist forelimb muscles from motor cortex sites in the awake monkey. *Journal of Neurophysiology, 53,* 805-820.

Corkin, S. (1968). Acquisition of motor skill after bilateral medial temporal lobe excision. *Neuropsychologia, 6,* 255-265.

Crowder, R. G. (1989). Modularity and dissociations in memory systems. In H. L. Roediger III & F. I. M. Craik (Eds.), *Varieties of memory and consciousness: Essays in honor of Endel Tulving* (pp. 271-294). Hillsdale, NJ: Erlbaum.

Day, B. L., Dick, J. P. R., & Marsden, C. D. (1984). Patients with Parkinson's disease can employ a predictive motor strategy. *Journal of Neurology, Neurosurgery and Psychiatry, 47,* 1299-1306.

Dick, J. P. R., Benecke, R., Rothwell, J. C., Day, B. L., & Marsden, C. D. (1986). Simple and complex movements in a patient with infarction of the right supplementary motor area. *Movement Disorders, 1,* 255-266.

Evarts, E. V., Teravainen, H., & Calne, D. B. (1981). Reaction time in Parkinson's disease. *Brain, 104,* 167-186.

Flowers, K. (1978a). Some frequency response characteristics of parkinsonism on pursuit tracking. *Brain, 101,* 19-34.

Flowers, K. (1978b). Lack of prediction in the motor behavior of parkinsonism. *Brain, 101,* 35-52.

Gauthier, G. M., Hofferer, J.-M., Hoyt, W. F., & Stark, L. (1979). Visual–motor adaptation: Quantitative demonstration in patients with posterior fossa involvement. *Archives of Neurology, 36,* 155-160.

Gaymard, B., Pierrot-Deseilligny, C., & Rivaud, S. (1990). Impairment of sequences of memory-guided saccades after supplementary motor area lesions. *Annals of Neurology, 28,* 622-626.

Glickstein, M., Cohen, J. L., Dixon, B., Gibson, A., Hollins, M., Labossiere, E., & Robinson, F. (1980). Corticopontine visual projections in macaque monkeys. *Journal of Comparative Neurology, 190,* 209-229.

Glickstein, M., May, J. G., III, & Mercier, B. E. (1985). Corticopontine projection in the macaque: The distribution of labelled cortical cells after large injections of horseradish peroxidase in the pontine nuclei. *Journal of Comparative Neurology, 235,* 343-359.

Godschalk, M., Lemon, R. N., Kuypers, H. G. J. M., & van der Steen, J. (1985). The involvement of monkey premotor cortex neurones in preparation of visually cued arm movements. *Behavioural Brain Research, 18,* 143-158.

Graf, P., Squire, L. R., & Mandler, G. (1984). The information that amnesic patients do not forget. *Journal of Experimental Psychology: Learning, Memory, and Cognition, 10,* 164-178.

Graybiel, A. M., & Ragsdale, C. W. (1979). Fiber connections of the basal ganglia. *Progress in Brain Research, 51,* 239-283.

Haaland, K. Y., & Harrington, D. L. (1990). Complex movement behavior: Toward understanding cortical and subcortical interactions in regulating control processes. In G. E. Hammond (Ed.), *Advances in psychology: Cerebral control of speech and limb movements* (pp. 169-200). Amsterdam: North-Holland.

Haaxma, R., & Kuypers, H. G. J. M. (1975). Intrahemispheric cortical connections and visual guidance of hand and finger movements in the rhesus monkey. *Brain, 98,* 239-260.

Halsband, U. (1987). Higher disturbances of movement in monkeys (*Macaca fascicularis*). In G. N. Gantchev, B. Dimitrov, & P. Gatev (Eds.), *Motor control* (pp. 79-85). New York: Plenum Press.

Halsband, U., & Freund, H.-J. (1990). Premotor cortex and conditional motor learning in man. *Brain, 113,* 207-222.

Halsband, U., & Passingham, R. E. (1982). The role of premotor and parietal cortex in the direction of action. *Brain Research, 240,* 368-372.

Harrington, D. L., & Haaland, K. Y. (1991). Sequencing in Parkinson's disease: Abnormalities in programming and controlling movement. *Brain, 114,* 99–115.

Harrington, D. L., Haaland, K. Y., Yeo, R. A., & Marder, E. (1990). Procedural memory in Parkinson's disease: Impaired motor but not visuoperceptual learning. *Journal of Clinical and Experimental Neuropsychology, 12,* 323–339.

Heindel, W. C., Butters, N., & Salmon, D. P. (1988). Impaired learning of a motor skill in patients with Huntington's disease. *Behavioral Neuroscience, 102,* 141–147.

Heindel, W. C., Salmon, D. P., Shults, C. W., Walicke, P. A., & Butters, N. (1989). Neuropsychological evidence for multiple implicit memory systems: A comparison of Alzheimer's, Huntington's, and Parkinson's disease patients. *Journal of Neuroscience, 9,* 582–587.

Hogan, N. (1984). An organizing principle for a class of voluntary movements. *Journal of Neuroscience, 4,* 2745–2754.

Holmes, G. (1939). The cerebellum of man. *Brain, 62,* 1–30.

Horak, F. B., & Nashner, L. M. (1986). Central programming of postural movements: Adaptation to altered support-surface configurations. *Journal of Neurophysiology, 55,* 1369–1381.

Humphrey, D. L. (1986). Representation of movements and muscles within the primate precentral motor cortex: Historical and current perspectives. *Federation Proceedings, 45,* 2687–2699.

Humphreys, M. S., Bain, J. D., & Pike, R. (1989). Different ways to cue a coherent memory system: A theory for episodic, semantic, and procedural tasks. *Psychological Review, 96,* 208–233.

Ivry, R. B., Keele, S. W., & Diener, H. C. (1988). Dissociation of the lateral and medial cerebellum in movement timing and movement execution. *Experimental Brain Research, 73,* 167–180.

Jeannerod, M. (1986). Mechanisms of visuomotor coordination: A study in normal and brain-damaged subjects. *Neuropsychologia, 24,* 41–78.

Knopman, D., & Nissen, M. J. (1991). Procedural learning is impaired in Huntington's disease: Evidence from the serial reaction time task. *Neuropsychologia, 29,* 245–254.

Kosslyn, S. M. (1987). Seeing and imaging in the cerebral hemispheres: A computational approach. *Psychological Review, 94,* 148–175.

Kunzle, H. (1977). Projections from primary somatosensory cortex to basal ganglia and thalamus in the monkey. *Experimental Brain Research, 30,* 481–492.

Lalonde, R., & Botez, M. I. (1990). The cerebellum and learning processes in animals. *Brain Research Reviews, 15,* 325–332.

Lamarre, Y., & Jacks, B. (1978). Involvement of the cerebellum in the initiation of fast ballistic movement in the monkey. In W. A. Cobb & H. Van Duijn (Eds.), *Contemporary clinical neurophysiology* (pp. 441–447). New York: Elsevier.

Lamotte, R. H., & Acuna, C. (1978). Defects in accuracy of reaching after removal of posterior parietal cortex in monkeys. *Brain Research, 139,* 309–326.

Luschei, F. S., & Goldberg, L. J. (1981). Neural mechanisms of mandibular control: Mastication and voluntary biting. In V. B. Brooks (Ed.), *Handbook of physiology: Section 1. The nervous system. Vol. 2. Motor control* (Part 2, pp. 1237–1274). Bethesda, MD: American Physiological Society.

Marr, D. (1982). *Vision.* New York: W. H. Freeman.

Mishkin, M., Malamut, B., & Bachevalier, J. (1984). Memories and habits: Two neural systems. In G. Lynch, J. L. McGaugh, & N. M. Weinberger (Eds.), *Neurobiology of learning and memory* (pp. 65–77). New York: Guilford Press.

Mitz, A. R., Godschalk, M., & Wise, S. P. (1991). Learning-dependent neuronal activity in the premotor cortex: Activity during the acquisition of conditional motor associations. *Journal of Neuroscience, 11,* 1855–1872.

Mountcastle, V. B., Lynch, J. C., Georgopoulos, A. P., Sakata, H., & Acuna, C. (1975). Posterior parietal association cortex of the monkey: Command functions for operations within extrapersonal space. *Journal of Neurophysiology, 38,* 871–908.

Mower, G., Gibson, A., Robinson, F. Stein, J., & Glickstein, M. (1980). Visual pontocerebellar projections in the cat. *Journal of Neurophysiology, 43,* 355–366.

Mushiake, H., Inase, M., & Tanji, J. (1990). Selective coding of motor sequence in the supplementary motor area of monkey cerebral cortex. *Experimental Brain Research, 82,* 208–210.

Nashner, L. M., & Grimm, R. J. (1978). Analysis of multiloop dyscontrol in standing cerebellar patients. In J. E. Desmedt (Ed.), *Progress in clinical neurophysiology: Vol. 5. Cerebral motor control in man: Long loop mechanisms* (pp. 300–319). Basel: Karger.

Nissen, M. J., & Bullemer, P. (1987). Attentional requirements of learning: Evidence from performance measures. *Cognitive Psychology, 19,* 1–32.

Passingham, R. E. (1985). Premotor cortex: Sensory cues and movement. *Behavioural Brain Research, 18,* 175-186.

Passingham, R. E. (1987). Two cortical systems for directing movement. In G. Bock, M. O'Connor, & J. Marsh (Eds.), *Motor areas of the cerebral cortex* (pp. 154-161). New York: Wiley.

Petrides, M. (1982). Motor conditional associative-learning after selective prefrontal lesions in the monkey. *Behavioural Brain Research, 5,* 407-413.

Petrides, M. (1985a). Deficits on conditional associative-learning tasks after frontal- and temporal-lobe lesions in man. *Neuropsychologia, 23,* 601-614.

Petrides, M. (1985b). Deficits in non-spatial conditional associative learning after periarcuate lesions in the monkey. *Behavioural Brain Research, 16,* 94-101.

Petrides, M. (1986). The effect of periarcuate lesions in the monkey on the performance of symmetrically and asymmetrically reinforced visual and auditory go, no-go tasks. *Journal of Neuroscience, 6,* 2054-2063.

Petrides, M., & Pandya, D. N. (1984). Projections to the frontal cortex from the posterior parietal region in the rhesus monkey. *Journal of Comparative Neurology, 228,* 105-116.

Pew, R. W., & Rosenbaum, D. A. (1988). Human movement control: Computation, representation, and implementation. In R. C. Atkinson, R. J. Herrnstein, G. Lindzey, & R. D. Luce (Eds.), *Stevens' handbook of experimental psychology: Vol. 2. Learning and cognition* (2nd ed., pp. 473-509). New York: Wiley.

Polit, A., & Bizzi, E. (1978). Processes controlling arm movements in monkeys. *Science, 201,* 1235-1237.

Rafal, R. D., Inhoff, A. W., Friedman, J. H., & Bernstein, E. (1987). Programming and execution of sequential movements in Parkinson's disease. *Journal of Neurology, Neurosurgery and Psychiatry, 50,* 1267-1273.

Richardson-Klavehn, A., & Bjork, R. A. (1988). Measures of memory. *Annual Review of Psychology, 39,* 475-543.

Roediger, H. L., III, Rajaram, S., & Srinivas, K. (1990). Specifying criteria for postulating memory systems. *Annals of the New York Academy of Sciences Press, 608,* 572-589.

Schacter, D. L. (1987). Implicit memory: History and current status. *Journal of Experimental Psychology: Learning, Memory, and Cognition, 13,* 501-518.

Schell, G. R., & Strick, P. L. (1984). The origin of thalamic inputs to the arcuate premotor and supplementary motor areas. *Journal of Neuroscience, 4,* 539-560.

Schmahmann, J. D., & Pandya, D. N. (1989). Anatomical investigation of projections to the basis pontis from posterior parietal association cortices in rhesus monkey. *Journal of Comparative Neurology, 289,* 53-73.

Schmidt, R. A. (1975). A schema theory of discrete motor skill learning. *Psychological Review, 82,* 225-260.

Sheridan, M. R., Flowers, K. A., & Hurrell, J. (1987). Programming and execution of movement in Parkinson's disease. *Brain, 110,* 1247-1271.

Shik, M. L., & Orlovsky, G. N. (1976). Neurophysiology of locomotor automatism. *Physiological Reviews, 56,* 465-501.

Stelmach, G. E., Worringham, C. J., & Strand, E. A. (1986). Movement preparation in Parkinson's disease. *Brain, 109,* 1179-1194.

Stelmach, G. E., Worringham, C. J., & Strand, E. A. (1987). The programming and execution of movement sequences in Parkinson's disease. *International Journal of Neuroscience, 36,* 55-65.

Stern, Y., Mayeux, R., Rosen, J., & Ilson, J. (1983). Perceptual motor dysfunction in Parkinson's disease: A deficit in sequential and predictive voluntary movement. *Journal of Neurology, Neurosurgery and Psychiatry, 46,* 145-161.

Taira, M., Mine, S. L., Georgopoulos, A. P., Murata, A., & Sakata, H. (1990). Parietal cortex neurons of the monkey related to the visual guidance of hand movement. *Experimental Brain Research, 83,* 29-36.

Thach, W. T., Goodkin, H. G., & Keating, J. G. (1992). Cerebellum and the adaptive coordination of movement. *Annual Review of Neuroscience, 15,* 403-442.

Thompson, P. D., Berardelli, A., Rothwell, J. C., Day, B. L., Dick, J. P. R., Benecke, R., & Marsden, C. D. (1988). The coexistence of bradykinesia and chorea in Huntington's disease and its implications for theories of basal ganglia control of movement. *Brain, 111,* 223-244.

Vercher, J.-L., & Gauthier, G. M. (1988). Cerebellar involvement in the coordination control of the oculomanual tracking system: Effects of cerebellar dentate nucleus lesion. *Experimental Brain Research, 73,* 155-166.

Warrington, E. K., & Weiskrantz, L. (1970). Amnesia: Consolidation or retrieval? *Nature, 228,* 628-630.

Weiner, M. J., Hallett, M., & Funkenstein, H. H. (1983). Adaptation to lateral displacement of vision in patients with lesions of the central nervous system. *Neurology, 33,* 766-772.

Weinrich, M., & Wise, S. P. (1982). The premotor cortex of the monkey. *Journal of Neuroscience, 2,* 1329-1345.

Willingham, D. B., & Koroshetz, W. J. (1990). Huntington's patients learn motor associations, but not motor sequences. *Society for Neuroscience Abstracts, 16,* 1239.

Wise, S. P. (1984). Non-primary motor cortex and its role in the cerebral control of movement. In G. Edelman, W. M. Gall, & W. M. Cowan (Eds.), *Dynamic aspects of neocortical function* (pp. 525–555). New York: Wiley.

Wise, S. P. (1985). The primate premotor cortex: Past, present, and preparatory. *Annual Review of Neuroscience, 8,* 1–19.

Wise, S. P., & Mauritz, K.-H. (1985). Set-related neuronal activity in the premotor cortex of rhesus monkeys: Effects of changes in premotor set. *Proceedings of the Royal Society of London: Behavioural and Biological Sciences, 223,* 331–354.

Worringham, C. J., & Stelmach, G. E. (1990). Practice effects on the preprogramming of discrete movements in Parkinson's disease. *Journal of Neurology, Neurosurgery and Psychiatry, 53,* 702–704.

Zola-Morgan, S. J., & Squire, L. R. (1985). Medial temporal lesions in monkeys impair memory on a variety of tasks sensitive to human amnesia. *Behavioral Neuroscience, 9,* 22–34.

15

Impaired Priming in Alzheimer's Disease: Neuropsychological Implications

DAVID P. SALMON and WILLIAM C. HEINDEL

A major development in the study of memory over the past decade has been the emphasis on relatively independent memory subsystems that differ from one another in the type of information stored and in the processes acting upon that information (Squire, 1987; Tulving & Schacter, 1990). One memory subsystem dichotomy that has recently generated considerable theoretical and empirical interest is the distinction between "explicit" and "implicit" forms of memory (Graf & Schacter, 1985, 1987; Schacter, 1987). Explicit memory is directed, conscious remembering of previous learning episodes, whereas implicit memory is unconscious remembering expressed only through the performance of the specific operations comprising a particular task. Priming, a prototypical form of implicit memory, involves the unconscious facilitation of a subject's ability to process stimuli as a result of prior exposure to the same or related stimulus material. For example, subjects are able to make more accurate and faster lexical decisions about previously presented words than about new words (Scarborough, Gerard, & Cortese, 1979). This increment in speed of lexical decision making occurs without the conscious awareness of the subject and without any attempt on the part of the subject to recollect or attend to the previously presented materials. It is this "unconscious" feature of the priming paradigm that characterizes its implicit nature.

The distinction between priming and explicit memory receives psychological and neurobiological validity from the differential impairment of these two forms of memory in patients with circumscribed amnesia (i.e., alcoholic Korsakoff [AK] patients, patients with bilateral hippocampal damage). Amnesic patients with profound deficits on explicit recall or recognition memory tests retain the capacity to benefit from the prior presentation of information in a priming task (Cermak, Talbot, Chandler, & Wolbarst, 1985; Gardner, Boller, Moreines, & Butters, 1973; Graf, Squire, & Mandler, 1984; Shimamura, 1986; Shimamura & Squire, 1984; Warrington & Weiskrantz, 1968, 1970). For example, Graf et al. (1984) observed that amnesic patients demonstrated as strong a tendency (relative to chance) as normal control subjects to complete three-letter word stems (e.g., "mot-") with previously presented words (e.g., "motel"), despite their failure to recall or recognize these words on standard memory tests. The amnesic patients apparently treated the stem completion task as a word puzzle and reported that the words seemed to "pop" into mind in response to the stems, even though they were not recognized as familiar.

Verbal Priming in Dementia

Because stem completion and other forms of priming are preserved in even severely impaired amnesic patients (Shimamura, 1986; Squire, 1987), the ability to prime must depend upon brain regions other than the medial temporal (hippocampal) and diencephalic structures known to be affected in amnesia. Thus, a deeper and more extensive understanding of the psychobiological bases of priming phenomena may only be possible through careful investigations with patients whose brain damage extends beyond those regions involved in circumscribed amnesia. Studies of the priming performance of patients with different forms of dementing illnesses (and different sites of neural damage), for example, may demonstrate unique patterns of preserved and impaired priming ability—patterns that reflect the particular brain pathology associated with each disease.

This approach to the study of the neuropsychological basis of priming has recently been adopted in several investigations (Heindel, Salmon, Shults, Walicke, & Butters, 1989; Salmon, Shimamura, Butters, & Smith, 1988; Shimamura, Salmon, Squire, & Butters, 1987) which compared the lexical priming performance of patients with dementia of the Alzheimer type (DAT), Huntington's disease (HD), and AK syndrome, as well as intact normal control subjects, on the word stem completion task previously used by Graf et al. (1984). Subjects were first exposed to a list of 10 target words (e.g., "motel," "abstain") and asked to rate each word in terms of its "likability." Following two presentations and ratings of the entire list, the subjects were shown three-letter stems (e.g., "mot-," "abs-") of words that were and were not on the presentation list, and were asked to complete the stems with the "first word that comes to mind." Half of the stems could be completed with previously presented words, while the other half were used to assess baseline guessing rates. Other lists of words were used to assess the subjects' ability at free recall and recognition.

Although all three patient groups were severely and equally impaired on free recall and recognition of presented words, the AK and HD patients exhibited intact stem completion priming. In comparison to the AK and HD patients, the DAT patients showed little or no tendency to complete the word stems with previously presented words. That is, for the DAT patients, the presentation–rating procedure failed to generate the transient activation of memory traces needed for this form of implicit memory or "memory without awareness" (Schacter, 1985).

Salmon et al. (1988) also compared the priming performance of DAT, HD, and intact control subjects on a semantic priming task that employed a paired-associate procedure. In this task, subjects were first asked to judge categorically or functionally related word pairs (e.g., "bird–robin," "needle–thread") and later to "free-associate" to the first words (e.g., "bird") of the previously presented pairs. The results with this priming task showed that DAT patients were significantly less likely to produce the second word of the semantically related pair than were the other two subject groups.

In fact, the priming score for the DAT patients did not differ from baseline guessing rates.

Verbal Priming and Semantic Memory

The studies of stem completion priming and paired-associate priming in DAT patients described above were among the earliest to demonstrate significant deficiencies in long-term priming in any neurologically impaired patient group, and suggest that verbal priming may be mediated by a neural system that is selectively disrupted in Alzheimer's disease. Since DAT patients, and not HD or AK patients, evidence marked pathology in temporal, parietal, and frontal association cortices (Brun, 1983; Terry and Katzman, 1983), it is possible that impaired priming ability is related to damage to those neocortical association regions that are presumed to store the representations of semantic memory. This brain dysfunction in DAT patients may result in a breakdown in the structure of semantic knowledge that is necessary to support stem completion priming and paired-associate priming. That is, the hierarchical associative network that forms the skeletal structure of semantic knowledge may have deteriorated sufficiently to greatly limit the capacity of available cues to activate traces of previously presented stimuli. For example, the cue "bird" may not evoke an unconscious activation of the categorical associate "robin" on the semantic priming task because the association between the two words has been greatly weakened. Similarly, the association in semantic memory between the word stem "mot-" and the word "motel" on the lexical priming task may be sufficiently disrupted to negate the facilitating effect of the word's presentation.

The interpretation of the priming findings presented above allows for the integration of the DAT patients' performance on tests of priming and their deficits on other traditional tests of semantic memory (for reviews, see Hart, 1988; Nebes, 1989). Like deficits in stem completion priming and paired-associate priming, the DAT patients' deficiencies in the effortful retrieval of specific exemplars of an abstract category may also reflect significant changes in the structure and organization of semantic memory (Butters, Granholm, Salmon, Grant, & Wolfe, 1987; Chertkow & Bub, 1990; Martin, 1987). As Martin and Fedio (1983) have noted using a supermarket fluency task, the number of specific exemplars associated with a given category is greatly reduced in DAT. Alzheimer patients can often name many of the general categories of items found in a supermarket (e.g., meats, vegetables, fruits), but are unable to produce specific examples (e.g., veal, beef, tomatoes, lettuce, apples). Further evidence of semantic memory dysfunction in DAT patients emanates from their impaired performance on tests of confrontation naming (Bayles & Tomoeda, 1983; Hart, 1988; Hodges, Salmon, & Butters, 1991; Huff, Corkin, & Growdon, 1986; Smith, Murdoch, & Chenery, 1989). An analysis of the types of errors committed on a confrontation-naming task (i.e., the Boston Naming Test) revealed that DAT patients produced a greater proportion of semantic–superordinate and semantic–associative errors than did HD patients who were equally deficient in overall naming ability (Hodges et al., 1991). This disproportionate production of semantic errors suggests that the DAT patients' naming deficits reflect a breakdown in semantic processes.

If the DAT patients' impairments in stem completion priming and paired-associate priming do indeed result from a deterioration in the organization of semantic memory, then a relationship should exist between performance on these tasks and performance on other measures of semantic knowledge. Only a weak relationship, at best, should exist between priming performance and performance on tests assessing other "nonsemantic" neuropsychological processes (e.g., tests of episodic memory, attention). To address this issue, we compared the stem completion priming and paired-associate priming scores (i.e., priming minus baseline guessing rate) of 30 mildly to moderately demented DAT patients with their scores on traditional neuropsychological tests of episodic and semantic memory, language, attention, and visuospatial processes (Salmon, Heindel, & Butters, 1992). Correlational analyses revealed that the stem completion priming score was not significantly related to any other neuropsychological measure, including scores on tests of semantic memory (e.g., Boston Naming Test, Number Information Test, Letter and Category Fluency Tests, Wechsler Adult Intelligence Scale—Revised Vocabulary subtest). To examine the relationship among these variables further, we subjected the priming scores and the scores on these other neuropsychological tests to a principal-components factor analysis with varimax rotation. Five factors emerged from this analysis: a semantic knowledge factor, an attention/memory factor, a general dementia factor, a memory factor, and a priming factor. The priming score loaded heavily only on the priming factor (and notably not on the semantic knowledge factor). Similar results were obtained in correlational and principal-components factor analyses of paired-associate priming scores and other neuropsychological test scores.

The results of these correlational and factor analyses cast doubt upon the notion that the priming deficit of DAT patients is mediated by the disruption of their semantic memory. They are also consistent with studies demonstrating normal semantic priming in DAT patients on priming tasks that do not require "effortful" retrieval from semantic memory (Nebes, Martin, & Horn, 1984). For example, in a study by Nebes et al. (1984), a given word was preceded (by approximately 500 milliseconds) either by a semantically related word (primed trials) or by an unrelated word (unprimed trials), and priming was measured by the difference in naming latencies on primed and unprimed trials. The results of this study showed that both the DAT patients and control subjects had a slight and equivalent facilitation in naming latency when a word was preceded by a semantic associate (i.e., semantic priming). From these data, Nebes et al. concluded that DAT patients' semantic memory is normal when it is assessed with techniques that rely solely upon "automatic" information processing. Nebes (1989) has reviewed additional evidence supporting his conclusion about DAT patients' semantic processing problems.

Possible Mechanisms of Verbal Priming

The results of the study by Nebes et al. (1984), in conjunction with our failure to find a significant relationship between the DAT patients' priming deficits and their impairment on traditional tests of semantic memory, suggest that the deficits in long-term priming exhibited by DAT patients may result from (or may at least be influenced by) some factor other than the breakdown of semantic memory. For example, DAT patients may fail to process the target words fully at a semantic level during the initial orienting (i.e., presentation) phase of the stem completion priming and paired-associate priming tasks. Partridge, Knight, and Freehan (1990) recently examined this alternative explanation by changing the nature of the orienting task in the stem completion paradigm to one that would increase the likelihood of semantic processing of the target words. Rather than judging the likability of the target words during the presentation phase of the task (as in the studies by Shimamura et al., 1987, and Salmon et al., 1988), DAT patients were required to supply the meaning of each word, thus ensuring that the semantic properties of the words had been analyzed. With this procedure, Partridge et al. (1990) observed normal levels of stem completion priming in DAT patients. Unfortunately, the "likability judgment" and "semantic processing" orienting tasks were not directly compared in this study, so alternative explanations for the differences in Partridge et al.'s results and those of Shimamura et al. (1987) and Salmon et al. (1988) (e.g., subject differences) cannot be ruled out.

Another possible mechanism underlying the priming deficit of DAT patients is a generalized disturbance in attention, arousal, or activation, which could lead to an inability to activate an otherwise intact representation in semantic memory at a level that would be sufficient to support long-term priming. Traces may still be sufficiently activated, however, to manifest intact priming over the very short (e.g., 500-millisecond) delay intervals used in the Nebes et al. (1984) paradigm. Partridge et al.'s (1990) demonstration that priming performance improves in DAT patients with increasing semantic encoding demands does not completely rule out deficient attention or activation as a source of these patients' priming deficit, since the proportion of attentional resources allocated to the task probably increases as well. Indeed, Partridge et al. pointed out that one major difference between their "definition" orientation task and the "liking" orientation task used by Salmon et al. (1988) is the level of attentional processing required.

Although not as extensively studied as other cognitive functions, attentional disturbances appear to be relatively common in patients with DAT (Cossa, Della Sala, & Spinnler, 1989; Freed, Corkin, Growdon, & Nissen, 1989; Grady et al., 1989; Nebes & Brady, 1989). Cossa et al. (1989), employing an automated visual search task, found that normal controls improved their performance when cues were available to direct attention (either actively or passively), whereas DAT patients did not. Nebes and Brady (1989) reported that DAT patients had greater difficulty than normal control subjects in distributing their attention across increasingly larger arrays of stimuli, even though their focused attention ability appeared relatively intact. A similar deficit in divided attention in DAT patients was reported by Grady et al. (1989). Using a dichotic listening task, these investigators observed an impairment in attention that could not be attributed to a perceptual processing deficit. Finally, Freed et al. (1989) found that a subgroup of DAT patients demonstrated anomalous performance on a task involving the covert orientation of visual attention.

As suggested by Freed et al. (1989), the selective attention impairments observed in some DAT patients may be the behavioral manifestation of a noradrenergic deficit that results from damage to the locus coeruleus. Locus coeruleus neuropathology is often observed in DAT patients at autopsy (Zweig et al., 1988), and both animal and human studies have demonstrated the importance of the noradrenergic system in selective attention processes (Clark, Geffen, & Geffen, 1989; Sara, 1985a, 1985b). In a review of the literature, Posner and Peterson (1990) concluded that the noradrenergic system is primarily concerned with maintaining vigilance and alertness, and provides critical support for the involvement of the posterior parietal system in visual orientation and selective attention. Sara (1985a) has similarly suggested that the noradrenergic innervation provided by the locus coeruleus modulates selective attention by enhancing the level of steady-state cortical activation, or "cortical tonus," which increases the efficiency of cortical information processing. During a priming task, the noradrenergic system may provide a level of "cortical tonus" necessary to initiate and maintain activation of a representation. In the DAT patient with damage to this system, stimuli presented in a priming task may be processed at a semantic level, but the representation of the stimulus cannot be normally activated (or the activation cannot be maintained), and priming does not occur.

Despite the evidence reviewed above, it is still possible that DAT patients' verbal priming impairments are strongly related to their deficits in semantic memory, but that this relationship is overshadowed by the variability contributed by some other cognitive process involved in performing the priming tasks. Several investigators (e.g., Tulving & Schacter, 1990; Keane, Gabrieli, Fennema, Growdon, & Corkin, 1991) have suggested that most priming tasks involve both a semantic and a presemantic perceptual processing component, but that the relative contribution of each component varies across tasks. Because of their verbal nature, the stem completion priming and paired-associate priming tasks appear to be more heavily weighted toward the semantic than the perceptual processing component. Although control subjects are able to perform these tasks using their intact semantic memory system, DAT patients may be forced to rely primarily upon their relatively preserved perceptual abilities, since their semantic system is impaired. For a DAT patient, the relative contribution of perceptual processes to stem completion priming may actually be greater than that of semantic processes. Thus, the DAT patients' verbal priming deficit may still result fundamentally from their semantic memory impairment, but the variability that is seen in these patients' residual priming performance is now related more to their perceptual than to their semantic abilities.

This interpretation of DAT patients' priming deficits, and of the lack of correlation between these deficits and semantic memory dysfunction, is dependent upon a relative preservation of presemantic perceptual priming ability in these patients. Preliminary evidence in support of this notion is found in a recent study by Keane et al. (1991), which examined both stem completion priming and perceptual priming in the same DAT patients. In the perceptual priming task, subjects were required to identify briefly presented words, half of which had been presented previously in an unrelated reading task. Priming was reflected in the shorter exposure time necessary to identify previously presented words than words not previously seen. The stem completion task was similar to that employed by Shimamura et al. (1987). Consistent with previous reports, Keane et al. found impaired stem completion priming in DAT patients. Despite this deficit, these same patients demonstrated preserved perceptual priming ability.

Summary and Conclusions

The identification of long-term priming deficits in patients with DAT provides an opportunity to examine the psychological and neurological determinants of the priming phenomenon—an opportunity that is not available with normal subjects or with strictly amnesic patients. Clearly, the priming impairment exhibited by DAT patients must *not* be the result of damage to neural structures affected in patients with circumscribed amnesia (e.g., hippocampus, midline thalamic nuclei) or other forms of dementia (e.g., caudate, putamen), or of a deficit in explicit memory processes. However, the particular neurological or psychological processes impaired in DAT that do mediate these patients' deficient priming have not yet been identified.

Although the mechanisms underlying the deficits in stem completion priming and paired-associate priming shown by patients with DAT are presently unknown, several possibilities can be identified. Among these possible mechanisms are a disruption of the organization of semantic memory due to damage in cortical association areas, an inability to spontaneously and fully encode verbal stimuli to a semantic level, and a dysfunction of cortical activation (i.e., attention and arousal) that results from damage to the ascending noradrenergic system. Further studies designed to elucidate the processes underlying DAT patients' priming deficits may lead to important information about the necessary and sufficient psychobiological conditions for the occurrence of priming.

ACKNOWLEDGMENTS

The preparation of this chapter was supported in part by National Institute on Aging grants No. AG-05131 and No. AG-08204 to the University of California at San Diego. We would like to thank Dr. Nelson Butters for contributing to the development of the ideas expressed in this chapter.

REFERENCES

Bayles, K., & Tomoeda, C. (1983). Confrontational naming impairment in dementia. *Brain and Language, 19*, 98–114.
Brun, A. (1983). An overview of light and electron microscopic changes. In B. Reisberg (Ed.), *Alzheimer's disease.* New York: Free Press.
Butters, N., Granholm, E., Salmon, D., Grant, I., & Wolfe, J. (1987). Episodic and semantic memory: A comparison of amnesic and demented patients. *Journal of Clinical and Experimental Neuropsychology, 9*, 479–497.
Cermak, L., Talbot, N., Chandler, K., & Wolbarst, L. (1985). The perceptual priming phenomenon in amnesia. *Neuropsychologia, 23*, 615–622.
Chertkow, H., & Bub, D. (1990). Semantic memory loss in dementia of Alzheimer's type. *Brain, 113*, 397–417.
Clark, C., Geffen, G., & Geffen, L. (1989). Catecholamines and the covert orientation of attention in humans. *Neuropsychologia, 27*, 131–139.
Cossa, F., Della Sala, S., & Spinnler, H. (1989). Selective visual attention in Alzheimer's and Parkinson's patients: Memory- and data-driven control. *Neuropsychologia, 27*, 887–892.
Freed, D., Corkin, S., Growdon, J., & Nissen, M. (1989). Selective attention and Alzheimer's disease: Characterizing cognitive subgroups of patients. *Neuropsychologia, 27*, 325–339.

Gardner, H., Boller, F., Moreines, J., & Butters, N. (1973). Retrieving information from Korsakoff patients: Effects of categorical cues and reference to the task. *Cortex, 9*, 165–175.

Grady, C., Grimes, A., Patronas, N., Sunderland, T., Foster, N., & Rapoport, S. (1989). Divided attention, as measured by dichotic speech performance, in dementia of the Alzheimer type. *Archives of Neurology, 46*, 317–320.

Graf, P., & Schacter, D. (1985). Implicit and explicit memory for new associations in normal and amnesic subjects. *Journal of Experimental Psychology: Learning, Memory, and Cognition, 11*, 501–518.

Graf, P., & Schacter, D. (1987). Selective effects of interference on implicit and explicit memory for new associations. *Journal of Experimental Psychology: Learning, Memory, and Cognition, 13*, 45–53.

Graf, P., Squire, L., & Mandler, G. (1984). The information that amnesic patients do not forget. *Journal of Experimental Psychology: Learning, Memory, and Cognition, 10*, 164–178.

Hart, S. (1988). Language and dementia: A review. *Psychological Medicine, 18*, 99–112.

Heindel, W., Salmon, D., Shults, C., Walicke, P., & Butters, N. (1989). Neuropsychological evidence for multiple implicit memory systems: A comparison of Alzheimer's, Huntington's and Parkinson's disease patients. *Journal of Neuroscience, 9*, 582–587.

Hodges, J., Salmon, D., & Butters, N. (1991). The nature of the naming deficit in Alzheimer's and Huntington's disease. *Brain, 114*, 1547–1558.

Huff, F., Corkin, S., & Growdon, J. (1986). Semantic impairment and anomia in Alzheimer's disease. *Brain and Language, 28*, 235–249.

Keane, M., Gabrieli, J., Fennema, A., Growdon, J., & Corkin, S. (1991). Evidence for a dissociation between perceptual and conceptual priming in Alzheimer's disease. *Behavioral Neuroscience, 105*, 326–342.

Martin, A. (1987). Representation of semantic and spatial knowledge in Alzheimer's patients: Implications for models of preserved learning in amnesia. *Journal of Clinical and Experimental Neuropsychology, 9*, 191–124.

Martin, A., & Fedio, P. (1983). Word production and comprehension in Alzheimer's disease: The breakdown in semantic knowledge. *Brain and Language, 19*, 124–141.

Nebes, R. (1989). Semantic memory in Alzheimer's disease. *Psychological Bulletin, 106*, 377–394.

Nebes, R., & Brady, C. (1989). Focused and divided attention in Alzheimer's disease. *Cortex, 25*, 305–315.

Nebes, R., Martin, D., & Horn, L. (1984). Sparing of semantic memory in Alzheimer's disease. *Journal of Abnormal Psychology, 93*, 321–330.

Partridge, F., Knight, R., & Freehan, M. (1990). Direct and indirect memory performance in patients with senile dementia. *Psychological Medicine, 20*, 111–118.

Posner, M., & Petersen, S. (1990). The attention system of the human brain. *Annual Review of Neuroscience, 13*, 25–42.

Salmon, D., Heindel, W., & Butters, N. (1992). *The relationship between neuropsychological deficits and impaired priming in Alzheimer's disease.* Manuscript in preparation.

Salmon, D., Shimamura, A., Butters, N., & Smith, S. (1988). Lexical and semantic priming deficits in patients with Alzheimer's disease. *Journal of Clinical and Experimental Neuropsychology, 10*, 477–494.

Sara, S. (1985a). The locus coeruleus and cognitive function: Attempts to relate noradrenergic enhancement of signal/noise in the brain to behavior. *Physiological Psychology, 13*, 151–162.

Sara, S. (1985b). Noradrenergic modulation of selective attention: Its role in memory retrieval. *Annals of the New York Academy of Sciences, 444*, 178–193.

Scarborough, D., Gerard, L., & Cortese, C. (1979). Accessing lexical memory: The transfer of word repetition effects across task and modality. *Memory and Cognition, 7*, 3–12.

Schacter, D. (1985). Priming of old and new knowledge in amnesic patients and normal subjects. *Annals of the New York Academy of Sciences, 444*, 41–53.

Schacter, D. (1987). Implicit memory: History and current status. *Journal of Experimental Psychology: Learning, Memory and Cognition, 13*, 501–517.

Shimamura, A. (1986). Priming effects in amnesia: Evidence for a dissociable memory function. *Quarterly Journal of Experimental Psychology, 38A*, 619–644.

Shimamura, A., Salmon, D., Squire, L., & Butters, N. (1987). Memory dysfunction and word priming in dementia and amnesia. *Behavioral Neurosciences, 101*, 347–351.

Shimamura, A., & Squire, L. (1984). Paired-associate learning and priming effects in amnesia: A neuropsychological study. *Journal of Experimental Psychology: General, 113*, 556–570.

Smith, S., Murdoch, B., & Chenery, H. (1989). Semantic abilities in dementia of the Alzheimer type: 1. Lexical semantics. *Brain and Language, 36*, 314–324.

Squire, L. (1987). *Memory and brain.* New York: Oxford University Press.

Terry, R., & Katzman, R. (1983). Senile dementia of the Alzheimer type. *Annals of Neurology, 14*, 497–506.

Tulving, E., & Schacter, D. (1990). Priming and human memory systems. *Science, 247*, 301-306.

Warrington, E., & Weiskrantz, L. (1968). New method of testing long-term retention with special reference to amnesic patients. *Nature, 217*, 972-974.

Warrington, E., & Weiskrantz, L. (1970). Amnesic syndrome: Consolidation or retrieval? *Nature, 228*, 628-630.

Zweig, R., Ross, C., Hedreen, J., Steele, C., Cardillo, J., Whitehouse, P., Folstein, M., & Price, D. (1988). The neuropathology of aminergic nuclei in Alzheimer's disease. *Annals of Neurology, 24*, 233-242.

16

The Mobilization of Procedural Learning: The "Key Signature" of the Basal Ganglia

J. A. SAINT-CYR and A. E. TAYLOR

Introduction

The concept of two functionally and perhaps anatomically distinct memory systems arose out of consideration that even densely amnesic individuals, such as Milner's case H. M., could demonstrate the ability to learn new skills (Corkin, 1965). Cohen and Squire (1980) later proposed that two independent systems—namely, the procedural and declarative—coexist and underlie different kinds of learning. Although volumes have been written about the declarative system, the procedural domain has almost been defined by default, being the sort of knowledge of "how to do" that is preserved in amnestics.

The present chapter is a brief overview of the theoretical basis for the assignment of portions of the basal ganglia (or striatal)–frontal lobe circuitry to a functional subset of the procedural domain. The hypothesis is advanced that these circuits are involved in the mobilization and selection of procedures in either the sensorimotor domain or the more general problem-solving domain. In our view, the declarative system, dedicated to conscious utilization of encoding and retrieval, is designed to be under continuous modification and susceptible to forgetting. In contrast, the procedural system is inaccessible to consciousness and is designed according to principles of sensorimotor developmental adaptation; it thus engenders robust strategies, which may be altered or built upon, but which appear to be more resistant to decay.

The interplay between these two memory systems is a fundamental anatomical and behavioral feature of complex learning and adaptive behavior. The idea therefore emerges that there may be a shifting of locus of control of certain behaviors between the striatum and the cortex, both during development and in different phases of learning in the adult. Three converging lines of evidence—neuroanatomical, developmental and behavioral, and cognitive—are presented in support of the present formulation.

Neuroanatomical Elements

There is general agreement, at least in a broad sense, concerning the anatomical substrate for the declarative system. This includes portions of the temporal lobe neocortex, the hippocampus, and, for some, the amygdala (Mishkin, 1982; Mishkin & Appenzeller, 1987; Zola-Morgan, Squire, & Amaral, 1989; Zola-Morgan, Squire, Amaral, & Suzuki, 1989). To be complete, this list would also have to include the mammillary bodies, the anterior and mediodorsal nuclei of the thalamus, and the important contribution of the frontal lobes (Friedman, Janas, & Goldman-Rakic, 1990; Milner, Petrides, & Smith, 1985). In contrast, the proposed anatomical substrate for the procedural or habit system is the basal ganglia or striatum (Mishkin, Malamut, & Bachevalier, 1984; Mishkin & Petrie, 1984). (See Figure 16.1.)

Another way to approach the dual-system concept is to ask what the striatum might contribute to higher-order behavioral control. In fact, given the massive cortical inputs to the striatum (Kemp & Powell, 1970; Saint-Cyr, Ungerleider, & Desimone, 1990; Selemon & Goldman-Rakic, 1985) and the focused output back to the frontal lobes (Alexander, DeLong, & Strick, 1986; Taylor, Saint-Cyr, & Lang, 1986), the idea of a complete anatomical dissociation of the procedural system from the structures contributing to the declarative system (cf. Rosvold, 1972) may be as misguided as the older notion of an extrapyramidal system divorced from the pyramidal system (cf. Brodal, 1963).

The basal ganglia have long been associated with movement disorders, as recognized by Kinnier Wilson at the beginning of this century (Wilson, 1925). It has never been clear, however, whether a unique or central role is played in motor control by these structures, as suggested by some (e.g., Denny-Brown, 1962), or whether we should propose multiple functions—for example, decompose striatal circuitry into multiple parallel loops, each with its own function, as suggested more recently (e.g., Alexander et al., 1986). With regard to the pathophysiology of motor control, these issues have recently been reviewed (Albin, Young, & Penney, 1989; Mitchell, Cross, Sambrook, & Crossman, 1986; Weiner & Lang, 1989), but the nonmotor contributions of the basal ganglia in health and disease remain more enigmatic (for a recent review, see Dubois, Boller, Pillon, & Agid, 1991).

Developmental and Behavioral Evidence

Bachevalier and Mishkin (1984) showed that cortical memory systems are not mature at birth in the rhesus monkey. They suggested that infant behavior is guided by the striatal system. The youngest monkeys in their study were rather slow to learn the memory tasks set to them (e.g., nonmatching-to-sample tasks), although relearning was much more rapid. These authors argued that the maturing cortical systems progressively acquire the capacity to cognitively recognize and to capitalize on conscious recall strategies, while the slower trial-and-error habit mechanism was responsible for the initial learning of the infant monkeys. In contrast, the ability of the infant monkeys to learn a concurrent object discrimination task (with 24-hour intertrial intervals) was

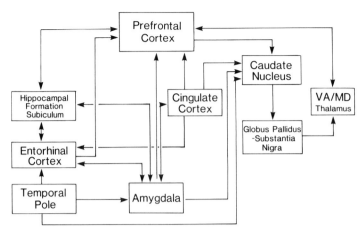

FIGURE 16.1. Major interrelations between striatal and limbic circuits. The left of this diagram depicts anatomical linkages between the major components of limbic structures identified as playing key roles in declarative memory. To the right are the essential striatal structures under consideration as candidate substrates for procedural learning. Although the relative independence of the entorhinal–hippocampal complex and the caudate–pallido-nigral circuits is evident, important links can be traced through prefrontal, cingulate, and temporal cortical regions as well as the amygdala. The reciprocal path, however, is limited to the prefrontal cortex. For the sake of simplicity, many known connections have been omitted, such as the traditional Papez circuit, the direct hippocampo-thalamic projection, and the pallido-subthalamo-pallidal loop, as well as the cortical and striatal circuits through the centre médian/parafascicular nuclei. For more complete anatomical information, the reader should refer to Amaral (1987) and Albin et al. (1989).

Recent anatomical studies have identified both the supplementary motor cortex and adjacent regions of the premotor and prefrontal cortical areas as the principal targets of outflow circuits involving the putamen and caudate, respectively. For the purposes of this chapter, the caudate–prefrontal circuit is emphasized; we do not consider the nucleus accumbens and so-called ventral striatal circuits, since adequate primate data about the functional relations of these areas are still sparse (see Heimer, Switzer, & Van Hoesen, 1982).

The anatomical exit pathways from the striatum are limited to virtually only two brainstem routes: the nucleus tegmenti pedunculo-pontinus pars compacta (TPC) or surrounding areas (cf. Rye, Saper, Lee, & Wainer, 1987) and the superior colliculus (Graybiel, 1978) (not illustrated), and an ascending thalamic route (i.e., mainly nucleus ventralis anterior [VA] and parts of ventralis lateralis and medialis dorsalis [MD]). Only VA and MD have been shown as thalamic relay nuclei for the striatum, for the sake of simplicity. The outflow to the vicinity of the TPC nucleus is not functionally understood, but the possible association with the mesencephalic locomotor region has been noted (Rye et al., 1987). The link with the superior colliculus is now known to support the control of saccadic eye movements, which may be guided from memory (Hikosaka & Wurtz, 1983; Hikosaka, Sakamoto, & Usui, 1989). However, when considering the extensive reascending pathways to the frontal lobes, we are only now beginning to understand what contribution striatal operations play in the nonmotor sphere.

judged equivalent to that of adult animals. Performance of that task is known not to be dependent on temporal lobe–hippocampal connections (Mishkin et al., 1984). The explanation of these findings is complex and entails consideration of rapidly maturing cortico-striate and cortico-limbic connections, as well as the ability to exploit both limbic and striatal mechanisms to solve tasks (Bachevalier, 1990).

In infant monkeys, Goldman and Rosvold (1972) showed that the striatum, unlike the overlying prefrontal cortex, is essential for the performance of delayed-response and delayed-alternation tasks (Goldman, 1971); this suggests that, at least in infants, the striatal circuits appear to be able to function somewhat independently. Whether these functions can be expressed through brainstem pathways (i.e., the superior colliculus or nucleus TPC; see Figure 16.1 caption) or whether alternate, perhaps transient pathways may be present, such as those that have been found between temporal area TEO and the amygdala (Webster, Bachevalier, & Ungerleider, 1988; Webster, Ungerleider, & Bachevalier, 1989), is not known.

Evidence from studies of experimentally induced striatal dysfunction supports the view of the importance of the striatum for noncognitive procedural learning. Monkeys with nigral lesions caused by the toxic drug 1-methyl-4-phenyl-1,2,3,6-tetrahydropyridine (MPTP) showed severely impaired ability to solve a detour-reaching problem (Saint-Cyr, Wan, Aigner, & Doudet, 1988; J. R. Taylor, Elsworth, Roth, Sladek, & Redmond, 1990). This is significant, because MPTP destroys virtually all of the dopaminergic innervation of the striatum (Elsworth, Deutch, Redmond, Sladek, & Roth, 1987; Elsworth et al., 1989; Mitchell et al., 1986) and thus mimics severe Parkinson's disease (Kopin & Markey, 1988). In these animals, other motor tasks could be performed after behavioral recovery, which suggests that their difficulty with the detour-reaching problem was indeed a problem-solving (i.e., procedural) failure and not a result of motor impairment. In a similar series of experiments, Schneider and Kovelowski (1990a) have demonstrated deficits in the performance of delayed-response tasks in animals judged to be motorically asymptomatic after chronic MPTP treatment. Subsequent histochemical analyses revealed significant striatal depletion of monoamines, with relatively greater reductions in the caudate than in the putamen (Schneider & Kovelowski, 1990b).

It is significant that the ability to perform the detour-reaching task has been shown by Diamond (1990) to mature during the first year of life in the cynomolgus monkey and that this behavior is independent of the temporal lobe–hippocampal system. We know from previous studies in the adult (Diamond, 1991; Moll & Kuypers, 1977) that the dorsolateral prefrontal cortex and supplementary motor cortical areas are necessary for the successful execution of this task. Both of those areas receive striatal influences via pallido-nigral and thalamic relays (Alexander et al., 1986). Thus, it appears that both the striatum and the prefrontal cortex participate in the solution of this task. In infancy, because of the relative immaturity of the prefrontal cortex, the striatum bears a heavier share of the work, although performance is not perfect. However, as the prefrontal areas come "on-line," performance reaches adult levels.

In failing this task, the MPTP monkeys appear to resort initially to direct visual guidance, a tactic that only succeeds when the reward is directly accessible through the open front of the Plexiglas box. However, when the opening is to either side or away from the MPTP monkeys, they will abandon the task after a few abortive attempts to grab the reward directly through the side of the box closest to them. This is an example of stimulus-bound or environmentally dependent behavior, as would be expected in animals and humans (Fuster, 1989) with frontal lobe lesions. The fact that the MPTP animals readily abandon a given trial suggests that they can conceive of no alternate strategy. If a chance movement is made that brings the hand around to the side of the box, this "insight" quickly leads to task mastery.

In similar MPTP monkeys, unit recording has revealed that pallidal neurons, which normally discharge conditionally in relation to single-limb movements in particular directions, fire in relation to several limbs and to several directions of movement (Filion, Tremblay, & Bédard, 1988). Therefore, in the intact animal each of these cells can potentially fire in conjunction with numerous movements, but the final allegiance is shaped conditionally (probably during the animal's maturation, training, or both). Importantly, the depletion of dopamine abolishes these privileged links or prevents these circuits from expressing such associations, thus reducing response contingencies to the undifferentiated state. Accordingly, at the striatal level, the parkinsonian monkey or human should also be unable to form or to maintain adaptive associations. The parkinsonian patient appears slow to resolve ambiguous choices in either the motor or problem-solving domains. This stagnation with regard to response selection (for established behaviors) or procedural mobilization (for novel situations) leads to delayed initiation of action and to impersistence of set.

Finally, Caan, Perrett, and Rolls (1984), in recording unit activity in the tail of the caudate nucleus of the behaving monkey, have shown that activity quickly habituates to repeated presentation of stimuli but that dishabituation requires only a single intervening novel trial. This system would be ideal if the striatum had the capacity to temporarily "hold" inputs while waiting for potentially contingent events, such as rewards or other consequences, to declare themselves. In the absence of such events, those inputs could be safely but selectively ignored. Since it is necessary for cortical mechanisms to play an important role in these transactions, the obligatory interplay between cortical and striatal circuits to shape response tendencies seems clear.

Cognitive Studies

Parkinson's disease (PD) and Huntington's disease (HD), in which major pathopysiological changes affect the basal ganglia, have provided the best available human model systems for pursuing hypotheses concerning the functional role of the basal ganglia in relation to behavior. Many authors have used perceptual or visuomotor tasks that are procedural or skill-based in nature, such as the pursuit rotor, mirror-image reading, or mirror-image tracing, to dissociate striatal from cortical functions (e.g., Butters, Wolfe, Martone, Granholm, & Cermak, 1985). It is problematic that these tasks make demands on hand or oculomotor control, both of which are impaired in basal ganglia disease (see Weiner & Lang, 1989). Nevertheless, both PD and HD patients seem to be procedurally impaired in the acquisition of a pursuit-rotor task, in contrast to amnesic patients and to patients suffering from dementia of the Alzheimer type (Bondi & Kazniak, 1991; Heindel, Butters, & Salmon, 1988; Heindel, Salmon, Shults, Walicke, & Butters, 1989). A double dissociation between cortically based (explicit) memory functions and putatively striatally based skill learning (or implicit memory) has been shown in these studies.

Outside of the motor skill domain, one of the earliest cognitive complaints of patients suffering from HD is difficulty in planning the day's activities (Brandt & Butters, 1986). This may be a result of their reported difficulty with the sequencing of information (Caine, Ebert, & Weingartner, 1977). PD patients have also been shown to have selective difficulty with temporal sequencing (Sagar, Sullivan, Gabrieli, Corkin, & Growdon, 1988; Taylor, Saint-Cyr, Lang, & Kenny, 1986). Implicit planning and sequencing could be considered as functions embedded in daily habits or routines, and thus as part of the procedural domain. If explicit, these are assigned to the domain of executive functions.

Many studies have shown that executive dysfunction is an especially prominent, if not exclusive, feature of the cognitive profile of PD patients (for reviews, see Dubois et al., 1991; Taylor & Saint-Cyr, in press). Our early studies confirmed the hypothesis that error messages sent from the malfunctioning striatum would disrupt those (and only those) cognitive and motor functions "classically" defined as frontally dependent (Taylor, Saint-Cyr, & Lang, 1986). Thus, patients showed uniform impairment on the Wisconsin Card-Sorting Test (WCST), on the Rey Auditory Verbal Learning Test, on the spatial series of a delayed-nonmatching-to-sample paradigm, and on Talland's bead-tapping task. What was particularly interesting in these results was the identification of the cognitive processes that failed in each task.

Unlike patients with structural lesions of the frontal lobes, PD patients were neither perseverative nor impulsive on the WCST; rather, the formulation of the necessary strategy to obtain the first set was inconsistent. Subsequently, performance became more nearly normal, but the total number of categories obtained was quite reduced. When retested 1 or more years later, these patients performed normally, thus demonstrating intact long-term recall for these procedures. On the Rey test, the patients showed normal primacy and recency effects, which again attested to intact mnemonic mechanisms. However, the central items in the 15-word list were not well encoded associatively, and hence were poorly retrieved in the free-recall phase of testing. In contrast, recognition memory proved to be normal.

On a paradigm adapted from Albert and Moss (1984) (based on the nonmatching-to-sample protocols devised for monkeys), PD patients performed normally when the stimuli were concrete nouns or even nameless geometric designs (up to 14 items), thus confirming the normal functioning of representational memory systems. However, in the spatial series, only the relative position of identical stimuli provided the cue to identify the nonmatching stimuli. Patients were unable to cluster the items spatially once a normal span of seven to nine had been surpassed. Talland's task requires the simultaneous execution of two motor actions: sorting beads of different shapes and repetitive finger tapping. This paradigm requires the subject to divide attention and to automatize the tapping task. Patients tended either to tap or to sort, but were incapable of performing both tasks smoothly. This type of difficulty is also expected with certain types of frontal dysfunction (Fisher, 1956; Luria, 1966). The essence of this impairment can be seen as the inability to automatize the tapping task, since the bead sorting, *a fortiori*, requires virtually full attentional focus and conscious decision making.

Subsequent studies, in which patients were subdivided according to their clinical response to levodopa therapy, revealed that therapeutic loss (which is taken as an indication of progressive deterioration of the dopaminergic striatal system) was associated with a more profound impairment of all executive capacities (Taylor, Saint-Cyr, & Lang, 1987). This finding heightens the importance of striatal input for the maintenance of normal frontal lobe operations.

Thus, only when external cues or guidance were provided, or familiar routines were called upon, could PD patients perform successfully (see also Brown & Marsden, 1988). However, when new procedures had to be mobilized (i.e., new strategies implicitly evolved) or the best old strategy rapidly selected, in either the motor or problem-solving sphere, PD patients experienced difficulty. It was nevertheless intriguing that they could eventually solve the problems put to them and achieve normal performance. This brought to mind the report by Frith, Bloxham, and Carpenter (1986), in which it was demonstrated that PD patients were impaired only in the early phases of the acquisition of a mirror-image drawing task.

This concept was further tested in a large series of experiments in which task conditions were selected for their novel and supraspan nature. Processes of interest included semantic relations in the organization of memory, source recall, interference effects, and priming (A. E. Taylor, Saint-Cyr, & Lang, 1990b). PD patients were not receiving medication, were in the early stages of disease, and could perform normally on a wide variety of declarative memory tasks. However, process analysis revealed subtle deficits in memory function. For example, in our version of the California Verbal Learning Test, a 16-item shopping list was not efficiently learned by the PD patients, who failed to profit from the embedded categories within the list and persisted in applying conscious rote methods, in keeping with the results obtained by Massman, Delis, Butters, Levin, and Salmon (1990). Although certain individuals (usually control subjects) sometimes volunteered their conscious realization of embedded categories, this information often remained implicit. The expectation that spontaneous clustering and the use of implicit cues would not be readily shaped by experience in the PD group was borne out. In addition, PD patients did not embed their new knowledge according to source, in keeping with previous observations (Sagar et al., 1988). Despite these inefficient strategies and relatively shallower depth of encoding, PD patients displayed no deficits in long-term retrieval, as demonstrated by free recall. Preserved priming was also demonstrated in our study using gradual unmasking of target words. This latter effect was expected on the basis of results reported in other centers (Heindel et al., 1989).

Finally, a simplified paradigm (4 × 4) of Petrides's (1985) conditional associative learning task using only spatial location was designed (A. E. Taylor et al., 1990b). Despite constant feedback, links between stimuli were very unstable, and unassigned options were not systematically chosen by PD patients. All options remained equally likely, suggesting poor access to implicit shaping procedures. In similar experiments, Vriezen and Moscovitch (1990) demonstrated that internally driven trial-and-error procedures such as those just described are unavailable to PD patients, but that the provision of externally supplied cues is sufficient to correct performance.

Prado-Alcala (1985) has proposed that the cholinergic striatal system is essential for guiding behavior through the early stages of learning. Upon mastery of a novel task, the locus of control is thought to be shifted to other brain regions (e.g., the cortex?), thus liberating the striatal circuits for new challenges. Evidence has been obtained that attributes certain cognitive deficits to cholinergic dysfunction both in PD (Dubois, Pillon, Lhermitte, & Agid, 1990) and in dystonia (Taylor, Lang, Saint-Cyr, Riley, & Ranawaya, 1991). Alternatively, these observations may testify more to the tight coupling between cortical and striatal functions required by certain cognitive routines.

Indeed, both Marsden's group (Gotham, Brown, & Marsden, 1988) and Pullman, Watts, Juncos, Chase, and Sanes (1988) have convincing evidence for a link between dopamine deficiency and the cognitive impairments documented in PD. Dopamine not only is considered to be essential for the maintenance of normal striatal operations in the adult, but may be even more important in the developing organism. For example, Graybiel and Hickey (1982) and Fishell and van der Kooy (1987) have shown the importance of dopamine in the anatomical formation of the striosomes. It may thus not be surprising that Leenders (1990) has reported that striatal tyrosine hydroxylase levels are most elevated at birth, declining until adult levels are reached at the end of the second decade (see also Wong et al., 1984). In addition, there is evidence of an age-dependent decrease of dopamine binding sites (Lai, Bowden, & Horita, 1987), with both dopamine and tyrosine hydroxylase levels decreasing with age while monoamine oxidase activity increases (Rogers & Bloom, 1985). During this period, the human organism is physically and intellectually growing, thus requiring a constant redefinition of motor and procedural approaches to new challenges. This may be accompanied by anatomical/neurochemical changes within the striatum, and ultimately in circuits involving the frontal lobes (cf. Diamond, 1991).

This raises the issue of whether the operations of the striatal system are directly accessible to consciousness, and, if not, whether they can interact with conscious cortical circuits. Neal Cohen suggested that the Tower of Hanoi might be the kind of task that could be done "procedurally" even by amnesic patients (Cohen, 1984; Cohen, Eichenbaum, DeAcedo, & Corkin, 1985). Unfortunately, Cohen (personal communication, 1986) required his subjects to provide a verbal protocol of their efforts, in keeping with the tradition of Simon and his colleagues at Carnegie-Mellon (Simon, 1975; Kotovsky, Hayes, & Simon, 1985). In our view, this effectively forces subjects to process the task consciously. After modifying the task (Saint-Cyr, Taylor, & Lang, 1988; see Figure 16.2), we administered it to PD, HD, and amnesic patients with appropriate control subjects. Simple rules were kept displayed, but no guidance was provided and verbalization was not encouraged.

The amnesic patients performed normally, whereas PD and most HD patients experienced difficulty. In sharp contrast, the PD patients performed normally on all semantic verbal learning tasks, whereas the amnesics were profoundly impaired; the results thus demonstrated a double dissociation. Results with the HD patients were mixed, with one group of early-stage patients performing like the PD patients and the other resembling the amnesics. The patients with advanced HD were impaired on both types of tasks, but were relatively worse on the Tower of Toronto. Similar findings were reported in an earlier study by Butters et al. (1985), although that group permitted either of two end points and used the traditional five-disk, size-coded tower.

The question arises as to whether such a complex task can really be solved nonconsciously. The answer appears to be that it can be and usually is by aged individuals or by those with significant memory impairment. There are other reports in the literature of apparently nonconscious solution of complex procedural tasks (e.g., Lewicki, Czyzewska, & Hoffman, 1987). In younger, healthier subjects, we have shown that a combination of conscious and nonconscious strategies is used (Saint-Cyr, Taylor, Trépanier, & Lang, in press; Trépanier, 1989; Trépanier & Saint-Cyr, 1990). Strategic retreats or backtracking tactics appear to require conscious, memory-dependent planning. In addition, rapid sequences of moves, separated by pauses, testify to conscious forward planning (cf. Karat, 1982). The alternation between con-

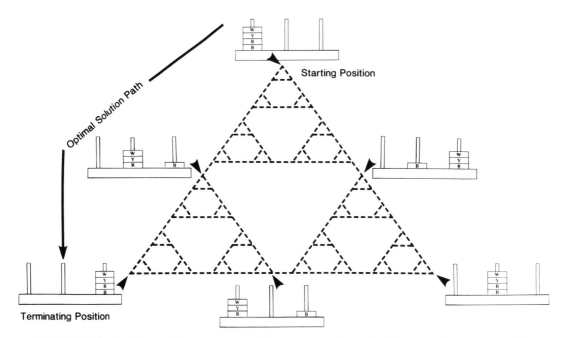

FIGURE 16.2. The Tower of Toronto puzzle and its state space. The goal of this puzzle is to reconstruct the tower on the right peg, while respecting the two rules of only moving one disk at a time and never placing a darker disk on top of a lighter one. Each intersect in this state space diagram represents a possible disk configuration in the puzzle. Three trials of a three-disk puzzle are first given to familiarize subjects with the rule structure and the task environment. Two blocks of five trials each are then given, with a 1½-hour hiatus between them. Inability to learn the three-disk task relatively efficiently is taken as evidence of impaired problem-solving ability and usually signifies cortical (especially frontal) dysfunction. At the starting position (peak of the pyramid), the four color-coded disks (W, white; Y, yellow; R, red; B, black) are stacked on the left peg. The optimal solution path, along the left diagonal, results in the stack's being reassembled on the right peg. Following the right limb of the pyramid (the least efficient route) necessitates the construction of an intermediary stack on the middle peg before a final reconstruction on the right peg.

PD patients very often follow the least efficient latter path rather than the optimal one. Along the way, there may be some attempts at corrective backtracking if the individual is capable of effortful, conscious planning. Some patients simply become lost in their attempts to solve the problem and engage in almost random disk displacements, which appear as closed loops or meanderings through the state space. After the first five trials, a 1½-hour interval is permitted to test for possible loss of acquired task mastery. Typically, PD patients maintain previous performance levels if they have relied largely on implicit procedural learning mechanisms. Those individuals who were able to elaborate conscious strategies typically experience a decrease in performance due to temporal decay of memory. In contrast, amnesics achieve smooth learning curves without loss over the interval. It is interesting to note that schizophrenics, while inefficient on the three-disk phase, nevertheless manage to learn the four-disk problem despite the distraction of repeated rule breaking and tangentiality in associative thinking. This task thus provides an environment in which the interplay between implicit and explicit memory mechanisms can interact and their relative contributions can be assessed (see Goldberg, Saint-Cyr, & Weinberger, 1990; Saint-Cyr, Taylor, & Lang, 1988; Saint-Cyr, Taylor, Trépanier, & Lang, in press).

scious hypothesis testing and intuitive trial-and-error procedures may result in wild fluctuations in efficiency. However, normal subjects will stabilize their performance to near-perfection within about eight trials, whereas PD subjects will, on average, cling to less efficient but nevertheless successful solutions. Patients of advanced age and lower IQ seem less able to call upon the effort-demanding backtracking corrective strategy available to younger and brighter individuals. This suggests that in older and more impaired PD patients, conscious cortical systems cannot participate as readily in the solution of this task, leaving the dopamine-poor striatal circuits to limp along inefficiently.

Conclusions

Our model of striatal function predicts that the striatum should only be transiently involved during the early stages of procedural learning (mobilization phase), and that this system is designed to function intuitively and nonconsciously. Direct evidence in support of this has recently been obtained in positron emission tomographic studies of motor learning (Seitz, Roland, Bohm, Greitz, & Stone-Elander, 1990). We have previously referred to this role as defining the "ballpark" of options, or as approximating the appropriate domain within which conscious cortical mechanisms should focus (Saint-Cyr et al., in press; A. E. Taylor, Saint-Cyr, & Lang, 1990a). The benefit of the striatal contribution is evident in situations that are novel and for which the organism has no prior experience on which to rely. If a given situation has been experienced, then a selection has to be made from the set of previous analogous solutions. This will be used to launch a strategic attack on the problem. Paradoxically, there appears to be little generalization between task environments in the procedural domain, perhaps forcing a more cautious trial-and-error approach; this may have conferred more survival value in evolutionary terms. From a developmental perspective, the sensorimotor strategies that have proved successful in similar past situations will surely fail, since body size and agility rapidly change. In the adult, the possible need to update or modify procedures is constantly under scrutiny; the loss of frontal control leads to decreased vigilance, to increasing concreteness and environmental dependency, and eventually to a regression to primitive behaviors (Goldstein, 1936; Lhermitte, 1983, 1986; Lhermitte, Pillon, & Seradu, 1986; Fuster, 1989).

We therefore suggest that the fundamental role of the striatum is to mobilize new procedures and to select among known procedures by acting as a procedural memory buffer. These procedures are amenable to instrumental shaping and serve to develop response tendencies or habits. They are designed to lead the organism to find the correct strategic domain or "ballpark" in which to formulate more detailed, perhaps conscious, algorithms to guide behavior. Once the organism is on the correct final path to solution, the striatum may be reassigned by frontal executive "order" to the next-priority open-ended situation (if one is present).

While fulfilling its procedural assignment, the striatum is subject to constant vigilance by conscious cortically based mechanisms geared to seizing opportunities for insightful solutions. If these "strategic leaps" are false alarms, performance suffers a setback, as we have seen in our data. The intrusive errors of motor sequences experienced by HD patients are a pathological example of striatal dysfunction. In PD, the inability to resolve seemingly equivalent choices leads to slowed initiation and to both bradykinesia and bradyphrenia (cf. Zimmermann, Sprengelmeyer, Fimm, & Wallesch, 1992). Normally, however, there may also be successful "intuitive leaps" that are accurately launched from the nonconscious strategic base of the striatum. Our vision of this dynamic interplay between cortex and striatum thus suggests elements of Alexander's model of parallel processing (Alexander & Crutcher, 1990a, 1990b; Crutcher & Alexander, 1990), but maintains the nested hierarchical relation proposed by Greene (1972).

In conclusion, we have proposed a model for the cooperative interaction between implicit and explicit memory systems, and have elaborated on the neuroanatomical bases for this. The role of the implicit striatal system is seen as the incremental mobilization of procedures and the selection of response strategies in the domains of both sensorimotor control and problem solving. In advancing the hypothesis of a unique role with regard to mobilization of procedures, we see this as the "lietmotif" or the "key signature" of the basal ganglia according to which all motor or behavioral programs are played out. Support from both developmental and cognitive studies has been presented to show the consistency of this theme; the available animal behavioral evidence is also consonant with this view.

ACKNOWLEDGMENTS

The preparation of this chapter was supported by grants from the Medical Research Council of Canada and the Parkinson Foundation of Canada to J. A. Saint-Cyr.

REFERENCES

Albert, M., & Moss, M. (1984). The assessment of memory disorders in patients with Alzheimer's disease. In L. R. Squires & N. Butters (Eds.), *Neuropsychology of memory* (1st ed., pp. 236-246). New York: Guilford Press.

Albin, R. L., Young, A. B., & Penney, J. B. (1989). The functional anatomy of basal ganglia disorders. *Trends in Neurosciences, 12*, 366-375.

Alexander, G. E., & Crutcher, M. D. (1990a). Preparation for movement: Neural representations of intended direction in three motor areas of the monkey. *Journal of Neurophysiology, 64*, 132-150.

Alexander, G. E., & Crutcher, M. D. (1990b). Neural representations of the target (goal) of visually-guided arm movements in three motor areas of the monkey. *Journal of Neurophysiology, 64*, 164-178.

Alexander, G. E., DeLong, M., & Strick, P. (1986). Parallel organization of functionally segregated circuits linking basal ganglia and cortex. *Annual Review of Neuroscience, 9*, 357-381.

Amaral, D. G. (1987). Memory: Anatomical organization of candidate brain regions. In F. Plum (Ed.), *Handbook of physiology: Section 1. The nervous system. Vol. 5. Higher functions of the brain* (Part 1, pp. 211-294). Bethesda, MD: American Physiological Society.

Bachevalier, J. (1990). Ontogenetic development of habit and memory formation in primates. *Annals of the New York Academy of Sciences, 608*, 457-477.

Bachevalier, J., & Mishkin, M. (1984). An early and a late developing system for learning and retention in infant monkeys. *Behavioral Neuroscience, 96*(5), 770-778.

Bondi, M. W., & Kaszniak, A. W. (1991). Implicit and explicit memory in Alzheimer's disease and Parkinson's disease. *Journal of Clinical and Experimental Neuropsychology, 13*, 339-358.

Brandt, J., & Butters, N. (1986). The neuropsychology of Huntington's disease. *Trends in Neurosciences, 9*, 118-120.

Brodal, A. (1963). Some data and perspectives on the anatomy of the so-called "extrapyramidal system." *Acta Neurologica Scandinavica, 39*(Suppl. 4), 17-38.

Brown, R. G., & Marsden, C. D. (1988). Internal versus external cues and the control of attention in Parkinson's disease. *Brain, 111*, 23-45.

Butters, N., Wolfe, J., Martone, M., Granholm, E., & Cermak, L. S. (1985). Memory disorders associated with Huntington's disease: Verbal recall, verbal recognition, and procedural memory. *Neuropsychologia, 23*, 729-743.

Caan, W., Perrett, D. I., & Rolls, E. T. (1984). Responses of striatal neurons in the behaving monkey: 2. Visual processing in the caudal neostriatum. *Brain Research, 290*, 53-65.

Caine, E. D., Ebert, M. H., & Weingartner, H. (1977). An outline for the analysis of dementia. *Neurology*, *27*, 1087–1092.

Cohen, N. J. (1984). Preserved learning capacity in amnesia: Evidence for multiple memory systems. In L. R. Squire & N. Butters (Eds.), *Neuropsychology of memory* (1st ed., pp. 83–103). New York: Guilford Press.

Cohen, N. J., Eichenbaum, H., DeAcedo, H., & Corkin, S. (1985). Different memory systems underlying acquisition of procedural and declarative knowledge. *Annals of the New York Academy of Sciences*, *444*, 54–71.

Cohen, N. J., & Squire, L. R. (1980). Preserved learning and retention of pattern-analyzing skill in amnesia: Dissociation of knowing how and knowing that. *Science*, *210*, 207–210.

Corkin, S. (1965). Tactually-guided maze learning in man: Effects of unilateral cortical excisions and bilateral hippocampal lesions. *Neuropsychologia*, *3*, 339–351.

Crutcher, M. D., & Alexander, G. E. (1990). Movement-related neuronal activity selectively coding either direction or muscle pattern in three motor areas of the monkey. *Journal of Neurophysiology*, *64*, 151–163.

Denny-Brown, D. (1962). *The basal ganglia and their relation to disorders of movement*. Oxford: Oxford University Press.

Diamond, A. (1990). Developmental time course in human infants and infant monkeys, and the neural bases of inhibitory control in reaching. *Annals of the New York Academy of Sciences*, *608*, 637–669.

Diamond, A. (1991). Frontal lobe involvement in cognitive changes during the first year of life. In K. R. Gibson, & A. C. Petersen (Eds.), *Brain maturation and cognitive development* (pp. 127–180). New York: Aldine/de Gruyter.

Dubois, B., Boller, F., Pillon, B., & Agid, Y. (1991). Cognitive deficits in Parkinson's disease. In F. Boller & J. Grafman (Eds.), *Handbook of neuropsychology* (Vol. 5, pp. 195–240). Amsterdam: Elsevier.

Dubois, B., Pillon, B., Lhermitte, F., & Agid, Y. (1990). Cholinergic deficiency and frontal dysfunction in Parkinson's disease. *Annals of Neurology*, *28*, 117–121.

Elsworth, J. D., Deutch, A. Y., Redmond, D. E., Jr., Sladek, J. R., Jr., & Roth, R. H. (1987). Differential responsiveness to 1-methyl-4-phenyl-1,2,3,6-tetrahydropyridine toxicity in subregions of the primate substantia nigra and striatum. *Life Sciences*, *40*, 193–202.

Elsworth, J. D., Deutch, A. Y., Redmond, D. E., Jr., Taylor, J .R., Sladek, J. R., Jr., & Roth, R. H. (1989). Symptomatic and asymptomatic 1-methyl-4-phenyl-1,2,3,6-tetrahydropyridine (MPTP)-treated primates: Biochemical changes in striatal regions. *Neuroscience*, *33*, 323–331.

Filion, M., Tremblay, L., & Bédard, P. J. (1988). Abnormal influences of passive limb movement on the activity of globus pallidus neurons in parkinsonian monkeys. *Brain Research*, *444*, 165–176.

Fishell, G., & van der Kooy, D. (1987). Pattern formation in the striatum: Developmental changes in the distribution of striatonigral neurons. *Journal of Neuroscience*, *7*(7), 1969–1978.

Fisher, M. (1956). Left hemiplegia and motor impersistence. *Journal of Nervous and Mental Disease*, *123*, 201–218.

Friedman, H. R., Janas, J. D., & Goldman-Rakic, P. S. (1990). Enhancement of metabolic activity in the diencephalon of monkeys: A 2-deoxyglucose study in behaving rhesus monkeys. *Journal of Cognitive Neuroscience*, *2*(1), 18–31.

Frith, C. A., Bloxham, C. A., & Carpenter, K. N. (1986). Impairments in learning and performance of a new manual skill in patients with Parkinson's disease. *Journal of Neurology, Neurosurgery and Psychiatry*, *49*, 661–668.

Fuster, J. M. (1989). *The prefrontal cortex: Anatomy, physiology and neuropsychology of the frontal lobe*. New York: Raven Press.

Goldberg, T. E., Saint-Cyr, J. A., & Weinberger, D. R. (1990). Assessment of procedural learning and problem-solving in schizophrenic patients by Tower of Hanoi type tasks. *Journal of Neuropsychiatry and Clinical Neurosciences*, *2*, 165–173.

Goldman, P. S. (1971). Functional development of the prefrontal cortex in early life and the problem of neuronal plasticity. *Experimental Neurology*, *32*, 366–387.

Goldman, P. S., & Rosvold, H. E. (1972). The effects of selective caudate lesions in infant and juvenile rhesus monkeys. *Brain Research*, *43*, 53–66.

Goldstein, K. (1936). The significance of the frontal lobes for mental performances. *Journal of Neurology and Psychopathology*, *17*, 27–40.

Gotham, A. M., Brown, R. G., & Marsden, C. D. (1988). 'Frontal' cognitive function in patients with Parkinson's disease 'on' and 'off' levodopa. *Brain*, *111*, 299–321.

Graybiel, A. . (1978). Organization of the nigrotectal connection: An experimental tracer study in the cat. *Brain Research*, *143*, 339–348.

Graybiel, A. M., & Hickey, T. L. (1982). Chemospecificity of ontogenetic units in the striatum: Demonstration by combining [³H]thymidine neuronography and histochemical staining. *Proceedings of the National Academy of Sciences USA, 79*, 198–202.

Greene, P. H. (1972). Problems of organization of motor systems. In R. Rosen & F. Snell (Eds.), *Progress in theoretical biology* (Vol. 2, pp. 303–338). New York: Academic Press.

Heimer, L., Switzer, R. D, & van Hoesen, G. W. (1982). Ventral striatum and ventral pallidum: Components of the motor system? *Trends in Neurosciences, 5*, 83–87.

Heindel, W. C., Butters, N., & Salmon, D. P. (1988). Impaired learning of a motor skill in patients with Huntington's disease. *Behavioral Neuroscience, 102*, 141–147.

Heindel, W. C., Salmon, D. P., Shults, C. W., Walicke, P. A., & Butters, N. (1989). Neuropsychological evidence for multiple implicit memory systems: A comparison of Alzheimer's, Huntington's, and Parkinson's disease patients. *Journal of Neuroscience, 9*(2), 582–587.

Hikosaka, O., Sakamoto, M., & Usui, S. (1989). Functional properties of monkey caudate neurons: I. Activities related to saccadic eye movements. *Journal of Neurophysiology, 61*(4), 780–832.

Hikosaka, O., & Wurtz, R. H. (1983). Visual and oculomotor functions of monkey substantia nigra pars reticulata: III. Memory-contingent visual and saccade responses. *Journal of Neurophysiology, 49*, 1268–1284.

Karat, J. A. (1982) A model of problem solving with incomplete constraint knowledge. *Cognitive Psychology, 14*, 538–559.

Kemp, J. M., & Powell, T. P. S. (1970). The corticostriate projection in the monkey. *Brain, 93*, 525–546.

Kopin, I. J., & Markey, S. P. (1988). MPTP toxicity: Implications for research in Parkinson's disease. *Annual Review of Neuroscience, 11*, 81–96.

Kotovsky, K., Hayes, J. R., & Simon, H. A. (1985). Why are some problems hard? Evidence from Tower of Hanoi. *Cognitive Psychology, 17*, 248–294.

Lai, H., Bowden, D. M., & Horita, A. (1987). Age-related decreases in dopamine receptors in the caudate nucleus and putamen of the rhesus monkey (*Macaca mulatta*). *Neurobiology of Aging, 8*, 45–49.

Leenders, K. L. (1990, August). *The striatal dopaminergic system in Parkinson's disease.* Paper presented at the conference on Basal Ganglia Mechanisms in Health and Disease, Santillana del Mar, Spain.

Lewicki, P., Czyzewska, M., & Hoffman, H. (1987). Unconscious acquisition of complex procedural knowledge. *Journal of Experimental Psychology, 13*(4), 523–530.

Lhermitte, F. (1983). 'Utilization behaviour' and its relation to lesions of the frontal lobes. *Brain, 106*, 237–255.

Lhermitte, F. (1986). Human autonomy and the frontal lobes: Part II. Patient behavior in complex and social situations: The 'environmental dependency syndrome.' *Annals of Neurology, 19*, 335–343.

Lhermitte, F., Pillon, B., & Seradu, M. (1986). Human autonomy and the frontal lobes: I. Imitation and utilization behavior: A neuropsychological study of 75 patients. *Annals of Neurology, 19*, 326–334.

Luria, A. R. (1966). *Higher cortical functions in man.* New York: Basic Books.

Massman, P. J., Delis, D. C., Butters, N., Levin, B. E., & Salmon, D. P. (1990). Are all subcortical dementias alike? Verbal learning and memory in Parkinson's and Huntington's disease patients. *Journal of Clinical and Experimental Neuropsychology, 12*, 729–744.

Milner, B., Petrides, M., & Smith, M. L. (1985). Frontal lobes and the temporal organization of memory. *Human Neurobiology, 4*, 137–142.

Mishkin, M. (1982). A memory system in the monkey. *Philosophical Transactions of the Royal Society of London, B298*, 85–95.

Mishkin, M., & Appenzeller, T. (1987). The anatomy of memory. *Scientific American, 256*, 80–89.

Miskhin, M., Malamut, B., & Bachevalier, J. (1984). Memories and habits: Two neural systems. In G. Lynch, J. L. McGaugh, & N. M. Weinberger (Eds.), *Neurobiology of learning and memory* (pp. 65–77). New York: Guilford Press.

Mishkin, M., & Petri, H. (1984). Memories and habits: Some implications for the analysis of learning and retention. In L. R. Squire & N. Butters (Eds.), *Neuropsychology of memory* (1st ed., pp. 287–296). New York: Guilford Press.

Mitchell, I. J., Cross, A. J., Sambrook, M. A., & Crossman, A. R. (1986). Neural mechanisms mediating 1-methyl-4-phenyl-1,2,3,6-tetrahydropyridine-induced parkinsonism in the monkey: Relative contributions of the striatopallidal and striatonigral pathways as suggested by 2-deoxyglucose uptake. *Neuroscience Letters, 63*, 61–65.

Moll, L., & Kuypers, H. G. J. M. (1977). Premotor cortical ablations in monkeys: Contralateral changes in visually-guided reaching behavior. *Science, 198*, 317–319.

Petrides, M. (1985). Deficits on conditional associative learning tasks after frontal- and temporal-lobe lesions in man. *Neuropsychologia, 23*, 601–614.

Prado-Alcala, R. A. (1985). Is cholinergic activity of the caudate nucleus involved in memory? *Life Sciences, 37*(23), 2135–2142.

Pullman, S. L., Watts, R. L., Juncos, J. L., Chase, T. N., & Sanes, J. N. (1988). Dopaminergic effects on simple and choice reaction time performance in Parkinson's disease. *Neurology, 38,* 249-254.

Rogers, J., & Bloom, F. E. (1985). Neurotransmitter metabolism and function in the aging central nervous system. In C. E. Finch & E. L. Schneider (Eds.), *Handbook of the biology of aging* (pp. 645-691). New York: Van Nostrand Reinhold.

Rosvold, H. E. (1972). The frontal lobe system: Cortical–subcortical interrelationships. *Acta Neurobiologica Experientia, 32,* 439-460.

Rye, D. B., Saper, C. B., Lee, H. J., & Wainer, B. H. (1987). Pedunculopontine tegmental nucleus of the rat: Cytoarchitecture, cytochemistry, and some extrapyramidal connections of the mesopontine tegmentum. *Journal of Comparative Neurology, 259,* 483-528.

Sagar, H. J., Sullivan, E. V., Gabrieli, J. D. E., Corkin, S., & Growden, J. H. (1988). Temporal ordering and short-term memory deficits in Parkinson's disease. *Brain, 111,* 525-539.

Saint-Cyr, J. A., Taylor, A. E., & Lang, A. E. (1988). Procedural learning and neostriatal dysfunction in man. *Brain, 111,* 941-959.

Saint-Cyr, J. A., Taylor, A. E., Trépanier, L., & Lang, A. E. (in press). The caudate nucleus: Head ganglion of the habit system. In C. Wallesch & G. Vallar (Eds.), *Neuropsychological disorders associated with subcortical lesions.* Oxford: Oxford University Press.

Saint-Cyr, J. A., Ungerleider, L. G., & Desimone, R. (1990). Organization of visual cortical inputs to the striatum and subsequent outputs to the pallido-nigral complex in the monkey. *Journal of Comparative Neurology, 298,* 129-156.

Saint-Cyr, J. A., Wan, R. Q., Aigner, T. G., & Doudet, D. (1988). Impaired detour reaching in rhesus monkeys after MPTP lesions. *Society for Neuroscience Abstracts, 14,* 389.

Schneider, J. S., & Kovelowski, C. J. (1990a). Chronic exposure to low doses of MPTP: I. Cognitive deficits in motor asymptomatic monkeys. *Brain Research, 519,* 122-128.

Schneider, J. S., & Kovelowski, C. J. (1990b). Chronic exposure to low doses of MPTP: II. Neurochemical and pathological consequences in cognitively-impaired motor asymptomatic monkeys. *Brain Research, 534,* 25-36.

Seitz, R. J., Roland, P. E., Bohm, C., Greitz, T., & Stone-Elander, S. (1990). Motor learning in man: A positron emission tomographic study. *NeuroReport, 1,* 17-20.

Selemon, L. D., & Goldman-Rakic, P. S. (1985). Longitudinal topography and interdigitation of corticostriatal projections in the rhesus monkey. *Journal of Neuroscience, 5,* 776-794.

Simon, H. A. (1975). The functional equivalence of problem-solving skills. *Cognitive Psychology, 7,* 268-288.

Taylor, A. E., Lang, A. E., Saint-Cyr, J. A., Riley, D. E., & Ranawaya, R. (1991). Cognitive processes in idiopathic dystonia treated with high dose anticholinergic therapy: Implications for treatment strategies. *Clinical Neuropharmacology, 14*(1), 62-77.

Taylor, A. E., & Saint-Cyr, J. A. (in press). Executive function. In J. L. Cummings & S. J. Huber (Eds.), *Parkinson's disease: Behavioural and neuropsychological aspects.* Oxford: Oxford University Press.

Taylor, A. E., Saint-Cyr, J. A., & Lang, A. E. (1986). Frontal lobe dysfunction in Parkinson's disease: The cortical focus of neostriatal outflow. *Brain, 109,* 279-292.

Taylor, A. E., Saint-Cyr, J. A., & Lang, A. E. (1987). Parkinson's disease: Cognitive changes in relation to treatment response. *Brain, 110,* 35-51.

Taylor, A. E., Saint-Cyr, J. A., & Lang, A. E. (1990a). Sub-cognitive processing in the frontocaudate "complex loop": The role of the striatum. *Journal of Alzheimer's Disease and Related Disorders, 13,* 150-160.

Taylor, A. E., Saint-Cyr, J. A., & Lang, A. E. (1990b). Memory and learning in early Parkinson's disease: Evidence for a "frontal lobe syndrome." *Brain and Cognition, 13,* 211-232.

Taylor, A. E., Saint-Cyr, J. A., Lang, A. E., & Kenny, F. T. (1986). Parkinson's disease and depression: A critical re-evaluation. *Brain, 109,* 279-292.

Taylor, J. R., Elsworth, J. D., Roth, R. H., Sladek, J. R., Jr., & Redmond, D. E., Jr. (1990). Cognitive and motor deficits in the acquisition of an object retrieval/detour task in MPTP-treated monkeys. *Brain, 113,* 617-637.

Trépanier, L. L. (1989). *Process analysis of the solution of the Tower of Toronto.* Unpublished master's thesis, University of Toronto.

Trépanier, L. L., & Saint-Cyr, J. A. (1990). Process analysis of a procedural/cognitive task. *Journal of Clinical and Experimental Neuropsychology* (INS Abstracts), *12,* 67.

Vriezen, E., & Moscovitch, M. (1990). Memory for temporal order and conditional associative-learning in patients with Parkinson's disease. *Neuropsychologia, 28*(12), 1283-1293.

Webster, M. J. Bachevalier, J., & Ungerleider, L. G. (1988). Plasticity of visual memory circuits in developing monkeys. *Society for Neuroscience Abstracts, 14,* 1.

Webster, M. J., Ungerleider, L. G., & Bachevalier, J. (1989). Projections from inferior temporal cortex to widespread perirhinal areas in infant monkeys. *Society for Neuroscience Abstracts, 15,* 342.

Weiner, W. J., & Lang, A. E. (1989). *Movement disorders: A comprehensive survey.* New York: Futura.

Wilson, S. A. K. (1925). The Croonian lectures on some disorders of motility and muscle tone with special reference to the corpus striatum. *Lancet, 2,* 1-10, 53-62, 169-178, 215-219, 268-276.

Wong, D. F., Wagner, H. N., Jr., Dannals, R. F., Links, J. M., Frost, J. J., Ravert, H. T., Wilson, A. A., Rosenbaum, A. E., Gjedde, A., Douglass, K. H., Petronis, J. E., Folstein, M. F., Toung, J. K. T., Burns, H. D., & Kuhar, M. J. (1984). Effects of age on dopamine and serotonin receptors measured by positron tomography in the living human brain. *Science, 226,* 1393-1396.

Zimmermann, P., Sprengelmeyer, R., Fimm, B., & Wallesch, C.-W. (1992). Cognitive slowing in decision tasks in early and advanced Parkinson's disease. *Brain and Cognition, 18,* 60-69.

Zola-Morgan, S., Squire, L.R ., & Amaral, D. G. (1989). Lesions of the amygdala that spare adjacent cortical regions do not impair memory or exacerbate the impairment following lesions of the hippocampal formation. *Journal of Neuroscience, 9*(6), 1922-1936.

Zola-Morgan, S., Squire, L. R., Amaral, D. G., & Suzuki, W. A. (1989). Lesions of perirhinal and parahippocampal cortex that spare the amygdala and hippocampal formation produce severe memory impairment. *Journal of Neuroscience, 9*(12), 4355-4370.

17

Procedural and Declarative Learning: Distinctions and Interactions

MARY JO NISSEN

In 1980, Cohen and Squire reported that amnesic patients could learn to read mirror-reversed words at a normal rate, despite their inability to remember the words they had read and their poor recollection of the experience itself. Although phenomena that were at some level similar to this one had been reported before (e.g., Brooks & Baddeley, 1976; Cermak, Lewis, Butters, & Goodglass, 1973; Corkin, 1965, 1968; Milner, 1962; Milner, Corkin, & Teuber, 1968; Warrington & Weiskrantz, 1968), the Cohen and Squire (1980) article had a special impact for at least two reasons. First, it emphasized that skill learning in amnesics could occur at a *normal* rate and was not limited to motor skills. Second, it applied to the phenomenon a theoretical framework borrowed from philosophy and artificial intelligence: the distinction between procedural and declarative knowledge.

Since 1980, research on preserved learning in amnesia has moved in a variety of directions, one of which has been the relation between skill learning and priming effects, which are also intact in amnesia (see Schacter, 1987; Shimamura, 1986; Tulving & Schacter, 1990, for treatments of priming effects in amnesia). It has seemed to my collaborators and me, however, that the investigation of preserved skill learning itself could provide a rich source of information about the organization of memory and the interaction of memory systems with other components of cognition. It also seemed that such an endeavor would be more likely to succeed if the empirical work were based on the use of a model task—one that was simple enough that the cognitive requirements of task performance could be relatively well defined; and one that could be used to address a variety of questions, such that a cumulative body of knowledge could be obtained with comparable methods. In addition, it seemed desirable to develop parallel versions of the model task: one that tapped procedural knowledge and another that reflected declarative knowledge.

In this chapter, I describe the task we have used and summarize what we have learned from it.

The Model Task and Its Validity

On each trial in the serial reaction time (SRT) task, a spot of light appears in one of four locations arranged horizontally, and subjects press a button corresponding to the position of the light. In a repeating-sequence condition, the lights appear repeatedly in a 10-trial sequence,[1] although this fact is never mentioned to subjects and the end of one cycle through the sequence and the beginning of the next is not marked in any way. In a random-sequence condition, the position of the lights is determined randomly. As subjects perform in the repeating-sequence condition, their responses become progressively faster. When they are then given the random-sequence condition, their reaction time increases sharply, indicating that they have learned the repeating sequence.

We have found that individuals with memory disorders of several etiologies demonstrate learning of the sequence. These groups include patients with Korsakoff's syndrome (Nissen & Bullemer, 1987; Nissen, Willingham, & Hartman, 1989); most patients with Alzheimer's disease (Knopman & Nissen, 1987; Knopman, 1991); ECT patients (Nissen & Mackenzie, 1991); healthy young adults given scopolamine, an anticholinergic drug that produces a temporary amnesia (Nissen, Knopman, & Schacter, 1987); and a woman with multiple personality disorder who, despite her interpersonality amnesia, showed transfer of knowledge of the sequence across personalities (Nissen, Ross, Willingham, Mackenzie, & Schacter, 1988). In addition, even though older adults are impaired relative to younger adults in learning serial patterns declaratively, the two groups show the same rate of learning on this task (Howard & Howard, 1989).

A parallel version of this task has allowed us to assess subjects' explicit declarative knowledge of the sequence following training on the SRT task. On each trial a spot of light appears, as before, but subjects are supposed to press the button corresponding to where they think the next light will appear. Accuracy rather than reaction time is the dependent variable in this "generate" task.

Even though the amnesic patients showed by their performance on the SRT task that they learned the repeating sequence, they either reported that they were not aware of the presence of a sequence, were significantly impaired on the generate task, or both. The learning that occurs on the SRT task can occur without awareness of what is learned; we take it as an example of procedural learning. When normal subjects were given the amount of training on the SRT task that we typically give to amnesics, most of them became aware of the sequence, but about a third of them were unaware of the sequence and performed at chance level on the generate task (Willingham, Nissen, & Bullemer, 1989). Those who had learned the sequence declaratively appeared to use this knowledge in performing the SRT task, by effectively anticipating the onset of the next stimulus. This finding represents an example of the interaction of procedural and declarative knowledge in task performance.

The Content of Procedural Knowledge

Despite the findings of Cohen and Squire (1980), there has been a tendency to equate procedural learning with motor learning. Motor skills certainly are a form of "knowing

---

[1] We have used other sequence lengths as well, with comparable results.

how," and it is easy to think of examples in which people carry out a particular motor skill (e.g., riding a bicycle) without conscious awareness of the steps involved in what they are doing. Although it may be true that most motor learning is a type of procedural learning, our work has led us to challenge the view that all procedural learning is motor learning.

In order to determine what subjects learned when they demonstrated that they had learned the repeating sequence, we (Willingham et al., 1989) devised three experimental conditions. Subjects in all three conditions responded according to the color of the stimulus that appeared on each trial, pressing one key if the stimulus was blue, another if it was green, another if it was orange, and a fourth if it was violet. The three conditions involved either (1) a repeating spatial perceptual sequence but no spatial motor sequence (i.e., the locations in which the colored stimuli appeared followed a repeating sequence); (2) a repeating spatial motor sequence but no spatial perceptual sequence (i.e., the sequence of colors and thus responses followed a repeating sequence); or (3) a control condition with neither motor nor perceptual sequences. In a study of normal subjects, we found that there was no learning in the first condition, but there was robust learning in the second condition, which included a motor sequence. This result argues for the view that the learning in this task basically involves learning a sequence of motor responses. Another aspect of the study, however, indicates that the learning was not entirely encapsulated within the motor system. After completing one of the three conditions just described, subjects were given a transfer task that was essentially the original SRT task, so that now responses were based on stimulus location rather than color. Even though this task employed exactly the same motor sequence as that used in the second condition described above, there was virtually no transfer of training.

We believe that what subjects learn in this task is central to and incorporates both perceptual and motor information. What is learned may be thought of as a series of condition–action statements mapping stimuli onto responses. The repetitious use of a series of productions would strengthen the associative connections between them, and performance would be facilitated by the spread of activation between productions (Hunt & Lansman, 1986).

In addition to the common tendency to equate procedural learning with motor learning, there is a tendency to equate verbal learning with declarative learning and to rule out the possibility of procedural learning within the verbal domain. The origins of this view may stem from the fact that the content of consciousness is often verbal, and more generally from the close association between verbal processes and conscious processes (Gazzaniga, 1985).

We tried to find evidence for procedural learning in the verbal domain by using a verbal version of the SRT task (Hartman, Knopman, & Nissen, 1989). On each trial one of four words was presented visually; the words appeared in either a 10-trial repeating sequence or a random sequence. When normal subjects read each word aloud as fast as possible and naming latencies were recorded, we found no evidence of implicit procedural learning. That is, subjects who became aware of the repetition showed by their naming latencies that they learned the sequence, but unaware subjects did not. In contrast, when normal subjects named the category to which each stimulus word belonged, the latency of responses indicated that even subjects who were not aware of the sequence learned it.

Although results from the categorization task show that procedural learning can occur in the verbal domain, the magnitude of the effects in that study were less than in tasks involving either spatially arranged motor responses to verbal stimuli or verbal responses to spatially arranged stimuli (Hartman et al., 1989). It is not entirely clear why the introduction of spatial components into the task enhances the degree of procedural learning. One possibility is that the spatial tasks, unlike the verbal tasks, can take advantage of simple patterns (such as spatial runs and trills) that are familiar pre-experimentally and that form part of the repeating sequence (Restle, 1970).

The Role of Attention and Awareness in Procedural Learning

Because procedural learning can occur without awareness, it has sometimes been assumed that it can occur without attention as well. In an effort to test this assumption, we (Nissen & Bullemer, 1987) trained normal subjects on the SRT task using the repeating sequence. We manipulated the allocation of attention during subjects' performance of the task by including a single-task condition, in which the SRT task was performed alone, and a dual-task condition, in which subjects discriminated and silently counted tones while performing the SRT task. We found that training under dual-task conditions produced no learning of the sequence: Subjects who had completed this dual-task training were no faster than completely unpracticed subjects in responding to the sequence in a single-task situation. The attentional requirements of procedural learning may contribute to the inability of some patients with Alzheimer's disease (Knopman & Nissen, 1987; Knopman, 1991) and Huntington's disease (Knopman & Nissen, 1991) to learn the sequence.

Our findings represent a separation of conscious awareness and attentional capacity. Learning the sequence required attentional capacity but not awareness. Bullemer (1988; Bullemer & Nissen, 1990) addressed the relation between awareness and another aspect of attention: attentional orienting. It seemed reasonable to suppose that when subjects learned the repeating sequence, they developed expectancies regarding the location of the next stimulus. The performance of amnesic patients, however, raised questions about the nature of those expectancies. Because amnesic patients showed by their performance that they learned the sequence, one might argue that they developed expectancies regarding where the next stimulus would appear. Yet if these were conscious expectancies, the amnesic patients should have been aware of the existence of the sequence and should have been able to generate it, but they were not.

The questions Bullemer addressed empirically were these: When subjects who have learned the repeating sequence "expect" a stimulus to appear at a certain location, does that expectancy involve the orienting of attention? And does the act of orienting depend on awareness? Normal subjects were trained on either a random sequence or a repeating sequence, and then performed a slightly modified version of the repeating-sequence condition in which there was an occasional out-of-sequence item. The question was whether subjects who had previously learned the repeating sequence would respond to these out-of-sequence items more slowly than subjects who had previously received the random sequence. The results showed that they did. As in the work of

Posner (1978; Posner & Snyder, 1975), the presence of this slowing or "cost" in response to unexpected items was taken as a symptom of the involvement of attention in these expectancies. This conclusion was supported by Bullemer's additional finding that cost disappeared in a divided-attention dual-task condition.

The part of these findings that was most intriguing was that although the appearance of cost depended on the amount of previous training on the repeating sequence, the appearance of cost was independent of awareness. Even subjects who were unaware of the sequence showed cost in responding to out-of-sequence events. Conscious awareness appears to be separable from both the capacity and orienting aspects of attention.

Theoretical Views

The memory structures and processes involved in this task can be characterized in the following way. As subjects are trained on the repeating sequence, associative procedural connections develop among representations of the productions involved in mapping the four stimuli onto the four responses. As these connections increase in strength, the occurrence of one item (stimulus–response pair) primes or provides early activation of the next item, thus decreasing the time required for the activation to reach some critical level when the next stimulus actually occurs. This early priming can also be great enough to pull attention to the next item. If this orienting of attention occurs, there will be cost in responding if an out-of-sequence stimulus occurs instead. The appearance and magnitude of cost depend on the amount of training subjects have received on the repeating sequence, because training affects the connection strengths and thus the likelihood of priming and attentional orienting.

Conscious awareness of the sequence does not directly affect its procedural representation. Instead, awareness is associated with the parallel development of a declarative representation of the sequence. Attention, in contrast, can be drawn by and oriented to either procedural or declarative representations.

As in Anderson's (1983) ACT° model, general-purpose productions can make use of the declarative representation of the sequence for generating responses. In our experiments, this process supports performance in the generate task (and perhaps anticipatory responses in the SRT task). Even though the priming of associated productions in procedural memory is adequate for pulling attention to the next item in the sequence, it is not adequate for triggering a response in the absence of a stimulus. For that, declarative knowledge is required.

This last point raises another question: What are the necessary and sufficient conditions for preserved learning in amnesia? Several things are clear from our research: (1) The consistent repetition of stimulus–response pairs appears to be necessary but is not sufficient. (2) The use of an implicit learning situation similarly appears to be necessary but not sufficient. (3) Not all "motor learning" tasks are preserved. (4) Preserved learning is not automatic learning (i.e., learning that does not require attention). Instead, it appears that amnesic patients learn normally in situations where the stimulus specifies or tightly constrains response selection. (Jacoby,

1983; Mishkin, Malamut, & Bachevalier, 1984; and Moscovitch, 1984, have presented similar views.)

We were led to this view in part by results obtained from patients with Korsakoff's syndrome on two versions of a tactual stylus maze task (Nissen et al., 1989). The ability to learn the route through a standard tactual stylus maze is impaired in amnesia (Cermak et al., 1973; Corkin, 1965; Milner et al., 1968), and our results replicated that finding: The mean number of errors per trial and the time required to complete the maze both decreased in our healthy and alcoholic control groups, but not among the Korsakoff patients.

We also tested performance on a modified version of the tactual stylus maze task, in which entrances to blind alleys were blocked, so that there was only one route through the maze. Korsakoff patients and healthy and alcoholic control subjects were asked to trace the route as fast as possible, and their completion times were measured. Because there was only one route through the maze, no errors were possible. This was an implicit learning task with no requirement to recollect prior experiences; it was a perceptual–motor learning task; and it included consistent repetition during training. Nevertheless, the Korsakoff patients were impaired relative to controls in showing learning on this task.

One way in which this modified maze task differs from the SRT task, in which the same patients showed learning of a spatial sequence, is that the modified maze provides no cues indicating which response should be made until a response has already been attempted, whereas the stimuli in the SRT task uniquely specify which response is to be made. Early interitem activation (priming) in the SRT task can facilitate performance because less time is required for activation to reach criterion when the triggering stimulus appears. It is possible that associative procedural connections allowing priming might develop in the maze task as well, at least if performance were consistent, but in the absence of the triggering stimulus (i.e., one that specifies the response) there is nothing to boost activation above criterion. Response selection in the maze task depends on declarative knowledge. Hence, any potential associative procedural learning cannot make itself evident in performance.

Conclusion

The surge of new studies of amnesia and associated research on implicit learning in normal subjects, triggered in part by Cohen and Squire's (1980) article, has stimulated new thinking about conscious awareness and has provided new opportunities for studying it empirically. Our work (Bullemer, 1988; Bullemer & Nissen, 1990; Nissen & Bullemer, 1987) suggests that the custom of equating awareness with attention is inappropriate. Recent findings by Posner and his colleagues, using positron emission tomography and other methods, also point to a separation of neural systems subserving attentional orienting from those associated with the control of action and the subjective experience of being aware of an event (Posner, Petersen, Fox, & Raichle, 1988; Posner & Petersen, 1990; Posner & Rothbart, 1990). The study of the amnesic syndrome thus not only has led to important changes in how we think about memory, but is now beginning to change theories of other components of cognition as well.

ACKNOWLEDGMENTS

The research described here was supported in part by Office of Naval Research Contract No. N00014-86-K-0277; by the Center for Research in Learning, Perception, and Cognition of the University of Minnesota; and by a faculty research fellowship from the University of Minnesota. The research described in this chapter was done in collaboration with Peter Bullemer, Marilyn Hartman, David Knopman, Thomas Mackenzie, James Ross, Daniel Schacter, and Daniel Willingham. I thank them all.

REFERENCES

Anderson, J. R. (1983). *The architecture of cognition*. Cambridge, MA: Harvard University Press.

Brooks, D. N., & Baddeley, A. (1976). What can amnesic patients learn? *Neuropsychologia, 14*, 111–122.

Bullemer, P. T. (1988). *On the relationship between attentional processes and memory systems in the expression of skill: A combined cost-benefit and dual-task approach*. Unpublished doctoral dissertation, University of Minnesota.

Bullemer, P., & Nissen, M. J. (1990, November). *Attentional orienting in the expression of procedural knowledge*. Paper presented at the meeting of the Psychonomic Society, New Orleans.

Cermak, L. S., Lewis, R., Butters, N., & Goodglass, H. (1973). Role of verbal mediation in performance of motor tasks by Korsakoff patients. *Perceptual and Motor Skills, 37*, 259–262.

Cohen, N. J., & Squire, L. R. (1980). Preserved learning and retention of pattern-analyzing skill in amnesia: Dissociation of knowing how and knowing that. *Science, 210*, 207–210.

Corkin, S. (1965). Tactually-guided maze learning in man: Effects of unilateral cortical excisions and bilateral hippocampal lesions. *Neuropsychologia, 3*, 339–351.

Corkin, S. (1968). Acquisition of motor skill after bilateral medial temporal-lobe excision. *Neuropsychologia, 6*, 255–265.

Gazzaniga, M. S. (1985). *The social brain*. New York: Basic Books.

Hartman, M., Knopman, D., & Nissen, M. J. (1989). Implicit learning of new verbal associations. *Journal of Experimental Psychology: Learning, Memory, and Cognition, 15*, 1070–1082.

Howard, D. V., & Howard, J. H. (1989). Age differences in learning serial patterns: Direct versus indirect measures. *Psychology and Aging, 4*, 357–364.

Hunt, E., & Lansman, M. (1986). Unified model of attention and problem solving. *Psychological Review, 93*, 446–461.

Jacoby, L. L. (1983). Remembering the data: Analyzing interactive processes in reading. *Journal of Verbal Learning and Verbal Behavior, 22*, 485–508.

Knopman, D. S. (1991). Long-term retention of implicitly acquired learning in patients with Alzheimer's disease. *Journal of Clinical and Experimental Neuropsychology, 13*, 880–894.

Knopman, D. S., & Nissen, M. J. (1987). Implicit learning in patients with probable Alzheimer's disease. *Neurology, 37*, 784–788.

Knopman, D. S., & Nissen, M. J. (1991). Procedural learning is impaired in Huntington's disease: Evidence from the serial reaction time task. *Neuropsychologia, 29*, 245–254.

Milner, B. (1962). Les troubles de la mémoire accompagnant des lésions hippocampiques bilatérales. In P. Passouant (Ed.), *Physiologie de l'hippocampe*. Paris: Centre National de la Recherche Scientifique.

Milner, B., Corkin, S., & Teuber, H.-L. (1968). Further analysis of the hippocampal syndrome: 14-year follow-up study of H. M. *Neuropsychologia, 6*, 215–234.

Mishkin, M., Malamut, B., & Bachevalier, J. (1984). Memories and habits: Two neural systems. In G. Lynch, J. L. McGaugh, & N. Weinberger (Eds.), *Neurobiology of learning and memory* (pp. 65–77). New York: Guilford Press.

Moscovitch, M. (1984). The sufficient conditions for demonstrating preserved memory in amnesia: A task analysis. In N. Butters & L. R. Squire (Eds.), *Neuropsychology of memory* (1st ed., pp. 104–114). New York: Guilford Press.

Nissen, M. J., & Bullemer, P. (1987). Attentional requirements of learning: Evidence from performance measures. *Cognitive Psychology, 19*, 1–32.

Nissen, M. J., Knopman, D. S., & Schacter, D. L. (1987). Neurochemical dissociation of memory systems. *Neurology, 37*, 789–794.

Nissen, M. J., & Mackenzie, T. B. (1991). [Procedural learning following electroconvulsive therapy]. Unpublished raw data.

Nissen, M. J., Ross, J. L., Willingham, D. B., Mackenzie, T. B., & Schacter, D. L. (1988). Memory and awareness in a patient with multiple personality disorder. *Brain and Cognition, 8,* 117–134.

Nissen, M. J., Willingham, D. B., & Hartman, M. (1989). Explicit and implicit remembering: When is learning preserved in amnesia? *Neuropsychologia, 27,* 341–352.

Posner, M. I. (1978). *Chronometric explorations of mind.* Hillsdale, NJ: Erlbaum.

Posner, M. I., & Petersen, S. E. (1990). The attention system of the human brain. *Annual Review of Neuroscience, 13,* 25–42.

Posner, M. I., Petersen, S. E., Fox, P. T., & Raichle, M. E. (1988). Localization of cognition operations in the human brain. *Science, 240,* 1627–1631.

Posner, M. I., & Rothbart, M. K. (1990). *Attentional mechanisms and conscious experience* (Tech. Rep. No. 90-17). Eugene: University of Oregon, Institute of Cognitive and Decision Sciences.

Posner, M. I., & Snyder, C. R. R. (1975). Attention and cognitive control. In R. L. Solso (Ed.), *Information processing and cognition: The Loyola Symposium* (pp. 55–85). Hillsdale, NJ: Erlbaum.

Restle, F. (1970). Theory of serial pattern learning: Structural trees. *Psychological Review, 77,* 481–495.

Schacter, D. L. (1987). Implicit memory: History and current status. *Journal of Experimental Psychology: Learning, Memory, and Cognition, 13,* 501–518.

Shimamura, A. P. (1986). Priming effects in amnesia: Evidence for a dissociable memory function. *Quarterly Journal of Experimental Psychology, 38A,* 619–644.

Tulving, E., & Schacter, D. L. (1990). Priming and human memory. *Science, 247,* 301–306.

Warrington, E. K., & Weiskrantz, L. (1968). New method of testing long-term retention with special reference to amnesic patients. *Nature, 217,* 972–974.

Willingham, D. B., Nissen, M. J., & Bullemer, P. (1989). On the development of procedural knowledge. *Journal of Experimental Psychology: Learning, Memory, and Cognition, 15,* 1047–1060.

18

The Assessment of Memory Disorders in Patients with Alzheimer's Disease

MARILYN S. ALBERT and MARK B. MOSS

Since the original description by Alois Alzheimer (1907) of the disorder that bears his name, there has been a widespread awareness that patients with Alzheimer's disease (AD) or dementia of the Alzheimer type have a prominent memory deficit. In recent years there has been a growing consensus that this memory impairment is likely to be the first symptom of disease. There is less agreement, however, on the nature of this memory impairment.

The present chapter discusses the evidence to date concerning the type of memory impairment that is most characteristic of AD patients early in the course of disease. If the nature of this memory impairment is understood, it will improve diagnostic accuracy for mildly impaired patients. This has considerable practical significance, as it pertains to both patient care and attempts to treat AD with a variety of pharmacological interventions. It has substantial theoretical importance as well, since it should shed light on the pathophysiology of AD. The longitudinal evaluation of questionable dementia cases also relates to the subject of early accurate diagnosis of AD patients. Recent data pertaining to this subject is therefore also reviewed.

The Memory Impairment in Alzheimer's Disease

Evidence has accumulated to suggest that the hippocampal formation is damaged in AD (Ball, 1977; Kemper, 1984; Hyman, Van Hoesen, Kromer, & Damasio, 1984). It was hypothesized that hippocampal damage should manifest itself in terms of rapid forgetting. Therefore recent studies have examined the loss of information over varying delay intervals in patients with AD, to determine whether these patients display an unusually rapid rate of forgetting. The results of these studies suggest that clinical and experimental measures that capitalize on loss of information over brief delays (about 2–10 minutes) are most useful for differentiating AD patients from controls and from other patient groups.

In the first such study (Moss, Albert, Butters, & Payne, 1986), we compared patients with AD to a group of amnesic patients who had alcoholic Korsakoff's (AK) syndrome, a group of dementing patients who had Huntington's disease (HD), and a group of normal controls (NC). The subjects were administered the Delayed Recognition Span Test. This task employs disks on which are placed a variety of stimuli (words, colors, faces, patterns, etc.). During the recognition portion of the task, the disks are placed on a board one at a time (there are 16 disks in all). As each disk is added, the board is hidden from view. The subject is then asked to point to the disk that was added during the delay interval. In order to do this, the subject must keep track of an increasingly long series of disks. There was no significant difference among the patient groups in their delayed-recognition span for spatial, color, pattern, or facial stimuli; patients with HD performed significantly better than the other groups when verbal stimuli were used. However, substantial differences among the groups were evident during the delayed-recall portion of the verbal version of the task. At both 15 seconds and 2 minutes after the completion of the verbal recognition span, each subject was asked to recall the words that had been on the disks. All three patient groups were equally impaired relative to NC subjects at the 15-second delay; only the AD group performed significantly worse at the longer as compared to the shorter interval. It was particularly notable that by the end of the 2-minute interval, 11 of the 12 patients in the AD group could recall fewer than 3 of the 16 words presented repeatedly during recognition testing. Of these 11 patients, 7 patients were unable to recall any of the 16 words at the longer interval. The savings score (i.e., the difference between immediate and delayed recall) best differentiated the groups. Whereas the AK, HD, and NC subjects lost an average of 10% to 15% of the verbal information between the 15-second and 2-minute delay intervals, patients with AD lost an average of 73% of the material.

A similar pattern of results was reported by Butters et al. (1988). They showed that AD patients could be distinguished from patients with HD and NC subjects on the basis of the differences between the Attention/Concentration and General Memory indices of the Wechsler Memory Scale—Revised. More specifically, savings scores calculated from the Logical Memory and Visual Reproduction subtests showed that the AD patients forgot verbal and figural materials more quickly than did the HD patients and NC subjects.

A recent study by Welsh, Butters, Hughes, Mohs, and Heyman (1991) found that among very mildly impaired AD patients (patients with Mini-Mental State Exam scores of 24 or greater), the memory measure that best differentiated patients and controls pertained to delayed recall. The memory tasks employed in this study were those in the battery developed by the Consortium to Establish a Registry for Alzheimer's Disease (CERAD). It includes three learning trials of a 10-word list, one delayed-recall trial of the list, two measures of delayed recognition, and the number of intrusions on each recall trial. The investigators found that 86% of the AD patients were correctly classified when the delayed-recall measure was used. A savings score, derived from subtracting the delayed-recall score from the score on the last immediate-recall trial, correctly classified 62% of the subjects. All other memory measures yielded even lower discrimination between the groups (e.g., on average, the intrusion scores differentiated 22% of the subjects, and the recognition score differentiated 21% of the subjects). However, a comparison of moderately and severely impaired patients indicated that a combination of recognition and intrusion measures provided the best discrimination between mild and moderately impaired patients (i.e, 66% accuracy), indicating that delayed-recall measures are not useful in staging AD patients as the disease progresses.

Other patient groups also appear to recall more information after a delay than patients with AD. Milberg and Albert (1989) have demonstrated that patients with progressive supranuclear palsy differ significantly from AD patients on measures of delayed recall. Similarly, we (Moss & Albert, 1988) have reported that patients with a frontal lobe dementia (FLD) have significantly better savings scores on the Delayed Recognition Span Test than AD patients equated for overall level of disease severity.

Although all of these studies emphasize the importance of delayed-recall measures in differentiating AD patients from other groups of subjects, they leave unanswered the question of the underlying nature of the memory impairment. That is, do AD patients recall less information over a delay because they cannot encode the information correctly, because they use poor retrieval strategies, or because the rate at which they forget information (i.e., their storage capacity) differs from that of other subject groups? This issue was addressed directly in a study by Hart, Kwentus, Harkin, and Taylor (1988). They administered a continuous-recognition task to AD patients and controls. Subjects were shown a large series of pictures of complex scenes; then they were shown these scenes again, mixed in with scenes that had not been previously shown. The subjects' task was to indicate whether or not each scene had been in the original set (i.e.,whether it was an old or new one). Adjusting the exposure time of each scene made it possible to equate both groups of subjects for retention of a subset of the items at 90 seconds after the completion of the task (retention levels were equated at about 85–90% accuracy). The subjects were then retested at delay intervals of 10 minutes, 2 hours, and 48 hours. The AD patients showed a rapid rate of forgetting between the 90-second interval and the 10-minute interval, but not between the 10-minute and 2-hour or 48-hour intervals.

Both Corkin et al. (1984) and Kopelman (1985) have also published studies employing a continuous-recognition task such as this with AD patients. They concluded that there was no difference in rate of forgetting beteen AD patients and controls. However, both groups of investigators had equated the two groups of subjects for recognition accuracy at 10 minutes and then looked for loss of information at subsequent delay periods (i.e., 24 hours and 72 hours or 24 hours and 7 days, respectively). Taken together, these three studies suggest that AD patients forget information at a more rapid rate during the first 10 minutes after initial learning; following this 10-minute period, their rate of loss of information cannot be distinguished from that of controls.

The pratical implication of the findings from all of the foregoing studies is that relatively brief delay intervals (about 2–10 minutes) should be best at differentiating AD patients from controls and from other patient groups. Delay intervals of longer duration should make it harder, rather than easier, to use memory testing to distinguish patients with differing disorders from one another and from controls.

The major clinical application of these findings is likely to pertain to the identification of patients with FLD. Reports of recent autopsy series from patients meeting clinical research criteria for AD (the so-called National Institute of Neurological and Communicative Disorders and Stroke/Alzheimer's Disease and Related Disorders

Association [NINCDS/ADRDA] criteria; McKhann et al., 1984) indicate that the majority of the patients who fail to have AD on autopsy but were thought to have AD during their lifetimes have FLD (Tierney et al., 1988; Joachim, Morris, & Selkoe, 1988). Thus, improving the differentiation of patients with AD and FLD should greatly improve the accuracy of diagnosis among patients with progressive dementing disorders.

The FLDs represent a constellation of disorders that affect primarily, but not exclusively, the frontal association areas. At least three different disorders are collectively referred to as FLD: Pick's disease (Pick, 1898); progressive subcortical gliosis (Neumann & Cohn, 1967) or Pick type II (Neumann, 1949); and FLD of the non-Alzheimer type (Gustafson, Brun, & Risberg, 1988), also referred to as dementia of the frontal lobe type (DFLT; Neary et al., 1986). As a group, they are characterized by the insidious onset of either a personality change or a language disturbance, with a concomitant impairment in executive function. Memory impairment is generally present, but it is not the predominant feature at the earliest stages of disease. As with AD, eventually all areas of cognitive function are compromised, so that in moderately or severely impaired patients the nature of the presenting symptoms can only be established in retrospect. The presentation among these three diseases is quite similar, and at the present time they are difficult to differentiate from one another during a patient's lifetime.

Although research studies pertaining to patients with FLD are extremely limited, those that exist indicate that FLD patients frequently show impaired immediate recall, but retain information quite well over a very brief delay (i.e., 2-10 minutes). For example, Gustafson (1987) describes the clinical presentation of five patients who had DFLT on autopsy. All of the patients presented with changes in personality and/or language, along with memory problems. However, the patients could typically recall information over brief delays until their disease was moderately advanced.

Neuropathological Underpinnings for the Memory Impairment in Alzheimer's Disease

There have been at least two major hypotheses concerning the relationship between the pathophysiology of AD and the memory dysfunction of AD patients. It was first hypothesized that the marked depletion of the cholinergic enzymes choline acetyltransferase and acetylcholinesterase were primarily responsible for the severe memory loss associated with the disease. This proposal, known as the cholinergic hypothesis (Bartus, Dean, Beer, & Lippa, 1982), was based in part on pharmacological evidence from both human and animal studies. Cholinergic antagonists, such as scopolamine, produce memory dysfunction when administered to normal adults and nonhuman primates (Drachman & Leavitt, 1974; Drachman & Sahakian, 1980; Bartus, 1978; Bartus, Dean, & Beer, 1980); while substances that are known to increase the amount of available acetylcholine, such as arecoline or physostigmine, improve memory (Bartus, 1978). In addition, neuropathological studies of patients with AD show a loss of cholinergic-positive neurons in the basal forebrain—neurons projecting to cortical and limbic areas that show cholinergic depletion. However, recent studies in animals indicate that lesions of the basal forebrain do not produce a severe or lasting impairment in new learning (Aigner et al., 1984; Moss & Rosene, 1985; Moss, Rosene, & Beason, 1991), thus casting doubt on the notion that a cholinergic deficit is primarily responsible for the anterograde memory loss seen in AD.

The second hypothesis concerning the relationship between the pathophysiology and cognitive impairment in AD proposes that neuropathological alterations in the amygdala and hippocampal formation are the critical changes responsible for the memory loss seen in AD patients. Combined damage to the amygdala and hippocampus (Mishkin, 1978; Mahut, Zola-Morgan, & Moss, 1982; Murray & Mishkin, 1984; Saunders, Murray, & Mishkin, 1984); damage to the hippocampus alone (Mahut et al., 1982; Zola-Morgan & Squire, 1986) or to the rhinal cortices alone (Moss, Mahut, & Zola-Morgan, 1981); or damage to the rhinal cortices in combination with the hippocampus or amygdala (Murray & Mishkin, 1986) produces impairments in learning and memory. In AD, neurofibrillary tangles and neuritic plaques are prevalent in the cortical association areas and regions of the medial temporal lobe—that is, the hippocampus, the amygdala, and the parahippocampal gyri (Ball et al., 1985; Herzog & Kemper, 1980; Hyman et al., 1984; Kemper, 1984). In the hippocampal formation, these alterations are seen primarily in the entorhinal cortex and subiculum (Hyman et al., 1984, 1991), the primary pathways that convey information into and out of the hippocampus (Rosene & Van Hoesen, 1987). These findings suggest that neuropathological damage to medial temporal structures—in particular, the amygdala and hippocampus—may be responsible for the marked impairment in delayed memory evident in the early stages of AD. The development of other symptoms in the patients, such as difficulty in set shifting or language function, may result from the destruction of cortico-cortical connections (Morrison et al., 1990), from the direct damage to cortical regions thought to underlie these functions, or from dysfunction in subcortical regions that project to these cortical areas (e.g., the basal forebrain).

Given the pathology of FLD, it is not surprising that the nature of the memory impairment differs substantially between AD and FLD. The focus of the cortical pathology is the frontal lobes and the hippocampal formation appears to be spared in FLD (Seitelberger, Gross, & Pilz, 1983; Neumann & Cohn, 1967; Gustafson, 1987).

Diagnosis of Patients with Questionable Dementia

As the nature of the memory impairment in AD patients has become better understood, it is increasingly likely that the findings regarding the importance of delayed-recall measures can be applied to patients who are so mildly impaired that it is unclear that a true dementia exists (so-called "questionable dementia" cases). If delayed-recall measures are most effective in differentiating mildly impaired AD patients from controls, then it is theoretically possible that from among those patients with a questionable dementia, the patients with a striking deficit in delayed recall are those who will go on to develop a true dementia. There are only a small number of studies concerning such cases that can be examined to determine the applicability of this hypothesis.

Some studies that examined questionable cases who subsequently developed confirmed AD have reported postmortem data on patients who were defined as questionable because they failed to meet cutoff criteria on a mental status screening test (Katzman et al., 1988) or a detailed neuropsychological battery (Crystal et al., 1988). There was, however, no information concerning whether reports from collateral sources (such as relatives or friends) indicated that the subjects' performance in everyday life had actually declined. It is therefore unclear that the subjects in these studies were in fact demonstrating declines from premorbid levels. A parallel concern pertains to studies reporting postmortem data on the brains of subjects who met pathological criteria for AD (Khatchaturian, 1985) and were reported to be normal during their lifetimes, but had not in fact been systematically examined prior to death (Ulrich, 1985; de la Monte, 1989; Miller, Hicks, Damato, & Landis, 1984).

A few recent studies, however, have performed comprehensive examinations on subjects who were questionably impaired and have followed them to autopsy. These studies utilized the Washington University Clinical Dementia Rating Scale (CDR; Hughes et al., 1982), as well as a structured clinical assessment by skilled clinicians, to classify subjects regarding the presence or absence of dementia. Subjects were classified as either controls (CDR = 0), questionably demented (CDR = 0.5), or demented (CDR = 1 or more). The first of these studies (Rubin, Morris, & Grant, 1989) reported that there was no significant difference in cognitive test performance between the questionable subjects who went on to develop a true dementia and the questionable subjects who did not. However, the questionable group as a whole differed from controls on a set of brief screening measures and on tasks included in a detailed neuropsychological battery. The second study (Morris et al., 1991), which contained some of the subjects from the first study, did not find a significant difference between the questionable subjects and controls on brief screening measures, but reported that some of the tasks on the more lengthy neuropsychological battery were significantly different between the groups. The test scores that differed between the questionable cases and the controls included two measures of immediate recall and a measure of general information: the Logical Memory and Associate Learning subtests of the Wechsler Memory Scale, and the Information subtest of the Wechsler Adult Intelligence Scale—Revised, respectively. There was, however, an overlap between the scores of the questionable cases and the controls. These data indicate that measures of immediate recall and general information cannot be used to reliably differentiate questionable cases who will go on to develop a true dementia from those who will not, or even all questionable cases from controls.

The structured assessments of the clinicians, however, yielded some intriguing information. First, all of the subjects who progressed from a CDR score of 0.5 to 1.0 or greater and came to autopsy had AD at postmortem (Morris et al., 1991). Second, all of the questionable subjects who were rated as having an impaired memory by the clinicians (i.e., received a score of 1 on the Memory subscale of the CDR) went on to develop a true dementia, whereas more than half of the questionable subjects who were not rated as having an impaired memory by the clinicians did not develop a true dementia during the 7-year course of the study (Rubin et al., 1989). These findings suggest that carefully screened questionable subjects with ratings of 1 on the Memory subscale of the CDR will develop AD. They also confirm the importance of a memory impairment as an early marker of AD. However, since neither of these studies measured delayed recall in their questionable subjects, it remains unclear whether tasks that assess delayed recall, or a savings score that is based on the difference between immediate and delayed recall, can differentiate questionable cases who will develop a true dementia from those who will not. Future studies that are designed with this goal in mind, and that employ delayed-recall measures designed to maximize the difference between mildly impaired AD patients and controls (e.g., Knopman & Ryberg, 1989), should answer this question.

REFERENCES

Aigner, T., Mitchell, S., Aggleton, J., DeLong, M., Struble, R., Wenk, G., Price, D., & Mishkin, M. (1984). Recognition memory in monkeys following neurotoxic lesions of the basal forebrain. *Society for Neuroscience Abstracts, 10*, 386.

Alzheimer, A. (1907). Über eine eigenartige Erkrankung der Hirnrinde. *Allgemeines Zeitschrift für Psychiatrie, 64*, 146-148.

Ball, M. J. (1977). Neuronal loss, neurofibrillary tangles, granulovacuolar degeneration in the hippocampus with aging and dementia. *Acta Neuropathologica, 37*, 111-118.

Ball, M. J., Fisman, H., Hachinski, V., Blume, W., Fox, A., Kral, V., Kirshen, A., Fox, H., & Merskey, H. (1985). A new definition of Alzheimer's disease: A hippocampal dementia. *Lancet, i*, 14-16.

Bartus, R. T. (1978). Evidence for direct cholinergic involvement in scopolamine-induced amnesia in monkeys: Effects of concurrent administration of physostigmine and methylphenidate with scopolamine. *Pharmacology, Biochemistry and Behavior, 9*, 833-836.

Bartus, R. T., Dean, R. L., & Beer, B. (1980). Memory deficits in aged cebus monkeys and facilitation with central cholinomimetics. *Neurobiology of Aging, 1*, 145-152.

Bartus, R. T., Dean, R. L., Beer, B., & Lippa, A. (1982). The cholinergic hypothesis of geriatric memory dysfunction. *Science, 217*, 408-416.

Butters, N., Salmon, D. P., Munro Cullum, C., Cairns, P., Tröster, A. I., & Jacobs, D. (1988). Differentiation of amnesic and demented patients with the Wechsler Memory Scale—Revised. *Clinical Neuropsychologist, 2*, 133-148.

Corkin, S., Growdon, J., Nissen, M. J., Huff, F., Freed, D., & Sagar, H. (1984). Recent advances in the neuropsychological study of Alzheimer's disease. In R. J. Wurtman, S. Corkin, & J. H. Growdon (Eds.), *Alzheimer's disease: Advances in basic research and therapies* (pp. 75-94). Boston: Center for Brain Sciences and Metabolism Trust.

Crystal, H., Dickson, D., Fuld, P., Masur, R., Scott, R., Mehler, M., Masdeu, J., Kawas, C., Aronson, M., & Wolfson, L. (1988). Clinico-pathologic studies in dementia: Nondemented subjects with pathologically confirmed Alzheimer's disease. *Neurology, 38*, 1682-1687.

de la Monte, S. M. (1989). Quantitation of cerebral atrophy in preclinical and end-stage Alzheimer's disease. *Annals of Neurology, 25*, 450-459.

Drachman, D. A., & Leavitt, J. (1974). Human memory and the cholinergic system: A relationship to aging? *Archives of Neurology, 30*, 113-121.

Drachman, D. A., & Sahakian, B. J. (1980). Memory and cognitive function in the elderly: Preliminary trial of physostigmine. *Archives of Neurology, 37*, 383-385.

Gustafson, L. (1987). Frontal lobe degeneration of the non-Alzheimer type: II. Clinical picture and differential diagnosis. *Archives of Gerontology and Geriatrics, 6*, 209-223.

Gustafson, L., Brun, A., & Risberg, J. (1988). Frontal lobe dementia of non-Alzheimer type. In R. J. Wurtman (Ed.), *Advances in neurology* (Vol. 51, pp. 65-71). New York: Raven Press.

Hart, R. P., Kwentus, J. A., Harkins, S. W., & Taylor, J. R. (1988). Rate of forgetting in mild Alzheimer's type dementia. *Brain and Cognition, 7*, 31-38.

Herzog, A. G., & Kemper, T. (1980). Amygdaloid changes in aging and dementia. *Archives of Neurology, 37*, 625-629.

Hughes, C. P., Berg, L., Danziger, W. L., Coben, L., & Martin, R. (1982). A new clinical scale for the staging of dementia. *British Journal of Psychiatry, 140*, 566-572.

Hyman, B. T., Arriagada, P. V., McKee, A., Ghika, J., Corkin, S., & Growdon, J. (1991). The earliest symptoms of Alzheimer's disease: Anatomic correlates. *Society for Neuroscience Abstracts, 17*, 352.

Hyman, B. T., Van Hoesen, G. W., Kromer, L. J., & Damasio, A. (1984). Perforant pathway changes and the memory impairment of Alzheimer's disease. *Annals of Neurology, 20*, 472-481.

Joachim, C. L., Morris, J. H., & Selkoe, D. J. (1988). Clinically diagnosed Alzheimer's disease: Autopsy results in 150 cases. *Annals of Neurology, 24*, 50-56.

Katzman, R., Terry, R., De Teresa, R., Brown, T., Davies, P., Fuld, P., Renbing, X., & Peck, A. (1988). Clinical, pathological and neurochemical changes in dementia: A subgroup with preserved mental status and numerous neocortical plaques. *Annals of Neurology, 23*, 138-144.

Kemper, T. (1984). Neuroanatomical and neuropathological changes in normal aging and dementia. In M. L. Albert (Ed.), *Clinical neurology of aging* (pp. 9-52). New York: Oxford University Press.

Khatchaturian, Z. S. (1985). Diagnosis of Alzheimer's disease. *Archives of Neurology, 42*, 1097-1105.

Knopman, D. S., & Ryberg, S. (1989). A verbal memory test with high predictive accuracy for dementia of the Alzheimer type. *Archives of Neurology, 46*, 141-145.

Kopelman, M. D. (1985). Rates of forgetting in Alzheimer-type dementia and Korsakoff's syndrome. *Neuropsychologia, 23*, 623-638.

Mahut, H., Zola-Morgan, S., & Moss, M. (1982). Recognition memory impairment after selective hippocampal resections in the monkey. *Journal of Neuroscience, 2*, 1214-1229.

McKhann, G., Drachman, D., Folstein, M., Katzman, R., Price, D., & Stadlan, E. (1984). Clinical diagnosis of Alzheimer's disease: Report of the NINCDS-ADRDA Work Group under the auspices of Department of Health and Human Services Task Force on Alzheimer's Disease. *Neurology, 34*, 939-944.

Milberg, W., & Albert, M. S. (1989) Cognitive differences between patients with progressive supranuclear palsy and Alzheimer's disease. *Journal of Clinical and Experimental Neuropsychology, 10*, 576-596.

Miller, F. D., Hicks, S. P., D'Amato, C. J., & Landis, J. (1984). A descriptive study of neuritic plaques and neurofibrillary tangles in an autopsy population. *American Journal of Epidemiology, 120*, 331-341.

Mishkin, M. (1978). Memory in monkeys severely impaired by combined but not separate removal of amygdala and hippocampus. *Nature, 273*, 297-298.

Morris, J. C., McKeel, D. W., Storandt, M., Rubin, E., Price, J., Grant, E., Ball, M., & Berg, L. (1991). Very mild Alzheimer's disease: Informant-based clinical, psychometric and pathologic distinction from normal aging. *Neurology, 41*, 469-478.

Morrison, J. H., Hof, P. R., Campbell, M. J., DeLima, A., Voight, T., Bouras, C., Cox, K., & Young, W. (1990). Cellular pathology in Alzheimer's disease: Implications for corticocortical disconnection and differential vulnerability. In S. R. Rappaport, H. Petit, D. Leys, & Y. Christen (Eds.), *Imaging, cerebral topography and Alzheimer's disease* (pp. 19-40). New York: Springer-Verlag.

Moss, M. B., & Albert, M. S. (1988). Alzheimer's disease and other dementing disorders. In M. S. Albert & M. B. Moss (Eds.), *Geriatric neuropsychology* (pp. 293-304). New York: Guilford Press.

Moss, M. B., Albert, M. S., Butters, N., & Payne, M. (1986). Differential patterns of memory loss among patients with Alzheimer's disease, Huntington's disease and alcoholic Korsakoff's syndrome. *Archives of Neurology, 43*, 239-246.

Moss, M. B., Mahut, H., & Zola-Morgan, S. (1981). Concurrent discrimination learning of monkeys after hippocampal, entorhinal or fornix lesions. *Journal of Neuroscience, 1*, 227-240.

Moss, M. B., & Rosene, D. (1985). A graded retrograde memory impairment after lesions of the basal forebrain in the rhesus monkey. *Society for Neuroscience Abstracts, 11*, 831.

Moss, M. B., Rosene, D. L., & Beason, L. L. (1991). *A mild and transient impairment in recognition memory following damage to the nucleus basalis of Meynert in the rhesus monkey.* Manuscript submitted for publication.

Murray, E. A., & Mishkin, M. (1984). Severe tactual as well as visual memory deficits follow combined removal of the amygdala and hippocampus in monkeys. *Journal of Neuroscience, 4*, 2565-2580.

Murray, E. A., & Mishkin, M. (1986). Visual recognition in monkeys following rhinal cortical ablations combined with either amygdalectomy or hippocampectomy. *Journal of Neuroscience, 6*, 1991-2003.

Neary, D., Snowden, J. S., Bowen, D. M., Sims, N., Mann, D., Benton, J., Northen, B., Yates, P., & Davison, A. (1986). Neuropsychological syndromes in presenile dementia due to cerebral atrophy. *Journal of Neurology, Neurosurgery and Psychiatry, 53*, 929-931.

Neumann, M. A. (1949). Pick's disease. *Journal of Neurology, Neurosurgery and Psychiatry, 8*, 255-282.

Neumann, M. A., & Cohn, R. (1967). Progressive subcortical gliosis: A rare form of presenile dementia. *Brain, 90*, 405-418.

Pick, A. (1898). *Beitrage zur pathologie und Pathologischen Anatomie des Zentralnervensystem.* Berlin: S. Karger.

Rosene, D. L., & Van Hoesen, G. W. (1987). The hippocampal formation of the primate brain. In E. G. Jones & A. Peters (Eds.), *Cerebral cortex* (Vol. 6, pp. 345-456). New York: Plenum.

Rubin, E., Morris, J. C., & Grant, E. A. (1989). Very mild senile dementia of the Alzheimer type. *Archives of Neurology, 46,* 379–382.

Saunders, R. C., Murray, E. A., & Mishkin, M. (1984). Further evidence that amygdala and hippocampus contribute equally to recognition memory. *Neuropsychologia, 22,* 785–796.

Seitelberger, F., Gross, H., & Pilz, P. (1983). Pick's disease: A neuropathologic study. In A. Hirano & K. Miyashi (Eds.), *Neuropsychiatric disorders in the elderly* (pp. 87–117). New York: Igaku-Shoin.

Tierney, M. C., Fisher, R. H., Lewis, A. J., Zorzitto, M., Snow, G., Reid, D., & Nieuwstraten, P. (1988). The NINCDS-ADRDA criteria for the clinical diagnosis of Alzheimer's disease: A clinico-pathologic study of 57 cases. *Neurology, 38,* 359–364.

Ulrich, J. (1985). Alzheimer changes in nondemented patients younger than sixty-five: Possible early stages of Alzheimer's disease and senile dementia of the Alzheimer type. *Annals of Neurology, 17,* 272–277.

Welsh, K., Butters, N., Hughes, J., Mohs, R., & Heyman, A. (1991). Detection of abnormal memory decline in mild cases of Alzheimer's disease using CERAD neuropsychological measures. *Archives of Neurology, 48,* 278–281.

Zola-Morgan, S., & Squire, L. (1986). Memory impairment in monkeys following lesions limited to the hippocampus. *Behavioral Neuroscience, 100,* 155–160.

19

Degraded Knowledge Representations in Patients with Alzheimer's Disease: Implications for Models of Semantic and Repetition Priming

ALEX MARTIN

Damage to the neocortex often results in an inability to perform tasks dependent on previously acquired knowledge and skills. Simply stated, patients with cortical lesions seem no longer to know what they used to know, and appear to be unable to do what they previously could do. The nature of these deficits is, of course, largely dependent on the specific location of damage within the cerebral hemispheres. Thus, the extensive literature on the myriad disorders of recognition (the agnosias), language (the aphasias), and action (the apraxias) provides compelling evidence that knowledge is stored or represented in the cerebral cortex. This supposition is further supported by the fact that bilateral damage limited to the hippocampus and other structures of the medial temporal lobe results in a profound inability to consciously recall and recognize all types of recently presented material (global amnesia), while having little or no effect on the retrieval and utilization of knowledge and skills acquired in the more distant past. Therefore, although recent evidence has confirmed that medial temporal lobe damage produces a retrograde amnesia, this deficit is temporally graded, with memory failures becoming less and less severe as one probes knowledge that was acquired further and further before the time of injury (Squire, Haist, & Shimamura, 1989; Zola-Morgan & Squire, 1990). Amnesic patients, for example, can perform normally on tests of object naming and visuospatial ability. In contrast, patients with Alzheimer's disease (AD) most often present with a global amnesia plus deficits in a variety of other cognitive domains, including object naming and visuospatial ability. As would be expected, this combination of deficits results from the fact that the characteristic pathology of AD is most common and most severe in the medial temporal region (especially the entorhinal cortex, hippocampus, and amygdala; Hyman, Van Hoesen, & Damasio, 1990) and in the association regions of the cerebral cortex (especially posterior temporal and parietal zones; Brun & Gustafson, 1976). These patients thus provide a unique opportunity to explore the deterioration of specific, cortically based knowledge systems, as well as the interaction between these systems and the medial temporal lobe structures responsible for the ability to learn and remember newly presented information.

Evidence for Degraded Knowledge Representations

A central issue in the neuropsychology of disorders of knowledge is whether deficits result from impaired access to otherwise intact knowledge bases or from an actual loss or degradation of knowledge stores (Shallice, 1988). As I have argued previously (Martin, 1987; Martin & Fedio, 1983), the pattern of impairment in AD seems to be more consistent with the degraded-store hypothesis. This argument is based on several related findings. First, as is often seen following damage to association cortex, the deficits in AD are not total. As a rule, these patients can provide some information when their knowledge of specific information is probed. For example, AD patients will often provide accurate but incomplete definitions of words on vocabulary tasks, and provide accurate but incomplete descriptions of objects on tests of confrontation naming. Second, their object-naming errors often consist of the name of an object from the same semantic category as the item presented, or the name of the category to which the target object belongs. Third, these patients have marked difficulty generating lists of items that belong to the same semantic category, and this category fluency deficit is disproportionately severe in comparison to their performance on fluency tasks more dependent on lexical than on semantic search (Butters, Granholm, Salmon, Grant, & Wolfe, 1987; Shuttleworth & Huber, 1988; Weingartner et al., 1981). Fourth, when asked to generate a list of items that have a more general relation to each other (e.g., items found in a supermarket), AD patients, like normal elderly controls, tend to sample from a variety of categories (e.g., fruits, vegetables), but produce fewer examples from each category. They also tend to produce an abnormally large ratio of category labels to specific item names (Martin & Fedio, 1983; Nebes & Brady, 1990; Ober, Dronkers, Koss, Delis, & Friedland, 1986; Tröster, Salmon, McCullough, & Butters, 1989). Finally, when their knowledge about specific objects is directly probed, it is found that AD patients can make accurate judgments concerning superordinate and specific category membership. However, these patients have difficulty answering simple yes–no questions concerning specific object attributes (e.g., "Is it used to hold things?", "Is it used to cut things?", "Does it have moving parts?" for pictures of tools), and this tendency to make attribute errors occurs most often with objects that the patients are unable to name (Chertkow & Bub, 1990; Chertkow, Bub, & Seidenberg, 1989; Martin, 1987; Martin & Fedio, 1983; Warrington, 1975).

This pattern of results has been interpreted as suggesting that semantic knowledge about objects is hierarchically organized, proceeding from knowledge of specific attributes to more global, superordinate information (Warrington, 1975). Furthermore, AD, and perhaps other disorders affecting more posterior regions of the left temporal lobe (see, e.g., Whitehouse, Caramazza, & Zurif, 1978), result in a loss of knowledge concerning those attributes that distinguish objects within the same semantic category. Thus, it is assumed that in response to either a picture of an object or presentation of the object's name, AD patients are limited to creating a semantic representation that is abnormally underspecified because of a lack of critical, object-specific attributes (i.e., those attributes that serve to distinguish similar objects within the same semantic category). It should be readily appreciated that an underspecified representation with regard to object-specific features is also an overgeneralized representation in relation to other objects within the same semantic category. If this is in fact the case, then it may be assumed that essentially the same semantic representation will be elicited in response to the presentation of objects that bear a close semantic relationship to each other.

This type of degraded-representation explanation is appealing because it seems to account for many of the features enumerated above concerning the performance of AD patients on semantic tasks. For example, when a patient is confronted with an object, an overgeneralized representation should lead to the normal activation of knowledge that is specific for the category to which the object belongs. This representation should be perfectly adequate for eliciting correct but incomplete object descriptions and for making judgments concerning superordinate and category membership. However, it should be insufficient for making judgments about object-specific attributes or features, or for consistently providing the object's name.

On-Line Repetition and Semantic Priming

Since the initial formulation of this hypothesis, not all investigations have provided supportive evidence. For example, Chertkow et al. (1989) were able to replicate our observations that AD patients could correctly answer yes–no questions concerning category membership but not object-specific attributes (Martin & Fedio, 1983), and that attribute knowledge was most impaired for objects that the patients could not name (Martin, 1987). However, Nebes and Brady (1988) and Bayles, Tomoeda, and Trosset (1990), using different paradigms, have obtained evidence suggesting that category knowledge may be as impaired as, or perhaps even more impaired than, attribute knowledge. Similarly, Grober, Buschke, Kawas, and Fuld (1985) found that AD patients could accurately distinguish those attributes that were associated with an object from those that were not, although their judgments of the relative importance or saliency of these attributes were abnormal. Even more troubling have been studies reporting intact semantic facilitation or priming when on-line semantic priming tasks were used, although again the findings have been rather inconsistent across laboratories.

The main assumption underlying these investigations is that the presentation of either a word or a picture of an object will automatically activate its representation in semantic memory. It is further assumed that this activation will spread to semantically related concepts, thus momentarily increasing their accessibility. Typically, when normal individuals are required to process a word (the target), either by reading it or judging whether it is a real word or a nonword (the lexical decision task), the time to perform this operation on the target item is decreased when it is immediately preceded by a semantically related word. For example, the time to read "hammer" will be faster if the preceding item is "screwdriver" (a semantically related prime) than if the preceding item is "dog" (an unrelated prime). Nebes and colleagues have argued that if the semantic system is disrupted in AD, then semantic activation should be substantially reduced or absent in these patients. Contrary to expectation, the AD patients in their initial study showed a normal amount of semantic priming (Nebes, Martin, & Horn, 1984). However, in subsequent studies Ober and Shenaut (1988) found no evidence of semantic priming, whereas Albert and Milberg (1989) reported highly variable performance, with some AD patients showing semantic priming and others showing inhibition rather than facilitation (slower performance with semantically related than with unrelated primes). More recently, both Nebes, Brady, and Huff (1989) and Chertkow et al. (1989) reported that AD patients actually show increased semantic facilitation or "hyperpriming" in comparison to normal elderly controls. It is likely that these discrepant and inconsistent findings will be traceable to important differences in methodology and in the types of patients studied. In fact, the magnitude of semantic priming in normal subjects is critically dependent on a host of experimental variables (see Neely, 1991, for a review), and it is well known that as a group, AD patients may be quite heterogeneous with regard to patterns of preserved and impaired cognitive functions (see Martin, 1990, for a review).

Nevertheless, the majority of studies do seem to be consistent in showing some degree of semantic facilitation in AD patients when variations of the on-line semantic priming paradigm are used. On the basis of this and other findings, Nebes has argued that the semantic system or network may be essentially intact in AD, and that their poor performance on other more effortful and demanding tasks of semantic knowledge results from a defect in intentional search of semantic memory (Nebes, 1989, in press). Nebes thus views the difficulties on semantic tasks such as object naming and verbal fluency as primarily a reflection of impaired access to, or deficient search of, a generally intact semantic store. This hypothesis is consistent with the seemingly preserved performance by AD patients on measures of automatic semantic activation, as opposed to their extremely poor performance on tests requiring retrieval of specific lexical entries. However, this, as well as other retrieval-based hypotheses, must be more constrained in order to account for the preservation of more general superordinate and category knowledge about objects, the production of semantic errors on naming tests, and a reversal of the normal superiority of category fluency (e.g., providing a list of animals) over lexical fluency (e.g., providing a list of words that begin with the letter C).

The primary data in support of the argument for an intact semantic system in AD are the findings of normal facilitation and perhaps hyperfacilitation on semantic priming tasks. Therefore, the critical question is whether this finding is inconsistent with the type of degraded-store model previously described. If patients with AD are restricted to the creation of an overgeneralized representation, then what would be the expected outcome on an on-line semantic priming task? To answer this question, we must specify a set of assumptions about normal semantic representations. For illustrative purposes, the present discussion is restricted to object naming. Most current models of object vision maintain that, when presented with an object, the visual system first creates a "viewer-centered" representation based on the pattern of light that impinges on the retina. This low-level representation is so named because it is totally dependent on the position of the viewer in relation to the object. To support object recognition, this representation must be transformed into an "object-centered" representation—that is, a representation that is invariant across retinal transformations. It is this object-centered representation that allows the viewer to recognize an object as the same object when it is viewed from different locations or in different orientations (see Humphreys & Bruce, 1989, for a review). Studies with nonhuman primates indicate that the creation of these representations is dependent on the functioning of a hierarchically organized occipital inferior temporal system (see Desimone & Ungerleider, 1989, for a review). This object-centered representation may then automatically activate a semantic object representation consisting of our stored knowledge about the object in question, including knowledge of both physical and functional features or attributes. This semantic representation should then activate the appropriate lexical entry for naming. An object-centered representation must be specific enough to allow the viewer to visually distinguish, for example, one type of chair from another type of chair on the basis of differences in physical form. In contrast, the semantic representation of both of these objects must be general enough to represent the concept of "chair," yet specific enough to represent only "chair" and not other objects that may share many of the same attributes (e.g., "desk").

Let us further assume that this semantic representation is instantiated in the brain as a distributed network of neuronal connections. Thus, in response to a picture of an object or an object's name, a specific neuronal network is activated. Because this network represents the specific attributes associated with the object, semantically related objects (e.g., chairs and desks) must normally be represented by overlapping networks, with the degree of overlap being equal to the number of shared attributes. Now, what would be the outcome of damage to these neuronal networks? Let us remember that, by definition, closely related objects share a large number of attributes, and thus are assumed to be represented by largely overlapping networks. If so, then any random pathological process (e.g., the development of plaques and tangles in the posterior temporal lobe) should tend to make these representations *more similar*. Over time, as the degree of pathology increases, so should the inability to distinguish, on a semantic level, objects from the same category. As a result, it is assumed that when an AD patient is confronted with an object, the semantic representation that is activated is no longer specific enough to activate only the object's name, but rather will activate a number of lexical entries (i.e., the names of all of the objects consistent with the patient's underspecified and thus overgeneralized representation). (See Dean, 1982, and Gaffan, Harrison, & Gaffan, 1986, for evidence consistent with overgeneralized representations in monkeys following damage to posterior temporal cortex.)

Now, let us return to the semantic priming paradigm. If this formulation is correct, then, for the AD patient, the presentation of a prime that bears a close semantic relationship to the target (semantic priming) should approach the degree of activation that occurs when the identical object is presented as both the prime and target (repetition priming). Thus, to the extent that direct repetition of a word or object normally produces a greater degree of facilitation than the presentation of a semantically related prime, then the presentation of semantically related primes should produce greater facilitation or hyperpriming, in AD patients than in normal controls.

My colleagues and I have recently obtained evidence in support of this possibility (Martin, Lalonde, Wertheimer, & Sunderland, 1991). On each trial subjects were presented with either a picture of an object (Snodgrass & Vanderwart, 1980) or a picture of a nonobject (Kroll & Potter, 1984). Subjects were required to respond as quickly as possible by pressing a key if the picture was of a real object (i.e., something that exists in the world) and to refrain from responding if the object was not real. Each target object or nonobject was preceded by the presentation of a prime consisting of either a neutral stimulus (a grid of intersecting lines), a nonobject, an unrelated real object, or exactly the same object. In addition, two types of semantic primes were presented; these consisted of closely and distantly related items based on category typicality ratings. For example, for the target picture of a bed, the closely related item was a picture of a table and the distantly related item was a picture of a vase. The prime was presented for 150 milliseconds (msec), and the subjects were told to attend to the picture but not to respond. The prime was then followed by the presentation of the target stimulus, which remained visible until the subject responded or until 2 seconds had elapsed. Depending on the experiment, the time interval between the onset of the prime and the onset of the target (the stimulus onset asynchrony, or SOA) varied from 250 to 2000 msec. On the basis of the discussion presented above, it was predicted that the AD patients would show normal priming when the prime was the same object as the target and greater-than-normal activation when the prime was semantically related to the target.

Our preliminary data have been highly supportive of these predictions, but only under certain conditions. As illustrated in Figure 19.1A, when an SOA of 250 msec was used, the AD patients showed robust facilitation when the target object was preceded by the brief presentation of the same object (repetition priming) relative to the neutral-prime condition. Moreover, the relative amount of repetition priming was equivalent for the patients and age-matched normal controls. However, the patients showed no evidence of semantic facilitation when the target was preceded by the semantically related prime. When this experiment was repeated under the identical conditions except for the use of a longer SOA (750 msec), the same group of patients again showed normal repetition priming and also significantly greater semantic priming than the normal subjects (see Figure 19.1B).

We have replicated this set of findings in an essentially identical study (Martin, Lalonde, et al., 1991), except that the SOA was randomly varied from 250 to 2000 msec from trial to trial. In comparison to normals, the AD patients showed no semantic facilitation at an SOA of 250 msec, equal facilitation at an SOA of 500 msec, significantly increased semantic facilitation or hyperpriming at 1000 msec, and no semantic priming at an SOA of 2000 msec (see Figure 19.2). The degree of facilitation that occurred when the same object served as the prime and target continued to be robust and equivalent for the patients and controls at SOAs of 1000 and 2000 msec. As would be expected, the patients responded significantly more slowly than controls and made more errors. However, the error rates were below 7% in each of the studies. These data replicate and extend the previously cited reports of hyperpriming by Nebes et al. (1989) and Chertkow et al. (1989), and are consistent with the hypothesis of degraded, overgeneralized semantic representations in patients with AD. These results also suggest that semantic activation is a dynamic process and that this process is qualitatively different in AD patients in comparison to normals. For the patients with AD, activation of the semantic system seems to develop slowly; once the system is stimulated, however, the degree of activation appears to be greater than that seen in normal individuals.

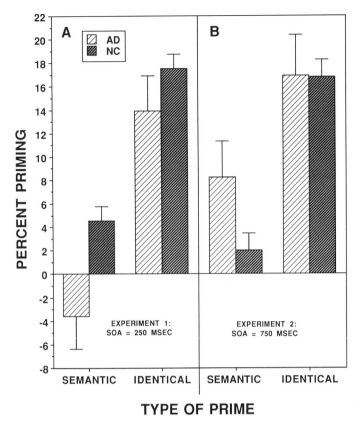

FIGURE 19.1. Performance by patients with Alzheimer's disease (AD; $n = 8$) and age- and education-matched normal controls (NC; $n = 13$) on an object decision task with primes that were semantically related or identical to the target object (repetition priming). Bars represent mean percentages of semantic and direct repetition priming ($\pm$ *SEM*), relative to the neutral-prime condition. In both studies, repetition priming was equivalent for the patients and controls. The AD patients showed significantly reduced semantic priming at an SOA of 250 msec and significantly increased semantic priming with an SOA of 750 msec.

It is noteworthy that increased semantic facilitation can be produced in normal subjects by perceptually *degrading* the target stimulus (see Neely, 1991, for a review). This occurs because target degradation produces relatively more slowing of responses when the target is preceded by an unrelated prime than when it is preceded by a semantically related prime. Thus, it appears that semantic activation normally provides relatively greater aid for processing degraded than for processing nondegraded information. I have argued that AD patients have degraded representations, albeit on a semantic as opposed to a perceptual level (however, see below). It therefore might be expected that AD patients would derive greater-than-normal benefit from semantically related primes.

Longer-Term Priming

Although these data are consistent with at least some of the previous reports of on-line priming in AD, they are clearly at odds with studies that have failed to find evidence of either semantic priming (Brandt, Spencer, McSorley, & Folstein, 1988; Salmon, Shimamura, Butters, & Smith, 1988) or direct priming (Heindel, Salmon, & Butters, 1990; Shimamura, Salmon, Squire, & Butters, 1987) in AD patients on implicit memory tasks. This is particularly puzzling with regard to the tests of direct priming. Our studies indicated that the AD patients show a normal degree of direct or repetition priming with SOAs as long as 2000 msec, suggesting that the patients are able to construct some form of object representation. However, line drawings of objects similar to the ones used in our studies were employed by Heindel et al. (1990); yet they were unable to obtain evidence of direct priming. If, as argued by Schacter, Cooper, and Delaney (1990), direct priming is dependent on the activation of a structural object description or object-centered representation, then why do these patients fail to show direct priming of objects on implicit memory tasks? One possibility is that the activated representation simply does not last long enough, since, in the implicit memory tasks, the delay between the first and second presentation of the item is usually several minutes. Alternatively, the problem may stem from the fact that the tests of longer-term direct priming required the patients to generate specific information about the objects (i.e., to name them). Even if such patients have intact structural descriptions of the previously presented objects, they may still fail to show direct priming because the semantic representation necessary for eliciting the correct name has become degraded. If so, then these patients should show normal direct priming over longer time intervals if the task is structured in such a way as to avoid reliance on object-specific semantic representations.

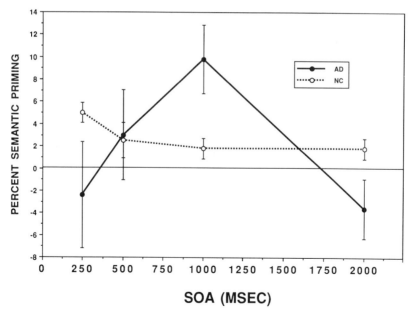

FIGURE 19.2. Percentage of semantic priming ($\pm$ *SEM*) on the object decision task for AD patients ($n = 6$) and NC subjects ($n = 15$), with SOA randomly varied from trial to trial. Semantic activation in AD patients was highly variable and significantly reduced relative to NC levels with SOAs of 250 msec and 2000 msec, equivalent to NC levels at 500 msec, and significantly increased at an SOA of 1000 msec.

A task that fulfills this criteria is the object decision task. Will AD patients fail to show evidence of direct priming on a task that requires the generation of object names, but show normal priming on a similar task that requires only a judgment on a global level? To explore this issue, we first attempted a replication of the Heindel et al. (1990) object priming study. In their task, the study phase consisted of the presentation of a series of pictures of common objects for naming. Approximately 10 minutes later, the subjects were presented with fragmented or incomplete versions of half of the previously seen pictures and an equal number of pictures of fragmented objects that they had not previously seen. Subjects were informed that this was a test of perceptual ability and were asked simply to guess what the fragment represented. Increasingly complete versions of the objects were presented until each object was identified (the implicit condition). Following this condition the subjects were presented with the remaining half of the previously studied object set, again in fragmented form, but were now informed that these were fragments of the objects seen during the study phase and that the subjects should use the fragments as cues for recall. Again, increasingly complete pictures were shown until the object was identified (the explicit condition). Our procedure was identical, except that during the study phase the AD patients were shown the complete version of the objects three times in order to avoid floor effects (Martin, Mack, Lalonde, & Sunderland, 1991). In addition, during the implicit and explicit memory conditions, the patients were shown pictures only at a single level of fragmentation based on previously determined perceptual identification thresholds (Snodgrass & Corwin, 1988).

As illustrated in Figure 19.3, we found a large priming effect for the elderly controls. For the AD patients, however, identification (naming) under the implicit and explicit conditions did not exceed their baseline guessing rate, even though during the study phase the patients had been given additional exposure to the pictures and were able to name them with little or no difficulty. These data thus replicated the Heindel et al. (1990) findings. However, a very different pattern of results was obtained using the object decision task. Again, AD patients studied pictures of objects as described above. Ten minutes later, implicit memory was tested by presenting complete objects and nonobjects, and asking the subjects to respond as quickly as possible by pressing a key if the object was real and not to respond to the nonobjects. Half of the real objects had been previously studied, while half had not previously been seen by the subjects. This condition was followed by a standard recognition task for the remaining half of the studied object pictures to assess explicit memory. As expected, the AD patients were markedly impaired on the explicit test of recognition memory. In contrast, as illustrated in Figure 19.4, the patients and controls showed an equivalent degree of priming (7.2% and 5.2% for the AD patients and controls, respectively; see also Moscovitch, 1982, and Ober & Shenaut, 1988, for evidence of intact repetition priming of visually presented words using lexical decision tasks).

Taken together, these data suggest that AD patients may show normal direct priming for objects over relatively long intervals, at least under certain conditions. These findings further suggest that AD patients may be able to create normal object-centered representations and that these representations can be primed at a later time, as long as the testing procedure does not require the utilization of a semantic representation needed for naming. Alternatively, the object representation may also be de-

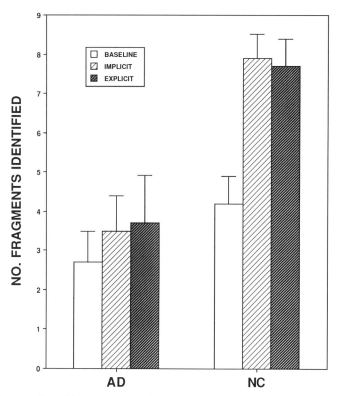

FIGURE 19.3. Mean number of fragments identified ($\pm$ *SEM*) by AD patients ($n = 12$) and normal controls ($n = 16$) on a test of object picture priming, using fragmented pictures as retrieval cues. Performance by the AD patients under the implicit and explicit test conditions did not differ significantly from their baseline perceptual identification rates.

graded in a manor similar to the type of degradation argued for the semantic representation. This degraded representation would be expected to be sufficient to support priming when only a general judgment is required (i.e., real vs. not real), but unable to support identification on an object-specific level (e.g., naming).

Conclusions

I have argued that the semantic representations in anomic patients with AD (and perhaps in other anomic patients with posterior damage to the left temporal cortex) are abnormally underspecified with regard to object-specific attributes that distinguish closely related items within the same semantic category. I have also argued that a consequence of degraded semantic representations should be hyperfacilitation from semantically related, but not identical, primes. Our studies provided support for this possibility and also provided evidence that the magnitude of semantic priming in AD is critically dependent on the duration between the prime and target. Additional studies will be needed to demonstrate that hyperpriming from semantically related primes is limited to patients with semantic deficits, rather than being a more general effect (e.g.,

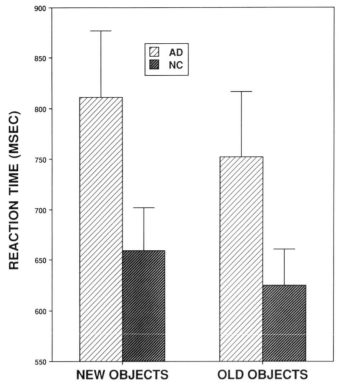

FIGURE 19.4. Mean reaction time ($\pm$ *SEM*) for OLD (previously studied) and NEW objects by AD patients ($n = 7$) and NC subjects ($n = 10$) when an object decision test was used to obtain evidence of priming. The time between study and test was approximately 10 minutes. Both the patients and controls showed a significant and equivalent speed advantage for objects that they had previously studied over objects that they had not previously seen.

reduced cortically mediated inhibition) of cortical lesions. Our implicit memory studies suggest that normal direct priming can occur in patients assumed to have widespread cortical damage, but only under certain conditions. It may occur because the object decision task bypasses the need for object-specific semantic knowledge, or because this task can be accomplished via access to a degraded representation. If this second alternative is correct, then the object-centered representations of AD patients may be disrupted in a fashion similar to that hypothesized for the representation of semantic information. Again, further study will be necessary before a choice can be made between these alternatives. On a more general level, these studies highlight the need to gain a fuller understanding of the demands of our tasks, in order to gain a more complete understanding of the nature of patterns of impaired and preserved abilities in brain-damaged individuals.

REFERENCES

Albert, M., & Milberg, W. (1989). Notes and discussion. *Brain and Language, 37,* 163–171.
Bayles, D. A., Tomoeda, C. K., & Trosset, M. W. (1990). Naming and categorical knowledge in Alzheimer's disease. *Brain and Language, 39,* 498–510.

Brandt, J., Spencer, M., McSorley, P., & Folstein, M. F. (1988). Semantic activation and implicit memory in Alzheimer disease. *Alzheimer Disease and Associated Disorders, 2*, 112–119.

Brun, A., & Gustafson, L. (1976). Distribution of cerebral degeneration in Alzheimer's disease: A clinico-pathological study. *Archives of Psychiatry and Neurological Sciences, 233*, 15–33.

Butters, N., Granholm, E., Salmon, D., Grant, I., & Wolfe, J. (1987). Episodic and semantic memory: A comparison of amnesic and demented patients. *Journal of Clinical and Experimental Neuropsychology, 9*, 479–497.

Chertkow, H., & Bub, D. (1990). Semantic memory in dementia of Alzheimer's type: What do various measures measure? *Brain, 113*, 397–417.

Chertkow, H., Bub, D., & Seidenberg, M. (1989). Priming and semantic memory loss in Alzheimer's disease. *Brain and Language, 36*, 420–446.

Dean, P. (1982). Analysis of visual behavior in monkeys with inferotemporal lesions. In D. J. Ingle, M. A. Goodale, & R. J. W. Mansfield (Eds.), *Analysis of visual behavior* (pp. 587–628). Cambridge, MA: MIT Press.

Desimone, R., & Ungerleider, L. G. (1989). Neural mechanisms of visual processing in monkeys. In F. Boller & J. Grafman (Eds), *Handbook of neuropsychology* (Vol. 2, pp. 267–299). Amsterdam: Elsevier Science.

Gaffan, D., Harrison, S., & Gaffan, E. A. (1986). Visual identification following inferotemporal ablation in the monkey. *Quarterly Journal of Experimental Psychology, 38B*, 5–30.

Grober, E., Buschke, H., Kawas, C., & Fuld, P. (1985). Impaired ranking of semantic attributes in dementia. *Brain and Language, 26*, 276–286.

Heindel, W. C., Salmon, D. P., & Butters, N. (1990). Pictorial priming and cued recall in Alzheimer's disease and Huntington's disease. *Brain and Cognition, 13*, 282–295.

Humphreys, G. W., & Bruce, V. (1989). *Visual cognition: Computation, experimental and neuropsychological perspectives*. Hillsdale, NJ: Erlbaum.

Hyman, B. T., Van Hoesen, G. W., & Damasio, A. R. (1990). Memory-related neural systems in Alzheimer's disease: An anatomic study. *Neurology, 40*, 1721–1730.

Kroll, J. F., & Potter, M. C. (1984). Recognizing words, pictures and concepts: A comparison of lexical, object, and reality decisions. *Journal of Verbal Learning and Verbal Behavior, 23*, 39–66.

Martin, A. (1987). Representation of semantic and spatial knowledge in Alzheimer's patients: Implications for models of preserved learning in amnesia. *Journal of Clinical and Experimental Neuropsychology, 9*, 191–224.

Martin, A. (1990). The neuropsychology of Alzheimer's disease: The case for subgroups. In M. Schwartz (Ed.), *Modular deficits in Alzheimer's-type dementia* (pp. 143–175). Cambridge, MA: Bradford Books/MIT Press.

Martin, A., & Fedio, P. (1983). Word production and comprehension in Alzheimer's disease: The breakdown of semantic knowledge. *Brain and Language, 19*, 124–141.

Martin, A., Lalonde, F., Wertheimer, S., & Sunderland, T. (1991). *Semantic and repetition priming of objects in patients with Alzheimer's disease and the normal elderly: Evidence for degraded representations.* Manuscript submitted for publication.

Martin, A., Mack, C., Lalonde, F., & Sunderland, T. (1991). *Implicit memory for objects but not visual patterns in normal subjects and patients with Alzheimer's disease.* Manuscript submitted for publication.

Moscovitch, M. (1982). A neuropsychological approach to perception and memory in normal and pathological aging. In F. I. M. Craik & S. Trehub (Eds.), *Aging and cognitive processes* (pp. 55–78). New York: Plenum Press.

Nebes, R. D. (1989). Semantic memory in Alzheimer's disease. *Psychological Bulletin, 106*, 377–394.

Nebes, R. D. (in press). Cognitive dysfunction in Alzheimer's disease. In F. I. M. Craik & T. Salthouse (Eds.), *Handbook of cognitive aging*. Hillsdale, NJ: Erlbaum.

Nebes, R. D., & Brady, C. B. (1988). Integrity of semantic fields in Alzheimer's disease. *Cortex, 24*, 291–299.

Nebes, R. D., & Brady, C. B. (1990). Preserved organization of semantic attributes in Alzheimer's disease. *Psychology and Aging, 5*, 574–579.

Nebes, R. D., Brady, C. B., & Huff, F. J. (1989). Automatic and attentional mechanisms of semantic priming in Alzheimer's disease. *Journal of Clinical and Experimental Neuropsychology, 11*, 219–230.

Nebes, R. D., Martin, D. C., & Horn, L. C. (1984). Sparing of semantic memory in Alzheimer's disease. *Journal of Abnormal Psychology, 93*, 321–330.

Neely, J. H. (1991). Semantic priming effects in visual word recognition: A selective review of current findings and theories. In D. Besner & G. W. Humphreys (Eds.), *Basic processes in reading: Visual word recognition* (pp. 264–336). Hillsdale, NJ: Erlbaum.

Ober, B. A., Dronkers, N. F., Koss, E., Delis, D. C., & Friedland, R. P. (1986). Retrieval from semantic memory in Alzheimer-type dementia. *Journal of Clinical and Experimental Neuropsychology, 8*, 75-92.

Ober, B. A., & Shenaut, G. K. (1988). Lexical decision and priming in Alzheimer's disease. *Neuropsychologia, 26*, 273-286.

Salmon, D. P. Shimamura, A. P., Butters, N., & Smith, S. (1988). Lexical and semantic priming deficits in patients with Alzheimer's disease. *Journal of Clinical and Experimental Neuropsychology, 10*, 477-494.

Schacter, D. L., Cooper, L. A., & Delaney, S. M. (1990). Implicit memory for unfamiliar objects depends on access to structural descriptions. *Journal of Experimental Psychology: General, 119*, 5-24.

Shallice, T. (1988). *From neuropsychology to mental structure.* Cambridge, England: Cambridge University Press.

Shimamura, A. P., Salmon, D. P., Squire, L. R., & Butters, N. (1987). Memory dysfunction and word priming in dementia and amnesia. *Behavioral Neuroscience, 101*, 347-351.

Shuttleworth, E. C., & Huber, S. J. (1988). The naming disorder of dementia of Alzheimer type. *Brain and Language, 34*, 222-234.

Snodgrass, J. G., & Corwin, J. (1988). Perceptual identification thresholds for 150 fragmented pictures from the Snodgrass and Vanderwart picture set. *Perceptual and Motor Skills, 67*, 3-36.

Snodgrass, J. G., & Vanderwart, M. (1980). A standardized set of 260 pictures: Norms for naming agreement, familiarity, and visual complexity. *Journal of Experimental Psychology: Human Learning and Memory, 6*, 174-215.

Squire, L. R., Haist, F., & Shimamura, A. P. (1989). The neurology of memory: Quantitative assessment of retrograde amnesia in two groups of amnesic patients. *Journal of Neuroscience, 9*(3), 828-839.

Tröster, A. I., Salmon, D. P., McCullough, D., & Butters, N. (1989). A comparison of category fluency deficits associated with Alzheimer's and Huntington's disease. *Brain and Language, 37*, 500-513.

Warrington, E. K. (1975). The selective impairment of semantic memory. *Quarterly Journal of Experimental Psychology, 27*, 635-657.

Weingartner, H., Kaye, W., Smallberg, S. A., Ebert, M. H., Gillin, J. C., & Sitaram, N. (1981). Memory failures in progressive idiopathic dementia. *Journal of Abnormal Psychology, 90*, 187-196.

Whitehouse, P., Caramazza, A., & Zurif, E. (1978). Naming in aphasia: Interacting effects of form and function. *Brain and Language, 6*, 63-74.

Zola-Morgan, S. M., & Squire, L. R. (1990). The primate hippocampal formation: Evidence for a time-limited role in memory storage. *Science, 250*, 288-290.

20

Semantic Memory Dysfunction in Alzheimer's Disease: Disruption of Semantic Knowledge or Information-Processing Limitation?

ROBERT D. NEBES

Although the memory of patients with Alzheimer's disease (AD) has long been a focus of intense study, one aspect of their memory function, "semantic memory," has recently received special attention. As conceptualized by Tulving (1986), semantic memory is the organized body of knowledge people possess about words, concepts, their meanings and associations, and the rules for manipulating these concepts and symbols. Information in semantic memory is thought to exist as a hierarchically organized network of concept nodes connected by labeled pathways (Collins & Loftus, 1975). Semantic memory is therefore thought to be quite different from the type of memory examined in traditional memory tests, in which subjects are given words or pictures that they are later to recall or recognize. Tulving calls this latter type of memory "episodic memory," which he views as an autobiographical record of events, encoded with respect to a spatiotemporal context. Thus, my memory of seeing a canary in a shop window at the mall last weekend is an example of an episodic memory, whereas my knowledge that a canary is alive, is a member of the category "birds," and possesses certain distinctive attributes (e.g., being small and yellow, having feathers, and flying) is an example of semantic memory.

The recent interest in the status of semantic memory in AD patients arises from evidence that normal older persons (Burke, White, & Diaz, 1987) and patients with other dementing diseases, such as Huntington's disease (Butters, Salmon, Heindel, & Granholm, 1988), perform relatively normally on most semantic memory tasks, whereas AD patients are often severely impaired. Thus, unlike many cognitive abilities (e.g., episodic memory, attention, problem solving, etc.), which show varying degrees of impairment in many pathological conditions, a semantic memory impairment may be a distinctive symptom of AD.

Variations in Alzheimer Patients' Performance as a Function of Task Requirements

Early in the course of their disease, AD patients begin to have difficulty on many tests of semantic memory function (see Nebes, 1989, for a recent review). However, it is still not clear whether these difficulties reflect a disruption of the patients' semantic knowledge base (i.e., an actual loss of semantic information) or whether they reflect deficits in the patients' ability to access or use this knowledge base. Is the poor performance of AD patients on a given semantic test the result of an actual semantic deficit, or does it stem from problems in more general-purpose cognitive operations that just happen to be involved in that task? For example, AD patients have substantial trouble naming objects. Is this because they have actually lost knowledge of the semantic features that define different lexical referents (Bayles & Tomoeda, 1983), or is it because they have a problem in carrying out the needed perceptual analysis of the object (Kirshner, Webb, & Kelly, 1984) or in accessing its name (Barker & Lawson, 1968)? Although the first of these potential mechanisms would involve a deficit in semantic knowledge, the latter two would represent situations in which a failure on a "semantic" test would result from limitations in nonsemantic cognitive operations necessary for appropriate use of an intact semantic knowledge base.

In order to avoid such interpretational ambiguities, tests of semantic memory should not require AD patients to engage in the type of self-initiated and controlled processing that is required for conscious recollection or manipulation of semantic information. Otherwise, if the patients do poorly on the task, it will not be clear whether this demonstrates the presence of a specific semantic deficit or a limitation in general information-processing abilities not limited to semantic memory. Thus, tasks that require AD patients to intentionally search their semantic memory for specific pieces of information (e.g., asking them to give definitions of words) or to make complex decisions about retrieved information (e.g., deciding which attribute of a concept is most important) could produce a distorted picture of the status of semantic knowledge in AD. Indirect or implicit memory measures might therefore appear to be especially appropriate for evaluating semantic memory in AD, since such measures do not require the subject to consciously recollect information (Richardson-Klavehn & Bjork, 1988). However, even if a particular task uses an indirect measure of memory, other aspects of that task may require cognitive operations on which AD patients are impaired. For example, Salmon, Shimamura, Butters, and Smith (1988) found AD patients to perform abnormally on an indirect memory measure (priming of stem completion), but a recent study by Partridge, Knight, and Feehan (1990) found normal stem completion priming in AD patients. Partridge et al. (1990) concluded that the crucial difference between their own study and that of Salmon et al. (1988) was that their own study ensured that the AD patients attended to the meaning of the stimuli during their initial exposure to the stimulus words. Partridge et al. suggest that the attentional and encoding deficits known to exist in AD patients may limit their performance on measures of indirect memory, unless special care is taken to ensure that their initial processing of the stimulus material is adequate. This emphasizes the need to pay careful attention to the cognitive demands imposed by all aspects of a task when designing studies to examine the semantic knowledge possessed by AD patients. For another excellent example of how variations in task demands can influence performance by AD patients on semantic memory tasks, see Bayles, Tomoeda, Kaszniak, and Trosset (1991).

What Do Alzheimer Patients Know about Semantic Concepts?

As an example of how changing the cognitive demands made by a task can alter semantic memory performance by AD patients, let us examine what AD patients know about semantic concepts. A number of investigators have suggested that AD patients' knowledge of concept meaning is impaired (Chertkow, Bub, & Seidenberg, 1989; Huff, Corkin, & Growdon, 1986; Martin & Fedio, 1983; Tröster, Salmon, McCullough, & Butters, 1989). They claim that although AD patients usually retain knowledge of the semantic category to which a concept belongs, they lose information about its specific attributes. This pattern of differential loss is thought to reflect a bottom-up deterioration in a hierarchical knowledge structure, in which specific attributes are at the bottom and category information at the top of the hierarchy. The attributes of a concept represent both perceptual and abstract knowledge about that concept (e.g., its physical features, functions, etc.), and thus are essential for understanding concept meaning. Any deterioration of concept meaning would have a major impact on AD patients' performance in other areas of cognition, such as language comprehension, object naming, memory encoding, and so forth.

One line of evidence used to support the existence of a differential disruption of attribute and category information in AD comes from studies examining the word-finding deficits that are such a prominent symptom of this disease. In confrontation naming, when AD patients misname an object they often call it by its category name (e.g., calling a trumpet a musical instrument) or by the name of another item from the same category (e.g., calling a hammer a saw). AD patients also have a great deal of difficulty recognizing the name of a pictured object in a multiple-choice task when the distractors are drawn from the same category as the object, but not when they are drawn from other categories (Huff et al., 1986; Chertkow et al., 1989). This pattern of performance has been interpreted as reflecting a preservation of category information, coupled with a loss of those specific attributes that make it possible to differentiate semantically related objects—thus, the confusion with other items from the same category. Similarly, on the "supermarket" test, in which subjects are asked to generate the names of as many items found in a supermarket as possible, AD patients often give the names of categories (e.g., vegetables) rather than specific category members (e.g., carrots, corn). Again, a loss of specific attribute information is postulated to be responsible for this pattern of disfluency (Martin & Fedio, 1983; Tröster et al., 1989). The most impressive evidence for a loss of specific attribute information in AD comes from several studies that have asked subjects direct questions about an item's category membership and its attributes. Martin and Fedio (1983) showed that AD patients could accurately answer a question about an object's category, but that they had a great deal of difficulty answering questions about its physical features or functions. Thus, when shown a saw, they could correctly answer the question "Is it a tool?", but were much less successful in answering questions such as "Is it made of metal?" or "Is it used for cutting?" Chertkow et al. (1989) replicated these results with a wider array of objects and questions. They showed that even when given multiple-choice questions (e.g., "Do you use this object to lift things or to cut things?"), AD patients were much more impaired on questions about an object's attributes than on questions about its category membership.

There is, however, other evidence suggesting that AD patients retain their knowledge of the semantic attributes of concepts. Grober, Buschke, Kawas, and Fuld (1985, Experiment 1) presented subjects with a target concept (e.g., the word "airplane") along with a number of stimulus words. The subject was to check off those words that were *related to* the target (i.e., were its attributes). Demented patients were quite accurate (95% correct) on this task. A colleague and I (Nebes & Brady, 1988) used a similar task, in which we measured the time it took normals and AD patients to decide whether a given stimulus word was related to a target word (e.g., "shirt"). On those trials in which the stimulus was related to the target, it was either the name of its category (e.g., "clothing"), a general associate (e.g., "tie"), a distinctive physical feature (e.g., "collar"), or a verb describing a characteristic action or function (e.g., "wear"). If AD patients have actually lost knowledge of the features and functions of objects, or find them differentially difficult to access, then they should be slower and less accurate in making decisions about a target's feature and action than about its category and associate. However, as can be seen in Table 20.1, the difference in response time between AD patients and the normal elderly was, if anything, smaller for decisions about features and actions than for decisions about categories and associates. As in the Grober et al. (1985) study, the AD patients made very few errors (fewer than 5%), and there was no evidence that decisions about a concept's action or feature were significantly more difficult for them than were decisions about its category or associate. These results, unlike those of Martin and Fedio (1983) and Chertkow et al. (1989), suggest that AD patients are aware of the relationship between concepts and their attributes, including physical features and actions.

Another related hypothesis about concept knowledge in AD is that even though knowledge of concept attributes is preserved in AD patients, the internal organization of these attributes is disrupted. Grober et al. (1985, Experiment 3) suggested that while AD patients remain aware of the relationship between a concept and its attributes, they no longer know the relative importance that the various attributes have for concept meaning. In their study, a subject was given a target concept along with three attributes, and was asked to select the most important attribute and then the next most

TABLE 20.1. Mean Response Time (in Milliseconds) for Decisions about Different Types of Relationships between a Stimulus Word and a Target Concept

	Relationship of stimulus to target concept			
	Function	Attribute	Associate	Category
Alzheimer	1041	1021	1050	1103
Normal old	684	668	684	685
Difference	357	353	366	418

important one. Thus, for the concept "airplane," if given the attributes "radar," "fly," and "luggage," the subject should first chose "fly" and then "radar." Grober et al. (1985) found that AD patients did poorly on this task; they concluded that although AD patients retain knowledge of the linkage between a concept and its attributes, they are not aware of the relative importance the various attributes have for the meaning of the concept. Such a disruption of the internal organization of a concept's attributes could be just as disabling as an actual loss of the attributes, leaving AD patients ignorant of which attributes are crucial for specifying concept meaning and which are merely incidental (e.g., they would not know that "feathers" is a more critical attribute of a bird than is "feet").

However, we recently completed a study (Nebes & Brady, 1990), the results of which suggest that information about attribute importance also remains intact in AD patients. As in the earlier (Nebes & Brady, 1988) study, we presented a target concept followed by a stimulus word, and measured the time it took subjects to decide whether the stimulus was related to the target. In this study, subjects' knowledge of attribute importance was investigated indirectly by examining how their decision time varied as a function of attribute importance. Normal individuals make decisions faster about important attributes than they do about less important attributes. If AD patients do not know the relative importance of various concept attributes, then, unlike normals, their decision time should be unaffected by attribute importance. We determined the relative importance of various concept attributes by presenting a concept in the form of a word to a large number of normal old persons and asking them to generate as many of its attributes as possible in 1 minute. We assumed that the more important an attribute was, the more likely subjects would be to generate it when given the concept. We therefore used response dominance (the percentage of the normative population generating that attribute) as our measure of attribute importance. High-dominant attributes were those generated by approximately 60% of the normative population; medium-dominant attributes were those generated by about 25%; and low-dominant attributes were those generated by fewer than 10%. For example, for the concept of "elephant," "trunk" was a high-dominant attribute and "memory" was a low-dominant attribute. If the internal organization of concept attributes is actually disrupted in AD, as suggested by Grober et al. (1985), then attribute dominance should not influence AD patients' decision time. It is clear from Figure 20.1 that for all subject groups, the more dominant the attribute, the faster the decision. If anything, the response time of AD patients was more affected by relative attribute dominance than was that of the normal young or old. Thus, when AD patients' knowledge of attribute importance was measured indirectly by assessing the effect it had on their decision time, rather than by directly asking them to judge relative importance, the results suggest that the patients retained their knowledge of attribute importance.

Reconciling the Findings

How are we to reconcile the contradictory conclusions about concept knowledge in AD reached by the studies described above? Martin and Fedio (1983) and Chertkow et al. (1989) have found evidence for a loss of attribute knowledge in AD, whereas

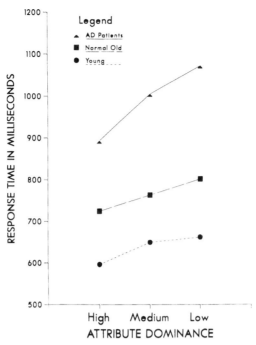

FIGURE 20.1. Average time (in milliseconds) that normal and demented subjects took to determine that an attribute was related to a concept, as a function of attribute dominance.

Grober et al. (1985, Experiment 1) and we ourselves (Nebes & Brady, 1988) have concluded that this information remains intact. One possible source for this discrepancy lies in the differing cognitive demands imposed by the experimental tasks. When AD patients are asked a direct question about a concept's attributes (e.g., for a knife, the question "Is it used for cutting?"), they perform poorly; by contrast, if they are asked merely to decide whether a concept and one of its attributes are related (e.g., "Is the word 'cut' related to the concept 'knife'?"), they do very well. We can contrast these different types of task within the context of the Collins and Loftus (1975) spreading-activation model of semantic memory. In this model, concepts exist as nodes within a network. The properties of a concept are represented as paths between that concept and related concepts, with the paths being labeled with the nature of the relationship (e.g., "is," "has a," "can," etc.). When a subject is asked a question about a concept and an attribute, activation spreads out in parallel along the network from each concept. If these two waves of activation should intersect, and the resultant activation at this intersection exceeds some threshold, a pathway connecting the two concepts has been found. This alone would be sufficient to answer the question posed by the Grober et al. (1985, Experiment 1) and by the Nebes and Brady (1988) tasks (i.e., "Is 'cut' related to 'knife'?"). However, if a specific type of relationship is specified in the question ("Is a knife used to cut?"), then the nature of the pathway must be evaluated by the subject to determine whether it meets the syntactic and semantic constraints specified by the question. The difficulty that AD patients have with such direct questions may therefore reflect a problem with consciously evaluating the nature of the pathway found, rather than a loss of the concept–attribute pathway itself.

The conflict between the results of Grober et al. (1985, Experiment 3) and our own findings (Nebes & Brady, 1990) as to whether AD patients still know the relative importance of the various attributes of concepts can also be examined in the context of the Collins and Loftus (1975) model. In this model, different pathways vary in their "criterality" (i.e., the esxtent to which a pathway is essential to the meaning of the concept), and a pathway's criterality determines how quickly activation spreads along it. The Nebes and Brady (1990) results would suggest that the varying criteralities of attribute pathways are preserved in AD, since our patients made decisions about more important (i.e., critical) attributes faster than about less important attributes. Thus, the problem that AD patients had on the Grober et al. (1985, Experiment 3) task may say more about the demands this task placed on their ability to make conscious comparisons than it does about their actual knowledge of attribute importance.

On the basis of these results, I would propose that what appears in some studies to be an impairment in the structure of semantic memory in AD (i.e., a loss of knowledge of concept attributes or their relative importance) instead reflects a failure of more general-purpose cognitive operations, such as those involved in intentionally accessing and evaluating information, making decisions, and so on. If the need for these cognitive operations is minimized in tests of semantic knowledge, then AD patients may show a pattern of performance similar to that seen in normals. Thus, before we attribute poor performance by AD patients on tests of semantic memory to an actual semantic deficit, it is important for us to be sure that their performance is not being limited by some nonsemantic processing impairment.

REFERENCES

Barker, M. G., & Lawson, J. S. (1968). Nominal aphasia in dementia. *British Journal of Psychiatry, 114*, 1351–1356.

Bayles, K. A., & Tomoeda, C. K. (1983). Confrontation naming in dementia. *Brain and Language, 19*, 98–114.

Bayles, K. A., Tomoeda, C. K., Kaszniak, A. W., & Trosset, M. W. (1991). Alzheimer's disease effects on semantic memory: Loss of structure or impaired processing. *Journal of Cognitive Neurosciences, 3*, 166–182.

Burke, D. M., White, H., & Diaz, D. L. (1987). Semantic priming in young and older adults: Evidence for age constancy in automatic and attentional processes. *Journal of Experimental Psychology: Human Perception and Performance, 13*, 79–88.

Butters, N., Salmon, D. P., Heindel, W., & Granholm, E. (1988). Episodic, semantic and procedural memory: Some comparisons of Alzheimer and Huntington disease patients. In R. D. Terry (Ed.), *Aging and the brain* (pp. 63–87). New York: Raven Press.

Chertkow, H., Bub, D., & Seidenberg, M. (1989). Priming and semantic memory loss in Alzheimer's disease. *Brain and Language, 36*, 420–446.

Collins, A. M., & Loftus, E. F. (1975). A spreading-activation theory of semantic processing. *Psychological Review, 82*, 407–428.

Grober, E., Buschke, H., Kawas, C., & Fuld, P. (1985). Impaired ranking of semantic attributes in dementia. *Brain and Language, 26*, 276–286.

Huff, F. J., Corkin, S., & Growdon, J. H. (1986). Semantic impairment and anomia in Alzheimer's disease. *Brain and Language, 28*, 235–249.

Kirshner, H. S., Webb, W. G., & Kelly, M. P. (1984). The naming disorder of dementia. *Neuropsychologia, 22*, 23–30.

Martin, A., & Fedio, P. (1983). Word production and comprehension in Alzheimer's disease: The breakdown of semantic knowledge. *Brain and Language, 19*, 124–141.

Nebes, R. D. (1989). Semantic memory in Alzheimer's disease. *Psychological Bulletin, 106,* 377–394.

Nebes, R. D., & Brady, C. B. (1988). Integrity of semantic fields in Alzheimer's disease. *Cortex, 24,* 291–300.

Nebes, R. D., & Brady, C. B. (1990). Preserved organization of semantic attributes in Alzheimer's disease. *Psychology and Aging, 5,* 574–579.

Partridge, F. M., Knight, R. G., & Feehan, M. (1990). Direct and indirect memory performance in patients with senile dementia. *Psychological Medicine, 20,* 111–118.

Richardson-Klavehn, A., & Bjork, R. A. (1988). Measures of memory. *Annual Review of Psychology, 39,* 475–543.

Salmon, D. P., Shimamura, A. P., Butters, N., & Smith, S. (1988). Lexical and semantic priming deficits in patients with Alzheimer's disease. *Journal of Clinical and Experimental Neuropsychology, 10,* 477–494.

Tröster, A. I., Salmon, D. P., McCullough, D., & Butters, N. (1989). A comparison of category fluency deficits associated with Alzheimer's and Huntington's disease. *Brain and Language, 37,* 500–513.

Tulving, E. (1986). What kind of hypothesis is the distinction between episodic and semantic memory? *Journal of Experimental Psychology: Learning, Memory, and Cognition, 12,* 307–311.

21

A Transfer-Appropriate Processing Account for Memory and Amnesia

PETER GRAF and KAREN A. GALLIE

The theoretical approach generally known as "transfer-appropriate processing" (TAP) guides our investigations of human memory. This chapter describes a TAP-based account for performance dissociations between implicit and explicit memory tests. To focus discussion, we review a small set of critical studies that have used implicit and explicit memory tests, illustrating how these forms of memory work in healthy young adults, how they change across the lifespan, and how they are affected when the brain is traumatized by an accident or disease. These findings from different subject groups serve to illustrate various aspects of our TAP-based account, thereby highlighting its potential as a general framework for theorizing about human memory and amnesia.

Explicit and Implicit Memory: Critical Findings

"Explicit" and "implicit" are labels for tests that index different ways of using memory (Graf & Schacter, 1985). Explicit memory tests (i.e., situations defined by test cues and instructions) require subjects to be aware of, to focus on, and to recollect information from specific prior events or experiences, whereas no such awareness and focusing are required for implicit memory tests. On the latter tests, changes in performance that are caused by memory for specific events or experiences are known as "priming effects." Although the fundamental difference between these two ways of using memory became widely recognized only in the past decade, it presents a fascinating puzzle that has captured the attention of memory researchers, cognitive psychologists, developmental psychologists, and neuropsychologists alike (for reviews, see Schacter, 1987; Shimamura, 1986; Squire, 1987; and various chapters in this book).

A decade of intense research has yielded a large collection of findings. One of the first to emerge, and one that is still fascinating, comes from experiments on patients with anterograde amnesia. A large number of studies have by now well established that in amnesic patients, implicit memory test performance can be entirely normal even when the ability for explicit remembering is severely impaired (see Shimamura, 1986; Squire, 1987; Tulving & Schacter, 1990). Normal priming effects have been found with different types of amnesic patients, with different materials, and across different study and test conditions. A second and similarly intriguing finding has emerged from studies assessing implicit and explicit memory test performance across the adult lifespan. They show that aging has no effect or has only a minimal effect on priming; at the same time, they reconfirm that explicit remembering declines in old age (for reviews, see Graf, 1990; Hultsch, Masson, & Small, 1991; Light, 1988).

The largest collection of findings, however, comes from mainstream cognitive psychology, from experiments on healthy young adults—which are most abundantly available. They show that a wide variety of materials, study tasks, and test manipulations have different effects on performance of implicit and explicit memory tests (for reviews, see Lewandowsky, Dunn, & Kirsner, 1989; Schacter, 1987). Two findings are especially noteworthy. The first is from experiments in which subjects studied words by attending either to their meaning or to their nonsemantic aspects (e.g., a word's sound, number of letters). They showed that levels-of-processing manipulations have a large effect on explicit memory tests, but only a minimal effect or no effect on priming (e.g., Graf, Mandler, & Haden, 1982; Jacoby & Dallas, 1981). A second core finding from experiments with healthy young adults is that priming effects are typically larger for words studied and tested in the same sensory modality (e.g., visual) than for words presented in different sensory modalities (e.g., auditory for study and visual for testing) (e.g., Kirsner, Milech, & Standon, 1983; Roediger & Blaxton, 1987; Schacter & Graf, 1989). By contrast, recall and recognition test performance typically shows minimal or no effects of such study–test modality manipulations.

This brief review of the literature is deliberately selective and shows only the tip of the iceberg. It features a few of the core findings from different subject populations that are well established in the literature. These findings set crucial but minimal constraints that must be met by any comprehensive account of implicit and explicit memory test performance. In this chapter, these findings are used to highlight various aspects of our TAP-based view of memory and amnesia.

Transfer-Appropriate Processing: A Framework for Human Memory Research

The concept of TAP was introduced by Morris, Bransford, and Franks (1977). It has roots in the work of Kolers and his colleagues, in the view that remembering is best understood in terms of the cognitive operations or processes that are engaged by different study and test activities (e.g., Kolers, 1975, 1979; Kolers & Ostry, 1974). Kolers argued that a task such as reading a word or sentence, for example, requires a particular set of sensory-perceptual and conceptual analyzing operations, and that engaging these operations has the same effect as practicing a skill—it increases the fluency and efficiency with which they can be carried out subsequently. By this reasoning, it follows that performance of a memory test will be facilitated to the extent that it engages the same set or a similar set of cognitive operations as that used for a preceding study task. Thus, TAP claims that remembering is determined by the degree of overlap between study and test processing.

We have argued elsewhere (Graf & Ryan, 1990) that in this form, TAP cannot explain differences between implicit and explicit memory test performance. This is because the general idea that performance is determined by the degree of overlap between study and test processing, in the absence of an independent index of processing, is consistent with *any* experimental outcome. For this reason, we view TAP as a basic assumption about human memory, as a general framework for theorizing; we also emphasize that any meaningful explanation of dissociations between implicit and explicit memory must at least specify the different processes that mediate performance on different types of tests.

Transfer-Appropriate Processing for Implicit and Explicit Memory

Two TAP-based accounts for implicit–explicit memory dissociations have been proposed in recent years, one by Roediger and his colleagues (e.g., Roediger & Blaxton, 1987; Weldon, Roediger, & Challis, 1989), and the other by us (Graf, 1991; Graf & Mandler, 1984; Graf & Ryan, 1990; Graf & Schacter, 1989). Roediger and his colleagues raised the possibility that implicit and explicit memory tests rely to different degrees on data-driven and conceptually driven processing, and that this difference mediates performance dissociations across tests. But more recent evidence now indicates that whereas the relative amount of data-driven and conceptually driven processing is a critical attribute of memory tests, it does not distinguish between implicit and explicit tests (see Graf & Ryan, 1990; Roediger, Srinivas, & Weldon, 1989). Thus, we have opted for another processing distinction to capture the critical difference between implicit and explicit memory test performance.

We believe that implicit and explicit memory tests tap two different memory-organizing processes, called "integration" and "elaboration," respectively (Graf & Mandler, 1984; Mandler, 1980, 1988). Integration results from processing that bonds the features of a target into a coordinated whole or unitized representation; it occurs when the subject either perceives coherence among separate stimulus components (e.g., under the top-down guidance of pre-existing representations or gestalt laws such as proximity or good continuation) or conceives a structure for processing target features concurrently (e.g., Graf, 1991; Graf & Schacter, 1989; Mandler, 1980, 1988). In a neural net, integration occurs when a collection of neurons in a network becomes mutually activating by virtue of the interconnections among them. Once established, activity in a subset of these neurons will suffice to reactivate the entire unit. Elaboration results from processing that associates a target with other mental contents; it occurs when a target is encoded in relation to the experimental situation (e.g., other targets, situational cues, and relevant prior knowledge), thereby embedding its unitized representation in a network of other representations.

Integration and elaboration typically occur together. To distinguish between them, let us consider a to-be-remembered target item. Processing is integrative if it increases the organization of features that constitute that target, and it is elaborative if it associates the target with other targets, prior knowledge, situational cues, or the like. This distinction holds when the target is a letter, a word, a word pair, or a bigger verbal or nonverbal unit.

We make two basic assumptions. The first is that each study or test task engages a combination of integrative and elaborative processing, and that tasks differ by emphasizing either one or the other type of processing. The precise combination in which processes are engaged by a particular task is determined by several factors, including the cues made available on the test form and by the test environment, the instructions given to the subject, and the mental or motivational state of each subject. The second assumption is that implicit memory tests engage primarily integrative processing, whereas explicit memory tests engage primarily elaborative processing. From these assumptions, and consistent with TAP, it follows that priming reflects primarily study–test overlaps in integrative processing, whereas explicit remembering reflects primarily study–test overlaps in elaborative processing.

An intuitive analysis of the processing requirements of different memory tests validates these assumptions. Implicit memory tests require subjects, for example, to name items in response to words or category labels, to complete words in response to word fragments (e.g., "gra _____"; "v _ l _ n"), or to identify briefly presented words. In all cases, performance requires perceiving or conceiving a structure that unitizes (i.e., converts into a unit) the cueing information, and thereby specifies a target or target set. Study trial integration facilitates this type of processing, because once unitized, a representation has an increased tendency to become completely reactivated even when only some of its components are subsequently reprocessed (Mandler, 1980, 1988; Horowitz & Prytulak, 1969). Priming effects are thus an index of the increased integration produced by study trial processing.

Explicit memory tests require subjects either to recollect previously studied items in response to cues (cued-recall tests) or in the absence of cues (free-recall tests), or to identify targets that had appeared in a previously studied list (recognition tests). In all cases, performance requires accessing information that associates a target with a specific prior episode. We assume that elaboration during the study trial facilitates explicit remembering because it involves encoding targets in relation to the experimental situation, thereby establishing the associations that identify each target as belonging to a specific learning episode.

Memory Dissociations in Healthy Young Adults

Our TAP-based view provides a parsimonious account for the findings outlined earlier. It explains differences in the size of priming effects, for example, by focusing on the contents of the unitized representations that are established in different experimental conditions. The finding of larger priming effects for targets studied and tested in the same modality than for those studied and tested in different modalities implicates modality specific sensory and perceptual processes. We maintain that priming is mediated by unitized representations that include modality-specific sensory and perceptual processes, as well as semantic-conceptual processes (i.e., all processes engaged at study). However, the cues provided by a test, such as visual word identification, recruit only a subset of these processes—mostly those that are modality-specific—and engaging these processes in turn triggers the reintegration or reactivation of representations established at study. By this view, modality effects occur in priming because modality-specific sensory and perceptual processing provides the most direct access routes to the particular representations established during the study trial (see Graf, 1991; Graf & Ryan, 1990; Graf & Schacter, 1989).

The finding of similar priming effects after semantic and nonsemantic study tasks[1] highlights an additional critical difference between the processes that mediate implicit and explicit test performance. The absence of a levels-of-processing effect—the fact that priming does not vary across such study tasks—suggests that integrative processing of familiar items such as common words is relatively automatic. This may be because for familiar items, integrative processing is initiated and guided primarily by pre-existing long-term memory representations and can thus be carried out independently of, and probably prior to, the subject-controlled elaborative processing that is guided by the study task constraints.

As these examples illustrate, we claim that the precise content of the unitized representations that underlie priming is determined by many factors, including various characteristics of the targets and of the test cues (e.g., modality, display format, familiarity, unusual appearance); the particular requirements of each study or test task (e.g., focus on appearance or meaning); and the general experimental context (including the mental set of the subject). By assuming that priming taps a large complex of factors, our TAP-based view can accommodate such diverse findings as differences in modality effects across different implicit memory tests (for reviews, see Kirsner et al., 1983; Roediger & Blaxton, 1987), and even variations in modality effects across study tasks that focus processing either on the specific appearance or on the meaning of target words (Graf & Ryan, 1990).

Even though we have so far focused entirely on priming, TAP also offers a parsimonious account of a wide range of findings from explicit memory tests. It explains the absence of modality effects on explicit memory tests by suggesting that elaborative processing typically does not focus on modality-specific attributes of targets—that modality-specific processes are usually not engaged to link targets with the study trial context. By contrast, the well-known finding of levels-of-processing effects on explicit memory tests is viewed as evidence that subjects usually do focus on semantic-conceptual attributes to forge links that identify targets with specific learning episodes.

Aging Effects

What accounts for an age-related decline in explicit memory test performance together with normal implicit memory test performance? Our TAP account suggests that priming remains intact because integrative activity is mediated by processing that occurs automatically (at least with familiar items such as common words). By contrast, explicit remembering declines in late adulthood because elaboration depends on attention-demanding processing, and aging reduces the attentional resources required

---

[1]A modified version of this view is required to explain implicit and explicit memory test performance when to-be-remembered items are not familiar and have no pre-existing long-term memory representation (see Graf & Schacter, 1985; Schacter & Graf, 1989).

for this type of processing. Such a view has been advocated by others, especially Craik (1983) and Salthouse (1982).

Instead of focusing on the declining availability of attentional resources, we speculate that performing any memory task involves a number of different components that must be initiated and executed in a coordinated manner. We further assume that elaborative processing—which is engaged for explicit remembering—involves coordinating a larger number of components than does the integrative processing required for priming. Finally, we maintain that aging is accompanied by a decrease in the ability to initiate and coordinate multiple processing components.

The focus on processing comes from Craik's (1983) insightful proposal that all memory tests can be arranged on a continuum that reflects the extent to which performance depends on subject-controlled activities, at one end, and the extent to which it is supported or guided by the test environment, at the other end. The total amount of *environmental support* provided by a test is defined by the cues and the instructions that are given to subjects. Craik has suggested that on average, implicit memory tests tend to be clustered at one end of the support continuum, whereas explicit tests are closer to the other, subject-initiated activities end. By this view, priming remains intact in old age because integrative processing is self-coordinating; it is mediated by sensory and perceptual processes that are initiated and guided by the cues and instructions provided for testing.

Amnesia Effects

Our account for age-related changes in memory can be extended to accommodate the main findings from amnesic patients: that anterograde amnesia impairs the ability for explicit remembering while sparing implicit memory test performance. The general notion—that priming is spared because integrative processing is self-coordinating (guided by study and test cues and instructions), and that explicit remembering is impaired because elaborative processing involves primarily subject-controlled activities—is consistent with various explanations of amnesia that are already in the neuropsychology literature (see Shallice, 1990; Squire, 1987; Tulving & Schacter, 1990).

Neuropsychological explanations for selectively spared memory functions highlight the role of the medial temporal region, especially the hippocampus and amygdala, which are typically compromised in patients with anterograde amnesia (see Damasio, 1990; Squire, 1987). It is known that the hippocampal formation projects to and receives input from the sensory-specific cortical areas and the multimodal association areas that serve as memory storage sites. These input and output connections allow the hippocampal formation to monitor cortical activity at memory storage sites. By virtue of these connections, the hippocampal formation may be involved in establishing something like a map that links the various components that define a memory episode. It is further assumed that new memories are held together by such maps (until they are replaced by more permanent synaptic changes), and thus these maps are critical for guiding the access to and the retrieval of new memories. By this view, it follows that damage to the hippocampal formation—the mapmaker—will impair subjects' ability to establish and retrieve new memories.

These ideas about the brain mechanisms that are involved in storing and retrieving new memories are consistent with our TAP model. We can view the hippocampal formation as the system module that coordinates the elaborative processing involved in explicit remembering. Damage to this module will thus impair explicit remembering. By contrast, hippocampal damage does not affect priming because integrative processing is self-coordinated—mediated by sensory and perceptual processes that are initiated and guided directly (without the maps produced by the hippocampal formation) by the cues and instructions provided for testing.

Concluding Remarks

We have outlined a TAP-based view for implicit–explicit memory dissociations and illustrated how it accounts for a few of the major findings from different subject populations. Although we see this view as complementing others that are already in the literature, we also want to underline that it makes a unique contribution to the field by asking different questions, and thereby guides research in new directions.

TAP focuses on the processing that is recruited by different study and test situations, and on the processing overlap between study and test. It recognizes unequivocally that every situation involves a large collection of cognitive processes (variously classified as perceptual and conceptual, data-driven and conceptually driven, integrative and elaborative, automatic and controlled), and that the precise makeup of the collection engaged for a particular test is determined by multiple factors. By so doing, TAP directs the investigator to analyze each study–test task, and to identify the processes that are recruited by it. A systematic investigation of these processes gives insight into performance differences between situations and tasks, as well as between subject groups.

ACKNOWLEDGMENTS

Preparation of this chapter was supported by grants from the Natural Sciences and Engineering Research Council of Canada and from Sigma Xi.

REFERENCES

Craik, F. I. M. (1983). On the transfer of information from temporary to permanent memory. *Philosophical Transactions of the Royal Society of London, B302*, 341–359.

Damasio, A. R. (1990). Synchronous activation in multiple cortical regions: A mechanism for recall. *Seminars in the Neurosciences, 2*, 287–296.

Graf, P. (1990). Life-span changes in implicit and explicit memory. *Bulletin of the Psychonomic Society, 28*, 353–358.

Graf, P. (1991). Implicit and explicit memory: An old model for new findings. In W. Kessen, A. Ortony, & F. Craik (Eds.), *Memories, thoughts, and emotions: Essays in honor of George Mandler* (pp. 135–147). Hillsdale, NJ: Erlbaum.

Graf, P., & Mandler, G. (1984). Activation makes words more accessible but not necessarily more retrievable. *Journal of Verbal Learning and Verbal Behavior, 23*, 553–568.

Graf, P., Mandler, G., & Haden, P. E. (1982). Simulating amnesic symptoms in normal subjects. *Science, 218*, 1243–1244.

Graf, P., & Ryan, L. (1990). Transfer-appropriate processing for implicit and explicit memory. *Journal of Experimental Psychology: Learning, Memory, and Cognition, 16,* 978–992.

Graf, P., & Schacter, D. L. (1989). Unitization and grouping mediate dissociations in memory for new associations. *Journal of Experimental Psychology: Learning, Memory, and Cognition, 15,* 930–940.

Graf, P., & Schacter, D. L. (1985). Implicit and explicit memory for new associations in normal and amnesic subjects. *Journal of Experimental Psychology: Learning, Memory, and Cognition, 11,* 501–518.

Horowitz, L. M., & Prytulak, L. S. (1969). Reintegrative memory. *Psychological Review, 76,* 519–531.

Hultsch, D. F., Masson, M. E. J., & Small, B. J. (1991). Adult age differences in direct and indirect tests of memory. *Journal of Gerontology, 46,* 22–30.

Jacoby, L. L., & Dallas, M. (1981). On the relationship between autobiographical memory and perceptual learning. *Journal of Experimental Psychology: General, 110,* 306–340.

Kirsner, K., Milech, D., & Standon, D. (1983). Common and modality-specific processes in the mental lexicon. *Memory and Cognition, 11,* 621–630.

Kolers, P. A. (1975). Memorial consequences of automatized encoding. *Journal of Experimental Psychology: Human Learning and Memory, 1,* 689–701.

Kolers, P. A. (1979). A pattern-analyzing basis of recognition. In L. S. Cermak & F. I. M. Craik (Eds.), *Levels of processing in human memory* (pp. 363–384). Hillsdale, NJ: Erlbaum.

Kolers, P. A., & Ostry, D. J. (1974). Time course of loss of information regarding pattern analyzing operations. *Journal of Verbal Learning and Verbal Behavior, 13,* 599–612.

Lewandowsky, S., Dunn, J. C., & Kirsner, K. (Eds.). (1989). *Implicit memory: Theoretical issues.* Hillsdale, NJ: Erlbaum.

Light, L. L. (1988). Preserved implicit memory in old age. In M. M. Gruneberg, P. E. Morris, & R. N. Sykes (Eds.), *Practical aspects of memory: Current research and issues* (Vol. 2, pp. 90–95). Chichester, England: Wiley.

Mandler, G. (1980). Recognizing: The judgment of previous occurrence. *Psychological Review, 87,* 252–271.

Mandler, G. (1988). Memory: Conscious and unconscious. In P. R. Solomon, G. R. Goethals, C. M. Kelly, & R. B. Stephens (Eds.), *Memory: Interdisciplinary approaches* (pp. 84–106). New York: Springer-Verlag.

Morris, C. D., Bransford, J. D., & Franks, J. J. (1977). Levels of processing versus transfer appropriate processing. *Journal of Verbal Learning and Verbal Behavior, 16,* 519–533.

Roediger, H. L., & Blaxton, T. A. (1987). Effects of varying modality, surface features, and retention interval on priming in word fragment completion. *Memory and Cognition, 15,* 379–388.

Roediger, H. L., Srinivas, K., & Weldon, M. S. (1989). Dissociations between implicit measures of retention. In S. Lewandowsky, J. C. Dunn, & K. Kirsner (Eds.), *Implicit memory: Theoretical issues* (pp. 67–84). Hillsdale, NJ: Erlbaum.

Salthouse, T. A. (1982). *Adult cognition.* New York: Springer-Verlag.

Schacter, D. L. (1987). Implicit memory: History and current status. *Journal of Experimental Psychology: Learning, Memory, and Cognition, 13,* 501–518.

Schacter, D. L., & Graf, P. (1989). Modality specificity of implicit memory for new associations. *Journal of Experimental Psychology: Learning, Memory, and Cognition, 15,* 3–12.

Shallice, T. (1990). *From neuropsychology to mental structure.* New York: Cambridge University Press.

Shimamura, A. P. (1986). Priming effects in amnesia: Evidence for a dissociable memory function. *Quarterly Journal of Experimental Psychology, 38A,* 619–644.

Squire, L. R. (1987). *Memory and brain.* New York: Oxford University Press.

Tulving, E., & Schacter, D. L. (1990). Priming and human memory systems. *Science, 247,* 301–305.

Weldon, M. S., Roediger, H. L., & Challis, B. H. (1989). The properties of retrieval cues constrain the picture superiority effect. *Memory and Cognition, 17,* 95–105.

22

Age-Related Changes in Explicit and Implicit Memory

HASKER P. DAVIS and PATRICIA A. BERNSTEIN

So we say, old age may reason well, but old age does not
remember well. This is a commonplace. It seems as if memory
were the most uncertain of all our faculties. (Burroughs, 1922,
p. 283)

Introduction

Burroughs's notion that memory is the cognitive faculty most vulnerable to the process
of aging is probably consistent with the modern popular view of how cognition
changes with age. Middle-aged persons may wonder whether age is beginning to affect
their memory when they forget an item at the grocery store, or the name of a person
just met. Despite the widely held belief that memory is adversely affected by the aging
process, relatively few investigations of memory and aging occurred prior to the last
few decades. For most of the 20th century, the psychology of aging has been a
relatively small field, with most studies of cognition concentrating on intellectual
development (Riegel, 1977). Indeed, Brumer (1977) reported that there were just over
200 publications in 1972 for the entire field of geropsychology. However, the last two
decades have witnessed a dramatic increase in the number of studies in the field of
geropsychology, including studies of memory. A computerized search of *Psychological Abstracts* using the key words "aged" or "aging" and "memory" showed a
marked growth in the number of reports on memory and aging. Figure 22.1 shows that
the number of reports on memory and aging now exceeds the number of publications
reported for the entire field of geropsychology in 1972.

There are a number of recent reviews of the effects of age on tests of recall and
recognition (Craik, 1977; Poon, 1985). In general, these reviews report that age has no
effect or only a slight effect on sensory memory, short-term memory, or remote
memory. However, the elderly are impaired on recall and recognition tests of long-
term memory. For the most part, memory deficits associated with age have been
explained in terms of information-processing deficits (i.e., encoding, storage, or retrieval), reduced semantic elaboration, or a decline in cognitive resources (Craik, 1985;

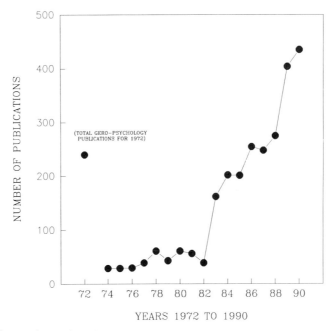

FIGURE 22.1. The rapid growth in the area of memory and aging during the last two decades, demonstrated by a plot of the publications per year in memory and aging relative to the total number of publications in the entire field of geropsychology for 1972.

Salthouse, 1985, 1988). Although there is little disagreement that the elderly demonstrate impairment on tests of recall and recognition, a number of investigators have recently reported that the elderly are not impaired or only slightly impaired on memory tests that do not require deliberate recollection (Howard, 1988; Light, Singh, & Capps, 1986; Mitchell, 1989). Other investigators report significant impairment by the elderly on memory tests that do not require deliberate recollection (Chiarello & Hoyer, 1988; Davis et al., 1990; Hultsch, Masson, & Small, 1991).

Tests of recall and recognition are frequently referred to in the aging literature as tests of "explicit memory," and tests that do not require deliberate recollection are referred to as tests of "implicit memory." These terms are used in a similar way to describe memory systems that were first investigated in normal subjects and amnesic patients (Schacter, 1987a; Squire, 1987). "Explicit memory" refers to a domain of memory that is usually associated with conscious awareness, includes memories for personal and temporal episodes, and is frequently measured with traditional tests of recall and recognition. "Implicit memory" or "indirect memory" refers to a domain of memory that is demonstrated by performance, can occur without conscious awareness, and includes skill learning and the phenomenon of priming. The dissociation demonstrated by the elderly on some tests of implicit and explicit memory has been taken as support for multiple memory systems, and has led some investigators to suggest that the memory impairment in the elderly may be qualitatively similar to that demonstrated by amnesic patients. That is, elderly subjects and amnesic patients demonstrate impairment on explicit memory tests, yet both may show little or no impairment on tests of implicit memory.

In this chapter we address the reported dissociation between implicit and explicit memory in the elderly by providing recent findings from our laboratory on memory change as a function of age. First, we report the performance of individuals in their 20s through their 80s on an explicit test of memory. We next provide a report of the performance of individuals from their 20s through their 80s on two implicit tests of memory—a lexical priming test and a cognitive skill test. Finally, we argue that age is likely to affect performance on tests of both implicit and explicit memory.

Explicit Memory Performance from the 20s through the 80s

It is well known that performance on explicit tests of memory declines with age (see Craik, 1977; Light, 1991; and Poon, 1985, for reviews). In our laboratory, subjects in their 20s through their 80s have been administered explicit memory tests, as reported in a previous study (Davis et al., 1990) and in several ongoing studies. Subjects in their 40s or younger were student volunteers. Older subjects were recruited from senior organizations or the Life-Long Learning program at the University of Colorado. Full Scale IQ scores and years of formal education for subjects in their 70s and 80s were equivalent to or greater than those demonstrated by subjects in their 20s or 30s. Performance by these subjects on Rey's Auditory Verbal Learning Test (Rey's AVLT) is presented here. This test consists of the verbal presentation of 15 concrete nouns, followed by an immediate-recall test after each of five presentations. The last immediate trial is followed by a recall trial 20 minutes later. The results from this test are presented because they illustrate changes across the lifespan, and show that differences in performance can be detected within subgroups of older subjects.

Figure 22.2 shows the performance of subjects in each decade of life from the 20s through the 80s on the immediate and delayed trials of Rey's AVLT. Subjects in all age conditions recalled significantly more words across the immediate trials, but subjects in their 50s and older recalled fewer words than subjects in their 40s or younger. Subjects in their 70s and 80s recalled fewer words than subjects in their 50s and 60s. For the delayed trial, subjects in their 50s and older showed a significant decline in the number of words recalled, relative to their performance on the last immediate test.

The explicit memory of subjects was further analyzed by examining primacy and recency effects on the first immediate trial of Rey's AVLT. The "primacy effect" reflects the recall of words from the beginning of a list that are thought to be stored in long-term memory. The "recency effect" refers to the recall of words from the end of a list that are thought to be recalled from short-term memory. For our purposes, the number of words recalled from the first four serial positions and the last four serial positions reflect primacy and recency effects, respectively. The primacy and recency scores for subjects in each decade of life are shown in Figure 22.3. Subjects showed a greater primacy than recency effect. Subjects in their 50s or older showed a significantly smaller primacy effect than younger subjects. There was no significant age-related change in the recency effect.

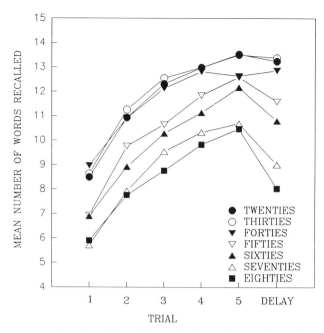

FIGURE 22.2. The mean number of words recalled on the immediate and delayed trials of the Rey AVLT for subjects in their 20s through their 80s. The *n* per age group ranged from 41 to 130; total $n = 474$.

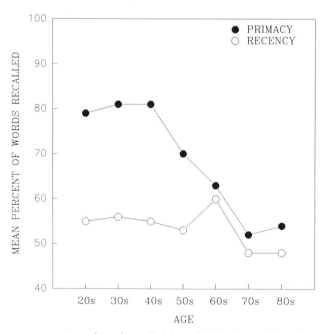

FIGURE 22.3. The mean percentage of words recalled from the first four positions (primacy effect) and last four positions (recency effect) of the first immediate trial of Rey's AVLT for subjects in their 20s through their 80s. Total $n = 474$.

These results are in general accord with previous findings. Specifically, the lack of a recency effect across age groups is consistent with reports that short-term memory is not impaired in the elderly. In addition, the age-related impairment in the primacy effect, the reduction in the number of words recalled across the immediate-recall trials by older subjects, and the age-related decline on the delayed-recall test are consistent with previous reports that long-term memory is impaired in old age. This deficit is typically detected in subjects 60 years of age and older. However, by pooling subjects from several experiments, we detected an impairment in explicit recall by 50-year-old subjects, and also found that subjects in their 70s and 80s were impaired relative to subjects in their 50s and 60s on a test of explicit verbal recall.

Word Stem Priming Performance from the 20s through the 80s

Our results with Rey's AVLT, along with those of other investigations (see Light, 1991, for a review), clearly document an age-related impairment on explicit memory tests. However, when tests of implicit memory are employed, the results are less clear (Chiarello & Hoyer, 1988; Howard, 1988; Howard, McAndrews, & Lasaga, 1981; Hultsch et al., 1991; Light & Singh, 1987; Light et al., 1986; Moscovitch, 1982; Rose, Yesavage, Hill, & Bower, 1986; Salmon, Shimamura, Butters, & Smith, 1988; Shimamura, Salmon, Squire, & Butters, 1987). The majority of studies of implicit memory in elderly subjects have focused on priming, a phenomenon that is considered to fall within the domain of implicit memory (Schacter, 1987a; Squire, 1987). Priming is inferred when a subject demonstrates a differential reaction to a test stimulus as a consequence of its prior presentation, and this may occur without conscious recollection of the prior presentation.

Normal priming in the elderly has been observed with a variety of experimental procedures. For example, both young and elderly subjects demonstrated facilitated reaction times in a lexical decision task that used repetition priming (Moscovitch, 1982). Similarly, Mitchell (1989) found no effect of age in a picture-naming version of repetition priming, and Rabbitt (1982) reported no effect of age on category membership judgments using repetition priming. Normal priming with elderly subjects has also been reported for a word stem completion task and a word fragment completion task (Light & Singh, 1987; Light et al., 1986). In these tasks, the subject is exposed to a list of words, and subsequently asked to complete word stems (e.g., "mot__") or word fragments (e.g., "__ss__ss__") with "the first word that comes to mind." Some of the partial words can be completed to form previously presented words, while others cannot. Young and elderly subjects have been shown to benefit equally from prior exposure. Normal priming in the elderly has also been reported for a homophone priming task (Howard, 1988). In this task, the subject is first exposed to text containing the uncommon member of homophone pairs (e.g.,"knight" in the homophone pair "knight-night"), and then priming is assessed in a subsequent spelling test. Priming effects may be inferred if the subject demonstrates a bias toward spelling the uncommon member of the homophone pair. The results of these studies have been interpreted as support for the view that elderly subjects and amnesic patients share a qualitatively similar memory impairment (Howard, 1988; Light & Singh, 1987; Light

et al., 1986). That is, both amnesic patients and elderly subjects show normal priming with impairment on explicit tests.

In contrast, priming has been reported in several studies to be impaired in the elderly (Chiarello & Hoyer, 1988; Hultsch et al., 1991). In these studies, the detection of impaired priming in elderly subjects was probably a result of the ability to detect small differences with large sample sizes. Chiarello and Hoyer (1988) detected an age-related impairment of priming in a word stem completion task with 144 subjects, and Hultsch et al. (1991) detected a similar impairment in another such task with 584 subjects.

Recently, we examined priming effects across the lifespan (Davis et al., 1990) with a word stem completion test used previously in studies of amnesic patients, young adults, and elderly adults (Salmon et al., 1988; Shimamura et al., 1987; Squire, Shimamura, & Graf, 1987). Rather than increase the sample size of the age groups and the statistical power for detecting small differences, we chose to assess priming in each decade of life from the 20s through the 80s. In this way, it is possible to obtain a finer analysis of implicit memory changes in an elderly population.

Subjects in their 20s through their 80s were presented with 15 words and instructed to rate each individual item on a 5-point scale (1 = "dislike extremely"; 5 = "like extremely"). The first three and last two words were filler words and were included to prevent primacy and recency effects. After the rating task, subjects were presented with 20 three-letter word stems and were asked to complete each with the first word that "popped" into mind. Ten of the stems could be completed to form the 10 primed words, and the remaining novel stems could be completed to form words from a frequency-matched list. Completion of the latter 10 stems provided the baseline guessing score. While each primed stem allowed for the formation of at least 10 different words, only one of the potential solutions spelled a word that had been presented on the rating task.

The mean percentages of word stems completed with previously primed words and baseline guessing rates for subjects are shown in Figure 22.4. No significant effect of age was detected for baseline scores, and all age groups demonstrated priming scores that were significantly above baseline scores. However, subjects in their 70s and 80s had significantly lower priming scores than subjects in all other age conditions.

The present results showing an age-related impairment in priming, and results from studies using large samples to detect impaired priming in older subjects (Chiarello & Hoyer, 1988; Hultsch et al., 1991), all support the view that implicit memory is impaired in the elderly. For the subjects in their 70s and 80s tested in our laboratory, the deficit in implicit memory is rather large. In fact, the magnitude of this deficit (subjects in their 70s and 80s completed approximately 25% fewer stems than subjects in their 20s; see Figure 22.4) is similar to the deficit detected on Rey's AVLT (subjects in their 70s and 80s recalled approximately 20% fewer words than subjects in their 20s; see Figure 22.2).

The frequent failure to detect age-related impairments in priming may result from several factors. For example, the detection of priming deficits in the elderly may depend on the age of the subjects tested (Davis et al., 1990), the size of the groups tested (Chiarello & Hoyer, 1988; Hultsch et al., 1991), the level of task difficulty (e.g., lexical decision vs. lexical completion), or task instructions.

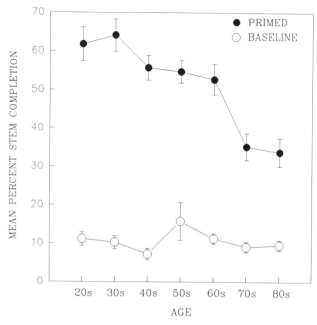

FIGURE 22.4. The mean percentages ($\pm$ *SEM*) of word stems completed with previously presented primed words and baseline guessing rates for individuals in their 20s through their 80s. Adapted from "Lexical Priming Deficits as a Function of Age" (p. 294) by H. P. Davis, A. Cohen, M. Gandy, P. Colombo, G. VanDusseldrop, N. Simolke, and J. Romano, 1990, *Behavioral Neuroscience, 104*, 288-297. Copyright 1990 by the American Psychological Association. Adapted by permission.

Tower of Hanoi Performance from the 20s through the 80s

Inconsistent results have also been obtained for motor, perceptual, and cognitive skill tasks purported to tap implicit memory when administered to the elderly. For example, elderly subjects demonstrated impaired performance in a mirror-image tracking task and in a pursuit-rotor task (Wright & Payne, 1985), a mirror-image reading task (Moscovitch, Winocur, & McLachlan, 1986), and a test of classical conditioning of the eyeblink response (Woodruff-Pak & Thompson, 1988). In contrast, elderly subjects are reported to acquire learning of a serial pattern task (Howard & Howard, 1989) and a video skill game (Salthouse & Somberg, 1982) at the same rate as young subjects.

We have investigated the acquisition of a cognitive skill in the elderly with the Tower of Hanoi puzzle. This puzzle is representative of tasks belonging to the category of puzzles known as transformation problems: A goal must be reached through a series of moves that are controlled by certain procedural rules. We chose this task because it has been carefully studied by investigators in the fields of cognitive psychology and artificial intelligence for its applications to the areas of problem solving and development of solution strategies (Anzai & Simon, 1979; Ewert & Lambert, 1932; Gagne & Smith, 1962; Karat, 1982; Simon, 1975). In general, the solution to the Tower of Hanoi puzzle requires the development of a cognitive strategy that develops slowly with practice and is not easily or accurately verbalized by subjects.

The Tower of Hanoi, a five-ring puzzle with its start and finish position, is illustrated in Figure 22.5. There is a single solution strategy that results in the minimal number of moves (minimal moves $= 2^n - 1$, where $n =$ the number of rings). The Tower of Hanoi can thus be solved in a minimum of 31 moves. For administration of the puzzle, the subject is instructed to move the rings from the left peg to the right peg, with the constraints that only one ring may be moved at a time and a larger ring cannot be placed on a smaller one.

In our investigation, subjects made four solution attempts per session for four sessions. To prevent the possibility of unintentional nonverbal cueing, the experimenter was positioned to the side and slightly behind the subject during all solution attempts. In order to avoid verbal cueing, interactions were limited to specific statements of encouragement, such as "I know this puzzle seems difficult, but it can be solved," and "I know this can be frustrating, but please keep trying." Statements of encouragement were offered when the subject failed to make a move within 1 minute. A subject's questions about the puzzle were answered directly only if they pertained to the rules for solving the puzzle. After each solution attempt the subject was told the number of moves made for that attempt. If the number of moves made was greater than the optimal solution number, the subject was told the optimal solution number of moves (31) and was encouraged to try for this best solution.

A single transfer test was given to subjects after the 16th solution attempt. For the transfer test, subjects were told that the rules for solving the puzzle were the same as before, but that the middle peg was now the goal peg. All subjects were in good health, and age groups were matched on Full Scale IQ.

Figure 22.6 shows the mean number of excess moves per session made beyond the optimal 31 moves for each decade of age between the 20s and 80s. As subjects acquired experience with the puzzle, fewer moves were required to achieve a successful solution. However, this improvement was not equivalent across age groups. For sessions 2 through 4, subjects in their 80s performed more poorly than subjects in their 40s or younger ($p < .05$). Subjects in their 70s made significantly more moves than subjects in their 20s during session 3.

The difficulty that older subjects experience on this task becomes more apparent when the goal peg is shifted for the transfer test. Figure 22.7 shows the mean number of excess moves ($\pm$ *SEM*) made on the transfer test for the different age conditions. Age significantly affected the number of moves required to accomplish the transfer test

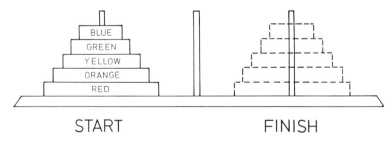

FIGURE 22.5. A schematic diagram of the Tower of Hanoi puzzle. Subjects are instructed to move the disks from the start position on the left peg to the finish position on the right peg.

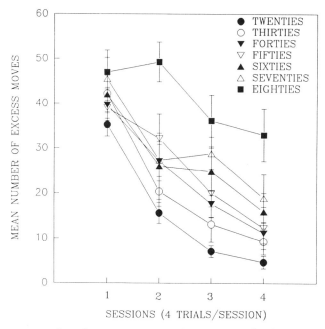

FIGURE 22.6. The mean number of excess moves per solution attempt for the Tower of Hanoi puzzle for subjects in their 20s through their 80s. The *n* per age group ranged from 15 to 37; total *n* = 132.

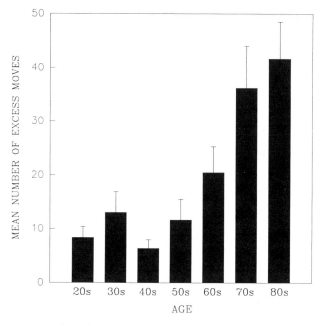

FIGURE 22.7. The mean number of excess moves (± *SEM*) for the transfer trial of the Tower of Hanoi puzzle for subjects in their 20s through their 80s. Total *n* = 132.

($p < .001$). Specifically, subjects in their 70s and 80s required more moves than subjects from all younger age groups ($p < .05$). Subjects in their 60s made significantly more moves than subjects in their 20s or 40s.

These results are in general accord with the results for priming reported in the previous section. Specifically, subjects in their 70s and 80s demonstrated a clear deficit in acquiring the strategy necessary for successfully solving the Tower of Hanoi puzzle. Older subjects in their 60s demonstrated a less severe deficit.

Conclusions and Directions

The demonstration of dissociations or double dissociations on tasks designed to assess different memory systems in amnesic patients (Schacter, 1987a; Squire, 1987) and neurological patients of differing etiologies (Heindel, Salmon, Shults, Walicke, & Butters, 1989) provides strong support for the existence of multiple memory systems. Dissociations on tests assessing implicit and explicit memory in elderly subjects have also been interpreted as support for the existence of multiple memory systems (Mitchell, 1989). In some cases, these dissociations have been further interpreted as evidence for a qualitatively similar memory impairment in elderly subjects and amnesic patients (Light & Singh, 1986; Light et al., 1987). Other investigators have failed to obtain clear dissociations with tests designed to assess implicit and explicit memory in the elderly (Chiarello & Hoyer, 1988; Davis et al., 1990; Hultsch et al., 1991).

In our view, studies of implicit memory in elderly subjects, because of inconsistent results, provide little support for the theoretical distinction between memory systems. This does not, of course, discount the dramatic and compelling evidence for multiple memory systems obtained in studies of amnesic patients. In the case of the proposed similarity between the memory impairment of the elderly and that of amnesic patients, studies that have detected impaired priming with large samples (Chiarello & Hoyer, 1988; Hultsch et al., 1991) and those that have included older groups of elderly subjects (Davis et al., 1990) provide evidence against this position. The inconsistent results for nonpriming tasks of implicit memory noted in the previous section also argue against this position. Furthermore, elderly subjects demonstrate deficits on tests sensitive to frontal lobe pathology (Craik, Morris, Morris, & Loewen, 1990; Davis et al., 1990; Mittenberg, Seidenberg, O'Leary, & DiGiulio, 1989; Veroff, 1980), a phenomenon that is not characteristic of all forms of amnesia (Janowsky, Shimamura, & Squire, 1989; Schacter, 1987b; Squire, 1987). Indeed, a consistent parallel in the memory performance of amnesic patients and elderly subjects would be somewhat surprising, given the differential neural changes associated with amnesia and aging. The elderly show heterogeneous neuronal changes, whereas amnesic patients may have brain damage restricted to medial temporal and/or diencephalic areas (Squire, 1987). Specifically, the elderly may experience neuronal changes that extend well beyond the areas of damage reported for amnesic patients. For example, age-related neuronal shrinkage has been observed in neocortex (Haug, 1985; Haug et al., 1983). Similarly, a significant decrease in large neurons in midfrontal, superior temporal, and inferior parietal cortex, with loss attributed to neuronal shrinkage, was detected in a clinically and neuropathologically normal sample of elderly subjects

(Terry, DeTeresa, & Hansen, 1987). More recently, age-related volume decreases in caudate, diencephalic structures, and most neocortical regions were detected in a magnetic resonance imaging study of normal subjects between 30 and 79 years of age (Jernigan et al., 1991). The greatest changes appeared to occur in cortical association areas and in medial temporal lobe structures.

Since aging is likely to produce diffuse damage to the brain that will affect both subcortical structures and neocortex, it is not surprising to find an impairment of both implicit and explicit memory in the elderly. However, since neuronal change does not occur evenly throughout the brain with age (Haug et al., 1983; Jernigan et al., 1991; Terry et al., 1987), performance on some tasks—particularly tasks that are relatively insensitive to neuronal loss—might be expected to be normal. Thus, the elderly can be expected to perform normally on some implicit memory tasks and to be impaired on other such tasks. Specifically, whether or not normal priming occurs in the elderly may depend on subtle differences in task difficulty, the degree to which instructions minimize memory aspects of the task (Graf, Squire, & Mandler, 1984), and the degree of impairment in brain areas subserving task performance (Heindel et al., 1989).

These factors make it difficult to predict the performance of elderly subjects on different types of memory tasks, with the notable exception of tests of recall and recognition. The theoretical formulation that characterizes the elderly as qualitatively similar to amnesic patients has not been supported by our findings, or our review of results from tests purported to measure implicit memory. Specifically, the results obtained with elderly subjects were inconsistent. Yet some results do provide a basis for speculation regarding the impairments in memory that may be expected in elderly subjects. If one considers the impaired performance of older subjects on frontal-lobe-dependent tasks, one might expect some degree of congruence with the performance of amnesic patients who demonstrate frontal lobe pathology (i.e., Korsakoff patients). It has been suggested that amnesic patients with frontal lobe signs are disproportionately impaired on memory for spatiotemporal information, relative to recall or recognition of specific item information (Schacter, 1987b; Squire, 1982). Thus, the elderly would be expected to be impaired on tests that assess memory for contextual information, such as place, time, and temporal order. Consistent with this prediction, elderly subjects have demonstrated poor retention of the context in which they learned new factual information (Craik et al., 1990). In addition, elderly subjects and Korsakoff patients are both reported to demonstrate normal acquisition of an implicit task that requires learning a serial pattern (Howard & Howard, 1989; Nissen & Bullemer, 1987). On the other hand, these two groups demonstrate dissimilar performance on a priming task: Korsakoff patients show normal priming when tested with a word stem completion task (Shimamura et al., 1987), but older elderly subjects do not (Davis et al., 1990). Thus, the comparison of elderly subjects with amnesic patients showing frontal signs should not be taken as a modification of the view that the elderly are qualitatively similar in memory performance to amnesic patients. Instead, it appears that the elderly will have their own unique pattern of memory deficits.

Our conclusion and expectation that age-related impairments will be detected on some implicit tests and not on others does not negate a memory systems approach. The use of a broad array of cognitive tests increases the likelihood of documenting and understanding age-related changes in cognition. That is, tests that share in the assessment of a particular attribute (e.g., frontal lobe function) should demonstrate a consistent pattern of results when administered to elderly subjects. Assessments across attributes may show conflicting results. Thus, the increased usage of neuropsychological tests designed to assess implicit memory in the elderly can only increase the opportunity for documenting and understanding age-related changes in cognition.

ACKNOWLEDGMENT

The research reported in this chapter was supported by Grant No. 1R15AG08317-01A1 from the National Institute on Aging.

REFERENCES

Anzai, Y., & Simon, H. A. (1979). The theory of learning by doing. *Psychological Review*, 86, 124–140.

Brumer, S. (1977). Some documentation for the history of psychological gerontology. In J. E. Birren & K. W. Schaie (Eds.), *Handbook of the psychology of aging* (1st ed., pp. 88–93). New York: Van Nostrand Reinhold.

Burroughs, J. (1922). *The last harvest*. Cambridge: Riverside Press.

Chiarello, C., & Hoyer, W. J. (1988). Adult age differences in implicit and explicit memory: Time course and encoding effects. *Psychology and Aging*, 3, 358–366.

Craik, F. I. M. (1977). Age differences in human memory. In J. E. Birren & K. W. Schaie (Eds.), *Handbook of the psychology of aging* (1st ed., pp. 384–420). New York: Van Nostrand Reinhold.

Craik, F. I. M. (1985). Paradigms in human memory research. In L. G. Nilsson & T. Archer (Eds.), *Perspectives on learning and memory* (pp. 197–221). Hillsdale, NJ: Erlbaum.

Craik, F. I. M., Morris, L. W., Morris, R. G., & Loewen, R. E. (1990). Relations between source amnesia and frontal lobe functioning in older adults. *Psychology and Aging*, 5, 148–151.

Davis, H. P., Cohen, A., Gandy, M., Colombo, P., VanDusseldorp, G., Simolke, N., & Romano, J. (1990). Lexical priming deficits as a function of age. *Behavioral Neuroscience*, 104, 288–297.

Ewert, P. H., & Lambert, J. F. (1932). Part II: The effect of verbal instructions upon the formation of a concept. *Journal of General Psychology*, 6, 400–413.

Gagne, R. M., & Smith, E. C. (1962). A study of the effects of verbalization on problem solving. *Journal of Experimental Psychology*, 63, 12–18.

Graf, P., Squire, L. R., & Mandler, G. (1984). The information that amnesic patients do not forget. *Journal of Experimental Psychology: Learning, Memory, and Cognition*, 10, 164–178.

Haug, H. (1985). Are neurons of the human cerebral cortex really lost during aging? A morphometric examination. In J. Traber & W. H. Gispen (Eds.), *Senile dementia of the Alzheimer type* (pp. 150–163). Berlin: Springer-Verlag.

Haug, H., Barmwater, U., Eggers, R., Fischer, D., Kuhl, S., & Sass, N. L. (1983). Anatomical changes in aging brain: Morphometric analysis of the human prosencephalon. In J. Cervos-Navarro & H. I. Sarkander (Eds.), *Aging: Vol. 21. Brain aging: Neuropathology and neuropharmacology* (pp. 1–12) New York: Raven Press.

Heindel, W. C., Salmon, D. P., Shults, C. W., Walicke, P. A., & Butters, N. (1989). Neuropsychological evidence for multiple implicit memory systems: A comparison of Alzheimer's, Huntington's, and Parkinson's disease patients. *Journal of Neuroscience*, 9, 582–587.

Howard, D. V. (1988). Implicit and explicit assessment of cognitive aging. In M. L. Howe & C. J. Brainerd (Eds.), *Progress in cognitive development research: Cognitive development in adulthood* (pp. 3–37). New York: Springer-Verlag.

Howard, D. V., & Howard, J. H., Jr. (1989). Age differences in learning serial patterns: Direct versus indirect measures. *Psychology and Aging*, 4, 357–364.

Howard, D. V., McAndrews, M. P., & Lasaga, M. I. (1981). Semantic priming of lexical decisions in young and old adults. *Journal of Gerontology*, 36, 707–714.

Hultsch, D. F., Masson, M. E. J., & Small, B. J. (1991). Adult age differences in direct and indirect tests of memory. *Journal of Gerontology: Psychological Sciences*, 46, P22–P30.

Janowsky, J. S., Shimamura, A. P., & Squire, L. R. (1989). Memory and metamemory: Comparisons between patients with frontal lobe lesions and amnesics. *Psychobiology*, 17, 3–11.

Jernigan, T. L., Archibald, S. L., Berhow, M. T., Sowell, E. R., Foster, D. S., & Hesselink, J. R. (1991). Cerebral structure on MRI: Part I. Localization of age-related changes. *Biological Psychiatry, 29*, 55–67.

Karat, J. (1982). A model of problem solving with incomplete constraint knowledge. *Cognitive Psychology, 14*, 538–559.

Light, L. L. (1991). Memory and aging: Four hypotheses in search of data. *Annual Review of Psychology, 42*, 333–376.

Light, L. L., & Singh, A. (1987). Implicit and explicit memory in young and older adults. *Journal of Experimental Psychology: Learning, Memory, and Cognition, 13*, 531–541.

Light, L. L., Singh, A., & Capps, J. L. (1986). Dissociation of memory and awareness in young and older adults. *Journal of Clinical and Experimental Neuropsychology, 8*, 62–74.

Mitchell, D. B. (1989). How many memory systems? Evidence from aging. *Journal of Experimental Psychology: Learning, Memory, and Cognition, 15*, 31–49.

Mittenberg, W., Seidenberg, M., O'Leary, D., & DiGiulio, D. V. (1989). Changes in cerebral functioning associated with normal aging. *Journal of Clinical and Experimental Neuropsychology, 11*, 918–932.

Moscovitch, M. (1982). A neuropsychological approach to perception and memory in normal and pathological aging. In F. I. M. Craik & S. Trehub (Eds.), *Aging and cognitive processes* (pp. 55–78). New York: Plenum Press.

Moscovitch, M., Winocur, G., & McLachlan, D. (1986). Memory as assessed by recognition and reading time in normal and memory-impaired people with Alzheimer's disease and other neurological disorders. *Journal of Experimental Psychology: General, 115*, 331–347.

Nissen, M. J., & Bullemer, P. (1987). Attentional requirements of learning: Evidence from performance measures. *Cognitive Psychology, 19*, 1–32.

Poon, L. W. (1985). Differences in human memory with aging: Nature, causes, and clinical implications. In J. E. Birren & K. W. Schaie (Eds.), *Handbook of the psychology of aging* (2nd ed., pp. 427–462). New York: Van Nostrand Reinhold.

Rabbitt, P. M. A. (1982). How do old people know what to do next? In F. I. M. Craik & S. Trehub (Eds.), *Aging and cognitive processes* (pp. 79–98). New York: Plenum Press.

Riegel, K. F. (1977). History of psychological gerontology. In J. E. Birren & K. W. Schaie (Eds.), *Handbook of the psychology of aging* (1st ed., pp. 70–102). New York: Van Nostrand Reinhold.

Rose, T. L., Yesavage, J. A., Hill, R. D., & Bower, G. H. (1986). Priming effects and recognition memory in young and elderly adults. *Experimental Aging Research, 12*, 31–37.

Salmon, D. P., Shimamura, A. P., Butters, N., & Smith, S. (1988). Lexical and semantic priming deficits in patients with Alzheimer's disease. *Journal of Clinical and Experimental Neuropsychology, 10*, 477–494.

Salthouse, T. A. (1985). *A theory of cognitive aging.* Amsterdam: Elsevier.

Salthouse, T. A. (1988). The role of processing resources in cognitive aging, In M. L. Howe & C. J. Brainerd (Eds.), *Progress in cognitive development research: Cognitive development in adulthood* (pp. 185–239). New York: Springer-Verlag.

Salthouse, T. A., & Somberg, B. L. (1982). Skilled performance: Effects of adult age and experience on elementary processes. *Journal of Experimental Psychology: General, 111*, 176–207.

Schacter, D. L. (1987a). Implicit memory: History and current status. *Journal of Experimental Psychology: Learning, Memory, and Cognition, 13*, 368–379.

Schacter, D. L. (1987b). Memory, amnesia, and frontal lobe dysfunction. *Psychobiology, 15*, 21–36.

Shimamura, A. P., Salmon, D. P., Squire, L. R., & Butters, N. (1987). Memory dysfunction and word priming in dementia and amnesia. *Behavioral Neuroscience, 101*, 347–351.

Simon, H. A. (1975). The functional equivalence of problem solving skill. *Cognitive Psychology, 7*, 268–288.

Squire, L. R. (1982). Comparisons between forms of amnesia: Some deficits are unique to Korsakoff's syndrome. *Journal of Experimental Psychology: Learning, Memory, and Cognition, 8*, 560–571.

Squire, L. R. (1987). *Memory and brain.* New York: Oxford University Press.

Squire, L. R., Shimamura, A. P., & Graf, P. (1987). Strength and duration of priming effects in normal subjects and amnesic patients. *Neuropsychologia, 25*, 195–210.

Terry, R. D., DeTeresa, R., & Hansen, L. A. (1987). Neocortical cell counts in normal human adult aging. *Annals of Neurology, 21*, 530–539.

Veroff, A. E. (1980). The neuropsychology of aging. *Psychological Research, 41*, 259–268.

Woodruff-Pak, D. S., & Thompson, R. F. (1988). Classical conditioning of the eyeblink response in the delay paradigm in adults aged 18–83 years. *Psychology and Aging, 3*, 219–229.

Wright, B. M., & Payne, R. B. (1985). Effects of aging on sex differences in psychomotor reminiscence and tracking proficiency. *Journal of Gerontology, 40*, 179–184.

23

Aging and Memory:
A Model Systems Approach

PAUL R. SOLOMON and WILLIAM W. PENDLEBURY

Among the primary characteristics of both normal and pathological aging are impairments of memory. Disordered memory can be associated with normal aging and is one of the primary features of age-related disorders such as Alzheimer's disease (AD). Because memory disorders can be debilitating, and because the general population is rapidly aging, considerable effort has been devoted to characterizing these disorders. Nevertheless, important questions remain unanswered, including the following:

1. Is memory decline a natural consequence of aging or a by-product of diseases and other insults to the nervous system that accompany aging? Although most studies find a decline in cognitive abilities between groups of aged and young subjects, many of these studies also report a subset of the aged subjects who perform within the range of young subjects. What distinguishes these subjects who age successfully from those who do not (Rowe & Kahn, 1987)?

2. What are the neural systems and mechanisms of plasticity that change during aging? This, of course, will be a difficult question to approach until the systems and mechanisms for normal memory are elucidated.

3. What is the best strategy for developing interventions (e.g., drugs) for disordered memory? Two basic approaches to this problem exist. The first involves testing drugs in clinical populations that alter systems that *may* be involved in memory. A current example of this strategy is the use of tetrahydroaminoacridine (THA) with AD patients. A second strategy involves attempting to fully understand the mechanisms of memory and then to develop agents for clinical trials based on these findings. The model systems approach described in this chapter is an example of this strategy. These strategies are not mutually exclusive and in practice often coexist, but in their pure forms they do represent fundamentally different approaches.

4. What is the nature of the pathology that accompanies disordered aging, and how does it develop? This is a particularly difficult question to address in clinical populations, because most tissue is harvested in end-stage disease. There is preliminary work using imaging techniques to correlate pathology with cognition, but until more sophisticated imaging techniques become available, these studies will continue to be difficult to interpret. To the extent that animal models can reproduce some of the

cognitive symptoms seen with aging, and to the extent that the neuropathology is similar, these models may prove useful.

There are many approaches to answering these and related questions. In this chapter, we would like to argue that one approach that has been underutilized and that may provide a framework for addressing questions related to age-related memory disorders (ARMDs) is the model systems approach.

The Model Systems Approach to Memory

The model systems approach to the neurobiology of memory advocates studying a well-characterized learned response in a relatively simple and well-controlled preparation. The ultimate goal of this approach is to (1) characterize the behavioral response, (2) trace the neural circuitry controlling the response, (3) identify the site(s) of plasticity, and (4) elucidate the mechanism(s) of plasticity. As several of the chapters in this volume attest, the model systems approach has provided valuable information concerning the possible neural systems and mechanisms involved in learning and memory. The work in invertebrates has progressed to the point of beginning to identify possible mechanisms (Abrams & Kandel, 1988; Alkon, 1986), and the work in mammalian preparations has made enormous strides in the past few years and is now at the point of identifying the circuitry for simple forms of learning (Thompson, 1988). As progress continues, it should be possible to begin to use the model systems approach to study other aspects of memory. For example, Marcus and Carew (1990) have used the *Aplysia* gill withdrawal reflex to study the development of simple forms of associative learning. Our work has also used the model systems approach, but has focused on the other end of the lifespan. We have argued that the advantages of the model systems approach for studying memory would also apply to the study of ARMDs. Using a well-developed model system should make it possible both to characterize the changes in learning and memory that accompany aging and to investigate their neural substrate. With this information in hand, it should be possible to begin to develop interventions.

The Model Systems Approach to Age-Related Memory Disorders

The rabbit's classically conditioned eyeblink (EB) response has become the most widely used model system for studying associative learning in mammals (Gormezano, Prokasy, & Thompson, 1987). Because so much is now known about both the behavioral and neurobiological aspects of this form of learning, it has become possible to use this approach to study ARMDs. There are a number of reasons why this model system may be especially well suited for this purpose. These have been reviewed in several recent papers (Graves & Solomon, 1985; Woodruff-Pak & Thompson, 1985; Solomon & Pendlebury, 1988; Solomon, Beal, & Pendlebury, 1988), but are briefly summarized here:

1. The behavioral aspects of this conditioned response (CR) are well defined for both humans and rabbits. Within certain boundaries, acquisition of the CR in both species appears to follow the same set of rules (Hilgard & Marquis, 1940). Because the

identical learned behaviors are used in the rabbit and human, human-to-animal extrapolation becomes more plausible.

2. There are significant age differences in both humans and rabbits in the ability to acquire the CR.

3. The neural circuitry for the CR is now beginning to be well understood. It now appears that the cerebellum is the essential site of plasticity for the simple delay CR in both rabbits (Thompson, 1988) and humans (Solomon, Stowe, & Pendlebury, 1989), whereas the hippocampus is involved in more complex types of learning such as trace conditioning (Moyer, Deyo, & Disterhoft, 1988; Solomon, Vander Schaaf, Thompson, & Weisz, 1986). It is interesting that the hippocampus is a primary site of pathology in disorders of memory that accompany human aging (Ball, 1977; Hyman, Van Hoesen, Damasio, & Barnes, 1984).

4. Although comparatively little is known about the pharmacology of this form of learning, what is known implicates the cholinergic system (Downs et al., 1972; Moore, Goodell, & Solomon, 1976). This may be of some significance because of the hypothesized role of the cholinergic system in ARMDs (Bartus, Dean, Beer, & Lippa, 1982; Collerton, 1986).

5. The rabbit provides an excellent preparation for studying the effects of experimentally induced neuropathology that may accompany ARMDs. Specifically, aluminum exposure produces neurofilamentous degeneration in rabbits that is similar to the neurofibrillary tangles seen in AD (Klatzko, Wisniewski, & Streicher, 1965; Terry & Penna, 1965).

6. The rabbit has also been used extensively to investigate potential mechanisms of memory such as long-term potentiation (LTP) (Bliss & Lomo, 1973).

7. One major problem often associated with studying ARMDs is that age-related decrements in performance can affect the CR. Using a relatively simple form of learning such as the EB response makes it possible to rule out many of these nonassociative factors, such as sensorimotor deficits, motivational differences, and fatigue (Graves & Solomon, 1985).

8. Although classical conditioning is a relatively simple form of learning, it has been argued that both the behavioral and neurobiological mechanisms underlying Pavlovian conditioning are directly applicable to more complex types of learning (Hawkins & Kandel, 1984).

9. Age-related deficits that are limited to certain conditioning tasks may help limit hypotheses about the underlying neurobiological basis of these deficits. For example, if trace conditioning were disrupted earlier in the lifespan than delay conditioning, this could have different implications for the underyling neurobiological substrate. As information regarding the neurobiological basis of conditioning in the rabbit becomes available, more precise statements about the anatomical substrates of ARMDs will be possible.

10. Most recently, the EB preparation in rabbits and in humans has been used to begin to evaluate pharmacological agents that may alter learning and memory (Deyo, Straube, & Disterhoft, 1989; Solomon, Groccia-Ellison, Edwards, & Stanton, 1991).

In summary, the advantages inherent to using a model systems approach to studying aging in young organisms may also apply to the study of age-related changes in learning and memory in aged organisms. Because the classically conditioned EB response is well characterized at the behavioral and neurobiological levels, it may be the model system of choice for studying ARMDs.

A Strategy for Using the Classically Conditioned Eyeblink Response for Studying Age-Related Memory Disorders

We have adopted a fourfold strategy for using the classically conditioned EB response to study aging. This approach includes investigating conditioning deficits in (1) rabbits across the lifespan, (2) humans across the lifespan, (3) AD patients, and (4) young animals with induced neuropathology that may accompany aging and disorders of aging. If similar deficits occur in each of these groups, it may be possible to begin to form hypotheses about the neurobiology of ARMD.

Conditioning in Rabbits across the Lifespan

AGE-RELATED DISRUPTION OF THE RABBIT EYEBLINK RESPONSE

The research on conditioning in aged rabbits is limited to a few published studies (Graves & Solomon, 1985; Powell, Buchanan, & Hernandez, 1981, 1984; Woodruff-Pak, Lavond, Logan, & Thompson, 1987). In one of these studies, we (Graves & Solomon, 1985) found that although aged (36- to 60-month-old) and young (6-month-old) rabbits acquired the CR in a delay conditioning paradigm in which the tone conditioned stimulus (CS) and airpuff unconditioned stimulus (US) overlapped in time, aged rabbits were severely retarded in acquisition of the CR in the trace paradigm in which there was a 500-millisecond delay between the offset of the CS and the onset of the US. Woodruff-Pak et al. (1987) have replicated this finding, while also showing that trace conditioning can be disrupted in rabbits as young as 2.5 years of age. Unfortunately, neither our study nor the Woodruff-Pak et al. study attempted to correlate behavioral changes with neuropathological or neurochemical changes.

We have recently completed an extensive study examining delay, trace, and long-delay conditioning in rabbits from 6 to 48 months of age. Although the results of the study are currently being analyzed, the behavioral data appear consistent with the previous studies in indicating that (1) both delay and trace conditioning decline in aged animals; (2) trace conditioning is impaired as early as 2 years; and (3) delay conditioning is impaired at 4 years (Figure 23.1). What may be particularly interesting in these data is that although aged animals showed deficits in conditioning on the average, some aged animals conditioned as well as young animals. It will be informative to correlate the anatomical and pathological changes with conditioning in these animals. These data may suggest that chronological aging may not be as important for memory as neurological aging. The data may also suggest crucial neurobiological structures and systems that can then be manipulated in young animals to begin to determine their contribution to conditioning.

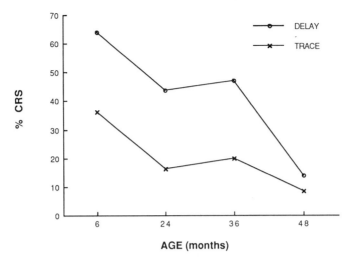

FIGURE 23.1. Mean percentage of CRs for delay and trace conditioning in 6-, 24-, 36-, and 48-month-old rabbits.

LONG-TERM POTENTIATION AS A POSSIBLE MECHANISM
OF AGE-RELATED MEMORY DISORDERS

LTP is an increase in the excitability of neurons caused by high-frequency electrical stimulation. LTP is considered to be a leading candidate mechanism for memory (Brown, Chapman, Kairiss, & Keenan, 1988; Landfield & Deadwyler, 1988; Teyler & Discenna, 1987) and has also been suggested to be important in ARMDs (Barnes, 1979; DeToledo-Morrell, Geinsman, & Morrell, 1988). In addition, LTP has been shown to be related to EB conditioning (Berger, 1984; Weisz, Clark, & Thompson, 1984).

We have recently completed a preliminary study examining LTP in the perforant path–dentate gyrus synapse in aged rabbits both before and after conditioning (Yang & Solomon, 1992). These preliminary results indicate that (1) synaptic efficacy in the rabbit declines with aging; (2) the decay of LTP is more rapid in aged animals; (3) the rate of conditioning in aged animals is related to the degree of synaptic efficacy (specifically, the old animals that condition at the same rate as young animals show LTP similar to that seen in young animals); and (4) following conditioning, there is an enhancement of synaptic efficacy that is significantly greater in young than in old animals (Figure 23.2).

Conditioning in Humans across the Lifespan

To our knowledge, only five studies have examined EB conditioning in aged human subjects. Three early studies all reported age-related deficits in EB conditioning (Braun & Geiselhart, 1959; Gakkel & Zinna, cited in Jerome, 1959; Kimble & Pennypacker, 1963). These studies, however, are subject to several alternative interpretations. For example, none of these studies attempted to determine whether the subjects had age-appropriate cognitive abilities; nor was there any attempt to determine whether nonassociative factors, such as sensitivity to the CS or US or spontaneous blink rate, could be contributing to the conditioning deficit.

We have recently completed a study on acquisition of the EB response in humans ranging in age from 18 to 85, using a tone CS and an airpuff US (Solomon, Pomerleau, Bennett, James, & Morse, 1989). We found a decline in percentage of CRs with age that was most pronounced in subjects over age 50 (Figure 23.3). Moreoever, we found a significant correlation ($r = .59$) between age and number of CRs (Figure 23.4). These differences could not be attributed to sensory or motor deficits or changes in spontaneous blink rates, nor were they related to general cognitive impairment. These findings are in near-perfect agreement with a study carried on simultaneously by Woodruff-Pak and Thompson (1988), using identical equipment. The results of these recent studies suggest that the deficits in EB conditioning over the age span are due to a disruption of a central associative process. To date, comparable data do not exist for the trace conditioning paradigm.

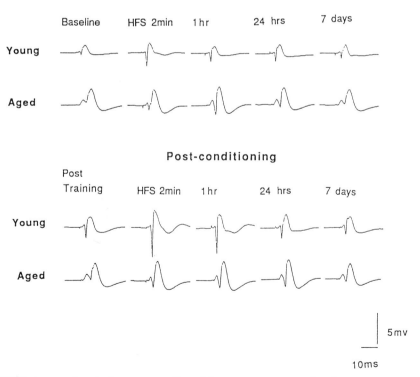

FIGURE 23.2. Averaged evoked responses collected from one young animal and one aged animal throughout the course of the experiment. Note: The aged animal was a "poor" learner. From B. Y. Yang and P. R. Solomon, 1992, manuscript in preparation.

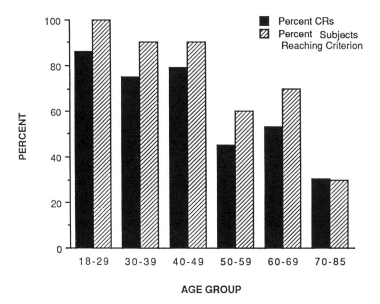

FIGURE 23.3. Percentage of CRs and percentage of subjects reaching a criterion of eight CRs in any block of nine trials for human subjects ranging in age from 18 to 85 years. From "Acquisition of the Classically Conditioned Eyeblink Response in Humans over the Lifespan" (p. 36) by P. R. Solomon, D. Pomerleau, L. Bennett, J. James, and D. L. Morse, 1989, *Psychology and Aging, 4*, 34–41. Copyright 1989 by the American Psychological Association. Reprinted by permission.

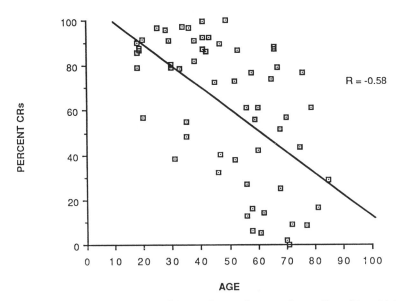

FIGURE 23.4. Correlation between percentage of CRs and age in human subjects. From "Acquisition of the Classically Conditioned Eyeblink Response in Humans over the Lifespan" (p. 37) by P. R. Solomon, D. Pomerleau, L. Bennett, J. James, and D. L. Morse, 1989, *Psychology and Aging, 4*, 34–41. Copyright 1989 by the American Psychological Association. Reprinted by permission.

Conditioning in Patients with Alzheimer's Disease

We are aware of only one study of EB conditioning in "demented" patients. In this study, Solyom and Barik (1965) compared elderly subjects (aged 70–81), young subjects (aged 20–43), and 17 hospitalized patients diagnosed as having either "senile dementia" or "cerebral arteriosclerosis." They found that young subjects conditioned most rapidly, followed by aged subjects, followed by "dementia/arteriosclerosis" patients.

We have recently collected data from 15 patients who meet the National Institutes of Health criteria for AD, and have found that delay conditioning is significantly disrupted in these patients compared to age-matched controls. As in our lifespan study, deficits in conditioning in the AD patients could not be attributed to nonassociative factors (Solomon, Levine, Bein, & Pendlebury, 1989, 1991) (Figure 23.5).

Modeling in Animals with Induced Neuropathology

Two primary strategies have been used to model ARMDs in animals: (1) disruption of the cholinergic system, and (2) aluminum-induced neurofibrillary degeneration (NFD). It is clear that neither of these produces a satisfactory model of normal aging, nor can either be considered a model of disorders of aging such as AD (see Solomon,

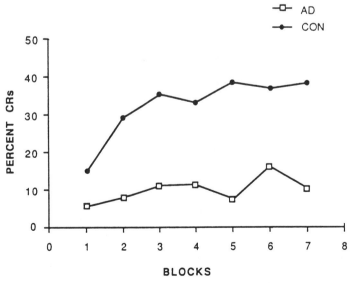

FIGURE 23.5. Mean percentage of CRs for AD patients and age-matched controls (CON). From "Disruption of Classical Conditioning in Patients with Alzheimer's Disease" (p. 285) by P. R. Solomon, B. Levine, T. Bein, and W. W. Pendlebury, 1991, *Neurobiology of Aging, 12*, 283–287. Copyright 1991 by Pergamon Press. Reprinted by permission.

Beal, & Pendlebury, 1988). Nevertheless, they both hold promise for modeling some aspects of the human disorder, and as such may warrant further investigation.

DISRUPTION OF THE CHOLINERGIC SYSTEM

There is evidence from both clinical studies and animal research that the cholinergic system is particularly vulnerable to disorders of aging and particularly to AD (Bartus et al., 1982; Coyle, Price, & DeLong, 1982; Sitaram, Weingartner, Caine, & Gillin, 1978). Because the cholinergic system has been implicated in memory in healthy subjects, and because the cholinergic deficits cannot explain fully the cognitive decline seen in AD, it is tempting to speculate that the cholinergic deficit may be primarily involved with the memory disorders that accompany pathological aging. The data from the rabbit EB preparation are consistent with this view.

A number of studies have reported that cholinergic blockade disrupts conditioning in rabbits (Downs et al., 1972; Moore et al., 1976; Harvey, Gormezano, & Cool-Hauser, 1983). Moreover, there are data to suggest that the septo-hippocampal cholinergic system is critical (Berry & Thompson, 1978; Solomon & Gottfried, 1981; Solomon, Solomon, Vander Schaaf, & Perry, 1983). Unfortunately, there are no studies that have investigated the effects of nucleus basalis of Mynert lesions on conditioning in the rabbit.

We have recently completed a study examining the effects of cholinergic blockade in human EB conditioning. Human volunteers who received 1.2 mg of scopolamine emitted significantly fewer CRs than subjects who received 0.6 mg of scopolamine, a vehicle, or peripheral control (Solomon, Groccia-Ellison, et al., 1991).

ALUMINUM-INDUCED NEUROFILAMENTOUS DEGENERATION

Intrathecal administration of aluminum salts in the rabbit produces an acute encephalopathy that is characterized pathologically by the formation of neuronal cytoplasmic structures resembling neurofibrillary tangles at the light-microscopic level (Klatzko et al., 1965). In order to characterize the aluminum-induced NFD, we have been involved in a series of studies investigating the behavioral, pathological, neurochemical, and immunocytochemical effects of aluminum intoxication in rabbits. These results have been reviewed elsewhere (Pendlebury, Beal, Kowall, & Solomon, 1988a, 1988b; Solomon & Pendlebury, 1988), but, briefly, we have found the following:

1. Intraventricular injection of aluminum chloride ($AlCl_3$) produces NFD (Figure 23.6) and disrupts both acquisition and retention of the CR (Pendlebury, Perl, Schwentker, Pingree, & Solomon, 1988; Solomon, Pingree, et al., 1988; Figure 23.7).

2. Disrupted learning and memory do not appear due to either sensory or motor deficits. Motor responses are intact. $AlCl_3$ rabbits are no different from controls in their ability to reflexively give the EB response when presented with an airpuff US (i.e., the response amplitudes do not differ from those of controls). Responses to the tone CS also appear unaltered. Threshold tests for tone are similar in control and $AlCl_3$ rabbits. We have also demonstrated that memory deficits are present when CSs from three different modalities are used (i.e., tone, light, and vibratory). Finally, memory is also disrupted in aluminum-treated rabbits when electrical brain stimulation to the medial

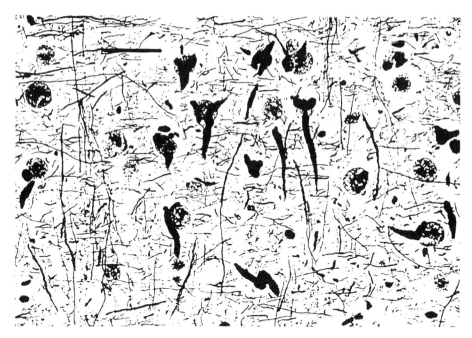

FIGURE 23.6. High-power photomicrograph of cingulate cortex from the brain of a New Zealand White rabbit exposed intraventricularly to 100 μl of 1% aluminum chloride. Shown are neurons from cortical layer V, with most cells showing perikaryal neurofilamentous degeneration. Bielschowsky silver impregnation stain. Calibration bar: 50 μm. From "A Model Systems Approach to Age-Related Memory Disorders" (p. 454) by P. R. Solomon and W. W. Pendlebury, 1988, *Neurotoxicology*, 9, 443–462. Copyright 1988 by Intox Press. Reprinted by permission.

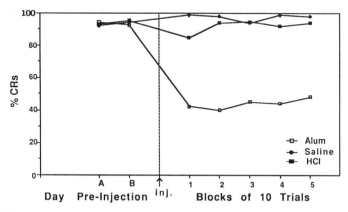

FIGURE 23.7. Mean percentage of CRs during retention testing for animals in the aluminum (Alum), hydrochloric acid (HCl), and saline conditions during preinjection acquisition of the CR (left panel) and the 50 trials of retention testing (right panel). Note the disruption of retention in aluminum-treated rabbits. From "Disrupted Retention of the Classically Conditioned Nictitating Membrane Response in Rabbits with Aluminum-Induced Neurofibrillary Degeneration" (p. 213) by P. R. Solomon, T. Pingree, D. Baldwin, D. Koota, D. P. Perl, and W. W. Pendlebury, 1988, *Neurotoxicology*, 9, 209–222. Copyright 1988 by Intox Press. Reprinted by permission.

geniculate body is used as a CS. This result indicates that memory deficits are not the results of pathology of the primary sensory pathway, as these pathways are bypassed with this technique (Solomon, Koota, Kessler, & Pendlebury, 1987).

3. There is no correlation between aluminum-induced illness and either acquisition or retention of the response (Pendlebury, Perl, et al., 1988; Solomon et al., 1988).

4. The deficits in learning and memory are correlated with the degree of pathology. We have evaluated the number of neurons containing neurofilamentous accumulation in five brain areas (frontal cortex, parietal cortex, ventral hippocampus, cerebellum, and pons) and have found that the overall degree of pathology is significantly correlated with the percentage of CRs (Pendlebury, Perl, et al., 1988; Solomon et al.,1988). This may be particularly interesting, given our data showing disrupted conditioning in rabbits and humans following scopolamine administration.

5. Using monoclonal antibodies directed against neuronal cytoskeletal components and the avidin–biotin immunocytochemical technique, we have shown that phosphorylated and nonphosphorylated neurofilament epitopes are present in $AlCl_3$-induced neurofilamentous accumulations (Munoz-Garcia, Pendlebury, Kessler, & Perl, 1986; Pendlebury, Beal, et al., 1988a, 1988b).

6. Quantitative neurochemical analysis of $AlCl_3$-exposed rabbits has revealed similarities to neurochemical deficts seen in AD (Table 23.1). The most striking parallel is the significant reduction in choline acetyltransferase activity in the entorhinal cortex and hippocampus in aluminum-exposed rabbits (Beal et al., 1989).

TABLE 23.1. Types of Neurochemical Depletion Seen in Aluminum Exposure and in Alzheimer's Disease (AD) and Senile Dementia of Alzheimer Type (SDAT)

Aluminum		AD/SDAT
↓	Acetylcholine	↓
↓	Serotonin	↓
↓	Norepinephrine	↓
—	GABA	↓
↓	Aspartate	↓ or —
↓	Glutamate	↓
↓	Taurine	—
—	Somatostatin	↓
—	Neuropeptide Y	↓ or —
↓	Substance P	↓ or —
—	Cholecystokinin	—
—	VIP	—

Note. GABA, γ-aminobutyric acid; VIP, vasoactive intestinal polypeptide. From "Neurochemical Characteristics of Aluminum-Induced Neurofibrillary Degeneration in Rabbits" (p. 341) by M. F. Beal, M. F. Mazurek, D. W. Ellison, N. W. Kowall, P. R. Solomon, and W. W. Pendlebury, 1989, *Neuroscience, 29,* 339–346. Copyright 1989 by Pergamon Press. Reprinted by permission.

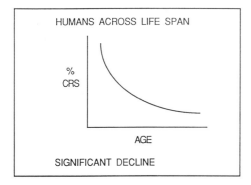

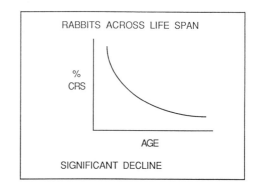

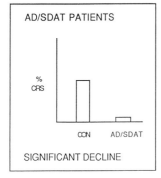

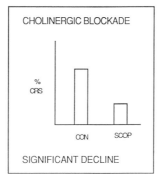

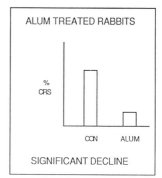

FIGURE 23.8. Summary of five lines of research.

Using Model Systems to Answer Questions about Age-Related Memory Disorders

We would argue that a model systems approach may be useful in addressing some of the questions regarding ARMDs raised at the beginning of this chapter. Figure 23.8 summarizes our findings using this approach.

As we have indicated at the beginning of the chapter, it will be difficult to specify the systems and mechanisms involved in plasticity that change with aging until these systems and mechanisms are elucidated for normal memory. The fortuitous findings that even simple and neurobiologically analyzable forms of memory are disrupted in aging may create opportunities for understanding these aspects of ARMDs. It seems to be particularly advantageous that we can investigate the same form of simple learning and memory in both humans and rabbits. Because this form of memory follows similar rules in both species, it is tempting to speculate that it is governed by similar neurobiological processes. As we are able to better delineate the neural mechanisms of learning in young rabbits, this should provide testable hypotheses regarding the neurobiological bases of ARMDs in both aged rabbits and humans.

Studying mechanisms of "successful aging" requires a model system in which a subset of the aged population being studied learns almost as well as the young subjects. The finding that a subset of both aged humans and aged rabbits condition within the range of young subjects raises the possibility of investigating the mechanisms of successful aging within this subgroup. LTP may be one such candidate mechanism. We are particularly encouraged by pilot data showing that the conditionability in aged rabbits is related to the degree of synaptic facilitation in the perforant path–dentate synapse.

The rapid progress in elucidating the neurobiological substrate of memory in young animals will lead to testable hypotheses regarding memory deficits in aged rabbits and, by extrapolation, in aged humans.

The work showing similar effects of drugs such as scopolamine in human and rabbit EB conditioning, and the work showing enhancement of conditioning with nimodipine, suggest that human EB conditioning may be a useful paradigm for evaluating pharmacological agents. The work of Disterhoft and his colleagues showing that nimodipine facilitates conditioning in aged rabbits was a direct outgrowth of their earlier work showing that rabbit EB conditioning was related to reduction of calcium-activated potassium channels (Disterhoft, Coulter, & Alkon, 1986). As additional information becomes available regarding synaptic mechanisms of plasticity in the EB preparation, additional pharmacological agents can be evaluated.

Finally, the possibility of correlating neuropathological and neurochemical changes with age-related changes in conditioning at various points in the lifespan should provide useful information regarding the development of the neurobiological basis of ARMDs.

ACKNOWLEDGMENTS

This work was supported by National Science Foundation Grant No. BNS 8616814, Environmental Protection Agency Grant No. CR 816043-01-0, a Faculty Research Grant from Williams College to Paul R. Solomon, and National Institute on Aging Grant No. AG-00258-03 to William W. Pendlebury. This chapter has been reviewed by the Health Effects Research Laboratory, U.S. Environmental Protection Agency, and approved for publication. Mention of trade names or commercial products does not constitute endorsement or recommendation for future use.

REFERENCES

Abrams, T. W., & Kandel, E. R. (1988). Is contiguity in classical conditioning a system or a cellular property? Learning in *Aplysia* suggests a possible molecular site. *Trends in Neurosciences, 11*(4), 128–135.

Alkon, D. L. (1986). Learning in a marine snail. *Scientific American, 249,* 70–89.

Ball, M. J. (1977). Neuronal loss, neurofibrillary tangles and granulovascular degeneration in the hippocampus with aging and dementia. *Acta Neuropathologica, 37,* 111–118.

Barnes, C. A. (1979). Memory deficits associated with senescence: A neuropsychological and behavioral study in the rat. *Journal of Comparative and Physiological Psychology, 93,* 74–104.

Bartus, R. T., Dean, R. L., Beer, B., & Lippa, A. S. (1982). The cholinergic hypothesis of geriatric memory dysfunction. *Science, 217,* 408–416.

Beal, M. F., Mazurek, M. F., Ellison, D. W., Kowall, N. W., Solomon, P. R., & Pendlebury, W. W. (1989). Neurochemical characteristics of aluminum-induced neurofibrillary degeneration in rabbits. *Neuroscience, 29,* 339–346.

Berger, T. W. (1984). Long term potentiation of hippocampal synaptic transmission affects rate of behavioral learning. *Science, 224,* 627–630.

Berry, S. D., & Thompson, R. F. (1978). Prediction of learning rate from the hippocampal electroencephalogram. *Science, 200,* 1298–1300.

Bliss, T. V. P., & Lomo, T. (1973). Long-lasting potentiation of synaptic transmission in the dentate area of the anesthetized rabbit following stimulation in the perforant path. *Journal of Physiology* (London), *232*, 331–356.

Braun, W. H., & Geiselhart, R. (1959). Age differences in the acquisition and extinction of the conditioned eyelid response. *Journal of Experimental Psychology, 57*, 386–388.

Brown, T. H., Chapman, P. F., Kairiss, E. W., & Keenan, C. L. (1988). Long-term synaptic potentiation. *Science, 242*, 724–728.

Collerton, D. (1986). Cholinergic function and intellectual decline in Alzheimer's disease. *Neuroscience, 19*, 1–28.

Coyle, J. T., Price, D. L., & DeLong, M. R. (1982). Alzheimer's disease: A disorder of cortical cholinergic innervation. *Science, 219*, 1184–1190.

DeToledo-Morrell, L., Geinsman, Y., & Morrell, F. (1988). Age dependent alterations in hippocampal synaptic plasticity: Relation to memory disorders. *Neurobiology of Aging, 9*(5–6), 581–590.

Deyo, R. A., Straube, K. T., & Disterhoft, J. F. (1989). Nimodipine facilitates associative learning in aging rabbits. *Science, 243*, 809–811.

Disterhoft, J. F., Coulter, D. A., & Alkon, D. A. (1986). Conditioning specific membrane changes of rabbit hippocampal neurons measured *in vitro. Proceedings of the National Academy of Sciences USA, 83*, 2733–2737.

Downs, D., Cardoza, C., Schneiderman, N., Yehle, A. L., Van Decar, D. H., & Zwilling, G. (1972). Central effects of atropine upon aversive classical conditioning in rabbits. *Psychopharmacology, 23*, 319–333.

Gormezano, I., Prokasy, W. F., & Thompson, R. F. (Eds.). (1987). *Classical conditioning III: Behavioral, physiological, and neurochemical studies in the rabbit.* Hillsdale, NJ: Erlbaum.

Graves, C. A., & Solomon, P. R. (1985). Age-related disruption of trace but not delay classical conditioning of the rabbit's nictitating membrane response. *Behavioral Neuroscience, 99*, 88–96.

Harvey, J. A., Gormezano, I., & Cool-Hauser, V. A. (1983). Effects of scopolamine and methylscopolamine on classical conditioning of the rabbit's nictitating membrane response. *Journal of Pharmacology and Experimental Therapeutics, 225*, 42–49.

Hawkins, R. D., & Kandel, E. R. (1984). Is there a cell biological alphabet for simple forms of learning? *Psychological Review, 91*, 375–391.

Hilgard, E. R., & Marquis, D. G. (1940). *Conditioning and learning.* New York: Appleton-Century-Crofts.

Hyman, B. T., Van Hoesen, G. W., Damasio, A. R., & Barnes, C. L. (1984). Alzheimer's disease: Cell-specific pathology isolates the hippocampal formation. *Science, 225*, 1168–1170.

Jerome, E. A. (1959). Age and learning: Experimental studies. In J. E. Birren (Ed.), *Handbook of aging and the individual.* Chicago: University of Chicago Press.

Kimble, B. A., & Pennypacker, H. S. (1963). Eyelid conditioning in young and aged subjects. *Journal of Genetic Psychology, 103*, 283–289.

Klatzko, I., Wisniewski, H., & Streicher, E. (1965). Experimental production of neurofibrillary degeneration: 1. Light microscopic observations. *Journal of Neuropathology and Experimental Neurology, 24*, 187–199.

Landfield, P. W., & Deadwyler, S. A. (Eds.). (1988). *Long-term potentiation: From biophysics to behavior.* New York: Alan R. Liss.

Marcus, E., & Carew, T. (1990). Ontogenetic analysis of learning in a simple system. *Annals of the New York Academy of Sciences, 608*, 212–238.

Moore, J. W., Goodell, N. A., & Solomon, P. R. (1976). Central cholinergic blockade by scopolamine and habituation, classical conditioning, and latent inhibition of the rabbit's nictitating membrane response. *Physiological Psychology, 4*(3), 395–399.

Moyer, J. R., Deyo, R. A., & Disterhoft, J. F. (1988). Effects of hippocampal lesions on acquisition and extinction of trace eye-blink in rabbit. *Society for Neuroscience Abstracts, 14*(1), 233.

Munoz-Garcia, D., Pendlebury, W. W., Kessler, J. B., & Perl, D. P. (1986). An immunocytochemical comparison of cytoskeletal proteins in aluminum-induced and Alzheimer-type neurofibrillary tangles. *Acta Neuropathologica, 70*, 243–248.

Pendlebury, W. W., Beal, M. F., Kowall, N. W., & Solomon, P. R. (1988a). Immunocytochemical, neurochemical, and behavioral studies in aluminum-induced neurofilamentous degeneration. *Journal of Neural Transmission, 24*, 213–217.

Pendlebury, W. W., Beal, M. F., Kowall, N. W., & Solomon, P. R. (1988b). Results of immunocytochemical, neurochemical, and behavioral studies in aluminum-induced neurofilamentous degeneration. In R. J. Wurtman, S. H. Corkin, & J. H. Growdon (Eds.), *Alzheimer's disease: Advances in basic research and therapies.* Boston: Center for Brain Sciences and Metabolism Charitable Trust.

Pendlebury, W. W., Perl, D. P., Schwentker, A., Pingree, T., & Solomon, P. R. (1988). Aluminum-induced neurofibrillary degeneration disrupts acquisition of the rabbit's classically conditioned nictitating membrane response. *Behavioral Neuroscience, 102*(5), 615–620.

Powell, D. A., Buchanan, S. L., & Hernandez L. L. (1981). Age-related changes in classical (Pavlovian) conditioning in the New Zealand albino rabbit. *Experimental Aging Research, 7,* 453–465.

Powell, D. A., Buchanan, S. L., & Hernandez, L. L. (1984). Age-related changes in Pavlovian conditioning: Central nervous system correlates. *Physiology and Behavior, 32,* 609–616.

Rowe, J. W., & Kahn, R. L. (1987). Human aging: Unusual and successful. *Science, 237,* 143–149.

Sitaram, N., Weingartner, H., Caine, E., & Gillin, C. (1978). Choline: Selective enhancement of serial learning and encoding of low imagery words in man. *Life Sciences, 22,* 1555–1560.

Solomon, P. R., Beal, M. F., & Pendlebury, W. W. (1988). Age-related disruption of classical conditioning: A model systems approach to age-related memory disorders. *Neurobiology of Aging, 9,* 935–946.

Solomon, P. R., & Gottfried, K. E. (1981). Disruption of acquisition of the classically conditioned rabbit nictitating membrane response following injection of scopolamine into the medial septal nucleus. *Journal of Comparative and Physiological Psychology, 95*(2), 322–330.

Solomon, P. R., Groccia-Ellison, M. E., Edwards, K. R., & Stanton, M. E. (1991). Central cholinergic blockade by scopolamine disrupts classical conditioning of the human eyeblink response. *Society for Neuroscience Abstracts, 17,* 642.

Solomon, P. R., Koota, D., Kessler, J. B., & Pendlebury, W. W. (1987). Disrupted retention of the classically conditioned eyeblink response in the aluminum intoxicated rabbit using brain stimulation as a conditioned stimulus. *Society for Neuroscience Abstracts, 13*(1), 642.

Solomon, P. R., Levine, E., Bein, T., & Pendlebury, W. W. (1989). Disrupted eyelid conditioning in patients with Alzheimer's disease. *Society for Neuroscience Abstracts, 15,* 888.

Solomon, P. R., Levine, E., Bein, T., & Pendlebury, W. W. (1991). Disruption of classical conditioning in patients with Alzheimer's disease. *Neurobiology of Aging, 12,* 283–287.

Solomon, P. R., & Pendlebury, W. W. (1988). A model systems approach to age-related memory disorders. *Neurotoxicology, 9,* 443–462.

Solomon, P. R., Pingree, T., Baldwin, D., Koota, D., Perl, D. P., & Pendlebury, W. W. (1988). Disrupted retention of the classically conditioned nictitating membrane response in rabbits with aluminum-induced neurofibrillary degeneration. *Neurotoxicology, 9,* 209–222.

Solomon, P. R., Pomerleau, D., Bennett, L., James, J., & Morse, D. L. (1989). Acquisition of the classically conditioned eyeblink response in humans over the lifespan. *Psychology and Aging, 4,* 34–41.

Solomon, P. R., Solomon, S. D., Vander Schaaf, E. R., & Perry, H. E. (1983). Altered activity in the hippocampus is more detrimental to conditioning than removal of the structure. *Science, 220,* 329–331.

Solomon, P. R., Stowe, G. T., & Pendlebury, W. W. (1989). Disrupted eyelid conditioning in a patient with damage to the cerebellar inputs. *Behavioral Neuroscience, 103,* 898–902.

Solomon, P. R., Vander Schaaf, E. R., Thompson, R. F., & Weisz, D. J. (1986). Hippocampus and trace conditioning of the rabbit's classically conditioned nictitating membrane response. *Behavioral Neuroscience, 100*(5), 729–744.

Solyom, L., & Barik, H. C. (1965). Conditioning in senescence and senility. *Journal of Gerontology, 20,* 483–488.

Terry, R. D., & Penna, C. (1965). Experimental production of neurofibrillary degeneration: 2. Electron microscopy, phosphatase histochemistry, and electron probe analysis. *Journal of Neuropathology and Experimental Neurology, 24,* 200–210.

Teyler, T. J., & Discenna, P. (1987). Long-term potentiation. *Annual Review of Neuroscience, 10,* 131–161.

Thompson, R. F. (1988). A model system approach to age and the neuronal bases of learning and memory. In M. W. Riley, J. D. Matarazzo, & A. Baum (Eds.), *Perspectives on behavioral medicine.* New York: Academic Press.

Weisz, D. J., Clark, G. A., & Thompson, R. F. (1984). Increased responsivity of dentate granule cells during nictitating membrane response conditioning in rabbit. *Behavioural Brain Research, 12,* 145–154.

Woodruff-Pak, D. S., Lavond, D. G., Logan, C. G., & Thompson, R. F. (1987). Classical conditioning in 3-, 30-, and 45-month-old rabbits: Behavioral learning and hippocampal unit activity. *Neurobiology of Aging, 8,* 101–108.

Woodruff-Pak, D. S., & Thompson, R. F. (1985). Classical conditioning of the eyelid response in rabbits as a model system for the study of brain mechanisms of learning and memory. *Experimental Aging Research, 11*(2), 109–122.

Woodruff-Pak, D. S., & Thompson, R. F. (1988). Classical conditioning of the eyeblink response in the delay paradigm in adults aged 18–83 years. *Psychology and Aging, 3,* 219–229.

Yang, B. Y., & Solomon, P. R. (1992). Manuscript in preparation.

24

Cholinomimetic Therapy in Alzheimer's Disease

LEON J. THAL

Introduction

In the United States, diseases of the aged are a major public health concern because of increased life expectancy. In 1990, 12.5% of the U.S. population was over the age of 65; by 2004, this is expected to increase to 22%. Approximately 15% of individuals over the age of 65 suffer from some form of acquired cognitive loss. Recent community surveys indicate that approximately 10%, or two-thirds of those with acquired cognitive loss, are afflicted with Alzheimer's disease (AD) (Evans et al., 1989), making AD the most prevalent form of acquired cognitive dysfunction. In addition, all prevalence studies indicate a marked increase in AD with aging, with the proportion of individuals afflicted with this disease doubling for each 5-year epoch after age 65.

Clinically, AD is characterized by insidious and progressive cognitive decline. While AD subjects invariably suffer from memory impairment, they are also frequently impaired in calculations, visuospatial relations, language, and abstract thinking. Personality changes and behavioral disturbances, including agitation, anxiety, depression, hallucinations, and sleep disorders, may also accompany the syndrome (American Psychiatric Association, 1980).

Pathology and Pathogenesis of Alzheimer's Disease

The etiology of AD remains unknown. Gross morphological changes include generalized cerebral atrophy and a decrease in brain weight. Microscopic changes include the loss of large neurons, as well as the presence of neurofibrillary tangles, plaques, and amyloid deposition (see Selkoe, 1990, and Terry & Katzman, 1983, for reviews). The number of senile plaques in the cortex is roughly correlated with the degree of dementia on bedside cognitive screening instruments (Blessed, Tomlinson, & Roth, 1968). More recently, a loss of cortical synapses has been described; this loss correlates very highly with cognitive decline as measured by standard screening instruments, such as the Blessed Information–Memory–Concentration Test, the Mini-Mental State

Examination, and the Dementia Rating Scale (Terry et al., 1991). Some investigators have postulated a direct causative role for amyloid, believing it to be a neurotoxic agent. However, this postulate remains unproven. In addition to morphometric changes, there are marked changes in neurotransmitter systems in AD. The most profound include a marked decrease in cortical choline acetyltransferase (ChAT), the synthetic enzyme for acetylcholine (ACh), a finding now replicated by more than 30 laboratory groups. The loss of ChAT has been correlated with both the number of senile plaques and the severity of the dementia (Perry et al., 1978).

The Initial Hypothesis: Cholinergic Involvement in Memory

Early observations with scopolamine, a cholinergic antagonist, revealed that this agent could lead to memory impairment in humans. Scopolamine was initially combined with analgesics in obstetrical anesthesia to produce a state of "twilight sleep." Women given scopolamine during labor and delivery were often amnesic for the details of the delivery. In young volunteers, scopolamine produced impaired acquisition of new information. Subjects tested had normal Verbal IQs but reduced Performance IQs (Drachman & Leavitt, 1974). This pattern is similar to that seen in the normal elderly. However, a recent study demonstrated that the pattern of neuropsychological deficits produced by scopolamine does not mirror the pattern observed in AD (Beatty, Butters, & Janowsky, 1986). The deficits in memory and learning in AD included many false-positive errors and intrusions, a pattern not observed in the young after scopolamine administration.

Animal studies using anticholinergic agents support the involvement of cholinergic neurotransmission in learning and memory. On a visual discrimination task, rats receiving injections of scopolamine into the hippocampus bilaterally were impaired when tested after intervals of 1 to 3 days between training and scopolamine administration; no effect was noted for intervals of 7 to 14 days (Deutsch, 1971). These results suggest that memory consolidation requires more than 1 but fewer than 7 days and is dependent upon cholinergic activity. Similar results have been noted with intraperitoneal scopolamine in rats (Hamburg, 1967) and aged monkeys (Bartus & Johnson, 1976). Although these experiments emphasize the particular importance of cholinergic systems in acquisition of memory, disruption of other neurotransmitter systems may also clearly impair memory.

In AD, neurons of the nucleus basalis, the major cholinergic input to the cortex, undergo degeneration (Whitehouse, Price, Clark, Coyle, & DeLong, 1981). In animals, lesions of the nucleus basalis and/or septum clearly impair learning and memory (see Dekker, Connor, & Thal, 1991, for a review) and result in reduced levels of cortical ChAT. Furthermore, these deficits can be ameliorated by the administration of cholinomimetic agents such as physostigmine (Mandel & Thal, 1988) or tetrahydroaminoacridine (THA) (Kwo-On-Yuen, Mandel, Chen, & Thal, 1990).

On the basis of these clinical and experimental observations, many investigators hypothesized that memory impairment in AD may be at least in part caused by alterations of cholinergic neurotransmission.

The Plot Thickens: Multiple Neurotransmitter Abnormalities

In addition to changes in the cholinergic system first noted in the mid-1970s, subsequent workers noted changes in other conventional transmitter systems, including loss of neurons containing noradrenaline and serotonin. Neuropeptide changes have also been reported, including decreases in somatostatin, substance P, neuropeptide Y, and corticotrophin-releasing factor (see Katzman, 1986, for a review). It is clear, then, that multiple neurotransmitter deficits occur in AD. At best, one might therefore expect improvement in the memory component of AD with cholinomimetics, but not improvement in other features (e.g., language, behavior, and visuospatial relations). Moreover, cholinergic hypofunctioning secondary to cell loss in the nucleus basalis occurs in other diseases, including Parkinson's disease, progressive supranuclear palsy, and spinocerebellar degeneration (see Chozick, 1987, for a review), suggesting that loss in this cholinergic projection system is not specific for AD.

The Empirical Evidence: Trials of Cholinomimetic Agents in Alzheimer's Disease

Despite the evidence of widespread cell loss and multiple neurotransmitter changes, recent therapeutic trials in AD have concentrated on cholinergic replacement therapy. Four strategies have been pursued, in part derived from the successful strategy used to treat Parkinson's disease. The first used ACh precursors in an attempt to increase the rate of synthesis of ACh. The second used inhibitors of cholinesterase to reduce the rate of degradation of ACh in the synaptic cleft. The third used agents to enhance the release of ACh. Finally, cholinergic agonists that act directly on postsynaptic muscarinic receptors have been tried.

Precursors

Choline-deficient rats fed a diet rich in either choline or lecithin were shown to have increased levels of ACh in their brains, compared to the levels measured while the rats were on the choline-deficient diet (Cohen & Wurtman, 1976). However, subsequent studies have shown that increasing dietary choline in animals on a normal diet did not lead to an increase in the concentration of brain ACh (Brunello, Cheney, & Costa, 1982; Wecker & Schmidt, 1979). As one might predict from these animal experiments, results of trials using choline and lecithin in AD patients have been disappointing. After choline administration, patients improved minimally on a word recognition task in one double-blind study (Fovall et al., 1980), but other double-blind trials reported no improvement on tests of verbal learning, verbal fluency, visuospatial functions, or motor speed (Christie et al., 1979; Renvoize & Jerram, 1979; Smith et al., 1978; Thal, Rosen, Sharpless, & Crystal, 1981). Trials of lecithin have been equally disappointing (Brinkman et al., 1982; Dysken, Fovall, Harris, Davis, & Noronha, 1982; Little, Levy, Chuaqui-Kidd, & Hand, 1985; Weintraub et al., 1983). The most likely reason for failure to improve cognition in AD with precursors is that the supply of choline is not the rate-limiting step for the synthesis of ACh in the human brain.

Cholinesterase Inhibitors

Cholinesterase inhibitors prolong the action of ACh at the postsynaptic cholinergic receptor by preventing its breakdown.

PHYSOSTIGMINE

Physostigmine is a tertiary amine that readily crosses the blood–brain barrier. Early studies used intravenous physostigmine to overcome the problem of poor gastrointestinal absorption. Five of six double-blind studies of parenteral physostigmine demonstrated some degree of improvement on tests of verbal and nonverbal memory (Christie, Shering, Ferguson, & Glen, 1981; Davis & Mohs, 1982; Peters & Levin, 1979; Schwartz & Kohlstaedt, 1986). Most negative studies included patients with severe dementia or used a low fixed dose without dose titration. Some studies also demonstrated an inverted U-shaped dose–response curve for physostigmine. Dose–response relationships of this type are fairly common and have been observed with many drugs that affect memory.

More recent studies of physostigmine have utilized an oral preparation. Six out of 11 double-blind trials in AD demonstrated cognitive improvement on verbal memory, either on the Buschke Selective Reminding Task (Beller, Overall, & Swann, 1985; Harrell et al., 1986; Stern, Sano, & Mayeux, 1988; Thal, Masur, Sharpless, Fuld, & Davies, 1986; Thal, Masur, Blau, Fuld, & Klauber, 1989) or on total scores for a composite assessment instrument, the Alzheimer Disease Assessment Scale (ADAS) (Mohs et al., 1985). Five double-blind trials failed to demonstrate improvement, including one study in which patients were severely demented (Wettstein, 1983). In a second brief 3-day crossover study, patients failed to respond (Stern, Sano, & Mayeux, 1987), but many of these same patients responded to longer treatment (Stern et al., 1988). Two additional well-controlled trials were negative (Mitchell, Drachman, O'Donnell, & Glasser, 1986; Schmechel et al., 1984). The true response rate to oral physostigmine has not yet been demonstrated.

It should be noted that there are many difficulties with the trials of oral physostigmine. Only two groups of investigators measured the entry of physostigmine into the brain by assaying cerebrospinal fluid (CSF) cholinesterase inhibition (Thal et al., 1986) or neuroendocrine function (Mohs et al., 1985). A strong correlation between retrieval of memory on the Selective Reminding Task and degree of cholinesterase inhibition in CSF has been reported ($r = .61$) (Thal et al., 1986), suggesting that negative results in some reports may have been due to failure to achieve an adequate degree of cholinesterase inhibition in the brain. Orally administered physostigmine has a very short half-life. Controlled-release preparations that produce sustained blood levels for up to 7 hours after ingesting a single dose (Thal, Lasker, et al., 1989) have been developed. A multicenter trial examining the efficacy of controlled-release physostigmine in AD is currently underway.

TETRAHYDROAMINOACRIDINE

A second cholinesterase inhibitor, THA, is also undergoing clinical testing. Two early double-blind studies in small groups of patients reported slight improvement in verbal memory (Kaye et al., 1982) and marked improvement in global functioning (Summers, Majorski, Marsh, Tachiki, & Kling, 1986). This latter study, however, has been heavily criticized for faulty methodology, and the magnitude of the results is in doubt. In contrast to these positive findings, negative results have recently been reported from three additional studies (Chatellier & Lacomblez, 1990; Fitten et al., 1990; Gauthier et al., 1990). The largest study of THA, a multicenter U.S. trial, has recently been completed, but results from this trial have not yet been reported. A preliminary presentation of the data to the Food and Drug Administration in early 1991 indicated that THA treatment resulted in less decline on the ADAS than did placebo treatment. However, the treatment effect was small, and a significant proportion of the patients developed side effects during treatment.

Drugs Increasing Acetylcholine Release

A single study of 4-aminopyridine, a compound known to enhance the release of ACh, failed to improve cognition in AD patients on the ADAS (Davidson et al., 1988).

Cholinergic Agonists

A number of drugs that act directly on postsynaptic muscarinic receptors exist. Their use in AD has often been hampered by the development of significant peripheral side effects. Slight improvement was reported on a picture recognition task after arecoline (Christie et al., 1981), but a more recent trial found no improvement in 12 AD patients (Tariot et al., 1988). Trials with other cholinergic agents, including oxotremorine, RS 86, and pilocarpine, have also been negative (Bruno, Mohr, Gillespie, Fedio, & Chase, 1986; Caine, 1980; Davis et al., 1987; Hollander et al., 1987; Mouradian, Mohr, Williams, & Chase, 1988; Wettstein & Spiegel, 1984). Moreover, a promising single-blind trial of intraventricular bethanechol in AD (Harbaugh, Roberts, Coombs, Saunders, & Reeder, 1984) was followed by a larger double-blind study in which cognition failed to improve (Penn, Martin, Wilson, Fox, & Savoy, 1988).

Why Has Cholinergic Therapy in Alzheimer's Disease Failed?

There are numerous difficulties and pitfalls in carrying out clinical trials in patients with AD. Reliable diagnostic criteria have not always been utilized. However, this criticism does not apply to most contemporary studies, which have utilized patients who meet the diagnosis of "probable AD" according to standardized National Institute of Neurological, Communicative Disorders, and Stroke/Alzheimer's Disease and Related Disorders Association (NINCDS/ADRDA) guidelines. When criteria equivalent to these guidelines are used, approximately 85% of individuals entered into clinical trials will have AD pathology at autopsy (Wade et al., 1987).

Many of the cholinomimetic drugs chosen for testing have not received appropriate pharmacokinetic attention. Many agents tested are poorly absorbed, do not cross the blood–brain barrier, have severe peripheral side effects, and have short half-lives. In order to determine whether cholinergic augmentation can enhance memory, it will be necessary to achieve an adequate understanding of central cholinergic functioning in the brain.

Perhaps most important to explaining the failure of cholinomimetic therapy is the widespread, diffuse pathology in AD. Numerous neurotransmitter systems are affected, and it is unlikely that correction of a single neurotransmitter abnormality could markedly enhance function. Given the marked and widespread pathology in AD, it seems likely that, at best, small improvements in learning and memory can occur with cholinergic augmentation. Whether these will translate into meaningful functional improvement in patients with widespread neuropathology remains to be empirically demonstrated.

REFERENCES

American Psychiatric Association. (1980). *Diagnostic and statistical manual of mental disorders* (3rd ed.). Washington, DC: Author.

Bartus, R. T., & Johnson, H. R. (1976). Short-term memory in the rhesus monkey: Disruption from the anticholinergic scopolamine. *Pharmacology, Biochemistry and Behavior, 5,* 39–46.

Beatty, W. W., Butters, N., & Janowsky, D. S. (1986). Patterns of memory failure after scopolamine treatment: Implications for cholinergic hypothesis of dementia. *Behavioral and Neural Biology, 45,* 196–211.

Beller, S. A., Overall, J. E., & Swann, A. C. (1985). Efficacy of oral physostigmine in primary degenerative dementia. *Psychopharmacology, 87,* 147–151.

Blessed, G., Tomlinson, E. E., & Roth, M. (1968). The association between quantitative measures of dementia and of senile change in the cerebral grey matter of elderly subjects. *British Journal of Psychiatry, 114,* 797–811.

Brinkman, S. D., Smith, R. C., Meyer, J. S., Vroulis, G., Shaw, T., Gordon, J. R., & Allen, R. H. (1982). Lecithin and memory training in suspected Alzheimer's disease. *Journal of Gerontology, 37,* 4–9.

Brunello, N., Cheney, D. L., & Costa, E. (1982). Increase in exogenous choline fails to elevate the content or turnover of cortical, striatal or hippocampal acetylcholine. *Journal of Neurochemistry, 38,* 1160–1163.

Bruno, G., Mohr, E., Gillespie, M., Fedio, P., & Chase, T. N. (1986). Muscarinic agonist therapy of Alzheimer's disease. *Archives of Neurology, 43,* 659–661.

Caine, E. (1980). Cholinomimetic treatment fails to improve memory disorders. *New England Journal of Medicine, 303,* 585–586.

Chatellier, G., & Lacomblez, L. (1990). Tacrine (tetrahydroaminoacridine; THA) and lecithin in senile dementia of the Alzheimer type: A multicenter trial. *British Journal of Medicine, 300,* 495–499.

Chozick, B. (1987). The nucleus basalis of Meynert in neurological dementing disease: A review. *International Journal of Neuroscience, 37,* 31–48.

Christie, J. E., Shering, A., Ferguson, J., & Glen, A. I. M. (1981). Physostigmine and arecoline: Effects of intravenous infusions in Alzheimer presenile dementia. *British Journal of Psychiatry, 138,* 46–50.

Christie, J. E., Blackburn, I. M., Glen, A. I. M., Zeiglel, S., Shering, A., & Yates, C. M. (1979). Effects of choline and lecithin on CSF choline levels and on cognitive function in patients with presenile dementia of the Alzheimer type. In A. Barbeau, J. H. Growdon, & R. J. Wurtman (Eds.), *Nutrition and the brain* (Vol. 5, pp. 377–387). New York: Raven Press.

Cohen, E. L., & Wurtman, R. J. (1976). Brain acetylcholine: Control by dietary choline. *Science, 191,* 561–562.

Davidson, M., Zemishlany, Z., Mohs, R. C., Horvath, T. B., Powchik, P., Blass, J. P., & Davis, K. L. (1988). 4-Aminopyridine in the treatment of Alzheimer's disease. *Biological Psychiatry, 23,* 485–490.

Davis, K. L., Hollander, E., Davidson, M., Davis, B. M., Mohs, R. C., & Horvath, T. B. (1987). Induction of depression with oxotremorine in patients with Alzheimer's disease. *American Journal of Psychiatry*, *144*, 468–471.

Davis, K. L., & Mohs, R. (1982). Enhancement of memory processes in Alzheimer's disease with multiple-dose intravenous physostigmine. *American Journal of Psychiatry, 139*, 1421–1424.

Dekker, A. J. A. M., Connor, D. M., & Thal, L. J. (1991). The role of cholinergic projections from the nucleus basalis in memory. *Neuroscience and Behavioral Review, 15*, 299–317.

Deutsch, D. A. (1971). The cholinergic synapse and the site of memory. *Science, 174*, 788–790.

Drachman, D. A., & Leavitt, J. (1974). Human memory and the cholinergic system: Relationship to aging? *Archives of Neurology, 30*, 113–121.

Dysken, M. W., Fovall, P., Harris, C. M., Davis, J. M., & Noronha, A. (1982). Lecithin administration in Alzheimer dementia. *Neurology, 32*, 1203–1204.

Evans, D. A., Funkenstein, H. H., Albert, M. S., Scherr, P. A., Cook, N. R., Chown, M. J., Hebert, L. E., Hennekensch, C. H., & Taylor, J. O. (1989). Prevalence of Alzheimer's disease in a community population of older persons. *Journal of the American Medical Association, 262*, 2551–2556.

Fitten, L. J., Perryman, K. M., Gross, P., Fine, H., Cummins, J., & Marshall, E. (1990). Treatment of Alzheimer's disease with short- and long-term oral THA and lecithin: A double-blind study. *American Journal of Psychiatry, 147*, 239–242.

Fovall, P., Dysken, M. W., Lazarus, L. W., Davis, J. M., Kahn, R. J., Jope, R., Rinkel, S., & Rattan, P. (1980). Choline bitartrate treatment of Alzheimer-type dementias. *Communications in Psychopharmacology, 4*, 141–145.

Gauthier, S., Bouchard, R., Lamontagne, A., Baily, P., Bergman, H., Ratner, J., Tesfaye, Y., Saint-Martin, M., Bacher, Y., Carrier, L., Charbonneau, R., Clarfield, A. M., Collier, B., Dastoor, D., Gauthier, L., Germain, M., Kissel, C., Krieger, M., Kushnir, S., Masson, H., Morin, J., Nair, V., Neirinck, L., & Suissa, S. (1990). Tetrahydroaminoacridine–lecithin combination treatment in patients with intermediate-stage Alzheimer's disease. *New England Journal of Medicine, 322*, 1272–1276.

Hamburg, M. D. (1967). Retrograde amnesia produced by intraperitoneal injection of physostigmine. *Science, 156*, 973–974.

Harbaugh, R. E., Roberts, D. W., Coombs, D. W., Saunders, R. L., & Reeder, T. M. (1984). Preliminary report: Intracranial cholinergic drug infusion in patients with Alzheimer's disease. *Neurosurgery, 15*, 514–518.

Harrell, L., Falgout, J., Leli, D., Jope, R., McClain, C., Spiers, M., Callaway, R., & Halsey, J. (1986). Behavioral effects of oral physostigmine in Alzheimer's disease patients. *Neurology, 36*(Suppl. 1), 269.

Hollander, E., Davidson, M., Mohs, R. C., Horvath, T. B., Davis, B. M., Zemishlany, Z., & Davis, K. L. (1987). RS 86 in the treatment of Alzheimer's disease: Cognitive and biological effects. *Biological Psychiatry, 22*, 1067–1078.

Katzman, R. D. (1986). Alzheimer's disease. *New England Journal of Medicine, 314*, 964–973.

Kaye, W. H., Sitaram, N., Weingartner, H., Ebert, M. H., Smallberg, G., & Gillin, J. C. (1982). Modest facilitation of memory in dementia with combined lecithin and anticholinesterase treatment. *Biological Psychiatry, 17*, 275–280.

Kwo-On-Yuen, P. F., Mandel, R., Chen, A. D., & Thal, L. J. (1990). Tetrahydroaminoacridine improves the spatial acquisition deficit produced by nucleus basalis lesions in rats. *Experimental Neurology, 108*, 221–228.

Little, A., Levy, R., Chuaqui-Kidd, P., & Hand, D. (1985). A double-blind, placebo controlled trial of high-dose lecithin in Alzheimer's disease. *Journal of Neurology, Neurosurgery and Psychiatry, 48*, 736–742.

Mandel, R. J., & Thal, L. J. (1988). Physostigmine improves water maze performance following nucleus basalis magnocellularis lesions in rats. *Psychopharmacology, 96*, 421–425.

Mitchell, A., Drachman, D., O'Donnell, B., & Glasser, G. (1986). Oral physostigmine in Alzheimer's disease. *Neurology, 36*, 295.

Mohs, R. C., Davis, B. M., Johns, C. A., Mathe, A. A., Greenwald, B. S., Horvath, T. B., & Davis, K. (1985). Oral physostigmine treatment of patients with Alzheimer's disease. *American Journal of Psychiatry, 142*, 28–33.

Mouradian, M. M., Mohr, E., Williams, J. A., & Chase, T. N. (1988). No response to high-dose muscarinic agonist therapy in Alzheimer's disease. *Neurology, 38*, 606–608.

Penn, R. D., Martin, E. M., Wilson, R. S., Fox, J. H., & Savoy, S. M. (1988). Intraventricular bethanechol infusion for Alzheimer's disease: Results of double-blind and escalating-dose trials. *Neurology, 38*, 219–222.

Perry, E. K., Tomlinson, B. E., Blessed, G., Perry, R. H., Cross, A. J., & Crow, T. J. (1978). Correlation of cholinergic abnormalities with senile plaques and mental test scores in senile dementia. *British Medical Journal, ii*, 1457–1459.

Peters, B., & Levin, H. S. (1979). Effects of physostigmine and lecithin on memory in Alzheimer's disease. *Annals of Neurology, 6,* 219-221.

Renvoize, E. B., & Jerram, T. (1979). Choline in Alzheimer's disease. *New England Journal of Medicine, 301,* 330.

Schmechel, D. E., Schmitt, F., Horner, J., Wilkinson, W. E., Hurwitz, B. J., & Heyman, A. (1984). Lack of effect of oral physostigmine and lecithin in patients with probable Alzheimer's disease. *Neurology, 34,* 280.

Schwartz, A. S., & Kohlstaedt, E. V. (1986). Physostigmine effects in Alzheimer's disease: Relationship to dementia severity. *Life Sciences, 38,* 1021-1028.

Selkoe, D. J. (1990). Deciphering Alzheimer's disease: The amyloid precursor protein yields new clues. *Science, 248,* 1058-1060.

Smith, C. M., Swase, M., Exton-Smith, A. N., Phillips, M. J., Overall, P. W., Piper, M. E., & Bailey, M. R. (1978). Choline therapy in Alzheimer's disease. *Lancet, ii,* 318.

Stern, Y., Sano, M., & Mayeux, R. (1987). Effects of oral physostigmine in Alzheimer's disease. *Annals of Neurology, 22,* 306-310.

Stern, Y., Sano, M., & Mayeux, R. (1988). Long-term administration of oral physostigmine in Alzheimer's disease. *Neurology, 38,* 1837-1841.

Summers, W. K., Majorski, L. V., Marsh, G. M., Tachiki, K., & Kling, A. (1986). Oral tetrahydroaminoacridine in long-term treatment of senile dementia, Alzheimer type. *New England Journal of Medicine, 315,* 1241-1245.

Tariot, P., Cohen, R., Welkowitz, J., Sunderland, T., Newhouse, P., Murphy, D., & Weingartner, H. (1988). Multiple-dose arecoline infusions in Alzheimer's Disease. *Archives of General Psychiatry, 45,* 901-905.

Terry, R. D., & Katzman, R. (1983). Senile dementia of the Alzheimer type. *Annals of Neurology, 14,* 497-506.

Terry, R. D., Masliah, E., Salmon, D. P., Butters, N., De Teresa, R., Hill, R., Hansen, L. A., & Katzman, R. (1991). Physical basis of cognitive alterations in Alzheimer disease: Synapse loss is the major correlate of cognitive impairment. *Annals of Neurology, 30,* 572-580.

Thal, L. J., Lasker, B., Sharpless, N. S., Bobotas, G., Schor, J. M., & Nigalye, A. (1989). Plasma physostigmine concentrations after controlled-release oral administration. *Archives of Neurology, 46,* 13.

Thal, L. J., Masur, D. M., Blau, A. D., Fuld, P. A., & Klauber, M. R. (1989). Chronic oral physostigmine without lecithin improves memory in Alzheimer's disease. *Journal of the American Geriatric Society, 37,* 42-48.

Thal, L. J., Masur, D. M., Sharpless, N. S., Fuld, P. A., & Davies, P. (1986). Acute and chronic effects of oral physostigmine and lecithin in Alzheimer's disease. *Progress in Neuropsychopharmacological and Biological Psychiatry, 10,* 627-636.

Thal, L. J., Rosen, W., Sharpless, S., & Crystal, H. (1981). Choline chloride fails to improve cognition in Alzheimer's disease. *Neurobiology of Aging, 2,* 205-208.

Wade, J. P., Mirsen, T. R., Hachinski, V. C., Fisman, M., Lau, C., & Mersky, H. (1987). The clinical diagnosis of Alzheimer's disease. *Archives of Neurology, 44,* 24-29.

Wecker, L., & Schmidt, D. E. (1979). Central cholinergic function: Relationship to choline administration. *Life Sciences, 25,* 375-384.

Weintraub, S., Mesulam, M.-M., Auty, R., Baratz, R., Cholakos, B. N., Ransil, B., Tellers, J. G., Albert, M. S., LoCastro, S., & Moss, M. (1983). Lecithin in the treatment of Alzheimer's disease. *Archives of Neurology, 40,* 527-528.

Wettstein, A. (1983). No effect from double-blind trial of physostigmine and lecithin in Alzheimer disease. *Annals of Neurology, 13,* 210-212.

Wettstein, A., & Spiegel, R. (1984). Clinical trials with the cholinergic drug RS 86 in Alzheimer's disease (AD) and senile dementia of the Alzheimer type (SDAT). *Psychopharmacology, 84,* 572-573.

Whitehouse, P. J., Price, D. L., Clark, A. W., Coyle, J. T., & DeLong, M. R. (1981). Alzheimer's disease: Evidence for selective loss of cholinergic neurons in the nucleus basalis. *Annals of Neurology, 10,* 122-126.

25

A Strategy for Studying Memory Disorders in Multiple Sclerosis

WILLIAM W. BEATTY

The purpose of this brief chapter is to describe a strategy for utilizing variability to analyze memory and other cognitive functions in neuropsychological studies. The approach grew out of studies conducted in my laboratory of patients with multiple sclerosis (MS), but it may be applicable to other populations, especially those that are characterized by large individual differences.

Multiple Sclerosis as Subcortical Dementia

The primary neuropathological changes in such diseases as Huntington's disease, Parkinson's disease, and progressive supranuclear palsy involve subcortical structures in the thalamus, basal ganglia, and related brainstem nuclei. The "subcortical" dementia associated with each of these diseases is said to be characterized by slowed information processing, impaired memory retrieval, deficient problem solving, and personality and mood disturbances in the absence of agnosia, aphasia, and apraxia (Cummings & Benson, 1984).

Although the plaques that represent areas of demyelination in MS can occur anywhere in the white matter of the central nervous system, there is a strong tendency for the subcortical paraventricular white matter to be involved (Raine, 1990). Furthermore, after a careful review of the neuropsychological literature, Rao (1986) proposed that MS might be a prototype of subcortical dementia.

My colleagues and I conducted a number of studies aimed at testing this hypothesis by comparing groups of MS patients to normal controls. The groups were carefully equated for age, education, and gender, and we attempted to choose tests that would make minimal demands on sensory and motor skills. In one study of patients with the "relapsing–remitting" form of the disease (Beatty, Goodkin, Monson, & Beatty, 1989), we administered a battery of tests aimed at measuring the core functions supposedly affected in subcortical dementia, as well as abilities that might be expected to be spared in subcortical dementia but compromised in a "cortical" dementia such as Alzheimer's disease.

The oral version of the Symbol Digit Modalities Test was used to measure information-processing speed; as expected, the MS patients produced fewer correct substitutions than controls. Qualitatively similar deficits have been observed in studies in which information-processing speed was assessed with the Paced Auditory Serial Addition Test (Litvan, Grafman, Vendrell, & Martinez, 1988) or Sternberg's memory-scanning procedure (Rao, St. Aubin-Faubert, & Leo, 1989).

We assessed problem solving with the Wisconsin Card-Sorting Test (WCST). In agreement with other studies using the WCST or the Category Test (Heaton, Nelson, Thompson, Burks, & Franklin, 1985; Peyser, Edwards, Poser, & Filskov, 1980), the MS patients were impaired; they achieved fewer categories and made more perseverative responses and errors.

Several different measures of memory were included. To study retention of information from primary memory, we used a version of the Brown–Peterson task. Consistent with the findings of two other studies of relapsing–remitting patients tested during remission (Litvan, Grafman, et al., 1988; Rao, Leo, & St. Aubin-Faubert, 1989), we found no deficits on this task.

Our patients were impaired, however, on the acquisition and delayed recall of a supraspan word list. In agreement with most other studies using verbal and nonverbal stimuli (see Grafman, Rao, & Litvan, 1990; Rao, 1990), the patients' performance was impaired on the first learning trial, but thereafter they improved at about the same rate as controls. Delayed recall was, of course, impaired in absolute terms, but forgetting rates for patients and controls were comparable. This finding is also consistent with most published studies (Rao, 1990). By contrast, the patients were not impaired on a delayed-recognition test over the same material. This finding is also consistent with most of the literature, which indicates that in MS recognition memory is much less seriously impaired than is recall (Grafman et al., 1990; Rao, 1990).

Letter and category fluency tests were included as measures of access to semantic memory. Consistent with other findings (Caine, Bamford, Schiffer, Shoulson, & Levy, 1986), the patients produced fewer correct responses than controls, but they did not show an increased tendency to make repetitive or intrusive errors (as Alzheimer patients often do). Likewise, the MS patients in this study performed normally on the Boston Naming Test.

The final memory test was an updated version of the Remote Memory Battery (Albert, Butters, & Levin, 1979). On this test the MS patients showed impaired recall but nearly normal recognition. The magnitude of their recall deficit was nearly the same for each of the decades sampled from the 1950s to the 1980s.

Considered together, the results of the various memory tests suggest that retrieval of information from secondary memory is the main source of the MS patients' difficulties.

Ostensibly, the results of this study, as well as most of the available literature, provide strong support for Rao's (1986) hypothesis that MS is a type of subcortical dementia. As a group, the MS patients displayed all of the cognitive characteristics associated with subcortical dementia and none of the characteristics of cortical dementia. Inspection of the data from individual patients, however, showed that very few patients exhibited clear-cut impairments in memory, problem solving, *and* information-processing speed (only 12% of this sample). That is, despite the highly significant differences between group means, very few patients actually exhibited subcortical dementia. The remaining patients either performed within normal limits on all of the cognitive tests or displayed relatively isolated deficits in some cognitive domains but not in others. In our experience, problem solving and information-procesing speed are the most sensitive measures for detecting deficits in MS, but patients with isolated memory impairments can be identified as well.

Partitioning Variability

Traditionally, neurologists have classified MS patients as "chronic progressive" or "relapsing–remitting," according to the course of their disease. Although on average chronic progressive patients perform more poorly than relapsing–remitting patients on a broad range of neuropsychological tests (Beatty et al., 1989; Heaton et al., 1985), there is considerable heterogeneity of cognitive performance within each of these diagnostic subtypes. In other words, knowing that a patient is chronic progressive or relapsing–remitting is only minimally helpful in predicting cognitive performance (Beatty, Goodkin, Hertsgaard, & Monson, 1990). Likewise, mental status tests such as the Mini-Mental State Examination are too insensitive to be of much use (Beatty & Goodkin, 1990).

Recently, we have attempted to exploit the natural variation in cognitive performance of MS patients to ask questions about the organization of cognitive functions in the brain. In one study, we examined metamemory in MS patients (Beatty & Monson, 1991). Previous research demonstrated marked impairment on metamemory tasks by amnesic patients with alcoholic Korsakoff's syndrome (Shimamura & Squire, 1986), but normally accurate metamemory performance by patients with amnesias of other etiologies. Suspecting that the impairments of Korsakoff patients might be related to their frontal lobe pathology and dysfunction, which are not present in other amnesics, Janowsky, Shimamura, and Squire (1989) studied metamemory in patients with frontal lobe lesions who were not amnesic or demented. Deficits in metamemory were observed, but only when memory was weakened by imposing a delay of 1–3 days. These findings implied that impairments in metamemory require disturbances in frontal lobe function and some degree of memory deficit. This leads to the prediction that only MS patients with evidence of frontal lobe dysfunction (as inferred from poor performance on the WCST) and memory disturbance (as inferred from poor performance on a recognition memory test) should exhibit impaired metamemory.

To test this hypothesis, we formed four groups of MS patients; the groups comprised the factorial combination of normal or impaired performance on the WCST and a test of delayed recognition memory. "Impairment" was defined as a score at or below the 5th percentile of normal controls. The task required subjects to predict their performance on a free-recall test. As shown in Table 25.1, the patients who performed poorly on the WCST *and* on the recognition memory test overestimated their recall by more than 50%. Patients who scored within normal limits on the WCST and the recognition memory test, or patients who were impaired on only one of the classification tests, were able to predict their performance as accurately as normal controls. Control analyses indicated that the deficits in metamemory were related to the specific

TABLE 25.1. Mean Number of Words Predicted and Actually Recalled

	Controls	MS patient groups[a]			
		NM, NW	LM, NW	NM, LW	LM, LW
Predicted	14.2	13.0	9.9	11.2	11.3
Actual	14.4	12.4	9.6	11.0	7.5
Predicted − actual	−0.2	0.6	0.3	0.2	3.8

Note. Adapted from "Metamemory in Multiple Sclerosis" (p. 319) by W. W. Beatty and N. Monson, 1991, *Journal of Clinical and Experimental Neuropsychology, 13,* 309–327. Copyright 1991 by Swets & Zeitlinger. Adapted by permission.

[a]NM, normal memory; NW, normal WCST; LM, low memory; LW, low WCST.

combination of WCST and recognition memory impairments, rather than to more global cognitive impairments.

The strategy of grouping patients according to patterns of cognitive impairment helped us to avoid an erroneous conclusion about the status of metamemory in MS, at least in this instance. Had we formed only a single group of MS patients, we would have concluded that metamemory was either intact or impaired, depending on the sample size. Either conclusion, as it turned out, would have been partially in error.

Future Directions

If the strategy described above is to be maximally useful in analyzing control of cognitive functions by the brain, it must be coupled with sophisticated analyses of brain structure and function, which are now possible with modern neuroimaging techniques. Because of its sensitivity to white matter lesions, MRI is the method of choice for studies of MS. To date, most of the MRI studies relating cognition to brain structure in MS have shown modest correlations between the severity of cognitive impairment and the overall degree of brain pathology (e.g., Franklin, Heaton, Nelson, Filley, & Seibert, 1988; Huber et al., 1987). In these studies, the use of gross measures of both behavior and structure may have precluded discovering more interesting relationships.

A recent study by Rao et al. (1989) indicates that more specific relationships can be established. They compared the performance of MS patients with significant atrophy of the corpus callosum to patients without such atrophy on a verbal dichotic listening task and on a task that required naming objects presented tachistoscopically to the left or right visual field. Both tasks are highly sensitive to commissurotomy. As predicted, only the patients with callosal atrophy showed significant left-ear suppression on the dichotic listening task and slowed naming of objects presented to the left visual field—classic signs of hemispheric disconnection.

Let us hope that the success of Rao's group will encourage other, similar efforts. For example, in my experience, the distribution of WCST scores by MS patients is essentially bimodal: About 55% of the patients perform normally, while 40% are severely impaired. The obvious prediction that the severity of damage to the connections of the dorsolateral frontal cortex is greater in the latter group remains to be tested.

REFERENCES

Albert, M. S., Butters, N., & Levin, J. (1979). Temporal gradients in the retrograde amnesia of patients with alcoholic Korsakoff's disease. *Archives of Neurology, 36*, 211-216.

Beatty, W. W., & Goodkin, D. E. (1990). Screening for cognitive impairment in multiple sclerosis: An evaluation of the Mini-Mental State Examination. *Archives of Neurology, 47*, 297-301.

Beatty, W. W., Goodkin, D. E., Hertsgaard, D., & Monson, N. (1990). Clinical and demographic predictors of cognitive performance in multiple sclerosis: Do diagnostic type, disease duration, and disability matter? *Archives of Neurology, 47*, 305-308.

Beatty, W. W., Goodkin, D. E., Monson, N., & Beatty, P. A. (1989). Cognitive disturbances in patients with relapsing remitting multiple sclerosis. *Archives of Neurology, 47*, 1113-1119.

Beatty, W. W., & Monson, N. (1991). Metamemory in multiple sclerosis. *Journal of Clinical and Experimental Neuropsychology, 13*, 309-327.

Caine, E. D., Bamford, K. A., Schiffer, R. B., Shoulson, I., & Levy, S. (1986). A controlled neuropsychological comparison of Huntington's disease and multiple sclerosis. *Archives of Neurology, 43*, 249-254.

Cummings, J. L., & Benson, D. F. (1984). Subcortical dementia: Review of an emerging concept. *Archives of Neurology, 41*, 874-879.

Franklin, G. M., Heaton, R. K., Nelson, L. M., Filley, C. M., & Seibert, C. (1988). Correlation of neuropsychological and MRI findings in chronic/progressive multiple sclerosis. *Neurology, 38*, 1826-1829.

Grafman, J., Rao, S. M., & Litvan, I. (1990). Disorders of memory. In S. M. Rao (Ed.), *Neurobehavioral aspects of multiple sclerosis* (pp. 102-117). New York: Oxford University Press.

Heaton, R. K., Nelson, L. M., Thompson, D. S., Burks, J. S., & Franklin, G. M. (1985). Neuropsychological findings in relapsing-remitting and chronic-progressive multiple sclerosis. *Journal of Consulting and Clinical Psychology, 53*, 103-110.

Huber, S. J., Paulson, G. W., Shuttleworth, E. C., Chakeres, D., Clapp, L. E., Pakalnis, A., Weiss, K., & Rammohan, K. Magnetic resonance imaging correlates of dementia in multiple sclerosis. *Archives of Neurology, 44*, 732-736.

Janowsky, J. S., Shimamura, A. P., & Squire, L. R. (1989). Memory and metamemory: Comparisons between patients with frontal lobe lesions and amnesic patients. *Psychobiology, 17*, 3-11.

Litvan, I., Grafman, J., Vendrell, P., & Martinez, J. M. (1988). Slowed information processing in multiple sclerosis. *Archives of Neurology, 45*, 281-285.

Litvan, I., Grafman, J., Vendrell, P., Martinez, J. M., Junque, C., Vendrell, J. M., & Barraquer-Bordas, L. (1988). Multiple memory deficits in patients with multiple sclerosis: Exploring the working memory system. *Archives of Neurology, 45*, 607-610.

Peyser, J. M., Edwards, K. R., Poser, C. M., & Filskov, S. B. (1980). Cognitive function in patients with multiple sclerosis. *Archives of Neurology, 37*, 577-579.

Raine, C. S. (1990). Neuropathology. In S. M. Rao (Ed.), *Neurobehavioral aspects of multiple sclerosis* (pp. 15-36). New York: Oxford University Press.

Rao, S. M. (1986). Neuropsychology of multiple sclerosis: A critical review. *Journal of Clinical and Experimental Neuropsychology, 8*, 503-542.

Rao, S. M. (1990). Multiple sclerosis. In J. L. Cummings (Ed.), *Subcortical dementia* (pp. 164-180). New York: Oxford University Press.

Rao, S. M., Bernardin, L., Leo, G. J., Ellington, L., Ryan, S. B., & Burg, L. S. (1989). Cerebral disconnection in multiple sclerosis: Relationship to atrophy of the corpus callosum. *Archives of Neurology, 46*, 918-921.

Rao, S. M., Leo, G. J., & St. Aubin-Faubert, P. (1989). On the nature of memory disturbance in multiple sclerosis. *Journal of Clinical and Experimental Neuropsychology, 11*, 699-712.

Rao, S. M., St. Aubin-Faubert, P., & Leo, G. J. (1989). Information processing speed in patients with multiple sclerosis. *Journal of Clinical and Experimental Neuropsychology, 11*, 471-477.

Shimamura, A. P., & Squire, L. R. (1986). Memory and metamemory: A study of the feeling-of-knowing phenomenon in amnesic patients. *Journal of Experimental Psychology: Learning, Memory, and Cognition, 12*, 452-460.

26

Posttraumatic and Retrograde Amnesia after Closed Head Injury

HARVEY S. LEVIN, MATTHEW A. LILLY,
ANDREW PAPANICOLAOU, and HOWARD M. EISENBERG

Head injury is the most common etiology of memory disorder, but it has attracted less investigative interest than alcoholic Korsakoff's syndrome or rare cases of medial temporal lobe surgery. Perhaps this apparent neglect of posttraumatic amnesia (PTA) reflects a reluctance to study memory problems that are frequently complicated by disturbed consciousness and attentional deficits. In this chapter, we assess the relationship between impaired consciousness and the gross amnesic defects characteristic of the early stages of recovery after head injury, and examine current methods of assessment for disorientation and memory deficits reflective of PTA. We also discuss characteristic patterns of recovery from PTA and review findings concerning the presence of a temporal gradient in retrograde amnesia (RA) produced by closed head injury (CHI). Auditory evoked potential correlates of subacute amnesia after head-injured patients emerge from coma are also presented. Lastly, we examine recent evidence concerning the preserved capacity to accomplish certain types of learning during PTA.

Subacute Amnesia in Relation to Impaired Consciousness and Attention

PTA (anterograde amnesia) is one of the most distinctive features of CHI, occurring even after mild head trauma that produces brief or no loss of consciousness (Russell, 1932; Yarnell & Lynch, 1970). RA for events before a head injury is relatively brief in relation to the duration of anterograde amnesia, typically spanning an interval measured in minutes or seconds in mild or moderate head injuries (Russell, 1935; Russell & Nathan, 1946). Consistent with clinical observations of amnesic periods in patients with relatively undisturbed consciousness after mild head injury, Ommaya and Gennarelli (1974) postulated that the structural irregularity and variation in tissue densities of the limbic and fronto-temporal cortices contribute to the vulnerability of these structures to injury, with resulting memory impairment, whereas the neural substrate for alertness (e.g., mesencephalic brainstem) is less vulnerable.

In contrast to amnesic disorders with an insidious onset (e.g., Korsakoff's syndrome), moderate or severe head injury is typically followed immediately by a period of anterograde amnesia concomitant with a variable degree of disturbance in level of consciousness. The anterograde amnesia observed in PTA is distinguished by rapid forgetting of information that has been learned through repeated exposure (Levin, High, & Eisenberg, 1988), whereas diencephalic amnesics exhibit a normal rate of forgetting. Lethargy, agitation, incoherent talkativeness, inappropriate behavior, hallucinations, euphoria, and fluctuations in autonomic functioning frequently accompany anterograde amnesia during the early stages of emergence from coma following CHI (Moore & Ruesch, 1944; Russell, 1932). In view of these marked behavioral aberrations, Moore and Ruesch referred to this phase of recovery as "posttraumatic psychosis" rather than PTA. This constellation of features raises the question of whether PTA is but one of numerous manifestations of globally impaired consciousness, or the most prominent cognitive deficit during this stage of recovery. PTA also differs from alcoholic Korsakoff's syndrome because surgical findings and neuroimaging techniques such as computed tomographic (CT) scanning and magnetic resonance imaging (MRI) permit antemortem clinicopathological correlation after head injury. Furthermore, current clinical gradings of coma provide a quantitative index of the severity of brain injury (Teasdale & Jennett, 1974).

Following publication of Russell's clinical data on estimates of PTA, Moore and Ruesch (1944) employed quantitative cognitive and psychomotor tasks to study impaired attention and other aspects of disturbed consciousness after CHI. While Russell and his colleagues focused on the amnesia characteristic of the early stage of recovery from head injury, they also acknowledged the presence of other early sequelae compatible with disturbed consciousness. Although recent research has emphasized the disruption of memory (cf. Schacter & Crovitz, 1977), there has been also a resurgence of interest in the contribution of attentional deficit to apparent memory disorder (Geschwind, 1982). The phenomenon of "islands" of intact memory—that is, preserved recall of isolated incidents during an otherwise amnesic period—may reflect the waxing and waning of attention.

Definition and Measurement of Posttraumatic Amnesia

Ritchie Russell reported the first systematic studies of early recovery from head injury in his 1932 paper. He initially characterized this interval as the duration of disturbed consciousness (i.e., the "loss of full consciousness"). Accordingly, there was no differentiation of anterograde amnesia from coma or impaired consciousness (see Figure 26.1). In fact, Russell and Nathan (1946) defined the duration of PTA as the interval of "impaired consciousness." In 1961, Russell and Smith revised the earlier formulation by emphasizing impaired memory. They defined PTA as the duration of disturbance (of consciousness) during which "current events have not been stored." This definition has gained wide acceptance as an index of severity of CHI (cf. Jennett & Teasdale, 1981). Other investigators, however, have preferred to measure the duration of anterograde amnesia apart from the period of impaired consciousness as defined by the Glasgow Coma Scale (Teasdale & Jennett, 1974).

EARLY STAGES OF RECOVERY FROM CLOSED HEAD INJURY

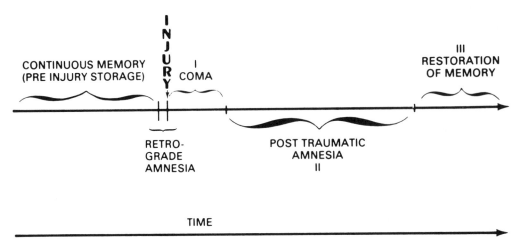

FIGURE 26.1. Sequence of acute alterations in memory after CHI. The periods of coma (I) and PTA (II) have been traditionally combined to yield a total interval of impaired consciousness that extends until continuous memory for ongoing events (III) is restored. From *Neurobehavioral Consequences of Closed Head Injury* (p. 74) by H. S. Levin, A. L. Benton, and R. G. Grossman, 1982, New York: Oxford University Press. Copyright 1982 by Oxford University Press. Reprinted by permission of the publisher.

Procedures to measure PTA resemble traditional techniques of the mental status examination and are typically constrained by the necessity for brief bedside testing. Russell and his colleagues studied head-injured patients who had been transferred to the Military Hospital for Head Injuries in Oxford. To develop a uniform index of severity of brain insult for a large series of patients who were initially treated in diverse field hospitals under wartime conditions, Russell employed a retrospective interview that yielded an estimate of the interval of impaired consciousness (i.e., the period of both coma and anterograde amnesia; see Figure 26.1). Although this strategy yields prognostically useful information, particularly when other indices of acute neurological impairment are not available (Russell & Smith, 1961), it assumes that patients can distinguish between "real memory" and repeated briefing by their families during the early stages of recovery. Moreover, retrospective estimates of the duration of PTA are frequently discrepant from estimates given by a patient during the early stage of recovery (Gronwall & Wrightson, 1980). Consequently, investigators have recently developed techniques to evaluate PTA directly, beginning when the patient emerges from coma (i.e., exhibits eye opening and obeys commands) (Fortuny, Briggs, Newcombe, Ratcliff, & Thomas, 1980; Levin, O'Donnell, & Grossman, 1979). Although patients in this stage of recovery from CHI usually utter comprehensible speech, intubation may require modification of standard procedures, such as substituting a multiple-choice recognition format for verbal recall.

The Galveston Orientation and Amnesia Test (GOAT) was derived from a brief questionnaire of temporal orientation (Benton, Van Allen, & Fogel, 1964) and was expanded to include items testing orientation to person, place, and circumstances, in addition to a detailed description of the first postinjury memory and the last event before the injury. Although these latter items are frequently difficult to verify, they provide traditional measures of PTA and RA. Based on the distribution of scores in young adults who recovered from mild CHI (intact eye opening, preserved ability to obey commands, and comprehensible speech on admission, with no neurological deficit or CT evidence of hematoma or contusion), various levels of performance were defined and applied to a prospective series of head injuries of varying severity.

Daily administration of the GOAT yields a recovery curve depicting the restoration of orientation and resolution of gross amnesia, as illustrated in Figure 26.2. We (Levin, Papanicolaou, & Eisenberg, 1984) operationally defined duration of PTA as the interval during which the GOAT score is below a borderline level of performance recorded in the standardization group ($\leq$75). We found a strong relationship between the severity of initial neurological impairment (Glasgow Coma Scale score) and the duration of PTA as defined by the GOAT. The duration of PTA, as measured by the GOAT, was also related to overall recovery at least 6 months postinjury.

Despite the established utility of the GOAT as a quantitative, objective index of recovery of orientation and continuous memory with good predictive validity in adults (Levin et al., 1979), until recently there existed no analogue of the GOAT that would

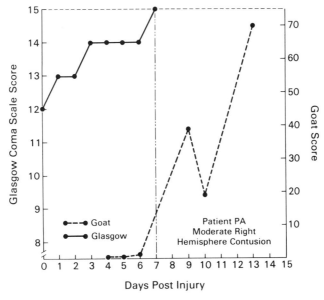

FIGURE 26.2. Recovery of orientation following a CHI of moderate severity. There was a 1-week delay in restoration of full orientation and resolution of gross amnesia after ratings of the patient's level of consciousness reached the ceiling of the Glasgow Coma Scale. From "Observations on Amnesia after Nonmissile Head Injury" (p. 250) by H. S. Levin, A. Papanicolaou, and H. M. Eisenberg, 1984, in L. R. Squire and N. Butters (Eds.), *Neuropsychology of Memory* (1st ed., pp. 247–257). New York: Guilford Press. Copyright 1984 by The Guilford Press. Reprinted by permission of the publisher.

allow reliable, objective assessment of PTA in children. We and our colleagues (Ewing-Cobbs, Levin, Fletcher, Miner, & Eisenberg, 1990) have introduced the Children's Orientation and Amnesia Test (COAT) as a practical means of obtaining objective, serial assessment of recovery of orientation and continuous memory in children and adolescents during the early stages of recovery from traumatic brain injury.

The COAT is comprised of 16 items assessing the areas of general orientation, temporal orientation, and memory. There are seven questions of general orientation that examine orientation to person and place, as well as recall of biographical information; five questions assessing temporal orientation; and four questions assessing memory (immediate, short-term, and remote). We also report norms for the COAT for children from ages 3 to 15. The norms were obtained from 146 children who were enrolled in standard academic programs and had no previous history of neurological difficulties.

We (Ewing-Cobbs et al., 1990) also examined the predictive validity of duration of PTA as measured by the COAT, by examining the relationship between duration of PTA and memory functioning assessed during the initial year postinjury. Verbal and nonverbal memory functioning was assessed after resolution of PTA and at 6 and 12 months postinjury. Verbal memory was assessed using the age-appropriate form of the Verbal Selective Reminding Test (Buschke, 1974; Buschke & Fuld, 1974; Morgan, 1981). This test involves orally presenting a list of words to the subject and asking the subject to repeat back to the examiner as many words as he or she can recall from the list in any order. The subject is subsequently reminded of only the words that he or she omitted upon recall, and is asked to repeat the entire list of words again. This procedure is repeated over six successive trials. The outcome measure selected for this study consisted of the total number of words consistently retrieved from long-term memory (consistent long-term retrieval, or CLTR). This measure is obtained by counting words that were recalled on two consecutive trials, and every trial thereafter. The findings presented in Figure 26.3 indicate that PTA duration as assessed by the COAT was significantly related to CLTR scores from the Verbal Selective Reminding Test. After significant overall effects were found, planned follow-up contrasts indicated significantly poorer outcome for PTA duration group 3 (PTA > 14 days) as compared to group 1 (PTA ≤ 7 days).

Similar results were observed on the Nonverbal Selective Reminding Test, an analogue of the Verbal Selective Reminding Test that involves remembering the location of target dots among a random array of eight dots (Fletcher, 1985). The pattern of results shown in Figure 26.4 reveals that impaired memory for spatial information was related to increased PTA duration. Follow-up contrasts to significant overall effects indicated significantly poorer performance among group 3 (PTA duration > 14 days) as compared to group 1 (PTA duration ≤ 7 days), and among groups 1 and 2 combined (PTA duration ≤ 14 days) as compared to group 3.

The objectivity of the COAT, combined with its associated high interrater reliability (98%) and initial indications of good predictive validity, suggests that this measure may prove to have significant functional utility. The brevity of the test and ease of training persons to administer the test properly make its use highly practical as well.

An alternative technique to measure PTA directly in adults was developed by Fortuny et al. (1980), who supplemented questions of orientation with a brief picture recall text and asked the patient to recall the examiner's name. The investigators defined the termination of PTA as the point when the patient had 3 consecutive days of correct recall. The authors found that this brief test yielded estimates of PTA that agreed closely with the results of clinical examination by neurosurgeons.

Consistent with the results of direct measurement of PTA, Russell (1971) recommended that the "return of orientation" be used to signal the end of PTA. Gronwall and Wrightson (1980) serially interviewed a consecutive series of patients with mild head injury, beginning in the emergency room (an average interval of less than 2 hours postinjury). The authors determined that PTA ended when a patient exhibited "return of continuous memory" (i.e., was able to recall ongoing events related to his or her treatment and the circumstances of injury). Although Gronwall and Wrightson found a significant overall relationship between recovery of orientation and return of continuous memory, the number of dissociations (e.g., impaired recall of ongoing events despite normal orientation) was sufficient to lead the authors to dispute the functional equivalence of disorientation and PTA. Whether such dissociations occur after more severe CHI awaits further study. Clinical experience, however, suggests that marked disorientation and impaired memory are closely related during the early stages of recovery following coma.

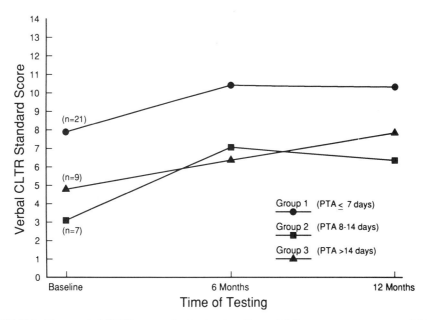

FIGURE 26.3. Mean verbal CLTR scores obtained at baseline and follow-up examinations in children and adolescents with PTA of varying duration. PTA persisting for at least 2 weeks was associated with significantly lower verbal memory scores than PTA persisting for less than 1 week. From "The Children's Orientation and Amnesia Test: Relationship to Severity of Acute Head Injury and to Recovery of Memory" (p. 688) by L. Ewing-Cobbs, H. S. Levin, J. M. Fletcher, M. E. Miner, and H. M. Eisenberg, 1990, *Neurosurgery, 27*(5), 683–691. Copyright 1990 by *Neurosurgery.* Reprinted by permission of the publisher.

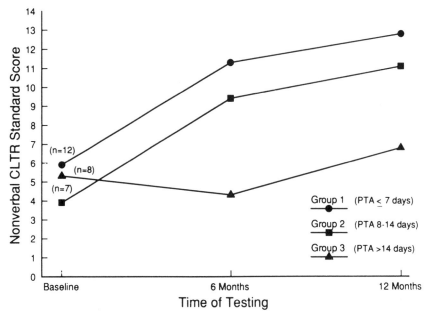

FIGURE 26.4. Mean nonverbal CLTR scores plotted against time of examination. Patients who had PTA for at least 2 weeks had significantly lower nonverbal memory scores, and showed less recovery during the first year after injury, than patients with PTA of shorter duration. From "The Children's Orientation and Amnesia Test: Relationship to Severity of Acute Head Injury and to Recovery of Memory" (p. 689) by L. Ewing-Cobbs, H. S. Levin, J. M. Fletcher, M. E. Miner, and H. M. Eisenberg, 1990, *Neurosurgery, 27*(5), 683–691. Copyright 1990 by *Neurosurgery*. Reprinted by permission of the publisher.

Duration of Posttraumatic Amnesia in Relation to the Duration of Coma

Direct measurement of PTA offers the opportunity to elucidate the early postcomatose stages of memory deficit following head injury. We have employed this technique to inquire about the relationship between the duration of coma and the period of PTA. Apart from the theoretical aspect of this relationship, it would be clinically useful to predict the duration of gross confusion and marked behavioral disturbance after patients emerge from coma. Jennett and Teasdale (1981) estimated from an international data bank that the duration of PTA is about four times the length of the interval until speech returns after CHI, but details of measuring PTA were not given.

The pilot phase of the Coma Data Bank Network, which was developed by the National Institute of Neurological and Communicative Disorders and Stroke (NINCDS), provided us (Levin et al., 1984) with an opportunity to study consecutive admissions at six university hospitals for severe CHI (i.e., Glasgow Coma Scale score ≤ 8, consistent with no eye opening, inability to obey commands, and failure to utter comprehensible words). The GOAT was administered serially to survivors while they were hospitalized, yielding a direct measure of PTA (number of days postcoma until the GOAT score reached a normal level of ≥ 75) in 50 cases.

Plotting the duration of PTA against the duration of coma (coma was considered to end when the eyes opened to some stimulus and the patient obeyed commands and uttered comprehensible speech) yielded a relationship characterized by excessive variability to permit linear prediction, despite statistical significance (Kendall rank-order correlation coefficient of .30, $p < .003$). Several atypical cases of markedly prolonged PTA despite relatively brief periods of coma were identified. There was no feature common to these atypical cases or to patients whose PTA resolved rapidly after an interval of coma. From these preliminary findings, we surmise that there are other important determinants of PTA duration, apart from duration of coma.

Retrograde Amnesia and Ribot's Law of Regression

Ribot (1882) reviewed the published case studies of his era, which included detailed descriptions of amnesia for events before and after head injury. From these cases and reports of other etiologies of amnesia, Ribot proposed the law of regression, which holds that the susceptibility of a memory to disruption is inversely proportional to its age. He considered those memories to be unstable that were the "most recent recollections," because they had been "rarely repeated" and were therefore without "permanent associations."

Consistent with this view, Russell and Nathan (1946) found that the retrograde effects of amnesia rarely exceeded 30 minutes, except in patients with more severe CHI as reflected by a duration of PTA exceeding 1 day. Furthermore, Russell (1935) described a CHI patient who initially exhibited an RA that extended 9 years into the past while he was in PTA. During the following 10 weeks, he gradually recollected events in the remote past, beginning with the earliest memories, until his recall for past events was restored to within a few minutes of the accident. Russell and Nathan (1946) confirmed the shrinkage of RA in a series of CHI patients in whom the chronological sequence of recovery of remote memory typically paralleled the resolution of PTA. Benson and Geschwind (1967) reported an impressive case of shrinking RA in a head-injured patient whose retrograde loss was reduced from 2 years to 24 hours during the first 3 months after injury.

A recent study by High, Levin, and Gary (1990), investigating the pattern of recovery of orientation to person, place, and time in association with resolving PTA, also yielded results consistent with Ribot's law of regression. This study examined recovery from PTA in 84 patients who were initially disoriented after sustaining CHI. The criteria for orientation to person, place, and time were as follows: For person, patients identified themselves and their birthdays on two consecutive testings; for place, they identified the city they were in and were aware of being in the hospital on two consecutive occasions; and for time, they estimated the date within 5 days on two consecutive testings. Figure 26.5 shows that orientation returned in the order of person, place, and time for a minimum of 60–70% of the cases in each severity group, and 70% of the cases overall. Person, time, and place represented the order of return to orientation for 13% of the cases overall.

High et al. (1990) suggest that return of orientation to person before orientation to time and place provides support for Ribot's (1885) theory that older memories are relatively resistant to disruption, since the knowledge of orientation to person represents older, overlearned information, whereas orientation to both time and place relies on retention of new information. Recovery of orientation to place before orientation to time is also consistent with this hypothesis, as geographical location remains constant during hospitalization, while the date changes daily. These findings are similar to results reported by Daniel, Crovitz, and Weiner (1987). However, in both of these studies the order of return of orientation with respect to person, place, and time was not invariant.

Since case reports of head-injured patients based on recall of autobiographical events and orientation have supported Ribot's law, we predicted that results of tests of remote memory given to patients in PTA would yield a temporal gradient (i.e., relative sparing of the oldest memories). To test this hypothesis, we conducted a pair of studies (Levin et al., 1985) investigating the possibility of a temporal gradient for RA associated with CHI.

In the first of these studies, a revised and expanded version of Squire and Slater's (1975) recognition memory test for titles of television programs was used to investigate remote memory for general information. This multiple-choice test required the subject to select which of four program names printed on an index card was actually the title of a program broadcast during the evening on a major network for a single season. Six test items were selected from each of five time periods: 1968–1971, 1971–1975, 1975–1977, 1977–1979, and 1979–1981. Subjects included two groups of 10 CHI patients who were studied during the course of inpatient rehabilitation. The first group of CHI patients was tested during PTA; the second group was normally oriented and no longer in PTA at the time of testing. The groups were closely matched in age, education, initial Glasgow Coma Scale score, and the interval of time during which the patient failed to follow simple commands. Severe CHI predominated in the PTA group (9 of 10

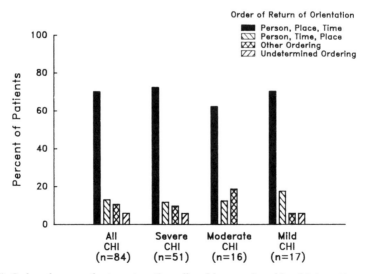

FIGURE 26.5. Order of return of orientation: Overall and by severity of head injury. From "Recovery of Orientation Following Closed Head Injury" (p. 706) by W. M. High, Jr., H. S. Levin, and H. E. Gary, Jr., 1990, *Journal of Clinical and Experimental Neuropsychology, 12*(5), 703–714. Copyright 1990 by Swets & Zeitlinger. Reprinted by permission of the publisher.

patients) and post-PTA group (10 of 10 patients). The remote memory test was also administered to 187 undergraduate students at a local university to obtain normative data.

As depicted in Figure 26.6, recognition of past television programs of the control subjects exceeded that of the PTA group for each time period and surpassed that of the post-PTA group for all but the earliest time period. A repeated-measures analysis of variance also indicated highly significant effects for the between-groups factor (PTA, post-PTA, and controls), the within-groups factor (time period), and the interaction between grouping and time period. A trend analysis performed to break down the interaction indicated a significant trend for the linear component in the control group, suggesting optimal retention for the most recent information, but no significant linear trend in either the PTA or post-PTA group. These findings failed to indicate a temporal gradient for RA in either of the CHI groups, as the presence of a linear component would be necessary to support the postulation that the dissolution of memory is inversely related to the recency of the event.

In a related study of RA, CHI patients were again selected from the same inpatient rehabilitation service (PTA group $n = 6$; post-PTA group $n = 17$). In this study, personally salient remote memories were investigated by means of an autobiographical inventory we developed for use with young head-injured adults. This inventory consisted of eight questions, including two from each of four different time periods (primary school, junior high school, high school, and young adult life). For example, the question "What was the name of your elementary school?" represented a test of memory for the developmental time period of primary school, whereas a high school era question was "On what car did you learn to drive?" This biographical information was corroborated by a collateral source (usually a relative).

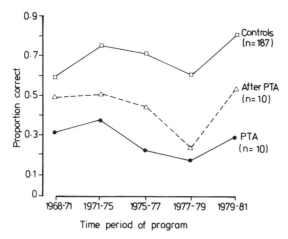

FIGURE 26.6. Mean proportion of correct recognition of television program titles plotted across the time period of broadcast for oriented (after PTA) and amnesic (PTA) head-injured patients and control subjects. From "Impairment of Remote Memory after Closed Head Injury" (p. 558) by H. S. Levin, W. M. High, Jr., C. A. Meyers, A. Von Laufen, M. E. Hayden, and H. M. Eisenberg, 1985, *Journal of Neurology, Neurosurgery and Psychiatry*, 48, 556–563. Copyright 1985 by the British Medical Association. Reprinted by permission of the publisher.

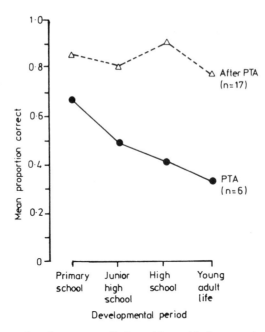

FIGURE 26.7. Mean proportion of correct recall of autobiographical events plotted across developmental periods for head-injured patients in PTA ($n = 6$) and after PTA ($n = 17$). From "Impairment of Remote Memory after Closed Head Injury" (p. 561) by H. S. Levin, W. M. High, Jr., C. A. Meyers, A. Von Laufen, M. E. Hayden, and H. M. Eisenberg, 1985, *Journal of Neurology, Neurosurgery and Psychiatry, 48*, 556–563. Copyright 1985 by the British Medical Association. Reprinted by permission of the publisher.

Results presented in Figure 26.7 reveal a trend of more accurate recall by the CHI group that had regained orientation. Furthermore, recall accuracy of the PTA group decreased monotonically from being rather well preserved for early childhood autobiographical information to a noticeable retrograde loss for autobiographical information of young adulthood. Trend analysis for all participants revealed a significant interaction of groups with a linear component; trend analysis for the separate groups indicated a significant linear decline for the PTA group, and no significant linear trend for the oriented group.

Findings from these studies indicate that moderate and severe CHI patients may frequently exhibit at least partial RA for events that occurred during the preceding decade. This amnesia can include both events in the public domain and personally salient events—a finding that precludes inadequate acquisition or lack of exposure as an explanation for this remote memory failure. Second, these studies found that remote memory for life events was more impaired in CHI patients still experiencing PTA than in patients with injuries of comparable severity who were no longer exhibiting disorientation. We posit that these findings support Benson and Geschwind's (1967) suggestion that "the retrieval process depends on the same system that is necessary for the laying down of new memories" (p. 542). Finally, the relative preservation of autobiographical memories despite impaired memories of the television programs can be seen as supporting Ribot's postulation that the repeated retrieval of memories increases their resistance to decay. We suggest that repeated reminiscence of early life events results in incorporation of these memories in a semantic memory structure relatively invulnerable to RA, whereas this effect is negligible for information such as the single-season program titles presented in the first study.

High et al. (1990) established further support for the argument that older memories are relatively better preserved following CHI by investigating the characteristics of temporal disorientation following CHI. These authors examined the magnitude and displacement of estimates of the current date provided by temporally disoriented patients. Their findings revealed that disoriented patients typically provided an estimate of the current date that was earlier than the testing date. The magnitude of this backwards displacement of time was generally greater in the more acute stages of recovery (see Figure 26.8). The initial backwards displacement of time estimates, and the corresponding shrinkage in the degree of displacement, were seen most clearly in severely injured patients.

The inconsistent observation of a temporal gradient associated with RA following CHI may initially seem to be at variance with previous studies showing a consistent temporal gradient in remote memory of patients with alcoholic Korsakoff's syndrome or medial temporal lobe damage (Albert, Butters, & Levin, 1979; Squire & Cohen, 1982). However, this disparity can be at least partially explained by the insidious onset of anterograde memory deficit, which disrupts storage of new information in patients with Korsakoff's syndrome, while access to previously acquired knowledge may be relatively preserved. In contrast, we presume that the young victims of CHI with no antecedent neuropsychiatric disorder had normal long-term memory consolidation during the preinjury time periods covered by the television questionnaire. Consequently, we infer that the RA of head-injured patients is primarily attributable to

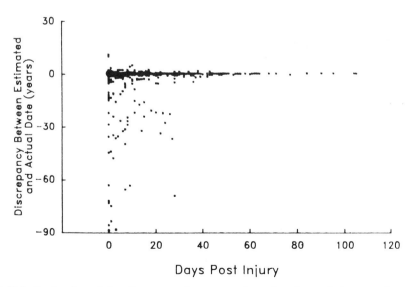

FIGURE 26.8. Scatterplot of the discrepancy between estimated and actual date in relation to days postinjury: All patients (*n* = 84). From "Recovery of Orientation Following Closed Head Injury" (p. 707) by W. M. High, Jr., H. S. Levin, and H. E. Gary, Jr., 1990, *Journal of Clinical and Experimental Neuropsychology*, *12*(5), 703–714. Copyright 1990 by Swets & Zeitlinger. Reprinted by permission of the publisher.

retrieval failure. Findings from the previously discussed studies indicating a temporal gradient for autobiographical information assessed with recall procedures, but no temporal gradient for recognition of titles of television programs (Levin et al., 1985), are consistent with this hypothesis. Further investigation is needed to clarify whether this inconsistency in observation of a temporal gradient is largely related to the type of information being assessed (autobiographical vs. personally nonsalient) or reflective of the type of assessment procedure (i.e., recall vs. recognition).

Evoked Potential Correlates of Posttraumatic Amnesia

Clinicians and investigators typically describe patients during the early stages of recovery from CHI as being "in" or "out" of PTA—expressions that denote a distinctive neurological condition. Although the cognitive and behavioral disturbances character-istic of PTA are more complex than the responses used to rate the depth of coma, this early stage of recovery can be distinguished from the behavioral characteristics of head-injured patients who have achieved full orientation and are no longer confused or grossly amnesic. As previously suggested (Levin, Benton, & Grossman, 1982), PTA may constitute a specific neurophysiological state in which learning does not transfer to the post-PTA stage of recovery (Overton, 1978).

We (Papanicolaou et al., 1984) postulated that aberrations in the P300, a late positive-going component of the auditory evoked potential (AEP) that purportedly reflects cognitive processing of a rare unpredictable stimulus (Pritchard, 1981), would parallel the resolution of PTA during the early stage of recovery from head injury. The appearance of this late AEP component after presentation of the rare tone is generally attributed to its greater salience, which engages focal attention and, presumably, more elaborate processing than the frequently occurring predictable stimulus. The precise nature of this processing, however, is unclear (see Pritchard, 1981, for an informative review).

Therefore, we (Papanicolaou et al., 1984) proposed that the appearance of the P300 requires at least that the patient recognize the salience of the rare stimulus as opposed to the frequent one. However, recognition can only occur if there is registra-tion in memory of both the physical parameters and the temporal features of both stimuli, as well as appreciation of their differences. As such, it would be expected that severely impaired attention and memory during PTA would preclude the possibility of recognition and differential processing of the rare stimulus and would be reflected by the absence of the P300. The failure to retain information about the frequent tone and to appreciate the distinctiveness of the rare tone would result in identical AEP wave-forms to both stimuli. We predicted that oriented CHI patients, who have emerged from PTA and therefore exhibit less severe deficits of attention and memory, should be capable of differentially processing the rare stimulus. A P300 should therefore appear in these head-injured patients, albeit a delayed one because of their inefficient speed of cognitive processing (see Squires, Goodin, & Starr, 1979) in comparison with normal subjects.

We (Papanicolaou et al., 1984) compared AEPs recorded from a train of frequent 500-Hz tones to AEPs recorded from rare 100-Hz tones that appear at random intervals (probability of .2). These stimuli were delivered binaurally through headphones at the same intensity level (65-dB sound pressure level). All recordings were made from the vertex (C_z) with linked-ear reference. A Nicolet Med-80 system was used for data collection and reduction. We obtained data from 7 normal adult volunteers, 8 disoriented or marginally oriented patients (GOAT score = 60–75), and 10 fully oriented CHI patients (GOAT score ≥ 80). All CHI patients were young adults studied during their initial hospitalization on our service. Both the patients and the normal subjects were asked to listen to the tones, but no response was requested.

The AEPs to the rare and frequent tones were characterized by major negative (N1) and positive (P2) peaks, whereas an additional third positive peak (P300) was present in the AEP to the rare and unpredictable tones. Representative waveforms to the rare and unpredictable tones from one subject in each group are shown in Figure 26.9, which indicates that the latency of the P300 to the rare tone increased from the normal subject to the oriented CHI patient and was delayed in the disoriented CHI patient who was in PTA. Statistical analysis confirmed that the P300 latency of the patients in PTA was delayed, whereas there was no significant difference between the oriented patients and normal subjects.

These data suggest that the AEP response to the rare tone consists of two positive peaks (P2 and P300), the first most likely representing preattentive and the second

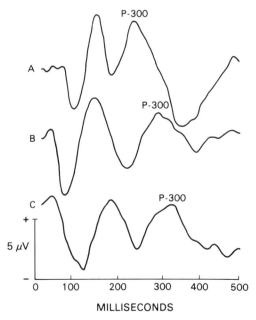

FIGURE 26.9. Evoked potential waveforms to the rare and unpredictable tone from a normal subject (**A**), an oriented patient whose PTA has resolved (**B**), and a disoriented patient in PTA (**C**) show progressive increases in the P300 latency that are representative of the latency means of their respective groups. From "Evoked Potential Correlates of Posttraumatic Amnesia after Closed Head Injury" (p. 677) by A. C. Papanicolaou, H. S. Levin, H. M. Eisenberg, B. D. Moore, K. E. Goethe, and W. M. High, Jr., 1984, *Neurosurgery, 14*(6), 676–678. Copyright 1984 by *Neurosurgery.* Reprinted by permission of the publisher.

attentive processing of the salient stimulus. In normal subjects the latter process is represented by the P300, as it is with the fully awake, oriented CHI patients. During PTA (GOAT score = 60–75), however, when CHI patients fail to recognize consistently the difference between the two tones and to appreciate the saliency of the rare one, the latency differences of the rare- and frequent-tone peaks tend to overlap. Consistent with the possibility of using this procedure as a direct physiological measure of recovering memory and attention during PTA, Onofrj et al. (1991) recently showed that the P300 latency decreased progressively during recovery from PTA in a group of 10 patients who had sustained mild to moderate CHI.

Preserved Learning during Posttraumatic Amnesia

The past decade has seen an expanding literature and accumulation of research indicating that amnesic patients of many different etiologies possess a preserved capacity to accomplish certain types of learning (Shimamura, 1986; Squire, 1987). Although these amnesic patients demonstrate a marked inability to learn on traditional neuropsychological tests of explicit recall, they maintain an intact ability to learn and retain certain perceptuomotor, perceptual, and cognitive skills with a strong rule-based component, often referred to as "skill learning" or "procedural learning" (Brooks & Baddeley, 1976; Cohen & Squire, 1980; Milner, 1962). They have also been shown to demonstrate intact priming effects; that is, prior exposure to stimulus materials facilitates (or biases) test performance under certain circumstances (Gardner, Boller, Moreines, & Butters, 1973; Shimamura & Squire, 1984; Warrington & Weiskrantz, 1974, 1978).

Schacter, Cooper, Tharan, and Rubens (1991) recently presented evidence of intact priming effects for six patients with memory disorders on an object decision task that involved identifying whether line drawings of three-dimensional objects that did not exist in the real world were structurally possible or impossible. Prior to introducing the structurally possible–impossible condition, subjects were asked to perform a structural encoding task (judging whether each object faced primarily to the right or the left) on half of the line drawings that were subsequently introduced for the possible–impossible decision. This served as a study condition that was designed to induce priming effects. Results indicated robust priming effects, which were similar in magnitude for the organic amnesia group and for groups of matched controls and student controls. Furthermore, despite the similar magnitude of priming effects for the three groups, a subsequent recognition test reliant on explicit memory skills yielded significant between-group effects, with the patient group performing significantly below the level of both the matched controls and the student controls.

Ewert, Levin, Watson, and Kalisky (1989) have conducted the sole study to date investigating preserved learning during PTA. These researchers investigated the possibility of procedural learning during PTA in 16 CHI patients in comparison to 16 control subjects, using mirror-image reading, mazes (Porteus, 1959), and the pursuit-rotor task (which involves tracking a moving target) (Corkin, 1968; Eslinger & Damasio, 1986; Heindel, Butters, & Salmon, 1988). For each task, learning was evaluated on 3 consecutive days during PTA (GOAT score ≤ 75) and in a fourth session following resolution of PTA. These subjects evidenced learning on all tasks administered across the initial three sessions, and demonstrated transfer of the learned skills to the fourth testing session. Similar to findings in other studies investigating procedural learning in amnesics (Brooks & Baddeley, 1976; Cohen & Squire, 1980), the PTA groups attained these skills despite impairment in declarative memory as compared to the control group on a recognition memory test for words presented during the mirror-image reading task, as well as on a questionnaire regarding details of previous testing sessions.

Results of the control and PTA groups' performance on the mirror-image reading task are presented in Figure 26.10. On this task, subjects were asked to read aloud three-letter words arranged in triads, presented on slides projected in mirror-reversed fashion. Thirty-nine word triads were developed and randomly divided into groups for the four sessions. In sessions 2 through 4, the learning sessions consisted of three trials with six triads per trial (three unique, three repeated in random sequence). Session 1 included only two trials, with four unique triads and two repeated triads per trial. Two CHI patients were excluded from analysis, as they failed to achieve a criterion cutoff time for correctly reading the word triads. Figure 26.10 shows that mirror-image

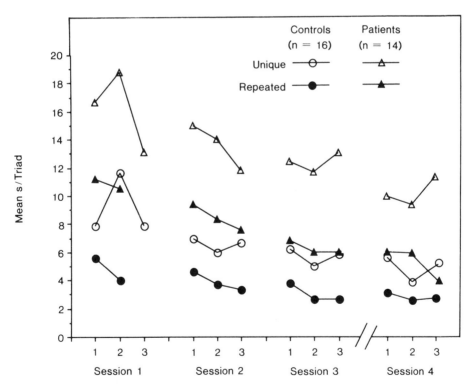

FIGURE 26.10. Latencies for mirror-image reading across trials plotted against sessions for CHI and control groups. Latencies for reading word triads presented only once (unique) and for triads presented in each trial (repeated) are plotted separately. Note that only two trials of repeated triads were given in session 1, whereas three trials were given under each condition in sessions 2–4. From "Procedural Memory during Posttraumatic Amnesia in Survivors of Severe Closed Head Injury: Implications for Rehabilitation" (p. 914) by J. Ewert, H. S. Levin, M. G. Watson, and Z. Kalisky, 1989, *Archives of Neurology, 46,* 911–916. Copyright 1989 by the American Medical Association. Reprinted by permission of the publisher.

reading latencies in the PTA group declined across the initial three sessions for both unique and repeated word triads. Further analysis indicated a linear trend of improvement across sessions for both the unique and repeated words. The decline in reading latencies for unique words was comparable between the PTA and control groups across sessions, whereas the reduction in reading latency for repeated words was greater in the PTA group. It can also be seen that mirror-image reading continued to improve in session 4, which was administered following resolution of PTA. Analysis indicated that reading times had indeed significantly declined for repeated word triads in session 4 as compared to session 3. These results indicate that the PTA group had clearly demonstrated acquisition of pattern-analyzing skills necessary for reading words presented in this mirror image. Ewert et al. (1989) postulated that the facilitative effect of repeated word triads for the PTA group may have been related to priming effects.

Further research on procedural learning and priming effects among PTA patients will be valuable in furthering our understanding of implicit learning in amnesic syndromes, since this population demonstrates a unique combination of disorientation, severely impaired cognitive functioning, and pathophysiology that frequently involves diffuse as well as focal injury.

Directions for Future Research

We anticipate application of information-processing paradigms and nonverbal measures to elucidate further the PTA and RA that characterize the early stages of recovery from nonmissile head injury. As we have shown, impaired consciousness is related to PTA duration, but other factors are also contributory. Concurrent assessment of various types of attention (e.g., selective vs. vigilant) could determine the contribution of nonretentive defects to PTA. In this connection, the P300 or other physiological measures may prove to be useful.

We also anticipate that amnesia resulting from brain injury will be studied more intensively to elucidate the neuropsychology of memory, and to evaluate the capacity for potential benefits associated with procedural learning and possible priming effects during PTA. Technological advances in activation and neuroimaging procedures could permit visualization of regional changes in cerebral metabolism that parallel the onset and resolution of traumatic amnesia.

ACKNOWLEDGMENTS

Our research reported in this chapter was supported by Grant No. NS 21889 from the National Institute of Neurologic Disorder and Stroke. We are grateful to Lori Bertolino for assistance in data analysis, and to Angela D. Thompson for manuscript preparation.

REFERENCES

Albert, M. S., Butters, N., & Levin, J. (1979). Temporal gradients in the retrograde amnesia of patients with alcoholic Korsakoff's disease. *Archives of Neurology, 36*, 211-216.

Benson, D. F., & Geschwind, N. (1967). Shrinking retrograde amnesia. *Journal of Neurology, Neurosurgery and Psychiatry, 30*, 539-544.

Benton, A. L., Van Allen, M. W., & Fogel, M. L. (1964). Temporal orientation in cerebral disease. *Journal of Nervous and Mental Disease, 139*, 110-119.

Buschke, H. (1974). Components of verbal learning in children: Analysis by selective reminding. *Journal of Experimental Child Psychology, 18*, 488-496.

Buschke, H., & Fuld, P. A. (1974). Evaluating storage, retention, and retrieval in disordered memory and learning. *Neurology, 24*, 1019-1025.

Brooks, D. N., & Baddeley, A. (1976). What can amnesic patients learn? *Neuropsychologia, 14*, 111-112.

Cohen, N. J., & Squire, L. R. (1980). Preserved learning and retention of pattern-analyzing skills in amnesia: The association of knowing how and knowing what. *Science, 210*, 207-210

Corkin, S. (1968). Acquisition of motor skill after bilateral mesial temporal-lobe excision. *Neuropsychologia, 6*, 255-265.

Daniel, W. F., Crovitz, H. F., & Weiner, R. D. (1987). Neuropsychological aspects of disorientation. *Cortex, 23*, 169-187.

Eslinger, P. E., & Damasio, A. R. (1986). Preserved motor learning in Alzheimer's disease: Implications for anatomy and behavior. *Journal of Neuroscience, 6*, 3006-3009.

Ewert, J., Levin, H. S., Watson, M. G., & Kalisky, Z. (1989). Procedural memory during posttraumatic amnesia in survivors of severe closed head injury: Implications for rehabilitation. *Archives of Neurology, 46*, 911-916.

Ewing-Cobbs, L., Levin, H. S., Fletcher, J. M., Miner, M. E., & Eisenberg, H. M. (1990). The Children's Orientation and Amnesia Test: Relationship to severity of acute head injury and to recovery of memory. *Neurosurgery, 27*(5), 683-691.

Fletcher, J. M. (1985). Memory for verbal and nonverbal stimuli in learning disability subgroups: Analysis by selective reminding. *Journal of Experimental Child Psychology, 40*, 244-259.

Fortuny, L. A. I., Briggs, M., Newcombe, F., Ratcliff, G., & Thomas, C. (1980). Measuring the duration of post traumatic amnesia. *Journal of Neurology, Neurosurgery and Psychiatry, 43*, 377-379.

Gardner, H., Boller, F., Moreines, J., & Butters, N. (1973). Retrieving information from Korsakoff's patients: Effect of categorical cues and reference to the test. *Cortex, 9*, 165-175.

Geschwind, N. (1982). Disorders of attention: A frontier in neuropsychology. *Philosophical Transactions of the Royal Society of London, B. 298*, 173-185.

Gronwall, C., & Wrightson, P. (1980). Duration of post-traumatic amnesia after mild head injury. *Journal of Clinical Neuropsychology, 2*, 51-60.

Heindel, W. C., Butters, N., & Salmon, D. P. (1988). Impaired learning of a motor skill in patients with Huntington's disease. *Behavioral Neuroscience, 102*, 141-147.

High, W. M., Jr., Levin, H. S., & Gary, H. E., Jr. (1990). Recovery of orientation following closed head injury. *Journal of Clinical and Experimental Neuropsychology, 12*, 703-714.

Jennett, B., & Teasdale, G. (1981). *Management of head injuries*. Philadelphia: F. A. Davis.

Levin, H. S., Benton, A. L., & Grossman, R. G. (1982). *Neurobehavioral consequences of closed head injury*. New York: Oxford University Press.

Levin, H. S., High, W. M., Jr., & Eisenberg, H. M. (1988). Learning and forgetting during posttraumatic amnesia in head injured patients. *Journal of Neurology, Neurosurgery, and Psychiatry, 51*, 14-20.

Levin, H. S., High, W. M., Jr., Meyers, C. A., Von Lau.fen, A., Hayden, M. E., & Eisenberg, H. M. (1985). Impairment of remote memory after closed head injury. *Journal of Neurology, Neurosurgery and Psychiatry, 48*, 556-563.

Levin, H. S., O'Donnell, V. M., & Grossman, R. G. (1979). The Galveston Orientation and Amnesia Test: A practical scale to assess cognition after head injury. *Journal of Nervous and Mental Disease, 167*, 675-684.

Levin, H. S., Papanicolaou, A., & Eisenberg, H. M. (1984). Observations on amnesia after nonmissile head injury. In L. R. Squire & N. Butters (Eds.), *Neuropsychology of memory* (1st ed., pp. 247-257). New York: Guilford Press.

Milner, B. (1962). Les troubles de la mémoire accompagnant des lesions hippocampiques bilatérales. In P. Passouant (Ed.), *Physiologie de l'hippocampe*. Paris: Centre National de la Recherche Scientifique.

Moore, B. E., & Ruesch, J. (1944). Prolonged disturbances of consciousness following head injury. *New England Journal of Medicine, 230*, 445-452.

Morgan, S. F. (1981). Measuring long-term memory storage and retrieval in children. *Journal of Clinical Neuropsychology, 4*, 77-86.

Ommaya, A. K., & Gennarelli, T. A. (1974). Cerebral concussion and traumatic unconsciousness: Correlation of experimental and clinical observations on blunt head injuries. *Brain, 97*, 633-654.

Onofrj, M., Curatola, L., Malatesta, G., Bazzano, S., Colamartino, P., & Fulgente, T. (1991). Reduction of P_3 latency during outcome from posttraumatic amnesia. *Acta Neurologica Scandinavica, 83,* 273-279.

Overton, D. A. (1978). Major theories of state dependent learning. In B. T. Ho, D. W. Richards III, & D. L. Chute (Eds.), *Drug discrimination and state dependent learning.* New York: Academic Press.

Papanicolaou, A. C., Levin, H. S., Eisenberg, H. M., Moore, B. D., Goethe, K. E., & High, W. M., Jr. (1984). Evoked potential correlates of posttraumatic amnesia after closed head injury. *Neurosurgery, 14*(6), 676-678.

Porteus, S. D. (1959). *The maze test and clinical psychology.* Palo Alto, CA: Pacific Books.

Pritchard, W. S. (1981). Psychophysiology of P300. *Psychological Bulletin, 89,* 506-540.

Ribot, T. (1882). *Diseases of memory: An essay in the positive psychology.* New York: Appleton.

Russell, W. R. (1932). Cerebral involvement in head injury. *Brain, 55,* 549-603.

Russell, W. R. (1935). Amnesia following head injuries. *Lancet, ii,* 762-763.

Russell, W. R. (1971). *The traumatic amnesias.* New York: Oxford University Press.

Russell, W. R., & Nathan, P. W. (1946). Traumatic amnesia. *Brain, 69,* 183-187.

Russell, W. R., & Smith, A. (1961). Post-traumatic amnesia in closed head injury. *Archives of Neurology, 5,* 4-17.

Schacter, D. L., & Crovitz, H. F. (1977). Memory function after closed head injury: A review of the quantitative research. *Cortex, 13,* 150-176.

Schacter, D. L., Cooper, L. A., Tharan, M., & Rubens, A. B. (1991). Preserved priming of novel objects in patients with memory disorders. *Journal of Cognitive Neuroscience, 3*(2), 117-130.

Shimamura, A. P. (1986). Priming effects in amnesia: Evidence for a dissociable memory function. *Quarterly Journal of Experimental Psychology, 38A,* 619-644.

Shimamura, A. P., & Squire, L. R. (1984). Paired-associate learning and priming effects in amnesia: A neuropsychological study. *Journal of Experimental Psychology: General, 113,* 556-573.

Squire, L. R. (1987). *Memory and brain.* New York: Oxford University Press.

Squire, L. R., & Cohen, N. J. (1982). Remote memory, retrograde amnesia, and the neuropsychology of memory. In L. S. Cermak (Ed.), *Human memory and amnesia.* Hillsdale, NJ: Erlbaum.

Squire, L. R., & Slater, P. C. (1975). Forgetting in very long-term memory as assessed by an improved questionnaire technique. *Journal of Experimental Psychology: Human Learning and Memory, 1,* 50-54.

Squires, K., Goodin, D., & Starr, A. (1979). Event related potentials in development, aging, and dementia. In D. Lehmann & E. Callaway (Eds.), *Human evoked potentials: Applications and problems.* New York: Plenum Press.

Teasdale, G., & Jennett, B. (1974). Assessment of coma and impaired consciousness: A practical scale. *Lancet, ii,* 81-84.

Warrington, E. K., & Weiskrantz, L. (1974). The effect of prior learning on subsequent retention in amnesic patients. *Neuropsychologia, 12,* 419-428.

Warrington, E. K., & Weiskrantz, L. (1978). Further analysis of the prior learning effect in amnesic patients. *Neuropsychologia, 16,* 169-177.

Yarnell, P. R., & Lynch, S. (1970). Progressive retrograde amnesia in concussed football players: Observation shortly postimpact. *Neurology, 20,* 416-417.

27

Implicit Memory and Errorless Learning: A Link between Cognitive Theory and Neuropsychological Rehabilitation?

ALAN D. BADDELEY

Over the past 20 years, our understanding of normal human memory has gained a great deal from the study of patients with neuropsychological deficits. The separation of working memory from long-term memory, the distinction between semantic and episodic memory, and more recently the contrast between implicit and explicit learning are all examples of this impact (Baddeley, 1990). However, while patients have helped the science of psychology, it is much less clear that the science has helped the patients (see Wilson & Patterson, 1990, for a more detailed discussion of this issue).

One might of course argue that more knowledge is always a good thing, and that in the long run it will enhance treatment. I think that one could begin to argue that theory, or at least good experimental practice, is beginning to improve methods of assessing memory. The Wechsler Memory Scale in its revised version does at least avoid its earlier practice of combining attentional measures with episodic memory measures to produce a single uninterpretable scale, although the changes seem to be pragmatic rather than theoretically based. The current interest in everyday cognition has had some influence on the development of more ecologically valid measures of memory outside the clinic, such as the Rivermead Behavioural Memory Test (Wilson, Cockburn, Baddeley, & Hiorns, 1989) and the Autobiographical Memory Interview (Kopelman, Wilson, & Baddeley, 1989). However, neither of these could strictly be regarded as involving the direct application of cognitive theory.

The picture is no more impressive in the area of treatment. Although there are good examples of the adaptation of single-case behavioral treatment designs to the enhancement of learning in amnesic patients (Wilson, 1987), these have typically used techniques ranging from imagery to the use of external aids and reminders—techniques that, with the one exception of the expanded rehearsal technique of Landauer and Bjork (1978), owe little to recent developments in cognitive psychology or neuropsychology. Studies have typically shown that methods that are effective in helping normal subjects to learn can also be adapted, given sufficient ingenuity, to help amnesic patients. The amnesics' rate of learning tends to be very slow, however, presumably because most such techniques rely on episodic memory, the very system that is impaired in the classic amnesic syndrome. Thus, although genuine progress has been made, it is limited and attributable at least as much to behavioral as to cognitive psychology.

This lack of direct applicability of cognitive psychology is particularly frustrating, since one of the major recent developments seems so directly relevant to rehabilitation. This concerns the apparent preservation of procedural or implicit learning in amnesia. Although the existence of preserved learning capacities in amnesia has been known since the last century (Parkin, 1982), it was initially thought that preservation was limited to one or two atypical forms of learning, such as conditioning and motor skill learning (Milner, 1962). However, in the late 1960s, Warrington and Weiskrantz (1968) demonstrated good learning of words and pictures when tested by fragment cueing. By the mid-1970s it was becoming clear that such preserved learning could be found in a range of perceptual, motor, and problem-solving tasks (Brooks & Baddeley, 1976; Kinsbourne & Wood, 1975). Since that time the range and variety of tasks showing preserved learning has proved to be remarkably large (Richardson-Klavehn & Bjork, 1988; Squire, 1987; Tulving & Schacter, 1990), suggesting very considerable untapped resources for learning in amnesic patients. However, despite one or two notable attempts to utilize implicit learning methods in the clinic, such resources remain largely untapped.

The one attempt with which I am familiar was made by Glisky, Schacter, and Tulving, who succeeded in using the word stem completion method of implicit learning to teach computing skills to amnesic patients (Glisky & Schacter, 1987; Glisky, Schacter, & Tulving, 1986). The rate of learning was much slower than that for subjects with normal memory, and the resultant learning appeared to be relatively inflexible, with little evidence of generalization. Although this was a notable achievement, it has not, to the best of my knowledge, so far had a clear impact either on cognitive theory or on the practice of rehabilitation.

Why has this important development in theory not been more readily applicable? As someone who has been frustrated by this issue for many years, my view is that it reflects our incomplete understanding of the phenomenon of implicit learning, and of its functional role in the adaptation of the organism to the environment. Despite the enormous amount of experimental work in this area over recent years, the area has been in a kind of pregnant chaos, with a number of terms, concepts, and frameworks being applied. All seem to be able to account for most of the results, but none seems totally satisfactory (Richardson-Klavehn & Bjork, 1988). I would like, in the remainder of this chapter, to make a possibly foolhardy attempt at producing a simple framework that allows a broad characterization of the existing evidence and provides some suggestions as to how such a framework might be used to help the amnesic patient.

A Speculative Framework

I want to begin by taking a speculative evolutionary perspective. Suppose one were trying to design an organism with the capacity to learn and to adapt to a complex and changing environment. What capacities would be useful? I suggest that, first of all, the organism would need a range of sensory channels through which it could monitor the environment. Since any given object will tend to have correlated visual, tactile, haptic, olfactory, and auditory characteristics, it would be useful to have a system that allowed these various associated sources of information to be integrated within a single system—a process that is likely to require at least a temporary form of storage. In short, it would be useful to give the organism the basis of a working memory, complete with a method of focusing attention on the resulting construction. Conscious awareness, perhaps?

Given that the environment is complex and changing, though coherent, it would be useful if the organism could learn. One form of learning might simply involve observing the frequency of objects and events, and of any correlation among such observations; such a learning mechanism could in principle be arranged to give more weight either to the frequency of events or to their recency, depending on whether that particular subsystem is mainly concerned with creating a stable model of the world or is more concerned with its current state. Learning where one can typically find food would be an example of the former; maintaining current orientation while wandering through a familiar environment would probably demand the latter, a system with a strong recency component.

The type of simple learning system I have so far described is essentially concerned with the accumulation and averaging of data. Such systems are not likely to be good at separately storing individual episodes in a form that allows them to be retrieved and used to predict the future. I suggest that these basic systems for learning by accumulation and averaging represent the many learning processes that have been labeled "implicit learning," "procedural learning," or "priming," and what they have in common is that they do not require the more complex system I shall describe next.

This is a system that allows specific individual episodes to be stored and subsequently retrieved. The need to have separable episodes means that a rich coding system is required—a system that is capable of linking arbitrary events that happen to occur together, possibly only on a single occasion. This is of course the system that is typically referred to as "episodic memory" or sometimes "autobiographical memory." It appears to be very sensitive to damage to a neural circuit involving the temporal lobes, hippocampi, thalamus, and mammillary bodies, but probably also depends for adequate retrieval on the executive functions of working memory, which may well depend critically on frontal lobe functioning.

The capacity to associate the various possible arbitrary features of a given episode, together with a content-addressable retrieval process, allows specific individual events to be retrieved. By providing appropriate temporal or contextual cues, the system can also answer questions of when an event occurred, or what happened at a specified time.

Semantic memory or knowledge retrieval is assumed to be based on the same system as episodic memory, but retrieval in this case is concerned with consistencies across episodes rather than with isolating a specific event. Semantic memory is based on the residue of multiple episodes; hence amnesic patients are likely to have relatively normal access to semantic memories formed before their illness, but to have difficulty in building new semantic systems.

My speculative framework clearly makes assumptions that are still not universally accepted, and one might therefore regard it as premature. Although I think all the assumptions can be defended strongly, lack of space prohibits that option. Instead, I shall try to make the case that the framework, whatever its ultimate fate, offers a possible way of applying advances in theory to the practice of neuropsychological rehabilitation.

Implicit Learning and Rehabilitation

The basic question is simple: Why is it apparently so hard to use implicit learning as a basis for rehabilitation?

One reason is that implicit learning may not necessarily lead to normal performance in amnesic patients. This was brought home to us in a study in which a range of neuropsychological patients attempted to learn to enter the date and time into an electronic calculator and memory aid (Wilson, Baddeley, & Cockburn, 1989). The operation involves about five simple steps and is mastered by normal subjects within two or three trials. It is a procedural task in which explicit recollection of the experience of learning is not necessary for performance, and yet it proved extremely difficult for our patients with defective episodic memory.

We suggested that the reason for this failure is that although the task itself is procedural, the number of steps to be mastered exceeds the capacity of working memory, typically producing at least one error on trial 1. Normal subjects on trial 2 are able to use episodic memory to recollect the error and correct it. Amnesic patients however, tend to repeat their earlier attempts, including errors that they fail to recall and correct.

I was reminded of one of the conclusions from an earlier paper (Brooks & Baddeley, 1976): that the tasks that showed preserved learning in our amnesic patients tended to be those in which errors were few, and in which learning was measured in terms of faster performance or more time on target. The potential importance of errors was further emphasized in a pilot study on implicit learning in amnesia patients by a research student at the Applied Psychology Unit, Robin Green (personal communication, 1990). She attempted to teach her subjects a list of words, using the stem completion cueing technique. However, instead of beginning by presenting the words whole, she began by presenting the stem and asking the subject to guess the word. The amnesic patients showed very poor learning, in contrast to the preserved learning typically found with the standard procedure in which the whole word is initially presented. Once again, this unexpected lack of learning in amnesic patients suggests a problem with error correction.

One final piece of encouraging evidence comes from the description by the husband of an amnesic patient of his success in helping his wife cope with a daily routine, despite a severe memory deficit (Moakes, 1988). He adopted a strategy of organizing and planning her routine with great precision, leaving extensive lists and cues so that initially she could go through the routine without error and without recourse to memory. She is now able to cook and run the house, albeit on a very rigid and stereotyped regimen. She is also able to drive a limited number of routes, including going to the school where she has resumed her job as a secretary. It appears that David Moakes has hit on a successful strategy—one of extensive practice and avoidance of errors.

Errorless Learning and Rehabilitation

Our current hypothesis is that one of the crucial roles of episodic memory is to allow errors to be eradicated; the subject is able to recollect the error, and preferably recall how it was corrected and can thus avoid repeating it. In the absence of such recollective information, the factors that made an error occur on trial 1 will have a similar effect on subsequent trials. I suggest that procedural or implicit learning systems are subject to the problem of local minima, short-term solutions that make the optimal long-term solution less probable; I assume that one very important function of episodic memory is to allow the system to escape from such blind alleys.

Such a view has implications for both cognitive theory and for the practice of rehabilitation. At a theoretical level, it suggests a re-examination of the concept of implicit or procedural learning; is it the case that all such tasks involve the strengthening or facilitation of already existing or evoked responses? If errorful implicit learning tasks occur, will amnesic patients fail to learn them? And if we can teach episodic memory tasks by errorless learning, will this optimize learning in memory-impaired patients?

At a practical level, our hypothesis suggests a possible principle for the practice of rehabilitation—that of errorless learning, a technique that has already been studied in the animal learning laboratory (Terrace, 1963). Even if our theoretical analysis is broadly correct, much work will be needed on ways in which it might be used clinically. This is one of the problems that we are tackling in the Applied Psychology Unit's recently founded rehabilitation research section. Preliminary results are encouraging (see Wilson, Chapter 28, this volume), but we are of course still a long way from being able to claim any substantial influence of cognitive theory on rehabilitation practice.

REFERENCES

Baddeley, A. D. (1990). *Human memory: Theory and practice*. Boston: Allyn & Bacon.

Brooks, D. N., & Baddeley, A. D. (1976). What can amnesic patients learn? *Neuropsychologia, 14*, 111–122.

Glisky, E. L., & Schacter, D. L. (1987). Acquisition of domain specific knowledge in organic amnesia: Training for computer related work. *Neuropsychologia, 25*, 893–906.

Glisky, E. L., Schacter, D., & Tulving, E. (1986). Computer learning by memory impaired patients: Acquisition and retention of complex knowledge. *Neuropsychologia, 24*, 313–328.

Kinsbourne, M., & Wood, F. (1975). Short-term memory processes and the amnesic syndrome. In D. Deutsch & J. A. Deutsch (Eds.), *Short-term memory* (pp. 258–293). New York: Academic Press.

Kopelman, M. D., Wilson, B. A., & Baddeley, A. D. (1989). The autobiographical memory interview: A new assessment of autobiographical and personal semantic memory in amnesic patients. *Journal of Clinical and Experimental Neuropsychology, 11*, 724–744.

Landauer, T. K., & Bjork, R. A. (1978). Optimum rehearsal patterns and name learning. In M. M. Gruneberg, P. E. Morris, & R. N. Sykes (Eds.), *Practical aspects of memory* (pp. 625–632). London: Academic Press.

Milner, B. (1962). Les troubles de mémoire accompagnant des lesions hippocampiques bilatérales. In P. Passouant (Ed.), *Physiologie de l'hippocampe* (Report No. 107). Paris: Centre National de la Recherche Scientifique.

Moakes, D. (1988). *The viewpoint of the carer*. Paper presented at the Amnesia Association Course on Memory and Amnesia, Isle of Thorns Conference Centre, East Sussex.

Parkin, A. J. (1982). Residual learning capability in organic amnesia. *Cortex, 18,* 417–440.

Richardson-Klavehn, A., & Bjork, R. A. (1988). Measures of memory. *Annual Review of Psychology, 39,* 475–543.

Squire, L. R. (1987). *Memory and the brain*. New York: Oxford University Press.

Terrace, H. S. (1963). Discrimination learning with and without "errors." *Journal of the Experimental Analysis of Behavior, 6,* 1–27.

Tulving, E., & Schacter, D. L. (1990). Priming and human memory systems. *Science, 247,* 301–306.

Warrington, E. K., & Weiskrantz, L. (1968). New methods of testing long-term retention with special reference to amnesic patients. *Nature, 217,* 972–974.

Wilson, B. A. (1987). *Rehabilitation of memory*. New York: Guilford Press.

Wilson, B. A., Baddeley, A. D., & Cockburn, J. M. (1989). How do old dogs learn new tricks: Teaching a technological skill to brain injured people. *Cortex, 27,* 115–119.

Wilson, B. A., Cockburn, J., Baddeley, A. D., & Hiorns, R. (1989). The development and validation of a test battery for detecting and monitoring everyday memory problems. *Journal of Clinical and Experimental Neuropsychology, 11,* 855–870.

Wilson, B. A., & Patterson, K. E. (1990). Theory and practice in rehabilitation. *Applied Cognitive Psychology, 4,* 247–260.

28

Rehabilitation and Memory Disorders

BARBARA A. WILSON

The Role of Rehabilitation

McLellan (1991) offers a definition of rehabilitation that is particularly suited to the field of memory disorders, where rehabilitation can seldom if ever be considered a cure in the sense that normal memory will return after treatment. He writes: "Rehabilitation is an active process whereby people who are disabled by injury or disease work together with professional staff, relatives and members of the wider community to achieve their optimum physical, psychological, social and vocational wellbeing" (p. 785). Although neuropsychologists do not claim to cure severe memory disorders, they can nevertheless work together with amnesic or memory-impaired people and their relatives to reduce the effects of memory problems as experienced in the everyday lives of both the injured and the members of their immediate community.

Memory rehabilitation rarely concentrates solely on restoration of function (probably impossible with severely amnesic patients). It is more uusually concerned with encouraging people to use their residual skills more efficiently; with teaching compensatory strategies; and with designing or restructuring environments to enable memory-impaired people to lead a more normal life, free from the emotional and behavioral concomitants associated with severe memory problems.

The Influence of Theory

Treatment programs that are aimed at rehabilitating memory disorders, and are encompassed within the framework implied by the definition above, will be influenced most broadly by the three disciplines of neuropsychology, cognitive psychology, and behavioral psychology. Neuropsychology provides a means of understanding the organization of the brain, as well as potential methodologies for assessing cognitive strengths and weaknesses of individuals. Knowledge thereby gained can be used to explain and predict memory difficulties after cerebral lesions, and can influence the design of programs that capitalize on intact areas of the brain. So, for example, a person whose problems are primarily verbal following left-hemisphere damage can be encouraged to turn verbal tasks into visuospatial ones, thus employing skills dependent on the intact right hemisphere.

Cognitive psychology, and cognitive neuropsychology, provide us with theoretical models of memory functioning. These models allow us to conceptualize disorders and encourage more precise analyses of memory functioning. The double dissociation between short-term memory and long-term learning, for example, might seem puzzling when viewed as an empirical phenomenon, but makes sense when viewed in the light of the working memory model created by Baddeley and Hitch (1974).

Although there is very little in the way of a direct relationship between neuropsychology or cognitive (neuro)psychology and actual treatment of patients, it is nevertheless true to say that principles and practices from these disciplines have enabled us to diagnose particular deficits with precision. In other words, these disciplines can accurately pinpoint what is wrong in terms of the actual cognitive deficit, but they cannot then tell us how to put things right. Of course, at this stage in the development of these disciplines we should not expect them to do this, even though the potential for achieving this may be there. Neither should we expect them to be able to comment on the social and environmental consequences of a cognitive deficit, even though these are part of the brief of rehabilitationists, given their role as defined above. After accurate assessment of cognitive deficit, then, the rehabilitationist will need to make connections between test results obtained while measuring cognitive deficit and the manifestation of consequent disability in the daily life of the patient.

It is at this stage that behavioral psychology plays such an important role, because this discipline can provide us with further assessment procedures that specify and measure problems as manifested in the everyday life of a patient, and can also offer behavioral treatments that might overcome these problems and lead to more desirable or comfortable behavior on the part of the patient within a community. A further benefit derived from behavioral psychology is that it offers us the means of evaluating treatment effectiveness. Obviously, treatment techniques from behavioral psychology, such as shaping, chaining, modeling, behavioral contracts, and others, may need to be modified for use with people with severe memory problems.

One of the most influential behavioral models is that designed by Kanfer and Saslow (1969), known as SORKC. The acronym stands for "stimulus–organism–response–contingencies–consequences," and can be used to plan memory rehabilitation programs. A major strength of this model is that it can take into account the neuropsychological and neurological status of the patient. For example, a 60-year-old right-hemisphere stroke patient, F. S. (Wilson, in press), was referred for memory therapy because (1) she could not pay attention in physiotherapy sessions and was unable to complete her physiotherapy exercises; (2) she kept forgetting the purpose of her actions in occupational therapy and was thus considered a danger to herself and others in the kitchen; and (3) she could not find her way around the rehabilitation center. By applying the SORKC model to one of these problems—getting lost in the rehabilitation center—we can demonstrate how it influenced selection of treatment strategies.

Stimulus   F. S. asked to return to her ward at the end of her physiotherapy session.

Organism	F. S. had hemianopia and unilateral neglect. Her verbal memory was unimpaired. Her poor topographical memory was (at least in part) secondary to visuospatial deficits.
Response	F. S. attempted to find the ward but failed to take the shortest route.
Contingency	Partial reinforcement in operation. Sometimes F. S. was guided by a therapist or fellow patient; sometimes she wandered aimlessly.
Consequences	F. S. was either taken to her ward or rescued. She had no opportunity to succeed on her own.

As a result of this analysis, it was decided to (1) use F. S.'s relatively intact verbal skills to teach her the route to the ward; and (2) provide an opportunity for her to learn the correct route, thus reinforcing success. The procedure was as follows: F. S. was met at the end of one physiotherapy session by the neuropsychologist, who then led the way to the ward while F. S. recorded directions on an audiocassette, avoiding visuospatial descriptions as far as possible (e.g., "Now I am going along the brick wall by physiotherapy; now I am going under the covered pathway"). F. S. was then required to listen to the recording each time she left physiotherapy for the ward with the psychologist. After three successful attempts, F. S. was asked to find her way without the recording. Learning was very rapid, and the same procedure was used to teach other routes.

The influence of all three disciplines is present in the program described above. Neuropsychology taught us to capitalize on the cognitive strengths of F. S.'s intact left hemisphere; cognitive psychology provided some of the procedures for assessing F. S.'s memory and perceptual deficits; and a structure for planning treatment was based on principles and techniques from behavioral psychology.

Practical Approaches

The fact that little evidence exists to suggest that restoration of memory powers can result from any of the treatments so far devised should not deter us from rehabilitating patients to their optimum levels of achievement. Given our previous definition of rehabilitation, many strategies can be pursued that will lead to improvements in patients' well-being and encourage reasonable adjustment to the demands of daily living. Memory-impaired people and their families need therapy that will enable them to understand and cope with difficulties that arise as a result of memory impairment. People can be taught strategies that will, if generalized to daily living, enable them to compensate for or bypass problems caused by impaired memory.

Providing information and explanations about the nature of memory deficit can improve the emotional well-being of both patients and carers. Amnesic patients may think that they are going crazy or having a psychiatric disorder, or that their difficulties are caused by some fault of their own. A simple logbook containing basic information that can be easily referred to may be a major comfort to a memory-impaired person. Relaxation exercises can also reduce anxiety, and role-playing exercises can teach people how to explain their memory problems to people with whom they interact.

For people with memory problems whose intellectual capacities are also significantly damaged (such as those suffering from Alzheimer's disease), perhaps the only realistic approach is to structure or adapt the environment so that it is possible for them to get through their daily lives without being dependent on memory. Reality orientation incorporates this latter approach by using labels, signposts, and color coding. Verbal environments can also be changed. If a particular question or statement triggers repetitions or outbursts on the part of the impaired person, then those who come into contact with that person must be encouraged not to use such questions or statements. A British musician, C. W., who became very densely amnesic in 1985 following herpes simplex encephalitis and who remains hospitalized at this writing, as deeply amnesic as ever, is less prone to outbursts of anxiety and aggression because those around him have learned to alter their behavior. For example, members of the staff usually greet him by his surname (Mr. W.) rather than by his first name, as is common with long-stay patients. This is because staff members are always seen as strangers by C. W., however long he has been treated by them. A more formal behavior on the staff's part is less unnerving for him than demonstrable affection from perceived strangers. A psychology trainee, Avi Schmueli, demonstrated that C. W.'s episodes of belching and minor seizures were associated with changes of activity, so efforts were made to reduce these behaviors by keeping a more constant environment.

Few people are as impaired as C. W. In a long-term follow-up study of 54 people originally referred for memory therapy 5 to 10 years earlier (Wilson, 1991a), only 9 were living in long-term care. Most were residing with relatives or friends, and most were making better use of memory aids and strategies than they were at the end of their previous rehabilitation.

External memory aids are often the lifelines of those memory-disordered people who have learned to use them effectively. One common response when a therapist or psychologist introduces such aids is for the patient to reject them in the belief that dependency on memory aids will impede natural recovery of memory functioning. It is also common for patients to forget to use the aids or to use them inefficiently. Therapists, doctors, nurses, and physiotherapists mistakenly expect patients to use the aids spontaneously when in fact programs are required to find aids that are suited to individuals, who are then taught how to use them effectively and constantly. Sohlberg and Mateer (1989), for example, describe a structured program they use to teach the use of personal organizers. The steps involved in designing a behavior modification program (Wilson, 1987) can be employed to teach the use of an external aid. An errorless learning procedure (see below) can also be incorporated. Generalization, or transfer of learning, must be built into the program. This means that the use of aids must be taught in several locations so that general use is encouraged, rather than usage that is merely specific to one location or situation. Indeed, it could be argued that failure to teach generalization is the most common cause for lack of success in many rehabilitation programs.

The long-term follow-up study referred to above also showed that subjects were more prepared to rely upon aids and strategies once they were back in their homes, where the need for such help became more obvious. On the basis of this finding, it could be argued that the teaching of reliance upon memory aids should occur in patients' homes rather than in hospitals or rehabilitation centers.

Finally, we can help people use their damaged residual memory skills more efficiently through the use of mnemonics and rehearsal strategies (Wilson, 1989). These will not improve memory functioning per se, but will enable people to learn more efficiently or quickly—as long as we do not expect memory-impaired people themselves to use mnemonics on their own. It should always be stressed that it is usual for a neuropsychologist, therapist, or relative to use mnemonics to enhance the learning of information for a patient; it is a mistake to regard mnemonics as tools used by patients themselves.

Future Developments

If real advances are to be made in rehabilitation of memory disorders, then rehabilitation itself must continue to be influenced by new theoretical principles and paradigms that are themselves the result of research carried out by experts in the three fields mentioned above. Current work in Cambridge, England, has important implications for broadening our approach to rehabilitation of memory-impaired people. This work has been influenced by studies of errorless discrimination learning from behavioral psychology (e.g., Terrace, 1963, 1966) and by the studies of implicit learning in memory-impaired people from cognitive neuropsychology (e.g., Brooks & Baddeley, 1976; Graf & Schacter, 1985).

Terrace's work in the 1960s showed that it was possible to teach pigeons to discriminate a red from a green key with very few (or no) errors. This was achieved by teaching a pecking response to the red key first. When this response was well established, the red key was darkened and shown very briefly while the pigeon was not in a good position to peck, thus preventing an incorrect response. The darkened key was shown for increasing lengths of time, as well as gradually changing color to green. The result of this experiment was that the pigeon only pecked at the red key. This fading-in procedure was also employed to teach the pigeon a more complex discrimination between horizontal and vertical lines. In 1967 Sidman and Stoddard taught mentally handicaped children to discriminate between circles and ellipses, using an errorless learning procedure similar to Terrace's.

Glisky and Schacter (1987, 1989) tried to use the implicit learning abilities of amnesic subjects to teach them computer technology. Although some success was achieved, it was at the expense of considerable time and effort. This and other attempts to build on the relatively intact skills of amnesic subjects have been disappointing so far. One reason for the failures and anomalies could be that once amnesic subjects have made an error, that error gets repeated. If procedural or implicit learning involves a simple incrementing of habit whenever a response is formed, then an erroneous response will tend to strengthen the error, making trial-and-error learning a slow and laborious process.

In a research project in progress, Alan Baddeley and I have posed this question: "Do amnesic subjects learn better when prevented from making errors during the learning process?" We have so far seen 16 patients with severe memory disorders and given each of them two lists of five-letter words. One list is presented in an errorful learning way and the other in an errorless way, with the order and condition counterbalanced across subjects. In the errorful condition, subjects are told, "I am thinking of a five-letter word beginning with 'br-.' Can you guess what it might be?" After three incorrect responses (or 25 seconds), in which the subject might say "brain," "bread," and "brown," the tester says, "No, good guesses, but the word is 'bring.' Please write that down." This is repeated for the remaining words, after which two further trials are conducted. So altogether the subject writes down each word three times; the incorrect guesses are not written down. In the errorless condition, the subject is told, "I am thinking of a five-letter word beginning with 'br-,' and the word is 'bring.' Please write that down." Again there are three trials. Thus, in one condition the subject is generating guesses, and in the other only correct responses are produced. This is followed in both conditions by a further nine trials over a 30-minute period. Each trial involves cueing with the first two letters and correcting any incorrect responses.

Of the 16 subjects we have seen so far, every single one of them has recalled more words in the errorless learning condition than in the errorful condition (see Table 28.1). This suggests that learning is indeed better when the subject is not allowed to guess during the learning process. The errorless learning in this study is far from perfect, however, and the results are quite unlike those from Terrace's studies. There may well be a number of reasons why results are not better. First, it is not good rehabilitation or learning practice to try to teach five items at once to anybody with learning difficulties. I have argued elsewhere that we should teach memory-impaired people one thing at a time (Wilson, 1991b). Second, words are not important or useful pieces of information for memory-impaired subjects to learn, in comparison with real-life tasks (Wilson, 1987). I would argue that we need to combine the errorless learning procedure with

TABLE 28.1. Results of 16 Memory-Impaired Subjects on Errorful and Errorless Learning (Total Correct Responses over Nine Trials)

Subject	Sex	Age	Diagnosis	Errorful	Errorless	Difference
1	M	23	Cerebral hemorrhage	15	37	22
2	M	58	Encephalitis	12	22	10
3	M	20	Carbon monoxide poisoning	26	43	17
4	M	63	Korsakoff	16	42	26
5	M	69	Encephalitis	11	35	24
6	F	44	ACoA aneurysm[a]	16	40	24
7	F	45	Encephalitis	36	41	5
8	M	67	Thalamic stroke	9	27	18
9	F	21	Head injury	18	30	12
10	M	54	Head injury	22	30	8
11	M	34	Encephalitis	18	32	14
12	F	35	Encephalitis	10	15	5
13	M	52	Encephalitis	20	27	7
14	M	34	Head injury	16	27	11
15	M	20	Head injury	16	35	19
16	F	68	ACoA aneurysm[a]	21	35	14

[a]ACoA aneurysm, anterior communicative artery aneurysm.

other principles from memory therapy such as expanding rehearsal (Landauer & Bjork, 1978; Moffat, 1989), as well as with principles from behavior modification (Alderman & Ward, 1991).

Nevertheless, the results so far are encouraging, with potential applications to the learning of names, routes, use of electronic organizers, and new skills.

REFERENCES

Alderman, N., & Ward, A. (1991). Behavioural treatment of the dysexecutive syndrome: Reduction of repetitive speech using response cost and cognitive overlearning. *Neuropsychological Rehabilitation, 1*, 65–80.

Baddeley, A. D., & Hitch, G. J. (1974). Working memory. In G. A. Bower (Ed.), *The psychology of learning and motivation* (Vol. 8). New York: Academic Press.

Brooks, D. N., & Baddeley, A. D. (1976). What can amnesics learn? *Neuropsychologia, 14*, 111–122.

Glisky, E. L., & Schacter, D. L. (1987). Acquisition of domain-specific knowledge in organic amnesia: Training for computer-related work. *Neuropsychologia, 25*, 893–906.

Glisky, E. L., & Schacter, D. L. (1989). Extending the limits of complex learning in organic amnesia: Computer training in a vocational domain. *Neuropsychologia, 27*, 107–120.

Graf, P., & Schacter, D. L. (1985). Implicit and explicit memory for new associations in normal and amnesic subjects. *Journal of Experimental Psychology: Learning, Memory, and Cognition, 11*, 501–518.

Kanfer, F. H., & Saslow, G. (1969). Behavioral diagnosis. In C. Franks (Ed.), *Behavior therapy: Appraisal and status* (pp. 417–444). New York: McGraw-Hill.

Landauer, T. K., & Bjork, R. A. (1978). Optimum rehearsal patterns and name learning. In M. M. Gruneberg, P. E. Morris, & R. N. Sykes (Eds.), *Practical aspects of memory* (pp. 625–632). London: Academic Press.

McLellan, D. L. (1991). Functional recovery and the principles of disability medicine. In M. Swash & J. Oxbury (Eds.), *Clinical neurology* (pp. 768–790). Edinburgh: Churchill Livingstone.

Moffat, N. (1989). Home based rehabilitation programs for the elderly. In L. Poon, D. Rubin, & B. Wilson (Eds.), *Everyday cognition in adult and later life* (pp. 659–680). Cambridge: Cambridge University Press.

Sidman, M., & Stoddard, L. T. (1967). The effectiveness of fading in programming simultaneous form discrimination for retarded children. *Journal of the Experimental Analysis of Behavior, 10*, 3–15.

Sohlberg, M. M., & Mateer, C. A. (1989). Training use of compensatory memory books: A three stage behavioral approach. *Journal of Clinical and Experimental Psychology, 11*, 871–891.

Terrace, H. S. (1963). Discrimination learning with and without "errors." *Journal of the Experimental Analysis of Behavior, 6*, 1–27.

Terrace, H. S. (1966). Stimulus control. In W. K. Honig (Ed.), *Operant behavior: Areas of research and application* (pp. 271–344). New York: Appleton-Century-Crofts.

Wilson, B. A. (1987). *Rehabilitation of memory*. New York: Guilford Press.

Wilson, B. A. (1989). Models of cognitive rehabilitation. In R. L. Wood & P. Eames (Eds.), *Models of brain injury rehabilitation* (pp. 117–141). London: Chapman & Hall.

Wilson, B. A. (1991a). Long term prognosis of patients with severe memory disorders. *Neuropsychological Rehabilitation, 1*, 117–134.

Wilson, B. A. (1991b). Behavior therapy in the treatment of neurologically impaired adults. In P. R. Martin (Ed.), *Handbook of behavior therapy and psychological science: An integrative approach* (pp. 227–252). Elmsford, NY: Pergamon Press.

Wilson, B. A. (in press). Rehabilitating memory disorders. In A. Mazzuchi (Ed.), *La riabilitazione neuropsicologica* (2nd ed.). Bologna: Societa Editrice il Mulino.

Studies of Monkeys and Rodents

This section consists of 16 chapters describing progress in the neuropsychology of memory based on studies of rodents and monkeys. One reason why the study of patients has been useful for understanding how the brain accomplishes learning and memory is that it is possible to carry out extensive and detailed analysis of cognition itself. Indeed, it could be said that were it not for information derived from patients with hippocampal damage, we would still be uncertain whether damage to the hippocampus in experimental animals should be understood in terms of a memory problem. Nevertheless, studies of experimental animals provide unique opportunities to extend our knowledge, and it is fair to say that most of what we currently know about the anatomy, pharmacology, and physiology of memory is based on studies of rats, monkeys, and other animals. Here, it is possible to ask directly about brain organization.

Chapters 29, 30, and 31 present anatomical, cognitive, and physiological data about the organization of memory based on studies of nonhuman primates. The remaining chapters in this section are based largely on work with rodents. Chapters 32 and 33 show how studies with rodents can illuminate issues of age-related cognitive impairment. Chapters 34 and 35 show how memory can be modulated by treatments that occur close to the time of learning. The second of these two chapters also considers related work with humans. Chapter 36 considers the function of the rodent hippocampus in memory, and Chapter 37 contrasts the roles of the hippocampus with the role of prefrontal cortex. Chapters 38 and 39 focus on diencephalic brain structures important for memory, and they indicate that considerable progress has been made toward the heretofore elusive goal of establishing an animal model of Korsakoff's syndrome. Chapter 40 considers brain systems that are important for the acquisition and storage of emotional memories. Chapter 41 also considers brain systems involved in emotional memories, by considering how fear modulates the startle response, which is subserved by a well-studied brain system.

The final three chapters in this section provide a more conceptual treatment of particular themes in the neuropsychology of learning and memory that have been developed from studies of experimental animals. Chapter 42 considers the idea of multiple forms of memory; Chapter 43 considers how the analysis of receptive fields has illuminated the function of neocortex during simple forms of conditioning; and Chapter 44 considers the kind of knowledge acquired during classical conditioning procedures.

29

The Components of the Medial Temporal Lobe Memory System

STUART ZOLA-MORGAN and LARRY R. SQUIRE

Studies of human amnesia and studies of an animal model of amnesia in the nonhuman primate have helped clarify which brain structures and connections in the temporal lobe are involved in memory functions. This chapter focuses on some of the work with monkeys that has been important in identifying the components of the medial temporal lobe memory system. This work has been guided by the facts of human amnesia and has depended, in large part, on the use of amnesia-sensitive tasks developed to study memory in monkeys. Findings from these tasks have helped characterize the effects on memory (e.g., the severity, duration, and pattern of impairment) that follow damage to specific structures. In this way, the animal model has allowed a systematic investigation of which structures in the medial temporal lobe are important for memory.

In our work with monkeys, we currently use five tasks to assess memory function. Three tasks (trial-unique delayed-nonmatching-to-sample, delayed retention of object discriminations, and eight-pair concurrent discrimination learning; Squire, Zola-Morgan, & Chen, 1988; Zola-Morgan & Squire, 1990b) are known to be sensitive to the kind of memory that is impaired in human amnesia (sometimes termed "declarative memory" or "explicit memory"), and two tasks (pattern discrimination learning and motor skill learning; Zola-Morgan & Squire, 1984) assess the kind of memory that is intact in amnesia ("nondeclarative memory" or "implicit memory"). The most widely used task for demonstrating impaired memory in monkeys is the trial-unique delayed-nonmatching-to-sample task. This task requires monkeys to identify which of two objects is the novel one (see Figure 29.2). In this chapter, the effects on memory of damage to different structures in the medial temporal lobe are described mainly in terms of performance on the nonmatching-to-sample task. Findings from the two other amnesia-sensitive tasks are described when appropriate.

Structures in the Medial Temporal Lobe That Are Important for Memory

It has been known for several decades that severe memory impairment in humans can result from bilateral damage to the medial temporal region (Scoville & Milner, 1957).

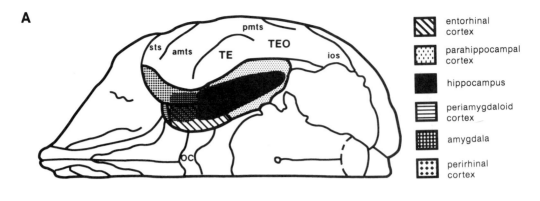

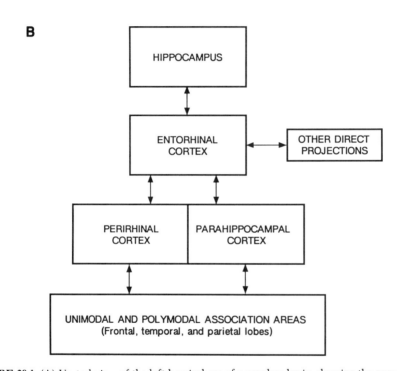

FIGURE 29.1. (A) Ventral view of the left hemisphere of a monkey brain, showing the components of the large H^+A^+ lesion that first established an animal model of human amnesia. This view shows the amygdala and hippocampus, and adjacent cortical regions included in the H^+A^+ surgery: perirhinal cortex; periamygdaloid cortex; entorhinal cortex; parahippocampal cortex. sts, superior temporal sulcus; amts, anterior middle temporal sulcus; ios, inferior occipito-temporal sulcus; TE, TEO, inferotemporal cortex. (B) A schematic view of the medial temporal lobe memory system. The entorhinal cortex is the major source of cortical projections to the hippocampus. Perirhinal and parahippocampal cortices account for approximately 60% of the cortical input to the entorhinal cortex, and they in turn receive projections from unimodal and polymodal areas in the frontal, temporal, and parietal lobes. The entorhinal cortex also receives other direct inputs from orbital frontal cortex, cingulate cortex, insular cortex, and superior temporal gyrus. As indicated, all these projections are reciprocal. From "The Neuropsychology of Memory: Parallel Findings from Humans and Nonhuman Primates" (p. 442) by S. Zola-Morgan and L. R. Squire, 1990, *Annals of the New York Academy of Sciences, 608*, 434–456. Copyright 1990 by the New York Academy of Sciences. Reprinted by permission.

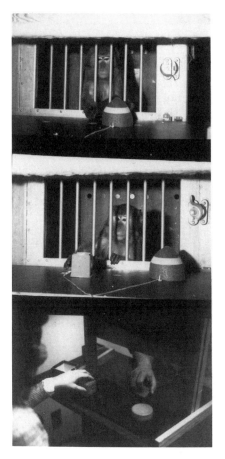

FIGURE 29.2. The trial-unique delayed-nonmatching-to-sample task. Monkeys are tested in a modified Wisconsin General Test Apparatus (WGTA; Harlow & Bromer, 1938). Top: The sample. The monkey first displaces a single object covering the middle well of a three-well food tray, and obtains a food reward. Middle: The choice. Approximately 8 seconds later, the monkey sees two objects, the original one and the novel one. The monkey must displace the novel object to obtain a food reward. New pairs of objects are used on every trial. Once the monkey learns the basic 8-second task, the interval between the sample and choice parts of the trial is increased in steps to 15 seconds, 60 seconds, and 10 minutes. This task is sensitive to medial temporal lobe damage in monkeys and humans. Bottom: The same task as it is administered to patients, using a table-top WGTA. An opaque door is raised, and the stimulus tray is moved toward the patient. A correct response uncovers a monetary reward. From "The Neuropsychology of Memory: Parallel Findings from Humans and Nonhuman Primates" (p. 440) by S. Zola-Morgan and L. R. Squire, 1990, *Annals of the New York Academy of Sciences, 608*, 434–456. Copyright 1990 by the New York Academy of Sciences. Reprinted by permission.

One of the best-studied cases of human amnesia (case H. M.) involved a patient who became severely amnesic after undergoing extensive bilateral removal of the medial temporal region, including the amygdala and the hippocampus as well as cortex adjacent to these structures. When monkeys sustained neurosurgically induced damage to the medial temporal lobe that approximated the damage sustained by patient H. M., they too exhibited severe memory impairment (Mishkin, 1982; Squire & Zola-Morgan, 1983; Mahut & Moss, 1984). The medial temporal lobe lesion in monkeys was intended to involve the amygdaloid complex and the hippocampal formation (including the hippocampus proper, the dentate gyrus, the subicular complex, and the entorhinal cortex), as well as adjacent cortex (Figure 29.1A). We have termed this lesion H^+A^+, where H refers to the hippocampus, A to the amygdala, and $^+$ to the adjacent cortical tissue.

The memory impairment following H^+A^+ lesions in monkeys is similar in many ways to the memory impairment in patients with medial temporal lobe damage (Table 29.1). In particular, monkeys with H^+A^+ lesions were severely impaired on the memory tasks that human amnesic patients also fail, including the delayed-nonmatching-to-sample task (Figure 29.3; Squire et al., 1988; Aggleton, Nicol, Huston, & Fairbairn, 1988); however, like amnesic patients, they were entirely normal at acquiring and retaining skills (Zola-Morgan & Squire, 1984).

TABLE 29.1. Characteristics of Human Amnesia That Have Been Produced in Monkeys with Large Bilateral Lesions of the Medial Temporal Lobe ($H^+ A^+$ Lesions)

Characteristic	Studies
1. Memory is impaired on several tasks, including ones identical to those failed by amnesic patients.	Zola-Morgan and Squire (1985); Zola-Morgan and Squire (1990b); Squire, Zola-Morgan, and Chen (1988)
2. Memory impairment is exacerbated by increasing the retention delay or the amount of material to be learned.	Mishkin (1978); Zola-Morgan and Squire (1985)
3. Memory impairment is exacerbated by distraction.	Zola-Morgan and Squire (1985)
4. Memory impairment is not limited to one sensory modality.	Murray and Mishkin (1984)
5. Memory impairment can be enduring.	Zola-Morgan and Squire (1985)
6. Memory for events prior to the onset of amnesia can be affected (retrograde amnesia).	Salmon, Zola-Morgan, and Squire (1987)
7. Skill-based memory is spared.	Zola-Morgan and Squire (1984); Malamut, Saunders, and Mishkin (1984)
8. Immediate memory is spared.	Overman, Ormsby, and Mishkin (1990)

Note. Adapted from "The Neuropsychology of Memory: Parallel Findings from Humans and Nonhuman Primates" (p. 438) by S. Zola-Morgan and L. R. Squire, 1990, *Annals of the New York Academy of Sciences, 608,* 434–456. Copyright 1990 by the New York Academy of Sciences. Adapted by permission.

Studies using monkeys with less extensive bilateral damage to the medial temporal region, involving primarily the hippocampal formation, also report significant memory impairment (Mahut, Zola-Morgan, & Moss, 1982; Mishkin, 1978; Zola-Morgan & Squire, 1986; Zola-Morgan, Squire, & Amaral, 1989a). We have termed this lesion H^+, and it includes the hippocampal formation (except for the anterior portion of entorhinal cortex) and the parahippocampal cortex. The H^+ lesion produces less severe memory impairment than the H^+A^+ lesion on the nonmatching-to-sample task (Figure 29.3), as well as on the other amnesia-sensitive tasks.

There are several possible explanations for the finding that the H^+A^+ lesion produces more severe memory impairment than the H^+ lesion. One possibility is that the more severe deficit occus because the amygdala is damaged in the H^+A^+ lesion but not in the H^+ lesion (Mishkin, 1978; Murray & Mishkin, 1986; Saunders, Murray, & Mishkin, 1984; Bachevalier, Parkinson, & Mishkin, 1985). A second possibility is that the H^+A^+ lesion, but not the H^+ lesion, damages cortical regions adjacent to the amygdala—that is, periamygdaloid, anterior entorhinal, and perirhinal cortices (Squire & Zola-Morgan, 1988; Zola-Morgan, Squire, & Amaral, 1989b; Zola-Morgan, Squire, Amaral, & Suzuki, 1989)—and that this cortical damage is responsible for the greater impairment. Recent experiments have addressed these two possibilities.

Monkeys with stereotaxic lesions of the amygdaloid complex (the A lesion) that spared adjacent areas of cortex (i.e., the periamygdaloid, entorhinal, and perirhinal cortices) exhibited normal performance on the delayed-nonmatching-to-sample task (Figure 29.3), as well as on other memory tasks administered during the 1.5 years after surgery (Zola-Morgan et al., 1989b). A second group of monkeys, with conjoint H^+ and A lesions (H^+A lesions), were impaired on the same memory tasks. However, the severity of impairment in the monkeys with H^+A lesions was no greater than in monkeys with H^+ lesions alone (Figure 29.3). Thus, circumscribed bilateral lesions of the amygdala did not impair memory, nor did they exacerbate the memory impairment that followed H^+ lesions alone. These findings suggested that one must look to damage other than in the amygdala to account for the severe memory impairment that follows large lesions of the medial temporal region.

In particular, these findings pointed to the importance for memory of the cortex surrounding the amygdala, which is necessarily damaged during H^+A^+ surgery but not during H^+ surgery. To help determine precisely the cortical damage that might be contributing to the impairment following H^+A^+ surgery, we re-evaluated the histological material from a previously studied H^+A^+ group (Zola-Morgan, Squire, & Mishkin, 1982; Zola-Morgan & Squire, 1984, 1985). We found that at least some of the white matter located lateral to the amygdaloid complex was damaged bilaterally. Moreover, we found significant damage to perirhinal cortex.

Recent neuroanatomical studies suggest why damage to perirhinal cortex could be important for memory (see Figure 29.1B). Specifically, perirhinal cortex and para-

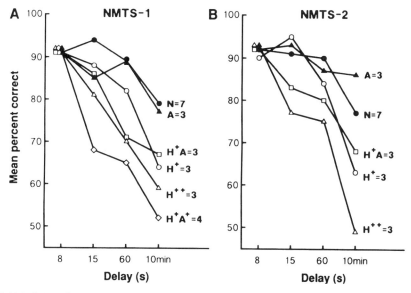

FIGURE 29.3. (A) Performance on the delayed-nonmatching-to-sample task 6 to 8 weeks after surgery by seven normal monkeys (N) and five groups of monkeys with lesions: A, circumscribed lesion of the amygdala sparing surrounding cortex; H^+, lesion of the hippocampal formation and parahippocampal cortex; H^+A, a combination of these two lesions; H^+A^+, lesion of the hippocampus, the amygdala, and adjacent cortical regions, that is, perirhinal, entorhinal, and parahippocampal cortex; H^{++}, lesion of the hippocampus and the same cortical regions damaged in the H^+A^+ lesion. The performance curve for the H^{++} group may underestimate the deficit, because one of the three animals in this group required a remedial procedure in which the sample object was presented twice instead of once. (B) Performance of the same normal monkeys as in (A) and four of the five groups with lesions on the same task 1 to 2 years later. The H^+A^+ group was not retested on this version of the nonmatching task. From "The Medial Temporal Lobe Memory System" (p. 1382) by L. R. Squire and S. Zola-Morgan, 1991, Science, 253, 1380–1386. Copyright 1991 by the American Association for the Advancement of Science. Reprinted by permission.

hippocampal cortex (the other major cortical area damaged in the H^+A^+ lesion) provide nearly two-thirds of the cortical input to entorhinal cortex (Insausti, Amaral, & Cowan, 1987). Thus, these two regions are essential for the normal exchange of information between the neocortex and the hippocampus.

We next investigated the possibility that extending the H^+ lesion forward to include the anterior entorhinal cortex and the perirhinal cortex (the H^{++} lesion) could exacerbate the impairment that follows H^+ lesions, and could produce a memory impairment as severe as that observed following H^+A^+ lesions. Monkeys with bilateral H^{++} lesions (which spared the amygdala) were as severely impaired on the delayed-nonmatching-to-sample task as monkeys with H^+A^+ lesions (Figure 29.3; Clower, Zola-Morgan, & Squire, 1990). In addition, at the longest retention inverval tested (10 minutes), monkeys with H^{++} lesions made significantly more errors than monkeys with either H^+ lesions or H^+A lesions. Moreover, the memory impairment exhibited by the monkeys with H^{++} lesions on this task persisted for 1 year after surgery. Monkeys with H^{++} and H^+A^+ lesions were also comparably impaired on a second amnesia-sensitive task (retention of object discriminations). On pattern discrimination and on the learning and retention of a motor skill task—two tasks analogous to ones amnesic patients perform well—monkeys in the H^{++} group performed normally. In a separate study (Zola-Morgan, Squire, Amaral, & Suzuki, 1989), monkeys with lesions that were limited to the perirhinal and parahippocampal cortex, and that spared the hippocampus, the amygdala, and the entorhinal cortex (PRPH lesions), exhibited impaired performance on all of the amnesia-sensitive tasks. Overall, the monkeys with PRPH lesions were as impaired or more impaired than monkeys with H^+A^+ lesions.

The findings from the H^{++} and PRPH lesions suggests that the cortical regions adjacent and anatomically related to the hippocampus are important for memory. Consistent with the idea that damage to the perirhinal cortex, and not damage to the amygdala, contributes to the H^+A^+ memory deficit was the finding that perirhinal damage was substantial in the monkeys with H^{++} lesions and PRPH lesions, but was minimal in monkeys with H^+ and H^+A lesions (Clower et al., 1990; Squire & Zola-Morgan, 1991). These findings indicate that the severe memory impairment associated with medial temporal (H^+A^+) lesions results from conjoint damage to the hippocampus and anatomically related cortex (entorhinal cortex, perirhinal cortex, and parahippocampal cortex), and not from conjoint damage to hippocampus and amygdala. Importantly, because the H^{++} and PRPH lesions produced more severe impairment than the H^+ lesion (Zola-Morgan & Squire, 1986; Zola-Morgan et al., 1989a), and because the perirhinal cortex is the only region damaged in the H^{++} and PRPH lesions but not in the H^+ lesion, it would appear that damage to the perirhinal cortex does not simply disconnect areas significant for memory. Rather, the perirhinal cortex and possibly other cortex adjacent to the hippocampus (e.g., parahippocampal cortex) may normally contribute to memory functions (Zola-Morgan, Squire, Amaral, & Suzuki, 1989; Zola-Morgan & Squire, 1990a; Squire & Zola-Morgan, 1991).

Another important conclusion from the work described thus far is that the amygdaloid complex does not contribute to the kind of memory (declarative or explicit memory) that depends on the medial temporal lobe memory system (Squire & Zola-Morgan, 1988; Zola-Morgan et al., 1989b; Zola-Morgan, Squire, Amaral, & Suzuki, 1989; Murray, 1992), although it is involved in other cognitive functions (Mishkin &

Aggleton, 1981; Murray & Mishkin, 1985; Gaffan & Harrison, 1987). Additional evidence that the amygdala is not involved in declarative memory, and that the hippocampus and the amygdala are indeed functionally distinct, comes from a study in which monkeys that sustained partial or complete damage to the amygdaloid complex exhibited less fearful behavior than normal and were unusually willing to touch and otherwise interact with novel stimuli (Zola-Morgan, Squire, Alvarez-Royo, & Clower, 1991). As long as there was no damage to the hippocampal formation or adjacent cortex, memory was intact. Conversely, monkeys with damage to hippocampal formation or associated cortex exhibited impaired memory. Unless there was also damage to the amygdala, however, emotional behavior was normal (Figure 29.4).

The Hippocampus

An additional issue concerns the effects in the monkey of lesions limited to the hippocampus alone. It is entirely possible that the memory impairment in monkeys

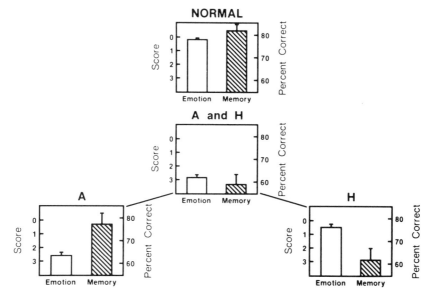

FIGURE 29.4. Memory impairment and abnormal emotional behavior are anatomically dissociable. The emotion score was obtained by measuring the responsiveness of monkeys to seven inanimate stimuli that could elicit investigatory or consummatory behavior. The memory score is the score on the delayed-nonmatching-to-sample task at a 10-minute delay. In both cases, high bars indicate normal performance (top panel). The A and H category (middle panel) includes two groups of monkeys with damage to both the hippocampal formation and the amygdala. The bottom panels include two groups with damage to the amygdala but not the hippocampal formation (A), and two groups with damage to the hippocampal formation and/or associated cortical areas but not the amygdala (H). Amygdala damage affected only emotional reactivity, and lesions of the hippocampal formation or related cortex affected only memory. Combined lesions affected both emotion and memory. From "Independence of Memory Functions and Emotional Behavior: Separate Contributions of the Hippocampal Formation and the Amygdala" (p. 217) by S. Zola-Morgan, L. R. Squire, P. Alvarez-Royo, and R. P. Clower, 1991, Hippocampus, 1, 207–220. Copyright 1991 by Churchill Livingstone, Inc. Reprinted by permission.

with H$^+$ lesions results from damage to the entorhinal cortex and parahippocampal cortex, and not to the hippocampus itself. Certainly, the relative role of the hippocampus could be illuminated by studying monkeys with circumscribed damage limited to this structure. The findings from patient R. B. (Zola-Morgan, Squire, & Amaral, 1986) showed that amnesia can be associated with a lesion limited to the hippocampus. Following an ischemic episode, patient R. B. exhibited an enduring memory impairment that resulted from a circumscribed bilateral lesion of the entire CA1 field of the hippocampus; the lesion spared the entorhinal, perirhinal, and parahippocampal cortices. Until recently, however, it has been difficult to make selective lesions limited to the hippocampus in monkeys. A direct surgical approach to the hippocampus necessarily damages the entorhinal and parahippocampal cortex, and a stereotaxic approach based on available monkey brain atlases is problematic because of the variability between monkeys in the size and shape of the hippocampus.

Recently, however, we were successful in combining stereotaxic neurosurgery with magnetic resonance (MR) imaging to make accurate surgical lesions within the hippocampus (Alvarez-Royo, Clower, Zola-Morgan, & Squire, 1991). Prior to surgery, small radio-opaque landmarks were anchored to each monkey's skull, and the monkey was then imaged (Figure 29.5). The landmarks, visible in the images, were then used to

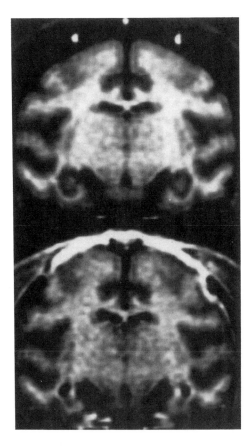

FIGURE 29.5. Top: Preoperative coronal image of a monkey brain, showing three beads filled with copper sulfate anchored to the skull, which were used as landmarks to establish stereotaxic coordinates for making hippocampal lesions. Bottom: Postoperative image of the same monkey in a plane perpendicular to the long axis of the hippocampus. The lesion of the hippocampus at this level appears virtually complete, and the surrounding cortex has been spared. From "Stereotaxic Lesions of the Hippocampus in Monkeys: Determination of Surgical Coordinates and Analysis of Lesions Using Magnetic Resonance Imaging" (p. 229) by P. Alvarez-Royo, R. P. Clower, S. Zola-Morgan, and L. R. Squire, 1991, *Journal of Neuroscience Methods, 38,* 223–232. Copyright 1991 by Elsevier Science Publishers. Reprinted by permission.

generate individualized stereotaxic coordinates for each monkey. Postoperative analysis of MR images for four monkeys prepared in this way shows that they sustained bilateral damage to the hippocampus, dentate gyrus, and subiculum (the H lesion). The perirhinal, entorhinal, and parahippocampal cortices were almost entirely spared. On the nonmatching-to-sample task, at delays of 10 minutes, monkeys with H lesions were as impaired as monkeys with H^+ lesions. Monkeys with H lesions were significantly less impaired than H^+ monkeys on the two other amnesia-sensitive tasks (retention of object discriminations and eight-pair concurrent discrimination learning).

We have also examined the effects on memory of selective hippocampal damage, using a noninvasive procedure to produce cerebral ischemia in the monkey. This procedure consistently results in significant bilateral cell loss in the hippocampus, involving the CA1 and CA2 fields and the hilar portion of the dentate gyrus (the ISC lesion; Zola-Morgan, Squire, Rempel, & Clower, in press). Detailed analysis of the CA1 field revealed that cell loss was greater in the posterior portion of the hippocampus than in the anterior portion. On the delayed-nonmatching-to-sample task, monkeys with ISC lesions performed similarly to monkeys with H^+ lesions. Moreover, their impairment on the task persisted during a period of 6–8 months after surgery. On the two other amnesia-sensitive tasks, monkeys with ISC lesions, like the monkeys with H lesions, performed better than monkeys with H^+ lesions ($p = .06$ for both tasks).

The findings from monkeys in the ISC and H groups, together with findings described earlier in the chapter, make several important points. First, even incomplete damage to the hippocampus (the ISC and the H groups) is sufficient to impair memory in monkeys, just as in humans (case R. B.). Second, the finding of enduring memory impairment after lesions limited to the hippocampus contrasts sharply with the transient effects on memory following damage to the fornix or mammillary nuclei (Zola-Morgan et al., 1989a). This finding emphasizes the importance for memory functions of the reciprocal connections between the hippocampus and adjacent cortical regions, rather than the subcortical projections of the hippocampus through the fornix to the mammillary nuclei. Finally, the finding that partial damage to the hippocampus can produce significant memory impairment contrasts dramatically with the finding that complete lesions of the amygdaloid complex produced no detectable memory impairment on any of the amnesia-sensitive memory tasks.

Conclusions

Cumulative and systematic work with monkeys suggests that in the medial temporal lobe, the hippocampus, together with adjacent, anatomically related areas of cortex (including the entorhinal, perirhinal, and parahippocampal cortices), performs a crucial role in establishing declarative (explicit) memory. Although the amygdaloid complex is likely to be importantly involved in other cognitive functions, including certain kinds of nondeclarative memory functions, it does not appear to be an essential component of the declarative memory system. Indeed, it now appears that the effects on declarative memory observed in previous studies involving the amygdaloid complex resulted from damage to the perirhinal cortex, which necessarily occurs during neurosurgical removal of the amygdala.

ACKNOWLEDGMENTS

The research reported in this chapter was supported by the Medical Research Service of the Department of Veterans Affairs, the Office of Naval Research, National Institutes of Health Grant No. NS19063, National Institute of Mental Health Grant No. MH24600, and the McKnight Foundation.

REFERENCES

Aggleton, J. P., Nicol, R. M., Huston, A. E., & Fairbairn, A. F. (1988). The performance of amnesic subjects on tests of experimental amnesia in animals: Delayed nonmatching-to-sample and concurrent learning. *Neuropsychologia, 26,* 265–272.

Alvarez-Royo, P., Clower, R. P., Zola-Morgan, S., & Squire, L. R. (1991). Stereotaxic lesions of the hippocampus in monkeys: Determination of surgical coordinates and analysis of lesions using magnetic resonance imaging. *Journal of Neuroscience Methods, 38,* 223–232.

Bachevalier, J., Parkinson, J. K., & Mishkin, M. (1985). Visual recognition in monkeys: Effects of separate versus combined transection of fornix and amydalofugal pathways. *Experimental Brain Research, 57,* 554–561.

Clower, R. P., Zola-Morgan, S., & Squire, L. R. (1990). Lesions of the perirhinal cortex, but not lesions of the amygdala, exacerbate memory impairment in monkeys following lesions of the hippocampal formation. *Society for Neuroscience Abstracts, 16,* 616.

Gaffan, D., & Harrison, S. (1987). Amygdalectomy and disconnection in visual learning for auditory secondary reinforcement by monkeys. *Journal of Neuroscience, 7,* 249–259.

Harlow, H., & Bromer, J. A. (1938). A test apparatus for monkeys. *Psychological Review, 19,* 434–438.

Insausti, R., Amaral, D. G., & Cowan, W. M. (1987). The entorhinal cortex of the monkey: II. Cortical afferents. *Journal of Comparative Neurology, 264,* 356–395.

Mahut, H., & Moss, M. (1984). Consolidation of memory: The hippocampus revisited. In L. R. Squire & N. Butters (Eds.), *Neuropsychology of memory* (1st ed., pp. 297–315). New York: Guilford Press.

Mahut, H., Zola-Morgan, S., & Moss, M. (1982). Hippocampal resections impair associative learning and recognition memory in the monkey. *Journal of Neuroscience, 1,* 227–240.

Malamut, B. L., Saunders, R. C., & Mishkin, M. (1984). Monkeys with combined amygdalo-hippocampal lesions succeed in object discrimination learning despite 24-hour intertrial intervals. *Behavioral Neuroscience, 98,* 759–769.

Mishkin, M. (1978). Memory in monkeys severely impaired by combined but not separate removal of the amygdala and hippocampus. *Nature, 273,* 297–298.

Mishkin, M. (1982). A memory system in the monkey. *Philosophical Transactions of the Royal Society of London, B298,* 85–89.

Mishkin, M., & Aggleton, J. P. (1981). Multiple functional contributions of the amygdala in the monkey. In Y. Ben-Ari (Ed.), *The amygdaloid complex* (pp. 409–420). Amsterdam: Elsevier.

Murray, E. A. (1992). Medial temporal lobe structures contributing to recognition memory: The amygdaloid complex versus the rhinal cortex. In J. Aggleton (Ed.), *Neurobiology of the amygdala* (pp. 453–470). New York: Wiley–Liss.

Murray, E. A., & Mishkin, M. (1984). Severe tactual as well as visual memory deficits follow combined removal of the amygdala and hippocampus in monkeys. *Journal of Neuroscience, 4,* 2565–2580.

Murray, E. A., & Mishkin, M. (1985). Amygdalectomy impairs cross-modal association in monkeys. *Science, 228,* 604–605.

Murray, E. A., & Mishkin, M. (1986). Visual recognition in monkeys following rhinal cortical ablations combined with either amygdalectomy or hippocampectomy. *Journal of Neuroscience, 6,* 1191–2003.

Overman, W. H., Ormsby, G., & Mishkin, M. (1990). Picture recognition versus picture discrimination learning in monkeys with medial temporal removals. *Experimental Brain Research, 79,* 18–24.

Salmon, D. P., Zola-Morgan, S., & Squire, L. R. (1987). Retrograde amnesia following combined hippocampus–amygdala lesions in monkeys. *Psychobiology, 15,* 37–47.

Saunders, R. C., Murray, E. A., & Mishkin, M. (1984). Further evidence that amygdala and hippocampus contribute equally to recognition memory. *Neuropsychologia, 22,* 785–796.

Scoville, W. B., & Milner, B. (1957). Loss of recent memory after bilateral hippocampal lesions. *Journal of Neurology, Neurosurgery and Psychiatry, 20,* 11–21.

Squire, L. R., & Zola-Morgan, S. (1983). The neurology of memory: The case for correspondence between the findings for humans and nonhuman primates. In J. A. Deutsch (Ed.), *The physiological basis of memory* (pp. 199-268). New York: Academic Press.

Squire, L. R., & Zola-Morgan, S. (1988). Memory: Brain systems and behavior. *Trends in Neurosciences, 11,* 170-175.

Squire, L. R., & Zola-Morgan, S. (1991). The medial temporal lobe memory system. *Science, 253,* 1380-1386.

Squire, L. R., Zola-Morgan, S., & Chen, K. S. (1988). Human amnesia and animal models of amnesia: Performance of amnesic patients on tests designed for the monkey. *Behavioral Neuroscience, 102,* 210-221.

Zola-Morgan, S., & Squire, L. R. (1984). Preserved learning in monkeys with medial temporal lesions: Sparing of cognitive skills. *Journal of Neuroscience, 4,* 1072-1085.

Zola-Morgan, S., & Squire, L. R. (1985). Medial temporal lesions in monkeys impair memory on a variety of tasks sensitive to human amnesia. *Behavioral Neuroscience, 99,* 22-34.

Zola-Morgan, S., & Squire, L. R. (1986). Memory impairment in monkeys following lesions of the hippocampus. *Behavioral Neuroscience, 100,* 165-170.

Zola-Morgan, & Squire, L. R. (1990a). Identification of the memory system damaged in medial temporal lobe amnesia. In L. R. Squire & E. Lindenlaub (Eds.), *The biology of memory* (pp. 509-525). Stuttgart: F. K. Schattauer Verlag.

Zola-Morgan, S., & Squire, L. R. (1990b). The neuropsychology of memory: Parallel findings from humans and nonhuman primates. *Annals of the New York Academy of Sciences, 608,* 434-456.

Zola-Morgan, S., Squire, L. R., Alvarez-Royo, P., & Clower, R. P. (1991). Independence of memory functions and emotional behavior: Separate contributions of the hippocampal formation and the amygdala. *Hippocampus, 1,* 207-220.

Zola-Morgan, S., Squire, L. R., & Amaral, D. G. (1986). Human amnesia and the medial temporal region: Enduring memory impairment following a bilateral lesion limited to field CA1 of the hippocampus. *Journal of Neuroscience, 10,* 2950-2967.

Zola-Morgan, S., Squire, L. R., & Amaral, D. G. (1989a). Lesions of the hippocampal formation but not lesions of the fornix or the mammillary nuclei produce long-lasting memory impairment in monkeys. *Journal of Neuroscience, 9,* 897-912.

Zola-Morgan, S., Squire, L. R., & Amaral, D. G. (1989b). Lesions of the amygdala that spare adjacent cortical regions do not impair memory or exacerbate the impairment following lesions of the hippocampal formation. *Journal of Neuroscience, 9,* 1922-1936.

Zola-Morgan, S., Squire, L. R., Amaral, D. G., & Suzuki, W. (1989). Lesions of perirhinal and parahippocampal cortex that spare the amygdala and hippocampal formation produce severe memory impairment. *Journal of Neuroscience, 9,* 4355-4370.

Zola-Morgan, S., Squire, L. R., & Mishkin, M. (1982). The neuroanatomy of amnesia: Amygdala-hippocampus vs. temporal stem. *Science, 218,* 1337-1339.

Zola-Morgan, S., Squire, L. R., Rempel, N. L., & Clower, R. P. (in press). Enduring memory impairment in monkeys after ischemic damage to the hippocampus. *Journal of Neuroscience.*

30

The Role of the Hippocampus-Fornix-Mammillary System in Episodic Memory

DAVID GAFFAN

In 1969, Delay and Brion put forward the hypothesis that the hippocampus, the fornix, and the mammillary bodies constitute a single functional system for memory, and that the same functional consequence (namely, amnesia) results from interruption of this system at any of its anatomical stages. In support of this hypothesis, they gave a comprehensive account of the clinical evidence then available on the neuropathological causes of amnesia. Since 1969, clinical evidence has continued to accumulate in favor of Delay and Brion's hypothesis. Particularly in the case of the fornix, recent evidence from patients who became amnesic after verified discrete surgical damage to the fornix (E. A. Gaffan, Gaffan, & Hodges, 1991; Hodges & Carpenter, 1991) and an evaluation of the available clinical evidence as a whole (Gaffan & Gaffan, 1991) make an overwhelming case in favor of Delay and Brion's view that fornix damage produces the same characteristic amnesic syndrome as is produced by damage to the other parts of the system they identified.

As is well known, the cardinal feature of amnesia is the impairment of episodic memory—that is, memory for discrete, personally experienced events (Cermak, 1984). Experimental investigations have supported the clinical data, in showing that a similar memory disorder in macaque monkeys results from lesions in Delay and Brion's system made under controlled experimental conditions. Furthermore, they have shown why episodic memory is so heavily dependent on the hippocampus-fornix-mammillary system. The present chapter reviews these developments.

Episodic Memory in the Monkey

Two experiments have examined the effect of fornix transection on monkeys' memory for complex naturalistic scenes. In one (Gaffan, 1977), a recognition memory task with projected photographs of complex scenes as the stimulus material was used; in the other (Gaffan, 1992b), a discrimination-learning task with still frames from a cinema film was used. In both experiments, fornix transection produced a severe impairment. A similar impairment has been seen in amnesic patients. Figure 30.1 (left) shows the

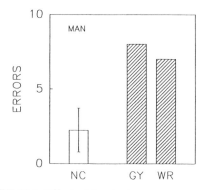
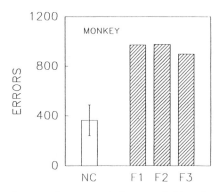

FIGURE 30.1. Effect of fornix damage on memory for complex scenes in humans (left) and monkeys (right). The averages of the groups of normal controls are shown with open bars, and those of the individuals with fornix damage are shown with hatched bars. The error bar for the normal controls (NC) shows ±2 standard errors of the mean. The data on the left are from E. A. Gaffan, Gaffan, and Hodges (1991); the data on the right are from Gaffan (1992b).

performance of two amnesic patients with fornix damage in a task of remembering 50 photographs of complex scenes (E. A. Gaffan et al., 1991). Figure 30.1 (right) shows the impairment of monkeys (Gaffan, 1992b) in an associative learning task with 320 scenes from a cinema film, each of which was associated with either food reward or no reward. The impairment was equally severe, relative to the performance of normal controls, in the two species.

Memory for complex naturalistic scenes is the basis of episodic memory. If a subject is taught the verbal association "apple–bicycle" in an experiment, the subject does not learn as a general principle to say "bicycle" whenever he or she sees the word "apple," but instead remembers a particular personally experienced complex event involving a psychologist in a laboratory and some word pairs. If a colleague inquires what questions were asked after a lecture you gave, you retrieve the target information (the questions) by a process of recall that reconstructs the whole scene of the event as you experienced it: the lecture theater as viewed from the podium, the position in the audience of the woman who asked about the statistics, and so on. These are familiar examples of episodic memory.

This whole-scene memory allows individuals to differentiate between the memories of similar events that might otherwise be confused with each other. You therefore use it in the example above, even though the memory task you have been set by your colleague's inquiry does not overtly require scene memory. Similarly, any memory task set by an experimenter takes place against the background of the very rich contents of extraexperimental long-term memory. Therefore, even if a task set by an experimenter does not, within its own confines, appear to require memory for complex scenes, normal subjects will nevertheless use the memory of the scene of the experiment to protect experimental memories from interference generated by extraexperimental memories. Thus, an impairment in memory for complex scenes will produce widespread episodic memory impairments, even in tasks that do not overtly require scene memory. This is what is observed in human amnesia. For example, amnesic patients with fornix damage were impaired in visual object discrimination learning (E. A.

Gaffan et al., 1991); this was a task in which discrete objects were associated with either a reward or no reward.

A similar phenomenon has been observed in monkeys. The fornix-transected monkeys in the Gaffan (1992b) experiment were impaired not only in scene memory (as described above), but also in visual object memory (associating visually presented objects with food reward or no reward). It is well established that this kind of visual associative learning with objects is not impaired by fornix transection in monkeys when the only visual associations with food reward that the animals learn are associations to objects presented in a single constant scene, such as the Wisconsin General Test Apparatus (WGTA) (Gaffan, Saunders, et al., 1984; Gaffan & Harrison, 1989a, 1989b; Zola-Morgan, Squire, & Amaral, 1989). Therefore, it is clear that the deficit of the Gaffan (1992b) monkeys in object associative learning was produced by an interaction between this task and the tasks with complex pictures that the animals had already learned. This interaction was caused by confusion among visual associations with food reward in the animals' long-term memory. Memory for the whole scene in which an object was rewarded could not reduce confusion between one object and another, in the case when all the objects associated with food reward were presented in the same scene—namely, the WGTA. When the WGTA was only one scene among many in which visual associations with reward were formed, however, memory for the whole scene in which an object was rewarded could protect the memories of events in the WGTA from confusion with other events. Such protection from interference was less available to the fornix-transected animals than to the controls, because of the deficit in scene memory that fornix transection produces.

Figure 30.2 shows the contrast in the monkey between the effects of fornix transection on object associative learning in the Gaffan and Harrison (1989a, p. 214, Table V) and Gaffan (1992b, Table 1) experiments.

The Basis of the Impairment in Memory for Complex Scenes: Memory for Spatial Organization

Several experiments have shown that fornix transection in the monkey produces a severe impairment in tasks that overtly require memory for the spatial position of the

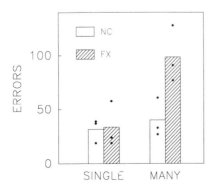

FIGURE 30.2. Object discrimination learning in the Wisconsin General Test Apparatus (WGTA) by four groups of monkeys. When the animals learned all visual associations with food reward in the single scene of the WGTA (left), fornix transection caused no impairment. When the WGTA was one scene among many in which the animals learned visual associations with food reward (right), animals with fornix transection were impaired. Each group contained three monkeys, and the dots show individuals in groups. The data are from Gaffan and Harrison (1989a) and Gaffan (1992b).

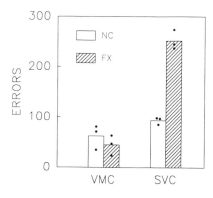

FIGURE 30.3. No impairment followed fornix transection in visuomotor conditional learning (VMC; left), in which an animal had to learn which of two motor responses to emit in response to a visual stimulus. Fornix transection did produce an impairment in spatiovisual conditional learning (SVC; right), in which an object was rewarded only if it was in a certain place in the scene. Each group contained three monkeys, and the dots show individuals in groups. The VMC data are from Gaffan and Harrison (1988); the SVC data are from Gaffan and Harrison (1989a).

objects in a scene. Unlike simple object associative learning, where spatial position within the scene is not overtly relevant, these object–place memory tasks show severe impairments even when there is only one learning task and it takes place in a single background scene. Thus, these impairments do not depend on interference between many different scenes, as the impairment in simple object associative learning does (see above).

For example, monkeys with fornix transection were impaired in learning that a particular object was rewarded only in a specific place—for instance, on the left but not on the right. (See Figure 30.3, right half. The data in the figure for this task, spatiovisual conditional learning [SVC], come from Gaffan & Harrison, 1989a, Table III, p. 212. Similar findings from another kind of spatiovisual task were also reported [Gaffan, Saunders, et al., 1984].) The same was true when the spatial organization of objects in the background, rather than the objects an animal chose between, was manipulated. Animals with fornix transection were impaired in learning that if objects A and B were presented with a distinctive wooden structure to the left of them, then A was rewarded, but if the wooden structure was to the right, then B was rewarded (Gaffan & Harrison, 1989b). A one-trial memory task that overtly required the monkeys to remember what position an object had previously appeared in also revealed severe impairments in fornix-transected monkeys (Gaffan & Saunders, 1985). Elsewhere (Gaffan, 1990), I review further examples of this kind of impairment.

Some important negative results show that these impairments should not be interpreted as representing a general impairment in learning to use contextual cues, or in putting together disparate sources of information. For example, fornix-transected monkeys were not impaired in learning visuomotor conditional problems, in which they had to learn for a series of visual stimuli whether to tap each stimulus or to hold it. (See Figure 30.3, left half. The data in the figure for this task, visuomotor conditional learning [VMC], come from Gaffan & Harrison, 1988.) There was also no impairment in learning that in white noise A was rewarded but in clicks B was rewarded—a particularly difficult task (Gaffan, Saunders, et al., 1984). In the visual modality, fornix-transected monkeys were able to learn normally about the presence or absence of a distinctive background object: On a white tray A was rewarded, whereas on an orange tray B was rewarded (Gaffan & Harrison, 1989b); with the doorknob in the background A was rewarded, but with the white coat in the background B was rewarded

(Gaffan & Harrison, 1989b). Thus, the impairment in memory for the spatial relation of objects to each other in complex scenes is a highly specific impairment. Nonetheless, as we have seen, it has widespread effects upon episodic memory.

These results make clear the functional link between remembering many complex naturalistic scenes, as in human episodic memory or analogous memory tasks for monkeys, and simple spatial tasks, as in many experiments on hippocampal and fornix function in primates and nonprimates (Murray, Davidson, Gaffan, Olton, & Suomi, 1989; Markowska, Olton, Murray, & Gaffan, 1989). Primates with fornix damage have difficulty remembering many complex naturalistic scenes, because without memory for their spatial organization, scenes are less distinct from one another in memory.

Recognition Memory Tasks

Two types of recognition memory tasks—delayed-matching-to-sample and delayed-nonmatching-to-sample tasks, which give monkeys objects to remember singly or in lists—have become generally familiar because of their extensive use in experiments on memory function in monkeys. Early suggestions (Gaffan, 1972, 1974, 1976) that these recognition memory tasks tested a form of memory representative of that which is impaired in human amnesia, whereas discrimination-learning tasks did not, have not been supported by subsequent evidence (as discussed by Cirillo, Horel, & George, 1989, pp. 65-66). For instance, the preceding discussion has shown that amnesic patients are impaired in object discrimination learning, as are monkeys with fornix transection under analogous conditions of interference in long-term memory. Nevertheless, a number of studies have clearly shown that fornix transection in the monkey disrupts either the acquisition of the basic principle of the recognition memory tasks of delayed matching or delayed nonmatching, or the level at which these tasks can be performed in tests with lists of objects (Bachevalier, Saunders, & Mishkin, 1985; Gaffan, 1974; Gaffan & Weiskrantz, 1980; Owen & Butler, 1981; Zola-Morgan et al., 1989). It is therefore important to consider what the role of the fornix is in these recognition memory tasks.

Experiments using delayed matching or delayed nonmatching have invariably employed a spatial cue to help the animal to differentiate between sample acquisition trials (at which the sample, a novel object to be remembered, is presented on the central well of a three-well board) and sample retention tests (at which the previously presented sample appears again on one of the side wells, with a novel object as foil on the other side well). It is important for the animal to differentiate between these two types of trials.

For example, my colleagues and I (Gaffan, Shields, & Harrison, 1984) demonstrated that one source of task difficulty in delayed matching arises from the fact that novelty is an inconsistent predictor of reward, since in the normal version of the task a novel object is rewarded when it is a sample at an acquisition trial, but not rewarded when it is a foil at a retention test. We showed that animals learned the principle of matching to sample faster when this particular difficulty was removed, by omitting to reward objects presented as samples at acquisition trials; in this version of the task, fornix transection produced no impairment. Equally, in nonmatching, one source of task difficulty in the normal procedure is that the association of the sample with reward at the acquisition trial is inconsistent with the same object's association with nonreward at the retention test. We (Gaffan, Gaffan, & Harrison, 1984) showed that both normal and fornix-transected monkeys learned nonmatching very rapidly and at the same rate when each sample was presented twice, the first presentation (as a novel object) being rewarded (just as the novel foil is rewarded at retention tests in nonmatching) but the second unrewarded. These data point to the specific requirements for the animal to differentiate clearly between acquisition trials and retention tests in the tasks of matching or nonmatching as normally administered.

One salient difference between aquisition trials and retention tests is the spatial position at which they are presented. The other difference is the number of objects presented, one as opposed to two; however, this may not be as salient to a monkey as one might imagine anthropomorphically, since there is strong evidence that monkeys focus their attention exclusively on one object at a time (Stollnitz, 1965; Eacott & Gaffan, 1989a, 1989b). We have seen (Figure 30.3) that fornix transection severely impairs monkeys' ability to utilize the spatial position of an object as a discriminative cue. Fornix-transected monkeys, being insensitive to the different spatial positions of objects in sample presentations and retention tests, will be impaired in learning to treat the two types of trial differently, as is clearly required in the normal versions of matching or nonmatching.

Strong support for this interpretation comes from related experiments with short-term associative memory tasks. These are similar to the recognition memory tasks discussed above, in that they are one-trial memory tasks in which objects appear at an acquisition trial on the central food well and subsequently at a retention test. In the associative tasks, however, neither of the objects at a retention test is a novel foil. Two objects appear in separate acquisition trials, each on the central well; then they are presented together at a retention test on the two side wells, and the animal's choice at the retention test is to be guided by the memory of the reward or nonreward that was associated with each object at its acquisition trial. We (Gaffan, Saunders, et al., 1984) examined two such tasks. Some animals learned a task we called Stay. Here, the rule was simply that the object that was rewarded at the acquisition trial was also rewarded at the retention test, while the object that was not to be rewarded at the retention test was presented unrewarded at its acquisition trial. Other animals learned the opposite memory task, which we called Shift: If an object was rewarded at its acquisition trial, it was not rewarded at its retention test, but if it had no reward at acquisition, then it was rewarded at retention. Figure 30.4 shows the contrasting effects of fornix transection upon the animals' performance when they were given lists of objects to remember in these two tasks. (The data in this figure come from Table II, p. 182, and Table IV, p. 185, of Gaffan, Saunders, et al., 1984. The slight improvement in Stay following fornix transection was an effect of practice at the task rather than of fornix transection, since the same degree of improvement was shown by control animals given the same training.) The contrast is not an effect of task difficulty, since normal animals learned the basic principle of Shift as easily as they learned that of Stay, and performed the two tasks equally well in tests with lists of objects (Gaffan, 1985). Rather, the contrast can be attributed to the importance of the spatial cue in differentiating acquisition trials from retention tests, since it is obvious that the ability to differentiate clearly between

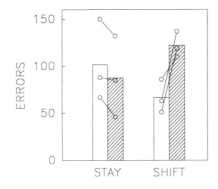

FIGURE 30.4. Results from two forms of one-trial associative memory task (Stay and Shift, described in the text), learned by separate groups of monkeys. Each task was tested before (open bars) and after (hatched bars) fornix transection. The circles and lines show results from individual monkeys within each group. The data are from Gaffan, Saunders, et al. (1984).

rewards at acquisition trials and rewards at retention tests is much more important in Shift than in Stay.

The results from these one-trial memory tasks appear to show, if taken at face value, that fornix transection can impair nonspatial memory—memory for having seen an object before, or memory for the reward that was associated with an object. As we have seen, however, the evidence is consistent with a reinterpretation of this evidence, stressing the importance of the animal's utilization of the spatial cue that differentiates acquisition trials from retention tests in these one-trial memory tasks. Thus, it may be that all impairments following fornix transection are fundamentally spatial impairments, in the particular sense explained above—namely, impaired memory for the spatial organization of complex scenes.

Hippocampal and Mammillary Lesions in Monkeys

Delay and Brion's (1969) hypothesis requires not only that fornix transection should produce amnesia, but also that amnesia of the same kind and severity should follow lesions of the hippocampus or the mammillary bodies. Experimentally, the effects of mammillary body lesions in monkeys have been investigated in regard to some simple spatial memory tasks and in recognition memory tasks; they have been found to be similar to those of fornix transection (Holmes, Butters, Jacobson, & Stein, 1983; Holmes, Jacobson, Stein, & Butters, 1983; Aggleton & Mishkin, 1985; Zola-Morgan et al., 1989). Hippocampal lesions also produce impairments in spatial tasks (Parkinson, Murray, & Mishkin, 1988) and in recognition memory tasks (Zola-Morgan et al., 1989). These data strongly suggest that the effects of these lesions are similar to those of fornix transection. However, it will be important to establish the effect of mammillary or hippocampal lesions in the monkey upon memory for complex scenes, since this task is more evidently related to human amnesia.

It will also be important for future research to investigate the effects of more selective hippocampal lesions than those that have so far been made in experimental studies in the monkey. These studies have made use of very extensive aspiration lesions, including the parahippocampal gyrus as well as all the parts of the hippocampal formation; these are much more extensive lesions than appear to be necessary to produce amnesia in humans (Zola-Morgan, Squire, & Amaral, 1986). Some of the behavioral effect of such extensive lesions results from the fact that they interrupt the blood supply to extrahippocampal visual association cortex, area TE (Gaffan & Lim, 1991). This extra effect on area TE may explain the observation by Zola-Morgan et al. (1989) that a more severe visual memory impairment followed large hippocampal aspiration lesions than followed mammillary body or fornix lesions. In this context, it is important to note that the effects of fornix transection that have been described above can be attributed with certainty to fornix transection rather than to extrafornical damage. Since the fornix is surrounded by ventricle, it can reliably be completely transected without damaging surrounding structures.

Exacerbation of Amnesia

It is clear that amnesia can be exacerbated by lesions outside the hippocampus–fornix–mammillary system. A particularly important example is the medial part of the medio-dorsal nucleus of the thalamus. The effects of lesions here in the monkey are not well understood, but they include effects on long-term memory (Gaffan & Watkins, 1991). This area of the thalamus is often damaged in alcoholic Korsakoff patients (Victor, Adams, & Collins, 1971). It sends a projection to prefrontal cortex (Giguere & Gold-man-Rakic, 1988), and the effects of lesions in it are in some ways functionally relatable to the effects of prefrontal cortex lesions (Gaffan & Murray, 1990). The severity of retrograde amnesia in Korsakoff patients is correlated with their signs of prefrontal cortex dysfunction (Kopelman, 1991). Retrograde amnesia in alcoholic Korsakoff psychosis can include some loss of semantic memory as well as of episodic memory (Butters & Cermak, 1986). For all these reasons, it is highly probable that damage to the mediodorsal nucleus is the cause of these additional impairments of semantic memory in many amnesic patients. However, clinical evidence indicates that mediodorsal thalamic lesions do not in isolation produce the characteristic amnesic syndrome (Kritchevsky, Graff-Radford, & Damasio, 1987; Graff-Radford, Tramel, Van Hoesen, & Brandt, 1990). Thus, in those amnesic patients who have such lesions in addition to lesions in the hippocampus–fornix–mammillary system, it is reasonable to think of mediodorsal thalamic lesions as exacerbating the central impairment of episodic memory in amnesia rather than as being a fundamental cause of it.

Similarly, amnesic patients with lesions of the hippocampal formation in the medial temporal lobe may also have varying degrees of additional damage to other structures in the temporal lobe, such as the medial temporal cortex or the amygdala. The cortex in the region of the rhinal sulcus, on the medial part of the inferior temporal lobe, is important for normal visual short-term memory (Horel, Pytko-Joiner, Voytko, & Salsbury, 1987; Murray, Bachevalier, & Mishkin, 1989; Gaffan & Murray, 1992). Patients may have severe amnesia without an impairment in visual short-term memory, however (Warrington & Taylor, 1973). Similarly, amygdalectomy produces powerful behavioral changes in monkeys, but these do not resemble those seen in human amnesia (Gaffan, 1992a). Thus, as in the case of mediodorsal thalamic lesions, it is reasonable to think of temporal lobe lesions outside the hippocampus, in those amnesic patients who have such lesions in addition to lesions in the hippocampus–fornix–

mammillary system, as exacerbating the central impairment of episodic memory in amnesia rather than as being a fundamental cause of it.

Conclusion

Modern evidence, both clinical and experimental, has supported Delay and Brion's (1969) hypothesis that the amnesic syndrome is always caused by interruption of the anatomically closely linked system that includes the fornix, hippocampus, and mammillary bodies. In addition, experimental work with monkeys has shown why episodic memory is so heavily dependent on this system. Episodic memory relies on memory for a whole complex scene—namely, the scene of an event as experienced by the person recalling it. Interruption of the Delay–Brion system impairs discrimination of the spatial organization of complex scenes, and hence makes complex scenes less distinct from one another in memory.

REFERENCES

Aggleton, J. P., & Mishkin, M. (1985). Mamillary-body lesions and visual recognition in monkeys. *Experimental Brain Research, 58,* 190–197.
Bachevalier, J., Saunders, R. C., & Mishkin, M. (1985). Visual recognition in monkeys: Effects of transection of fornix. *Experimental Brain Research, 57,* 547–553.
Butters, N., & Cermak, L. S. (1986). A case study of the forgetting of autobiograpical knowledge: Implications for the study of retrograde amnesia. In D. Rubin (Ed.), *Autobiographical memory* (pp. 253–272). Cambridge, England: Cambridge University Press.
Cermak, L. S. (1984). The episodic–semantic distinction in amnesia. In L. R. Squire & N. Butters (Eds.), *Neuropsychology of memory* (1st ed., pp. 55–62). New York: Guilford Press.
Cirillo, R. A., Horel, J. A., & George, P. J. (1989). Lesions of the anterior temporal stem and the performance of delayed match-to-sample and visual discriminations in monkeys. *Behavioural Brain Research, 34,* 55–69.
Delay, J., & Brion, S. (1969). *Le syndrome de Korsakoff.* Paris: Masson.
Eacott, M. J., & Gaffan, D. (1989a). Interhemispheric transfer of visual learning in monkeys with intact optic chiasm. *Experimental Brain Research, 74,* 348–352.
Eacott, M. J., & Gaffan, D. (1989b). Reaching to a rewarded visual stimulus: Interhemispheric conflict and hand use in monkeys with forebrain commissurotomy. *Brain, 112,* 1215–1230.
Gaffan, D. (1972). Loss of recognition memory in rats with lesions of the fornix. *Neuropsychologia, 10,* 327–341.
Gaffan, D. (1974). Recognition impaired and association intact in the memory of monkeys after transection of the fornix. *Journal of Comparative and Physiological Psychology, 86,* 1100–1109.
Gaffan, D. (1976). Recognition memory in animals. In J. Brown (Ed.), *Recall and recognition* (pp. 229–242). London: Wiley.
Gaffan, D. (1977). Monkeys' recognition memory for complex pictures and the effect of fornix transection. *Quarterly Journal of Experimental Psychology, 29,* 505–514.
Gaffan, D. (1985). Hippocampus: Memory, habit and voluntary movement. In L. Weiskrantz (Ed.), *Animal intelligence* (pp. 87–99). Oxford: Clarendon Press.
Gaffan, D. (1990). Behavioral analysis of the spatial learning impairment in fornix-transected monkeys, with some comments on its relation to impairments of apparently non-spatial memory. In L. R. Squire, M. Mishkin, & A. Shimamura (Eds.), *Discussions in neuroscience: Vol. 6, Nos. 3 and 4. Learning and memory* (Report of the 1989 FESN Study Group, pp. 52–55). Amsterdam: Elsevier.
Gaffan, D. (1992a). Amygdala and the memory of reward. In J. P. Aggleston (Ed.), *The amygdala: Neurobiological aspects of emotion, memory and mental dysfunction* (pp. 471–483). New York: Wiley.
Gaffan, D. (1992b). Amnesia for complex naturalistic scenes and for objects following fornix transection in the monkey. *European Journal of Neuroscience, 4,* 381–388.

Gaffan, D., & Gaffan, E. A. (1991). Amnesia in man following transection of the fornix: A review. *Brain, 114,* 2611–2618.

Gaffan, D., Gaffan, E. A., & Harrison, S. (1984). Effects of fornix transection on spontaneous and trained non-matching by monkeys. *Quarterly Journal of Experimental Psychology, 36B,* 285–303.

Gaffan, D., & Harrison, S. (1988). Inferotemporal–frontal disconnection and fornix transection in visuomotor conditional learning by monkeys. *Behavioural Brain Research, 31,* 149–163.

Gaffan, D., & Harrison, S. (1989a). A comparison of the effects of fornix transection and sulcus principalis ablation upon spatial learning by monkeys. *Behavioural Brain Research, 31,* 207–220.

Gaffan, D., & Harrison, S. (1989b). Place memory and scene memory: Effects of fornix transection in the monkey. *Experimental Brain Research, 74,* 202–212.

Gaffan, D., & Lim, C. (1991). Hippocampus and the blood supply to TE: Parahippocampal pial section impairs visual discrimination learning in monkeys. *Experimental Brain Research, 87,* 227–231.

Gaffan, D., & Murray, E. A. (1990). Amygdalar interaction with the mediodorsal nucleus of the thalamus and the ventromedial prefrontal cortex in stimulus–reward associative learning in the monkey. *Journal of Neuroscience, 10,* 3479–3493.

Gaffan, D., & Murray, E. A. (1992). Monkeys with rhinal cortex lesions succeed in object discrimination learning despite 24-hour intertrial intervals and fail at match to sample despite double sample presentations. *Behavioral Neuroscience, 106,* 1–8.

Gaffan, D., & Saunders, R. C. (1985). Running recognition of configural stimuli by fornix-transected monkeys. *Quarterly Journal of Experimental Psychology, 37B,* 61–71.

Gaffan, D., Saunders, R. C., Gaffan, E. A., Harrison, S., Shields, C., & Owen, M. J. (1984). Effects of fornix transection upon associative memory in monkeys: Role of the hippocampus in learned action. *Quarterly Journal of Experimental Psychology, 36B,* 173–221.

Gaffan, D., Shields, S., & Harrison, S. (1984). Delayed matching by fornix-transected monkeys: The sample, the push and the bait. *Quarterly Journal of Experimental Psychology, 36B,* 305–317.

Gaffan, D., & Watkins, S. (1991). Mediodorsal thalamic lesions impair long term visual associative memory in macaques. *European Journal of Neuroscience, 3,* 615–620.

Gaffan, D., & Weiskrantz, L. (1980). Recency effects and lesion effects in delayed non-matching to randomly baited samples by monkeys. *Brain Research, 196,* 373–386.

Gaffan, E. A., Gaffan, D., & Hodges, J. R. (1991). Amnesia following damage to the left fornix and to other sites: A comparative study. *Brain, 114,* 1297–1313.

Giguere, M., & Goldman-Rakic, P. S. (1988). Mediodorsal nucleus: Areal, laminar and tangential distribution of afferents and efferents in the frontal lobe of rhesus monkeys. *Journal of Comparative Neurology, 227,* 195–213.

Graff-Radford, N. R., Tramel, N., Van Hoesen, G. W., & Brandt, J. P. (1990). Diencephalic amnesia. *Brain, 113,* 1–25.

Hodges, J. R., & Carpenter, K. (1991). Anterograde amnesia with fornix damage following removal of IIIrd ventricle colloid cyst. *Journal of Neurology, Neurosurgery and Psychiatry, 54,* 633–638.

Holmes, E. J., Butters, N., Jacobson, S., & Stein, B. M. (1983). An examination of the effects of mammillary-body lesions on reversal learning sets in monkeys. *Physiological Psychology, 11,* 159–165.

Holmes, E. J., Jacobson, S., Stein, B. M., & Butters, N. (1983). Ablations of the mammillary nuclei in monkeys: Effects on post-operative memory. *Experimental Neurology, 81,* 97–113.

Horel, J. A., Pytko-Joiner, D. E., Voytoko, M. L., & Salsbury, K. (1987). The performance of visual tasks while segments of the inferotemporal cortex are suppressed by cold. *Behavioural Brain Research, 23,* 29–42.

Kopelman, M. D. (1991). Frontal dysfunction and memory deficits in the alcoholic Korsakoff syndrome and Alzheimer-type dementia. *Brain, 114,* 117–137.

Kritchevsky, M., Graff-Radford, N. R., & Damasio, A. R. (1987). Normal memory after damage to medial thalamus. *Archives of Neurology, 44,* 959–962.

Markowska, A. L., Olton, D. S., Murray, E. A., & Gaffan, D. (1989). A comparative analysis of the role of the fornix and cingulate cortex in memory: Rats. *Experimental Brain Research, 74,* 187–201.

Murray, E. A., Bachevalier, J., & Mishkin, M. (1989). Effects of rhinal cortical lesions on visual recognition memory in rhesus monkeys. *Society for Neuroscience Abstracts, 15,* 342.

Murray, E. A., Davidson, M., Gaffan, D., Olton, D. S., & Suomi, S. J. (1989). Effects of fornix transection and cingulate cortical ablation on spatial memory in rhesus monkeys. *Experimental Brain Research, 74,* 173–186.

Owen, M. J., & Butler, S. R. (1981). Amnesia after transection of the fornix in monkeys: Long-term memory impaired, short-term memory intact. *Behavioural Brain Research, 3,* 115–123.

Parkinson, J. K., Murray, E. A., & Mishkin, M. (1988). A selective mnemonic role for the hippocampus in monkeys: Memory for the location of objects. *Journal of Neuroscience, 8,* 4159–4167.

Stollnitz, F. (1965). Spatial variables, observing responses, and discrimination learning sets. *Psychological Review*, 72, 247-261.

Victor, M., Adams, R. D., & Collins, G. H. (1971). *The Wernicke-Korsakoff syndrome*. Philadelphia: F. A. Davis.

Warrington, E. K., & Taylor, A. M. (1973). Immediate memory for faces: Long or short-term memory? *Quarterly Journal of Experimental Psychology*, 25, 316-322.

Zola-Morgan, S., Squire, L. R., & Amaral, D. G. (1986). Human amnesia and the medial temporal region: Enduring memory impairment following a bilateral lesion limited to field CA1 of the hippocampus. *Journal of Neuroscience*, 6, 2950-2967.

Zola-Morgan, S., Squire, L. R., & Amaral, D. G. (1989). Lesions of the hippocampal formation but not lesions of the fornix or the mammillary nuclei produce long-lasting memory impairment in monkeys. *Journal of Neuroscience*, 9, 898-913.

31

A Hypothesis on Primal Long-Term Memory: Neurophysiological Evidence in the Primate Temporal Cortex

YASUSHI MIYASHITA, HAN SOO CHANG, and KOICHI MORI

Long-Term Memory Has Stages with Distinguishable Localizations

Memory has stages. The distinction between short-term memory and long-term memory (LTM) has been supported not only with respect to their capacity, optimal code, and time paramaters, but also by the double dissociation of neuropsychological deficits (Milner, Corkin, & Teuber, 1968; Warrington, 1982). LTM itself has been claimed to have at least two components; one is the recently acquired, labile memory that can be readily disrupted by head injury, as retrograde amnesia demonstrates clinicallly (Russell, 1971). The other is the remote, fully consolidated memory (Squire, Slater, & Chace, 1975). Drug applications selectively depress or facilitate the labile component (McGaugh & Herz, 1972).

Bilateral damage to the medial temporal region, which includes the hippocampus, amygdala, and adjacent cortex, accompanied a short-span retrograde amnesia in one patient (Milner et al., 1968). Bilateral lesions of the hippocampal CA1 field in another patient produced little retrograde amnesia, although the possibility remains that the patient could have suffered some retrograde amnesia for a period of a few years prior to his surgery (Zola-Morgan, Squire, & Amaral, 1986). Monkeys also suffered retrograde amnesia after bilateral amygdalo-hippocampal ablations (Mishkin, Spiegler, Saunders, & Malamut, 1982). When the effects of hippocampal lesions (including the entorhinal and parahippocampal cortex) on the retention of 100 object discrimination problems were tested, monkeys were severely impaired at remembering recently learned objects, but they remembered objects learned more than 8 weeks earlier as well as normal monkeys did (Zola-Morgan & Squire, 1990).

These data suggest that the labile component of the LTM is localized in the hippocampus and/or adjacent cortex, or is strongly influenced by these structures. Possible contributions of the hippocampal neural circuits have been examined previously (Miyashita, Rolls, Cahusac, Niki, & Feigenbaum, 1989). In this chapter, I propose a hypothesis that the anterior ventral temporal cortex, lateral to the hippocampal formation, contains a group of neurons that encodes one component of the visual LTM.

The Primal Long-Term Memory

We have found a neuronal correlate of visual LTM in the anteroventral temporal cortex of monkeys. Response selectivity to visual objects is acquired in these neurons, and the selectivity represents a recently learned visual–visual association (Miyashita, 1988a; Sakai & Miyashita, 1991). The neurons have limited spatial distribution along the border between area 35 and visual association cortex (Miyashita, Cho, & Mori, 1987; Miyashita, Masui, & Higuchi, 1991), and in this area they are organized into unique functional columns (Higuchi, Sakai, & Miyashita, 1991).

This border area overlaps with the perirhinal and parahippocampal (PRPH) area (Zola-Morgan, Squire, Amaral, & Suzuki, 1989; Horel & Pytko, 1982). Monkeys with PRPH lesions were as impaired or more impaired on a delayed-nonmatching-to-sample task than the comparison group of monkeys with H^+A^+ lesions (which include the hippocampal formation, amygdala, and adjacent cortex). This area is tightly connected with the hippocampus via the entorhinal cortex (area 28) and via area 35 (Herzog & Van Hoesen, 1976; Insausti, Amaral, & Cowan, 1987), or directly with the CA1 field (Suzuki & Amaral, 1990).

We propose to name the mnemonic code on these neurons "primal LTM." Figure 31.1 depicts a hypothetical structure of the visual memory system of the primate. The physical properties of a visual object (such as its size, color, texture, and shape) are analyzed in the multiple subdivisions of the prestriate–posterior temporal complex (Mishkin, 1982; Zeki & Shipp, 1988). The anterior part of the inferior temporal cortex (AIT) synthesizes the analyzed attributes into a unique configuration and forms a central image of the object (Gross, 1972; Mishkin, 1982). The primal LTM neurons are presumed to receive synthesized perceptual images of the object from this part of AIT, since the neurons' activity is highly selective for coded pictorial information and is

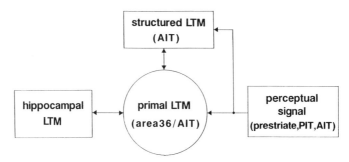

FIGURE 31.1. A hypothesis: The primal LTM and related visual memory systems of the primate. PIT, posterior inferior temporal cortex; AIT, anterior inferior temporal cortex.

independent of the object's physical attributes, such as size, orientation, color, or position (Miyashita & Chang, 1988; see below). The region where the primal LTM neurons are located indeed receives afferent projections from more lateral part of AIT (Jones & Powell, 1990; Van Hoesen & Pandya, 1975).

Since localization of the primal LTM neurons is limited to a region not far from the rhinal sulcus, neuropsychological data on retrograde amnesia suggest that the LTM system has another group of neurons to store the remote, fully consolidated LTM (Milner, 1968). The idea is supported by recent findings that the primal LTM neurons have unique columnar organizations that can provide an interface between visual cortical columns and hippocampal associative networks (Higuchi et al., 1991; see below).

In the following, I describe evidence supporting the brief sketch given above. Recording the activities of the primal LTM neurons in monkeys that learn and perform visual memory tasks will give vivid concrete shape to the presumed multiple representation of LTM, complementary to that obtained by neuropsychological observations.

Behavioral Task and Recording of Neural Activities

In a trial of our visual memory task (a delayed-matching-to-sample task), sample and match stimuli were successively presented on a video monitor, each for 0.2 seconds (sec) at a 16-sec delay interval. Monkeys (*Macaca fuscata*) had to memorize the sample stimulus during a delay period and then to decide whether the match stimulus was the same as the sample. A set of 97 color patterns was generated by a fractal algorithm with a 32-bit seed of random numbers (Miyashita, Higuchi, Sakai, & Masui, 1991; Miyashita, 1988b); the set was repeatedly used during a training session ("learned stimuli") in a fixed sequence according to an arbitrary attached number (serial position number, or SPN). While extracellular discharges of a neuron were recorded, a sample stimulus was selected not only from the 97 learned patterns but also from a new set of 97 patterns ("new stimuli"). Different sets of new stimuli were created for each neuron, using the same algorithm but a different seed. The learned stimuli and new stimuli were used at random, independently of the SPNs.

Selectivity of Neural Discharges Is Acquired through Learning

A few of the 97 learned stimuli reproducibly activated a particular neuron in the anterior ventral temporal cortex during the sample period or during the delay period of the task. The optimal picture differed from cell to cell, and the entire population of optimal pictures for the tested cells covered a substantial part of the repertory of the pictorial stimuli (Miyashita & Chang, 1988).

Intuition told us that learning but not genetic determinants had formed the stimulus selectivity of these neurons, since (1) the optimal stimuli were computer-generated artificial patterns (fractal patterns), which the monkeys would rarely have seen in their lives before the experiments; and (2) the responsive neurons were not scattered randomly in the temporal cortex, but formed a high-density cluster in a limited area related to the hippocampus.

We obtained several lines of experimental evidence supporting our intuition. First, we compared the discharge selectivity of a neuron for two different sets of the fractal stimuli: the learned stimuli that the monkeys stored in their LTM through the training sessions, and the new stimuli that they had never seen before the recording session. Figure 31.2 shows a result. A few of the 97 learned stimuli were effective in activating high-frequency sustained delay discharges in a cell (Figure 31.2a). By contrast, the 97 new patterns produced only weak delay responses. The distribution of the delay discharge rate to the new stimuli (Figure 31.2b) lacked the small population of high-frequency responses (>2 impulses/sec) that characterized the distribution to the learned stimuli (Figure 31.2a). Most of the tested neurons had similar response selectivity, which was characterized by the following three properties.

1. The maximum delay discharge for learned stimuli (e.g., the arrow in Figure 31.2a) was larger than that for new stimuli (e.g., the arrow in Figure 31.2b).
2. When the selectivity of a neuron to a set of 97 patterns was represented by the sharpness of the response distribution (the kurtosis of the distribution), the selectivity to the learned patterns was higher than that to the new patterns.
3. In spite of the presence of a few effective pictures in the learned stimuli, there was no difference between the median responses to the learned and new stimuli (e.g., the double arrows in Figure 31.2).

These results suggest that the sharpness of the response selectivity of these neurons to the learned patterns was formed throughout the course of training.

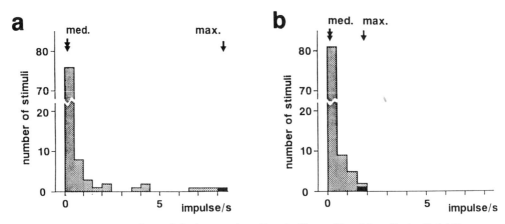

FIGURE 31.2. Selectivity of neural discharges of a cell to the "learned" and "new" stimuli. (a) Frequency distribution of the average firing rate measured during the delay period following 97 "learned" sample pictures. ↓ max. and ↓ med., maximum and median values in the distribution. (b) Similar illustration to a, but "new" pictures were used as sample stimuli in the same cell. From "Neuronal Correlate of Visual Associative Long-Term Memory in the Primate Temporal Cortex" (p. 818) by Y. Miyashita, 1988, *Nature, 335,* 817–820. Copyright 1988 by Macmillan Magazines Ltd. Reprinted by permission.

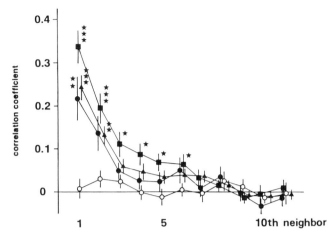

FIGURE 31.3. Stimulus–stimulus association among the learned fractal patterns. Ordinate, autocorrelations of the delay discharge rate along the SPN of the stimuli. Filled circles and open circles, average autocorrelograms for the learned and new stimuli, respectively, in the 17 cells. Filled triangles, average autocorrelogram for the learned stimuli in the 57 cells. Filled squares, average autocorrelogram for the learned stimuli in the 28 cells for which the nearest-neighbor correlation along the SPN was significant ($p < .05$) according to Kendall's test. Error bars, standard errors. $^{\circ\circ\circ}p < .001$, $^{\circ\circ}p < .01$, and $^{\circ}p < .05$, according to the Kolmogorov–Smirnov test in comparison with the value for new stimuli. From "Neuronal Correlate of Visual Associative Long-Term Memory in the Primate Temporal Cortex" (p. 819) by Y. Miyashita, 1988, *Nature, 335,* 817–820. Copyright 1988 by Macmillan Magazines Ltd. Reprinted by permission.

Acquired Selectivity Represents an Association among Memorized Objects

In human LTM, ideas and concepts become associated through learning. We may ask whether the neurons with acquired selectivity can code such associations. To be more specific, is it possible that training determines not only how sharply the effective learned patterns are represented in each neuron (as shown above), but also which patterns are conjointly chosen as the few optimal stimuli? We examined the effect of a fixed-order presentation of the patterns during the training session, according to an arbitrarily assigned SPN (Miyashita, 1988a). If the consecutively presented patterns tended to be associated together, and if the association was fixed in the choice of effective patterns for a cell, we could expect to find the effective patterns correlated along the SPN, in spite of a random presentation of the stimuli during the unit-recording session.

Figure 31.3 shows the results. The effective responses to the learned stimuli indeed clustered along the SPNs (filled circles), and the clustering was not due to an artifact in the testing procedure because the responses simultaneously obtained from the new stimuli were not clustered (open circles). Thus, we conclude that these neurons are good candidates for one of the visual associative LTM stores (the primal LTM).

It is interesting to ask how many times the monkey should see and memorize the fractal pattern that eventually develops the neural representation of the stimulus–stimulus associations. Unfortunately, no direct answer is available from the experimental procedure described above, because two factors were confounded in the training; one was to learn the rule of the delayed-matching-to-sample task, and the other to learn the association. We roughly estimate the upper limit to be about a few hundred trials (500 trials/day/100 patterns $\times$ 30 days).

Recently we developed a new memory task, the visual paired-associate learning task, to tackle the problem (Sakai & Miyashita, 1991). In this task 24 computer-generated pictures were prepared for each macaque monkey, and geometrically distinct patterns were sorted into pairs. The combinations of the paired associates are not predictable unless they are memorized beforehand. In each trial, a cue stimulus was shown on a video monitor. After the delay period, the monkeys were presented with a choice of two stimuli—the paired associate of the cue and one from a different pair—and obtained fruit juice as a reward for correctly touching the paired associate. Picture-selective neural responses during the cue period were found in the anterior inferior temporal cortex. The neurons of this type responded reproducibly to only a few pictures. It might be that the cells responded to geometrically similar patterns, but in many cases the strongest and the second strongest responses were ascribed to a particular pair that had no apparent geometrical similarity. These responsive cells tended to be located near one another (1–2 mm in width). It was concluded that the selectivity of these neurons was acquired through learning of the paired-associate task. Lesion studies have demonstrated that monkeys with bilateral removal of the medial temporal region could not learn the paired-associate task (Murray, Gaffan, & Mishkin, 1988), and the type of memory these tasks employed would therefore correspond to one that relies on the integrity of the medial temporal lobe. These results not only confirm the previous ones with the delayed-matching-to-sample task but also provide new approaches for dissecting the primal and the structured LTM.

A Categorized Percept of a Picture Is Memorized

The anterior ventral temporal cortex has been designed as the last link from the visual system to the hippocampus (Van Hoesen & Pandya, 1975; Insausti et al., 1987; Yukie & Iwai, 1988; Suzuki & Amaral, 1990). Thus the primal LTM neurons should receive final-stage information in serial visual processing along occipito-temporal cortices (Figure 31.1). Indeed, the primal LTM neurons encode highly abstract pictorial properties of the stimulus, as demonstrated by the following analyses of triggering features of the delay responses (Miyashita & Chang, 1988). Sample pictures were manipulated in three different manners: (1) the stimulus size was reduced by half, (2) the stimuli were rotated by 90 degrees in a clockwise direction, or (3) colored stimuli were transformed into monochrome by referring to a color conversion table. Figure 31.4 illustrates the responses of a neuron that consistently fired during the delay after one particular picture but not after others, regardless of stimulus size (Figure 31.4b), orientation (Figure 31.4c), or color (Figure 31.4d).

Functional Architecture

Functional architecture was studied by recording each of a succession of cells encountered through several closely spaced (~100-μm interval) parallell microelectrode pene-

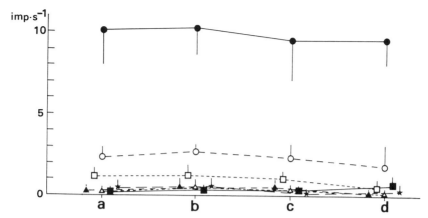

FIGURE 31.4. Response tolerance under stimulus transformation in size, orientation, or color. (**a**) Control responses. (**b**) The effects of stimulus size reduction by half. (**c**) The effects of stimulus rotation by 90 degrees in a clockwise direction. (**d**) The effects of color-to-monochrome transformation. Ordinate, average delay spike frequencies as a function of stimulus transformation. Responses to seven different sample pictures are plotted with different symbols. Error bars indicate standard deviations for 4–15 trials. From "Neuronal Correlate of Pictorial Short-Term Memory in the Primate Temporal Cortex" (p. 70) by Y. Miyashita and H. S. Chang, 1988, *Nature, 331*, 68–70. Copyright 1988 by Macmillan Magazines Ltd. Reprinted by permission.

trations (Hubel & Wiesel, 1962, 1963). Each electrode position was determined on the X-ray image that was superimposed on histological serial sections with reference to electrolytic lesions. Typically, in a few electrode penetrations confined within 0.5 mm between the rhinal sulcus and the anterior middle temporal sulcus, almost all neurons encountered were selectively activated by some fractal patterns (Higuchi, Sakai, & Miyashita, 1991). Many of the neurons exhibited sustained activity during the delay period of the delayed-matching-to-sample task. In other electrode tracks, a few neurons fired weakly, but only during the sample period. The firing magnitude during the sample period, as well as the number of responsive neurons, declined sharply in the electrode tracks that were placed more than 1 mm apart from the highly responsive tracks. In one typical example, the maximum firing rate to an optimal fractal pattern was 71.5 impulses/sec (averaged during the sample period after subtraction of spontaneous firing rates) in the responsive cell cluster, but 0.0, 23.4, and 21.3 impulses/sec in more medial tracks (from medial to lateral) and 22.0 and 13.5 impulses/sec in more lateral tracks (adjacent tracks within 0.5 mm were lumped together). Successively recorded pictorial neurons in the cluster did not indicate a common preference for an identical fractal pattern and for geometrically similar patterns. Thirteen clusters from four hemispheres were studied, and optimum patterns were collected in each cluster to test any preference to a specific picture, but no bias was detected in any of the 13 clusters.

Interface between Visual Cortices and Hippocampus

The modular organization found in the anteroventral temporal cortex presents a striking contrast to functional architectures reported in two other memory-related areas: one in the hippocampus and the other in the dorsolateral part of the temporal cortex. In the monkey hippocampus, there have been reports on neural activity responding selectively to a delayed-response task (Watanabe & Niki, 1985), a visually guided conditional-response task (Miyashita, Rolls, et al., 1989), and an object–place memory task (Cahusac, Miyashita, & Rolls, 1989; Rolls et al., 1989). In all of these tasks, however, responsive cells were scattered over wide areas in the hippocampus and had no clear local column-like structures. In the rat hippocampus, place units also had a widely distributed organization, and did not show any apparent trend for neighboring units to code the nearby locations of the place field (O'Keefe, 1976; Muller, Kubie, & Ranck, 1987).

Unlike the hippocampus, the dorsolateral part of the temporal cortex, which contains neurons selectively responsive to particular visual patterns, has been reported to have column-like structures. However, a common preference for geometrically similar objects characterized vertical clustering of cells in these reports. In the bank of the superior temporal sulcus, cells responding to the frontal faces and to the profile faces formed distinct vertical clumps (Perrett, Mistlin, & Chitty, 1987; Perrett et al., 1984), and in the lateral inferotemporal cortex between the superior temporal sulcus and the anterior middle temporal sulcus, spatially adjacent cells simultaneously recorded by a single microelectrode showed similar selectivity for visual patterns (Fujita, Cheng, & Tanaka, 1990). This architecture is essentially similar to that in other visual cortices where cells work as feature detectors. In the experiments described in this chapter, the pictorial memory neurons in the anteroventral temporal cortex also formed a cluster, but closely adjacent neurons did not indicate a common preference for a fractal pattern. Rather, the neurons in the column were characterized by associative representation of pictures. This unique architecture, together with bidirectional neural connections of this cortex, meets the requirement for an interface between visual cortical columns for feature detection and hippocampal associative memory circuits.

Conclusion

In this chapter, I have proposed a hypothesis that the anterior ventral temporal cortex contains a group of neurons that encodes one component of the LTM, named the primal LTM (Figure 31.1). Highly abstract visual information is inputted to the primal LTM through the occipito-temporal visual cortices. Unique functional architecture, limited spatial localization near the rhinal sulcus, and bidirectional communication with the hippocampal system all support the hypothesis that the primal LTM is an important stage in memory consolidation. However, in the present stage of investigation, we know nothing about how the formation of the primal LTM depends on the hippocampal LTM. Nor is it clear how the primal LTM and hippocampal LTM are related to the labile component of LTM, which can be revealed with electric shock or with application of drugs after learning. Since a hippocampal neuron also encodes a newly formed association (Miyashita, Rolls, et al., 1989), it is necessary to compare the susceptibilities to electric shock and/or convulsant drugs between the hippocampal and anteroventral temporal cortical neurons. It will be possible to confirm or reject the present hypothesis on the primal LTM (Figure 31.1) by an appropriate combination of neuropsychological and electrophysiological experiments.

ACKNOWLEDGMENT

This work was supported by a grant from the Japanese Ministry of Education, Science and Culture (No. 02102008).

REFERENCES

Cahusac, P. M. B., Miyashita, Y., & Rolls, E. T. (1989). Responses of hippocampal formation neurons in the monkey related to delayed spatial response and object–place memory tasks. *Behavioural Brain Research, 33,* 229-240.

Fujita, I., Cheng, K., & Tanaka, K. (1990). Stimulus selectivity of inferotemporal cortex neurons: Simultaneous recording from adjacent cells. *Society for Neuroscience Abstracts, 16,* 1220.

Gross, C. G. (1972). Visual functions of inferotemporal cortex. In R. Jung (Ed.), *Handbook of sensory physiology* (Vol. 8, Section 3B, pp. 451-482). Berlin: Springer-Verlag.

Herzog, A. G., & Van Hoesen, G. W. (1976). Temporal neocortical afferent connections to the amygdala in the rhesus monkey. *Brain Research, 115,* 57-69.

Higuchi, S., Sakai, K., & Miyashita, Y. (1991). Functional architecture of pictorial memory neurons in the primate anteroventral temporal cortex. *Neuroscience Research, 14,* 61.

Horel, J. A., & Pytko, D. E. (1982). Behavioral effects of local cooling in temporal lobe of monkeys. *Journal of Neurophysiology, 47,* 11-22.

Hubel, D. H., & Wiesel, T. N. (1962). Receptive fields, binocular interaction and functional architecture in the cat's visual cortex. *Journal of Physiology* (London), *160,* 106-154.

Hubel, D. H., & Wiesel, T. N. (1963). Shape and arrangement of columns in cat's striate cortex. *Journal of Physiology* (London), *165,* 559-568.

Insausti, R., Amaral, D. G., & Cowan, W. M. (1987). The entorhinal cortex of the monkey: II. Cortical afferents. *Journal of Comparative Neurology, 264,* 356-395.

Jones, E. G., & Powell, T. P. S. (1970). An anatomical study of converging sensory pathways within the cerebral cortex of the monkey. *Brain, 93,* 793-820.

McGaugh, J. L., & Herz, M. J. (1972). *Memory consolidation.* San Francisco: Albion.

Milner, B. (1968). Visual recognition and recall after right temporal-lobe excision in man. *Neuropsychologia, 6,* 191-209.

Milner, B., Corkin, S., & Teuber, H. L. (1968). Further analysis of the hippocampal amnesic syndrome: 14-year follow-up study of H. M. *Neuropsychologia, 6,* 215-234.

Mishkin, M. (1982). A memory system in the monkey. *Philosophical Transactions of the Royal Society of London, B298,* 85-95.

Mishkin, M., Spiegler, B. J., Saunders, R. C., & Malamut, B. L. (1982). An animal model of global amnesia. In S. Corkin, K. L. Davis, J. H. Growden, E. Usdin, & R. J. Wurtman (Eds.), *Alzheimer's disease: A report of progress in research* (pp. 235-247). New York: Raven Press.

Miyashita, Y. (1988a). Neuronal correlate of visual associative long-term memory in the primate temporal cortex. *Nature, 335,* 817-820.

Miyashita, Y. (1988b). Neuronal representation of pictorial working memory in the primate temporal cortex. In M. A. Arbib & S. Amari (Eds.), *Dynamic interactions in neural networks: Models and data* (pp. 183-192). Berlin: Springer-Verlag.

Miyashita, Y., & Chang, H. S. (1988). Neuronal correlate of pictorial short-term memory in the primate temporal cortex. *Nature, 331,* 68-70.

Miyashita, Y., Cho, K., & Mori, K. (1987). Selective pictorial information is retained by neurons in the ventral temporal cortex of the monkey during the delay period of a matching-to-sample task. *Society for Neuroscience Abstracts, 13,* 608.

Miyashita, Y., Higuchi, S., Sakai, K., & Masui, N. (1991). Generation of fractal patterns for probing the visual memory. *Neuroscience Research, 12,* 307-311.

Miyashita, Y., Masui, N., & Higuchi, S. (1991). Primal long-term memory in the primate temporal cortex: Linkage between visual perception and memory. In A. Gorea (Ed.), *Representation of vision* (pp. 141–152). Cambridge: Cambridge University Press.

Miyashita, Y., Rolls, E. T., Cahusac, P. M. B., Niki, H., & Feigenbaum, J. D. (1989). Activity of hippocampal neurons in the monkey related to a stimulus–response association task. *Journal of Neurophysiology, 61,* 669–678.

Miyashita, Y., Sakai, K., & Highuchi, S. (1989). Memorized objects mutually interfere on delay discharges for pictorial short-term memory in neurons of primate temporal cortex. *Society for Neuroscience Abstracts, 15,* 303.

Muller, R. U., Kubie, J. L., & Ranck, J.B., Jr. (1987). Spatial firing patterns of hippocampal complex-spike cells in a fixed environment. *Journal of Neuroscience, 7,* 1935–1950.

Murray, E. A., Gaffan, D., & Mishkin, M. (1988). Role of the amygdala and hippocampus in visual–visual associative memory in rhesus monkeys. *Society for Neuroscience Abstracts, 14,* 2.

O'Keefe, J. (1976). Place units in the hippocampus of the freely moving rat. *Experimental Neurology, 51,* 78–109.

Perrett, D. I., Mistlin, A. J., & Chitty, A. J. (1987). Visual neurones responsive to faces. *Trends in Neurosciences, 10,* 358–364.

Perrett, D. I., Smith, P. A. J., Potter, D.D., Mistlin, A. J., Head, A. S., Milner, A. D., & Jeeves, M. A. (1984). Neurones responsive to faces in the temporal cortex: Studies of functional organization, sensitivity to identity and relation to perception. *Human Neurobiology, 3,* 197–208.

Rolls, E. T., Miyashita, Y., Cahusac, P. M. B., Kesner, R. P., Niki, H., Feigenbaum, J. D., & Bach, L. (1989). Hippocampal neurons in the monkey with activity related to the place in which a stimulus is shown. *Journal of Neuroscience, 9,* 1835–1845.

Russell, W. R. (1971). *The traumatic amnesias.* London: Oxford University Press.

Sakai, K., & Miyashita, Y. (1991). Neural organization for the long-term memory of paired associates. *Nature, 354,* 152–155.

Squire, L. R., Slater, P. C., & Chace, P. M. (1975). Retrograde amnesia: Temporal gradient in very long term following electroconvulsive therapy. *Science, 187,* 77–79.

Suzuki, W. A., & Amaral, D. G. (1990). Cortical inputs to the CA1 field of the monkey hippocampus originate from the perirhinal and parahippocampal cortex but not from area TE. *Neuroscience Letters, 115,* 43–48.

Van Hoesen, G. W., & Pandya, D. N. (1975). Some connections of the entorhinal (area 28) and perirhinal (area 35) cortices of the rhesus monkey: I. Temporal lobe afferents. *Brain Research, 95,* 1–24.

Warrington, E. K. (1982). The double dissociation of short- and long-term memory deficits. In L. S. Cermak (Ed.), *Human memory and amnesia* (pp. 61–70). Hillsdale, NJ: Erlbaum.

Watanabe, T., & Niki, H. (1985). Hippocampal unit activity and delayed response in the monkey. *Brain Research, 325,* 241–254.

Yukie, M., & Iwai, E. (1988). Direct projections from the ventral TE area of the inferotemporal cortex to hippocampal field CA1 in the monkey. *Neuroscience Letters, 88,* 6–10.

Zeki, S., & Shipp, S. (1988). The functional logic of cortical connections. *Nature, 335,* 311–317.

Zola-Morgan, S., Squire, L. R., & Amaral, D. G. (1986). Human amnesia and the medial temporal region: Enduring memory impairment following a bilateral lesion limited to field CA1 of the hippocampus. *Journal of Neuroscience, 6,* 2950–2967.

Zola-Morgan, S., Squire, L. R., Amaral, D. G., & Suzuki, W. A. (1989). Lesions of perirhinal and parahippocampal cortex that spare the amygdala and hippocampal formation produce severe memory impairment. *Journal of Neuroscience, 9,* 4355–4370.

Zola-Morgan, S., & Squire, L. R. (1990). The primate hippocampal formation: Evidence for a time-limited role in memory storage. *Science, 250,* 288–290.

32

Aging, Memory, and Cholinergic Systems: Studies Using Delayed-Matching and Delayed-Nonmatching Tasks in Rats

STEPHEN B. DUNNETT

Background to a Personal Interest

My interest in developing a task to assess short-term memory in the rat arose by a somewhat circuitous route. In collaboration with Anders Björklund and colleagues in Sweden, my colleagues and I had found that dopamine-rich nigral grafts could reinnervate the dopamine-depleted neostriatum of 6-hydroxydopamine-lesioned rats and ameliorate their profound impairments in simple motor behaviors (Dunnett, Björklund, Gage, & Stenevi, 1985). How general were these results? We sought to address this issue by considering whether neural tissues implanted into other systems of the brain might be equally effective functionally.

Fimbria–Fornix Lesions and Cholinergic Grafts

A logical second system for investigation was the hippocampus. This structure had been much studied anatomically as a suitable target site for implantation of cholinergic, adrenergic, and serotonergic tissues (Björklund, Stenevi, & Svendgaard, 1976), and the role of the hippocampus in mediating learning, memory, and spatial functions was the subject of much discussion at the time (O'Keefe & Nadel, 1978; Olton, Becker, & Handelman, 1979)—as indeed it still is. The work of David Gaffan, David Olton, and others (e.g., Gaffan, 1972; Olton, Walker, & Gage, 1978) had shown that transection of the fimbria–fornix (FF) could induce functional impairments that were as profound as those induced by destruction of the hippocampus itself. Such FF lesions remove regulatory cholinergic, adrenergic, and serotonergic afferents arising in the basal forebrain and brainstem, as well as destroying subcortical efferents of the hippocampus. At the same time, these lesions leave intact the neocortical–entorhinal–dentate–hippocampal–subicular–neocortical circuit, which is most probably necessary for relaying the complex information utilized by the hippocampus in processing cognitive tasks.

In a first study of the functional effects of transplantation of cholinergic neurons, we found that septal grafts could reverse the deficits of rats with FF lesions in learning a T-maze alternation task (Dunnett, Low, Iversen, Stenevi, & Björklund, 1982), and that reformation of a cholinergic innervation of the hippocampus was a necessary condition for recovery to take place. Subsequent studies have confirmed the viability of septal grafts in rats with FF lesions tested on a variety of maze-learning tasks (Daniloff, Bodony, Low, & Wells, 1985; Low et al., 1982; Nilsson, Shapiro, Gage, Olton, & Björklund, 1987; Shapiro et al., 1989). In general, septal grafts had a moderate beneficial effect, although it was sometimes necessary to promote cholinergic activity with physostigmine to yield significant effects, and the grafted rats never achieved the level of performance observed in unlesioned control rats. More recent studies indicate that grafts that combine cholinergic and serotonergic neurons are even more effective than grafts of cholinergic neurons alone, at least when assessed in spatial water mazes (Nilsson, Brundin, & Björklund, 1990; see also Richter-Levin & Segal, 1989). By contrast, locus coeruleus grafts, which formed a new noradrenergic innervation of the hippocampus, were ineffective against the rats' maze deficits, but did ameliorate their spontaneous locomotor hyperactivity (Dunnett, Gage, et al., 1982). Thus, the pattern of graft activity is dependent on the neuronal specificity of the graft tissue, with cholinergic reinnervation being necessary for restoring the animals' ability to learn complex spatial mazes.

Aging and Cholinergic Grafts

Although an association among cholinergic systems, aging, and memory dysfunction had been suggested in a number of previous studies (e.g., Deutsch, 1971; Drachman & Sahakian, 1980; Perry et al., 1978), the hypothesis that neurodegenerative decline in forebrain cholinergic systems is fundamental to the memory impairments associated with aging and dementia only attracted widespread attention following the publication of two influential reviews by Bartus, Dean, Beer, and Lippa (1982) and by Coyle, Price, and DeLong (1983). This association stimulated us to consider whether cholinergic grafts might be effective against some of the deficits that aged rats show on learning tasks (Barnes, 1979; Kubanis & Zornetzer, 1981; Wallace, Steinert, Scobie, & Spear, 1980). Septal grafts were found to survive transplantation into the hippocampus of otherwise intact aged rats, and the profound age-related impairments in learning the Morris water maze recovered almost to a youthful level of performance in the old animals after transplantation (Gage, Björklund, Stenevi, Dunnett, & Kelly, 1984). Fred Gage has gone on to show that the recovery in grafted old rats is sustained by an atropine-sensitive mechanism, suggesting that the age-related deficit in the water maze is indeed cholinergic in nature (Gage & Björklund, 1986).

Basal Forebrain Lesions and Cholinergic Grafts

In addition to the septo-hippocampal projection, a second major forebrain cholinergic system projects from the nucleus basalis magnocellularis (NBM) of the basal forebrain to the neocortical mantle. The cholinergic hypothesis of aging involved the idea that degeneration of the NBM contributes to age-related impairments in memory to as great an extent as the septo-hippocampal circuitry (Bartus et al., 1982; Coyle et al., 1983). If this is so, then destruction of the NBM in experimental animals should disrupt their mnemonic capacities. A series of studies soon found that basal forebrain lesions made with a variety of toxins disrupted the acquisition and performance of rats in a variety of avoidance and maze tasks (Fisher & Hanin, 1986; Hagan & Morris, 1988; Smith, 1988; Wenk & Olton, 1987). This then provided the rationale for our first investigation of the effects of cholinergic grafts in the neocortex, in which we found that the grafts could improve the retention capacity of animals with basal forebrain lesions in a passive avoidance task (Dunnett, Toniolo, et al., 1985; Fine, Dunnett, Björklund, & Iversen, 1985).

Is the Deficit Cholinergic?

Although the reversal of passive avoidance deficits by cholinergic grafts appears at first sight to support the cholinergic hypothesis, several aspects of the data relating to the specificity of the effects have worried us. The first concern relates to whether the deficits are actually cholinergic in nature. Although basal forebrain lesions do indeed destroy the cholinergic neurons of the NBM, they destroy many other noncholinergic neurons as well. Parallel deficits induced by anticholinergic drugs, and reversal of lesion deficits with cholinomimetic drugs, for a while supported the view that the lesion deficits were attributable to cholinergic damage. However, a fundamental challenge to this specificity arose when the efficacy of different toxins was compared (Dunnett, Whishaw, Jones, & Bunch, 1987). In particular, lesions of the basal forebrain made with kainic acid or ibotenic acid induce profound deficits on a variety of learning and memory tasks, even in animals with relatively mild destruction of the cortical cholinergic projection. By direct contrast, quisqualic acid lesions, which are far more destructive of NBM neurons, induce at most mild impairments on the same tasks (Dunnett et al., 1987; Etherington, Mittleman, & Robbins, 1987; Markowska, Wenk, & Olton, 1990; Robbins et al., 1989; Wenk, Markowska, & Olton, 1989). This double dissociation strongly suggests that the deficits in many (if not all) learning and memory tasks must be attributable to destruction of noncholinergic systems in the basal forebrain, rather than to destruction of the cholinergic neurons of the NBM per se.

Although a partial resolution can be obtained by systematic covariation of the anatomical and functional consequences of alternative toxins, the problem of lesion specificity will only be adequately resolved with the development of toxins that permit selective destruction of the cholinergic neurons alone, in the basal forebrain or elsewhere.

Is the Deficit Mnemonic?

A second concern relates to whether the deficits are actually mnemonic in nature. Although maze-learning and avoidance tasks are dependent upon normal learning processes for their acquisition and upon intact memory for their adequate performance, it is not at all clear that the rats' impairments following basal forebrain lesions (or indeed in aging) are specifically due to a disturbance of learning or memory processes per se. Similar impairments might result from disturbances in response selection, motivation, spatial mapping abilities, or attention to the relevant discriminative stimuli (Collerton, 1986; Hagan & Morris, 1988). Indeed, detailed psychopharmacological studies have tended to characterize the effects of anticholinergic drugs in terms of a disturbance of attention or stimulus discrimination rather than a disturbance of memory per se (Heise, 1975; Warburton, 1974). Moreover, NBM lesions produce profound neurological and sensorimotor as well as learning impairments (Dunnett et al., 1987; Whishaw, O'Connor, & Dunnett, 1985; Wozniak, Stewart, Finger, & Olney, 1989). Some of these noncognitive impairments are also reversed by cholinergic grafts implanted in the neocortex (Dunnett, Toniolo, et al., 1985), which suggests that the functional contribution of the cholinergic neurons of the basal forebrain may be essentially nonmnemonic in nature.

We have attempted to address the issue of the specific involvement of memory systems by developing a delayed-matching task for use in rats, with the intention that analyses of rates of forgetting might permit specific mnemonic effects to be distinguished from other nonmnemonic interpretations.

Delayed-Matching and Delayed-Nonmatching Tasks

Delayed-Matching-to-Sample and Delayed-Nonmatching-to-Sample Tasks

The theoretical power of discrete-trial delayed response tasks is that the memory challenge can be varied from trial to trial by variation of the delay interval over which the to-be-remembered information must be retained. In such paradigms, if an experimental animal manifests normal performance at the shortest delays (when the memory load is minimal), then it can be inferred that the animal has no primary sensory or motor impairments in performing the task, is attending to the relevant task stimuli, has learned the decision rule, and is motivated to work for the task reward. If the experimental animal then manifests progressive impairments when the memory load is increased (which is achieved by extending the delay interval), we can have greater confidence that the animal's deficit is indeed specifically mnemonic, with the increased slope of the delay–performance curve representing an increased rate of forgetting.

The most widely used versions of such discrete-trial delayed response tasks are the delayed-matching-to-sample (DMTS) and delayed-nonmatching-to-sample (DNMTS) tests. DMTS and DNMTS tasks have long provided a powerful way of assessing short-term memory function in primates. For example, the observation of mnemonic deficits in humans following temporal lobectomy stimulated further studies of short-term memory function in primates using DMTS and DNMTS tasks. These have included investigations of the effect of lesions of the hippocampus, the amygdala, and overlying temporal cortex (Mishkin, 1978; Zola-Morgan, Squire, & Mishkin, 1982); the contrasts between the capacities of young and old animals (Bartus, Fleming, & Johnson, 1978); the effects of cholinergic blockade with the muscarinic antagonist scopolamine (Bartus & Johnson, 1976; Glick & Jarvik, 1970); and most recently the effects of NBM lesions

(Aigner et al., 1987; Ridley, Murray, Johnson, & Baker, 1986). Among these reports, the hippocampal–amygdala lesion studies and the studies of aged monkeys reveal clear delay-dependent deficits, indicating a specific disturbance of memory function. By contrast, the effects of scopolamine and of NBM lesions are more controversial; at least some studies indicate that both these and other cholinergic drugs induce nonspecific disturbances at all delay intervals, even the shortest (e.g., Glick & Jarvik, 1970).

Delayed-Matching-to-Position and Delayed-Nonmatching-to-Position Tasks

Whereas training rats to learn DMTS and DNMTS tasks has been achieved in open mazes (Aggleton, 1985; Alexinsky & Chapouthier, 1978; Rothblat & Hayes, 1987), it has proved more difficult to train rats on similar tasks in an operant test apparatus, which would enable greater experimental control of performance (Wallace et al., 1980; Dunnett, 1985). A possible reason is that the visual modality does not provide salient stimuli for rats, which learn olfactory or spatial cues much more readily (Hodos, 1970). We have therefore developed two versions of a paired-trial operant task based on spatial sample stimuli (the "delayed-matching-to-position" [DMTP] task and the "delayed-nonmatching-to-position" [DNMTP] task), which were designed to be closely analogous to primate DMTS and DNMTS tasks (Dunnett, 1985; see also Kesner, Bierley, & Peebles, 1981, and van Haaren & van Hest, 1989). The elements of the DMTP paradigm are illustrated schematically in Figure 32.1. In both the DMTP and DNMTP tasks, one of two retractable levers in the operant chamber is presented at the start of each trial as the sample to which the rat must respond. Then, after a variable delay, the rat is confronted with a choice: Both levers are presented simultaneously, and the rat must respond to either the same (in DMTP) or the opposite (in DNMTP) lever as the sample to gain reward. The distinctive feature of this task is that during the delay interval the animal must respond to the central panel in order to obtain insertion of the choice levers into the chamber. Panel responding (on a variable-interval schedule) provides a supplementary distractor task during the delay interval and keeps the rat centralized between the two choice levers, thereby preventing the adoption of position or orienting strategies to solve the task without recourse to memory.

The DMTP and DNMTP tasks provide a paradigm within which it has proved possible to compare systematically a variety of different pharmacological and surgical manipulations in rats that have been proposed to provide animal models of aging. These are summarized in Table 32.1, and provide the topic for the remainder of the present chapter.

The Nature of Age-Related Impairments

The Effects of Aging

As in monkeys, so also aged rats have been reported to show deficits in a variety of maze and other learning tasks dependent upon memory for correct performance

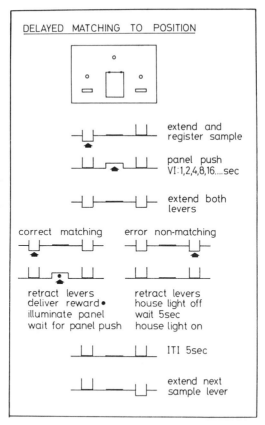

FIGURE 32.1. Schematic illustration of the delayed-matching-to-position (DMTP) task. Above is shown the side wall of the operant chamber (Campden Instruments, U.K.), built with a hinged square Perspex panel covering the central food well, and a retractable response lever on either side. Illumination is provided by a house light in the ceiling and a panel light behind the Perspex panel. Additional stimulus lights above the panel and each response lever are not used at any stage of the task. Below is shown each stage of a trial viewed from above, with each response made by the rat indicated by a filled arrow. On each trial the side of the sample lever and the variable-interval delay (VI; range 0–16 seconds, 0–24 seconds, or 0–32 seconds in the different experiments) are selected at random. The delayed-nonmatching-to-position (DNMTP) task is identical, apart from the one difference that the "error" contingencies follow a matching response and the "correct" contingencies follow a nonmatching response. Redrawn from Dunnett (1987).

(Barnes, 1979; Bartus, Flicker, & Dean, 1983; Gage, Dunnett, & Björklund, 1984; Gage, Kelly, & Björklund, 1984; Kubanis & Zornetzer, 1981). In order to identify the extent to which short-term memory was specifically implicated in these impairments, we investigated separate groups of young, middle-aged, and old rats (aged 6, 15, and 24 months, respectively) on both the DMTP and the DNMTP versions of our task (Dunnett, Evenden, & Iversen, 1988). Performance in the DNMTP task is shown in Figure 32.2. All groups showed near-perfect performance at the shortest delays of 0, 1, or 2 seconds, and a progressive decline in performance at longer delays. However, the rate of decline was greater in the 24-month group than in the 6-month group on both versions of the task. The middle-aged (15-month) group was unimpaired on the DNMTP version (see Figure 32.2), although significant deficits were apparent by this age on the DMTP version of the task. These data indicate that old rats do indeed have

TABLE 32.1. Treatments That Do (and Do Not) Mimic Aging in the DMTP and DNMTP Tasks

Delay-dependent effects on STM	Delay-independent effects	No effects on task performance
Aging		
Aging[1,2]		
Septal grafts in aged HPC[2]		Arecoline in aged rats[1]
Septal grafts in aged PFC[2]		Physostigmine in aged rats[1]
Lesions		
FF lesion[3,5]	NBM lesion (ibo)[3]	NBM lesion (quis)[4,a]
Rostral PFC aspiration[5]	Caudal PFC aspiration[5]	Motor cortex aspiration[5]
Nucleus accumbens lesion[5]	Caudate–putamen lesion[5]	Parietal cortex aspiration[5]
Drugs		
Clonidine i.p.[6]	Scopolamine i.p.[3,4]	Nicotine i.p.[6,a]
	Physostigmine i.p.[3,6]	
	Amphetamine[3]	
Scopolamine in HPC[7]	Scopolamine in PFC[7]	

Note. STM, short-term memory; HPC, hippocampus; PFC, prefrontal cortex; FF, fimbria–fornix; NBM, nucleus basalis magnocellularis; ibo, ibotenic acid; quis, quisqualic acid.

[a]Although these treatments did not influence basic task performance, they did have effects on task acquisition or susceptibility to interference.

[1]Dunnett, Evenden, and Iversen (1988); [2]Dunnett, Badman, et al. (1988); [3]Dunnett (1985); [4]Dunnett et al. (1989); [5]Dunnett (1990); [6]Dunnett and Martel (1990); [7]Dunnett et al. (1990).

specific delay-dependent impairments in their short-term memory capacity. Moreover, the pattern of impairment revealed by sensitive delayed-matching tasks in rats is directly comparable with the pattern of impairment observed in aged monkeys (Bartus et al., 1978) and humans (Flicker, Ferris, Bartus, & Crook, 1984; Irle, Kessler, & Markowitsch, 1987; Sahakian et al., 1988).

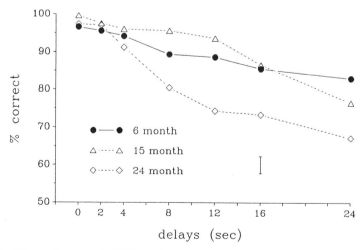

FIGURE 32.2. Effects of aging on DNMTP performance. Percentage correct at each delay (0–24 seconds) by rats 6, 15, and 24 months of age, collapsed over 7 days of testing at asymptotic levels of performance. The vertical bar indicates 2 *SEM*. The data are from Dunnett, Evenden, and Iversen (1988).

Cholinergic Replacement with Drugs

It has been suggested that if declining memory capacity in aging is attributable to a decline in cholinergic activation in the cortex, then cholinergic replacement therapies might be effective (Bartus et al., 1982, 1983). In particular, Bartus et al. (1983) suggested that both the cholinergic agonist arecoline and the cholinesterase inhibitor physostigmine can improve aged rats' performance on passive avoidance tests. We therefore administered both of these drugs over a range of doses to our young and aged rats trained in the DMTP and DNMTP tasks. However, we were unable to find any dose of either drug that produced either a general improvement of performance in all groups, or indeed any selective benefit to the aged rats (Dunnett, Evenden, & Iversen, 1988). These pharmacological treatments do not, therefore, support the hypothesis that generalized pharmacological activation of cholinergic systems can ameliorate short-term memory deficits in aged rats.

Cholinergic Replacement with Grafts

Although cholinergic replacement by pharmacological therapy was ineffective in our old rats, the synaptic reinnervation and greater integration provided by cholinergic grafts in young animals warranted investigation of similar grafts in the aged brain. We therefore compared the effects of cholinergic grafts implanted either into the neocortex or into the hippocampus on the ability of old rats to learn the DNMTP task (Dunnett, Badman, Rogers, Evenden, & Iversen, 1988). As shown in Figure 32.3, the previous demonstration of an increased rate of forgetting in old rats was replicated. Moreover, the delay-dependent deficits of old rats were significantly improved by the

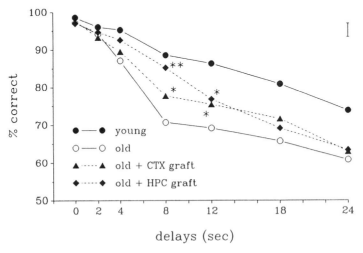

FIGURE 32.3. Effects of cholinergic grafts on DNMTP performance by old rats. Percentage correct at each delay (0–24 seconds) by old rats with cortical (CTX) or hippocampal (HPC) grafts, collapsed over 7 days of training at asymptotic levels of performance. The vertical bar indicates 2 *SEM*. The data are from Dunnett, Badman, Rogers, Evenden, and Iversen (1988).

grafts at intermediate delays, when the memory load was moderate. Of particular interest is the fact that grafts implanted in the neocortex were almost as effective as grafts implanted into the hippocampus. These observations suggest that the cholinergic innervation of both cortical and hippocampal systems may be implicated in the age-related decline in short-term memory. Moreover, whereas diffuse or tonic receptor activation by drugs is insufficient to reverse the hypothesized cholinergic dysfunction, cholinergic reinnervation by grafts does appear to be effective.

Do Cholinergic Manipulations Model Aging?

The transplantation data give credence to the hypothesis that age-related deficits in the DMTP and DNMTP tasks (1) reflect impairments in short-term memory and (2) involve cholinergic systems, at least in part. We therefore have the basis to start considering whether experimental manipulations of central cholinergic systems can provide valid models of aging. One major determinant of the validity of each experimental model will be the extent to which the characteristic delay-dependent pattern of deficit manifested by aged animals is reproduced.

Peripherally Administered Drugs

In an early experiment (Dunnett, 1985), 12 rats were trained on the DMTP task. Once stable baseline performance had been achieved, four doses of scopolamine (0.125, 0.25, 0.5, and 1.0 mg/kg) were administered in counterbalanced order. Scopolamine induced a dose-dependent disruption of performance on the task. In particular, as shown in Figure 32.4 for the 0.5 mg/kg dose, the drug induced impairments at all delays (including the shortest). By contrast, injections of methylscopolamine, which does not cross the blood–brain barrier and so controls for the peripheral effects of scopolamine, had no significant effect on choice accuracy. The generalized nonspecific disturbance induced by scopolamine has been subsequently replicated in a larger study (Dunnett, Rogers, & Jones, 1989). Thus, central cholinergic blockade by scopolamine appears to disrupt the animals' discriminative capacities for accurate performance of the task contingencies, rather than specifically influencing mnemonic capacity per se (see also e.g., Heise, 1975; Warburton, 1974).

A similar conclusion was reached from injections of the cholinomimetic drug physostigmine. In the first study of this drug, a low dose of physostigmine (0.05 mg/kg) was seen to produce a small but significant enhancement of performance across all delays (Dunnett, 1985). The lack of any significant dose × delay interaction was again not compatible with an action on memory processes per se, but rather suggested improved attention to the relevant stimuli. Similarly, in a subsequent study that compared the effects of several drugs, physostigmine again had no significant delay-dependent effect, although in this case the significant drug effects were attributable to higher doses impairing performance at all delays (Dunnett & Martel, 1990).

By contrast with the cholinergic drugs scopolamine and physostigmine, the noradrenergic α_2 agonist clonidine disrupted performance (Dunnett & Martel, 1990) in

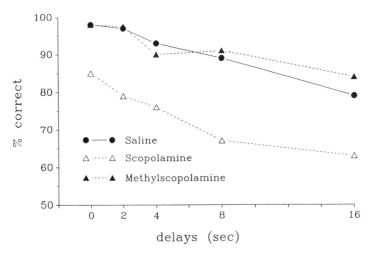

FIGURE 32.4. Effect of the muscarinic antagonist scopolamine on the DMTP task. Scopolamine (0.5 mg/ kg, i.p.) disrupted performance at all delays, whereas methylscopolamine had no effect, demonstrating that the scopolamine effect resulted from a central action of the drug. The data are from Dunnett (1985).

a delay-dependent manner, which was compatible with an influence on short-term memory function. However, the effect of clonidine was to impair performance progressively at each ascending dose, in contrast to the beneficial effects of low doses reported by Arnsten and Goldman-Rakic (1985). The most likely reason for this discrepancy is that the present experiments were conducted on young animals whose performance was perhaps already optimal, whereas Arnsten and Goldman-Rakic conducted their tests on impaired aged monkeys.

Of course, the problem with all pharmacological studies, especially when the effects are to cause generalized, nonspecific impairments, is that peripherally administered drugs act throughout the nervous system. Consequently, cholinergic drugs for instance will influence all cholinergic neurons in the brainstem, diencephalon, and basal ganglia, in addition to the basal forebrain cells of present interest. These additional sites of action may induce nonspecific deficits—that is, disturbance in nonmnemonic systems such as attention or motor initiation—which would mask any effects of the drugs on memory systems per se. Resolution of this issue requires the use of experimental manipulations that are restricted to identified populations of cholinergic neurons in the brain.

Fimbria–Fornix and Basal Forebrain Lesions

In the first study of operant DMTP in rats (Dunnett, 1985), following the drug treatments described above, the animals were divided into three matched groups (1) to receive basal forebrain lesions by stereotaxic injection of 0.4 μl 0.06 M ibotenic acid into the vicinity of the NBM cholinergic cells in the ventral pallidum–substantia innominata; (2) to receive FF lesions by aspirative transection of the fiber bundle under visual guidance; or (3) to remain as unoperated controls. Training on the DMTP task recommenced 5 weeks later.

As shown in Figure 32.5, both NBM and FF lesions impaired postoperative retention of task performance. Although the deficit was greater in the NBM group in the first few days of postoperative testing, these rats rapidly relearned the task up to control levels within approximately 15 days. By contrast, although the FF lesions initially induced a somewhat less severe impairment, that impairment did not decline with further training. Inspection of performance at different delay intervals (see Figure 32.5) indicated that whereas the deficit in the rats with FF lesions was delay-dependent, akin to that seen in the aged rats (compare with Figure 32.2), the deficit induced by NBM lesions was constant across all delays (including the shortest), akin to that induced by a moderate dose of scopolamine (compare with Figure 32.4).

The characteristic delay-dependent deficit induced by FF lesions has been replicated several times (e.g., Dunnett, 1990). However, although the FF lesion appears to provide a potential model of aging, these lesions are not specific to cholinergic neurons. Rather, the FF lesion transects all subcortical afferent and efferent connections of the hippocampus, and it is not possible to determine from such data whether the cholinergic component or some other component of the circuitry is central to the mnemonic deficit. We have therefore sought to provide regionally specific cholinergic disturbance by central administration of cholinergic antagonist drugs.

Centrally Administered Drugs

In order to determine whether cholinergic neurons of the hippocampus are specifically implicated in the delay-dependent deficits induced by nonspecific distur-

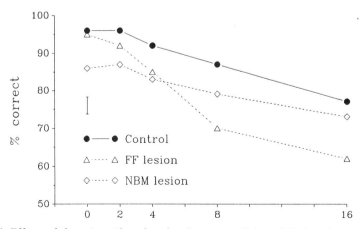

FIGURE 32.5. Effects of ibotenic acid nucleus basalis magnocellularis (NBM) and aspirative fimbria-fornix (FF) lesions on DMTP performance in young rats. Percentage correct at each delay (0–16 seconds), collapsed across 18 days of testing. The vertical bar indicates 2 *SEM*. The data are from Dunnett (1985).

bance of the hippocampal circuitry, we prepared groups of pretrained rats with cannulae implanted bilaterally in the dorsal hippocampus (Dunnett, Wareham, & Torres, 1990). These animals then received counterbalanced doses of the muscarinic antagonist scopolamine injected bilaterally via the cannulae. The effect of ascending doses of the drug on DNMTP performance are shown in Figure 32.6. The low dose of scopolamine had a small effect that was just detectable at the longest delays; a moderate dose induced a more extensive deficit at all but the shortest delays; and the highest dose disrupted performance at all delays, although again this was less marked at the shortest delays.

Thus, scopolamine does induce delay-dependent deficits when it is administered to the specific area—the hippocampus—implicated as being involved in short-term memory by the neurochemically nonspecific lesion study.

Role of Cortical Cholinergic Systems

Basal Forebrain Lesions

As indicated earlier, the cholinergic hypothesis emphasized the involvement of the NBM–cortical cholinergic system in the memory dysfunctions associated with aging. And yet the study in which the DMTP paradigm was first developed (Dunnett, 1985) indicated that ibotenic acid lesions of the basal forebrain (including NBM) had at best a nonspecific effect on short-term memory performance, as reflected by the significant delay-independent disturbance (see Figure 32.5). This situation is made even more complex by further analysis of the effects of different basal forebrain

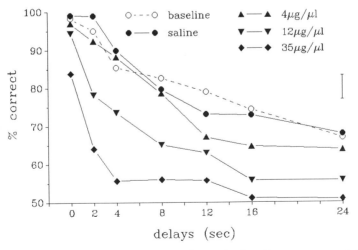

FIGURE 32.6. Effects of scopolamine injected bilaterally into the dorsal hippocampus on DNMTP performance. The vertical bar indicates 2 *SEM*. The data are from Dunnett, Wareham, and Torres (1990).

lesions made by different toxins. In particular, as described earlier for other tasks, quisqualic acid lesions induced no detectable disturbance whatsoever in rats' capacities to perform either the DMTP or the DNMTP task, even though the lesions were effective in producing extensive depletion of cholinergic innervation of the whole dorsal and lateral neocortical mantle (Dunnett et al., 1989). This is not to say that quisqualate lesions of the basal forebrain are without effect—indeed, they do produce profound deficits in the animals' acquisition of the DNMTP nonmatching contingency rule, and in reversal learning between matching and nonmatching versions of the task. Rather, the pattern of results indicates that whereas these lesions may profoundly disturb certain aspects of discrimination learning, they have no effect whatsoever on the animals' mnemonic capacities.

At first sight, these results might suggest that the NBM cortical cholinergic innervation is not involved in short-term memory functions. However, such a conclusion is premature. In particular, what are we then to make of the apparent benefit provided by grafts that result in a cholinergic reinnervation of the neocortex in aged animals (see Figure 32.3; Dunnett, Badman, et al., 1988)?

A possible resolution of these discrepancies arises from consideration of the topography of denervation induced by NBM lesions. Most studies of the effects of NBM lesions simply report a single measure of the extent of cortical denervation, such as a decline in choline acetyltransferase activity in cortical slabs dissected from the dorsal or lateral fronto-parietal neocortex. By contrast, the few studies that have reported biochemical or histochemical descriptions of the *pattern* of denervation are consistent in indicating that the denervation is not uniform. Rather, NBM lesions typically induce profound loss of the ascending cholinergic innervation of the dorsal and lateral quadrants of the whole neocortical mantle throughout its rostrocaudal extent, but leave intact the innervation in the limbic borders (i.e., the medial and orbital prefrontal, piriform, and entorhinal areas). And yet it is just these areas, particularly the prefrontal cortex, that we might predict *a priori* to be implicated in short-term memory function.

Cortical Lesions

I have sought to test this hypothesis by assessing whether the prefrontal cortex is indeed critical for short-term memory, as assessed by DMTP performance (Dunnett, 1990). A large group of rats was pretrained on the DMTP task prior to receiving lesions of (1) the prefrontal cortex (PFC), (2) the motor cortex, (3) the dorsal parietal cortex, or (4) the FF, or to remaining as unoperated controls. As shown in Figure 32.7, lesions of the motor and parietal areas (which are both extensively denervated by NBM lesions) had no effect whatsoever on DMTP performance. Lesions of the FF induced a delay-dependent disruption of short-term memory function, replicating the earlier observations (compare with Figure 32.5; Dunnett, 1985). The results of the PFC group were initially disappointing: The lesion appeared to disrupt performance at all delays, suggesting a nonspecific impairment. However, more careful inspection of the data indicated that the seven PFC lesion rats fell into two distinct subgroups: Three had a

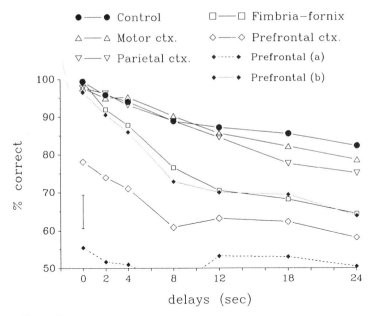

FIGURE 32.7. Effects of aspirative lesions in different regions of the neocortex or allocortex on DMTP performance. The prefrontal cortex lesion group has been divided into two subgroups on both behavioral and histological criteria (see text). The vertical bar indicates 2 *SEM*. The data are from Dunnett (1990).

completely nonspecific impairment (subgroup a), whereas four had a delay-dependent impairment that was indistinguishable from the effects of the FF lesion (subgroup b).

The situation became clarified when it was found that two PFC subgroups were discriminable on the basis of histological reconstruction of the lesions. The lesions in the rats with the delay-dependent deficit (subgroup b) were all restricted to the rostral medial wall of the PFC. By contrast, the lesions in the rats with the nonspecific deficit (subgroup a) were all more extensive and involved bilateral invasion of the anterior cingulate cortex (Cg3). These results therefore not only are compatible with the hypothesis that discrete areas of the rostral PFC are critically involved in mnemonic function, but also suggest that the PFC is itself subdivided into multiple systems implicated in different aspects of spatial and temporal planning, including (but not limited to) mnemonic functions (Rosenkilde, 1979).

The confirmation of the importance of a topographic perspective on NBM–cortical functions poses two further issues that require resolution:

1. If the rostral part of medial PFC is indeed involved in short-term memory, does the ascending cholinergic innervation play any role in this function?

2. If the NBM projects to motor and parietal cortical areas that are not involved in DMTP performance, and the (relatively) more selective quisqualic acid lesions of the NBM (which remove the cortical cholinergic innervation from these cortical areas) also have no effect on DMTP, what then is the substrate for the deficits induced by ibotenic acid lesions of the basal forebrain?

Prefrontal Cholinergic Involvement

Naturally, our first approach to this issue was to attempt to find a site for injecting quisqualic acid or some other neurotoxin that would result in cholinergic deafferentation of the medial PFC. Mindful of the suggestion that the prefrontal innervation may arise not from the NBM itself but from the horizontal limb of the diagonal band of Broca (e.g., Luiten, Gaykema, Traber, & Spencer, 1987), we have made several series of trial lesions, injecting quisqualic acid, ibotenic acid, or N-methyl-D-aspartate into a variety of basal forebrain sites. Although horizontal limb lesions will give mild denervation of the cingulate cortex and dorsomedial lip of the PFC, we have not as yet found a set of coordinates that will yield reliable and extensive cholinergic deafferentation extending into the depths of the medial wall of the PFC. It is possible that this approach is essentially doomed to fail, however, since it is now apparent that this particular area of neocortex receives an additional cholinergic input from brainstem cholinergic cell groups (Vincent, Satoh, Armstrong, & Fibiger, 1983). Consequently, it will be necessary either to employ an approach using multiple subcortical lesion sites at different levels of the neuraxis or to develop an alternative lesion strategy targeting the cortical terminals or receptors.

We have attempted this latter approach by investigating the consequences of bilateral infusions of the muscarinic antagonist scopolamine into the PFC. The first study was conducted on the same animals that received infusions into the hippocampus (Dunnett et al., 1990; see Figure 32.6). The results of this initial study were disappointing: Scopolamine produced a modest disruption of DNMTP performance, but equally at all delay intervals, suggesting a relatively nonspecific impairment. However, as it is now clear that distinct subdivisions with the PFC may be important, the delay-independent nature of the deficit in this first study could equally have resulted from spread of the pharmacological blockade into the more caudal cingulate margins of the prefrontal cortex. Consequently, the precise contribution of the cholinergic innervation of rostral PFC remains ambiguous. Further studies are currently underway to refine our understanding of this local topography.

Prefrontal Efferent Systems

The remaining issue that requires clarification is the identification of the substrates for the variety of deficits induced by ibotenic acid lesions or by other basal forebrain lesions that cause extensive nonspecific damage (Abrogast & Kozlowski, 1988; Everitt et al., 1987). Although the quisqualic acid lesion data rule out a destruction of the cholinergic neurons of the NBM as the primary basis of the full ibotenic acid syndrome, there are nevertheless many parallels with the effects of aging, cholinergic blockade, and cortical disturbance. Clarification may arise from the realisation that the ventral pallidum–substantia innominata area damaged by these lesions is a relay site for the major cortico-striato-pallido-thalamic circuits involved in the translation of cortical plans of action into effective motor programs. Consequently, although much research interest has focused on the involvement of ascending cholinergic systems, many of the

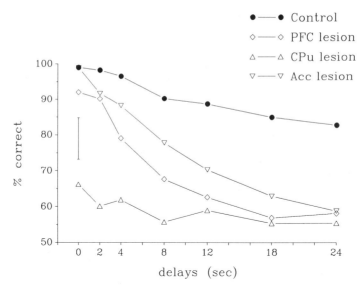

FIGURE 32.8. Effects of aspirative lesions of prefrontal cortex (PFC) and quinolinic acid lesions of the anterior medial caudate nucleus (CPu) or nucleus accumbens (Acc) on DMTP performance. The vertical bar indicates 2 *SEM*. The data are from Dunnett (1990).

effects observed after basal forebrain lesions may result from damage not of cortical afferent pathways but of cortical efferent pathways returning through the same area.

In order to evaluate this idea further, I (Dunnett, 1990) have considered the effects of lesions to the first-order subcortical targets of PFC efferents in the nucleus accumbens and medial parts of the head of the caudate nucleus (Christie, Summers, Stephenson, Cook, & Beart, 1987; McGeorge & Faull, 1989). As shown in Figure 32.8, these two lesions induced deficits that were directly comparable to the deficits induced by lesions in the rostral and caudal PFC, respectively (compare with Figure 32.7). It is noteworthy that delay-dependent deficits are obtained from the nucleus accumbens lesions, since this nucleus received converging inputs not only from the rostral PFC but also from the hippocampus (Kelley & Domesick, 1982), whereas the less-specific impairments were obtained from the medial caudate nucleus, which may be more closely related with inputs from the Cg3 area of the anterior cingulate cortex. It may also be expected that more or less specific delay-dependent and delay-independent deficits will be obtained from lesions in circumscribed areas in the globus pallidus, ventral pallidum, or substantia innominata, depending primarily on the precise output system that is disturbed, along the lines envisaged by Rosvold (1972) and Divac (1972) in their earlier formulation of the concept of prefrontal systems.

Summary and Conclusions

The effects of the variety of experimental manipulations on performance in the DMTP and DNMTP tasks have already been summarized in Table 32.1. From these observations, we can draw a number of conclusions about the involvement of cortical and other cholinergic systems in the mediation of normal short-term memory functions, and in the deficits that accumulate with aging.

1. Aged rats manifest a delay-dependent deficit in performance on both the DMTP and DNMTP tasks; this is suggestive of a fundamental impairment in the short-term retention of to-be-remembered information.

2. The delay-dependent deficit of aged rats can be ameliorated by cholinergic-rich grafts implanted in either the hippocampus or the neocortex (including PFC), suggesting a role of central cholinergic pathways in the age-related impairments in memory.

3. An equivalent benefit in DMTP/DNMTP performance has not been achieved with cholinomimetic drugs in aged rats. It is not resolved whether this difference is due to an essential limitation in pharmacological delivery systems or to the inadequate determination of optimal pharmacological treatments.

4. Bilateral lesions of the FF, disrupting subcortical connections of the hippocampus, induce delay-dependent deficits that are remarkably similar to the deficits seen in aging.

5. Cholinergic blockade by bilateral infusion of scopolamine into the hippocampus produces clear dose- and delay-dependent deficits in DNMTP performance, indicating that cholinergic afferents contribute to hippocampal mediation of short-term memory function.

6. Lesions of NBM-cortical cholinergic projections (e.g., with quisqualic acid) do not disrupt short-term memory function. This may be because they leave intact the cholinergic innervation in critical (PFC) cortical areas.

7. Aspirative lesions of the PFC (as of the FF) can induce delay-dependent deficits in short-term memory, provided that the lesion is targeted on the critical rostral subarea. Moreover, lesions of the major subcortical target of projections from the PFC to the nucleus accumbens produce similar delay-dependent deficits.

8. It has not yet been possible to make selective subcortical lesions that destroy cholinergic afferents to the medial PFC area, and cholinergic blockade by bilateral infusion of scopolamine into this cortical area has so far produced ambiguous deficits. Consequently, the role of PFC cholinergic systems in short-term memory functions remains unresolved.

Thus, at the time of this writing, a coherent story is beginning to emerge, although there remain several discrepancies for further investigation and resolution. The delay-dependent deficits in DMTP/DNMTP performance that have been interpreted in terms of short-term memory dysfunction appear to implicate two distinct neural circuits in the hippocampus and rostral PFC. These circuits are not independent; in addition to well-documented interconnections between them, their efferents also converge on the nucleus accumbens–ventral pallidal output system. The relative involvement of prefrontal and hippocampal systems in the deficits of aged rats has not been resolved, nor the extent to which the deficits of aged animals are *primarily* related to cholinergic dysfunction.

In conclusion, the operant delayed response paradigm using DMTP and DNMTP tasks is providing a powerful complement to conventional tests in rats for disentangling the role of central neurotransmitter pathways in the control of short-term memory functions, and their dysfunction in aging.

ACKNOWLEDGMENTS

The studies described in this chapter have been supported by grants from the Mental Health Foundation and the Medical Research Council.

REFERENCES

Abrogast, R. E., & Kozlowski, M. R. (1988). Quantitative morphometric analysis of the neurotoxic effects of the excitotoxin ibotenic acid on the basal forebrain. *Neurotoxicology, 9*, 39–46.

Aggleton, J. P. (1985). One-trial object recognition by rats. *Quarterly Journal of Experimental Psychology, 37B*, 279–294.

Aigner, T. G., Mitchell, S. J., Aggleton, J. P., DeLong, M. R., Struble, R. G., Price, D. L., Wenk, G. L., & Mishkin, M. (1987). Effects of scopolamine and physostigmine on recognition memory in monkeys with ibotenic-acid lesions of the nucleus basalis of Meynert. *Psychopharmacology, 92*, 292–300.

Alexinsky, T., & Chapouthier, G. (1978). A new behavioral model for studying delayed response in rats. *Behavioral Biology, 24*, 442–456.

Arnsten, A. F. T., & Goldman-Rakic, P.S. (1985). α_2- Adrenergic mechanisms in prefrontal cortex associated with cognitive decline in aged nonhuman primates. *Science, 230*, 1273–1276.

Barnes, C. A. (1979). Memory deficits associated with senescence: A neurophysiological and behavioral study in the rat. *Journal of Comparative and Physiological Psychology, 93*, 74–104.

Bartus, R. T., Dean, R. L., Beer, B., & Lippa, A. S. (1982). The cholinergic hypothesis of geriatric memory dysfunction. *Science, 217*, 408–417.

Bartus, R. T., Fleming, D., & Johnson, H. R. (1978). Aging in the rhesus monkey: Debilitating effects on short-term memory. *Journal of Gerontology, 33*, 858–871.

Bartus, R. T., Flicker, C., & Dean, R. L. (1983). Logical principles for the development of animal models of age-related memory impairments. In T. Crook, S. Ferris & R. T. Bartus (Eds.), *Assessment in geriatric psychopharmacology* (pp. 263–299). New Canaan, CT: Mark Powley Associates.

Bartus, R. T., & Johnson, H. R. (1976). Short-term memory in the rhesus monkey: Disruption from the anti-cholinergic scopolamine. *Physiology and Behavior, 11*, 571–575.

Björklund, A., Stenevi, U., & Svendgaard, N.-A. (1976). Growth of transplanted monoaminergic neurones into the adult hippocampus along the perforant path. *Nature, 262*, 787–790.

Christie, M. J., Summers, R. J., Stephenson, J. A., Cook, C. J., & Beart, P. M. (1987). Excitatory amino acid projections to the nucleus accumbens septi in the rat: A retrograde transport study utilizing D[^{3}H]aspartate and [^{3}H]GABA. *Neuroscience, 22*, 425–439.

Collerton, D. (1986). Cholinergic function and intellectual decline in Alzheimer's disease. *Neuroscience, 19*, 1–28.

Coyle, J. T., Price, D. L., & DeLong, M. R. (1983). Alzheimer's disease: A disorder of cortical cholinergic innervation. *Science, 219*, 1184–1190.

Daniloff, J. K., Bodony, R. P., Low, W. C., & Wells, J. (1985). Cross-species embryonic septal transplants: restoration of conditioned learning behavior. *Brain Research, 346*, 176–180.

Deutsch, J. A. (1971). The cholinergic synapse and the site of memory. *Science, 174*, 788–794.

Divac, I. (1972). Neostriatum and functions of prefrontal cortex. *Acta Neurobiologica Experimentalis (Warsaw), 32*, 461–471.

Drachman, D. A., & Sahakian, B. J. (1980). Memory, aging and pharmacosystems. In D. Stein (Ed.), *The psychobiology of aging: Problems and perspectives* (pp. 347–368). Amsterdam: Elsevier.

Dunnett, S. B. (1985). Comparative effects of cholinergic drugs and lesions of nucleus basalis or fimbria-fornix on delayed matching in rats. *Psychopharmacology, 87*, 357–363.

Dunnett, S. B. (1987). Anatomical and behavioural consequences of cholinergic-rich grafts to the neocortex of rats with lesions of the nucleus basalis magnocellularis. *Annals of the New York Academy of Sciences, 495*, 415–430.

Dunnett, S. B. (1990). Role of prefrontal cortex and striatal output systems in short-term memory deficits associated with ageing, basal forebrain lesions, and cholinergic-rich grafts. *Canadian Journal of Psychology, 44*, 210–232.

Dunnett, S. B., Badman, F., Rogers, D. C., Evenden, J. L., & Iversen, S. D. (1988). Cholinergic grafts in the neocortex or hippocampus of aged rats: reduction of delay-dependent deficits in the delayed non-matching to position task. *Experimental Neurology, 102*, 57–64.

Dunnett, S. B., Björklund, A., Gage, F. H., & Stenevi, U. (1985). Transplantation of mesencephalic dopamine neurones to the striatum of adult rats. In A. Björklund & U. Stenevi (Eds.), *Neural grafting in the mammalian CNS* (pp. 451–469). Amsterdam: Elsevier.

Dunnett, S. B., Evenden, J. L., & Iversen, S. D. (1988). Delay-dependent short-term memory impairments in aged rats. *Psychopharmacology, 96*, 174–180.

Dunnett, S. B., Gage, F. H., Björklund, A., Stenevi, U., Low, W. C., & Iversen, S. D. (1982). Hippocampal deafferentation: Transplant-derived reinnervation and functional recovery. *Scandanavian Journal of Psychology* (Suppl. 1), 104–111.

Dunnett, S. B., Low, W. C., Iversen, S. D., Stenevi, U., & Björklund, A. (1982). Septal transplants restore maze learning in rats with fornix-fimbria lesions. *Brain Research, 251*, 335–348.

Dunnett, S. B., & Martel, F. L. (1990). Proactive interference effects on short-term memory in rats. I. Basic parameters and drug effects. *Behavioral Neuroscience, 104*, 655–665.

Dunnett, S. B., Rogers, D. C., & Jones, G. H. (1989). Effects of nucleus basalis magnocellularis lesions on delayed matching and nonmatching to position tasks: disruption of conditional discrimination learning but not of short-term memory. *European Journal of Neuroscience, 1*, 395–406.

Dunnett, S. B., Toniolo, G., Fine, A., Ryan, C. N., Björklund, A., & Iversen, S. D. (1985). Transplantation of embryonic ventral forebrain neurons to the neocortex of rats with lesions of nucleus basalis magnocellularis: II. Sensorimotor and learning impairments. *Neuroscience, 16*, 787–797.

Dunnett, S. B., Wareham, A. T., & Torres, E. M. (1990). Cholinergic blockade in prefrontal cortex and hippocampus disrupts short-term memory in rats. *NeuroReport, 1*, 61–64.

Dunnett, S. B., Whishaw, I. Q., Jones, G. H., & Bunch, S. T. (1987). Behavioural, biochemical and histochemical effects of different neurotoxic amino acids injected into nucleus basalis magnocellularis of rats. *Neuroscience, 20*, 653–669.

Etherington, R., Mittleman, G., & Robbins, T. W. (1987). Comparative effects of nucleus basalis and fimbria-fornix lesions on delayed matching and alternation tests of memory. *Neuroscience Research Communications, 1*, 135–143.

Everitt, B. J., Robbins, T. W., Evenden, J. L., Marston, H. M., Jones, G. H., & Sirkiä, T. E. (1987). The effects of excitotoxic lesions of the substantia innominata, ventral and dorsal globus pallidus on the acquisition and retention of a conditional visual discrimination: Implications for cholinergic hypotheses of learning and memory. *Neuroscience, 22*, 441–469.

Fine, A., Dunnett, S. B., Björklund, A., & Iversen, S. D. (1985). Cholinergic ventral forebrain grafts into the neocortex improve passive avoidance memory in a rat model of Alzheimer's disease. *Proceedings of the National Academy of Sciences USA, 82*, 5227–5230.

Fisher, A., & Hanin, I. (1986). Potential animal models for senile dementia of Alzheimer's type, with an emphasis on AF64A-induced toxicity. *Annual Review of Pharmacology and Toxicology, 26*, 161–181.

Flicker, C., Ferris, S. F., Bartus, R. T., & Crook, T. (1984). Effects of aging and dementia upon recent visuo-spatial memory. *Neurobiology of Aging, 5*, 75–83.

Gaffan, D. (1972). Loss of recognition memory in rats with lesions of the fornix. *Neuropsychologia, 10*, 327–341.

Gage, F. H., & Björklund, A. (1986). Cholinergic grafts into the hippocampal formation improve spatial learning and memory in aged rats by an atropine sensitive mechanism. *Journal of Neuroscience, 6*, 2837–2847.

Gage, F. H., Björklund, A., Stenevi, U., Dunnett, S. B., & Kelly, P. A. T. (1984). Intrahippocampal septal grafts ameliorate learning impairments in aged rats. *Science, 225*, 533–536.

Gage, F. H., Dunnett, S. B., & Björklund, A. (1984). Spatial learning and motor deficits in aged rats. *Neurobiology of Aging, 5*, 43–48.

Gage, F. H., Kelly, P. A. T., & Björklund, A. (1984). Regional changes in brain glucose metabolism reflect cognitive impairments in aged rats. *Journal of Neuroscience, 4*, 2856–2866.

Glick, S. D., & Jarvik, M. E. (1970). Differential effects of amphetamine and scopolamine on matching performance of monkeys with lateral frontal lesions. *Journal of Comparative and Physiological Psychology, 73*, 307–313.

Hagan, J. J., & Morris, R. G. M. (1988). The cholinergic hypothesis of memory: A review of animal experiments. In L. L. Iversen, S. D. Iversen, & S. Y. Snyder (Eds.), *Handbook of psychopharmacology* (Vol. 20, pp. 237–323). New York: Plenum Press.

Heise, G. A. (1975). Discrete trial analysis of drug action. *Federation Proceedings, 34*, 1898–1903.

Hodos, W. (1970). Evolutionary interpretation of neural and behavioral studies of living vertebrates. In F. O. Schmitt (Ed.), *The neurosciences: Second study program* (pp. 26–39). New York: Rockefeller University Press.

Irle, E., Kessler, J., & Markowitsch, H. J. (1987). Primate learning tasks reveal strong impairments in patients with presenile or senile dementia of the Alzheimer type. *Brain and Cognition, 6*, 429–449.

Kelley, A. E., & Domesick, V. B. (1982). The distribution of the projection from the hippocampal formation to the nucleus accumbens in the rat: An anterograde and retrograde horseradish peroxidase study. *Neuroscience, 7*, 2321–2335.

Kesner, R. P., Bierley, R. A., & Pebbles, P. (1981). Short-term memory: The role of *d*-amphetamine. *Pharmacology, Biochemistry and Behavior, 15*, 673–676.

Kubanis, P., & Zornetzer, S. F. (1981). Age-related behavioral and neurobiological changes: A review with an emphasis on memory. *Behavioral and Neural Biology, 31*, 115–172.

Low, W. C., Lewis, P. R., Bunch, S. T., Dunnett, S. B., Thomas, S. R., Iversen, S. D., Björklund, A., & Stenevi, U. (1982). Functional recovery following neural transplantation of embryonic septal nuclei in adult rats with septohippocampal lesions. *Nature, 300*, 260–262.

Luiten, P. G. M., Gaykema, R. P. A., Traber, J., & Spencer, D. G. (1987). Cortical projection patterns of magnocellular basal nucleus subdivisions as revealed by anterogradely transported phaseolus vulgaris leucoagglutinin. *Brain Research, 413*, 229–250.

Markowska, A. L., Wenk, G. L., & Olton, D. S. (1990). Nucleus basalis magnocellularis and memory: Differential effects of two neurotoxins. *Behavioral and Neural Biology, 54*, 13–26.

McGeorge, A. J., & Faull, R. L. M. (1989). The organization of the projection from the cerebral cortex to the striatum in the rat. *Neuroscience, 29*, 503–537.

Mishkin, M. (1978). Memory in monkeys severely impaired by combined but not separate removal of amygdala and hippocampus. *Nature, 273*, 297–298.

Nilsson, O. G., Brundin, P., & Björklund, A. (1990). Amelioration of spatial memory impairment by intrahippocampal grafts of mixed septal and raphe tissue in rats with combined cholinergic and serotonergic denervation of the forebrain. *Brain Research, 515*, 193–206.

Nilsson, O. G., Shapiro, M. L., Gage, F. H., Olton, D. S., & Björklund, A. (1987). Spatial learning and memory following fimbria–fornix transection and grafting of fetal septal neurons to the hippocampus. *Experimental Brain Research, 67*, 195–215.

O'Keefe, J., & Nadel, L. (1978). *The hippocampus as a cognitive map.* Oxford: Clarendon Press.

Olton, D. S., Becker, J. T., & Handelmann, G. E. (1979). Hippocampus, space and memory. *Behavioral and Brain Sciences, 2*, 313–365.

Olton, D. S., Walker, J. A., & Gage, F. H. (1978). Hippocampal connections and spatial discrimination. *Brain Research, 139*, 295–308.

Perry, E. K., Tomlinson, B. E., Blessed, G., Bergmann, K., Gibson, P. H., & Perry, R. H. (1978). Correlation of cholinergic abnormalities with senile plaques and mental test scores in senile dementia. *British Medical Journal, ii*, 1457–1459.

Richter-Levin, G., & Segal, M. (1989). Raphe cells grafted into the hippocampus can ameliorate spatial memory deficits in rats with combined serotonergic/cholinergic deficiencies. *Brain Research, 478*, 184–186.

Ridley, R. M., Murray, T. K., Johnson, J. A., & Baker, H. F. (1986). Learning impairment following lesion of the basal nucleus of Meynert in the marmoset: Modification by cholinergic drugs. *Brain Research, 376*, 108–116.

Robbins, T. W., Everitt, B. J., Ryan, C. N., Marston, H. M., Jones, G. H., & Page, K. J. (1989). Comparative effects of quisqualic and ibotenic acid-induced lesions of the substantia innominata and globus pallidus on the acquisition of a conditional visual discrimination: Differential effects on cholinergic mechanisms. *Neuroscience, 28*, 337–352.

Rosenkilde, C. E. (1979). Functional heterogeneity of the prefrontal cortex in the monkey: A review. *Behavioral and Neural Biology, 25*, 301–345.

Rosvold, H. E. (1972). The frontal lobe system: Cortical–subcortical relationships. *Acta Neurobiologica Experimentalis (Warsaw), 32*, 439–460.

Rothblat, L. A., & Hayes, L. L. (1987). Short-term object recognition memory in the rat: Nonmatching with trial-unique junk objects. *Behavioral Neuroscience, 101*, 587–590.

Sahakian, B. J., Morris, R. G., Evenden, J. L., Heald, A., Levy, R., Philpot, M., & Robbins, T. W. (1988). A comparative study of visuospatial memory and learning in Alzheimer-type dementia and Parkinson's disease. *Brain, 111*, 695–718.

Shapiro, M. L., Simon, D. K., Olton, D. S., Gage, F. H., Nilsson, O. G., & Björklund, A. (1989). Intrahippo-campal grafts of fetal basal forebrain tissue alter place fields in the hippocampus of rats with fimbria-fornix lesions. *Neuroscience, 32*, 1–18.

Smith, G. (1988). Animal models of Alzheimer's disease: Experimental cholinergic denervation. *Brain Research Reviews, 13*, 103–118.

van Haaren, F., & van Hest, A. (1989). Spatial matching and nonmatching in male and female Wistar rats: Effects of delay-interval duration. *Animal Learning and Behavior, 17*, 355–360.

Vincent, S. R., Satoh, K., Armstrong, D. M., & Fibiger, H. C. (1983). Substance P in the ascending cholinergic reticular system. *Science, 306,* 688–690.

Wallace, J., Steinert, P. A., Scobie, S. R., & Spear, N. E. (1980). Stimulus modality and short-term memory in rats. *Animal Learning and Behavior, 8,* 10–16.

Warburton, D. M. (1974). The effects of scopolamine on a two-cue discrimination. *Quarterly Journal of Experimental Psychology, 26,* 395–404.

Wenk, G. L., Markowska, A. L., & Olton, D. S. (1989). Basal forebrain lesions and memory: Alterations in neurotensin, not acetylcholine, may cause amnesia. *Behavioral Neuroscience, 103,* 765–769.

Wenk, G. L., & Olton, D. S. (1987). Basal forebrain cholinergic neurons and Alzheimer's disease. In J. T. Coyle (Ed.), *Animal models of dementia: A synaptic neurochemical perspective* (pp. 81–101). New York: Alan R. Liss.

Whishaw, I. Q., O'Connor, W. T., & Dunnett, S. B. (1985). Disruption of central cholinergic systems in the rat by basal forebrain lesions or atropine: Effects on feeding, sensorimotor behaviour, locomotor activity and spatial navigation. *Behavioural Brain Research, 17,* 103–115.

Wozniak, D. F., Stewart, G. R., Finger, S., & Olney, J. W. (1989). Comparison of behavioral effects of nucleus basalis magnocellularis lesions and somatosensory cortex ablation in the rat. *Neuroscience, 32,* 685–700.

Zola-Morgan, S., Squire, L. R., & Mishkin, M. (1982). The neuroanatomy of amnesia: Amygdala–hippocampus versus temporal stem. *Science, 218,* 1337–1339.

33

The Aging Septo-Hippocampal System: Its Role in Age-Related Memory Impairments

DAVID S. OLTON and ALICJA L. MARKOWSKA

The aging process brings with it an increased susceptibility to impaired memory. This chapter discusses two issues that are important in the analysis of age-related memory impairments and their neural bases. The first is the accurate description of memory impairments in the aged population. Most populations of aged individuals have greater variability in performance than a similar population of young individuals. The major question here is whether the age-related increase in variance results from the presence of two distinct subpopulations of individuals, or whether it reflects a continuous distribution. Although empirical steps can divide an aged population into two subpopulations—one that has impaired memory and one that does not—the actual distribution of scores suggests that this division is artificial and does not accurately reflect the true distribution of performance. It may be useful to answer some experimental questions, but it is not optimal to answer other questions.

The second issue concerns the neural bases of these age-related memory impairments. The major question here is the accurate interpretation of correlations between age-related neuropathology and mnemonic impairments. Age-related changes in the basal forebrain cholinergic system and the hippocampus are correlated with the magnitude of age-related mnemonic impairments. However, the age-related neuropathology involves only a portion of the affected system. Although detailed information is lacking, the available data suggest that the parametric functions relating the magnitude of a behavioral impairment to the magnitude of neuropathology are not linear, and may have different shapes for different combinations of behavior and pathology. Interpreting the significance of these correlations requires more detailed information about the exact shape of these functions.

In this discussion, the terms "young" and "aged" are often used without indicating a specific age. Considerable debate has focussed on the question of the appropriate use of the terms "young" and "aged," as well as the number of different age groups that should be included in an analysis of age-related changes (Coleman, 1989; Coleman, Finch, & Joseph, 1990). As is often the case, no particular approach is absolutely right or wrong in every circumstance, and the question being addressed strongly influences the ability of any given approach to provide meaningful information. For the present analysis, the requirements are simple: If any two groups of individuals that differ in age have the characteristics discussed here, then these two issues have significant implications for our understanding of age-related changes in both cognitive and neural processes. The exact ages of these two groups are not important for this analysis.

Individual Differences in Aged Populations: Independent Subpopulations or a Continuum?

Although considerable information is available about the effects of aging on average performance, much less information has been gathered about its effects on the variability of performance. In many studies measures of variance may be lacking. If present, these measures usually include only the standard error of the mean; it is assumed that the variance is normally distributed, which is probably not the case. Occasionally, data from individual animals are presented so that post hoc analyses can be done by the reader. Only rarely have statistical analyses tested the significance of the difference in variability (Gage, Dunnett, & Björklund, 1989). Consequently, the points made here are usually supported by post hoc analyses of individual data, without statistical support for the significance of the differences. However, the differences in variance are typically large, and should be significant both statistically and scientifically.

Whereas some aged individuals perform within the range of young individuals, some have substantial impairments; their performance is often at the levels expected by chance, and many standard deviations away from the mean of the young group. Some examples of increased variability in aged populations are provided in Table 33.1, which presents, in order: the mnemonic task, the ages of the animals, and the reference for each study.

In a series of publications, Fred Gage has developed two different approaches to the analysis of this increased variability, and indicated the conditions in which each approach is most effective. Both of these are described in the following sections.

TABLE 33.1. Age-Related Increases in the Variability of Performance in Mnemonic Tasks

| Task | Age (months) | | Reference |
	Young	Old	
Place discrimination in water	4–5	25–26	Gallagher and Burwell (1989)
maze	3	21–23	Gage, Kelly, and Björklund (1984)
Place discrimination on circular platform	4–5	25–26	Gallagher and Burwell (1989)
Working memory in radial arm maze	4	26	Geinismann, de Toledo-Morrell, and Morrell (1986b)
Inhibitory avoidance	3	24	Stone, Wenk, Olton, and Gold (1990)

Therapeutic Interventions

One analysis divides the aged populations into two subgroups. The unimpaired subgroup is composed of individuals with scores close to those of young individuals, usually within two standard deviations of the mean of the young group. The impaired subgroup is composed of individuals with scores indicating a greater impairment. Statistical analyses of the difference in performance of the impaired and unimpaired subgroups support the effectiveness of this division. The usual pattern of results is what would be expected, given this quantitative manipulation. One difference (between the young group and the aged unimpaired subgroup) is statistically insignificant, whereas two other differences (between the aged unimpaired subgroup and the aged impaired subgroup, and between the young group and the aged impaired subgroup) are statistically significant. Given the empirical operation used to perform the two aged subgroups, this statistical pattern is almost inevitable.

This division into subgroups is appropriate for the development of therapeutic interventions to alleviate age-related behavioral impairments. In the context of memory, the development of cognitive enhancers to reduce or prevent the memory decline associated with aging has received intensive analysis (Bartus, 1990; Olton & Wenk, 1990). The sensitivity of behavioral tests to detect the cognition-enhancing properties of any particular intervention can be influenced heavily by task parameters (Olton, 1989). One of those parameters is the magnitude of the amnesic syndrome in the impaired individuals. Of particular importance is the possibility that the intervention may help to alleviate an impairment, but may not produce better-than-normal performance. If such is the case, then including unimpaired individuals in the experiment is a waste of resources and reduces the sensitivity of the behavioral procedures to detect cognition enhancement, because part of the treated group may be refractory to the intervention. Elimination of unimpaired individuals can help to minimize these problems (Gage, Björklund, Stenevi, Dunnett, & Kelly, 1984).

Even in this instance, further consideration of the entire range of performance may be beneficial. An intervention may be ineffective not only in unimpaired individuals, but also in severely impaired individuals. The mnemonic impairment may be so substantial that the intervention does not have sufficient power to produce a noticeable improvement, or some change in the cognitive system as a whole may limit the ability of the individual to express a mnemonic improvement. Thus, a division into two subpopulations is certainly appropriate, but further consideration of the entire range of variance may provide maximum sensitivity to potential beneficial effects of the intervention, and give information about some of the parameters that influence the power of the intervention to alter memory.

Describing Mnemonic Performance in Aged Populations

Describing the mnemonic characteristics of an aged population, as compared to a young population, addresses another question about age-related mnemonic impairments. For this research endeavor, multivariate analyses that consider the entire range of performance are important (Gage, Kelly, & Björklund, 1984; Gage et al., 1989).

Although the division of the aged population into two subgroups emphasizes the relatively greater variability in the aged group as compared to the young group, it has three potential difficulties: (1) It does not accurately reflect the actual distribution of scores in the aged population; (2) it may lead to erroneous inferences about the effects of aging on both memory and its neural bases; and (3) it encourages the use of dichotomous comparisons rather than multivariate analyses, and the latter may be better able to detect age-related changes in both mnemonic and neural variables. Each of these points is addressed in turn.

1. The division into two subpopulations suggests a bimodal distribution of scores, with one mode near or within the range of performance of young individuals, and the other mode at some distance from that value. Although the appropriate statistical tests have not yet been conducted to determine the extent to which aged populations have scores that are bimodally distributed, examination of the available data does not suggest a bimodal distribution. Rather, scores typically have a continuous but skewed distribution, with the mode relatively near the value for the young group, and the tail stretching toward an impairment. (The actual location of the mode and the shape of the distribution of scores will vary, depending on the mnemonic difficulty of the experimental procedure.)

2. Although it may not necessarily do so, a division into two subpopulations can encourage certain lines of reasoning. For example, consider the following. Aging is a dichotomous process, affecting some individuals but not others. Normal aging may be benign, and only some individuals, who either are inherently susceptible to age-related pathological processes or get exposed to certain environmental insults, develop cognitive impairments. If the distribution of scores in the aged group is really continuous, this line of thinking may be inappropriate.

3. Finally, the division of the aged population into two subgroups discourages the use of multivariate analyses. Particularly in the aged impaired group, the variance in performance may still be very large after the subdivision. As a result, group comparisons may be statistically insignificant because of the large variance. A multivariate analysis does not rely on an artificial distinction imposed by the experimenter, and should be a more sensitive test of the statistical significance of age-related changes in mnemonic function (Gage, Dunnett, & Björklund, 1984; Gage, Chen, Buzsaki, & Armstrong, 1988; Gage et al., 1989; Ingram, 1985; Olton et al., 1991).

Neural Correlates of Age-Related Memory Impairments

Age-related changes in memory provide a natural experiment to examine the neural bases of these changes (Gage et al., 1988). In young animals, lesions of the septo-hippocampal system impair performance in a variety of mnemonic tasks, indicating that the integrity of these structures is necessary for normal performance. Pathological changes in the septo-hippocampal system correlate with the magnitude of age-related memory impairments in these same tasks (Table 33.2). This pattern of results is consistent with the hypothesis that age-related changes in the septo-hippocampal system are responsible for these mnemonic impairments.

Two problems complicate this conclusion. The first concerns the imperfect

TABLE 33.2. Age-Related Mnemonic Impairments and Neuropathology: Positive Correlations

| Behavioral task | Neural measure | Age (months) | | Reference |
		Young	Old	
Place discrimination on circular platform	Long-term enhancement in hippocampus	10–16	28–34	Barnes (1979), Barnes and McNaughton (1985)
Working memory in a radial arm maze	Perforated synapses in hippocampus	4	26	Geinisman, de Toledo-Morrell, and Morrell (1986a, 1986b)
Working memory in a radial arm maze	Kindling in the hippocampus	4	26	de Toledo-Morrell, Morrell, and Fleming (1984)
Place discrimination in water maze	Brain glucose metabolism in hippocampus, medial septal area, dentate gyrus	3	24	Gage, Kelly, and Björklund (1984)
T-maze avoidance	Frequency potentiation in the hippocampus	4–6	24–25	Landfield (1988)
Place discrimination in water maze	Size and number of cells in medial septum	3	23–25	Fischer, Gage, and Björklund (1989)

selectivity of these tasks as a means to identify precisely the functional state of the septo-hippocampal system. Although lesions of the septo-hippocampal system in young animals do impair choice accuracy in these tasks, lesions in other brain structures may have similar effects. Consequently, the directional logic of the neural–behavioral correlation is asymmetrical. Increasingly severe pathological changes in the septo-hippocampal system should produce increasingly severe memory impairments. However, increasingly severe memory impairments may not reflect increasingly severe pathology in the septo-hippocampal system because the behavioral impairments may be caused by pathology in other neural systems. As a result, any correlation will probably underestimate the extent to which any given age-related neuropathology is responsible for any given age-related mnemonic impairment.

An analysis of the distribution of the data can help provide insights into the extent to which a low correlation between any given neuropathology and any given behavior creates a problem for a particular hypothesis. Any individual with substantial neuropathology but minimal mnemonic impairment obviously poses problems for the hypothesis that this neuropathology is responsible for the mnemonic impairment. The opposite dissociation is not so difficult for the hypothesis; an individual with a substantial mnemonic impairment but minimal neuropathology in the system being considered may reflect the imperfect selectivity of the mnemonic task, and neuropathology in some other system may be responsible for the mnemonic impairment. Scatterplots showing the relevant data from all individuals can help identify the influence of these two patterns of mnemonic–pathological correlations on the overall result.

A second challenge to identifying the neural bases of age-related memory impairments concerns the parametric shape of the function relating the magnitude of the memory impairment to the magnitude of the neuropathology. In drug experiments, the experimental design usually includes at least four groups; one group receives no drug, while each of the other three groups receives a different dose of a drug. This type of dose–response curve is usually considered a prerequisite for appropriate interpretation because the behavioral effects of a drug may differ substantially at different doses.

In a similar fashion, the completeness of a lesion can have a significant effect on memory. For example, complete lesions of the fornix reduced choice accuracy to the level expected by chance in a test of cued working memory (Rafaelle & Olton, 1988). Lesions that destroyed half of the fornix, however, had only a minimal impact on choice accuracy, which returned to normal levels after a few weeks of testing. The effects of lesions of the dopaminergic system on motor behavior are notoriously nonlinear. Lesions of as much as 80% of the system had almost no behavioral effects, whereas lesions of 95% of the system produced profound and enduring behavioral impairments (Zigmond & Stricker, 1987; Zigmond, Berger, Grace, & Stricker, 1989). In contrast to drug experiments, however, most lesion experiments do not manipulate the size of the lesion, and little systematic information is available about the shape of the function relating the completeness of the lesion to the severity of the mnemonic impairment.

Age-related neuropathology usually involves a relatively small portion of the affected system. In young animals, lesions of an equivalent magnitude would probably produce a minimal mnemonic impairment. If such is the case, then the "dose-response" curve for the aged population may be shifted relative to that for the young population, complicating any attempt to relate a specific type of neuropathology to a specific mnemonic impairment.

This conclusion must be tentative for two reasons. The first is the relative absence of information about the parametric functions relating lesion size and mnemonic impairment in young animals. The second is the difficulty of obtaining an informative measure to compare the functional equivalence of two very different types of lesions— those produced experimentally in young animals, and those occurring naturally in old animals. Without the empirical data and conceptual frameworks to enable us to assess the scientific significance of any given magnitude of correlation, the interpretation of that correlation is difficult. Consider the following example. In old animals, the correlation between the number of cells lost in a given structure and the size of the mnemonic impairment is about .60. In young animals with lesions produced by a neurotoxin, the correlation may be lower, higher, or the same. How does the interpretation of the correlation in the old animals change as a result of the three different results from young animals? A positive correlation of some magnitude might seem to lend support to the hypothesis that the measured neuropathology is related to the measured behavioral impairment. However, the absence of a standard for comparison in young animals complicates this interpretation. Without this standard, any given correlation may be either higher or lower than expected, and interpretation of these two different patterns may be substantially different. The extent to which a particular value for a positive correlation in an aged individual should be taken as supporting the hypothesis that the neuropathology is responsible for the mnemonic impairment depends in part on the expected value for young individuals.

Summary

The analysis of age-related memory impairments and their neural bases can make three important contributions to our understanding of the neuropsychology of memory: (1) Aging is a natural experiment, so that age-related mnemonic impairments can be correlated with age-related neuropathological changes to indicate the neural systems that are required for normal memory; (2) an increased understanding of the ways in which aging affects neural and cognitive processes should have significant implications for practical approaches to aging in humans; and (3) identification of the age-related neuropathological changes involved in mnemonic impairments should help us to design therapeutic interventions to alleviate them. All three of these endeavors can be assisted by an accurate description of the variability inherent in aged populations, and of the parametric function relating the magnitude of neuropathology to the magnitude of mnemonic impairment.

ACKNOLWEDGMENTS

We thank Fred Gage for helpful comments on this chapter, and Anu Dürr for preparation of the manuscript.

REFERENCES

Barnes, C. A. (1979). Memory deficits associated with senescence: A neurophysiological and behavioral study in the rat. *Journal of Comparative and Physiological Psychology, 93*, 74-104.

Barnes, C. A., & McNaughton, B. L. (1985). An age comparison of the rates of acquisition and forgetting of spatial information in relation to long-term enhancement of hippocampal synapses. *Behavioral Neuroscience, 99*, 1040-1048.

Bartus, R. T. (1990). Drugs to treat age-related neurodegenerative problems. *Geriatric Bioscience, 38*, 680-695.

Coleman, P. D. (1989). How old is old? *Neurobiology of Aging, 10*, 115.

Coleman, P. D., Finch, C., & Joseph, J. (1990). The need for multiple time points in aging studies. *Neurobiology of Aging, 11*, 1-2.

de Toledo-Morrell, L., Morrell, F., & Fleming, S. (1984). Age dependent deficits in spatial memory are related to impaired hippocampal kindling. *Behavioral Neuroscience, 98*, 902-907.

Fischer, W., Gage, F. H., & Björklund, A. (1989). Degenerative changes in forebrain cholinergic nuclei correlate with cognitive impairments in aged rats. *European Jounal of Neuroscience, 1*, 34-45.

Gage, F. H., Björklund, A., Stenevi, U., Dunnett, S. B., & Kelly, P. A. T. (1984). Intrahippocampal septal grafts ameliorate learning impairments in aged rats. *Science, 225*, 533-536.

Gage, F. H., Chen, K. S., Buzsaki, G., & Armstrong, D. (1988). Experimental approaches to age-related cognitive impairments. *Neurobiology of Aging, 9*, 645-655.

Gage, F. H., Dunnett, S. B., & Björklund, A. (1984). Spatial learning and motor deficits in aged rats. *Neurobiology of Aging, 5*, 43-48.

Gage, F. H., Dunnett, S. B., & Björklund, A. (1989). Age-related impairments in spatial memory are independent of those of sensorimotor skills. *Neurobiology of Aging, 10*, 347-352.

Gage, F. H., Kelly, P. A. T., & Björklund, A. (1984). Regional changes in brain glucose metabolism reflect cognitive impairments in aged rats. *Journal of Neuroscience, 4*(11), 2856-2865.

Gallagher, M., & Burwell, R. D. (1989). Relationship of age-related decline across several behavioral domains. *Neurobiology of Aging, 10*, 691-708.

Geinisman, Y., de Toledo-Morrell, L., & Morrell, F. (1986a). Loss of perforated synapses in the dentate gyrus: Morphological substrate of memory deficit in aged rats. *Neurobiology, 83*, 3027-3031.

Geinisman, Y., de Toledo-Morrell, L., & Morrell, F. (1986b). Aged rats need a preserved complement of perforated axospinous synapses per hippocampal neuron to maintain good spatial memory. *Brain Research, 398*, 266-275.

Ingram, D. K. (1985). Analysis of age-related impairments in learning and memory in rodent models. *Annals of the New York Academy of Sciences, 444*, 312-331.

Landfield, P. W. (1988). Hippocampal neurobiological mechanisms of age-related memory dysfunction. *Neurobiology of Aging, 9*, 571-579.

Olton, D. S. (1989). Dimensional mnemonics. In G. H. Bower (Ed.), *The psychology of learning and motivation* (pp. 1-23). San Diego: Academic Press.

Olton, D. S., Markowska, A. L., Breckler, S., Pang, K., Koliatsos, V., & Price, D. L. (1991). Individual differences in aging: Behavioral and neural analyses. *Biomedical and Environmental Sciences, 4*, 166-172.

Olton, D. S., & Wenk, G. L. (1990). The development of behavioral tests to assess the effects of cognitive enhancers. *Pharmacopsychiatry, 23*, 65-69.

Raffaele, K. C., & Olton, D. S. (1988). Hippocampal and amygdaloid involvement in working memory for nonspatial stimuli. *Behavioral Neuroscience, 102*, 349-355.

Stone, W. S., Wenk, G. L., Olton, D. S., & Gold, P. E. (1990). Poor blood glucose regulation predicts sleep and memory deficits in normal aged rats. *Journal of Gerontology: Biological Sciences, 45*(5), B169-B173.

Zigmond, M. J., Berger, T. W., Grace, A. A., & Stricker, E. M. (1989). Compensatory responses to nigrostriatal bundle injury studies with 6-hydroxydopamine in an animal model of parkinsonism. *Molecular and Chemical Neuropathology, 10*, 185-200.

Zigmond, M. J., & Stricker, E. M. (1987). Parkinsonism: Insights from animal models utilizing neurotoxic agents. In J. P. Coyle (Ed.), *Animal models of dementia* (pp. 1-38). New York: Alan R. Liss.

34

Neuromodulatory Systems and the Regulation of Memory Storage

JAMES L. McGAUGH

Considerable experimental as well as clinical evidence indicates that postlearning memory storage processes are susceptible to influences affecting brain functioning. Retrograde amnesia is readily produced by a variety of treatments, including electrical stimulation of the brain, as well as drugs (McGaugh, 1966; McGaugh & Herz, 1972); moreover, retention can be enhanced by posttraining electrical stimulation of specific brain regions, as well as by many drugs affecting neuromodulatory systems (Bloch, 1970; McGaugh & Petrinovich, 1965; McGaugh, 1973, 1989a, 1989b; McGaugh & Gold, 1976). Evidence indicating that the memory-enhancing effects of such posttraining treatments are time-dependent provides strong support for the view that the treatments influence retention by modulating processes underlying memory consolidation (McGaugh, 1966; McGaugh & Herz, 1972). Furthermore, the experimental findings are consistent with the hypothesis that memory storage processes may normally be regulated by the actions of neuromodulatory systems activated by training experiences (Gold & McGaugh, 1975).

Recent research in my laboratory has focused on the involvement of adrenergic, opioid peptidergic, and cholinergic γ-aminobutyric acid-ergic (GABAergic) systems in the regulation of memory storage. It is now well documented that in rats and mice, retention assessed in many types of training tasks is affected by posttraining injections of drugs affecting these systems. Furthermore, recent evidence indicates that treatments affecting these neuromodulatory systems affect memory through influences involving the amygdala.

Adrenergic Influences on Memory Storage

The adrenergic hormone epinephrine is released from the adrenal medulla during and immediately after stressful stimulation of the kinds typically used in training rats and mice. Gold and van Buskirk's (1975) finding that retention of an inhibitory (passive) avoidance task is enhanced by posttraining systemic injections of low doses of epinephrine has since been replicated and extended in subsequent experiments using many types of training tasks, including inhibitory avoidance, active avoidance, discrimination learning, and appetitively motivated tasks (Borrell, de Kloet, Versteeg, & Bohus, 1983; Gold, van Buskirk, & Haycock, 1977; Introini-Collison & McGaugh, 1986; Izquierdo & Dias, 1983; Sternberg, Isaacs, Gold, & McGaugh, 1985; Liang, Bennett, & McGaugh, 1985). As would be expected on the assumption that epinephrine enhances the consolidation of long-term memory, the memory-enhancing effects of epinephrine are long-lasting. Memory-enhancing effects produced by posttraining systemic injections of epinephrine are found on retention tests given at intervals of up to a month following training (Introini-Collison & McGaugh, 1986). Findings (Gold & McCarty, 1981) indicating that the plasma levels of epinephrine measured following the administration of memory-enhancing doses of epinephrine are comparable to those found in untreated animals given training that results in good retention support the view that endogenously released epinephrine modulates postlearning memory storage processes.

It is unlikely that the memory-modulating effects of epinephrine result from direct influences on brain activity, as it is known that epinephrine passes the blood–brain barrier (BBB) poorly (Weil-Malherbe, Axelrod, & Tomchick, 1959). Recent findings suggest that epinephrine influences on memory are initiated by activation of peripheral β-adrenergic receptors (Introini-Collison, Saghafi, Novack, & McGaugh, 1992). Systemic injections of the β-adrenergic antagonist sotalol, which does not pass the BBB, block the memory-enhancing effects of epinephrine (see Figure 34.1A). However, sotalol does not block the retention-enhancing effects of posttraining systemic injections of dipivalyl epinephrine (DPE), a drug that is less polar than epinephrine (see Figure 34.1B) and that, thus, more readily enters the brain. DPE effects on memory are, however, blocked by propranolol, a β-adrenergic antagonist that readily passes the BBB when administered systemically.

These findings suggest that both epinephrine and DPE enhance memory through effects involving the activation of central adrenergic receptors. DPE effects on memory appear to result directly from activation of central adrenergic receptors, as DPE readily enters the brain and the memory-enhancing effects of DPE are not attenuated by blockade of peripheral adrenergic receptors. Epinephrine effects seem likely to result from activation of a central noradrenergic system by stimulation of peripheral adrenergic receptors on visceral afferents projecting to the brain. This conclusion is consistent with earlier evidence indicating that systemic injections of epinephrine induce the release of brain norepinephrine (NE) (Gold & van Buskirk, 1978a, 1978b).

Gold (1986) has suggested that epinephrine effects on memory may involve adrenergic activation of the release of glucose. The findings of a number of experiments indicate that posttraining injections of glucose have effects of retention that are highly comparable to those induced by epinephrine (Gold, 1988). Findings suggesting that glucose effects on memory involve enhancement of cholinergic systems (see Gold, Chapter 35, this volume) are of particular interest, in view of evidence (discussed below) suggesting that the memory-modulating effects of hormones and drugs involve influences on cholinergic systems (Baratti, Introini, & Huygens, 1984; Introini-Collision & McGaugh, 1988; Castellano & McGaugh, 1991).

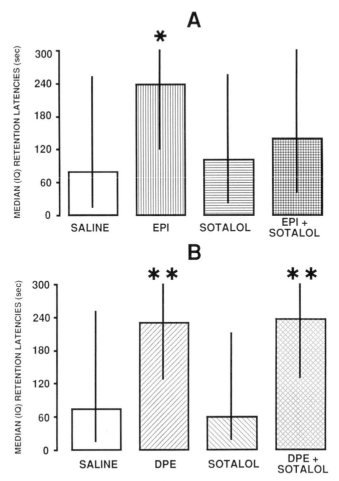

FIGURE 34.1. Effects of posttraining (i.p.) injections of epinephrine (**A**) and dipivalyl epinephrine (DPE; **B**) on 24-hour retention of an inhibitory avoidance response (median and interquartile range). The peripherally acting β-adrenergic antagonist sotalol blocked the memory-enhancing effects of epinephrine, but did not block the effects of DPE. °$p < .05$ and °°$p < .01$ compared with saline controls and groups given only sotalol. From "Memory-Enhancing Effects of Posttraining Dipivefrin and Epinephrine: Involvement of Peripheral and Central Adrenergic Receptors" (p. 83) by I. B. Introini-Collison, D. Saghafi, G. Novack, and J. L. McGaugh, 1992, *Brain Research*, *572*, 81–86. Copyright 1992 by Elsevier Science Publishers. Reprinted by permission.

Involvement of the Amygdala

There is extensive evidence suggesting that epinephrine influences memory storage through effects involving noradrenergic activation within the amygdala. It is well known that posttraining electrical stimulation of the amygdala can produce enhancement as well as impairment of memory (Kesner & Wilburn, 1974; McGaugh & Gold, 1976). It is also known that lesions of the amygdala impair learning of tasks when emotionally arousing training conditions are used (Cahill & McGaugh, 1990; Hitchcock & Davis, 1987; Kesner, Walser, & Winzenried, 1989; LeDoux, Iwata, Cicchetti, & Reis,

1988; Weiskrantz, 1956). Such findings suggest the possibility that epinephrine released in response to arousing stimulation may influence learning by activating the amygdala. Experiments examining the memory-modulating effects of electrical stimulation of the amygdala in adrenal-demedullated rats were the first to address this possibility. Posttraining stimulation of the amygdala that impaired memory in intact rats was found to enhance memory in adrenal-demedullated rats (Bennett, Liang, & McGaugh, 1985). However, retrograde amnesia was induced in adrenal-demedullated rats if systemic injections of epinephrine were administered immediately before the brain stimulation (Liang et al., 1985). Thus, effects initiated by peripheral epinephrine appear to modulate amygdala sensitivity to brain stimulation.

Such findings suggest that epinephrine may have a more general influence on amygdala functioning in memory. If this is the case, lesions of the amygdala or amygdala pathways would be expected to attenuate the effects of epinephrine on memory. The findings of several experiments are consistent with this implication. N-methyl-D-aspartate-induced lesions of the amygdala block the memory-enhancing effects of posttraining systemic injections of epinephrine (Cahill & McGaugh, 1991). Furthermore, lesions of the stria terminalis (ST) block the memory-enhancing effects of both epinephrine and clenbuterol, a β-adrenergic agonist that passes the BBB (Liang & McGaugh, 1983; Introini-Collison, Miyazaki, & McGaugh, 1991). These findings provide strong support for the view that epinephrine influences memory storage through influences involving activation of the amygdala.

Experiments examining the effects of intra-amygdala injections of NE agonists and antagonists have provided more direct evidence supporting the hypothesis that epinephrine influences on memory result from activation of the amygdala. Gallagher and her colleagues reported that posttraining intra-amygdala injections of the β-adrenergic antagonists propranolol and alprenolol impaired retention, and that the impairment was blocked by NE administered concurrently (Gallagher, Kapp, Pascoe, & Rapp, 1981). Furthermore, as is shown in Figure 34.2, propranolol administered to rats intra-amygdally immediately after training in an inhibitory avoidance task attenuated the memory-enhancing effect of systemically administered epinephrine (Liang, Juler, & McGaugh, 1986). These findings are consistent with the evidence summarized above suggesting that epinephrine influences on memory involve noradrenergic activation of the amygdala, as well as the finding that stressful stimulation initiates the release of NE within the amygdala (Tanaka et al., 1991).

A major implication of the hypothesis that epinephrine enhancement of memory results from the release of NE within the amygdala is that direct intra-amygdala administration of noradrenergic agonists should enhance retention. The findings of several experiments strongly support this implication. Posttraining intra-amygdala injections of NE (see Figure 34.3) or clenbuterol enhance retention of inhibitory avoidance training (Liang et al., 1986; Liang, McGaugh, & Yao, 1990; Introini-Collison et al., 1991). In addition, as is shown in Figure 34.3, lesions of the ST block the memory modulating effects of intra-amygdala injections of NE. These findings, considered together with findings indicating that ST lesions block the memory-enhancing effects of systemically administered epinephrine (Liang & McGaugh, 1983), suggest that the amygdala is involved in regulating memory storage in brain regions activated via the ST.

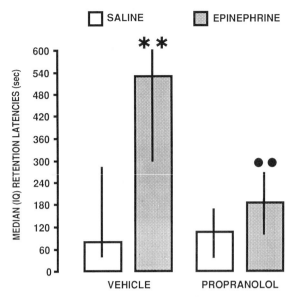

FIGURE 34.2. Effects of posttraining intra-amygdala injections of propranolol (0.2 µg) on epinephrine-induced enhancement of 24-hour retention of an inhibitory avoidance response (median and interquartile range). Epinephrine (0.1 mg) was administered s.c. $^{\circ\circ}p < .01$ as compared with the vehicle-injected control group. Filled circles, $p < .001$ as compared with the epinephrine-injected control group. From "Modulating Effects of Posttraining Epinephrine on Memory: Involvement of the Amygdala Noradrenergic System" (p. 130) by K. C. Liang, R. Juler, and J. L. McGaugh, 1986, *Brain Research, 368,* 125–133. Copyright 1986 by Elsevier Science Publishers. Reprinted by permission.

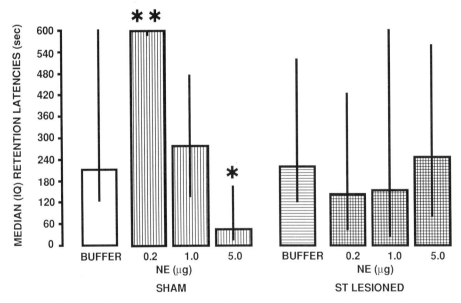

FIGURE 34.3. Effects of posttraining intra-amygdala injections of NE on inhibitory avoidance retention (24 hours) in sham-lesioned controls and ST-lesioned rats (median and interquartile range). ST lesions blocked NE-induced enhancement and impairment of memory. $^{\circ}p < .05$ and $^{\circ\circ}p < .01$ compared with the buffer-injected control group. From "Involvement of Amygdala Pathways in the Influence of Posttraining Amygdala Norepinephrine and Peripheral Epinephrine on Memory Storage" (p. 229) by K. C. Liang, J. L. McGaugh, and H. Y. Yao, 1990, *Brain Research, 508,* 225–233. Copyright 1990 by Elsevier Science Publishers. Reprinted by permission.

Opioid Peptidergic and GABAergic Influences on Memory Storage

Other experiments in my laboratory have examined the memory-modulating effects of drugs affecting opioid peptidergic and GABAergic systems. The findings of these experiments have provided extensive evidence suggesting that the effects of these drugs, like those produced by epinephrine, are mediated by the activation of NE receptors within the amygdala (McGaugh, 1989a; Castellano, Brioni, & McGaugh, 1990).

It is well established that in rats and mice, posttraining systemic as well as intra-amygdala injections of opiate antagonists such as naloxone and naltrexone enhance retention of a variety of training tasks (Gallagher & Kapp, 1978; Introini-Collison & McGaugh, 1987; Introini-Collison, Nagahara, & McGaugh, 1989; Izquierdo, 1979; Messing et al., 1979). Naloxone influences on memory, like those of epinephrine, are blocked by lesions of the ST (McGaugh, Introini-Collison, Juler, & Izquierdo, 1986). The findings indicating that the effects of opiate antagonists on memory are highly similar to those of epinephrine suggest that adrenergic and opiate influences on memory may work through a common mechanism. This view is further supported by findings indicating that the memory-enhancing effects of posttraining systemic injections of naloxone and epinephrine are additive when these are administered concurrently in low doses (Introini-Collison & McGaugh, 1987).

The findings of several experiments suggest that the common effect of adrenergic and opiate influences on memory may involve the release of brain NE. Abercrombie and Jacobs (1988) reported that in animals subjected to stressful stimulation, systemic injections of naloxone potentiated the activity of noradrenergic neurons in the locus coeruleus. In addition, opioid peptides are known to inhibit the release of NE (Arbilla & Langer, 1978; Montel, Starke, & Weber, 1974; Nakamura, Tepper, Young, Ling, & Groves, 1982; Werling, Brown, & Cox, 1987; Werling, McMahon, Portoghese, Takemori, & Cox, 1989). If, as this evidence suggests, naloxone effects on memory result from antagonism of opioid inhibition of NE release, the effects, like those of epinephrine (Liang et al., 1986), should be blocked by treatments that impair NE release or block NE receptors. Findings indicating that memory-enhancing effects of naloxone are blocked in animals treated with the β-adrenergic antagonist propranolol (Izquierdo & Graudenz, 1980) or with DSP4, an adrenergic neurotoxin (Introini-Collison & Baratti, 1986), provide strong support for this implication.

The memory-modulating effects of opioid peptidergic agonists and antagonists appear to be mediated, at least in part, by activation of the amygdala. The effects obtained with intra-amygdala injections of opiate agonists and antagonists are comparable to those found with systemic injections: Retention is enhanced by opiate antagonists and impaired by opiate agonists (Gallagher, 1982, 1985; Gallagher & Kapp, 1978; Gallagher et al., 1981). Furthermore, findings indicating that the memory-enhancing effects of peripheral as well as intra-amygdala injections of naloxone are blocked in animals with 6-hydroxydopamine-induced lesions of the dorsal noradrenergic pathway clearly suggest that the effects are mediated by influences involving NE (Fanelli, Rosenberg, & Gallagher, 1985; Gallagher, Rapp, & Fanelli, 1985). Additional evidence suggests that naloxone effects on memory involve the release of NE within the amygdala. As is shown in Figure 34.4, posttraining intra-amygdala injections of β-adrenergic

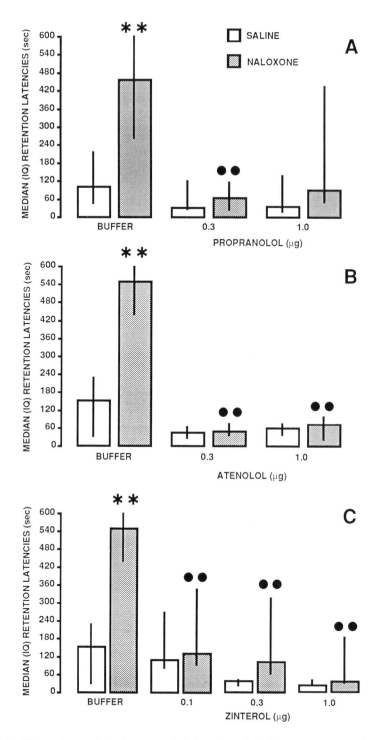

FIGURE 34.4. Effects of posttraining intra-amygdala injections of β-adrenoceptor antagonists on naloxone-induced enhancement of retention of an inhibitory avoidance response (median and interquartile range). Naloxone (3.0 mg/kg) was administered i.p. Retention was tested 1 week after training. $^{\circ\circ}p < .01$ as compared with the saline-injected control group. Filled circles, $p < .01$ as compared with the naloxone-injected group. Adapted from "Memory-Enhancing Effects of Posttraining Naloxone: Involvement of β-Noradrenergic Influences in the Amygdaloid Complex" (pp. 43, 44) by J. L. McGaugh, I. B. Introini-Collison, and A. H. Nagahara, 1988, *Brain Research, 446,* 37–49. Copyright 1988 by Elsevier Science Publishers. Adapted by permission.

antagonists block the memory-enhancing effects of systemically administered naloxone (McGaugh, Introini-Collison, & Nagahara, 1988). In addition, as is shown in Figure 34.5, the retention-enhancing effects of intra-amygdala injections of naloxone are blocked by propranolol injected concurrently with the naloxone (Introini-Collison et al., 1989).

The findings summarized above suggest that the interactions of neuromodulatory influences on memory storage are integrated within the amygdala. The results of other recent experiments suggest that the memory-modulating effects of GABAergic drugs (Castellano et al., 1990), like those of adrenergic and opiate influences, involve NE receptors within the amygdala. The findings of an early experiment (Breen & McGaugh, 1961) indicated that posttraining injections of the GABAergic antagonist picrotoxin enhanced maze learning in rats. This effect has been replicated and extended in many subsequent experiments using a variety of training tasks (Bovet, McGaugh, & Oliverio, 1966; Brioni & McGaugh, 1988; McGaugh, Castellano, & Brioni, 1990). When administered posttraining, GABAergic antagonists (picrotoxin and bicuculline) enhance retention, and GABAergic agonists (muscimol and baclofen) impair retention (Brioni & McGaugh, 1988; Castellano & McGaugh, 1989; Castellano, Brioni, Nagahara, & McGaugh, 1989; Swartzwelder, Tilson, McLamb, & Wilson, 1987).

The findings of other experiments indicating that low doses of GABAergic antagonists and opiate antagonists injected together after training are additive in their memory-enhancing effects (Castellano, Introini-Collison, Pavone, & McGaugh, 1989) suggest that these two systems influence memory storage through a common mechanism. Accordingly, on the basis of findings summarized above indicating that the amygdala is involved in opiate influences on memory, lesions of the amygdala should block the effects of GABAergic drugs, and intra-amygdala injections of GABAergic agonists and antagonists should produce effects on memory comparable to those induced by opiate agonists and antagonists. Recent experimental findings are consistent with these implications. As is shown in Figure 34.6, amygdala lesions block the memory-enhancing effects of posttraining systemic injections of bicuculline and mus-

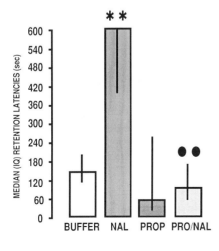

FIGURE 34.5. Effects of posttraining intra-amygdala injections of naloxone (0.1 μg) and propranolol (0.3 μg) on retention of an inhibitory avoidance response (median and interquartile range). Retention was tested 1 week after training. Propranolol blocked naloxone-induced enhancement of memory when the drugs were injected concurrently into the amygdala. $^{\circ\circ}p < .01$ as compared with the buffer group. Filled circles, $p < .01$ as compared with the naloxone-injected group. From "Memory-Enhancement with Intra-Amygdala Posttraining Naloxone Is Blocked by Concurrent Administration of Propranolol" (p. 99) by I. B. Introini-Collison, A. H. Nagahara, and J. L. McGaugh, 1989, *Brain Research, 476,* 94–101. Copyright 1989 by Elsevier Science Publishers. Reprinted by permission.

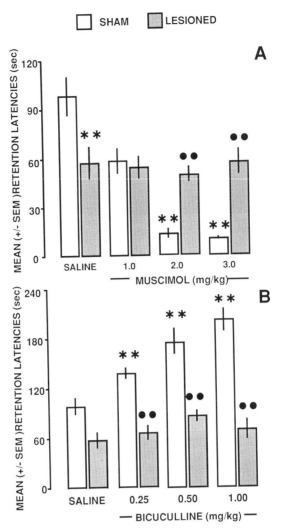

FIGURE 34.6. Effects of muscimol (**A**) and bicuculline (**B**) on 24-hour inhibitory avoidance retention in animals with amygdala lesions. The lesions blocked muscimol-induced impairment of memory as well as bicuculline-induced enhancement of memory. $^{\circ\circ}p < .01$ as compared with the saline-injected control group. Filled circles, $p < .01$ as compared with the sham group receiving the same drug treatment. From "Amygdala and Dorsal Hippocampus Lesions Block the Effects of GABAergic Drugs on Memory Storage" (p. 106) by M. Ammassari-Teule, F. Pavone, C. Castellano, and J. L. McGaugh, 1991, *Brain Research, 551*, 104–109. Copyright 1991 by Elsevier Science Publishers. Reprinted by permission.

cimol (Ammassari-Teule, Pavone, Castellano, & McGaugh, 1991). Furthermore, post-training intra-amygdala injections of bicuculline enhance memory, whereas intra-amygdala injections of baclofen and muscimol impair memory (Brioni, Nagahara, & McGaugh, 1989; Castellano, Brioni, et al., 1989). Other recent findings indicate that GABAergic influences on memory, like those of adrenergic and opiate influences, involve noradrenergic activation within the amygdala. Propranolol administered either systemically or intra-amygdally blocks the retention-enhancing effects of bicuculline (unpublished findings).

Interactions of adrenergic, opioid peptidergic, and GABAergic influences on memory storage suggested by the experimental evidence are summarized in Figure 34.7. The evidence suggests that epinephrine activates a central NE system projecting to the amygdala, and that GABAergic and opioid peptidergic influences regulate the release of NE. The findings strongly support the hypothesis that the influences of several neuromodulatory systems on memory are integrated by interactions occurring within the amygdala, and that the amygdala regulates memory storage in other brain regions through influences mediated, at least in part, by the ST.

Examination of State Dependency in GABAergic and Opiate Influences on Memory

Izquierdo (1984) reported that the retention impairment produced by some posttraining treatments may be based on state dependency. These findings raise the question of whether retention enhancement produced by GABAergic and opiate drugs might reflect the induction of state dependency. A state-dependent interpretation of posttraining drug enhancement of retention would require an assumption that the state normally occurring at the time of the retention test is similar to that induced by the drugs following the training. Thus, injection of the same drug prior to the retention test should decrease the similarity of the states and block the retention enhancement.

Experiments examining this implication have provided no evidence of state dependency in the memory-modulating effects of posttraining and effects of picrotoxin,

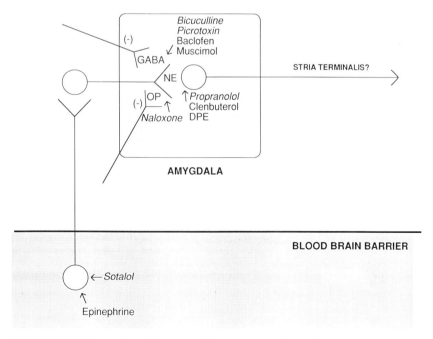

FIGURE 34.7. Interactions of neuromodulatory systems in regulating memory storage.

bucuculline, and muscimol in an inhibitory avoidance task (Castellano & McGaugh, 1989, 1990). The dose-dependent memory-enhancing effects of posttraining injections of these drugs were not affected by drug injections administered prior to the retention test. We also found that the memory-impairing effects of posttraining injections of the opiate agonists morphine and dynorphin were not state-dependent (Castellano & McGaugh, 1989; Introini-Collison, Cahill, Baratti, & McGaugh, 1987). These findings are consistent with the view that the drug effects on memory summarized in this chapter reflect influences on neuromodulatory systems involved in regulating memory storage.

Interactions Involving Cholinergic Actions

The findings of several previous studies suggest that opiate as well as adrenergic influences on memory storage are mediated through cholinergic influences. The memory-enhancing effects of naloxone are blocked by atropine, and the memory-impairing effects of morphine and β-endorphin are attenuated by oxotremorine (Baratti et al., 1984). Furthermore, as is shown in Figure 34.8, atropine also blocks the memory-enhancing effects of epinephrine when both treatments are administered posttraining (Introini-Collison & McGaugh, 1988). Other findings indicate that low (and ineffective) doses of epinephrine injected together posttraining are additive in their memory-enhancing effects (Introini-Collison & McGaugh, 1988). In view of the evidence discussed above indicating that adrenergic and opiate influences on memory are due to

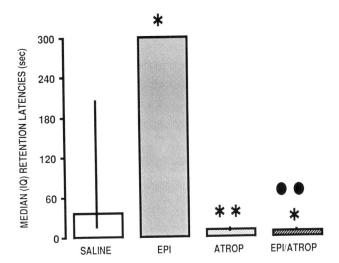

FIGURE 34.8. Effects of posttraining injections (i.p.) of atropine (10.0 mg/kg) and epinephrine (10.0 μg/kg) on 24-hour retention of an inhibitory avoidance response. $^{\circ}p < .05$ and $^{\circ\circ}p < .01$ versus saline control group; filled circles, $p < .01$ versus group given only epinephrine. From "Modulation of Memory by Posttraining Epinephrine: Involvement of Cholinergic Mechanisms" (p. 381) by I. B. Introini-Collison and J. L. McGaugh, 1988, *Psychopharmacology, 94,* 379–385. Copyright 1988 by Springer-Verlag. Reprinted by permission.

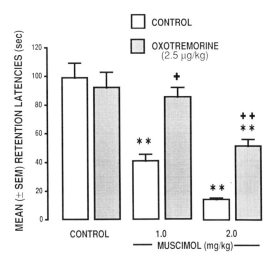

FIGURE 34.9. Effects of posttraining injections (i.p.) of a low dose of the cholinergic agonist oxotremorine (2.5 μg/kg) administered concurrently with memory-impairing doses (1.0 and 2.0 mg/kg) of the GABA-A agonist muscimol on 24-hour retention of an inhibitory avoidance task. $^{\circ\circ}p < .01$ versus oxotremorine-injected group. $^{+}p < .05$ and $^{++}p < .01$ versus saline control plus muscimol groups (1.0 and 2.0 mg/kg, respectively). From "Oxotremorine Attenuates Retrograde Amnesia Induced by Posttraining Administration of the GABAergic Agonists Muscimol and Baclofen" (p. 29) by C. Castellano and J. L. McGaugh, 1991, *Behavioral and Neural Biology*, *56*, 25–31. Copyright 1991 by Academic Press. Reprinted by permission.

a common effect on the release of NE in the amygdala, these findings suggest that NE release in the amygdala activates the release of acetylcholine (ACh). As discussed above, there is evidence suggesting that GABAergic influences on memory storage also involve the release of amygdala NE. Thus, the evidence indicating that cholinergic drugs override the effects of drugs that influence memory through effects on the release of NE suggests that cholinergic drugs should also attenuate the effects of GABAergic drugs. This implication is strongly supported by the findings shown in Figure 34.9: The retention-impairing effects of posttraining systemic injections of the GABA-A agonist muscimol are attenuated by a low and otherwise ineffective dose of oxotremorine administered concurrently with the muscimol (Castellano & McGaugh, 1991).

Experiments have not as yet examined the locus of the interaction of noradrenergic and cholinergic systems in regulating memory storage. Because there are muscarinic cholinergic receptors within the amygdala, the interaction may occur within the amygdala. However, as it is known that the amygdala projects to several brain regions that are rich in cholinergic neurons, including the nucleus basalis and the caudate nucleus, it seems equally likely that the interactions of noradrenergic and cholinergic influences may be mediated by amygdala projections to these systems.

Concluding Comments

The findings summarized in this chapter provide strong support for the view that neuromodulatory systems activated by learning play an important role in regulating memory storage processes. Furthermore, they provide extensive evidence suggesting that the influences of noradrenergic, opiate, and GABAergic systems on memory storage are integrated by interactions within the amygdala, and that such interactions converge in regulating the release of NE. Finally, the findings suggest that these systems influence memory through an NE-mediated release of ACh. Determination of the locus of the suggested NE-ACh interaction should provide additional clarification of the role of neuromodulatory systems in regulating memory storage.

ACKNOWLEDGMENTS

The research described in this chapter was supported by U.S. Public Health Service Research Grant No. MH12526 from the National Institute of Mental Health and the National Institute of Drug Abuse, and by Office of Naval Research Contract No. N00014-90-J-1626. I thank Jorge Brioni, Larry Cahill, Claudio Castellano, Ines Introini-Collison, K. C. Liang, and Alan Nagahara for their contributions to the experimental findings summarized in this chapter, and Nancy Collett for assistance in the preparation of the manuscript.

REFERENCES

Abercrombie, E. D., & Jacobs, J. L. (1988). Systemic naloxone administration potentiates locus coeruleus noradrenergic neuronal activity under stressful but not non-stressful conditions. *Brain Research, 441,* 362–366.

Ammassari-Teule, M., Pavone, F., Castellano, C., & McGaugh, J. L. (1991). Amygdala and dorsal hippocampus lesions block the effects of GABAergic drugs on memory storage. *Brain Research, 551,* 104–109.

Arbilla, S., & Langer, S. Z. (1978). Morphine and beta-endorphin inhibit release of noradrenaline from cerebral cortex but not of dopamine from rat striatum. *Nature, 271,* 559–561.

Baratti, C. M., Introini, I. B., & Huygens, P. (1984). Possible interaction between central cholinergic muscarinic and opioid peptidergic systems during memory consolidation in mice. *Behavioral and Neural Biology, 40,* 155–169.

Bennett, C., Liang, K. C., & McGaugh, J. L. (1985). Depletion of adrenal catecholamines alters the amnestic effect of amygdala stimulation. *Behavioural Brain Research, 15,* 83–91.

Bloch, V. (1970). Facts and hypotheses concerning memory consolidation. *Brain Research, 24,* 561–575.

Borrell, J., de Kloet, E. R., Versteeg, D. H. G., & Bohus, B. (1983). Inhibitory avoidance deficit following short-term adrenalectomy in the rat: The role of adrenal catecholamines. *Behavioral and Neural Biology, 39,* 241–258.

Bovet, D., McGaugh, J. L., & Oliverio, A. (1966). Effects of posttrial administration of drugs on avoidance learning of mice. *Life Sciences, 5,* 309–1315.

Breen, R. A., & McGaugh, J. L. (1961). Facilitation of maze learning with posttrial injections of picrotoxin. *Journal of Comparative and Physiological Psychology, 54,* 498–501.

Brioni, J. D., & McGaugh, J. L. (1988). Posttraining administration of GABAergic antagonists enhance retention of aversively motivated tasks. *Psychopharmacology, 96,* 505–510.

Brioni, J. D., Nagahara, A. H., & McGaugh, J. L. (1989). Involvement of the amygdala GABAergic system in the modulation of memory storage. *Brain Research, 487,* 105–112.

Cahill, L., & McGaugh, J. L. (1990). Amygdaloid complex lesions differentially affect retention of tasks using appetitive and aversive reinforcement. *Behavioral Neuroscience, 104,* 523–543.

Cahill, L., & McGaugh, J. L. (1991). NMDA-induced lesions of the amygdaloid complex block the retention enhancing effect of posttraining epinephrine. *Psychobiology, 19,* 206–210.

Castellano, C., Brioni, J. D., & McGaugh, J. L. (1990). GABAergic modulation of memory. In L. R. Squire & E. Lindenlaub (Eds.), *Biology of memory* (pp. 361–378). Stuttgart: Schattauer Verlag.

Castellano, C., Brioni, J. D., Nagahara, A. H., & McGaugh, J. L. (1989). Posttraining systemic and intra-amygdala administration of the GABA-B agonist baclofen impair retention. *Behavioral and Neural Biology, 52,* 170–179.

Castellano, C., Introini-Collison, I. B., Pavone, F., & McGaugh, J. L. (1989). Effects of naloxone and naltrexone on memory consolidation in CD1 mice: Involvement of GABAergic mechanisms. *Pharmacology, Biochemistry and Behavior, 32,* 563–567.

Castellano, C., & McGaugh, J. L. (1989). Retention enhancement with posttraining picrotoxin: Lack of state dependency. *Behavioral and Neural Biology, 51,* 165–170.

Castellano, C., & McGaugh, J. L. (1990). Effects of post-training bicuculline and muscimol on retention: Lack of state dependency. *Behavioral and Neural Biology, 54,* 156–164.

Castellano, C., & McGaugh, J. L. (1991). Oxotremorine attenuates retrograde amnesia induced by posttraining administration of the GABAergic agonists muscimol and baclofen. *Behavioral and Neural Biology*, 56, 25–31.

Fanelli, R. J., Rosenberg, R. A., & Gallagher, M. (1985). Role of noradrenergic function in the opiate antagonist facilitation of spatial memory. *Behavioral Neuroscience*, 99(4), 751–755.

Gallagher, M. (1982). Naloxone enhancement of memory processes: Effects of other opiate antagonists. *Behavioral and Neural Biology*, 35, 375–382.

Gallagher, M. (1985). Reviewing modulation of learning and memory. In N. M. Weinberger, J. L. McGaugh, & G. Lynch (Eds.), *Memory systems of the brain: Animal and human cognitive processes* (pp. 311–334). New York: Guilford Press.

Gallagher, M., & Kapp, B. S. (1978). Manipulation of opiate activity in the amygdala alters memory processes. *Life Sciences*, 23, 1973–1978.

Gallagher, M., Kapp, B. S., Pascoe, J. P., & Rapp, P. R. (1981). A neuropharmacology of amygdaloid systems which contribute to learning and memory. In Y. Ben-Ari (Ed.), *The amygdaloid complex* (pp. 343–354). Amsterdam: Elsevier/North Holland.

Gallagher, M., Rapp, P. R., & Fanelli, R. J. (1985). Opiate antagonist facilitation of time-dependent memory processes: Dependence upon intact norepinephrine function. *Brain Research*, 347, 284–290.

Gold, P. E. (1986). Glucose modulation of memory storage processing. *Behavioral and Neural Biology*, 45, 342–349.

Gold, P. E. (1988). Plasma glucose regulation of memory storage processes. In C. D. Woody, D. L. Alkon, & J. L. McGaugh (Eds.), *Cellular mechanisms of conditioning and behavioral plasticity* (pp. 329–341). New York: Academic Press.

Gold, P. E., & McCarty, R. (1981). Plasma catecholamines: Changes after footshock and seizure-producing frontal cortex stimulation. *Behavioral and Neural Biology*, 31, 247–260.

Gold, P.E., & McGaugh, J. L. (1975). A single-trace, two process view of memory storage processes. In D. Deutsch & J. A. Deutsch (Eds.), *Short-term memory* (pp. 355–378). New York: Academic Press.

Gold, P. E., & van Buskirk, R. (1975). Facilitation of time-dependent memory processes with posttrial amygdala stimulation: Effect on memory varies with footshock level. *Brain Research*, 86, 509–513.

Gold, P. E., & van Buskirk, R. (1978a). Posttraining brain norepinephrine concentrations: Correlation with retention performance of avoidance training with peripheral epinephrine modulation of memory processing. *Behavioral Biology*, 23, 509–520.

Gold, P.E., & van Buskirk, R. (1978b). Effects of alpha and beta adrenergic receptor antagonists on post-trial epinephrine modulation of memory: Relationship to posttraining brain norepinephrine concentrations. *Behavioral Biology*, 24, 168–184.

Gold, P.E., van Buskirk, R., & Haycock, J. (1977). Effects of posttraining epinephrine injections on retention of avoidance training in mice. *Behavioral Biology*, 20, 197–207.

Hitchcock, J. M., & Davis, M. (1987). Fear-potentiated startle using an auditory conditioned stimulus: Effect of lesions of the amygdala. *Physiology and Behavior*, 39, 403–408.

Introini-Collison, I. B., & Baratti, C. M. (1986). Opioid peptidergic systems modulate the activity of beta-adrenergic mechanisms during memory consolidation processes. *Behavioral and Neural Biology*, 46, 227–241.

Introini-Collison, I. B., Cahill, L., Baratti, C. M., & McGaugh, J. L. (1987). Dynorphin induces task-specific impairment of memory. *Psychobiology*, 15, 171–174.

Introini-Collison, I. B., & McGaugh, J. L. (1986). Epinephrine modulates long-term retention of an aversively-motivated discrimination task. *Behavioral and Neural Biology*, 45, 358–365.

Introini-Collison, I. B., & McGaugh, J. L. (1987). Naloxone and beta-endorphin alter the effects of posttraining epinephrine on retention of an inhibitory avoidance response. *Psychopharmacology*, 92, 229–235.

Introini-Collison, I. B., & McGaugh, J. L. (1988). Modulation of memory by posttraining epinephrine: Involvement of cholinergic mechanisms. *Psychopharmacology*, 94, 379–385.

Introini-Collison, I. B., Miyazaki, B., & McGaugh, J. L. (1991). Involvement of the amygdala in the memory-enhancing effects of clenbuterol. *Psychopharmacology*, 104, 541–544.

Introini-Collison, I. B., Nagahara, A. H., & McGaugh, J. L. (1989). Memory-enhancement with intra-amygdala posttraining naloxone is blocked by concurrent administration of propranolol. *Brain Research*, 476, 94–101.

Introini-Collison, I. B., Saghafi, D., Novack, G., & McGaugh, J. L. (1992). Memory-enhancing effects of posttraining dipivefrin and epinephrine: Involvement of peripheral and central adrenergic receptors. *Brain Research*, 572, 81–86.

Izquierdo, I. (1979). Effect of naloxone and morphine on various forms of memory in the rat: Possible role of endogenous opiate mechanisms in memory consolidation. *Psychopharmacology*, 66, 199–203.

Izquierdo, I. (1984). Endogenous state dependency: Memory depends on the relation between the neuro-humoral and hormonal states present after training and at the time of testing. In G. Lynch, J. L. McGaugh & N. M. Weinberger (Eds.), *Neurobiology of learning and memory* (pp. 333–350). New York: Guilford Press.

Izquierdo, I., & Dias, R. D. (1983). Effect of ACTH, epinephrine, β-endorphin, naloxone, and of the combination of naloxone or B-endorphin with ACTH or epinephrine on memory consolidation. *Psychoneuroendocrinology, 8,* 81–87.

Izquierdo, I., & Graudenz, M. (1980). Memory facilitation by naloxone is due to release of dopaminergic and beta-adrenergic systems from tonic inhibition. *Psychopharmacology, 67,* 265–268.

Kesner, R. P., Walser, R. D., & Winzenried, G. (1989). Central but not basolateral amygdala mediates memory for positive affective experiences. *Behavioural Brain Research, 33,* 189–195.

Kesner, R. P., & Wilburn, M. W. (1974). A review of electrical stimulation of the brain in context of learning and retention. *Behavioral Biology, 10,* 259–293.

LeDoux, J. E., Iwata, J., Cicchetti, P., & Reis, D. J. (1988). Different projections of the central amygdaloid nucleus mediate autonomic and behavioral correlates of conditioned fear. *Journal of Neuroscience, 8,* 2517–2529.

Liang, K. C., Bennett, C., & McGaugh, J. L. (1985). Peripheral epinephrine modulates the effects of posttraining amygdala stimulation on memory. *Behavioural Brain Research, 15,* 93–100.

Liang, K. C., Juler, R., & McGaugh, J. L. (1986). Modulating effects of posttraining epinephrine on memory: Involvement of the amygdala noradrenergic system. *Brain Research, 368,* 125–133.

Liang, K. C., & McGaugh, J. L. (1983). Lesions of the stria terminalis attenuate the enhancing effect of posttraining epinephrine on retention of an inhibitory avoidance response. *Behavioural Brain Research, 9,* 49–58.

Liang, K. C., McGaugh, J. L., & Yao, H. Y. (1990). Involvement of amygdala pathways in the influence of posttraining amygdala norepinephrine and peripheral epinephrine on memory storage. *Brain Research, 508,* 225–233.

McGaugh, J. L. (1966). Time-dependent processes in memory storage. *Science, 153,* 1351–1358.

McGaugh, J. L. (1973). Drug facilitation of learning and memory. *Annual Review of Pharmacology, 13,* 229–241.

McGaugh, J. L. (1983). Hormonal influences on memory. *Annual Review of Psychology, 34,* 297–323.

McGaugh, J. L. (1989a). Involvement of hormonal and neuromodulatory systems in the regulation of memory storage. *Annual Review of Neuroscience, 12,* 255–287.

McGaugh, J. L. (1989b). Dissociating learning and performance: Drug and hormone enhancement of memory storage. *Brain Research Bulletin, 23,* 339–345.

McGaugh, J. L., Castellano, C., & Brioni, J. D. (1990). Picrotoxin enhances latent extinction of conditioned fear. *Behavioral Neuroscience, 104,* 262–265.

McGaugh, J. L., & Gold, P. E. (1976). Modulation of memory by electrical stimulation of the brain. In M. R. Rosenzweig & E. L. Bennett (Eds.), *Neural mechanisms of learning and memory* (pp. 549–560). Cambridge, MA: MIT Press.

McGaugh, J. L., & Herz, M. J. (1972). *Memory consolidation.* San Francisco: Albion.

McGaugh, J. L., Introini-Collison, I. B., Juler, R. G., & Izquierdo, I. (1986). Stria terminalis lesions attenuate the effects of posttraining naloxone and β-endorphin on retention. *Behavioral Neuroscience, 100,* 839–844.

McGaugh, J. L., Introini-Collison, I. B., & Nagahara, A. H. (1988). Memory-enhancing effects of posttraining naloxone: Involvement of β-noradrenergic influences in the amygdaloid complex. *Brain Research, 446,* 37–49.

McGaugh, J. L., & Petrinovich, L. F. (1965). Effects of drugs on learning and memory. *International Review of Neurobiology, 8,* 139–196.

Messing, R. B., Jensen, R. A., Martinez, J. L., Jr., Spiehler, V. R., Vasquez, B. J., Soumireu-Mourat, B., Liang, K. C., & McGaugh, J. L. (1979). Naloxone enhancement of memory. *Behavioral and Neural Biology, 27,* 266–275.

Montel, H., Starke, K., & Weber, F. (1974). Influence of morphine and naloxone on the release of noradrena-line from rat brain cortex slices. *Naunyn-Schmiedeberg's Archives of Pharmacology, 283,* 283–369.

Nakamura, S., Tepper, J. M., Young, S. J., Ling, N., & Groves, P. M. (1982). Noradrenergic terminal excitability: Effects of opioids. *Neuroscience Letters, 30,* 57–62.

Sternberg, D. B., Isaacs, K., Gold, P. E., & McGaugh, J. L. (1985). Epinephrine facilitation of appetitive learning: Attenuation with adrenergic receptor antagonists. *Behavioral and Neural Biology, 44,* 447–453.

Swartzwelder, H. S., Tilson, H. A., McLamb, R. L., & Wilson, W. A. (1987). Baclofen disrupts passive avoidance retention in rats. *Psychopharmacology, 92*, 398–401.

Tanaka, T., Yokoo, H., Mizoguichi, K., Yoshida, M., Tsuda, A., & Tanaka, M. (1991). Noradrenaline release in the rat amygdala is increased by stress: Studies with intracerebral microdialysis. *Brain Research, 544*, 174–176.

Weil-Malherbe, H., Axelrod, J., & Tomchick, R. (1959). Blood–brain barrier for adrenaline. *Science, 129*, 1226–1228.

Weiskrantz, L. (1956). Behavioral changes associated with ablation of the amygdaloid complex in monkeys. *Journal of Comparative and Physiological Psychology, 49*, 381–391.

Werling, L. L., Brown, S. R., & Cox, B. M. (1987). Opioid receptor regulation of the release of norepinephrine in brain. *Neuropharmacology, 26*, 987–996.

Werling, L. L., McMahon, P. N., Portoghese, P. S., Takemori, A. E., & Cox, B. M. (1989). Selective opioid antagonist effects on opioid-induced inhibition of release of norepinephrine in guinea pig cortex. *Neuropharmacology, 28*, 103–107.

35

Modulation of Memory Processing: Enhancement of Memory in Rodents and Humans

PAUL E. GOLD

Memories appear to be most robust for events that are particularly salient to an animal and appear to be transitory for events that are relatively trivial (see Gold, 1991, in press). This intuitive statement suggests that there may be biological systems and processes responsible for regulating the mechanisms of memory formation (Livingston, 1967; Kety, 1976). In combination with evidence that pharmacological and other treatments can retroactively enhance memory storage processing, many investigators have addressed the possibility that neuroendocrine responses to experience may be an early step in a sequence of biological responses responsible for regulating the formation of memory for that experience (e.g., Gold & McGaugh, 1975; McGaugh, 1989; Gold, 1991, in press).

An understanding of the mechanisms by which hormones regulate memory offers promise of fulfilling two goals. The first is that a full understanding of the mechanisms underlying hormonal control of the brain mechanisms responsible for storing information will direct investigators to specific forms of neural plasticity that mediate memory formation. The mechanisms by which hormones regulate memory storage may lead directly to the mechanisms of memory storage. The second is that deficiencies in hormonal systems that regulate memory formation may contribute to memory pathologies. Instances of memory dysfunction—aging, dementia, brain damage—may reflect loss of brain elements and systems that store the representations of new memories. In addition, however, memory dysfunction might also (or, in some cases, instead) be a consequence of a loss of brain processes necessary for regulating the formation of the substrates of memory. Thus, identification of the mechanisms underlying hormonal effects on memory may lead to development of treatment strategies directed at ameliorating memory dysfunctions. This chapter deals with each of these issues in turn; it first describes evidence for epinephrine and glucose enhancement of memory, as well as early findings relevant to their mechanisms of action, and then discusses epinephrine and glucose attenuation of memory impairments in animals and humans during aging and after brain injury.

Enhancement of Memory by Epinephrine and Glucose

Of those hormones tested for effects on memory, epinephrine has been examined in the greatest detail. Epinephrine is released into the circulation from the adrenal medulla in response to acute stressors, including release after footshock at levels used in training procedures with experimental animals (McCarty & Gold, 1981; Gold & McCarty, 1981). Thus, release of this hormone is accomplished during typical training episodes in rodents, offering the potential at least for regulating memory storage. In animals trained on an inhibitory avoidance task with quite low footshock intensities and durations, at levels that release epinephrine only in small amounts, posttraining administration of epinephrine enhances later retention (see McGaugh, 1989). These findings are not restricted to inhibitory avoidance tasks, but have broad generality across tasks, including discriminated avoidance, classical conditioning, and appetitive procedures (reviewed in McGaugh, 1989; McGaugh & Gold, 1989; Gold, 1991).

Thus, the basic findings are that epinephrine is released during training with procedures resulting in good retention at later tests, and that posttraining epinephrine administration enhances memory for training situations that themselves would be inadequate to produce optimal retention. In considering the mechanisms by which epinephrine enhances memory, it is necessary to bring the behavioral findings into agreement with the substantial evidence that circulating epinephrine is largely excluded from the central nervous system (CNS); that is, epinephrine does not cross the blood–brain barrier (Axelrod, Weil-Malherbe, & Tomchick, 1959). Epinephrine does, however, have significant influences on CNS functions. For example, systemic injections of epinephrine result in electroencephalographic activation (Baust, Niemczyk, & Vieth, 1963), increased cerebral oxygen consumption and blood flow (Dahlgren, Rosen, Sakabe, & Siesjo, 1980), and activation of central noradrenergic systems (Gold & van Buskirk, 1978). With specific regard to modulation of memory storage processing, such findings may be related to the substantial evidence that epinephrine enhancement of memory is mediated through the amygdala (see McGaugh, Chapter 34, this volume; Liang & McGaugh, 1983; Introini-Collison, Miyazaki, & McGaugh, 1991), possibly via mechanisms including noradrenergic influences within the amygdala (Gallagher, Kapp, Pascoe, & Rapp, 1981; Liang, Juler, & McGaugh, 1986).

Since epinephrine does not appear to have direct actions on the CNS, it is likely that peripheral actions may also contribute to epinephrine effects on behavior. One peripheral action of epinephrine is to produce an increase in circulating glucose levels (Ellis, Kennedy, Eusebi, & Vincent, 1967). A growing body of evidence indicates that, as with epinephrine, posttraining increases in circulating glucose levels are correlated with performance on later memory tests, and posttraining administration of glucose enhances memory storage processing (see Gold, 1991, in press; White, 1991). For example, both epinephrine and glucose exhibit inverted-U dose–response curves for enhancement of memory, with parallel dose–effect curves (peak memory-enhancing doses for epinephrine, 0.1 mg/kg; for glucose, 100 mg/kg) noted for subsequent circulating glucose levels (Gold, 1986; Figure 35.1). Both treatments also have similar interactions with neurotransmitter functions, discussed below.

One difference in the findings obtained with epinephrine and glucose is particularly revealing. Like the effects of many other memory-modulating treatments, epi-

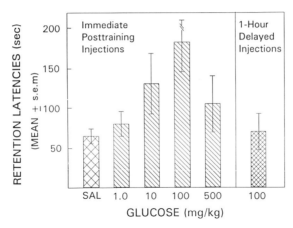

FIGURE 35.1. Glucose enhancement of memory for inhibitory avoidance training. Retention was tested 24 hours after training and treatment. From "Glucose Modulation of Memory Storage Processing" (p. 345) by P. E. Gold, 1986, *Behavioral and Neural Biology, 45*, 342–349. Copyright 1986 by Academic Press. Reprinted by permission.

nephrine's effects on memory are blocked in the presence of peripherally administered adrenergic antagonists (e.g., Gold & Sternberg, 1978). However, glucose effects on memory are not blocked by adrenergic antagonists (Gold, Vogt, & Hall, 1986). These findings suggest that epinephrine enhancement of memory requires peripheral adrenergic receptor activation, but that glucose enhancement of memory does not. Peripheral adrenergic receptor activation is important in determining the extent of increases in circulating glucose levels, but is not a component of similar increases after glucose administration (Hall & Gold, 1992; Figure 35.2). These findings suggest that increases in glucose levels subsequent to peripheral epinephrine actions contribute to enhancement of memory storage processing. Importantly, the magnitude of the increase in blood glucose levels necessary (and optimal) for memory enhancement is not large (e.g., 140 mg/dl vs. baseline values near 110 mg/dl) and is well within normal physiological limits. For example, diabetic rats would attain blood glucose levels well above 200 mg/dl after a dose of glucose sufficient to enhance memory in healthy rats.

Unlike epinephrine, glucose has ready access to the CNS via a facilitated glucose transport mechanism (Crone, 1965; Pardridge & Oldendorf, 1975; Lund-Anderson, 1979). Initial evidence indicates that direct central injections of glucose (into lateral ventricle) also enhance memory when administered shortly after inhibitory avoidance training (Lee, Graham, & Gold, 1988) and reverse scopolamine-induced deficits (see below) in spontaneous alternation performance (Parsons & Gold, 1992). Such findings are consistent with the view that increases in circulating epinephrine result in enhancement of memory via a sequence of events that includes increases in circulating glucose, which acts on the brain to augment the processes responsible for memory formation.

The inverted-U dose–response curve for glucose enhancement of memory is not the full description of the findings. In addition to one peak effective glucose dose at 100 mg/kg, White and colleagues (see White, 1991) have reported a second, higher inverted-U curve for glucose effects on memory, with a peak dose of 2 g/kg enhancing memory. This higher dose–response function apparently involves a different mechanism from the one underlying the lower dose levels; this mechanism may include peripheral glucose actions. For example, fructose and other simple sugars, which do not act directly on the CNS, enhance memory at high (2 g/kg) doses but not at low (100 mg/kg) doses. Furthermore, removal of peripheral afferents to the CNS from the coeliac ganglion block the higher but not the lower dose–response functions. It will be necessary to determine in the future how these different mechanisms, peripheral and central glucose actions, interact to enhance memory.

Glucose Interactions with Central Nervous System Neurotransmitters

The robust effects of glucose on memory storage point to the need for development of a pharmacological basis for understanding glucose effects on brain function. To address this issue, my colleagues and I began by examining glucose interactions with the

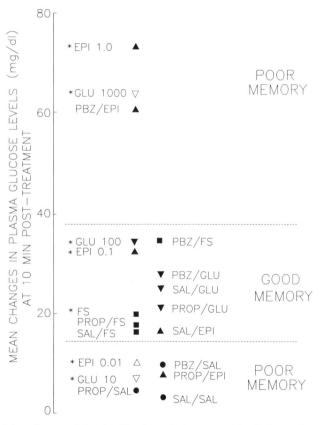

FIGURE 35.2. Ranking of posttraining (at 10 minutes) changes in blood glucose levels. Note that good performance on later retention tests was seen in groups of animals with increases in blood glucose levels between 15 and 40 mg/dl. In studies of pretreatment with phenoxybenzamine (PBZ) or propranolol (PROP), the glucose (GLU) and epinephrine (EPI) doses were 100 and 0.1 mg/kg, respectively. FS, foot shock; SAL, saline. The data are from Hall and Gold (1986, 1992).

effects of several classes of drugs with major influences on memory storage and extended these interactions to neural and behavioral measures other than memory. The drug classes examined have included treatments that act on opiate, γ-aminobutyric acid (GABA), acetylcholine, and excitatory amino acid receptors. These pharmacological systems were selected for initial examination because manipulation of each of them has large effects on memory. Opiate and GABA receptor agonists generally impair, and antagonists enhance, memory (see McGaugh & Gold, 1989; Martinez, Weinberger, & Schulteis, 1988). Cholinergic agonists generally enhance memory, whereas cholinergic receptor antagonists, as well as antagonists at the N-methyl-D-aspartate (NMDA) class of excitatory amino acid receptors, impair memory (see McGaugh, 1989; Cotman, Monaghan, & Ganong, 1988). Furthermore, there is considerable evidence that, of these neurotransmitters, at least opiate and cholinergic systems exhibit interactive influences on memory. For example, the cholinergic (muscarinic) receptor antagonist atropine blocks enhancement of memory with an opiate antagonist, naloxone (Baratti, Introini, & Huygens, 1984); conversely, naloxone blocks scopolamine-induced memory impairment (Rush, 1986). Similarly, the cholinergic agonists oxotremorine and physostigmine block amnesia produced by the opiate, β-endorphin (Introini & Baratti, 1984). These behavioral findings are consistent with evidence that systemic injections of morphine reduce, and injections of naloxone increase, neocortical and striatal acetylcholine release (see Lamour & Epelbaum, 1988). Also, direct injections of opiate agonists into medial septum, a brain area containing cholinergic cell bodies that project to hippocampus, result in decreases on several measures of hippocampal cholinergic activity (e.g., Moroni, Cheney, & Costa, 1977; Costa, Panula, Thompson, & Cheney, 1983; Botticelli & Wurtman, 1982). Such findings on both behavioral and neurochemical measures suggest that opiates inhibit cholinergic activity in several brain regions, including the septo-hippocampal system.

When glucose's interactions with drugs acting at opiate and cholinergic receptors are examined, the results are very consistent across the large domain of neural and behavioral measures listed in Figure 35.3: Glucose acts in a manner suggesting increased activation of cholinergic receptors and decreased activation of opiate receptors. For example, glucose attenuates impairments produced by muscarinic antagonists (atropine, scopolamine) and an opiate agonist (morphine) on inhibitory avoidance and spontaneous alternation performance (Stone, Walser, Gold, & Gold, 1991); naloxone has similar effects on these measures (Walker, McGlynn, Grey, Ragozzino, & Gold, 1991). Glucose also attenuates the increases in locomotor activity seen after scopolamine or morphine administration, attenuates decreases in rapid eye movement (REM) sleep after atropine, and attenuates decreases in 2-deoxyglucose uptake after scopolamine (see Gold, 1991). Furthermore, animals pretreated with glucose exhibit increased sensitivity to physostigmine-induced tremors, with shorter latency to tremor onset and increased severity of the tremors after physostigmine (Stone, Cottrill, Walker, & Gold, 1988). Preliminary evidence suggests that glucose also attenuates decreased spontaneous alternation levels produced by an NMDA antagonist (NPC 12626) (Walker, Stone, & Gold, 1990).

As noted above, one brain area in which opiates appear to inhibit cholinergic neurons, possibly through GABA interneurons (Wood, Cheney, & Costa, 1979), is the medial septum. We therefore investigated the effects of medial septum injections of

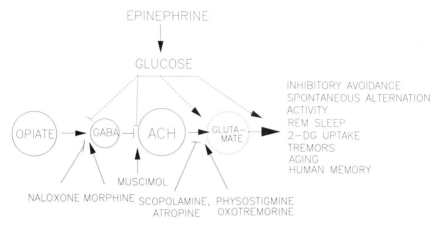

FIGURE 35.3. Working model incorporating the pharmacological evidence obtained thus far regarding glucose interactions with central neurotransmitter systems. Several points at which glucose might enter the scheme are noted. In studies where they have been tested, the results are consistent for the several measures on the right. Not all drug conditions have been investigated for all measures. ACh, acetylcholine; 2-DG, 2-deoxyglucose.

morphine on spontaneous alternation performance and inhibitory avoidance learning (Ragozzino, Parker, & Gold, 1990). Septal injections of morphine impaired performance on both tasks; moreover, both peripheral and medial septum injections of glucose attenuated these deficits. Thus, like systemic injections, direct septal injections of glucose antagonized the effects on behavior of direct septal injections of morphine.

The substantial projection of medial septum cholinergic neurons to hippocampus suggests that, as seen with neurochemical measures of hippocampal activity, septal injections of an opiate may inhibit cholinergic activity in hippocampus—an effect apparently attenuated by concomitant septal administration of glucose. The morphine-induced impairments are similar to those we and others have observed after lesions of the medial septum. If the medial septum is a target site for glucose actions on memory, systemic glucose should be ineffective if administered to rats with septal lesions. We (McGlynn, Lennartz, Gold, & Gold, 1992) observed this to be the case. Rats were prepared with ibotenic acid lesions; at the conclusion of the experiment, these lesions were found to have significantly decreased acetylcholinesterase staining in widespread regions of the hippocampal formation. Rats tested on a spontaneous alternation task 1–2 weeks after surgery exhibited significant deficits in performance (Figure 35.4). Although glucose enhances spontaneous alternation performance under several other conditions, as noted above, glucose was ineffective in reversing the deficits after septal damage. Interestingly, the indirect cholinergic agonist physostigmine also failed to reverse the deficit, suggesting that the loss of cholinergic terminals in hippocampus was sufficient to block physostigmine's actions. However, the direct agonist oxotremorine returned spontaneous alternation performance to levels near those of controls.

These results may be important in several respects. First, because glucose does not reverse memory deficits after medial septal lesions, the medial septum may be one site of glucose action. Further support for this possibility comes from the findings that intraseptal injections of glucose reverse memory impairments produced by septal

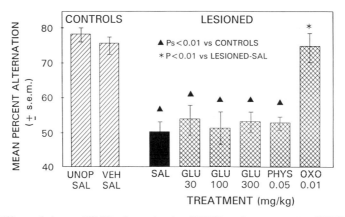

FIGURE 35.4. Effects of glucose (GLU), physostigmine (PHYS), and oxotremorine (OXO) on spontaneous alternation performance in rats with ibotenic lesions of medial septum. Note that oxotremorine, but not glucose or physostigmine, reversed the lesion-induced deficit. From *Ibotenic Lesions of Medial Septum: Reversal of Spontaneous Alternation Deficits with Oxotremorine, but Not Glucose or Physostigmine* by T. J. McGlynn, R. L. Lennartz, S. D. Gold, and P. E. Gold, 1992, manuscript submitted for publication.

injections of morphine. Still, the specific cell type (e.g., by neurotransmitter) or mechanism by which glucose acts within the medial septum is not known. Second, the ability of a direct cholinergic receptor agonist, oxotremorine, but not an indirect agonist, physostigmine, to reverse deficits after medial septum lesions suggests that the behavioral impairment probably reflects interference with cholinergic functions within the hippocampal formation; if activation of other (nonhippocampal) cholinergic systems were sufficient to explain the reversal of the lesion-induced deficit, physostigmine should also be effective. Furthermore, there is a curious aspect of the oxotremorine results. Traditional views of neurotransmitter action would seem to obviate the possibility that a drug, which cannot match the exquisite spatial and temporal specificity of a classic neurotransmitter, could replace a (indeed, any) neurotransmitter function. Because oxotremorine can apparently do so, one possible explanation of the results is that some afferent activity projected to the hippocampal formation controls the activity of the hippocampus by specifying different processing modes under different environmental conditions. For example, the oxotremorine findings suggest that activation of cholinergic receptors within the hippocampus may place the structure in a state appropriate for spatial processing, resulting in relatively normal performance in the spontaneous alternation task by rats with medial septum damage.

   In summary, the findings of studies of interactions between glucose and several pharmacological agents, on memory and several other measures, indicate that glucose attenuates behavioral actions of opiate agonists and has marked similarities of action to naloxone, an opiate antagonist. Furthermore, glucose potentiates the actions of cholinergic agonists and attenuates the actions of an NMDA antagonist. On the other hand, glucose does not reverse the effects on memory of medial septum lesions.

   Comparisons of instances in which glucose does and does not attenuate deficits are likely to be very important in determining the mechanisms by which glucose acts. In terms of glucose's acting through particular neurotransmitter systems, more direct assessments of transmitter release after glucose administration—for example, *in vivo* microdialysis assessments—will be necessary components of a complete profile of glucose action on brain functions.

Glucose Attenuation of Age-Related Deficits in Memory

Memory pathologies are generally assumed to reflect deficits in memory storage mechanisms; that is, brain areas or systems in which memory storage occurs in normal subjects are thought to be damaged. Neuroendocrine regulation of memory storage opens a second possibility, though not a mutually exclusive one: Some forms of memory pathology may be the result of a loss of hormones or their targets that are important in promoting memory storage mechanisms. According to the latter view, deficits in neuroendocrine responses to an experience may contribute to impaired memory storage for that experience. Aged rodents, like other mammals (including humans), exhibit age-related memory deficits that are most readily characterized as the inability to retain recent information, or, more concisely, rapid forgetting of new information. For example, under conditions in which young rats retain memory for inhibitory avoidance training for up to 6 weeks, 2-year-old rats retain the memories for less than 24 hours (Gold, McGaugh, Hankins, Rose, & Vasquez, 1981). Aged rats also exhibit decreased release of epinephrine after footshock (McCarty, 1981). Thus, the animals have both a memory deficit and a deficit in a neuroendocrine response important for regulation of memory storage processes. Both epinephrine and glucose can attenuate age-related memory deficits in rats and mice. A single injection of epinephrine, administered immediately after training in an inhibitory avoidance task, enhances memory when tested 1 week later (Sternberg, Martinez, McGaugh, & Gold, 1985). Rats also exhibit age-related deficits in spontaneous alternation performance when a 1-minute intertrial interval is employed; glucose injections shortly before spontaneous alternation tests reverse this deficit (Stone & Gold, 1992).

Age-related impairments of brain function, and the effects of glucose in aged rats, are not limited to memory tests. Aged rats also exhibit significant deficits in sleep; these are particularly evident with measures of REM (paradoxical) sleep. Moreover, sleep and memory deficits are significantly correlated in individual aged animals; those aged rats with memory deficits are likely also to be the rats with sleep deficits (Stone & Gold, 1988; Stone, Altman, Berman, Caldwell, & Kilbey, 1989; for review, see Stone, Manning, & Gold, 1989). Glucose injections attenuate the sleep deficits in aged rats, returning the measures to values near those of young rats. The coappearance of REM sleep and memory deficits, and the susceptibility of both measures to enhancement with glucose administration, raise the possibility that a brain system or process impaired during aging may contribute to both impairments.

The broad range of glucose effects on several tests of memory and other measures, together with the safety of employing glucose as a treatment, led us to determine whether glucose might be an effective treatment with which to ameliorate memory impairments during aging and after brain damage. The results of several experiments indicate that administration of glucose (by ingestion in a fruit drink; saccharin control) can enhance memory in elderly humans. The subjects in these studies were generally healthy individuals aged 60–80 years. The experiments employed a double-blind crossover design. When alternate forms of standardized tests are used, this design enables within-subject comparisons of subjects under glucose or control conditions. The findings have been remarkably consistent with those observed in animal studies. Using repeated measures with alternate forms of the Logical Memory test from the Wechsler Memory Scale, we tested subjects over several weeks (no more than one session/week). Glucose (10, 25, or 50 g) was ingested about 30 minutes prior to presentation of the material to be learned; when recall was tested 45 minutes later, the glucose enhanced memory in an inverted-U dose–response manner, as shown in Figure 35.5 (Parsons & Gold, in press). Moreover, the most effective glucose dose in this experiment (25 g) resulted in increases in blood glucose levels in humans similar to those for the most effective dose in rats (compare with Figure 35.2).

As in animals, posttraining administration of glucose also enhances memory in elderly people (Manning, Parsons, & Gold, 1992). Subjects received glucose or saccharin shortly before or immediately after hearing the Logical Memory test paragraph. When recall was tested 24 hours later, retention was significantly better with both pre- and posttraining glucose administration (vs. saccharin). These findings add to the relatively small literature demonstrating posttraining enhancement of memory in humans. Furthermore, the findings indicate that the enhanced memory formed when blood glucose levels are elevated near the time of training is maintained for at least 24 hours. Also, because blood glucose levels return to baseline within the 24-hour interval, elevated blood glucose levels are not necessary for the enhanced memory seen at the time of retrieval tests.

We (Manning, Hall, & Gold, 1990; Manning, Parsons, Cotter, & Gold, 1992) have begun to characterize the aspects of cognitive function most susceptible to enhancement by glucose. Glucose has no apparent effects on tests of primary memory,

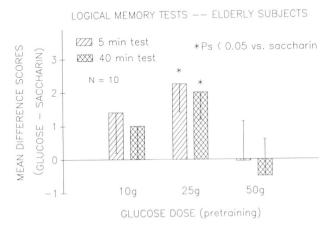

FIGURE 35.5. Inverted-U dose–response curve for glucose enhancement of memory (Logical Memory test) in elderly humans. Glucose (or saccharin matched to taste) was administered in a fruit-flavored drink. Results are shown as differences from baseline (saccharin control) performance. From "Glucose Enhancement of Memory in Elderly Humans: An Inverted-U Dose–Response Curve" by M. W. Parsons and P. E. Gold, in press, *Neurobiology of Aging.* Copyright by Pergamon Press. Reprinted by permission.

attention, or motor abilities. In addition to repeatedly finding that glucose enhances performance on the Logical Memory test (a test of contextual verbal declarative memory), we have also found that glucose enhances memory on a selective reminding test (a test of noncontextual verbal declarative memory). Moreover, we (Manning, Parsons, Cotter, & Gold, 1992) tested the efficacy of glucose in enhancing performance on a priming test, a word stem completion test of implicit memory. Glucose did not affect performance on the priming test itself; that is, glucose did not affect implicit memory. However, when the subjects were then asked to recall freely the words employed in the task (a measure of declarative memory), the subjects performed significantly better under glucose than under saccharin. Thus, in generally healthy elderly subjects, glucose appears to have its largest effects on declarative memory tests. However, in a case study of an individual with global amnesia after extensive telencephalic damage (gunshot wound), glucose appeared to enhance memory on nondeclarative tests as well (Manning, Jane, & Gold, 1992).

Thus, the cognitive processes on which glucose can act are still in early stages of identification. Defining the cognitive elements susceptible to enhancement by glucose may be as simple as determining those tests on which there is a deficit permitting the greatest room for improvement. The extent to which the cognitive elements will correspond to those elegantly defined in individuals with selective brain damage (Squire, 1987) remains to be determined. An important question here is whether studies of pharmacological enhancement of memory in humans will lead to memory taxonomies similar to or different from those previously developed in studies of individuals with brain injury.

Conclusions

In animals, glucose enhances memory and other neural and behavioral measures under several experimental circumstances. Although the primary mechanisms by which glucose acts are not yet known, the interactions with drugs that augment or impair neurotransmitter functions—and the instances in which glucose effects on memory are blocked—suggest that one system through which glucose acts may include the medial septum, possibly by regulating cholinergic projections to the hippocampal formation.

The findings obtained in studies of human memory indicate that glucose is an effective treatment with which to enhance memory, particularly in individuals with impairments. Glucose might best be seen as a primitive early step in the development of pharmacological cognitive enhancers (see Wenk, 1989). Furthermore, we should be cautious in assuming that the reliability of these findings, in contrast to that seen with other treatments such as nootropics or cholinergic agonists, reflects greater potency of glucose than these other treatments; more simply, it may reflect greater sensitivity of the tests and designs (e.g., within-subject comparisons) employed. To the extent that the findings obtained with glucose will lead to development of pharmacological treatments targeted at enhancement of cognitive functions, the future treatments are likely to require prior understanding of the cognitive, anatomical, and neurochemical mechanisms by which glucose acts.

ACKNOWLEDGMENTS

Research described in this chapter from my laboratory was supported by grants from the Office of Naval Research (No. N0001489-J-1216), the National Institute on Aging (No. AG 07648), and the National Science Foundation (No. BNS-9012239).

REFERENCES

Axelrod, J., Weil-Malherbe, H., & Tomchick, R. (1959). The physiological disposition of 3H-epinephrine and its metabolite metanephrine. *Journal of Pharmacology and Experimental Therapeutics, 127*, 251-256.

Baratti, C. M., Introini, I. B., & Huygens, P. (1984). Possible interaction between central cholinergic muscarinic and opioid peptidergic systems during memory consolidation in mice. *Behavioral and Neural Biology, 40*, 155-169.

Baust, W., Niemczyk, H., & Vieth, K. (1963). The action of blood pressure on the ascending reticular activating system with special reference to adrenalin-induced EEG arousal. *Electroencephalography and Clinical Neurophysiology, 15*, 63-72.

Botticelli, L. J., & Wurtman, R. J. (1982). Septohippocampal cholinergic neurons are regulated trans-synaptically by endorphin and corticotrophin neuropeptides. *Journal of Neuroscience, 2*, 1316-1321.

Costa, E., Panula, P., Thompson, H. K., & Cheney, D. L. (1983). The transynaptic regulation of the septal-hippocampal cholinergic neurons. *Life Sciences, 32*, 165-179.

Cotman, C. W., Monaghan, D. T., & Ganong, A. H. (1988). Excitatory amino acid neurotransmission: NMDA receptors and Hebb-type synaptic plasticity. *Annual Review of Neuroscience, 11*, 61-80.

Crone, C. (1965). Facilitated transfer of glucose from blood into brain tissue. *Journal of Physiology, 181*, 103-113.

Dahlgren, N., Rosen, I., Sakabe, T., & Siesjo, B. K. (1980). Cerebral functional, metabolic and circulatory effects of intravenous infusion of adrenaline in the rat. *Brain Research, 184*, 143-152.

Ellis, S., Kennedy, B. L., Eusebi, A. J., & Vincent, N. H. (1967). Autonomic control of metabolism. *Annals of the New York Academy of Sciences, 139*, 826-832.

Gallagher, M., Kapp, B. S., Pascoe, J. P., & Rapp, P. R. (1981). A neuropharmacology of amygdaloid systems which contribute to learning and memory. In Y. Ben-Ari (Ed.), *The amygdaloid complex* (pp. 343-354). Amsterdam: Elsevier/North-Holland.

Gold, P. E. (1986). Glucose modulation of memory storage processing. *Behavioral and Neural Biology, 45*, 342-349.

Gold, P. E. (1991). An integrated memory regulation system: From blood to brain. In R. C. A. Frederickson, J. L. McGaugh, & D. L. Felten (Eds.), *Peripheral signaling of the brain: Role in neural–immune interactions and learning and memory* (pp. 421-441). Toronto: Hogrefe & Huber.

Gold, P. E. (in press). A proposed neurobiological basis for regulating memory storage for significant events. In E. Winograd & U. Neisser (Eds.), *Affect and accuracy in recall: The problem of "flashbulb" memories*. New York: Cambridge University Press.

Gold, P. E., & McCarty, R. (1981). Plasma catecholamines: Changes after footshock and seizure-producing frontal cortex stimulation. *Behavioral and Neural Biology, 31*, 247-260.

Gold, P. E., & McGaugh, J. L. (1975). A single-trace, two process view of memory storage processes. In D. Deutsch & J. A. Deutsch (Eds.), *Short-term memory* (pp. 355-390). New York: Academic Press.

Gold, P. E., McGaugh, J. L., Hankins, L. L., Rose, R. P., & Vasquez, B. J. (1981). Age dependent changes in retention in rats. *Experimental Aging Research, 8*, 53-58.

Gold, P. E., & Sternberg, D. B. (1978). Retrograde amnesia produced by several treatments: Evidence for a common neurobiological mechanism. *Science, 201*, 367-369.

Gold, P. E., & van Buskirk, R. B. (1978). Effects of alpha- and beta-adrenergic receptor antagonists on posttrial epinephrine modulation of memory: Relationship to posttraining brain norepinephrine concentrations. *Behavioral Biology, 24*, 168-184.

Gold, P. E., Vogt, J., & Hall, J. L. (1986). Posttraining glucose effects on memory: Behavioral and pharmacological characteristics. *Behavioral and Neural Biology, 46*, 145-155.

Hall, J. L., & Gold, P. E. (1986). The effects of training, epinephrine, and glucose injections on plasma glucose levels in rats. *Behavioral and Neural Biology, 46*, 156-176.

Hall, J. L., & Gold, P. E. (1992). *Plasma glucose levels predict the susceptibility of memory enhancement to disruption by adrenergic antagonists.* Manuscript submitted for publication.

Introini, I. B., & Baratti, C. M. (1984). The impairment of retention induced by β-endorphin in mice may be mediated by reduction of central cholinergic activity. *Behavioral and Neural Biology, 41*, 152-163.

Introini-Collison, I. B., Miyazaki, B., & McGaugh, J. L. (1991). Involvement of the amygdala in the memory-enhancing effects of clenbuterol. *Psychopharmacology*, *104*, 541–544.

Kety, S. S. (1976). Biological concomitants of affective states and their possible roles in memory processes. In M. R. Rosenzweig & E. L. Bennett (Eds.), *Neural mechanisms of learning and memory* (pp. 321–326). Cambridge, MA: MIT Press.

Lamour, Y., & Epelbaum, J. (1988). Interactions between cholinergic and peptidergic systems in the cerebral cortex and hippocampus. *Progress in Neurobiology*, *31*, 109–148.

Lee, M., Graham, S., & Gold, P. E. (1988). Memory enhancement with posttraining intraventricular glucose injections in rats. *Behavioral Neuroscience*, *102*, 591–595.

Liang, K. C., Juler, R., & McGaugh, J. L. (1986). Modulating effects of posttraining epinephrine on memory: Involvement of the amygdala noradrenergic system. *Brain Research*, *368*, 125–133.

Liang, K. C., & McGaugh, J. L. (1983). Lesions of the stria terminalis attenuate the enhancing effect of posttraining epinephrine on retention of an inhibitory avoidance response. *Behavioural Brain Research*, *9*, 49–58.

Livingston, R. B. (1967). Reinforcement. In G. C. Quarton, T. Melnick, & F. O. Schmitt (Eds.), *The neurosciences* (pp. 568–576). New York: Rockefeller University Press.

Lund-Anderson, H. (1979). Transport of glucose from blood to brain. *Physiology Reviews*, *59*, 305–352.

Manning, C. A., Hall, J. L., & Gold, P. E. (1990). Glucose effects on memory and other neuropsychological tests in elderly humans. *Psychological Science*, *1*, 307–311.

Manning, C. A., Jane, J., & Gold, P. E. (1992). *Glucose facilitation of memory on a middle-aged, head-injured male: A case study*. Unpublished findings.

Manning, C. A., Parsons, M. W., & Gold, P. E. (1992). *Pre- and post-training glucose enhances memory in elderly humans*. Manuscript submitted for publication.

Manning, C. A., Parsons, M. W., Cotter, E. M., & Gold, P. E. (1992). *Glucose enhancement of free recall but not priming task in elderly humans*. Manuscript in preparation.

Martinez, J. L., Weinberger, S. B., & Schulteis, G. (1988). Enkephalins and learning and memory: A review of evidence for a site of action outside the blood-brain barrier. *Behavioral and Neural Biology*, *49*, 192–221.

McCarty, R. (1981). Aged rats: Diminished sympathetic–adrenal medullary response to acute stress. *Behavioral and Neural Biology*, *33*, 204–212.

McCarty, R., & Gold, P. E. (1981). Plasma catecholamines: Effects of footshock level and hormonal modulators of memory storage. *Hormones and Behavior*, *15*, 168–182.

McGaugh, J. L. (1989). Involvement of hormonal and neuromodulatory systems in the regulation of memory storage. *Annual Review of Neuroscience*, *12*, 255–287.

McGaugh, J. L., & Gold, P. E. (1989). Hormonal modulation of memory. In R. Brush & S. Levine (Eds.), *Psychoendocrinology* (pp. 305–339). New York: Academic Press.

McGlynn, T. J., Lennartz, R. L., Gold, S. D., & Gold, P. E. (1992). *Ibotenic lesions of medial septum: Reversal of spontaneous alternation deficits with oxotremorine, but not glucose or physostigmine*. Manuscript submitted for publication.

Moroni, F., Cheney, D. L., & Costa, E. (1977). Inhibition of acetylcholine turnover in rat hippocampus by intraseptal injections of β-endorphin and morphine. *Naunyn-Schmiedeberg's Archives of Pharmacology*, *299*, 149–153.

Pardridge, W. M., & Oldendorf, W. H. (1975). Kinetics of blood-brain barrier transport of hexoses. *Biochimica Biophysica Acta*, *382*, 377–392.

Parsons, M. W., & Gold, P. E. (1992). Scopolamine-induced deficits in spontaneous alternation performance: Attenuation with lateral ventricle injections of glucose. *Behavioral and Neural Biology*, *57*, 90–92.

Parsons, M. W., & Gold, P. E. (in press). Glucose enhancement of memory in elderly humans: An inverted-U dose–response curve. *Neurobiology of Aging*.

Ragozzino, M. E., Parker, M. E., & Gold, P. E. (1990). *Memory impairments with medial septal morphine injections: Attenuation with peripheral glucose injections*. Paper presented at the 20th Annual Meeting of the Society for Neuroscience, St. Louis.

Rush, D. K. (1986). Reversal of scopolamine-induced amnesia of passive avoidance by pre and post training naloxone. *Psychopharmacology*, *89*, 296–300.

Squire, L. R. (1987). *Memory and brain*. New York: Oxford University Press.

Sternberg, D. B., Martinez, J., McGaugh, J. L., & Gold, P. E. (1985). Age-related memory deficits in aged mice and rats: Enhancement with peripheral epinephrine. *Behavioral and Neural Biology*, *44*, 213–220.

Stone, W. S., Altman, H. J., Berman, R. F., Caldwell, D. F., & Kilbey, M. M. (1989). Association of sleep parameters and memory in intact old and nucleus basalis lesioned young rats. *Behavioral Neuroscience*, *103*, 755–764.

Stone, W. S., Cottrill, K., Walker, D., & Gold, P. E. (1988). Blood glucose and brain function: Interactions with CNS cholinergic systems. *Behavioral and Neural Biology, 50*, 325–334.

Stone, W. S., & Gold, P. E. (1988). Sleep and memory relationships in intact old and amnestic young rats. *Neurobiology of Aging, 9*, 719–727.

Stone, W. S., & Gold, P. E. (1992). *Glucose effects on scopolamine-induced and age-induced deficits in spontaneous alternation behavior and in regional brain [³H]-2-deoxyglucose uptake.* Manuscript submitted for publication.

Stone, W. S., Manning, C. A., & Gold, P. E. (1989). Relationships between circulating glucose levels and memory storage processes. In H. J. Altman & B. N. Altman (Eds.), *Alzheimer's and Parkinson's disease: Recent advances in research and clinical management* (pp. 167–189). New York: Plenum Press.

Stone, W. S., Walser, B., Gold, S. D., & Gold, P. E. (1991). Scopolamine- and morphine-induced impairments of spontaneous alternation behavior in mice: Reversal with glucose and with cholinergic and adrenergic agonists. *Behavioral Neuroscience, 105*, 264–271.

Walker, D. L., McGlynn, T., Grey, C., Ragozzino, M., & Gold, P. E. (1991). Naloxone modulates the behavioral effects of cholinergic agonists and antagonists. *Psychopharmacology, 105*, 57–62.

Walker, D. L., Stone, W. S., & Gold, P. E. (1990). *Parallel effects of the NMDA antagonist NPC 12626 on sleep and memory: Reversal of the memory deficit with glucose injections.* Paper presented at the 20th Annual Meeting of the Society for Neuroscience, St. Louis.

Wenk, G. L. (1989). An hypothesis on the role of glucose in the mechanism of action of cognitive enhancers. *Psychopharmacology, 99*, 431–438.

White, N. (1991). Peripheral and central memory-enhancing actions of glucose. In R. C. A. Frederickson, J. L. McGaugh, & D. L. Felten (Eds.), *Peripheral signaling of the brain: Role in neural-immune interactions and learning and memory* (pp. 421–441). Toronto: Hogrefe & Huber.

Wood, P. L., Cheney, D. L., & Costa, E. (1979). An investigation of whether septal g-amino-butyrate-containing interneurones are involved in the reduction in the turnover rate of acetylcholine elicited by substance P and β-endorphin in the hippocampus. *Neuroscience, 4*, 1479–1484.

36

Toward a Comprehensive Account of Hippocampal Function: Studies of Olfactory Learning Permit an Integration of Data across Multiple Levels of Neurobiological Analysis

TIM OTTO and HOWARD EICHENBAUM

The past three decades have witnessed a tremendous surge of effort toward defining and characterizing the neural substrates of learning and memory. One important catalyst that initiated several current lines of research was the neuropsychological study of the patient H. M., whose medial temporal lobes were removed bilaterally in an effort to treat chronic, severe epilepsy (Scoville & Milner, 1957). Subsequent to this procedure H. M. demonstrated normal perceptual, motor, and cognitive abilities, but suffered a profound anterograde memory disturbance characterized by an inability to form new, lasting memories of facts and events. Other aspects of H. M.'s memory capacity, however, were spared by this surgery. In particular, his remote memories for information acquired well before the surgery remained intact. H. M. also retained the ability for immediate recall of information and the capacity for many forms of perceptual and motor learning. Thus the pattern of H. M.'s impaired and intact memory capacities defined the general role played by medial temporal structures in mediating the permanent consolidation of most new memories elsewhere in the brain (e.g., Corkin, 1984; Squire, Cohen, & Nadel, 1984). Although there is still some debate on the subject, numerous subsequent studies assessing the consequences of more limited medial temporal lobe damage in humans, nonhuman primates, and rats all indicate that the hippocampus in particular plays a pivotal role in memory formation.

Progress in further understanding the nature of the hippocampal contribution to memory has been made along three largely separate avenues, each representing a different level of analysis. One line of research has sought to further specify the type of memory encoded by the hippocampus. As mentioned above, even the early work on H. M. demonstrated that there were certain "exceptions" to his otherwise "global" amnesic disorder. Subsequent studies of amnesic patients have revealed that these exceptions were representative of a large domain of preserved memory capacity in amnesia (reviewed in Squire & Cohen, 1984). Recent studies in animals with hippocampal system damage have also dissociated domains of impaired and preserved learning capacities (reviewed in Squire, 1987). Emerging from these neuropsychological studies are a number of accounts suggesting that the brain supports multiple memory systems; each account distinguishes one form of memory dependent upon hippocampal circuitry from others that are not. A second line of research has attempted to reveal the nature of hippocampal memory representation by examining the functional correlates of hippocampal neuronal activity with respect to critical behavioral events associated with learning. Many of these studies have focused on characterizing hippocampal "place cells"—principal neurons that have been observed to fire selectively when the rat occupies a particular spatial location, regardless of ongoing behavior (O'Keefe, 1979). Other studies indicate that the activity of these cells may be determined by specific behavioral, contextual, or perceptual events during learning and cannot be accounted for by spatial location alone (e.g., Eichenbaum & Wiener, 1989). Emerging from this work on the behavioral physiology of the hippocampus is considerable controversy over the fundamental nature of the mnemonic events reflected in its cellular activity (reviewed in Eichenbaum & Cohen, 1988). A third avenue of investigation has focused on identifying physiological and biochemical mechanisms of plasticity in the hippocampus. Of particular promise in this regard are the electrophysiological and behavioral data indicating that hippocampal long-term potentiation (LTP), a selective strengthening of synaptic efficacy, has induction and maintenance characteristics that parallel those of behaviorally defined memory (Lynch, 1986; Otto & Eichenbaum, 1992a; Teyler, 1986). Emerging from this work on hippocampal synaptic plasticity are findings suggesting that cellular events closely approximating characteristics of the induction and expression of LTP occur during and as a result of learning, respectively.

Thus impressive progress has been made in our understanding of the neuropsychology, behavioral physiology, and synaptic plasticity of the hippocampus. Unfortunately, success in integrating the findings across these three levels of analysis has been relatively limited, perhaps because the preparations typically employed across approaches involve different species and behavioral paradigms. In our view, the development of a comprehensive theory of hippocampal function might benefit from the use of a "model system" that would permit the collection and assimilation of data from a single species and behavioral paradigm across levels of analysis. We suggest that rodent olfaction provides such a model system, for several reasons (see also Otto & Eichenbaum, 1992a; Lynch, 1986). First, when trained with olfactory cues, rats exhibit a remarkable facility for both simple discrimination learning (Eichenbaum, Fagan, & Cohen, 1986; Slotnick & Katz, 1974; Staubli, Fraser, Faraday, & Lynch, 1987; Otto, Schottler, Staubli, Eichenbaum, & Lynch, 1991) and a variety of complex forms of learning, including serial ordering (Wible, Eichenbaum, & Otto, 1990), the oddity principle (Langworthy & Jennings, 1972), delayed nonmatching to sample (Otto & Eichenbaum, in press), and category formation (Granger et al., 1991). Thus, when trained using olfactory stimuli, rodents exhibit capacities for higher-order learning previously thought to be unique to primates. Second, the olfactory–hippocampal pathway is fully evolved in rodents and parallels the neocortical–hippocampal pathways of dominant sense modalities in primates, thereby permitting direct anatomical comparisons across species (Otto & Eichenbaum, 1992a). Third, olfactory inputs to the hippocampus are organized in a well-described (see Switzer, de Olmos, & Heimer, 1985), relatively accessible pathway, thereby facilitating the application of both anatomical and electrophysiological techniques for investigation. With these advantages in mind, we have focused our efforts on examining several aspects of the neurobiology of rodent olfactory learning and memory, and in the course of our investigations have explored this system across each of the three levels of analysis described above. The purpose of the present chapter is twofold: (1) to support the notion that rodent olfactory learning provides a fruitful domain in which to investigate the mnemonic functions of the hippocampus across behavioral and biological levels of analysis, and in doing so, (2) to offer evidence in favor of a particular account of hippocampal processing in memory.

Olfactory Learning and the Neuropsychology of the Hippocampus

Our current understanding of the role of the hippocampus in memory is based primarily on studies of human amnesia and on experiments assessing the effects of hippocampal system lesions on visual memory in primates and on spatial memory in rats. As alluded to above, the results of these studies collectively suggest that the hippocampus is critical to the encoding of only a certain type of memory; a precise characterization of the memory processes supported by the hippocampus, however, remains the source of considerable debate. Much of the work on human amnesia supports the view that the hippocampal system is selectively involved in "declarative memory"—the memory for facts and events that is based on comparing and contrasting information from various sources, and, correspondingly, can be accessed in a variety of contexts outside the original learning situation (Cohen & Squire, 1980). Much of the work on rats has led some investigators to a fundamentally different sort of characterization; they have suggested that hippocampal processing is selectively involved in memory for spatial relations (O'Keefe & Nadel, 1978; Nadel, 1991). This view remains quite popular, despite the findings on human amnesia and the results of experiments on rats and monkeys indicating that hippocampal involvement is not limited to any specific domain of learning materials (see Cohen & Eichenbaum, 1991). Our work seeks support for an account of hippocampal function in memory that is consistent both with the views on the structure of declarative memory in humans and with demonstrations that the hippocampus is critical to most forms of spatial learning in animals. Our hypothesis is that the hippocampal system processes memories that involve comparisons among, and encoding of relevant relations between, multiple, perceptually independent cues (for a detailed discussion, see Eichenbaum, Cohen, Otto, & Wible, in press). This notion can be explored directly by comparing the performance of intact animals and animals with hippocampal system damage on tasks that employ identical learning materials but differ in their requirement for cue comparison. Indeed, this approach has been used successfully to dissociate hippocampal-dependent and hippocampal-independent memory representations in spatial (Eichenbaum, Stewart, & Morris, 1990) and in nonspatial olfactory (Eichenbaum, Fagan, Mathews, & Cohen, 1988) tasks in rats. We focus on two strategies used in this approach, both of which exploit the advantages of the rodent olfactory system.

One strategy used successfully in characterizing impaired and spared memory capacities following hippocampal system damage has involved designing different odor discrimination paradigms in which identical stimuli are employed, but which differentially *encourage* or *discourage* the comparison between cues and thus favor or hinder, respectively, a representation based on relevant relations among cues. These studies have revealed that when explicit comparison between odor stimuli is encouraged by presenting multiple stimuli simultaneously and in close juxtaposition, damage to either of the major hippocampal afferent and efferent fiber systems (produced by lesions of the fornix or entorhinal cortex) results in the pattern of impaired acquisition of new information (Eichenbaum et al., 1988) and intact memory of preoperatively learned cues (Staubli, Ivy, & Lynch, 1984) that characterizes human amnesia. Conversely, when comparison between the odor cues is discouraged by presenting them separately across successive trials, the same damage produces no observable deficit, and in some cases even facilitates learning (Eichenbaum et al., 1988; Otto, Schottler, et al., 1991).

The hypothesis that the hippocampus participates in a representation of significant relations between stimuli was further supported by investigations revealing qualitative differences in odor memory representations of normal rats and rats with hippocampal system damage. Eichenbaum, Mathews, and Cohen (1989) found that even when animals with fornix lesions successfully acquired a simultaneous olfactory discrimination, they failed to differentiate, compare, and encode the relevant relations among odor cues. Analyses of stimulus-sampling strategies indicated that, unlike normal subjects, rats with hippocampal system damage executed accurate discriminative responses without investigating each odor individually, suggesting that their performance was based on separate representations for each distinct stimulus compound (i.e., each left–right juxtaposition of an odor pair) presented. Confirming this hypothesis, subsequent probe tests revealed that rats with fornix lesions could not recognize a set of familiar odor elements when they were presented in novel pairings. It appeared that rats with hippocampal system damage acquired an individual association for each odor pair compound, employing a representational strategy much like that used more appropriately in successive odor discrimination.

Another strategy for investigating the role of the hippocampus in encoding the relations among items in memory is to develop odor-guided tasks that might *require* (rather than merely encourage or hinder) direct comparison of a discriminative stimulus to a representation of a stimulus that was presented previously. Accordingly, we have recently developed an odor-guided continuous delayed-nonmatching-to-sample (cDNM) task, conceptually similar in memory demands to the visually guided delayed-nonmatching-to-sample task often used to investigate the neural substrates of primate memory. On each trial, rats are presented with one odor chosen randomly from a relatively large set. Successful performance requires that they remember across an intertrial interval the odor presented on the immediately preceding trial, and respond for water reinforcement only if the odor presented on the current trial is *different* (i.e., a nonmatch). Thus correct performance in this task demands the direct comparison of current information to a stored representation of information presented previously.

The results from a recent study examining the effect of hippocampal system damage on performance in the cDNM task further support the hypothesis that the

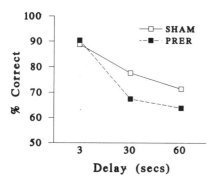

FIGURE 36.1. The effect of damage to perirhinal and entorhinal cortex on performance of an odor-guided delayed-nonmatching-to-sample task. Percentage of correct performance within 50-trial sessions is plotted at each of three intertrial intervals for a group of rats with aspiration of perirhinal and entorhinal cortex (PRER, $n = 6$) and a group of sham-operated control subjects (SHAM, $n = 10$). A two-way analysis of variance with repeated measures revealed a significant effect of delay, $F(3, 32) = 63.8$, $p < .001$, as well as a significant condition $\times$ delay interaction, $F(2, 32) = 4.6$, $p < .02$, due to poorer performance of PRER rats relative to SHAM rats at the 30- and 60-second intertrial intervals.

hippocampus participates in the encoding of relations among cues (Otto & Eichenbaum, in press). Rats with aspiration of perirhinal and entorhinal cortex performed as well as normal subjects when the memory delay was very brief, thus demonstrating an intact immediate memory capacity. In contrast, the same rats were markedly impaired relative to controls when longer memory delays were introduced (see Figure 36.1). These data parallel the observation of delay-dependent memory deficits characteristic of hippocampal system damage in humans and nonhuman primates (Squire, 1987).

Collectively, these neuropsychological data support the notion that the hippocampus is critical to a representation of relationships among items in memory. Rats with hippocampal system damage were impaired either when the odor cues were presented simultaneously in a discrimination paradigm that encouraged their comparison across space, or when they were presented successively in a matching task that required comparison of odors across time. In contrast, rats with hippocampal system damage were either unimpaired or superior to normal rats in successive discrimination, a task that discourages specific comparisons between the odor cues. Moreover, this pattern of impaired and spared memory in rats with hippocampal system damage closely parallels that in humans and nonhuman primates with similar damage.

Olfactory Learning and the Behavioral Physiology of the Hippocampus

The above-described studies support the view that the hippocampus participates critically in encoding the relations among multiple cues. To reveal the way in which these features of memory are encoded by cellular activity within the hippocampus, we have employed a second line of investigation seeking to characterize hippocampal processing during performance of odor-guided tasks. These studies involve two approaches to exploring the behavioral physiology of the hippocampus.

One approach has focused on the behavioral correlates of the hippocampal EEG during olfactory discrimination. Initial analyses revealed that cycles of hippocampal information processing and stimulus sampling become entrained during odor discrimination. Macrides, Eichenbaum, & Forbes (1982) found that the theta rhythm, a 4- to 12-Hz sinusoidal EEG pattern reflecting cycles of excitation within the hippocampus (Rudell, Fox, & Ranck, 1980), synchronized with the sniffing cycle as the rats sampled the odors they were required to discriminate. Further analyses indicated that the degree of this entrainment was maximal just prior to the acquisition of a discrimination or just after a reversal of stimulus valence. These data suggested that olfactory stimulus sampling engaged hippocampal function in such a way that cycles of information acquisition and its central processing in the hippocampus were precisely time-locked.

A second approach has focused on detailed characterizations of the way in which individual hippocampal pyramidal cells encode features of hippocampal-dependent memory in rats performing each of the three odor-guided tasks described above. In a series of studies, we have identified a class of CA1 pyramidal cells that are maximally active during the odor sampling period in olfactory discrimination and the cDNM task (Eichenbaum, Kuperstein, Fagan, & Nagode, 1987; Wiener, Paul, & Eichenbaum, 1989; Otto & Eichenbaum, 1992b). In simultaneous odor discrimination, some of these cells responded selectively during sampling of particular configurations of odor cues; these same cells were relatively quiescent during the presentation of other configurations of the same odors or of other odors (Wiener et al., 1989). In successive odor discrimination, the activity of some of these cells was dependent upon specific odor sequences; for example, some cells responded during the odor-sampling period only on S+ trials that were preceded by S− trials (Eichenbaum et al., 1987). Thus in each of the two variants of olfactory discrimination, the behavioral correlates of hippocampal unit firing reflected processing of the task-relevant relationships among odor cues.

Further data supporting the hypothesis that the hippocampus participates in the processing of relationships among cues come from a recent study (Otto & Eichenbaum, 1992b) examining CA1 pyramidal cell activity during performance of the odor-guided cDNM task described above. These analyses revealed that some cells fired differentially during the odor sampling period on match versus nonmatch trials, regardless of the particular odors involved (see Figure 36.2). Thus the firing of these cells could not be accounted for by the perceptual qualities of the individual stimuli that were the subject of specific comparisons, and therefore does not reflect the encoding of a unique combination of odors; rather, the activity of these cells reflects the *outcome* of comparisons (i.e., "same" or "different") between stimuli.

Finally, although cells that are maximally active during odor sampling are the best understood and most directly relevant to the present discussion of the mnemonic functions of the hippocampus, it should be noted that each of our studies also identified a number of other behavioral correlates of hippocampal unit activity. For example, in all three tasks other hippocampal cells fired maximally as the rat approached the odor-sampling area or executed its discriminative response. Indeed, virtually every identifiable behavioral event in all three odor-guided tasks was represented by neural activity within the hippocampus. In addition, many of these same cells fired in relation to the rat's spatial location when it performed a place memory task (Wiener et al., 1989). Thus, a wide variety of behavioral correlates of hippocampal neuronal activity can be demonstrated in multiple behavioral situations. The olfactory paradigm is particularly useful, in that it allows the critical memory cues to be identified and systematically manipulated; the results most clearly demonstrate the fundamentally *relational* aspect of hippocampal neuronal coding.

NON-MATCH TRIALS

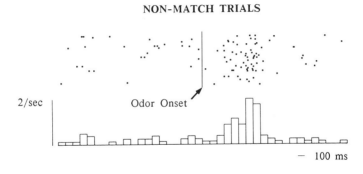

MATCH TRIALS

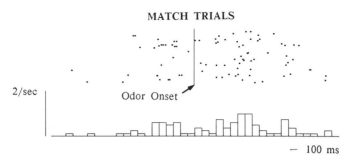

FIGURE 36.2. Raster displays and cumulative histograms of hippocampal unit firing during the odor-sampling period of the cDNM task. An analysis of firing rates within the odor-sampling period indicated that this cell fired far more often on nonmatch trials than on match trials, t (135) = 2.5, p <.02.

Olfactory Learning and Hippocampal Synaptic Plasticity

To this point, we have outlined the accumulated neuropsychological and electrophysiological evidence indicating that the hippocampus participates in an encoding of the relevant relations among multiple cues. Although these findings have helped us understand the nature of memory representations encoded by the hippocampus, they do not address directly the mechanisms of cellular plasticity underlying these representations. Indeed, revealing the precise physiological mechanism(s) by which memories are made permanent in the brain has been a daunting problem for decades. This problem is particularly difficult to confront with regard to hippocampal-dependent memory, because although it is clear that the hippocampus participates in memory consolidation (Zola-Morgan & Squire, 1990), it is still unclear whether storage within the hippocampus per se is critical to the consolidation process. An additional obstacle to identifying memory-dependent plastic changes in the hippocampus (if indeed they do occur) is that one might reasonably expect the fraction of synapses involved in the storage of a particular memory to be infinitesimal, which would make it infeasible to detect their associated lasting neurochemical and neurophysiological changes. Accordingly, the search for the physiological substrate of memory storage may benefit from a system with a dense source of afferent fibers projecting to a brain area known to play a critical role in memory consolidation. This is indeed the case for the rodent olfactory–hippocampal pathway. Primary olfactory information reaches the hippocampus in as few as two synapses via a dense projection from entorhinal cortex (see Lynch, 1986). Correspondingly, as described above, hippocampal physiology is strongly engaged during odor learning, entrained to the cycle of stimulus sampling, and involved in encoding virtually every aspect of the learning event. Moreover, because we can identify particular cells activated during each of these events, we may be able to reveal, at the single-cell level, mnemonic (storage) mechanisms associated with identified integrative (encoding) processes.

In evaluating the plausibility of any physiological phenomenon as a mnemonic storage device, we must first consider whether its operating characteristics match those of behaviorally defined memory. Thus, like memory itself, a physiological memory mechanism must be rapidly induced, long-lasting, strengthened by repetition, associative, and selective. Furthermore, this mechanism must be found within brain regions critical to memory formation, and must be blocked by manipulations that also impair memory. Accumulating evidence suggests that LTP, a selective strengthening of synaptic efficacy, meets each of these criteria. As originally described by Bliss and colleagues (Bliss & Lomo, 1973; Bliss & Garner-Medwin, 1973), LTP reflects an increase in synaptic strength, and is typically characterized by an increase in amplitude and slope of monosynaptic field potentials evoked by orthodromic stimulation. LTP in the hippocampus has been well documented and characterized (Teyler, 1986), is induced rapidly by brief bouts of afferent stimulation (Larson & Lynch, 1986; Rose & Dunwiddie, 1986), and can be strengthened by repetition (Barnes, 1979). Furthermore, LTP is both associative and selective with respect to the specific fibers inducing and exhibiting potentiation, respectively (McNaughton, Douglas, & Goddard, 1978). Finally, blocking hippocampal LTP induction by pharmacological (Morris, Anderson, Lynch, & Baudry, 1986) or electrophysiological (Castro, Silbert, McNaughton, & Barnes, 1989) manipulations interferes with several forms of learning that are dependent on hippocampal function. Thus LTP has quickly become the leading candidate as a physiological mechanism for memory storage.

The discovery of LTP initiated two important lines of research attempting to relate LTP directly to memory. One approach has focused on evaluating whether the conditions optimal for LTP induction are characteristic of natural patterns of hippocampal activity. A second approach has sought to determine whether naturally occurring alterations of hippocampal excitability occur as a result of learning.

With regard to the first of these, recent efforts have revealed that hippocampal LTP is most easily induced by a specific combination of three electrical stimulation parameters: (1) high-frequency bursts that are (2) delivered near the positive peak of the ongoing dentate theta rhythm (Pavlides, Greenstein, Grudman, & Winson, 1988) and (3) preceded by either single-pulse or burst stimulation at a latency of 100–200 milliseconds (Larson, Wong, & Lynch, 1986; Rose & Dunwiddie, 1986). In an attempt to determine whether any or all of these patterns of activity occur naturally during odor learning, we (Otto, Eichenbaum, Wiener, & Wible, 1991) examined in detail the temporal firing patterns of hippocampal neurons in rats engaged in simultaneous odor discrimination. These analyses revealed that the three activation parameters described above are reflected simultaneously in the endogenous firing patterns of CA1 pyramidal cells, and that these patterns emerge preferentially during episodes of likely mnemonic processing (Figure 36.3). Specifically, CA1 pyramidal cells that fired selectively during the period of stimulus sampling and analysis often discharged in high-frequency bursts. Furthermore, for the overwhelming majority of these cells, the bursts occurred near the positive peak of the ongoing dentate theta rhythm. Finally, these bursts were typically preceded by neural activity at latencies of 100–200 milliseconds. For these cells, all three aspects of temporal patterning, collectively referred to as "theta-bursting" (Lynch, Muller, Seubert, & Larson, 1988), were observed to occur far more often during odor sampling than during any other behavioral event. Thus, at least in the hippocampus, the conditions appropriate for inducing LTP commonly occur during

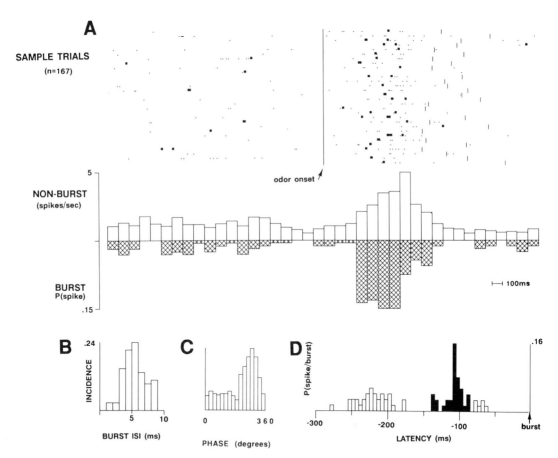

FIGURE 36.3. Analyses of a CA1 neuron that showed theta-bursting during odor sampling. (**A**) Raster diagram of single spike (small dots) and burst (large dots) firing across trials. Summary histograms indicate average firing rates for nonburst (spikes/second) and burst (probability of a spike/bin) activity. (**B**) Distribution of interspike intervals (ISIs) within identified bursts. (**C**) Distribution of spikes within the theta cycle (0 = dentate theta peak). Bursts tend to occur just before the dentate theta peak. (**D**) Distribution of firing preceding a burst. The darkened portion represents latencies corresponding to frequencies between 7 and 12.5 Hz. A chi-square analysis revealed a significant tendency for firing to precede bursts at latencies within this interval ($\chi^2 = 139.0$, $p < .001$). The data are from Otto, Eichenbaum, et al. (1991).

olfactory learning, time-locked to behavioral events associated with mnemonic processing.

Although it may be considered likely that theta-bursting would induce alterations in synaptic strength, it is at present unclear whether naturally occurring synaptic enhancement actually accompanies these patterns, and, if so, what the specific anatomical locus of this change is. With respect to the locus of synaptic enhancement associated with theta-bursting, two possibilities come immediately to mind. First, it is possible that theta-bursting in CA1 cells reflects the result of afferent (CA3) activity and, by hypothesis, an enhancement of synaptic efficacy in the CA1 region itself. This account is consistent with views suggesting that synaptic enhancement within the hippocampus serves as a memory "buffer," temporarily storing memory prior to (or perhaps in addition to) its permanent storage elsewhere (Rawlins, 1985), or as an "index" to the location of long-term memories stored in neocortex (Teyler & DiScenna, 1986). Alternatively, theta-bursting might reflect processes leading to potentiation in targets of CA1 output—for example, the anterior olfactory nucleus (Van Groen & Wyss, 1990), parahippocampal cortex (Deacon, Eichenbaum, Rosenberg, & Eckmann, 1983), or neocortex (Jay, Glowinski, & Thierry, 1989).

The findings described above provide compelling evidence that conditions suitable for the natural enhancement of synaptic strength are found in the hippocampus during olfactory learning, and that these patterns of neural activity emerge preferentially during periods of mnemonic processing. It is at present unclear, however, whether these or other patterns of neural activity are associated with observable, learning-dependent increases in synaptic efficacy within the hippocampus or any other locus. The answer to this important question awaits further study.

Toward a Comprehensive Account of Hippocampal Function: Conclusions

Rodent olfactory learning provides a suitable domain in which the mnemonic functions of the hippocampus can be studied in detail at three separate levels of analysis. At each level our findings are consistent with, and help elucidate, results of other studies that employ other behavioral or anatomical systems. At the neuropsychological level, studies of the effects of discrete medial temporal lesions on memory in humans and nonhuman primates indicate that the hippocampus is critically involved in establishing declarative representations based on explicit comparisons among items. Unlike hippocampal-independent memory, declarative representations are accessible outside the context of original acquisition. These findings have served as the template against which we have successfully matched the neuropsychological findings obtained in the studies of rodent olfactory learning described above. Collectively, the data suggest an account by which in humans, nonhuman primates, and rats, hippocampal-dependent memory is based on the encoding of relations among multiple cues (see Eichenbaum, Otto, & Cohen, 1992).

Like our own findings, other studies on the behavioral physiology of the hippocampus support the notion that individual hippocampal cells participate in the encoding of features relevant to declarative memory. For example, studies involving delayed-matching tasks based on memory for visual cues in rats (Wible et al., 1986) and monkeys (Rolls et al., 1989) have demonstrated that the firing of many CA1 cells is determined by particular configurations of visual cues. Thus, consistent with our findings on simultaneous odor discrimination, the activity of these cells, like those exhibiting spatial correlates (O'Keefe & Conway, 1978), reflects not simply the appearance of a particular cue or its spatial location, but rather the demands for processing cue configurations. Other studies have identified hippocampal cells whose activity depends on the sequence of cues during successive auditory discrimination (Foster, Christian, Hampson, Campbell, & Deadwyler, 1987) and auditory cDNM tasks (Sakurai, 1988). As in our findings on successive odor discrimination and the cDNM task, the activity of these cells reflects not simply the presentation of a particular cue or its reward value, but rather the demand for comparing previous and current cues. These studies provide converging evidence that, across species, behavioral paradigms, and cue modalities, hippocampal unit activity reflects the demand for comparison of cues appropriate to each task. Furthermore, these findings extend our understanding of the coding of declarative memories to the cellular level.

Finally, our findings on theta-bursting in CA1 principal cells indicate clearly that the hippocampus supports activity patterns suitable for the induction of synaptic changes that might support learning. Although it is unclear whether theta-bursting actually results in learning-specific alterations in synaptic efficacy, other investigators have reported synaptic enhancement bearing at least a superficial similarity to LTP at the perforant path–dentate gyrus synapse following brief bouts of exploratory activity (Sharp, McNaughton, & Barnes, 1985; Green, McNaughton, & Barnes, 1990) or instrumental learning (Ruthrich, Matthies, & Ott, 1982; Skelton, Scarth, Wilkie, Miller, & Phillips, 1987). Collectively, these data suggest that hippocampal synaptic plasticity as revealed in *in vitro* studies of LTP may indeed participate in the storage of at least some forms of memory.

Thus at each level of analysis, the data from studies of the neurobiology of olfactory learning are consistent with and extend those from studies employing other systems. Moreover, studies on the rodent olfactory–hippocampal pathway permit an integration of data collected across these levels, thereby promoting the development of a comprehensive account of hippocampal involvement in memory. Collectively, the results of these studies indicate that the hippocampus participates critically in constructing a representation of relations among cues, and that the critical relationships among cues may be stored as a result of the coding properties and temporal patterns of naturally occurring neural activity of hippocampal output cells.

ACKNOWLEDGMENTS

Preparation of this chapter was supported in part by National Institutes of Health Grant No. NS26402, and by National Science Foundation Grants No. BNS-8721157 and No. BNS-8810095 to Howard Eichenbaum. Much of the theoretical analysis discussed here was developed in conjunction with Neal J. Cohen. We would like also to acknowledge the work of Sidney Wiener, Patricia Mathews, Cynthia Wible, Jean Piper, and Matthew Shapiro, who participated in many of the experiments described herein.

REFERENCES

Barnes, C. A. (1979). Memory deficits associated with senescence: A neurophysiological and behavioral study in the rat. *Journal of Comparative and Physiological Psychology, 93,* 74-104.

Bliss, T. V. P., & Garner-Medwin, R. (1973). Long-lasting potentiation of synaptic transmission in the dentate area of the unanaesthetized rabbit following stimulation of the perforant path. *Journal of Physiology, 232,* 357-374.

Bliss, T. V. P., & Lomo, T. (1973). Long-lasting potentiation of synaptic transmission in the dentate area of the anaesthetized rabbit following stimulation of the perforant path. *Journal of Physiology, 232,* 331-356.

Castro, C. A., Silbert, L. H., McNaughton, B. L., & Barnes, C. A. (1989). Recovery of spatial learning following decay of experimental saturation of LTE at perforant path synapses. *Nature, 342,* 545-548.

Cohen, N. J., & Eichenbaum, H. (1991). The theory that wouldn't die: A critical look at the spatial mapping theory of hippocampal function. *Hippocampus, 1,* 265-268.

Cohen, N. J., & Squire, L. R. (1980). Preserved learning and retention of a pattern-analyzing skill in amnesia: Dissociation of knowing how and knowing that. *Science, 210,* 207-210.

Corkin, S. (1984). Lasting consequences of bilateral medial temporal lobectomy: Clinical course and experimental findings in H. M. *Seminars in Neurology, 4,* 249-259.

Deacon, T. W., Eichenbaum, H., Rosenberg, P., & Eckmann, K. W. (1983). Afferent connections of the perirhinal cortex in the rat. *Journal of Comparative Neurology, 220,* 168-190.

Eichenbaum, H., & Cohen, N. J. (1988). Representation in the hippocampus: What do the neurons code? *Trends in Neurosciences, 11,* 244-248.

Eichenbaum, H., Cohen, N. J., Otto, T., & Wible, C. G. (in press). Memory representation in the hippocampus: Functional domain and functional organization. In L. R. Squire, G. Lynch, N. Weinberger, & J. McGaugh (Eds.), *Memory: Organization and locus of change.* New York: Oxford University Press.

Eichenbaum, H., Fagan, A., & Cohen, N. J. (1986). Normal olfactory discrimination learning set and facilitation of reversal learning after medial-temporal damage in rats: Implications for an account of preserved learning abilities in amnesia. *Journal of Neuroscience, 6,* 1876-1884.

Eichenbaum, H., Fagan, A., Mathews, P., & Cohen, N. J. (1988). Hippocampal system dysfunction and odor discrimination learning in rats: Impairment or facilitation depending on representational demands. *Behavioral Neuroscience, 102,* 331-339.

Eichenbaum, H., Kuperstein, M., Fagan, A., & Nagode, J. (1987). Cue-sampling and goal-approach correlates of hippocampal unit activity in rats performing an odor-discrimination task. *Journal of Neuroscience, 7,* 716-732.

Eichenbaum, H., Mathews, P., & Cohen, N. J. (1989). Further studies of hippocampal representation during odor discrimination learning. *Behavioral Neuroscience, 103,* 1207-1216.

Eichenbaum, H., Otto, T., & Cohen, N. J. (1992). The hippocampus: What does it do? *Behavioral and Neural Biology, 57,* 1-35.

Eichenbaum, H., Stewart, C., & Morris, R. G. M. (1990). Hippocampal representation in spatial learning. *Journal of Neuroscience, 10,* 3531-3542.

Eichenbaum, H., & Wiener, S. I. (1989). Is place the (only) functional correlate? *Psychobiology, 17,* 217-220.

Foster, T. C., Christian, E. P., Hampson, R. E., Campbell, K. A., & Deadwyler, S. A. (1987). Sequential dependencies regulate sensory evoked responses of single units in the rat hippocampus. *Brain Research, 40,* 86-96.

Granger, R., Staubli, U., Powers, H., Otto, T., Ambros-Ingerson, J., & Lynch, G. (1991). Behavioral tests of a prediction from a cortical network simulation. *Psychological Science, 2,* 116-118.

Green, E. J., McNaughton, B. L., & Barnes, C. A. (1990). Exploration-dependent modulation of evoked responses in fascia-dentata: Dissociation of motor, EEG, and sensory factors and evidence for a synaptic efficacy change. *Journal of Neuroscience, 10,* 1455-1471.

Jay, T. M., Glowinski, J., & Thierry, A. M. (1989). Selectivity of the hippocampal projection to the prelimbic area of the prefrontal cortex in the rat. *Brain Research, 202,* 337-340.

Langworthy, R. A., & Jennings, J. W. (1972). Odd ball, abstract, olfactory learning in laboratory rats. *Psychological Record, 22,* 487-490.

Larson, J., & Lynch, G. (1986). Induction of synaptic potentiation in hippocampus by patterned stimulation involves two events. *Science, 232,* 985-988.

Larson, J., Wong, D., & Lynch, G. (1986). Patterned stimulation at the theta frequency is optimal for the induction of hippocampal long-term potentiation. *Brain Research, 441,* 111-118.

Lynch, G. (1986). *Synapses, circuits, and the beginnings of memory.* Cambridge, MA: MIT Press.

Lynch, G., Muller, D., Seubert, P., & Larson, J. (1988). Long-term potentiation: Persisting problems and recent results. *Brain Research Bulletin, 21,* 363-372.

Macrides, F., Eichenbaum, H. B., & Forbes, W. B. (1982). Temporal relationship between sniffing and the limbic theta rhythm during odor discrimination reversal learning. *Journal of Neuroscience, 2*, 1705–1717.

McNaughton, B. L., Douglas, R. M., & Goddard, G. V. (1978). Synaptic enhancement in fascia dentata: Cooperativity among coactive afferents. *Brain Research, 157*, 277–293.

Morris, R. G. M., Anderson, E., Lynch, G. S., & Baudry, M. (1986). Selective impairment of learning and blockade of long-term potentiation by an N-methyl-D-aspartate receptor antagonist, AP5. *Nature, 319*, 774–776.

Nadel, L. (1991). The hippocampus and space revisited. *Hippocampus, 1*, 221–229.

O'Keefe, J. A. (1979). A review of hippocampal place cells. *Progress in Neurobiology, 13*, 419–439.

O'Keefe, J. A., & Conway, D. H. (1978). Hippocampal place units in the freely-moving rat: Why they fire when they fire. *Experimental Brain Research, 31*, 573–590.

O'Keefe, J. A., & Nadel, L. (1978). *The hippocampus as a cognitive map.* Oxford: Oxford University Press.

Otto, T., & Eichenbaum, H. (1992a). Olfactory learning and memory in the rat: A "model system" for studies of the neurobiology of memory. In K. Chobor & M. Serby (Eds.), *The science of olfaction* (pp. 213–244). New York: Springer-Verlag.

Otto, T., & Eichenbaum, H. (1992b). Neuronal activity in the hippocampus during delayed non-match to sample performance in rats: Evidence for hippocampal processing in recognition memory. *Hippocampus, 2*(3), 329–340.

Otto, T., & Eichenbaum, H. (in press). Complementary roles of orbital prefrontal cortex and the perirhinal/entorhinal cortices in an odor-guided delayed non-matching to sample task. *Behavioral Neuroscience.*

Otto, T., Eichenbaum, H., Wiener, S. I., & Wible, C. G. (1991). Learning-related patterns of CA1 spike trains parallel stimulation parameters optimal for inducing hippocampal long term potentiation. *Hippocampus, 1*, 181–192.

Otto, T., Schottler, F., Staubli, U., Eichenbaum, H., & Lynch, G. (1991). The hippocampus and olfactory discrimination learning: Effects of entorhinal cortex lesions on learning-set acquisition and on odor memory in a successive-cue, go/no-go task. *Behavioral Neuroscience, 105*, 111–119.

Pavlides, C., Greenstein, Y. J., Grudman, M., & Winson, J. (1988). Long-term potentiation in the dentate gyrus is induced preferentially on the positive phase of theta rhythm. *Brain Research, 439*, 383–387.

Rawlins, J. N. P. (1985). Associations across time: The hippocampus as a temporary memory store. *Behavioral and Brain Sciences, 8*, 479–496.

Rolls, E. T., Miyashita, Y., Cahusac, P., Kesner, R. P., Niki, H. D., Feigenbaum, J. D., & Bach, L. (1989). Hippocampal neurons in the monkey with activity related to the place where a stimulus is shown. *Journal of Neuroscience, 9*, 1835–1846.

Rose, G. M., & Dunwiddie, T. V. (1986). Induction of hippocampal long-term potentiation using physiologically-patterned stimulation. *Neuroscience Letters, 69*, 244–248.

Rudell, A., Fox, S., & Ranck, J. B., Jr. (1980). Hippocampal excitability phase-locked to the theta rhythm in walking rats. *Experimental Neurology, 68*, 87–96.

Ruthrich, H., Matthies, H., & Ott, T. (1982). Long-term changes in synaptic excitability of hippocampal cell populations as a result of training. In C. A. Marsan & H. Matthies (Eds.), *International Brain Research Organization Monograph Series: Vol. 9. Neuronal plasticity and memory formation* (pp. 289–294). New York: Raven Press.

Sakurai, Y. (1988). Thalamocortical, hippocampus, and auditory neuronal activity related to auditory working memory processes in the rat. *Society for Neuroscience Abstracts, 14*, 862.

Scoville, W. B., & Milner, B. (1957). Loss of recent memory after bilateral hippocampal lesions. *Journal of Neurology, Neurosurgery and Psychiatry, 20*, 11–21.

Sharp, P. E., McNaughton, B. L., & Barnes, C. A. (1985). Enhancement of hippocampal field potentials in rats exposed to a novel, complex environment. *Brain Research, 339*, 361–365.

Skelton, R. W., Scarth, A. S., Wilkie, D. M., Miller, J. J., & Phillips, A. G. (1987). Long-term increases in dentate granule cell responsivity accompany operant conditioning. *Journal of Neuroscience, 7*, 3081–3087.

Slotnick, B. M., & Katz, H. M. (1974). Olfactory learning-set formation in rats. *Science, 185*, 796–798.

Squire, L. R. (1987). *Memory and brain.* New York: Oxford University Press.

Squire, L. R., & Cohen, N. J. (1984). Human memory and amnesia. In G. Lynch, J. L. McGaugh, & N. M. Weinberger (Eds.), *Neurobiology of learning and memory* (pp. 3–64). New York: Guilford Press.

Squire, L. R., Cohen, N. J., & Nadel, L. (1984). The medial temporal region and memory consolidation: A new hypothesis. In H. Weingartner & E. Parker (Eds.), *Memory consolidation* (pp. 185–210). Hillsdale, NJ: Erlbaum.

Staubli, U., Fraser, D., Faraday, R., & Lynch, G. (1987). Olfaction and the "data" memory system in rats. *Behavioral Neuroscience, 101*, 757–765.

Staubli, U., Ivy, G., & Lynch, G. (1984). Hippocampal denervation causes rapid forgetting of olfactory information in rats. *Proceedings of the National Academy of Sciences USA, 81,* 5885-5887.

Switzer, R. C., de Olmos, J., & Heimer, L. (1985). Olfactory system. In G. Paxinos (Ed.), *The rat nervous system: Vol. 1. Forebrain and midbrain* (pp. 1-36). Orlando, FL: Academic Press.

Teyler, T. J. (1986). Memory: Electrophysiological analogs. In J. L. Martinez & R. P. Kesner (Eds.), *Learning and memory: A biological view* (pp. 237-266). San Diego, CA: Academic Press.

Teyler, T. J., & DiScenna, P. (1986). The hippocampal memory indexing theory. *Behavioral Neuroscience, 100,* 147-154.

Van Groen, T., & Wyss, J. M. (1990). Extrinsic projections from area CA1 of the rat hippocampus: Olfactory, cortical, subcortical, and bilateral hippocampal formation projections. *Journal of Comparative Neurology, 303,* 1-14.

Wible, C. G., Eichenbaum, H., & Otto, T. (1990). A task designed to demonstrate a declarative memory representation of odor cues in rats. *Society for Neuroscience Abstracts, 16,* 605.

Wible, C. G., Findling, R. L., Shapiro, M., Lang, E. J., Crane, S., & Olton, D. S. (1986). Mnemonic correlates of unit activity in the hippocampus. *Brain Research, 399,* 97-110.

Wiener, S. I., Paul, C. A., & Eichenbaum, H. (1989). Spatial and behavioral correlates of hippocampal neuronal activity. *Journal of Neuroscience, 9,* 2737-2763.

Zola-Morgan, S., & Squire, L. R. (1990). The primate hippocampal formation: Evidence for a time-limited role in memory storage. *Science, 250,* 160-163.

37

The Hippocampus and Prefrontal Cortex in Learning and Memory: An Animal Model Approach

GORDON WINOCUR

In humans, a clear distinction can be drawn between the effects of lesions to the hippocampus (HPC) and to the prefrontal cortex (PFC) on cognitive function. Patients with HPC damage reliably suffer a profound anterograde amnesia for events experienced within particular contexts and for specific items on tests of explicit memory. There is also evidence that the deficit may extend to premorbid experiences that occurred during a limited time period before injury, resulting in a temporally graded retrograde amnesia. In contrast, memory of a semantic or procedural nature, assessed by implicit tests of memory, is relatively preserved, as are cognitive abilities related, for example, to general intelligence or linguistic functions (see Squire, 1987).

Patients with damage to PFC show a very different pattern. Their ability to recall straightforward personal experiences and their performance on tests of explicit memory are usually normal. On the other hand, they are severely impaired on tests of learning and memory that require, for example, the temporal ordering of information, response sequencing, and the acquisition of certain types of rule-based behaviors. In humans, the PFC is widely associated with executive-like functions that control the organization of information and the planning of behavior (see Stuss & Benson, 1986).

The contrasting effects of PFC and HPC lesions, while readily seen in humans, are less clearly defined in animal models. In animals, lesions to either structure produce similar results in a surprising number of behavioral paradigms. For example, selective damage to the HPC or PFC in several species has little effect on most forms of simultaneous discrimination learning, but consistently impairs reversal discrimination learning. Other tests that reliably yield similar deficits in animals with PFC or HPC lesions include spatial alternation learning, complex maze learning, and delayed-matching-to-sample tasks. (The reader is directed to O'Keefe & Nadel, 1978, and Gray, 1982, for reviews of the relevant animal HPC literature, and to Markowitsch & Pritzel, 1977, Fuster, 1989, and Kolb, 1984, for reviews of the corresponding animal PFC literature.)

In general, studies of animals with HPC or PFC lesions have not provided satisfactory models of the types of behavioral dissociations reliably observed in humans with comparable lesions. One possibility, of course, is that the functions of the

HPC and PFC are more similar than is generally thought to be the case. Or perhaps this is only true for animals, and functional differences emerge in advanced stages of the structures' phylogenetic development. Neither of these explanations is appealing, particularly in view of a third alternative that focuses on the nature of the tests used in animal experimentation.

An analysis of tasks that are sensitive to effects of HPC or PFC lesions reveals that they usually assess multiple functions. For example, on many tests, the animal is required to remember highly specific information and to use that information in making appropriate response selections. The ability to recall specific events is widely identified with HPC function, whereas the process of selecting responses on the basis of previous events may be seen as a form of behavioral planning under PFC control. Thus, it would appear that the tests measure functions of the HPC *and* PFC, and that successful performance depends on the contributions of both structures. According to this view, lesions to either structure can be expected to impair performance on the various tasks, but for different reasons. The problem, in terms of assessing the structures' respective functions, appears to reside with the tests' measures that fail to differentiate between the deficits produced by either lesion.

Consider, for example, tests of delayed alternation (DA) or delayed matching (DM), on which animals with PFC or HPC damage are reliably impaired. In DA testing, animals learn a response alternation sequence; in DM testing, they compare successively presented stimuli and respond in terms of similarities or differences in features of the stimuli. On these tasks, animals must choose responses that were cued by previously performed responses or previously presented stimuli. Deficits may result from a failure to recall the previous events, as might be expected following HPC damage. Or the animal may remember the events, but may fail to integrate the relevant information with demands of the current trial. A deficit in using, rather than in recalling, information may reflect impaired PFC function. However, in terms of the behavioral measures usually employed in such tests, the deficits produced by both lesions would appear very similar.

These examples highlight the need for tests of animal learning and memory that are capable of distinguishing between effects of HPC and PFC damage. Accordingly, an attempt was made to design tasks with this need in mind. Several tasks emerged from this effort, enabling a series of studies aimed at dissociating and describing the respective functions of the HPC and PFC. These studies were guided by the hypothesis that HPC lesions selectively affect memory for highly specific information, while sparing the type of nonspecific memory involved in learning and remembering various skills and rules of behavior. Conversely, if the PFC is involved in using rather than recalling information, damage to this structure should disrupt new learning in which information must be organized and applied in a strategic manner. The following sections review some of this research.

Delayed Alternation

Early work in this series utilized a variation of a nonspatial DA task that was introduced by Walker, Messer, Freund, and Means (1972). In previous work, this task proved to be useful in dissociating behavioral effects of lesions to the hippocampus and the dorsomedial thalamus (Winocur, 1985). The task was administered in a Skinner box that contained a centrally located retractable lever. Daily test sessions consisted of reinforced ("go") trials that alternated with an equal number of nonreinforced ("no-go") trials. The lever was always present during the go and no-go trials, which were 20 seconds (sec) long. Each lever press during the go trials produced a food pellet, whereas lever presses during the no-go trials were never rewarded. The lever was retracted during the intertrial intervals (ITIs) which varied between 0 and 80 sec. Thus, to perform successfully on each trial, rats had to recall, over a variable interval, specific events of the preceding trial and then use that information in selecting an appropriate response.

Figure 37.1 compares the performance of groups of rats with HPC or PFC lesions and an operated control (OC) group after 12 days of DA testing. The measure reported at each ITI was a latency ratio, calculated by dividing the mean latency to the first response in the go trials by the mean latency to the first response in the no-go trials. By this measure, a low ratio signified good performance. The HPC group learned the basic alternation rule as well as controls and responded normally at relatively short ITIs. However, the performance of this group deteriorated markedly when the ITI reached 20 sec. The HPC deficit was directly related to the length of time that events of immediately preceding trials must be retained. The PFC group exhibited a different

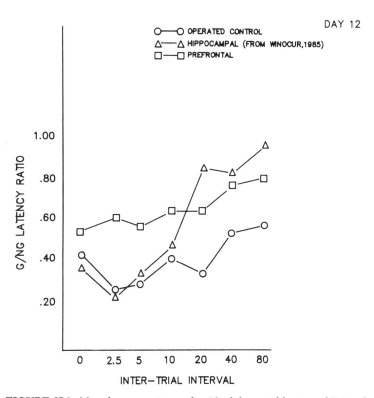

FIGURE 37.1. Mean latency ratios on day 12 of the variable-interval DA task.

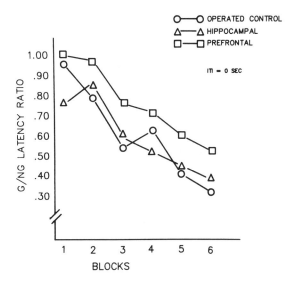

FIGURE 37.2. Mean latency ratios at ITI_0 of the variable-interval DA task, expressed over blocks of two test sessions.

pattern of behavior. These rats were impaired at all intervals, including ITI_0, where demands on specific or episodic memory were minimal. Of particular interest was the fact that the rate of decline for the PFC group paralleled that of the OC group.

In contrast to the HPC group, the problem for the PFC group was not one of remembering events of previous trials, but of using that information to learn or apply the alternation rule. To assess basic alternation learning in the three groups, the data for ITI_0 were isolated and compared over the 12 days of testing. This analysis showed that the HPC and OC groups learned the alternation rule at the same rate, but that the PFC group progressed much more slowly (see Figure 37.2). These results suggest that the PFC group's failure to utilize the available information resulted in impaired learning of the alternation habit.

Conditional Discrimination Learning

In the next study, similar questions were addressed using a conditional-discrimination-learning (CDL) paradigm, a test known to be highly sensitive to the effects of PFC damage in humans (Petrides, 1985). To adapt this test for rats, a Skinner box was outfitted with a panel of six lights on the front wall and two retractable levers positioned below the panel on either side of a food well. Rats were trained to press the left bar in response to any combination of lights on the left side of the panel, and the right bar when lights appeared on the right side. Stimuli and levers were simultaneously present for the first 30 trials. Then, to increase memory load, successive delays of 5 and 15 sec were introduced between the stimuli and the appearance of the levers. Fifteen sessions were conducted at each of these delays (see Winocur, 1991, for a more detailed description of this task).

As can be seen in Figure 37.3, there was no difference between the HPC and OC groups on the CDL task in the zero-delay condition. However, the performance of the HPC rats deteriorated as the length of the interval increased. In fact, increasing the delay to 5 sec produced a near-total collapse in this group, and at 15 sec its performance was at chance level.

In contrast, the PFC group was severely impaired on this task at all delays. The poor performance of this group at zero delay, where there was no challenge to specific memory, is particularly interesting, in that the ability to learn associations between specific stimuli and responses is not usually impaired by PFC lesions (Fuster, 1989). Rats could solve the CDL task simply by learning to press the lever that was closest to the light. However, a feature that may be unique to this task is that on any trial, the discriminanda could take one of three forms. The task could pose special problems to animals if they failed to ignore irrelevant differences between the stimuli.

The PFC deficit in the zero-delay condition also relates to Fuster's (1989) contention that temporal factors are crucial in determining the involvement of PFC in new learning. No temporal ordering was required at zero delay, so that impaired performance in this condition would most likely result from a failure to perform those essential operations that are inherent to the task. The present findings suggest that the crucial factors may relate more directly to the requirement that information from various sources be integrated with current task demands. Furthermore, a comparison of the PFC and OC groups' overall performance revealed no group × delay interac-

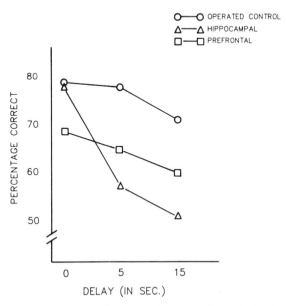

FIGURE 37.3. Percentage correct scores in the CDL task, averaged over the last five sessions in each delay condition. From "Functional Dissociation of the Hippocampus and Prefrontal Cortex in Learning and Memory" (p. 17) by G. Winocur, 1991, *Psychobiology, 19*, 11–20. Copyright 1991 by Psychonomic Society Publications. Reprinted by permission.

tion, indicating that the deficit did not increase with the length of the ITI. The deficit of the PFC group seems to have resulted from an inability to organize available information for purposes of learning the conditional discrimination.

Delayed Matching

In DM testing, the typical procedure is to present a sample stimulus for study, followed by a test in which that stimulus is presented together with a new comparison stimulus. In the matching-to-sample version of the test, subjects are rewarded for responding to the sample; and in the nonmatching-to-sample version, a response to the comparison stimulus is correct. Milner (1964) developed a nonspatial version of this test in which the sample and comparison stimuli are presented successively, and subjects must respond one way when the stimuli are the same and another way when they are different.

Milner (1972) found that damage to HPC did not affect performance on the delayed-comparison task, at least when intervals between the stimuli were relatively short. On the other hand, monkeys (Stamm & Rosen, 1969) and humans (Milner, 1964) with PFC lesions were severely impaired on this test. It is not clear whether DM performance following HPC or PFC lesions is directly affected by the length of the stimulus interval. If HPC damage causes rapid forgetting of specific memories, a deficit following such lesions would be expected at longer intervals. As for PFC, the results of previous studies in this series suggest that lesions to this region should produce a deficit on DM performance that is independent of temporal factors.

To address this issue, a version of Milner's paired-comparison test was adapted for the rat. A Skinner box was outfitted with a single light, centrally located in the front wall, just above a single retractable lever. On each trial, the light was illuminated twice in succession. If the two lights were identical, the rat was to press the lever for food; if the second light was brighter or dimmer than the first, the rat was to refrain from bar pressing. Initially, the stimuli were presented as close in time as possible, to assess the rat's basic ability to make the necessary comparisons and apply the conditional rule. In subsequent tests, delays of 5 and 15 sec were introduced to determine whether performance was affected by having to recall the sample stimulus over extended intervals.

The results of this test virtually mirrored those of the CDL study (Figure 37.4). The HPC and OC groups did not differ at the shortest delay, but thereafter, at 5- and 15-sec delays, HPC rats barely performed at chance level. The PFC group was severely impaired at all delays, but its performance was disproportionately affected by the length of the interval. The results confirm the time-dependent memory deficit of rats with hippocampal lesions, and provide another example of the critical involvement of PFC in organizing information for purposes of conditional learning.

Transfer of Learning

In showing that lesions to PFC seriously impair learning on DA, CDL, and DM tasks, the studies discussed above highlight the widespread effects of such lesions. The fact

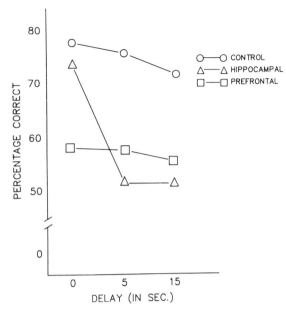

FIGURE 37.4. Percentage correct scores in the DM task, averaged over the last three sessions in each delay condition.

that the deficits were independent of demands on specific memory implicates the structure in nonspecific memory functions that are essential to the acquisition of rule-based behaviors. PFC involvement in nonspecific aspects of learning and memory is not restricted to rule learning; indeed, it extends to a wide range of tasks, including some that involve skill learning (Winocur & Moscovitch, 1990) and problem solving (Moscovitch, 1989). Once again, in these examples PFC lesions did not impair memory for specific aspects of the tasks.

The question arises as to whether the PFC is important for all types of rule learning, and the answer appears to be that it is not. In transfer-of-learning tests, where a series of problems share a common element, normal subjects progressively improve their performance by transferring a general rule to successive problems. Studies have shown that monkeys with PFC damage were as good as controls at transferring learning within a series of visual discrimination problems (French, 1964).

This finding was confirmed recently, in my laboratory, in a test that involved transfer of a size discrimination rule between pairs of stimuli that changed on every trial. For some rats, the correct response was to the larger of two stimuli, while for others it was the smaller. HPC, PFC, and OC groups showed equal transfer of the rule in reaching a criterion of 80% accuracy during learning and when tested weeks later on new stimulus pairs (see Table 37.1).

These results showed that PFC lesions do not affect all forms of rule-governed learning. The transfer test differs from the previous rule-learning tests in many ways, but one notable feature that distinguishes the transfer test is the absence of a *conditional* learning requirement. This may be a significant difference, particularly in view of Petrides's (1985) argument that the PFC is critically involved in forming

TABLE 37.1. Transfer of a Size Discrimination Rule between Constantly Changing Stimulus Pairs

	HPC	PFC	OC
Original learning (trials to criterion)	132.9	162.1	120.5
Retest (% correct)	80.6	71.2	84.6

Note. The measure in original learning is the number of trials required to reach 80% accuracy in daily performance. At retest, the measure was percentage of correct responses in a 20-trial test session.

conditional associations. However, while there is little doubt that PFC lesions impair conditional learning, this does not appear to have been the crucial factor in the transfer-of-learning deficit.

In a variation of the preceding test that also involved nonconditional rule learning, rats with PFC lesions were found to be severely impaired in transferring that rule. In the latter study, instead of being presented with a different pair of stimuli on each training trial, rats initially learned to discriminate between a single pair of stimuli (circles) of different size. When a preset learning criterion was reached, they were tested with the same pair of stimuli, or with a new pair of stimuli (triangles) that also varied in terms of size. All groups quickly learned the discrimination and performed well on the retention test. The transfer test in this study was more difficult for all groups than was the case in the previous study. However, the deficit was clearly greatest for the PFC group, which required three times as many trials as the OC group to re-establish criterion on this test (see Table 37.2).

Although the tasks in both experiments measured rule learning and transfer, it is worth considering the procedural differences that contributed to differences in the way that the rules were acquired and in the demands of the transfer tests. These variations provide valuable insights into the conditions under which PFC lesions impair transfer of learning, and, indeed, into the nature of PFC participation in learning and memory generally.

TABLE 37.2. Retention and Transfer of a Size Discrimination Acquired Originally with One Pair of Stimuli

	Retention			Transfer		
	HPC	PFC	OC	HPC	PFC	OC
Original learning	55.7	62.8	51.3	57.8	61.4	53.3
Test	8.6	11.4	7.4	51.1	111.3	34.4
	(85%)	(82%)	(85%)	(12%)	(−81%)	(35%)

Note. The measure in original learning and test is the number of trials to reach a criterion of 80% accuracy in daily performance. The numbers in parentheses represent percentages of savings at test.

In the first study, because different stimuli were presented on every trial, rats were forced to respond exclusively to differences in the size of the stimuli. Attention was directed away from the specific features of the stimuli. Learning a size discrimination in this way was more difficult than when only a single pair of stimuli were presented, but it was equally so for all groups. The transfer test was essentially an extension of the training condition, in that after a few weeks, rats were presented with a new series of stimulus pairs that differed only in size. The animals merely had to remember the learned rule and, in a straightforward manner, apply it to the larger (or smaller) of the stimuli. Under these conditions, all groups exhibited excellent transfer.

In the second study, where animals learned the size discrimination in relation to a single pair of stimuli, the stimuli themselves were an integral part of the learned discrimination. In comparison with the previous study, all groups transferred the learned discrimination less readily to unfamiliar stimuli. The relatively slow learning undoubtedly reflected the additional processing that was necessary to overcome the interference and deal with the significant change in the test situation. To transfer successfully, animals must first compare training and test conditions, isolate similarities and differences, and learn to attend to the critical similarities while ignoring irrelevant differences. This strategic operation enabled effective integration of previous learning with the new task and appropriate behavioral planning. The disproportionate impairment of the PFC group on this aspect of the task points to a fundamental deficit in performing such operations.

The excellent performance of the HPC group in the transfer conditions of both tasks appears to be at variance with reports of impaired transfer of discrimination learning following HPC lesions (e.g., Winocur & Salzen, 1968). However, animals with HPC lesions are often quite sensitive to changes in context or in the salient features of discriminative stimuli. In transfer tests, where training and test conditions differed in this way, animals with HPC have shown good transfer of learning (Winocur & Gilbert, 1984). The present results are consistent with those findings.

Conclusions

It is now possible to conclude that functional differences between effects of HPC and PFC lesions in the rat are similar to those reported for humans with comparable brain damage. An important point that emerges from the present research is that to demonstrate these differences in the rat model, tasks must be suitably designed to yield separate measures of the functions respectively controlled by the two structures.

On a variety of tasks that incorporated independent measures of memory function, rats with damage to the HPC were consistently impaired in their recall of highly specific events. The deficit was time-dependent and affected the retention of new information beyond a certain interval. The ability to remember nonspecific information, as part of the process of learning and applying rules of behavior, was not affected by HPC lesions.

These results are consistent with a large body of evidence that links the HPC to the process of forming long-term representations of new experiences, and with the view that emphasizes the structure's involvement in consolidation processes (Milner,

1972; Squire, Cohen, & Nadel, 1984; Winocur, 1985; Moscovitch & Umilta, 1990). The hippocampus is seen as being essential for assembling relevant information and creating new and permanent memory traces. This process and the amount of time it takes are influenced by several factors, including the nature and complexity of the information involved. Damage to the structure will necessarily prevent the efficient organization of coherent memory traces and will result in poor memory at retrieval. However, the HPC is not seen as performing primarily a retrieval function, nor is it regarded as the permanent site of stored information. The ability of humans (Milner, 1972) and animals (Winocur, 1990; Zola-Morgan & Squire, 1990) with HPC damage to display excellent memory for well-established premorbid experiences strongly supports this position.

The effects of PFC damage were very different and provided evidence that this region is implicated in nonspecific memory function. Rats with PFC lesions exhibited severe deficits on several rule-learning tasks, but they did not differ from controls on measures of specific memory. The deficits seemed to result from a failure to effectively use task-related information derived from previous experience to facilitate the selection of correct responses or the development of appropriate behavioral strategies.

Although the PFC is not essential to the process of laying down a memory trace or recalling information, the structure clearly draws on memory of past events to perform its function (Moscovitch, 1989). Its role seems to be related to the strategic use of memory, and investigators have used the term "working memory" to describe this function (Goldman-Rakic, 1984; Passingham, 1985). This general position has considerable appeal, but the term itself poses a problem, in that it has been applied in rather different ways and consequently is associated with several meanings. The confusion is especially apparent when its uses in the animal and human literatures are compared. For example, Baddeley (1986) describes working memory as a limited-capacity storage system and uses the term in ways that closely resemble traditional notions of human short-term memory. In contrast, animal investigators (e.g., Goldman-Rakic, 1984; Passingham, 1985) use it to describe the process of transferring trial-specific information in responding to current task demands.

To avoid confusion, we (Moscovitch & Winocur, in press) have coined the term "working-with memory" to describe the PFC's basic function. The intent is to convey the sense that the PFC uses information from previously experienced events to plan new activities. The sources of information can vary and are not restricted to the immediately preceding trial in a learning test or to a specific period of time. Emphasizing the PFC's involvement in the strategic use of memory makes it possible to explain not only the learning deficits of PFC rats reviewed in this chapter, but the general pattern of cognitive impairment reliably observed following PFC damage in animal and human populations.

ACKNOWLEDGMENTS

Research reported in this chapter was supported by grants from the Natural Sciences and Engineering Research Council of Canada and from the Medical Research Council of Canada. The excellent technical assistance provided by Taru Freeman in preparing this chapter is gratefully acknowledged.

REFERENCES

Baddeley, A. (1986). *Working memory*. Oxford: Oxford University Press.

Fuster, J. M. (1989). *The prefrontal cortex: Anatomy, physiology, and neuropsychology of the frontal lobe* (2nd ed.). New York: Raven Press.

French, G. B. (1964). The frontal lobes and association. In J. M. Warren & K. Akert (Eds.), *The frontal granular cortex and behavior* (pp. 56-73). New York: McGraw-Hill.

Goldman-Rakic, P. S. (1984). Modular organization of prefrontal cortex. *Trends in Neurosciences, 7*, 419-429.

Gray, J. A. (1982). *The neuropsychology of anxiety: An inquiry into the functions of the septo-hippocampal system*. Oxford: Oxford University Press.

Kolb, B. (1984). Functions of the frontal cortex of the rat: A comparative review. *Brain Research Reviews, 8*, 65-98.

Markowitsch, H. J., & Pritzel, M. (1977). Comparative analysis of prefrontal learning functions in rats, cats, and monkeys. *Psychological Bulletin, 84*, 817-837.

Milner, B. (1964). Some effects of frontal lobectomy in man. In J. M. Warren & K. Akert (Eds.), *The frontal granular cortex and behavior* (pp. 313-334). New York: McGraw-Hill.

Milner, B. (1972). Disorders of learning and memory after temporal lobe lesions in man. *Clinical Neuropsychology, 19*, 421-446.

Moscovitch, M. (1989). Confabulation and the frontal system: strategic versus associative retrieval in neuropsychological theories of memory. In H. L. Roediger III & F. I. M. Craik (Eds.), *Varieties of memory and consciousness: Essays in honor of Endel Tulving* (pp. 133-160). Hillsdale, NJ: Erlbaum.

Moscovitch, M., & Umilta, C. (1990). Modularity and neuropsychology: Modular and central processes in attention and memory. In M. F. Schwartz (Ed.), *Modular deficits in Alzheimer type dementia* (pp. 1-59). Cambridge, MA: MIT Press.

Moscovitch, M., & Winocur, G. (in press). A neuropsychological analysis of cognitive change in old age. In F. I. M. Craik & T. Salthouse (Eds.), *Aging and cognition*. New York: Plenum Press.

O'Keefe, J., & Nadel, L. (1978). *The hippocampus as a cognitive map*. Oxford: Oxford University Press.

Passingham, R. E. (1985). Memory of monkeys (*Macaca mulatta*) with lesions in prefrontal cortex. *Behavioral Neuroscience, 99*, 3-21.

Petrides, M. (1985). Deficits on conditional associative-learning tasks after frontal- and temporal-lobe lesions in man. *Neuropsychologia, 23*, 601-614.

Squire, L. R. (1987). *Memory and brain*. Oxford: Oxford University Press.

Squire, L. R., Cohen, N. J., & Nadel, L. (1984). The medial temporal region and memory consolidation: A new hypothesis. In H. Weingartner & E. Parker (Eds.), *Memory consolidation* (pp. 185-210). Hillsdale, NJ: Erlbaum.

Stamm, J. S., & Rosen, S. T. (1969). Electrical stimulation and steady potential shifts and prefrontal cortex in the monkey. *Acta Biologica Experimentalis, 29*, 385-399.

Stuss, D. T., & Benson, D. F. (1986). *The frontal lobes*. New York: Raven Press.

Walker, D. W., Messer, L. G., Freund, G., & Means, L. W. (1972). Effect of hippocampal lesions and intertrial interval on single-alteration performance in the rat. *Journal of Comparative and Physiological Psychology, 80*, 469-477.

Winocur, G. (1985). The hippocampus and thalamus: Their roles in short- and long-term memory and the effects of interference. *Behavioural Brain Research, 16*, 135-152.

Winocur, G. (1990). Anterograde and retrograde amnesia in rats with dorsal hippocampal or dorsomedial thalamic lesions. *Behavioural Brain Research, 38*, 145-154.

Winocur, G. (1991). Functional dissociation of the hippocampus and prefrontal cortex in learning and memory. *Psychobiology, 19*, 11-20.

Winocur, G., & Gilbert, M. (1984). The hippocampus, context, and information processing. *Behavioral and Neural Biology, 40*, 27-43.

Winocur, G., & Moscovitch, M. (1990). Hippocampal and prefrontal cortex contributions to learning and memory: Analysis of lesion and aging effects on maze learning in rats. *Behavioral Neuroscience, 104*, 544-551.

Winocur, G., & Salzen, E. A. (1968). Hippocampal lesions and transfer behavior in the rat. *Journal of Comparative and Physiological Psychology, 65*, 303-310.

Zola-Morgan, S. M., & Squire, L. R. (1990). The primate hippocampal formation: Evidence for a time-limited role in memory storage. *Science, 25*, 288-290.

38

Role of Diencephalic Lesions and Thiamine Deficiency in Korsakoff's Amnesia: Insights from Animal Models

PHILIP J. LANGLAIS

Introduction

A major interest in studying memory disturbances associated with brain damage is the potential for understanding the neural substrates responsible for normal memory. Amnesia in humans is frequently observed following destruction of structures in the medial temporal lobe or the diencephalon. Temporal lobe amnesia is observed in patients following bilateral surgical removal of the anterior one-third of the temporal pole (e.g., patient H. M.), a severe anoxic episode, or encephalitis. Diencephalic amnesia is seen in patients with Wernicke–Korsakoff disease, or selective focal destruction of the thalamus produced by infarction, tumors, or neoplasms.

It has been argued that the patterns of memory impairment produced by destruction of the temporal lobe and diencephalon are different and support the idea that these structures represent two anatomically distinct memory systems (Huppert & Piercy, 1979; Squire, 1982). Others have argued that these two brain regions are integral parts of a more unitary memory system (Mishkin, 1982). This latter view is based on the existence of two anatomical pathways connecting the temporal lobe with the diencephalon. Destruction of either pathway reportedly produces a detectable memory deficit, but severe amnesia requires interruption of both pathways connecting temporal and diencephalic structures.

Although few would disagree that damage to any of these structures can result in impaired memory, there is relatively little agreement as to which cognitive and mnemonic impairments observed in the human amnesias can be attributed to destruction of these temporal lobe–diencephalic pathways. This lack of knowledge reflects, in part, inadequate localization and detection of damage in human amnesics, the variability in memory deficits within and between types of human amnesias, and the lack of adequate animal models. This uncertainty regarding the critical lesion or lesions and their relationship to specific memory deficits is most apparent in the human diencephalic amnesias.

Human Diencephalic Amnesia: Neural Substrates

Evidence that diencephalic structures are critical to normal human memory have been derived mostly from observations of Wernicke-Korsakoff subjects. Korsakoff's disease is the most common form of human amnesia; it is characterized by an inability to form new memories (anterograde amnesia), the loss of old memories formed prior to onset of disease (retrograde amnesia), and a relative preservation of short-term memory, intellect, and cognition. Postmortem studies have demonstrated bilateral symmetric lesions of structures in medial thalamus, mammillary bodies (MBs), periacqueductal grey, periventricular regions of brainstem, and cerebellar vermis of Korsakoff subjects. The importance of the diencephalic lesions, particularly of the medial thalamus, to the amnesic symptoms is supported by reports of memory disturbances in patients with diencephalic tumors (McEntee, Biber, Perl, & Benson, 1976) and thalamic infarcts (von Cramon, Hebel, & Shuri, 1985; Graff-Radford, Damasio, Yamada, Eslinger, & Damasio, 1985), as well as by experimental thalamic lesions in monkeys (Aggleton & Mishkin, 1983a, 1983b; Zola-Morgan & Squire, 1985). On the other hand, damage to frontal cortex (Butters, 1985), the cholinergic nucleus basalis–neocortical and septo-hippocampal pathways (Arendt, Bigl, Arendt, & Tennstedt, 1983), and the noradrenergic locus coeruleus (LC)–cortical pathway (Mayes, Mendell, Mann, & Pickering, 1988; Victor, Adams, & Collins, 1971) has also been observed in Korsakoff postmortem brains. These structures are also important to learning and memory, and suggest that damage outside of the diencephalon may contribute to Korsakoff's amnesia.

At present there are several hypotheses regarding the critical lesion(s) in Korsakoff's and other forms of diencephalic amnesia. One hypothesis considers damage to the mediodorsal (MD) nucleus of thalamus as sufficient to cause the memory loss (Victor et al., 1971), whereas a second hypothesis argues that damage of the MB nuclei is critical to the amnesia (Malamud & Skillikorn, 1956). Another study of two Korsakoff cases (Mair, Warrington, & Weiskrantz, 1979) observed relative sparing of the MD nucleus and concluded that a lesion of the anterior paratenial nucleus, alone or in combination with MB damage, was critical to the memory disturbances. A third hypothesis, derived primarily from experimental studies of monkeys, suggests that severe amnesia occurs when a lesion damages two limbic–diencephalic memory pathways (Mishkin, 1982). The first pathway projects from the hippocampus via the fornix to the MB and from MB via the mammillo-thalamic tract (MTT) to the anterior nuclei of the thalamus. The second pathway projects from the amygdala via the inferior thalamic peduncle/internal medullary lamina (IML) to the MD. According to this hypothesis, a severe amnesia will result from a lesion of the diencephalon that damages both fiber tracts (IML and MTT), or both MD and anterior thalamic nuclei, or any combination of either a fiber tract and nucleus involved in the two memory systems.

In addition to disruption of these temporal lobe–diencephalic memory pathways, my colleagues and I have suggested that interruption of the monoamine pathways, particularly the LC noradrenergic system, plays a role in the anterograde memory deficits of Korsakoff's amnesia. We have observed significant reduction in cerebrospinal fluid (CSF) levels of 3-methoxy-4-hydroxyphenyl glycol (MHPG), homovanillic acid (HVA), and 5-hydroxyindoleacetic acid (5-HIAA) in a large number of Korsakoff amnesics (McEntee, Mair, & Langlais, 1984). Performance of Korsakoff subjects on memory tasks is highly and inversely correlated with CSF MHPG, whereas performance on motor skill tasks is significantly correlated with CSF HVA levels (McEntee, Mair, & Langlais, 1987). These observations have led to our hypothesis that the verbal and visual memory deficits of Korsakoff's amnesia may be related to disruptions of brain norepinephrine (NE) systems and that psychomotor skill learning may be related to dopamine (DA) activity. Treatment of Korsakoff subjects with the noradrenergic agonists clonidine (McEntee, Mair, & Langlais, 1981) and DL-threo-3,4-dihydroxyphenyl serine (DOPS; Langlais, Mair, Walen, McCourt, & McEntee, 1988) has improved their performance on several measures of anterograde memory. Further support for the role of noradrenergic loss in the memory impairments of Korsakoff's disease is provided by the recent report of a significant loss of neurons in LC, but not MD or MB nuclei, of two Korsakoff subjects with well-documented anterograde and retrograde amnesia (Mayes et al., 1988).

Korsakoff's Amnesia: Etiological Issues

An important and unresolved issue regarding Korsakoff's disease is the relative role of acute thiamine deficiency and chronic alcoholism in the etiology of the pathological lesions, and therefore in the cognitive and memory disturbances. Wernicke–Korsakoff syndrome is generally accepted as caused by acute thiamine deficiency, although the more severe and long-lasting cognitive and memory deficits are usually seen only in chronic alcoholics (Lishman, 1986; Victor et al., 1971). Two recent reports, however, describe Korsakoff's amnesia without chronic alcoholism (Beatty, Bailly, & Fisher, 1989; Becker, Furman, Panisset, & Smith, 1990). In experimental animals, acute thiamine deficiency produces midline diencephalic, mesencephalic, and brainstem lesions (Troncoso, Johnston, Hess, Griffin, & Price, 1981), whereas chronic alcohol treatment results in cortical atrophy and loss of neurons in hippocampus and basal forebrain cholinergic nuclei (Arendt et al., 1988; Walker, Hunter, & Abraham, 1981). These observations have led to the hypothesis that ethanol-induced damage of nondiencephalic structures may be an important etiological factor in both Korsakoff's amnesia and the milder cognitive and memory impairments of the non-Korsakoff "alcoholic amnesic syndrome" (Butters, 1985; Grant, 1987; Lishman, 1986).

The questions of which structures are damaged by thiamine deficiency versus alcohol and which lesions contribute to the profile of cognitive and memory deficits remain unanswered because of a lack of adequate animal models. Several laboratories using stereotaxic lesions have demonstrated a significant role of hippocampus, amygdala, and related temporal lobe structures in learning and memory. On the other hand, not enough work has been done with respect to the role of the diencephalon in cognitive and memory functions. Furthermore, studies directed at the neuroanatomical bases of alcohol- or thiamine-deficiency-related memory disturbances have been inadequate and inconsistent.

The Pyrithiamine-Induced Thiamine Deficiency Model in Rats

In an attempt to determine the neural substrates responsible for the various anterograde and retrograde memory deficits associated with the Wernicke–Korsakoff syndrome, our group has conducted a series of pathological, biochemical, and behavioral studies of a rat model of acute thiamine deficiency. These animal studies have intentionally *excluded* chronic alcohol treatment, so that the findings from these studies could be unequivocally related to the effects of thiamine deficiency. Additional studies have been conducted on rats with stereotaxic lesions of discrete thalamic structures, to further explore the role of diencephalic lesions in thiamine-deficiency-induced learning and memory deficits. These studies suggest that the pyrithiamine-induced thiamine deficiency (PTD) rat model is a useful model of Wernicke–Korsakoff syndrome, but raise important questions regarding the role of diencephalic lesions in the retrograde memory deficits of Korsakoff's amnesia.

Pathological and Biochemical Changes

Our studies, as well as those from other laboratories (Armstrong-James, Ross, Chen, & Ebner, 1988; Papp et al., 1981; Troncoso et al., 1981), have shown that within 2 weeks of receiving daily pyrithiamine injections and eating a thiamine-deficient chow (PTD treatment), rats develop a consistent pattern of acute neurological symptoms that predictably mark the onset of lesions within the diencephalon, periacqueductal grey, vestibular nuclei, and brainstem nuclei. Four regions of the diencephalon are consistently damaged in recovered PTD rats: (1) IML and thalamic intralaminar nuclei (paracentral, central median, anteromedial, interanteromedial, rhomboideus, and central lateral nuclei); (2) ventral portion of the MD nucleus of thalamus; (3) posterior nuclear group and parafascicular nucleus of thalamus; and (4) medial MB nuclei (Langlais & Mair, 1990; Langlais, Mandel, & Mair, 1992; Mair, Knoth, Rabchenuk, & Langlais, 1991). Careful light-microscopic examination has failed to detect any pathological change within hippocampus, amygdala, medial septum, or basal forebrain regions of several groups of PTD rats (Langlais & Mair, 1990; Mair, Anderson, Langlais, & McEntee, 1988). Choline acetyltransferase activity in neocortical regions and hippocampus is similar in PTD and pair-fed controls (Mair, Knoth, et al., 1991). Thus, biochemical measures also suggest that cholinergic projections from basal forebrain to neocortex and from septum to hippocampus are relatively intact in PTD rats.

The pathophysiological mechanism responsible for the selective lesions within the diencephalon following PTD treatment is unclear, but excitotoxicity mediated by glutamate receptors may be involved (Langlais, Mair, Anderson, & McEntee, 1988; Langlais & Mair, 1990). Treatment with MK-801, a blocker of the N-methyl-D-aspartate (NMDA) subtype of glutamate receptor, reduces damage to the diencephalon (Langlais & Mair, 1990) and prevents the behavioral impairments caused by PTD treatment in rats (Robinson & Mair, 1991).

This pattern of pathological change in recovered rats is similar but not identical to that of Korsakoff's disease. The overall size of the thalamic destruction is typically larger and extends to more lateral regions in the PTD rat. In addition, necrotic lesions within periacqueductal grey and periventricular regions, typically seen in human Korsakoff brains, are observed only in severely debilitated PTD rats. However, comparisons of pathological changes in the PTD rat and human Korsakoff's is made difficult by obvious differences in anatomical organization and the typically longer recovery period in human Wernicke–Korsakoff cases.

Damage to the region of the intralaminar nuclei and IML observed in PTD rats is consistently associated with anterograde learning and memory deficits (Langlais, Mandel, & Mair, 1992; Mair et al., 1988; Mair, Knoth, et al., 1991; Mair, Otto, Knoth, Rabchenuk, & Langlais, 1991). In several studies, PTD animals without damage to this region have performed similarly to controls. The reason why intralaminar damage is so closely associated with PTD-induced anterograde memory deficits is not known. However, these behavioral impairments may be related to damage of the IML fibers that are part of the limbic–diencephalic memory pathway connecting amygdala and MD nuclei. These nuclei also play a major role in the nonspecific thalamo-cortical projection system and are proposed to be involved in alerting, selective attention, and the enhancement of cortical cognitive processing (Rafal & Posner, 1987; Steriade & Glenn, 1982; Steriade, Domich, & Oakson, 1986). The difficulty PTD animals demonstrate in learning new tasks and retaining trial-specific information over long delay periods may be caused by disruption of cortical activation and information processing following intralaminar damage. Although damage to ventral portion of the MD is observed in PTD rats, this lesion is probably not critical to the anterograde memory deficits, since many behaviorally impaired PTD animals have had total sparing of this thalamic nucleus.

Contrary to our observations in human Korsakoff subjects, studies of behaviorally impaired PTD rats have failed to provide biochemical evidence of a loss of central nervous system noradrenergic activity within cortex or hippocampus (Langlais, Mair, Anderson, & McEntee, 1987, 1988). However, these studies were limited to measurement of tissue NE concentration in large brain regions and did not measure turnover or synthesis rates, which are better indices of the physiological activity of noradrenergic neurons. We have recently obtained more direct evidence of PTD-induced damage to the noradrenergic system (Langlais, Van Luyn, & Weiller, unpublished observations). The brainstems of PTD animals previously shown to be impaired on a nonmatching-to-sample (NMTS) task (Langlais & Van Luyn, 1990) were sectioned and the number and size of LC neurons counted. In PTD rats too impaired to be tested on an NMTS task, there were significantly fewer neurons (42.7 ± 5.0 cells/field; mean ± 1 SD) than in pair-fed controls (68.6 ± 12.9). The average size of LC neurons was also significantly smaller (Scheffe F test) in the PTD group (164 ± 23.5) than in the controls (248.2 ± 47.5). Neurons in various stages of degeneration but not included in the cells counts were observed throughout the LC of the PTD brains. Loss of LC neurons was also evident in PTD rats that were significantly impaired in learning an NMTS task and demonstrated an accelerated decline in performance on delayed trials of the NMTS task (see below). Post hoc comparison of the number of LC neurons in these behaviorally impaired PTD rats (55.9 ± 5.5) with controls approached significance ($p = .067$). In addition, the mean neuronal size (308.2 ± 54.1) was significantly greater (Scheffe F test) than that of controls (248.2 ± 47.5), suggesting that many of the surviving LC neurons had undergone metabolic changes and may not have been functioning normally. In fact, many cells were swollen and contained abnormal mitochondria and desnse chromatin material.

The behavioral importance of these observations is suggested by the high correlation ($r = .701$) between the number of LC neurons and performance (percentage correct) of the PTD group on the first 3 days of training on the NMTS task. In the behaviorally tested PTD rats, tissue NE was unchanged in cortex and hippocampus, whereas in the more severely affected PTD rats, NE was significantly reduced in cortex and significantly elevated in hippocampus (Langlais & Van Luyn, 1990). Loss of LC neurons following PTD parallels reports of LC loss in a large series of Korsakoff brains (Victor et al., 1971), and more recently in two well-studied Korsakoff patients (Mayes et al., 1988). Studies are currently underway to monitor *in vivo* release of NE in regions of cortex and hippocampus of PTD rats during learning. These data will provide a more direct examination of NE utilization and its relationship to the anterograde memory impairment following PTD treatment.

Behavioral Changes: Anterograde Memory

PTD rats display a variety of anterograde learning and memory deficits similar to those observed in human Korsakoff subjects. Difficulty in performing delayed-alternation and delayed-response tasks is commonly observed in Korsakoff subjects (Oscar Berman, Zola-Morgan, Oberg, & Bonner, 1982; Squire, Zola-Morgan, & Chen, 1988). Recovered PTD rats also demonstrate significant impairments on delayed-alternation tasks (Mair, Anderson, Langlais, & McEntee, 1985) and delayed responding on matching-to-sample and NMTS tasks (Langlais & Van Luyn, 1990; Mair et al., 1988; Mair, Knoth, et al., 1991; Mair, Otto, et al., 1991). The impairment of PTD rats appears to be related to an inability to utilize and retain specific information within and between trials, and suggests a deficit primarily of working memory. Reference memory, on the other hand, appears to be relatively intact, since with repeated training recovered PTD rats can perform at a criterion or a level comparable to that of pair-fed controls on a variety of tasks (Langlais, Mandel, & Mair, 1992; Mair et al., 1988; Mair, Knoth, et al., 1991; Mair, Otto, et al., 1991).

This learning deficit is clearly evident when PTD rats are trained on a paired-run NMTS task (Langlais & Van Luyn, 1990). In this task, a trial consists of two runs: a forced-choice information run, and a free-choice sample run (Thomas & Spafford, 1984). Training trials are conducted in a distributed rather than massed fashion and with a minimal (3- to 5-second) delay between the information and sample runs. PTD rats can learn this task, but require significantly more trials than pair-fed controls to attain a criterion of 90% correct responses on 2 out of 3 successive days (Langlais & Van Luyn, 1990). The inability of PTD rats to retain trial-specific information (i.e., the goal box reinforced on the current information run) in working memory becomes evident when the delay between the information and choice runs is increased. At an interrun delay of 180 seconds, the performance of PTD animals falls to a near-chance level (64% correct), whereas control performance at the same delay is much higher (80%). The rapid decline in performance at longer delays is probably a result of impaired working memory, since both PTD and control animals continue to achieve >90% on blocks of zero-delay trials administered between each block of delay trials. These observations suggest that PTD rats have difficulty in retaining place and proprioceptive information in short-term memory over long delays—a phenomenon characteristic of anterograde amnesia in humans.

The importance of PTD-induced lesions of the intralaminar nuclei and IML to the learning and working memory deficits on the NMTS task is further demonstrated by studies of animals with selective thalamic lesions (Henderson & Langlais, 1990). Rats with bilateral lesions that destroy MD but spare the intralaminar nuclei and IML demonstrate a mild acquisition deficit on the paired-run NMTS task, but their performance is indistinguishable from controls at delays up to 600 seconds. Rats with bilateral electrolytic destruction of MD and intralaminar nuclei, on the other hand, have a severe deficit in learning the NMTS task and display an accelerated decline in performance at increasingly longer interpair delays. Similar studies have demonstrated that radiofrequency lesions of the lateral intralaminar nuclei, but not the MBs or fornix, produce a behavioral impairment on an automated delayed NMTS task that is indistinguishable from that observed in PTD rats on the same task (see Mair, Robinson, & Koger, Chapter 39, this volume).

The anterograde memory impairment of PTD rats is not restricted to food-reinforced T-maze tasks. Rats recovered from PTD treatment are impaired in their ability to learn an aversively motivated (shock escape) spatial NMTS task (Mair, Otto, et al., 1991). PTD rats are also impaired in learning the location of a hidden platform int he Morris water maze (Langlais, Mandel, & Mair, 1992). The latency of PTD rats to find the platform on the initial days of training is significantly longer than that of pair-fed controls. The difficulty in finding the platform does not appear to be related to a motor impairment, since no significant differences are observed in swim speed of the PTD and control groups. Difficulty in integrating and retaining information about spatial, extramaze cues, or an inability to shift strategies, is suggested by the observation that PTD rats swim less in the annulus and quadrant containing the platform than controls. PTD rats continue to swim along the perimeter of the tank and make fewer excursions to the interior of the pool in the first several days of training. Despite this initial impairment, PTD animals eventually learn to find the platform and attain latencies similar to controls. When tested 5 weeks following the last training trial, PTD rats demonstrate latencies very similar to those of controls (Langlais, Mandel, & Mair, 1992). Thus, PTD animals appear to have stable reference memory for spatial, extramaze cues as well as for kinethetic, intramaze cues.

Behavioral Changes: Retrograde Memory

The effect of PTD treatment on retrograde memory has also been examined. Rats pretrained on the Morris water maze and then subjected to PTD treatment show no memory loss of the platform location (Langlais, Mandel, & Mair, 1992). Latencies of

PTD rats on retention trials are very similar to those of controls, despite extensive damage to medial thalamus and loss of neurons in medial MB nuclei. These observations suggest that damage of medial thalamus and/or MBs following thiamine deficiency may not affect a spatial memory acquired 2 weeks prior to the insult. This possibility is also suggested by reports that only the most recent memories are affected and that older and more remote memories are preserved in patients with severe anterograde amnesia following thalamic infarction (von Cramon et al., 1985; Michel, Laurent, Foyatier, Blanc, & Portafaix, 1982; Schott, Mauguiere, Laurent, Serclerat, & Fischer, 1980; Winocur, Oxbury, Roberts, Agnetti, & Davis, 1984). These observations suggest that the retrograde amnesia of Korsakoff's disease may be caused by damage to structures outside of the diencephalon, perhaps in cortical association areas, frontal cortex, or temporal lobe.

This hypothesis is supported by our observation that rats with extensive destruction of medial thalamus display normal retention of a passive avoidance task. Retention of a previously acquired passive avoidance response is a useful task for studies of retrograde amnesia, because the memory is acquired in a single trial and is retained for several weeks without further training. Furthermore, retention of the passive avoidance task is severely disrupted by pharmacological and electroconvulsive treatments, and the retrograde amnesia is relatively stable and temporally graded (Spanis & Squire, 1987). In our study (Langlais, Sheffield, Nicholson, & Henderson, 1992), a large number of rats ($n = 96$) were trained on a one-trial passive avoidance task, underwent surgery for bilateral electrolytic destruction of the entire medial thalamus, and subsequently were tested for retention of passive avoidance at 7 or 21 days following surgery. Separate groups of sham control and thalamic lesion animals underwent surgery at 1, 7, 14, and 28 days following the one training trial. As shown in Figure 38.1, rats with thalamic lesions displayed retention latencies comparable to those of sham-operated controls. For both lesion and control groups, the longest latencies were observed when surgery was conducted 28 days after training and were shortest when surgery was conducted 1 day following training. The control and lesion groups demonstrated a comparable improvement in retention when tested for retention after a 21-day versus 7-day postsurgery recovery period. Despite the failure of medial thalamic destruction to produce a retrograde amnesia for this passive avoidance task, the lesion animals demonstrated a severe anterograde memory impairment. Following the retention trial of the passive avoidance task, groups of 12 control and 12 lesion animals

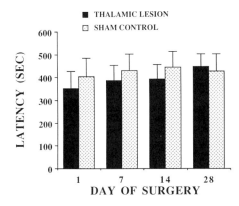

FIGURE 38.1. Latency (mean ± SD) to enter the dark end of a passive avoidance chamber on retention trial of groups of 12 rats receiving electrolytic destruction of medial thalamus (thalamic lesion) or the identical surgical procedure without insertion of electrode (sham control). Surgery was conducted 1, 7, 14, or 28 days following a one-trial acquisition of the passive avoidance task. Retention trials were conducted 7 or 21 days after each of the four posttraining surgical periods. Since recovery period had no effect on retention at any of the surgical periods, the data are presented as a single value.

were trained on the food-reinforced paired-run NMTS task described earlier. The control group attained criterion by the third day of training, but the lesion group could not exceed 75% correct even after 150 trials. Histological examination demonstrated total destruction of all nuclei and fiber tracts medial to IML (i.e., the midline, intralaminar, MD, and parafascicular nuclei).

Conclusions

Acute thiamine deficiency in the rat results in a significant impairment of working memory, but not reference memory, for a variety of tasks involving different sensory modalities, procedures, and types of reinforcement. Lesions of medial thalamus, especially in the region of the intralaminar nuclei and IML, appear to be critical to the PTD-induced anterograde learning and working memory deficits. The nature of this PTD-induced anterograde memory deficit remains unclear, but impairments of selective attention, hypothesis formation and shifting, and response selection–inhibition are possible. Disruptions of these cognitive processes are consistent with PTD-induced damage of the intralaminar–neocortical activation pathway. However, PTD-induced lesions of medial thalamus certainly disrupt other pathways coursing into and through this region. Further studies, therefore, will be needed to indentify the relative contribution of these structures and pathways to the various cognitive and mnemonic impairments that underlie PTD-induced anterograde amnesia. These studies further suggest that thiamine deficiency and the resulting damage to diencephalic structures are critical in the anterograde memory disturbances observed in Korsakoff's amnesia.

Retrograde amnesia, on the other hand, has not been observed in rats following PTD or stereotaxically placed electrolytic lesions of medial thalamus. It is possible that the tasks examined in these studies involved memories different from those lost in human retrograde amnesia. This seems unlikely, since location of a hidden platform would appear to involve formation of specific memories relating the position of several extramaze objects to the platform location and the tank environment. Medial thalamic lesions have also failed to produce any measurable loss of a socially transmitted food preference acquired 1 day prior to lesion (Winocur, 1990). This task purportedly assesses memory for an event that is identified with a specific time period and location. At present, there appears to be little support from animal studies for a critical role of diencephalic lesions in retrograde amnesia. Our studies with the PTD rat model suggest that the retrograde amnesia of Korsakoff's disease may be more closely related to alcohol-induced damage of structures outside of the diencephalon. Further studies are needed to examine the effects of combined alcohol and thiamine deficiency on both retrograde and anterograde memory in rats.

ACKNOWLEDGMENTS

I am grateful to Steve Henderson, Jan Weiler, Beth Sheffield, and Karen Nicholson for their skillfull assistance in conducting various behavioral and histological procedures. This research was supported by funds from the Department of Veterans Affairs and National Institutes of Health Grant No. NS29481.

REFERENCES

Aggleton, J. P., & Mishkin, M. (1983a). Visual recognition impairment following medial thalamic lesions in monkeys. *Neuropsychologia, 21,* 189-197.

Aggleton, J. P., & Mishkin, M. (1983b). Memory impairments following restricted medial thalamic lesions in monkeys. *Experimental Brain Research, 52,* 199-209.

Arendt, T., Allen, Y., Sinden, J., Schugens, M. M., Marchbanks, R. M., Lantos, P. L., & Gray, J. A. (1988). Cholinergic-rich brain transplants reverse alcohol-induced memory deficits. *Nature, 332,* 448-450.

Arendt, T., Bigl, V., Arendt, A., & Tennstedt, A. (1983). Loss of neurons in the nucleus basalis of Meynert in Alzheimer's disease, paralysis agitans and Korsakoff's disease. *Acta Neuropathologica, 61,* 101-108.

Armstrong-James, M., Ross, D. T., Chen, F., & Ebner, F. F. (1988). The effect of thiamine deficiency on the structure and physiology of the rat forebrain. *Metabolic Brain Disease, 3,* 91-124.

Beatty, W. W., Bailly, R. C., & Fisher, L. (1989). Korsakoff-like amnesic syndrome in a patient with anorexia and vomiting. *International Journal of Clinical Neuropsychology, 11,* 55-65.

Becker, J. T., Furman, M. M. R., Panisset, M., & Smith, C. (1990). Characteristics of the memory loss of a patient with Wernicke-Korsakoff's syndrome without alcoholism. *Neuropsychologia, 28,* 171-179.

Butters, N. (1985). Alcoholic Korsakoff's syndrome: Some unresolved issues concerning etiology, neuropathology, and cognitive deficits. *Journal of Clinical and Experimental Neuropsychology, 7,* 181-210.

Graff-Radford, N. R., Damasio, H., Yamada, T., Eslinger, P. J., & Damasio, A. R. (1985). Nonhaemorrhagic thalamic infarction: Clinical, neuropsychological and electrophysiological findings in four anatomical groups defined by computerized tomography. *Brain, 108,* 485-516.

Grant, I. (1987). Alcohol and the brain: Neuropsychological correlates. *Journal of Consulting and Clinical Psychology, 55,* 310-324.

Henderson, S., & Langlais, P. J. (1990). Differences in spatial learning and memory abilities following mediodorsal versus posterior thalamic lesions in rat. *Society for Neuroscience Abstracts, 16,* 609.

Huppert, F. A., & Piercy, M. (1979). Normal and abnormal forgetting in organic amnesia. *Cortex, 15,* 385-390.

Langlais, P. J., & Mair, R. G. (1990). Protective effects of the glutamate antagonist MK-801 on pyrithiamine induced lesions and amino acid changes in rat brain. *Journal of Neuroscience, 10,* 1664-1674.

Langlais, P. J., Mair, R. G., Anderson, C. D., & McEntee, W. J. (1987). Monoamines and metabolites in cortex and subcortical strucures: Normal regional distribution and the effects of thiamine deficiency in the rat. *Brain Research, 421,* 140-149.

Langlais, P. J., Mair, R. G., Anderson, C. D., & McEntee, W. J. (1988). Long-lasting changes in regional brain amino acids and monoamines in recovered pyrithiamine treated rats. *Neurochemical Research, 13,* 1199-1206.

Langlais, P. J., Mair, R. G., Walen, P., McCourt, W., & McEntee, W. J. (1988). Memory effect of DL-threo-3,4-dihydroxyphenyl serine (DOPS) in human Korsakoff's disease. *Psychopharmacology, 95,* 250-254.

Langlais, P. J., Mandel, R. J., & Mair, R. G. (1992). Diencephalic lesions, learning impairments, and intact retrograde memory following acute thiamine deficiency in the rat. *Behavioural Brain Research, 48,* 177-185.

Langlais, P. J., Sheffield, B., Nicholson, K., & Henderson, S. (1992). *Anterograde but not retrograde memory deficits following medial thalamic lesions in rats.* Paper presented at the 4th Annual Meeting of the American Psychological Society, San Diego, CA.

Langlais, P. J., & Van Luyn, J. (1990). *Learning deficit and neurotransmitter disturbances in a rat model of diencephalic amnesia.* Paper presented at the 2nd Annual Meeting of the American Psychological Society, Dallas, TX.

Langlais, P. J., Van Luyn, J., & Weiller, J. Unpublished observations.

Lishman, W. A. (1986). Alcoholic dementia: A hypothesis. *Lancet, i,* 1184-1186.

Mair, R. G., Anderson, C. D., Langlais, P. J., & McEntee, W. J. (1985). Thiamine deficiency depletes cortical norepinephrine and impairs learning processes in the rat. *Brain Research, 360,* 273-284.

Mair, R. G., Anderson, C. D., Langlais, P. J., & McEntee, W. J. (1988). Behavioral impairments, brain lesions and monoaminergic activity in the rat following recovery from a bout of thiamine deficiency. *Behavioural Brain Research, 27,* 233-239.

Mair, R. G., Knoth, R. L., Rabchenuk, S. A., & Langlais, P. J. (1991). Impairment of olfactory, auditory, and spatial serial reversal learning in rats recovered from pyrithiamine induced thiamine deficiency. *Behavioral Neuroscience, 105,* 351-359.

Mair, R. G., Otto, T. A., Knoth, R. L., Rabchenuk, S. A., & Langlais, P. J. (1991). An analysis of aversively conditioned learning and memory in rats recovered from pyrithiamine induced thiamine deficiency. *Behavioral Neuroscience, 105,* 360-374.

Mair, W G. P., Warrington, E. K., & Weiskrantz, L. (1979). Memory disorder in Korsakoff's psychosis: A neuropathological and neuropsychological investigation of two cases. *Brain, 102*, 749–783.

Malamud, N., & Skillikorn, S. A. (1956). Relationship between the Wernicke and the Korsakoff syndrome. *Archives of Neurology and Psychiatry, 76*, 585–596.

Mayes, A. R., Meudell, P. R., Mann, D., & Pickering, A. (1988). Location of lesions in Korsakoff's syndrome: Neuropsychological and neuropathological data on two patients. *Cortex, 24*, 367–388.

McEntee, W. J., Biber, M. P., Perl, D. P., & Benson, F. D. (1976). Diencephalic amnesia: A reappraisal. *Journal of Neurology, Neurosurgery and Psychiatry, 39*, 436–441.

McEntee, W. F., Mair, R. G., & Langlais, P. J. (1981). Clonidine in Korsakoff disease: Pathophysiologic and therapeutic implications. In H. Lal & S. Fielding (Eds.), *Psychopharmacology of clonidine* (pp. 211–223). New York: Alan R. Liss.

McEntee, W. F., Mair, R. G., & Langlais, P. J. (1984). Neurochemical pathology in Korsakoff's psychosis. *Neurology, 34*, 648–652.

McEntee, W. F., Mair, R. G., & Langlais, P. J. (1987). Neurochemical specificity of learning: Dopamine and motor learning. *Yale Journal of Biology and Medicine, 20*, 187–193.

Michel, D., Laurent, B., Foyatier, N., Blanc, A., & Portafaix, M. (1982). Infarctus thalamique paramedian gauche: Etude de la mémoire et du langage. *Revue Neurologique, 138*, 533–550.

Mishkin, M. (1982). A memory system in the monkey. *Philosophical Transactions of the Royal Society of London, B298*, 85–95.

Oscar-Berman, M., Zola-Morgan, S. M., Oberg, R. G. E., & Bonner, R. T. (1982). Comparative neuropsychology and Korsakoff's syndrome: III. Delayed response, delayed alternation and DRL performance. *Neuropsychologia, 20*, 187–202.

Papp, M., Tarczy, M., Takats, A., Auguszt, A., Komoly, S., & Tulok, I. (1981). Symmetric central thalamic necrosis in experimental thiamine deficient encephalopathy. *Acta Neuropathologica* (Berlin), Suppl. 7, 48–49.

Rafal, R. D., & Posner, M. I. (1987). Deficits in human visual spatial attention following thalamic lesions. *Proceedings of the National Academy of Sciences USA, 84*, 7349–7353.

Robinson, J. K., & Mair, R. G. (1991). MK-801 protects rats from brain lesions and behavioral impairments following pyrithiamine-induced thiamine deficiency (PTD). *Society for Neuroscience Abstracts, 17*, 481.

Schott, B., Mauguiere, F., Laurent, B., Serclerat, O., & Fischer, C. (1980). L'amnésie thalamique. *Revue Neurologique, 136*, 117–130.

Spanis, C. W., & Squire, L. R. (1987). Stability of long temporal gradients of retrograde amnesia in mice. *Behavioral and Neural Biology, 48*, 237–245.

Squire, L. R. (1982). Comparisons between forms of amnesia: Some deficits are unique to Korsakoff's syndrome. *Journal of Experimental Psychology: Learning, Memory, and Cognition, 8*, 560–561.

Squire, L. R., Zola-Morgan, S., & Chen, K. S. (1988). Human amnesia and animal models of amnesia: Performance of amnesic patients on tests designed for the monkey. *Behavioral Neuroscience, 102*, 210–221.

Steriade, M., Domich, L., & Oakson, G. (1986). Reticularis thalami neurons revisited: Activity changes during shifts in states of vigilance. *Journal of Neuroscience, 6*, 68–81.

Steriade, M., & Glenn, L. L. (1982). Neocortical and caudate projections of intralaminar thalamic neurons and their synaptic excitation from midbrain reticular core. *Journal of Neurophysiology, 48*, 352–371.

Thomas, G. J., & Spafford, P. S. (1984). Deficits for representational memory induced by septal and cortical lesions (singly and combined) in rats. *Behavioral Neuroscience, 98*, 394–404.

Troncoso, J. C., Johnston, M. V., Hess, K. M., Griffin, J. W., & Price, D. L. (1981). Model of Wernicke's encephalopathy. *Archives of Neurology, 38*, 350–354.

Victor, M., Adams, R. D., & Collins, G. H. (1971). *The Wernicke-Korsakoff syndrome.* Philadelphia: F. A. Davis.

von Cramon, D. Y., Hebel, N., & Schuri, U. (1985). A contribution to the anatomical basis of thalamic amnesia. *Brain, 108*, 993–1008.

Walker, D. W., Hunter, B. E., & Abraham, W. C. (1981). Neuroanatomical and functional deficits subsequent to chronic ethanol administration in animals. *Alcoholism: Clinical and Experimental Research, 5*, 267–282.

Winocur, G. (1990). Anterograde and retrograde amnesia in rats with dorsal hippocampal or dorsomedial thalamic lesions. *Behavioural Brain Research, 38*, 145–154.

Winocur, G., Oxbury, S., Roberts, R., Agnetti, V., & Davis, C. (1984). Amnesia in a patient with bilateral lesions to the thalamus. *Neuropsychologia, 22*, 123–143.

Zola-Morgan, S., & Squire, L. R. (1985). Amnesia in monkeys after lesions of the mediodorsal nucleus of the thalamus. *Annals of Neurology, 17*, 558–564.

39

Thiamine Deficiency as an Animal Model of Diencephalic Amnesia

ROBERT G. MAIR, JOHN K. ROBINSON, and SUSAN M. KOGER

Amnesias attributed to diencephalic pathology are most commonly associated with Korsakoff's disease (Malamud & Skillicorn, 1956; Victor, Adams, & Collins, 1989), although they have also been reported in cases of trauma (Squire et al., 1989), tumors (McEntee, Biber, Perl, & Benson, 1976; Williams & Pennybacker, 1954), and thalamic infarct (von Cramon, Hebel, & Schuri, 1985). Beginning with Gudden in 1896, neuropathologists have recognized that Korsakoff's disease is inevitably accompanied by lesions surrounding the walls and floor of the third ventricle (Victor et al., 1989). Careful clinical analyses have demonstrated a consistent coincidence between the amnesic symptoms of this disease and lesions occurring bilaterally in medial thalamus and the mammillary bodies (Mair, Warrington, & Weiskrantz, 1979; Mayes, Meudell, Mann, & Pickering, 1988; Shimamura, Jernigan, & Squire, 1988; Squire, Amaral, & Press, 1990; Victor et al., 1989).

Although clinico-anatomical studies have identified consistent sites of pathology associated with memory impairment, there is still considerable uncertainty over the precise neurological basis of diencephalic amnesia. At least three different systems have been considered as the basis of these memory disorders. Some investigators have noted that the mammillary bodies are consistently involved in the Wernicke–Korsakoff syndrome, and have argued that the amnesic symptoms of this disease result from disruption of limbic system pathways from hippocampus through the fornix and mammillary nuclei to anterior thalamus (Barbizet, 1963; Brion & Mikol, 1978; Delay, Brion, & Elissalde, 1958; Malamud & Skillicorn, 1956). More recently, von Cramon et al. (1985) reviewed CT findings in 11 cases of amnesia associated with thalamic infarct and argued that vascular thalamic amnesia results from lesions affecting the mammillo-thalamic tract as well as amygdalo-thalamic pathways. Victor et al. (1989) argued against this view, basing their argument on evidence that thalamic lesions alone can impair memory and on observations of patients documented as being free of amnesia prior to death who showed signs of extensive, old pathology of mammillary bodies at postmortem.

A second possibility is that diencephalic amnesia results from lesions affecting the mediodorsal thalamic nucleus (MDn) and its connections with prefrontal cortex (see

Goldman-Rakic, 1987; Victor et al., 1989). Victor et al. (1989) carefully analyzed a large series of clinical cases and reported that although the mammillary bodies are the most frequent site of pathology in the Wernicke–Korsakoff syndrome, lesions involving the MDn correspond most consistently with the occurrence of amnesia. Similarly, radiological studies have shown signs of bilateral thalamic pathology in patients with Korsakoff's disease that correlate significantly with performance on memory tests (Shimamura et al., 1988). Other reports have questioned the importance of the MDn, because several cases of Korsakoff's disease proved at autopsy to have lesions of midline thalamus that apparently spared MDn (Mair et al., 1979; Mayes et al., 1988). Mair et al. (1979) argued that Korsakoff's amnesia results from concurrent lesions of midline thalamus and mammillary bodies. There are reports of amnesia associated with lesions affecting medial thalamus, including MDn and the internal medullary lamina (IML), produced by trauma (Squire et al., 1989), tumors (McEntee et al., 1976), and infarct (von Cramon et al., 1985; Victor et al., 1989). However, none of these cases have shown clear evidence of pathology restricted to MDn and not affecting limbic-related pathways within the diencephalon.

A third possibility is that amnesia can result from lesions disrupting neurochemical systems that arise from nuclei in the brainstem and diencephalon and that innervate widespread areas of cerebral cortex (Joyce, 1987; Kopelman, 1987; McEntee & Mair, 1984, 1990). McEntee et al. (1976) first considered this possibility, based on cases of amnesia observed in association with diencephalic tumors. Subsequent studies of patients with Korsakoff's disease have provided evidence relating signs of amnesia to measures of neurotransmitter function (McEntee & Mair, 1984, 1990). However, no evidence has been presented that amnesia can result from neurotransmitter deficits in patients free of other brain pathology.

Defining a Syndrome of Diencephalic Amnesia

One approach to defining the critical pathology of diencephalic amnesia is to analyze the effects of experimental lesions in animals on tasks measuring learning and memory. The extent to which observations of an animal model can be generalized to human amnesia (the external validity of the model) depends on the extent to which that model (1) affects systems known to be disrupted by disease processes; and (2) produces behavioral deficits that are consistent with the symptoms of amnesia. Animal models of diencephalic amnesia face several threats to their external validity. Diseases that produce diencephalic amnesia are not associated with lesions that are as circumscribed or tissue damage that is as complete as lesions produced by experimental surgical procedures. Thus experimental lesions may produce misleading results by totally disrupting pathways that are only partially affected by disease, or, at the other extreme, by failing to produce pathology that is sufficiently widespread to impair memory. Furthermore, comparisons between human amnesia and animal models are limited by anatomical differences between species, as well as uncontrolled aspects of human disease (including alterations in tissue associated with healing, agonal changes in brain tissue unrelated to amnesia, and histological artifacts related to postmortem handling of tissue and clinical fixation procedures).

The behavioral validity of an animal model can be evaluated by at least three criteria. First, does the model exhibit behavioral deficits that are qualitatively similar to impairments associated with amnesia? Second, is the extent of impairment quantitatively sufficient to account for amnesia? Third, is the overall syndrome of impairment comparable to global amnesia? In recent years, investigators have been successful in meeting the first criterion by demonstrating that human amnesics are impaired on tasks used to assess memory in animal models of amnesia (Aggleton, Nicol, Huston, & Fairbairn, 1988; Oscar-Berman, 1984; Oscar-Berman & Bonner, 1985; Squire, Zola-Morgan, & Chen, 1988). The second and third criteria are more problematic. It is difficult to compare the severity of memory impairment in humans and animals, particularly rodents. It is also hard to assess in animals the full range of psychological functions that are impaired or spared by amnesia in humans.

With our collaborators, we have developed a two-phase approach to developing an animal model of diencephalic amnesia. In the first phase, we have tried to develop a neurologically valid model of Korsakoff's disease by using thiamine deficiency to produce a syndrome of diencephalic amnesia. In a series of pilot studies (Mair, Anderson, & McEntee, 1982), we compared a number of methods to induce thiamine deficiency involving various combinations of dietary restriction, thiamine antagonists, loading with ethanol and glucose, and single versus multiple bouts of thiamine deprivation. We settled on a subacute treatment with dietary restriction and daily injections of pyrithiamine, which produced a remarkably consistent pattern of impairment from which animals could be recovered for chronic behavioral training.

We have since conducted a series of experiments (discussed below) in which rats ($n = 206$) have been given this pyrithiamine-induced thiamine deficiency (PTD) treatment and studied, for these purposes: (1) to describe the syndrome of behavioral impairment that results from this treatment; (2) to describe the histological lesions produced by this treatment; (3) to measure indices of neurochemical function in local brain areas among rats recovered from this treatment; and (4) to learn about the biochemical basis of this lesioning process. In the second phase of our research, we have attempted to fractionate the PTD model by comparing the behavioral consequences of PTD treatment to those of experimental lesions intended to reproduce selective aspects of PTD-induced pathology.

The Pyrithiamine-Induced Thiamine Deficiency Model

In PTD treatment, rats are placed on a thiamine-deficient diet and given daily intraperitoneal injections of pyrithiamine. The dose of pyrithiamine has been reduced from 0.5 mg/kg in earlier studies to 0.25 mg/kg body weight in more recent studies, without apparently altering the outcome of the treatment. Animals undergoing this treatment show a fixed progression of neurological signs: decreased food consumption (after 7 to 10 days); vigorous grasping at the floor of the home cage when lifted (1 to 2 days later); muscular discoordination and a flattened, prone posture (1 to 2 days later); and seizure-like activity (10 to 14 hours later) that progresses within 10 to 14 hours into opisthotonos, a tetanic spasm marked by dorsoflexion of the head, arching of the back, and loss of righting reflexes. PTD treatment is ended by a large injection of thiamine (100 mg/

kg). During the course of our experiments, we have shortened the period of PTD treatment by about 6 hours; we now end treatment after 6 to 8 hours of seizure-like activity in more recent studies, compared with 1 hour of opisthotonos in the earliest study. This decrease in time of treatment was associated with an increase in the number of animals surviving into chronic recovery (100% vs. 53%), as well as the number of treated animals surviving chronically and meeting the procedural demands of a pretrained delayed-alternation or delayed-nonmatching-to-sample (DNMTS) task (94% vs. 20%).

Behavioral Impairments

Behavioral analyses have been restricted to animals chronically recovered from PTD treatment that show no apparent signs of sensory, motor, or motivational impairment. We have observed deficits among PTD animals on a variety of delayed-conditional-response tasks based on spatial cues (Knoth & Mair, 1991; Mair, Anderson, Langlais, & McEntee, 1985, 1988; Mair, Knoth, Rabchenuk, & Langlais, 1991; Mair, Otto, Knoth, Rabchenuk, & Langlais, 1991; Robinson & Mair, in press). These have included tasks with and without pretreatment training, reinforced by aversive as well as appetitive contingencies, and requiring matching as well as nonmatching response strategies.

Analysis of DNMTS tasks trained prior to treatment have produced several notable findings (Knoth & Mair, 1991; Robinson & Mair, in press). First, PTD treatment has no apparent effect on the performance of the relatively complex procedural demands of the task. Second, PTD rats tend to be slow in executing DNMTS choice responses. Since slow DNMTS responses tend to be less accurate than fast ones, it is likely that this increase in response latency contributes to the overall DNMTS deficit. Third, when long-latency responses (> 2.9 seconds [sec]) are excluded from analyses, PTD animals remain significantly impaired on the DNMTS task. This indicates that the tendency to make relatively few short-latency responses cannot account entirely for this deficit.

The relationship between retention and DNMTS performance can also be delineated by varying the retention interval according to a staircase procedure, to determine the critical interval at which animals perform with 75% accuracy (Mair & Lacourse, in press). With extensive training on a staircase procedure, Robinson and Mair (in press) found that 13 of 14 PTD-treated animals performed at 90% accuracy or better at short retention intervals. This provides evidence of a preserved capacity to perform DNMTS when the effects of memory decay are minimized. Like the performance of controls, the performances of PTD-treated animals on the staircase showed consistent inverse relationships with retention interval, decreasing at longer delays. PTD animals, however, fell below 75% accuracy at significantly shorter retention intervals than did controls (mean of 6.0 vs, 14.8 sec). This deficit is consistent with an impairment of working memory, or the capacity to remember information that must be updated on a trial-by-trial basis (i.e., the side reinforced on the sample run preceding a given choice response). Other results have suggested that the working memory deficits produced by PTD treatment may be task-dependent. When Robinson and Mair (in press) trained rats to perform a radial arm maze task, they found that PTD animals made significantly more errors in learning to avoid entering arms never baited (a discrimination task), as well as arms that had been entered previously within a given trial (a working memory task). Nevertheless, with continued training (mean of 19.2 vs. 11.7 trials for controls), 13 of 14 PTD animals were able to reach a criterion of three consecutive errorless trials. This indicates that when given sufficient training, PTD animals are able to utilize working memory to discriminate between alleyways that have and have not yet been entered in a radial arm maze trial. These results are consistent with evidence that rats with medial thalamic lesions can be trained to perform to criterion on radial arm maze tasks without imposed delays (Kessler, Markowitsch, & Otto, 1982; Kolb, Pittman, Sutherland, & Whishaw, 1982).

PTD rats have been shown to have a spared capacity to perform discrimination tasks, in which a correct response is predicated on the same stimulus across trials, on the basis of visual (light-dark), place, olfactory, and auditory cues (Mair et al., 1985, 1988; Mair, Knoth, et al., 1991; Mair, Otto, et al., 1991). Although they eventually mastered these tasks, PTD animals were deficient in the *rate* at which they learned all but the light-dark discrimination tasks. For spatial serial reversal learning, PTD rats exhibited normal rates of positive transfer across a problem set, although they made significantly more errors in mastering each problem (Mair, Knoth, et al., 1991). The capacity to master discrimination problems or to exhibit normal transfer across a problem set denotes a spared capacity for reference memory, or the ability to respond based on a consistent rule or a fixed stimulus-response relationship, *once acquired*. The slow rate at which many of these discriminations are learned may reflect impairments in any of a number of processes.

Neuropathology

In various studies, brain tissue has been analyzed to study pathological lesions and indices of neurochemical activity in local brain regions following chronic recovery from PTD treatment. Histological analyses have described lesions in two common sites. The larger is a bilaterally symmetric lesion of medial thalamus that follows the course of the IML, involving tissue in adjacent thalamic nuclei, and extending in cases to involve regions lateral and posterior to the IML site (Figure 39.1). Mair, Ferguson, Knoth, and Langlais (1989) have shown that this thalamic lesion produces bilaterally symmetric denervation of layer IV in a number of areas of cortex, including all targets of the MDn. The second common site of pathology is centered on the medial mammillary nuclei and is accompanied by an enlargement of the mammillary recess of the third ventricle.

Pathophysiological analyses have demonstrated a consistent association between the occurrence of behavioral impairment and lesions in the IML site (Knoth & Mair, 1991; Mair et al., 1988; Mair, Knoth, et al., 1991; Mair, Otto, et al., 1991; Robinson & Mair, in press). However, given the high frequency of mammillary body pathology, it has not been possible to determine by correlational analyses whether lesions in either thalamus or mammillary bodies alone can account for the DNMTS impairments of the PTD model.

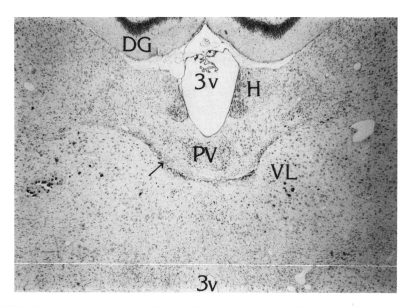

FIGURE 39.1. Coronal section through thalamus (about 6 mm anterior to the interaural line) showing typical IML lesion of the PTD model. The lesion appears as a band of gliosis, nerve cell loss, and apparent calcification (indicated by arrow) that crosses the midline in a bilaterally symmetric fashion. The relatively short distance between dorsal and ventral portions of the third ventricle is typical and represents the extent of tissue loss in chronically recovered animals. DG, dentate gyrus; H, habenula; PV, paraventricular thalamic nucleus; VL, ventrolateral thalamic nucleus; 3v, third ventricle.

Neurochemical studies have provided evidence that cortical norepinephrine (NE) is diminished, whereas serotonin (5-HT) is increased in midbrain–thalamus and striatum, in some groups of rats after chronic recovery from PTD treatment. Indices of NE, 5-HT, and dopamine function in other brain regions have been comparable to those of controls (Langlais, Mair, Anderson, & McEntee, 1987, 1988; Mair et al., 1985). However, there are several reasons to doubt the importance of altered neurochemical activity as a cause of the working memory deficits in the PTD model. First, substantial alterations in these local measures of monoamine function have been observed only in animals too severely impaired to be tested behaviorally. Second, normal indices of cortical monoaminergic and cholinergic function have been found in rats exhibiting significant behavioral impairments following less severe PTD treatment (Mair, Knoth, et al., 1991). Third, rats depleted of cortical NE by injection of 6-hydroxydopamine (6-OHDA) into the dorsal nonadrenergic bundle are not impaired on DMNTS measures that have been shown to be disrupted by the PTD treatment (Koger & Mair, in press) (see Figure 39.2, below).

Analyses of amino acids have provided evidence that PTD treatment results in a chronic decrease in glutamate and γ-aminobutyric acid that is restricted to midbrain–thalamus (Heroux & Butterworth, 1988; Langlais & Mair, 1990; Langlais, et al., 1988; Thompson & McGeer, 1985). Langlais and Mair (1990) showed that treatment with the glutamate blocker MK-801 at the end of PTD treatment attenuated the size of thalamic lesions and the extent of some of the amino acid abnormalities associated with this treatment. On the basis of these findings and the histological appearance of the acute PTD lesion, Langlais and Mair (1990) hypothesized that the thalamic lesion produced by this treatment resulted from a glutaminergic excitotoxic process. More recently, Robinson and Mair (in press) showed that intervention with MK-801 earlier in PTD treatment can protect rats entirely from the DNMTS deficits, as well as from lesions in both thalamus and mammillary bodies.

Experimental Analyses of the Model

The PTD rat model can make several claims to neurological validity as an animal model of Korsakoff's disease (see Knoth & Mair, 1991). These include (1) an etiology based on thiamine deficiency; (2) similarities in neuropathology; and (3) similarities in behavioral deficits. Over the past several years, we have conducted a series of experiments using more selective lesioning procedures in an attempt to identify the critical neural substrates of the behavioral impairments produced by PTD treatment. In this research, we use the PTD model as both a guide for the placement of lesions and a quantitative benchmark against which we can compare measures of behavioral function.

In the interests of brevity, we restrict ourselves to analyses of DNMTS performance at delays varying from 0.1 to 18.0 sec. In each of the experiments shown in Figure 39.2, animals were pretrained with standard procedures on a DNMTS task. Those performing at criterion were then matched for performance, assigned by block randomization to experimental treatments, recovered, and retrained first for 400 trials of the DNMTS task at a retention interval of 3.0 sec and then for a series of trials (100 to 150 in different studies) at each of the delays indicated in Figure 39.2. The procedures differed between studies in the amount of pretreatment training (affecting the overall level of performance) and the retention intervals tested. To compensate for differences in response latency, the analyses in Figure 39.2 exclude responses made at latencies of 3.0 sec or longer. For purposes of comparison, panel A shows the effects of PTD treatment on this task (data from Robinson & Mair, in press).

Panels B, C, and E show the results from animals with histologically verified radiofrequency (RF) lesions involving the medial zone of the IML lesion ($\pm$ 0.5 mm from midline) (M-IML); the lateral zone of the IML lesion (0.5 to 1.5 mm from midline) (L-IML); the medial mammillary body nuclei (MBodies); the medial IML and mammillary body sites combined (MT/MB); and fornix (data from Mair & Lacourse, in press). Only the L-IML and fornix lesions impaired DNMTS performance, and only the L-IML site produced a deficit comparable in severity to that of recovered PTD animals. The animals shown in panels B, C, and E were also trained with a staircase procedure, in which retention intervals were varied according to performance to determine the critical delay at which individual animals were 75% accurate on the DNMTS task. By this measure, only the L-IML group was impaired, responding at 75% accuracy at a significantly shorter delay (mean = 7.5 sec), than controls (mean = 17.8 sec), animals with M-IML lesions (mean = 18.0 sec), animals with MBody lesions

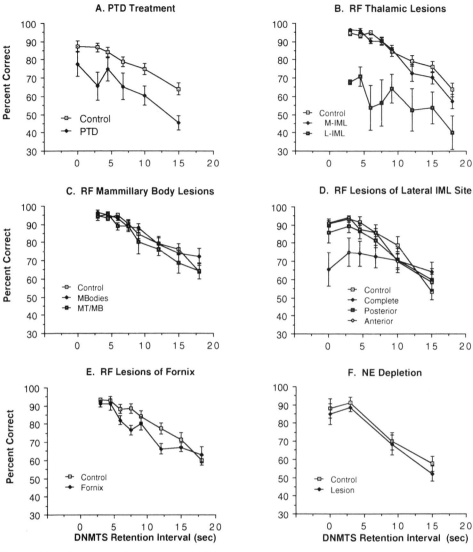

FIGURE 39.2. DNMTS performance (mean ± *SEM*) as a function of memory retention interval. Results are shown for choice responses made at short latency (0 to 2.9 sec after end of delay interval) in a series of trials (100 to 150 in different studies) at each of the delays indicated on the individual graphs. Panel **A** shows the impairment of the PTD group, compared to pair-fed controls. Panels **B**, **C**, **D**, and **E** show the effects of radiofrequency lesions (histologically verified in **B**, **C**, and **E**). The studies shown in **B** and **C** used a common control group and demonstrated impairment following lesions of the lateral IML site (L-IML) but not midline IML site (M-IML), mammillary body site (MBodies), or combined midline and mammillary body sites (MT/MB). Panel **E** shows the effects of fornix lesions. This group showed a deficit that was statistically significant, but not as severe as that observed following either PTD treatment or L-IML lesions. Panel **D** shows results from a study that verified the effects of the L-IML lesion and showed that DNMTS performance was not impaired by lesions of either the anterior or posterior half of the L-IML site. Panel **F** shows that 6-OHDA depletion of cortical NE, far more extensive than reported for any recovered PTD animal, does not affect DNMTS performance. The data are from the following sources: Panel **A**, Robinson and Mair (in press); panels **B**, **C**, and **E**, Mair and Lacourse (in press); panel **D**, Mair, Robinson, Koger, Fox, and Zhang (in press); and panel **F**, Koger and Mair (in press).

(mean = 16.7 sec), animals with MT/MB lesions (mean = 19.3 sec), and animals with fornix lesions (mean = 14.7 sec). By all measures examined, the L-IML lesion reproduced the DNMTS deficit observed (and described above) for animals recovered from PTD treatment.

The failure of fornix lesions to produce a substantial DNMTS deficit is compatible with at least two possibilities. First, the fornix lesions produced in our studies may have been insufficient to disrupt working memory, although they were comparable to those reported by others to disrupt radial arm maze performance (Olton, Becker, & Handelmann, 1979). Second, the working memory impairments produced by lesions of medial thalamus and fornix may depend on the type of information required to perform a task. Successful performance on radial arm maze tasks requires that information be stored to recall which alleys have already been entered on a single daily trial, but not the order in which they were entered. Failure on this task may reflect an inability to recall stimulus information (or spatial relationships) by which alleys may be distinguished. These are functions that others have ascribed to the hippocampal system (see Eichenbaum, Otto, & Cohen, in press) and that might be expected to be particularly sensitive to fornix lesions. The success of PTD animals on the radial arm maze may reflect a preserved capacity to store information by which alleyways can be distinguished. In the DNMTS task we use, animals visit each of the two choice ports repeatedly (50 times/session), and a successful choice response requires discriminating which of the two ports was visited most recently (on the preceding sample trial). Failure on this task may result from an inability to discriminate temporal recency or to hold stimulus information "on-line." These are functions that others have ascribed to frontal cortex (see Fuster, 1980; Goldman-Rakic, 1987) and that might be expected to be disrupted by lesions of MDn and IML that denervate these areas (Mair et al., 1989). The relatively preserved performance of fornix-lesioned animals on this task may reflect the effects of extensive pretreatment training and the limited sensory information required to distinguish between the two ports in this task.

We have recently replicated the effect of the L-IML lesion on DNMTS in a study (Figure 39.2), panel D; data from Mair, Robinson, Koger, Fox, & Zhang, in press) comparing the effects of complete L-IML lesions to lesions limited to the anterior or posterior half of this site. Animals with either anterior or posterior lesions performed at a level comparable to that of controls, and significantly better than animals with complete IML lesions. Taken together, our experimental analyses support the following conclusions:

1. A lesion of the L-IML site (involving the mediodorsal, central lateral, and paracentral nuclei) produces a DNMTS deficit that is indistinguishable from that produced by PTD treatment.

2. Animals receiving PTD treatment, but protected from the IML lesion by MK-801, are unimpaired on the DNMTS task.

3. Lesions destroying tissue in either the anterior or posterior halves of the L-IML site are without effect on DNMTS performance.

4. DNMTS performance is not affected by lesions of midline thalamus, or by depletion of forebrain NE systems through dorsal bundle 6-OHDA treatment (Figure 39.2, panel F; data from Koger & Mair, in press).

5. DNMTS performance is not affected by lesions of mammillary bodies and is only marginally impaired by fornix lesions. This indicates that disruption of limbic pathways through mammillary bodies to thalamus cannot account for the DNMTS deficit of the PTD model.

6. The L-IML lesions undoubtedly affect a number of pathways. Determining the critical substrate of this DNMTS deficit awaits further experimentation.

ACKNOWLEDGMENTS

The work described in this chapter was supported by Grant No. RO-1 NS26855 from the National Institute of Neurological and Communicative Disorders and Stroke, and by Medical Research funds from the Department of Veterans Affairs to Robert G. Mair.

REFERENCES

Aggleton, J. P., Nicol, R. M., Huston, A. E., & Fairbairn, A. F. (1988). The performance of amnesic subjects on tests of experimental amnesia in animals: Delayed matching to sample and concurrent learning. *Neuropsychologia, 26*(2), 265–272.

Barbizet, J. (1963). Defect of memorizing of hippocampal–mammillary origin: A review. *Journal of Neurology, Neurosurgery and Psychiatry, 26,* 127–135.

Brion, S., & Mikol, J. (1978). Atteinte du noyau lateral dorsal du thalamus et syndrome de Korsakoff alcoolique. *Journal of the Neurological Sciences, 38,* 249–261.

Delay, J., Brion, S., & Elissalde, B. (1958). Corps mammillaires et syndrome Korsakoff: Etude anatomique de huit cas de syndrome Korsakoff d'origine alcoolique sans altérations significatives du cortex cérébral. *Press Médicale, 66,* 1849–1852, 1965–1968.

Eichenbaum, H., Otto, T., & Cohen, N. J. (in press). The hippocampus: What does it do? *Annual Review of Neuroscience, 15.*

Fuster, J. M. (1980). *The prefrontal cortex.* New York: Raven Press.

Goldman-Rakic, P. S. (1987). Circuitry of primate prefrontal cortex and regulation of behavior by representational memory. In F. Plum (Ed.), *Handbook of physiology: Section 1. The nervous system Vol. 5. Higher functions of the brain* (pp. 373–417). Bethesda, MD: American Physiological Society.

Heroux, M., & Butterworth, R. F. (1988). Reversible alterations of cerebral g-aminobutyric acid in pyrithiamine-treated rats: Implications for the pathogenesis of Wernicke's encephalopathy. *Journal of Neurochemistry, 33,* 575–577.

Joyce, E. M. (1987). The neurochemistry of Korsakoff's syndrome. In S. M. Stahl, S. D. Iversen, & E. C. Goodman (Eds.), *Cognitive neurochemistry* (pp. 327–345). Oxford: Oxford University Press.

Kessler, J., Markowitsch, H., & Otto, B. (1982). Subtle but distinct impairments of rats with chemical lesions in the thalamic mediodorsal nucleus, tested in a radial arm maze. *Journal of Comparative and Physiological Psychology, 96,* 712–720.

Knoth, R. L., & Mair, R. G. (1991). Rats recovered from pyrithiamine-induced thiamine deficiency (PTD) treatment respond more slowly and less accurately in a pre-trained non-matching to sample task. *Behavioral Neuroscience, 105,* 375–385.

Koger, S. M., & Mair, R. G. (in press). Depletion of cortical norepinephrine in rats by 6-OHDA does not impair performance on a pretrained delayed non-matching to sample task. *Behavioral Neuroscience.*

Kolb, B., Pittman, K., Sutherland, R. J., & Whishaw, I. Q. (1982). Dissociation of the contributions of the prefrontal cortex and dorsomedial thalamic nucleus to spatially guided behavior in the rat. *Behavioural Brain Research, 6,* 365–378.

Kopelman, M. D. (1987). How far could cholinergic depletion account for the memory deficits of Alzheimer-type dementia or the alcoholic Korsakoff syndrome? In S. M. Stahl, S. D. Iversen, & E. C. Goodman (Eds.), *Cognitive Neurochemistry* (pp. 303–326). Oxford: Oxford University Press.

Langlais, P. J., & Mair, R. G. (1990). Protective effects of the glutamate antagonist MK-801 on pyrithiamine induced lesions and amino acid changes in rat brain. *Journal of Neuroscience, 10,* 1664–1674.

Langlais, P. J., Mair, R. G., Anderson, C. D. & McEntee, W. J. (1987). Monoamines and metabolites in cortex and subcortical structures: Normal distribution and the effects of thiamine deficiency in the rat. *Brain Research, 421,* 140–149.

Langlais, P. J., Mair, R. G., Anderson, C. D., & McEntee, W. J. (1988). Long-lasting changes in regional brain amino acids and monoamines in recovered pyrithiamine treated rats. *Neurochemical Research, 13,* 1199–1206.

Mair, R. G., Anderson, C. D., Langlais, P. J., & McEntee, W. J. (1985). Thiamine deficiency depletes cortical norepinephrine and impairs learning processes in the rat. *Brain Research, 360,* 273–284.

Mair, R. G., Anderson, C. D., Langlais, P. J., & McEntee, W. J. (1988). Behavioral impairments, brain lesions, and monoaminergic activity in the rat following recovery from a bout of thiamine deficiency. *Behavioural Brain Research, 27,* 223–239.

Mair, R. G., Anderson, C. D., & McEntee, W. J. (1982). Unpublished observations.

Mair, R. G., Ferguson, A. E., Knoth, R. L., & Langlais, P. J. (1989). Widespread cortical denervation following recovery from thiamine deficiency. *Society for Neuroscience Abstracts, 15,* 1104.

Mair, R. G., Knoth, R., Rabchenuk, S., & Langlais, P. J. (1991). Impairment of olfactory, auditory, and spatial serial reversal learning in rats recovered from pyrithiamine induced thiamine deficiency (PTD) treatment. *Behavioral Neuroscience, 105,* 360–374.

Mair, R. G., & Lacourse, D. M. (in press). Radiofrequency lesions of thalamus produce delayed non-matching to sample impairments comparable to pyrithiamine-induced thiamine deficiency. *Behavioral Neuroscience.*

Mair, R. G., Otto, T., Knoth, R., Rabchenuk, S., & Langlais, P. J. (1991). An analysis of aversively conditioned learning and memory in rats recovered from pyrithiamine induced thiamine deficiency (PTD) treatment. *Behavioral Neuroscience, 105,* 351–359.

Mair, R. G., Robinson, J. K., Koger, S. M., Fox, G. D., & Zhang, Y. P. (in press). Delayed non-matching to sample is impaired by extensive, but not by limited lesions of thalamus in the rat. *Behavioral Neuroscience.*

Mair, W. P. G., Warrington, E. K., & Weiskrantz, L. (1979). Memory disorders in Korsakoff's psychosis: A neuropathological and neuropsychological investigation of two cases. *Brain, 102,* 749–783.

Malamud, N., & Skillicorn, S.A. (1956). Relationship between the Wernicke and Korsakoff syndrome. *Archives of Neurology and Psychiatry, 76,* 585–596.

Mayes, A. R., Meudell, P. R., Mann, D., & Pickering, A. (1988). Location of lesion in Korsakoff's syndrome: Neuropsychological and neuropathological data on two patients. *Cortex, 24,* 367–388.

McEntee, W. J., Biber, M. P., Perl, D. P., & Benson, D. F. (1976). Diencephalic amnesia: A reappraisal. *Journal of Neurology, Neurosurgery and Psychiatry, 39,* 436–441.

McEntee, W. J., & Mair, R. G. (1984). Some behavioral consequences of neurochemical deficits in Korsakoff psychosis. In L. R. Squire & N. Butters (Eds.), *Neuropsychology of memory* (1st ed., pp. 224–235). New York: Guilford Press.

McEntee, W. J., & Mair, R. G. (1990). The Korsakoff syndrome: A neurochemical perspective. *Trends in Neurosciences, 13,* 340–344.

Olton, D. S., Becker, J. T., & Handelmann, G. E. (1979). Hippocampus, space, and memory. *Behavioral and Brain Sciences, 2,* 313–322.

Oscar-Berman, M. (1984). Comparative neuropsychology and alcoholic Korsakoff disease. In L. R. Squire & N. Butters (Eds.), *Neuropsychology of memory* (1st ed., pp. 194–202). New York: Guilford Press.

Oscar-Berman, M., & Bonner, R. T. (1985). Matching and delayed matching to sample performance as measures of visual processing, selective attention, and memory in aging and alcoholic individuals. *Neuropsychologia, 23*(5), 639–651.

Robinson, J. K., & Mair, R. G. (in press). MK-801 prevents brain lesions and delayed non-matching to sample deficits produced by pyrithiamine-induced encephalopathy in rats. *Behavioral Neuroscience.*

Shimamura, A. P., Jernigan, T. L., & Squire, L. R. (1988). Korsakoff's syndrome: Radiological (CT) findings and neuropsychological correlates. *Journal of Neuroscience, 8,* 4400–4410.

Squire, L. R., Amaral, D. G., & Press, G. A. (1990). Magnetic resonance imaging of the hippocampal formation and mammillary nuclei distinguish medial temporal lobe and diencephalic amnesia. *Journal of Neuroscience, 10,* 3106–3117.

Squire, L. R., & Amaral, D. G., Zola-Morgan, S., Kritchevsky, M., Press, G. A., & Moore, R. Y. (1989). Description of brain injury in the amnesic patient N.A. based on magnetic resonance imaging. *Experimental Neurology, 105,* 23–35.

Squire, L. R., Zola-Morgan, S., & Chen, K. S. (1988). Human amnesia and animals models of amnesia: Performance of amnesic patients on tests designed for the monkey. *Behavioral Neuroscience, 102*(2), 210–221.

Thompson, S. G., & McGeer, E. G. (1985). GABA-transaminase and glutamic acid decarboxylase changes in the brain of rats treated with pyrithiamine. *Neurochemical Research, 10*, 1653–1660.

Victor, M., Adams, R. D., & Collins, G. H. (1989). *The Wernicke–Korsakoff syndrome* (rev. ed.). Philadelphia: F. A. Davis.

von Cramon, D. Y., Hebel, N., & Schuri, U. (1985). A contribution to the anatomical basis of thalamic amnesia. *Brain, 108*, 993–1008.

Williams, M., & Pennypacker, J. (1954). Memory disturbances in third ventricle tumors. *Journal of Neurology, Neurosurgery and Psychiatry, 17*, 115–123.

40

Emotional Memories in the Brain

JOSEPH LeDOUX

Introduction

Animals (including people) need to remember many things about their environment. To do this, they draw upon one or more of the various learning (information acquisition) and memory (information storage) mechanisms that nature has provided their species with. In some instances, learning requires multiple encounters with the relevant information in order to firmly establish a long-lasting memory, whereas in others the learning is accomplished in a single encounter (or very few). Included in the class of rapidly learned experiences are those resulting from exposure to stimuli that cause bodily harm or threaten to do so. It only takes one touch of a hot stove to make one forever cautious in the kitchen. Slow learning about harmful situations is potentially so costly that any species lacking such a mechanism would probably not fare well.

Aversive classical conditioning (fear conditioning) procedures are useful for examining the neural mechanisms underlying memories about painful and otherwise dangerous situations. For example, a laboratory rat, when placed in a small test chamber, will at first orient to a novel sound, but quickly begins to ignore the sound with repeated presentations. However, if the same sound now being ignored is followed by a brief exposure to electric current through the grid floor of the chamber, subsequent presentations of the sound are no longer ignored. The rat will now exhibit characteristic signs of fear when the sound comes on ("freezing" behavior, piloerection, changes in blood pressure and heart rate, release of adrenal hormones into the circulation, etc.). One pairing of the sound, or conditioned stimulus (CS), with the footshock, or unconditioned stimulus (US), is often sufficient to endow the CS with emotion-arousing properties. And once established, such emotional associations, stored in the brain as memories of the experience-dependent affective significance of the CS, are difficult to eliminate through traditional extinction processes.

Fear conditioning can be studied in many ways. Some of the more common methods involve "simple conditioning," where an explicit CS is paired with the US; "discriminated conditioning," where two CSs are used (one paired with the US and the other not); "contextual conditioning," where the conditioning apparatus serves as a background or continuously present CS; and various other design complications, such as "blocking," "overshadowing," or "latent inhibition."

Experimental studies by several laboratories have contributed greatly to our understanding of the neuroanatomy of various forms of fear conditioning in mammalian species (e.g., Kapp, Pascoe, & Bixler, 1984; Kapp, Wilson, Pascoe, Supple, & Whalen, 1990; Davis, Hitchcock, & Rosen, 1987; LeDoux, 1986, 1990; Jarrell, Gentile, Romanski, McCabe, & Schneiderman, 1987; Smith, Astley, Devito, Stein, & Walsh, 1980). In this chapter, work from my laboratory on the neurobiology of simple fear conditioning is described.

Simple Fear Conditioning: The Procedure

In most of our work, my colleagues and I have studied the consequences of pairing a neutral auditory stimulus with footshock in laboratory rats. The pairing typically takes place in a standard rodent conditioning chamber on one day. The following day, the rat is exposed to the auditory CS in the absence of the US and in a test box that is physically different from the conditioning chamber. This allows us to examine the effects of CS-US pairing independently of contamination from contextual cues that were also present during the pairing. We measure changes in autonomic activity (arterial pressure) and emotional behavior (freezing) produced by the CS, and use these as indices of the efficacy of conditioning. In order to distinguish associatively conditioned responses from sensitized responses, we use appropriate controls for pseudoconditioning (see Iwata, LeDoux, Meeley, Arneric, & Reis, 1986; Iwata & LeDoux, 1988).

Neuroanatomy of Simple Fear Conditioning

The long-term goal of our research is to understand the cellular mechanisms underlying the formation of emotional memories, as typified by memories established experimentally through fear conditioning in the rat. Our working hypothesis is that the critical cellular changes underlying fear conditioning involve physiological modifications in the activity of neurons in one or more stations of the CS processing system, and that these are produced by the convergence of inputs from the US processing system. As a first step in our effort to understand the mechanisms of fear conditioning, we have therefore focused on the identification of the CS pathway.

The CS pathway necessarily involves the primary sensory system that transmits the CS centrally from the peripheral receptor organs that receive the stimulus. We first asked this question: Which components of the sensory projection system—in this case, the auditory system—are involved in CS transmission during simple fear conditioning (LeDoux et al., 1984)? We found that destruction of the auditory cortex bilaterally had little effect on the conditioning process. In contrast, bilateral electrolytic lesions of the thalamo-cortical relay nucleus, the medial geniculate body (MGB), or the main auditory relay station in the midbrain, the inferior colliculus (IC), interfered with conditioning (LeDoux et al., 1984). Thus, the CS is transmitted from the ear through the auditory system to the MGB, but the main known output projection from the MGB, the projection to the auditory cortex, is not the next link.

Anatomical tracing studies demonstrated that in addition to its projection to the auditory cortex, the MGB projects to subcortical areas of the forebrain, including the amygdala and striatum (LeDoux et al., 1984; LeDoux, Ruggiero, & Reis, 1985). Although excitotoxic lesions of the striatum had no effect on the development of the conditioned associations, excitotoxic lesions of the amygdala were as disruptive as lesions of the MGB (Iwata et al., 1986).

Earlier, Kapp, Frysinger, Gallagher, and Haselton (1979) found that lesions of the central nucleus of the amygdala (ACE) interfered with fear conditioning. ACE was thus the targeted area in our lesion study, and the effective lesions consistently damaged ACE (Iwata et al., 1986). In order to determine whether ACE might be the direct recipient of inputs from the auditory thalamus, we injected a retrograde axonal tracer into ACE. The thalamic cells of origin of the projection turned out to be displaced medially with respect to the MGB. This medial area does not receive projections from IC (LeDoux, Ruggiero, Forest, Stornetta, & Reis, 1987), and thus is unlikely to be part of an auditory transmission pathway. However, injections in the lateral nucleus of the amygdala (AL) produced retrograde transport to the medial division of MGB (MGM) and in the adjacent posterior intralaminar nucleus (PIN), both of which receive inputs from the IC (LeDoux et al., 1987; LeDoux, Farb, & Ruggiero, 1990).

Given that AL is the terminal field of a colliculo-thalamo-amygdala auditory projection, we examined whether lesions of AL would replicate the effects of MGB lesions (LeDoux, Cicchetti, Xagoraris, & Romanski, 1990). This was in fact found. Interestingly, AL projects to ACE by several routes: directly (Krettek & Price, 1978a; Nitecka & Frotscher, 1989), as well as by intermediate stops in the basolateral (Pitkänen & Amaral, 1991; Krettek & Price, 1978a) and intercalated nuclei of the amygdala (Millhouse, 1986). ACE has widespread connections with brainstem areas controlling somatomotor and autonomic response systems (Schwaber, Kapp, Higgins, & Rapp, 1982; Krettek & Price, 1978b; Price & Amaral, 1981). Thus, on anatomical grounds, AL appears to be the sensory interface of the amygdala and ACE the motor interface.

The involvement of ACE as an interface with response control systems was confirmed in studies examining the effects of lesions of different projections of ACE (LeDoux, Iwata, Cicchetti, & Reis, 1988). Lesions of the lateral hypothalamic area interfered with the arterial pressure but not the freezing response, whereas lesions of the midbrain central gray interfered with the freezing but not the arterial pressure response. Descending connections of these areas suggest that they serve as premotor links in the expression of autonomic and somatomotor conditioned responses.

In additional studies, we have shown that this general scheme involving the subcortical transmission of sensory inputs to the amygdala also applies to simple fear conditioning with a visual CS (LeDoux, Romanski, & Xagoraris, 1989). The exact origin of the subcortical visual inputs to the amygdala remains to be identified.

The neural pathway through which an auditory CS elicits changes in arterial pressure and freezing behavior following simple fear conditioning is summarized in Figure 40.1. The identification of such a pathway suggests important functional distinctions among the various structures it includes. Thus, the amygdaloid nuclei are in a

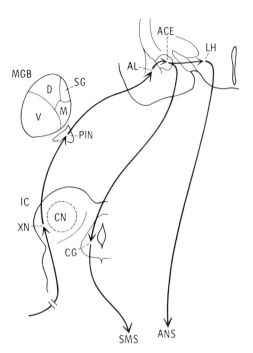

FIGURE 40.1. Neural pathways underlying fear conditioning with an auditory CS. Acoustic inputs are relayed through the auditory system to the level of the medial geniculate body (MGB). The posterior intralaminar nucleus (PIN), which is adjacent to and possibly related to the medial division (M) of MGB, transmits the signal to the lateral nucleus of the amygdala (AL). By way of connections from AL to the central nucleus of the amygdala (ACE), the CS comes to control emotional responses. Projections from ACE to the lateral nucleus of the hypothalamus (LH) are involved in the expression of autonomic conditioned responses, whereas projections from ACE to the central gray (CG) are involved in the expression of conditioned emotional behavior. These circuits bypass the neocortex and may mediate certain aspects of emotional processing, independently of the higher cognitive processes organized at the cortical level.

pivotal position in this pathway, as they stand between the sensory systems on the one hand and the motor systems on the other. Unit recording studies suggest that physiological changes are likely to occur throughout the circuit (Ryugo & Weinberger, 1978; Disterhoft & Stuart, 1976; Gabriel, Slatwick, & Miller, 1976; Pascoe & Kapp, 1985; LeGal LaSalle & Ben-Ari, 1981; Ono, Nakamura, Nishijo, & Fukuda, 1986; Linseman & Olds, 1973). However, while changes in the sensory system are likely to be involved in the sharpening of sensory responsivity to the CS and changes in the motor systems in the shaping of the conditioned responses, the changes occurring in the amygdala are sensory and motor-independent, and are likely to involve some integrated emotional learning and memory function. The exact nature of this integrative function is still unknown, but its elucidation will no doubt be a key to understanding the nature of emotional learning and memory processes.

Cellular Mechanisms: First Steps

The foregoing suggests that projections from the MGB to the amygdala are involved in the conversion of sensory into emotional information and may be a locus of cellular plasticity. We have therefore begun to examine the cellular basis of information processing in this projection system.

Anatomical investigations have revealed the cells of origin of the geniculo-amygdala projection contain the excitatory amino acid glutamate (Farb, LeDoux, & Milner, 1989; LeDoux & Farb, 1991). Glutamate is also present in presynaptic terminals in the amygdala (Farb et al., 1989). Furthermore, the presynaptic terminals of the geniculo-amygdala projection make asymmetric synaptic contacts on dendritic spines (LeDoux, Farb, & Milner, 1991). Asymmetric synaptic morphology is believed to be indicative of excitatory synaptic transmission (Gray, 1969). Electrical stimulation of the MGB produces short-latency unit responses in the lateral amygdala (Clugnet, LeDoux, & Morrison, 1990), and high-frequency stimulation of this pathway results in a long-lasting enhancement of synaptic efficacy (Clugnet & LeDoux, 1990).

The neurotransmitter systems underlying synaptic transmission and plasticity in the geniculo-amygdala projection aer unknown at present. However, the presence of the excitatory amino acid glutamate in the projection raises the possibility that gluta-mate mediates excitatory synaptic transmission and synaptic plasticity in this system. Recent studies have in fact shown that injections of hte excitatory amino acid antago-nist AP5 into the lateral/basolateral amygdala disrupts fear conditioning (Miserendino, Sananes, Melia, & Davis, 1990). This is of special significance, since AP5 blocks N-methyl-D-aspartate receptors, which are critically involved in the establishment of long-term synaptic plasticity in hippocampus produced by tetanization of input fibers (e.g., Cotman, Monaghan, & Ganong, 1988). The advantage of the geniculo-amygdala system as a model for studying synaptic plasticity is that it has a known involvement in a well-characterized memory function that has properties similar to those of long-term potentiation: rapid learning produced by stimulation of a discrete neural pathway.

The Information Cascade to the Amygdala: Implications for Emotional Memory

In addition to receiving inputs from sensory thalamus, AL also receives inputs from sensory association cortex. Lesion studies in rabbits have shown the necessity of the auditory cortex for conditioning a discrimination between two auditory stimuli (Jarrell et al., 1987). Moreover, the amygdala is reciprocally connected with the hippocampus (Amaral, 1987). Given that the hippocampus receives integrated, multimodal sensory inputs and is importantly involved in spatial and contextual processing, interconnec-tions between the hippocampus and amygdala might mediate multimodal contextual fear conditioning and other forms of fear learning that depend on higher cognitive functions. Indeed, new evidence suggests that damage to the dorsal hippocampus inteferes selectively with contextual conditioning, leaving the conditioning to an ex-plicit CS (such as the acoustic stimuli usually paired with the US in fear conditioning studies) intact (Phillips & LeDoux, 1992; Kim & Fanselow, 1992). The main difference between explicit CS conditioning and contextual conditioning is that the latter involves the association between the US and continuously present background stimuli that are not "paired" with the US in a time-dependent manner. Contextual stimuli thus predict the general situation in which the US might occur, but, unlike an explicit CS, do not predict the onset of any particular US. It is not known whether these lesion effects reflect the relay of inputs from the amygdala to hippocampus or from hippocampus to amygdala, or perhaps even to a neural loop between these structures. Nevertheless, the demonstration of differential involvement of amygdala and hippocampus in cued and contextual fear conditioning offers a new model for understanding how these limbic forebrain regions interact in the mediation of higher brain functions.

Conclusion

AL is a focal point in an emotional learning network. It is interconnected with sensory (thalamic), perceptual (neocortical), and higher cognitive (hippocampal) processing areas, and may be a locus where plastic changes can be generated in association with information transfer from each of these regions. Our hope is that through studies of the organization of this system of emotional memory in animals, we can glean some insights into the nature of emotional memory function and dysfunction in humans.

REFERENCES

Amaral, D. G. (1987). Memory: Anatomical organization of candidate brain regions. In F. Plum (Ed.), *Handbook of physiology: Section 1. The nervous system. Vol. 5. Higher functions of the brain* (pp. 211–294). Bethesda, MD: American Physiological Society.

Clugnet, M. C., & LeDoux, J. E. (1990). Synaptic plasticity in fear conditioning circuits: Induction of LTP in the lateral nucleus of the amygdala by stimulation of the medial geniculate body. *Journal of Neuroscience, 10,* 2818–2824.

Clugnet, M. C., LeDoux, J. E., & Morrison, S. F. (1990). Unit responses levoked in the amygdala and striatum by electrical stimulation of the medial geniculate body. *Journal of Neuroscience, 10,* 1055–1061.

Cotman, C. W., Monaghan, D. T., & Ganong, A. H. (1988). Excitatory amino acid neurotransmission: NMDA receptors and Hebb-type synaptic plasticity. *Annual Review of Neuroscience, 11,* 61–80.

Davis, M., Hitchcock, J. M., & Rosen, J. B. (1987). Anxiety and the amygdala: Pharmacological and anatomical analysis of the fear-potentiated startle paradigm. In G. H. Bower (Ed.), *The psychology of learning and motivation* (pp. 263–305). San Diego: Academic Press.

Disterhoft, J., & Stuart, D. (1976). Trial sequence of changed unit activity in auditory system of alert rat during conditioned response acquisition and extinction. *Journal of Neurophysiology, 39,* 266–281.

Farb, C. F., LeDoux, J. E., & Milner, T. A. (1989). Glutamate is present in medial geniculate body neurons that project to lateral amygdala and in lateral amygdala presynaptic terminals. *Society for Neuroscience Abstracts, 15,* 354.16.

Gabriel, M., Slatwick, S. E., & Miller, J. D. (1976). Multiple unit activity of the rabbit medial geniculate nucleus in conditioning, extinction, and reversal. *Physiological Psychology, 4,* 124–134.

Gray, E. G. (1969). Electron microscopy of excitatory and inhibitory synapses: A brief review. In K. Akert & P. G. Waser (Eds.), *Progress in brain research: Vol. 31. Mechanisms of synaptic transmission* (pp. 141–155). Amsterdam: Elsevier.

Iwata, J., & LeDoux, J. E. (1988). Dissociation of associative and nonassociative concommitants of classical fear conditioning in the freely behaving rat. *Behavioral Neuroscience, 102,* 66–76.

Iwata, J., LeDoux, J. E., Meeley, M. P., Arneric, S., & Reis, D. J. (1986). Intrinsic neurons in the amygdaloid field projected to by the medial geniculate body mediate emotional responses conditioned to acoustic stimuli. *Brain Research, 383,* 195–214.

Jarrell, T. W., Gentile, C. G., Romanski, L. M., McCabe, P. M., & Schneiderman, N. (1987). Involvement of cortical and thalamic auditory regions in retention of differential bradycardia conditioning to acoustic conditioned stimulii in rabbits. *Brain Research, 412,* 285–294.

Kapp, B. S., Frysinger, R. C., Gallagher, M., & Haselton, J. (1979). Amygdala central nucleus lesions: Effect on heart rate conditioning in the rabbit. Physiology and Behavior, 23, 1109–1117.

Kapp, B. S., Pascoe, J. P., & Bixler, M. A. (1984). The amygdala: A neuroanatomical systems approach to its contribution to aversive conditioning. In L. R. Squire & N. Butters (Eds.), *Neuropsychology of memory* (1st ed., pp. 473–488). New York: Guilford Press.

Kapp, B. S., Wilson, A., Pascoe, J., Supple, W., & Whalen, P. J. (1990). A neuroanatomical systems analysis of conditioned bradycardia in the rabbit. In M. Gabriel & J. Moore (Eds.), *Learning and computational neuroscience: Foundations of adaptive networks* (pp. 53–90). Cambridge, MA: MIT Press.

Kim, J. J., & Fanselow, M. S. (1992). Modality-specific retrograde amnesia of fear. *Science, 256,* 675–677.

Krettek, J. E., & Price, J. L. (1978a). A description of the amygdaloid complex in the rat and cat with observations on intra-amygdaloid axonal connections. *Journal of Comparative Neurology, 178,* 255–280.

Krettek, J. E., & Price, J. L. (1978b). Amygdaloid projections to subcortical structures within the basal forebrain and brainstem in the rat and cat. *Journal of Comparative Neurology, 178,* 225–254.

LeDoux, J. E. (1986). Sensory systems and emotion. *Integrative Psychiatry, 4,* 237–248.

LeDoux, J. E. (1987). Emotion. In F. Plum (Ed.), *Handbook of physiology: Section 1. The nervous system. Vol. 5. Higher functions of the brain* (pp. 419–460). Bethesda, MD: American Physiological Society.

LeDoux, J. E. (1990). Information flow from sensation to emotion: Plasticity in the neural computation of stimulus value. In M. Gabriel & J. Moore (Eds.), *Learning and computational neuroscience: Foundations of adaptive networks* (pp. 3–51). Cambridge, MA: Bradford Books/MIT Press.

LeDoux, J. E., Cicchetti, P., Xagoraris, A., & Romanski, L. R. (1990). The lateral amygdaloid nucleus: Sensory interface of the amygdala in fear conditioning. *Journal of Neuroscience, 10,* 1062–1069.

LeDoux, J. E., & Farb, C. R. (1991). Neurons of the acoustic thalamus that project to the amygdala contain glutamate. *Neuroscience Letters, 134,* 145–149.

LeDoux, J. E., Farb, C. R., & Milner, T. A. (1991). Ultrastructure and synaptic associations of auditory thalamo-amygdala projections in the rat. *Experimental Brain Research, 85,* 577–586.

LeDoux, J. E., Farb, C. F., & Ruggiero, D. A. (1990). Topographic organization of neurons in the acoustic thalamus that project to the amygdala. *Journal of Neuroscience, 10,* 1043–1054.

LeDoux, J. E., Iwata, J., Cicchetti, P., & Reis, D. J. (1988). Different projections of the central amygdaloid nucleus mediate autonomic and behavioral correlates of conditioned fear. *Journal of Neuroscience, 8,* 2517–2529.

LeDoux, J. E., Romanski, L. M., & Xagoraris, A. E. (1989). Indelibility of subcortical emotional memories. *Journal of Cognitive Neuroscience, 1,* 238–243.

LeDoux, J. E., Ruggiero, D. A., Forest, R., Stornetta, R., & Reis, D. J. (1987). Topographic organization of convergent projections to the thalamus from the inferior colliculus and spinal cord in the rat. *Journal of Comparative Neurology, 264,* 123–146.

LeDoux, J. E., Ruggiero, D. A., & Reis, D. J. (1985). Projections to the subcortical forebrain from anatomically defined regions of the medial geniculate body in the rat. *Journal of Comparative Neurology, 242,* 182–213.

LeDoux, J. E., Sakaguchi, A., & Reis, D. J. (1984). Subcortical efferent projections of the medial geniculate nucleus mediate emotional responses conditioned by acoustic stimuli. *Journal of Neuroscience, 4*(3), 683–698.

Le Gal La Salle, G., & Ben-Ari, Y. (1981). Unit activity in the amygdaloid complex: A review. In Y. Ben-Ari (Ed.), *The amygdaloid complex* (pp. 227–237). Amsterdam: Elsevier/North-Holland.

Linseman, M., & Olds, J. (1973). Activity changes in rat hypothalamus, preoptic area, and striatum associated with Pavlovian conditioning. *Journal of Neurophysiology, 36,* 1038–1050.

Millhouse, O. E. (1986). The intercalated cells of the amygdala. *Journal of Comparative Neurology, 247,* 246–271.

Miserendino, M. J. D., Sananes, C. B., Melia, K. R., & Davis, M. (1990). Blocking of acquisition but not expression of conditioned fear-potentiated startle by NMDA antagonists in the amygdala. *Nature, 345,* 716–718.

Nitecka, L., & Frotscher, M. (1989). Organization and synaptic interconnections of GABAergic and cholinergic elements in the rat amygdaloid nuclei: Single- and double-immunolabeling studies. *Journal of Comparative Neurology, 279,* 470–488.

Ono, T., Nakamura, K., Nishijo, H., & Fukuda, M. (1986). Hypothalamic neuron involvement in integration of reward, aversion, and cue signals. *Journal of Neurophysiology, 56,* 63–79.

Pascoe, J. P., & Kapp, B. S. (1985). Electrophysiological characteristics of amygdaloid central nucleus neurons during Pavlovian fear conditioning in the rabbit. *Behavioural Brain Research, 16,* 117–133.

Phillips, R. G., & LeDoux, J. E. (1992). Differential contribution of the amygdala and hippocampus to cued and contextual fear conditioning. *Behavioral Neuroscience, 106,* 274–285.

Pitkänen, A., & Amaral, D. G. (1991). Demonstration of projections from the lateral nucleus to the basal nucleus of the amygdala: A PHA-L study in the monkey. *Experimental Brain Research, 83,* 465–470.

Price, J. L., & Amaral, D. G. (1981). An autoradiographic study of the projections of the central nucleus of the monkey amygdala. *Journal of Neuroscience, 1,* 1242–1259.

Ryugo, D. K., & Weinberger, N. M. (1978). Differential plasticity of morphologically distinct neuron populations in the medial geniculate body of the cat during classical conditioning. *Behavioral Biology, 22,* 275–301.

Schwaber, J. S., Kapp, B. S., Higgins, G. A., & Rapp, P. R. (1982). Amygdaloid and basal forebrain direct connections with the nucleus of the solitary tract and the dorsal motor nucleus. *Journal of Neuroscience, 2* 1424–1438.

Smith, O. A., Astley, C. A., Devito, J. L., Stein, J. M., & Walsh, R. E. (1980). Functional analysis of hypothalamic control of the cardiovascular responses accompanying emotional behavior. *Federation Proceedings, 29,* 2487–2494.

41

Analysis of Aversive Memories Using the Fear-Potentiated Startle Paradigm

MICHAEL DAVIS

Introduction

I can't get the memories out of my mind! The images come flooding back in vivid detail, triggered by the most inconsequential things, like a door slamming or the smell of stir-fried pork. Last night, I went to bed, was having a good sleep for a change. Then in the early morning a storm front passed through and there was a bolt of crackling thunder. I awoke instantly, frozen in fear. I am right back in Vietnam, in the middle of the monsoon season at my guard post. I am sure I'll get hit in the next volley and convinced I will die. My hands are freezing, yet sweat pours from my entire body. I feel each hair on the back of my neck standing on end. I can't catch my breath and my heart is pounding. I smell a damp sulfur smell. Suddenly I see what's left of my buddy Troy, his head on a bamboo platter, sent back to our camp by the Viet Cong. Propaganda messages are stuffed between his clenched teeth. The next bolt of lightning and clap of thunder makes me jump so much that I fall to the floor. . . . (Paraphrased from conversations with Dr. R. L. Gelman, Department of Psychiatry, Yale University School of Medicine)

Perhaps there are no more vivid memories than those stored in the brains of soldiers who have experienced excruciatingly horrible combat situations. Witness the account above of the 49-year-old Vietnam veteran who cannot hear a clap of thunder, see an Oriental woman, or touch a bamboo placemat without re-experiencing the sight of his decapitated friend. Even though this occurred in a faraway place more than 27 years ago, the memory is still vivid in every detail and continues to produce the same state of hyperarousal and fear as it did on that fateful day.

Once called "combat fatigue," "war neurosis," or "shell shock," intense trauma of this sort is now known to produce vivid memories that can last a lifetime. They can be triggered by stimuli that were associated with the original traumatic event, and in some individuals the memories are so intrusive that normal functioning is no longer possible.

What is conditioned fear, and what are the neural mechanisms that allow aversive experiences to result in permanent memories? What parts of the brain are activated by conditioned fear, and what symptoms of the above-described syndrome, now generally called "posttraumatic stress disorder," would be useful to study in the laboratory?

What Is Conditioned Fear?

Conditioned fear is a hypothetical construct that is used to explain the cluster of behavioral effects that are produced by a stimulus formerly associated with an aversive situation. In the example above, the smell of stir-fried pork, formerly associated with severe combat in Vietnam, is sufficient to elicit a state of intense fear. In the laboratory, conditioned fear can be demonstrated by pairing an initially neutral stimulus, such as a light, with an aversive stimulus, such as a footshock. Following a small number of pairings, the light alone comes to elicit a constellation of behaviors that are typically used to define a state of fear in animals. To explain these findings, it is generally assumed (see McAllister & McAllister, 1971) that during light–shock pairings (training session), the shock elicits a variety of behaviors that can be used to infer a central state of fear (unconditioned responses—Figure 41.1). After pairing, the light can now produce the same central fear state and thus the same set of behaviors formerly produced by the shock. When fear is viewed in this way, one can study it with any of several markers, and this is exactly what is done. Some laboratories measure fear by examining freezing; others note changes in blood pressure or heart rate. Our laboratory studies fear conditioning by measuring the elevation in a simple reflex in the presence of a fear-eliciting stimulus. Heightened startle is one of the most prominent symptoms

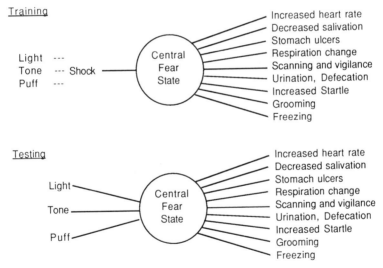

FIGURE 41.1. General scheme believed to occur during classical conditioning using an aversive conditioned stimulus. During training, the aversive stimulus (e.g., shock) activates a central fear system, which produces a constellation of behaviors generally associated with aversive stimuli (unconditioned responses). After consistent pairings of some neutral stimulus (e.g., a light, tone, or puff of air) with shock during the training phase, the neutral stimulus is now capable of producing a similar fear state and hence the same set of behaviors (conditioned responses) formerly only produced by the shock. From "Animal Models of Anxiety Based on Classical Conditioning: The Conditioned Emotional Response (CER) and the Fear-Potentiated Startle Effect" (p. 148) by M. Davis, 1991, in S. E. File (Ed.), *The International Encyclopedia of Pharmacology and Therapeutics* (pp. 147–165). Elmsford, NY: Pergamon Press. Copyright 1991 by Pergamon Press. Reprinted by permission.

of posttraumatic stress disorder, and elevated startle in a state of fear, first described by Brown, Kalish, and Farber in 1951, can be readily studied in both animals and humans. Using this paradigm, my colleagues and I have found that the amygdala is critically involved in the expression of conditioned fear through its direct projection to the brainstem nuclei involved in mediating the startle reflex. The amygdala may also be a site where neural activity produced by conditioned and unconditioned stimuli converge. Hence, the amygdala, and its many efferent projections, may represent a central fear system involved in both the expression and acquisition of conditioned fear.

The Fear-Potentiated Startle Paradigm

In the fear-potentiated startle paradigm, rats are first trained to be fearful of a neutral stimulus, such as a light, by consistently pairing it with an aversive stimulus, such as a footshock (Figure 41.2). Following this training session, the startle reflex is elicited in the presence or the absence of the light. Fear-potentiated startle is said to occur if startle is larger in amplitude when elicited in the presence versus the absence of the light. Potentiated startle occurs only following paired versus unpaired or "random" presentations of the conditioned stimulus and the shock; this indicates that it is a valid measure of classical conditioning (Davis & Astrachan, 1978). In rats, increased startle in the presence of the conditioned stimulus still occurs very reliably at least 1 month after original training, making it appropriate for the study of long-term memory as well (Campeau, Liang, & Davis, 1990; Cassella & Davis, 1985).

Neural Systems Involved in Fear-Potentiated Startle

A major advantage of the fear-potentiated startle paradigm is that fear is measured by a change in a simple reflex. Hence, with potentiated startle, fear is expressed through some neural circuit that is activated by the conditioned stimulus and ultimately impinges on the startle circuit. Figure 41.3 shows a schematic summary diagram of the neural pathways that we believe are required for fear-potentiated startle. These pathways involve convergence of the conditioned visual stimulus and the unconditioned shock stimulus at the lateral and basal amygdala nuclei, which then project to the central nucleus of the amygdala, which then projects directly to a particular nucleus in the acoustic startle pathway.

THE ACOUSTIC STARTLE PATHWAY

In the rat, the latency of acoustic startle is 6 milliseconds (msec) recorded electromyographically in the foreleg, and 8 msec in the hindleg (Ison, McAdam, & Hammond, 1973). This very short latency indicates that only a few synapses may be involved in mediating acoustic startle. Using a variety of techniques (Davis, Gendelman, Tischler, & Gendelman, 1982; Cassella & Davis, 1986), we have proposed that the acoustic startle reflex is mediated by the ventral cochlear nucleus; an area just medial to

TRAINING: LIGHT and SHOCK PAIRED

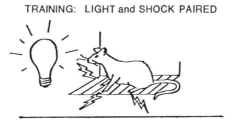

TESTING:

NOISE-ALONE
TRIALS

NORMAL STARTLE (in dark)

LIGHT-NOISE
TRIALS

POTENTIATED STARTLE (in light)

FIGURE 41.2. Cartoon depicting the fear-potentiated startle paradigm. During training a neutral stimulus (conditioned stimulus) such as a light is consistently paired with a footshock. In training, a 3700-msec light is typically paired with a 500-msec, 0.6-mA shock presented 3200 msec after the light onset. During testing, startle is elicited by an auditory stimulus (e.g., a 100-dB burst of white noise) in the presence (light–noise trial type) or absence (noise-alone trial type) of the conditioned stimulus. In testing, the noise burst is typically presented 3200 msec after light onset (i.e., at the same time as the shock was presented in training). It is important to note that the rat does not react with startle to light onset, but only to the noise burst presented alone or 3200 msec after light onset. This is simply a cartoon, so the positions and postures that are pictured may not mimic the actual behavior of the animals. From "Anxiety and the Amygdala: Pharmacological and Anatomical Analysis of the Fear-Potentiated Startle Paradigm" (p. 264) by M. Davis, J. M. Hitchcock, and J. B. Rosen, 1987, in G. H. Bower (Ed.), *The Psychology of Learning and Motivation: Advances in Research and Theory* (Vol. 21, pp. 263–305). Orlando, FL: Academic Press. Copyright 1987 by Academic Press. Reprinted by permission.

the ventral nucleus of the lateral lemniscus (the paralemniscal zone or the central nucleus of the acoustic tract); an area just dorsal to the superior olives in the nucleus reticularis pontis caudalis; as well as motoneurons in the spinal cord. Bilateral lesions using ibotenic acid in each of these nuclei eliminate startle, whereas lesions in a variety of other auditory or motor areas do not. Startle-like responses can be elicited electrically from each of these nuclei, with progressively shorter latencies as the electrode is moved down the pathway.

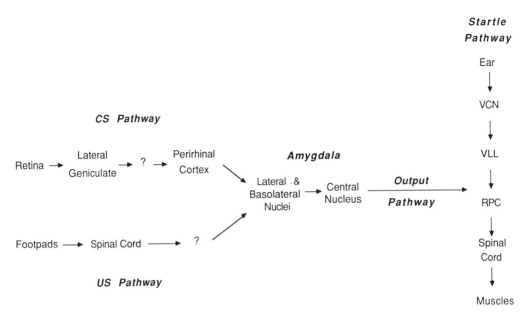

FIGURE 41.3. Proposed neural pathways involved in fear-potentiated startle using a visual conditioned stimulus (CS). Inputs from both the retina, via a projection involving the ventral lateral geniculate nucleus and the perirhinal cortex, and pain afferents in the spinal cord may converge at the lateral and basal nuclei of the amygdala. After being paired with a shock, the light may activate the lateral and basal amygdaloid nuclei, which in turn project to the central amygdaloid nucleus. Activation of the central nucleus of the amygdala may be both necessary and sufficient to facilitate startle through a direct connection to the nucleus reticularis pontis caudalis (RPC), an obligatory part of the acoustic startle pathway. US, unconditioned stimulus; VCN, ventral cochlear nucleus; VLL, ventral nucleus of the lateral lemniscus. From "The Role of the Amygdala in Conditioned Fear" (p. 263) by M. Davis, 1992, in J. Aggleton (Ed.), *The Amygdala: Neurobiological Aspects of Emotion, Memory, and Mental Dysfunction* (pp. 255–305). New York: Wiley-Liss. Copyright 1991 by Wiley–Liss. Reprinted by permission.

THE POINT IN THE STARTLE PATHWAY WHERE FEAR ALTERS
NEURAL TRANSMISSION

We have attempted to determine the point within the startle circuit where the visual conditioned stimulus ultimately modulates transmission following conditioning. To do this, we elicited startle-like responses electrically from various points along the startle pathway before and after presentation of a light that was either paired or not paired with a shock in different groups of rats (Berg & Davis, 1985). These experiments showed that startle elicited electrically from either the ventral cochlear nucleus or the paralemniscal zone was potentiated by a conditioned fear stimulus, whereas elicitation of startle in the nucleus reticularis pontis caudalis or beyond was not. On the basis of these and other data (see below), we have concluded that fear ultimately alters transmission at the nucleus reticularis pontis caudalis.

THE ROLE OF THE AMYGDALA IN FEAR-POTENTIATED STARTLE

In addition to its role in appetitive and perhaps attentional processes (e.g., Gallagher, Graham, & Holland, 1990; Gallagher & Holland, 1991; Kapp, Wilson,

Pascoe, Supple, & Whalen, 1990), converging evidence now indicates that the amygdala, and its many efferent projections, may represent a central fear system involved in
both the expression and acquisition of conditioned fear (Davis, 1992; Gray, 1989;
Gloor, 1960; Kapp & Pascoe, 1986; Kapp, Pascoe, & Bixler, 1984; Kapp et al., 1990;
Sarter & Markowitsch, 1985). Most sensory information enters the amygdala through its
lateral and basal nuclei (Amaral, 1987; LeDoux, Cicchetti, Xagoraris, & Romanski,
1990; Ottersen, 1980; Turner, 1981; Van Hoesen, 1981), which in turn project to the
central nucleus of the amygdala (Amaral, 1987; Aggleton, 1985; Krettek & Price, 1978b;
Millhouse & DeOlmos, 1983; Nitecka & Frotscher, 1989; Nitecka, Amerski, & Narkiewicz, 1981; Ottersen, 1982; Roberts, Woodhams, Polak, & Crow, 1982; Russchen, 1982;
Smith & Millhouse, 1985). The lateral nucleus of the amygdala appears to provide a
critical link involved in fear conditioning using an auditory conditioned stimulus for
relaying auditory information to the central nucleus of the amygdala (LeDoux et al.,
1990).

Lesions of the Amygdala Block Fear-Potentiated Startle. Figure 41.4 shows that
selective destruction of cell bodies in the lateral and basal amygdaloid nuclei following
training caused a complete blockade of fear-potentiated startle using a visual stimulus
(Sananes & Davis, 1992). This was accomplished by local infusion of N-methyl-D-
aspartate (NMDA) into the basal nucleus (Lewis et al., 1989; Crooks, Robinson,
Hatfield, Graham, & Gallagher, 1989), according to procedures generously supplied us
by Dr. Michela Gallagher. In addition, we have found that electrolytic lesions of the
central nucleus of the amygdala (Hitchcock & Davis, 1986) or ibotenic-acid-induced
destruction of cell bodies in the central nucleus (Hitchcock & Davis, 1983) completely

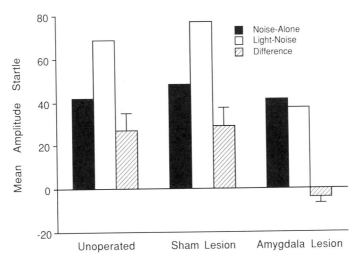

FIGURE 41.4. Mean amplitude startle response on noise-alone trials (black bars) and light–noise trials (white
bars), and the difference between these two trial types (± standard error of the mean), in rats given bilateral
NMDA lesions of the lateral and basal nuclei of the amygdala. From "NMDA Lesions of the Lateral and
Basolateral Nuclei of the Amygdala Block Fear-Potentiated Startle and Shock Sensitization of Startle" (p. 77)
by C. B. Sananes and M. Davis, 1992, *Behavioral Neuroscience, 106,* 72–80. Copyright 1992 by the American
Psychological Association. Reprinted by permission.

block fear-pontentiated startle. A visual prepulse test indicated that the blockade of potentiated startle observed in animals with lesions of the amygdala could not be attributed to the visual impairment. Blockade of fear-potentiated startle by amygdala lesions is not specific to the visual modality, because lesions of the central nucleus of the amygdala also blocked fear-potentiated startle when an auditory conditioned stimulus was used (Hitchcock & Davis, 1987).

Electrical Stimulation of the Amygdala Increases Acoustic Startle. Electrical stimulation of the amygdala has been reported to produce fear-like behaviors in many animals, including humans (see Davis, 1991). We have found that startle is an extremely sensitive index of amygdala stimulation, because low-level electrical stimulation of the amygdala (e.g., 40- to 400-μA, 25-msec trains of 0.1-msec square-wave cathodal pulses) markedly increases acoustic startle amplitude (Rosen & Davis, 1988a), with no obvious signs of behavioral activation during stimulation at these stimulation currents and durations. Moreover, the duration of stimulation is well below that used to produce kindling in rats (Handforth, 1984), so that the effects on startle are not associated with convulsions.

With electrical stimulation of the amygdala, the excitatory effect on startle appears to develop very rapidly. By eliciting startle at various times before and after electrical stimulation of the amygdala, we estimate a transit time of about 5 msec from the amygdala to the startle pathway (Rosen & Davis, 1988b), comparable to the very short latency (2–5 msec) of facilitation of trigeminal motoneurons following amygdala stimulation reported by Ohta (1984). The rapidity of action means that the increase in startle is not secondary to autonomic or hormonal changes that might be produced by amygdala stimulation, because these would have a much longer latency. In addition, electrical stimulation of the amygdala alone does not elicit startle at these currents. Moreover, electrical stimulation of several other nearby brain areas, such as the endopiriform nucleus, fundus striati, internal capsule, or some sites in the basal nucleus of the amygdala, does not increase startle. Finally, using electrically elicited startle, we have found that electrical stimulation of the amygdala appears to modulate startle at the level of the nucleus reticularis pontis caudalis (Rosen & Davis, 1990), as conditioned fear does.

The Role of Various Amygdala Projection Areas in Fear-Potentiated Startle. The central nucleus of the amygdala projects to a variety of brain regions via two major efferent pathways: the stria terminalis and the ventral amygdalo-fugal pathway. The caudal part of the ventral amygdalo-fugal pathway is known to project directly to many parts of the pons, medulla, and spinal cord (Krettek & Price, 1978a; Mizuno, Takahashi, Satoda, & Matsushima, 1985; Post & Mai, 1980; Price & Amaral, 1981; Sandrew, Edwards, Poletti, & Foote, 1986; Schwaber, Kapp, Higgins, & Rapp, 1982). Inagaki, Kawai, Matsuzak, Shiosaka, and Tohyama (1983) reported direct connections between the central nucleus of the amygdala and the exact part of the nucleus reticularis pontis caudalis that is critical for startle (an area just dorsal to the superior olives). We have confirmed this direct connection using anterograde (*Phaseolus vulgaris* leucoagglutin [PHA-L]) and retrograde (Fluro-Gold) tracing techniques (Rosen, Hitchcock, Sananes, Miserendino, & Davis, 1991). In addition, we have found that electrolytic lesions at various points along the output pathway of the amygdala to the startle circuit completely block fear-potentiated startle (Hitchcock & Davis, 1991). In contrast, lesions of the other major output of the amygdala through the stria terminalis and bed nucleus of the stria terminalis do not block fear-potentiated startle.

The output pathways of the central nucleus of the amygdala, and the effects of lesions at various points along this pathway, are summarized in Figure 41.5. Lesions of the stria terminalis itself, or the bed nucleus of the stria terminalis (a major projection

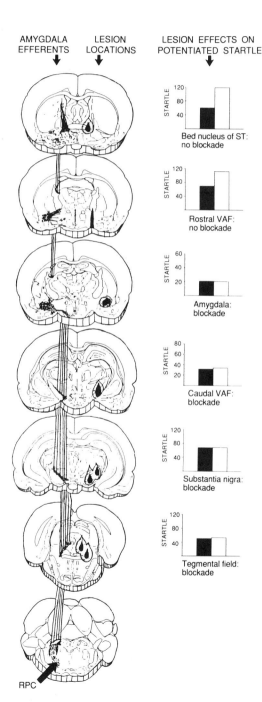

FIGURE 41.5. Lesions interrupting the pathway from the central nucleus of the amygdala to the nucleus reticularis pontis caudalis (RPC), but not lesions interrupting other central nucleus efferent pathways, block fear-potentiated startle. Left panel: A series of coronal rat brain sections, with the top section being the most rostral. The left sides of the sections show a schematic representation, based on PHA-L tracing studies, of the efferent pathways of the central nucleus of the amygdala. The right sides of the sections show representative lesions that interrupted the central nucleus efferent pathways at various levels. The black areas represent the cavities produced by the lesions and the stippled areas represent the surrounding gliosis. Right panel: Graphs showing the effects of bilateral lesions in each area on fear-potentiated startle. The graphs show the mean amplitude startle response on noise-alone trials (black bars) and light–noise trials (white bars) in rats given bilateral lesions in the locations shown in the corresponding brain section to the left of the graph. ST, stria terminalis; VAF, ventral amygdalofugal pathway. Adapted from "The Efferent Pathway of the Amygdala Involved in Conditioned Fear as Measured with the Fear-Potentiated Startle Paradigm" (p. 838) by J. M. Hitchcock & M. Davis, 1991, *Behavioral Neuroscience, 105*, 826–842. Copyright 1991 by the American Psychological Association. Adapted by permission.

area of this pathway), do not block potentiated startle. Knife cuts of the rostral part of the ventral amygdalo-fugal pathway, which would interrupt its projections to the rostral lateral hypothalamus and substantia innominata, also fail to block potentiated startle. On the other hand, lesions of the caudal part of the ventral amygdalo-fugal pathway, at the point where it passes through the subthalamic area and cerebral peduncles, completely block potentiated startle. Lesions of the substantia nigra, which receives central amygdaloid nucleus projections as well as fibers of passage from the central nucleus of the amygdala to more caudal brainstem regions, also block potentiated startle. This blockade does not seem to involve dopamine cells in the zona compacta, because infusion of the dopamine neurotoxin 6-hydroxydopamine into the substantia nigra does not block potentiated startle, despite over a 90% depletion of dopamine in the caudate nucleus. Finally, lesions of the lateral tegmental field, caudal to the substantia nigra, also block fear-potentiated startle.

THE VISUAL PATHWAY INVOLVED IN FEAR-POTENTIATED STARTLE

The data outlined thus far suggest that visual input critical for fear-potentiated startle using a visual conditioned stimulus may enter the amygdala through the lateral and/or basal nuclei, which then project to the central nucleus, which in turn projects to the startle pathway. At the present time, however, the visual pathway or pathways that are critical for fear-potentiated startle using a visual conditioned stimulus and that link the retina to these basal nuclei are unclear. Recently, we have found that complete removal of all primary and secondary visual cortex does not block the expression of fear-potentiated startle using a visual conditioned stimulus (Rosen et al., in press). In contrast, relatively small lesions of the perirhinal cortex completely block fear-potentiated startle, provided that the lesion includes an area of perirhinal cortex just dorsal and ventral to the rhinal sulcus (Rosen et al., in press). McDonald and Jackson (1987) have found heavy retrograde and anterograde labeling in the basal, accessory basal, and especially the lateral nuclei of the amygdala after deposits of horseradish peroxidase conjugated to wheatgerm agglutinin in the perirhinal cortex. Thus, it is possible that visual information is relayed from the perirhinal cortex to the amygdala, forming the last part of the conditioned stimulus pathway to the amygdala. Currently, we are using retrograde tracing techniques to evaluate how subcortical visual information might reach this area of the perirhinal cortex.

The Role of NMDA Receptors in the Amygdala in Conditioned Fear

One of the most promising models of learning in vertebrates is long-term potentiation (LTP). The finding that NMDA receptor antagonists such as 2-amino-5-phosphonovalerate (AP5) block the induction or acquisition of LTP in certain hippocampal synapses, but not the expression of LTP, has led to very powerful biochemical models of learning in vertebrates (see Brown, Chapman, & Kairiss, & Keenan, 1988; Collingridge & Bliss, 1987; Nicoll, Kauer, & Malenka, 1988). Moreover, a number of behavioral studies have now shown that competitive as well as noncompetitive NMDA antagonists attenuate or block various measures of learning (see Davis, 1992; Morris,

Halliwell, & Bowery, 1989). Recent studies have shown that LTP can occur in amygdala brain slices (Chapman, Kairiss, Keenan, & Brown, 1990) or *in vivo* following tetanic stimulation of the part of the medial geniculate nucleus that projects to the lateral nucleus of the amygdala (Clugnet & LeDoux, 1990). If convergence between the light and shock occurs at the amygdala, and an NMDA-dependent process is involved in the acquisition of conditioned fear, then local infusion of NMDA antagonists into the amygdala should block the acquisition of conditioned fear measured with the fear-potentiated startle effect.

EFFECTS OF NMDA ANTAGONISTS ON THE ACQUISITION OF FEAR-POTENTIATED STARTLE

Consistent with this, we found that local infusion of the NMDA antagonist AP5 caused a dose-related attentuation of fear-potentiated startle acquisition, with a total blockade at the higher doses (Miserendino, Sananes, Melia, & Davis, 1990; Figure 41.6). Observation of the animals during training provided no evidence of catalepsy or ataxia (e.g., Leung & Descorough, 1988). The effect did not seem to result from a decrease in sensitivity to footshock, because local infusion of AP5 into the amygdala did not alter either overall reactivity to footshock or the slope of reactivity as a function of different footshock intensities. In contrast to the blockade of acquisition, AP5 did not block the

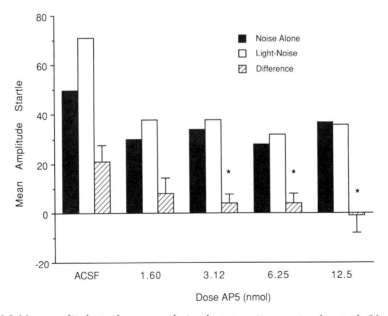

FIGURE 41.6. Mean amplitude startle response during the test session on noise-alone trials (black bars) and light–noise trials (white bars), and the difference between these two trial types (± standard error of the mean), following bilateral infusion of various doses of the NMDA antagonist AP5 into the amygdala during the training session, which occurred 1 week before the test session. From "Blocking of Acquisition but Not Expression of Conditioned Fear-Potentiated Startle by NMDA Antagonists in the Amygdala" (p. 717) by M. J. D. Miserendino, C. B. Sananes, K. R. Melia, & M. Davis, 1990, *Nature*, *345*, 716–718. Copyright 1990 by Macmillan Magazines Ltd. Reprinted by permission.

expression of fear-potentiated startle, because infusion of AP5 immediately before testing did not block potentiated startle in animals previously trained in the absence of the drug. Other studies showed that propranolol, which has local anesthetic effects (Weiner, 1985) and alters one-trial inhibitory avoidance conditioning (Liang, Juler, & McGaugh, 1986), did not block or even attenuate fear conditioning after local infusion into the amygdala prior to training. In addition, AP5 given after training but 1 week before testing did not block potentiated startle, ruling out any permanent damage to the amygdala or blockade caused by residual drug during testing. Local infusion of AP5 did not affect visual prepulse inhibition, a sensitive measure of vision in rats (Wecker & Ison, 1986). Finally, infusion of AP5 into deep cerebellar nuclei did not block acquisition, even at a dose eight times that required to block acquisition after local infusion into the amygdala.

EFFECTS OF NMDA ANTAGONISTS ON THE EXTINCTION OF
FEAR-POTENTIATED STARTLE

Clinically, the inability to eliminate the memory of prior traumatic events ranks as one of the major problems in psychiatry. The soldier mentioned at the beginning of this chapter has had the same nightmare almost every night for the last 27 years! In the laboratory, following light–shock pairings, presentation of a light in the absence of shock eventually leads to a loss of the fear reaction to the light. This phenomenon is called "experimental extinction." Several experiments indicate that the loss of fear to the light probably does not result from an erasure of the old memory, but instead results from learning a new memory that somehow inhibits or competes with the original one. For example, following extinction, presentation of a shock without explicit pairing with the light can restore fear of the light to its original level (e.g., Rescorla & Heth, 1975).

Although a good deal is known about neural systems involved in the acquisition of fear, much less is known about the neural systems that might be involved in extinction of conditioned fear (see LeDoux, Romanski, & Xagoraris, 1989). Recently, we have found that local infusion of the NMDA antagonist AP5 into the amygdala blocks extinction of fear-potentiated startle (Falls, Miserendino, & Davis, 1992). This suggests that extinction may be an active learning process and that an NMDA-dependent process in the amygdala may be importantly involved in extinction of conditioned fear. Patients suffering from posttraumatic stress disorder clearly have difficulty in extinction. We hope that further analysis of the neural mechanisms and brain systems involved in extinction of conditioned fear will lead to the development of better treatments for the alleviation of chronic anxiety disorders and the elimination of intrusive, unwanted aversive memories.

The Role of the Amygdala in Fear

As mentioned earlier, conditioned fear is a hypothetical construct that is used to explain the cluster of behavioral effects produced by a stimulus that was formerly associated with an aversive situation. Figure 41.7 shows a summary of the direct anatomical

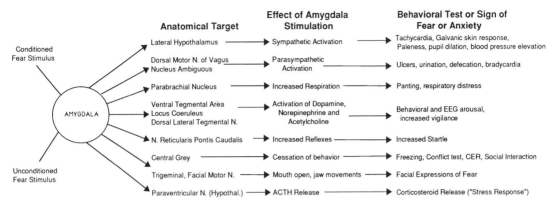

FIGURE 41.7. Schematic diagram showing direct connections between the central nucleus of the amygdala and a variety of hypothalamic and brainstem target areas that may be involved in different animal tests of fear and anxiety. ACTH, adrenocorticotrophic hormone; CER, conditioned emotional response. From "The Role of the Amygdala in Conditioned Fear" (p. 280) by M. Davis, 1992, in J. Aggleton (Ed.), *The Amygdala: Neurobiological Aspects of Emotion, Memory, and Mental Dysfunction* (pp. 255–305). New York: Wiley–Liss. Copyright 1991 by Wiley–Liss. Reprinted by permission.

outputs of the central nucleus of the amygdala projecting to brainstem and hypothalamic target areas that are involved in the signs of fear and anxiety (see Davis, 1992). Electrical stimulation of the amygdala elicits the entire constellation of behaviors used to define a state of fear, whereas stimulation of selected targets areas produce more selective effects. Conditioned fear may result when a formerly neutral stimulus now comes to activate the amygdala by virtue of pairing it with aversive stimulation. In fact, the amygdala may be the actual site of plasticity where aversive memories are stored, at least initially, because treatments that alter amygdala function have profound effects on aversive conditioning (cf. McGaugh, Chapter 34, this volume). Pharmacological treatments that selectively and directly inhibit the amygdala, or that activate brain systems inhibiting the amygdala, may thus be particularly effective in alleviating disorders characterized by intrusive memories of aversive events.

ACKNOWLEDGMENTS

Research reported in this chapter was supported by National Institute of Mental Health Grants No. MH-25642 and No. MH-47840; National Institute of Neurological and Communicative Disorders and Stroke Grant No. NS-18033; Research Scientist Development Award No. MH-00004, a grant from the Air Force Office of Scientific Research; and the State of Connecticut. My sincere thanks are extended to Lee Schlesinger, who tested many of the animals used for these studies, and to Leslie Fields for help in typing the chapter.

REFERENCES

Aggleton, J. P. (1985). A description of intra-amygdaloid connections in the Old World monkeys. *Experimental Brain Research, 57,* 390–399.

Amaral, D. (1987). Memory: Anatomical organization of candidate brain regions. In F. Plum (Ed.), *Handbook of physiology: Section 1. The nervous system. Vol. 5. Higher functions of the brain* (pp. 211–294). Bethesda, MD: American Physiological Society.

Berg, W. K., & Davis, M. (1985). Associative learning modifies startle reflexes at the lateral lemniscus. *Behavioral Neuroscience, 99,* 191–199.

Brown, J. S., Kalish, H. I., & Farber, I. E. (1951). Conditioned fear as revealed by magnitude of startle response to an auditory stimulus. *Journal of Experimental Psychology, 41,* 317–328.

Brown, T. H., Chapman, P. F., Kairiss, E. W., & Keenan, C. L. (1988). Long-term synaptic potentiation. *Science, 242,* 724–728.

Campeau, S., Liang, K. C., & Davis, M. (1990). Long-term retention of fear-poentiated startle following a short training session. *Animal Learning and Behavior, 18,* 462–468.

Cassella, J. V., & Davis, M. (1985). Fear-enhanced acoustic startle is not attenuated by acute or chronic imipramine treatment in rats. *Psychopharmacology, 87,* 278–282.

Cassella, J. V., & Davis, M. (1986). Neural structures mediating acoustic and tactile startle reflexes and the acoustically-elicited pinna response in rats: Electrolytic and ibotenic acid studies. *Society for Neuroscience Abstracts, 12,* 1273.

Chapman, P. F., Kairiss, E. W., Keenan, C. L., & Brown, T. H. (1990). Long-term synaptic potentiation in the amygdala. *Synapse, 6,* 271–278.

Clugnet, M. C., & LeDoux, J. E. (1990). Synaptic plasticity in fear conditioning circuits: Induction of LTP in the lateral nucleus of the amygdala by stimulation of the medial geniculate body. *Journal of Neuroscience, 10,* 2818–2824.

Collingridge, G. L., & Bliss, T. V. P. (1987). NMDA receptors: Their role in long-term potentiation. *Trends in Neuroscience, 10,* 288–293.

Crooks, G. B., Jr., Robinson, G. S., Hatfield, T. J., Graham, P. W., & Gallagher, M. (1989). Intraventricular administration of the NMDA antagonist APV disrupts learning of an odor aversion that is potentiated by taste. *Society for Neuroscience Abstracts, 15,* 464.

Davis, M. (1992). The role of the amygdala in conditioned fear. In J. Aggleton (Ed.), *The amygdala: Neurobiological aspects of emotion, memory, and mental dysfunction* (pp. 255–305). New York: Wiley–Liss.

Davis, M., & Astrachan, D. I. (1978). Conditioned fear and startle magnitude: Effects of different footshock or backshock intensities used in training. *Journal of Experimental Psychology: Animal Behavior Processes, 4,* 95–103.

Davis, M., Gendelman, D. S., Tischler, M. D., & Gendelman, P. M. (1982). A primary acoustic startle circuit: Lesion and stimulation studies. *Journal of Neuroscience, 6,* 791–805.

Falls, W. A., Miserendino, M. J. D., & Davis, M. (1992). Extinction of fear-potentiated startle: Blockade by infusion of an NMDA antagonist into the amygdala. *Journal of Neuroscience, 12,* 854–863.

Gallagher, M., Graham, P. W., & Holland, P. C. (1990). The amygdala central nucleus and appetitive Pavlovian conditioning: Lesions impair one class of conditioned behavior. *Journal of Neuroscience, 10,* 1906–1911.

Gallagher, M., & Holland, P. C. (1991). Understanding the function of central nucleus: Is simple conditioning enough? In J. Aggleton (Ed.), *The amygdala: Neurobiological aspects of emotion, memory, and mental dysfunction* (pp. 307–321). New York: Wiley–Liss.

Gloor, P. (1960). Amygdala. In J. Field, H. W. Magoun, & V. E. Hall (Eds.), *Handbook of physiology: Section 1. Neurophysiology* (Vol. 2, pp. 1395–1420). Washington, DC: American Physiological Society.

Gray, T. S. (1989). Autonomic neuropeptide connections of the amygdala. In Y. Tache, J. E. Morley, & M. R. Brown (Eds.), *Neuropeptides and stress* (Vol. 1, pp. 92–106). New York: Springer-Verlag.

Handforth, A. (1984). Implication of stimulus factors governing kindled seizure threshold. *Experimental Neurology, 86,* 33–39.

Hitchcock, J. M., & Davis, M. (1983). *Ibotenic acid induced lesions of the central nucleus of the amygdala block pear-potentiated startle.* Unpublished observations.

Hitchcock, J. M., & Davis, M. (1986). Lesions of the amygdala, but not of the cerebellum or red nucleus, block conditioned fear as measured with the potentiated startle paradigm. *Behavioral Neuroscience, 100,* 11–22.

Hitchcock, J. M., & Davis, M. (1987). Fear-potentiated startle using an auditory conditioned stimulus: Effect of lesions of the amygdala. *Physiology and Behavior, 39,* 403–408.

Hitchcock, J. M., & Davis, M. (1991). The efferent pathway of the amygdala involved in conditioned fear as measured with the fear-potentiated startle paradigm. *Behavioral Neuroscience, 105,* 826–842.

Inagaki, S., Kawai, Y., Matsuzak, T., Shiosaka, S., & Tohyama, M. (1983). Precise terminal fields of the descending somatostatinergic neuron system from the amygdala complex of the rat. *Journal für Hirnforschung, 24,* 345–365.

Ison, J. R., McAdam, D. W., & Hammond, G. R. (1973). Latency and amplitude changes in the acoustic startle reflex of the rat produced by variation in auditory prestimulation. *Physiology and Behavior, 10,* 1035–1039.

Kapp, B. S., & Pascoe, J. P. (1986). Correlation aspects of learning and memory: Vertebrate model systems. In J. L. Martinez & R. P. Kesner (Eds.), *Learning and memory: A biological view* (pp. 399–440). New York: Academic Press.

Kapp, B. S., Pascoe, J. P., & Bixler, M. A. (1984). The amygdala: A neuroanatomical systems approach to its contribution to aversive conditioning. In L. S. Squire & N. Butters (Eds.), *Neuropsychology of memory* (1st ed., pp. 473–488). New York: Guilford Press.

Kapp, B. S., Wilson, A., Pascoe, J. P., Supple, W. F., & Whalen, P. J. (1990). A neuroanatomical systems analysis of conditioned bradycardia in the rabbit. In M. Gabriel & J. Moore (Eds.), *Learning and computational neuroscience: Foundations of adaptive networks* (pp. 53–90). Cambridge, MA: Bradford Books/MIT Press.

Krettek, J. E., & Price, J. L. (1978a). Amygdaloid projections to subcortical structures within the basal forebrain and brainstem in the rat and cat. *Journal of Comparative Neurology, 178,* 225–254.

Krettek, J. E., & Price, J. L. (1978b). A description of the amygdaloid complex in the rat and cat with observations on intra-amygdaloid axonal connections. *Journal of Comparative Neurology, 178,* 255–280.

LeDoux, J. E., Cicchetti, P., Xagoraris, A., & Romanski, L. M. (1990). The lateral amygdaloid nucleus: Sensory interface of the amygdala in fear conditioning. *Journal of Neuroscience, 10,* 1062–1069.

LeDoux, J. E., Romanski, L., & Xagoraris, A. (1989). Indelibility of subcortical emotional memories. *Journal of Cognitive Neuroscience, 1,* 238–243.

Leung, L. W. S., & Desborough, K. A. (1988). APV, an *N*-methyl-D-aspartate receptor antagonist, blocks the hippocampal theta rhythm in behaving rats. *Brain Research, 463,* 148–152.

Lewis, S. J., Verberne, A. J. M., Robinson, T. G., Jarrott, B., Louis, W. J., & Beart, P. M. (1989). Excitotoxin-induced lesions of the central bu not basolateral nucleus of the amygdala modulate the baroreceptor heart rate reflex in conscious rats. *Brain Research, 494,* 232–240.

Liang, K. C., Juler, R. C., & McGaugh, J. L. (1986). Modulating effects of posttraining epinephrine on memory: Involvement of the amygdala noradrenergic systems. *Brain Research, 368,* 125–133.

McAllister, W. R., & McAllister, D. E. (1971). Behavioral measurement of conditioned fear. In F. R. Brush (Ed.), *Aversive conditioning and learning* (pp. 105–179). New York: Academic Press.

McDonald, A. J., & Jackson, T. R. (1987). Amygdaloid connections with posterior insular and temporal neocortical areas in the rat. *Journal of Comparative Neurology, 262,* 59–77.

Millhouse, O. E., & DeOlmos, J. (1983). Neuronal configurations in lateral and basolateral amygdala. *Neuroscience, 10,* 1269–1300.

Miserendino, M. J. D., Sananes, C. B., Melia, K. R., & Davis, M. (1990). Blocking of acquisition but not expression of conditioned fear-potentiated startle by NMDA antagonists in the amygdala. *Nature, 345,* 716–718.

Mizuno, N., Takahashi, O., Satoda, T., & Matsushima, R. (1985). Amygdalospinal projections in the macaque monkey. *Neuroscience Letters, 53,* 327–330.

Morris, R. G. M., Halliwell, R., & Bowery, N. (1989). Synaptic plasticity and learning: II. Do different kinds of plasticity underlie different kinds of learning? *Neuropsychologia, 27,* 41–59.

Nicoll, R. A., Kauer, J. A., & Malenka, R. C. (1988). The current excitement in long-term potentiation. *Neuron, 1,* 97–103.

Nitecka, L., Amerski, L., & Narkiewicz, O. (1981). The organization of intraamygdaloid connections: An HRP study. *Journal Hirnforsch, 22,* 3–7.

Nitecka, L., & Frotscher, M. (1989). Organization and synaptic interconnections of GABAergic and cholinergic elements in the rat amygdaloid nuclei: Single- and double-immunolabeling studies. *Journal of Comparative Neurology, 279,* 470–488.

Ohta, M. (1984). Amygdaloid and cortical facilitation or inhibition of trigeminal motoneurons in the rat. *Brain Research, 291,* 39–48.

Ottersen, O. P. (1980). Afferent connections to the amygdaloid complex of the rat and cat: II. Afferents from the hypothalamus and the basal telencephalon. *Journal of Comparative Neurology, 194,* 267–289.

Ottersen, O. P. (1982). Connections of the amygdala of the rat: IV. Corticoamygdaloid and intraamygdaloid connections as studied with axonal transport of horseradish peroxidase. *Journal of Comparative Neurology, 205,* 30–48.

Post, S., & Mai, J. K. (1980). Contribution to the amygdaloid projection field in the rat: A quantitative autoradiographic study. *Journal für Hirnforschung, 21,* 199–225.

Price, J. L., & Amaral, D. G. (1981). An autoradiographic study of the projections of the central nucleus of the monkey amygdala. *Journal of Neuroscience, 1,* 1242–1259.

Rescorla, R. A., & Heth, D. C. (1975). Reinstatement of fear to an extinguished conditioned stimulus. *Journal of Experimental Psychology: Animal Behavior Processes, 104,* 88–96.

Roberts, G. W., Woodhams, P. L., Polak, J. M., & Crow, T. J. (1982). Distribution of neuropeptides in the limbic system of the rat: The amygdaloid complex. *Neuroscience, 7,* 99–131.

Rosen, J. B., & Davis, M. (1988a). Enhancement of acoustic startle by electrical stimulation of the amygdala. *Behavioral Neuroscience, 102,* 195–202.

Rosen, J. B., & Davis, M. (1988b). Temporal characteristics of enhancement of startle by stimulation of the amygdala. *Physiology and Behavior, 44,* 117–123.

Rosen, J. B., & Davis, M. (1990). Enhancement of electrically elicited startle by amygdaloid stimulation. *Physiology and Behavior, 48,* 343–349.

Rosen, J. B., Hitchcock, J. M., Miserendino, M. J. D., Falls, W. A., Campeau, S., & Davis, M. (in press). Lesions of the perirhinal cortex, but not of the frontal, visual or insular cortex block fear-potentiated startle using a visual conditioned stimulus. *Journal of Neuroscience.*

Rosen, J. B., Hitchcock, J. M., Sananes, C. B., Miserendino, M. J. D., & Davis, M. (1991). A direct projection from the central nucleus of the amygdala to the acoustic startle pathway: Anterograde and retrograde tracing studies. *Behavioral Neuroscience, 105,* 817–825.

Russchen, F. T. (1982). Amygdalopetal projections in the cat: II. Subcortical afferent connections. A study with retrograde tracing techniques. *Journal of Comparative Neurology, 207,* 157–176.

Sananes, C. B., & Davis, M. (1992). NMDA lesions of the lateral and basolateral nuclei of the amygdala block fear-potentiated startle and shock sensitization of startle. *Behavioral Neuroscience, 106,* 72–80.

Sandrew, B. B., Edwards, D. L., Poletti, C. E., & Foote, W. E. (1986). Amygdalospinal projections in the cat. *Brain Research, 373,* 235–239.

Sarter, M., & Markowitsch, H. J. (1985). Involvement of the amygdala in learning and memory: A critical review, with emphasis on anatomical relations. *Behavioral Neuroscience, 99,* 342–380.

Schwaber, J. S., Kapp, B. S., Higgins, G. A., & Rapp, P. R. (1982). Amygdaloid and basal forebrain direct connections with the nucleus of the solitary tract and the dorsal motor nucleus. *Journal of Neuroscience, 2,* 1424–1438.

Smith, B. S., & Millhouse, O. E. (1985). The connections between basolateral and central amygdaloid nuclei. *Neuroscience Letters, 56,* 307–309.

Turner, B. J. (1981). The cortical sequence and terminal distribution of sensory related afferents to the amygdaloid complex of the rat and monkey. In Y. Ben-Ari (Ed.), *The amygdaloid complex* (pp. 51–62). Amsterdam: Elsevier/North-Holland.

Van Hoesen, G. W. (1981). The differential distribution, diversity and sprouting of cortical projections to the amygdala in the Rhesus monkey. In Y. Ben-Ari (Ed.), *The amygdaloid complex* (pp. 77–90). Amsterdam: Elsevier/North-Holland.

Wecker, J. R., & Ison, J. R. (1986). Visual function measured by reflex modification in rats with inherited retinal dystrophy. *Behavioral Neuroscience, 100,* 679–684.

Weiner, N. (1985). Drugs that inhibit adrenergic nerves and block adrenergic receptors. In A. Gilman, L. S. Goodman, T. W. Rall, & F. Murad (Eds.), *The pharmacological basis of therapeutics* (pp. 181–214). New York: Macmillan.

42

Memory: A Behavioristic and Neuroscientific Approach

GARTH J. THOMAS and J. M. ORDY

At the empirical level, it is presumed that memory is not a datum. Instead, it is regarded as a descriptive and abstract concept, inferred from observed discriminations that are crucially influenced by past experience. This influence from past experience on current discriminations is attributed to different but interactive types of memory, which have been designated "dispositional" and "representational." Furthermore, it is hypothesized that the memory types involve different underlying neural mechanisms. We have reported experimental results based on these presumptions. Two studies discussed in the latter part of this chapter are particularly appropriate because they concern the hypothesis about the relation of memory types to brain structures.

Olton's (1983) summary paper and this chapter demonstrate a marked convergence (and some differences) as regards empirical and theoretical issues concerning memory. The convergent views and facts from different laboratories enhance persuasiveness.

A Scientific View (Objective) of Memory

The concept of memory must be behaviorally specified, but psychology is not the only science concerned with this. The independent and dependent variables (and associated measurement techniques) of neuroscience are not limited to psychology's molar behavior. Behavioristic psychology's formulation, which is restricted to the elucidation of relations between events antecedent to sensory end organs and responses mediated by effector organs, cannot completely account for memory. Memory is mediated by many "under-the-skin" mechanisms. Within neuroscience, studies of memory now include molecular as well as molar perspectives. Memory is, indeed, a neurobehavioral concept.

Memorial events are essentially dependent for explanation on physiological events for the simple reason that the brain's output is limited to two classes of effector organs (muscles and exocrine glands) and its input is limited to several specific sensory systems. Anything accomplished behaviorally must be mediated by those brain-controlled effectors and sensory inputs. Thus, behavioral analysis can establish *what* an organism can remember under various environmental circumstances, but only physiological events, primarily in the brain as the "operator" of the effectors and "mediator" of sensory inputs, can establish *how* those memorial processes are accomplished. However, the complexity of explanations in terms of physiology would be overwhelming and beyond easy grasp or technical elucidation. For that reason, for example, the trajectory of artillery shells is not usually "explained" in terms of subatomic physics. (See Doty, 1976, for an account of the muscles and their patterns of contraction involved in even the simple response of reflex swallowing.) For the most part, an explanation of memory in terms of underlying neural mechanisms is only an explanation "in principle." Objective formulation of the phenomena of memory ensures this "in-principle" relationship to biological processes by eschewing animistic explanations that assume a "ghost in the machine"—that is, introduction of dualistic forces from a metaphysical realm beyond the world of public data. Memory by organisms could be explained, in principle, in the language of transmitters, receptor types, membrane and synaptic potentials, neuropeptides, anatomical connections, and so forth; however, except in rare instances for theoretical *tours de force*, explanations of memory are usually couched in terms of stimuli, discriminations, motivations, retrieval, response classes, traces, and the like, and these concepts can in turn (although some are hypothetical constructions) be defined in terms of publicly denotable events. That is, the behavioral analysis of memory is restricted to the same levels of discourse as that of other sciences. Problems of the memory phenomena that ultimately will have to be explained in terms of under-the-skin events must nonetheless be characterized first by behavioral analysis.

The rather cryptic characterizations above ride roughshod over many subtle and complex conceptual issues. These characterizations would appear banal and self-evident to most empirically minded scientists, who ignore such metaphysical implications of their everyday research. However, we think it is necessary to disavow explicitly the attribution of metaphysical forces acting on the nervous system (or behavior) from another realm—forces that are, by definition, publicly unobservable—in order to "explain" aspects of complex behavior. Such a tendency is a common remnant of animism in behavioral analysis. Perhaps it needs to be explicitly asserted in behavioral science that the language of data must be restricted to *stimuli* (i.e., physical events that are objective and antecedent to sense organs—although it sometimes takes considerable research to discover what the effective stimuli are) and *responses* (i.e., events that are also physical, objectively observed, and, in behavioral neuroscience, mediated by effector organs). At the behavioral level, we must restrict independent and dependent variables to events that are publicly denotable. We must also require that any hypothetical (fictional) processes necessary to relate stimulus–response (S-R) events at least not be contradicted by known neural processes, and also that these hypothetical processes be definable in terms of public events. That being so, neurobehavioral interpretation of the so-called "higher mental processes" (of which memory is one) should emerge without the metaphysical dualism that has plagued this topic for centuries. To be a practicing behavioral scientist in a field as conditional as brain–behavior relations is indeed fraught with many conceptual difficulties.

Types of Memory

For approximately a century, scholars and researchers have noted that memory (past experience influencing current discriminations) seems to be composed of at least two types. Squire (1987) has arranged some of these distinctions into a functional hierarchy; our view is somewhat different. All the dichotomies seem to slice the memory "pie" in similar but slightly different ways. Some dichotomies are based on philosophy; some stem from a specific theory or hypothesis about memory; some are seemingly defined in terms of linguistic responses of humans (and require some "metaphorical stretching" if the definitions are to be applied to the behavior of nonhuman animals); and some are based on scientific criteria that are not general enough. They all express the notion that there exist both a simpler type of memory and a more complex type of memory that mediates the past's influence on present behavior in terms of specific events (episodes) that have been experienced in the past. The significant hypothesis in this chapter is that these types of memory are mediated by different neural mechanisms; however, before that hypothesis can be evaluated, the types of memory must be experimentally unconfounded at the behavioral level. In our opinion, the preponderance of the available neurobehavioral evidence supports the hypothesis.

Dispositional Memory

Recently, Sherry and Schacter (1987) have discussed the selective pressures that may have led to evolutionary development of the brain's ability to modify present behavior by means of past stimuli and responses. They lump together various characterizations of memory types into two categories: System I designates the evolutionarily older (more primitive) memory type, and System II designates the more developed and the evolutionarily more recent type. Similar designations were proposed earlier by Thomas (1984), but they were defined in terms of observable behavioral events (discriminations).

Sherry and Schacter's System I belongs in our "dispositional memory." As a result of past experience, an organism develops a disposition (tendency) to respond in a specific way to a certain stimulus. Without the unique past experience, that specific response would not be made to that specific stimulus. The memory is based on what is called "associative learning" or on habituation. The learned behavior depends on memory because the likelihood of a correct (appropriate) response accumulates from trial to trial, and because, once established, the behavioral S-R connection lasts for some time without further or continuous practice. Experience-dependent changes in conductivity in different neural pathways that subserve different cue stimuli and associated responses comprise the neural basis for the learned (remembered) discrimination. The idea is at least as old as Descartes, but nowadays we suspect that the critical neural mechanisms would more likely be "synaptic plasticity" or perhaps the opening and closing of ion channels in membranes, rather than experience-dependent enlargement of the pores in nerves to facilitate the flow of animal spirits, as Descartes speculated.

Representational Memory

The more complex "representational memory" is exemplified by the capacity for *event* memory; presumably, it can be found in only some organisms. Sherry and Schacter (1987) refer to this type of memory as depending on System II, and it was designated as "representational memory" by Thomas (1984). Representational memory is instantiated by making correct discriminations when the response options are indicated sensorially at the time of choice, but there are no sensory cues available to indicate which response option should be chosen. However, such crucial stimulus cues are known by the experimenter to have been contingently reinforced in the past. Stimulus inputs at the time of choice provide no differential cues for the differential respondings that show memory. Only a brain-constructed "cognition" (memory) can correctly guide choice. There must be experience-dependent alterations of neural mechanisms similar to those underlying dispositional memories, but, for representational memory, the alterations must be independent of current sensory inputs. At present the representations are clearly hypothetical and are most often called "traces." They must be maintained by the brain, and they must be "retrievable" to help guide current discriminative responses.

The distinction between representational and dispositional memories is based on denotable cue stimuli at the time of choice in the memory-indicating discrimination, rather than defined in terms of other words (as in dictionary definitions), as are many older and similar distinctions between memory types. "Dispositional" and "representational," as terms for types of memories, are very similar to Honig's (1978) widely cited "reference" and "working" memories, but they differ in several respects. First, the former are defined in terms of discriminations and the latter are defined in terms of trials (across and within trials). "Trials" did not exist in the environment in which memory capacities evolved. Discriminations in nature often occur in series, but seldom with the regularity and similarity seen in trials in the behavior laboratory. Second, at least as regards the subsequently described "double-run procedure" in the T-maze, an animal may make errors because it is unable to remember which way it was forced during the previous "information" run (i.e., it depends on representational memory), or because it has forgotten the strategy under which it is working (to alternate [shift] relative to the direction of the previous run, or to perseverate [stay]). Memory for the stay-or-shift strategy was obviously learned over several contingently reinforced previous trials and would be classified as an instance of "reference memory" by Honig's criteria. On the other hand, by the present definition in terms of differentially available sensory stimuli at the time of the memory-indicating discrimination, it would be classified as an instance of representational memory (i.e., "working memory" in Honig's typology). Thus, the discrimination confounds two representational memories. However, in many laboratory experiments, the two memory types are essentially the same.

The concepts of representational and dispositional memories were derived from Hunter's (1913) classic paper on delayed response. (He never gave a name to what here is called dispositional memory; he simply called it "memory of the commonest kind.") Obviously, performance of any form of delayed conditional discrimination provides an instance of what is called representational memory. (The word "representational" is his usage.) Further distinctions within conditional discriminations are often made, ranging from (1) classical delayed response, in which monkeys must discriminate between two identical objects in different spatial locations in terms of the location of the sample stimulus (seeing the experimenter place the reward), to (2) delayed non-matching to sample of trial-unique stimulus objects that differ not only in their spatial location, but also in terms of visual characteristics. They must be distinguished in terms of novelty—that is, choosing the one that is different from the remembered sample stimulus. They all depend on representational memory.

Given the undifferentiated nature of rats' visual system, it is doubtful that they could learn to make the required visual discriminations with any facility in the usual conditional response situation. However, there are several commonly used tests for rats that require representational memory abilities, such as T-maze alternation and the radial arm maze.

Although speculations and theories abound, little has been established regarding neural mechanisms subserving representational memory. We scarcely know more than what can be learned by inferences from behavior–lesion studies; that is, the ability for representational-memory-dependent discrimination seems to depend more on some specific structures in the brain than on others. It must be presumed that the ability to make representational-memory-dependent discriminations depends on some process (hypothetical and inferred from behavior) of the brain ability called "retrieval," whereby a memory trace (the "enlarged pore" of Descartes) can be made functional and used by the brain to guide an appropriate choice response. Dispositional-memory-dependent discriminations require no retrieval. The sensory presence of the critical conditioned stimulus (CS) at the time of choice does the "retrieving"—makes the connections with the past.

Behavioral Procedure for Testing Spatial Dispositional and Representational Memories in Rats

In natural circumstances and in the usual laboratory tasks used to evaluate memory, dispositional and representational memories are closely interdependent, so separate evaluations of the effects of various neurobehavioral independent variables (e.g., lesions, drugs, age, etc.) on the two types of memory cannot be conducted. To separate the effects on the two types of memory and to control for anticipated performance effects, the procedures described by Thomas (1984) have proved useful for the relatively small-brained laboratory rat. The procedures require the conventional reten-tion paradigm and provide excessive (postcriterion) preoperative practice, which strongly establishes many discriminative responses that are not used in evaluating memory but that are critical for making the discriminative responses used to indicate memory (e.g., the rat must learn where the start-box door is so that it can orient itself properly before the door is opened). The main aspect of the test is called the "double-run procedure," which is essentially the same as that used by Grant (1986). The double-run procedure faces the rat with a spatial delayed-matching [or nonmatching]-to-sample conditional discrimination, which it masters quickly. There are two runs per trial. The first run is forced, in that only one of the two possible response sites (goal boxes) is available in the T-maze. The rat makes no discrimination as to right or left location. The maze is simply a runway with a right-angle turn. This is the information (I) run, and it is reinforced by about 8–10 seconds (sec) of exposure to wet mash. The rat is then replaced by hand into the start box and given its choice (C) run. An interrun interval can be interposed before the start-box door is opened. In the C run, both goal-box doors are open and the rat must choose which goal box to enter. It is reinforced only for correct choices (i.e., the *same* goal box [for stay] or the goal box *opposite* the one entered on the previous run [for shift]). Dispositional memory can be indicated by adaptation to the maze shown by response times, but in some studies (see below), a specific dispositional-memory-dependent test based on associative learning has been added in the T-maze stem, so that both dispositional and representational memories can be tested in the same T-maze in a "within-subject" design.

Illustrative Empirical Research Indicating Different Neural Mechanisms for Dispositional and Representational Memories

A number of neurobehavioral studies using the above-described procedures have been published. The studies described here illustrate procedures to instantiate the behaviorally defined memory types. Also, it is well established that the hippocampus is critically related to memory, so it and some related structures were selected for restricted lesions to determine any differential effects on the two types of memory.

The first study (Thomas & Gash, 1986) contained a control experiment that clearly demonstrated that rats were not using stimuli concurrent with the choice response for cues when we presumed they were making truly representational-memory-dependent discriminations; that is, the study showed that the rats were not using intramaze cues to discriminate the goal boxes on C runs. Very similar procedures of goal-box reversals were used much earlier by Squire (1969) in connection with spontaneous alternation.

After overlearning the ability to do correct discriminations of "opposite" (shift) relative to the goal box they were forced into on the preceding I run, the rats received 3 days (always 12 trials/day) under their original conditions (10-sec interrun intervals and no reversals); then they did another set of 3 days with longer interrun intervals (30 sec) but no reversal; next they received 36 trials (3 days) with 30-sec interrun intervals *and* with reversals between the I runs and the C runs (the reversals of the arms and goal boxes were accomplished during the interrun intervals while the rats were confined in the start box); and, finally, the rats experienced 36 trials under the regular conditions of 10-sec interrun intervals with no reversals. Surprisingly, testing with the 30-sec interrun intervals and no reversals had no effect on C-run accuracy, compared with performance with the regular (short) interrun intervals. Institution of the reversals temporarily increased running times on C runs, but the reversals had no effect on accuracy of choices. That is, the rats chose the goal box on C runs that was opposite in space to the one they had been forced into on the previous I run, even though, because of the reversal, they now had to enter the same goal box. It was not established what cues the rats were using to identify the goal boxes in order to choose the one *not* entered on the previous I run, but they could not have been using any intramaze cues (including their own odor trails), because the reversals had no effect on accuracy of goal-box choice. It is difficult to imagine any effective *extramaze* cues, because the maze used was a trough T-maze with solid walls and a solid but transparent roof that only permitted a view of the undifferentiated ceiling of the room. (We might guess that in this situation the rats may have been remembering *turns*, and some response-produced complex may have provided the critical "cue.")

The main point of this neurobehavioral study was to determine the effects of small electrolytic lesions in the posterodorsal septum, which presumably were effective because they severed septo-hippocampal connections. Twelve rats, later used in the reversal study, first learned preoperatively to do representational-memory-dependent discriminations—that is, to discriminate the goal boxes in terms of a memory of the goal box they had been forced into on the previous run, but with no sensory cues now present to indicate which goal box that was. The ability was acquired rapidly. The rats started off on the first session at about the level of spontaneous alternation (75% correct), and a median of 100% correct was reached by the 36th trial (third 12-trial session). They then received 144 postcriterion trials (these included the reversal trials). Next, they were divided into two matched groups for surgery; five operated control rats and six rats with posterodorsal septal lesions survived. After 2 weeks of postoperative recovery, all 11 rats were given three sessions (36 trials) under preoperative conditions. The median of the five control rats was 100% correct, but the median for the six rats with posterodorsal septal lesions was only 61% (no overlap). The representational-memory-dependent task was easy (acquired in a few trials); it was sensitive to the lesions; and extensive overtraining did not protect the memory from the lesion effects. That is, the animals with posterodorsal septal lesions could not readily remember their trial-specific learnings (i.e., which goal box to choose).

A second group of 12 rats worked preoperatively on a simple sensory discrimination. The two arms of the T-maze contained either rough (and white) or smooth (and black) floor inserts, and the rats had to choose the side containing their CS+, regardless of its position (right or left). This too proved to be an easy task. On the first session (12 trials), the median correct was 54% (slightly above chance); by the sixth session (72 trials), they achieved a median of 100% correct. They were given two more sessions during which the median percentage correct remained at 100% before the group was divided into two matched subgroups of six rats each for surgery. The operated controls received no brain lesions, and the experimental animals received small electrolytic lesions in posterodorsal septum. After 14 days of postoperative recovery, all rats received three sessions (36 trials) of testing in the T-maze with the same procedures used preoperatively. Both the operated control group and the experimental group with posterodorsal septal lesions achieved medians of 100% correct in each 12-trial session during these postoperative trials. Clearly, neither the "vacation" from testing during postoperative recovery, the control surgery, nor the limbic lesions negatively affected the rats' ability to remember the behavioral significance of the discriminative cues. They could still remember dispositional-memory-dependent discriminations.

The third group of 12 rats faced a simultaneous conditional discrimination. When the whole T-maze floor (start box, choice area, and both goal-box arms) was rough and white, the rats had to turn one way. When the whole maze floor was smooth and black, they had to turn the other way. This task required a condition*al* discrimination (if–

then), but the conditional stimuli (floor inserts) were sensorially present at the time of choice. This problem turned out to be very difficult for the rats. Even after 17 days (204 trials), the daily median was not consistently at 100% correct; it was 100% in two of the last three sessions, but it fell to 92% on the last session. Then two matched subgroups of six rats each were formed. One group got control surgery, and the other group received small posterodorsal septal lesions. After the 2-week postoperative recovery, all rats received three sessions (12 trials each) of discrimination testing. The control group achieved a median of 92% correct, whereas the group with septal lesions achieved 89% correct (the difference was not significant). Histologically, the lesions in all three experimental groups were very similar.

The neurobehavioral results show that (1) small electrolytic lesions in posterodorsal septum have a strongly deleterious effect on a very easy representational-memory-dependent discrimination, even after extensive preoperative experience; (2) the lesions have no effect on an easy dispositional-memory-dependent discrimination; and (3) they have no significant effect on a very difficult dispositional-memory-dependent task that involves conditional discriminations when the conditional cue is sensorially present at the time of choice. It appears that the conditionality of a discrimination is not what makes it sensitive to the effects of these limbic lesions. It is the delay that makes it dependent on representational memory.

The second experiment to be discussed (Thomas & Gash, 1988) is notable because it clearly shows in the same animals that near-total hippocampectomy has a devastating and long-lasting effect on representational-memory-dependent discriminations, but only a mild and temporary effect on dispositional-memory-dependent discriminations. A modification of the procedure used by Lowy et al. (1985) was adopted: The T-maze was revised to eliminate the reversals and to incorporate two parallel alleys in the stem to be used for making a simple sensory discrimination (dispositional-memory-dependent), while the same rats made a representational-memory-dependent spatial discrimination in the cross arm of the T-maze. As a rat made its way from the start box to the cross arm to make the representational-memory-dependent discrimination, it had to make a nonspatial dispositional-memory-dependent discrimination under the correction procedure in the stem alleys by going through the alley with its CS+ floor cues (rough and white or smooth and black). Thus, it made two discriminations on every trial.

As usual, preoperative acquisition of the spatial delayed-nonmatching-to-sample problem in the cross arms (representational-memory-dependent discriminations) was rapid. Preoperatively (all rats intact), the median 12-trial block ($n = 15$) reached 100% correct by the 48th trial. The rats were given 24 more preoperative trials of overtraining; from 48 trials through 72 trials, the medians of 12-trial blocks remained at 100% correct. Then the rats were divided into two matched groups: One group of six rats received only control operations (no brain damage); the other group of nine rats received multiple electrolytic lesions aimed at destroying the hippocampus on both sides. After 14 days of postoperative recovery, all rats received 72 trials (six trials/day for 12 days) under the same conditions as preoperatively. For the controls, the median of every 12-trial block (2 days) was 100% correct except one, and on that one the median was 92% correct. Every 12-trial block median of the rats that had sustained near-total hippocampectomy was 50% (chance). During the 12 days of postoperative testing, there was no evidence of recovery, as there is after lesions in other limbic-related areas.

As regards the simultaneous dispositional-memory-dependent discrimination in the stem by the same rats, and only on I runs, the problem was easy. Before surgery, all 15 rats (intact) learned rapidly; the 12-trial block median reached 100% correct after only 36 trials. After surgery, the six control rats achieved a median of 100% correct on every 12-trial block. The comparable medians for the nine hippocampectomized rats were somewhat (but significantly) below those of the control rats for the first three 12-trial blocks, but for the last three 12-trial blocks their medians were 100% correct, the same as the controls.

The near-total hippocampectomy reduced the experimental animals to chance levels of discrimination on a representational-memory-dependent discrimination. On the other hand, the performance of the same animals on the dispositional-memory-dependent discrimination in the stem of the T-maze was only slightly and temporarily affected. Nonquantitative observations of the hippocampectomized animals in the stem suggested that their temporary impairment was not a result of amnesia for the correct floor cue. Rather, their exploratory tendencies seemed disinhibited: They often "wandered" into the blind alley as if they were exploring, but it cost them an error! The tendency habituated to nonsignificance after only one 12-trial block.

Implications

The speculative background to these studies suggests that there may be marked species differences in memorial capabilities. Relatively small-brained animals, such as rats, are likely to be restricted not only to spatial attributes of stimulus events in the environment, but also as regards responses that can be used to indicate representational memories. (See Thomas & Gash, 1990, for a study showing the importance of response-generated factors in developing and using representational memories.) On the other hand, animals with relatively larger (and more differentiated) brains will have more options for forming and using representational memories. Of course, *Homo sapiens* seemingly can develop and use representational memories with regard to almost any attribute of stimulation in connection with almost any response. Although the hippocampal formation is somewhat "progressive" in evolution across a wide spectrum of mammals (West, 1990), its development is nowhere near as "progressive" as the relatively great evolutionary development of neocortex (neocorticalization) in the same spectrum of mammals. It seems a likely (though speculative) hypothesis that the hippocampal formation comprises a "bottleneck" through which all sensory information must be processed in order to become representational memories. It does not form a "bottleneck" for dispositional memories. Actual "storage" of memory traces (however this is done) will take place in other anatomical sites. For that reason, one expects to see large species differences in what types of information can be remembered representationally (and with what facility). Extensive connections between hippocampus (for instance) and other brain regions, especially sensory and multimodal association cortex in nonhuman primates (monkeys) (e.g., see Van Hoesen, 1985), strongly support that notion.

On the other hand, the parallelism between comparable findings in humans and rats is remarkable. Zola-Morgan, Squire, and Amaral (1986) presented a detailed report of a human case (R. B.) who suffered a cardiac dysfunction that resulted in a period of brain ischemia. For 5 years after recovery from the acute phase of his illness, he underwent extensive neuropsychological testing with a wide battery of tests to evaluate his cognitive and other capacities. Only an impairment of memory was found; there was no impairment of other cognitive or motor abilities. A subsequent and thorough postmortem anatomical analysis of his brain revealed very circumscribed, bilateral lesions in the CA1 region of his hippocampi. We (Ordy, Thomas, Volpe, Dunlap, & Columbo, 1988) and others have found that experimental ischemia of rat forebrain induced by temporary four-vessel occlusion (Pulsinelli & Brierly, 1979) produces a very similar brain lesion in the CA1 region of rats' hippocampi *and* also results in impairment of representational memory, as measured in a T-maze with the double-run procedure described above. Perhaps, in spite of the obvious differenes in behavioral characteristics (especially linguistic capabilities) and the obvious differences in size and complexity of brains between humans and rats, the basic properties of memory mechanisms in the two species may be much the same.

Most importantly, however, further research with other organisms and with memory tests specifically designed to differentiate dispositional from representational memories will be needed to see whether in the words of Squire (1982), the nervous system will continue to "honor the distinction" as it appears to do now in regard to spatial discrimination made by rats.

REFERENCES

Doty, R. W., Sr. (1976). The concept of neural centers. In J. C. Fentress (Ed.), *Simpler networks and vertebrate behavior* (pp. 251-265). Sunderland, MA: Sinauer.

Grant, D. S. (1986). Delayed alternation and short-term memory in the rat. In D. F. Kendrick, M. E. Rilling, & M. R. Denny (Eds.), *Theories of animal memory* (pp. 153-171). Hillsdale, NJ: Erlbaum.

Honig, W. K. (1978). Studies of working memory in the pigeon. In S. H. Hulse, H. Fowler, & W. K. Honig (Eds.), *Cognitive processes in animal behavior* (pp. 211-248). Hillsdale, NJ: Erlbaum.

Hunter, W. S. (1913). The delayed reaction in animals and children. *Behavioral Monographs, 2*, 1-86.

Lowy, A. M., Ingram, D. K., Olton, D. S., Walker, S. B., Reynolds, M. A., & London, E. D. (1985). Discrimination learning requiring different memory components in rats: Age and neurochemical comparisons. *Behavioral Neuroscience, 99*, 638-651.

Olton, D. S. (1983). Memory functions and the hippocampus. In W. Seifert (Ed.), *Neurobiology of the hippocampus* (pp. 335-373). New York: Academic Press.

Ordy, J. M., Thomas, G. J., Volpe, B. T., Dunlap, W. P., & Columbo, P. M. (1988). An animal model of human-type memory loss based on aging, lesion, forebrain ischemia and drugs with the rat. *Neurobiology of Aging, 9*, 667-683.

Pulsinelli, W. A., & Brierly, J. B. (1979). A new model of bilateral hemispheric ischemia in the unanesthetized rat. *Stroke, 10*, 267-272.

Sherry, D. F., & Schacter, D. L. (1987). The evolution of multiple memory systems. *Psychological Review, 94*, 439-454.

Squire, L. R. (1969). Effects of pretrial and posttrial administration of cholinergic and anticholinergic drugs on spontaneous alternation. *Journal of Comparative and Physiological Psychology, 69*, 69-75.

Squire, L. R. (1982). The neuropsychology of memory. *Annual Review of Neuroscience, 5*, 241-273.

Squire, L. R. (1987). Memory: Neural organization and behavior. In F. Plum (Ed.), *Handbook of physiology: Section 1. The nervous system: Vol. 5. Higher functions of the brain* (Part I, pp. 295-371). Bethesda, MD: American Physiological Society.

Thomas, G. J. (1984). Memory: Time binding in organisms. In L. R. Squire & N. Butters (Eds.), *Neuropsychology of memory* (1st. ed., pp. 374–384). New York: Guilford Press.

Thomas, G. J., & Gash, D. M. (1986). Differential effects of posterior septal lesions on dispositional and representational memory. *Behavioral Neuroscience, 100,* 712–719.

Thomas, G. J., & Gash, D. M. (1988). Differential effects of hippocampal ablations on dispositional and representational memory in the rat. *Behavioral Neuroscience, 102,* 635–642.

Thomas, G. J., & Gash, D. M. (1990). Movement-associated neural excitation as a factor in spatial representational memory in rats. *Behavioral Neuroscience, 104,* 552–563.

Van Hoesen, G. W. (1985). Neural systems of the non-human primate forebrain implicated in memory. *Annals of the New York Academy of Sciences, 444,* 97–112.

West, M. J. (1990). Stereological studies of the hippocampus: A comparison of the hippocampal subdivisions of diverse species including hedgehogs, laboratory rodents, wild mice, and men. *Progress in Brain Research, 83,* 13–36.

Zola-Morgan, S., Squire, L. R., & Amaral, D. (1986). Human amnesia and the medial temporal region: Enduring memory impairment following a bilateral lesion limited to field CA1 of the hippocampus. *Journal of Neuroscience, 10,* 2950–2967.

43

Beyond Neuronal Excitability: Receptive Field Analysis Reveals That Association Specifically Modifies the Representation of Auditory Information

NORMAN M. WEINBERGER

Introduction

This chapter explains how the application of receptive field (RF) analysis has solved an important problem in the neurobiology of learning and memory. To the best of my knowledge, no previous adequate solution of this problem has been published. Because the critical data have been provided by members of my laboratory, I make use of these data here. However, this chapter is not an overview of either our findings or our model of the acquisition and storage of information; these have been set forth elsewhere (Weinberger, Ashe, Diamond, et al., 1990; Weinberger, Ashe, Metherate, et al., 1990). Rather, this chapter focuses on the logic of RF analysis in learning and memory, and gives examples of empirical verification of this line of inquiry. The rationale transcends a particular set of data, and I hope that it will be applied broadly.

The views that follow are clearly subject to personal bias. This is always a problem, but is exacerbated by the multiple claims that we have (1) identified subtle but critical errors in logic of previous approaches, (2) applied an experimental approach that is novel in the field of the neurobiology of learning and memory, and (3) obtained crucial data that have solved the problem. The only justifications I can offer for this potentially self-indulgent exercise is that the problem is important, no other explicit solution of the problem is known, and the editors of this volume have provided the opportunity.

The Problem

There exists a lengthy, well-documented experimental literature showing that learning, especially Pavlovian conditioning, is accompanied by the rapid development of physiological plasticity of neuronal responses to a conditioned stimulus (CS), particularly in the sensory neocortex of the modality of the CS (see Weinberger & Diamond, 1987, for a review of auditory cortex). In general, relative to control periods, visual CSs evoke larger responses in the visual cortex, somatosensory CSs in the somatosensory cortex, and auditory CSs in the auditory cortex.[1] The literature includes more than ample documentation, based upon extensive and exhaustive controls, that the sensory cortical plasticity is a result of associative processes.

The problem to which I refer can be stated fairly simply. I phrase it in terms of the auditory system, with which the bulk of the research has been concerned:

> *Do facilitated CS evoked responses in the auditory cortex that are caused by association index a general increase in neuronal excitability, or do they index an actual change in the way auditory information is processed and represented?*

If learning simply facilitates sensory responses because the animal is more excited, even if that excited state is produced by associative processes, then these facilitated responses may be viewed merely as an indirect way to index the state of arousal and are likely to be of no particular importance for understanding the neural bases of learning and memory. In short, with reference to learning, they maybe considered to be trivial.

In this brief chapter, I focus on apparently critical tests of this issue performed by Hall and Mark (Hall & Mark, 1967; Mark & Hall, 1967). These are exemplars of strategies that have been used to examine the critical factors in sensory evoked plasicity during learning.[2] Hall and Mark rejected the claim that auditory system plasticity during conditioning indexes a change in the processing or representation of information about the CS. Rather, they concluded that such facilitated CS evoked responses were the results of a general increase in neuronal excitability induced by fear.

In what follows, I try to make evident the assumptions of these important experiments, as well as to show how RF analysis has provided critical data that reveal the opposite to be true: Association of a CS with another stimulus does indeed involve an actual, systematic, highly specific modification of the processing and representation of acoustic information. In short, learning produces profound changes in sensory cortex, which go beyond changes in neuronal excitability to changes in the representation of the external world—that is, modification of actual information.

Evidence That Auditory Cortical Plasticity during Learning Is Trivial

Hall and Mark performed two tightly linked studies. They recorded evoked potentials (EPs) to a click stimulus throughout the auditory system and in the reticular formation while rats were trained in several paradigms. In the following presentation, I confine my remarks to the data from the auditory cortex and the thalamic auditory system, the

---

[1]These findings do not imply that CS evoked plasticity develops only in sensory cortex. Full consideration of the complete distribution of such plasticity is far beyond the scope and purposes of this chapter.

[2]A study by Kitzes, Farley, and Starr (1978) addressed this issue more recently but less effectively. We have previously provided a thorough critique of their findings and conclusions (Diamond & Weinberger, 1989).

medial geniculate body (MGB). Although our own RF data are presently limited to these structures, our analysis of the involved logic is applicable throughout the nervous system.

Experiment 1 (Mark & Hall, 1967): "Acoustically Evoked Potentials in the Rat during Conditioning"

The salient features of Experiment 1 were as follows. Rats were trained to press a bar for food, and a conditioned emotional response (CER) was established by presenting clicks repetitively (one per second) for about 1 minute (the CS), followed by unavoidable footshock (the unconditioned stimulus, or the US). Strength of the CER was quantified in terms of the amount of suppression of bar pressing during presentation of the clicks. Prior to training, animals were highly habituated to the presentation of continuous clicks (4–10 sessions) during which click EPs were recorded; these EPs were used to establish a baseline with which to compare the click EPs during conditioning sessions.

The major results were as follows:

1. The amplitude of EPs in the auditory cortex and MGB was greater during conditioning sessions than during habituation sessions.
2. EP amplitude decreased during behavioral extinction sessions to pretraining (habituation) levels, and increased again during subsequent reconditioning sessions.
3. The amplitude of click EPs showed the same effects when a photic stimulus was used as the CS in conditioning; in this case, the clicks were presented continually as background stimuli.

The authors concluded that "observed changes in evoked potentials during aversive conditioning were not related to associative factors, acquired conditional or discriminative properties of the acoustic stimulus, but to some more general factor that is frequently correlated with the CER" (Mark & Hall, 1967, p. 890).

Experiment 2 (Hall & Mark, 1967): "Fear and the Modification of Acoustically Evoked Potentials during Conditioning"

Experiment 2 concerned the general factor responsible for increased responses to click, both when clicks were the CS and when they were not the CS. CER conditioning was also used. In addition, the authors focused on the possible role of movement in the facilitation of click EPs. Controls included using electrical stimulation of the cochlea or ventral cochlear nucleus as the CS, and training animals to freeze.[3] The major findings were as follows:

---

[3]Some animals were trained in an appetitive task. Because the vast majority of conditioning studies are defensive rather than appetitive, and because RF analysis to date has been used in defensive conditioning, data from the appetitive task are not discussed. In any event, they are not crucial either to the present analysis or to the major points of this chapter.

4. EPs in the auditory cortex and MGB to electrical CS stimulation increased during conditioning.
5. EPs to background clicks were increased during conditioning to a photic CS while subjects learned to freeze.

The authors concluded that increased EPs to clicks were not due to movement.

The results of the two studies together were taken as conclusive evidence that the increased responses to clicks in the auditory cortex and MGB were not caused by the association between clicks and shock, but rather reflected the nonassociative factor of fear, which was common to conditioning both with photic and with click CSs. As the authors stated, "these changes are not a function of the acquired conditional or discriminative properties of the CS. Or to put it another way, they are not related to what may be considered the neural substrate of conditioning" (Mark & Hall, 1967, p. 876).

An Analysis of the Logic of the Hall and Mark Experiments

The logic of the Hall and Mark experiments seems to be straightforward and clear. I explicitly state their findings (I), that which seems to be implicit in their experimental designs and interpretations (II), and the conclusion that follows (III):

   I. *The amplitudes of click EPs in the auditory cortex and MGB are greater than those during habituation in two different training circumstances: when the clicks serve as a CS and when a photic stimulus serves as the CS.*
  II. *The increases in the amplitude of click EPs under these two circumstances represent the same neural phenomenon.*
 III. *If two different training circumstances produce the same neural phenomenon, then that phenomenon is not restricted to either one of the circumstances.*

Statements I and III are above question. Statement I summarizes the major findings. Although neither paper included statistical analysis of the data, some quantitative data were presented, and the illustrations provided are quite clear. Thus, we may fully accept the findings as summarized in statement I.

Statement III follows logically from statements I and II. The conclusion that the increases in click EPs cannot be due to their signal value as a CS is clearly based on the conclusion that the increases are not limited to training in which the clicks serve as the CS.

Statement II is not made explicitly in either paper. I infer this proposition from the logic of the experimental designs and from the authors' conclusions based on these designs. If statement II is not implicit and is not the logical basis for the conclusion that rejects facilitation of click EPs as indexing the effective associative value of the CS, then the following discussion is wrong-minded and irrelevant. The reader is asked to consider this point carefully and reach his or her own conclusion.

In my view, statement II is essential for the authors' conclusions. Moreover, as obviously true as it may appear to be, I argue that acceptance of proposition II requires empirical verification, not logical justification. Furthermore, until and unless someone can demonstrate that statement II is true, the findings *do not support the conclusion that facilitation of EPs to click CSs results from fear rather than from the specific associative value of the clicks as predictors of shock.*

Receptive Field Analysis Can Distinguish between State-Based, General Increases in Response versus Associatively Based, Highly Specific Increases in Neuronal Response

How is it possible to determine whether increased responses to an acoustic CS represent the same or different processes for different training circumstances? Two steps are necessary: conceptual and empirical.

The conceptual step is to think of the problem in terms of sensory system function as well as in terms of learning. Elsewhere, I have discussed in detail the fact that two separate disciplines focus on information processing in the brain: the neurobiology of learning and memory, on the one hand, and the field of sensory physiology, on the other hand (Weinberger & Diamond, 1988). Moreover, there has been minimal cross-fertilization between the fields, despite the fact that they share some common goals. As more evidence of experience-based plasticity in sensory systems accumulates, far transcending developmental plasticity and including adult plasticity (e.g., Kaas et al., 1990), workers in sensory neurobiology are being drawn more closely to learning and memory (e.g., Delacour, Houcine, & Talbi, 1987; Recanzone, Merzenich, Jenkins, Grajski, & Dinse, in press). Whether the reverse trend occurs remains to be seen. Behavioral studies have discovered that the representation of a CS is changed by learning (Holland, 1990). Furthermore, there is reason to believe that the storage of information may occur where it is processed (Squire, 1987). I believe that a rapprochement between the two fields would be symbiotic.

When behavioral manipulations that modify sensory system activity are viewed from a sensory as well as a learning perspective, then a fundamental construct of sensory physiology becomes prominent; this is the RF. The RF of a cell is that part of the relevant sensory epithelium that, when stimulated, affects the activity of a given sensory system neuron. Common RFs are orientation RFs in the visual cortex, patches of skin in the somatosensory system, and frequency RFs in the auditory system. With the RF construct in mind, it becomes easier to see that understanding the effects of behavioral manipulations on physiological responses in sensory systems requires the use of many stimuli along a dimension rather than a single stimulus value, that of the CS.

Seen from this perspective, it is obvious that behavioral training that produces *increased evoked response to a sound may change RFs in either of two ways: (1) a general increase in response across the RFs or (2) a highly specific change, perhaps centered on the CS. The former would reflect (1) a general increase in neuronal excitability, whereas the latter would indicate (2) a highly specific change in the coding and representation of stimuli.*

To make this explicit, Figure 43.1 illustrates the two possibilities. Shown are cartoon RFs at pre- and posttraining. The top panel shows that response to the CS

General Increase in RF

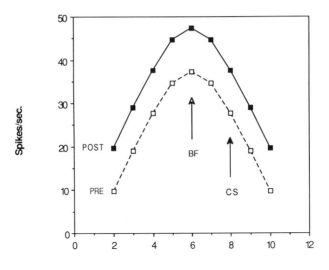

CS-Specific RF Plasticity

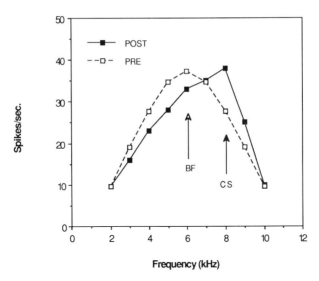

Frequency (kHz)

FIGURE 43.1. Examples of possible changes in RFs. Top: General increase: Responses to all frequencies are increased equally. Bottom: CS-specific RF plasticity: Responses to the CS frequency (solid arrow) are increased to the same extent as in the top panel; however, responses to most other frequencies, including that of the pretraining best frequency (BF; open arrow), are reduced.

frequency (8.0 kHz) is increased at posttraining compared to pretraining. Note, however, that this is but one of many increased responses across the frequency domain; this type of RF plasticity is a general increase in response. The lower panel illustrates the same magnitude of increase to the CS frequency. However, increases are restricted to the CS and an adajacent frequency (9.0 kHz). Responses to other frequencies are decreased, including that of the best frequency (BF; 6.0 kHz).

Given a sensory perspective centered on the RF, the empirical step follows directly: Determine the RFs of neurons before and after a behavior manipulation. If the increased response at the CS actually reflects nonassociative, general increases in some state of the organism, then responses to non-CS frequencies should also be increased. In contrast, if the increased response at the CS actually reflects the associative value of the CS, then responses to other frequencies will not be increased to the same extent, and may show no change or even a decrease.

In short, a critical test of the problem raised by Hall and Mark is possible through the use of RF analysis when used in a hybrid learning–sensory physiology experimental design.

Resolution of the Problem

Within the past 6 years, my laboratory has performed experiments on the auditory cortex and the MGB in which RFs for frequency have been obtained before and at various times following classical conditioning and sensitization training.[4]

Classical Conditioning

Findings for classical conditioning unequivocally demonstrate that associative processes produce highly specific plasticity of RFs at both the auditory cortex and MGB. The first study reported this effect for two nonprimary auditory cortical fields in the cat, the secondary and ventral ectosylvian fields. Maximal changes were evident at the frequency that served as the CS during rapidly developing pupillary conditioning. Moreover, the CS-specific plasticity was maintained unless behavioral extinction was accomplished, in which case the plasticity was reversed (Diamond & Weinberger, 1986, 1989).

More recently, we have extended these studies to the primary auditory cortical fields (Bakin & Weinberger, 1990) and the MGB of the guinea pig (Edeline and Weinberger, 1991a, 1991b, 1992) during cardiac conditioning or sensitization training (CS = tone at a non-BF; pawshock at CS offset in conditioning or unpaired in sensitization training). At both levels of the thalamo-cortical auditory system, Pavlovian conditioning produced highly specific modification of RFs. Responses to the frequency that had been used as the CS were markedly increased, whereas responses to other frequencies were increased little, did not change at all, or were decreased. This combination of changes across frequency was often sufficient to retune cells; thus, the frequency used as the CS often became the new BF. Moreover, the highly specific modifications in RFs were maintained for the duration of recording (up to 24 hours tested in the auditory cortex).

In summary, the use of RF analysis during classical conditioning revealed that behavioral training does not simply produce an increased response to any stimulus, but

---

[4]We have also studied habituation. Findings for habituation are not discussed in this chapter; suffice it to say that the findings reveal that habituation produces highly specific decreases in response to the habituated tonal frequency (Condon & Weinberger, 1990, 1991).

can be specific to the CS. This finding by itself establishes increased neuronal responses to the CS in the auditory system as indexing changes in the coding and representation of information, rather than general changes in neuronal excitability. *In short, learning does more than generally increase excitability; it alters the pattern of excitability, increasing responses to the CS, but decreasing responses to non-CS stimuli.*

This finding probably explains why Hall and Mark found increased responses to their CS during aversive conditioning. But it does not explain why they found increased responses to background acoustic stimuli when a photic stimulus was the CS. To understand this final facet of the problem, we must turn to our data for sensitization training.

Sensitization

What happens to the RF when a tone and shock are unpaired, so that animals do not learn a tone–shock association? The answer is surprisingly simple: Sensitization training also increases responses to the CS frequency. It does so because *it increases responses to many or all frequencies. That is, sensitization produces a general increase in neuronal excitability!* Therefore, if the experimenter restricts his or her investigation to only one stimulus value, that of the CS, then he or she will observe increased responses to the CS, whether the behavioral training produces an associative or a sensitized effect on responses to the CS.

To put it another way, statement II (see above) is *not* supported. The findings of RF analysis, as summarized above, invalidate the crucial assumption that increased responses to the same stimulus in two training circumstances represent the same neural phenomenon. Quite the contrary, the two training processes produce different phenomena *that appear to be similar at the frequency of the CS, but are revealed to be different across the frequency RF.* Figures 43.2–43.4 provide illustrations of the effects of Pavlovian conditioning and sensitization training on RFs in the auditory cortex and MGB (Edeline & Weinberger, 1991a; Bakin & Weinberger, 1990).

In summary, we explain the findings of Hall and Mark in the following manner. First, increased responses to click CSs during aversive conditioning indexed a highly specific change in the way that acoustic information was processed, as a function of associative effects. Second, the increased responses to clicks as background stimuli during presentation of a photic stimulus as the CS indexed a general increase in excitability as a result of sensitization. Additional support for this conclusion is based on ongoing studies in our laboratory. We have trained animals in a sensitization paradigm in which the CS is a photic stimulus instead of an acoustic tone. RFs for frequency were obtained in the auditory cortex before and following this training. This "cross-modality" sensitization paradigm produces general increases in the auditory frequency RF. Moreover, these general increases are indistinguishable from those produced by auditory sensitization training (Bakin & Weinberger, 1990). If one of the effects of sensitization caused by the presence of shock is considered to be fear, then Hall and Mark may have been correct when they invoked fear as the cause of facilitated click EPs in the cross-modality conditioning situation (photic CS, back ground clicks); however, because aversive stimuli have many effects, even this conclusion cannot be accepted in the absence of appropriate critical data.

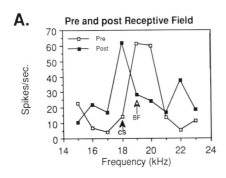

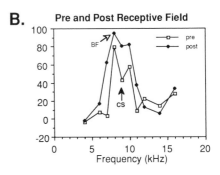

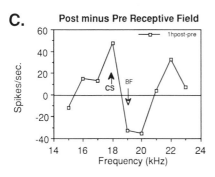

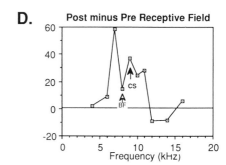

FIGURE 43.2. RFs obtained from MGB cells obtained during conditioning (**A, C**) and sensitization training (**B, D**). For conditioning, the posttraining RF was shifted with respect to the pretraining RF, so that the frequency of the CS became the new BF (**A**). The quantitative effects of conditioning are seen in **C**, in which the pretraining RF is subtracted from the posttraining RF. Note that the maximal increase is at the CS frequency and that responses to the pretraining BF were greatly reduced. This constitutes a CS-specific change in the RF. For sensitization, responses to most frequencies were increased. Note that the largest increase was not at the CS frequency (**D**). This is an example of a general increase in the RF, which was always found for sensitization training. From "Subcortical Adaptive Filtering in the Auditory System: Associative Receptive Field Plasticity in the Dorsal Medial Geniculate Body" (pp. 165, 171) by J.-M. Edeline and N. M. Weinberger, 1991, *Behavioral Neuroscience, 105,* 154–175. Copyright 1991 by the American Psychological Association. Reprinted by permission.

In any event, the issue is not simply whether nonassociative processes (in the sense of the absence of an association between background clicks and shock during pairing of photic and shock stimuli) can facilitate evoked sensory responses under some circumstances. *Rather, it is whether the actual processing and representation of the CS is altered by associative processes within its sensory modality. The answer to this question is* "Yes."

Perspective

Hall and Mark asked the critical question at an appropriate time. Moreover, their experimental approach was thoughtful and apparently incisive. In fact, within the context of their studies and the time period in which they were performed, their experiments and conclusions are not easy to fault. Nonetheless, we cannot ignore later developments and broader conceptualizations. Hall and Mark believed they had solved the problem, as we now believe we have done. We may well be proven to be wrong. But for now, we think that both convincing logical and empirical bases exist for accepting the conclusion that associative learning does indeed involve CS-specific modification of frequency RFs within the auditory cortex and thalamus. It follows that this finding goes beyond mere increased excitability to an important higher level of cerebral physiology, that of the representation of information itself.

Final Comment: On the Function of the Auditory Cortex in Learning and Memory

This concluding section is intended to provide a context within which to consider the findings provided by RF analysis in learning, particularly as they pertain to the auditory cortex. It cannot be comprehensive, and indeed may be somewhat misleading, because some findings may not apply to all species. But as the goal here is to promote the questioning of assumptions implicit in certain critiques of cortical physiological plasticity in learning and memory, the material reviewed (however briefly) should serve the purpose.

Although it has been established that learning involves systematic and highly specific modification of the neural coding and representation of sensory stimulation within the auditory cortex and thalamus, it might be argued nonetheless that these

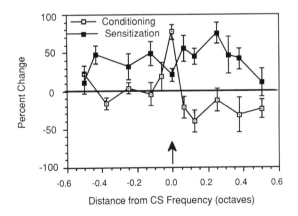

Medial Geniculate Body

FIGURE 43.3. Group data for the MGB. This presents the average of RF difference functions (as seen in Figures 43.2C and 43.2D), normalized across cells and expressed as percentage of change from pretraining and distance in octaves from the CS frequency. Note that conditioning produces a highly specific and marked increased response at the CS frequency; actual sideband suppression due to conditioning is seen for frequencies higher than the CS. In contrast, sensitization produces a broad increase across frequency. From "Subcortical Adaptive Filtering in the Auditory System: Associative Receptive Field Plasticity in the Dorsal Medial Geniculate Body" (p. 171) by J.-M. Edeline and N. M. Weinberger, 1991, *Behavioral Neuroscience*, *105*, 154–175. Copyright 1991 by the American Psychological Association. Reprinted by permission.

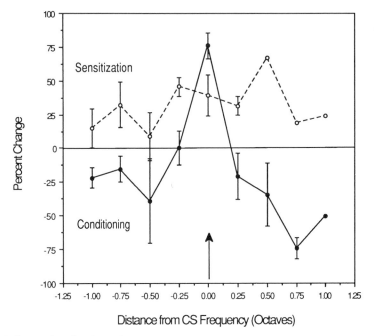

FIGURE 43.4. Group data for the auditory cortex. As in the case of the MGB, conditioning produces a marked and highly specific increase to the CS frequency. At the cortex, there is marked sideband suppression for almost all other frequencies. In contrast, sensitization training produces a general increase across frequency. From "Classical Conditioning Induces CS-Specific Receptive Field Plasticity in the Auditory Cortex of the Guinea Pig" (p. 281) by J. S. Bakin and N. M. Weinberger, 1990, *Brain Research, 536,* 271–286. Copyright 1990 by Elsevier Science Publishers. Reprinted by permission.

events are unimportant for learning—indeed, that the auditory cortex is not needed for learning. The rationale for this view is based upon findings that ablation of the auditory cortex apparently does not prevent learning or retention.

Regarding retention, the nictitating membrane (eyeblink) conditioned response model survives decerebration (Mauk & Thompson, 1987). As for learning, it has long been known that animals can learn many auditory tasks in the absence of auditory cortex, particularly those based on fairly simple acoustic parameters—for example, detecting the onset of a sound or changes in the intensity or frequency of continual sounds, including testing situations that are based on fear conditioning (Neff, Diamond, & Casseday, 1975). Consistent with these results, LeDoux (Chapter 40, this volume) has found that auditory-based fear conditioning, expressed as cardiovascular and freezing conditioned responses, is not impaired by destruction of auditory cortex. On the other hand, the auditory cortex appears to be necessary for learning tasks that involve localization of sound, change in frequency pattern, change in temporal pattern, change in duration of sounds, identification of temporal order, detection of absolute threshold, change in attribute of a signal (e.g., frequency) as a function of duration, change in sounds of complex spectra, comparison of signals involving recent memory, frequency discrimination learning, and extinction (Neff et al., 1975; Teich et al., 1988; Jenkins & Merzenich, 1984).

One can only conclude that some learning does not require the auditory cortex and other learning does require the auditory cortex. This same type of statement is also applicable to most if not all other brain structures. The problem is to formulate an adequate account that reduces lists of tasks to, one would hope, a small number of basic functions. There is little general agreement on or understanding of the functions of most brain structures; perhaps this attests to conceptual difficulties as well as lack of data. The auditory cortex is no exception. But "nonstandard" conceptions of sensory cortex in general and the auditory cortex in particular offer some promising lines of thought and inquiry.

Auditory cortex has been viewed traditionally in purely sensory terms. But even within this realm, it is becoming increasingly evident that the auditory cortex is involved in abstractions that form the basis of perceptions rather than sensations. For example, the frequency representation on the auditory cortex appears actually to be a representation of pitch, which is an abstraction based on stimulus frequency (Whitfield, 1985). Diamond (1979) has questioned the purely sensory-perceptual nature of sensory cortex on anatomical, physiological, and behavioral grounds. He has provided a strong case for the reinterpretation of sensory cortex as being equally associative and motor in function. Finally, apparently long forgotten is the interpretation, based on an extensive review of the ablation–learning literature, that the auditory cortex is essential for the retention of information so that comparisons of acoustic stimuli can be made over time (Neff et al., 1975).

Given this expanded context, there remains for RF analysis and learning the fact that RF plasticity in the auditory cortex develops during fear conditioning, but acquisition of the behavioral expression of conditioned fear to a sound does not require the auditory cortex. Is this a problem? No, except within one particular conceptual framework. This framework includes the following assumptions: (1) that learning can be completely accounted for by reflex circuits, and (2) that the importance of these circuits is to produce a particular behavioral conditioned reflex at the time of presentation of the conditioned stimulus. Although one can accept the findings of experiments done within this framework, one need not accept the assumptions, for they are indeed far too narrow and circumscribed to account for more than a fragment of learning, as has been well established in the history of the psychology of learning (e.g., Rescorla, 1988).

Elsewhere, we have discussed possible, not verified, functions for learning-induced RF plasticity (Weinberger & Diamond, 1987; Weinberger, Ashe, Diamond, et al., 1990). We view conditioned reflexes as a convenient tool to understand some aspects of learning, but we take as fundamental the fact that to understand learning, one must understand the acquisition and storage of information. Once the organism has acquired information, overt behaviors may be made immediately or at any time in the indefinite future, depending upon the situation. It is this flexibility, based on information, that we view as the hallmark of learning and the major challenge. It is to the questions of how information is acquired, represented, and stored that RF plasticity in learning can make important contributions.

ACKNOWLEDGMENTS

The research described in this chapter was supported by the following grants: Office of Naval Research Grants No. N00014-84-K-0391, No. N00014-87-K-0043, and No. N00014-91-J-1193, and Defense Advanced Research Projects Agency Grant No. N00014-89-J-3178. I wish to give special acknowledgment to Jon Bakin, Dave Diamond, Jean-Marc Edeline, and Jacquie Weinberger, and to gratefully acknowledge the technical support of Ann Markham, Manprit Dhillon, Duc Pham, Branko Lepan, Phuc Pham, Thu Huynh, and Gabriel Hui for computer programming and support. I also wish to give special thanks to Jeff Winer for his advice on the morphological organization of the auditory system.

REFERENCES

Bakin, J. S., & Weinberger, N. M. (1990). Classical conditioning induces CS-specific receptive field plasticity in the auditory cortex of the guinea pig. *Brain Research, 536,* 271-286.

Condon, C. D., & Weinberger, N. M. (1990). Frequency-specific receptive field plasticity in auditory cortex during habituation. *Society for Neuroscience Abstracts, 16,* 762.

Condon, C. D., & Weinberger, N. M. (1991). Habituation produces frequency-specific plasticity of receptive field plasticity in the auditory cortex. *Behavioral Neuroscience, 105,* 416-430.

Delacour, J., Houcine, O., & Talbi, B. (1987). "Learned" changes in the responses of the rat barrel field neurons. *Neuroscience, 23,* 63-71.

Diamond, D. M., & Weinberger, N. M. (1986). Classical conditioning rapidly induces specific changes in frequency receptive fields of single neurons in secondary and ventral ectosylvian auditory cortical fields. *Brain Research, 372,* 357-360.

Diamond, D. M., & Weinberger, N. M. (1989). Role of context in the expression of learning-induced plasticity of single neurons in auditory cortex. *Behavioral Neuroscience, 103,* 471-494.

Diamond, I. T. (1979). The subdivisions of the neocortex: A proposal to revise the traditional view of sensory, motor and associational areas. *Progress in Psychobiology and Psychology, 8,* 1-43.

Edeline, J.-M., & Weinberger, N. M. (1991a). Subcortical adaptive filtering in the auditory system: Associative receptive field plasticity in the dorsal medial geniculate body. *Behavioral Neuroscience, 105,* 154-175.

Edeline, J.-M., & Weinberger, N. M. (1991b). Thalamic short term plasticity in the auditory system: Associative retuning of receptive fields in the ventral medial geniculate body. *Behavioral Neuroscience, 105,* 618-639.

Edeline, J.-M., & Weinberger, N. M. (1992). Associative retuning in the thalamic source of input to the amygdala and auditory cortex: Receptive field plasticity in the medial geniculate division of the medial geniculate body. *Behavioral Neuroscience, 106,* 81-105.

Hall, R. D., & Mark, R. G. (1967). Fear and the modification of acoustically evoked potentials during conditioning. *Journal of Neurophysiology, 30,* 893-910.

Holland, P. C. (1990). Forms of memory in Pavlovian conditioning. In J. L. McGaugh, N. M. Weinberger, & G. Lynch (Eds.), *Brain organization and memory: Cells, systems, and circuits* (pp. 78-105). New York: Oxford University Press.

Jenkins, W. M., & Merzenich, M. M. (1984). Role of cat primary auditory cortex for sound localization behavior. *Journal of Neurophysiology, 53,* 819-847.

Kaas, J. H., Krubitzer, L., Chino, Y., Langston, A. Polley, E., & Blair, N. (1990). Reorganization of retinotopic cortical maps in adult mammals after lesions of the retina. *Science, 248,* 229-231.

Kitzes, L. N., Farley, G. R., & Starr, A. (1978). Modulation of auditory cortex unit activity during performance of a conditioned response. *Experimental Neurology, 62,* 678-796.

Mark, R. G., & Hall, R. D. (1967). Acoustically evoked potentials in the rat during conditioning. *Journal of Neurophysiology, 30,* 875-892.

Mauk, M. D., & Thompson, R. F. (1987). Retention of classically conditioned eyelid responses following acute decerebration. *Brain Research, 403,* 89-95.

Neff, W. D., Diamond, I. T., & Casseday, J. H. (1975). Behavioral studies of auditory discrimination: Central nervous system. In W. D. Keidel & W. D. Neff (Eds.), *Handbook of sensory physiology: Vol. 2. Auditory system* (pp. 307-401). New York: Springer-Verlag.

Recanzone, G. H., Merzenich, M. M., Jenkins, W. M., Grajski, K. A., & Dinse, H. A. (in press). Topographic reorganization of the hand representation in cortical area 3b of owl monkeys trained in a frequency discrimination task. *Journal of Neurophysiology.*

Rescorla, R. A. (1988). Behavioral studies of Pavlovian conditioning. *Annual Review of Neuroscience, 11,* 329–352.

Squire, L. R. (1987). *Memory and brain.* New York: Oxford University Press.

Teich, A. H., McCabe, P. M., Gentile, C. G., Jarrell, T. W., Winters, R. W., Liskowsky, D. R., & Schneiderman, N. (1988). Role of auditory cortex in the acquisition of differential heart rate conditioning. *Physiology and Behavior, 44,* 405–412.

Weinberger, N. M., & Diamond, D. M. (1987). Physiological plasticity of single neurons in auditory cortex: Rapid induction by learning. *Progress in Neurobiology, 29,* 1–55.

Weinberger, N. M., & Diamond, D. M. (1988). Dynamic modulation of the auditory system by associative learning. In G. M. Edelman, W. E. Gall, & W. M. Cowan (Eds.), *Auditory function: The neurobiological bases of hearing* (pp. 485–512). New York: Wiley.

Weinberger, N. M., Ashe, J. H., Diamond, D. M., Metherate, R., McKenna, T. M., & Bakin, J. (1990). Retuning auditory cortex by learning: A preliminary model of receptive field plasticity. *Concepts in Neuroscience, 1,* 91–132.

Weinberger, N. M., Ashe, J. H., Metherate, R., McKenna, T. M., Diamond, D. M., Bakin, J. S., Lennartz, R. C., & Cassady, J. M. (1990). Neural adaptive information processing: A preliminary model of receptive field plasticity in auditory cortex during Pavlovian conditioning. In M. Gabriel & J. Moore (Eds.), *Learning and computational neuroscience: Foundations of adaptive networks* (pp. 91–138). Cambridge, MA: Bradford Books/MIT Press.

Whitfield, I. C. (1985). The role of auditory cortex in behavior. In A. Peters & E. G. Jones (Eds.), *Cerebral cortex: Vol. 4. Association and auditory cortex* (pp. 329–349). New York: Plenum.

44

Knowledge Structures in Temporally Adaptive Conditioned Responding

JOHN W. MOORE

Introduction

One of the outstanding problems of cognitive science is that of understanding how experience assigns meaning to events. How does one set of stimulus attributes become symbolic of another set of stimulus attributes? This is the question of semantics. Neuropsychologists are interested in this question because of its implications for a wide variety of cognitive and performance dysfunction. Classical conditioning provides a set of tools for investigating, at both the behavioral and neurophysiological levels, how semantic relations among events are established and how these relationships determine behavior. Classical conditioning provides a set of coherent theories, typically mathematical models, which are capable of detailed descriptions of phenomenology. Recently, there has been progress in determining how these models might be aligned with specific neural circuits and processes (Commons, Grossberg, & Staddon, 1991; Gabriel & Moore, 1990). This chapter considers the kinds of knowledge instilled by classical conditioning procedures and the ways in which this knowledge is expressed in behavior. My approach is both experimental and theoretical. Its focus is the classically conditioned eyeblink/nictitating membrane response of the rabbit (Gormezano, Prokasy, & Thompson, 1987).

Conditioning and Knowledge

Although everyone recognizes that conditioning procedures instill (or modulate) stimulus–response relationships, contemporary treatments of classical conditioning emphasize its propositional character: Conditioning procedures produce knowledge about stimulus–response *relationships* from which, with the addition of performance rules, the observed relationships between a conditioned stimulus (CS) and a conditioned response (CR) can be deduced (Rescorla, 1988). Here are some examples of such propositions:

• *The CS predicts the unconditioned stimulus (US)*. The CS predicts the US because its capacity to control behavior depends on the extent to which it is an informative (reliable and nonredundant) signal that the US will occur. Subjects learn to ignore potential CSs that are poor predictors of the US, and they learn to suppress CRs to stimuli (conditioned inhibitors) that predict that the US will not occur.

• *The CS is equivalent to the US*. The CS is equivalent to the US because it can serve as a US surrogate, as in Pavlovian second-order conditioning, as long as the original CS retains its status as a good predictor of the original US.

• *The CS causes the US*. The CS causes the US because subjects will work to produce it if it predicts an agreeable US and to avert it if it predicts a disagreeable US, as in demonstrations of conditioned reinforcement.

Thus, the existence and validity of these statements are forced by the outcome of experiments. We would not say that the subjects learn that a CS predicts the US, were it not for studies showing that predictive informational content is the *sine qua non* of conditioning. We would not say that the CS is equivalent to the US, were it not for the fact that second-order conditioning is a proven associative phenomenon. We would not say that the CS causes the US, were it not for the fact that subjects work as though they *believe* that the CS causes the US. (Some theorists would claim that conditioned reinforcement in instrumental learning reflects acquired intrinsic value, and not the CS's predictive relationship to the US. If this were true, a CS would be an instrumental reinforcer, despite extinction or deflation of its relationship to the US.)

To say that conditioning procedures produce knowledge seems to contradict the view that a CR is a creature of unconscious brain processes. Although such an appraisal goes against contemporary views of the relationship between cognitive and the consciousness (Kihlstrom, 1987), let us review the evidence.

• Human subjects with severe (declarative) memory deficits can acquire an eyeblink CR (Weiskrantz & Warrington, 1979), although perhaps more slowly than normal.

• In particular, H. M., whose anterograde amnesia is too well known to be reviewed here, has been able to acquire and retain an eyeblink CR, while at the same having no recollection of having been trained (D. Woodruff-Pak, personal communication, January 1991).

• Studies of eyeblink conditioning with normal human subjects have shown that they are generally quite poor at describing (declaring) what went on during training. Moreover, correlations between speed and level of conditioning, on the one hand, and the degree of conscious awareness of the contingencies between the CS and the US, on the other, are weak at best (Kwaterski & Moore, 1969; Moore, Newman, & Glasgow, 1969).

• These observations appear to be consistent with studies showing that eyeblink CRs can be acquired and performed by rabbits that have had most of their cerebral neocortex or hippocampus removed (Moore, 1979).

In addition to expressing knowledge, a CR often possesses the basic elements of ski. Its topographical features—latency, rise time, peak amplitude—typically vary from one set of procedures to the next in such a way that they are appropriate to the "task demands" imposed by training parameters (Levey & Martin, 1968). In this sense, CRs express adaptation. The main evidence for this adaptive character of the CR is that its topographically features (latency, rise time, peak amplitude) vary systematically with the CS-US interval employed in training. In particular, eyeblink CRs are "temporally adaptive." Temporal adaptability simply means that the peak amplitudes of CRs occur within a restricted temporal window that also contains the US. In this sense, CRs reflect the knowledge that the US occurs at a specific time after the CS. Recent evidence for this assertion is reviewed later. For now, it suffices to say that subjects learn not only to expect the US in the presence of the CS (*The CS predicts [causes] the US*), but also when to expect it (*The US occurs [CS-US interval] after the CS*). Once again, the consequences of conditioning can be stated as a knowledge structure.

In light of the evidence, then, it is not the case that the ability to express this knowledge verbally is necessary for eyeblink conditioning in humans. In animals, it is not the case that brain structures such as the hippocampus, often cited as being essential for declarative memory in humans, are essential for conditioning to occur. It is not the case that conditioning without these structures is functionally attenuated, as, for example, in the case of blindsight, where some residual "vision" exists of which the subject has little or no conscious awareness. Although the knowledge formed in conditioning is unconscious or implicit, its existence cannot be doubted. The words chosen to express learned propositions ("causes," "predicts," "is equivalent to," and the like) have more than heuristic value and metatheoretical content.

Mechanisms of Knowledge Acquisition and Expression

Classical conditioning procedures establish propositional statements about relationships among events. What are the mechanisms that bring this about? What happens in the brain that might explain the temporally adaptive properties of the eyeblink CR, for example? Propositions about conditioning procedures and accompanying rules for generating CRs arise from "associative mechanisms." For psychologists, associative mechanisms are captured by mathematical models. These models take the form of rules for changing the strength of the connection between the CS and the US. Such rules consist of two factors: One factor is the level of CS processing, and the other factor is the level of US process (Desmond, 1990; Dickinson & Mackintosh, 1978; Sutton & Barto 1990; Rescorla, 1988). For physiologists, associative mechanisms refer to events within the nervous system. Our goal has been to unite these two domains by finding implementations of mathematical models within real brains. Some examples follow:

• A colleague and I (Moore & Stickney, 1980) presented a real-time computational version of a model originally proposed by Mackintosh (1975). By combining the predictions of this model with results of lesion experiments, we proposed that the hippocampus could be aligned with computations determining the level of CS processing. Brain implementations of models of this general class have been proposed by Schmajuk and his associates (e.g., Schmajuk & DiCarlo, 1991).

• We (Moore & Blazis, 1989) proposed a brain implementation of Sutton and Barto's (1981) "one-element" model of classical conditioning. The implementation was derived from two sets of considerations: (1) the parameter values of the model that produced the most realistic simulations of phenomena such as CS-US interval functions and response topography; (2) knowledge of the anatomy and physiology of the cerebellum and its demonstrated essential role in the behavior.

• We (Desmond & Moore, 1988) presented a "two-element" real-time model that describes behavioral phenomena with greater accuracy than the parameterized Sutton and Barto (1981) model. This model can also be implemented in the cerebellum (as described later), although details of the implementation differ significantly from that proposed (Moore & Blazis, 1989) for the Sutton–Barto model.

Response Topography and Conditioned Stimulus–Unconditioned Stimulus Intervals

CR topography is a function of the CS-US interval used in training. Long CS-US intervals give rise to "inhibition of delay," which Pavlov assumed to result from an active countervailing force that persists until the US is imminent. In fact, there is little evidence to support Pavlov's explanation of the delayed temporal placement of CRs. Instead of an inhibiting countervailing force, the phenomenon of delayed CR placement is more likely due to fact that the CR generated by a long CS-US interval is a *different* response from that generated by a shorter CS-US interval.

That a CR generated with one CS-US interval can be regarded as being a different response from one generated with a different CS-US interval is attested to by studies in which subjects are trained with a short CS-US interval and then shifted to a longer CS-US interval. Typically, the CR in the temporal window defined by the short CS-US interval undergoes extinction, while a new CR emerges in a window defined by the longer CS-US interval. It is *not* the case that the original CR migrates to the new temporal window; it remains within its original window but progressively loses amplitude, while at the same time the new CR emerges in the time window defined by the new US locus.

Additional evidence for the temporal specificity of CRs comes from a widely cited study by Millenson, Kehoe, and Gormezano (1977). Their training protocol consisted of mixing two CS-US intervals, one of 400 milliseconds (msec) and another of 700 msec. One 400-msec probes, response topography showed a peak appropriate to the 400-msec CS-US interval. On 700-msec probes, response topography revealed two peaks—one appropriate for the shorter interval, and another appropriate for the longer interval. This finding is consistent with the following proposition (among others): *If the CS extends beyond 400 msec, make another CR; if it does not, do nothing.* However one chooses to phrase this proposition, the implication remains that subjects learned not one CR but two, one appropriate for each CS-US interval it experienced.

The Millenson et al. (1977) experiment used a forward-delay paradigm, which is technical jargon for the fact that, on training trials, CS onset preceded the US and stayed "on" until the US occurred, at which time it went "off." Because the CS and US terminated together, another valid proposition for this protocol would be this one: *The US never occurs after CS offset.*

But what of trace conditioning paradigms, in which CS onset precedes the US but goes off beforehand? Where do subjects place their CRs: during the CS's "on" phase or during its "off" phase? As in the case of forward-delay paradigms, CRs occur within the temporal window defined by the CS-US interval, so the answer is that CRs occur during the off phase.

In trace conditioning there are two possible CS-US intervals, one defined by CS onset and the other defined by CS offset. Hence, two propositions are valid:

- *The US follows CS onset.*
- *The US follows CS offset.*

Which proposition is learned? Which CS-US interval defines the temporal window in which to place CRs? The answer is both, although this is constrained by such details as the CS's duration and the time between its offset and the US, the so-called "trace interval."

We (Desmond & Moore, 1991a) trained rabbits using a trace conditioning protocol in which the CS was a 150-msec tone followed 200 msec later by the US, giving a nominal CS-US interval of 350 msec. After training, subjects were given probe trials (without the US). These consisted of presentations of the tone for durations of 150, 400, and 600 msec. The two longer duration tones often resulted in bimodal (double-peaked) response topographies. The initial peak was located 350 msec after tone onset, within the temporal window defined by the interval between CS onset and the US. The second peak was located 200 msec after tone offset, within the temporal window defined by the interval between CS offset and the US. This second peak, though inappropriate for the nominal CS-US interval of 350 msec, is appropriate for the CS-US interval of 200 msec defined in terms of tone offset. Thus, for example, on a typical 600-msec probe trial, one peak appeared 350 msec after tone onset and the other appeared 800 msec after tone onset. Hence, the following knowledge structures were learned:

- *The US follows CS onset by* x *amount of time.*
- *The US follows CS offset by* y *amount of time.*

A Model for Conditioned Response Topography

All of the foregoing facts about response topography and CS-US intervals are encompassed by the Desmond and Moore (1988) model, which is here summarized:

- Both stimulus onset and offset trigger propagated activity in the nervous system, which provides time-tagged information to putative sites where learning occurs. In its simplest form, this activation can be represented by a tapped-delay line. Each tap off the delay line represents a unique input element. Each such element encodes the time after stimulus onset or the time after stimulus offset, but not both.
- In addition to time-tagged stimulus elements, there are two nodal processing elements where learning occurs. One nodal element associates active stimulus elements with the US and passes this information to the other nodal element, which uses this information to generate appropriate (adaptively time) CR topographies.

Neuropsychologists occurred with memory processes would ask where these ingredients for learning about the timing of the CS and the US and the expression of appropriate CR topography exist in the brain. I briefly review the status of research on this question for eyeblink conditioning in the rabbit.

The Desmond and Moore (1991a) experiment forces the conclusion that subjects learn how to generate adaptively timed CRs. This implies the existence of knowledge structures such as the following: *Initiate a CR such that the peak amplitude corresponds to the time of the US*. How is this "motor program" derived from the proposition *The US follows CS onset by* x *amount of time?* According to evidence reviewed previously, the mechanisms for generating the motor commands from the corresponding proposition need not engage brain processes involved in conscious awareness.

Our (Desmond & Moore, 1988) two-element neural network model, which prompted our trace conditioning experiment, suggests and answer. Recall that the model consists of two processing units that both receive parallel time-tagged input from the CS. The assumed delay-line representation of CS onset and offset enables these two processing units, which are thought to reside within cerebellar cortex, to treat CS-initiated input as a sequence of discrete events. One processing unit, which we have postulated as being a Golgi cell, learns when the US is expected. The other processing unit, which we have postulated as being a Purkinje cell, uses this information (through simple Hebbian rules such as association) to generate an output that ultimately produces a temporally adaptive CR. In brief, the Golgi cell learns when USs occur in relation to CS onsets and offsets, and the Purkinje cell learns how to generate the appropriate CR topography (Moore, Desmond, & Berthier, 1989).

What about the basic knowledge about conditioning, such as *The CS predicts the US?* Where does this knowledge arise, and what role does it play in the development of adaptively timed CRs? We have suggested that acquisition of this knowledge comes about through simple Hebbian learning among brainstem neurons that project to the cerebellum. Activation of these brainstem neurons is conveyed to cerebellar cortex, where it interacts with the Golgi and Purkinje cells in such a way as to achieve the appropriate CR waveform.

The activation or firing of the brain stem neuron encodes the knowledge that *The CS [predicts, is equivalent to, causes] the US*. There is no temporal specificity in these structures. We have proposed that the Golgi cell interacts with the activation from brainstem neurons, within the cerebellum, in such a way as to provide the temporal specificity needed to instruct the Purkinje cell to *Initiate a CR such that the peak amplitude occurs at the time of the US*. Thus, the Golgi cell, acting as the intermediary, encodes *The US follows the CS by* x *amount of time*.

Conditioned Response Topography and the Brain

The foregoing explanatory scheme raises several questions, which are now being addressed experimentally.

• Where in the brain does CR topography become manifest? As anticipated by the model, Purkinje cells in cerebellar cortex change firing in relation to CRs. Changes from base-rate firing occur up to 200 msec before the CR is observed at the periphery (Berthier & Moore, 1986). The Purkinje cells project to cerebellar deep nuclei. Firing patterns of CR-related deep nuclear cells predict the peripheral CR with an average lead time of 50 msec (Berthier & Moore, 1990), and the activity of some of these cells accounts for over 80% of the variation in CR waveforms (Berthier, Barto, & Moore, 1991). Deep nuclear cells project to red nucleus and form there to the motoneurons that mediate the CR.

• Is there any evidence to support the idea that brainstem neurons fire in a way consistent with the scheme's assumption that such cells encode *The CS predicts the US?* Furthermore, are such neurons located in structures that could project this information to cerebellar cortex? Some red nucleus cells fire in the CR-dependent manner required by the model (Desmond & Moore, 1991b), and some red nucleus sends a weak projection to the portion of cerebellar cortex implicated in this behavior. Some neurons of the sensory trigeminal system (which forms the US–unconditioned response reflex pathway) fire in a CR-dependent manner (Desmond & Moore, 1986; Richards, Ricciardi, & Moore, 1991), and some neurons of this system project to the relevant portion of the cerebellum. In neither case, however, has it been proven that a given red nucleus or sensory trigeminal neuron, with the requisite firing characteristics, actually projects to cerebellar cortex.

Summary

Classical conditioning is related to the general problem of semantics because it is concerned with the formation of knowledge about the relationships among events. In the case of classical eyeblink conditioning, there is good evidence that three propositions are learned and that the learning of one is propaedeutic to the next. The first thing learned is that *The CS predicts the US*. This knowledge, expressed in the activity of brainstem structures such as red nucleus, enables learning of the next proposition—namely, *The US follows the onset (or offset) of the CS by a specific amount of time*. My colleagues and I have proposed that this learning involves Golgi cells of cerebellar cortex. This knowledge then allows the cerebellar Purkinje cells to learn the motor program *Initiate a CR such that the peak amplitude occurs at the time of the US*.

This scheme, which is largely consistent with cerebellar physiology and anatomy, must be regarded as provisional. Indeed, others have suggested that learning occurs in the red nucleus under the guidance of positive feedback through a circuit that includes the lateral reticular nucleus and cerebellar deep nuclei (Houk, 1989). By this account, CRs are triggered by the direction action of the CS on red nucleus, instead of by the action of the CS on a Purkinje cell. That is, the red nucleus encodes not only the initial learning (*The CS predicts the US*), but also the motor program for generating CRs (procedural knowledge). The cerebellar cortex nevertheless participates in shaping these motor programs so that they are temporally adaptive. Our (Desmond & Moore, 1991b) study of single-unit activity in red nucleus supports the view that this structure's contribution to classical conditioning is more complex than that of merely relaying motor commands from the cerebellum to the motoneurons.

ACKNOWLEDGMENTS

My research program and preparation of this chapter were supported by grants from the Air Force Office of Scientific Research and the National Science Foundation.

REFERENCES

Berthier, N. E., Barto, A. G. & Moore, J. W. (1991). Linear systems analysis of the relationships between firing of deep cerebellar neurons and the classically conditioned nictitating membrane response. *Biological Cybernetics, 65*, 99–105.

Berthier, N. E., & Moore, J. W. (1990). Cerebellar Purkinje cell activity related to the classically conditioned nictitating membrane response. *Experimental Brain Research, 63*, 341–350.

Berthier, N. E., & Moore, J. W. (1990). Activity of deep cerebellar nuclear cells during classical conditioning of the nictitating membrane response. *Experimental Brain Research, 83*, 44–54.

Commons, M. L., Grossberg, S., & Staddon, J. E. R. (Eds.). (1991). *Neural network models of conditioning and action*. Hillsdale, NJ: Erlbaum.

Desmond, J. E. (1990). Temporally adaptive responses in neural models: The stimulus trace. In M. Gabriel & J. Moore (Eds.), *Learning and computational neuroscience: Foundations of adaptive networks* (pp. 421–456). Cambridge, MA: Bradford Books/MIT Press.

Desmond, J. E., & Moore, J. W. (1986). Dorsolateral pontine tegmentum and the classically conditioned nictitating membrane response: Analysis of CR-related activity. *Experimental Brain Research, 65*, 59–74.

Desmond, J. E., & Moore, J. W. (1988). Adaptive timing in neural networks: The conditioned response. *Biological Cybernetics, 58*, 405–415.

Desmond, J. E., & Moore, J. W. (1991a). Altering the synchrony of stimulus trace processes: Tests of a neural-network model, *Biological Cybernetics, 65*, 161–169.

Desmond, J. E., & Moore, J. W. (1991b). Single-unit activity in red nucleus during the classically conditioned rabbit nictitating membrane response. *Neuroscience Research, 10*, 260–279.

Dickinson, A., & Mackintosh, N. J. (1978). Classical conditioning in animals. *Annual Review of Psychology, 29*, 587–612.

Gabriel, M., & Moore, J. (Eds.). (1990). *Learning and computational neuroscience: Foundations of adaptive networks*. Cambridge, MA: Bradford Books/MIT Press.

Gormezano, I., Prokasy, W. F., & Thompson, R. F. (Eds.). (1987). *Classical conditioning* (3rd ed.). Hillsdale, NJ: Erlbaum.

Houk, J. C. (1989). Cooperative control of limb movements by the motor cortex, brainstem and cerebellum. In R. M. J. Cotterill (Ed.), *Models of brain function* (pp. 309–325). Cambridge, England: Cambridge University Press.

Kihlstrom, J. F. (1987). The cognitive unconscious. *Science, 237*, 1445–1452.

Kwaterski, S. E., & Moore, J. W. (1969). Differential eyelid conditioning based on opposing instrumental contingencies. *Journal of Experimental Psychology, 79*, 547–551.

Levey, A. B., & Martin, I. (1968). Shape of the conditioned eyelid response. *Psychological Review, 75*, 398–408.

Mackintosh, N. J. (1975). A theory of attention: Variations in the associability of stimuli with reinforcements. *Psychological Review, 82*, 276–298.

Millenson, J. R., Kehoe, E. J., & Gormezano, I. (1977). Classical conditioning of the rabbit's nictitating membrane response under fixed and mixed CS-US intervals. *Learning and Motivation, 8*, 351–366.

Moore, J. W. (1979). Brain processes in conditioning. In A. Dickinson & R. A. Boakes (Eds.), *Mechanisms of learning and motivation: A memorial volume to Jerzy Konorski* (pp. 111–142). Hillsdale, NJ: Erlbaum.

Moore, J. W., & Blazis, D. E. J. (1989). Cerebellar implementation of a computational model of classical conditioning. In P. Strata (Ed.), *The olivocerebellar system in motor control* (pp. 387–399). Berlin: Springer-Verlag.

Moore, J. W., Desmond, J. E., & Berthier, N. E. (1989). Adaptively timed conditioned responses and the cerebellum: A neural network approach. *Biological Cybernetics, 62*, 17–28.

Moore, J. W., Newman, F. L., & Glasgow, B. (1969). Intertrial cues as discriminative stimuli in human eyelid conditioning. *Journal of Experimental Psychology, 79*, 319–326.

Moore, J. W., & Stickney, K. J. (1980). Formation of attentional-associative networks in real-time: Role of the hippocampus and implications for conditioning. *Physiological Psychology, 8*, 207–217.

Rescorla, R. A. (1988). Behavioral studies of Pavlovian conditioning. *Annual Review of Neuroscience, 11,* 329-352.

Richards, W. G., Ricciardi, T. N., & Moore, J. W. (1991). Activity of spinal trigeminal pars oralis and adjacent reticular formation units during differential conditioning of the rabbit nictitating membrane response. *Behavioural Brain Research, 44,* 195-204.

Schmajuk, N. A., & DiCarlo, J. J. (1991). Neural dynamics of hippocampal modulation of classical conditioning. In M. L. Commons, S. Grossberg, & J. E. R. Staddon (Eds.), *Neural network models of conditioning and action* (pp. 149-180). Hillsdale, NJ: Erlbaum.

Sutton, R. S., & Barto, A. G. (1981). Toward a modern theory of adaptive networks: Expectation and prediction. *Psychological Review, 88,* 135-170.

Sutton, R. S., & Barto, A. G. (1990). Time-derivative models of Pavlovian reinforcement. In M. Gabriel & J. Moore (Eds.), *Learning and computational neuroscience: Foundations of adaptive networks* (pp. 497-537). Cambridge, MA: Bradford Books/MIT Press.

Weiskrantz, L., & Warrington, E. K. (1979). Conditioning in amnesic patients, *Neuropsychologia, 17,* 187-194.

Studies in Birds and Invertebrates

Some animals provide unique opportunities to ask specific questions about the organization of memory. For example, some species of birds store and later retrieve food by remembering the locations of multiple hiding places. This behavior in the natural environment has been a topic of much study in the past decade, and more recently the food-storing adaptation itself has been related to brain anatomy (Chapter 45). In addition, young chicks can rapidly acquire and retain a simple kind of learning. This learning has served as a model system for study of the anatomy and neurochemistry of memory formation (Chapters 46 and 47). Invertebrates have proved especially advantageous for some kinds of studies, because their relatively simple nervous systems are amenable to cellular and molecular studies. Both short- and long-lasting forms of several kinds of learning have been demonstrated, including habituation, sensitization, and classical conditioning, and all of these are under investigation at the cellular–synaptic level of analysis. The invertebrate animal that has contributed the most to this enterprise is the sea slug *Aplysia* (Chapter 48). Similar studies are also underway in another invertebrate, *Hermissenda* (Chapter 49). Chapter 50 considers what is being learned from both species.

45

Memory, the Hippocampus, and Natural Selection: Studies of Food-Storing Birds

DAVID F. SHERRY

Animals that make unusual demands on memory have unusual memories. The best known of these specialized memory systems are those responsible for the rather different phenomena of song production (Nottebohm, 1987) and imprinting (Horn, 1985) in birds. The simplest explanation for the existence of such adaptively specialized memory systems is that natural selection is capable of modifying memory to perform particular functions. Across the animal kingdom, memory probably consists of a diversity of systems and mechanisms that rivals the more apparent diversity in the structure and form of animals. There are clear implications for human memory. Human memory almost certainly possesses many properties that are adaptations to the social and physical environment in which humans evolved. Furthermore, human memory, like animal memory, may consist of a collection of systems specialized to varying degrees, each an adaptation to serve a particular function (Sherry & Schacter, 1987).

Food-storing birds provide an illustration of the evolutionary modification of memory, with some interesting complexities. These birds establish large numbers of widely scattered caches and later retrieve their stored food by remembering the spatial location of each cache (for reviews, see Sherry, 1989; Shettleworth, 1990; Vander Wall, 1990). A black-capped chickadee (*Parus atricapillus*) can create several hundred separate caches in a winter day and can recall the locations of these sites for at least several weeks. It is a remarkable feat. The complexities arise in attempting to determine exactly how memory has been modified to solve the problem of remembering large numbers of dispersed spatial locations. Comparative studies of food-storing chickadees and tits (in the family Paridae) give rather little indication that food-storing and non-food-storing species differ in their performance of memory tasks in the laboratory (Krebs, Healy, & Shettleworth, 1990). Studies of food-storing nutcrackers and jays (in the family Corvidae) show, in contrast, differences among species in the performance of such tasks as delayed-nonmatching-to-sample, and performance is correlated with the degree to which these species store food (Balda & Kamil, 1989; Olson, 1991). Although the behavioral data do not present a simple picture, recent neuroanatomical work shows clear evidence of adaptive modification of memory function in many food-storing birds. The hippocampal complex of chickadees, tits, jays, and other food-storing birds is over twice the size of the hippocampal complex of comparable non-food-storing species (Sherry, Vaccarino, Buckenham, & Herz, 1989; Krebs, Sherry, Healy, Perry, & Vaccarino, 1989). In what follows, I present a brief description of food storing as it occurs in the wild, then discuss experimental studies of memory in food-storing birds. This is followed by an examination of recent research on the role of the hippocampus in cache recovery, homing by pigeons, and orientation by voles, emphasizing what species differences in the hippocampus can tell us about the evolution of memory.

The Behavioral Ecology of Food Storing

A variety of birds store for later consumption a good deal of the food they encounter. Food storing occurs in all of the North American chickadees and titmice (Sherry, 1989; Hampton & Sherry, in press) and in most of the European tits, although it is absent in two European species, the blue tit (*Parus caeruleus*) and the great tit (*Parus major*). Most jays and crows store food, as do nuthatches and a variety of nonpasserines such as woodpeckers and raptors. Chickadees, jays, and nuthatches do not concentrate their supply of stored food into a single larder, but instead disperse it over a large number of small caches, each containing only a few food items. The European marsh tit (*Parus palustris*), for example, is capable of storing several hundred seeds, insects, and invertebrate prey per day. It places only one item at each cache, and spreads its caches over a territory a few hectares (4–5 acres) in size (Cowie, Krebs, & Sherry, 1981). Neighboring caches are spaced several meters apart, and cache sites are never reused. Each stored food item goes to a new location in the bark of a tree, in a hollow stem, in a patch of moss, in a leaf bud, or in some other small crevice or cavity. Field and laboratory studies of marsh tits, black-capped chickadees, Clark's nutcrackers (*Nucifraga columbiana*), and other food-storing birds show that stored food is recovered by remembering the spatial locations of caches (Bunch & Tomback, 1986; Kamil & Balda, 1985; Sherry, Krebs, & Cowie, 1981; Sherry, 1984; Shettleworth & Krebs, 1982; Vander Wall, 1982). For chickadees and tits, which retrieve their stored food within a few days after caching it, this means remembering a hundred or more novel spatial locations for several days. For Clark's nutcrackers, which may not retrieve until spring food stored the previous fall, it means remembering several thousand spatial locations for many months.

Cache Site Memory in the Laboratory

Laboratory studies examining memory for cache sites have taken several different approaches to the problem. Black-capped chickadees in captivity will readily store food in small holes in tree branches in an indoor aviary. In a 15-minute trial, a chickadee will store 4 to 5 sunflower seeds, placing them in the eligible cache sites in its artificial forest. Later, after intervals ranging from a few hours to many days, chicka-dees can find their caches quickly and accurately (Sherry, 1984; Figure 45.1). Their retrieval performance is more accurate than would be expected by chance, which can be calculated assuming random search among the potential cache sites. The birds do not need to be able to see or smell the stored seeds, because they can return accurately to cache sites where the stored food has been experimentally removed prior to searching. If, however, the birds have been allowed to remove the stored food themselves, they do not revisit these already harvested caches. Birds do not perform above chance level in finding food placed at other sites by the experimenter or by another bird (Shettleworth & Krebs, 1982; Baker et al., 1988). There is no systematic relation between the sequence in which the caches were made and the sequence of retrieving them, and no indication that the birds mark cache sites in any way to aid in relocating them.

In the laboratory, black-capped chickadees can remember the locations of their caches for at least 28 days, though accuracy declines over this time (Hitchcock & Sherry, 1990). In the wild, a good deal of stored food is lost to other birds and to rodents. Chickadees and tits are able to monitor this loss of cached food. They will shift their caching activity away from areas where cache pilfering is high, although

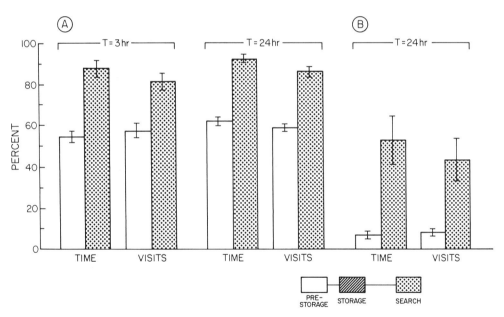

FIGURE 45.1. Cache recovery by marsh tits (**A**) and black-capped chickadees (**B**). Shown are the amount of time spent at sites used for caching and the number of visits to these sites, as a percentage of total time at all possible sites and total visits to all sites. Behavior was recorded prior to storing ("prestorage") and during search for caches ("search"). T is the time interval between storage and search. Both species spent more time searching cache sites than might be expected from pre-existing biases or preferences to search these sites, shown by prestorage behavior. Marsh tits created a mean of 4.9 caches in the 12 sites available, for a chance success rate of 40.8%. Chickadees created a mean of 4.4 caches in the 72 sites available, for a chance rate of 6.1%. All differences between prestorage and search were significant by t test ($p < .05$). The data in **A** are from Sherry, Krebs, and Cowie (1981); the data in **B** are from Sherry (1984).

they appear unable to avoid sites with distinctive cues that predict cache loss (Stevens, 1984; Hampton & Sherry, 1992).

A number of studies have examined the kinds of information used by food-storing birds to relocate their caches. As we shall see, hippocampal lesions that disrupt cache recovery leave simple associations intact, indicating that caches are not relocated by remembering cues common to all cache sites. The clearest demonstration that the information used to relocate caches is spatial comes from Vander Wall's (1982) work with Clark's nutcrackers. Nutcrackers stored pine seeds in the gravel-covered floor of a large aviary, on which had been placed a variety of rocks and logs. Before allowing the birds to search for their caches, Vander Wall displaced all of the objects on one side of the aviary 20 cm in the same direction. When the birds returned to search for stored food, they were accurate with respect to the landmarks, not the caches. On the side of the aviary where the objects had been moved, the birds missed their caches by about 20 cm. On the side of the aviary where objects had been left in place, their search attempts produced the hidden seeds. In the middle of the aviary, where the birds might be expected to have used as landmarks some objects that were later moved and some that were not, the displacement error in their search attempts ranged from 0 to 20 cm. Recent comparative work has shown that food-storing chickadees use landmarks and prominent edges to identify spatial locations in much the same way that non-food-storing birds use these spatial features (Cheng & Sherry, in press).

Comparative Studies of Memory

As noted earlier, comparative analyses of memory in food-storing and non-food-storing birds have produced equivocal results. Studies with chickadees and tits show better performance by food storers on some tasks, such as discriminating sites where food was previously encountered from sites where food was never found (Krebs et al., 1990), but better performance by non-food-storing birds on other tasks, such as an analogue of the radial arm maze (Krebs, Hilton, & Healy, 1990). Among corvids, however, the situation is different. Clark's nutcracker and the scrub jay (*Aphelocoma coerulescens*) both store food, but to different degrees. Nutcrackers store food to a greater extent, depend more on stored food, and show greater morphological specialization for transporting food to storage sites (Vander Wall & Balda, 1981). Scrub jays store less and depend less on stored food than do nutcrackers. In laboratory tests, nutcrackers are more accurate in recovering caches than are scrub jays (Balda & Kamil, 1989). On a delayed-nonmatching-to-sample task, nutcrackers achieve a higher level of performance that do scrub jays over a range of delays between presentation of the sample stimulus and the nonmatching test, and both perform better than do pigeons (Olson, 1991).

The Avian Hippocampus

Birds possess a hippocampus, though the anatomical differences between this structure and the mammalian hippocampus are striking. As shown in Figure 45.2, the avian

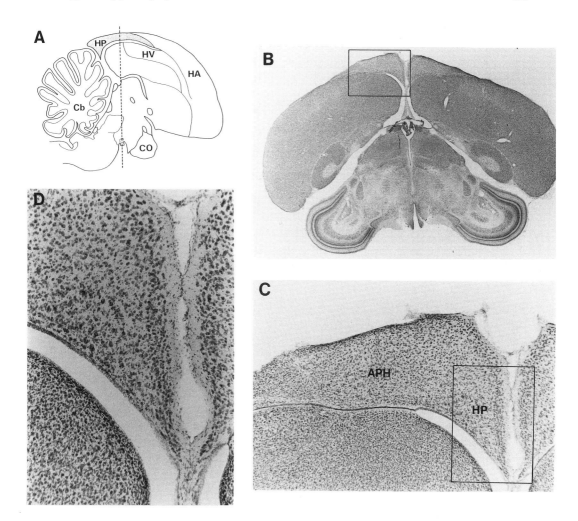

FIGURE 45.2. The brain and hippocampus of the black-capped chickadee. Boxed regions in **B** and **C** are shown enlarged in **C** and **D**, respectively. Clockwise from upper left: (**A**) Sagittal section showing the hippocampus (shaded) and the plane of section for photographs. (**B**) Coronal section at a point between the anterior and posterior commissures. (**C**) The hippocampus (HP) and area parahippocampalis (APH). (**D**) The ventromedial hippocampus. Cb, cerebellum; CO, optic chiasm; HA, hyperstriatum accessorium; HV, hyperstriatum ventrale. Photomicrographs by G. Ivy and M. Khurgel.

hippocampal complex consists of two regions in the dorsomedial forebrain, the hippocampus (HP in the figure) and the area parahippocampalis (APH). In birds there are no clear cell fields of the kind that characterize Ammon's horn, and no obvious dentate gyrus in HP-APH. Instead, there is a fairly uniform distribution of cells bounded by the midline, the dorsal surface of the brain, the ventricle, and the lateral boundary with hyperstriatum accessorium. Nevertheless, ontogenetic studies show that the hippocampal complex of birds develops from the same pallial precursors as does the mammalian hippocampus (Källén, 1962). The avian hippocampus is also comparable to the mammalian hippocampus in its connections with other parts of the brain. Both receive afferents from the contralateral hippocampus, the nucleus of the diagonal band, the lateral hypothalamus, and locus coeruleus, and send efferents to the septum, the nucleus of the diagonal band, and the hypothalamus (Benowitz & Karten, 1976; Casini, Bingman, & Bagnoli, 1986; Krayniak & Siegel, 1978). One distinctive avian feature is a V-shaped concentration of cells in the most ventromedial region of the hippocampus. Similarities in the distribution of neuropeptides in the avian and mammalian hippocampus have led Erichsen, Bingman, and Krebs (1991) to propose a homology between this V-shaped region and Ammon's horn.

The Hippocampus and Memory in Birds

The structural homology between the avian and mammalian hippocampal complexes raises the question of functional homology. Does the avian hippocampus serve any of the memory functions associated with the mammalian hippocampus? Experiments with black-capped chickadees have shown that it does. Hippocampal lesions disrupt cache recovery, other spatial tasks, and working memory, but leave intact the ability to form simple associations.

In an early study, Krushinskaya (1966) showed that ablations of the hyperstriatum that included the hippocampal complex disrupted the ability of Eurasian nutcrackers (*Nucifraga caryocatactes*) to find their hidden food caches. Nutcrackers continued to search for cedar seeds they had stored, but their search attempts were misplaced with respect to the true locations of the caches they had made. In other ways, their behavior was normal.

Black-capped chickadees suffer very similar deficits following aspiration lesions of HP-APH (Sherry & Vaccarino, 1989). Although they continue to eat and cache food normally, their cache recovery attempts are more or less random with respect to the locations of caches (Figure 45.3). Birds with control lesions of the hyperstriatum accessorium, rostral and lateral to the site of hippocampal lesions, relocate their caches as accurately as do unoperated control birds.

The effects of hippocampal lesions in black-capped chickadees were not limited to cache recovery (Sherry & Vaccarino, 1989). Birds that had been trained over a series of trials to find food at particular spatial locations ceased to perform this task accurately following hippocampal aspiration. The task required the birds to learn that 6 of the 60 sites on tree branches in the aviary contained a single piece of food. The same six places were baited on each trial, and birds learned this "place" task relatively quickly. Hippocampal lesions produced a deficit in performance of this task. By contrast, birds that had been trained to associate a cue with the presence of food performed normally. In this latter task, birds were required to learn that small colored cards placed on the tree branches signaled the presence of food. Six different sites were baited on each trial, but the presence of food was always indicated by a cue. Although this "cue" task was acquired more slowly than the place task and appeared more difficult, its performance was not disrupted by lesions. This is the kind of outcome predicted by O'Keefe and Nadel's (1978) proposed "cognitive mapping" function of the hippocampus—namely, that hippocampal damage has a selective effect on tasks with a spatial component—although other theoretical accounts predict a similar dissociation (Eichenbaum, Fagan, Mathews, & Cohen, 1988; Squire & Cave, 1991; Sutherland & Rudy, 1989).

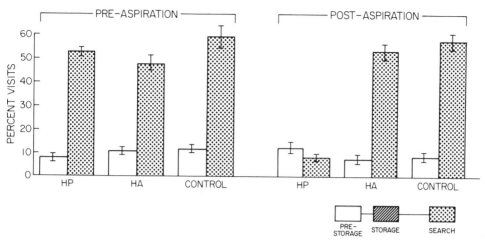

FIGURE 45.3. The effects of hippocampal aspiration lesions on cache recovery by black-capped chicka-dees. "Prestorage" and "search" are as in Figure 45.1. Shown are visits to cache sites as a percentage of visits to all sites for birds with aspiration lesions of HP-APH (HP), aspiration lesions of the same size in hyperstriatum accessorium (HA), and unoperated birds (CONTROL). All differences between prestorage and search behavior were significant by Tukey's HSD ($p < .01$), except for HP birds after aspiration. These birds did not relocate their caches at a rate above that expected from pre-existing biases or preferences to visit those sites. Chance rates of cache encounter ranged from 6% to 9% for different groups. The data are from Sherry and Vaccarino (1989).

Performance on both the place task and the cue task were affected in a further way by hippocampal aspiration. Normally, birds make few revisits to sites they have searched for food. When recovering stored food, black-capped chickadees can avoid searching previously emptied caches (Sherry, 1984), and on the place and cue tasks they made few revisiting errors. Following hippocampal lesions, however, chickadees made large numbers of revisiting errors on both tasks. This is the kind of disruption predicted by the working memory theory of hippocampal function (Olton, Becker, & Handelmann, 1979). The working memory model proposes that the hippocampus plays a central role in *working* memory (memory for performance of the current task; Honig, 1978), but is not involved in *reference* memory (memory for the nature of the task). Revisiting errors by chickadees with HP-APH lesions show that performance of the current task depends on hippocampal function, whether or not the task is spatial in nature; they also show that disruptions in working memory can occur even on prob-lems such as the cue task, for which reference memory is intact. Similar results supporting both the spatial orientation and working memory models of hippocampal function have been obtained in mammals (Jarrard, Okaichi, Steward, & Goldschmidt, 1984).

Hippocampus and the Homing Behavior of Pigeons

Homing by pigeons provides further information on the role of the avian hippocampus in memory, and shows a number of parallels with the role of HP-APH in cache recovery by food-storing birds. Experienced homing pigeons released several kilometers away from a familiar home loft can normally fly home, even if they have no previous experience of the release site. Performance in these experiments is measured by the accuracy of homeward orientation at the release site and by the time required to reach home. Hippocampal lesions produce deficits in homing performance in pigeons, and produce an interesting dissociation of the components of homing performance (Bingman, Bagnoli, Ioalè, & Casini, 1984; Bingman, Ioalè, Casini, & Bagnoli, 1985). Lesioned birds are correctly homeward-oriented at the release site, but fail to arrive home. In fact, lesioned birds released within sight of their home loft do not reach home. Hippocampal damage appears not to disrupt the navigational mechanisms used at the release site, and many such mechanisms have been proposed, including the use of solar, geomagnetic, and olfactory information. The pigeons can choose the correct homeward bearing even after complete hippocampal ablation. What is disrupted by hippocampal ablation is the ability to use familiar local landmarks to identify the home loft.

Several conclusions can be drawn from this result. First, pigeons normally return home by a two-stage process, and the mechanism that permits selection of a homeward bearing at the release site can operate independently of the mechanism responsible for home loft recognition. Second, there are kinds of orientation—such as selection of a homeward bearing at the release site—in which the hippocampus plays no apparent role, at least not in experienced adult birds. The qualification "experienced adult birds" is necessary, because recent results (Bingman, Ioalè, Casini, & Bagnoli, 1990) have shown that young pigeons given hippocampal lesions before being placed in what will be their home loft never do acquire the ability to fly home from distant unfamiliar sites. The hippocampus therefore plays a crucial role in development of the ability to orient correctly at distant sites, but plays no further role in this component of homing once the ability has been acquired.

Comparative Studies of the Avian Hippocampus

Not all passerine birds store food. As noted earlier, chickadees, jays, and nuthatches are avid food storers, but most other species of birds are not. The avian hippocampus reflects this interspecific variation in behavior. A comparison of the volume of the hippocampus, relative to telencephalon size and body weight, for 13 North American families and subfamilies of birds showed the hippocampus to be larger in food-storing than in non-food-storing birds (Sherry et al., 1989). Telencephalic volume accounted for a considerable proportion of the variance in hippocampal volume: Birds with a larger brain have a larger hippocampus. But the occurrence of food storing accounted for a significant proportion of the remaining variance (Figure 45.4). None of this variance could be accounted for by whether the birds are omnivorous or specialized in their diet, are migratory or nonmigratory, or are social or solitary. The same study showed no relation among long-distance migrants between hippocampal size and the distance traveled during migration—a result that might with hindsight be expected from the results of Bingman and his colleagues with homing pigeons. A comparison of European food-storing and non-food-storing species showed the same phenomenon found in North American birds: a clear increase in hippocampal volume in food storers (Krebs et al., 1989).

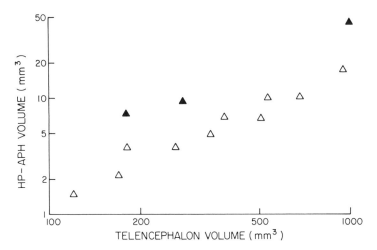

FIGURE 45.4. The relation between hippocampal size (HP-APH volume) and telencephalon size in 3 families of food-storing birds (filled triangles) and 10 families and subfamilies of non-food-storing birds (open triangles). Both axes are logarithmic. In increasing order of telencephalon volume, the food-storing families are Sittidae, Paridae, and Corvidae. Non-food-storing families and subfamilies are Sylviinae, Troglodytidae, Parulinae, Fringillidae, Emberizinae, Passeridae, Mimidae, Cardinalinae, Turdinae, and Sturnidae. The data are from Sherry et al. (1989).

The difference in size of the hippocampal complex between food-storing and non-food-storing birds has an important evolutionary implication. The three families of birds that show the effect—the chickadees and tits, the jays and crows, and the nuthatches—are no more closely related to each other than they are to other, non-food-storing families and subfamilies. Food storers are thus not all descendants of some ancestral species that both stored food and possessed a large hippocampus. The increase in hippocampal size they exhibit has occurred independently and convergently. This shows not only that there existed in several taxonomic groups sufficient heritable variation in hippocampal size to provide the raw material on which natural selection could act, but also that the selective consequences of improved memory function are sufficiently great among food-storing birds to produce comparable modifications of the hippocampus. Artificial selection on homing pigeons also makes this point. Rehkämper, Haase, and Frahm (1988) have shown that the hippocampus of homing pigeons is significantly larger than it is in nonhoming breeds of the same species.

Sexual Selection and Hippocampal Size in Voles

Food-storing birds and homing pigeons are not the only species in which unusual demands on memory have produced neuroanatomical modifications of the hippocampus. Voles are small, plump, short-tailed rodents in the family Cricetidae; various species are found in grassland habitat throughout most of North America. Voles show considerable variation in mating system and social organization. Meadow voles

(*Microtus pennsylvanicus*) are polygynous, and during the breeding season the home ranges of males expand to encompass the home ranges of several females. The pine vole (*M. pinetorum*) and prairie vole (*M. ochrogaster*) are monogamous, and the home ranges of males and females are roughly equal in size throughout the year. Gaulin and Fitzgerald (1986, 1989) have shown in a series of studies that a sex difference in spatial ability accompanies the polygynous mating system and home range size of the meadow vole: Males perform better than females on a number of laboratory spatial tasks. No sex difference in spatial ability occurs in the two monogamous species. This difference in spatial ability is a product of sexual selection. In a polygynous mating system, male reproductive success is highly variable and depends on the number of mates a male encounters. Polygynous male voles compete by ranging widely in search of females. Sexual selection for male competitive ability—in this case, a cognitive competitive ability—has led to greater spatial skills in males than in females. For monogamous male voles, reproductive success does not depend on encountering additional females, and there is no difference between male and female spatial skills. When the volume of the hippocampus was determined (the sum of the volumes of Ammon's horn and the dentate gyrus), a greater hippocampal volume was found in the animals making greater demands on memory. Males of the polygynous meadow vole had a greater hippocampal volume than did females, whereas no sex difference was found in monogamous pine voles (Jacobs, Gaulin, Sherry, & Hoffman, 1990).

The Evolution of Memory

The evolutionary changes in the hippocampus that accompany food storing in birds and polygyny in voles show that the neural substrates of memory can readily be modified by natural selection. Indeed, the difference observed between chickadees and tits on one hand, and nutcrackers on the other, in their ability to perform nonstoring memory problems suggests that there may be more than one way in which memory has been modified to deal with the requirements of remembering large numbers of spatial locations for long durations. The nutcracker solution seems to confer greater facility with other cognitive problems, whereas the chickadee and tit solution does not.

Such variability in outcome is not unusual or unexpected, given the opportunistic way in which natural selection acts. Jacob (1977) has described evolution as a tinkerer, rather than an engineer: It is always forced to modify existing structures for new functions and is forever denied the opportunity of redesigning systems from scratch. Both specialized systems and general systems of broad domain occur in animal and human memory (Sherry & Schacter, 1987). The principal conclusion that can be drawn from the research described here is that the ecological selection pressures that promote food storing have had a cascade of cognitive and neuroanatomical consequences. The operation of memory has been modified, and a major change in a neuroanatomical region that plays an important role in memory has occurred. This research began by asking an ecological question—namely, how do food-storing birds find their hidden caches? It has shown that this approach makes it possible to identify some of the cognitive and neuroanatomical conseqences of using memory to solve specific ecological problems.

ACKNOWLEDGMENTS

I would like to thank Jon Erichsen, Robert Hampton, Christine Hitchcock, and Sara Shettleworth for much helpful discussion. This research was supported by grants from the Natural Sciences and Engineering Research Council of Canada.

REFERENCES

Balda, R. P., & Kamil, A. C. (1989). A comparative study of cache recovery by three corvid species. *Animal Behaviour, 38,* 486-495.

Baker, M. C., Stone, E., Baker, A. E. M., Shelden, R. J., Skillicorn, P., & Mantych, M. D. (1988). Evidence against observational learning in storage and recovery of seeds by black-capped chickadees. *Auk, 105,* 492-497.

Benowitz, L. I., & Karten, H. J. (1976). The tractus infundibuli and other afferents to the parahippocampal region of the pigeon. *Brain Research, 102,* 174-180.

Bingman, V. P., Bagnoli, P., Ioalè, P., & Casini, G. (1984). Homing behavior of pigeons after telencephalic ablations. *Brain, Behavior and Evolution, 24,* 94-108.

Bingman, V. P., Ioalè, P., Casini, G., & Bagnoli, P. (1985). Dorsomedial forebrain ablations and home loft association behavior in homing pigeons. *Brain, Behavior and Evolution, 26,* 1-9.

Bingman, V. P., Ioalè, P., Casini, G., & Bagnoli, P. (1990). The avian hippocampus: Evidence for a role in the development of the homing pigeon navigational map. *Behavioral Neuroscience, 104,* 906-911.

Bunch, K. G., & Tomback, D. F. (1986). Bolus recovery by gray jays: An experimental analysis. *Animal Behaviour, 34,* 754-762.

Casini, G., Bingman, V. P., & Bagnoli, P. (1986). Connections of the pigeon dorsomedial forebrain studied with WGA-HRP and ^{3}H-proline. *Journal of Comparative Neurology, 245,* 454-470.

Cheng, K., & Sherry, D. F. (in press). Landmark-based spatial memory in birds: The use of edges and distances in representing spatial location. *Journal of Comparative Psychology.*

Cowie, R. J., Krebs, J. R., & Sherry, D. F. (1981). Food storing by marsh tits. *Animal Behaviour, 29,* 1252-1259.

Eichenbaum, H., Fagan, A., Mathews, P., & Cohen, N. J. (1988). Hippocampal system dysfunction and odor discrimination learning in rats: Impairment or facilitation depending on representational demands. *Behavioral Neuroscience, 102,* 331-339.

Erichsen, J. T., Bingman, V. P., & Krebs, J. R. (1991). The distribution of neuropeptides in the dorsomedial telencephalon of the pigeon (*Columba livia*): A basis for regional subdivisions. *Journal of Comparative Neurology, 314,* 478-492.

Gaulin, S. J. C., & Fitzgerald, R. W. (1986). Sex differences in spatial ability: An evolutionary hypothesis and test. *American Naturalist, 127,* 74-88.

Gaulin, S. J. C., & Fitzgerald, R. W. (1989). Sexual selection for spatial-learning ability. *Animal Behaviour, 37,* 322-331.

Hampton, R. R., & Sherry, D. F. (in press). Food storing by Mexican chickadees and bridled titmice. *Auk.*

Hampton, R. R., & Sherry, D. F. (1992). *Memory for the outcome of caching.* Manuscript submitted for publication.

Hitchcock, C. L., & Sherry, D. F. (1990). Long-term memory for cache sites in the black-capped chickadee. *Animal Behaviour, 40,* 701-712.

Honig, W. K. (1978). Studies of working memory in the pigeon. In S. H. Hulse, H. Fowler, & W. K. Honig (Eds.), *Cognitive processes in animal behavior* (pp. 211-248). Hillsdale, NJ: Erlbaum.

Horn, G. (1985). *Memory, imprinting, and the brain.* Oxford: Clarendon Press.

Jacob, F. (1977). Evolution and tinkering. *Science, 196,* 1161-1166.

Jacobs, L. F., Gaulin, S. J. C., Sherry, D. F., & Hoffman, G. E. (1990). Evolution of spatial cognition: Sex-specific patterns of spatial behavior predict hippocampal size. *Proceedings of the National Academy of Sciences USA, 87,* 6349-6352.

Jarrard, L. E., Okaichi, H., Steward, O., & Goldschmidt, R. B. (1984). On the role of hippocampal connections in the performance of place and cue tasks: Comparisons with damage to hippocampus. *Behavioral Neuroscience, 98,* 946-954.

Källén, B. (1962). Embryogenesis of brain nuclei in the chick telencephalon. *Ergebnisse der Anatomie und Entwicklungsgeschichte, 36,* 62-82.

Kamil, A. C., & Balda, R. P. (1985). Cache recovery and spatial memory in Clark's nutcrackers (*Nucifraga columbiana*). *Journal of Experimental Psychology: Animal Behavior Processes, 11,* 95-111.

Krayniak, P. F., & Siegel, A. (1978). Efferent connections of the hippocampus and adjacent regions in the pigeon. *Brain, Behavior and Evolution, 15*, 372–388.

Krebs, J. R., Healy, S. D., & Shettleworth, S. J. (1990). Spatial memory of Paridae: Comparison of a storing and a non-storing species, the coal tit, *Parus ater*, and the great tit, *Parus major*. *Animal Behaviour, 39*, 1127–1137.

Krebs, J. R., Hilton, S. C., & Healy, S. D. (1990). Memory in food-storing birds: Adaptive specialization in brain and behavior? In G. M. Edelman, W. E. Gall, & W. M. Cowan (Eds.) *Signal and sense: Local and global order in perceptual maps* (pp. 475–498). New York: Wiley–Liss.

Krebs, J. R., Sherry, D. F., Healy, S. D., Perry, V.H., & Vaccarino, A. L. (1989). Hippocampal specialization of food-storing birds. *Proceedings of the National Academy of Sciences USA, 86*, 1388–1392.

Krushinskaya, N. L. (1966). Some complex forms of feeding behaviour of nutcracker *Nucifraga caryocatactes*, after removal of old cortex. *Zhurnal Evoluzionni Biochimii y Fisiologgia, 2*, 563–568.

Nottebohm, F. (1987). Plasticity in adult avian central nervous system: Possible relation between hormones, learning and brain repair. In F. Plum (Ed.), *Handbook of physiology: Section 1. The nervous system. Vol. 5. Higher functions of the brain* (pp. 85–108). Bethesda, MD: American Physiological Society.

O'Keefe, J., & Nadel, L. (1978). *The hippocampus as a cognitive map*. Oxford: Clarendon Press.

Olson, D. J. (1991). Species differences in spatial memory among Clark's nutcrackers, scrub jays, and pigeons. *Journal of Experimental Psychology: Animal Behavior Processes, 17*, 363–376.

Olton, D. S., Becker, J. T., & Handelmann, G. E. (1979). Hippocampus, space, and memory. *Behavioral and Brain Sciences, 2*, 313–365.

Rehkämper, G., Haase, E., & Frahm, H. D. (1988). Allometric comparison of brain weight and brain structure volumes in different breeds of the domestic pigeon, *Columba livia f.d.* (fantails, homing pigeons, strassers). *Brain, Behavior and Evolution, 31*, 141–149.

Sherry, D. F. (1984). Food storage by black-capped chickadees: Memory for the location and contents of caches. *Animal Behaviour, 32*, 451–464.

Sherry, D. F. (1989). Food storing in the Paridae. *Wilson Bulletin, 101*, 289–304.

Sherry, D. F., Krebs, J. R., & Cowie, R. J. (1981). Memory for the location of stored food in marsh tits. *Animal Behaviour, 29*, 1260–1266.

Sherry, D. F., & Schacter, D. L. (1987). The evolution of multiple memory systems. *Psychological Review, 94*, 439–454.

Sherry, D. F., & Vaccarino, A. L. (1989). Hippocampus and memory for food caches in black-capped chickadees. *Behavioral Neuroscience, 103*, 308–318.

Sherry, D. F., Vaccarino, A. L., Buckenham, K., & Herz, R. S. (1989). The hippocampal complex of food-storing birds. *Brain, Behavior and Evolution, 34*, 308–317.

Shettleworth, S. J. (1990). Spatial memory in food-storing birds. *Philosophical Transactions of the Royal Society of London, B329*, 143–151.

Shettleworth, S. J., & Krebs, J. R. (1982). How marsh tits find their hoards: The roles of site preference and spatial memory. *Journal of Experimental Psychology: Animal Behavior Processes, 8*, 354–375.

Squire, L. R., & Cave, C. B. (1991). The hippocampus, memory, and space. *Hippocampus, 1*, 269–271.

Stevens, T. A. (1984). *Food storing by marsh tits*. Unpublished doctoral dissertation, Oxford University.

Sutherland, R. J., & Rudy, J. W. (1989) Configural association theory: The role of the hippocampal formation in learning, memory, and amnesia. *Psychobiology, 17*, 129–144.

Vander Wall, S. B. (1982). An experimental analysis of cache recovery in Clark's nutcracker. *Animal Behaviour, 30*, 84–94.

Vander Wall, S.B. (1990). *Food hoarding in animals*. Chicago: University of Chicago Press.

Vander Wall, S. B., & Balda, R. P. (1981). Ecology and evolution of food-storage behavior in conifer-seed-caching corvids. *Zeitschrift für Tierpsychologie, 56*, 217–242.

46

Studying Stages of Memory Formation with Chicks

MARK R. ROSENZWEIG, EDWARD L. BENNETT,
JOE L. MARTINEZ, JR., PAUL J. COLOMBO, DIANE W. LEE,
and PETER A. SERRANO

Our overall aim is to test and extend hypotheses about the neurochemical brain processes that must occur between the input of information and its eventual recall. This is the same aim that we stated in the first edition of this book (Rosenzweig & Bennett, 1984), where we described our attempts "to investigate the basic processes and modulatory influences in the stages of memory formation in nonhuman vertebrates" (p. 555), using both laboratory rodents and young chicks. At that time, we were using chiefly rodents, but had begun to work with chicks as well. Now we are working principally with chicks, and we confine this chapter to our methods and findings with them.

As more and more work is accomplished on neural mechanisms of learning and memory, it becomes apparent that many different processes are involved. Many workers (some of whom are represented in this volume) have tried to develop schemata to encompass a number of sequential processes in the formation of memory. Understandably, most of them focus on sections of the total sequence, such as presynaptic or postsynaptic events, events related to receptors and ion channels, events related to phosphorylation, or events leading to synthesis of proteins (including the involvement of immediate early genes). A few workers—including Horn, Rose (Chapter 47, this volume), and we ourselves—are also interested in the possible changes in sites of memory storage processes over time.

There is a consensus that formation of long-term memory (LTM) requires the synthesis of proteins shortly after training; this synthesis may be involved in altering characteristics of existing synapses, in forming new synaptic junctions, or in altering characteristics of the neuronal membrane. Our research has contributed to this consensus in two main ways: (1) by demonstrating that either formal training or experience in differential environments leads to changes in synaptic numbers and dimensions and to increases of brain proteins (e.g., Bennett, Diamond, Krech, & Rosenzweig, 1964; Rosenzweig, Bennett, & Diamond, 1972), and (2) by demonstrating that inhibition of protein synthesis shortly after learning prevents formation of LTM, although it does not interfere with short-term memory (STM) (e.g., Bennett, Orme, & Hebert, 1972; Bennett, Rosenzweig, & Flood, 1977; Flood, Rosenzweig, Bennett, & Orme, 1973).

We then turned our attention to the study of neurochemical processes involved in the earlier stages of memory formation: STM and intermediate-term memory (ITM). We have concentrated on research with young chicks because of the advantages they offer for the study of the sequence of neurochemical processes involved in formation of STM, ITM, and LTM. Research with peck avoidance training in chicks now spans much of the gamut of cellular processes that lead to protein synthesis, as can be seen in Table 46.1. This table lists several known signal transduction pathways within a neuron that may lead to gene activation and to memory storage. The table, although incomplete, is a convenient compilation and is more inclusive than most schemata. We have indicated a dozen pathways that have been studied with the chick system; the underlined items show over 30 agents that we have demonstrated to have a significant effect on the formation of memory in the chick. It seems clear that the chick learning-memory system can be used to investigate many aspects of the neural events involved in memory storage, and that with this system one can attempt to form an integrated account of the main processes required to accomplish memory storage. The study of further hypothesized mechanisms is likely to be fruitful in the chick system, whose wide relevance has already been demonstrated in so many ways. Advantages of the chick system are discussed further at the end of this chapter.

Promising models of memory formation hold that several sequentially linked stages are required for formation of memory, and that different neurochemical processes underlie the different stages provisionally identified as STM, ITM, and LTM. The importance of stages of memory and their investigation at different levels of analysis was stressed by Simon (1986, p. 301): "The two components of the memory system that appear to play the most critical roles in complex cognitive performance are short-term memory and long-term memory." He added, "Information-processing psychologists must look forward to, but must not wait for, the happy day when we will be able to link up our data and theories with the data and theories developed by physiological psychologists." Linkages between behavioral and physiological studies of stages of memory formation are exactly what our research aims to provide.

Our recent research has focused on testing and extending the following hypotheses:

1. There are at least three main stages of memory formation, each with its own specific neurochemical processes. Gibbs and Ng (1977) stated specific hypotheses about the neurochemical processes involved in each stage, and we have been testing and extending these hypotheses.

2. The three stages are sequentially linked, so that preventing formation of any one also prevents formation of the following stage(s).

3. Specific brain regions are the sites of the processes necessary for one or more stages; that is, a given brain region may not be involved in memory formation, or it may be involved in the formation of one, two, or three stages of memory.

In working on these hypotheses, we have been following three specific aims:

1. Perform behavioral–pharmacological tests of the hypotheses, attempting both to enhance and to impair memory formation with agents of defined activities. This includes testing the precise times at which enhancement or impairment of memory occurs, in order to test the three-stage hypothesis.

TABLE 46.1. Known Signal Transduction Pathways in Neurons That May Lead to Gene Activation and Memory Storage

Steps tested, or to be tested, in the chick learning–memory model.

Coding of agents:

_____ Agents that we have demonstrated to have significant effects are shown underlined; we are doing further work with some of these agents.

( ) Agents whose administration in our experiments does not appear to affect memory formation are shown in parentheses.

/ / Agents with which we have done only preliminary work are shown between slashes.

* Agents that we propose to test are marked with an asterisk.

Neurotransmitters and receptors
(only some specific examples are shown here)

  Acetylcholine (ACh)
    Scopolamine
    ACh receptors
      Muscarinic-M1
        Pirenzepine
      Nicotinic
        (Gallamine)

  Glutamate
    Glutamate
      NMDA receptors
        AP5
        MK-801
      AMPA receptors
        *CNQX
        DNQX

  Opioid agonists and antagonists
    Naloxone
    β-endorphin
    [Leu]enkephalin
    ICI-174,864
    DPLPE
    Dynorphin$_{1-13}$
    (Dynorphin$_{1-8}$)
    Nor-BNI
    U-50,488

Regulation of ion channels in the neuronal membrane
  Ca^{2+} channels
    $LaCl_3$
    (Amiloride)

  Na^+ and K^+ channels
    Na^+ channels
      (Amiloride)
    Na^+-K^+ ATPase
      Ouabain

Second messengers
  Adenylate cyclase
    Forskolin
  Diacylglycerol
    Bradykinin

Protein kinases (PKs)
  PKC
    Arachidonic acid
    Phorbol esters such as PDBu and *TPA
    *Chelcrythrine
    *Calphostin C
  PKs, nonspecific
    A-3
    H-7
    H-8
    H-9
    HA-156
    HA-1004
    /Polymyxin-B/
    *Iso-H-7
  Note: Learning induces increase of PKC.

Nucleic acid synthesis
  Nucleic acid inhibitors
    Actinomycin D
    Alpha-amanitin
    Chloramphenicol

Protein synthesis
  Inhibitors
    Anisomycin
    Emetine
    Cycloheximide
    Chloramphenicol

  Note: Learning induces increases of brain proteins and glycoproteins, as well as of immediate early genes.

(continued)

TABLE 46.1. (*continued*)

Calmodulin	*Transport mechanisms in axons and dendrites*
TFP	Agents that inhibit transport mechanisms
W-13	Vinblastine
ML-7	Colchicine
ML-9	
W-9	
Melittin	
/Polymyxin-B/	
/W-7/	
*KN-62	

Note. Identification of some of the agents abbreviated above:
A-3: *N*(2-aminoethyl)-5-chloro-1-naphthalene sulfonamide, hydrochloride
CNQX: 6-cyano-7-nitroquinoxaline-2, 3-dione
DNQX: 6, 7-dinitroquinoxaline-2, 3-dione
H-7: 1-[5-isoquinolinesulfonyl-(2-methylpiperazine)]
Iso-H-7: 1-[5-isoquinolinesulfonyl-(3-methylpiperazine)]
KN-62: 1-[*N*,*O*-bis(5-isoquinolinesulfonyl)-*N*-methyl-L-tyrosyl]-4-phenylpiperazine
MK-801: [(+)-5-methyl-10,11-dihydro-5H-dibenzo[*a*,*d*]cyclohepten-5,10-imine malate]
ML-7: 1-(5-iodonaphthalene-1-sulfonyl)-*H*-hexahydro-1,4-diazepine, hydrochloride
ML-9: 1-(5-chloronaphthalenesulfonyl)-1*H*-hexahydro-1,4-diazepine, hydrochloride
TFP: trifluoperazine
W-7: *N*-(6-aminohexyl)-5-chloro-1-naphthalene sulfonamide, hydrochloride
W-9: *N*-(6-aminohexyl)-5-chloro-2-naphthalene sulfonamide, hydrochloride
W-13: *N*-(6-aminobutyl)-5-chloro-2-naphthalene sulfonamide, hydrochloride

2. Test the involvement of specific regions of chick brain in stages of memory formation by injecting into these brain regions amnestic (amnesia-causing) or memory-enhancing agents that do not spread far from the site of injection.

3. Perform neurochemical determinations to parallel the behavioral–pharmacological experiments by investigating in chick brains the localization–diffusion and persistence of agents we employ and the neurochemical actions of selected pharmacological agents. The results of the neurochemical determinations are used to test interpretations of the behavioral–pharmacological findings.

Methods

Behavioral Tests

In most of our experiments, the chicks are trained in a one-trial peck avoidance (passive avoidance) task originally described by Cherkin and Lee-Teng (1965). In other experiments, they are trained in an appetitive visual discrimination task. Both tasks are described briefly next.

PECK AVOIDANCE TASK

In initial trials with a drug, chicks are injected with saline or drug intracerebrally (i.c.) 5 minutes (min) prior to training. Various brain sites are used in order to map regions involved in memory formation. A frequently used site is the intermediate medial hyperstriatum ventrale (IMHV). Training for the peck avoidance task consists of one 10-second (sec) exposure to a 3-mm stainless steel bead attached to a thin wire. The bead is dipped in a solution of methylanthranilate (MeA), an aversive liquid. After pecking the bead, chicks display a disgust response consisting of distress peeps, head shaking, and bill wiping. Chicks trained with a bead dipped in 100% MeA avoid the dry bead at test at a very high level of avoidance; we therefore refer to training with 100% MeA as "strong" training. To allow for enhancement as well as impairment of memory, some of the studies use "moderate" training. For this we dip the bead in 10% MeA/90% ethanol (v./v.). Only 40% of chicks trained with a 10% MeA bead avoid the test bead 24 hours later (Rosenzweig, Lee, Means, Bennett, & Martinez, 1989; Lee et al., 1989). The latency to peck, the number of pecks, and the display of the disgust response are recorded.

Testing consists of one 10-second exposure to a similar but dry bead at various training–test intervals. Latency to peck and number of pecks are recorded. A different group of chicks is tested for each time point and condition; an individual chick is tested only once. Chicks that do not peck the bead during the test trial are scored as remembering; those that do peck are scored as amnesic. Retention is therefore measured as the percentage of chicks avoiding the dry bead at test. "Blind" procedures are used in all experiments; experimenters do not know which drug treatment an animal has received at either training or testing.

APPETITIVE DISCRIMINATION TASK

Most of our work to date with chicks has been done with the one-trial peck avoidance task. It is not yet known to what extent the results can be extended from this aversive training to appetitive training. For this reason, we have begun to employ appetitive training with a visual discrimination task similar to that of Rogers, Drennen, and Mark (1974). Variations of this paradigm, in which the chick learns to discriminate bits of food from pebbles, are currently being used by Deyo, Conner, and Panksepp (1987) and Anokhin and Rose (1991). Gibbs and Ng (1978) reported that three agents that impaired memory formation on the peck avoidance task also impaired memory for appetitive training, and with similar doses. We plan to extend this work to include additional agents that we have found to affect memory formation for peck avoidance training.

The appetitive visual discrimination task is designed to facilitate learning in chicks by using pebbles and bits of food that are easily discriminated visually. Preliminary work shows that chicks learn this appetitive visual discrimination in 1–2 min, so this task will be useful in characterizing further the temporal aspects of memory formation.

Determining Dose–Response Curves, Susceptibility Gradients, and Time Courses of Changes in Strength of Memory

To characterize an agent's effect on memory formation, three series of experiments are performed. First, a dose–response function is determined, to provide us with the dose or doses that effectively impair or enhance performance on the learning task. Second, a susceptibility gradient (time window of effectiveness) is obtained, to characterize the effectiveness of administration at various pre- and posttraining times. And third, the time course of the change in the strength of memory (either impairment or enhancement) is obtained, to determine the stage of memory formation that is being affected. For examples of these experiments, see Patterson, Alvarado, Warner, Bennett, and Rosenzweig (1986).

Survey of Progress

We have accomplished quite a bit on each of our principal aims, as we review briefly under the next headings.

Behavioral–Pharmacological Experiments

We have tested effects of several of the agents used by Gibbs and Ng, and we have added other agents with defined activities to test proposed neurochemical mechanisms more thoroughly. We have found that several agents do cause memory to decline at times that conform with one of the three hypothesized stages, but some further results suggest that the hypotheses must be extended to accommodate still other stages or substages; we give in turn examples of both sorts of results. First are some results reported in our publications (e.g., Patterson et al., 1986; Rosenzweig, 1990; Rosenzweig et al., 1991) that support the hypotheses of Gibbs and Ng: Some agents cause memory to decline by about 10 min posttraining and thus interfere with formation of STM; these agents are L-glutamate and lanthanum chloride. Other agents do not affect STM, but all cause memory to decline by 30 min posttraining; these include ouabain, scopolamine, trifluoperazine (TFP), and dynorphin$_{1-13}$. A third group of agents does not impair ITM, but all cause memory to decline by 60 min posttraining; these include the protein synthesis inhibitors anisomycin, cycloheximide, and emetine. Inhibition of formation of STM prevents appearance of ITM and LTM; inhibition of formation of ITM prevents appearance of LTM. These observations support the hypothesis that the three stages are linked sequentially.

Some exceptions that we have found to the set of time courses described by Gibbs and Ng appear to concern all stages—STM, ITM, and LTM. Thus we have shown that the N-methyl-D-aspartate (NMDA) receptor is probably involved in peck avoidance learning in the chick, because memory for this is prevented by use of the NMDA receptor antagonist 2-amino-5-phosphonovalerate (AP5) (Patterson, Scharre, Bennett, & Rosenzweig, 1987). Importantly, AP5 caused early onset of amnesia; although memory was intact at 10 sec posttraining, it was seriously impaired at 30 sec posttraining. As another problem with short-term effects, it is not clear why a glutamate receptor agonist (glutamate) and antagonist (AP5) should both cause amnesic effects in chicks. The time courses of memory impairment following administration of some opioid peptides also do not support the hypotheses of Gibbs and Ng. We (Bennett, Patterson, Schulteis, Martinez, & Rosenzweig, 1988) found that β-endorphin caused amnesia to develop by 30 sec posttraining. In the case of long-term effects, we found that [leu]enkephalin (LEU) caused memory to decline 3–4 hours posttraining, much later than do inhibitors of protein synthesis (Colombo, Tsai, Bennett, Rosenzweig, & Martinez, 1989). This is one of several indications that LTM formation has two or more phases.

Reports of effects of inhibitors of protein kinase C (PKC) on long-term potentiation (LTP) suggested to us in 1988 that it would be worthwhile to compare the amnestic and neurochemical properties of a number of PKC inhibitors that have different inhibitory characteristics with respect to PKC and cyclic adenosine monophosphate (cAMP)-dependent or calmodulin-dependent kinases (Hidaka, Inagaki, Kawamoto, & Sasaki, 1984; Kawamoto & Hidaka, 1984). We have found that protein kinase inhibitors (PKIs), when injected into the region of the IMHV 5 min pretraining, produce significant amnesia at a 24-hour test. Thus far, we have investigated 14 different PKIs with different selectivities for protein kinase activity. Of the 11 PKIs that produce amnesia, five of these agents (A-3, HA-1004, TFP, W-9, and W-13) were found to disrupt ITM formation; that is, they all produced amnesia between 15 and 30 min posttraining. The times of onset of amnesia induced by these agents were not found to differ significantly from each other. These five PKIs are also known to inhibit calcium or calmodulin kinase activity. Five additional PKIs tested (HA-156, H-7, H-8, H-9, and ML-9) were found to disrupt the formation of LTM; that is, these agents produced amnesia with onset around 60 min posttraining. Our statistical analysis showed that these five time courses did not differ significantly from each other. These PKIs were found to inhibit PKC and/or PKG and PKA. The remaining PKI that produced amnesia is melittin. Although melittin is a calmodulin kinase inhibitor, and from our other findings would be expected to produce amnesia during ITM, it was found to produce amnesia 45 min posttraining, between the ITM and LTM stages of memory. Since melittin is a large polypeptide, it may not be entering the neuron as quickly as these other, smaller agents can and so may be producing an amnesic effect later posttraining than other calmodulin inhibitors (Serrano, Oxonian, Rodriguez, Rosenzweig, & Bennett, 1992). Interestingly, none of these PKIs disrupts the formation of STM. We propose that protein kinase activity plays an important role during the formation of two stages of memory, ITM and LTM.

Recently we have found that agents that stimulate PKC activity (e.g., bradykinin, arachidonic acid, and PDBu) can enhance memory for a weakly learned task. But forskolin, which stimulates cAMP, did not enhance memory formation. However, injection of either bradykinin or forskolin with H-7 can attenuate the amnesia produced by an injection of H-7 alone. Likewise, the amnesia produced by melittin can be attenuated by the simultaneous administration of either bradykinin or forskolin. These results suggest that the activation of cAMP is a pertinent mechanism during learning in chicks. Further research on enhancement not only helps us to understand the mechanisms of memory, but may also lead to practical means of improving memory that is deficient because of aging or disease.

Experiments with weaker training have also yielded a serendipitous finding— what appears to be *behavioral* evidence that there are more than two stages of memory formation; this supplements the evidence from effects of pharmacological treatments. When chicks are given weaker training with diluted MeA, the detailed curves of retention measured at several intervals over the first 2 hours after training present a complex function with several cusps; see Figure 46.1 for a schematic presentation. This function appears to correspond with the distinct stages of memory that we have hypothesized. The function shows four components: (1) An initial limb that falls steeply to a low point at about 1 min posttraining; this may correspond to the hypothesized sensory buffer stage. (2) A hump that peaks about 10 min posttraining and falls off to a dip at about 15–20 min; this time course corresponds to so-called STM for peck avoidance in the chick. (3) A hump that peaks at about 45 min and declines by about 60 min; this corresponds to the so-called ITM for this task. (4) Finally, a broad hump that rises after the 60-min cusp; this appears to correspond to LTM (Rosenzweig et al., 1989). We do not claim that these stages will necessarily be of the same length for all tasks and for all species.

Recently we have tested the identification of the components of this complex function by using agents that are believed to inhibit, respectively, formation of STM (glutamate), ITM (ouabain and scopolamine), and LTM (anisomycin). As shown by the broken curves in Figure 46.1, both glutamate and anisomycin prevented occurrence of the corresponding part of the retention function as well as the subsequent parts, as would be expected of sequentially dependent stages (Lee, Murphy, Bennett, & Rosenzweig, 1990). However, preliminary results in our laboratory with either ouabain or scopolamine have not prevented occurrence of the ITM part of the function, although they do prevent ITM after stronger training. We reported early results on retention after moderate training at the 1988 Sussex Conference (Rosenzweig et al., 1991) and at subsequent meetings (Rosenzweig et al., 1989; Rosenzweig, 1990; Lee

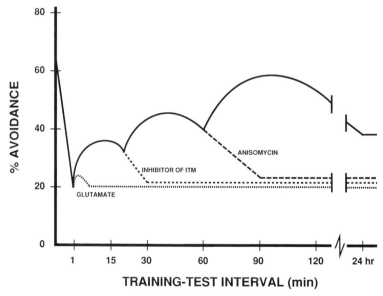

FIGURE 46.1. Schematic figure of retention after training with 10% methylanthranilate (———). Use of anisomycin prevents formation of LTM (— — — —). Use of certain agents prevents formation of ITM and therefore also prevents formation of LTM (- - - -). Use of L-glutamate prevents formation of STM and therefore also prevents formation of ITM and LTM (- - - -).

et al., 1990). Crowe, Ng, and Gibbs (1989) have also reported on retention after weak training; in their case, only STM and ITM occur, with a dip between these two stages at 15 min.

Another major aim of our research is to localize in the chick brain regions important for memory formation by injecting agents into specific regions. This work is made possible by our discovery (Patterson et al., 1986) that certain amnestic agents appear to affect only a small volume of tissue around the site of the injection. We subsequently confirmed this finding by neurochemical experiments on recovery of radioactivity (see "Neurochemical Experiments," below). Among such agents are L-glutamate, ouabain, and emetine. Injecting any of these agents into the region of the IMHV or the lateral neostriatum (LNS) causes amnesia to occur at the relevant time (STM, ITM, or LTM). The importance of the IMHV for memory formation was first reported by Horn, McCabe, and Bateson (1979) for imprinting, and work on IMHV with peck avoidance has been done by Rose and collaborators (e.g., Rose & Csillag, 1985). We have found that *unilateral* injections yield evidence of hemispheric asymmetry that is opposite for IMHV and LNS. Injections into the region of the left IMHV cause amnesia, whereas injections into the region of the right IMHV are without effect; on the contrary, injections into the region of the left LNS are without effect, whereas those into the right LNS cause amnesia (Patterson, Alvarado, Rosenzweig, & Bennett, 1988). Research with injections into the lobus parolfactorius (LPO) revealed the surprising fact that this region is involved in formation of ITM, but not of STM or LTM. Injection of ouabain into the region of the LPO causes inhibition of formation of ITM, but injection of glutamate, which impairs formation of STM when injected into other regions, does not cause amnesia when injected into the LPO; similarly, injection of inhibitors of protein synthesis such as emetine, which impairs formation of LTM when injected into other regions, does not cause amnesia when injected into the region of the LPO. Recent work shows that injection of scopolamine into the region of the LPO also causes amnesia, and the time course of decline of memory is the same as for ouabain; this supports the conclusion that the LPO is involved in formation of ITM (Serrano, Oxonian, Bennett, & Rosenzweig, 1990). Recent results show that ouabain will prevent formation of ITM after weaker training when the injections are made into LPO instead of IMHV. We have also found that unilateral injection of ouabain into the LPO shows significant hemispheric asymmetry; the amnesic effect is stronger with injection into the left than into the right LPO.

Our work comparing the roles of the IMHV and LPO in memory formation can be related to other hypotheses about the roles of different brain structures in maintaining memories at successive times after acquisition. Thus, work with mammals has shown that the hippocampus is necessary for days, weeks, or (in the case of humans) months or even a few years, but the hippocampus is not the site of long-term or at least of permanent storage of memory. In the chick, Horn (1985) has presented evidence that the memory store moves from the IMHV to an as yet unlocated secondary site of storage. Rose (Chapter 47, this volume; Gilbert, Patterson, & Rose, 1991) has shown that the LPO may be such a secondary store. Our findings (Serrano, 1990; Serrano, Ramus, Bennett, & Rosenzweig, 1992) that the LPO appears to be involved in the formation of ITM but not of other stages may be related to its function as a secondary store, following primary storage in the IMHV.

Neurochemical Experiments

We have also performed neurochemical determinations to parallel the behavioral–pharmacological experiments. One set of these studies was an extensive series of experiments to determine how much of radioactive drugs could be recovered close to the site of injection. Radioactive L-glutamate, ouabain, and LEU were used in these experiments; injections were made into the region of the IMHV. Over 80% of the recovered ouabain or LEU and 65% of the L-glutamate were found near the site of the injection. For LEU and ouabain, less than 10% of the recovered activity was in the opposite hemisphere, brainstem, or tectum (Rosenzweig et al., 1991).

We have attempted to find whether direct measurements of inhibition of PKC activity parallel the behavioral effects caused by inhibitors of PKC. Many investigators have implicated PKC and F1 (B-50) in learning and memory-related processes in numerous species (including *Aplysia*, rats, and chicks) and in several model systems, such as conditioning in *Aplysia*, LTP in rodents, and peck avoidance in chicks. In addition to behavioral experiments, we have done neurochemical experiments to investigate the effectiveness of PKC inhibitors on the *in vitro* phosphorylation of proteins in the synaptic plasma membrane (SPM) fraction isolated from chick brain. When the SPM fraction was incubated with adenosine triphosphate (ATP)–gamma ^{32}P and separated by polyacrylamide gel electrophoresis (according to the method of Ali, Bullock, & Rose, 1988), the radioactive band at the location expected for F1 contained 60–70% of the radioactivity. About a dozen additional bands contained most of the remainder of the incorporated radioactivity. The major radioactive protein has therefore been tentatively identified as F1.

Ali et al. (1988) have reported selective inhibition of phosphorylation of F1 by melittin and polymyxin-B in a chick brain preparation. Unexpectedly, in our laboratory melittin had no apparent effect on phosphorylation at 20 μM, but appeared to *stimulate* phosphorylation at 50 μM. To date, we have not been able to obtain evidence that phosphorylation of F1 is *selectively* inhibited by any of the agents that we have tried. Thus, although these agents are all amnestic, it is not clear whether the amnesic effect is caused by specific inhibition of PKC or by inhibition of phosphorylation in general. The results to date with melittin are perplexing and call for further work. Preliminary experiments have shown that forskolin will partially overcome the inhibition of phosphorylation of F1 by HA-1004 and H-7; forskolin potentiates the stimulation of phosphorylation by melittin.

Experiments with Endogenous Opioids

To extend hypotheses about the modulation of memory formation, we have examined the effects of administration of endogenous opioid peptides and agents selective for different opioid receptors. Endogenous opioid peptides bind to at least three opioid receptor subtypes: the mu, delta, and kappa receptors. We demonstrated that administration of the endogenous mu receptor ligand β-endorphin impaired memory formation in the chick, and that this effect was reversed by the opioid antagonist naloxone (Patterson et al., 1989). In the same report, we also showed that the endogenous delta opioid receptor ligand LEU or a highly selective agonist for the delta receptor, DPLPE, impaired memory formation; furthermore, these effects were reversed by a highly selective antagonist for the delta receptor, ICI-174,864. Although ICI alone did not enhance memory, enhancement probably could not have been detected in those experiments because the saline-injected control group was near ceiling performance. Recently we have examined the role of the kappa opioid receptor in memory formation. The endogenous kappa receptor ligand dynorphin and the highly selective kappa agonist U-50,488 both impaired memory formation; the selective kappa receptor antagonist nor-BNI enhanced memory formation (Colombo, Martinez, Bennett, & Rosenzweig, in press). Therefore, memory formation in the chick can be either attenuated or enhanced by activity at each of the three classes of receptors for endogenous opioid peptides. Pretraining administration of dynorphin has no effect on memory 5 min after training, but causes amnesia by 15 min posttraining, during the intermediate-term stage (Colombo, Everill, Martinez, Bennett, & Rosenzweig, 1990). Additionally, $dynorphin_{1-13}$ impairs memory formation for both appetitive visual discrimination and peck avoidance training. Our investigation of the other classes of opioid peptides is being extended to determine if they, too, impair memory formation for both aversively and appetitively motivated learning.

We have measured the concentrations of LEU (Bennett et al., 1990) and [met]enkephalin (MET) in five main regions of chick brain and have begun examining enkephalin concentrations in the IMHV and LPO, using radioimmunoassays (RIA); we plan also to measure concentrations of dynorphin and β-endorphin. These assays suggest brain regions to be studied in regard to opioid modulation of learning and memory formation. A region that is high in concentrations of endogenous opioids may not be involved in learning and memory, but one that has very low concentrations is unlikely to be involved. We found the concentration of MET to be approximately three to eight times that of LEU, depending upon the brain region examined. The concentrations of MET varied from a high of 13.4 pmol/mg protein in ventral forebrain to 0.32 pmol/mg in the cerebellum (Colombo, Schulteis, Bennett, Martinez, & Rosenzweig, 1991). We have also investigated the hydrolysis of opioids in chick plasma (Shibanoki, Weinberger, Ishikawa, & Martinez, 1990; Shibanoki, Weinberger, Beniston, Nudelman, et al., 1991) and in chick brain tissue (Shibanoki, Weinberger, Beniston, Schulteis, et al., 1991). The half-life of LEU in chick plasma was found to be 0.7–1 min, clearly shorter than its half-life in rat and mouse plasma (Shibanoki, Weinberger, Ishikawa, & Martinez, 1991). Aminopeptidase M accounts for 95–97% of the hydrolysis of LEU by chick plasma *in vitro*. Aminopeptidase MII and angiotensin converting enzyme are chiefly responsible for hydrolysis of LEU in chick brain. The half-life measures vary less than twofold among brain regions, the greatest difference being between ventral forebrain and cerebellum; this parallels the differences in concentrations of LEU and MET observed with RIA.

Advantages of the Chick System

Having worked with chick systems since 1985 and having communicated with other investigators who use chicks as subjects, we have found the chick system to possess several advantages, which we plan to exploit in our continuing research (Rosenzweig, 1990). Some of these advantages are the following:

1. The chick system is more convenient than most for study of the stages of memory formation and storage, because chicks can be trained rapidly and can be tested within seconds after training. Detailed study of the temporal aspects of memory storage is a focus of our research that differentiates it from that of most other teams.

2. A relatively large number of subjects can be studied in a single run, so one can compare critically the effects of several agents within the same batch of subjects. One can also readily screen effects over a wide dose-response range. Finally, both enhancement and impairment of memory can be tested within the same experiment.

3. Unlike invertebrate preparations or tissue-slice preparations, the chick learning–memory system can be used to study the roles of different brain structures in learning and memory and to investigate questions of cerebral asymmetry in learning and memory.

4. With the chick system, learning and memory of intact animals is studied, whereas the relevance to learning and memory of certain models, such as LTP or kindling, is still a matter of controversy.

5. Since many hatcheries sell only the females (hens), males (cockerels) are usually destroyed shortly after hatching. Therefore hatcheries are willing to sell these excess male chicks in large quantities at a relatively low price. By using cockerels as our experimental subjects, we gain scientific knowledge from animals that would otherwise be sacrificed soon after hatching.

6. The cost of purchasing chicks is relatively low, and costs of maintenance are low because chicks are used within a few days after delivery (often the day after delivery).

7. The final advantage to be mentioned here was pointed out by investigators who had used rats in previous research: Chicks do not bite! (Kastin, Honour, & Coy, 1981).

ACKNOWLEDGMENTS

This research was supported by National Science Foundation Grant No. BNS 88-10528 and by National Institute on Drug Abuse Grant No. 5 R01 DA04795.

REFERENCES

Ali, S. M., Bullock, S., & Rose, S. P. R. (1988). Protein kinase C inhibitors prevent long-term memory formation in the one-day-old chick. *Neuroscience Research Communications, 3*(3), 133–140.

Anokhin, K. V., & Rose, S. P. R. (1991). Learning-induced increase of immediate early gene messenger RNA in the chick forebrain. *European Journal of Neuroscience, 3*, 162–167.

Bennett, E. L., Colombo, P. J., Sun, J., Schulteis, G., Rosenzweig, M. R., & Martinez, J. L. Jr., (1990). Determination of the distribution of leucine-enkephalin in brain regions of the two-day-old chick by radioimmunoassay. *Society for Neuroscience Abstracts, 16*, 391.

Bennett, E. L., Diamond, M. C., Krech, D., & Rosenzweig, M. R. (1964). Chemical and anatomical plasticity of brain. *Science, 146*, 610–619.

Bennett, E. L., Orme, A., Hebert, M. (1972). Cerebral protein synthesis inhibition and amnesia produced by scopolamine, cycloheximide, streptovitacin A, anisomycin and emetine in rat. *Federation Proceedings, 31*, 838.

Bennett, E. L., Patterson, T. A., Schulteis, G., Martinez, J. L., & Rosenzweig, M. R. (1988). β-Endorphin impairs acquisition in the chick. *Society for Neuroscience Abstracts, 14,* 1029.

Bennett, E. L., Rosenzweig, M. R., & Flood, J. F. (1977). Protein synthesis and memory studied with anisomycin. In S. Roberts, A. Lajtha, & W. H. Gispen (Eds.), *Mechanisms, regulation and special function of protein synthesis in the brain* (pp. 319-330). Amsterdam: Elsevier/North-Holland.

Cherkin, A., & Lee-Teng, E. (1965). Interruption by halothane of memory consolidation in chicks. *Federation Proceedings, 24,* 328.

Colombo, P. J., Everill, H. A., Martinez, J. L., Jr., Bennett, E. L., & Rosenzweig, M. R. (1990). Kappa agonists can cause amnesia for one-trial passive-avoidance training in the two-day-old chick. *Society for Neuroscience Abstracts, 16,* 1329.

Colombo, P. J., Martinez, J. L., Jr., Bennett, E. L., & Rosenzweig, M. R. (in press). Kappa opioid receptor activity modulates memory for peck-avoidance training in the 2-day-old chick. *Psychopharmacology.*

Colombo, P. J., Schulteis, G., Bennett, E. L., Martinez, J. L., Jr., & Rosenzweig, M. R. (1991). Distribution of [leu]enkephalin and [met]enkephalin in brain regions of the 2-day-old chick. *Society for Neuroscience Abstracts, 17,* 964.

Colombo, P. J., Tsai, J., Bennett, E. L., Rosenzweig, M. R., & Martinez, J. L., Jr., (1989). Delayed development of amnesia following intracranial injection of [leu]enkephalin in two-day-old chicks. *Society for Neuroscience Abstracts, 15,* 1169.

Crowe, S. F., Ng, K. T., & Gibbs, M. E. (1989). Memory formation processes in weakly reinforced learning. *Pharmacology, Biochemistry and Behavior, 33,* 881-887.

Deyo, R. A., Conner, R. L., & Panksepp, J. (1987). Perinatal leupeptin retards subsequent acquisition of a visual discrimination task in chicks. *Behavioral and Neural Biology, 53,* 149-152.

Flood, J. F., Rosenzweig, M. R., Bennett, E. L., & Orme, A. E. (1973). The influence of duration of protein synthesis inhibition on memory. *Physiology and Behavior, 10,* 555-562.

Gibbs, M. E., & Ng, K. T. (1977). Psychobiology of memory: Towards a model of memory formation. *Biobehavioral Reviews, 1,* 113-136.

Gibbs, M. E., & Ng, K. T. (1978). Memory formation for an appetitive visual discrimination task in young chicks. *Pharmacology, Biochemistry and Behavior, 8,* 271-276.

Gilbert, D. B., Patterson, T. A., & Rose, S. P. R. (1991). Dissociation of brain sites necessary for registration and storage of one-trial passive avoidance learning task in chicks. *Behavioral Neuroscience, 105,* 553-561.

Hidaka, H., Inagaki, M., Kawamoto, S., & Sasaki, Y. (1984). Isoquinolinesulfonamides, novel and potent inhibitor of cyclic nucleotide dependent protein kinase and protein kinase C. *Biochemistry, 23,* 5036-5041.

Horn, G. (1985). *Memory, imprinting, and the brain.* Oxford: Clarendon Press.

Horn, G., McCabe, B. J., & Bateson, P. P. G. (1979). An autoradiographic study of the chick brain after imprinting. *Brain Research, 168,* 361-373.

Kastin, A. J., Honour, L. C., & Coy, D. H. (1981). Kyotorphins affect aversive pecking in chicks. *Physiology and Behavior, 27,* 1073-1076.

Kawamoto, S., & Hidaka, H. (1984). H-7 is a selective inhibitor of protein kinase C in rabbit platelets. *Biochemical and Biophysical Research Communications, 125,* 258-264.

Lee, D. W., Means, M. D., Afinowicz, D. J., Bennett, E. L., Martinez, J. L., Jr., & Rosenzweig, M. R. (1989). Enhancement of memory for a one-trial passive avoidance task in chicks given peripheral and central injections of naloxone. *Society for Neuroscience Abstracts, 15,* 1171.

Lee, D. W., Murphy, G. G., Bennett, E. L., & Rosenzweig, M. R. (1990). Effects of glutamate, ouabain, and anisomycin on memory for weak training in chicks. *Society for Neuroscience Abstracts, 16,* 769.

Patterson, T. A., Alvarado, M. C., Warner, I. T., Bennett, E. L., & Rosenzweig, M. R. (1986). Memory stages and brain asymmetry in chick learning. *Behavioral Neuroscience, 100,* 856-865.

Patterson, T. A., Alvarado, M. C., Rosenzweig, M. R., & Bennett, E. L. (1988). Time courses of amnesia development in two areas of the chick forebrain. *Neurochemical Research, 13*(7), 643-647.

Patterson, T. A., Schulteis, G., Alvarado, M. C., Martinez, J. L., Jr., Bennett, E. L., Rosenzweig, M. R., & Hruby, V. J. (1989). Influence of opioid peptides on learning and memory processes in the chick. *Behavorial Neuroscience, 103,* 429-437.

Patterson, T. A., Scharre, K. L., Bennett, E. L., & Rosenzweig, M. R. (1987). Influence of AP5 on memory formation in the chick. *Society for Neuroscience Abstracts, 14,* 244.

Rogers, L. J., Drennen, H. D., & Mark, R. F. (1974). Inhibition of memory formation in the imprinting period: Irreversible action of cycloheximide in young chickens. *Brain Research, 79,* 213-233.

Rose, S. P. R., & Csillag, A. (1985). Passive avoidance training results in lasting changes in deoxyglucose metabolism in left hemisphere regions of chick brain. *Behavioral and Neural Biology, 44,* 315-324.

Rosenzweig, M. R. (1990). The chick as a model system for studying neural processes in learning and memory. In L. Erinoff (Ed.), *Behavior as an indicator of neuropharmacological events: Learning and memory* (NIDA Research Monograph No. 97, DHHS Pub. No. (ADM)90-1677, pp. 1–20). Washington, DC: U.S. Government Printing Office.

Rosenzweig, M. R., & Bennett, E. L. (1984). Studying stages of memory formation with chicks and rodents. In L. R. Squire & N. Butters (Eds.), *Neuropsychology of memory* (1st ed., pp. 555–565). New York: Guilford Press.

Rosenzweig, M. R., Bennett, E. L., & Diamond, M. C. (1972). Cerebral effects of differential environments occur in hypophysectomized rats. *Journal of Comparative and Physiological Psychology, 79*, 56–66.

Rosenzweig, M. R., Bennett, E. L., Martinez, J. L., Jr., Beniston, D., Colombo, P. J., Lee, D. W., Patterson, T. A., Schulteis, G., & Serrano, P. A. (1991). Stages of memory formation in the chick: Findings and problems. In R. J. Andrew (Ed.), *Neural and behavioural plasticity: The use of the domestic chick as a model* (pp. 394–418). Oxford: Oxford University Press.

Rosenzweig, M. R., Lee, D. W., Means, M. K., Bennett, E. L., & Martinez, J. L., Jr. (1989). Effects of varying training strength on short-, intermediate-, and long-term formation of memory (STM, ITM, LTM) for a one-trial passive avoidance task in chicks. *Society for Neuroscience Abstracts, 15*, 1171.

Serrano, P. A. (1990). *Evidence supporting the involvement of multiple areas of the chick brain during the three stages of memory formation.* Unpublished master's thesis, University of California at Berkeley.

Serrano, P. A., Oxonian, M. G., Rodriguez, W., Rosenzweig, M. R., & Bennett, E. L. (1992). *Molecular mechanisms of learning and memory in the two-day-old chick: The role of PKC and other kinases.* Manuscript submitted for publication.

Serrano, P. A., Oxonian, M. G., Bennett, E. L., & Rosenzweig, M. R. (1990). Selected PKC inhibitors disrupt long-term memory formation in the two-day-old chick for a peck aversion task; Forskolin attenuates the amnesia. *Society for Neuroscience Abstracts, 16*, 769.

Serrano, P. A., Ramus, S. J., Bennett, E. L., & Rosenzweig, M. R. (1992). Comparative study of roles of the lobus parolfactorius and intermediate medial hyperstriatum ventrale in memory formation in the chick brain. *Pharmacology, Biochemistry and Behavior, 41*, 761–766.

Shibanoki, S., Weinberger, S. B., Beniston, D., Nudelman, K. A., Schulteis, G., Bennett, E. L., Rosenzweig, M. R., Ishikawa, K., & Martinez, J. L., Jr. (1991). Hydrolysis of [leu]enkephalin by chick plasma in vitro. *Journal of Pharmacology and Experimental Therapeutics, 256*, 650–655.

Shibanoki, S., Weinberger, S. B., Beniston, D., Schulteis, G., Bennett, E. L., Rosenzweig, M. R., Ishikawa, K., & Martinez, J. L., Jr. (1991). Hydrolysis of [leu]enkephalin by chick brain in vitro. *Comparative Biochemistry and Pharmacology, 99B*, 301–306.

Shibanoki, S., Weinberger, S. B., Ishikawa, I., & Martinez, J. L., Jr. (1990). A sensitive method for measuring hydrolysis of enkephalins in plasma, using high performance liquid chromatography with electrochemical detection. *Journal of Chromatography: Biomedical Applications, 532*, 249–259.

Shibanoki, S., Weinberger, S. B., Ishikawa, K., & Martinez, J. L., Jr. (1991). Further characterization of the in vitro hydrolysis of [leu] and [met]enkephalin in rat plasma: HPLC-ECD measurements of substrate and metabolite concentrations. *Regulatory Peptides, 32*, 267–278.

Simon, H. (1986). The parameters of human memory. In F. Klix & H. Hagendorf (Eds.), *Human memory and cognitive capabilities: Symposium in memoriam Hermann Ebbinghaus* (Vol. A, pp. 299–309). Amsterdam: Elsevier.

47

On Chicks and Rosetta Stones

STEVEN P. R. ROSE

Close inside the neoclassical entrance to the British Museum in London lies a slab of black stone, its flat surface covered with white marks. The marks in the top third are ancient Egyptian hieroglyphs; those in the middle are in a cursive script, demotic Egyptian; those in the lower third are Greek. This is the Rosetta stone, the text of a decree passed by a general council of Egyptian priests who assembled at Memphis on the Nile on the first anniversary of the coronation of King Ptolemy in 196 B.C.E.. The importance of the Rosetta stone lies not in the content of this ancient decree, but in the fact that its three scripts each carry the same message. Nineteenth-century scholars could read the Greek, and hence could begin to decipher the hitherto incomprehensible hieroglyphs. The simultaneous translation offered by the Rosetta stone became a code-breaking device, a metaphor for the task of translation that we face in understanding the relationships between mind and brain. The neuroscientist, struggling to translate between the Greek of mind and the hieroglyphs of brain, needs a Rosetta stone—some inscription in which the two languages can be read in parallel and the interpretation rules deciphered (Rose, 1992).

I believe that the study of memory can provide just such a code breaker, because in biology as in other sciences, it is always easier to measure change than stasis. When learning occurs and memories are formed, the behavior of an animal changes in a time-dependent and predictable way, to which there must correspond an appropriate set of brain changes. I use the word "correspond" to emphasize that I am not arguing that the brain changes "cause" the behavioral ones, or that they are merely correlates of them, but that they *are identical with*—another way of describing—the behavioral changes, albeit described within a different language. The task of the memory researcher within this paradigm is to identify the correspondences between the brain and behavioral changes and to derive from them the translation rules between the two languages. Redefining the task within this more dialectical framework does not, of course, automatically dissolve either the experimental or the theoretical problems that the field confronts; it merely recasts them. In the first edition of this book, I discussed the work of my own laboratory in the context of the criteria necessary to verify such correspondences (Rose, 1984).

At what level of brain process and structure should we seek the translation for "memory"? Is it written in the language of single synapses and their biochemistry and biophysics (cellular alphabets), of small ensembles of synapses and their modified connectivity (connectionism), or of global field properties (chaos models)? All have had their protagonists over recent years, yet they cannot all be right; unification is not simply a question of letting a hundred flowers bloom, but of defining the right level at which to identify brain memory. The follies of an earlier period's enthusiasm for genetic and immunological metaphors for memory and the hunt for specific memory molecules should be a warning of the importance of defining levels correctly. Yet sometimes it seems as if we choose our level and model of memory by the techniques at our disposal. For physiologists and PET imagers, memories are essentially fluid and dynamic—the fluctuating records from shifting ensembles of neurons measured either directly or by way of the surrogates given by blood flow or radioactive accumulation. By contrast, biochemists and morphologists seem to offer linear sequences of processes in single synapses or cells, which fix memories as rigidly as the blackened images of an autoradiogram. Are memories local or global—or, as I argue below, mobile?

In the search for appropriate levels of analysis of memory, how are we to interpret the many proposed taxonomies of "procedural" and "declarative," "semantic" and "episodic," "recognition" and "recall"? One feature that these dichotomies share is that they all seem to be time-dependent; there is no space within them for the stage theories, the transitions between long and short term, that the multitudinous pharmacological studies with animals seem empirically to indicate. Is "memory" then an omnibus term embracing a multitude of different mechanisms, or can we identify general cellular processes that subserve all or most of memory, the only distinction being the addresses of the cells whose connectivity is being modulated during the learning? Does localism conflict with globalism, or is it embraced within it? Do long-term habituation in the gill withdrawal reflex in *Aplysia*, classical conditioning of a dog to salivate to the sound of a bell, hippocampal place learning in a rat swimming in a water maze, imprinting in chicks, and Proustian memory in humans all translate into similar cell mechanisms, differing only in the addresses and connectivities of the cells concerned? Or are they fundamentally different in biological kind, united only by an imposed terminological identity within mind language? Is memory a special case of neural plasticity, in which case seizures, enriched experience, environmental deprivation during development, even transplant technology all have something to say as to mechanism, or is it *sui generis*? Does Hebb universally rule? Is what is true for *H-ermissenda* also the case for *H. sapiens*? The ubiquity of the phenomena of habituation, sensitization, and association, at least at the behavioral level, argues for unity theories. Aesthetically, I favor such a universalism, but we lack the evidence. Yet does not the richness of human experience suggest multiplicity rather than unity?

I address some of these questions more precisely by way of work from our own laboratory, based on studies of early learning in the domestic chick. Chick shown small, bright objects will quickly peck at them. If the object is a colored bead dipped in a bitter-tasting liquid (we use methylanthranilate), the chick will subsequently avoid pecking at even a dry bead of that color and shape, although its general pecking activity is unimpaired. It will continue to avoid such a bead for at least a week after the initial experience, though as it grows older it ceases to peck spontaneously at small objects any more, and other forms of behavior supervene. This behavior forms the basis of the one-trial passive avoidance learning task introduced by Cherkin more than two decades ago, and can be reliably induced in more than 75% of day-old birds (Cherkin, 1969). It is but one of the large repertoire of forms of early learning about key features of its environment—such as mother (imprinting; Horn, 1985) and edible food—which the naive but precocial young chick, hatched with a large brain and considerable behavioral competence, must achieve rapidly if it is to survive. Avian learning, from canaries' song to marsh tits' food caching, is becoming increasingly popular as offering model systems in which to study vertebrate memory formation (Horn & Krebs, 1990); the chick, with its repertoire of strongly ontogenetically driven learning, is particularly attractive (Andrew, 1991).

Learning to suppress pecking at the bitter bead initiates an intracellular cascade of cellular processes, which, beginning with pre- and postsynaptic membrane transients and proceeding by way of genomic activation to the lasting structural modification of these membranes, occurs in identified regions of the chick forebrain. I believe that these synaptic modifications form in some way the neural representations of the aversive bead-pecking experience and encode the instructions for the changed behavior ("Avoid pecking a bead of these characteristics") that follows. The key stages of this cascade have been reviewed recently (Rose, 1991a, 1991b; Stewart, 1991), and I only summarize them briefly here before turning to some recent, seemingly paradoxical findings and their implications for theories of vertebrate memory storage.

In the basic experimental design, day-old chicks are trained on either a methylanthranilate- or a water-colored bead, and their subsequent behavior and biochemistry are compared. Controls such as induction of amnesia can be made to distinguish between the effects of the experience (taste, etc.) of the bitter bead and the act of remembering to avoid it. Using 2-deoxyglucose (2-DG), we identified two particular regions of the forebrain as showing enhanced activity during and just after training on this task: the intermediate medial hyperstriatum ventrale (IMHV) and lobus parolfactorius (LPO); the regions are shown diagrammatically in the figures below (Rose & Csillag, 1985). Interestingly, and of considerable relevance to our subsequent studies, there was also evidence of lateralization, with the greatest changes being seen in the left-hemisphere regions. The IMHV is an area that had previously been implicated as showing cellular plasticity during visual imprinting (Horn, 1985). However, it is important to emphasize in the context of some of the later argument that there are no known direct connections between IMHV and LPO.

Having identified IMHV and LPO as sites of enhanced neural activity in the minutes following training on the passive avoidance task, in subsequent experiments we have followed biochemical, physiological, and morphological changes in these regions. In brief, within the first 30 minutes after training there is an activation of both cholinergic and N-methyl-D-aspartate (NMDA) receptors, and an altered phosphorylation rate in a 52-kD presynaptic membrane protein known as B-50 or GAP43. This phosphorylation is modulated by the translocation of cytoplasmic protein kinase C (PKC) to the cell membrane. Amnesia is induced by inhibitors of PKC or NMDA channel blockers such as MK-801 (Burchuladze, Potter, & Rose, 1990; Burchuladze & Rose, in press).

These transient membrane processes result, presumably by way of intracellular second and third messengers, in genomic activation and enhanced protein synthesis.

The initial steps in this genomic activation involve members of the immediate early gene family, the protein oncogenes c-fos and c-jun, which show increased expression in IMHV 30 minutes after training. This increase is not a response to stress or the aversive situation, but is directly correlated with the learning process itself. In the hours that follow this initial genomic activation, there is enhanced synthesis of a number of proteins, including the microtubular protein tubulin and, most importantly, a number of glycoproteins (in particular, a presynaptic component of molecular weight around 50 kD and postsynaptic components of molecular weight 100–120 and 150–180 kD) that are exported from the cell body and within 24 hours become inserted into pre- and postsynaptic sites in both IMHV and LPO. We have raised antibodies to some of these glycoproteins and are currently studying them in detail. They are of particular relevance because of the major role that several glycoprotein families (e.g., the neural cell adhesion molecules, whose role is discussed extensively by Edelman, 1987) play as cell recognition molecules in stabilizing intercellular connections. Inhibitors of glycoprotein synthesis such as the antimetabolite 2-deoxygalactose (2-DGal) produce amnesia, if injected either at the time of training or between 5 and 8 hours later. There thus appears to be a "second wave" of memory-related glycoprotein synthesis occurring some hours downstream of the first.[1]

Between 12 and 24 hours after training, this intracellular cascade translates into measurable alterations in pre- and postsynaptic morphology. There is a large (60%) increase in the density of dendritic spines on the projection neurons of the left IMHV in the trained birds; there are also increases in synapse numbers in both left and right LPO, and a 60% increase in the numbers of synaptic vesicles per synapse in the left IMHV and left LPO (reviewed in Stewart, 1991).

What might these biochemical and structural changes to the synapse "mean" in terms of changed physiology? The IMHV of the young chick shows a number of interesting neurophysiological properties, the most relevant of which is perhaps its capacity to express long-term potentiation (LTP)-like phenomena *in vivo* and *in vitro* (Bradley, Burns, & Webb, 1991; Mason & Gigg, 1991). Extracellular recordings from the IMHV and LPO of anesthetized chicks in the hours after training with the bitter bead show dramatic, several-fold increases in the incidence of bouts of high-frequency neuronal firing (bursting activity; Mason & Rose, 1987)—learning-related increases that show two peaks of intensity, one at 3–4 hours after training, the second at 6–7 hours after training. Whereas the first peak occurs in both left and right IMHV, the second is confined to the right IMHV and both LPOs (Gigg, 1991).

The story so far is in accord with relatively straightforward cellular association models of memory formation, best summarized as those offered by Hebb rules and their variants. One could argue that, in an association region of the chick brain like the IMHV, convergent inputs from pathways associated on the one hand with visual signals

---

[1]Similar results, both as to biochemistry and as to the effects of pharmacological intervention, have been observed in parallel studies made by the Berkeley group of Rosenzweig, Bennett, and their collaborators. These are reviewed by Rosenzweig et al. (Chapter 46, this volume; see particularly their Table 46.1), and are not discussed in any further detail here. Their chapter also makes the case for there being a further transitional stage between short- and long-term memory. Our work does not address the question of these intermediate stages, but instead has largely focused on the longer-term processes (persisting for hours to days after training) presumably involved in encoding long-term memory.

from the bead and on the other with its bitter and aversive taste result in modifying an output pathway (perhaps directly or indirectly via LPO) so that the original peck response is switched to a no-peck one. Within individual IMHV cells, a linear set of processes passes smoothly through the molecular steps associated with short- to intermediate- and long-term stages of memory.

In accordance with this hypothesis, chicks given either bilateral or unilateral left IMHV lesions (Figure 47.1) on the day of hatch and trained the next day can learn the avoidance response, showing the usual disgust response and immediate avoidance. However, they are amnesic when tested 3 or more hours subsequently (Patterson, Gilber, & Rose, 1990). Right IMHV lesions are without effect. The strong interpretation of this result is that the left IMHV is necessary for memory formation, in accord with the biochemical and structural observations. A weaker conclusion would be simply that the left IMHV is necessary for the expression of the memory. However, if the chicks are first trained, and the IMHV lesions are made an hour or more after training, the birds are not amnesic when tested 24 hours later. Thus, once the animals have learned the task, IMHV is no longer necessary. This rules out the weaker interpretation of the pretraining lesions, but suggests that within a short time after the memory has been formed, it relocates to some alternative storage site.

Could this site be the LPO? If this were so, then lesions of the LPO made an hour after training should cause amnesia, and indeed such bilateral LPO lesions result in loss of memory (Figure 47.2) (Gilbert, Patterson, & Rose, 1991). Paradoxically, though, as Figure 47.2 also shows, *pretraining* LPO lesions are without effect on either learning or memory. This apparent paradox could be explained by a simple mechanistic assumption that in the intact animal there is some "flow" of memory from IMHV to LPO; then,

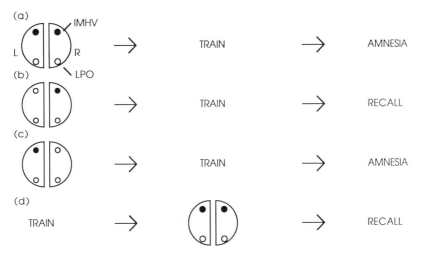

FIGURE 47.1. Effects of IMHV lesions on recall for passive avoidance. Pretraining lesions were made on the day of hatch, and the chicks were trained the following day and tested 3 hours subsequently. For posttraining lesions, chicks were trained at a day old, and lesions were made 1 hour subsequently; they were tested after recovery on the following day. Open circles, unlesioned sites; filled circles, lesioned sites. Recall occurred if chicks avoided the bead on test; amnesia was signified by pecking the bead. The data are from Patterson, Gilbert, and Rose (1990).

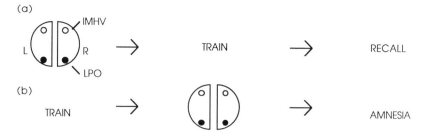

FIGURE 47.2. Effects of LPO lesions on recall for passive avoidance. Pre- and posttraining lesions were made according to the schedule of Figure 47.1. The data are from Gilbert, Patterson, and Rose (1991).

if there is no LPO present at training, the memory "trace" should remain in the IMHV. A prediction from this simple model is that in the absence of the LPO, posttraining lesions of the IMHV, which do *not* cause amnesia in the presence of an intact LPO, should result in amnesia, because there should be nowhere for the trace to relocate. And in fact such lesions cause amnesia—but now, just as the flow model would predict, it is the *right* IMHV that is essential. This sequence is shown in the sequence of Figures 47.3a–47.3c. By an analogous argument, with a pretraining right IMHV lesion, which does not of course itself cause amnesia, the "trace" should not be able to leave the left IMHV at all; therefore, posttraining LPO lesions, which *should* cause amnesia in the intact animal, should no longer do so. Figure 47.3d shows that this prediction is correct; pretraining lesions of the right IMHV prevent posttraining LPO lesions from producing amnesia, as if by blocking the "memory flow."

So, with a right IMHV lesion, does the "trace" stay permanently in the left IMHV? If this were so, then the model would predict that in animals with a pretraining

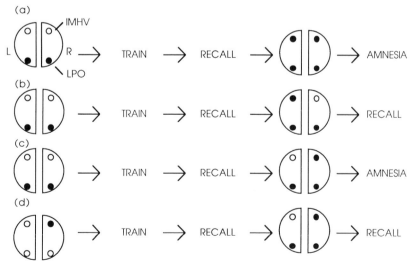

FIGURE 47.3. Testing the "memory flow" model. Conventions as in Figures 47.1 and 47.2. Time between first test and second set of lesions was 1 hour, after which chicks were left for a further 24 hours to recover before the final test. The data are from Gilbert et al. (1991).

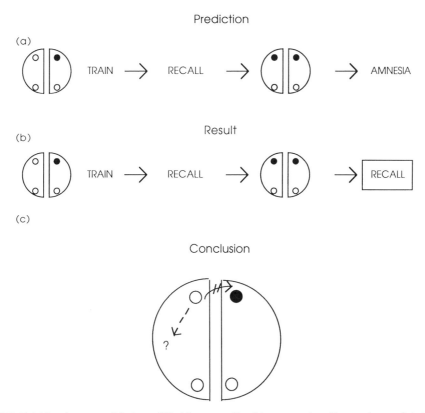

FIGURE 47.4. More lesions and their modified "memory flow" interpretation. Conventions and timings as in Figure 47.3. The data are from Gilbert et al. (1991).

right IMHV lesion, a posttraining left IMHV lesion should cause amnesia, because the memory has become somehow "stranded" in left IMHV (Figure 47.4a). As Figure 47.4b shows, however, this does *not* happen; the product of this set of dissociations is still recall. In the absence of the right IMHV, there must be yet another route out of the left IMHV to some as yet unspecified locus (Figure 47.4c).

What do these data have to say about how memories are stored in the brain? The observed biochemical and cellular cascade implies, as do most cellular models of memory formation, that a linear sequence of processes in a pair of neurons (or, more realistically, in a small ensemble of such neurons) results in lasting modification of synaptic connectivity within the ensemble—a modulation that is the brain representation of some association of events and experiences whose consequences are changed behaviors. The lesion studies, however, cast doubt on such a simplistic sequential model. Memory traces are not, it would appear, stably located within a single neuronal ensemble, but are (at least in their early phases) dynamic and fluid, moving from site to site within the brain, though not necessarily by simple pathways. This does not mean that Lashley was right and that memories are at once everywhere and nowhere, for the effect of the lesions is specific, localized, and time-dependent. Nor can this fluidity be simply interpreted as an artifact of the lesion approach—the classic Gregory transistor fallacy implicit in inferring function from dysfunction. The fact that biochemical, neurophysiological, and morphological changes occur following training in just those regions in which lesions can result in amnesia indicates that in the intact animal too, these regions have significant functions in making the brain representations required for the avoidance response. It seems more likely that representations are multiple, and that the very concept of a fixed locus may be misleading, as Skarda and Freeman (1990), basing their argument on different premises, have contended.

In this context, it becomes important to return from the cell biology to the behavior itself. What is meant by saying that the chick "remembers" the bead? When the dry bead is presented the second time, the chick must be in a position to compare the present sense data derived from the bead with the past representation of the bead and its associated bitter taste. But what form might the representation take? There are several features of the bead by which it might be recognized, including color, size, and shape, and young chicks classify objects according to all these criteria. One could imagine that, following an initial "registration" of the bead in the left IMHV (assuming that the experience is important enough to be stored at all), it is then "filed" under several different classifiers, perhaps in different brain regions. Any one of these classifiers could subsequently provide the cue for the recall when the second presentation of the bead occurs. If, for example, the left IMHV remembers color, but the other classifiers are represented elsewhere, this would explain why biochemical, morphological, and physiological changes occurring in the left IMHV continue up to 24 hours after training, even though the region is no longer necessary for memory of the avoidance.

This hypothesis also has something to say about the surprising magnitude of the changes we find—up to a 60% increase in dendritic spine density and vesicle number; a fourfold increase in neuronal bursting. Perhaps the importance of the aversive experience in the life of the young chick is so great that it is initially dramatically overrepresented in the brain. As the memory recedes, and other aspects of the young animal's experience supervene, the excess of representation declines; thus one would expect spine numbers to be pruned as in normal development, as has indeed been found by Wallhauser and Scheich (1987) in the context of auditory imprinting. Furthermore, it also answers a question frequently asked about our data—if one trained a chick to avoid first a chrome bead, then, say, a red bead, then a blue bead, and so on, would one expect that the cellular changes would increase in magnitude or distribution *pari passu*? The answer is no, because the question assumes that the chick does not know how to classify and generalize. The bird may decide that the decisive feature of "bitter-tasting" is associated not with a bead of a specific color, but instead of a particular size, and readjust its representational criteria accordingly. Chicks, unlike computers, are after all intelligent systems.

Let me return to the phenomenon of the "double wave" of glycoprotein synthesis described above and consider its implications for this model. I have long been struck by the disturbing implications of the phenomenon of conditioned taste aversion, first described by Garcia (Garcia, Ervin, & Keolling, 1966), for the "temporal contiguity" models of learning that dominate both association psychology and its cellular manifestation, the famous Hebb rules. It turns out that one can obtain a strong Garcia-type effect in the chick by simply offering it a dry green bead to peck, and 30 minutes to an hour later making it mildly sick by injecting lithium chloride intraperitoneally. The chick will avoid the green bead on presentation 3 hours later. Thus it must form some representation of the bead in its brain even without explicit pairing with a contiguous aversive or appetitive stimulus (unlike early attempts to explain away the Garcia effect when animals were trained on colored or flavored water by claiming that some residual taste was being paired with the lithium chloride).

This intriguing result in itself presents some challenges to simple cellular memory models, but the point I wish to make here is that inhibition of glycoprotein synthesis at the time of pecking the bead by injecting 2-DGal prevents the subsequent association of the lithium-chloride-induced sickness with the beadpeck. As a result, birds that have been made sick with the lithium chloride nevertheless peck the bead when it is offered 3 hours later. The 2-DGal must be injected at the time of bead peck; there is no amnesia when it is injected at the time of administering the lithium chloride, nor is the phenomenon a state-dependent effect. Thus, not only does the chick make a brain representation of the bead without specifically associating it with either appetitive or aversive consequences, but making that representation requires macromolecular—or at least glycoprotein—synthesis (Barber, Gilbert, & Rose, 1990).

Unlike the memory for the bitter-tasting bead, however, such simple representations, if unassociated with any strongly aversive or rewarding experience, soon fade; the chick cannot associate bead peck with sickness if the lithium chloride is given more than an hour after the bead. And weak aversive associations—such as pairing the bead peck not with methylanthranilate, but with the taste of quinine, which is remembered only for a few hours—do not produce any increase in glycoprotein synthesis over and above that found for pecking at the water bead alone (Bourne, Davis, Stewart, & Cooper, 1991). I suggest that in these cases of weak learning only a first wave of glycoprotein synthesis is involved, and the memory is thus impermanent. Only if the memory is to be more permanently represented does the "second wave" of glycoprotein synthesis occur. The initial representation, and the first wave of glycoprotein synthesis, may occur in the left IMHV; during the subsequent processing, classifying, distributing, and stabilizing of the trace, there may be a sequential activation of right IMHV and LPO. This is why, at about 6 hours after training (the time of the second wave), the neuronal bursting is no longer found in the left IMHV, but only in the right IMHV and in the LPO. It is the second wave, then, that is responsible for producing the glycoproteins that stabilize the changed synaptic connectivities, by creating new synapses or dendritic structures or by altering the locations of pre-existing ones.

I do not know whether this is a universally generalizable model—true for LTP and *Aplysia* as much as for chicks, for procedural as well as declarative memory. What does seem to be sure, however, is that the time has come to discard cellular alphabet or simple connectionist models, at least for real vertebrate learning. Memory may be the brain's Rosetta stone, but in order to translate its scripts we will find that it is global functional systems, and not simply Hebb, that rule.

ACKNOWLEDGMENTS

The experiments described in this chapter have been based on collaborative work by many members of the Brain and Behaviour Research Group over the past decade; I thank all who are cited—and those whose work forms part of the essential background to the results foregrounded here. Our research has been funded through the Open University, the Medical Research Council and the Science and Engineering Research Council of the United Kingdom, the Royal Society, the Wellcome Foundation, and the United Kingdom Department of Health.

REFERENCES

Andrew, R. J. (Ed.). (1991). *Neural and behavioural plasticity: The use of the domestic chick as a model.* Oxford: Oxford University Press.

Barber, A. J., Gilbert, D. B., & Rose, S. P. R. (1990). Glycoprotein synthesis is necessary for memory of sickness-induced learning in chicks. *European Journal of Neuroscience, 1,* 673-677.

Bourne, R., Davies, C., Stewart, M. G., & Cooper, W. (1991). Cerebral glycoprotein synthesis and long-term memory formation in the chick (*Gallus domesticus*) following passive avoidance training depends on the nature of the aversive stimulus. *European Journal of Neuroscience, 3,* 243-248.

Bradley, P. M., Burns, B. D., & Webb, A. C. (1991). Potentiation of synaptic responses in slices from the chick forebrain. *Proceedings of the Royal Society of London, B243,* 19-24.

Burchuladze, R., Potter, J., & Rose, S. P. R. (1990). Memory formation for passive avoidance in the chick depends on membrane-bound protein kinase C. *Brain Research, 535,* 131-138.

Burchuladze, R., & Rose, S. P. R. (in press). Memory formation in chicks requires NMDA but not non-NMDA receptors. *European Journal of Neuroscience.*

Cherkin, A. (1969). Kinetics of memory consolidation: Role of amnestic treatment parameters. *Proceedings of the National Academy of Sciences USA, 63,* 1094-1100.

Edelman, G. (1987). *Neural Darwinism.* New York: Basic Books.

Garcia, J., Ervin, F. R., & Keolling, R. (1966). Learning with prolonged delay of reinforcement. *Psychonomic Science, 5,* 121-122.

Gigg, J. (1991). *An investigation of the neurophysiological correspondents of learning and memory in two forebrain regions of the day old chick.* PhD thesis, Open University, Milton Keynes, England.

Gilbert, D. B., Patterson, T. A., & Rose, S. P. R. (1991). Discussion of brain sites necessary for registration and storage of a one-trial passive avoidance learning task in chicks. *Behavioral Neuroscience, 105,* 553-561.

Horn, G. (1985). *Memory, imprinting and the brain.* Oxford: Oxford University Press.

Horn, G., & Krebs, J. R. (Eds.). (1990). Behavioural and neural aspects of learning and memory. *Philosophical Transactions of the Royal Society of London, B329,* 97-227.

Mason, R. J., & Gigg, J. (1991). Paper presented at the meeting of the European Neurosciences Association, Cambridge, England.

Mason, R. J., & Rose, S. P. R. (1987). Lasting changes in spontaneous multi-unit activity in the chick brain following passive avoidance training. *Neuroscience, 21,* 931-941.

Patterson, T. A., Gilbert, D. B., & Rose, S. P. R. (1990). Pre- and post-training lesions of the intermediate medial hyperstriatum ventrale and passive avoidance learning in the chick. *Experimental Brain Research, 80,* 189-195.

Rose, S. P. R. (1984). Strategies in studying the cell biology of learning and memory. In L. R. Squire & N. Butters (Eds.), *Neuropsychology of memory* (1st ed., pp. 547-554). New York: Guilford Press.

Rose, S. P. R. (1991a). Biochemical mechanisms of memory formation in the chick. In R. J. Andrew (Ed.), *Neural and Behavioural Plasticity: The use of the domestic chicks a model* (pp. 277-304). Oxford: Oxford University Press.

Rose, S. P. R. (1991b). How chicks make memories. *Trends in Neuroscience, 14,* 390-397.

Rose, S. P. R. (1992). *Memories are made of this.* New York: Bantam.

Rose, S. P. R., & Csillag, A. (1985). Passive avoidance training results in lasting changes in deoxyglucose metabolism in left hemisphere regions of chick brain. *Behavioral Neural Biology, 44,* 315-324.

Skarda, C. A., & Freeman, W. J. (1990). Chaos and the new science of the brain. *Concepts in Neuroscience, 1,* 275-286.

Stewart, M. G. (1991). Changes in dendritic and synaptic structure in chick forebrain consequent on passive avoidance learning. In R. J. Andrew (Ed.), *Neural and behavioural plasticity: The use of the domestic chick as a model* (pp. 305-328). Oxford: Oxford University Press.

Wallhauser, E., & Scheich, H. (1987). Auditory imprinting leads to differential 2-deoxyglucose uptake and dendritic spine loss in the chick rostral forebrain. *Developmental Brain Research, 31,* 29-44.

48

Molecular Interrelationships between Short- and Long-Term Memory

TIMOTHY E. KENNEDY, ROBERT D. HAWKINS,
and ERIC R. KANDEL

A striking feature of memory in human beings and in experimental animals is that for most learning tasks memory appears to be a single, graded, continuous process whose duration is a function of the number of training trials (Weiskrantz, 1970; Wickelgren, 1973; Craik & Lockhart, 1972). As Ebbinghaus (1885/1963) first demonstrated experimentally in the 19th century, repetition of a task usually increases both the strength and the duration of the memory for that task. As a result, long-term memory has often been thought to be a graded extension of short-term memory. Yet clinical studies and observations derived from experimental animals indicate that memory is probably not a unitary process, but has at least two forms, each of which subserves a family of time courses: a short-term form that can last seconds, minutes, or hours; and a long-term form that can last days, weeks, or years. For example, in humans, a number of clinical conditions clearly dissociate short-term from long-term memory (Squire & Zola-Morgan, 1988). A similar dissociation has been demonstrated in experimental animals, using inhibitors of protein synthesis (Davis & Squire, 1984; Agranoff, 1972; Barondes, 1975; Flexner, Flexner, & Stellar, 1983; Castellucci, Blumenfeld, Goelet, & Kandel, 1989). In this chapter we explore the apparent similarities and the fundamental differences between short- and long-term memory at the behavioral, cellular, and molecular levels, using an invertebrate animal (the marine snail *Aplysia*). In this relatively simple nervous system, synaptic changes can be compared to and correlated with behavioral changes. Because synaptic plasticity is readily reflected in behavioral change, memory and synaptic plasticity can be directly compared and causally related.

In *Aplysia*, a tactile stimulus to the siphon evokes gill and siphon withdrawal, two simple defensive reflexes. This stimulus activates siphon sensory neurons, which relay the information to interneurons and gill and siphon motor neurons (Castellucci, Pinsker, Kupfermann, & Kandel, 1970; Byrne, Castellucci, & Kandel, 1974, 1978). These reflexes exhibit several types of learned associative and nonassociative behavioral changes, including sensitization, habituation, and classical conditioning (Hawkins, Clark, & Kandel, 1987). We focus here on sensitization of the gill and siphon withdrawal reflexes, and specifically on the similarities and differences between their short-

and long-term forms. Sensitization is a nonassociative form of learning in which an animal enhances its defensive responses to a variety of eliciting stimuli following presentation of a noxious stimulus. In *Aplysia*, sensitization of the gill and siphon withdrawal reflexes can be induced by a strong stimulus applied to another site, such as the tail. This activates facilitatory interneurons, which synapse onto the presynaptic terminals of the sensory neurons and other neurons (Hawkins, Castellucci, & Kandel, 1981; Hawkins & Schacher, 1989; Mackey, Kandel, & Hawkins, 1989). One result of activating these modulatory interneurons is to strengthen the synaptic connection between the sensory and the motor neurons.

Behaviorally, sensitization of these reflexes exhibits both short- and long-term forms of memory. A single stimulus to the tail gives rise to short-term sensitization lasting minutes to hours. Repetition of the stimulus produces long-term behavioral sensitization that can last days to weeks (see Figure 48.1) (Pinsker, Hening, Carew, & Kandel, 1973; Frost, Castellucci, Hawkins, & Kandel, 1985). As is the case with learning in vertebrates, memory for sensitization in *Aplysia* is graded, and retention of the memory is proportional to the number of training trials.

Both short- and long-term sensitization are represented in the monosynaptic pathway of these reflexes, the sensory neurons and their connections to the motor

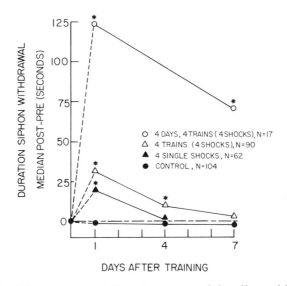

FIGURE 48.1. Behavioral long-term sensitization. A summary of the effects of long-term sensitization training on the duration of siphon withdrawal in *Aplysia californica*. The retention of the memory for sensitization is a graded function proportional to the number of training trials. Experimental animals received either four single shocks for 1 day (filled triangles), four trains of shocks for 1 day (open triangles), or four trains of shocks a day for 4 days (open circles). Control animals were not shocked (filled circles). A pretest determined the mean duration of siphon withdrawal for all animals before training. Posttraining testing was carried out 1, 4, or 7 days after the last day of training. The asterisks indicate a significant difference between the duration of siphon withdrawal for the trained and control animals (Mann–Whitney U tests; $p < .01$). N represents the number of animals per group. From "Monosynaptic Connections from the Sensory Neurons of the Gill- and Siphon-Withdrawal Reflex in *Aplysia* Participate in the Storage of Long-Term Memory for Sensitization" (p. 8267) by W. N. Frost, V. G. Castellucci, R. D. Hawkins, and E. R. Kandel, 1985, *Proceedings of the National Academy of Sciences USA, 82*, 8266–8269.

neurons (Frost et al., 1985). This monosynaptic pathway, the sensory-neuron-to-motor-neuron connection, can be reconstituted in dissociated cell culture, where it has been used as a model for the cellular changes underlying the learned changes in behavior (Rayport & Schacher, 1986; Montarolo et al., 1986). In cell culture, serotonin (5-HT), a modulatory transmitter released by sensitizing stimuli (Glanzman et al., 1989; Mackey et al., 1989), can substitute for the reinforcing stimulus used during behavioral training of the intact animal, shock to the tail (Rayport & Schacher, 1986; Montarolo et al., 1986). A single application of 5-HT produces short-term changes in synaptic effectiveness, whereas four or five applications of 5-HT over 1.5 hours (or continuous application of 5-HT for 1.5 to 2 hours) produce long-term changes lasting 1 or more days (Montarolo et al., 1986). This common site of both short- and long-term neuromodulation has allowed us to focus on the sensory-neuron-to-motor-neuron component, because we have identified here, in what is essentially a two-neuron system, one critical component of both the short- and the long-term processes.

Electrophysiological studies of this component have indicated that both the similarities and the differences in memory at the behavioral level reflect, at least in part, intrinsic cellular mechanisms of the nerve cells participating in memory storage. Thus, studies of the connections between sensory and motor neurons, both in the intact animal and on cells in culture, indicate that the long-term changes are surprisingly similar to the short-term changes (Frost et al., 1985; Montarolo et al., 1986; Dale, Kandel, & Schacher, 1987). The increase in synaptic strength observed during both the short- and long-term changes reflects enhanced release of transmitter by the sensory neuron. This is accompanied by an increase in the excitability and a broadening of the action potential of the sensory neurons, attributable in part to the depression of a specific potassium channel (Klein & Kandel, 1980; Hochner, Klein, Schacher, & Kandel, 1985; Dale et al., 1987; Scholz & Byrne, 1987; Dale, Schacher, & Kandel, 1988).

However, despite these similarities, the short-term changes in *Aplysia* differ from the long-term changes in two important ways. First, short-term behavioral sensitization in the animal and short-term facilitation in dissociated cell culture do not require ongoing macromolecular synthesis; the short-term change is not blocked by inhibitors of transcription or translation (Montarolo et al., 1986; Schwartz, Castellucci, & Kandel, 1971). By contrast, these inhibitors selectively block the induction of the long-term changes, both in the semi-intact animal and in primary cell culture (Montarolo et al., 1986; Castellucci et al., 1989). In addition, the inhibition must be present during training or 5-HT application, and thus the induction of long-term facilitation exhibits a time window in its requirement for protein and ribonucleic acid (RNA) synthesis characteristic of that necessary for learning in both vertebrate and invertebrate animals (Montarolo et al., 1986; Agranoff, 1972; Barondes, 1975; Davis & Squire, 1984; Flexner et al., 1983). Thus, the long-term behavioral and cellular changes may require the expression of genes and proteins not required for the short-term changes. Second, both Bailey and Chen (1983, 1988a, 1988b, 1989) and Glanzman, Kandel, and Schacher (1990) have found that the long-term but not the short-term changes are associated with growth of new synaptic contacts by the sensory neurons. These structural changes in the connectivity between the sensory and motor neurons may be the cellular correlates of the retention phase of the long-term memory. Furthermore, the structural changes may be dependent on, and induced by, changes in gene and protein expression in the neurons involved.

Long-Term Sensitization and Persistent Protein Phosphorylation

What molecular mechanisms account for the similarity of long- and short-term memory—a similarity that gives memory its apparently graded and continuous properties? What accounts for the distinct susceptibility of long-term memory to inhibitors of protein and RNA synthesis?

Bernier, Castellucci, Kandel, and Schwartz (1982) demonstrated that short-term facilitation of sensory neurons is accompanied by an increase in the intracellular concentration of cyclic adenosine monophosphate (cAMP). This increase in cAMP following 5-HT application presumably activates a cAMP-dependent protein kinase as an early step in the cascade of events leading to facilitation. The involvement of the cAMP-dependent protein kinase was further implicated by the demonstration that intracellular injection of the purified catalytic subunit produced a broadening of the sensory neuron action potential and facilitation of transmitter release (Castellucci et al., 1980). In addition, intracellular injection of a specific inhibitor of the cAMP-dependent protein kinase blocked the facilitatory effects of 5-HT on sensory neurons (Castellucci, Nairn, Greengard, Schwartz, & Kandel, 1982).

To explore similarities and differences in 5-HT-induced kinase activation during the induction and maintenance of short- and long-term sensitization, Sweatt and Kandel (1989) used high-resolution analytical two-dimensional (2-D) gels to identify proteins whose phosphorylation was altered following 5-HT application to isolated *Aplysia* sensory neurons. They found that long-term facilitation produced by repeated or prolonged exposure to 5-HT or cAMP induced increased phosphorylation of the same 17 substrate proteins that were similarly phosphorylated during short-term facilitation (Figure 48.2). But, whereas the increased phosphorylation of the substrate proteins following a single pulse of 5-HT or cAMP is transient and does not require new protein synthesis, the increased phosphorylation of the same substrates following repeated or prolonged exposure persists for at least 24 hours and is blocked by inhibitors of protein or RNA synthesis applied during the period of 5-HT application (Figure 48.2). Thus, the induction of the persistent phosphorylation of substrate proteins requires active transcription and translation. These data suggest that one of the functions of the proteins required for long-term facilitation is to maintain actively, in the sensory cells, an increased phosphorylation of a set of substrate proteins capable of eliciting physiological effects that resemble those seen in the short term. Insofar as these data reflect events occurring in the intact animal, they also illustrate that although the behavioral and cellular effects of sensitization appear to be graded, they are in fact the result of distinct biochemical mechanisms for the induction of short- and long-term responses.

What protein kinase, or set of kinases, mediates these persistent effects? Both brief application and prolonged application of a cell-permeable analogue of cAMP produce an increase in the phosphorylation of the same 17 proteins as those altered following 5-HT application. In addition, the long-term change in protein phosphoryla-

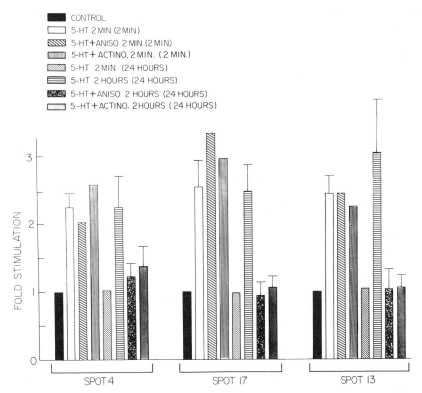

FIGURE 48.2. Short- and long-term effects of 5-HT on the phosphorylation of individual proteins. The incorporation of phosphate into the same set of 17 proteins was increased during both short- and long-term facilitation of isolated *Aplysia* sensory neurons. Representative data are shown for three proteins. The protein synthesis inhibitor anisomycin or the RNA synthesis inhibitor actinomycin D applied during the period of 5-HT application had no effect on phosphorylation increases associated with short-term facilitation, but blocked the persistence of phosphorylation during long-term facilitation. From "Persistent and Transcriptionally-Dependent Increase in Protein Phosphorylation upon Long-Term Faciliation of *Aplysia* Sensory Neurons" (p. 53) by J. D. Sweatt and E. R. Kandel, 1989, *Nature*, *339*, 51–54. Copyright 1989 by Macmillan Magazines Ltd. Reprinted by permission.

tion induced by cAMP showed the same dependence on macromolecular synthesis for its induction. The effects of cAMP in eukaryotic cells have been proposed to be mediated by the cAMP-dependent protein kinases (Kuo & Greengard, 1969; Greengard, 1978; Rall, 1979; Walsh, Perlans, & Koch, 1968). Since cAMP can initiate the long-term process (Schacher, Castellucci, & Kandel, 1988), and since the substrates phosphorylated in the long term are identical to those phosphorylated by cAMP activation in the short term, it is possible that the long-term process may also be maintained by the cAMP-dependent kinase. Bernier et al. (1982) had earlier examined the level of cAMP, and found that it does not persistently increase following behavioral training or exposure to 5-HT. Thus, a kinase must either continue to be active or the phosphate moiety must be maintained on the protein, perhaps by the suppression of a specific phosphatase. The possibility that the cAMP-dependent protein kinase remains active emerged initially from the work of Greenberg, Castellucci, Bayley, and Schwartz (1987), who found that behavioral training for long-term sensitization leads to a depression in the level of the regulatory subunits of the cAMP-dependent kinase. Bergold, Sweatt, Kandel, and Schwartz (1990) next found that this depression in the level of the regulatory subunits of the cAMP-dependent kinase could be produced by repeated exposure of isolated sensory neurons to 5-HT. Moreover, Bergold et al. (1990) found that this depression requires active protein synthesis with the same time window of sensitivity as the long-term facilitation requires, and that the depression is not regulated by changes in the level of messenger RNA (mRNA). These findings suggest that training leads to the activation of a protein (perhaps a specific protease), resulting in the functional loss of the regulatory subunit of the cAMP-dependent protein kinase, which allows the catalytic subunit to function in a constitutive manner in the absence of cAMP.

The Induction of Long-Term Sensitization Requires the Activation of One or More cAMP-Dependent Transcription Factors

The observation that the cAMP-dependent protein kinase is involved in the induction of long-term facilitation suggested a specific model for the early molecular events that initiate the long-term process. The nature of this molecular switch has been examined by Dash, Hochner, and Kandel (1990). The cAMP-dependent protein kinase is responsible for the activation of cAMP-induced gene expression by phosphorylation of cAMP-responsive-element-binding proteins (CREBPs), which bind to an upstream enhancer sequence, the cAMP-responsive element (CRE) (Comb, Birnberg, Seasholtz, Herbert, & Goodman, 1986; Jones & Jones, 1989; Montminy, Sevarino, Wagner, Mandel, & Goodman, 1986; Montminy & Bilezikjian, 1987; Yamamoto, Gonzalez, Bigg, Montminy, 1988). Using deoxyribonuclease (DNase) 1 footprinting, Dash et al. (1990) demonstrated the presence of an activity in *Aplysia* central nervous system protein extract that binds to the CRE sequence. They then showed that competition for the CREBP in sensory neurons, induced by direct microinjection of an oligonucleotide containing the CRE sequence into the nucleus, blocked the induction of long-term facilitation. This suggests that in addition to the immediate effects of 5-HT mediated by the kinase, the kinase may also translocate to the nucleus of the sensory neuron, initiating changes in gene expression via the CREBP. These changes in gene expression may be important both for changes in the expression of early effector proteins, and also for much later events resulting from the activation of early gene regulatory proteins, which initiates a temporal cascade of later-expressed regulatory and effector proteins.

Long-Term Sensitization and Neuronal Growth

In addition to the induction of persistent phosphorylation, what other cellular changes might the newly synthesized proteins required for long-term memory bring about? Morphological studies by Bailey and Chen (1983, 1988a, 1988b, 1989) have demonstrated that long-term behavioral sensitization is accompanied by significant structural changes in the sensory neurons. Using horseradish peroxidase to visualize the terminals of the sensory neurons, they examined the number of synaptic varicosities, the number and size of the active zones, and the distribution of the synaptic vesicles in abdominal ganglia from control animals and animals given long-term sensitization training. Bailey and Chen (1983, 1988a, 1989) found that following long-term sensitization training, the number of varicose expansions doubled (Figure 48.3), and that within the synaptic varicosities there was an increase in the number and size of the active zones and in the total number of vesicles associated with each release site. This modulation of the connectivity between the sensory neuron and motor neuron may provide a long-term structural mechanism underlying the persistence of reflex strength observed following long-term behavioral sensitization. Bailey and Chen's findings also suggest that varicosities and active zones are not fixed neuronal elements, but rather that learning modulates these structures to alter synaptic effectiveness.

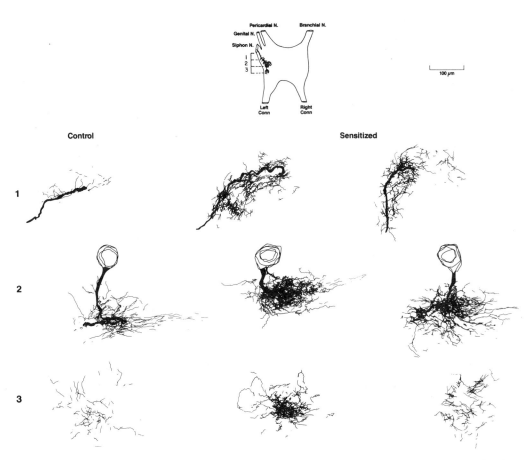

FIGURE 48.3. Serial reconstructions of sensory neurons from control and long-term sensitized animals. The neuropil arbors of individual sensory neurons injected with horesradish peroxidase were reconstructed by the superimposition of camera lucida tracings of serial sections. The sizes of the arbors of long-term sensitized animals were increased with respect to controls. Rows 1, 2, and 3 refer to similar regions of each sensory neuron, as indicated on the inset of the abdominal ganglion at the top of the figure. From "Long-Term Memory in *Aplysia* Modulates the Total Number of Varicosities of Single Identified Sensory Neurons" (p. 2375) by C. H. Bailey and M. Chen, 1988, *Proceedings of the National Academy of Sciences USA, 85,* 2373–2377.

Glanzman et al. (1990) have extended these findings, using low-light-level video microscopy. This has allowed them to observe similar structural changes in cell culture following application of 5-HT to isolated pairs of sensory and motor neurons. Sensory neurons cultured alone (or with inappropriate target cells) have fewer defasciculated processes and varicosities than those cocultured with L7 motor cells, suggesting that some interaction with the target motor neuron, an interaction related to synaptic contact, may regulate the growth of sensory neurons. Moreover, Glanzman et al. (1990) found a good correlation between the number of varicosities on a sensory neuron and the strength of its synaptic connection with the motor neuron when sensory neurons were cocultured with L7 cells. This correlation suggests that the varicosities, particularly those associated with the initial segment of the major neurite of the motor neuron, represent synaptic release sites. Repeated applications of 5-HT to cultures of sensory and motor neurons produced an increase in the number of sensory neuron synaptic varicosities on the initial segment of the motor neuron axon. This increase paralleled the long-term facilitation of synaptic strength. Interestingly, unlike the long-term changes in the biophysical properties of the sensory neuron following 5-HT application to sensory neurons cultured alone, 5-HT-stimulated growth requires the presence of the postsynaptic motor neuron for its expression.

In addition to characterizing the structural changes that occur during the onset and establishment of sensitization, Bailey and Chen (1989) have examined the decay of these changes during forgetting, the period during which reflex strength returns to baseline levels. A week after training, the increase in the number of synaptic varicosities was still present; however, the number and size of the active zone release sites had returned to baseline levels. This suggests that a week after training (during the late maintenance phase of long-term sensitization), although there are now more synapses, each individual synapse may have available to it all the mechanisms of plasticity that were present before training. The neurons have therefore passed from a baseline pretrained state, to a transient growth state induced by training, to a new baseline state in which long-term sensitization has been established and is maintained. At this new baseline the neuron again has multiple mechanisms of plasticity available to it, and new parameters of plasticity have been established.

What Proteins Contribute to the Long-Term Change?

Using analytical 2-D gels and [^{35}S]methionine incorporation to identify changes in protein synthesis following long-term facilitation, we (Barzilai, Kennedy, Sweatt, & Kandel, 1989) found that application of 5-HT to primary cultures of sensory neurons leads to a transcriptionally dependent induction of at least three major rounds of specific protein synthesis (Figure 48.4). First, peaking at approximately 30 minutes after 5-HT application, 10 proteins rapidly and transiently increase and 5 decrease their incorporation of [^{35}S]methionine. These early changes are followed by at least two further rounds of changes in the expression of specific protein synthesis, some of which are transient and some of which persist for at least 24 hours. The time course and sequence of the induced changes suggest that application of 5-HT may produce its long-term effects by the activation of a cascade of gene expression, in which regulatory

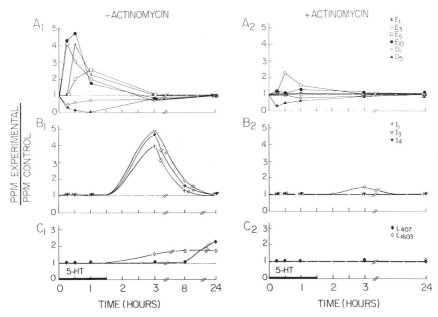

FIGURE 48.4. The effects of 5-HT and actinomycin D on the incorporation of [^{35}S]methionine into specific proteins of isolated *Aplysia* sensory neurons in primary cell culture. Each plot represents the ratio of the average parts per million (PPM) of 5-HT-treated clusters over the average PPM for the control for a specific protein at the indicated time points. (**A$_1$**) Early increases and decreases in the net synthesis of specific proteins. (**B$_1$**) Intermediate increases peaking at 3 hours. (**C$_1$**) Late increases in the net synthesis of specific proteins. (**A$_2$**, **B$_2$**, **C$_2$**). All of the changes in protein expression were either partially or completely blocked by the addition of actinomycin D 1 hour prior to the application of 5-HT. From "5-HT Modulates Protein Synthesis and the Expression of Specific Proteins during Long-Term Facilitation in *Aplysia* Sensory Neurons" (p. 1582) by A. Barzilai, T. E. Kennedy, J. D. Sweatt, and E. R. Kandel, 1989, *Neuron, 2,* 1577–1586. Copyright 1989 by Cell Press. Reprinted by permission.

genes expressed early modify the expression of multiple rounds of late regulatory and effector genes. We are testing these ideas, and also attempting to determine whether some of the later proteins might contribute to the neuronal growth coincident with long-term sensitization (for similar results, see Eskin, Garcia, & Byrne, 1989).

In addition to changes in the specific expression of individual proteins, we (Barzilai et al., 1989) observed three temporally distinct alterations in overall protein synthesis following 5-HT application: a decrease at ½ hour, a small increase at 1 hour, and a second and larger increase at 3 hours (Figure 48.5). In these two respects— alterations in specific protein expression, and modulation of overall protein synthesis— the action of 5-HT on sensory neurons resembles the changes in protein expression observed in mammalian cell culture when stimulated to grow by serum or by peptide growth factors such as platelet-derived growth factor or nerve growth factor (Angeletti, Gardini-Attardi, Tosehi, Salvi, & Levi-Montalcini, 1965; Garrels & Schubert, 1979) and by second messengers (Brostrom, Chin, Cade, Gmitter, & Brostrom, 1987).

As a first step toward understanding the contribution of these changes to the long-term process, we are attempting to characterize and identify each of the proteins observed to be specifically altered in expression during long-term sensitization. Four of the proteins described in the Barzilai et al. (1989) study, which transiently decrease

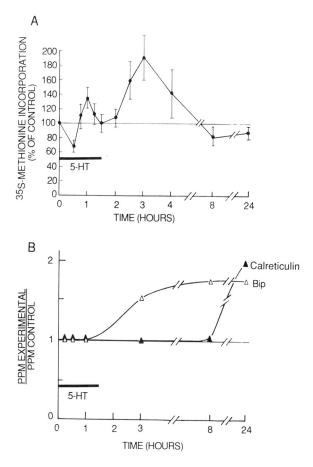

FIGURE 48.5. The specific increase in synthesis of BiP coincides with the peak of an increase in total protein synthesis. This general increase in protein synthesis may contribute to the structural changes observed in long-term sensitization and long-term facilitation. BiP may be regulated by the sensory neurons as part of the cellular machinery to process the general increase in protein synthesis. From "5-HT Modulates Protein Synthesis and the Expression of Specific Proteins during Long-Term Facilitation in *Aplysia* Sensory Neurons" (p. 1580) by A. Barzilai, T. E. Kennedy, J. D. Sweatt, and E. R. Kandel, *Neuron, 2*, 1577–1586. Copyright 1989 by Cell Press. Reprinted by permission.

following 5-HT application to isolated sensory neurons in primary cell culture, have been found to cross-react with two monoclonal antibodies generated by Keller and Schacher (1990) against an *Aplysia* synaptosomal fraction. These antibodies have allowed Mayford, Barzilai, Keller, Schacher, and Kandel (1992) to identify them as the *Aplysia* homologues of the mammalian neural cell adhesion molecules (NCAMs), the apCAMs, and to clone their corresponding mRNAs. The antibodies have also allowed Keller and Schacher (1990), Mayford et al. (1992), and Bailey, Chen, Keller, and Kandel (1992) to implicate the apCAMs as being functionally involved in the regulation of neurite fasciculation. The neurites of sensory neurons, which usually grow in tightly fasciculated bundles, defasciculate and grow as much thinner neuritic processes when exposed to the antibody in culture. This suggests that the down-regulation of the apCAMs observed following 5-HT application to sensory neurons may function as a preliminary and permissive step for the neuron to grow and form the new synaptic arbors associated with long-term sensitization and long-term facilitation.

Electron microscopy and gold-labeled apCAM antibodies have allowed Bailey et al. (1992) to demonstrate that following 5-HT application, not only does the synthesis of apCAM decrease, but apCAM is internalized from the surface of the sensory neuron into compartment for the uncoupling of receptor and ligand (CURL)-like structures in the cytoplasm. This activation of the endocytic pathway removes the cell adhesion molecule from the surface, which may be permissive for growth, and also provides a source of membrane available to be rapidly inserted at new sites of neuronal growth and synapse formation.

Coincident with the internalization of apCAM, the protein E4 was shown (Barzilai et al., 1989) to increase its incorporation of [^{35}S]methionine early following 5-HT application to isolated sensory neurons. E4 has been identified by Hu, Bailey, Chen, Kandel, and Barzilai (1992) as an *Aplysia* homologue of clathrin light chain. Clathrin forms a cage-like structure around coated vesicles during receptor-mediated endocytosis (for a review, see Brodsky et al., 1991). This up-regulation of clathrin light chain synthesis may be a component in the activation of the endocytic cycle required for the internalization of apCAM.

What Changes in Protein Synthesis Are Involved in the Later Phases of the Induction and Maintenance of Long-Term Sensitization?

In addition to the early changes observed following 5-HT application to isolated sensory neurons, later changes in protein synthesis were also observed following 5-HT application to isolated sensory neurons (Barzilai et al., 1989), as well as following long-term sensitization training of the intact animal (Castellucci, Kennedy, Kandel, & Goelet, 1988). We (Kennedy, Gawinowicz, Barzilai, Kandel, & Sweatt, 1988; Kennedy, Wager-Smith, Barzilai, Kandel, & Sweatt, 1988) therefore developed a method to obtain amino acid sequences of proteins isolated directly from 2-D gels, and used it to identify and clone two proteins observed to increase 24 hours after both behavioral training and 5-HT application to isolated primary cultures of sensory neurons. Such amino acid sequence data and further 2-D gel expression analysis have indicated that one of these proteins is the *Aplysia* homologue of GRP78/BiP (Kennedy, Kuhl, Barzilai, Kandel, & Sweatt, 1989; Kuhl, Kennedy, Barzilai, & Kandel, 1992). BiP, the member of the HSP 70 family localized within the lumen of the endoplasmic reticulum, is thought to function as a molecular chaperone of newly synthesized proteins (Pelham, 1988). The increase in *Aplysia* BiP expression is first detected 3 hours after 5-HT application to isolated sensory neurons (Kennedy et al., 1989; Barzilai et al., 1989). This increase is coincident with the 3-hour increase in overall protein synthesis observed in the Barzilai et al. (1989) study (Figure 48.5). This change in the expression of *Aplysia* BiP may represent a response by the sensory neuron to meet the posttranslational demands of the general increase in protein synthesis. Furthermore, the increase in general protein synthesis may in part underlie the structural growth-related change in the sensory-neuron-to-motor-neuron connections observed during the maintenance phase of long-term sensitization.

Parallel findings by Brostrom et al. (1987; Brostrom, Cades, Prostko, Gmitter-Yellen, & Brostrom, 1990) have shown that the application of cAMP or phorbol esters to GH3 cells, which induce an increase in total protein synthesis, similarly induce a coincident increase in BiP synthesis. This suggests that modulation of BiP expression may be a general response of cells to an increased posttranslational load on the endoplasmic reticulum, which results from increased protein synthesis.

The amino acid sequence of a second protein that increases its incorporation of [^{35}S]methionine 24 hours after behavioral training and following 5-HT application to isolated sensory neurons has allowed us (Kennedy et al., 1989; Kennedy, Kuhl, Barzilai, & Kandel, 1992) to clone its corresponding mRNA and identify it as the *Aplysia* homologue of calreticulin. Calreticulin is thought to be the major Ca^{2+}-binding protein of the lumen of the endoplasmic reticulum, binding approximately 25 moles of calcium per mole of protein (Ostwald & MacLennan, 1974; Fliegel, Burns, MacLennan, Reith-meier, & Michalak, 1989; Smith & Koch, 1989; Treves et al., 1990). Copurification of calreticulin with the Ins(1,4,5)P$_3$-sensitive Ca^{2+} store (Krause, Simmerman, Jones, & Campbell, 1990), and the presence of the Ins(1,4,5)P$_3$-receptor in presynaptic terminals (Ross et al., 1989; Mignery, Sudhof, Takei, & DeCamilli, 1989; Peng, Sharp, Snyder, & Yau, 1991), suggest that the regulation of calreticulin expression may be involved in the long-term regulation and modulation of calcium levels in the presynaptic terminals.

Regulation of mRNA Expression during Learning

Are the levels of specific mRNAs regulated during learning? To address this question, we (Kennedy et al., 1992) and Kuhl et al. (1992) have measured the steady-state levels of calreticulin and BiP mRNA in naive animals and in animals following long-term sensitization training, using quantitative S1 nuclease analysis. Significant increases in the mRNA-encoding calreticulin and BiP were found in sensory neurons following long-term sensitization training. This is the first demonstration of the modulation of specific mRNA levels following behavioral training in cells known to be involved in the neuronal plasticity underlying the behavioral modification of a reflex. It is also the first direct test and confirmation of a prediction of the model proposed by Goelet, Castellucci, Schacher, and Kandel (1986)—namely, that neuromodulatory changes underlying learning involve changes in gene expression, and hence the regulation of the steady-state level of specific mRNAs.

Summary

These studies of neuronal changes accompanying long-term memory for sensitization, as well as the earlier studies on the regulation of tyrosine hydroxylase, proenkephalin, and c-fos in sympathetic neurons or PC12 cells, illustrate a new class of transmitter action—regulation by neurotransmitters of translation and transcription (Comb et al., 1986; Black et al., 1987; Chalazonitis & Zigmond, 1980; Greenberg et al., 1987; for reviews, see Goelet et al., 1986; Mattson, 1988). These data suggest that with repeated or prolonged application, modulatory transmitters activate not only a cytoplasmic second-messenger system involved in the short-term action, but also a nuclear messenger (or third-messenger) system in which the transmitter exerts a long-term modulatory control over the excitability and connectivity of the neuron through changes in gene expression. In that view, the distinction between short- and long-term memory in the sensory neurons would derive, in part, from the ability of the modulatory neurotransmitter to select between a program involving only cytoplasmic mechanisms of regulation and one involving the induction of additional mechanisms altering cell state via regulation in the nucleus. A corollary to this finding is that the conventional distinction between transmitters and growth factors is not exclusive. Certain transmitters and second messengers have been shown to influence neurite outgrowth and synapse formation in culture (Haydon, McGobb, & Kater, 1984; Nirenberg et al., 1983; for a review, see Mattson, Lee, Adams, Guthrie, & Kater, 1988). Furthermore, the observation of sequential, transcriptionally dependent increases and decreases in specific protein expression following 5-HT application to sensory neurons (Barzilai et al., 1989; Eskin et al., 1989) may be directly analogous to the dynamic changes in RNA and protein synthesis induced in mammalian cell culture following stimulation by growth factors, serum, or second-messenger application (Garrels & Schubert, 1979; Nevins, 1985; Schneider, King, & Philipson, 1988; Lau & Nathans, 1985).

Figure 48.6 illustrates our current understanding of the signaling systems involved in the activation of long-term facilitation in *Aplysia* sensory neurons. In this model, 5-HT, a transmitter released by modulatory neurons, acts on the presynaptic element of a sensory neuron to initiate separate memory processes with different durations. Short-term memory, which has a time course of minutes to hours, involves the covalent modification of pre-existing proteins. Transmembrane and cytoplasmic signaling mechanisms, including membrane receptor proteins, adenylate cyclase, and cAMP, transduce the extracellular signal and initiate the modification of target proteins such as the 5-HT-sensitive potassium channel. The duration of these modifications determines the time course of short-term memory retention.

Unlike these short-term mechanisms, the acquisition of long-term memory depends in this model on the induced synthesis of new proteins (filled rectangle and triangle, Figure 48.6). This induction is initiated by the same second messengers involved in the induction of short-term memory, which modify transacting regulators of gene expression such as CREBP (open circles in pathway 3, Figure 48.6). These may activate both early effector genes, such as clathrin light chains and a specific protease, and also early transacting regulatory genes. Induced early effector genes such as clathrin may be involved in the removal of apCAM from the cell surface through activation of the endocytic pathway, and may contribute to the early stages of structural changes involved in the growth of new synaptic connections. The induced regulatory genes may in turn initiate further rounds of transcriptional activation, which generate a cascade of sequential gene expression affecting genes encoding proteins, such as calreticulin and BiP. Memory lasting hours is retained by the half-life of the effector proteins or by the functional modifications, such as phosphorylation, of these proteins. Certain of the early effector proteins may serve to reinforce and maintain the initial response—for example, by proteolytic activation of a protein kinase. Memory lasting, days, weeks and months, longer than the half-life of effector proteins, may be initiated by the early regulatory genes whose protein products trigger the maintained

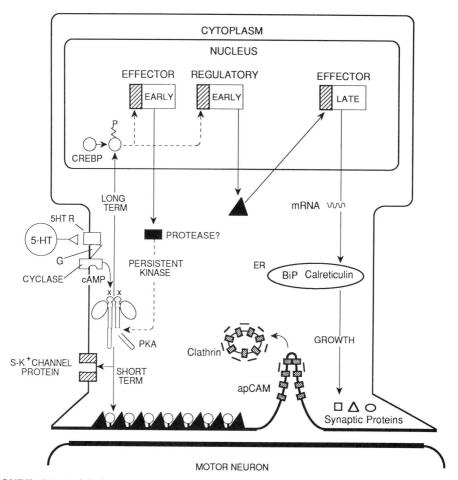

FIGURE 48.6. Model of the macromolecular events underlying long-term sensitization in an *Aplysia* sensory neuron. 5-HT, released from facilitatory interneurons that synapse presynaptically onto the sensory neurons, binds to its transmembrane receptor, activating the adenylyl cyclase to generate cAMP and activating the A kinase. Kinase activation produces short-term effects that are independent of new macromolecular synthesis, such as the closure of the 5-HT-sensitive potassium channel. In addition to the short-term effects, repeated activation of facilitatory interneurons triggers the induction of long-term sensitization. Transcription factors such as CREBP initiate a cascade of regulatory and effector gene expression. These changes in gene expression may involve both effector and regulatory gene products. Early effectors may include the induction of a protease specific for the regulatory subunit of the A kinase, thereby generating persistent kinase activation, or clathrin light chains involved in the endocytic pathway. Induction of early regulatory genes triggers the expression of later effector genes such as calreticulin and BiP, as well as the proteins necessary for the construction of the new synaptic arbors associated with long-term sensitization. Although the initiating response is transient, it triggers a cascade of changes in regulatory and effector gene expression—changes that move the cells from a baseline state, to a growth state, to a sensitized but new baseline state. The time course of synaptic enhancement is determined by a coherent contribution of all the mechanisms of plasticity operating in the cell, from early events (such as closure of the S-K$^+$ channel) to very late events (such as the changes in structural connectivity that may underlie the longest phase of memory retention). In this way, multiple mechanisms with different time courses underlie a graded enhancement of the connectivity between cells lasting from periods of seconds to weeks.

expression of late effector genes, which may underlie the morphological and anatomical changes coincident with the maintenance phase of long-term memory. Through the induction of transient changes in the activity of gene regulatory proteins, a cascade of both transient and persistent changes in gene expression is generated. Through their effects at the cellular and behavioral levels, these different molecular mechanisms with their multiple time courses contribute in concert to the generation of a cellular program of neuronal short- and long-term plasticity.

ACKNOWLEDGMENTS

We thank K. Hilten and S. Mack for preparing the figures, and H. Ayers and A. Krawetz for typing the manuscript. This work was supported in part by a Natural Sciences and Engineering Research Council of Canada postgraduate scholarship to Timothy E. Kennedy, and by the Howard Hughes Medical Institute.

REFERENCES

Agranoff, B. W. (1972). *The chemistry of mood motivation and memory*. New York: Plenum Press.

Angeletti, P. U., Gardini-Attardi, D., Tosehi, G., Salvi, M. L., & Levi-Montalcini, R. (1965). Metabolic aspects of the effect of nerve growth factor on sympathetic and sensory ganglia: Protein and ribonucleic acid synthesis. *Biochimica et Biophysica Acta, 95,* 111–120.

Bailey, C. H., & Chen, M. (1983). Morphological basis of long-term habituation and sensitization in *Aplysia*. *Science, 220,* 91–93.

Bailey, C. H., & Chen, M. (1988a). Long-term memory in *Aplysia* modulates the total number of varicosities of single identified sensory neurons. *Proceedings of the National Academy of Sciences USA, 85,* 2373–2377.

Bailey, C. H., & Chen, M. (1988b). Long-term sensitization in *Aplysia* increases the number of presynaptic contacts onto the identified gill motor neuron L7. *Proceedings of the National Academy of Sciences USA, 85,* 9356–9359.

Bailey, C. H., & Chen, M. (1989). Time course of structural changes at identified sensory neuron synapses during long-term sensitization in *Aplysia*. *Journal of Neuroscience, 9,* 1774–1780.

Bailey, C. H., Chen, M., Keller, F., & Kandel, E. R. (1992). Serotonin-mediated endocytosis of apCAM: An early step of learning-related synaptic growth in *Aplysia*. *Science, 256,* 645–649.

Barondes, S. H. (1975). Protein synthesis dependent and protein synthesis independent memory storage processes. In D. Deutsch & J. A. Deutsch (Eds.), *Short-term memory* (pp. 379–390). New York: Academic Press.

Barzilai, A., Kennedy, T. E., Sweatt, J. D., & Kandel, E. R. (1989). 5-HT modulates protein synthesis and the expression of specific proteins during long-term facilitation in *Aplysia* sensory neurons. *Neuron, 2,* 1577–1586.

Bergold, P. J., Sweatt, J. D., Kandel, E. R., & Schwartz, J. H. (1990). Protein synthesis during acquisition of long-term facilitation is needed for the persistent loss of regulatory subunits of the *Aplysia* cAMP-dependent protein kinase. *Proceedings of the National Academy of Sciences USA, 87,* 3788–3791.

Bernier, L., Castellucci, V. F., Kandel, E. R., & Schwartz, J. H. (1982). Facilitatory transmitter causes a selective and prolonged increase in adenosine 3′:5′-monophosphate in sensory neurons mediating the gill and siphon withdrawal reflex in *Aplysia*. *Journal of Neuroscience, 2,* 1682–1691.

Black, I. B., Alder, J. E., Dreyfus, C. F., Friedman, W. F., Lagamma, E. F., & Roach, A. H. (1987). Biochemistry of information storage in the nervous system. *Science, 236,* 1263–1268.

Brodsky, F. M., Hill, B. L., Acton, S. L., Nathke, I., Wong, D. H., Ponnambalam, S., & Parham, P. (1991). Clathrin light chains: Arrays of protein motifs that regulate coated-vesicle dynamics. *Trends in Biochemical Sciences, 16,* 208–213.

Brostrom, M. A., Cades, C., Prostko, C. R., Gmitter-Yellen, D., & Brostrom, C. O. (1990). Accommodation of protein synthesis to chronic deprivation of intracellular sequestered calcium, a putative role for GRP78. *Journal of Biological Chemistry, 265,* 20539–20546.

Brostrom, M. A., Chin, K.-V., Cade, C., Gmitter, D., & Brostrom, C. O. (1987). Stimulation of protein synthesis in pituitary cells by phorbol esters and cyclic AMP. *Journal of Biological Chemistry, 262,* 16515–16523.

Byrne, J., Castellucci, V., & Kandel, E. R. (1974). Receptive fields and response properties of mechanoreceptor neurons innervating skin and mantle shelf of *Aplysia. Journal of Neurophysiology, 37,* 1041–1064.

Byrne, J. H., Castellucci, V. F., & Kandel, E. R. (1978). Contribution of individual mechanoreceptor sensory neurons to defensive gill-withdrawal reflex in *Aplysia. Journal of Neurophysiology, 41,* 418–431.

Castellucci, V. F., Blumenfeld, H., Goelet, P., & Kandel, E. R. (1989). Inhibitor of protein synthesis blocks long-term behavioral sensitization in the isolated gill-withdrawal reflex of *Aplysia. Journal of Neurobiology, 20,* 1–9.

Castellucci, V. F., Kandel, E. R., Schwartz, J. H., Wilson, F. D., Nairn, A. C., & Greengard, P. (1980). Intracellular injection of the catalytic subunit of cyclic AMP-dependent protein kinase simulates facilitation of transmitter release underlying behavioral sensitization in *Aplysia. Proceedings of the National Academy of Sciences USA, 77,* 7492–7496.

Castellucci, V. F., Kennedy, T. E., Kandel, E. R., & Goelet, P. (1988). A quantitative analysis of 2-D gels identifies proteins in which labeling is increased following long-term sensitization in *Aplysia. Neuron, 1,* 321–328.

Castellucci, V. F., Nairn, A., Greengard, P., Schwartz, J. H., & Kandel, E. R. (1982). Inhibitor of adenosine 3′:5′-monophosphate-dependent protein kinase blocks presynaptic facilitation in *Aplysia. Journal of Neuroscience, 2,* 1673–1681.

Castellucci, V. F., Pinsker, H., Kupfermann, I., & Kandel, E. R. (1970). Neuronal mechanisms of habituation and dishabituation of the gill-withdrawal reflex in *Aplysia. Science, 167,* 1745–1748.

Chalazonitis, A., & Zigmond, R. E. (1980). Effects of synaptic and antidromic stimulation of tyrosine hydroxylase activity in the rat superior cervical ganglion. *Journal of Neurophysiology* (London), *300,* 525–538.

Comb, M., Birnberg, N. C., Seasholtz, A, Herbert, E., & Goodman, H. M. (1986). A cyclic AMP and phorbol-ester inducible DNA element. *Nature, 323,* 353–356.

Craik, F. I. M., & Lockhart, R. S. (1972). Levels of processing: A framework for memory research. *Journal of Verbal Learning and Verbal Behavior, 11,* 671–684.

Dale, N., Kandel, E. R., & Schacher, S. (1987). Serotonin produces long-term changes in the excitability of *Aplysia* sensory neurons in culture that depend on new protein synthesis. *Journal of Neuroscience, 7,* 2232–2238.

Dale, N., Schacher, S., & Kandel, E. R. (1988). Long-term facilitation in *Aplysia* involves increases in transmitter release. *Science, 239,* 282–285.

Dash, P. K., Hochner, B., & Kandel, E. R. (1990). Injection of the cAMP-responsive element into the nucleus of *Aplysia* sensory neurons blocks long-term facilitation. *Nature, 345,* 718–721.

Davis, H. P., & Squire, L. R. (1984). Protein synthesis and memory: A review. *Psychological Bulletin, 96,* 518–559.

Ebbinghaus, H. (1963) *Memory: A contribution to experimental psychology.* New York: Dover. (Original work published 1885)

Eskin, A., Garcia, K. S., & Byrne, J. H. (1989). Information storage in the nervous system of *Aplysia:* Specific proteins affected by serotonin and cAMP. *Proceedings of the National Academy of Sciences USA, 86,* 2458–2462.

Flexner, J. B., Flexner, L. B., & Stellar, E. (1983). Memory in mice as affected by intracerebral puromycin. *Science, 141,* 57–59.

Fliegel, L., Burns, K., MacLennan, D. H., Reithmeier, R. A. F., & Michalak, M. (1989). Molecular cloning of the high affinity calcium-binding protein (calreticulin) of skeletal muscle sarcoplasmic reticulum. *Journal of Biological Chemistry, 264,* 21522–21528.

Frost, W. N., Castellucci, V. G., Hawkins, R. D., & Kandel, E. R. (1985). Monosynaptic connections from the sensory neurons of the gill- and siphon-withdrawal reflex in *Aplysia* participate in the storage of long-term memory for sensitization. *Proceedings of the National Academy of Sciences USA, 82,* 8266–8269.

Garrels, J. I., & Schubert, D. (1979). Modulation of protein synthesis by nerve growth factor. *Journal of Biological Chemistry, 254,* 7978–7985.

Glanzman, D. L., Kandel, E. R., & Schacher, S. (1990). Target-dependent structural changes accompanying long-term synaptic facilitation in *Aplysia* neurons. *Science, 249,* 799–802.

Glanzman, D. L., Mackey, S. L., Hawkins, R. D., Dyke, A., Lloyd, P. E., & Kandel, E. R. (1989). Depletion of serotonin in the nervous system of *Aplysia* reduces the behavioral enhancement of gill withdrawal as well as the heterosynaptic facilitation produced by tail shock. *Journal of Neuroscience, 9,* 4200–4213.

Goelet, P., Castellucci, V. F., Schacher, S., & Kandel, E. R. (1986). The long and short of long-term memory: A molecular framework. *Nature, 322,* 419–422.

Greenberg, S. M., Castellucci, V. F., Bayley, H., & Schwartz, J. H. (1987). A molecular mechanism for long-term sensitization in *Aplysia*. *Nature, 329*, 62–65.

Greengard, P. (1978). *Cyclic nucleotides, phosphorylated proteins and neuronal function*. New York: Raven Press.

Hawkins, R. D., Castellucci, V. F., & Kandel, E. R. (1981). Interneurons involved in mediation and modulation of gill-withdrawal reflex in *Aplysia*: II. Identified neurons produce heterosynaptic facilitation contributing to behavioral sensitization. *Journal of Neurophysiology, 45*, 315–326.

Hawkins, R. D., Clark, G. A., & Kandel, E. R. (1987). Cell biological studies of learning in simple vertebrates and invertebrate systems. In F. Plum (Ed.), *Handbook of physiology: Section 1. The nervous system. Vol. 5. Higher functions of the brain* (Part 1, pp. 25–83). Bethesda, MD: American Physiological Society.

Hawkins, R. D., & Schacher, S. (1989). Identified facilitator neurons L29 and L28 are excited by cutaneous stimuli used in dishabituation, sensitization, and classical conditioning of *Aplysia*. *Journal of Neuroscience, 9*, 4236–4245.

Haydon, P. G., McGobb, D. P., & Kater, S. B. (1984). Serotonin selectively inhibits growth cone motility and synaptogenesis of specific identified neurons. *Science, 226*, 561–564.

Hochner, B., Klein, M., Schacher, S., & Kandel, E. R. (1986). Action-potential duration and the modulation of transmitter release from the sensory neurons of *Aplysia* in presynaptic facilitation and behavioral sensitization. *Proceedings of the National Academy of Sciences USA, 83*, 8410–8414.

Hu, Y., Bailey, C. H., Chen, M., Kandel, E. R., & Barzilai, A. (1992). *Long-term facilitation stimulates expression of clathrin light chain and functions of coated pits in* Aplysia *sensory neurons*. Manuscript in preparation.

Jones, R. H., & Jones, N. C. (1989). Mammalian cAMP-responsive element can activate transcription in yeast and binds a yeast factor(s) that resembles the mammalian transcription factor ATF. *Proceedings of the National Academy of Sciences USA, 86*, 2176–2180.

Keller, F., & Schacher, S. (1990). Neuron-specific membrane glycoproteins promoting neurite fasciculation in *Aplysia californica*. *Journal of Cell Biology, 111*, 2637–2650.

Kennedy, T. E., Gawinowicz, M. A., Barzilai, A., Kandel, E. R., & Sweatt, J. D. (1988). Sequencing of proteins from two-dimensional gels using in situ digestion and transfer of peptides to polyvinylidene difluoride membranes: Application to proteins associated with sensitization in *Aplysia*. *Proceedings of the National Academy of Sciences USA, 85*, 7008–7012.

Kennedy, T. E., Kuhl, D., Barzilai, A., Kandel, E. R., & Sweatt, J. D. (1989). Characterization of changes in late protein and mRNA expression during the maintenance phase of long-term sensitization. *Society for Neuroscience Abstracts, 15*, 1117.

Kennedy, T. E., Kuhl, D., Barzilai, A., Sweatt, J. D., & Kandel, E. R. (1992). *Long-term sensitization training in* Aplysia *leads to an increase in calreticulin, a major presynaptic calcium binding protein*. Manuscript in preparation.

Kennedy, T. E., Wager-Smith, K., Barzilai, A., Kandel, E. R., & Sweatt, J. D. (1988). Sequencing proteins from acrylamide gels. *Nature, 336*, 499–500.

Klein, M., & Kandel, E. R. (1980). Mechanism of calcium current modulation underlying presynaptic facilitation and behavioral sensitization in *Aplysia*. *Proceedings of the National Academy of Sciences USA, 77*, 6912–6916.

Krause, K.-H., Simmerman, H. K. B., Jones, L. R., & Campbell, K. P. (1990). Sequence similarity of calreticulin with a Ca^{2+} binding protein that co-purifies with an $Ins(1,4,5)P_3$-sensitive Ca^{2+} store in HL-60 cells. *Biochemical Journal, 270*, 545–548.

Kuhl, D., Kennedy, T. E., Barzilai, A., & Kandel, E. R. (1992). *Long-term sensitization training in* Aplysia *leads to an increase in the expression of BiP, the major protein chaperon of the endoplasmic reticulum*. Manuscript in preparation.

Kuo, J. F., & Greengard, P. (1969). Cyclic nucleotide-dependent protein kinases: IV. Widespread occurrence of adenosine 3',5'-monophosphate-dependent protein kinase in various tissues and phyla of the animal kingdom. *Proceedings of the National Academy of Sciences USA, 64*, 1349–1355.

Lau, L. F., & Nathans, D. (1985). Identification of a set of genes expressed during Go/Gi transition of cultured mouse cells. *European Molecular Biology Organization Journal, 4*, 3145–3151.

Mackey, S. L., Kandel, E. R., & Hawkins, R. D. (1989). Identified serotonergic neurons LCB1 and RCB1 in the cerebral ganglia of *Aplysia* produce presynaptic facilitation of siphon sensory neurons. *Journal of Neuroscience, 9*, 4227–4235.

Mattson, M. P. (1988). Neurotransmitters in the regulation of neuronal cytoarchitecture. *Brain Research Reviews, 13*, 179–212.

Mattson, M. P., Lee, R. E., Adams, M. E., Guthrie, P. B., & Kater, S. B. (1988). Interaction between enthorinal axons and target hippocampal neurons: A role for glutamate in the development of hippocampal circuitry. *Neuron, 1*, 865–876.

Mayford, M., Barzilai, A., Keller, F., Schacher, S., & Kandel, E. R. (1992). Modulation of an NCAM-related adhesion molecule with long-term synaptic plasticity in *Aplysia*. *Science*, *256*, 638-644.

Mignery, G. A., Sudhof, T. C., Takei, K., & DeCamilli, P. (1989). Putative receptor for inositol, 1,4,5-trisphosphate similar to ryanodine receptor. *Nature*, *342*, 192-195.

Montarolo, P. G., Goelet, P., Castellucci, V. F., Morgan, J., Kandel, E. R., & Schacher, S. (1986). A critical period for macromolecular synthesis in long-term heterosynaptic facilitation in *Aplysia*. *Science*, *234*, 1249-1254.

Montminy, M. R., & Biezikjian, L. M. (1987). Binding of a nuclear protein to the cyclic-AMP response element of the somatostatin gene. *Nature*, *328*, 175-178.

Montminy, M. R., Sevarino, K. A., Wagner, J. A., Mandel, G., & Goodman, R. H. (1986). Identification of a cyclic-AMP-responsive element within the rat somatostatin gene. *Proceedings of the National Academy of Sciences USA*, *83*, 6682-6686.

Nevins, J. R. (1985). Control of cellular and viral transcription during adenovirus infection. *CRC Critcal Reviews in Biochemistry*, *12*, 307-322.

Nirenberg, M., Wilson, S., Higashida, H., Rotter, A., Kruger, K., Busis, N., Ray, R., Kenimer, K., Adler, M., & Fukui, H. (1983). Synapse formation by neuroblastoma cells. *Cold Spring Harbor Symposium on Quantitative Biology*, *48*, 707-715.

Ostwald, T. J., & MacLennan, D. H. (1974). Isolation of a high affinity calcium-binding protein from sarcoplasmic reticulum. *Journal of Biological Chemistry*, *249*, 974-979.

Pelham, H. (1988). Heat shock proteins: Coming in from the cold. *Nature*, *332*, 776-777.

Peng, Y.-W., Sharp, A. H., Synder, S. H., & Yau, K.-W. (1991). Localization of the inositol 1,4,5-trisphosphate receptor in synaptic terminals in the vertebrate retina. *Neuron*, *6*, 525-531.

Pinsker, H. M., Hening, W. A., Carew, T. J., & Kandel, E. R. (1973). Long-term sensitization of a defensive withdrawal reflex in *Aplysia*. *Science*, *182*, 1039-1042.

Rall, T. W. (1979). General regulatory role of cyclic nucleotides in hormone and neurohormone action. In F. O. Schmitt & F. G. Worden (Eds.), *The neurosciences: Fourth study program* (pp. 858-872). Cambridge, MA: MIT Press.

Rayport, S. G., & Schacher, S. (1986). Synaptic plasticity in vitro: Cell culture of identified *Aplysia* neurons mediating short-term habituation and sensitization. *Journal of Neuroscience*, *6*, 759-763.

Ross, C. A., Meldolesi, J., Milner, T. A., Saitoh, T., Supattapone, S., & Snyder, A. (1989). Inositol 1,4,5,-trisphosphate receptor localized to endoplasmic reticulum in cerebellar Purkinje neurons. *Nature*, *339*, 468-470.

Schacher, S., Castellucci, V. F., & Kandel, E. R. (1988). Cyclic AMP evokes long-term facilitation in *Aplysia* sensory neurons that requires new protein synthesis. *Science*, *240*, 1667-1669.

Schneider, C., King, R. M., & Philipson, L. (1988). Genes specifically expressed at growth arrest of mammalian cells. *Cell*, *54*, 787-793.

Scholz, K. P., & Byrne, J. H. (1987). Long-term sensitization in *Aplysia*: Biophysical correlates in tail sensory neurons. *Science*, *235*, 685-687.

Schwartz, J. H., Castellucci, V. F., & Kandel, E. R. (1971). Functions of identified neurons and synapses in abdominal ganglion of *Aplysia* in absence of protein synthesis. *Journal of Neurophysiology*, *34*, 939-953.

Smith, M. J., & Koch, G. L. E. (1989). Multiple zones in the sequence of calreticulin (CRP55, calregulin, HACBP), a major calcium binding ER/SR protein. *European Molecular Biology Organization Journal*, *8*, 3581-3586.

Squire, L. R., & Zola-Morgan, S. (1988). Memory: Brain systems and behavior. *Trends in Neurosciences*, *11*, 170-175.

Sweatt, J. D., & Kandel, E. R. (1989). Persistent and transcriptionally-dependent increase in protein phosphorylation upon long-term facilitation of *Aplysia* sensory neurons. *Nature*, *339*, 51-54.

Treves, S., De Mattei, M., Lanfredi, M., Villa, A., Green, M., MacLennan, D. H., Meldolesi, J., & Pozzan, T. (1990). Calreticulin is a candidate for a calsequestrin-like function in Ca^{2+}-storage compartments (calciosomes) of liver and brain. *Biochemical Journal*, *271*, 473-480.

Walsh, D. A., Perlans, J. P, & Kochs, E. G. (1968). An adenosine 3'5'-monophosphate-dependent protein kinase from rabbit skeletal muscle. *Journal of Biological Chemistry*, *243*, 3763-3765.

Weiskrantz, L. (1970). A long-term view of short-term memory in psychology. In G. Horn & R.A. Hinde (Eds.), *Short-term changes in neural activity and behavior* (pp. 63-74). Cambridge, England: Cambridge University Press.

Wickelgren, W. A. (1973). The long and the short of memory. *Psychological Bulletin*, *80*, 425-438.

Yamamoto, K. K., Gonzalez, G. A., Bigg, W. H., & Montminy, M. R. (1988). Phosphorylation-induced binding and transcriptional efficacy of nuclear factor CREB. *Nature*, *334*, 494-498.

49

Analysis of Short- and Long-Term Enhancement Produced by One-Trial Conditioning in *Hermissenda*: Implications for Mechanisms of Short- and Long-Term Memory

TERRY J. CROW

Introduction

The nudibranch mollusk *Hermissenda crassicornis* is one invertebrate preparation that has contributed to the study of associative learning at the behavioral, cellular, and molecular levels of analysis. *Hermissenda* normally exhibits a positive phototaxis when stimulated with light. The phototactic response is expressed in behavior by various measures of visually influenced locomotion that have been examined in detail (Crow, 1983, 1985; Crow & Alkon, 1978; Crow & Offenbach, 1983; Farley, 1987; Harrigan & Alkon, 1985). The conditioning procedure used to modify phototactic behavior consists of light (the conditioned stimulus, or CS) paired with high-speed rotation (the unconditioned stimulus, or US). Stimulation of the animal's visual and vestibular systems with paired light and rotation produces a long-term behavioral suppression of the normal positive phototactic response evoked by light, lasting from days (Crow & Alkon, 1978) to several weeks (Harrigan & Alkon, 1985). In addition to the effects upon phototactic behavior, conditioning also produces a pairing-specific shortening of the foot, first described by Lederhendler, Gart, and Alkon (1986). Normally, dark-adapted animals respond to the CS by lengthening the foot, while the US elicits a shortening of the foot. Following conditioning, the CS elicits a shortening of the foot. Behavioral studies have shown that the suppression of phototactic behavior produced by the conditioning procedure exhibits most of the features of classical conditioning as described for vertebrates (for recent reviews, see Crow, 1988, 1989). The change in phototactic behavior is dependent upon the temporal association of the two sensory stimuli. Animals that received the CS and US paired exhibited significant phototactic suppression, as compared to the groups that received the CS and US each programmed on independent random schedules, or the CS and US explicitly unpaired. Suppression of phototactic behavior is specific to the presentation of the CS. Conditioned animals show suppressed locomotor behavior in the presence of the CS; however, their locomotor behavior in the dark is not significantly changed (Crow & Offenbach, 1983). Although nonassociative factors may contribute to the suppression of phototactic behavior in the initial phase of conditioning, such factors appear to follow a different time course. A recent study of the nonassociative contribution to conditioned modification of phototaxis showed that nonassociative changes in phototactic behavior decrease within 1 hour following the conclusion of training and do not significantly contribute to long-term changes in phototactic behavior (Crow, 1983).

Cellular neurophysiological studies have identified one site for intrinsic changes produced by classical conditioning: the primary sensory neurons (photoreceptors) of the CS pathway. Current-clamp studies of isolated Type B photoreceptors showed that conditioning produced conductance changes and alterations in excitability, expressed by changes in the CS evoked generator potential (Crow & Alkon, 1980). Voltage-clamp studies of isolated Type B photoreceptors showed that two K^+ currents were reduced in conditioned animals (Alkon, Lederhendler, & Shoukimas, 1982; Alkon et al., 1985). One K^+ current (I_A) has similar properties to the A current described previously in mollusks. The second K^+ current ($I_{K,Ca}$) is primarily activated by intracellular Ca^{2+} (Alkon, Shoukimas, & Heldman, 1982; Alkon et al., 1985; Alkon, 1984). Recent voltage-clamp studies have also characterized the delayed rectifier ($I_{K(v)}$) and an inward rectifier (I_{ir}) not previously described in Type B photoreceptors (Acosta-Urquidi & Crow, 1990). Both K^+ currents are modulated by serotonin (5-HT), and thus could contribute to plasticity produced by one-trial conditioning (see section in *in vivo* conditioning). In addition to the biophysical results, evidence has been presented from changes in the phosphorylation of proteins that may be associated with reductions of K^+ currents in conditioned animals (Neary, Crow, & Alkon, 1981). Several second-messenger systems and protein kinases have been implicated in mediating the reductions in K^+ currents produced by conditioning (Acosta-Urquidi, Alkon, & Neary, 1984; Alkon, Acosta-Urguidi, Olds, Kuzma, & Neary, 1983; Sakakibara et al., 1986). However, the Ca-phospholipid-dependent kinase, protein kinase C (PKC), has received the most experimental attention (Alkon et al., 1986; Crow, Forrester, Williams, Waxham, & Neary, 1991; Farley & Auerbach, 1986; Neary, Naito, & Alkon, 1985; Neary, Naito, DeWeer, & Alkon, 1986).

The cellular and molecular analysis of correlates of conditioning detected in Type B photoreceptors has produced several possible mechanisms for long-term changes in the nervous system. Mechanisms for long-term information storage in the nervous system have been studied at the conclusion of multiple-trial conditioning, where changes in phototactic behavior are well established. However, little is known concerning the initial cellular events that are important for the induction of both short- and long-term memory of the associative experience and cellular mechanisms associated with the transition between short- and long-term memory. As a first step in this analysis, a one-trial conditioning procedure was developed to provide for the opportunity to examine the induction of cellular changes produced by conditioning in Type B photoreceptors, and to study how such cellular events develop over time.

One-Trial *In Vivo* Conditioning

Since all of the second-messenger pathways that have been implicated in conditioning of *Hermissenda* can be activated by transmitters, an obvious question is whether there is evidence that a transmitter or neuromodulator is involved in producing long-lasting changes in the photoreceptors of conditioned *Hermissenda*. Recent studies have suggested a possible role for a modulatory transmitter, since the action of a number of biogenic amines can mimic some of the correlates observed in Type B photoreceptors following conditioning (Crow & Bridge, 1985; Farley & Auerbach, 1986; Sakakibara et al., 1987). Heldman and Alkon (1978) had previously reported that both dopamine and 5-HT are synthesized in the nervous system of *Hermissenda*. Histofluorescence studies identified neurons containing catecholamines in the optic ganglion (Heldman, Grossman, Jerussi, & Alkon, 1979) and in the cerebropleural and pedal ganglia (Sakakibara et al., 1987). An immunohistochemical study (Land & Crow, 1985) revealed 5-HT-immunoreactive fibers and varicosities on the optic nerve and in the synaptic region of the neuropil near the synaptic terminals of the photoreceptors. This finding provides a potential 5-HT pathway for direct interaction with photoreceptors within the eye.

If a modulatory transmitter is released by stimulation of the US pathway and is involved in conditioned modification of phototactic behavior, then substituting the direct application of the modulatory transmitter for stimulation of the US pathway should produce similar changes in behavior. To test this hypothesis, a one-trial *in vivo* conditioning procedure was developed. Light (the CS) was paired with direct application of several modulatory transmitters (dopamine, octopamine, 5-HT) to the exposed nervous system of otherwise intact *Hermissenda* (Crow & Forrester, 1986; see Figure 49.1). One 5-minute conditioning trial, consisting of the CS paired with 5-HT, produced significant suppression of phototactic behavior when the animals were tested 24 hours after the end of the training session. As shown in Figure 49.2A, the two other putative neuromodulators, dopamine and octopamine, did not produce significant suppression of phototactic behavior when paired with the CS. If the CS and 5-HT pairings are analogous to the conditioning procedure used to modify phototactic behavior, then the change in behavior should be dependent upon the temporal pairing of the CS and 5-HT. Pairing specificity was shown by comparing the group that received the CS paired with 5-HT to a group that received the CS and 5-HT unpaired, and a group that only received 5-HT. The group that received the CS paired with 5-HT showed phototactic suppression as compared to the two control groups when tested the next day (Figure 49.2B). As an additional control, one control group that had initially received the unpaired CS and 5-HT was tested again after receiving the application of the CS paired with 5-HT. Following the paired procedure, the animals showed behavioral suppression when tested 24 hours later (see Figure 49.2C).

One-Trial *In Vivo* Conditioning Produces Short- and Long-Term Enhancement in Identified Neurons

In addition to the change in phototactic behavior produced by one-trial *in vivo* conditioning, cellular correlates were also detected in identified Type B photorecep-

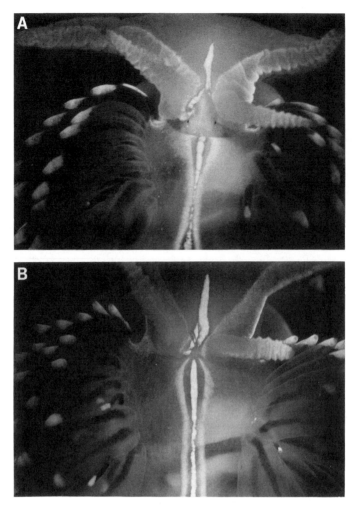

FIGURE 49.1. Photograph of the experimental preparation used to study short- and long-term enhancement following one-trial *in vivo* conditioning. (**A**) An example of a *Hermissenda* immediately following completion of a dorsal–lateral incision to expose the circumesophageal nervous system. The *in vivo* conditioning procedure consists of pairing light with the direct application of 5-HT to the exposed nervous system of otherwise intact animals. (**B**) A photograph of a preparation as shown in **A** taken 24 hours after exposure of the nervous system, showing that the wound margins have closed and the animal appears normal. Intracellular recordings are collected from identified photoreceptors within the eyes of preparations that have recovered as indicated here. From "Light Paired with Serotonin *In Vivo* Produces Both Short- and Long-Term Enhancement of Generator Potentials of Identified B-Photoreceptors in *Hermissenda*" (p. 610) by T. Crow and J. Forrester, 1991, *Journal of Neuroscience, 11,* 608–617. Copyright 1991 by the Society for Neuroscience. Reprinted by permission.

tors. Animals were trained with the one-trial *in vivo* conditioning procedure (see above), and neural correlates were examined in isolated Type B photoreceptors at 1 hour and 24 hours after training (Crow & Forrester, 1991). Pairing light (the CS) with 5-HT produced both a short-term enhancement and a long-term enhancement of the generator potentials recorded from identified Type B photoreceptors. The *in vivo* conditioning procedure resulted in an enhanced generator potential when Type B photoreceptors were examined 1 hour after training. However, photoreceptors from

A

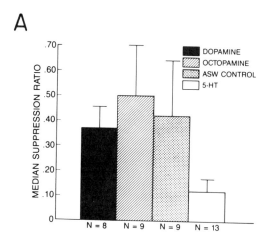

B

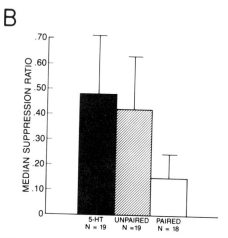

C

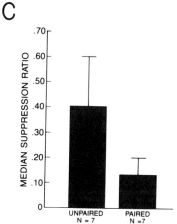

FIGURE 49.2. The one-trial *in vivo* conditioning procedure consists of substitution of normal activation of the US pathway with the direct application of neuromodulators to the exposed central nervous system. (**A**) Different groups of *Hermissenda* received light (the CS) paired with several putative neurotransmitters/neuromodulators applied directly to the exposed nervous system. Animals were tested before training and 24 hours after one-trial conditioning to assess suppression of phototactic behavior. The ordinate represents the measure of learning (median suppression ratios ± semi-interquartile range). Only the group that received light (the CS) paired with 5-HT exhibited significant suppression of phototactic behavior. ASW, artificial seawater. (**B**) Pairing-specific effect of light and 5-HT. Light paired with 5-HT results in suppression of phototactic behavior when tested 24 hours after one-trial conditioning. Unpaired light and 5-HT, and 5-HT applied in the dark, do not produce statistically significant suppression of phototactic behavior. (**C**) Within-group comparison of the effects on behavior of unpaired light and 5-HT and paired light and 5-HT. The unpaired group represents the behavior of a control group that initially received unpaired light and 5-HT. When the group that had previously received the unpaired control procedure was trained with light paired with 5-HT, a significant suppression of phototactic behavior was observed. Adapted from "Light Paired with Serotonin Mimics the Effects of Conditioning on Phototactic Behavior in *Hermissenda*" (pp. 7976, 7977) by T. Crow and J. Forrester, 1986, *Proceedings of the National Academy of Sciences USA, 83*, 7975–7978.

both the paired and unpaired control groups showed an enhanced generator potential, indicating that the short-term enhancement was not specific to pairing. In contrast to the non-pairing-specific nature of short-term enhancement, long-term enhancement was found to be pairing-specific. Recordings from lateral Type B photoreceptors exhibited enhanced generator potentials only for the group that received the CS paired with 5-HT (see Figure 49.3A).

Long-Term Enhancement Depends upon Protein Synthesis

The finding that one-trial *in vivo* conditioning produces both suppression of phototaxis and short- and long-term enhancement in identified Type B photoreceptors has pro-

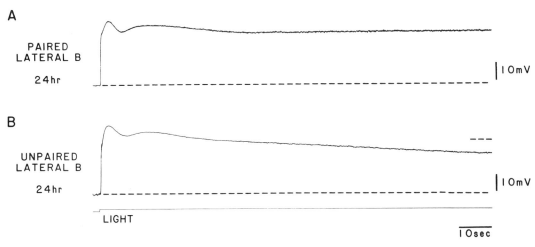

FIGURE 49.3. Long-term enhancement of light-evoked generator potentials recorded from surgically isolated lateral Type B photoreceptors 24 hours following one-trial *in vivo* conditioning. (**A**) Generator potential from an isolated lateral Type B photoreceptor evoked by light 24 hours following the presentation of light paired with 5-HT. (**B**) Generator potential recorded from a lateral Type B photoreceptor 24 hours following unpaired light and 5-HT. The generator potential in **A** exhibits an enhanced plateau as compared to the example shown in **B**. The peak of the generator potential recorded from lateral Type B photoreceptors does not show long-term enhancement. The short dashed line in **B** represents the amplitude of the generator potential plateau shown in **A**. From "Light Paired with Serotonin *In Vivo* Produces Both Short- and Long-Term Enhancement of Generator Potentials of Identified B-Photoreceptors in *Hermissenda*" (p. 614) by T. Crow and J. Forrester, 1991, *Journal of Neuroscience, 11*, 608–617. Copyright 1991 by the Society for Neuroscience. Reprinted by permission.

vided a convenient tool to study the cellular mechanisms of time-dependent processes that may be related to both short- and long-term memory. The hypothesized mechanisms for associative interactions between the activation of kinases and the consequences of the presentation of the CS (as summarized in Figure 49.6, below) may account for the short-term reduction of K^+ currents observed in conditioned animals. However, it is attractive to propose a role for protein synthesis in the induction of long-term enhancement produced by conditioning. Historically, it has been proposed that short- and long-term memory represent different components of memory with distinct qualitative and quantitative features. Previous studies of memory in vertebrates suggested that long-term memory requires the synthesis of new protein, whereas short-term memory does not (for a review, see Davis & Squire, 1984).

In *Hermissenda, in vivo* conditioning in the presence of the protein synthesis inhibitor anisomycin did not block short-term enhancement (Crow & Forrester, 1990). In contrast to the lack of an effect upon short-term enhancement, long-term enhancement of the generator potential was blocked if the one-trial *in vivo* conditioning procedure was applied in the presence of anisomycin, as shown in Figure 49.4A2. Moreover, inhibition of protein synthesis was only effective when applied during the presentation of the conditioning trial. For example, when anisomycin was applied 1 hour after the conditioning trial, long-term enhancement was not blocked (Figure 49.4A1). A derivative of anisomycin, deacetylanisomycin, which is inactive in inhibiting protein synthesis, also failed to block long-term enhancement produced by *in vivo*

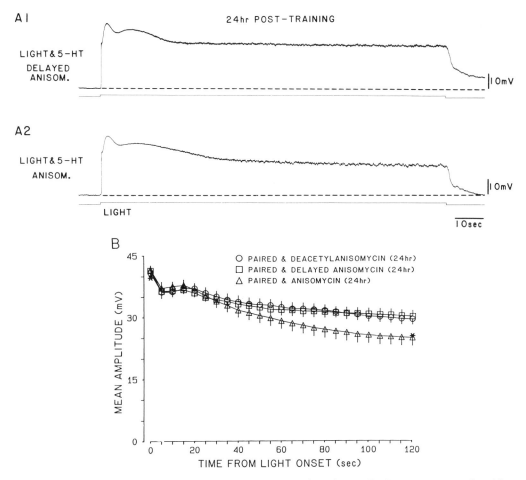

FIGURE 49.4. Anisomycin blocks long-term enhancement in lateral Type B photoreceptors produced by one-trial *in vivo* conditioning. (**A1**) Intracellular recording of a generator potential from an isolated lateral Type B photoreceptor evoked by a 2-minute light step 24 hours after the termination of one-trial *in vivo* conditioning. The application of 1 μM anisomycin was delayed 1 hour after the conditioning trial. (**A2**) Generator potential evoked by the light step recorded from an isolated lateral Type B photoreceptor 24 hours after the termination of one-trial *in vivo* conditioning. The conditioning trial was presented in the presence of 1 μM anisomycin. The dashed lines in **A1** and **A2** represent the dark-adapted resting membrane potential. Delaying the application of anisomycin resulted in long-term enhancement of the generator potential, whereas pretreatment with anisomycin blocked long-term enhancement. (**B**) Group data showing the mean amplitude of the generator potential $\pm$ *SEM* (in millivolts) evoked by a 2-minute light step recorded 24 hours after the conditioning trial for the groups that received light paired with 5-HT in the presence of deacetylanisomycin ($n = 11$), light paired with 5-HT with anisomycin delayed 1 hour after one-trial conditioning ($n = 12$), or light paired with 5-HT in the presence of anisomycin ($n = 15$). The mean amplitudes of the transient peak and plateau phase of the generator potential for an unpaired control group ($n = 5$) in the presence of anisomycin are denoted by the asterisks at time 0 and 120 seconds from light onset. The plateau phase of the generator potential was significantly enhanced for both the paired-with-deacetyla-nisomycin and paired-with-delayed-anisomycin groups as compared to the group that received the light paired with 5-HT or the unpaired light and 5-HT in the presence of anisomycin ($p < .01$). The amplitudes of the transient peak and plateau phase of the generator potential were not significantly different for the paired and unpaired groups in the presence of anisomycin. Pretreatment with anisomycin blocked long-term enhancement (plateau phase of the generator potential) recorded from lateral Type B photoreceptors. From "Inhibition of Protein Synthesis Blocks Long-Term Enhancement of Generator Potentials Produced by One-Trial *In Vivo* Conditioning in *Hermissenda*" (p. 4493) by T. Crow and J. Forrester, 1990, *Proceedings of the National Academy of Sciences USA, 87*, 4490–4494.

conditioning (Figure 49.4B). In addition, anisomycin by itself did not cause any change in the amplitude of generator potentials. These findings indicate that ongoing protein synthesis is necessary for the induction and maintenance of long-term enhancement, but it is also likely that this process requires transcription. Thus, long-term enhancement may depend upon an independent and parallel signaling system, or, alternatively, both short- and long-term enhancement may occur in series and depend upon the same steps for induction.

Protein Kinase C Is Important for the Induction of Enhancement, but Not Its Expression or Maintenance

Since PKC has been implicated in conditioning of *Hermissenda*, my colleagues and I have examined its possible role in one-trial conditioning. As a first step, we substituted an activator of PKC—12-*O*-tetradecanoyl-phorbol-13-acetate (TPA), a phorbol ester—for 5-HT. Pairing the CS (light) with TPA produced both short- and long-term enhancement of generator potentials recorded from Type B photoreceptors (Crow & Forrester, 1988). In addition, pairing the CS with diacylglycerol analogues produced enhancement. Consistent with the results from the 5-HT research, the CS and TPA did not produce a short-term pairing-specific enhancement. However, the long-term enhancement was dependent upon pairing the CS with TPA. Moreover, an inactive phorbol, 4α-phorbol, did not produce either short- or long-term enhancement. These results show that pairing the CS with activation of PKC is sufficient to produce both short- and long-term enhancement.

We next used kinase inhibitors to further examine the role of PKC in enhancement. Applying the kinase inhibitors H-7 or sphingosine prior to the presentation of the CS and 5-HT was sufficient to block the induction of short-term enhancement (Crow & Forrester, 1988). The concentration of the two kinase inhibitors that was used did not produce changes in the generator potential of Type B photoreceptors recorded from normal controls. Although these results are consistent with the hypothesis that PKC is involved in induction of enhancement, the lack of specificity of the kinase inhibitors complicates the interpretation of the results. Sphingosine has been shown to affect Ca^{2+}/calmodulin-dependent kinases (Jefferson & Schulman, 1988), and H-7 inhibits cyclic AMP-dependent kinase (Hidaka, Inagaki, Kawamoto, & Sasaki, 1984). As an alternative to the use of kinase inhibitors, we examined the effect of down-regulation of PKC on the induction of short-term enhancement. Prolonged exposure of the nervous system to TPA results in a decrease in the activity of the enzyme PKC. Following down-regulation of PKC, the presentation of the CS and 5-HT did not produce enhancement (Figure 49.5 and 5C). Animals that received an equal exposure of 4α-phorbol exhibited normal enhancement to the CS and 5-HT (Figure 49.5B and 5C). These results indicate that activation of PKC is an important step in the induction of short-term enhancement produced by the CS and 5-HT (Crow et al., 1991).

Is persistent activation of a kinase essential for the maintenance or expression of enhancement? Previous studies of long-term potentiation have suggested that potentiation could be reversed by the application of kinase inhibitors (Malinow, Madison, & Tsien, 1988). Following the induction of enhancement, we applied either H-7 or

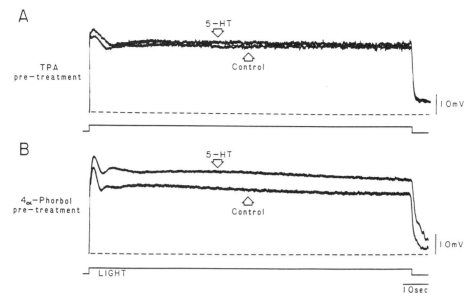

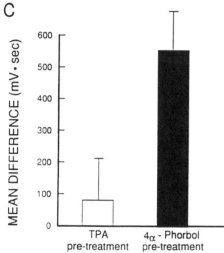

FIGURE 49.5. Down-regulation of PKC by TPA pretreatment blocks induction of short-term enhancement. Representative examples of light-evoked generator potentials recorded from surgically isolated type B photoreceptors after an 8-hour pretreatment in TPA (1 μM) or the inactive phorbol ester 4α-phorbol (1 μM). (**A**) TPA pretreatment: Superimposed generator potentials elicited by a 2-minute light step recorded before (control) and after the application of 5-HT (0.1 mM). (**B**) 4α-phorbol pretreatment: Superimposed generator potentials elicited by a 2-minute light step before (control) and after the application of 5-HT (0.1 mM). Down-regulation of PKC by the 8-hour TPA pretreatment blocked the induction of short-term enhancement. In contrast, pretreatment with 4α-phorbol did not block short-term enhancement produced by 5-HT. (**C**) Group data showing the mean difference in the computed area of light-evoked generator potentials for TPA pretreatment ($n = 18$) and 4α-phorbol pretreatment ($n = 12$). The area of each generator potential was approximated by digitizing the response and summing the amplitudes over successive time periods. Difference scores were generated for groups that received either TPA or 4α-phorbol pretreatment by subtracting the area computed for generator potentials elicited by light in control periods before 5-HT application from responses elicited after 5-HT application. Pretreatment with TPA blocked short-term enhancement produced by light and 5-HT. The increase in the area of the generator potentials after 5-HT application was significant for the 4α-phorbol pretreatment group ($p < .0025$), whereas the TPA pretreatment group's response was not significantly different from pre-5-HT-application control responses. The short-term enhancement produced by 5-HT was significantly larger for the 4α-phorbol control group as compared to the TPA pretreatment group ($p < .025$). From "Down-Regulation of Protein Kinase C Blocks 5-HT-Induced Enhancement in *Hermissenda* B-Photoreceptors" (p. 109) by T. Crow, J. Forrester, M. Williams, N. Waxham, and J. Neary, 1991, *Neuroscience Letters, 121,* 107–110. Copyright 1991 by Elsevier Science Publishers. Reprinted by permission.

sphingosine at concentrations that were sufficient to block induction (Forrester & Crow, 1989). Neither H-7 nor sphingosine reversed short-term enhancement produced by the CS and 5-HT. The same kinase inhibitors were used to determine whether long-term enhancement could be reversed. Consistent with the short-term enhancement findings, long-term enhancement was not reversed by the application of H-7 and sphingosine at concentrations that were sufficient to block the induction of short-term enhancement. These results indicate that activation of PKC is an important step in the induction of enhancement; however, the continued activity of the kinase is not required for the expression or maintenance of either short- or long-term enhancement.

Short-Term and Long-Term Enhancement May Be Parallel and Independent Processes

The cellular mechanisms responsible for the induction of long-term enhancement may be similar to the mechanism important for the induction of short-term enhancement. The biochemical steps involved in induction may be in series or sequential, such that long-term enhancement is derived from short-term enhancement. Alternatively, long-term enhancement may depend upon events that are independent and involve a parallel signaling system different from the system essential for the induction of short-term enhancement. Although little is known about whether short-term and long-term memory occur in series or in parallel, recent evidence from *Hermissenda* suggests that long-term enhancement may be independent of short-term enhancement. Using kinase inhibitors and down-regulation of PKC, we found that the conditions that were sufficient to block the induction of short-term enhancement did not block the induction of long-term enhancement detected 24 hours after one-trial *in vivo* conditioning (Forrester & Crow, 1988). Since long-term enhancement can be expressed without the induction of short-term enhancement, different biochemical pathways may be involved, including the possibility that different kinase systems may contribute to short- and long-term enhancement.

Summary and Conclusions

The development of one-trial conditioning in *Hermissenda* has provided a useful tool to study cellular processes related to short- and long-term memory. The evidence suggests that there are a number of similarities between cellular correlates detected following one-trial conditioning and multiple-trial conditioning procedures. One-trial conditioning produces changes in identified neurons that have been implicated as loci for long-term memory storage following multiple-trial classical conditioning (see Figure 49.6). In addition, one-trial conditioning results in a long-term suppression of normal phototactic behavior—a change in behavior that mimics changes produced by multiple-trial classical conditioning. Cellular studies of one-trial conditioning have provided evidence for both short- and long-term enhancement detected in identified neurons. Consistent with work in other nervous systems, long-term enhancement depends upon protein synthesis, while short-term enhancement does not. The activa-

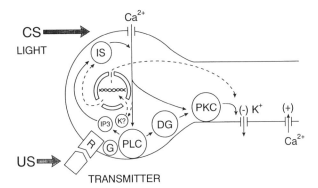

FIGURE 49.6. A cellular model for associative memory in Type B photoreceptors of *Hermissenda*. Short-term enhancement produced by one-trial conditioning involves activation and amplification of protein kinase C (PKC). Transmitter released by stimulation of the US pathway binds to a specific receptor (R). The receptor-activated signal is transmitted through a G protein to the enzyme phospholipase C (PLC). PLC splits PIP^2 (not shown) into inositol trisphosphate and diacylglycerol (DG). The DG, Ca^{2+} influx produced by the CS and Ca^{2+} released by inositol trisphosphate from internal stores (IS) activates PLC and PKC, which reduces K^+ currents and results in enhanced excitability of the photoreceptors. The presentation of the CS results in increased levels of intracellular Ca^{2+} produced by the depolarizing generator potential activating voltage-dependent Ca^{2+} channels and light-induced release of Ca^{2+} from IS. Pairing specificity results from the amplification provided by Ca^{2+} acting on PLC and PKC. Long-term memory in this model is dependent upon protein synthesis and gene products dependent upon Ca^{2+} activating an unidentified kinase (K?) or long-term changes in Ca^{2+} buffering. The evidence suggests that short-term and long-term memory in this system involve independent parallel pathways (see text).

tion of second messengers and protein kinases is important for the induction of enhancement. Recent evidence has shown that the activation of PKC is an important step in the induction of short-term enhancement in this system. However, persistent kinase activity is not necessary for the expression or maintenance of either short- or long-term enhancement. Finally, the recent results showing that the conditions sufficient to block short-term enhancement do not block long-term enhancement measured 24 hours after one-trial conditioning indicate that different pathways may be involved in the induction of short- and long-term enhancement. Taken collectively, these results show that short- and long-term memory in this nervous system may be independent, parallel, and involve different mechanisms for induction. The study of short-term and long-term enhancement produced by one-trial conditioning of *Hermissenda* now provides for the opportunity to determine if short-term and long-term memory occur in series or in parallel.

REFERENCES

Acosta-Urquidi, J., Alkon, D. L., & Neary, J. T. (1984). Ca^{2+}-dependent protein kinase injection in a photoreceptor mimics biophysical effects of associative learning. *Science, 224*, 1254–1275.

Acosta-Urquidi, J., & Crow, T. (1990). 5-HT modulates two distinct K^+ currents in *Hermissenda* type B photoreceptors. *Society for Neuroscience Abstracts, 16*, 20.

Alkon, D. L. (1984). Calcium-mediated reduction of ionic currents: A biophysical memory trace. *Science, 226*, 1037–1045.

Alkon, D. L., Acosta-Urquidi, J., Olds, J., Kuzma, G., & Neary, J. T. (1983). Protein kinase activity reduces voltage-dependent K^+ currents. *Science, 219*, 303–306.

Alkon, D. L., Lederhendler, I., & Shoukimas, J. J. (1982). Primary changes of membrane currents during retention of associative learning. *Science, 275*, 693-695.

Alkon, D. L., Rubota, M., Neary, J. T., Naito, S., Coulter, D., & Rasmussen, H. (1986). C-kinase activation prolongs Ca^{2+}-dependent inactivation of K^+ currents. *Biochemical and Biophysical Research Communications, 134*, 1215-1222.

Alkon, D. L., Sakakibara, M., Forman, R., Harrigan, J., Lederhendler, I., & Farley, J. (1985). Reduction of two voltage-dependent K^+ currents mediates retention of a learned association. *Behavioral and Neural Biology, 44*, 278-300.

Alkon, D. L., Shoukimas, J. J., & Heldman, E. (1982). Calcium-mediated decrease of a voltage-dependent potassium current. *Biophysical Journal, 40*, 245-250.

Crow, T. (1983). Conditioned modification of locomotion in *Hermissenda crassicornis*: Analysis of time dependent associative and nonassociative components. *Journal of Neuroscience, 3*, 2621-2628.

Crow, T. (1985). Conditioned modification of phototactic behavior in *Hermissenda*: 1. Analysis of light intensity. *Journal of Neuroscience, 5*, 209-214.

Crow, T. (1988). Cellular and molecular analysis of associative learning and memory in *Hermissenda*. *Trends in Neuroscience, 11*, 136-142.

Crow, T. (1989). Associative learning, memory, and neuromodulation in *Hermissenda*. In J. H. Byrne & W. O. Berry (Eds.), *Neural models of plasticity* (pp. 1-21). New York: Academic Press.

Crow, T., & Alkon, D. L. (1978). Retention of an associative behavioral change in *Hermissenda*. *Science, 201*, 1239-1241.

Crow, T., & Alkon, D. L. (1980). Associative behavioral modification in *Hermissenda*: Cellular correlates. *Science, 209*, 412-414.

Crow, T., & Bridge, M. S. (1985). Serotonin modulates photoresponses in *Hermissenda* type-B photoreceptors. *Neuroscience Letters, 60*, 83-88.

Crow, T., & Forrester, J. (1986). Light paired with serotonin mimics the effects of conditioning on phototactic behavior in *Hermissenda*. *Proceedings of the National Academy of Sciences USA, 83*, 7975-7978.

Crow, T., & Forrester, J. (1988). Light paired with activators of protein kinase C produces short- and long-term enhancement of light responses. *Society for Neuroscience Abstracts, 14*, 839.

Crow, T., & Forrester, J. (1990). Inhibition of protein synthesis blocks long-term enhancement of generator potentials produced by one-trial *in vivo* conditioning in *Hermissenda*. *Proceedings of the National Academy of Sciences USA, 87*, 4490-4494.

Crow, T., & Forrester, J. (1991). Light paired with serotonin *in vivo* produces both short and long-term enhancement of generator potentials of identified B-photoreceptors in *Hermissenda*. *Journal of Neuroscience, 11*, 608-617.

Crow, T., Forrester, J., Williams, M., Waxham, N., & Neary, J. (1991). Down-regulation of protein kinase C blocks 5-HT-induced enhancement in *Hermissenda* B-photoreceptors. *Neuroscience Letters, 121*, 107-110.

Crow, T., & Offenbach, N. (1983). Modification of the initiation of locomotion in *Hermissenda*: Behavioral analysis. *Brain Research, 271*, 301-310.

Davis, H. P., & Squire, L. R. (1984). Protein synthesis and memory: A review. *Psychological Bulletin, 96*, 518-559.

Farley, J. (1987). Contingency learning and casual detection in *Hermissenda*: 1. Behavior. *Behavioral Neuroscience, 101*, 13-27.

Farley, J., & Auerbach, S. (1986). Protein kinase C activation induces conductance changes in *Hermissenda* photoreceptors like those seen in associative learning. *Nature, 319*, 220-223.

Forrester, J., & Crow, T. (1988). Protein kinase C inhibition prevents short-term but not long-term light 5-HT-induced enhancement of generator potentials in *Hermissenda* B-photoreceptors. *Society for Neuroscience Abstracts, 14*, 839.

Forrester, J., & Crow, T. (1989). Kinase inhibitors do not reverse short or long-term enhancement of light responses in identified *Hermissenda* B-photoreceptors. *Society for Neuroscience Abstracts, 15*, 1274.

Harrigan, J. F., & Alkon, D. L. (1985). Individual variation in associative learning of the nudibranch mollusc *Hermissenda crassicornis*. *Biological Bulletin, 168*, 222-238.

Heldman, E., & Alkon, D. L. (1978). Neurotransmitter synthesis in the nervous system of the mollusc *Hermissenda*. *Comparative Biochemistry and Physiology, 59*, 117-125.

Heldman, E., Grossman, Y., Jerussi, T. P., & Alkon, D. L. (1979). Cholinergic features of photoreceptor synapses in *Hermissenda*. *Journal of Neurophysiology, 43*, 153-165.

Hidaka, H., Inagaki, M., Kawamoto, S., & Sasaki, Y. (1984). Isoquinolinesulfonamides, novel and potent inhibitors of cyclic nucleotide dependent protein kinase and protein kinase C. *Biochemistry, 23*, 5036-5041.

Jefferson, A. B., & Schulman, H. (1988). Sphingosine inhibits calmodulin-dependent enzymes. *Journal of Biological Chemistry, 263*, 15241–15244.

Land, P. W., and Crow, T. (1985). Serotonin immunoreactivity in the circumesophageal nervous system of *Hermissenda crassicornis*. *Neuroscience Letters, 3*, 199–205.

Lederhendler, I., Gart, S., & Alkon, D. L. (1986). Classical conditioning of *Hermissenda*: Origin of a new response. *Journal of Neuroscience, 6*, 1325–1331.

Malinow, R., Madison, D. V., & Tsien, R. W. (1988). Persistent protein kinase activity underlying long-term potentiation. *Nature, 335*, 820–824.

Neary, J. T., Crow, T. J., & Alkon, D. L. (1981). Changes in a specific phosphoprotein band following associative learning in *Hermissenda*. *Nature, 293*, 658–660.

Neary, J. T., Naito, S., & Alkon, D. L. (1985). Ca^{2+}-activated phospholipid protein kinase (C-kinase) activity in *Hermissenda* nervous system. *Society for Neuroscience Abstracts, 11*, 746.

Neary, J. T., Naito, S., DeWeer, A., & Alkon, D. L. (1986). Ca^{2+}/diacylglycerol-activated phospholipid-dependent protein kinase in the *Hermissenda* CNS. *Journal of Neurochemistry, 47*, 1405–1411.

Sakakibara, M., Alkon, D. L., DeLorenzo, R., Goldenring, J. R., Neary, J. T., & Heldman, E. (1986). Modulation of calcium-mediated inactivation of ionic currents by Ca^{2+}/calmodulin-dependent protein kinase II. *Biophysical Journal, 50*, 319–327.

Sakakibara, M., Collin, C., Kuzirian, A., Alkon, D. L., Heldman, E., Naito, S., & Lederhendler, I. (1987). Effects of α_2-adrenergic agonists and antagonists on photoreceptor membrane currents. *Journal of Neurochemistry, 48*, 405–416.

50

Snails' Tales: Initial Comparisons of Synaptic Plasticity Underlying Learning in *Hermissenda* and *Aplysia*

GREGORY A. CLARK and ERIN M. SCHUMAN

In the last decade, it has become increasingly possible to examine the processes of learning and memory on a cellular and molecular level. Much of this progress has come through the use of invertebrate preparations such as *Aplysia* and *Hermissenda*, which have relatively simple nervous systems containing large, identifiable neurons of known behavioral function. The use of these simple systems has been driven by the goal of finding general principles of cellular plasticity that might be phylogenetically conserved. Somewhat surprisingly, however, analyses of neural learning mechanisms in *Aplysia* and *Hermissenda* have led to apparently different views regarding the cellular processes mediating learning—or, at least, so it might seem at first to those not working directly in the field. Thus, initial studies in *Aplysia* showed that habituation, sensitization, and classical conditioning of the gill and siphon withdrawal responses all involve changes in synaptic strength (e.g., changes in the amount of transmitter a neuron releases per action potential). During habituation, synaptic transmission from siphon sensory cells is depressed, and the reflexes are weakened; during sensitization and classical conditioning, synaptic transmission and the resulting behaviors are enhanced (see Kennedy, Hawkins, & Kandel, Chapter 48, this volume). Similar behavioral and cellular processes are also evident in the *Aplysia* tail withdrawal response (e.g., Walters & Byrne, 1983). In contrast, classically conditioned suppression of phototaxis in *Hermissenda* has been shown to involve increases in cellular excitability (e.g., changes in the number of action potentials elicited in a neuron by a constant input; see Crow, Chapter 49, this volume). As described in more detail below, after training the conditioned stimulus (CS), light, elicits a larger discharge in the inhibitory Type B photoreceptors, thereby attenuating the normal positive phototactic behavioral response. These initial findings have raised some questions about the relationship between these two forms of neuronal plasticity, as well as questions about the model systems approach itself. After all, it might be asked, if one cannot generalize from one mollusk to another, then how can one hope to generalize from mollusk to mammal, or mollusk to man?

Despite their obvious phenotypic differences, however, changes in synaptic strength and changes in neuronal excitability are not necessarily mutually exclusive, and may even share aspects of a common underlying molecular process. In support of this notion, recent work in *Aplysia* has indicated that some of the same extracellular and intracellular signals that facilitate transmitter release from sensory cells also render these same cells more excitable (Baxter & Byrne, 1990; Billy & Walters, 1989; Klein, Hochner, & Kandel, 1986; Walters, 1987). We were therefore interested in exploring whether these principles hold true in *Hermissenda* as well. In other words, do the same experimental procedures and cellular processes that increase the excitability of Type B photoreceptors also enhance synaptic transmission at connections of Type B cells onto follower neurons?

In this chapter, we describe some of our initial investigations that indicate this is indeed the case. We have found that the Type B photoreceptors exhibit synaptic facilitation in addition to the excitability changes previously described, and furthermore, that this facilitation is mediated by the same first messenger (serotonin, or 5-HT) and second messenger (protein kinase C) that mediate the increased excitability (Schuman & Clark, 1990). Thus, in *Hermissenda* as in *Aplysia*, changes in synaptic strength and changes in neuronal excitability can work together to enhance the output of the relevant neural pathways during learning. Because synaptic facilitation may contribute importantly to behavioral learning, these experiments may provide new insights into the mechanisms underlying conditioning in *Hermissenda*. In the larger sense, these studies may also help reconcile the somewhat disparate views of learning mechanisms that have emerged from the analysis of different model systems, and thereby highlight fundamental principles of neural learning mechanisms common to a wide variety of species.

Previous Behavioral and Biological Analyses of Conditioning in *Hermissenda*

One of the first convincing findings of associative learning in an invertebrate was the demonstration of conditioned suppression of phototactic behavior in *Hermissenda*. Naive untrained *Hermissenda* normally locomote toward light. However, following an associative conditioning paradigm involving pairings of light (the CS) and rotation (the unconditioned stimulus, or US), the normally positive phototactic behavior of *Hermissenda* is suppressed (Crow & Alkon, 1978). This behavioral change has been shown to involve an increase in the excitability of the Type B photoreceptors; following training, these cells exhibit depolarized membrane potentials, an increased input resistance, and an enhanced light response (Crow & Alkon, 1980; Farley & Alkon, 1982; West, Barnes, & Alkon, 1982). Ultimately, this *enhancement* of excitability to light in Type B cells translates into a *suppression* of phototactic behavior, because the B photoreceptors inhibit other photoreceptors (the Type A photoreceptors) and other neural elements that connect to motor circuitry mediating phototaxis (Goh & Alkon, 1984; Goh, Lederhendler, & Alkon, 1985).

A great deal of work over the last decade by Alkon, Crow, Farley, and their colleagues has identified many of the cellular processes underlying these training-induced enhancement of Type B cell excitability. On a biophysical level, excitability changes involve underlying reductions in two potassium currents—the A current, I_A

(Alkon, Lederhendler, & Shoukimas, 1982), and a Ca^{2+}-activated K^+ current, I_{K-Ca} (Alkon et al., 1985; Farley, 1988)—and possibly a change in a Ca^{2+} current (Collin, Ikeno, Harrigan, Lederhendler, & Alkon, 1988; Farley, Richards, & Alkon, 1983; Farley, 1988). These conditioning-produced ionic conductance changes render Type B photoreceptors more excitable to light and result in greater impulse frequency for a given light stimulus. What mechanisms mediate these biophysical changes on a biochemical and molecular level? According to one class of models (e.g., Crow, 1988; Farley & Auerbach, 1986), the rotational US activates neuromodulatory interneurons utilizing 5-HT (Auerbach, Grover, & Farley, 1989; Crow & Bridge, 1985; Crow & Forrester, 1986, 1991; Farley & Wu, 1989; Grover, Farley, & Auerbach, 1989; Land & Crow, 1985). 5-HT, in conjunction with a rise in intracellular Ca^{2+} triggered by the light CS, leads to the activation of protein kinase C in Type B photoreceptors; through a series of biochemical steps, protein kinase C then phosphorylates K^+ channels or closely associated proteins, and induces the aforementioned conductance changes (Alkon et al., 1986, 1988; Farley & Auerbach, 1986; Farley & Schuman, 1991; Forrester & Crow, 1988, 1989; Matzel, Lederhendler, & Alkon, 1990; Neary, Naito, DeWeer, & Alkon, 1986). However, agreement on all these points is not complete, and other models exist. For example, according to Alkon and colleagues (Alkon, 1989; Alkon & Nelson, 1990), the effects of the US on Type B cells are mediated primarily by depolarization and subsequent Ca^{2+} influx, rather than by 5-HT. This depolarization of Type B cells is proposed to arise from various network interactions, including excitation by the silent/excitatory (S/E) optic ganglion cell, and release from inhibition by the caudal hair cells (Alkon, 1979; Farley & Alkon, 1987; Tabata & Alkon, 1982). Other questions remain regarding whether protein kinase C is involved in long-term neural changes (Farley & Schuman, 1991) as well as short-term neural changes (Forrester & Crow, 1988), and whether it is involved in maintenance (Farley & Schuman, 1991; Matzel et al., 1990) as well as induction (Forrester & Crow, 1989) of these changes.

Regardless of these particular issues, however, there are a number of striking similarities between these proposed mechanisms for learning in *Hermissenda* and those proposed for learning in *Aplysia*. Both involve intrinsic changes in the primary sensory neurons mediating the CS; reductions in particular (although different) potassium conductances; modulation by 5-HT; phosphorylation events mediated by particular (although different) second messengers; the enhancement of this second-messenger cascade via elevation of intracellular calcium elicited by the CS; and the involvement of ribonucleic acid (RNA) and protein synthesis in long-term neural changes. Given that synaptic plasticity is known to play such an important role in learning in *Aplysia* and possibly other systems, these similarities suggested that it might prove worthwhile to assess its possible contribution to conditioning in *Hermissenda*. We also hoped that the demonstration of synaptic plasticity in *Hermissenda* might provide an additional tool to investigate the unresolved mechanistic issues in this preparation.

Synaptic Plasticity in *Hermissenda*

Because previous research had focused primarily on the changes in Type B photoreceptor excitability, at the outset it was important to determine simply whether Type B photoreceptors could exhibit synaptic plasticity in addition to the excitability changes previously described. As an expeditious first step, we assessed whether the same neuromodulatory transmitter system (5-HT) and, as described in the following experiments, the same second messenger (protein kinase C) that produce Type B cell excitability changes also increase the magnitude of the inhibitory postsynaptic potential (IPSP) elicited by Type B cell stimulation (Schuman & Clark, 1990).

To examine the effects of 5-HT on synaptic strength, we recorded from a presynaptic Type B photoreceptor (usually an intermediate Type B cell) and a postsynaptic Type A photoreceptor (usually a lateral Type A cell) intracellularly *in vitro* (Figure 50.1). We then monitored the IPSP elicited by the Type B cell in the Type A cell before and after either exposure to 10^{-6} M 5-HT, or sham solution exchanges with artificial seawater (ASW). We also measured the initial input resistance in both the Type B cell and the Type A cell as a rough index of cellular excitability. To minimize possible secondary influences on the IPSP size and input resistance measurements, the baseline membrane potential was held constant throughout this and other experiments by manually varying the holding current.

We found that 5-HT could indeed produce synaptic facilitation at Type B cell connections, in addition to the excitability changes previously described (Schuman & Clark, 1990). As shown in Figure 50.2, acute application of 5-HT dramatically enhanced the size of the IPSP elicited by the Type B cells in the Type A cells. In contrast,

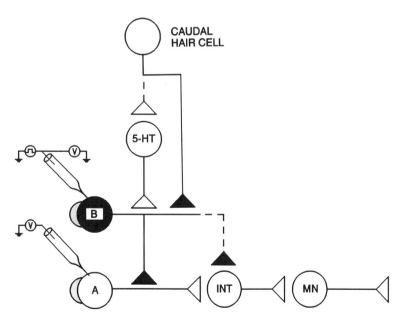

FIGURE 50.1. Experimental arrangement for examining synaptic facilitation at connections of Type B photoreceptors onto Type A photoreceptors. In the present *in vitro* experiments, we examined the inhibitory postsynaptic potentials (IPSPs) elicited in Type A photoreceptors by individual action potentials evoked by intracellular stimulation of Type B photoreceptors. In the intact animal, the inhibitory influences of the Type B cells are believed to be responsible for the conditioned suppression of phototaxis. Open triangles indicate excitatory synaptic connections; closed triangles indicate inhibitory synaptic connections. Only selected relevant connections are depicted. 5-HT, serotonin; INT, interneuron; MN, motor neuron.

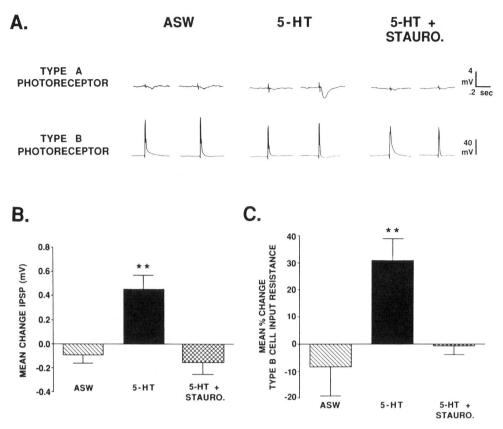

FIGURE 50.2. Acute application of 5-HT facilitates synaptic transmission at Type B to Type A photoreceptor synapses. (**A**) Sample simultaneous recordings from Type A photoreceptors (top traces) and Type B
photoreceptors (bottom traces) in three preparations. Examples are from before (left) and after (right) three
different experimental treatments. Bath application of 10^{-6} M 5-HT produced an immediate and dramatic
enhancement of the IPSP elicited by the Type B cell (middle traces), whereas control preparations receiving
exchanges of artificial seawater (ASW) (left traces) showed relatively little change. In addition, preincuba-
tion with 10^{-7} M staurosporine (STAURO.), an inhibitor of protein kinase C, blocked the facilitation normally
produced by 5-HT (right traces). (**B**) Group data indicating the mean change in IPSP amplitude following
each of the experimental treatments. An analysis of variance followed by Newman–Keuls tests for individual
comparisons indicated that the increased IPSP amplitude following 5-HT treatment ($n = 15$) was significantly different from effects in the ASW group ($n = 11$; $p < .01$) and the staurosporine group ($n = 11$;
$p < .01$), $F (2, 34) = 11.0$. (**C**) Group data indicating mean change in Type B cell input resistance following
each of the three experimental treatments. Again, effects observed in response to 5-HT ($n = 14$) were
significantly greater than those in the ASW group ($n = 11$; $p < .01$) or the staurosporine group ($n = 11$;
$p < .01$), $F (2, 33) = 6.2$. Note that 5-HT enhanced both IPSP amplitude and Type B cell input resistance in
roughly equivalent fashion.

sham exchanges with normal ASW produced no effect. Consistent with previous work,
5-HT also caused a significant increase in the input resistance of the Type B cell, but
had no effect on Type A cell input resistance, suggesting (though not proving) that
facilitation was due to presynaptic changes in the B cell. The close fit evident between
resistance changes in Type B cells and synaptic facilitation further suggests that these
two processes may be mechanistically related. These findings indicate that Type B

photoreceptors in *Hermissenda* are capable of exhibiting synaptic facilitation, and further suggest that such synaptic changes are mediated by the same neuromodulatory transmitter (5-HT) as the excitability changes previously described in these cells.

Does synaptic facilitation at connections of Type B photoreceptors also involve the same intracellular second messenger as the excitability changes? As indicated above, protein kinase C is believed to be an important intracellular second messenger underlying learning-dependent excitability changes in *Hermissenda* Type B photoreceptors (Alkon et al., 1986, 1988; Farley & Auerbach, 1986; Farley & Schuman, 1991; Forrester & Crow, 1988, 1989; Matzel et al., 1990; Neary et al., 1986). If protein kinase C is involved in synaptic facilitation as well, then inhibition of protein kinase C should block the facilitation normally produced by 5-HT. In addition, activation of protein kinase C (but not other kinases) should produce synaptic facilitation at connections of the Type B photoreceptors. We have found both of these hypotheses to be true (Schuman & Clark, 1990).

As an initial test for the involvement of protein kinase C in synaptic plasticity, we examined whether staurosporine, an inhibitor of protein kinase C (Tamaokie et al., 1986) and other kinases (Ruegg & Burgess, 1989), blocks the synaptic facilitation normally produced by 5-HT. In brief, we preincubated the preparations with 10^{-7} M staurosporine, and then examined the effects of applying 5-HT at synaptic connections from Type B cells to Type A cells, as previously. As shown in Figure 50.2, staurosporine did in fact block the effects of 5-HT on synaptic facilitation and on increased cellular excitability, suggesting that 5-HT exerts its modulatory effects on these cells through a protein kinase, possibly protein kinase C.

Another important test for potential involvement of a kinase is its ability to induce the relevant neuronal changes. Accordingly, we next determined whether activation of protein kinase C, or, alternatively, activation of the cyclic adenosine monophosphate (cAMP)-dependent protein kinase, would elicit synaptic facilitation at Type B cell connections. As before, we recorded simultaneously from a Type B photoreceptor and a Type A photoreceptor. We measured the magnitude of the IPSP at Type B–Type A synaptic connections, as well as the input resistance of both cells. The bathing solution was then exchanged to ASW containing one of the following: (1) 10^{-7} M phorbol 12-myristate 13-acetate (PMA), a phorbol ester that activates protein kinase C; (2) 4α-phorbol, an inactive phorbol ester; or (3) a combination of 10^{-4} M 8-benzylthio cAMP (8-BT cAMP, a membrane-permeable cAMP analogue) and 10^{-4} M 3-isobutyl-1-methyl-xanthine (IBMX), a phosphodiesterase inhibitor. Following a 5- to 10-minute incubation period, the magnitude of the IPSP was again monitored, and input resistance measurements were taken.

We found that activation of protein kinase C, but not the cAMP-dependent kinase, facilitated Type B cell synaptic transmission (Figure 50.3). Application of PMA, a phorbol ester that activates protein kinase C, produced a marked facilitation in the amplitude of the IPSP evoked by Type B cell stimulation. In contrast, both the inactive phorbol ester 4α-phorbol and 8-BT cAMP had little or no effect. In addition, PMA increased the input resistance of Type B photoreceptors, whereas the inactive 4α-phorbol and 8-BT cAMP did not. None of the agents produced a significant change in the Type A photoreceptor input resistance. The fact that cAMP was ineffective in

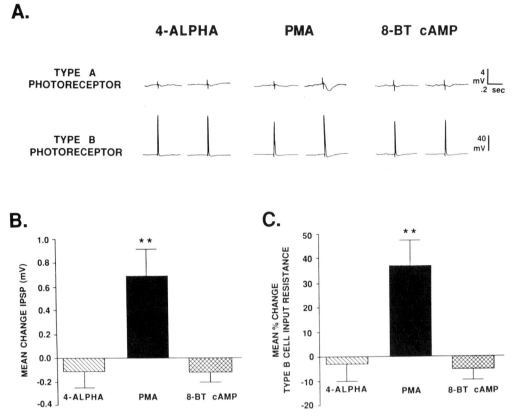

FIGURE 50.3. Activation of protein kinase C, but not the cAMP-dependent protein kinase, facilitates synaptic transmission at Type B to Type A photoreceptor synapses. (**A**) Sample intracellular recordings from Type A photoreceptors (top traces) and Type B photoreceptors (bottom traces) in three preparations. Examples are from before (left) and after (right) application of either 10^{-7} M 4α-phorbol (an inactive phorbol ester), 10^{-7} M PMA (a phorbol ester that activates protein kinase C), or 10^{-4} M 8-BT cAMP (a membrane-permeable cAMP analogue) given in combination with IBMX (a phosphodiesterase inhibitor). Note synaptic facilitation occurring after exposure to PMA, but not after the other two treatments. (**B**) Group data indicating the mean change in IPSP amplitude following each of the experimental treatments. PMA produced a significant increase in IPSP amplitude ($n = 13$) relative to preparations receiving 4α-phorbol ($n = 10$; $p < .01$) or cAMP plus IBMX ($n = 12$; $p < .01$), $F(2, 32) = 7.9$. (**C**) Group data indicating mean change in input resistance of Type B photoreceptors following each of the three experimental treatments. Type B cell input resistances observed following PMA ($n = 13$) were significantly increased relative to changes observed following 4α-phorbol application ($n = 10$; $p < .01$) or cAMP plus IBMX ($n = 12$; $p < .02$). Like 5-HT, PMA enhanced both IPSP amplitude and Type B cell input resistance in roughly equivalent fashion.

producing synaptic plasticity suggests that the effects of staurosporine in blocking synaptic facilitation described above resulted from staurosporine's inhibition of protein kinase C, rather than from inhibition of the cAMP-dependent kinase. Taken together, these results corroborate our earlier findings that Type B cells exhibit synaptic facilitation, and suggest that the same first messenger (5-HT) and the same second messenger (protein kinase C) are involved in mediating both the changes in synaptic strength and cellular excitability.

Conclusions

Synaptic facilitation represents a previously undocumented form of plasticity in *Hermissenda* Type B photoreceptors that may contribute importantly to behavioral learning. Previously, excitability changes have been proposed to be causally involved in behavioral learning (Farley, Richards, Ling, Liman, & Alkon, 1983), and computational models explicitly lacking synaptic changes have been forwarded (Tesauro, 1988). One earlier study suggesting possible synaptic changes in Type B cells is the recent description of a reduction of the terminal arborizations of Type B cells following conditioning (Alkon et al., 1990). Because the loss of synaptic contacts on these processes might be expected to result in a decrease (rather than the anticipated increase) of inhibitory Type B cell influences, Alkon and colleagues suggested that there might have been an undetected anatomical augmentation restricted to relevant Type B cell synapses. More recently, Lederhendler, Etcheberrigaray, Yamoah, Matzel, and Alkon (1990) have shown that activation of protein kinase C can produce process outgrowth from Type B cell somata. In addition, response changes that appeared to arise from alterations in afferent input have been observed in various other circuit elements, including motor neurons (Crow & Alkon, 1980; Farley & Alkon, 1982; Goh et al., 1985; Richards & Farley, 1987). Although these response changes in downstream cells might have resulted from increased transmission at connections of Type B cells, they might in principle have arisen from any of several mechanisms, including increased firing in Type B cells and primary alterations in other cell types altogether. Our current experiments provide the first direct evidence that synaptic facilitation at connections of Type B cells can indeed occur. Obviously, these experiments represent only a preliminary exploration of synaptic facilitation underlying conditioned suppression of phototaxis in *Hermissenda*. It will be essential to determine whether synaptic facilitation also arises as a result of behavioral conditioning in the intact animal, and if so, whether it is mediated by the mechanisms described herein. The fact that 5-HT and protein kinase C—the cellular signals employed in our current studies—have previously been implicated in conditioning in the intact animal strongly encourages this possibility.

We also need to determine more precisely the mechanistic relationship between the excitability changes on the one hand, and synaptic facilitation on the other (Figure 50.4). It is possible that the same biophysical conductance changes that enhance cellular excitability also enhance synaptic transmission; for example, the previously observed reductions in potassium conductances might alter the waveform of the action potential, and thereby indirectly modify transmitter release. Alternatively, protein kinase C or other intracellular signals might directly modulate other processes, such as transmitter mobilization, independently of membrane conductance changes. These two possibilities are not necessarily mutually exclusive, as analyses of similar questions in *Aplysia* sensory neurons indicate. In *Aplysia* sensory cells, closure of 5-HT-sensitive potassium channels can lead to both enhanced excitability and action potential broadening, which results in increased calcium influx and increased transmitter release per action potential (Baxter & Byrne, 1990; Billy & Walters, 1989; Hochner, Klein, Schacher, & Kandel, 1986a; Klein & Kandel, 1978, 1980; Klein et al., 1986; Siegelbaum, Camardo, & Kandel, 1982; Walters, 1987). But an additional second process, as yet not

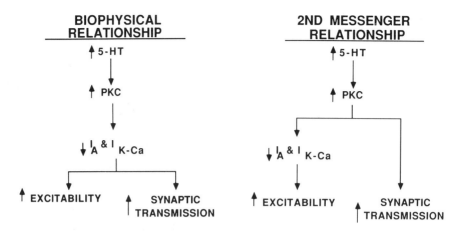

FIGURE 50.4. Possible mechanistic relationships between increased excitability and synaptic facilitation in Type B photoreceptors. Serotonin (5-HT) and/or other signals are proposed to activate protein kinase C (PKC), which in turn elicits both enhanced excitability and synaptic facilitation. Two different relationships between these forms of plasticity are depicted. One possibility (biophysical relationship, left) is that PKC produces synaptic facilitation via the same ionic conductance changes that enhance cellular excitability (e.g., a decrease in two potassium conductances, I_A and I_{K-Ca}), by modifying the duration or other parameters of the action potential. Alternatively (second-messenger relationship, right), PKC might induce synaptic facilitation via other processes, such as transmitter mobilization, not mediated by these conductance changes. The two possibilities are not mutually exclusive.

fully understood, can also facilitate transmitter release through an independent mechanism not involving ionic conductance changes, particularly when the synapse has previously been depressed (Braha et al., 1990; Hochner, Klein, Schacher, & Kandel, 1986b).

Regardless of the precise nature of these relationships in *Hermissenda* neurons, it is clear that Type B photoreceptors can exhibit changes in both cellular excitability and synaptic strength. We do not yet know on a quantitative level the relative contributions of these two forms of plasticity to behavioral learning in *Hermissenda* (or, for that matter, in *Aplysia*). Moreover, these two forms of plasticity need not always occur together, given that different regions of the cell may be modulated independently (Clark & Kandel, 1984). Nonetheless, because increases in excitability will enhance the number of action potentials in response to a given input, and synaptic facilitation will enhance transmitter release per action potential, these two changes can operate synergistically to increase the output of the cell (Figure 50.5).

These findings also bear on general attempts to characterize learning as either a presynaptic or postsynaptic process. One can find occasional proposals in the literature that cellular mechanisms of learning are presynaptic in *Aplysia*, but postsynaptic in *Hermissenda*. Similarly, learning-related excitability changes recorded from cell bodies in mammalian brain have sometimes been categorized as postsynaptic changes. These abstract depictions can be misleading in several ways. For one, changes in excitability are often better characterized as nonsynaptic (rather than presynaptic or postsynaptic) modifications. For example, changes can occur in baseline "spontaneous" firing rates that appear to be independent of afferent synaptic input (e.g.,

INCREASED NEURONAL EXCITABILITY AND SYNAPTIC TRANSMISSION

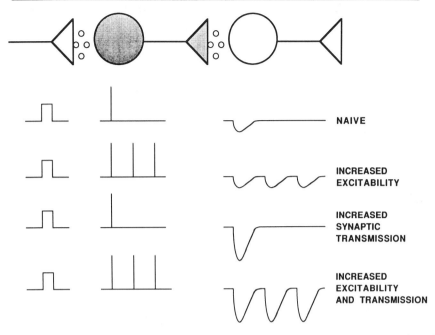

NAIVE

INCREASED EXCITABILITY

INCREASED SYNAPTIC TRANSMISSION

INCREASED EXCITABILITY AND TRANSMISSION

FIGURE 50.5. Single cells can exhibit both increased excitability, leading to an increased number of action potentials elicited by a constant input, and increased synaptic transmission, leading to an increase in transmitter release per action potential. Shading in middle cell indicates plasticity occurring in somatic-dendritic regions (producing increased excitability), and in synaptic regions (producing synaptic facilitation). Different traces below indicate particular functional consequences of each of these modifications for the various cells. Top trace: In the naive state, stimulation of an afferent input (left cell, square wave) evokes a single action potential in the middle cell, which in turn elicits a modest IPSP in its own postsynaptic target (right cell). Second trace: Changes occurring in somatic–dendritic regions of the middle cell would give rise to enhanced excitability, leading to an increase in the number of action potentials elicited in the middle cell by a constant input, and consequently to an increase in the number of IPSPs evoked in cells downstream. Third trace: Changes occurring in synaptic terminal regions of the middle cell would enhance transmitter release, and consequently enhance the magnitude of the IPSP elicited in its postsynaptic target. Bottom trace: Changes occurring simultaneously in *both* somatic-dendritic regions and synaptic terminal regions of the shaded cell would produce both increased excitability (more action potentials) and synaptic facilitation (a larger IPSP elicited by each action potential). These two types of changes would operate in concert to increase the output of the cell. Note that, depending on which set of synapses is being considered, the cellular changes occurring in the shaded neuron might be viewed as either "postsynaptic" modifications, involving enhanced responsiveness to a constant input (from the left cell), or as "presynaptic" modifications, involving increased transmitter release from the shaded neuron onto its own postsynaptic target (right cell).

Woollacott & Hoyle, 1977). Likewise, strictly speaking, changes in firing frequency that occur in both *Aplysia* and *Hermissenda* sensory neurons in response to a sensory stimulus are nonsynaptic modifications, because transmission across a synapse is not involved in activating primary sensory neurons.

Moreover, it is important to keep in mind that "presynaptic" and "postsynaptic" are relative, not absolute terms, as others have also pointed out (Billy & Walters, 1989; Carew, Hawkins, Abrams, & Kandel, 1984; Klein et al., 1986; Walters, 1987). These labels describe the nature of an alteration across a particular synapse, and so may not accurately characterize the change in a particular cell, which may show alterations in both input and output functions, and may be both afferent and efferent to other cells. For example, consider a neuron that has been modulated both in somatic–dendritic regions and in synaptic terminal regions (Figure 50.5). Plasticity in dendritic and somatic regions (such as decreased K^+ conductances) might decrease accommodation of action potential firing, as well as enhance the propagation of synaptic potentials to spike-generating regions via increased membrane resistance; both these changes could result in an increase in the number of action potential discharges elicited by a constant afferent input. Consequently, an experimenter recording increased firing from the cell body region of this plastic neuron might be tempted to categorize learning as post-synaptic, because the cell in question shows an increase in responding while the afferent input remains constant. But at the same time, changes in synaptic terminal regions of the same plastic cell might yield increased transmitter release per action potential; and another experimenter recording an enhanced synaptic potential evoked by this cell in a target neuron downstream might be tempted to categorize learning as presynaptic, because the synaptic facilitation observed results from enhanced transmitter release. Thus, modification of the same neuron may appear as either "presynaptic," involving increased transmitter release, or "postsynaptic," involving increased responsiveness, depending on which synapses are being considered. Such labels are understandable and, if not taken too literally, even useful. But, as in the folk tale of the blind men describing an elephant from opposite ends, we must be careful to realize that our characterizations may reflect the limitations of our vantage points as much as the true nature of the beast.

In closing, we wish to indicate quite explicitly that our current findings do not in any way detract from the previous results in *Hermissenda*, or fundamentally alter their interpretation. Our findings on synaptic plasticity complement, rather than contradict, the excitability changes previously described. Indeed, because synaptic facilitation in Type B photoreceptors appears to involve some of the same cellular processes as the excitability changes, our results may allow investigators to extend many of the conclusions obtained from previous mechanistic analyses of excitability changes to the processes of synaptic plasticity, and so increase the relevance of this previous work in *Hermissenda* to investigations of synaptic plasticity in other invertebrate and vertebrate systems.

This is by no means to say that all learning can be accounted for by a single cellular mechanism, or even that the plasticity in *Aplysia* and *Hermissenda* is identical. It is not, and should not be expected to be. In this chapter we have highlighted many of the similarities between the two systems, as we feel these have not always been fully appreciated. But it is also important to remember the distinctions (Figure 50.6). Compared with plasticity in *Aplysia* siphon sensory cells, plasticity in *Hermissenda* Type B photoreceptors involves a different sensory modality (light rather than touch), different types of potassium conductances (I_A and I_{K-Ca}, rather than I_S), primarily a different second-messenger system (protein kinase C, rather than the cAMP-dependent kinase), and an inhibitory rather than an excitatory synaptic potential, among other differences. These are meaningful distinctions, and their existence suggests that each preparation will provide unique insights into cellular mechanisms of learning. In addition, because the two preparations do differ in these regards, they provide a

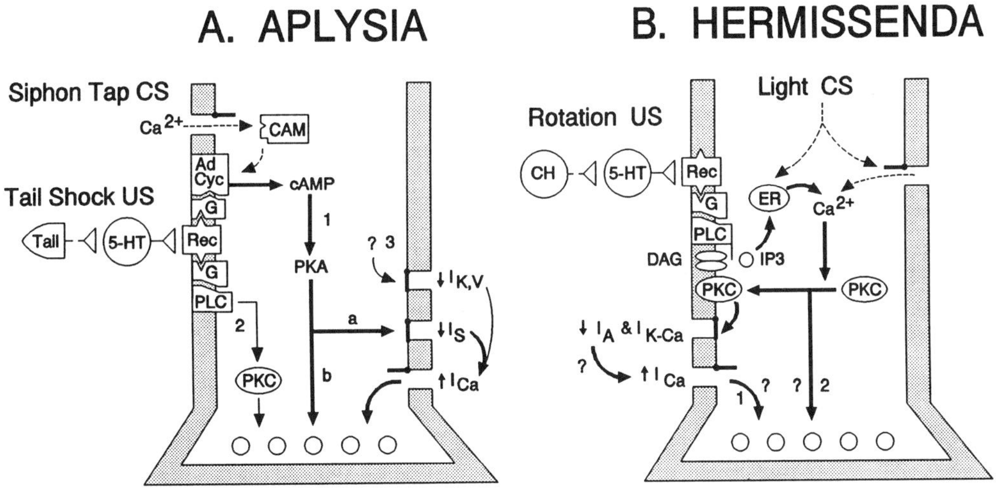

FIGURE 50.6. Comparison of cellular mechanisms for learning in *Aplysia* and *Hermissenda* sensory neurons. (**A**) Cellular modifications involved in sensitization and classical conditioning in *Aplysia* siphon sensory cells. In sensitization, tail shock activates facilitatory interneurons (some of which are serotonergic) that synapse onto sensory neurons, causing multiple effects. In the most well-documented biochemical cascade (arrow 1a), stimulation of the 5-HT receptor–adenylate cyclase complex leads to the production of cAMP, activation of the cAMP-dependent protein kinase (PKA), and closure of the S (and possibly I_{K-Ca}) potassium channels. Closure of these channels leads both to increased cellular excitability, yielding more action potentials for a given depolarization, and to broadening of the action potential, which in turn prolongs Ca^{2+} entry and consequently enhances transmitter release. cAMP may also enhance transmitter release through a second process (arrow 1b), perhaps vesicle mobilization, that is independent of ionic conductance changes, particularly in synapses that have undergone homosynaptic depression. In addition (arrow 2), 5-HT can also cause translocation and activation of protein kinase C (PKC), which acts in concert with cAMP to promote transmitter mobilization (some intermediate steps of the PKC cascade are omitted for clarity; see **B** for details). 5-HT may also close a delayed, voltage-dependent potassium conductance ($I_{K,V}$) via an unidentified second messenger other than cAMP (arrow 3); closure of this channel contributes primarily to spike broadening and consequently enhances neurotransmitter release. Other actions of 5-HT (not shown) may include modulation of an L-type Ca^{2+} channel (via cAMP) and possibly changes in Ca^{2+} handling by the cell. Classical conditioning involves many of the same cellular mechanisms that occur in sensitization, but the steps are enhanced by action potential activity elicited in the sensory neurons by the tactile siphon conditioned stimulus (CS, dashed arrows). This activity-dependent enhancement may arise from Ca^{2+} entry during depolarization and the subsequent activation of calmodulin (CAM), which may interact with the cyclase and/or at other steps to amplify the biochemical cascades elicited by tail shock. (**B**) Working model for cellular changes occurring in *Hermissenda* Type B cells. The rotation unconditioned stimulus (US) activates caudal hair cells (CH) and ultimately serotonergic interneurons (as yet unidentified) that contact Type B photoreceptors. The binding of 5-HT to the receptors activates a G protein, which in turn activates phospholipase C (PLC), yielding diacylglycerol (DAG) and inositol trisphosphate (IP_3) from the hydrolysis of phosphatidylinositol (not shown). IP_3 then diffuses to the endoplasmic reticulum (ER), where it, along with the light CS, causes release of Ca^{2+} from intracellular stores. Ca^{2+} promotes the translocation of cytosolic PKC to the cell membrane, where PKC can interact with membrane-associated phospholipid to become fully activated. Once activated, PKC then phosphorylates K^+ channels or associated proteins, resulting in their closure, and thereby enhances cellular excitability. PKC also promotes synaptic facilitation through mechanisms not yet determined for these cells. In principle, facilitation might arise as a consequence of some of the same ionic conductance changes that mediate excitability (e.g., via closure of K^+ channels, action potential broadening, and enhanced Ca^{2+} influx, arrow 1). Direct modulation of Ca^{2+} channels (not shown) might also enhance release. Alternatively, PKC might facilitate transmitter release via steps independent of conductance changes (arrow 2). The light CS is proposed to enhance the PKC cascade via depolarization-induced Ca^{2+} influx and release of Ca^{2+} from intracellular stores (dashed arrows).

meaningful opportunity to search for common general principles of mnemonic mechanisms that transcend the particular details of any individual species. We hope that these initial studies prove to be a step in this direction.

ACKNOWLEDGMENTS

This work was supported by Office of Naval Research Grant No. N00014-89-J-1954, and by a Pew Biomedical Scholars Award and Alfred P. Sloan Research Fellowship to Gregory A. Clark.

REFERENCES

Alkon, D. L. (1979). Voltage-dependent calcium and potassium ion conductances: A contingency mechanism for an associative learning model. *Science, 205,* 810–816.

Alkon, D. L. (1989). Memory storage and neural systems. *Scientific American, 261*(1), 42–50.

Alkon, D. L., Ikeno, H., Dworkin, J., McPhie, D. L., Olds, J. L., Lederhendler, I., Matzel, L., Schreurs, B. G., Kuzirian, A., Collin, C., & Yamoah, E. (1990). Contraction of branching volume: An anatomic correlate of Pavlovian conditioning. *Proceedings of the National Academy of Sciences USA, 87,* 1611–1614.

Alkon, D. L., Kubota, M., Neary, J. T., Naito, S., Coulter, D., & Rasmussen, H. (1986). C-kinase activation prolongs Ca^{2+}-dependent inactivation of K^+ currents. *Biochemical and Biophysical Research Communications, 134,* 1245–1253. (Published erratum: *Biochemical and Biophysical Research Communications, 1986, 140,* 774.)

Alkon, D. L., Lederhendler, I., & Shoukimas, J. (1982). Primary changes of membrane currents during retention of associative learning. *Science, 215,* 693–695.

Alkon, D. L., Naito, S., Kubota, M., Chen, C., Bank, B., Smallwood, J., Gallant, P., & Rasmussen, H. (1988). Regulation of *Hermissenda* K^+ channels by cytoplasmic and membrane associated C-kinase. *Journal of Neurochemistry, 51,* 903–917.

Alkon, D. L., & Nelson, T. J. (1990). Specificity of molecular changes in neurons involved in memory storage. *FASEB Journal, 4,* 1567–1576.

Alkon, D. L., Sakakibara, M., Forman, R., Harrigan, J., Lederhendler, I., & Farley, J. (1985). Reduction of two voltage-dependent K^+ currents mediates retention of a learned association. *Behavioral and Neural Biology, 44,* 278–300.

Auerbach, S., Grover, L., & Farley, J. (1989). Neurochemical and immunohistochemical studies of serotonin in the *Hermissenda* central nervous system. *Brain Research Bulletin, 22,* 353–361.

Baxter, D. A., & Byrne, J. H. (1990). Differential effects of cAMP and serotonin on membrane current, action potential duration, and excitability in somata of pleural sensory neurons of *Aplysia*. *Journal of Neurophysiology, 64,* 978–990.

Billy, A. J., & Walters, E. T. (1989). Long-term expansion and sensitization of mechanosensory receptive fields in *Aplysia* support an activity-dependent model of whole-cell plasticity. *Journal of Neuroscience, 9,* 1254–1262.

Braha, O., Dale, N., Hochner, B., Klein, M., Abrams, T. W., & Kandel, E. R. (1990). Second messengers involved in the two processes of presynaptic facilitation that contribute to sensitization and dishabituation in *Aplysia* sensory neurons. *Proceedings of the National Academy of Sciences USA, 87,* 2040–2044.

Carew, T. J., Hawkins, R. D., Abrams, T. W., & Kandel, E. R. (1984). A test of Hebb's postulate at identified synapses which mediate classical conditioning in *Aplysia*. *Journal of Neuroscience, 4,* 1217–1224.

Clark, G. A., & Kandel, E. R. (1984). Branch-specific heterosynaptic facilitation in *Aplysia* siphon sensory cells. *Proceedings of the National Academy of Sciences USA, 81,* 2577–2581.

Collin, C., Ikeno, H., Harrigan, J. F., Lederhendler, I., & Alkon, D. L. (1988). Sequential modification of membrane currents with classical conditioning. *Biophysical Journal, 54,* 955–60.

Crow, T. (1988). Cellular and molecular analysis of associative learning and memory in *Hermissenda*. *Trends in Neurosciences, 11,* 136–142.

Crow, T., & Alkon, D. L. (1978). Retention of an associative behavioral change in *Hermissenda*. *Science, 201,* 1239–1241.

Crow, T., & Alkon, D. L. (1980). Associative behavioral modification in *Hermissenda*: Cellular correlates. *Science, 209,* 412–414.

Crow, T., & Bridge, M. S. (1985). Serotonin modulates photoresponses in *Hermissenda* Type-B photoreceptors. *Neuroscience Letters, 60*, 83–88.
Crow, T., & Forrester, J. (1986). Light paired with serotonin mimics the effect of conditioning on phototactic
   behavior of *Hermissenda*. *Proceedings of the National Academy of Sciences USA, 83*, 7975–7978.
Crow, T., & Forrester, J. (1991). Light paired with serotonin *in vivo* produces both short- and long-term
   enhancement of generator potential of identified B-photoreceptors in *Hermissenda*. *Journal of Neuroscience, 11*, 608–617.
Farley, J. (1988). Associative training results in persistent reductions in a calcium-activated potassium current
   in *Hermissenda* Type B photoreceptors. *Behavioral Neuroscience, 102*, 784–802.
Farley, J., & Alkon, D. L. (1982). Associative and behavioral change in *Hermissenda*: Consequences of
   nervous system orientation for light- and pairing specificity. *Journal of Neurophysiology, 48*, 785–807.
Farley, J., & Alkon, D. L. (1987). In vitro associative conditioning of *Hermissenda*: Cumulative depolarization of Type B photoreceptors and short-term associative behavioral change. *Journal of Neurophysiol-
   ogy, 57*, 1639–1668.
Farley, J., & Auerbach, S. (1986). Protein kinase C activation induces conductance changes in *Hermissenda*
   photoreceptors like those seen in associative learning. *Nature, 319*, 220–223. (Published erratum,
   Nature, 1986, *324*, 702.)
Farley, J., Richards, W. G., & Alkon, D. L. (1983). Evidence for an increased voltage-dependent Ca^{2+} current
   during retention of associative learning. *Biophysical Journal, 41*, 294a.
Farley, J., Richards, W. G., Ling, L. J., Liman, E., & Alkon, D. L. (1983). Membrane changes in a single
   photoreceptor cause associative learning in *Hermissenda*. *Science, 221*, 1201–1203.
Farley, J., & Schuman, E. (1991). Protein kinase C inhibitors prevent induction and continued expression of
   cell memory in *Hermissenda* Type B photoreceptors. *Proceedings of the National Academy of Sciences
   USA, 88*, 2016–2020.
Farley, J., & Wu, R. (1989). Serotonin modulation of *Hermissenda* Type B photoreceptor light responses and
   ionic currents: Implications for mechanisms underlying associative learning. *Brain Research Bulletin,
   22*, 335–351.
Forrester, J., & Crow, T. (1988). Protein kinase C inhibition prevents short-term but not long-term light-
   5-HT-induced enhancement of generator potentials in *Hermissenda*. *Society for Neuroscience Abstracts, 14*, 839.
Forrester, J., & Crow, T. (1989). Kinase inhibitors do not reverse short- or long-term enhancement of light
   responses in identified *Hermissenda* B-photoreceptors. *Society for Neuroscience Abstracts, 15*, 1284.
Goh, Y., & Alkon, D. L. (1984). Sensory, interneuronal, and motor interactions within the *Hermissenda* visual
   pathway. *Journal of Neurophysiology, 52*, 156–169.
Goh, Y., Lederhendler, I., & Alkon, D. L. (1985). Input and output changes of an identified neural pathway
   are correlated with associative learning in *Hermissenda*. *Journal of Neuroscience, 5*, 536–543.
Grover, L. M., Farley, J., & Auerbach, S. B. (1989). Serotonin involvement during *in vitro* conditioning of
   Hermissenda. *Brain Research Bulletin, 22*, 363–372.
Hochner, B., Klein, M., Schacher, S., & Kandel, E. R. (1986a). Action potential duration and the modulation
   of transmitter release from the sensory neurons of *Aplysia* in presynaptic facilitation and behavioral
   sensitization. *Proceedings of the National Academy of Sciences USA, 83*, 8410–8414.
Hochner, B., Klein, M., Schacher, S., & Kandel, E. R. (1986b). Additional component in the cellular
   mechanism of presynaptic facilitation contributes to behavioral dishabituation in *Aplysia*. *Proceedings
   of the National Academy of Sciences USA, 83*, 8794–8798.
Klein, M., Hochner, B., & Kandel, E. R. (1986). Facilitatory transmitters and cAMP can modulate accommodation as well as transmitter release in *Aplysia* sensory neurons: Evidence for parallel processing in a
   single cell. *Proceedings of the National Academy of Sciences USA, 83*, 7994–7998.
Klein, M., & Kandel, E. R. (1978). Presynaptic modulation of a voltage-dependent Ca^{2+} current: Mechanism
   for behavioral sensitization. *Proceedings of the National Academy of Sciences USA, 75*, 3512–3516.
Klein, M., & Kandel, E. R. (1980). Mechanism of calcium current modulation underlying presynaptic
   facilitation and behavioral sensitization in *Aplysia*. *Proceedings of the National Academy of Sciences
   USA, 77*, 6912–6916.
Land, P. W., & Crow, T. (1985). Serotonin immunoreactivity in the circumesophageal nervous system of
   Hermissenda crassicornis. *Neuroscience Letters, 62*, 199–205.
Lederhendler, I., Etcheberrigaray, R., Yamoah, E. N., Matzel, L. D., & Alkon, D. L. (1990). Outgrowths from
   Hermissenda photoreceptor somata are associated with activation of protein kinase C. *Brain Research,
   534*, 195–200.
Matzel, L. D., Lederhendler, I. I., & Alkon, D. L. (1990). Regulation of short-term associative memory by
   calcium-dependent protein kinase. *Journal of Neuroscience, 10*, 2300–2307.

Neary, J. T., Naito, S., DeWeer, A., & Alkon, D. L. (1986). Ca^{2+}/diacylglycerol-activated, phospholipid-dependent protein kinase in the *Hermissenda* CNS. *Journal of Neurochemistry, 47*, 1405-1411.

Richards, W. G., & Farley, J. (1987). Motor correlates of phototaxis and associative learning in *Hermissenda crassicornis*. *Brain Research Bulletin, 19*, 175-189.

Ruegg, U. T., & Burgess, G. M. (1989). Staurosporine, K-252 and UCN-01: Potent but nonspecific inhibitors of protein kinases. *Trends in Pharmacological Sciences, 10*, 218-220.

Schuman, E. M., & Clark, G. A. (1990). *Hermissenda* photoreceptors exhibit synaptic facilitation as well as enhanced excitability. *Society for Neuroscience Abstracts, 16*, 21.

Siegelbaum, S. A., Camardo, J. S., & Kandel, E. R. (1982). Serotonin and cyclic AMP close single K^+ channels in *Aplysia* sensory neurons. *Nature, 299*, 413-417.

Tabata, M., & Alkon, D. L. (1982). Positive synaptic feedback in visual system of nudibranch mollusk *Hermissenda crassicornis*. *Journal of Neurophysiology, 48*, 174-191.

Tamaokie, T., Nomoto, H., Takahashi, I., Kato, Y., Morimoto, M., & Tomita, F. (1986). Staurosporine, a potent inhibitor of phospholipid/Ca^{++} dependent protein kinase. *Biochemical and Biophysical Research Communications, 135*, 397-402.

Tesauro, G. (1988). A plausible neural circuit for classical conditioning without synaptic plasticity. *Proceedings of the National Academy of Sciences USA, 85*, 2830-2833.

Walters, E. T. (1987). Multiple sensory neuronal correlates of site-specific sensitization in *Aplysia*. *Journal of Neuroscience, 7*, 408-417.

Walters, E. T., & Byrne, J. H. (1983). Associative conditioning of single sensory neurons suggests a cellular mechanism for learning. *Science, 219*, 405-408.

West, A., Barnes, E., & Alkon, D. L. (1982). Primary changes of voltage responses during retention of associative learning. *Journal of Neurophysiology, 48*, 1243-1255.

Woollacott, M., & Hoyle, G. (1977). Neural events underlying learning in insects: Changes in pacemaker. *Proceedings of the Royal Society of London, B, 195*, 395-415.

Index